Tax Formula for Individuals

Income (broadly conceived)	$xx,xxx
Less: Exclusions..	(x,xxx)
Gross income	$xx,xxx
Less: Deductions *for* adjusted gross income	(x,xxx)
Adjusted gross income....................................	$xx,xxx
Less: The greater of— Total itemized deductions *or* standard deduction	(x,xxx)
Less: Personal and dependency exemptions	(x,xxx)
Taxable income	$xx,xxx
Tax on taxable income	$ x,xxx
Less: Tax credits (including Federal income tax withheld and other prepayments of Federal income taxes)	(xxx)
Tax due (or refund)......................................	$ xxx

Basic Standard Deduction Amounts

	Standard Deduction Amount	
Filing Status	**2007**	**2008**
Single	$ 5,350	$ 5,450
Married, filing jointly	10,700	10,900
Surviving spouse	10,700	10,900
Head of household	7,850	8,000
Married, filing separately	5,350	5,450

Amount of Each Additional Standard Deduction

Filing Status	**2007**	**2008**
Single	$1,300	$1,350
Married, filing jointly	1,050	1,050
Surviving spouse	1,050	1,050
Head of household	1,300	1,350
Married, filing separately	1,050	1,050

Personal and Dependency Exemption

2007	**2008**
$3,400	$3,500

SOUTH-WESTERN
FEDERAL TAXATION

Individual
Income Taxes

2009 EDITION

General Editors

William H. Hoffman, Jr.
J.D., Ph.D., CPA

James E. Smith
Ph.D., CPA

Eugene Willis
Ph.D., CPA

Contributing Authors

James H. Boyd
Ph.D., CPA
Arizona State University

D. Larry Crumbley
Ph.D., CPA
Louisiana State University

Steven C. Dilley
J.D., Ph.D., CPA
Michigan State University

William H. Hoffman, Jr.
J.D., Ph.D., CPA
University of Houston

David M. Maloney
Ph.D., CPA
University of Virginia

Gary A. McGill
Ph.D., CPA
University of Florida

William A. Raabe
Ph.D., CPA
The Ohio State University

Boyd C. Randall
J.D., Ph.D.
Brigham Young University

W. Eugene Seago
J.D., Ph.D., CPA
Virginia Polytechnic
Institute and State University

James E. Smith
Ph.D., CPA
College of William and Mary

Eugene Willis
Ph.D., CPA
University of Illinois,
Urbana-Champaign

SOUTH-WESTERN
CENGAGE Learning™

Australia • Brazil • Japan • Korea • Mexico • Singapore • Spain • United Kingdom • United States

**South-Western Federal Taxation:
Individual Income Taxes, 2009 Edition**

William H. Hoffman, Jr., James E. Smith, Eugene Willis

Vice President of Editorial, Business: Jack W. Calhoun

Editor-in-Chief: Rob Dewey

Senior Developmental Editor: Craig Avery

Marketing Manager: Kristen Hurd

Marketing Communications Manager: Libby Shipp

Senior Content Project Manager: Tim Bailey

Media Editor: Robin Browning

Website Project Manager: Brian Courter

Senior Frontlist Buyer: Doug Wilke

Production Service: LEAP Publishing Services, Inc.

Compositor: Cadmus Communications

Senior Art Director: Michelle Kunkler

Internal Designer: Diane Gliebe/Design Matters

Cover Designer: Craig Ramsdell

Cover Image: © Getty Images, Inc.

For product information and technology assistance, contact us at
Cengage Learning Academic Resource Center, 1-800-423-0563

For permission to use material from this text or product, submit all requests online at **www.cengage.com/permissions**
Further permissions questions can be emailed to
permissionrequest@cengage.com

Exam*View*® is a registered trademark of eInstruction Corp. Windows is a registered trademark of the Microsoft Corporation used herein under license.

Cengage Learning WebTutor™ is a trademark of Cengage Learning.

Student Edition ISBN 13: 978-0-324-66016-6
Student Edition ISBN 10: 0-324-66016-2
Student Edition with CD ISBN 13: 978-0-324-66020-3
Student Edition with CD ISBN 10: 0-324-66020-0
Instructor's Edition with CD ISBN 13: 978-0-324-66132-3
Instructor's Edition with CD ISBN 10: 0-324-66132-0
Loose Leaf Edition with CD ISBN 13: 978-0-324-66134-7
Loose Leaf Edition with CD ISBN 10: 0-324-66134-7

ISSN: 0272-0329
2009 Annual Edition

South-Western Cengage Learning
5191 Natorp Boulevard
Mason, OH 45040
USA

Cengage Learning products are represented in Canada by Nelson Education, Ltd.

For your course and learning solutions, visit **academic.cengage.com**

Purchase any of our products at your local college store or at our preferred online store **www.ichapters.com**

Printed in the United States of America
1 2 3 4 5 6 7 12 11 10 09 08

To the Student
The Leadership You Trust—The Innovation You Expect—The Service You Deserve

◆

South-Western Federal Taxation is the most trusted and largest selling brand in college taxation. We are focused exclusively on providing the most useful, comprehensive, and up-to-date tax texts, online study aids, tax preparation tools, and print study guides to help you succeed in your tax courses and beyond.

◆

More than just a textbook, *Individual Income Taxes, 2009 Edition* provides a dynamic learning experience in and out of the classroom. Built around the areas students have identified as the most important, our complete study system will offer you options in the way you learn.

Online Resources and Study Tools

TaxCut® software automatically comes with this textbook to provide you with an additional tax preparation tool!

    TaxCut. More than software. Put the experience of H&R Block tax professionals on your side.

Thomson/RIA's Checkpoint® **Student Edition** is an **optional item** your instructor may have ordered, offering six-month access to a leading online tax research database.

    3 Simple Ways Checkpoint® **Helps You Make Sense of All Those Taxes:**

- Intuitive Web-based design makes it fast and simple to find what you need.
- A comprehensive collection of primary tax law, cases, and rulings along with analytical insight you simply can't find anywhere else.
- Checkpoint® has built-in productivity tools such as calculators to make research more efficient—a resource more tax pros use than any other.

Book Companion Web Site—academic.cengage.com/taxation/swft—contains updates, quizzes, and a rich array of **free learning aids**:

- **Free interactive quizzes.** These short, self-graded quizzes help you brush up on chapter topics. Many more self-quizzes are available in the Study Guide—see below.
- **Flashcards** use chapter terms and definitions to aid you in learning tax terminology for each chapter.
- **Online glossary** for each chapter provides terms and definitions from the text in alphabetical order for easy reference.
- **Learning objectives** are downloadable for each chapter to keep you on track.
- **Tax Tips for the Recent Graduate** introduce the college graduate to some common tax considerations that could be beneficial in reducing the dreaded "tax-bite."
- **Tax Updates** provide the most recent tax information and major changes to the tax law.
- **Tax tables** used in the textbook are downloadable for reference.
- **Download a Study Guide Chapter FREE Before You Buy!** Get one chapter of the print Study Guide free online. The Study Guide contains questions and problems with solutions for self-study, as well as chapter highlights that point you to the right place in the text for further study. Order it from your bookstore (**ISBN 0-324-66119-3**) or buy it online by chapter at **ichapters.com**.

iChapters.com

Visit **iChapters.com** to receive 25 percent off on more than 10,000 print, digital, and audio study tools that allow you to:

- **Practice, review, and master course concepts** ... *by purchasing the study guide or practice sets that work hand-in-hand with this textbook.*
- **Join the thousands of students who've benefited from iChapters.com**. Just search by author, title, or ISBN; then filter the results by "Study Tools" and select the format best suited for you.

Additional Student Resources

Study Guide, ISBN 0-324-66119-3
Do you need more help studying for your taxation class? Order the Study Guide to receive:

- Study Highlights—an outline of key topics for each chapter.
- Key Terms used in the chapter.
- Self-Quizzing with helpful, annotated answers that are keyed to pages in the 2009 Edition.

Check with your bookstore or order on **iChapters.com**.

Individual Practice Sets, ISBN 0-324-66120-7
Ask your instructor about assigning these practice sets.
Written specifically for Individual Income Taxes, 2009 Edition, practice sets are comprehensive and designed to be completed near the end of the course using tax preparation software such as TaxCut®.

Check with your instructor before ordering practice sets—solutions are available to instructors only in a separate volume.

For over 30 years, the **South-Western Federal Taxation** Series has guided more than 1.5 million students through the ever-changing field of Federal taxation.

With commitment to leadership, innovation, and service, we have a stake in your success both now and in the future.

About the Editors

William H. Hoffman Jr. earned B.A. and J.D. degrees from the University of Michigan and M.B.A. and Ph.D. degrees from the University of Texas. He is a licensed CPA and attorney in Texas. His teaching experience includes the University of Texas (1957–1961), Louisiana State University (1961–1967), and the University of Houston (1967–1999). Professor Hoffman has addressed many tax institutes and conferences and has published extensively in academic and professional journals. His articles appear in *The Journal of Taxation, The Tax Adviser, Taxes—The Tax Magazine, The Journal of Accountancy, The Accounting Review,* **and** *Taxation for Accountants.*

James E. Smith is the John S. Quinn Professor of Accounting at the College of William and Mary. He has been a member of the Accounting Faculty for over 30 years. He received his Ph.D. degree from the University of Arizona. Professor Smith has served as a discussion leader for Continuing Professional Education programs for the AICPA, Federal Tax Workshops, and various state CPA societies. He has conducted programs in more than 40 states for approximately 25,000 CPAs. He has been the recipient of the AICPA's Outstanding Discussion Leader Award and the American Taxation Association/Arthur Andersen Teaching Innovation Award. Among his other awards are the Virginia Society of CPAs' Outstanding Accounting Educator Award and the James Madison University's Outstanding Accounting Educator Award. He was the President of the Administrators of Accounting Programs Group (AAPG) in 1991–1992. He was the faculty adviser for the William and Mary teams that received first place in the Andersen Tax Challenge in 1994, 1995, 1997, 2000, and 2001 and in the Deloitte Tax Case Study Competition in 2002, 2004, 2005, and 2006

Eugene Willis is the Arthur Andersen Alumni Professor of Accountancy Emeritus at the University of Illinois (Urbana-Champaign). He joined the Illinois faculty in 1975 after receiving his Ph.D. from the University of Cincinnati. His articles have appeared in leading academic and professional journals, including *The Accounting Review, The Journal of the American Taxation Association, The Journal of Accountancy,* and *The Journal of Taxation.* Professor Willis is co-director of the National Tax Education Program, a continuing education program co-sponsored by the American Institute of CPAs and the University of Illinois.

CONTENTS IN BRIEF

PART 1: INTRODUCTION AND BASIC TAX MODEL

CHAPTER 1   AN INTRODUCTION TO TAXATION AND
UNDERSTANDING THE FEDERAL TAX LAW   1–1

CHAPTER 2   WORKING WITH THE TAX LAW   2–1

CHAPTER 3   TAX DETERMINATION; PERSONAL
AND DEPENDENCY EXEMPTIONS; AN
OVERVIEW OF PROPERTY TRANSACTIONS   3–1

PART 2: GROSS INCOME

CHAPTER 4   GROSS INCOME: CONCEPTS
AND INCLUSIONS   4–1

CHAPTER 5   GROSS INCOME: EXCLUSIONS   5–1

PART 3: DEDUCTIONS

CHAPTER 6   DEDUCTIONS AND LOSSES: IN GENERAL   6–1

CHAPTER 7   DEDUCTIONS AND LOSSES: CERTAIN
BUSINESS EXPENSES AND LOSSES   7–1

CHAPTER 8   DEPRECIATION, COST RECOVERY,
AMORTIZATION, AND DEPLETION   8–1

CHAPTER 9   DEDUCTIONS: EMPLOYEE AND
SELF-EMPLOYED-RELATED EXPENSES   9–1

CHAPTER 10   DEDUCTIONS AND LOSSES: CERTAIN ITEMIZED DEDUCTIONS   10–1

CHAPTER 11   INVESTOR LOSSES   11–1

PART 4: SPECIAL TAX COMPUTATION METHODS, PAYMENT PROCEDURES, AND TAX CREDITS

CHAPTER 12   ALTERNATIVE MINIMUM TAX   12–1

CHAPTER 13   TAX CREDITS AND PAYMENT PROCEDURES   13–1

PART 5: PROPERTY TRANSACTIONS

CHAPTER 14   PROPERTY TRANSACTIONS: DETERMINATION OF GAIN OR LOSS AND BASIS CONSIDERATIONS   14–1

CHAPTER 15   PROPERTY TRANSACTIONS: NONTAXABLE EXCHANGES   15–1

CHAPTER 16   PROPERTY TRANSACTIONS: CAPITAL GAINS AND LOSSES   16–1

CHAPTER 17   PROPERTY TRANSACTIONS: § 1231 AND RECAPTURE PROVISIONS   17–1

PART 6: ACCOUNTING PERIODS, ACCOUNTING METHODS, AND DEFERRED COMPENSATION

CHAPTER 18   ACCOUNTING PERIODS AND METHODS   18–1

CHAPTER 19   DEFERRED COMPENSATION   19–1

PART 7: CORPORATIONS AND PARTNERSHIPS

CHAPTER 20   CORPORATIONS AND PARTNERSHIPS   20–1

APPENDIXES   A–1

SUBJECT INDEX   I–1

CONTENTS

PART 1: INTRODUCTION AND BASIC TAX MODEL

CHAPTER 1
AN INTRODUCTION TO TAXATION AND UNDERSTANDING THE FEDERAL TAX LAW 1–1

HISTORY OF U.S. TAXATION	**1–2**
Early Periods	1–2
Revenue Acts	1–3
Historical Trends	1–3
CRITERIA USED IN THE SELECTION OF A TAX STRUCTURE	**1–4**
THE TAX STRUCTURE	**1–5**
Tax Base	1–5
Tax Rates	1–5
Tax in the News: *Adam Smith Stopped Too Soon*	1–5
Incidence of Taxation	1–6
MAJOR TYPES OF TAXES	**1–6**
Property Taxes	1–6
Tax in the News: *How a Few Cows and Birdhouses Can Save on Property Taxes*	1–7
Transaction Taxes	1–8
Ethical and Equitable Considerations: *Making Good Use of Out-of-State Relatives*	1–10
Death Taxes	1–10
Gift Taxes	1–12
Income Taxes	1–13
Tax in the News: *Using the Income Tax Return as a "Use Tax" Reminder*	1–15
Employment Taxes	1–15
Other U.S. Taxes	1–17
Proposed U.S. Taxes	1–17
TAX ADMINISTRATION	**1–19**
Internal Revenue Service	1–19
The Audit Process	1–19
Tax in the News: *One Way to Collect Taxes: Internet Shaming*	1–21
Statute of Limitations	1–21
Interest and Penalties	1–22
Tax Practice	1–23
Ethical and Equitable Considerations: *When the IRS Does Not Know*	1–23
UNDERSTANDING THE FEDERAL TAX LAW	**1–24**
Revenue Needs	1–24
Global Tax Issues: *Outsourcing of Tax Return Preparation*	1–25
Economic Considerations	1–25
Social Considerations	1–26
Equity Considerations	1–27
Tax in the News: *Treating Everyone the Same*	1–28
Political Considerations	1–30
Influence of the Internal Revenue Service	1–31
Ethical and Equitable Considerations: *Claiming a Bad Debt Deduction*	1–31
Influence of the Courts	1–32
Summary	1–33
PROBLEM MATERIALS	**1–34**

CHAPTER 2
WORKING WITH THE TAX LAW 2–1

TAX SOURCES	**2–2**
Statutory Sources of the Tax Law	2–2
Tax in the News: *Tax Freedom Day*	2–3
Tax in the News: *Underreporting Income*	2–4
Administrative Sources of the Tax Law	2–7
Ethical and Equitable Considerations: *The President and the IRS*	2–7
Judicial Sources of the Tax Law	2–12
Tax in the News: *Closing the Tax Gap*	2–13

Other Sources of the Tax Law   2–20
Global Tax Issues: *Tax Treaties*   2–20

WORKING WITH THE TAX LAW—TAX RESEARCH TOOLS   **2–22**
Electronic versus Paper Tax Research Tools   2–22
Tax Services   2–23
Electronic Services   2–23

WORKING WITH THE TAX LAW—TAX RESEARCH   **2–26**
Global Tax Issues: *Data Warehousing Reduces Global Taxes*   2–28
Identifying the Problem   2–28
Refining the Problem   2–28
Locating the Appropriate Tax Law Sources   2–29
Assessing the Validity of the Tax Law Sources   2–30
Tax in the News: *Internal Revenue Code: Interpretation Pitfalls*   2–31
Tax in the News: *Baseball and Tax Research*   2–33
Arriving at the Solution or at Alternative Solutions   2–33
Communicating Tax Research   2–34

WORKING WITH THE TAX LAW—TAX PLANNING   **2–34**
Nontax Considerations   2–35
Tax Avoidance and Tax Evasion   2–35
Ethical and Equitable Considerations: *Twist and Shout, But Pay Your Taxes*   2–37
Tax in the News: *The Disappearing Taxpayers*   2–38
Follow-up Procedures   2–38
Tax Planning—A Practical Application   2–38

TAXATION ON THE CPA EXAMINATION   **2–39**

PROBLEM MATERIALS   **2–40**

CHAPTER 3
TAX DETERMINATION; PERSONAL AND DEPENDENCY EXEMPTIONS; AN OVERVIEW OF PROPERTY TRANSACTIONS   **3–1**

TAX FORMULA   **3–3**
Components of the Tax Formula   3–3
Global Tax Issues: *Citizenship Is Not Tax-Free*   3–5
Application of the Tax Formula   3–9
Individuals Not Eligible for the Standard Deduction   3–9
Special Limitations for Individuals Who Can Be Claimed as Dependents   3–9

PERSONAL EXEMPTIONS   **3–10**

DEPENDENCY EXEMPTIONS   **3–11**
Qualifying Child   3–11
Ethical and Equitable Considerations: *Whose Qualifying Child Is He?*   3–13
Qualifying Relative   3–13
Ethical and Equitable Considerations: *Discovering Lost Dependency Exemptions*   3–16
Other Rules for Dependency Exemptions   3–17
Comparison of Categories for Dependency Exemptions   3–18
Phaseout of Exemptions   3–18
Child Tax Credit   3–19

TAX DETERMINATION   **3–20**
Tax Table Method   3–20
Tax in the News: *How to Subtly Pluck the Chicken*   3–20
Tax Rate Schedule Method   3–21
Computation of Net Taxes Payable or Refund Due   3–22
Unearned Income of Children under Age 19 Taxed at Parents' Rate   3–23

FILING CONSIDERATIONS   **3–25**
Filing Requirements   3–25
Tax in the News: *IRS versus USCIS*   3–27
Tax in the News: *Special Rules for Certain Military Personnel*   3–28
Filing Status   3–28
Tax in the News: *"Charge It"—Convenient But Not Cheap!*   3–29
Global Tax Issues: *Filing a Joint Return*   3–30

GAINS AND LOSSES FROM PROPERTY TRANSACTIONS—IN GENERAL   **3–32**

GAINS AND LOSSES FROM PROPERTY TRANSACTIONS—CAPITAL GAINS AND LOSSES   **3–33**
Definition of a Capital Asset   3–33
Taxation of Net Capital Gain   3–33
Determination of Net Capital Gain   3–34
Treatment of Net Capital Loss   3–34

TAX PLANNING CONSIDERATIONS   **3–35**
Maximizing the Use of the Standard Deduction   3–35
Dependency Exemptions   3–35
Taking Advantage of Tax Rate Differentials   3–37
Ethical and Equitable Considerations: *A Tax Benefit from Nondependents*   3–37
Income of Certain Children   3–38

PROBLEM MATERIALS   **3–38**

PART 2: GROSS INCOME

CHAPTER 4
GROSS INCOME: CONCEPTS AND INCLUSIONS   **4–1**

GROSS INCOME—WHAT IS IT?   **4–2**
Definition   4–2

Global Tax Issues: *From "All Sources" Is a Broad Definition*   4–3
Economic and Accounting Concepts   4–3
Tax in the News: *The Tax Gap*   4–4
Tax in the News: *Academy Awards Presenters must "Walk the Line"*   4–5
Comparison of the Accounting and Tax Concepts of Income   4–5

Tax in the News: *Barry Bonds Made Matt Murphy and the Federal Government Richer* — 4–6

Form of Receipt — 4–6

Recovery of Capital Doctrine — 4–6

Ethical and Equitable Considerations: *A Business Made Possible by eBay* — 4–7

YEAR OF INCLUSION — 4–7

Taxable Year — 4–7

Accounting Methods — 4–7

Ethical and Equitable Considerations: *The CPAs' Accounting Method* — 4–9

Exceptions Applicable to Cash Basis Taxpayers — 4–10

Global Tax Issues: *Tax Credit Neutralizes Foreign Income Taxes* — 4–12

Exceptions Applicable to Accrual Basis Taxpayers — 4–13

INCOME SOURCES — 4–14

Personal Services — 4–14

Income from Property — 4–15

Ethical and Equitable Considerations: *Enhancing Lottery Winnings* — 4–17

Income Received by an Agent — 4–17

Income from Partnerships, S Corporations, Trusts, and Estates — 4–17

Tax in the News: *The Attorney's Fee was the Plaintiff's Income* — 4–18

Income in Community Property States — 4–18

ITEMS SPECIFICALLY INCLUDED IN GROSS INCOME — 4–20

Alimony and Separate Maintenance Payments — 4–20

Ethical and Equitable Considerations: *Avoiding Front-Loading with Equal Payments* — 4–23

Imputed Interest on Below-Market Loans — 4–23

Tax in the News: *Loans to Executives Prohibited* — 4–26

Income from Annuities — 4–27

Prizes and Awards — 4–31

Group Term Life Insurance — 4–31

Unemployment Compensation — 4–32

Social Security Benefits — 4–33

Tax in the News: *A Taxpayer Learns about the "Quirky" Social Security Benefits Taxation Formula* — 4–33

TAX PLANNING CONSIDERATIONS — 4–34

Nontaxable Economic Benefits — 4–34

Tax Deferral — 4–34

Shifting Income to Relatives — 4–36

Accounting for Community Property — 4–37

Alimony — 4–37

PROBLEM MATERIALS — 4–38

CHAPTER 5
GROSS INCOME: EXCLUSIONS — 5–1

ITEMS SPECIFICALLY EXCLUDED FROM GROSS INCOME — 5–2

Tax in the News: *Avoiding a Natural Disaster can Create a Tax Burden* — 5–4

STATUTORY AUTHORITY — 5–4

GIFTS AND INHERITANCES — 5–4

General — 5–4

Tax in the News: *Begging as a Tax-Disfavored Occupation* — 5–5

Gifts to Employees — 5–5

Employee Death Benefits — 5–6

Tax in the News: *Frequent-Flyer Miles will not be Taxed* — 5–6

LIFE INSURANCE PROCEEDS — 5–6

General Rule — 5–6

Accelerated Death Benefits — 5–7

Ethical and Equitable Considerations: *Should the Terminally Ill Pay Social Security Taxes?* — 5–8

Transfer for Valuable Consideration — 5–8

SCHOLARSHIPS — 5–9

General Information — 5–9

Timing Issues — 5–10

Disguised Compensation — 5–10

Qualified Tuition Reduction Plans — 5–10

COMPENSATION FOR INJURIES AND SICKNESS — 5–11

Damages — 5–11

Tax in the News: *The Tax on a Whistle-Blower's Damages Award Declared Unconstitutional—for a Short While* — 5–11

Ethical and Equitable Considerations: *Negotiating a Damages Award* — 5–12

Workers' Compensation — 5–13

Accident and Health Insurance Benefits — 5–13

EMPLOYER-SPONSORED ACCIDENT AND HEALTH PLANS — 5–13

Global Tax Issues: *When Jobs Leave the Country, So Do the Health Insurance Benefits* — 5–14

Medical Reimbursement Plans — 5–14

Long-Term Care Insurance Benefits — 5–15

MEALS AND LODGING — 5–15

Furnished for the Convenience of the Employer — 5–15

Other Housing Exclusions — 5–17

OTHER EMPLOYEE FRINGE BENEFITS — 5–18

Specific Benefits — 5–18

Tax in the News: *Employee Tuition Assistance Offers Benefits to Employers Too* — 5–19

Cafeteria Plans — 5–19

Flexible Spending Plans — 5–20

General Classes of Excluded Benefits — 5–20

Taxable Fringe Benefits — 5–24

FOREIGN EARNED INCOME — 5–25

Global Tax Issues: *U.S. Taxpayers Abroad Are Gone but Not Forgotten* — 5–27

Ethical and Equitable Considerations: *Who Should Benefit from the Foreign Earned Income Exclusion?* — 5–27

Tax in the News: *To Qualify for the Foreign Earned Income Exclusion, You Must Work in a "Country"* — 5–28

INTEREST ON CERTAIN STATE AND LOCAL GOVERNMENT OBLIGATIONS — 5–28

DIVIDENDS — 5–29
General Information — 5–29
Ethical and Equitable Considerations: *Beneficiaries and Victims of Changes in Dividend Taxation* — 5–30
Stock Dividends — 5–30

EDUCATIONAL SAVINGS BONDS — 5–30

QUALIFIED TUITION PROGRAMS (§ 529 PLANS) — 5–31
Tax in the News: *Section 529 Plans are more Appealing after Changes in the "Kiddie Tax"* — 5–32

TAX BENEFIT RULE — 5–32

INCOME FROM DISCHARGE OF INDEBTEDNESS — 5–33
Tax in the News: *Is it an Appropriate Time to Tax?* — 5–34

TAX PLANNING CONSIDERATIONS — 5–34
Life Insurance — 5–34
Employee Benefits — 5–34
Investment Income — 5–35

PROBLEM MATERIALS — 5–36

PART 3: DEDUCTIONS

CHAPTER 6
DEDUCTIONS AND LOSSES: IN GENERAL — 6–1

CLASSIFICATION OF DEDUCTIBLE EXPENSES — 6–2
Tax in the News: *Proper Treatment of Your Voice* — 6–3
Deductions for Adjusted Gross Income — 6–3
Itemized Deductions — 6–4
Trade or Business Expenses and Production of Income Expenses — 6–5
Business and Nonbusiness Losses — 6–7
Reporting Procedures — 6–7

DEDUCTIONS AND LOSSES—TIMING OF EXPENSE RECOGNITION — 6–8
Importance of Taxpayer's Method of Accounting — 6–8
Cash Method Requirements — 6–9
Accrual Method Requirements — 6–10

DISALLOWANCE POSSIBILITIES — 6–11
Public Policy Limitation — 6–11
Ethical and Equitable Considerations: *Knowing the Right People* — 6–12
Global Tax Issues: *Disallowance of Deduction for Bribes in Other Countries* — 6–13
Political Contributions and Lobbying Activities — 6–13
Excessive Executive Compensation — 6–14
Tax in the News: *Decreasing the Difference between CEO Compensation and that of Other Employees* — 6–14
Investigation of a Business — 6–15
Hobby Losses — 6–16
Tax in the News: *IRS Doing Poorly in Policing Hobby Loss Deductions* — 6–17
Rental of Vacation Homes — 6–19
Tax in the News: *Vacation Home Facts* — 6–19
Expenditures Incurred for Taxpayer's Benefit or Taxpayer's Obligation — 6–22
Tax in the News: *NASCAR and Another Taxpayer's Obligations* — 6–24
Disallowance of Personal Expenditures — 6–24
Disallowance of Deductions for Capital Expenditures — 6–24

Ethical and Equitable Considerations: *Expensing Too Early: A Problem for Self-Constructed Buildings* — 6–25
Transactions between Related Parties — 6–26
Substantiation Requirements — 6–27
Expenses and Interest Relating to Tax-Exempt Income — 6–28

TAX PLANNING CONSIDERATIONS — 6–29
Time Value of Tax Deductions — 6–29
Unreasonable Compensation — 6–29
Excessive Executive Compensation — 6–29
Shifting Deductions — 6–31
Hobby Losses — 6–31
Capital Expenditures — 6–32

PROBLEM MATERIALS — 6–32

CHAPTER 7
DEDUCTIONS AND LOSSES: CERTAIN BUSINESS EXPENSES AND LOSSES — 7–1

BAD DEBTS — 7–3
Ethical and Equitable Considerations: *A Bad Debt Deduction?* — 7–3
Specific Charge-Off Method — 7–3
Business versus Nonbusiness Bad Debts — 7–4
Global Tax Issues: *Writing Off Bad Debts in Australia* — 7–5
Loans between Related Parties — 7–5
Tax in the News: *Higher Taxes and Small Business Owners?* — 7–6

WORTHLESS SECURITIES — 7–6
Small Business Stock — 7–6

LOSSES OF INDIVIDUALS — 7–8
Events That Are Not Casualties — 7–8
Theft Losses — 7–9
When to Deduct Casualty Losses — 7–9
Measuring the Amount of Loss — 7–10
Statutory Framework for Deducting Losses of Individuals — 7–13
Personal Casualty Gains and Losses — 7–13

Ethical and Equitable Considerations: *The Amount of a Casualty Loss*   7–15

RESEARCH AND EXPERIMENTAL EXPENDITURES   **7–15**
Expense Method   7–15
Deferral and Amortization Method   7–16

DOMESTIC PRODUCTION ACTIVITIES DEDUCTION   **7–17**
Operational Rules   7–17
Eligible Taxpayers   7–18

NET OPERATING LOSSES   **7–19**
Tax in the News: *Tax Savings from NOLs*   7–20
Carryback and Carryover Periods   7–20
Global Tax Issues: *New NOL Incentives*   7–21
Computation of the Net Operating Loss   7–21
Recomputation of Tax Liability for Year to Which Net Operating Loss Is Carried   7–23
Calculation of the Remaining Net Operating Loss   7–24

TAX PLANNING CONSIDERATIONS   **7–25**
Tax Consequences of the *Groetzinger* Case   7–25
Documentation of Related-Taxpayer Loans, Casualty Losses, and Theft Losses   7–26
Worthless Securities   7–26
Small Business Stock   7–26
Casualty Losses   7–26
Net Operating Losses   7–27
Tax in the News: *When is a Security Worthless?*   7–27

PROBLEM MATERIALS   **7–28**

CHAPTER 8
DEPRECIATION, COST RECOVERY, AMORTIZATION, AND DEPLETION   **8–1**

OVERVIEW   **8–2**
General   8–2
Concepts Relating to Depreciation   8–3

MODIFIED ACCELERATED COST RECOVERY SYSTEM (MACRS)   **8–4**
Global Tax Issues: *Simplified Depreciation for Small Business*   8–5
Personalty: Recovery Periods and Methods   8–5
Tax in the News: *Use of Tax Incentives for Wind Energy*   8–7
Realty: Recovery Periods and Methods   8–10
Tax in the News: *Frozen Capital Gain Rates on Depreciation*   8–11
Straight-Line Election   8–11
Farm Property   8–11
Leasehold Improvement Property   8–12
Election to Expense Assets   8–13
Business and Personal Use of Automobiles and Other Listed Property   8–15
Ethical and Equitable Considerations: *Substantiation Requirements*   8–20
Alternative Depreciation System (ADS)   8–20

ACCELERATED COST RECOVERY SYSTEM (ACRS)   **8–22**

AMORTIZATION   **8–22**
Ethical and Equitable Considerations: *Allocation of Purchase Price to Covenant not to Compete*   8–23

DEPLETION   **8–24**
Intangible Drilling and Development Costs (IDC)   8–25
Depletion Methods   8–25
Tax in the News: *Depletion of Landfill Sites*   8–25
Tax in the News: *Depletion for Marginal Oil and Gas Wells*   8–27

REPORTING PROCEDURES   **8–28**

TAX PLANNING CONSIDERATIONS   **8–31**
Cost Recovery   8–31
Amortization   8–32
Depletion   8–32

COST RECOVERY TABLES   **8–33**

PROBLEM MATERIALS   **8–37**

CHAPTER 9
DEDUCTIONS: EMPLOYEE AND SELF-EMPLOYED-RELATED EXPENSES   **9–1**

EMPLOYEE VERSUS SELF-EMPLOYED   **9–2**

EMPLOYEE EXPENSES—IN GENERAL   **9–4**

TRANSPORTATION EXPENSES   **9–4**
Qualified Expenditures   9–4
Computation of Automobile Expenses   9–6

TRAVEL EXPENSES   **9–7**
Definition of Travel Expenses   9–7
Away-from-Home Requirement   9–7
Restrictions on Travel Expenses   9–8
Combined Business and Pleasure Travel   9–9
Global Tax Issues: *Conventions in Faraway Lands*   9–10

MOVING EXPENSES   **9–11**
Distance Test   9–11
Time Test   9–11
Treatment of Moving Expenses   9–12
Global Tax Issues: *Expatriates and the Moving Expense Deduction*   9–13
Ethical and Equitable Considerations: *Manipulating the Real Estate Market*   9–13

EDUCATION EXPENSES   **9–13**
General Requirements   9–13
Requirements Imposed by Law or by the Employer for Retention of Employment   9–14
Maintaining or Improving Existing Skills   9–14
Classification of Specific Items   9–14
A Limited Deduction Approach   9–15
Tax in the News: *Is an MBA Degree Deductible?*   9–15
Other Provisions Dealing with Education   9–16

ENTERTAINMENT EXPENSES   **9–17**
Cutback Adjustment   9–18

Classification of Expenses   9–19
Restrictions upon Deductibility   9–19
Tax in the News: *Do Casinos Receive Special Treatment?*   9–20
Ethical and Equitable Considerations: *Your Turn or Mine?*   9–20

OTHER EMPLOYEE EXPENSES   **9–21**
Office in the Home   9–21
Miscellaneous Employee Expenses   9–23
Tax in the News: *"Home Sourcing" Can Generate Substantial Cost Savings*   9–24

CONTRIBUTIONS TO RETIREMENT ACCOUNTS   **9–25**
Employee IRAs   9–25
Self-Employed Keogh (H.R. 10) Plans   9–25

CLASSIFICATION OF EMPLOYEE EXPENSES   **9–25**
Accountable Plans   9–26
Nonaccountable Plans   9–27
Reporting Procedures   9–27
Ethical and Equitable Considerations: *A Sanitized Expense Account*   9–28

LIMITATIONS ON ITEMIZED DEDUCTIONS   **9–28**
Miscellaneous Itemized Deductions Subject to the 2 Percent Floor   9–28
Miscellaneous Itemized Deductions Not Subject to the 2 Percent Floor   9–29

TAX PLANNING CONSIDERATIONS   **9–29**
Self-Employed Individuals   9–29
Tax in the News: *Relief for Members of the Armed Forces Reserves*   9–30
Shifting Deductions between Employer and Employee   9–30
Transportation and Travel Expenses   9–31
Moving Expenses   9–31
Education Expenses   9–31
Tax in the News: *Even the Smithsonian Can't Get It Right*   9–32
Entertainment Expenses   9–32
Unreimbursed Employee Business Expenses   9–33

PROBLEM MATERIALS   **9–33**

CHAPTER 10
DEDUCTIONS AND LOSSES: CERTAIN ITEMIZED DEDUCTIONS   **10–1**

GENERAL CLASSIFICATION OF EXPENSES   **10–2**

MEDICAL EXPENSES   **10–2**
General Requirements   10–2
Medical Expenses Defined   10–3
Tax in the News: *The President and Vice President Itemize*   10–3
Ethical and Equitable Considerations: *Pigging Out to Get a Deduction*   10–5
Capital Expenditures for Medical Purposes   10–5
Medical Expenses Incurred for Spouse and Dependents   10–6
Transportation, Meal, and Lodging Expenses for Medical Treatment   10–6
Amounts Paid for Medical Insurance Premiums   10–7
Year of Deduction   10–8

Reimbursements   10–8
Health Savings Accounts   10–9
Tax in the News: *Promoters' Enthusiasm for HSAs Is Tempered by Users' Dissatisfaction*   10–9

TAXES   **10–11**
Deductibility as a Tax   10–11
Property Taxes   10–11
Global Tax Issues: *Deductibility of Foreign Taxes*   10–13
State and Local Income Taxes and Sales Taxes   10–13

INTEREST   **10–14**
Allowed and Disallowed Items   10–14
Restrictions on Deductibility and Timing Considerations   10–17
Classification of Interest Expense   10–18

CHARITABLE CONTRIBUTIONS   **10–18**
Criteria for a Gift   10–19
Qualified Organizations   10–20
Time of Deduction   10–20
Global Tax Issues: *Choose the Charity Wisely*   10–21
Record-Keeping and Valuation Requirements   10–21
Ethical and Equitable Considerations: *A Second Appraisal*   10–22
Limitations on Charitable Contribution Deduction   10–22
Tax in the News: *Congress Challenges Questionable Contribution Deductions*   10–23

MISCELLANEOUS ITEMIZED DEDUCTIONS   **10–27**
Ethical and Equitable Considerations: *Job Hunting in Ski Country: A Deductible Expense?*   10–27

OTHER MISCELLANEOUS DEDUCTIONS   **10–28**

COMPREHENSIVE EXAMPLE OF SCHEDULE A   **10–28**

OVERALL LIMITATION ON CERTAIN ITEMIZED DEDUCTIONS   **10–28**
Tax in the News: *The First Family and Itemized Deduction Phaseouts*   10–31
Ethical and Equitable Considerations: *Between a Rock and a Hard Place*   10–32

TAX PLANNING CONSIDERATIONS   **10–32**
Effective Utilization of Itemized Deductions   10–32
Utilization of Medical Deductions   10–32
Timing the Payment of Deductible Taxes   10–33
Protecting the Interest Deduction   10–33
Assuring the Charitable Contribution Deduction   10–34

PROBLEM MATERIALS   **10–36**

CHAPTER 11
INVESTOR LOSSES   **11–1**

THE TAX SHELTER PROBLEM   **11–2**

AT-RISK LIMITS   **11–4**

PASSIVE LOSS LIMITS   **11–5**
Classification and Impact of Passive Income and Losses   11–5
Taxpayers Subject to the Passive Loss Rules   11–8

Tax in the News: *Beware of Passive Loss Restrictions That Apply to Investments in Publicly Traded Partnerships*   11–9

Passive Activities Defined   11–10

Interaction of the At-Risk and Passive Activity Limits   11–18

Tax in the News: *Newly Developed Tax Shelter Strategies Now Protected by Patents—but for How Long?*   11–19

Special Passive Activity Rules for Real Estate Activities   11–19

Tax in the News: *Record Keeping Involves Creative Writing for Some!*   11–20

Ethical and Equitable Considerations: *Punching the Time Clock at Year-End*   11–22

Dispositions of Passive Interests   11–22

Ethical and Equitable Considerations: *How Much Latitude Can a Taxpayer Take in Setting Fair Market Value?*   11–23

INVESTMENT INTEREST   **11–24**

Tax in the News: *Proving Real Estate Professional Status Can Be a Big Deal*   11–26

OTHER INVESTMENT LOSSES   **11–26**

TAX PLANNING CONSIDERATIONS   **11–27**

Utilizing Passive Losses   11–27

PROBLEM MATERIALS   **11–29**

PART 4: SPECIAL TAX COMPUTATION METHODS, PAYMENT PROCEDURES, AND TAX CREDITS

CHAPTER 12
ALTERNATIVE MINIMUM TAX   **12–1**

INDIVIDUAL ALTERNATIVE MINIMUM TAX   **12–2**

AMT Formula for Alternative Minimum Taxable Income (AMTI)   12–2

Tax in the News: *The Growing Tentacles of the AMT*   12–3

AMT Formula: Other Components   12–6

Ethical and Equitable Considerations: *The Case of the Disappearing Inflation Adjustments*   12–8

AMT Adjustments   12–8

Tax in the News: *Who Pays the AMT?*   12–17

AMT Preferences   12–20

Tax in the News: *Tax-Free Municipal Bonds: Market Reaction to Being Taxed*   12–21

Illustration of the AMT Computation   12–23

AMT Credit   12–24

CORPORATE ALTERNATIVE MINIMUM TAX   **12–26**

Repeal of AMT for Small Corporations   12–26

Ethical and Equitable Considerations: *A Small Corporation Elects S Status*   12–27

AMT Adjustments   12–27

Tax Preferences   12–29

Exemption Amount   12–29

Other Aspects of the AMT   12–29

TAX PLANNING CONSIDERATIONS   **12–30**

Responding to Bob and Carol   12–30

Avoiding Preferences and Adjustments   12–30

Controlling the Timing of Preferences and Adjustments   12–30

Taking Advantage of the AMT/Regular Tax Rate Differential   12–30

PROBLEM MATERIALS   **12–31**

CHAPTER 13
TAX CREDITS AND PAYMENT PROCEDURES   **13–1**

TAX POLICY CONSIDERATIONS   **13–3**

Tax in the News: *Federal Tax Law Is a Key Component of U.S. Energy Policy*   13–4

OVERVIEW AND PRIORITY OF CREDITS   **13–4**

Refundable versus Nonrefundable Credits   13–4

General Business Credit   13–5

Treatment of Unused General Business Credits   13–6

SPECIFIC BUSINESS-RELATED TAX CREDIT PROVISIONS   **13–7**

Tax Credit for Rehabilitation Expenditures   13–7

Ethical and Equitable Considerations: *The Rehabilitation Tax Credit*   13–8

Work Opportunity Tax Credit   13–9

Research Activities Credit   13–10

Ethical and Equitable Considerations: *When Does "Research" Qualify as R&D?*   13–12

Low-Income Housing Credit   13–13

Disabled Access Credit   13–13

Credit for Small Employer Pension Plan Startup Costs   13–14

Credit for Employer-Provided Child Care   13–14

OTHER TAX CREDITS   **13–15**

Earned Income Credit   13–15

Tax in the News: *The Earned Income Credit: A Boost to the Working Poor and Merchants, Too!*   13–17

Tax Credit for Elderly or Disabled Taxpayers   13–17

Foreign Tax Credit   13–18

Global Tax Issues: *Sourcing Income in Cyberspace— Getting It Right When Calculating the Foreign Tax Credit*   13–19

Tax in the News: *IRS Targets Foreign Tax Credit Generators*   13–20

Adoption Expenses Credit   13–20

Child Tax Credit   13–21

Credit for Child and Dependent Care Expenses | 13–21
Ethical and Equitable Considerations: *Using the Credit for Child and Dependent Care Expenses* | 13–23
Education Tax Credits | 13–24
Credit for Certain Retirement Plan Contributions | 13–25
Recovery Rebate Credit | 13–26

PAYMENT PROCEDURES | **13–26**
Procedures Applicable to Employers | 13–26
Tax in the News: *Will Social Security Be There for You When You Need It?* | 13–33

Global Tax Issues: *Foreign "Withholding Tax" Performs an Important Role* | 13–38
Procedures Applicable to Self-Employed Persons | 13–38

TAX PLANNING CONSIDERATIONS | **13–42**
Foreign Tax Credit | 13–42
Credit for Child and Dependent Care Expenses | 13–42
Adjustments to Increase Withholding | 13–44
Adjustments to Avoid Overwithholding | 13–44

PROBLEM MATERIALS | **13–45**

PART 5: PROPERTY TRANSACTIONS

CHAPTER 14
PROPERTY TRANSACTIONS: DETERMINATION OF GAIN OR LOSS AND BASIS CONSIDERATIONS | 14–1

DETERMINATION OF GAIN OR LOSS | **14–3**
Realized Gain or Loss | 14–3
Ethical and Equitable Considerations: *Whose Property Tax Bill?* | 14–4
Recognized Gain or Loss | 14–6
Nonrecognition of Gain or Loss | 14–6
Recovery of Capital Doctrine | 14–7

BASIS CONSIDERATIONS | **14–8**
Determination of Cost Basis | 14–8
Tax in the News: *What is Your Stock Basis?* | 14–9
Tax in the News: *Frequent-Flyer Miles and Basis* | 14–11
Gift Basis | 14–11
Property Acquired from a Decedent | 14–14
Disallowed Losses | 14–16
Tax in the News: *Effect of 2001 Tax Legislation on the Basis of Inherited Property: Bad News/Good News!* | 14–16
Ethical and Equitable Considerations: *Drying Out a Wash Sale* | 14–18
Conversion of Property from Personal Use to Business or Income-Producing Use | 14–19
Additional Complexities in Determining Realized Gain or Loss | 14–20
Tax in the News: *Where to Invest: Growth Stock versus Income Stock* | 14–21
Summary of Basis Adjustments | 14–22

TAX PLANNING CONSIDERATIONS | **14–22**
Tax Consequences of Alice's Proposed Transaction | 14–22
Cost Identification and Documentation Considerations | 14–24
Selection of Property for Making Gifts | 14–24
Selection of Property for Making Bequests | 14–25
Disallowed Losses | 14–25

PROBLEM MATERIALS | **14–26**

CHAPTER 15
PROPERTY TRANSACTIONS: NONTAXABLE EXCHANGES | 15–1

GENERAL CONCEPT OF A NONTAXABLE EXCHANGE | **15–2**

LIKE-KIND EXCHANGES—§ 1031 | **15–3**
Like-Kind Property | 15–3
Tax in the News: *Is The Like-Kind Exchange Provision of § 1031 Being Abused?* | 15–4
Ethical and Equitable Considerations: *An Assumption for a Related-Party Exchange* | 15–5
Tax in the News: *Doing a Like-Kind Exchange Twice* | 15–6
Exchange Requirement | 15–6
Tax in the News: *Be Careful When Selecting A Qualified Intermediary* | 15–7
Ethical and Equitable Considerations: *A Delayed § 1031 Like-Kind Exchange: Identifying More than One Property* | 15–7
Boot | 15–7
Basis and Holding Period of Property Received | 15–8
Reporting Considerations | 15–11

INVOLUNTARY CONVERSIONS—§ 1033 | **15–11**
Involuntary Conversion Defined | 15–11
Computing the Amount Realized | 15–12
Replacement Property | 15–12
Tax in the News: *A Court Upholds the Government's Taking of Property* | 15–13
Time Limitation on Replacement | 15–13
Nonrecognition of Gain | 15–14
Involuntary Conversion of a Personal Residence | 15–15
Reporting Considerations | 15–16

SALE OF A RESIDENCE—§ 121 | **15–16**
Requirements for Exclusion Treatment | 15–16
Exceptions to the Two-Year Ownership Rule | 15–17
Tax in the News: *A Tax Break for Those Who Serve* | 15–18
Tax in the News: *Living in a High-Crime Neighborhood* | 15–19
Calculation of the Amount of the Exclusion | 15–19
Principal Residence | 15–22
Involuntary Conversion and Using §§ 121 and 1033 | 15–22

OTHER NONRECOGNITION PROVISIONS 15–23
Exchange of Stock for Property—§ 1032 15–23
Certain Exchanges of Insurance Policies—§ 1035 15–23
Exchange of Stock for Stock of the Same
Corporation—§ 1036 15–23
Certain Reacquisitions of Real Property—§ 1038 15–23
Transfers of Property between Spouses or Incident to
Divorce—§ 1041 15–23
Rollovers into Specialized Small Business Investment
Companies—§ 1044 15–24
Rollover of Gain from Qualified Small Business Stock
into Another Qualified Small Business Stock—§ 1045 15–24

TAX PLANNING CONSIDERATIONS 15–24
Like-Kind Exchanges 15–24
Involuntary Conversions 15–25
Sale of a Principal Residence 15–25
Tax in the News: *Sale of a Residence and the Home
Office Deduction* 15–26

PROBLEM MATERIALS 15–27

**CHAPTER 16
PROPERTY TRANSACTIONS: CAPITAL
GAINS AND LOSSES** 16–1

GENERAL CONSIDERATIONS 16–2
Rationale for Separate Reporting of Capital Gains
and Losses 16–2
Tax in the News: *A Private Entity Becomes a Public
Corporation* 16–3
General Scheme of Taxation 16–3

CAPITAL ASSETS 16–3
Definition of a Capital Asset 16–3
Ethical and Equitable Considerations: *Inventory
or Capital Asset?* 16–5
Effect of Judicial Action 16–6
Statutory Expansions 16–6

SALE OR EXCHANGE 16–8
Worthless Securities and § 1244 Stock 16–8
Tax in the News: *Know Your Losses* 16–8
Special Rule—Retirement of Corporate Obligations 16–9
Options 16–9
Patents 16–11
Franchises, Trademarks, and Trade Names 16–12
Lease Cancellation Payments 16–13

HOLDING PERIOD 16–14
Review of Special Holding Period Rules 16–15
Tax in the News: *How Long Was the Holding Period
for That Property?* 16–15
Special Rules for Short Sales 16–16
Global Tax Issues: *Trading ADRs on U.S. Stock
Exchanges* 16–17

**TAX TREATMENT OF CAPITAL GAINS AND
LOSSES OF NONCORPORATE TAXPAYERS** 16–19
Capital Gain and Loss Netting Process 16–20
Ethical and Equitable Considerations: *How Much Gain
Has to Be Reported?* 16–23

Qualified Dividend Income 16–23
Alternative Tax on Net Capital Gain 16–23
Treatment of Capital Losses 16–24
Tax in the News: *Costless Capital Gains* 16–26
Reporting Procedures 16–27

**TAX TREATMENT OF CAPITAL GAINS AND
LOSSES OF CORPORATE TAXPAYERS** 16–31

TAX PLANNING CONSIDERATIONS 16–31
Importance of Capital Asset Status 16–31
Planning for Capital Asset Status 16–31
Effect of Capital Asset Status in Transactions Other
Than Sales 16–32
Global Tax Issues: *Capital Gain Treatment in the
United States and Other Countries* 16–32
Stock Sales 16–33
Maximizing Benefits 16–33
Year-End Planning 16–34

PROBLEM MATERIALS 16–34

**CHAPTER 17
PROPERTY TRANSACTIONS: § 1231 AND
RECAPTURE PROVISIONS** 17–1

SECTION 1231 ASSETS 17–3
Relationship to Capital Assets 17–3
Tax in the News: *Capital Gain Confusion* 17–3
Justification for Favorable Tax Treatment 17–4
Property Included 17–4
Property Excluded 17–5
Special Rules for Certain § 1231 Assets 17–5
Tax in the News: *Tornado Blows in a Nondeductible "Loss"* 17–6
Global Tax Issues: *Canadian Slow Depreciation* 17–8
Ethical and Equitable Considerations: *Determining
How Long an Asset Has Been Held* 17–8
General Procedure for § 1231 Computation 17–8

SECTION 1245 RECAPTURE 17–11
Tax in the News: *Ask The CPA About Recapture* 17–12
Section 1245 Property 17–13
Observations on § 1245 17–14

SECTION 1250 RECAPTURE 17–14
Computing Recapture on Nonresidential Real Property 17–15
Computing Recapture on Residential Rental Housing 17–16
Section 1250 Recapture Situations 17–16
Unrecaptured § 1250 Gain (Real Estate 25% Gain) 17–17
Global Tax Issues: *Exchange for Foreign Property Yields
Recognized Recapture Gain* 17–19

CONSIDERATIONS COMMON TO §§ 1245 AND 1250 17–19
Exceptions 17–19
Other Applications 17–20

SPECIAL RECAPTURE PROVISIONS 17–21
Special Recapture for Corporations 17–21
Gain from Sale of Depreciable Property between
Certain Related Parties 17–21
Intangible Drilling Costs 17–21

REPORTING PROCEDURES   **17–22**
Global Tax Issues: *Depreciation Recapture in Other Countries*   17–23
Ethical and Equitable Considerations: *To Depreciate or Not to Depreciate*   17–25

TAX PLANNING CONSIDERATIONS   **17–25**
Timing of § 1231 Gain   17–25

Timing of Recapture   17–25
Postponing and Shifting Recapture   17–29
Avoiding Recapture   17–30
PROBLEM MATERIALS   **17–30**

PART 6: ACCOUNTING PERIODS, ACCOUNTING METHODS, AND DEFERRED COMPENSATION

CHAPTER 18
ACCOUNTING PERIODS AND METHODS   18–1
Tax in the News: *Domestic Production Activities Deduction Created Tax Planning Opportunities*   18–2

ACCOUNTING PERIODS   **18–3**
In General   18–3
Specific Provisions for Partnerships, S Corporations, and Personal Service Corporations   18–3
Ethical and Equitable Considerations: *Who Benefits from the Change in Tax Year?*   18–5
Making the Election   18–6
Changes in the Accounting Period   18–6
Taxable Periods of Less Than One Year   18–7
Mitigation of the Annual Accounting Period Concept   18–9

ACCOUNTING METHODS   **18–10**
Permissible Methods   18–10
Cash Receipts and Disbursements Method—Cash Basis   18–10
Tax in the News: *Who Wants to Be a Producer?*   18–11
Global Tax Issues: *Tax Accounting Methods as an Incentive to Go Foreign*   18–13
Accrual Method   18–13
Global Tax Issues: *Changes in the Tax Rates Lead to Income Shifting*   18–14
Tax in the News: *Payment Is Not Economic Performance*   18–16
Hybrid Method   18–16
Change of Method   18–16
Ethical and Equitable Considerations: *Change in Accounting Method*   18–18

SPECIAL ACCOUNTING METHODS   **18–19**
Installment Method   18–19
Disposition of Installment Obligations   18–24
Interest on Deferred Taxes   18–24
Electing Out of the Installment Method   18–24
Ethical and Equitable Considerations: *Electing Out of Electing Out of the Installment Sale Method*   18–25
Long-Term Contracts   18–25
Ethical and Equitable Considerations: *Intentional Delay*   18–28

INVENTORIES   **18–29**
Determining Inventory Cost   18–30
Global Tax Issues: *Inventory Acquired from a Foreign Subsidiary*   18–32
Tax in the News: *LIFO as a Source of Earnings*   18–34

Ethical and Equitable Considerations: *Preserving the LIFO Reserve*   18–35
The LIFO Election   18–35
Special Inventory Methods Relating to Farming and Ranching   18–36

TAX PLANNING CONSIDERATIONS   **18–36**
Taxable Year   18–36
Cash Method of Accounting   18–36
Installment Method   18–36
Completed Contract Method   18–37
Inventories   18–37

PROBLEM MATERIALS   **18–38**

CHAPTER 19
DEFERRED COMPENSATION   19–1

QUALIFIED PENSION, PROFIT SHARING, AND STOCK BONUS PLANS   **19–4**
Types of Plans   19–4
Tax in the News: *Compensation and Performance*   19–5
Ethical and Equitable Considerations: *Do Cash Balance Plans Discriminate Against Older Employees?*   19–7
Qualification Requirements   19–7
Tax in the News: *Defined Benefit Plans Declining?*   19–11
Tax Consequences to the Employee and Employer   19–12
Global Tax Issues: *Covering Expatriate Employees*   19–12
Limitations on Contributions to and Benefits from Qualified Plans   19–13
§ 401(k) Plans   19–15
Global Tax Issues: *Global Remuneration Approach*   19–16

RETIREMENT PLANS FOR SELF-EMPLOYED INDIVIDUALS   **19–19**
Coverage Requirements   19–19
Contribution Limitations   19–19

INDIVIDUAL RETIREMENT ACCOUNTS (IRAS)   **19–20**
General Rules   19–20
Tax in the News: *Roth 401 (k) Plan Adoptions Rising*   19–23
Penalty Taxes for Excess Contributions   19–26
Taxation of Benefits   19–26

NONQUALIFIED DEFERRED COMPENSATION PLANS   **19–29**
Underlying Rationale for Tax Treatment   19–29

Tax Treatment to the Employer and Employee   19–30

Ethical and Equitable Considerations: *Uneven Compensation Playing Field*   19–33

RESTRICTED PROPERTY PLANS   **19–33**
General Provisions   19–33
Substantial Risk of Forfeiture   19–34
Special Election Available   19–34
Employer Deductions   19–35

STOCK OPTIONS   **19–36**
In General   19–36
Incentive Stock Options   19–36
Nonqualified Stock Options   19–38
Tax in the News: *The Dual Reporting System in the United States*   19–39

TAX PLANNING CONSIDERATIONS   **19–39**
Deferred Compensation   19–39
Qualified Plans   19–40
Self-Employed Retirement Plans   19–40
Individual Retirement Accounts   19–40
Comparison of § 401(k) Plan with IRA   19–40
Nonqualified Deferred Compensation (NQDC) Plans   19–41
Stock Options   19–42
Flexible Benefit Plans   19–43
Liquidating Retirement Assets   19–43

PROBLEM MATERIALS   **19–44**

PART 7: CORPORATIONS AND PARTNERSHIPS

CHAPTER 20
CORPORATIONS AND PARTNERSHIPS   **20–1**

WHAT IS A CORPORATION?   **20–2**
Compliance with State Law   20–2
Entity Classification prior to 1997   20–3
Entity Classification after 1996   20–4

INCOME TAX CONSIDERATIONS   **20–4**
General Tax Consequences of Different Forms of Business Entities   20–4
Individuals and Corporations Compared—An Overview   20–4
Global Tax Issues: *Are Corporate Taxes Too High?*   20–6
Specific Provisions Compared   20–6
Tax in the News: *Variations in Mitigating the Effect of Multiple Taxation*   20–11
Deductions Available Only to Corporations   20–11
Determination of Corporate Tax Liability   20–14
Corporate Filing Requirements   20–14
Reconciliation of Corporate Taxable Income and Accounting Income   20–15

FORMING THE CORPORATION   **20–17**
Capital Contributions   20–17
Transfers to Controlled Corporations   20–17
Ethical and Equitable Considerations: *Selective Incorporation*   20–21

OPERATING THE CORPORATION   **20–21**
Dividend Distributions   20–21
Global Tax Issues: *Transferring Assets to Foreign Corporations—Forget § 351?*   20–22
Stock Redemptions   20–24

LIQUIDATING THE CORPORATION   **20–24**
General Rule of § 331   20–24
Ethical and Equitable Considerations: *Eliminating Burdensome Paperwork*   20–25
Exception to the General Rule   20–25
Basis Determination—§§ 334 and 338   20–25
Effect of the Liquidation on the Corporation   20–26

THE S ELECTION   **20–26**
Qualification for S Status   20–26
Operational Rules   20–28
Tax in the News: *S Corporations and Salaries: More Trauma On the Way!*   20–29

PARTNERSHIPS   **20–31**
Nature of Partnership Taxation   20–31
Partnership Formation   20–32
Partnership Operation   20–34

TAX PLANNING CONSIDERATIONS   **20–36**
Corporate versus Noncorporate Forms of Business Organization   20–36
Global Tax Issues: *Taxing the Income of Foreign Corporations*   20–37
Ethical and Equitable Considerations: *A Year-End Change in Corporate Policy*   20–38
Regular Corporation versus S Status   20–38
Use of an Entity to Reduce the Family Income Tax Burden   20–39
Ethical and Equitable Considerations: *Sharing the Family Business*   20–39

PROBLEM MATERIALS   **20–40**

APPENDIXES

TAX RATE SCHEDULES AND TABLES	A–1	**CITATOR EXAMPLE**	E–1
TAX FORMS	B–1	**COMPREHENSIVE TAX RETURN PROBLEMS**	F–1
GLOSSARY OF TAX TERMS	C–1	**TABLE OF CASES CITED**	G–1
TABLE OF CODE SECTIONS CITED	D–1	**DEPRECIATION**	H–1
TABLE OF REGULATIONS CITED	D–10	**INDEX**	I–1
TABLE OF REVENUE PROCEDURES AND REVENUE RULINGS CITED	D–13		

PART 1

Introduction and Basic Tax Model

Part I provides an introduction to taxation in the United States. Although the primary orientation of this text is income taxation, other types of taxes are also discussed briefly. The purposes of the Federal tax law are examined, and the legislative, administrative, and judicial sources of Federal tax law, including their application to the tax research process, are analyzed. Part I concludes with the introduction of the basic tax model for the individual taxpayer.

CHAPTER 1
An Introduction to Taxation and
Understanding the Federal Tax Law

CHAPTER 2
Working with the Tax Law

CHAPTER 3
Tax Determination; Personal and
Dependency Exemptions; An Overview
of Property Transactions

An Introduction to Taxation and Understanding the Federal Tax Law

LEARNING OBJECTIVES

After completing Chapter 1, you should be able to:

LO.1

Understand some of the history and trends of the Federal income tax.

LO.2

Know some of the criteria for selecting a tax structure; understand the components of a tax structure.

LO.3

Identify the different taxes imposed in the United States at the Federal, state, and local levels.

LO.4

Understand the administration of the tax law, including the audit process utilized by the IRS.

LO.5

Know some of the ethical guidelines involved in tax practice.

LO.6

Recognize the economic, social, equity, and political considerations that justify various aspects of the tax law.

LO.7

Describe the role played by the IRS and the courts in the evolution of the Federal tax system.

OUTLINE

History of U.S. Taxation, 1–2
Early Periods, 1–2
Revenue Acts, 1–3
Historical Trends, 1–3
Criteria Used in the Selection of a Tax Structure, 1–4
The Tax Structure, 1–5
Tax Base, 1–5
Tax Rates, 1–5
Incidence of Taxation, 1–6
Major Types of Taxes, 1–6
Property Taxes, 1–6
Transaction Taxes, 1–8
Death Taxes, 1–10
Gift Taxes, 1–12
Income Taxes, 1–13
Employment Taxes, 1–15

Other U.S. Taxes, 1–17
Proposed U.S. Taxes, 1–17
Tax Administration, 1–19
Internal Revenue Service, 1–19
The Audit Process, 1–19
Statute of Limitations, 1–21
Interest and Penalties, 1–22
Tax Practice, 1–23
Understanding the Federal Tax Law, 1–24
Revenue Needs, 1–24
Economic Considerations, 1–25
Social Considerations, 1–26
Equity Considerations, 1–27
Political Considerations, 1–30
Influence of the Internal Revenue Service, 1–31
Influence of the Courts, 1–32
Summary, 1–33

The primary objective of this chapter is to provide an overview of the Federal tax system. Among the topics discussed are the following:

- The history of the Federal income tax in brief.
- The types of taxes imposed at the Federal, state, and local levels.
- Some highlights of tax law administration.
- Tax concepts that help explain the reasons for various tax provisions.
- The influence that the Internal Revenue Service (IRS) and the courts have had in the evolution of current tax law.

Why does a text devoted primarily to the Federal individual income tax discuss state and local taxes? A simple illustration shows the importance of non-Federal taxes.

EXAMPLE 1

Rick is employed by Flamingo Corporation in San Antonio, Texas, at a salary of $64,000. Rick's employer offers him a chance to transfer to its New York City office at a salary of $82,000. A quick computation indicates that the additional taxes (Federal, state, and local) involve approximately $12,000. ∎

Although Rick must consider many nontax factors before he decides on a job change, he should also evaluate the tax climate. How do state and local taxes compare? For example, neither Texas nor San Antonio imposes an income tax, but New York State and New York City both do. Consequently, what appears to be an $18,000 pay increase is only $6,000 when the additional taxes of $12,000 are taken into account.

LO.1

Understand some of the history and trends of the Federal income tax.

History of U.S. Taxation

Early Periods

The concept of an income tax can hardly be regarded as a newcomer to the Western Hemisphere. An income tax was first enacted in 1634 by the English colonists in the Massachusetts Bay Colony, but the Federal government did not adopt this form of taxation until 1861. In fact, both the Federal Union and the Confederate

States of America used the income tax to raise funds to finance the Civil War. Although modest in its reach and characterized by broad exemptions and low rates, the income tax generated $376 million of revenue for the Federal government during the Civil War.

When the Civil War ended, the need for additional revenue disappeared, and the income tax was repealed. Once again the Federal government was able to finance its operations almost exclusively from customs duties (tariffs). It is interesting to note that the courts held that the Civil War income tax was not contrary to the Constitution.

When a new Federal income tax on individuals was enacted in 1894, its opponents were prepared and were able to successfully challenge its constitutionality. The U.S. Constitution provided that "No Capitation, or other direct, Tax shall be laid, unless in Proportion to the Census or Enumeration herein before directed to be taken." In *Pollock v. Farmers' Loan and Trust Co.*, the U.S. Supreme Court found that taxes on the income of real and personal property were the legal equivalent of a tax on the property involved and, therefore, required apportionment.[1]

A Federal corporate income tax, enacted by Congress in 1909, fared better in the judicial system. The U.S. Supreme Court found this tax to be constitutional because it was treated as an excise tax.[2] In essence, it was a tax on the right to do business in the corporate form. As such, it was likened to a form of the franchise tax.[3] The corporate form of doing business had been developed in the late nineteenth century and was an unfamiliar concept to the framers of the U.S. Constitution. Since a corporation is an entity created under law, jurisdictions possess the right to tax its creation and operation. Using this rationale, many states still impose franchise taxes on corporations.

The ratification of the Sixteenth Amendment to the U.S. Constitution in 1913 sanctioned both the Federal individual and corporate income taxes and, as a consequence, neutralized the continuing effect of the *Pollock* decision.

Revenue Acts

Following ratification of the Sixteenth Amendment, Congress enacted the Revenue Act of 1913. Under this Act, the first Form 1040 was due on March 1, 1914. The law allowed various deductions and personal exemptions of $3,000 for a single individual and $4,000 for married taxpayers. Rates ranged from a low of 2 percent to a high of 6 percent. The 6 percent rate applied only to taxable income in excess of $500,000![4]

Various revenue acts were passed between 1913 and 1939. In 1939, all of these revenue laws were codified into the Internal Revenue Code of 1939. In 1954, a similar codification of the revenue law took place. The current law is entitled the Internal Revenue Code of 1986, which largely carries over the provisions of the 1954 Code. To date, the Code has been amended numerous times since 1986. This matter is discussed further in Chapter 2 under Origin of the Internal Revenue Code.

Historical Trends

The income tax has proved to be a major source of revenue for the Federal government. Figure 1–1, which contains a breakdown of the major revenue sources,[5] demonstrates the importance of the income tax. *Estimated* income tax collections from individuals and corporations amount to 59 percent of the total receipts.

---

[1] 3 AFTR 2602, 15 S.Ct. 912 (USSC, 1895). See Chapter 2 for an explanation of the citations of judicial decisions.

[2] *Flint v. Stone Tracy Co.*, 3 AFTR 2834, 31 S.Ct. 342 (USSC, 1911).

[3] See the discussion of state franchise taxes later in the chapter.

[4] This should be contrasted with the highest 2008 tax rate of 35%, which applies once taxable income exceeds $357,700.

[5] Budget of the United States Government for Fiscal Year 2008, Office of Management and Budget (Washington, D.C.: U.S. Government Printing Office, 2007).

FIGURE 1–1	Federal Budget Receipts—2008
Individual income taxes	47%
Corporation income taxes	12
Social insurance taxes and contributions	35
Excise taxes	2
Other	4
	100%

The need for revenues to finance the war effort during World War II converted the income tax into a *mass tax*. For example, in 1939, less than 6 percent of the U.S. population was subject to the Federal income tax. In 1945, over 74 percent of the population was subject to the Federal income tax.[6]

Certain changes in the income tax law are of particular significance in understanding the Federal income tax. In 1943, Congress passed the Current Tax Payment Act, which provided for the first pay-as-you-go tax system. A pay-as-you-go income tax system requires employers to withhold for taxes a specified portion of an employee's wages. Persons with income from other than wages may have to make quarterly payments to the IRS for estimated taxes due for the year.

One trend that has caused considerable concern is the increasing complexity of the Federal income tax laws. In the name of tax reform, Congress has added to this complexity by frequently changing the tax laws. Most recent legislation continues this trend. Increasingly, this complexity forces many taxpayers to seek the assistance of tax professionals. At this time, therefore, substantial support exists for tax law simplification.

<table>
<tr><td>LO.2</td></tr>
<tr><td>Know some of the criteria for selecting a tax structure; understand the components of a tax structure.</td></tr>
</table>

Criteria Used in the Selection of a Tax Structure

In the eighteenth century, Adam Smith identified the following *canons of taxation*, which are still considered when evaluating a particular tax structure:[7]

- *Equality.* Each taxpayer enjoys fair or equitable treatment by paying taxes in proportion to his or her income level. Ability to pay a tax is the measure of how equitably a tax is distributed among taxpayers.
- *Convenience.* Administrative simplicity has long been valued in formulating tax policy. If a tax is easily assessed and collected and its administrative costs are low, it should be favored. An advantage of the withholding (pay-as-you-go) system is its convenience for taxpayers.
- *Certainty.* A tax structure is *good* if the taxpayer can readily predict when, where, and how a tax will be levied. Individuals and businesses need to know the likely tax consequences of a particular type of transaction.
- *Economy.* A *good* tax system involves only nominal collection costs by the government and minimal compliance costs on the part of the taxpayer. Although the government's cost of collecting Federal taxes amounts to less than one-half of 1 percent of the revenue collected, the complexity of our current tax structure imposes substantial taxpayer compliance costs.

By these canons, the Federal income tax is a contentious product. *Equality* is present as long as one accepts ability to pay as an ingredient of this component.

---

[6]Richard Goode, *The Individual Income Tax* (The Brookings Institution, Washington, D.C.: 1964), pp. 2–4.

[7]*The Wealth of Nations*, Book V, Chapter II, Part II (Dutton, New York: 1910).

TAX *in the News*   **ADAM SMITH STOPPED TOO SOON**

On July 2, 2001, the American Institute of Certified Public Accountants (AICPA) issued suggestions on Federal tax policy. Titled *Guiding Principles of Good Tax Policy: A Framework for Evaluating Tax Proposals*, the monograph sets forth 10 tax principles that are commonly used as indicators of desirable tax policy.

The first four principles are adapted from Adam Smith's *The Wealth of Nations*. The other six are summarized below:

- The tax system should be simple.
- The tax should be neutral in terms of its effect on business decisions.

- The tax system should not reduce economic growth and efficiency.
- The tax should be clear and readily understood so that taxpayers know about it and when it applies.
- The tax should be structured so as to minimize non-compliance.
- The tax system should enable the IRS to predict the amount and timing of revenue production.

Source: *Adapted from a Tax Policy Concept Statement issued by the Tax Division of the AICPA.*

Convenience exists due to a heavy reliance on pay-as-you-go procedures. *Certainty* probably generates the greatest controversy. In one sense, certainty is present since a mass of administrative and judicial guidelines exists to aid in interpreting the tax law. In another sense, however, certainty does not exist since many questions remain unanswered and frequent changes in the tax law by Congress lessen stability. Particularly troublesome in this regard are tax provisions that are given a limited life (e.g., 2007 and 2008). If not extended by Congress, the provisions expire. All too often, Congress does not give the necessary approval in time, and the extension has to be applied retroactively. *Economy* is present if only the collection procedure of the IRS is considered. Economy is not present, however, if one focuses instead on taxpayer compliance efforts and costs.

The Tax Structure

Tax Base

A tax base is the amount to which the tax rate is applied. In the case of the Federal income tax, the tax base is *taxable income*. As noted later in the chapter (Figure 1–2), taxable income is gross income reduced by certain deductions (both business and personal).

Tax Rates

Tax rates are applied to the tax base to determine a taxpayer's liability. The tax rates may be proportional or progressive. A tax is *proportional* if the rate of tax remains constant for any given income level. Examples of proportional taxes include most excise taxes, general sales taxes, and employment taxes (FICA, FUTA).

EXAMPLE 2

Bill has $10,000 of taxable income and pays a tax of $3,000, or 30%. Bob's taxable income is $50,000, and the tax on this amount is $15,000, or 30%. If this constant rate is applied throughout the rate structure, the tax is proportional. ■

A tax is *progressive* if a higher rate of tax applies as the tax base increases. The Federal income tax, Federal gift and estate taxes, and most state income tax rate structures are progressive.

EXAMPLE 3

If Cora, a married individual filing jointly, has taxable income of $10,000, her tax for 2008 is $1,000 for an average tax rate of 10%. If, however, Cora's taxable income is $50,000, her tax will be $6,698 for an average tax rate of 13.4%. The tax is progressive since higher rates are applied to greater amounts of taxable income. ∎

Incidence of Taxation

The degree to which various segments of society share the total tax burden is difficult to assess. Assumptions must be made concerning who absorbs the burden of paying the tax. For example, since dividend payments to shareholders are not deductible by a corporation and are generally taxable to shareholders, the same income is subject to a form of double taxation. Concern over double taxation is valid to the extent that corporations are *not* able to shift the corporate tax to the consumer through higher commodity prices. Many research studies have shown a high degree of shifting of the corporate income tax, converting it into a consumption tax that is borne by the ultimate purchasers of goods.

The progressiveness of the Federal income tax rate structure for individuals has varied over the years. As late as 1986, for example, there were 15 rates, ranging from 0 to 50 percent. These later were reduced to two rates of 15 and 28 percent. Currently, there are six rates ranging from 10 to 35 percent.

LO.3

Identify the different taxes imposed in the United States at the Federal, state, and local levels.

Major Types of Taxes

Property Taxes

Correctly referred to as **ad valorem taxes** because they are based on value, property taxes are a tax on wealth, or capital. In this regard, they have much in common with death taxes and gift taxes discussed later in the chapter. Although property taxes do not tax income, the income actually derived (or the potential for any income) may be relevant insofar as it affects the value of the property being taxed.

Property taxes fall into *two* categories: those imposed on realty and those imposed on personalty, or assets other than land and buildings. Both have added importance since they usually generate a deduction for Federal income tax purposes (see Chapter 10).

Ad Valorem Taxes on Realty.
Property taxes on realty are used exclusively by states and their local political subdivisions, such as cities, counties, and school districts. They represent a major source of revenue for *local* governments, but their importance at the *state* level has waned over the past few years. Some states, for example, have imposed freezes on upward revaluations of residential housing.

How realty is defined can have an important bearing on which assets are subject to tax. This is especially true in jurisdictions that do not impose ad valorem taxes on personalty. Primarily a question of state property law, **realty** generally includes real estate and any capital improvements that are classified as fixtures. Simply stated, a *fixture* is something so permanently attached to the real estate that its removal will cause irreparable damage. A built-in bookcase might well be a fixture, whereas a movable bookcase would not be a fixture. Certain items such as electrical wiring and plumbing cease to be personalty when installed in a building and become realty.

The following are some of the characteristics of ad valorem taxes on realty:

- Property owned by the Federal government is exempt from tax. Similar immunity usually is extended to property owned by state and local governments and by certain charitable organizations.
- Some states provide for lower valuations on property dedicated to agricultural use or other special uses (e.g., wildlife sanctuaries). Reductions in appraised

TAX *in the News*	**HOW A FEW COWS AND BIRDHOUSES CAN SAVE ON PROPERTY TAXES**

Property tax exemptions for the agricultural use (including the raising of livestock) of land are quite common in the United States. So are wildlife exemptions designed to encourage the development and maintenance of natural habitat. Such exemptions result in lower valuations and thus reduce the ad valorem taxes imposed on the land. Although these exemptions were not intended to benefit multinational corporations or their CEOs, some recent examples show that they do.

According to the 2006 wildlife plan filed with Travis County (home of Austin, Texas) for the 185-acre ranch belonging to Michael Dell (the founder of Dell, Inc.), as long as the ranch sprays for fire ants, maintains six water stations

and 11 turkey feeders, and builds 100 birdhouses for bluebirds, the annual property taxes on the property are reduced from $580,780 to $1,355. In addition, Dell and his family and guests can conduct "habitat control" by selective hunting of the white-tailed deer on the property.

In Harris County (home of Houston, Texas), 3,909 acres of old oil fields owned by ExxonMobil qualify for exemptions. By growing trees and grazing cattle on the land, the company was able to have the appraised value of the property reduced to $1.2 million from $38 million.

As these examples show, property tax exemptions need to be carefully defined, or they will produce unintended consequences.

Source: *Adapted from Jennifer Levitz, "Why Texas Firms Are Keeping Cattle on the Back Forty,"* Wall Street Journal, *July 28–29, 2007, pp. A1 and A10.*

valuations may also be available when the property is subject to a conservation easement (e.g., a limitation on further development).

- Some states partially exempt the homestead, or personal residence, portion of property from taxation. Additionally, modern homestead laws normally protect some or all of a personal residence (including a farm or ranch) from the actions of creditors pursuing claims against the owner.
- Lower taxes may apply to a residence owned by a taxpayer age 65 or older.
- When non-income-producing property (e.g., a personal residence) is converted to income-producing property (e.g., a rental house), typically the appraised value increases.
- Some jurisdictions extend immunity from tax for a specified period of time (a *tax holiday*) to new or relocated businesses. A tax holiday can backfire, however, and cause more harm than good. If it is too generous, it can damage the local infrastructure (e.g., less funding for public works and education).

Unlike the ad valorem tax on personalty (see below), the tax on realty is difficult to avoid. Since real estate is impossible to hide, a high degree of taxpayer compliance is not surprising. The only avoidance possibility that is generally available is associated with the assessed value of the property. For this reason, the assessed value of the property—particularly, a value that is reassessed upward—may be subject to controversy and litigation.

The history of the ad valorem tax on realty has been marked by inconsistent application due to a lack of competent tax administration and definitive guidelines for assessment procedures. In recent years, however, some significant improvements have occurred. Some jurisdictions, for example, have computerized their reassessment procedures so that they will immediately affect all property located within the jurisdiction.

Several jurisdictions provide homeowners with a measure of protection from increased property taxes by "freezing" existing assessments and limiting future upward adjustments. Such restrictions on reassessments, however, do not carry over to the new owner when the property is sold. Thus, such measures tend to lock in ownership and restrict the mobility of those who might otherwise change residences.

Ad Valorem Taxes on Personalty. **Personalty** can be defined as all assets that are not realty. It may be helpful to distinguish between the *classification* of an asset (realty or personalty) and the *use* to which it is put. Both realty and personalty can be either business use or personal use property. Examples include a residence (realty that is personal use), an office building (realty that is business use), surgical instruments (personalty that is business use), and regular wearing apparel (personalty that is personal use).[8]

Personalty can also be classified as tangible property or intangible property. For ad valorem tax purposes, intangible personalty includes stocks, bonds, and various other securities (e.g., bank shares).

The following generalizations may be made concerning the ad valorem taxes on personalty:

- Particularly with personalty devoted to personal use (e.g., jewelry, household furnishings), taxpayer compliance ranges from poor to zero. Some jurisdictions do not even attempt to enforce the tax on these items. For automobiles devoted to personal use, many jurisdictions have converted from value as the tax base to arbitrary license fees based on the weight of the vehicle. Some jurisdictions also consider the vehicle's age (e.g., automobiles six years or older are not subject to the ad valorem tax because they are presumed to have little, if any, value).
- For personalty devoted to business use (e.g., inventories, trucks, machinery, equipment), taxpayer compliance and enforcement procedures are measurably better.
- Which jurisdiction possesses the authority to tax movable personalty (e.g., railroad rolling stock) always has been and continues to be a troublesome issue.
- A few states levy an ad valorem tax on intangibles such as stocks and bonds. Taxpayer compliance may be negligible if the state lacks a means of verifying security transactions and ownership.

Transaction Taxes

Transaction taxes, which characteristically are imposed at the manufacturer's, wholesaler's, or retailer's level, cover a wide range of transfers. Like many other types of taxes (e.g., income taxes, death taxes, and gift taxes), transaction taxes usually are not within the exclusive province of any level of taxing authority (Federal, state, local government). As the description implies, these levies place a tax on transfers of property and normally are determined by multiplying the value involved by a percentage rate.

Federal Excise Taxes. Long one of the mainstays of the Federal tax system, Federal **excise taxes** had declined in relative importance until recently. In recent years, Congress substantially increased the Federal excise taxes on such items as tobacco products, fuel and gasoline sales, and air travel. Other Federal excise taxes include the following:

- Manufacturers' excise taxes on trucks, trailers, tires, firearms, sporting equipment, and coal and the gas guzzler tax on automobiles.[9]
- Alcohol taxes.
- Miscellaneous taxes (e.g., the tax on wagering).

The list of transactions covered, although seemingly impressive, has diminished over the years. At one time, for example, there was a Federal excise tax on

---

[8]The distinction, important for ad valorem and for Federal income tax purposes, often becomes confused when personalty is referred to as "personal" property to distinguish it from "real" property. This designation does not give a complete picture of what is involved. The description "personal" residence, however, is clearer, since a residence can be identified as being realty. What is meant, in this case, is realty that is personal use property.

[9]The gas guzzler tax is imposed on the manufacturers of automobiles and increases in amount as the mileage ratings per gallon of gas decrease.

admission to amusement facilities (e.g., theaters) and on the sale of such items as leather goods, jewelry, furs, and cosmetics.

When reviewing the list of both Federal and state excise taxes, one should recognize the possibility that the tax laws may be trying to influence social behavior. For example, the gas guzzler tax is intended as an incentive for the automobile companies to build fuel-efficient cars.

State and Local Excise Taxes. Many state and local excise taxes parallel the Federal version. Thus, all states tax the sale of gasoline, liquor, and tobacco products; however, unlike the Federal version, the rates vary significantly. For gasoline products, for example, compare the 36 cents per gallon imposed by the state of Washington with the 7.5 cents per gallon levied by the state of Georgia. For tobacco sales, contrast the 7 cents per pack of 20 cigarettes in effect in South Carolina with the $2.575 per pack applicable in the state of New Jersey. Given the latter situation, is it surprising that the smuggling of cigarettes for resale elsewhere is so widespread?

Other excise taxes found at some state and local levels include those on admission to amusement facilities, on the sale of playing cards, and on prepared foods. Most states impose a transaction tax on the transfer of property that requires the recording of documents (e.g., real estate sales).[10] Some extend the tax to the transfer of stocks and other securities.

Over the last few years, two types of excise taxes imposed at the local level have become increasingly popular: the hotel occupancy tax and the rental car "surcharge." Since they tax the visitor who cannot vote, they are a political windfall and are often used to finance special projects that generate civic pride (e.g., convention centers, state-of-the-art sports arenas). These levies can be significant, as demonstrated by Houston's hotel tax of 17 percent and the car rental tax and fees of 35 percent at the Kansas City, Missouri airport.

General Sales Taxes. The distinction between an excise tax and a general **sales tax** is easy to make. One is restricted to a particular transaction (e.g., the 18.4 cents per gallon Federal excise tax on the sale of gasoline), while the other covers a multitude of transactions (e.g., a 5 percent tax on *all* retail sales). In actual practice, however, the distinction is not always that clear. Some state statutes exempt certain transactions from the application of the general sales taxes (e.g., sales of food to be consumed off the premises, sales of certain medicines and drugs). Also, it is not uncommon to find that rates vary depending on the commodity involved. Many states, for example, allow preferential rates for the sale of agricultural equipment or apply different rates (either higher or lower than the general rate) to the sale of automobiles. With many of these special exceptions and classifications of rates, a general sales tax can take on the appearance of a collection of individual excise taxes.

A **use tax** is an ad valorem tax, usually at the same rate as the sales tax, on the use, consumption, or storage of tangible property purchased outside the state but used within the state. The purpose of a use tax is to prevent the avoidance of a sales tax. Every state that imposes a general sales tax levied on the consumer also has a use tax. Alaska, Delaware, Montana, New Hampshire, and Oregon have neither tax. There is no Federal general sales or use tax.

EXAMPLE 4

The state where Susan resides imposes a 5% general sales tax, but the neighboring state has no sales tax. Susan purchases an automobile for $20,000 from a dealer located in the neighboring state. Has she saved $1,000 in sales taxes? No, because the state use tax will pick up

---

[10]This type of tax has much in common with the stamp tax levied by Great Britain on the American colonies during the pre-Revolutionary War period in U.S. history.

the difference between the tax paid in the neighboring state (none here) and what would have been paid in the state in which Susan resides. ∎

The use tax is difficult to enforce for many purchases and is therefore often avoided. In some cases, for example, it may be worthwhile to make purchases through an out-of-state mail-order business or the Web sites of local vendors. In spite of shipping costs, the avoidance of the local sales tax that otherwise might be incurred can lower the cost of such products as computer components. Some states are taking steps to curtail this loss of revenue. For items such as automobiles (refer to Example 4), the use tax probably will be collected when the purchaser registers the item in his or her home state.

ETHICAL and EQUITABLE *Considerations*   MAKING GOOD USE OF OUT-OF-STATE RELATIVES

Marcus, a resident of Texas, has found the ideal gift for his wife in celebration of their upcoming wedding anniversary— a $22,000 diamond tennis bracelet. However, Marcus is appalled at the prospect of paying the state and local sales tax of $1,815 (combined rate of 8.25 percent). He, therefore, asks his aunt, a resident of Montana, to purchase the bracelet. The jewelry store lists the aunt as the buyer and ships the bracelet to her. Prior to the anniversary, Marcus receives the bracelet from his aunt. Is Marcus able to save $1,815 on the present for his wife? What can go wrong?

Local general sales taxes, over and above those levied by the state, are common. It is not unusual to find taxpayers living in the same state but paying different general sales taxes due to the location of their residence.

EXAMPLE 5

Pete and Sam both live in a state that has a general sales tax of 3%. Sam, however, resides in a city that imposes an additional general sales tax of 2%. Even though Pete and Sam live in the same state, one is subject to a rate of 3%, while the other pays a tax of 5%. ∎

For various reasons, some jurisdictions will suspend the application of a general sales tax. New York City does so to stimulate shopping. Illinois has permanently suspended the tax on construction materials used to build power-generating plants. Texas and numerous other states do so annually on clothing right before the beginning of the school year. Such suspensions are similar to the tax holidays granted for ad valorem tax purposes. As state revenues have declined in recent years, many states have had misgivings about the advisability of scheduling further sales tax holidays. Turning off the spigot could be political suicide, however. These holidays are extremely popular with both merchants and shoppers, so their termination could cause severe voter backlash at the polls.

Severance Taxes. **Severance taxes** are transaction taxes that are based on the notion that the state has an interest in its natural resources (e.g., oil, gas, iron ore, coal). Therefore, a tax is imposed when the natural resources are extracted.

For some states, severance taxes can be a significant source of revenue. Due to the severance tax on oil production, Alaska has been able to avoid both a state income tax and a state general sales tax.

Death Taxes

A **death tax** is a tax on the right to transfer property or to receive property upon the death of the owner. Consequently, a death tax falls into the category of an excise tax. If the death tax is imposed on the right to pass property at death, it is classified as an **estate tax**. If it taxes the right to receive property from a decedent, it is termed an **inheritance tax**. As is typical of other types of excise taxes, the value of the property transferred provides the base for determining the amount of the death tax.

The Federal government imposes only an estate tax. Many state governments, however, levy inheritance taxes, estate taxes, or both. Some states (e.g., Florida, Texas) levy neither tax.

E X A M P L E   6

At the time of her death, Wilma lived in a state that imposes an inheritance tax but not an estate tax. Mary, one of Wilma's heirs, lives in the same state. Wilma's estate is subject to the Federal estate tax, and Mary is subject to the state inheritance tax. ∎

The Federal Estate Tax. The Revenue Act of 1916 incorporated the estate tax into the tax law. Never designed to generate a large amount of revenue, the tax was originally intended to prevent large concentrations of wealth from being kept within a family for many generations. Whether this objective has been accomplished is debatable. Like the income tax, estate taxes can be reduced through various planning procedures.

The gross estate includes property the decedent owned at the time of death. It also includes property interests, such as life insurance proceeds paid to the estate or to a beneficiary other than the estate if the deceased-insured had any ownership rights in the policy. Quite simply, the gross estate represents property interests subject to Federal estate taxation.[11] All property included in the gross estate is valued as of the date of death or, if the alternate valuation date is elected, six months later.[12]

Deductions from the gross estate in arriving at the taxable estate include funeral and administration expenses, certain taxes, debts of the decedent, casualty losses[13] incurred during the administration of the estate, transfers to charitable organizations, and, in some cases, the marital deduction. The *marital deduction* is available for amounts actually passing to a surviving spouse (a widow or widower).

Once the taxable estate has been determined and certain taxable gifts made by the decedent during life have been added to it, the estate tax can be computed. From the amount derived from the appropriate tax rate schedules, various credits should be subtracted to arrive at the tax, if any, that is due.[14] Although many other credits are also available, probably the most significant is the *unified transfer tax credit*. The main reason for this credit is to eliminate or reduce the estate tax liability for modest estates. For 2008, the amount of the credit is $780,800. Based on the estate tax rates, the credit exempts a tax base of $2 million.

E X A M P L E   7

Ned made no taxable gifts before his death in 2008. If Ned's taxable estate amounts to $2 million or less, no Federal estate tax is due because of the application of the unified transfer tax credit. Under the tax law, the estate tax on a taxable estate of $2 million is $780,800. ∎

The Federal estate tax has been criticized by some for imposing a hardship on small businesses and, in particular, on family farms. Many believe that the need to pay the estate tax on the death of a major owner often forces the heirs to dissolve and liquidate the family business. In the Tax Relief Reconciliation Act of 2001, Congress responded to this criticism and scheduled a phaseout of the Federal estate

---

[11]For further information on these matters, see *South-Western Federal Taxation: Corporations, Partnerships, Estates, and Trusts.*

[12]See the discussion of the alternate valuation date in Chapter 14.

[13]For a definition of "casualty losses," see the Glossary of Tax Terms in Appendix C.

[14]For tax purposes, it is always crucial to appreciate the difference between a deduction and a credit. A *credit* is a dollar-for-dollar reduction of tax liability.

A *deduction*, however, only benefits the taxpayer to the extent of his or her tax bracket. An estate in a 50% tax bracket, for example, would need $2 of deductions to prevent $1 of tax liability. In contrast, $1 of credit neutralizes $1 of tax liability.

tax, to be accomplished over a 10-year period by increasing the amount of the credit at periodic intervals. Consequently, the Federal estate tax is due to be eliminated in 2010. For budgetary reasons, the Act included a "sunset" provision that reinstates the Federal estate tax (as it was prior to the phaseout) as of January 1, 2011. Although some in Congress have tried to enact legislation that would repeal the sunset provision, their efforts have not been successful. As it stands now, therefore, the Federal estate tax is scheduled to end and then begin again. Obviously, this is a situation that cannot last, as it makes meaningful estate planning impossible. (Sunset provisions are discussed further later in the chapter.)

State Death Taxes. As noted earlier, most states levy an inheritance tax, an estate tax, or both. The two forms of death taxes differ according to whether the tax is imposed on the heirs or on the estate.

Characteristically, an inheritance tax divides the heirs into classes based on their relationship to the decedent. The more closely related the heir, the lower the rates imposed and the greater the exemption allowed. Some states completely exempt from taxation amounts passing to a surviving spouse.

Gift Taxes

Like a death tax, a **gift tax** is an excise tax levied on the right to transfer property. In this case, however, the tax is imposed on transfers made during the owner's life and not at death. A gift tax applies only to transfers that are not offset by full and adequate consideration.

EXAMPLE 8

Carl sells property worth $20,000 to his daughter for $1,000. Although property worth $20,000 has been transferred, only $19,000 represents a gift, since this is the portion not supported by full and adequate consideration. ■

The Federal Gift Tax. First enacted in 1932, the Federal gift tax was intended to complement the estate tax. If lifetime transfers by gift were not taxed, it would be possible to avoid the estate tax and escape taxation entirely.

Only taxable gifts are subject to the gift tax. For this purpose, a taxable gift is measured by the fair market value of the property on the date of transfer less the *annual exclusion per donee* and, in some cases, less the *marital deduction,* which allows tax-free transfers between spouses. Each donor is allowed an annual exclusion of $12,000 in 2008 (also $12,000 in 2007) for each donee.[15]

EXAMPLE 9

On December 31, 2007, Louise (a widow) gives $12,000 to each of her four married children, their spouses, and her eight grandchildren. On January 2, 2008, she repeats the procedure, giving $12,000 to each recipient. Due to the annual exclusion, Louise has not made a taxable gift, although she transferred $192,000 [$12,000 (annual exclusion) × 16 (donees)] in 2007 and $192,000 [$12,000 (annual exclusion) × 16 (donees)] in 2008, for a total of $384,000 ($192,000 + $192,000). ■

A special election applicable to married persons allows one-half of the gift made by the donor-spouse to be treated as being made by the nondonor-spouse (*gift splitting*). This election to split the gifts of property made to third persons has the effect of increasing the number of annual exclusions available. Also, it allows the use of the nondonor-spouse's unified transfer tax credit and may lower the tax rates that will apply.

---

[15]The purpose of the annual exclusion is to avoid the need to report and pay a tax on *modest* gifts. Without the exclusion, the IRS could face a real problem of taxpayer noncompliance. The annual exclusion is indexed as the level of inflation warrants. The exclusion was $3,000 through 1981, $10,000 from 1982 to 2000, and $11,000 from 2001 through 2005.

The gift tax rate schedule is the same as that applicable to the estate tax. The schedule is commonly referred to as the *unified transfer tax schedule.*

The Federal gift tax is *cumulative* in effect. What this means is that the tax base for current taxable gifts includes past taxable gifts. Although a credit is allowed for prior gift taxes, the result of adding past taxable gifts to current taxable gifts could be to force the donor into a higher tax bracket.[16] Like the Federal estate tax rates, the Federal gift tax rates are progressive (see Example 3 earlier in this chapter).

The unified transfer tax credit is available for all taxable gifts; the amount of this credit for 2008 is $345,800. There is, however, only one unified transfer tax credit, and it applies both to taxable gifts and to the Federal estate tax. In a manner of speaking, therefore, once the unified transfer tax credit has been exhausted for Federal gift tax purposes, it is no longer available to insulate a decedent's transfers from the Federal estate tax, except to the extent of the excess of the credit amount for estate tax purposes over that for gift tax purposes.

As noted above, the Tax Relief Reconciliation Act of 2001 proposes to phase out the Federal estate tax. The reason for the elimination of the estate tax does not apply to the gift tax. Unlike death, which is involuntary, the making of a gift is a voluntary parting of ownership. Thus, the ownership of a business can be transferred gradually without incurring drastic and immediate tax consequences. As a result, the Federal gift tax is to be retained with the unified transfer tax credit frozen at $345,800 (which covers a taxable gift of $1 million).

Even though a larger unified transfer tax credit is available for transfers by death ($780,800 for 2008), lifetime gifts continue to be attractive. If income-producing property is involved (e.g., marketable securities, rental real estate), a gift may reduce income taxes for the family unit by shifting subsequent income to lower-bracket donees. If the gift involves property that is expected to appreciate in value (e.g., life insurance policies, real estate, artworks), future increases in value will be assigned to the donee and will not be included in the donor's estate. Also important is that due to the annual exclusion ($12,000 per donee in 2008), some of the gift is not subject to any gift tax. Recall that the gift-splitting election enables married donors to double up on the annual exclusion.

State Gift Taxes. The states currently imposing a state gift tax are Connecticut, Louisiana, North Carolina, and Tennessee. Most of the laws provide for lifetime exemptions and annual exclusions. Like the Federal gift tax, the state taxes are cumulative in effect. But unlike the Federal version, the amount of tax depends on the relationship between the donor and the donee. Like state inheritance taxes, larger exemptions and lower rates apply when the donor and donee are closely related to each other.

Income Taxes

Income taxes are levied by the Federal government, most states, and some local governments. The trend in recent years has been to place greater reliance on this method of taxation. This trend is not consistent with what is happening in other countries, and in this sense, our system of taxation is somewhat different.

Income taxes generally are imposed on individuals, corporations, and certain fiduciaries (estates and trusts). Most jurisdictions attempt to assure the collection of income taxes by requiring pay-as-you-go procedures, including withholding requirements for employees and estimated tax prepayments for all taxpayers.

Federal Income Taxes. Chapters 3 through 19 deal with the application of the Federal income tax to individuals. The procedure for determining the Federal income tax applicable to individuals is summarized in Figure 1–2.

---

[16]For further information on the Federal gift tax, see *South-Western Federal Taxation: Corporations, Partnerships, Estates, and Trusts.*

FIGURE 1–2   Formula for Federal Income Tax on Individuals

Income (broadly conceived)	$ xx,xxx
Less: Exclusions (income that is not subject to tax)	(x,xxx)
Gross income (income that is subject to tax)	$ xx,xxx
Less: Certain deductions (usually referred to as deductions *for* adjusted gross income)	(x,xxx)
Adjusted gross income	$ xx,xxx
Less: The greater of certain personal and employee deductions (usually referred to as *itemized deductions*)	
or	
The standard deduction (including any additional standard deduction)	(x,xxx)
and	
Less: Personal and dependency exemptions	(x,xxx)
Taxable income	$ xx,xxx
Tax on taxable income (see the Tax Tables and Tax Rate Schedules in Appendix A)	$ x,xxx
Less: Tax credits (including Federal income tax withheld and other prepayments of Federal income taxes)	(xxx)
Tax due (or refund)	$ xxx

Like its individual counterpart, the Federal corporate income tax is progressive in nature. But its application does not require the computation of adjusted gross income (AGI) and does not provide for the standard deduction and personal and dependency exemptions. All allowable deductions of a corporation fall into the business-expense category. In effect, therefore, the taxable income of a corporation is the difference between gross income (net of exclusions) and deductions.

Chapter 20 summarizes the rules relating to corporations. For an in-depth treatment of the Federal income tax as it affects corporations, estates, and trusts, see *South-Western Federal Taxation: Corporations, Partnerships, Estates, and Trusts,* 2009 Edition, Chapters 2 through 9, 12, and 19.

State Income Taxes. All but the following states impose an income tax on individuals: Alaska, Florida, Nevada, South Dakota, Texas, Washington, and Wyoming.

Some of the characteristics of state income taxes are summarized as follows:

- With few exceptions, all states require some form of withholding procedures.
- Most states use as the tax base the income determination made for Federal income tax purposes.
- A minority of states go even further and impose a flat rate upon AGI as computed for Federal income tax purposes. Several apply a rate to the Federal income tax liability. This is often referred to as the piggyback approach to state income taxation. Although the term *piggyback* does not lend itself to precise definition, in this context, it means making use, for state income tax purposes, of what was done for Federal income tax purposes.
- Some states are somewhat eroding the piggyback approach by "decoupling" from selected recent tax reductions passed by Congress. The purpose of the decoupling is to retain state revenue that would otherwise be lost. In other words, the state cannot afford to allow its taxpayers the same deductions for state purposes that are allowed for Federal purposes.

- Because of the tie-ins to the Federal return, a state may be notified of any changes made by the IRS upon audit of a Federal return. In recent years, the exchange of information between the IRS and state taxing authorities has increased. Lately, some states (e.g., California) are playing a major role in revealing tax shelter abuses to the IRS.
- Most states allow a deduction for personal and dependency exemptions. Some states substitute a tax credit for a deduction.
- A diminishing minority of states allow a deduction for Federal income taxes.
- Most states allow their residents some form of tax credit for income taxes paid to other states.
- The objective of most states is to tax the income of residents and those who regularly conduct business within the state (e.g., nonresidents who commute to work). These states also purport to tax the income of nonresidents who earn income within the state on an itinerant basis. Usually, however, the only visitors actually taxed are highly paid athletes and entertainers. This so-called *jock tax* has been much criticized as being discriminatory due to its selective imposition.
- The due date for filing generally is the same as for the Federal income tax (the fifteenth day of the fourth month following the close of the tax year).
- Some states have occasionally instituted amnesty programs that allow taxpayers to pay back taxes (and interest) on unreported income with no (or reduced) penalty. In many cases, the tax amnesty has generated enough revenue to warrant the authorization of follow-up programs covering future years—one state has had four amnesty periods, and seven states have had at least three.[17] Amnesties usually include other taxes as well (e.g., sales, franchise, severance). One major advantage of amnesty programs is that they uncover taxpayers that were previously unknown to the taxing authority.

Nearly all states have an income tax applicable to corporations. It is difficult to determine those that do not because a state franchise tax sometimes is based in part on the income earned by the corporation.[18]

Local Income Taxes. Cities imposing an income tax include, but are not limited to, Baltimore, Cincinnati, Cleveland, Detroit, Kansas City (Missouri), New York, Philadelphia, and St. Louis. The application of a city income tax is not limited to local residents.

Employment Taxes

Classification as an employee usually leads to the imposition of **employment taxes** and to the requirement that the employer withhold specified amounts for income

---

[17]Although the suggestion has been made, no comparable amnesty program has been offered for the Federal income tax.

[18]See the discussion of franchise taxes later in the chapter.

taxes. The rules governing the withholding for income taxes are discussed in Chapter 13. The material that follows concentrates on the two major employment taxes: FICA (Federal Insurance Contributions Act—commonly referred to as the Social Security tax) and FUTA (Federal Unemployment Tax Act). Both taxes can be justified by social and public welfare considerations: FICA offers some measure of retirement security, and FUTA provides a modest source of income in the event of loss of employment.

Employment taxes come into play only if two conditions are satisfied. First, is the individual involved an *employee* (as opposed to *self-employed*)? The differences between an employee and a self-employed person are discussed in Chapter 9. Second, if the individual involved is an employee, is he or she covered under FICA or FUTA or both? The coverage of both of these taxes is summarized in Exhibit 13–2 in Chapter 13.[19]

FICA Taxes. The **FICA tax** rates and wage base have increased steadily over the years. It is difficult to imagine that the initial rate in 1937 was only 1 percent of the first $3,000 of covered wages. Thus, the maximum tax due was only $30!

Currently, the FICA tax has two components: Social Security tax (old age, survivors, and disability insurance) *and* Medicare tax (hospital insurance). The Social Security tax rate is 6.2 percent for 2007 and 2008, and the Medicare tax rate is 1.45 percent for these years. The base amount for Social Security is $97,500 for 2007 and $102,000 for 2008. There is no limit on the base amount for the Medicare tax. The employer must match the employee's portion for both the Social Security tax and the Medicare tax.

A spouse employed by another spouse is subject to FICA. However, children under the age of 18 who are employed in a parent's unincorporated trade or business are exempted.

Taxpayers who are not employees (e.g., sole proprietors, independent contractors) may also be subject to Social Security taxes. Known as the self-employment tax, the rates are 12.4 percent for Social Security and 2.9 percent for Medicare, or twice that applicable to an employee. The tax is imposed on net self-employment income up to a base amount of $97,500 for 2007 and $102,000 for 2008.

FUTA Taxes. The purpose of the **FUTA tax** is to provide funds that the states can use to administer unemployment benefits. This leads to the somewhat unusual situation of one tax being handled by both Federal and state governments. The end result of such joint administration is to compel the employer to observe two sets of rules. Thus, state and Federal returns must be filed and payments made to both governmental units.

In 2008, FUTA is 6.2 percent on the first $7,000 of covered wages paid during the year to each employee. The Federal government allows a credit for FUTA paid (or allowed under a merit rating system) to the state. The credit cannot exceed 5.4 percent of the covered wages. Thus, the amount required to be paid to the IRS could be as low as 0.8 percent (6.2% − 5.4%).

States follow a policy of reducing the unemployment tax on employers who experience stable employment. Thus, an employer with little or no employee turnover might find that the state rate drops to as low as 0.1 percent or, in some states, even to zero. The reason for the merit rating credit is that the state has to pay fewer unemployment benefits when employment is steady.

FUTA differs from FICA in the sense that the incidence of taxation falls entirely upon the employer. A few states, however, levy a special tax on employees to

---

[19]Chapter 13 includes coverage of the self-employment tax (the Social Security and Medicare taxes for self-employed persons). See also Circular E, *Employer's Tax Guide,* issued by the IRS as Publication 15.

provide either disability benefits or supplemental unemployment compensation, or both.

Other U.S. Taxes

To complete the overview of the U.S. tax system, some missing links need to be covered that do not fit into the classifications discussed elsewhere in this chapter.

Federal Customs Duties.
One tax that has not yet been mentioned is the tariff on certain imported goods.[20] Generally referred to as customs duties or levies, this tax, together with selective excise taxes, provided most of the revenues needed by the Federal government during the nineteenth century. In view of present times, it is remarkable to note that tariffs and excise taxes alone paid off the national debt in 1835 and enabled the U.S. Treasury to pay a surplus of $28 million to the states.

In recent years, tariffs have served the nation more as an instrument for carrying out protectionist policies than as a means of generating revenue. Thus, a particular U.S. industry might be saved from economic disaster, so the argument goes, by imposing customs duties on the importation of foreign goods that can be sold at lower prices. Protectionists contend that the tariff thereby neutralizes the competitive edge held by the producer of the foreign goods.[21]

Protectionist policies seem more appropriate for less-developed countries whose industrial capacity has not yet matured. In a world where a developed country should have everything to gain by encouraging international free trade, such policies may be of dubious value. History shows that tariffs often lead to retaliatory action on the part of the nation or nations affected.

Miscellaneous State and Local Taxes.
Most states impose a franchise tax on corporations. Basically, a **franchise tax** is levied on the right to do business in the state. The base used for the determination of the tax varies from state to state. Although corporate income considerations may come into play, this tax most often is based on the capitalization of the corporation (either with or without certain long-term indebtedness).

Closely akin to the franchise tax are **occupational fees** applicable to various trades or businesses, such as a liquor store license, a taxicab permit, or a fee to practice a profession such as law, medicine, or accounting. Most of these are not significant revenue producers and fall more into the category of licenses than taxes. The revenue derived is used to defray the cost incurred by the jurisdiction in regulating the business or profession in the interest of the public good.

Proposed U.S. Taxes

Considerable dissatisfaction with the U.S. Federal income tax has led to several recent proposals that, to say the least, are rather drastic in nature. One proposal would retain the income tax but with substantial change. Two other proposals would replace the Federal income tax with an entirely different system of taxation.

The Flat Tax.
One proposal is for a **flat tax** that would replace the current graduated income tax with a single rate of 17 percent. Large personal exemptions (e.g., approximately $30,000 for a family of four) would allow many low- and

---

[20]Less-developed countries that rely principally on one or more major commodities (e.g., oil, coffee) are prone to favor *export* duties as well.

[21]The North American Free Trade Agreement (NAFTA), enacted in 1993, substantially reduced the tariffs on trade between Canada, Mexico, and the United States. The General Agreement on Tariffs and Trade (GATT) legislation enacted in 1994 also reduced tariffs on selected commodities among 124 signatory nations.

middle-income taxpayers to pay no tax. All other deductions would be eliminated, and no tax would be imposed on income from investments.

Various other versions of the flat tax have been suggested that would retain selected deductions (e.g., interest on home mortgages and charitable contributions) and not exclude all investment income from taxation.

The major advantage of the flat tax is its simplicity. Everyone agrees that the current Federal income tax is inappropriately complex. Consequently, compliance costs are disproportionately high. Proponents of the flat tax further believe that simplifying the income tax will significantly reduce the current "tax gap" (i.e., the difference between the amount of taxes that *should be paid* and what is *actually paid*).

Political considerations are a major obstacle to the enactment of a flat tax in its pure form. Special interest groups, such as charitable organizations and mortgage companies, are not apt to be complacent over the elimination of a tax deduction that benefits their industry. In addition, there is uncertainty as to the economic effects of the tax.

It is interesting to note that Russia's attempt at a progressive income tax was quite disastrous. Not only did high rates drive capital out of the country but also failure to report income was rampant. In early 2000, the income tax was repealed and replaced with a 13 percent flat tax. To date, the flat tax has worked quite well. Several Baltic states (Estonia, Latvia, and Lithuania) have followed Russia's example. Albania, Romania, Slovakia, Georgia, Ukraine, and Serbia have also adopted a flat tax.

Value Added Tax. The **value added tax (VAT)** is one of two proposals that would replace the Federal income tax. Under the VAT, a business would pay the tax (approximately 17 percent) on all of the materials and services required to manufacture its product. In effect, the VAT taxes the increment in value as goods move through production and manufacturing stages to the marketplace. Moreover, the VAT paid by the producer will be reflected in the selling price of the goods. Thus, the VAT is a tax on consumption.

The United States is the only country in the OECD (Organization for Economic Cooperation and Development) that does not have a VAT. Approximately 136 countries around the world use a VAT, ranging from 5 percent in Japan to 25 percent in Denmark. Instead, the United States relies heavily on income taxes.

Sales Tax. A **national sales tax** differs from a VAT in that it would be collected on the final sale of goods and services. Consequently, it is collected from the consumer and not from businesses that add value to the product. Like the VAT, the national sales tax is intended to replace the Federal income tax.

A current proposal for a national sales tax, called the "Fair Tax," would tax all purchases, including food and medicine, at approximately 23 percent. Exempt items include business expenses, used goods, and the costs of education. The "Fair Tax" would replace not only the income tax (both individual and corporate) but also payroll taxes (including the self-employment tax) and the gift and estate taxes. Current sponsors of this proposal, which is reintroduced in each new Congress, include Saxby Chambliss (R–Ga.) in the Senate and John Linder (R–Ga.) in the House.

Critics contend that both forms of consumption taxes, a VAT and a national sales tax, are regressive. They impose more of a burden on low-income taxpayers who must spend larger proportions of their incomes on essential purchases. The proposals attempt to remedy this inequity by granting some sort of credit, rebate, or exemption to low-income taxpayers.

In terms of taxpayer compliance, a value added tax is preferable to a national sales tax. Without significant collection efforts, a national sales tax could easily be circumvented by resorting to a barter system of doing business. Its high rate would also encourage smuggling and black market activities.

Tax Administration

LO.4

Understand the administration of the tax law, including the audit process utilized by the IRS.

Internal Revenue Service

The responsibility for administering the Federal tax laws rests with the Treasury Department. Administratively, the IRS is part of the Department of the Treasury and is responsible for enforcing the tax laws. The Commissioner of Internal Revenue is appointed by the President and is responsible for establishing policy and supervising the activities of the IRS.

The Audit Process

Selection of Returns for Audit. Due to budgetary limitations, only a small minority of tax returns are audited. For the fiscal year ended September 30, 2006, the IRS audited only 1 percent of all individual income tax returns (about one in every 103 returns filed). Nevertheless, the number of individual income tax returns audited has increased significantly over the past five years.

The IRS utilizes mathematical formulas and statistical sampling techniques to select tax returns that are most likely to contain errors and to yield substantial amounts of additional tax revenues upon audit. The mathematical formula yields what is called a Discriminant Information Function (DIF) score. It is the DIF score given to a particular return that may lead to its selection for audit.

To update the DIF components, the IRS selects a cross section of returns, which are subject to various degrees of inspection (i.e., information return verification, correspondence, and face-to-face audits with filers). The results of these audits highlight areas of taxpayer noncompliance and enable the IRS to use its auditors more productively. In recent years, IRS audits have resulted in an increasing number of "no change" results (see below). This indicates that the IRS is not always choosing the right returns to audit (i.e., the ones with errors).

Though the IRS does not openly disclose all of its audit selection techniques, the following observations may be made concerning the probability of selection for audit:

- Certain groups of taxpayers are subject to audit much more frequently than others. These groups include individuals with large amounts of gross income, self-employed individuals with substantial business income and deductions, and taxpayers with prior tax deficiencies. Also vulnerable are businesses that receive a large proportion of their receipts in cash (e.g., cafés and small service businesses) and thus have a high potential for tax avoidance.

EXAMPLE 10

Jack owns and operates a liquor store on a cash-and-carry basis. Since all of Jack's sales are for cash, he might well be a prime candidate for an audit by the IRS. Cash transactions are easier to conceal than those made on credit. ∎

- If information returns (e.g., Form 1099, Form W–2) are not in substantial agreement with reported income, an audit can be anticipated.
- If an individual's itemized deductions are in excess of norms established for various income levels, the probability of an audit is increased.
- Filing of a refund claim by the taxpayer may prompt an audit of the return.
- Information obtained from other sources (e.g., informants, news items) may lead to an audit. Recently, for example, the IRS advised its agents by Internet to be on the alert for newspaper accounts of large civil court judgments. The advice was based on the assumption that many successful plaintiffs were not reporting as income the taxable punitive damages portion of awards.

The tax law permits the IRS to pay rewards to persons who provide information that leads to the detection and punishment of those who violate the tax laws. The rewards may not exceed 30 percent of the taxes, fines, and penalties recovered as a result of such information.

EXAMPLE 11

After 15 years of service, Rita is discharged by her employer, Dr. Smith. Shortly thereafter, the IRS receives an anonymous letter stating that Dr. Smith keeps two separate sets of books and that the one used for tax reporting substantially understates his cash receipts. ■

EXAMPLE 12

During a divorce proceeding, it is revealed that Leo, a public official, kept large amounts of cash in a shoe box at home. This information is widely disseminated by the news media and comes to the attention of the IRS. Needless to say, the IRS is interested in knowing whether these funds originated from a taxable source and, if so, whether they were reported on Leo's income tax returns. ■

Types of Audits. Once a return is selected for audit, the taxpayer is notified. If the issue involved is minor, the matter often can be resolved simply by correspondence (a **correspondence audit**) between the IRS and the taxpayer.

EXAMPLE 13

During 2006, Janet received dividend income from Green Corporation. In early 2007, Green Corporation reported the payment on Form 1099–DIV (an information return for reporting dividend payments), the original being sent to the IRS and a copy to Janet. When preparing her income tax return for 2006, Janet apparently overlooked this particular Form 1099–DIV and failed to include the dividend on Schedule B, Interest and Dividend Income, of Form 1040. In 2008, the IRS sends a notice to Janet calling her attention to the omission and requesting a remittance for additional tax, interest, and penalty. Janet promptly mails a check to the IRS for the requested amount, and the matter is closed. ■

Other examinations are generally classified as either office audits or field audits. An **office audit** usually is restricted in scope and is conducted in the facilities of the IRS. In contrast, a **field audit** involves an examination of numerous items reported on the return and is conducted on the premises of the taxpayer or the taxpayer's representative.

Upon the conclusion of the audit, the examining agent issues a Revenue Agent's Report (RAR) that summarizes the findings. The RAR will result in a refund (the tax was overpaid), a deficiency (the tax was underpaid), or a *no change* (the tax was correct) finding. If, during the course of an audit, a special agent accompanies (or takes over from) the regular auditor, this means the IRS suspects fraud. If the matter has progressed to an investigation for fraud, the taxpayer should retain competent counsel.

Settlement Procedures. If an audit results in an assessment of additional tax and no settlement is reached with the IRS agent, the taxpayer may attempt to negotiate a settlement with a higher level of the IRS. If an appeal is desired, an appropriate request must be made to the Appeals Division of the IRS. The Appeals Division is authorized to settle all disputes based on the *hazard of litigation* (the probability of favorable resolution of the disputed issue or issues if litigated). In some cases, a taxpayer may be able to obtain a percentage settlement or a favorable settlement of one or more disputed issues.

If a satisfactory settlement is not reached within the administrative appeal process, the taxpayer can litigate the case in the Tax Court, a Federal District Court, or the Court of Federal Claims. However, litigation is recommended only as a last resort because of the legal costs involved and the uncertainty of the final outcome. Tax litigation considerations are discussed more fully in Chapter 2.

| **TAX** *in the News* | **ONE WAY TO COLLECT TAXES: INTERNET SHAMING** |

In tax administration, the first and major hurdle is to discover tax delinquencies. Once tax scofflaws are uncovered, however, making them "pay up" may require costly and time-consuming legal proceedings. A number of states have found that they can use the Internet to collect the taxes due from some tax-payers without such procedures. Typically, the taxpayers are notified that their names will be posted on the Internet as "tax delinquents" unless payment is made. Most often the embarrassment that would result from such exposure is enough to motivate payment, so the names never need to be posted.

Source: *Adapted from Tom Herman, "Deadbeats Risk Cybershame" Wall Street Journal, June 27, 2007, p. D2.*

Statute of Limitations

A **statute of limitations** is a provision in the law that offers a party a defense against a suit brought by another party after the expiration of a specified period of time. The purpose of a statute of limitations is to preclude parties from prosecuting stale claims. The passage of time makes the defense of such claims difficult since witnesses may no longer be available or evidence may have been lost or destroyed. Found at the state and Federal levels, such statutes cover a multitude of suits, both civil and criminal.

For our purposes, the relevant statutes deal with the Federal income tax. The two categories involved cover both the period of limitations applicable to the assessment of additional tax deficiencies by the IRS and the period that deals with claims for refunds by taxpayers.

Assessment by the IRS.
Under the general rule, the IRS may assess an additional tax liability against a taxpayer within *three years* of the filing of the income tax return. If the return is filed early, the three-year period begins to run from the due date of the return (usually April 15 for a calendar year individual taxpayer). If the taxpayer files the return late (i.e., beyond the due date), the three-year period begins to run on the date filed.

If a taxpayer omits an amount of gross income in excess of 25 percent of the gross income reported on the return, the statute of limitations is increased to six years.

EXAMPLE 14

For 2008, Mark, a calendar year taxpayer, reported gross income of $400,000 on a timely filed income tax return. If Mark omitted more than $100,000 (25% × $400,000), the six-year statute of limitations would apply to the 2008 tax year. ∎

The six-year provision on assessments by the IRS applies only to the omission of income and does not cover other factors that might lead to an understatement of tax liability, such as overstatement of deductions and credits.

There is *no* statute of limitations on assessments of tax if *no return* is filed or if a *fraudulent* return is filed.

Limitations on Refunds.
If a taxpayer believes that an overpayment of Federal income tax was made, a claim for refund should be filed with the IRS. A *claim for refund,* therefore, is a request to the IRS that it return to the taxpayer excessive income taxes paid.[22]

A claim for refund generally must be filed within *three years* from the date the return was filed *or* within *two years* from the date the tax was paid, whichever is later. Income tax returns that are filed early are deemed to have been filed on the date the return was due.

---
[22]Generally, an individual filing a claim for refund should use Form 1040X.

Interest and Penalties

Interest rates are determined quarterly by the IRS based on the existing Federal short-term rate. Currently, the rates for tax refunds (overpayments) for individual taxpayers are the same as those applicable to assessments (underpayments). For the first quarter (January 1–March 31) of 2008, the rates are 7 percent for refunds and assessments.[23]

For assessments of additional taxes, the interest begins running on the unextended due date of the return. With refunds, however, no interest is allowed if the overpayment is refunded to the taxpayer within 45 days of the date the return is filed. For this purpose, returns filed early are deemed to have been filed on the due date.

In addition to interest, the tax law provides various penalties for lack of compliance by taxpayers. Some of these penalties are summarized as follows:

- For a *failure to file* a tax return by the due date (including extension—see Chapter 3), a penalty of 5 percent per month up to a maximum of 25 percent is imposed on the amount of tax shown as due on the return. Any fraction of a month counts as a full month.
- A penalty for a *failure to pay* the tax due as shown on the return is imposed in the amount of 0.5 percent per month up to a maximum of 25 percent. Again, any fraction of a month counts as a full month. During any month in which both the failure to file penalty and the failure to pay penalty apply, the failure to file penalty is reduced by the amount of the failure to pay penalty.

EXAMPLE 15

Adam files his tax return 18 days after the due date of the return. Along with the return, he remits a check for $1,000, which is the balance of the tax he owed. Disregarding the interest element, Adam's total penalties are as follows:

Failure to pay penalty (0.5% × $1,000)		$ 5
Plus:		
Failure to file penalty (5% × $1,000)	$50	
Less failure to pay penalty for the same period	(5)	
Failure to file penalty		45
Total penalties		$50

Note that the penalties for one full month are imposed even though Adam was delinquent by only 18 days. Unlike the method used to compute interest, any part of a month is treated as a whole month. ■

- A *negligence* penalty of 20 percent is imposed if any of the underpayment was for intentional disregard of rules and regulations without intent to defraud. The penalty applies to just that portion attributable to the negligence.

EXAMPLE 16

Cindy underpaid her taxes for 2007 in the amount of $20,000, of which $15,000 is attributable to negligence. Cindy's negligence penalty is $3,000 (20% × $15,000). ■

- Various penalties may be imposed in the case of *fraud*. Fraud involves specific intent on the part of the taxpayer to evade a tax. In the case of *civil* fraud, the penalty is 75 percent of the underpayment attributable to fraud. In the case of *criminal* fraud, the penalties can include large fines as well as prison sentences.

---

[23]The rates applicable after March 31, 2008, were not available when this text went to press.

The difference between civil and criminal fraud is one of degree. Criminal fraud involves the presence of willfulness on the part of the taxpayer. Also, the burden of proof, which is on the IRS in both situations, is more stringent for criminal fraud than for civil fraud. The negligence penalty is not imposed when the fraud penalty applies. For possible fraud situations, refer to Examples 11 and 12.

Tax Practice

The area of tax practice is largely unregulated. Virtually anyone can aid another in complying with the various tax laws. If a practitioner is a member of a profession, such as law or public accounting, he or she must abide by certain ethical standards. Furthermore, the Internal Revenue Code imposes penalties upon the preparers of Federal tax returns who violate proscribed acts and procedures.

Ethical Guidelines.

Ethical Guidelines. The American Institute of CPAs has issued numerous pronouncements dealing with CPAs engaged in tax practice. Originally called "Statements on Responsibilities in Tax Practice," these pronouncements were intended to be only *guides* to action. In 2000, however, the AICPA redesignated the pronouncements as "Statements on Standards for Tax Services" and made them *enforceable* as part of its Code of Professional Conduct. They include the provisions summarized below.

> **LO.5**
>
> Know some of the ethical guidelines involved in tax practice.

- Do not take questionable positions on a client's tax return in the hope that the return will not be selected for audit by the IRS. Any positions taken should be supported by a good-faith belief that they have a realistic possibility of being sustained if challenged. The client should be fully advised of the risks involved and of the penalties that will result if the position taken is not successful.
- A practitioner can use a client's estimates if they are reasonable under the circumstances. If the tax law requires receipts or other verification, the client should be so advised. In no event should an estimate be given the appearance of greater accuracy than is the case. For example, an estimate of $1,000 should not be deducted on a return as $999.
- Every effort should be made to answer questions appearing on tax returns. A question need not be answered if the information requested is not readily available, the answer is voluminous, or the question's meaning is uncertain. The failure to answer a question on a return cannot be justified on the grounds that the answer could prove disadvantageous to the taxpayer.
- Upon learning of an error on a past tax return, advise the client to correct it. Do not, however, inform the IRS of the error. If the error is material and the client refuses to correct it, consider withdrawing from the engagement. This will be necessary if the error has a carryover effect and prevents the current year's tax liability from being determined correctly.

ETHICAL and EQUITABLE *Considerations*

WHEN THE IRS DOES NOT KNOW

Al Garth is a longtime client and a golfing companion as well. In reviewing the information he furnishes you to prepare his income tax return for 2007, you find no reference to the Honda SUV he won in the annual club tournament. When you inquire about the matter, Al tells you that the club treasurer says that the club does not report these awards to the IRS and has told him to "proceed accordingly." What course of action should you take?

Statutory Penalties Imposed on Tax Return Preparers. In addition to ethical constraints, a tax return preparer may be subject to certain statutorily sanctioned penalties, including the following:

- Various penalties involving procedural matters. Examples include failing to furnish the taxpayer with a copy of the return; endorsing a taxpayer's refund check; failing to sign the return as a preparer; failing to furnish one's identification number; and failing to keep copies of returns or maintain a client list.
- Penalty for understatement of a tax liability based on a position that lacks any realistic possibility of being sustained. If the position is not frivolous, the penalty can be avoided by disclosing it on the return.
- Penalty for any willful attempt to understate taxes. This usually results when a preparer disregards or makes no effort to obtain pertinent information from a client.
- Penalty for failure to exercise due diligence in determining eligibility for, or the amount of, an earned income tax credit.

<table>
<tr><td>LO.6</td></tr>
<tr><td>Recognize the economic, social, equity, and political considerations that justify various aspects of the tax law.</td></tr>
</table>

Understanding the Federal Tax Law

The Federal tax law is a mosaic of statutory provisions, administrative pronouncements, and court decisions. Anyone who has attempted to work with this body of knowledge would have to admit to its complexity. For the person who has to trudge through a mass of rules to find the solution to a tax problem, it may be of some consolation to know that the law's complexity can generally be explained. Whether sound or not, there is a reason for the formulation of every rule. Knowing these reasons, therefore, is a considerable step toward understanding the Federal tax law.

The Federal tax law has as its *major objective* the raising of revenue. But although the fiscal needs of the government are important, other considerations explain certain portions of the law. Economic, social, equity, and political factors also play a significant role. Added to these factors is the marked impact the IRS and the courts have had and will continue to have on the evolution of Federal tax law. These matters are treated in the remainder of the chapter, and, wherever appropriate, the discussion is referenced to subjects covered later in the text.

Revenue Needs

The foundation of any tax system has to be the raising of revenue to cover the cost of government operations. Ideally, annual outlays should not exceed anticipated revenues, thereby leading to a balanced budget with no resulting deficit.

When enacting tax legislation, a deficit-conscious Congress often has been guided by the concept of **revenue neutrality**. Also referred to as "pay-as-you-go" ("paygo"), the concept means that every new tax law that lowers taxes must include a revenue offset that makes up for the loss. Revenue neutrality does not mean that any one taxpayer's tax liability will remain the same. Since the circumstances involved will differ, one taxpayer's increased tax liability could be another's tax savings. Although revenue-neutral tax reform does not reduce deficits, at least it does not aggravate the problem.

In addition to making changes in the tax law revenue neutral, several other procedures can be taken to mitigate any revenue loss. When tax reductions are involved, the full impact of the legislation can be phased in over a period of years.[24] Or, as an alternative, the tax reduction can be limited to a period of years. When the period expires, the prior law is reinstated through a **sunset provision**. Most of the major tax bills recently passed by Congress have contained numerous sunset

---

[24]An example of a gradual phase-in is the increase in the unified transfer tax credit (discussed earlier in this chapter), which does not become fully implemented at $3.5 million until year 2009.

OUTSOURCING OF TAX RETURN PREPARATION

The use of foreign nationals to carry out certain job assignments for U.S. businesses is an increasingly popular practice. Outsourcing such activities as telemarketing to India, for example, usually produces the same satisfactory result but at a much lower cost.

Outsourcing is also being applied to the preparation of tax returns. Not only can this practice be expected to continue, but it probably will increase in volume. Outsourcing tax return preparation does not violate Federal law and is compatible with accounting ethical guidelines as long as three safeguards are followed: First, the practitioner must make sure that client confidentiality is maintained. Second, the practitioner must verify the accuracy of the work that has been outsourced. Third, the practitioner must inform clients, preferably in writing, when any third-party contractor is used to provide professional services.

Practitioners justify the outsourcing practice as a means of conserving time and effort that can be applied toward more meaningful tax planning on behalf of their clients.

GLOBAL
Tax Issues

provisions. They provide some semblance of revenue neutrality as some of the bills include tax cuts that were not offset by new sources of revenue. It remains to be seen, however, whether Congress will allow the sunset provisions to take effect and, thereby, kill the tax cuts that were enacted.

Economic Considerations

Using the tax system in an effort to accomplish economic objectives has become increasingly popular in recent years. Generally, proponents of this goal use tax legislation to amend the Internal Revenue Code in ways designed to help control the economy or encourage certain activities and businesses.

Control of the Economy. Congress has used depreciation write-offs as a means of controlling the economy. Theoretically, shorter asset lives and accelerated methods should encourage additional investment in depreciable property acquired for business use. Conversely, longer asset lives and the required use of the straight-line method of depreciation dampen the tax incentive for capital outlays.

Another approach that utilizes depreciation as a means of controlling capital investment is the amount of write-off allowed upon the acquisition of assets. This is the approach followed by the § 179 election to expense assets.

A change in the tax rate structure has a more immediate impact on the economy. With lower tax rates, taxpayers are able to retain additional spendable funds. If lower tax rates are accompanied by the elimination of certain deductions, exclusions, and credits, however, the overall result may not be lower tax liabilities.

Encouragement of Certain Activities. Without passing judgment on the wisdom of any such choices, it is quite clear that the tax law encourages certain types of economic activity or segments of the economy. For example, the favorable treatment allowed research and development expenditures can be explained by the desire to foster technological progress. Under the tax law, such expenditures can be either deducted in the year incurred or capitalized and amortized over a period of 60 months or more. In terms of the timing of the tax savings, these options usually are preferable to capitalizing the cost with a write-off over the estimated useful life of the asset created. If the asset developed has an indefinite useful life, no write-off would be available without the two options allowed by the tax law.

Part of the tax law addresses the energy crisis—in terms of both our reliance on foreign oil and the need to ease the problem of global warming. For example, tax credits are available to those who purchase motor vehicles that operate on alternative (i.e., nonfossil) fuels. Residential energy credits are allowed for home improvements that conserve energy or make its use more efficient. Ecological considerations justify a tax provision that permits a more rapid expensing of the costs of installing pollution control facilities. Measures such as these that aid in maintaining a clean air environment and conserving energy resources can also be justified under social considerations.

Is it wise to stimulate U.S. exports of services? Along this line, Congress has deemed it advisable to establish incentives for U.S. citizens who accept employment overseas. Such persons receive generous tax breaks through special treatment of their foreign-source income.

Is saving desirable for the economy? Saving leads to capital formation and thereby makes funds available to finance home construction and industrial expansion. The tax law encourages saving by according preferential treatment to private retirement plans. Not only are contributions to Keogh (H.R. 10) plans and certain Individual Retirement Accounts (IRAs) deductible, but income from the contributions accumulates free of tax. As noted below, the encouragement of private-sector pension plans can also be justified under social considerations.

Encouragement of Certain Industries.

No one can question the proposition that a sound agricultural base is necessary for a well-balanced national economy. Undoubtedly, this can explain why farmers are accorded special treatment under the Federal tax system. Among the benefits are the election to expense rather than capitalize certain soil and water conservation expenditures and fertilizers and the election to defer the recognition of gain on the receipt of crop insurance proceeds.

To stimulate the manufacturing industry, in 2005 Congress enacted a domestic production activities deduction. The provision provides a tax benefit in the form of a deduction for profits derived from manufacturing activities conducted within the United States. By restricting the deduction to manufacturing income attributable to wages reportable to the IRS, new U.S. jobs will result, and the outsourcing of labor is discouraged. Thus, the tax system is used to encourage both domestic manufacturing and job growth.

Encouragement of Small Business.

At least in the United States, a consensus exists that what is good for small business is good for the economy as a whole. Whether valid or not, this assumption has led to a definite bias in the tax law favoring small business.

In the corporate tax area, several provisions can be explained by the desire to benefit small business. One provision permits the shareholders of a small business corporation to make a special election that generally will avoid the imposition of the corporate income tax.[25] Furthermore, such an election enables the corporation to pass through its operating losses to its shareholders.

Social Considerations

Some provisions of the Federal tax law, particularly those dealing with the income tax of individuals, can be explained by social considerations. Some notable examples and their rationales include the following:

- Certain benefits provided to employees through accident and health plans financed by employers are nontaxable to employees. Encouraging such plans is considered socially desirable since they provide medical benefits in the event of an employee's illness or injury.

---

own as the S election, it is discussed in Chapter 20.

- Most premiums paid by an employer for group term insurance covering the life of the employee are nontaxable to the employee. These arrangements can be justified on social grounds in that they provide funds for the family unit to help it adjust to the loss of wages caused by the employee's death.
- A contribution made by an employer to a qualified pension or profit sharing plan for an employee may receive special treatment. The contribution and any income it generates are not taxed to the employee until the funds are distributed. Such an arrangement also benefits the employer by allowing a tax deduction when the contribution is made to the qualified plan. Private retirement plans are encouraged to supplement the subsistence income level the employee otherwise would have under the Social Security system.[26]
- A deduction is allowed for contributions to qualified charitable organizations. The deduction attempts to shift some of the financial and administrative burden of socially desirable programs from the public (the government) to the private (the citizens) sector.
- A tax credit is allowed for amounts spent to furnish care for certain minor or disabled dependents to enable the taxpayer to seek or maintain gainful employment. Who could deny the social desirability of encouraging taxpayers to provide care for their children while they work?
- Various tax credits, deductions, and exclusions are designed to encourage taxpayers to obtain additional education.[27]
- A tax deduction is not allowed for certain expenditures deemed to be contrary to public policy. This disallowance extends to such items as fines, penalties, illegal kickbacks, bribes to government officials, and gambling losses in excess of gains. Social considerations dictate that the tax law should not encourage these activities by permitting a deduction.

Many other examples could be cited, but the conclusion would be unchanged. Social considerations do explain a significant part of the Federal tax law.

Equity Considerations

The concept of equity is relative. Reasonable persons can, and often do, disagree about what is fair or unfair. In the tax area, moreover, equity is most often tied to a particular taxpayer's personal situation. To illustrate, compare the tax positions of those who rent their personal residences with those who own their homes. Renters receive no Federal income tax benefit from the rent they pay. For homeowners, however, a large portion of the house payments they make may qualify for the Federal interest and property tax deductions. Although renters may have difficulty understanding this difference in tax treatment, the encouragement of home ownership can be justified on both economic and social grounds.

In the same vein, compare the tax treatment of a corporation with that of a partnership. Although the two businesses may be of equal size, similarly situated, and competitors in the production of goods or services, they are not treated comparably under the tax law. The corporation is subject to a separate Federal income tax; the partnership is not. Whether the differences in tax treatment can be justified logically in terms of equity is beside the point. The point is that the tax law can and does make a distinction between these business forms.

Equity, then, is not what appears fair or unfair to any one taxpayer or group of taxpayers. Some recognition of equity does exist, however, and explains part of the law. The concept of equity appears in tax provisions that alleviate the effect of multiple taxation and postpone the recognition of gain when the taxpayer lacks the ability or wherewithal to pay the tax. Provisions that mitigate the effect of the

---

[26]The same rationale explains the availability of similar arrangements for self-employed persons (the H.R. 10, or Keogh, plan). See Chapter 19.

[27]These provisions can also be justified under the category of economic considerations. No one can take issue with the conclusion that a better educated workforce carries a positive economic impact.

TAX *in the News*   TREATING EVERYONE THE SAME

As noted in the text, a Federal income tax deduction for state and local income taxes paid is allowed to mitigate the effect of having the same income taxed more than once. But what if a state does not impose an income tax and, instead, derives comparable amounts of revenue from a general sales tax? Is it fair to deny a deduction to residents of this state just because the state imposes a tax on sales rather than on income?

Recent legislation resolved this purported inequity by allowing a Federal income tax deduction for state and local general sales taxes. However, a taxpayer who is subject to both state income and sales taxes must make a choice. One or the other, but not both, can be claimed as a deduction.

application of the annual accounting period concept and help taxpayers cope with the eroding results of inflation also reflect equity considerations.

Alleviating the Effect of Multiple Taxation.

The income earned by a taxpayer may be subject to taxes imposed by different taxing authorities. If, for example, the taxpayer is a resident of New York City, income might generate Federal, state of New York, and city of New York income taxes. To compensate for this apparent inequity, the Federal tax law allows a taxpayer to claim a deduction for state and local income taxes. The deduction does not, however, neutralize the effect of multiple taxation, since the benefit derived depends on the taxpayer's Federal income tax rate. Only a tax credit, rather than a deduction, would eliminate the effects of multiple taxation on the same income.

Equity considerations can explain the Federal tax treatment of certain income from foreign sources. Since double taxation results when the same income is subject to both foreign and U.S. income taxes, the tax law permits the taxpayer to choose between a credit and a deduction for the foreign taxes paid.

The Wherewithal to Pay Concept.

The **wherewithal to pay** concept recognizes the inequity of taxing a transaction when the taxpayer lacks the means with which to pay the tax. It is particularly suited to situations in which the taxpayer's economic position has not changed significantly as a result of the transaction.

An illustration of the wherewithal to pay concept is the provision of the tax law dealing with the treatment of gain resulting from an involuntary conversion. An involuntary conversion occurs when property is destroyed by a casualty or taken by a public authority through condemnation. If gain results from the conversion, it need not be recognized if the taxpayer replaces the property within a specified period of time. The replacement property must be similar or related in service or use to that involuntarily converted.

EXAMPLE 17

Some of the pasture land belonging to Ron, a rancher, is condemned by the state for use as a game preserve. The condemned pasture land cost Ron $120,000, but the state pays him $150,000 (its fair market value). Shortly thereafter, Ron buys more pasture land for $150,000. ∎

In Example 17, Ron has a realized gain of $30,000 [$150,000 (condemnation award) − $120,000 (cost of land)]. It would be inequitable to force Ron to pay a tax on this gain for two reasons. First, without disposing of the property acquired (the new land), Ron would be hard-pressed to pay the tax. Second, his economic position has not changed.

A warning is in order regarding the application of the wherewithal to pay concept. If the taxpayer's economic position changes in any way, tax consequences may result.

EXAMPLE 18

Assume the same facts as in Example 17, except that Ron reinvests only $140,000 of the award in new pasture land. Now, Ron has a taxable gain of $10,000. Instead of ending up with only replacement property, Ron now has $10,000 in cash. ■

Mitigating the Effect of the Annual Accounting Period Concept. For purposes of effective administration of the tax law, all taxpayers must report to and settle with the Federal government at periodic intervals. Otherwise, taxpayers would remain uncertain as to their tax liabilities, and the government would have difficulty judging revenues and budgeting expenditures. The period selected for final settlement of most tax liabilities, in any event an arbitrary determination, is one year. At the close of each year, therefore, a taxpayer's position becomes complete for that particular year. Referred to as the annual accounting period concept, its effect is to divide each taxpayer's life, for tax purposes, into equal annual intervals.

The finality of the annual accounting period concept could lead to dissimilar tax treatment for taxpayers who are, from a long-range standpoint, in the same economic position.

EXAMPLE 19

José and Alicia, both sole proprietors, have experienced the following results during the past three years:

	Profit (or Loss)	
Year	José	Alicia
2006	$50,000	$150,000
2007	60,000	60,000
2008	60,000	(40,000)

Although José and Alicia have the same profit of $170,000 over the period from 2006 to 2008, the finality of the annual accounting period concept places Alicia at a definite disadvantage for tax purposes. The net operating loss procedure offers Alicia some relief by allowing her to apply some or all of her 2008 loss to the earlier profitable years (in this case, 2006). Thus, with a net operating loss carryback, Alicia is in a position to obtain a refund for some of the taxes she paid on the $150,000 profit reported for 2006. ■

The same reasoning used to support the deduction of net operating losses can explain the special treatment the tax law accords to excess capital losses and excess charitable contributions.[28] Carryback and carryover procedures help mitigate the effect of limiting a loss or a deduction to the accounting period in which it was realized. With such procedures, a taxpayer may be able to salvage a loss or a deduction that might otherwise be wasted.

The installment method of recognizing gain on the sale of property allows a taxpayer to spread tax consequences over the payout period.[29] The harsh effect of taxing all the gain in the year of sale is thereby avoided. The installment method can also be explained by the wherewithal to pay concept since recognition of gain is tied to the collection of the installment notes received from the sale of the property. Tax consequences, then, tend to correspond to the seller's ability to pay the tax.

Coping with Inflation. Because of the progressive nature of the income tax, a wage adjustment to compensate for inflation can increase the income tax bracket

---

[28]The tax treatment of these items is discussed in Chapters 7, 10, and 16.
[29]Under the installment method, each payment received by the seller represents both a recovery of capital (the nontaxable portion) and profit from the sale (the taxable portion). The tax rules governing the installment method are discussed in Chapter 18.

of the recipient. Known as *bracket creep*, its overall impact is an erosion of purchasing power. Congress recognized this problem and began to adjust various income tax components, such as tax brackets, standard deduction amounts, and personal and dependency exemptions, through an indexation procedure. Indexation is based upon the rise in the consumer price index over the prior year.

Political Considerations

A large segment of the Federal tax law is made up of statutory provisions. Since these statutes are enacted by Congress, is it any surprise that political considerations influence tax law? For purposes of discussion, the effect of political considerations on the tax law is divided into the following topics: special interest legislation, political expediency situations, and state and local government influences.

Special Interest Legislation.

There is no doubt that certain provisions of the tax law can largely be explained by the political influence some pressure groups have had on Congress. Is there any other realistic reason that, for example, prepaid subscription and dues income is not taxed until earned while prepaid rents are taxed to the landlord in the year received?

The American Jobs Creation Act of 2004 included several good examples of special interest legislation. One provision, sponsored by former Senator Zell Miller (D–Ga.), suspended the import duties on ceiling fans. The nation's largest seller of ceiling fans is Home Depot, which is based in Atlanta, Georgia. Another provision, sponsored by then House Speaker Dennis Hastert (R–Ill.), reduced the excise taxes on fishing tackle boxes. Representative Hastert's district includes Plano Molding, a major manufacturer of tackle boxes. The justification for this change was that it placed tackle boxes on a more level playing field with toolboxes (which are not subject to tax). Allegedly, fishermen had been buying and converting toolboxes to avoid the excise tax!

Special interest legislation is not necessarily to be condemned if it can be justified on economic, social, or some other utilitarian grounds. In most cases, however, it is objectionable in that it adds further complexity to an already cluttered tax law. At any rate, it is an inevitable product of our political system.

Political Expediency Situations.

Various tax reform proposals rise and fall in favor with the shifting moods of the American public. That Congress is sensitive to popular feeling is an accepted fact. Therefore, certain provisions of the tax law can be explained by the political climate at the time they were enacted.

Measures that deter more affluent taxpayers from obtaining so-called preferential tax treatment have always had popular appeal and, consequently, the support of Congress. Provisions such as the alternative minimum tax, the imputed interest rules, and the limitation on the deductibility of interest on investment indebtedness can be explained on this basis.

Other changes explained at least partially by political expediency include the lowering of individual income tax rates, the increase in the personal and dependency exemptions, and the increase in the amount of the earned income credit.

State and Local Government Influences.

Political considerations have played a major role in the nontaxability of interest received on state and local obligations. In view of the furor that has been raised by state and local political figures every time any modification of this tax provision has been proposed, one might well regard it as next to sacred.

Somewhat less apparent has been the influence state law has had in shaping our present Federal tax law. Such was the case with community property systems. The nine states with community property systems are Louisiana, Texas, New Mexico, Arizona, California, Washington, Idaho, Nevada, and Wisconsin. The rest of the states are classified as common law jurisdictions.[30] The difference between common law and community property systems centers around the property rights possessed by married persons. In a common law system, each spouse owns whatever he or she earns. Under a community property system, one-half of the earnings of each spouse is considered owned by the other spouse.

Al and Fran are husband and wife, and their only income is the $80,000 annual salary Al receives. If they live in New Jersey (a common law state), the $80,000 salary belongs to Al. If, however, they live in Arizona (a community property state), the $80,000 is divided equally, in terms of ownership, between Al and Fran. ■

At one time, the tax position of the residents of community property states was so advantageous that many common law states adopted community property systems. Needless to say, the political pressure placed on Congress to correct the disparity in tax treatment was considerable. To a large extent this was accomplished in the Revenue Act of 1948, which extended many of the community property tax advantages to residents of common law jurisdictions.

The major advantage extended was the provision allowing married taxpayers to file joint returns and compute their tax liability as if the income had been earned one-half by each spouse. This result is automatic in a community property state, since half of the income earned by one spouse belongs to the other spouse. The income-splitting benefits of a joint return are now incorporated as part of the tax rates applicable to married taxpayers. See Chapter 3.

Influence of the Internal Revenue Service

The influence of the IRS is apparent in many areas beyond its role in issuing the administrative pronouncements that make up a considerable portion of our tax law. In its capacity as the protector of the national revenue, the IRS has been instrumental in securing the passage of much legislation designed to curtail the most flagrant tax avoidance practices (to close *tax loopholes*). As the administrator of the tax law, the IRS has sought and obtained legislation to make its job easier (to attain administrative feasibility).

The IRS as Protector of the Revenue. Innumerable examples can be given of provisions in the tax law that stem from the direct influence of the IRS. Usually, such provisions are intended to prevent a loophole from being used to avoid the tax consequences intended by Congress. Working within the letter of existing law, ingenious taxpayers and their advisers devise techniques that accomplish indirectly what cannot be accomplished directly. As a consequence, legislation is enacted to close the loopholes that taxpayers have located and exploited. Some tax law can be explained in this fashion and is discussed in the chapters to follow.

ETHICAL and EQUITABLE *Considerations*   **CLAIMING A BAD DEBT DEDUCTION**

Dr. Dewey is a cash basis, calendar year taxpayer who maintains a dental practice as a sole proprietor. For tax year 2008, she claims $32,900 as a bad debt deduction. After performing the dental procedures and billing the patients involved repeatedly, she has been unable to collect the amounts due. She is quite certain that those patients will never pay their bills. Comment on the propriety of Dr. Dewey's deduction.

---

[30]In Alaska, spouses can choose to have the community property rules apply. Otherwise, property rights are determined under common law rules.

In addition, the IRS has secured from Congress legislation of a more general nature that enables it to make adjustments based on the substance, rather than the formal construction, of what a taxpayer has done. For example, one such provision permits the IRS to make adjustments to a taxpayer's method of accounting when the method used by the taxpayer does not clearly reflect income.[31]

EXAMPLE 21

Tina, a cash basis taxpayer, owns and operates a pharmacy. All drugs and other items acquired for resale, such as cosmetics, are charged to the purchases account and written off (expensed) for tax purposes in the year of acquisition. As this procedure does not clearly reflect income, it would be appropriate for the IRS to require that Tina establish and maintain an ending inventory account. ∎

Administrative Feasibility. Some tax law is justified on the grounds that it simplifies the task of the IRS in collecting the revenue and administering the law. With regard to collecting the revenue, the IRS long ago realized the importance of placing taxpayers on a pay-as-you-go basis. Elaborate withholding procedures apply to wages, while the tax on other types of income may be paid at periodic intervals throughout the year. The IRS has been instrumental in convincing the courts that accrual basis taxpayers should in most cases pay taxes on prepaid income in the year received and not when earned. The approach may be contrary to generally accepted accounting principles, but it is consistent with the wherewithal to pay concept.

Of considerable aid to the IRS in collecting revenue are the numerous provisions that impose interest and penalties on taxpayers for noncompliance with the tax law. Provisions such as the penalties for failure to pay a tax or to file a return that is due, the negligence penalty for intentional disregard of rules and regulations, and various penalties for civil and criminal fraud serve as deterrents to taxpayer noncompliance.

One of the keys to an effective administration of our tax system is the audit process conducted by the IRS. To carry out this function, the IRS is aided by provisions that reduce the chance of taxpayer error or manipulation and therefore simplify the audit effort that is necessary. An increase in the amount of the standard deduction, for example, reduces the number of individual taxpayers who will choose the alternative of itemizing their personal deductions.[32] With fewer deductions to check, the audit function is simplified.[33]

Influence of the Courts

In addition to interpreting statutory provisions and the administrative pronouncements issued by the IRS, the Federal courts have influenced tax law in two other respects.[34] First, the courts have formulated certain judicial concepts that serve as guides in the application of various tax provisions. Second, certain key decisions have led to changes in the Internal Revenue Code.

Judicial Concepts Relating to Tax. A leading tax concept developed by the courts deals with the interpretation of statutory tax provisions that operate to benefit taxpayers. The courts have established the rule that these relief provisions are to be narrowly construed against taxpayers if there is any doubt about their application.

---

[31]See Chapter 18.

[32]For a discussion of the standard deduction, see Chapter 3.

[33]The same justification was given by the IRS when it proposed to Congress the $100 limitation on personal casualty and theft losses. Imposition of the limitation eliminated many casualty and theft loss deductions and, as a consequence, saved the IRS considerable audit time. Later legislation, in addition to retaining the $100 feature, limits deductible losses to those in excess of 10% of a taxpayer's adjusted gross income. See Chapter 7.

[34]A great deal of case law is devoted to ascertaining congressional intent. The courts, in effect, ask: What did Congress have in mind when it enacted a particular tax provision?

Important in this area is the *arm's length* concept. Particularly in dealings between related parties, transactions may be tested by looking to whether the taxpayers acted in an arm's length manner. The question to be asked is: Would unrelated parties have handled the transaction in the same way?

Rex, the sole shareholder of Silver Corporation, leases property to the corporation for a yearly rent of $60,000. To test whether the corporation should be allowed a rent deduction for this amount, the IRS and the courts will apply the arm's length concept. Would Silver Corporation have paid $60,000 a year in rent if it had leased the same property from an unrelated party (rather than from Rex)? Suppose it is determined that an unrelated third party would have paid an annual rent for the property of only $50,000. Under these circumstances, Silver Corporation will be allowed a deduction of only $50,000. The other $10,000 it paid for the use of the property represents a nondeductible dividend. Accordingly, Rex will be treated as having received rent income of $50,000 and dividend income of $10,000. ■

Judicial Influence on Statutory Provisions.

Some court decisions have been of such consequence that Congress has incorporated them into statutory tax law. For example, many years ago the courts found that stock dividends distributed to the shareholders of a corporation were not taxable as income. This result was largely accepted by Congress, and a provision in the tax statutes now covers the issue.

On occasion, however, Congress has reacted negatively to judicial interpretations of the tax law.

Nora leases unimproved real estate to Wade for 20 years. At a cost of $400,000, Wade erects a building on the land. The building is worth $150,000 when the lease terminates and Nora takes possession of the property. Does Nora have any income either when the improvements are made or when the lease terminates? In a landmark decision, a court held that Nora must recognize income of $150,000 upon the termination of the lease. ■

Congress felt that the result reached in Example 23 was inequitable in that it was not consistent with the wherewithal to pay concept. Consequently, the tax law was amended to provide that a landlord does not recognize any income either when the improvements are made (unless made in lieu of rent) or when the lease terminates.

Summary

In addition to its necessary revenue-raising objective, the Federal tax law has developed in response to several other factors:

- *Economic considerations.* The emphasis here is on tax provisions that help regulate the economy and encourage certain activities and types of businesses.
- *Social considerations.* Some tax provisions are designed to encourage (or discourage) certain socially desirable (or undesirable) practices.
- *Equity considerations.* Of principal concern in this area are tax provisions that alleviate the effect of multiple taxation, recognize the wherewithal to pay concept, mitigate the effect of the annual accounting period concept, and recognize the eroding effect of inflation.
- *Political considerations.* Of significance in this regard are tax provisions that represent special interest legislation, reflect political expediency, and exhibit the effect of state and local law.
- *Influence of the IRS.* Many tax provisions are intended to aid the IRS in the collection of revenue and the administration of the tax law.
- *Influence of the courts.* Court decisions have established a body of judicial concepts relating to tax law and have, on occasion, led Congress to enact statutory provisions to either clarify or negate their effect.

These factors explain various tax provisions and thereby help in understanding why the tax law developed to its present state. The next step involves learning to work with the tax law, which is the subject of Chapter 2.

KEY TERMS

Ad valorem taxes, 1–6	Franchise tax, 1–17	Revenue neutrality, 1–24
Correspondence audit, 1–20	FUTA tax, 1–16	Sales tax, 1–9
Death tax, 1–10	Gift tax, 1–12	Severance taxes, 1–10
Employment taxes, 1–15	Inheritance tax, 1–11	Statute of limitations, 1–21
Estate tax, 1–11	National sales tax, 1–18	Sunset provision, 1–24
Excise taxes, 1–8	Occupational fees, 1–17	Use tax, 1–9
FICA tax, 1–16	Office audit, 1–20	Value added tax (VAT), 1–18
Field audit, 1–20	Personalty, 1–8	Wherewithal to pay, 1–28
Flat tax, 1–17	Realty, 1–6	

PROBLEM MATERIALS

DISCUSSION QUESTIONS

1. Irene, a middle management employee, is offered a pay increase by her employer. As a condition of the offer, Irene must move to another state. What tax considerations should Irene weigh before making a decision on whether to accept the offer?

2. The Federal income tax was first enacted during the Civil War, but it was never challenged in the U.S. Supreme Court until the mid-1890s. Comment on whether this statement is correct, incorrect, or misleading.

3. The effect of the Sixteenth Amendment to the U.S. Constitution was to affirm what the U.S. Supreme Court had held in its prior decisions regarding the Federal income tax. Do you agree?

4. World War II converted the Federal income tax into a *mass tax*. Explain.

5. How does the pay-as-you-go procedure apply to wage earners? To persons who have income from other than wages?

6. In terms of Adam Smith's canon of *certainty*, how does the Federal income tax fare?

7. Are the following taxes *proportional* or *progressive*?
   a. FICA tax.
   b. Federal corporate income tax.
   c. Federal gift tax.
   d. General sales tax.

Issue ID

8. Until recently, Hunter College has relied on privately owned dormitories to provide housing for its out-of-state students. After a successful fund-raising campaign, the board of regents is considering purchasing and operating most of the privately owned dormitories. The city where Hunter College is located opposes the project. Why?

Issue ID

9. The Adams Independent School District desires to sell a parcel of unimproved land that it does not need. Its three best offers are as follows: from State Department of Public Safety (DPS), $2.3 million; from Second Baptist Church, $2.2 million; and from Baker Chevrolet Company, $2.1 million. DPS would use the property for a new state highway patrol barracks; Second Baptist would start a church school; and Baker would open a car

dealership. If you are the financial adviser for the school district, which offer would you prefer? Why?

10. Several years ago, Scott purchased the former parsonage of St. Anne's Church to use as his personal residence. To date, Scott has not received any ad valorem property tax assessments from either the city or the county tax authorities.

    Issue ID

    a. What is a reasonable explanation for this oversight?
    b. What should Scott do?

11. The commissioners for Colby County are actively negotiating with Eagle Industries regarding the location of a new manufacturing facility in the county. As Eagle is considering several other sites, a "generous tax holiday" may be needed to influence its choice. The local school district is opposed to any "generous tax holiday."
    a. In terms of a "generous tax holiday," what might the proposal entail?
    b. Why should the school district be opposed?

12. The Warren family made significant improvements to their personal residence and then converted it to a bed and breakfast facility. They were surprised when the property taxes on the residence were raised twice. Explain what probably happened.

13. Franklin County is in dire financial straits and is considering a number of sources for additional revenue. Evaluate the following possibilities in terms of anticipated taxpayer compliance:
    a. A property tax on business inventories.
    b. A tax on intangibles (i.e., stocks and bonds) held as investments.
    c. A property tax on boats used for recreational purposes.

14. After his first business trip to a major city, Herman is alarmed when he reviews his credit card receipts. Both the hotel bill and the car rental charge are in excess of the price he was quoted. Was Herman overcharged, or is there an explanation for the excess amounts?

15. Jared wants to give his wife a $30,000 diamond necklace for her birthday. To avoid the state and local general sales tax of 8.5%, he asks his aunt (who lives in New Hampshire) to make the purchase. Has Jared saved $2,550 (8.5% × $30,000)?

    Issue ID

16. a. What is a sales tax holiday? What purpose might it serve?
    b. If a state anticipates a revenue shortfall, an easy solution is to cancel any scheduled sales tax holidays. Please assess the validity of this statement.

17. Velma lives in Wilson County, which is adjacent to Grimes County. Although the retail stores in both counties are comparable, Velma drives an extra 10 miles to do all of her shopping in Grimes County. Why might she do this?

    Issue ID

18. During a social event, Muriel and Earl are discussing the home computer each recently purchased. Although the computers are identical makes and models, Muriel is surprised to learn that she paid a sales tax, while Earl did not. Comment as to why this could happen.

    Issue ID

19. On a recent shopping trip to a warehouse discount store, Ruby bought goods worth $400. Although the state and local general sales tax is 7%, she was charged less than $28 (7% × $400) in tax. Why?

20. Winston, age 70, wants all of his property to eventually pass to his granddaughter, Becky, age 20. From a tax standpoint, would it be cheaper for Winston to make the transfers to Becky by gift or at death? Explain.

21. Jake (age 72) and Jessica (age 28) were recently married. To avoid any transfer taxes, Jake has promised to leave Jessica all of his wealth when he dies. Is Jake under some misconception about the operation of the Federal gift and estate taxes? Explain.

    Issue ID

22. a. What is the purpose of the unified transfer tax credit?
    b. Is the same amount available for both the Federal gift tax and the estate tax? Explain.
    c. Does the use of the credit for a gift affect the amount of credit available for the estate tax? Explain.

23. Austin and Lila are husband and wife and have six married children and 15 minor grandchildren. For tax year 2008, what is the maximum amount they can give to the family (including the sons- and daughters-in-law) without using any of their unified transfer tax credit?

24. As the Federal estate tax is scheduled to be phased out, making lifetime gifts unnecessarily incurs a transfer tax that could have been avoided by passing the property by death.
    a. Evaluate this statement. In what way is it correct? Incorrect? Misleading?
    b. What could be some justifications for lifetime giving?

25. Compare the Federal income tax on corporations with that applicable to individual taxpayers in terms of the following:
    a. Determination of AGI.
    b. Availability of the standard deduction.
    c. Nature of deductions allowed.

Issue ID 26. Mike Barr was an outstanding football player in college and expects to be drafted by the NFL in the first few rounds. Mike has let it be known that he would prefer to sign with a club located in Florida, Texas, or Washington. Mike sees no reason why he should have to pay state income tax on his player's salary! Is Mike under any delusions? Explain.

27. A state that uses a "piggyback" approach to its income tax has "decoupled" from a recent change in the Internal Revenue Code.
    a. What does this mean?
    b. Why might it have occurred?

Issue ID 28. A question on a state income tax return asks the taxpayer if he or she made any out-of-state Internet or mail-order catalog purchases during the year. The question requires a yes or no answer, and if the taxpayer answers yes, the amount of such purchases is to be listed.
    a. Does such an inquiry have any relevance to the state income tax? If not, why is it being asked?
    b. Your client, Harriet, wants to leave the question unanswered. As the preparer of her return, how do you respond?

29. As to those states that impose an income tax on individuals, comment on the following:
    a. Use of withholding procedures.
    b. Treatment of Federal income taxes paid.
    c. Due date for filing.
    d. Handling of personal and dependency exemptions.
    e. Credit for income taxes paid to other states.
    f. Exchange of tax information between a state and the IRS.

30. a. What is the justification for a state adopting an amnesty program for its income taxes?
    b. What do such programs cover?
    c. Are they ever repeated?

31. Contrast FICA and FUTA as to the following:
    a. Purpose of the tax.
    b. Upon whom imposed.
    c. Governmental administration of the tax.
    d. Reduction of tax based on a merit rating system.

32. One of the tax advantages of hiring family members to work in your business is that FICA taxes are avoided. Do you agree with this statement? Explain.

Issue ID 33. Clarence, a highly paid CEO, declares, "After I received my salary for January, I was finished with FICA for this year!"
    a. Interpret Clarence's remark.
    b. Is Clarence correct? Explain.

34. Regarding the proposal for a "flat tax," comment on the following:
    a. Justification for.
    b. Major obstacles to enactment.

35. Regarding the value added tax (VAT), comment on the following:
    a. Popularity of this type of tax.
    b. Nature of the tax.

36. Both a value added tax (VAT) and a national sales tax have been criticized as being *regressive* in their effect.
    a. Explain.
    b. How could this shortcoming be remedied in the case of a national sales tax?

37. Serena operates a lawn maintenance service in southern California. As most of her employees are itinerant, they are paid on a day-to-day basis. Because of cash-flow problems, Serena requires her customers to pay cash for the services she provides.
    a. What are some of the tax problems Serena might have?
    b. Assess Serena's chances of audit by the IRS.

Issue ID

38. Assess the probability of an audit in each of the following independent situations:
    a. As a result of a jury trial, Linda was awarded $3.5 million because of job discrimination. The award included $3 million for punitive damages.
    b. Mel operates a combination check-cashing service and pawnshop. He recently broke up with his companion of 18 years and married her teenage daughter.
    c. Cindy has annual AGI in excess of $300,000 and recently donated $40,000 to her church building fund.
    d. Pierre is the maître d' at a five star restaurant and also manages the valet parking concession.
    e. Giselle is a cocktail waitress at an upscale night club. She has been audited several times in past years.
    f. Marcus was recently assessed a large *state* income tax deficiency by the state of California for his utilization of an abusive tax shelter.

39. With regard to the IRS audit process, comment on the following:
    a. Percentage of individual returns audited.
    b. Availability of an "informant's fee."
    c. DIF score.
    d. Relevance of information returns (e.g., Form 1099).
    e. Type of audit (i.e., correspondence, office, field).
    f. RAR.
    g. Special agent joins the audit team.
    h. Function of the Appeals Division.

40. Regarding the statute of limitations on additional assessments of tax by the IRS, determine the applicable period in each of the following situations. Assume a calendar year individual with no fraud or substantial omission involved.
    a. The income tax return for 2007 was filed on February 22, 2008.
    b. The income tax return for 2007 was filed on June 27, 2008.
    c. The income tax return for 2007 was prepared on April 7, 2008, but was never filed. Through some misunderstanding between the preparer and the taxpayer, each expected the other to file the return.
    d. The income tax return for 2007 was never filed because the taxpayer thought no additional tax was due.

41. Brianna, a calendar year taxpayer, files her income tax return for 2007 on February 7, 2008. Although she makes repeated inquiries, she does not receive her refund from the IRS until May 28, 2008. Is Brianna entitled to interest on the refund? Explain.

42. On a Federal income tax return filed five years ago, Andy inadvertently omitted a large amount of gross income.
    a. Andy seeks your advice as to whether the IRS is barred from assessing additional income tax in the event he is audited. What is your advice?
    b. Would your advice differ if you are the person who prepared the return in question? Explain.
    c. Suppose Andy asks you to prepare his current year's return. Would you do so? Explain.

43. Arlene files her income tax return 70 days after the due date of the return without obtaining an extension from the IRS. Along with the return, she remits a check for

$20,000, which is the balance of the tax she owes. Disregarding the interest element, what are Arlene's penalties for failure to file and for failure to pay?

44. For tax year 2000, the IRS assesses a deficiency against Elmer for $200,000. Disregarding the interest component, what is Elmer's penalty if the deficiency is attributable to:
   a. Negligence?
   b. Fraud?

45. What is the difference between civil fraud and criminal fraud?

46. In March 2008, Jim asks you to prepare his Federal income tax returns for tax years 2005, 2006, and 2007. In discussing this matter with him, you discover that he also has not filed for tax year 2004. When you mention this fact, Jim tells you that the statute of limitations precludes the IRS from taking any action as to this year.
   a. Is Jim correct about the application of the statute of limitations? Why?
   b. If Jim refuses to file for 2004, should you prepare returns for 2005 through 2007?

47. With regard to the concept of revenue neutrality, comment on the following:
   a. A tax cut that is accompanied by a revenue offset.
   b. A tax cut that is phased in over a period of years.
   c. A tax cut that contains a sunset provision.

48. Some tax rules can be justified on multiple grounds (e.g., economic, social, etc.). In this connection, comment on the possible justification for the rules governing the following:
   a. Energy conservation and pollution control.
   b. Pension plans.
   c. Education.
   d. Home ownership.

49. Discuss the probable justification for each of the following provisions of the tax law:
   a. The § 179 election to expense certain business assets upon their acquisition.
   b. Favorable treatment accorded to research and development expenditures.
   c. A deduction allowed for income resulting from U.S. production (manufacturing) activities.
   d. Election to expense certain soil and water conservation and fertilizer expenditures.
   e. The deduction allowed for contributions to qualified charitable organizations.

50. Discuss the probable justification for each of the following provisions of the tax law:
   a. An election that allows certain corporations to avoid the corporate income tax and pass losses through to their shareholders.
   b. A tax credit for amounts spent to furnish care for minor children while the parent works.
   c. An election that allows the deferral of gain recognition on the receipt of crop insurance proceeds.
   d. The tax rates applicable to married persons who file a joint return.
   e. Provisions in the tax law that allow taxpayers to carry over to future years unused capital losses and charitable contributions.

51. In 2004, Congress enacted a provision that allows a deduction for state and local sales taxes. Why?

52. A provision in the tax law allows gain from an involuntary conversion to be postponed.
   a. Under what circumstances does this provision apply?
   b. What is the justification for the provision?

53. Discuss the probable justification for each of the following aspects of the tax law:
   a. Prepaid income is taxed to the recipient in the year received and not in the year it is earned.
   b. A taxpayer that sells property on an installment basis can recognize gain on the sale over the period the payments are received.
   c. Every year the tax brackets and the amounts of the standard deduction and dependency exemptions are adjusted by the IRS.
   d. Like toolboxes, fishing tackle boxes are not subject to the Federal excise taxes on sporting goods.
   e. The deduction for personal casualty losses is subject to dollar and percentage limitations.

CHAPTER 2

Working with the Tax Law

LEARNING OBJECTIVES

After completing Chapter 2, you should be able to:

LO.1
Distinguish between the statutory, administrative, and judicial sources of the tax law and understand the purpose of each source.

LO.2
Locate and work with the appropriate tax law sources.

LO.3
Have an awareness of electronic and paper tax services.

LO.4
Understand the tax research process.

LO.5
Communicate the results of the tax research process in a client letter and a tax file memorandum.

LO.6
Apply tax research techniques and planning procedures.

LO.7
Be aware of taxation on the CPA examination.

OUTLINE

Tax Sources, 2–2
Statutory Sources of the Tax Law, 2–2
Administrative Sources of the Tax Law, 2–7
Judicial Sources of the Tax Law, 2–12
Other Sources of the Tax Law, 2–20
Working with the Tax Law—Tax Research Tools, 2–22
Electronic versus Paper Tax Research Tools, 2–22
Tax Services, 2–23
Electronic Services, 2–23
Working with the Tax Law—Tax Research, 2–26
Identifying the Problem, 2–28

Refining the Problem, 2–28
Locating the Appropriate Tax Law Sources, 2–29
Assessing the Validity of the Tax Law Sources, 2–30
Arriving at the Solution or at Alternative Solutions, 2–33
Communicating Tax Research, 2–34
Working with the Tax Law—Tax Planning, 2–34
Nontax Considerations, 2–35
Tax Avoidance and Tax Evasion, 2–35
Follow-up Procedures, 2–38
Tax Planning—A Practical Application, 2–38
Taxation on the CPA Examination, 2–39

LO.1

Distinguish between the statutory, administrative, and judicial sources of the tax law and understand the purpose of each source.

Tax Sources

Understanding taxation requires a mastery of the sources of the *rules of tax law.* These sources include not only legislative provisions in the form of the Internal Revenue Code, but also congressional Committee Reports, Treasury Department Regulations, other Treasury Department pronouncements, and court decisions. Thus, the *primary sources* of tax information include pronouncements from all three branches of government: legislative, executive, and judicial.

In addition to being able to locate and interpret the sources of the tax law, a tax professional must understand the relative weight of authority within these sources. The tax law is of little significance, however, until it is applied to a set of facts and circumstances. This chapter, therefore, both introduces the statutory, administrative, and judicial sources of tax law and explains how the law is applied to individual and business transactions. It also explains how to apply research techniques and use planning procedures effectively.

A large part of tax research focuses on determining the intent of Congress. Although Congress often claims simplicity as one of its goals, a cursory examination of the tax law indicates that it has not been very successful in achieving this objective. Commenting on his 48-page tax return, James Michener, the author, said, "It is unimaginable in that I graduated from one of America's better colleges, yet I am totally incapable of understanding tax returns." David Brinkley, the television news commentator, observed that "settling a dispute is difficult when our tax regulations are all written in a foreign tongue whose language flows like damp sludge leaking from a sanitary landfill."

Frequently, uncertainty in the tax law causes disputes between the Internal Revenue Service (IRS) and taxpayers. Due to these *gray areas* and the complexity of the tax law, a taxpayer may have more than one alternative for structuring a business transaction. In structuring business transactions and engaging in other tax planning activities, the tax adviser must be cognizant that the objective of tax planning is not necessarily to minimize the tax liability. Instead a taxpayer should maximize his or her after-tax return, which may include maximizing nontax as well as noneconomic benefits.

Statutory Sources of the Tax Law

Origin of the Internal Revenue Code. Before 1939, the statutory provisions relating to Federal taxation were contained in the individual revenue acts enacted by Congress. Because dealing with many separate acts was inconvenient and confusing,

---

TAX *in the News*   **TAX FREEDOM DAY**

In income tax history, 1913 was an important year. In that year, the Sixteenth Amendment to the Constitution was ratified:

> The Congress shall have power to tax and collect taxes on incomes, from whatever source derived, without apportionment among the several States, and without regard to any census or enumeration.

The first income tax legislation that definitely was constitutional was passed that same year.

According to the Tax Foundation, in 2007 Tax Freedom Day fell on April 30. Tax Freedom Day is the date on which an average taxpayer through working has paid off his or her taxes for the year. Of course, if you lived in Connecticut with the heaviest total tax burden, Tax Freedom Day fell on May 20, 2007. Alabamaians and Oklahomians paid the least and finished paying off their tax burden on April 12, 2007.

Source: *Tax Foundation, "America Celebrates Tax Freedom Day," http://www.taxfoundation.org/taxfreedomday.html.*

---

in 1939 Congress codified all of the Federal tax laws. Known as the Internal Revenue Code of 1939, the codification arranged all Federal tax provisions in a logical sequence and placed them in a separate part of the Federal statutes. A further rearrangement took place in 1954 and resulted in the Internal Revenue Code of 1954, which continued in effect until 1986 when it was replaced by the Internal Revenue Code of 1986. Although Congress did not recodify the law in the Tax Reform Act (TRA) of 1986, the magnitude of the changes made by TRA of 1986 did provide some rationale for renaming the Federal tax law the Internal Revenue Code of 1986.

The following observations help clarify the codification procedure:

- Neither the 1939 nor the 1954 Code substantially changed the tax law existing on the date of its enactment. Much of the 1939 Code, for example, was incorporated into the 1954 Code; the major change was the reorganization and renumbering of the tax provisions.
- Although the 1986 Code resulted in substantial changes, only a minority of the statutory provisions were affected.[1]
- Statutory amendments to the tax law are integrated into the Code. For example, the Taxpayer Relief Act (TRA) of 1997, the Internal Revenue Service Restructuring and Reform Act of 1998, the Tax Relief Reconciliation Act of 2001, the Job Creation and Worker Assistance Act of 2002, the Jobs and Growth Tax Relief Reconciliation Act (JGTRRA) of 2003, the Working Families Tax Relief Act of 2004, the American Jobs Creation Act of 2004, the Energy Tax Incentives Act of 2005, the Tax Increase Prevention Act of 2005 (TIPRA), the Pension Protection Act of 2006, the Tax Relief and Health Care Act of 2006, and the Small Business and Work Opportunity Tax Act of 2007 all became part of the Internal Revenue Code of 1986. In view of the frequency with which tax legislation has been enacted in recent years, it appears that the tax law will continue to be amended frequently.

The Legislative Process. Federal tax legislation generally originates in the House of Representatives, where it is first considered by the House Ways and Means Committee. Tax bills originate in the Senate when they are attached as riders to other legislative proposals.[2] If acceptable to the House Ways and Means Committee, the proposed bill is referred to the entire House of Representatives for approval or disapproval. Approved bills are sent to the Senate, where they are considered by the Senate Finance Committee.

---

[1]This point is important in assessing judicial decisions interpreting provisions of the Internal Revenue Code of 1939 and the Internal Revenue Code of 1954. If the same provision was included in the Internal Revenue Code of 1986 and has not been subsequently amended, the decision has continuing validity.

[2]The Tax Equity and Fiscal Responsibility Act of 1982 originated in the Senate, and its constitutionality was unsuccessfully challenged in the courts. The Senate version of the Deficit Reduction Act of 1984 was attached as an amendment to the Federal Boat Safety Act.

TAX *in the News*   **UNDERREPORTING INCOME**

According to the Government Accountability Office, 61 percent of sole proprietors underreported their income in 2001. One of these underreporters was Darryl Strawberry, a former Major League Baseball All-Star, who failed to pay almost half a million dollars in taxes, interest, and penalties. Much of the $481,656.86 that Strawberry owes results from his failure to report income from autograph shows and other promotional appearances from 1986 to 1992. Sole proprietors like Darryl Strawberry are responsible for a large portion of the so-called tax gap of $345 billion.

Source: *Adapted from Dustin Stamper, "GAO Says 6 in 10 Sole Proprietors Underreport Income," Tax Notes, August 20, 2007, pp. 623–624.*

The next step is referral from the Senate Finance Committee to the entire Senate. Assuming no disagreement between the House and Senate, passage by the Senate results in referral to the President for approval or veto. The passage of legislation in 2003 required the vote of Vice President Dick Cheney to break a 50–50 tie in the Senate. If the bill is approved or if the President's veto is overridden, the bill becomes law and part of the Internal Revenue Code of 1986.

House and Senate versions of major tax bills frequently differ. One reason bills are often changed in the Senate is that each individual senator has considerable latitude to make amendments when the Senate as a whole is voting on a bill referred to it by the Senate Finance Committee.[3] In contrast, the entire House of Representatives either accepts or rejects what is proposed by the House Ways and Means Committee, and changes from the floor are rare. When the Senate version of the bill differs from that passed by the House, the Joint Conference Committee, which includes members of both the House Ways and Means Committee and the Senate Finance Committee, is called upon to resolve the differences. The deliberations of the Joint Conference Committee usually produce a compromise between the two versions, which is then voted on by both the House and the Senate. If both bodies accept the bill, it is referred to the President for approval or veto. Former Senator Daniel Patrick Moynihan observed that it is common in the last hours of Congress for the White House and lawmakers to agree on a "1,200-page monster, we vote for it; nobody knows what is in it." Figure 2–1 summarizes the typical legislative process for tax bills.

The role of the Joint Conference Committee indicates the importance of compromise in the legislative process. As an example of the practical effect of the compromise process, consider Figure 2–2, which shows what happened to a limitation on contributions by taxpayers to their education Individual Retirement Accounts (now Coverdell Education Savings Accounts) in the Taxpayer Relief Act of 1997.

Referrals from the House Ways and Means Committee, the Senate Finance Committee, and the Joint Conference Committee are usually accompanied by Committee Reports. These Committee Reports often explain the provisions of the proposed legislation and are therefore a valuable source for ascertaining the *intent of Congress*. What Congress had in mind when it considered and enacted tax legislation is, of course, the key to interpreting such legislation by taxpayers, the IRS, and the courts. Since Regulations normally are not issued immediately after a statute is enacted, taxpayers often look to Committee Reports to determine congressional intent.

---

[3]During the passage of the Tax Reform Act of 1986, Senate leaders tried to make the bill *amendment proof* to avoid the normal amendment process.

FIGURE 2–1   Legislative Process for Tax Bills

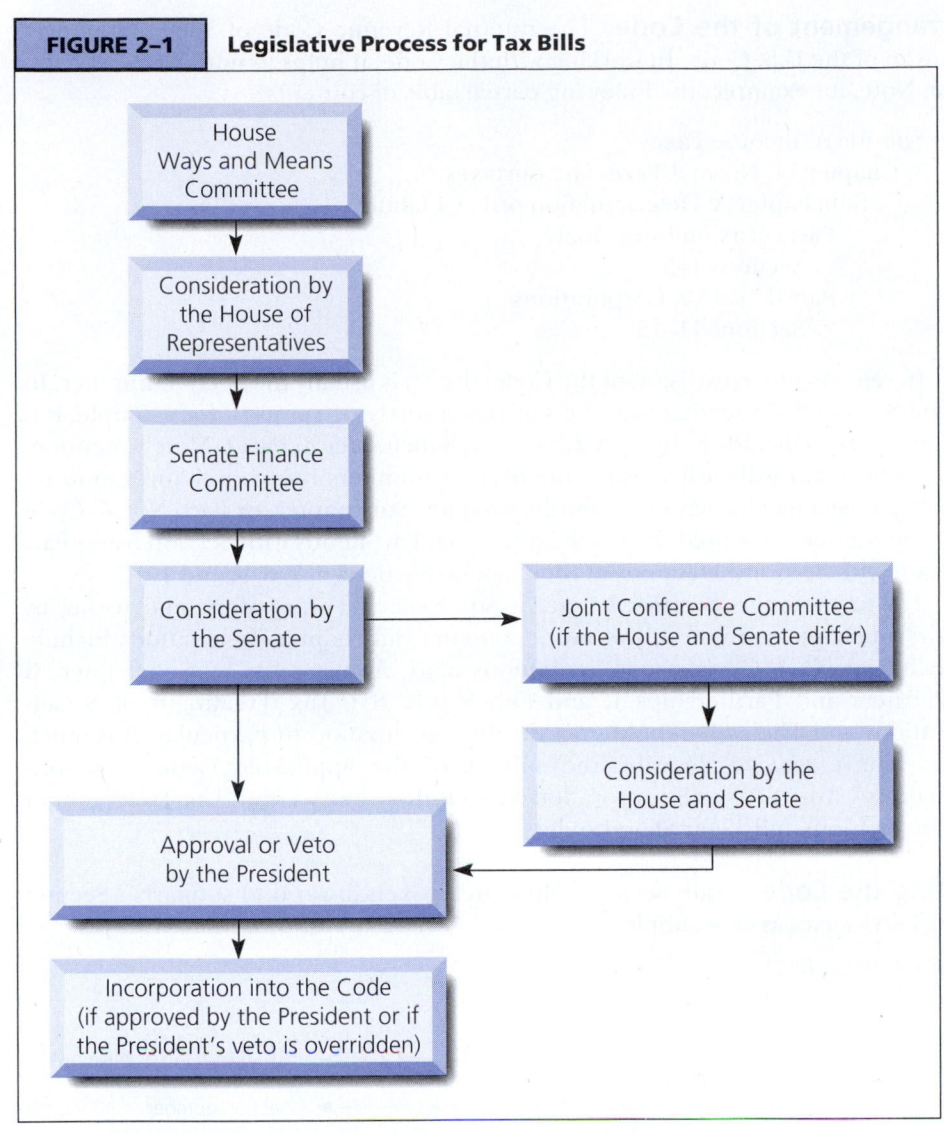

FIGURE 2–2   Example of Compromise in the Joint Conference Committee

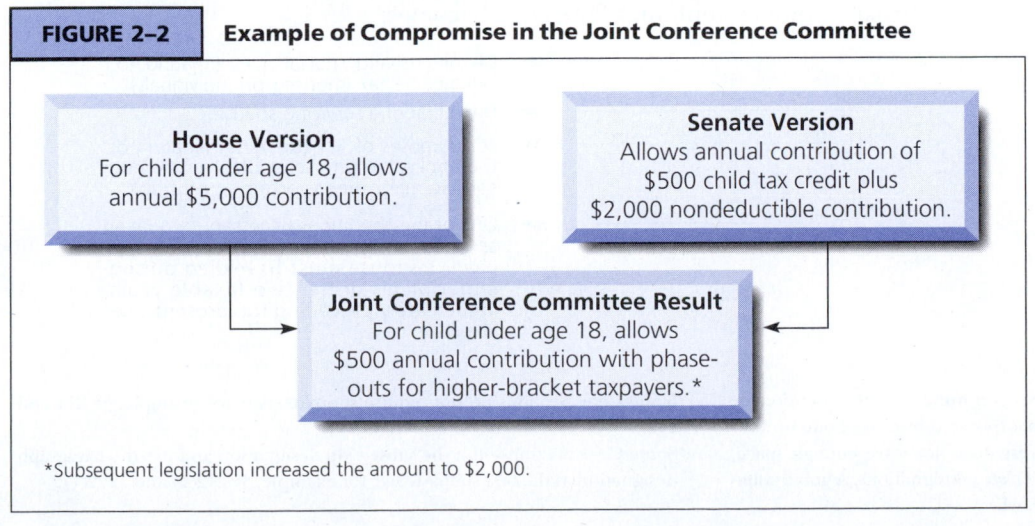

Arrangement of the Code. The Internal Revenue Code of 1986 is found in Title 26 of the U.S. Code. In working with the Code, it helps to understand the format. Note, for example, the following partial table of contents:

Subtitle A. Income Taxes
    Chapter 11. Normal Taxes and Surtaxes
        Subchapter A. Determination of Tax Liability
            Part I. Tax on Individuals
                Sections 1–5
            Part II. Tax on Corporations
                Sections 11–12

In referring to a provision of the Code, the *key* is usually the Section number. In citing Section 2(a) (dealing with the status of a surviving spouse), for example, it is unnecessary to include Subtitle A, Chapter 1, Subchapter A, Part I. Merely mentioning Section 2(a) will suffice, since the Section numbers run consecutively and do not begin again with each new Subtitle, Chapter, Subchapter, or Part. Not all Code Section numbers are used, however. Notice that Part I ends with Section 5 and Part II starts with Section 11 (at present there are no Sections 6, 7, 8, 9, and 10).[4]

Tax practitioners commonly refer to some specific areas of income tax law by their Subchapters. Some of the more common Subchapter designations include Subchapter C ("Corporate Distributions and Adjustments"), Subchapter K ("Partners and Partnerships"), and Subchapter S ("Tax Treatment of S Corporations and Their Shareholders"). In the last situation in particular, it is much more convenient to describe the subject of the applicable Code provisions (Sections 1361–1379) as S corporation status rather than as the "Tax Treatment of S Corporations and Their Shareholders."

Citing the Code. Code Sections often are broken down into subparts.[5] Section 2(a)(1)(A) serves as an example.

Broken down by content, § 2(a)(1)(A) becomes:

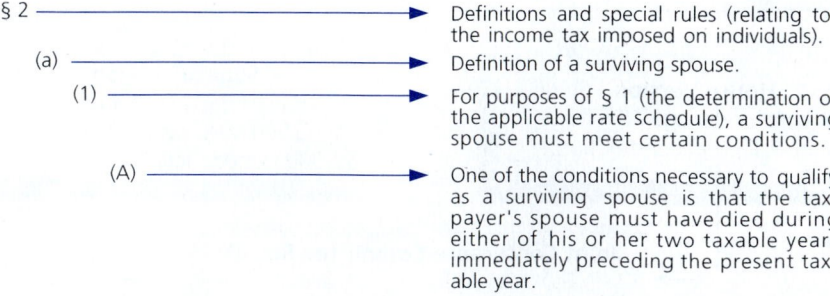

§ 2 ———————————————► Definitions and special rules (relating to the income tax imposed on individuals).

(a) ———————————————► Definition of a surviving spouse.

(1) ———————————————► For purposes of § 1 (the determination of the applicable rate schedule), a surviving spouse must meet certain conditions.

(A) ———————————————► One of the conditions necessary to qualify as a surviving spouse is that the taxpayer's spouse must have died during either of his or her two taxable years immediately preceding the present taxable year.

---

[4]When the 1954 Code was drafted, some Section numbers were intentionally omitted so that later changes could be incorporated into the Code without disrupting its organization. When Congress does not leave enough space, subsequent Code Sections are given A, B, C, etc., designations. A good example is the treatment of §§ 280A through 280H.

[5]Some Code Sections do not require subparts. See, for example, §§ 211 and 241.

[6]Some Code Sections omit the subsection designation and use the paragraph designation as the first subpart. See, for example, §§ 212(1) and 1222(1).

Throughout the text, references to the Code Sections are in the form given above. The symbols "§" and "§§" are used in place of "Section" and "Sections." Unless otherwise stated, all Code references are to the Internal Revenue Code of 1986. The following table summarizes the format that will be used:

Complete Reference	Text Reference
Section 2(a)(1)(A) of the Internal Revenue Code of 1986	§ 2(a)(1)(A)
Sections 1 and 2 of the Internal Revenue Code of 1986	§§ 1 and 2
Section 2 of the Internal Revenue Code of 1954	§ 2 of the Internal Revenue Code of 1954
Section 12(d) of the Internal Revenue Code of 1939[7]	§ 12(d) of the Internal Revenue Code of 1939

Administrative Sources of the Tax Law

The administrative sources of the Federal tax law can be grouped as follows: Treasury Department Regulations, Revenue Rulings and Revenue Procedures, and various other administrative pronouncements (see Exhibit 2–1). All are issued by either the U.S. Treasury Department or the IRS.

ETHICAL and EQUITABLE *Considerations*

THE PRESIDENT AND THE IRS

President Franklin Delano Roosevelt once said, "I am wholly unable to figure out the amount of tax." In a letter to the then Commissioner of the IRS, Roosevelt said, "As this is a problem in higher mathematics, may I ask the Bureau [IRS] to let me know the amount of the balance due."

When a friend of FDR was ordered to pay $420,000 in tax penalties, the President called the Commissioner within earshot of reporters and told him to cut the penalties to $3,000. One listener, David Brinkley, recalled years later: "Nobody seemed to think it was news or very interesting." Evaluate the President's actions.

Treasury Department Regulations. Regulations are issued by the U.S. Treasury Department under authority granted by Congress.[8] Interpretive by nature, they provide taxpayers with considerable guidance on the meaning and application of the Code. Regulations may be issued in *proposed, temporary,* or *final* form. Regulations carry considerable authority as the official interpretation of tax statutes. They are an important factor to consider in complying with the tax law.

Since Regulations interpret the Code, they are arranged in the same sequence as the Code. A number is added at the beginning, however, to indicate the type of tax or administrative, procedural, or definitional matter to which they relate. For example, the prefix 1 designates the Regulations under the income tax law. Thus, the Regulations under Code § 2 are cited as Reg. § 1.2 with subparts added for further identification. The numbering patterns of these subparts often have no correlation with the Code subsections. The prefix 20 designates estate tax Regulations; 25 covers gift tax Regulations; 31 relates to employment taxes; and 301 refers to procedure and administration. This list is not all-inclusive.

---

[7]§ 12(d) of the Internal Revenue Code of 1939 is the predecessor to § 2 of the Internal Revenue Code of 1954 and the Internal Revenue Code of 1986. Keep in mind that the 1954 Code superseded the 1939 Code and the 1986 Code has superseded the 1954 Code. Footnote 1 of this chapter explains why references to the 1939 or 1954 Code are included.

[8]§ 7805.

EXHIBIT 2–1	Administrative Sources

Source	Location	Authority**
Regulations	*Federal Register**	Force and effect of law.
Temporary Regulations	*Federal Register*** *Internal Revenue Bulletin* *Cumulative Bulletin*	May be cited as a precedent.
Proposed Regulations	*Federal Register*** *Internal Revenue Bulletin* *Cumulative Bulletin*	Preview of final Regulations.
Revenue Rulings Revenue Procedures Treasury Decisions Actions on Decisions	*Internal Revenue Bulletin* *Cumulative Bulletin*	Do not have the force and effect of law.
General Counsel Memoranda Technical Advice Memoranda	Tax Analysts' *Tax Notes*; RIA's *Internal Memoranda of the IRS*; CCH's *IRS Position Reporter*	May not be cited as a precedent.
Letter Rulings	Research Institute of America and Commerce Clearing House tax services	Applicable only to taxpayer addressed. No precedential force.

*Finalized, Temporary, and Proposed Regulations are published in soft-cover form by several publishers.

**Each of these sources may be substantial authority for purposes of the accuracy-related penalty in § 6662. Notice 90–20, 1990–1 C.B. 328.

New Regulations and changes to existing Regulations are usually issued in proposed form before they are finalized. The interval between the proposal of a Regulation and its finalization permits taxpayers and other interested parties to comment on the propriety of the proposal. **Proposed Regulations** under Code § 2, for example, are cited as Prop.Reg. § 1.2. The Tax Court indicates that Proposed Regulations carry little weight—no more than a position advanced in a written brief prepared by a litigating party before the Tax Court. **Finalized Regulations** have the force and effect of law.[9]

Sometimes the Treasury Department issues **Temporary Regulations** relating to matters where immediate guidance is important. These Regulations are issued without the comment period required for Proposed Regulations. Temporary Regulations have the same authoritative value as final Regulations and may be cited as precedents. Temporary Regulations must also be issued as Proposed Regulations and automatically expire within three years after the date of issuance.[10] Temporary Regulations and the simultaneously issued Proposed Regulations carry more weight than traditional Proposed Regulations. An example of a Temporary Regulation is Temp.Reg. § 1.199–8T, which covers computer software for purposes of the domestic production activities deduction.

Proposed, Temporary, and final Regulations are published in the *Federal Register*, in the *Internal Revenue Bulletin* (I.R.B.), and by major tax services. Final Regulations are issued as Treasury Decisions (TDs).

Regulations may also be classified as *legislative, interpretive,* or *procedural*. This classification scheme is discussed under Assessing the Validity of a Treasury Regulation later in the chapter.

Revenue Rulings and Revenue Procedures. **Revenue Rulings** are official pronouncements of the National Office of the IRS.[11] They typically provide one or

---

[9]*F. W. Woolworth Co.*, 54 T.C. 1233 (1970); *Harris M. Miller*, 70 T.C. 448 (1978); and *James O. Tomerlin Trust*, 87 T.C. 876 (1986).

[10]§ 7805(e).

[11]§ 7805(a).

more examples of how the IRS would apply a law to specific fact situations. Like Regulations, Revenue Rulings are designed to provide interpretation of the tax law. However, they do not carry the same legal force and effect as Regulations and usually deal with more restricted problems. Regulations are approved by the Secretary of the Treasury, whereas Revenue Rulings generally are not.

Although letter rulings (discussed below) are not the same as Revenue Rulings, a Revenue Ruling often results from a specific taxpayer's request for a letter ruling. If the IRS believes that a taxpayer's request for a letter ruling deserves official publication because of its widespread impact, the letter ruling will be converted into a Revenue Ruling and issued for the information and guidance of taxpayers, tax practitioners, and IRS personnel. Names, identifying descriptions, and money amounts are changed to conceal the identity of the requesting taxpayer. Revenue Rulings also arise from technical advice to District Offices of the IRS, court decisions, suggestions from tax practitioner groups, and various tax publications.

Revenue Procedures are issued in the same manner as Revenue Rulings but deal with the internal management practices and procedures of the IRS. Familiarity with these procedures can increase taxpayer compliance and help the IRS administer the tax laws more efficiently. A taxpayer's failure to follow a Revenue Procedure can result in unnecessary delay or, in a discretionary situation, can cause the IRS to decline to act on behalf of the taxpayer.

Both Revenue Rulings and Revenue Procedures serve an important function by providing *guidance* to IRS personnel and taxpayers in handling routine tax matters. Revenue Rulings and Revenue Procedures generally apply retroactively and may be revoked or modified by subsequent rulings or procedures, Regulations, legislation, or court decisions.

Revenue Rulings and Revenue Procedures are published weekly by the U.S. Government in the *Internal Revenue Bulletin* (I.R.B.). Semiannually, the bulletins for a six-month period are gathered together and published in a bound volume called the *Cumulative Bulletin* (C.B.).[12] The proper form for citing Revenue Rulings and Revenue Procedures depends on whether the item has been published in the *Cumulative Bulletin* or is only available in I.R.B. form. Consider, for example, the following transition:

| Temporary Citation | Rev.Rul. 2007–49, I.R.B. No. 31, 237. |
| | *Explanation:* Revenue Ruling Number 49, appearing on page 237 of the 31st weekly issue of the *Internal Revenue Bulletin* for 2007. |

| Permanent Citation | Rev.Rul. 2007–49, 2007–2 C.B. 237. |
| | *Explanation:* Revenue Ruling Number 49, appearing on page 237 of Volume 2 of the *Cumulative Bulletin* for 2007. |

Note that the page reference of 237 is the same for both the I.R.B. (temporary) and C.B. (permanent) versions of the ruling. The IRS numbers the pages of the I.R.B.s consecutively for each six-month period so as to facilitate their conversion to C.B. form. Revenue Rulings and other tax resources may be found on Tax Almanac, a free online resource from Intuit at **http://www.taxalmanac.org**.

Revenue Procedures are cited in the same manner, except that "Rev.Proc." is substituted for "Rev.Rul." Some recent Revenue Procedures dealt with the following matters:

- How the IRS issues Technical Advice Memoranda (TAMs) to a director or appeals officer.

---

[12]Usually, only two volumes of the *Cumulative Bulletin* are published each year. However, in the past, when Congress has enacted major tax legislation, other volumes have been published containing the congressional Committee Reports supporting the Revenue Act. See, for example, the two extra volumes for 1984 dealing with the Deficit Reduction Act of 1984. The 1984–3 *Cumulative Bulletin*, Volume 1, contains the text of the law itself; 1984–3, Volume 2, contains the Committee Reports. There are a total of four volumes of the *Cumulative Bulletin* for 1984: 1984–1; 1984–2; 1984–3, Volume 1; 1984–3, Volume 2.

- The areas in which the IRS will not issue letter rulings or determination letters.
- The requirements for preparing acceptable substitutes for official IRS forms.

Letter Rulings. **Letter rulings** are issued for a fee upon a taxpayer's request and describe how the IRS will treat a *proposed* transaction for tax purposes. They apply only to the taxpayer who asks for and obtains the ruling, but post-1984 letter rulings may be substantial authority for purposes of the accuracy-related penalty.[13] Letter rulings can be useful to taxpayers who wish to be certain of how a transaction will be taxed before proceeding with it. Letter rulings also allow taxpayers to avoid unexpected tax costs. Although the procedure for requesting a ruling can be quite cumbersome, sometimes requesting a ruling is the most effective way to carry out tax planning. Nevertheless, the IRS limits the issuance of individual rulings to restricted, preannounced areas of taxation. The main reason the IRS will not rule in certain areas is that they involve fact-oriented situations. Thus, a ruling may not be obtained on many of the problems that are particularly troublesome for taxpayers.[14] The IRS issues over 2,000 letter rulings each year.

The law now requires the IRS to make individual rulings available for public inspection after identifying details are deleted.[15] Published digests of private letter rulings can be found in *Private Letter Rulings* (published by RIA), BNA *Daily Tax Reports,* and Tax Analysts & Advocates *Tax Notes. IRS Letter Rulings Reports* (published by Commerce Clearing House) contains both digests and full texts of all letter rulings. *Letter Ruling Review* (published by Tax Analysts) is a monthly publication that selects and discusses the more important letter rulings issued each month. In addition, computerized databases of letter rulings are available through several private publishers.

Letter rulings are issued multidigit file numbers, which indicate the year and week of issuance as well as the number of the ruling during that week. Consider, for example, Ltr.Rul. 200731021, dealing with the exclusion from gross income of certain contributions by an employer to accident and health plans.

2007	31	021
Year 2007	31st week of issuance	21st ruling issued during the 31st week

Other Administrative Pronouncements. *Treasury Decisions* (TDs) are issued by the Treasury Department to promulgate new Regulations, amend or otherwise change existing Regulations, or announce the position of the Government on selected court decisions. Like Revenue Rulings and Revenue Procedures, TDs are published in the *Internal Revenue Bulletin* and subsequently transferred to the *Cumulative Bulletin.*

The IRS also publishes other administrative communications in the *Internal Revenue Bulletin* such as Announcements, Notices, IRs (News Releases), and Prohibited Transaction Exemptions.

---

[13]Notice 90–20, 1990–1 C.B. 328. In this regard, letter rulings differ from Revenue Rulings, which are applicable to *all* taxpayers. A letter ruling may later lead to the issuance of a Revenue Ruling if the holding affects many taxpayers. In its Agents' Manual, the IRS indicates that letter rulings may be used as a guide with other research materials in formulating a District Office position on an issue. The IRS is required to charge a taxpayer a fee for letter rulings, determination letters, etc.

[14]Rev.Proc. 2008–1, I.R.B. No. 1, 1 contains a list of areas in which the IRS will not issue advance rulings. From time to time, subsequent Revenue Procedures are issued that modify or amplify Rev.Proc. 2008–1.

[15]§ 6110.

Like letter rulings, **determination letters** are issued at the request of taxpayers and provide guidance on the application of the tax law. They differ from letter rulings in that the issuing source is the Area Director rather than the National Office of the IRS. Also, determination letters usually involve *completed* (as opposed to proposed) transactions. Determination letters are not published and are made known only to the party making the request.

The following examples illustrate the distinction between letter rulings and determination letters:

EXAMPLE 1

The shareholders of Red Corporation and Green Corporation want assurance that the consolidation of the corporations into Blue Corporation will be a nontaxable reorganization. The proper approach is to request the National Office of the IRS to issue a letter ruling concerning the income tax effect of the proposed transaction. ■

EXAMPLE 2

Chris operates a barber shop in which he employs eight barbers. To comply with the rules governing income tax and payroll tax withholdings, Chris wants to know whether the barbers working for him are employees or independent contractors. The proper procedure is to request a determination letter on their status from the appropriate Area Director. ■

Several internal memoranda that constitute the working law of the IRS now must be released. These General Counsel Memoranda (GCMs), Technical Advice Memoranda (TAMs), and Field Service Advices (FSAs) are not officially published, and the IRS indicates that they may not be cited as precedents by taxpayers.[16] However, these working documents do explain the IRS's position on various issues.

The National Office of the IRS releases **Technical Advice Memoranda (TAMs)** weekly. TAMs resemble letter rulings in that they give the IRS's determination of an issue. However, they differ in several respects. Letter rulings deal with proposed transactions and are issued to taxpayers at their request. In contrast, TAMs deal with completed transactions. Furthermore, TAMs arise from questions raised by IRS personnel during audits and are issued by the National Office of the IRS to its field personnel. TAMs are often requested for questions relating to exempt organizations and employee plans. TAMs are not officially published and may not be cited or used as precedent.[17] They are assigned file numbers according to the same procedure used for letter rulings. For example, TAM 200734026 refers to the 26th TAM issued during the 34th week of 2007.

The Office of Chief Counsel prepares Field Service Advice (FSAs) to help IRS employees. They are issued in response to requests for advice, guidance, and analysis on difficult or significant tax issues. FSAs are not binding on either the taxpayer to whom they pertain or on the IRS. For example, FSA 200233016 states that § 269 may be used to disallow foreign tax credits and deductions that arise from a series of reorganizations if the underlying transaction's principal purpose is to secure tax benefits.

Field Service Advices are being replaced by a new form of field guidance called Technical Expedited Advice Memoranda (TEAMs). The purpose of TEAMs is to expedite legal guidance to field agents as disputes are developing. FSAs are reverting to their original purpose of case-specific development of facts.

A TEAM guidance differs from a TAM in several ways, including a mandatory presubmission conference involving the taxpayer. In the event of a tentatively adverse conclusion for the taxpayer or the field, a conference of right is offered to the taxpayer and to the field; once the conference of right is held, no further conferences are offered.

---

[16]These are unofficially published by the publishers listed in Exhibit 2–1. Such internal memoranda for post-1984 may be substantial authority for purposes of the accuracy-related penalty. Notice 90–20, 1990–1 C.B. 328.

[17]§ 6110(j)(3). Post-1984 TAMs may be substantial authority for purposes of avoiding the accuracy-related penalty. Notice 90–20, 1990–1 C.B. 328.

FIGURE 2–3   Federal Judicial System

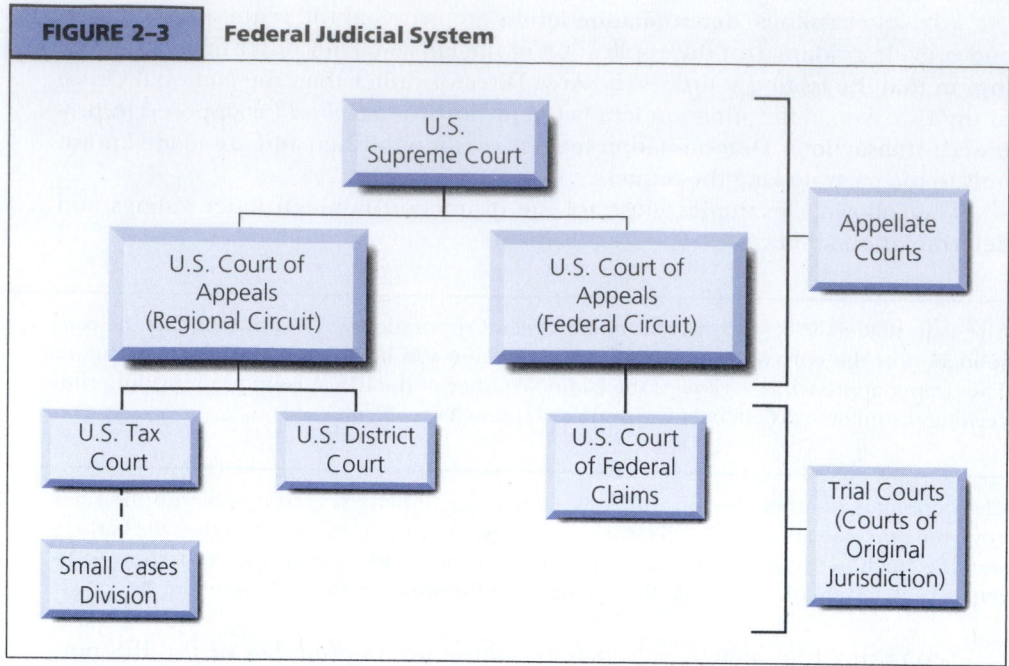

Judicial Sources of the Tax Law

The Judicial Process in General. After a taxpayer has exhausted some or all of the remedies available within the IRS (i.e., no satisfactory settlement has been reached at the agent or at the Appeals Division level), the dispute can be taken to the Federal courts. The dispute is first considered by a **court of original jurisdiction** (known as a trial court) with any appeal (either by the taxpayer or the IRS) taken to the appropriate appellate court. In most situations, the taxpayer has a choice of any of *four trial courts:* a **Federal District Court**, the **U.S. Court of Federal Claims**, the **U.S. Tax Court**, or the **Small Cases Division** of the U.S. Tax Court. The trial and appellate court system for Federal tax litigation is illustrated in Figure 2–3.

The broken line between the U.S. Tax Court and the Small Cases Division indicates that there is no appeal from the Small Cases Division. The jurisdiction of the Small Cases Division is limited to cases involving amounts of $50,000 or less. The proceedings of the Small Cases Division are informal (e.g., no necessity for the taxpayer to be represented by a lawyer or other tax adviser). Special trial judges rather than Tax Court judges preside over these proceedings. The decisions of the Small Cases Division are not precedents for any other court decision and are not reviewable by any higher court. Proceedings can be more timely and less expensive in the Small Cases Division. Some of these cases can now be found on the U.S. Tax Court Internet Web site.

American law, following English law, is frequently *made* by judicial decisions. Under the doctrine of *stare decisis*, each case (except in the Small Cases Division) has precedential value for future cases with the same controlling set of facts. Most Federal and state appellate court decisions and some decisions of trial courts are published. More than 6 million judicial opinions have been published in the United States; over 130,000 cases are published each year.[18] Published court decisions are organized by jurisdiction (Federal or state) and level of court (trial or appellate).

A decision of a particular court is called its holding. Sometimes a decision includes dicta or incidental opinions beyond the current facts. Such passing

---

[18]Mersky and Dunn, *Fundamentals of Legal Research*, 8th ed. (Westbury, N.Y.: The Foundation Press, 2002), p. 11.

TAX *in the News*   **CLOSING THE TAX GAP**

Every year Federal income tax evasion results in at least $290 billion of taxes going unpaid. Professor Jay A. Soled suggests that by eliminating cash our government could recapture at least 10 percent of this lost revenue. Since the use of cash by taxpayers leaves no paper or electronic trail, requiring buyers to use noncash alternatives would cause the underground economy to shrink dramatically. For example, Congress could prohibit buyers from using cash for transactions exceeding $500.

Source: *Adapted from Jay A. Soled, "To Close the Tax Gap, Eliminate Cash," Tax Notes, April 23, 2007, p. 379.*

---

remarks, illustrations, or analogies are not essential to the current holding. Although the holding has precedential value under *stare decisis*, dicta are not binding on a future court.

Trial Courts. The differences among the various trial courts (courts of original jurisdiction) can be summarized as follows:

- *Number of courts.* There is only one Court of Federal Claims and only one Tax Court, but there are many Federal District Courts. The taxpayer does not select the District Court that will hear the dispute but must sue in the one that has jurisdiction where the taxpayer resides.
- *Number of judges.* District Courts have various numbers of judges, but only one judge hears a case. The Court of Federal Claims has 16 judges, and the Tax Court has 19 regular judges. The entire Tax Court, however, reviews a case (the case is sent to court conference) only when more important or novel tax issues are involved. Most cases are heard and decided by one of the 19 judges.
- *Location.* The Court of Federal Claims meets most often in Washington, D.C., whereas a District Court meets at a prescribed seat for the particular district. Each state has at least one District Court, and many of the more populous states have more than one. Choosing the District Court usually minimizes the inconvenience and expense of traveling for the taxpayer and his or her counsel. Although the Tax Court is officially based in Washington, D.C., the various judges travel to different parts of the country and hear cases at predetermined locations and dates. This procedure eases the distance problem for the taxpayer, but it can mean a delay before the case comes to trial and is decided.
- *Jurisdiction of the Court of Federal Claims.* The Court of Federal Claims has jurisdiction over any claim against the United States that is based upon the Constitution, any Act of Congress, or any regulation of an executive department. Thus, the Court of Federal Claims hears nontax litigation as well as tax cases. This forum appears to be more favorable for issues having an equitable or pro-business orientation (as opposed to purely technical issues) and for those requiring extensive discovery.[19]
- *Jurisdiction of the Tax Court and District Courts.* The Tax Court hears only tax cases and is the most popular forum. The District Courts hear a wide variety of nontax cases, including drug crimes and other Federal violations, as well as tax cases. Some Tax Court judges have been appointed from IRS or Treasury Department positions. For these reasons, some people suggest that the Tax Court has more expertise in tax matters.

---

[19]T. D. Peyser, "The Case for Selecting the Claims Court to Litigate a Federal Tax Liability," *The Tax Executive* (Winter 1988): 149.

CONCEPT SUMMARY 2–1

Federal Judicial System: Trial Courts

Issue	U.S. Tax Court	U.S. District Court	U.S. Court of Federal Claims
Number of judges per court	19*	Varies	16
Payment of deficiency before trial	No	Yes	Yes
Jury trial available	No	Yes	No
Types of disputes	Tax cases only	Most criminal and civil issues	Claims against the United States
Jurisdiction	Nationwide	Location of taxpayer	Nationwide
IRS acquiescence policy	Yes	Yes	Yes
Appeal route	U.S. Court of Appeals	U.S. Court of Appeals	U.S. Court of Appeals for the Federal Circuit

*There are also 14 special trial judges and 9 senior judges.

- *Jury trial.* The only court in which a taxpayer can obtain a jury trial is a District Court. But since juries can only decide questions of fact and not questions of law, even taxpayers who choose the District Court route often do not request a jury trial. In that event, the judge will decide all issues. Note that a District Court decision is controlling only in the district in which the court has jurisdiction.
- *Payment of deficiency.* For the Court of Federal Claims or a District Court to have jurisdiction, the taxpayer must pay the tax deficiency assessed by the IRS and sue for a refund. A taxpayer who wins (assuming no successful appeal by the Government) recovers the tax paid plus appropriate interest. For the Tax Court, however, jurisdiction is usually obtained without first paying the assessed tax deficiency. In the event the taxpayer loses in the Tax Court (and does not appeal or an appeal is unsuccessful), the deficiency must be paid with appropriate interest. With the elimination of the deduction for personal (consumer) interest, the Tax Court route of delaying payment of the deficiency can become expensive. For example, to earn 7 percent after tax in 2008, a taxpayer with a 35 percent marginal tax rate would have to earn 10.77 percent. By paying the tax, a taxpayer limits underpayment interest and penalties on the underpayment.
- *Termination of running of interest.* A taxpayer who selects the Tax Court may deposit a cash bond to stop the running of interest. The taxpayer must deposit both the amount of the tax and any accrued interest. If the taxpayer wins and the deposited amount is returned, the Government does not pay interest on the deposit.
- *Appeals.* Appeals from a District Court or a Tax Court decision are to the U.S. Court of Appeals for the circuit in which the taxpayer resides. Appeals from the Court of Federal Claims go to the Court of Appeals for the Federal Circuit. Few Tax Court cases are appealed, and when appeals are made, most are filed by the taxpayer rather than the IRS.
- *Bankruptcy.* When a taxpayer files a bankruptcy petition, the IRS, like other creditors, is prevented from taking action against the taxpayer. Sometimes a bankruptcy court may settle a tax claim.

For a summary of the Federal trial courts, see Concept Summary 2–1.

FIGURE 2–4 | **The Federal Courts of Appeals**

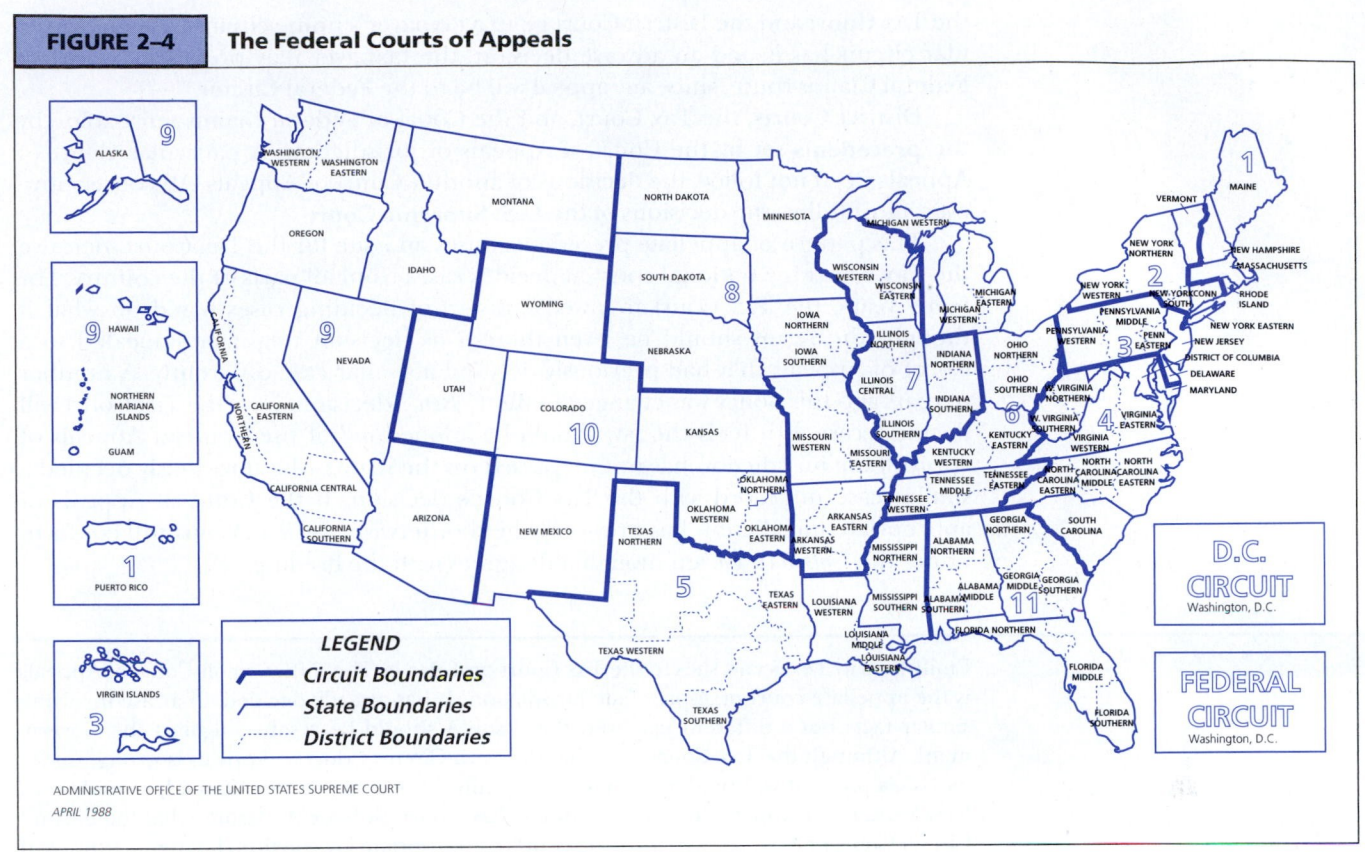

ADMINISTRATIVE OFFICE OF THE UNITED STATES SUPREME COURT

APRIL 1988

Appellate Courts. The losing party can appeal a trial court decision to a **Circuit Court of Appeals**. The 11 geographic circuits, the circuit for the District of Columbia, and the Federal Circuit[20] appear in Figure 2–4. The appropriate circuit for an appeal depends on where the litigation originated. For example, an appeal from New York goes to the Second Circuit.

If the Government loses at the trial court level (District Court, Tax Court, or Court of Federal Claims), it need not (frequently does not) appeal. The fact that an appeal is not made, however, does not indicate that the IRS agrees with the result and will not litigate similar issues in the future. The IRS may decide not to appeal for a number of reasons. First, if the current litigation load is heavy, the IRS may decide that available personnel should be assigned to other, more important cases. Second, the IRS may determine that this case is not a good one to appeal. Perhaps the taxpayer is in a sympathetic position or the facts are particularly strong in his or her favor. In that event, the IRS may wait to test the legal issues involved with a taxpayer who has a much weaker case. Third, if the appeal is from a District Court or the Tax Court, the Court of Appeals of jurisdiction could have some bearing on whether the IRS chooses to go forward with an appeal. Based on past experience and precedent, the IRS may conclude that the chance for success on a particular issue might be more promising in another Court of Appeals. If so, the IRS will wait for a similar case to arise in a different jurisdiction.

The Federal Circuit at the appellate level provides the taxpayer with an alternative forum to the Court of Appeals for his or her home circuit. Appeals from both

---

[20]The Court of Appeals for the Federal Circuit was created, effective October 1, 1982, by P.L. 97–164 (4/2/82) to hear decisions appealed from the Claims Court (now the Court of Federal Claims).

the Tax Court and the District Court go to a taxpayer's home circuit. When a particular circuit has issued an adverse decision, the taxpayer may prefer the Court of Federal Claims route, since any appeal will be to the Federal Circuit.

District Courts, the Tax Court, and the Court of Federal Claims must abide by the **precedents** set by the Court of Appeals of jurisdiction. A particular Court of Appeals need not follow the decisions of another Court of Appeals. All courts, however, must follow the decisions of the **U.S. Supreme Court**.

This pattern of appellate precedents raises an issue for the Tax Court. Because the Tax Court is a national court, it decides cases from all parts of the country. For many years, the Tax Court followed a policy of deciding cases based on what it thought the result should be, even though its decision might be appealed to a Court of Appeals that had previously decided a similar case differently. A number of years ago this policy was changed in the *Golsen*[21] decision. Now the Tax Court will decide a case as it feels the law should be applied *only* if the Court of Appeals of appropriate jurisdiction has not yet passed on the issue or has previously decided a similar case in accord with the Tax Court's decision. If the Court of Appeals of appropriate jurisdiction has previously held otherwise, the Tax Court will conform under the *Golsen* rule even though it disagrees with the holding.

EXAMPLE 3	Emily lives in Texas and sues in the Tax Court on Issue A. The Fifth Circuit Court of Appeals is the appellate court of appropriate jurisdiction. It has already decided, in a case involving similar facts but a different taxpayer, that Issue A should be resolved against the Government. Although the Tax Court feels that the Fifth Circuit Court of Appeals is wrong, under its *Golsen* policy it will render judgment for Emily. Shortly thereafter, Rashad, a resident of New York, in a comparable case, sues in the Tax Court on Issue A. Assume that the Second Circuit Court of Appeals, the appellate court of appropriate jurisdiction, has never expressed itself on Issue A. Presuming the Tax Court has not reconsidered its position on Issue A, it will decide against Rashad. Thus, it is entirely possible for two taxpayers suing in the same court to end up with opposite results merely because they live in different parts of the country. ■

Appeal to the U.S. Supreme Court is by **Writ of Certiorari**. If the Court agrees to hear the case, it will grant the Writ (*Cert. granted*). Most often, it will deny jurisdiction (*Cert. denied*). For whatever reason or reasons, the Supreme Court rarely hears tax cases. The Court usually grants certiorari to resolve a conflict among the Courts of Appeals (e.g., two or more appellate courts have assumed opposing positions on a particular issue) or where the tax issue is extremely important. The granting of a Writ of Certiorari indicates that at least four members of the Supreme Court believe that the issue is of sufficient importance to be heard by the full Court.

The *role* of appellate courts is limited to a review of the record of trial compiled by the trial courts. Thus, the appellate process usually involves a determination of whether the trial court applied the proper law in arriving at its decision. Rarely will an appellate court disturb a lower court's fact-finding determination.

Both the Code and the Supreme Court indicate that Federal appellate courts are bound by findings of facts unless they are clearly erroneous.[22] This aspect of the appellate process is illustrated by a decision of the Court of Appeals for the District of Columbia involving whether a taxpayer was engaged in an activity for profit under § 183.[23] This appeals court specifically held that the "Tax Court's findings of facts are binding on Federal courts of appeals unless clearly erroneous." The court

[21]*Jack E. Golsen*, 54 T.C. 742 (1970).

[22]§§ 7482(a) and (c). *Comm. v. Duberstein*, 60–2 USTC ¶9515, 5 AFTR2d 1626, 80 S.Ct. 1190 (USSC, 1960). See Rule 52(a) of the Federal Rules of Civil Procedure.

[23]*Dreicer v. Comm.*, 81–2 USTC ¶9683, 48 AFTR2d 5884, 665 F.2d 1292 (CA–DC, 1981).

applauded the Tax Court for the thoroughness of its factual inquiry but could "not place the stamp of approval upon its eventual legal outcome." In reversing and remanding the decision to the Tax Court, the appellate court said that "the language of § 183, its legislative history and the applicable Treasury regulation combine to demonstrate that the court's [Tax Court's] standard is erroneous as a matter of law." The appeals court held that this taxpayer's claims of deductibility were to be evaluated by proper legal standards.

An appeal can have any of a number of possible outcomes. The appellate court may approve (affirm) or disapprove (reverse) the lower court's finding, or it may send the case back for further consideration (remand). When many issues are involved, a mixed result is not unusual. Thus, the lower court may be affirmed (*aff'd*) on Issue A and reversed (*rev'd*) on Issue B, while Issue C is remanded (*rem'd*) for additional fact finding.

When more than one judge is involved in the decision-making process, disagreements are not uncommon. In addition to the majority view, one or more judges may concur (agree with the result reached but not with some or all of the reasoning) or dissent (disagree with the result). In any one case, of course, the majority view controls. But concurring and dissenting views can have an influence on other courts or, at some subsequent date when the composition of the court has changed, even on the same court.

Knowledge of several terms is important in understanding court decisions. The term *plaintiff* refers to the party requesting action in a court, and the *defendant* is the party against whom the suit is brought. Sometimes a court uses the terms *petitioner* and *respondent*. In general, "petitioner" is a synonym for "plaintiff," and "respondent" is a synonym for "defendant." At the trial court level, a taxpayer is normally the plaintiff (or petitioner), and the Government is the defendant (or respondent). If the taxpayer wins and the Government appeals as the new petitioner (or appellant), the taxpayer becomes the new respondent.

Judicial Citations—General. Having briefly described the judicial process, it is appropriate to consider the more practical problem of the relationship of case law to tax research. As previously noted, court decisions are an important source of tax law. The ability to cite and locate a case is, therefore, a must in working with the tax law. Judicial citations usually follow a standard pattern: case name, volume number, reporter series, page or paragraph number, court (where necessary), and the year of the decision.

LO.2

Locate and work with the appropriate tax law sources.

Judicial Citations—The U.S. Tax Court. A good starting point is with the Tax Court. The Tax Court issues two types of decisions: Regular and Memorandum. The Chief Judge decides whether the opinion is issued as a Regular or Memorandum decision. The distinction between the two involves both substance and form. In terms of substance, *Memorandum* decisions deal with situations necessitating only the application of already established principles of law. *Regular* decisions involve novel issues not previously resolved by the court. In actual practice, however, this distinction is not always preserved. Not infrequently, Memorandum decisions will be encountered that appear to warrant Regular status and vice versa. At any rate, do not conclude that Memorandum decisions possess no value as precedents. Both represent the position of the Tax Court and, as such, can be relied on.

The Regular and Memorandum decisions issued by the Tax Court also differ in form. Memorandum decisions are made available but are not published by the government. Regular decisions are published by the U.S. Government in a series entitled *Tax Court of the United States Reports* (T.C.). Each volume of these *Reports* covers a six-month period (January 1 through June 30 and July 1 through December 31) and is given a succeeding volume number. But, as is true of the *Cumulative Bulletin*, there is usually a time lag between the date a decision is rendered and the date it appears in bound form. A temporary citation may be necessary to help the researcher locate a recent Regular decision. Consider, for example, the temporary and permanent citations for *CRSO*, a decision filed on April 30, 2007:

Temporary Citation
$\begin{cases} \textit{CRSO}, 128 \text{ T.C. \_\_\_, No. 12 (2007).} \\ \textit{Explanation:} \text{ Page number left blank because not yet known.} \end{cases}$

Permanent Citation
$\begin{cases} \textit{CRSO}, 128 \text{ T.C. 153 (2007).} \\ \textit{Explanation:} \text{ Page number now available.} \end{cases}$

Both citations tell us that the case will ultimately appear in Volume 128 of the *Tax Court of the United States Reports*. But until this volume is bound and made available to the general public, the page number must be left blank. Instead, the temporary citation identifies the case as being the 12th Regular decision issued by the Tax Court since Volume 127 ended. With this information, the decision can easily be located in either of the special Tax Court services published by Commerce Clearing House (now owned by the Dutch company Wolters Kluwer) or Research Institute of America (formerly by Prentice-Hall). Once Volume 128 is released, the permanent citation can be substituted and the number of the case dropped. Starting in 1999, both Regular decisions and Memorandum decisions are published on the U.S. Tax Court Web site (**http://www.ustaxcourt.gov**).

Before 1943, the Tax Court was called the Board of Tax Appeals, and its decisions were published as the *United States Board of Tax Appeals Reports* (B.T.A.). These 47 volumes cover the period from 1924 to 1942. For example, the citation *Karl Pauli*, 11 B.T.A. 784 (1928), refers to the 11th volume of the *Board of Tax Appeals Reports*, page 784, issued in 1928.

If the IRS loses in a decision, it may indicate whether it agrees or disagrees with the results reached by the court by publishing an **acquiescence** ("A" or "*Acq.*") or **nonacquiescence** ("NA" or "*Nonacq.*"), respectively. Until 1991, acquiescences and nonacquiescences were published only for certain Regular decisions of the Tax Court, but the IRS has expanded its acquiescence program to include other civil tax cases where guidance is helpful. The acquiescence or nonacquiescence is published in the *Internal Revenue Bulletin* and the *Cumulative Bulletin* as an *Action on Decision*. The IRS can retroactively revoke an acquiescence.

Most often the IRS issues nonacquiescences to adverse decisions that are not appealed. In this manner, the Government indicates that it disagrees with the result reached, despite its decision not to seek review of the matter in an appellate court. A nonacquiescence provides a warning to taxpayers that a similar case cannot be settled administratively. A taxpayer will incur fees and expenses appealing within the IRS even though the IRS may be unwilling to litigate a fact pattern similar to a nonacquiescence decision.[24]

Although Memorandum decisions were not published by the U.S. Government until recently (they are now published on the U.S. Tax Court Web site), they were—and continue to be—published by Commerce Clearing House (CCH) and Research Institute of America (RIA [formerly by Prentice-Hall]). Consider, for example, the three different ways that *Jack D. Carr* can be cited:

Jack D. Carr, T.C.Memo. 1985–19
The 19th Memorandum decision issued by the Tax Court in 1985.
Jack D. Carr, 49 TCM 507
Page 507 of Vol. 49 of the CCH *Tax Court Memorandum Decisions*.
Jack D. Carr, RIA T.C.Mem.Dec. ¶85,019
Paragraph 85,019 of the RIA *T.C. Memorandum Decisions*.

---

[24]G. W. Carter, "Nonacquiescence: Winning by Losing," *Tax Notes* (September 19, 1988): 1301–1307.

Note that the third citation contains the same information as the first. Thus, ¶85,019 indicates the following information about the case: year 1985, 19th T.C. Memo. decision.[25] Although the RIA citation does not specifically include a volume number, the paragraph citation indicates that the decision can be found in the 1985 volume of the RIA Memorandum decision service.

U.S. Tax Court Summary Opinions relate to decisions of the Tax Court's Small Cases Division. These opinions are published commercially, and on the U.S. Tax Court Web site, with the warning that they may not be treated as precedent for any other case. For example, *James A. Nielsen*, filed on April 2, 2007, is cited as follows:

James A. Nielsen, T.C. Summary Opinion, 2007–53.

In 2005, the U.S. Supreme Court held that decisions of the Small Cases Division must be made public.

Judicial Citations—The U.S. District Court, Court of Federal Claims, and Courts of Appeals.

District Court, Court of Federal Claims, Courts of Appeals, and Supreme Court decisions dealing with Federal tax matters are reported in both the CCH *U.S. Tax Cases* (USTC) and the RIA *American Federal Tax Reports* (AFTR) series. Federal District Court decisions, dealing with *both* tax and nontax issues, also are published by West Publishing Company in its *Federal Supplement Series* (F.Supp.). Volume 999, published in 1998, is the last volume of the *Federal Supplement Series*. It is followed by the *Federal Supplement Second Series* (F.Supp.2d). The following examples illustrate three different ways of citing a District Court case:

Simons-Eastern Co. v. U.S., 73–1 USTC ¶9279 (D.Ct. Ga., 1972).
Explanation: Reported in the first volume of the *U.S. Tax Cases* (USTC) published by Commerce Clearing House for calendar year 1973 (73–1) and located at paragraph 9279 (¶9279).

Simons-Eastern Co. v. U.S., 31 AFTR2d 73–640 (D.Ct. Ga., 1972).
Explanation: Reported in the 31st volume of the second series of the *American Federal Tax Reports* (AFTR2d) published by RIA and beginning on page 640. The "73" preceding the page number indicates the year the case was published but is a designation used only in recent decisions.

Simons-Eastern Co. v. U.S., 354 F.Supp. 1003 (D.Ct. Ga., 1972).
Explanation: Reported in the 354th volume of the *Federal Supplement Series* (F.Supp.) published by West Publishing Company and beginning on page 1003.

In all of the preceding citations, note that the name of the case is the same (Simons-Eastern Co. being the taxpayer), as is the reference to the Federal District Court of Georgia (D.Ct. Ga.) and the year the decision was rendered (1972).[26]

Decisions of the Court of Federal Claims[27] and the Courts of Appeals are published in the USTCs, AFTRs, and a West Publishing Company reporter called the *Federal Second Series* (F.2d). Volume 999, published in 1993, is the last volume of the *Federal Second Series*. It is followed by the *Federal Third Series* (F.3d). Beginning with October 1982, the Court of Federal Claims decisions are published in another West Publishing Company reporter entitled the *Claims Court Reporter* (abbreviated Cl.Ct.). Beginning with Volume 27 on October 30, 1992, the name of the reporter changed to the *Federal Claims Reporter* (abbreviated as Fed.Cl.). The following examples illustrate the different forms:

---

[25]In this text, the RIA citation for Memorandum decisions of the U.S. Tax Court is omitted. Thus, *Jack D. Carr* would be cited as 49 TCM 507, T.C.Memo. 1985–19.

[26]In this text, the case would be cited in the following form: *Simons-Eastern Co. v. U.S.*, 73–1 USTC ¶9279, 31 AFTR2d 73–640, 354 F.Supp. 1003 (D.Ct. Ga., 1972). Prentice-Hall Information Services is now owned by Research

Institute of America. Although recent volumes contain the RIA imprint, many of the older volumes continue to have the P-H imprint.

[27]Before October 29, 1992, the Court of Federal Claims was called the Claims Court. Before October 1, 1982, the Court of Federal Claims was called the Court of Claims.

GLOBAL Tax Issues

TAX TREATIES

The United States has entered into treaties with most of the major countries of the world in order to eliminate possible double taxation. For example, nonresident alien students wishing to claim exemption from taxation are required to provide an information statement as set forth in several Revenue Procedures. The withholding agent must also certify the form.

Chinese students are required to prepare a four-part statement. Part 3 of the student's statement is as follows:

I will receive compensation for personal services performed in the United States. This compensation qualifies for exemption from withholding of Federal income tax under the tax treaty between the United States and the People's Republic of China in an amount not in excess of $5,000 for any taxable year.

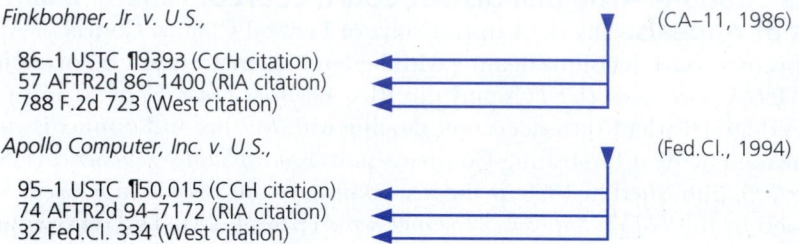

Finkbohner, Jr. v. U.S.,   (CA–11, 1986)

86–1 USTC ¶9393 (CCH citation)
57 AFTR2d 86–1400 (RIA citation)
788 F.2d 723 (West citation)

Apollo Computer, Inc. v. U.S.,   (Fed.Cl., 1994)

95–1 USTC ¶50,015 (CCH citation)
74 AFTR2d 94–7172 (RIA citation)
32 Fed.Cl. 334 (West citation)

Note that *Finkbohner, Jr.* is a decision rendered by the Eleventh Circuit Court of Appeals in 1986 (CA–11, 1986), while *Apollo Computer, Inc.* was issued by the Court of Federal Claims in 1994 (Fed.Cl., 1994).

Judicial Citations—The U.S. Supreme Court.

Like all other Federal tax decisions (except those rendered by the Tax Court), Supreme Court decisions are published by Commerce Clearing House in the USTCs and by RIA (formerly by Prentice-Hall) in the AFTRs. The U.S. Government Printing Office also publishes these decisions in the *United States Supreme Court Reports* (U.S.) as does West Publishing Company in its *Supreme Court Reporter* (S.Ct.) and the Lawyer's Co-operative Publishing Company in its *United States Reports, Lawyer's Edition* (L.Ed.). The following illustrates the different ways the same decision can be cited:

U.S. v. The Donruss Co.,   (USSC, 1969)

69–1 USTC ¶9167 (CCH citation)
23 AFTR2d 69–418 (RIA citation)
89 S.Ct. 501 (West citation)
393 U.S. 297 (U.S. Government Printing Office citation)
21 L.Ed.2d 495 (Lawyer's Co-operative Publishing Co. citation)

The parenthetical reference (USSC, 1969) identifies the decision as having been rendered by the U.S. Supreme Court in 1969. In this text, the citations of Supreme Court decisions will be limited to the CCH (USTC), RIA (AFTR), and West (S.Ct.) versions. For a summary, see Concept Summary 2–2.

Other Sources of the Tax Law

Other sources of tax information that a tax practitioner may need to consult include tax treaties and tax periodicals.

Tax Treaties. The United States signs certain tax treaties (sometimes called tax conventions) with foreign countries to render mutual assistance in tax enforcement

CONCEPT SUMMARY 2–2

Judicial Sources

Court	Location	Authority
U.S. Supreme Court	S.Ct. Series (West)	Highest authority
	U.S. Series (U.S. Gov't.)	
	L.Ed.2d (Lawyer's Co-op.)	
	AFTR (RIA)	
	USTC (CCH)	
U.S. Courts of Appeal	Federal 3d (West)	Next highest appellate court
	AFTR (RIA)	
	USTC (CCH)	
Tax Court (Regular decisions)	U.S. Gov't. Printing Office	Highest trial court*
	RIA/CCH separate services	
Tax Court (Memorandum decisions)	RIA T.C.Memo. (RIA)	Less authority than Regular T.C. decision
	TCM (CCH)	
U.S. Court of Federal Claims**	Federal Claims Reporter (West)	Similar authority as Tax Court
	AFTR (RIA)	
	USTC (CCH)	
U.S. District Courts	F.Supp.2d Series (West)	Lowest trial court
	AFTR (RIA)	
	USTC (CCH)	
Small Cases Division of Tax Court	U.S. Tax Court Web site***	No precedent value

*Theoretically, the Tax Court, Court of Federal Claims, and District Courts are on the same level of authority. But some people believe that since the Tax Court hears and decides tax cases from all parts of the country (i.e., it is a national court), its decisions may be more authoritative than a Court of Federal Claims or District Court decision.

**Before October 29, 1992, the U.S. Claims Court.

***Starting in 2001.

and to avoid double taxation. Tax legislation enacted in 1988 provided that neither a tax law nor a tax treaty takes general precedence. Thus, when there is a direct conflict, the most recent item will take precedence. A taxpayer must disclose on the tax return any position where a treaty overrides a tax law.[28] There is a $1,000 penalty per failure to disclose for individuals and a $10,000 per failure penalty for corporations.[29]

Tax Periodicals. The various tax periodicals are another source of tax information. The easiest way to locate a journal article pertinent to a tax problem is through Commerce Clearing House's *Federal Tax Articles*. This multivolume service includes a subject index, a Code Section number index, and an author's index. The RIA (formerly P-H) tax service also has a topical "Index to Tax Articles" section that is organized using the RIA paragraph index system. Also, beginning in 1992, *The Accounting & Tax Index* is available in three quarterly issues plus a cumulative year-end volume covering all four quarters. The original *Accountant's Index* started in 1921 and ended in 1991.

---

[28]§ 7852(d).

[29]Reg. §§ 301.6114–1, 301.6712–1, and 301.7701(b)(7).

The following are some of the more useful tax periodicals:

Journal of Taxation
Journal of International Taxation
Practical Tax Strategies
Estate Planning
Corporate Taxation
Business Entities
ria.thomson.com/Journals

The Tax Executive
www.tei.org

The Tax Adviser
aicpa.org/pubs/taxadv

Practical Accountant
webcpa.com/publications.cfm

Tax Law Review
www.law.nyu.edu/programs/tax/review.html

Journal of the American Taxation Association
atasection.org/jata.html

The ATA Journal of Legal Tax Research
aaahq.org/ata/_ATAMenu/ATAPubJLTR.html

Oil, Gas & Energy Quarterly
bookstore.lexis.com/bookstore/product/10462.html

Trusts and Estates
trustsandestates.com

Journal of Passthrough Entities
TAXES—The Tax Magazine
tax.cchgroup.com/Books

National Tax Journal
ntj.tax.org

Tax Notes
taxanalysts.com/TaxNotes

The Tax Lawyer
www.law.georgetown.edu/journals/tax

LO.3

Have an awareness of electronic and paper tax services.

Working with the Tax Law—Tax Research Tools

As the later discussion of tax research makes clear, a crucial part of the research process is the ability to locate appropriate sources of the tax law. Both electronic and paper-based research tools are available to aid in this search.

Electronic versus Paper Tax Research Tools

Computerized tax research tools have replaced paper resources in most tax practices. As will be described shortly, there are two chief ways to conduct tax research using computer resources: (1) online and CD-ROM subscription services and (2) online free Internet sites.

Accessing tax documents through electronic means offers a number of advantages over a strictly paper-based approach:

- Materials generally are available to the practitioner faster through an electronic system, as delays related to typesetting, proofreading, production, and distribution of the new materials are substantially reduced. Online services are updated daily and can be accessed from remote locations.
- Some tax documents, such as so-called slip opinions of trial-level court cases and interviews with policymakers, are available only through electronic means.
- Commercial subscriptions to electronic tax services are likely to provide, at little or no additional cost, additional tax sources to which the researcher would not have access through stand-alone purchases of traditional paper resources. For example, the full texts of letter rulings are quite costly to acquire in a paper-based format, but electronic publishers may bundle the rulings with other material for a reasonable cost.
- When consulting a topical or annotated paper tax service, a user is relying on someone else's judgment while searching the topical index. The keyword that the researcher is searching for may not have been used by the editor.
- A computerized tax service allows a user to create his or her own keywords and indexes. The software will electronically scan entire files and retrieve all of the documents that contain those words.

- A computerized tax service may retrieve documents that are no longer in print and may obtain regularly published documents to which a researcher does not otherwise have access.
- Most computerized services allow a user to retrieve documents in order of relevance or in the order listed by database sources. Although this can be useful, just because a document is placed high on the relevance list does not mean it is valid law. Reading the primary sources, validating their authority, and checking the citator are essential in reaching a correct answer.

As indicated above, computerized tools allow the tax library to reflect the tax law itself, including its dynamic and daily changes. Nevertheless, electronic research should not become an end in itself. Using electronic means to locate tax sources cannot substitute for developing and maintaining a thorough knowledge of the tax law or for logical and analytical review in addressing open tax research issues.

Tax Services

Whether in electronic or paper form, tax services are key research tools for the tax practitioner. The major tax services available are as follows:

Standard Federal Tax Reporter, Commerce Clearing House.

United States Tax Reporter, Research Institute of America (entitled *Federal Taxes* prior to July 1992).

Federal Tax Coordinator 2d, Research Institute of America.

Tax Management Portfolios, Bureau of National Affairs.

Federal Income, Gift and Estate Taxation, Warren, Gorham and Lamont.

CCH's Tax Research Consultant, Commerce Clearing House.

Mertens Law of Federal Income Taxation, Callaghan and Co.

In this text, it is not feasible to teach the use of any particular tax service; this ability can be obtained only by practice.[30] However, several important observations about the use of tax services cannot be overemphasized. First, always check for current developments. The main text of any paper-based service is not revised frequently enough to permit reliance on that portion as the *latest* word on any subject. Where current developments can be found depends, of course, on which service is being used. Commerce Clearing House's *Standard Federal Tax Reporter* service contains a special volume devoted to current matters. Both RIA's *United States Tax Reporter* and *Federal Tax Coordinator 2d* integrate the new developments into the body of the service throughout the year. Second, when dealing with a tax service synopsis of a Treasury Department pronouncement or a judicial decision, remember there is no substitute for the original source.

To illustrate, do not base a conclusion solely on a tax service's commentary on a potentially relevant court case such as *Simons-Eastern Co. v. U.S.* If the case is vital to the research, look it up. The facts of the case may be distinguishable from those involved in the problem being researched. This is not to say that the case synopsis contained in the tax service is wrong; it might just be misleading or incomplete.

Electronic Services

Virtually all of the major commercial tax publishers and most of the primary sources of the law itself, such as the Supreme Court and some of the Courts of Appeals, provide tax materials in electronic formats. Competitive pressures have

---

[30]The representatives of the various tax services are prepared to provide the users of their services with printed booklets and individual instruction on the use of the materials.

EXHIBIT 2–2	Electronic Tax Services

Electronic Tax Service	Description
CCH	Includes the CCH tax service, primary sources including treatises, and other subscription materials. Ten to 20 discs and online.
RIA	Includes the RIA topical *Federal Tax Coordinator 2d* and the annotated tax service formerly provided by Prentice-Hall. The citator has elaborate document-linking features, and major tax treatises are provided. One to 10 discs and online.
WESTLAW	Code, Regulations, *Cumulative Bulletins*, cases, citators, and editorial material. About a dozen discs and online.
Kleinrock's	A single disc with tax statutory, administrative, and judicial law. Another single disc provides tax forms and instructions for Federal and state jurisdictions.

rewarded tax practitioners who have developed computer literacy skills, and the user-friendliness of the best of the tax research software is of great benefit to both the daily and the occasional user. Exhibit 2–2 summarizes the most popular of the electronic tax services on the market today.

In using these resources, usually the law is found using one of the following strategies:

- *Search* various databases using keywords that are likely to be found in the underlying documents, as written by Congress, the judiciary, or administrative sources.
- *Link* to tax documents for which all or part of the proper citation is known (e.g., Code Section, court decision).
- *Browse* the tax databases, examining various tables of contents and indexes in a traditional manner or using cross-references in the documents to jump from one tax law source to another.

CD-ROM Services. The CD has been a major source of electronic tax data for more than a decade. Data compression techniques continue to allow more tax materials to fit on a single disc every year. CCH, RIA, WESTLAW, and others offer vast tax libraries to the practitioner, often in conjunction with a subscription to traditional paper-based resources or accompanied by newsletters, training seminars, and ongoing technical support.

At its best, a CD-based tax library provides the archival data that make up a permanent, core library of tax documents. For about $300 a year, the tax CD is updated quarterly, providing more comprehensive tax resources than the researcher is ever likely to need. The CD is comparable in scope to a paper-based library of a decade ago costing perhaps $20,000 to establish and $5,000 per year in perpetuity to maintain. If the library is contained on a small number of discs, it also can offer portability through use on notebook computers.

Online Systems. An online research system allows a practitioner to obtain virtually instantaneous use of tax law sources by accessing the computer of the service provider. Online services may employ price-per-search cost structures, which can be as much as $200 per hour, significantly higher than the cost of CD materials. Thus, unless a practitioner can pass along related costs to

EXHIBIT 2–3	Online Tax Services

Online Service	Description
LEXIS/NEXIS	Federal and state statutory, administrative, and judicial material. Extensive libraries of newspapers, magazines, patent records, and medical and economic databases, both U.S. and foreign-based.
RIA	Includes the RIA tax services, major tax treatises, Federal and state statutes, administrative documents, and court opinions. Extensive citator access, editorial material, and practitioner aids.
CCH	Includes the CCH tax service, primary sources including treatises, and other subscription materials. Tax and economic news sources, extensive editorial material, and practitioner support tools.
WESTLAW	Federal and state statutes, administrative documents, and court opinions. Extensive citator access, editorial material, and gateways to third-party publications. Extensive government document databases.

clients or others, online searching generally is limited to the most important issues and to the researchers with the most experience and training in search techniques.

Perhaps the best combination of electronic tax resources is to conduct day-to-day work on a CD system, so that the budget for the related work is known in advance, and augment the CD search with online access where it is judged to be critical. Exhibit 2–3 provides details on the contents of the most commonly used commercial online tax services.

The Internet. The Internet provides a wealth of tax information in several popular forms, sometimes at no direct cost to the researcher. Using so-called browser software that often is distributed with new computer systems and their communication devices, the tax professional can access information provided around the world that can aid the research process.

- *Home pages (sites) on the World Wide Web (WWW)* are provided by accounting and consulting firms, publishers, tax academics and libraries, and governmental bodies as a means of making information widely available or of soliciting subscriptions or consulting engagements. The best sites offer links to other sites and direct contact to the site providers. One of the best sites available to the tax practitioner is the Internal Revenue Service's *Digital Daily*, illustrated in Exhibit 2–4. This site offers downloadable forms and instructions, "plain English" versions of Regulations, and news update items. Exhibit 2–5 lists some of the Web sites that may be most useful to tax researchers and their Internet addresses as of press date.
- *Newsgroups* provide a means by which information related to the tax law can be exchanged among taxpayers, tax professionals, and others who subscribe to the group's services. Newsgroup members can read the exchanges among other members and offer replies and suggestions to inquiries as desired. Discussions address the interpretation and application of existing law, analysis of proposals and new pronouncements, and reviews of tax software.
- *E-mail capabilities* are available to most tax professionals through an employer's equipment or by a subscription providing Internet access at a low and usually

EXHIBIT 2–4   The IRS's *Digital Daily*

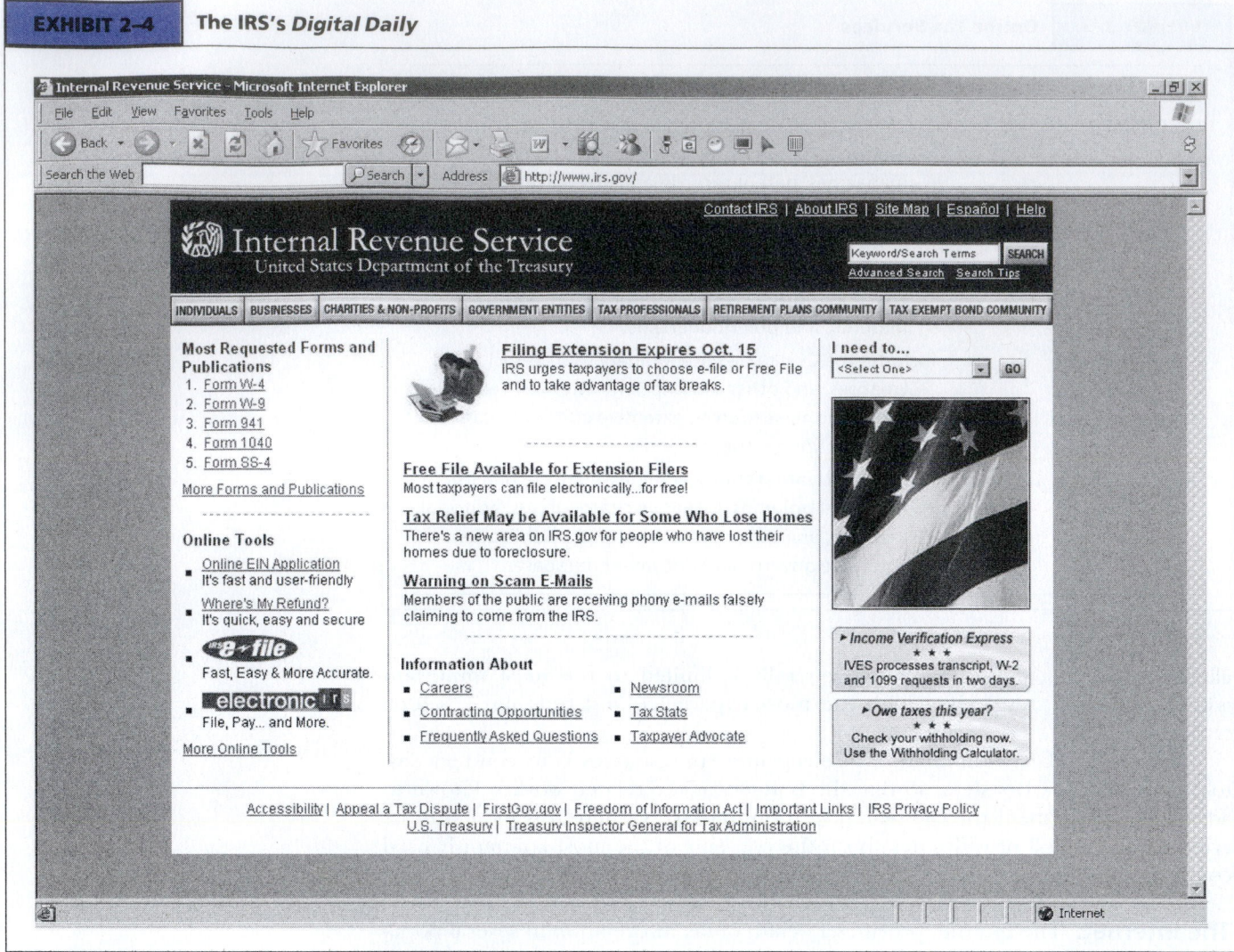

fixed cost for the period. E-mail allows for virtually instantaneous sending and receiving of messages, letters, tax returns and supporting data, spreadsheets, and other documents necessary to solve tax problems.

In many situations, solutions to research problems benefit from, or require, the use of various electronic tax research tools. A competent tax professional must become familiar and proficient with these tools and be able to use them to meet the expectations of clients and the necessities of work in the modern world.[31]

LO.4

Understand the tax research process.

Working with the Tax Law—Tax Research

Tax research is the method by which a tax practitioner, student, or professor determines the best available solution to a situation that possesses tax consequences. In other words, it is the process of finding a competent and professional conclusion to a tax problem. The problem may originate from completed or proposed transactions. In the case of a completed transaction, the objective of the research is to determine the tax result of what has already taken place. For example, was the

---

[31]For a more detailed discussion of the use of electronic tax research in the modern tax practice, see Raabe, Whittenburg, Sanders, and Bost, *South-Western's Federal Tax Research*, 8th ed. (Cengage Learning South-Western, 2008).

EXHIBIT 2–5	Tax-Related Web Sites

Web Site	WWW Address at Press Date (Usually preceded by http://www.)	Description
Tax Almanac	**taxalmanac.org**	Smorgasbord of tax research resources
Internal Revenue Service	**irs.gov/**	News releases, downloadable forms and instructions, tables, and e-mail
Court opinions	The site at **law.emory.edu/caselaw** allows the researcher to link to the site of the jurisdiction (other than the Tax Court) that is the subject of the query.	
Tax Analysts	**taxanalysts.com**	Policy-oriented readings on the tax law and proposals to change it, moderated bulletins on various tax subjects
Tax Sites Directory	**taxsites.com**	References and links to tax sites on the Internet, including state and Federal tax sites, academic and professional pages, tax forms, and software
Tax laws online	Regulations are at **cfr.law.cornell.edu/cfr/** and the Code is at **uscode.house.gov/search/criteria.shtml** and **www4.law.cornell.edu/uscode/**	
Commercial tax publishers	For instance, **tax.com** and **cch.com**	Information about products and services available for subscription and newsletter excerpts
Large accounting firms and professional organizations	For instance, the AICPA's page is at **aicpa.org**, Ernst and Young is at **ey.com**, and KPMG is at **kpmg.com**	Tax planning newsletters, descriptions of services offered and career opportunities, and exchange of data with clients and subscribers
Cengage Learning South-Western	**academic.cengage.com/taxation/SWFT**	Informational updates, newsletters, support materials for students and adopters, and continuing education
U.S. Tax Court decisions	**ustaxcourt.gov**	Recent U.S. Tax Court decisions

NOTE: Caution: addresses change frequently.

expenditure incurred by the taxpayer deductible or not deductible for tax purposes? When dealing with proposed transactions, the tax research process is directed toward the determination of possible alternative tax consequences. To the extent that tax research leads to a choice of alternatives or otherwise influences the future actions of the taxpayer, it becomes the key to effective tax planning.

Tax research involves the following procedures:

- Identifying and refining the problem.
- Locating the appropriate tax law sources.
- Assessing the validity of the tax law sources.
- Arriving at the solution or at alternative solutions with due consideration given to nontax factors.
- Effectively communicating the solution to the taxpayer or the taxpayer's representative.
- Following up on the solution (where appropriate) in light of new developments.

DATA WAREHOUSING REDUCES GLOBAL TAXES

Many global companies are using data warehouses to collect data, which can be analyzed and used to minimize their global tax liabilities. "You take all of your tax data and dump it into a data warehouse," says Michael S. Burke of KPMG's e-tax solutions. "Next, it's applying a tool to define user requirements—compliance, real time analysis, etc." The company can then manipulate all of this information to reduce compliance costs, facilitate planning for value added taxes, and minimize time spent dealing with international tax problems.

For example, a company wishes to implement an e-procurement technique that would save it $100 million in expenses and increase taxable income. That could mean that about $40 million in additional taxes would go to the U.S. Treasury and state treasuries. By looking at the tax laws worldwide, the company may decide to base the operation in Bermuda, Ireland, or the Philippines where the tax will be only $20 million. That's a savings of $20 million, which is not taxable.

Source: *Adapted from Jay Weinstein, "Internet Tax Solutions Proliferate,"* Global Finance, *January 2001, pp. 74–75.*

This process is depicted schematically in Figure 2–5. The broken lines reflect the steps of particular interest when tax research is directed toward proposed, rather than completed, transactions.

Identifying the Problem

Problem identification must start with a compilation of the relevant facts involved.[32] In this regard, *all* of the facts that may have a bearing on the problem must be gathered because any omission could modify the solution reached. To illustrate, consider what appears to be a very simple problem.

EXAMPLE 4

Early in December 2008, Fred and Megan review their financial and tax situation with their son, Sam, and daughter-in-law, Dana, who live with them. Fred and Megan are in the 28% tax bracket in 2008. Both Sam and Dana are age 21. Sam, a student at a nearby university, owns some publicly traded stock that he inherited from his grandmother. A current sale would result in approximately $8,000 of gross income ($19,000 amount realized − $11,000 adjusted basis). At this point, Fred and Megan provide about 55% of Sam and Dana's support. Although neither is now employed, Sam has earned $960 and Dana has earned $900. The problem: Should the stock be sold, and would the sale prohibit Fred and Megan from claiming Sam and Dana as dependents? Would the stock sale in 2008 result in a tax liability for Sam and Dana? ■

Refining the Problem

Initial reaction is that Fred and Megan in Example 4 could *not* claim Sam and Dana as dependents if the stock is sold, since Sam would then have gross income of more than the exemption amount under § 151(d).[33] However, after 2004, the test for whether a child qualifies for dependency status is first conducted under the *qualifying child* requirements. Only if these requirements cannot be satisfied is the test for dependency status conducted under the *qualifying relative* requirements. The gross

---

[32]For an excellent discussion of the critical role of facts in carrying out tax research, see R. L. Gardner, D. N. Stewart, and R. G. Worsham, *Tax Research Techniques* (The American Institute of Certified Public Accountants, New York: 2000), Chapter 2.

[33]§ 152(d)(2). See the related discussion in Chapter 3.

FIGURE 2–5   **Tax Research Process**

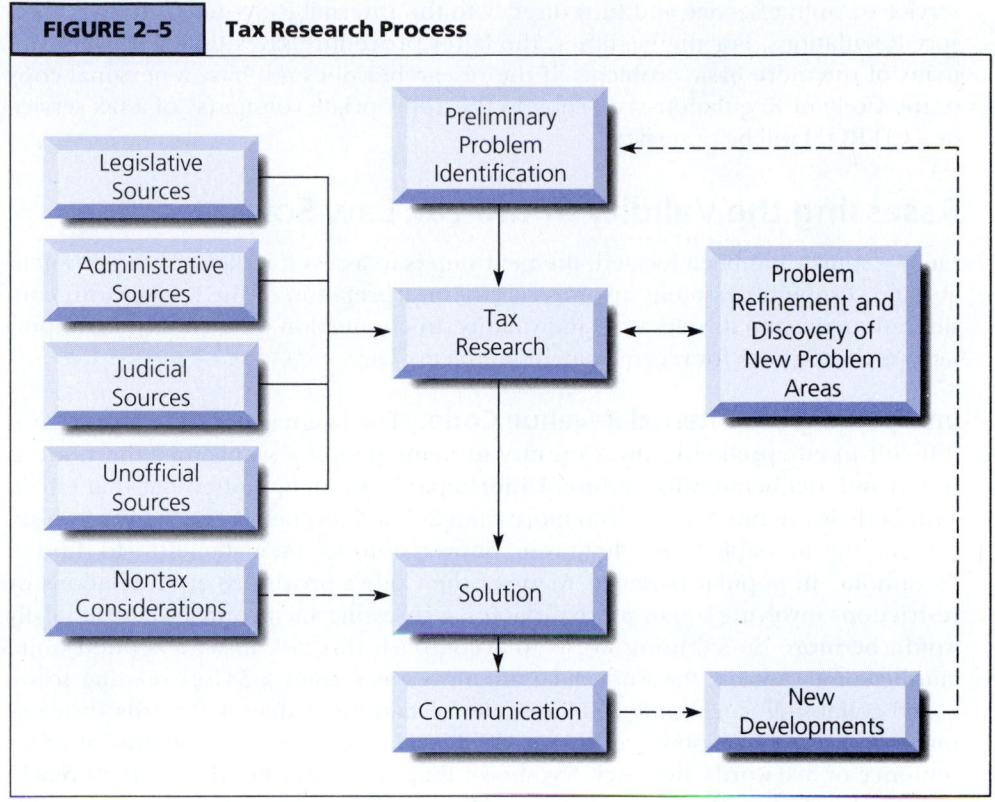

income test is applicable only under the qualifying relative status.[34] Thus, Sam could sell the stock without penalizing the parents with respect to the gross income test. Under the qualifying child provision, however, Sam must not have provided more than one-half of his own support.[35] Hence, the $19,000 of proceeds from the sale of the stock might lead to the failure of the not self-supporting requirement, depending on how much Sam spends for his support.

Assume, however, that further fact gathering reveals the following additional information:

- Sam does not really need to spend the proceeds from the sale of the stock.
- Sam receives a sizable portion of his own support from a scholarship.

With these new facts, additional research leads to § 152(f)(5) and Regulation § 1.152–1(c), which indicate that a scholarship received by a student is not included for purposes of computing whether Sam is self-supporting under the qualifying child provision. Further, if Sam does not spend the proceeds from the sale of the stock, the unexpended amount is not counted for purposes of the not self-supporting test. Thus, it appears that the parents would not be denied the dependency exemptions for Sam and Dana, as the qualifying child requirements appear to be satisfied for Sam and the qualifying relative requirements appear to be satisfied for Dana.

Locating the Appropriate Tax Law Sources

Once the problem is clearly defined, what is the next step? Although the next step is a matter of individual judgment, most tax research begins with the index volume of the tax service, a keyword search on an online tax service, or a CD-ROM search as described earlier. If the problem is not complex, the researcher may bypass the tax

---

[34]Compare § 152(c) for qualifying child with § 152(d) for qualifying relative.   [35]§ 152(c)(1)(D).

service or online service and turn directly to the Internal Revenue Code and Treasury Regulations. For the beginner, the latter procedure saves time and will solve many of the more basic problems. If the researcher does not have a personal copy of the Code or Regulations, resorting to the appropriate volume(s) of a tax service or a CD-ROM will be necessary.[36]

Assessing the Validity of the Tax Law Sources

Once a source has been located, the next step is to assess it in light of the problem at hand. Proper assessment involves careful interpretation of the tax law with consideration given to its relevance and validity. In connection with validity, an important step is to check for recent changes in the tax law.

Interpreting the Internal Revenue Code.
The language of the Code often is difficult to comprehend fully. Contrary to many people's suspicions, the Code is not written deliberately to confuse. Unfortunately, though, it often has that effect. The Code is intended to apply to more than 200 million taxpayers, many of whom are willing to exploit any linguistic imprecision to their benefit—to find a "loophole" in popular parlance. Many of the Code's provisions are limitations or restrictions involving two or more variables. Expressing such concepts algebraically would be more direct; using words to accomplish this task instead is often quite cumbersome. Among the worst such attempts was former § 341(e) relating to so-called collapsible corporations. One sentence had more than 450 words (twice as many as in the Gettysburg Address). Within this same subsection was another sentence of 300 words. Research has shown that in one-third of the conflicts reaching the Tax Court, the court could not discern the intent of Congress by simply reading the statute. Yet the overriding attitude of the Tax Court judges is that the statute comes first. Even when the statute is unworkable, the court will not rewrite the law.[37]

Assessing the Validity of a Treasury Regulation.
Treasury Regulations are the official interpretation of the Code and are entitled to great deference. Occasionally, however, a court will invalidate a Regulation or a portion thereof on the grounds that the Regulation is contrary to the intent of Congress. Usually, the courts do not question the validity of Regulations because of the belief that "the first administrative interpretation of a provision as it appears in a new act often expresses the general understanding of the times or the actual understanding of those who played an important part when the statute was drafted."[38]

Keep the following observations in mind when assessing the validity of a Regulation:

- IRS agents must give the Code and the Regulations issued thereunder equal weight when dealing with taxpayers and their representatives.
- Proposed Regulations provide a preview of future final Regulations, but they are not binding on the IRS or taxpayers.
- In a challenge, the burden of proof is on the taxpayer to show that the Regulation varies from the language of the statute and has no support in the Committee Reports.
- If the taxpayer loses the challenge, a 20 percent negligence penalty may be imposed.[39] This accuracy-related penalty applies to any failure to make a

---

[36]Several of the major tax services publish paperback editions of the Code and Treasury Regulations that can be purchased at modest prices. These editions are usually revised twice each year. For an annotated and abridged version of the Code and Regulations that is published annually, see James E. Smith, *South-Western Federal Taxation: Internal Revenue Code of 1986 and Treasury Regulations: Annotated and Selected* (Cengage Learning South-Western, 2009).

[37]T. L. Kirkpatrick and W. B. Pollard, "Reliance by the Tax Court on the Legislative Intent of Congress," *The Tax Executive* (Summer 1986): 358–359.

[38]*Augustus v. Comm.*, 41–1 USTC ¶9255, 26 AFTR 612, 118 F.2d 38 (CA–6, 1941).

[39]§§ 6662(a) and (b)(1).

TAX *in the News* | **INTERNAL REVENUE CODE: INTERPRETATION PITFALLS**

One author has noted 10 common pitfalls in interpreting the Code:

1. Determine the limitations and exceptions to a provision. Do not permit the language of the Code Section to carry greater or lesser weight than was intended.
2. Just because a Section fails to mention an item does not necessarily mean that the item is excluded.
3. Read definitional clauses carefully.
4. Do not overlook small words such as *and* and *or*. There is a world of difference between these two words.
5. Read the Code Section completely; do not jump to conclusions.
6. Watch out for cross-referenced and related provisions, since many Sections of the Code are interrelated.
7. At times Congress is not careful when reconciling new Code provisions with existing Sections. Conflicts among Sections, therefore, do arise.
8. Be alert for hidden definitions; terms in a particular Code Section may be defined in the same Section or in a separate Section.
9. Some answers may not be found in the Code; therefore, a researcher may have to consult the Regulations and/or judicial decisions.
10. Take careful note of measuring words such as *less than 50 percent*, *more than 50 percent*, and *at least 80 percent*.

Source: Adapted by permission from Henry G. Wong, "Ten Common Pitfalls in Reading the Internal Revenue Code," Journal of Business Strategy (July–August 1972): 30–33. Reprinted with permission by Faulkner & Gray, Inc., 11 Penn Plaza, New York, NY 10001.

---

reasonable attempt to comply with the tax law and any disregard of rules and Regulations.[40]

- Final Regulations can be classified as procedural, interpretive, or legislative. **Procedural Regulations** neither establish tax laws nor attempt to explain tax laws. Procedural Regulations are *housekeeping-type instructions* indicating information that taxpayers should provide the IRS as well as information about the internal management and conduct of the IRS itself.

- Some **interpretive Regulations** rephrase and elaborate what Congress stated in the Committee Reports that were issued when the tax legislation was enacted. Such Regulations are *hard* and *solid* and almost impossible to overturn because they clearly reflect the intent of Congress. An interpretive Regulation is given less deference than a legislative Regulation, however. The Supreme Court has told lower courts to analyze Treasury Regulations carefully before accepting the Treasury's interpretation.[41]

- In some Code Sections, Congress has given the *Secretary or his delegate* the authority to prescribe Regulations to carry out the details of administration or to otherwise complete the operating rules. Under such circumstances, Congress effectively is delegating its legislative powers to the Treasury Department. Regulations issued pursuant to this type of authority possess the force and effect of law and are often called **legislative Regulations** (e.g., consolidated return Regulations).

- Courts tend to apply a legislative reenactment doctrine. A particular Regulation is assumed to have received congressional approval if the Regulation was finalized many years earlier and Congress has not amended the Code Section pertaining to that Regulation.

---

[40]§ 6662(c).

[41]*U.S. v. Vogel Fertilizer Co.*, 82–1 USTC ¶9134, 49 AFTR2d 82–491, 102 S.Ct. 821 (USSC, 1982); *National Muffler Dealers Assn., Inc.*, 79–1 USTC ¶9264, 43 AFTR2d 79–828, 99 S.Ct. 1304 (USSC, 1979).

Assessing the Validity of Other Administrative Sources of the Tax Law. Revenue Rulings issued by the IRS carry less weight than Treasury Department Regulations. Revenue Rulings are important, however, in that they reflect the position of the IRS on tax matters. In any dispute with the IRS on the interpretation of tax law, therefore, taxpayers should expect agents to follow the results reached in any applicable Revenue Rulings. A 1986 Tax Court decision, however, indicated that Revenue Rulings "typically do not constitute substantive authority for a position."[42] Most Revenue Rulings apply retroactively unless a specific statement indicates the extent to which a ruling is to be applied without retroactive effect.[43]

Actions on Decisions further tell the taxpayer the IRS's reaction to certain court decisions. Recall that the IRS follows a practice of either acquiescing (agreeing) or nonacquiescing (not agreeing) with selected judicial decisions. A nonacquiescence does not mean that a particular court decision is of no value, but it does indicate that the IRS may continue to litigate the issue involved.

Assessing the Validity of Judicial Sources of the Tax Law. The judicial process as it relates to the formulation of tax law has already been described. How much reliance can be placed on a particular decision depends upon the following variables:

- The higher the level of the court that issued a decision, the greater the weight accorded to that decision. A decision rendered by a trial court (e.g., a Federal District Court) carries less weight than one issued by an appellate court (e.g., the Fifth Circuit Court of Appeals). Unless Congress changes the Code, decisions by the U.S. Supreme Court represent the last word on any tax issue.
- More reliance is placed on decisions of courts that have jurisdiction in the area where the taxpayer's legal residence is located. If, for example, a taxpayer lives in Texas, a decision of the Fifth Circuit Court of Appeals means more than one rendered by the Second Circuit Court of Appeals. This result occurs because any appeal from a U.S. District Court or the Tax Court would be to the Fifth Circuit Court of Appeals and not to the Second Circuit Court of Appeals.[44]
- A Tax Court Regular decision carries more weight than a Memorandum decision since the Tax Court does not consider Memorandum decisions to be binding precedents.[45] Furthermore, a Tax Court *reviewed* decision carries even more weight. All of the Tax Court judges participate in a reviewed decision.
- A Circuit Court decision where certiorari has been requested and denied by the U.S. Supreme Court carries more weight than a Circuit Court decision that was not appealed. A Circuit Court decision heard *en banc* (all the judges participate) carries more weight than a normal Circuit Court case.
- A decision that is supported by cases from other courts carries more weight than a decision that is not supported by other cases.
- The weight of a decision also can be affected by its status on appeal. For example, was the decision affirmed or overruled?

In connection with the last two variables, the use of a citator is invaluable to tax research.[46] A **citator** provides the history of a case and lists subsequently published opinions that refer to the case being assessed. Reviewing these references enables the tax researcher to determine whether the decision in question has been reversed, affirmed, followed by other courts, or distinguished in some way. If one

---

[42] *Nelda C. Stark*, 86 T.C. 243 (1986). See also *Ann R. Neuhoff*, 75 T.C. 36 (1980). For a different opinion, however, see *Industrial Valley Bank & Trust Co.*, 66 T.C. 272 (1976).

[43] Rev.Proc. 87–1, 1987–1 C.B. 503.

[44] Before October 1, 1982, an appeal from the then-named U.S. Court of Claims (the other trial court) was directly to the U.S. Supreme Court.

[45] *Severino R. Nico, Jr.*, 67 T.C. 647 (1977).

[46] The major citators are published by Commerce Clearing House, RIA, and Shepard's Citations, Inc. These citators are available in published and electronic formats. WESTLAW has a citator that is available only in electronic format. See Appendix E.

TAX *in the News*   **BASEBALL AND TAX RESEARCH**

An analogy based on the philosophy of Sandy Koufax, a great pitcher for the Los Angeles Dodgers in the late 1950s and 1960s, is appropriate for a tax researcher. Koufax is one of only some 17 baseball players to pitch a perfect game. He said that whenever he started a game, he tried to pitch a perfect game. If he was not successful, he tried for a no-hitter and then a shutout (no runs), and if he failed at all of these, he tried to win the game.

In researching a tax problem, the researcher tries first to find a Code Section, a tax treaty, or a committee report to support his or her position. If not successful in doing this, the researcher tries to find a Regulation, then a Revenue Ruling, and then a court decision (in this order). If no primary authority can be found, the researcher looks for a Bluebook passage, letter ruling, a learned book or article, or a comment from a tax service.

intends to rely on a judicial decision to any significant degree, "running" the case through a citator is imperative. Citators and their use are discussed in Appendix E.

Assessing the Validity of Other Sources. *Primary sources* of tax law include the Constitution, legislative history materials, statutes, treaties, Treasury Regulations, IRS pronouncements, and judicial decisions. In general, the IRS considers only primary sources to constitute substantial authority. However, a researcher might wish to refer to *secondary materials* such as legal periodicals, treatises, legal opinions, General Counsel Memoranda, and written determinations. In general, secondary sources are not authority.

Although the statement that the IRS regards only primary sources as substantial authority generally is true, there is one exception. In Notice 90–20,[47] the IRS expanded the list of substantial authority *for purposes of* the accuracy-related penalty in § 6662 to include a number of secondary materials (e.g., letter rulings, General Counsel Memoranda, the Bluebook). "Authority" does not include conclusions reached in treatises, legal periodicals, and opinions rendered by tax professionals.

A letter ruling or determination letter is substantial authority *only* for the taxpayer to whom it is issued, except as noted above with respect to the accuracy-related penalty.

Upon the completion of major tax legislation, the staff of the Joint Committee on Taxation (in consultation with the staffs of the House Ways and Means and Senate Finance Committees) often will prepare a General Explanation of the Act, commonly known as the Bluebook because of the color of its cover. The IRS will not accept this detailed explanation as having legal effect, except as noted above with respect to the accuracy-related penalty. The Bluebook does, however, provide valuable guidance to tax advisers and taxpayers until Regulations are issued. Some letter rulings and General Counsel Memoranda of the IRS cite Bluebook explanations.

Arriving at the Solution or at Alternative Solutions

Example 4 raised the question of whether a taxpayer would be denied dependency exemptions for a son and a daughter-in-law if the son sold some stock near the end of the year. A refinement of the problem supplies additional information:

- Sam and Dana anticipate filing a joint return.

Section 152(b)(2) indicates that a taxpayer is not permitted a dependency exemption for a married dependent if the married individual files a joint return. Initial reaction is that a joint return by Sam and Dana would be disastrous to the parents. However, more research uncovers two Revenue Rulings that provide an exception if neither the dependent nor the dependent's spouse is required to file a

---

[47]1990–1 C.B. 328; see also Reg. § 1.6661–3(b)(2).

return but does so solely to claim a refund of tax withheld. The IRS asserts that each spouse must have gross income of less than the exemption amount.[48] Therefore, if Sam sells the stock and he and Dana file a joint return, the parents would lose the dependency exemption for both Sam and Dana.

If the stock is not sold until January 2009, both dependency exemptions are available to the parents in 2008 even if Sam and Dana file a joint return. However, under § 151(d)(2) a personal exemption is not available to a taxpayer who can be claimed as a dependent by another taxpayer (whether actually claimed or not). Thus, if the parents can claim Sam and Dana as dependents, Sam and Dana would lose their personal exemptions on their tax return.

<table>
<tr><td>**LO.5**</td></tr>
<tr><td>Communicate the results of the tax research process in a client letter and a tax file memorandum.</td></tr>
</table>

Communicating Tax Research

Once the problem has been researched adequately, the researcher may need to prepare a memo, letter, or oral presentation setting forth the result. The form such a communication takes could depend on a number of considerations. For example, does the employer or professor recommend a particular procedure or format for tax research memos? Is the memo to be given directly to the client, or will it first go to the researcher's employer? Who is the audience for the oral presentation? How long should you talk? Whatever form it takes, a good tax research communication should contain the following elements:

- A clear statement of the issue.
- In more complex situations, a short review of the fact pattern that raises the issue.
- A review of the pertinent tax law sources (e.g., Code, Regulations, Revenue Rulings, judicial authority).
- Any assumptions made in arriving at the solution.
- The solution recommended and the logic or reasoning supporting it.
- The references consulted in the research process.

In short, a good tax research communication should tell the audience what was researched, the results of that research, and the justification for the recommendation made.[49]

Illustrations of the memos for the tax file and the client letter associated with Example 4 appear in Figure 2–6, Figure 2–7, and Figure 2–8.

<table>
<tr><td>**LO.6**</td></tr>
<tr><td>Apply tax research techniques and planning procedures.</td></tr>
</table>

Working with the Tax Law—Tax Planning

Tax research and tax planning are inseparable. The *primary* purpose of effective *tax planning* is to reduce the taxpayer's total tax bill. This statement does not mean that the course of action selected must produce the lowest possible tax under the circumstances. The minimization of tax liability must be considered in context with the legitimate business goals of the taxpayer.

A *secondary* objective of effective tax planning is to reduce or defer the tax in the current tax year. Specifically, this objective aims to accomplish one or more of the following: eradicating the tax entirely; eliminating the tax in the current year; deferring the receipt of income; converting ordinary income into capital gains; converting active to passive income; converting passive to active expense; proliferating taxpayers (i.e., forming partnerships and corporations or making lifetime gifts to family members); eluding double taxation; avoiding ordinary income; or creating, increasing, or accelerating deductions. However, this second objective should

---

[48]Rev.Rul. 54–567, 1954–2 C.B. 108; Rev.Rul. 65–34, 1965–1 C.B. 86.

[49]See Chapter 6 of the publication cited in Footnote 32. For oral presentations, see W. A. Raabe and G. E. Whittenburg, "Talking Tax: How to Make a Tax Presentation," *The Tax Adviser* (March 1997): 179–182.

FIGURE 2–6	**Tax File Memorandum**

August 16, 2008

TAX FILE MEMORANDUM

FROM: John J. Jones
SUBJECT: Fred and Megan Taxpayer
              Engagement: Issues

Today I talked to Fred Taxpayer with respect to his August 12, 2008 letter requesting tax assistance. He wishes to know if his son, Sam, can sell stock worth $19,000 (basis = $11,000) without the parents losing the dependency exemptions for Sam and Sam's wife, Dana. Fred would also like to know the effect on Sam and Dana's tax liability in 2008 if the stock is sold.

Fred Taxpayer is married to Megan, and Sam is a full-time student at a local university. Sam inherited the stock from his grandmother about five years ago. If he sells the stock, he will save the proceeds from the sale. Sam does not need to spend the proceeds if he sells the stock because he receives a $5,500 scholarship that he uses for his own support (i.e., to pay for tuition, books, and fees). Although neither Sam nor Dana is currently employed, Sam has earned income of $960, and Dana has earned income of $900. Fred and Megan are in the 28% tax bracket and furnish approximately 55% of Sam and Dana's support.

ISSUES: If the stock is sold, would the sale prohibit Fred and Megan from claiming Sam and Dana as dependents? What is the effect on Sam and Dana's tax liability if the stock is sold in 2008? I told Fred that we would have an answer for him within two weeks.

be approached with considerable reservation and moderation. For example, a tax election in one year may reduce taxes currently, but saddle future years with a disadvantageous tax position.

Nontax Considerations

There is an honest danger that tax motivations may take on a significance that does not correspond to the true values involved. In other words, tax considerations may impair the exercise of sound business judgment by the taxpayer. Thus, the tax planning process can become a medium through which to accomplish ends that are socially and economically objectionable. All too often, planning seems to lean toward the opposing extremes of placing either too little or too much emphasis on tax considerations. The happy medium—a balance that recognizes the significance of taxes, but not beyond the point where planning detracts from the exercise of good business judgment—turns out to be the promised land that is too infrequently reached.

The remark is often made that a good rule is to refrain from pursuing any course of action that would not be followed were it not for certain tax considerations. This statement is not entirely correct, but it does illustrate the desirability of preventing business logic from being *sacrificed at the altar of tax planning.*

Tax Avoidance and Tax Evasion

A fine line exists between legal tax planning and illegal tax planning—tax avoidance versus tax evasion. **Tax avoidance** is merely tax minimization through legal techniques. In this sense, tax avoidance is the proper objective of all tax planning. Tax evasion, while also aimed at the elimination or reduction of taxes, connotes the use of subterfuge and fraud as a means to an end. Popular usage—probably because of the common goals involved—has so linked these two concepts that many individuals are no longer aware of the true distinctions between them. Consequently, some taxpayers have been deterred from properly taking advantage of planning possibilities. The now classic words of Judge Learned Hand in *Commissioner v. Newman* reflect the true values the taxpayer should have:

FIGURE 2–7   Tax File Memorandum

August 26, 2008

TAX FILE MEMORANDUM

FROM: John J. Jones
SUBJECT: Fred and Megan Taxpayer
          Engagement: Conclusions

See the Tax File Memorandum dated August 16, 2008, which contains the facts and identifies the tax issues.

Section 152(a) provides that in order for a taxpayer to take a dependency exemption, the potential dependent must satisfy either the qualifying child requirements or the qualifying relative requirements (see Chapter 3). Fred and Megan provide about 55% of the support of their son, Sam, and their daughter-in-law, Dana. If Sam should sell the stock in 2008, he would not need to spend the proceeds for support purposes (i.e., would save the proceeds). Thus, the stock sale would not affect his qualifying as not self-supporting under § 152(c)(1)(D). In calculating the percentage of support provided by Fred and Megan, a $5,500 scholarship received by Sam is not counted in determining the amount of support Sam provides for himself [see § 152(f)(5) and Reg. § 1.152–1(c)]. Note, however, that if the $5,500 had been provided by student loans, it would have been included in calculating support [*Philip J. McCauley*, 56 T.C. 48 (1971)].

Section 152(d)(1)(B) provides that in order to qualify for a dependency exemption as a qualifying relative, the potential dependent's gross income must be less than the exemption amount (i.e., $3,500 in 2008). Without the stock sale, the gross income of both Sam ($960) and Dana ($900) will be below the exemption amount in 2008. The $5,500 Sam receives as a scholarship is excluded from his gross income under § 117(a) because he uses the entire amount to pay for his tuition, books, and fees at a local university.

Although the gross income test is not applicable to Sam (as a qualifying child), it is applicable to Dana, the daughter-in-law (a qualifying relative). [See Concept Summary 3–1.] A key issue is whether the stock sale that will produce $8,000 of recognized gain for Sam and Dana will cause the gross income test to be violated for Dana. Since the $8,000 recognized gain is from the sale of Sam's separately owned asset and they do not live in a community property state, Dana should qualify as a dependent because her gross income would be only $900.

Sam must not be self-supporting under the qualifying child requirements. So, if the stock is sold, he must limit his spending of the sales proceeds such that he continues to be supported by his parents. Since he plans on not spending any of the sales proceeds, this should not be an issue.

The stock sale would result in the parents' loss of the dependency exemptions for Sam and Dana if they file a joint return for 2008 [see § 152(b)(2)]. The joint return requirement does not apply, however, if the dependent files a joint return solely to claim a refund and neither spouse had a tax liability on a separate return (Rev.Rul. 65–34, 1965–1 C.B. 86). However, sale of the stock would keep this exception from applying.

From a tax planning perspective, Sam can choose to sell the stock in 2008. However, if this choice is made, Sam and Dana need to file separate returns so as not to violate the absence of a joint return provision. Under these circumstances, the sale will not interfere with Fred and Megan's ability to claim dependency exemptions for Sam and Dana on their 2008 return. Note, however, that neither Sam nor Dana will be permitted to take a personal exemption deduction on their 2008 tax return since they are claimed as dependents on someone else's return [see § 151(d)(2)]. This disallowance of the personal exemption deduction will not produce any significant negative tax consequences for Dana since her tax liability would be $0. However, Sam's tax liability would now be $930 (see the kiddie tax in Chapter 3). Alternatively, Sam could delay the sale of the stock until 2009. In this case, Sam and Dana's tax liability in 2008 would be $0. The disallowance of the personal exemption deductions by Sam and Dana will not produce any negative tax consequences since both Sam and Dana's tax liability would be $0.

Over and over again courts have said that there is nothing sinister in so arranging one's affairs as to keep taxes as low as possible. Everybody does so, rich or poor; and all do right, for nobody owes any public duty to pay more than the law demands: taxes are enforced extractions, not voluntary contributions. To demand more in the name of morals is mere cant.[50]

As Denis Healy, a former British Chancellor, once said, "The difference between tax avoidance and tax evasion is the thickness of a prison wall."

The Government Accountability Office estimates that U.S. taxpayers spend at least $107 billion each year on tax compliance costs. The Treasury Department estimates that individuals spend at least 6.4 billion hours preparing Federal income tax

---

[50]*Comm. v. Newman*, 47–1 USTC ¶9175, 35 AFTR 857, 159 F.2d 848 (CA–2, 1947).

FIGURE 2–8   Client Letter

Hoffman, Smith, and Willis, CPAs
5191 Natorp Boulevard
Mason, Ohio 45040

August 30, 2008

Mr. and Ms. Fred Taxpayer
111 Boulevard
Williamsburg, Virginia 23185

Dear Mr. and Ms. Taxpayer:

This letter is in response to your request for us to review your family's financial and tax situation. Our conclusions are based upon the facts as outlined in your August 12th letter. Any change in the facts may affect our conclusions.

You provide over 50% of the support for your son, Sam, and his wife, Dana. The scholarship Sam receives is not included in determining support. If the stock is not sold, you will qualify for a dependency exemption for both Sam and Dana.

If the stock is sold, a gain of approximately $8,000 will result. If Sam and Dana then file a joint return, you would lose the dependency exemption for Sam as a qualifying child and would lose the dependency exemption for Dana as a qualifying relative. You can avoid the loss of these two dependency exemptions if Sam and Dana file separate returns. This would result in a tax liability of $0 for Dana and $930 for Sam.

From a family tax planning and tax avoidance perspective, Sam should not sell the stock in 2008. Delaying the stock sale will enable you to claim dependency exemptions for both Sam and Dana and will enable Sam and Dana to have a $0 tax liability for 2008.

Should you need more information or need to clarify our conclusions, do not hesitate to contact me.

Sincerely yours,

John J. Jones, CPA
Partner

ETHICAL and EQUITABLE *Considerations*

TWIST AND SHOUT, BUT PAY YOUR TAXES

Failing to file Federal income tax returns, failing to make voluntary payments to the IRS from 1976 to 1996, spending millions of dollars of unreported cash payments from performances on a yacht and two houses, and cashing royalty checks belonging to your dead brother are not tax avoidance schemes. These were the activities that led to the conviction of soul legend Ronald Isley, of "Twist and Shout" fame, for income tax evasion. Isley and his siblings, known as the Isley Brothers, rose to fame in the 1950s with such hits as "This Old Heart of Mine." In sentencing Isley to three years in Federal prison, the judge agreed with the description of Isley as a "serial tax avoider." Did the judge really mean "serial tax evader"?

Sources: *Adapted from "Ronald Isley Gets 3 Years for Tax Evasion," Reuters, September 2, 2006; "Ronald Isley Sentenced for Tax Evasion," USA Today, September 5, 2006, p. 10.*

TAX *in the News*   THE DISAPPEARING TAXPAYERS

Should income taxes be increased, not decreased, especially on the bottom 60 percent of taxpayers? Should the tax base be expanded? Recent tax data lend credence to such unpopular opinions.

In 2004, 99 percent of the individual Federal income tax was received from 40 percent of the taxpayers. The top 10 percent of taxpayers paid 71 percent of all Federal income taxes while the bottom 50 percent of taxpayers paid less than 4 percent. Of the 136 million returns processed, at least 44 million owed no tax, and many of those received an earned income credit. Add to this figure the 15 million households and individuals who file no Federal income tax returns, and it

appears that about 41 percent of the U.S. population fell outside the Federal income tax system.

Another problem is that the Internet is helping taxpayers to disappear. In a recent *New Yorker* magazine cartoon, two dogs are sitting in front of a computer screen: one tells the other, "On the Internet, nobody knows that you are a dog." Similarly, in order to collect a tax, the government must know who is liable to pay the tax. Taxpayers are becoming increasingly more difficult to identify as anonymous electronic money and uncrackable encryption techniques are developed.

If too many taxpayers disappear via the Internet, will the government's deficit grow larger?

---

returns. Small businesses, self-employed persons, and taxpayers with the highest marginal tax rates have the highest levels of tax evasion.[51]

Follow-up Procedures

Because tax planning usually involves a proposed (as opposed to a completed) transaction, it is predicated upon the continuing validity of the advice based upon the tax research. A change in the tax law (either legislative, administrative, or judicial) could alter the original conclusion. Additional research may be necessary to test the solution in light of current developments (refer to the broken lines at the right in Figure 2–5).

Tax Planning—A Practical Application

Returning to the facts of Example 4, what could be done to protect the dependency exemptions for the parents? If Sam and Dana refrain from filing a joint return, both could be claimed by the parents.

An obvious tax planning tool is the installment method. Could the securities be sold using the installment method under § 453 so that most of the gain is deferred into the next year? Under the installment method, certain gains may be postponed and recognized as the cash proceeds are received. The problem is that the installment method is not available for stock traded on an established securities market.[52]

A little more research, however, indicates that Sam might be able to sell the stock and postpone the recognition of gain until the following year by selling short an equal number of substantially identical shares and covering the short sale in the subsequent year with the shares originally held. Selling short means that Sam sells borrowed stock (substantially identical) and repays the lender with the stock held on the date of the short sale. This *short against the box* technique would allow Sam to protect his $8,000 profit and defer the closing of the sale until the following year.[53] However, additional research indicates that 1997 tax legislation provides that the short against the box technique will no longer produce the desired postponement of recognized gain. That is, at the time of the short sale, Sam will have a recognized gain of $8,000 from a constructive sale. Note the critical role of obtaining the correct facts in attempting to resolve the proper strategy for the taxpayers.

---

[51]Adapted from J. A. Tackett, Joe Antenucci, and Fran Wolf, "A Criminological Perspective of Tax Evasion," *Tax Notes* (February 6, 2006): 654–658; L. E. Burman, "Tax Evasion, IRS Priorities, and the EITC," *Statement before the*

United States House of Representatives Committee on the Budget; On Waste, Fraud, and Abuse in Federal Mandatory Programs (July 9, 2003).

[52]See Chapter 18 for a discussion of installment sales.

[53]§§ 1233(a) and 1233(b)(2). See Chapter 16 for a discussion of short sales.

Throughout this text, most chapters include observations on Tax Planning Considerations. Such observations are not all-inclusive but are intended to illustrate some of the ways in which the material covered can be effectively utilized to minimize taxes.

Taxation on the CPA Examination

The CPA examination has changed from a paper-and-pencil exam to a computer-based exam with increased emphasis on information technology and general business knowledge. The 14-hour exam has four sections, and taxation is included in the 3-hour Regulation section. The taxation part of the Regulation section covers:

- Federal tax procedures and accounting issues.
- Federal taxation of property transactions.
- Federal taxation—individuals.
- Federal taxation—entities.

The Regulation section of the CPA examination had the lowest pass rate for 2006 at 42.33, with the highest being FAR at 44.54. The CPA examination is not curved to produce a designated pass rate. In theory, if all candidates are well prepared, they will all pass. Of course, if all are unprepared, all could fail.

Each exam section includes both multiple-choice questions and case studies called simulations. The multiple-choice part consists of three sequential testlets, each containing 24 to 30 questions. These testlets are groups of questions prepared to appear together. In addition, each exam section includes a testlet that consists of two simulations. A candidate may review and change answers within each testlet but cannot go back after exiting a testlet. Candidates take different, but equivalent exams.

Simulations are small case studies designed to test a candidate's tax knowledge and skills using real-life work-related situations. The simulations range from 30 to 50 minutes in length and complement the multiple-choice questions. Simulations include a four-function pop-up calculator, a blank spreadsheet with some elementary functionality, and authoritative literature appropriate to the subject matter. The taxation database includes authoritative excerpts that are necessary to complete the tax case study simulations (e.g., Internal Revenue Code and Federal tax forms). Examples of such simulations follow.

EXAMPLE 5

The *tax citation type* simulation requires the candidate to research the Internal Revenue Code and enter a Code Section and subsection. For example, Amber Company is considering using the simplified dollar-value method of pricing its inventory for purposes of the LIFO method that is available to certain small businesses. What Code Section is the relevant authority in the Internal Revenue Code to which you should turn to determine whether the taxpayer is eligible to use this method? To be successful, the candidate needs to find § 474. ■

EXAMPLE 6

A *tax form completion* simulation requires the candidate to fill out a portion of a tax form. For example, Green Company is a limited liability company (LLC) for tax purposes. Complete the income section of the 2007 IRS Form 1065 for Green Company using the values found and calculated on previous tabs along with the following data:

Ordinary income from other partnerships	$ 5,200
Net gain (loss) from Form 4797	2,400
Management fee income	12,000

The candidate is provided with page 1 of Form 1065 on which to record the appropriate amounts. ■

Candidates can learn more about the CPA examination at **http://www.cpa-exam.org**. This online tutorial site reviews the exam's format, navigation functions, and tools. A 30- to 60-minute sample exam will familiarize a candidate with the types of questions on the examination.

KEY TERMS

Acquiescence, 2–18

Circuit Court of Appeals, 2–15

Citator, 2–32

Court of original jurisdiction, 2–12

Determination letters, 2–11

Federal District Court, 2–12

Finalized Regulations, 2–8

Interpretive Regulations, 2–31

Legislative Regulations, 2–31

Letter rulings, 2–10

Nonacquiescence, 2–18

Precedents, 2–16

Procedural Regulations, 2–31

Proposed Regulations, 2–8

Revenue Procedures, 2–9

Revenue Rulings, 2–8

Small Cases Division, 2–12

Tax avoidance, 2–35

Tax research, 2–26

Technical Advice Memoranda (TAMs), 2–11

Temporary Regulations, 2–8

U.S. Court of Federal Claims, 2–12

U.S. Supreme Court, 2–16

U.S. Tax Court, 2–12

Writ of Certiorari, 2–16

PROBLEM MATERIALS

DISCUSSION QUESTIONS

1. What is an outcome of the many gray areas in the tax laws?

2. Did Congress recodify the Internal Revenue Code in 1986?

3. Tax legislation generally originates in the Senate Finance Committee. Discuss the validity of this statement.

4. In order for a tax bill to become law, the President must sign or approve the changes in the law. Discuss the validity of this statement.

5. In which Title of the U.S. Code is the Internal Revenue Code of 1986 found?

Communications

6. Paul Bishop operates a small international firm named Teal, Inc. A new treaty between the United States and France conflicts with a Section of the Internal Revenue Code. Paul asks you for advice. If he follows the treaty position, does he need to disclose this on his tax return? If he is required to disclose, are there any penalties for failure to disclose? Prepare a letter in which you respond to Paul. Teal's address is 100 International Drive, Tampa, FL 33620.

7. Interpret this Regulation citation: Reg. § 1.702–1(a)(8).

8. Explain how Regulations are arranged. How would the following Regulations be cited?
   a. Finalized Regulations under § 265.
   b. Proposed Regulations under § 707.
   c. Temporary Regulations under § 125.
   d. Legislative Regulations under § 1001.

9. Distinguish between legislative, interpretive, and procedural Regulations.

10. In the citation Notice 97–9, 1997–1 C.B. 365, to what do the 9 and the 365 refer?

11. Rank the following items from the highest authority to the lowest in the Federal tax law system:
    a. Interpretive Regulation.
    b. Legislative Regulation.
    c. Letter ruling.
    d. Revenue Ruling.

e. Internal Revenue Code.

f. Proposed Regulation.

12. Interpret each of the following citations:

a. Prop.Reg. § 1.280A–3(c)(4).

b. Rev.Rul. 67–74, 1967–1 C.B. 194.

c. Ltr.Rul. 200409001.

13. Barbara Brown calls you on the phone. She says that she has found a 1991 letter ruling that agrees with a position she wishes to take on her tax return. She asks you about the precedential value of a letter ruling. Draft a memo for the tax files outlining what you told Barbara.

Communications

14. Sammie is considering writing the IRS to determine whether a retirement plan maintained by an association of churches qualifies as a church plan under § 414(e). Outline some relevant tax issues Sammie faces in making this decision.

Issue ID

15. Are General Counsel Memoranda (GCM) officially published? Can they be cited as precedents by taxpayers?

16. What are the differences between Technical Advice Memoranda (TAMs) and Technical Expedited Advice Memoranda (TEAMs)?

17. Caleb receives a 90-day letter after his discussion with an appeals officer. He is not satisfied with the $92,000 settlement offer. Identify the relevant tax research issues facing Caleb.

Issue ID

18. Which of the following would be considered advantages of the Small Cases Division of the Tax Court?

a. Appeal to the U.S. Tax Court is possible.

b. A hearing of a deficiency of $65,000 is considered on a timely basis.

c. Taxpayer can handle the litigation without using a lawyer or certified public accountant.

d. Taxpayer can use other Small Cases Division decisions for precedential value.

e. The actual hearing is conducted informally.

f. Travel time will probably be reduced.

19. List an advantage and a disadvantage of using the U.S. District Court as the trial court for Federal tax litigation.

20. Dwain Toombs is considering litigating a tax deficiency of approximately $311,000 in the court system. He asks you to provide him with a short description of his alternatives indicating the advantages and disadvantages of each. Prepare your response to Dwain in the form of a letter. His address is 200 Mesa Drive, Tucson, AZ 85714.

Communications

21. List an advantage and a disadvantage of using the U.S. Court of Federal Claims as the trial court for Federal tax litigation.

22. A taxpayer lives in Michigan. In a controversy with the IRS, the taxpayer loses at the trial court level. Describe the appeal procedure under the following different assumptions:

a. The trial court was the Small Cases Division of the U.S. Tax Court.

b. The trial court was the U.S. Tax Court.

c. The trial court was a U.S. District Court.

d. The trial court was the U.S. Court of Federal Claims.

23. Why is the U.S. Tax Court sometimes called the "poor person's court"?

24. Suppose the U.S. Government loses a tax case in the U.S. Tax Court but does not appeal the result. What does the failure to appeal signify?

25. For the U.S. Tax Court, U.S. District Court, and U.S. Court of Federal Claims, indicate the following:

a. Number of regular judges per court.

b. Availability of a jury trial.

c. Whether the deficiency must be paid before the trial.

26. In which of the following states could a taxpayer appeal the decision of a U.S. District Court to the Eleventh Circuit Court of Appeals?

a. Alaska.

b. Arkansas.

    c. Florida.

    d. New York.

    e. Kansas.

27. What precedents must each of these courts follow?
    a. U.S. Tax Court.
    b. U.S. Court of Federal Claims.
    c. U.S. District Court.

28. What determines the appropriate Circuit Court of Appeals for a particular taxpayer?

29. In assessing the validity of a prior court decision, discuss the significance of the following on the taxpayer's issue:
    a. The decision was rendered by the U.S. District Court of Wyoming. Taxpayer lives in Wyoming.
    b. The decision was rendered by the U.S. Court of Federal Claims. Taxpayer lives in Wyoming.
    c. The decision was rendered by the Second Circuit Court of Appeals. Taxpayer lives in California.
    d. The decision was rendered by the U.S. Supreme Court.
    e. The decision was rendered by the U.S. Tax Court. The IRS has acquiesced in the result.
    f. Same as (e) except that the IRS has issued a nonacquiescence as to the result.

30. In the citation *D. L Evans*, 54 T.C. 40 (1970), what do the 54 and the 40 refer to?

31. What is the difference between a Regular decision, a Memorandum decision, and a Summary Opinion of the U.S. Tax Court?

32. Referring to the citation only, determine which court issued these decisions:
    a. *Julia A. Strauss*, 2 B.T.A. 598 (1925).
    b. *James v. U.S.*, 81 S.Ct. 1052 (USSC, 1961).
    c. *Evelyn M. Martin*, T.C.Memo. 2000–346..
    d. *Zarin v. Comm.*, 916 F.2d 110 (CA–3, 1990).

33. Interpret each of the following citations:
    a. 54 T.C. 1514 (1970).
    b. 408 F.2d 1117 (CA–2, 1969).
    c. 69–1 USTC ¶9319 (CA–2, 1969).
    d. 23 AFTR2d 69–1090 (CA–2, 1969).
    e. 293 F.Supp. 1129 (D.Ct. Miss., 1967).
    f. 67–1 USTC ¶9253 (D.Ct. Miss., 1967).
    g. 19 AFTR2d 647 (D.Ct. Miss., 1967).
    h. 56 S.Ct. 289 (USSC, 1935).
    i. 36–1 USTC ¶9020 (USSC, 1935).
    j. 16 AFTR 1274 (USSC, 1935).
    k. 422 F.2d 1336 (Ct.Cls., 1970).

34. Explain the following abbreviations:

a. CA–2.	g. *acq.*	m. USSC.
b. Fed.Cl.	h. B.T.A.	n. S.Ct.
c. *aff'd.*	i. USTC.	o. D.Ct.
d. *rev'd.*	j. AFTR.	
e. *rem'd.*	k. F.3d.	
f. *Cert. denied.*	l. F.Supp.	

35. Give the Commerce Clearing House citation for the following courts:
    a. Small Cases Division of the Tax Court.
    b. Federal District Court.
    c. U.S. Supreme Court.
    d. U.S. Court of Federal Claims.
    e. Tax Court Memorandum decision.

36. Where can you locate a published decision of the U.S. Court of Federal Claims?

37. Which of the following items can probably be found in the *Cumulative Bulletin?*
    a. Action on Decision.
    b. Small Cases Division of the U.S. Tax Court decision.
    c. Letter ruling.
    d. Revenue Procedure.
    e. Finalized Regulation.
    f. U.S. Court of Federal Claims decision.
    g. Senate Finance Committee Report.
    h. Acquiescences to Tax Court decisions.
    i. U.S. Circuit Court of Appeals decision.

38. Ashley has to prepare a research paper discussing the tax aspects of child support payments for her tax class. Explain to Ashley how she can research this topic.

    Issue ID

39. Where can a researcher find the current Internal Revenue Code of 1986?

40. Which of the following would be considered differences between the Research Institute of America and Commerce Clearing House citators?
    a. Distinguishes between the various issues in a particular court decision.
    b. Lists all court decisions that cite the court decision being researched.
    c. Allows a researcher to determine the validity of a Revenue Ruling.
    d. Indicates whether a court decision is explained, criticized, followed, or overruled by a subsequent decision.
    e. Pinpoints the exact page on which a decision is cited by another case.

41. You inherit a tax problem that was researched five months ago. You believe the answer is correct, but you are unfamiliar with the general area. How would you find some recent articles dealing with the subject area? How do you evaluate the reliability of the authority cited in the research report? How do you determine the latest developments pertaining to the research problem?

    Decision Making

42. Discuss the advantages of computerized tax research versus paper tax research.

43. What are the three ways that most electronic tax services can be entered?

PROBLEMS

44. Tom, an individual taxpayer, has just been audited by the IRS and, as a result, has been assessed a substantial deficiency (which has not yet been paid) in additional income taxes. In preparing his defense, Tom advances the following possibilities:
    a. Although a resident of Kentucky, Tom plans to sue in a U.S. District Court in Oregon that appears to be more favorably inclined toward taxpayers.
    b. If (a) is not possible, Tom plans to take his case to a Kentucky state court where an uncle is the presiding judge.
    c. Since Tom has found a B.T.A. decision that seems to help his case, he plans to rely on it under alternative (a) or (b).
    d. If he loses at the trial court level, Tom plans to appeal either to the U.S. Court of Federal Claims or to the U.S. Second Circuit Court of Appeals because he has relatives in both Washington, D.C., and New York. Staying with these relatives could save Tom lodging expense while his appeal is being heard by the court selected.
    e. Whether or not Tom wins at the trial court or appeals court level, he feels certain of success on an appeal to the U.S. Supreme Court.

    Evaluate Tom's notions concerning the judicial process as it applies to Federal income tax controversies.

45. Using the legend provided, identify the governmental unit that produces the following tax sources:

Legend

T = U.S. Treasury Department
NO = National Office of the IRS
AD = Area Director of the IRS
NA = Not applicable

---

a. Proposed Regulations.
b. Revenue Procedures.
c. Letter rulings.
d. Determination letters.
e. Technical Advice Memoranda.
f. Treasury Decisions.
g. Revenue Rulings.
h. Small Cases Division decisions.

46. Using the legend provided, classify each of the following statements (more than one answer per statement may be appropriate):

Legend

D = Applies to the U.S. District Court
T = Applies to the U.S. Tax Court
C = Applies to the U.S. Court of Federal Claims
A = Applies to the U.S. Circuit Court of Appeals
U = Applies to the U.S. Supreme Court
N = Applies to none of the above

---

a. Decides only Federal tax matters.
b. Decisions are reported in the F.3d Series.
c. Decisions are reported in the USTCs.
d. Decisions are reported in the AFTRs.
e. Appeal is by Writ of Certiorari.
f. Court meets most often in Washington, D.C.
g. A jury trial is available.
h. Trial court.
i. Appellate court.
j. Appeal is to the Federal Circuit and bypasses the taxpayer's particular circuit court.
k. Has a Small Cases Division.
l. The only trial court where the taxpayer does not have to pay the tax assessed by the IRS first.

47. Using the legend provided, classify each of the following citations as to the type of court:

Legend

D = Applies to the U.S. District Court
T = Applies to the U.S. Tax Court
C = Applies to the U.S. Court of Federal Claims
A = Applies to the U.S. Circuit Court of Appeals
U = Applies to the U.S. Supreme Court
N = Applies to none of the above

---

a. Rev.Proc. 71–21, 1971–2 C.B. 249.
b. *Garwood Irrigation Co. v. Comm.*, T.C.Memo. 2004–195.
c. *J. W. Yarbro v. Comm.*, 737 F.2d 479 (CA–5, 1984).
d. *Harris v. Comm.*, 71 S.Ct. 181 (1950).
e. *Argo Sales Co. v. Comm.*, 105 T.C. 86 (1995).
f. *Whittington v. Jones*, 96 F.Supp. 967 (W.D. Okla., 1951).
g. *Jack D. Carr*, T.C.Memo. 1985–19.

h. Ann. 93–42, 1993–11 I.R.B. 55.

i. *Jerry Washington*, T.C. Summary Opinion, 2006–31.

48. Using the legend provided, classify each of the following tax sources:

Legend
P = Primary tax source
S = Secondary tax source
B = Both
N = Neither

a. Sixteenth Amendment to the Constitution.

b. Tax treaty between the United States and France.

c. Revenue Ruling.

d. General Counsel Memoranda (1989).

e. U.S. District Court decision.

f. *Tax Notes* article.

g. Temporary Regulations (issued 2004).

h. U.S. Tax Court Memorandum decision.

i. Small Cases Division of the U.S. Tax Court decision.

j. Senate Finance Committee report.

49. Using the legend provided, classify each of the following citations as to publisher:

Legend
RIA = Research Institute of America
CCH = Commerce Clearing House
W   = West Publishing Company
U.S. = U.S. Government
O   = Others

a. 64 T.C. 203.

b. 30 TCM 817.

c. 434 F.Supp. 206.

d. 89 AFTR2d 2002–1314.

e. 74–1 USTC ¶9306.

f. RIA T.C.Mem.Dec. ¶80,582.

g. Rev.Proc. 93–27, 1993–2 C.B. 343.

h. Rev.Rul. 81–300, 1981–2 C.B. 143.

i. 71 S.Ct. 181.

j. 544 U.S. 336.

50. Using the legend provided, classify each of the following statements:

Legend
A = Tax avoidance
E = Tax evasion
N = Neither

a. Terry writes a $250 check for a charitable contribution on December 28, 2008, but does not mail the check to the charitable organization until January 10, 2009. She takes a deduction in 2008.

b. Robert decides not to report interest income from a bank because the amount is only $11.75.

c. Jim pays property taxes on his home in December 2008 rather than waiting until February 2009.

d. Jane switches her investments from taxable corporate bonds to tax-exempt municipal bonds.

e.   Ted encourages his mother to save most of her Social Security benefits so that he will be able to claim her as a dependent.

RESEARCH PROBLEMS

Note: Solutions to Research Problems can be prepared by using the **RIA Checkpoint®** **Student Edition** online research product, which is available to accompany this text. It is also possible to prepare solutions to the Research Problems by using tax research materials found in a standard tax library.

Research Problem 1.   Locate Chief Counsel Advice 200333043. What does it say?

Research Problem 2.   Determine what is covered in the following subchapters in Chapter 1, Subtitle A of the Internal Revenue Code of 1986:
a.   B.
b.   D.
c.   C.
d.   S.
e.   P.

Research Problem 3.   Locate the following items and give a brief summary of the results.
a.   Prop.Reg. § 1.864(b)–1(b)(2)(ii)(E).
b.   Rev.Proc. 2005–50, I.R.B. No. 32,272.
c.   FSA 200228005.
d.   IRC § 32(c)(2)(A).
e.   *Ramirez-Ota v. Comm.*, T.C. Summary Opinion, 2002–27.

Research Problem 4.   Determine how the term *person* is defined in the Internal Revenue Code of 1986. Specify the Code Section in which the term is defined.

Research Problem 5.   Locate the June 2006 issue of *The Tax Adviser* and find the article by Professors Godfrey, Guinn, and Malmgren. What are the title and page numbers of their article? Into which two categories do below-market loans fit?

Research Problem 6.   Determine the reliability of the following items:
a.   *FRGC Investment, LLC*, T.C.Memo. 2002–276.
b.   *Donald L. Evans*, 54 T.C. 40 (1970).
c.   Rev.Rul. 77–137, 1977–1 C.B. 178.

Research Problem 7.   Locate the following tax services in your library and indicate the name of the publisher and whether the service is organized by topic or Code Section:
a.   *United States Tax Reporter.*
b.   *Standard Federal Tax Reporter.*
c.   *Federal Tax Coordinator 2d.*
d.   *Mertens Law of Federal Income Taxation.*
e.   *Tax Management Portfolios.*
f.   *Federal Income, Gift and Estate Taxation.*
g.   *Tax Research Consultant.*

Research Problem 8.   In the following tax publications matrix, place an X if a court decision can be found in the publication. There may be more than one X in a row for a particular court.

| Court | U.S. Govt. Printing Office | West Publishing Company | | | | Research Institute of America | | | Commerce Clearing House | |
		Federal Supp.2d	Federal 3d	Federal Claims Reporter	S.Ct.	BTA Memo.	T.C.Memo.	AFTR	T.C. Memo.	USTC
U.S. Supreme Court										
Circuit Court of Appeals										
Court of Federal Claims										
District Court										
Tax Court (Regular decisions)										
Tax Court (Memo decisions)										
Board of Tax Appeals										
BTA Memo.										

Research Problem 9. Supply the missing information for these court decision citations:
  a. *Scott v. U.S.*, 91 AFTR2d 2003–2100, 328 F.3d 132 (_____, 2003), *aff'g* 89 AFTR2d 2002–1314, 186 F.Supp.2d 664 (D.Ct. Va., _____).
  b. *Maac v. Resource Design & Construction, Inc.*, 875 P.2d _____ (Utah, 1994).
  c. *U.S. v. Grabske*, 260 F.Supp.2d _____ (N.D. Cal, 2002).
  d. *Broudo v. Dura Pharmaceutical, Inc.*, 339 F.3d 933 (CA–9, _____).
  e. *William L. Rudkin Testamentary Trust*, 98 AFTR2d 2006–7368, 467 F.3d _____ (CA–2, 2006), *aff'g* 124 T.C. _____ (2005).

Research Problem 10. Supply the missing information for these court decision citations:
  a. *U.S. v. Adelson*, 441 F.Supp.2d _____ (S.D.N.Y., 2006).
  b. *Dura Pharmaceuticals, Inc. v. Broudo*, 544 U.S. 336 (_____).
  c. *U.S. v. Olis*, 429 F.3d 540 (_____, 2005).
  d. *Flora*, 1 AFTR2d 1925, 357 U.S. ____ (_____).
  e. *Mellon Bank v. U.S.*, 88 AFTR2d 2001–5800, 265 F.3d 1275 (_____, _____).

Research Problem 11. Determine whether these items are still reliable.
  a. Rev.Rul. 73–300, 1973–2 C.B. 215.
  b. Rev.Rul. 60–345, 1960–2 C.B. 211.
  c. *William J. O'Neill*, 98 T.C. 227 (1992).
  d. *Hospital Corporation of America*, 107 T.C. 116 (1996).

Research Problem 12. When Oprah gave away Pontiac G6 sedans to her TV audience, was the value of the cars taxable? On Labor Day weekend in 2006, World Furniture Mall in Plano, Illinois, gave away $275,000 of furniture because the Chicago Bears shut out the Green Bay Packers in their football season opener at Lambeau Field in Green Bay (26–0). Was the free furniture in the form of a discount or rebate taxable, or should the furniture company hand the customers a Form 1099–MISC?

Research Problem 13. During 2007, Frank lived with and supported a 20-year-old woman who was not his wife. He resides in a state that has a statute that makes it a misdemeanor for a man and woman who are not married to each other to live together. May Frank claim his *friend* as a dependent assuming he satisfies the normal tax rules for the deduction? Should Frank consider moving to another state?

Decision Making

Partial list of research aids:
§ 152(f)(3).
John T. Untermann, 38 T.C. 93 (1962).
S.Rept. 1983, 85th Cong., 2d Sess., reprinted in the 1958 Code Cong. & Adm. News 4791, 4804.

Internet
Activity

Use the tax resources of the Internet to address the following questions. Do not restrict your search to the World Wide Web, but include a review of newsgroups and general reference materials, practitioner sites and resources, primary sources of the tax law, chat rooms and discussion groups, and other opportunities.

Research Problem 14.   Go to each of the following Internet locations:
   a. Several primary sources of the tax law, including the U.S. Supreme Court, a Circuit Court of Appeals, the Internal Revenue Service, and final Regulations.
   b. Sources of proposed Federal tax legislation.
   c. A collection of tax rules for your state.

Research Problem 15.   Go to the U.S. Tax Court Internet site:
   a. What different types of cases can be found on the site?
   b. What is a Summary Opinion? Find one.
   c. What is a Memorandum Opinion? Find one.
   d. Find the "Rules and Practices and Procedures."
   e. Is the site user-friendly? E-mail suggested improvements to the webmaster.

Tax Determination; Personal and Dependency Exemptions; An Overview of Property Transactions

LEARNING OBJECTIVES

After completing Chapter 3, you should be able to:

LO.1
Understand and apply the components of the Federal income tax formula.

LO.2
Apply the rules for arriving at personal exemptions.

LO.3
Apply the rules for determining dependency exemptions.

LO.4
Use the proper method for determining the tax liability.

LO.5
Identify and report kiddie tax situations.

LO.6
Recognize the filing requirements and the proper filing status.

LO.7
Possess an overview of property transactions.

LO.8
Identify tax planning opportunities associated with the individual tax formula.

OUTLINE

Tax Formula, 3–3
Components of the Tax Formula, 3–3
Application of the Tax Formula, 3–9
Individuals Not Eligible for the Standard Deduction, 3–9
Special Limitations for Individuals Who
    Can Be Claimed as Dependents, 3–9
Personal Exemptions, 3–10
Dependency Exemptions, 3–11
Qualifying Child, 3–11
Qualifying Relative, 3–13
Other Rules for Dependency Exemptions, 3–17
Comparison of Categories for Dependency
    Exemptions, 3–18
Phaseout of Exemptions, 3–18
Child Tax Credit, 3–19
Tax Determination, 3–20
Tax Table Method, 3–20
Tax Rate Schedule Method, 3–21
Computation of Net Taxes Payable or Refund Due, 3–22

Unearned Income of Children under Age 19 Taxed
    at Parents' Rate, 3–23
Filing Considerations, 3–25
Filing Requirements, 3–25
Filing Status, 3–28
Gains and Losses from Property Transactions—In General, 3–32
Gains and Losses from Property Transactions— Capital Gains and Losses, 3–33
Definition of a Capital Asset, 3–33
Taxation of Net Capital Gain, 3–33
Determination of Net Capital Gain, 3–34
Treatment of Net Capital Loss, 3–34
Tax Planning Considerations, 3–35
Maximizing the Use of the Standard Deduction, 3–35
Dependency Exemptions, 3–35
Taking Advantage of Tax Rate Differentials, 3–37
Income of Certain Children, 3–38

Individuals are subject to Federal income tax based on taxable income. This chapter explains how taxable income and the income tax of an individual taxpayer are determined.

To compute taxable income, it is necessary to understand the tax formula in Figure 3–1. Although the tax formula is rather simple, determining an individual's taxable income can be quite complex. The complexity stems from the numerous provisions that govern the determination of gross income and allowable deductions.

FIGURE 3–1	Tax Formula	
Income (broadly conceived)		$xx,xxx
Less: Exclusions		(x,xxx)
Gross income		$xx,xxx
Less: Deductions *for* adjusted gross income		(x,xxx)
Adjusted gross income		$xx,xxx
Less: The greater of total itemized deductions		
or the standard deduction		(x,xxx)
Personal and dependency exemptions		(x,xxx)
Taxable income		$xx,xxx
Tax on taxable income (see Tax Tables or		
Tax Rate Schedules)		$ x,xxx
Less: Tax credits (including income		
taxes withheld and prepaid)		(xxx)
Tax due (or refund)		$ xxx

After computing taxable income, the appropriate rates must be applied. This requires a determination of the individual's filing status, since different rates apply for single taxpayers, married taxpayers, and heads of household. The basic tax rate structure is progressive, with rates for 2008 ranging from 10 percent to 35 percent.[1] For comparison, the lowest rate structure, which was in effect in 1913–1915, ranged from 1 to 7 percent, and the highest, in effect during 1944–1945, ranged from 23 to 94 percent.

Once the individual's tax has been computed, prepayments and credits are subtracted to determine whether the taxpayer owes additional tax or is entitled to a refund.

When property is sold or otherwise disposed of, a gain or loss may result, which can affect the determination of taxable income. Although property transactions are covered in detail in Chapters 14–17, an understanding of certain basic concepts helps in working with some of the materials to follow. The concluding portion of this chapter furnishes an overview of property transactions, including the distinction between realized and recognized gain or loss, the classification of such gain or loss (ordinary or capital), and the treatment for income tax purposes.

Tax Formula

> **LO.1**
>
> Understand and apply the components of the Federal income tax formula.

Most individuals compute taxable income using the tax formula shown in Figure 3–1. Special provisions govern the computation of taxable income and the tax liability for certain minor children who have unearned income in excess of specified amounts. These provisions are discussed later in the chapter.

Before illustrating the application of the tax formula, a brief discussion of its components is helpful.

Components of the Tax Formula

Income (Broadly Conceived). This includes all the taxpayer's income, both taxable and nontaxable. Although it is essentially equivalent to gross receipts, it does not include a return of capital or receipt of borrowed funds.

EXAMPLE 1

Dan decides to quit renting and move into a new house. Consequently, the owner of the apartment building returns to Dan the $600 damage deposit he previously made. In order to make a down payment on the house, Dan sells stock for $20,000 (original cost of $8,000) and borrows $50,000 from a bank. Only the $12,000 gain from the sale of the stock is income to Dan. The $600 damage deposit and the $8,000 cost of the stock are a return of capital. The $50,000 bank loan is not income as Dan has an obligation to repay that amount. ■

Exclusions. For various reasons, Congress has chosen to exclude certain types of income from the income tax base. The principal income exclusions are discussed in Chapter 5. A partial list of these exclusions is shown in Exhibit 3–1.

Gross Income. The Internal Revenue Code defines gross income broadly as "except as otherwise provided . . . , all income from whatever source derived."[2] The "except as otherwise provided" refers to exclusions. Gross income includes, but is not limited to, the items in the partial list in Exhibit 3–2. It does not include unrealized gains. Gross income is discussed in Chapters 4 and 5.

---

[1]Prior to the Tax Relief Reconciliation Act of 2001, the tax rates ranged from 15% to 39.6%. The Act established 10% as the new lowest bracket. Later legislation lowered the top rate to 35%.

[2]§ 61(a).

EXHIBIT 3–1	Partial List of Exclusions from Gross Income

Accident insurance proceeds	Meals and lodging (if furnished for employer's convenience)
Annuities (cost element)	
Bequests	Military allowances
Child support payments	Minister's dwelling rental value allowance
Cost-of-living allowance (for military)	
Damages for personal injury or sickness	Railroad retirement benefits (to a limited extent)
Gifts received	
Group term life insurance, premium paid by employer (for coverage up to $50,000)	Scholarship grants (to a limited extent)
	Social Security benefits (to a limited extent)
Inheritances	Veterans' benefits
Interest from state and local (i.e., municipal) bonds	Welfare payments
	Workers' compensation benefits
Life insurance paid on death	

EXHIBIT 3–2	Partial List of Gross Income Items

Alimony	Hobby income
Annuities (income element)	Interest
Awards	Jury duty fees
Back pay	Living quarters, meals (unless furnished for employer's convenience)
Bargain purchase from employer	
Bonuses	
Breach of contract damages	Mileage allowance
Business income	Military pay (unless combat pay)
Clergy fees	Notary fees
Commissions	Partnership income
Compensation for services	Pensions
Death benefits	Prizes
Debts forgiven	Professional fees
Director's fees	Punitive damages
Dividends	Rents
Embezzled funds	Rewards
Employee awards (in certain cases)	Royalties
Employee benefits (except certain fringe benefits)	Salaries
	Severance pay
Estate and trust income	Strike and lockout benefits
Farm income	Supplemental unemployment benefits
Fees	Tips and gratuities
Gains from illegal activities	Travel allowance (in certain cases)
Gains from sale of property	Treasure trove (found property)
Gambling winnings	Wages
Group term life insurance, premium paid by employer (for coverage over $50,000)	

CITIZENSHIP IS NOT TAX-FREE

Gross income from "whatever source derived" includes income from both U.S. and foreign sources. This approach to taxation, where the government taxes its citizens and residents on their worldwide income regardless of where earned, is referred to as a *global system*. Income earned by U.S. citizens outside the United States can be subject to additional taxes, however, because all countries maintain the right to tax income earned within their borders. Consequently, the U.S. tax law includes various mechanisms to alleviate the double taxation that arises when income is subject to tax in multiple jurisdictions. These mechanisms include the foreign tax deduction, the foreign tax credit, the foreign earned income exclusion for U.S. citizens and residents working abroad, and various tax treaty provisions.

Most industrialized countries use variants of the global system. An alternative approach is the *territorial system*, where a government taxes only the income earned within its borders. Hong Kong and Guatemala, for example, use a territorial approach.

EXAMPLE 2

Beth received the following amounts during the year:

Salary	$30,000
Interest on savings account	900
Gift from her aunt	10,000
Prize won in state lottery	1,000
Alimony from ex-husband	12,000
Child support from ex-husband	6,000
Damages for injury in auto accident	25,000
Ten $50 bills in an unmarked envelope found in an airport lounge (airport authorities could not locate anyone who claimed ownership)	500
Increase in the value of stock held for investment	5,000 ■

Review Exhibits 3–1 and 3–2 to determine the amount Beth must include in the computation of taxable income and the amount she may exclude. Then check your answer in footnote 3.[3]

Deductions for Adjusted Gross Income. Individual taxpayers have two categories of deductions: (1) deductions *for* adjusted gross income (deductions to arrive at adjusted gross income) and (2) deductions *from* adjusted gross income.

Deductions *for* adjusted gross income (AGI) are sometimes known as *above-the-line* deductions because on the tax return they are taken before the "line" designating AGI. They are also referred to as *page 1 deductions* since they are claimed, either directly or indirectly (i.e., through supporting schedules), on page 1 of Form 1040. Deductions *for* AGI include, but are not limited to, the following:[4]

- Expenses incurred in a trade or business.
- One-half of self-employment tax.
- Unreimbursed moving expenses.
- Contributions to traditional Individual Retirement Accounts (IRAs) and certain other retirement plans.
- Fees for college tuition and related expenses.

---

[3]Beth must include $44,400 in computing taxable income ($30,000 salary + $900 interest + $1,000 lottery prize + $12,000 alimony + $500 found property). She can exclude $41,000 ($10,000 gift from aunt + $6,000 child support + $25,000 damages). The unrealized gain on the stock held for investment also is not included in gross income. Such gain will be included in gross income only when it is realized upon disposition of the stock.

[4]§ 62.

- Contributions to Health Savings Accounts (HSAs).
- Penalty for early withdrawal from savings.
- Interest on student loans.
- Excess capital losses.
- Alimony payments.

The principal deductions *for* AGI are discussed in Chapters 6, 7, 8, 9, and 11.

Adjusted Gross Income (AGI). AGI is an important subtotal that serves as the basis for computing percentage limitations on certain itemized deductions, such as medical expenses, charitable contributions, and certain casualty losses. For example, medical expenses are deductible only to the extent they exceed 7.5 percent of AGI, and charitable contribution deductions may not exceed 50 percent of AGI. These limitations might be described as a 7.5 percent *floor* under the medical expense deduction and a 50 percent *ceiling* on the charitable contribution deduction.

EXAMPLE 3			

Keith earned a salary of $66,000 in 2008. He contributed $5,000 to his traditional Individual Retirement Account (IRA) and sustained a $1,000 capital loss on the sale of Wren Corporation stock. His AGI is computed as follows:

Gross income		
Salary		$66,000
Less: Deductions *for* AGI		
IRA contribution	$5,000	
Capital loss	1,000	(6,000)
AGI		$60,000

EXAMPLE 4	

Assume the same facts as in Example 3, and that Keith also had medical expenses of $5,800. Medical expenses may be included in itemized deductions to the extent they exceed 7.5% of AGI. In computing his itemized deductions, Keith may include medical expenses of $1,300 [$5,800 medical expenses − $4,500 (7.5% × $60,000 AGI)]. ∎

Itemized Deductions. As a general rule, personal expenditures are disallowed as deductions in arriving at taxable income. However, Congress allows specified personal expenses as **itemized deductions**. Such expenditures include medical expenses, certain taxes and interest, and charitable contributions.

In addition to these personal expenses, taxpayers are allowed itemized deductions for expenses related to (1) the production or collection of income and (2) the management of property held for the production of income.[5] These expenses, sometimes referred to as *nonbusiness expenses,* differ from trade or business expenses (discussed previously). Trade or business expenses, which are deductions *for* AGI, must be incurred in connection with a trade or business. Nonbusiness expenses, on the other hand, are expenses incurred in connection with an income-producing activity that does not qualify as a trade or business. Such expenses are itemized deductions.

EXAMPLE 5	

Leo is the owner and operator of a video game arcade. All allowable expenses he incurs in connection with the arcade business are deductions *for* AGI. In addition, Leo has an extensive portfolio of stocks and bonds. Leo's investment activity is not treated as a trade or business. All allowable expenses that Leo incurs in connection with these investments are itemized deductions. ∎

[5]§ 212.

EXHIBIT 3–3	**Partial List of Itemized Deductions**

Medical expenses in excess of 7.5% of AGI
State and local income or sales taxes
Real estate taxes
Personal property taxes
Interest on home mortgage
Investment interest (to a limited extent)
Charitable contributions (within specified percentage limitations)
Casualty and theft losses in excess of 10% of AGI
Miscellaneous expenses (to the extent such expenses exceed 2% of AGI)
> Union dues
> Professional dues and subscriptions
> Certain educational expenses
> Tax return preparation fee
> Investment counsel fees
> Unreimbursed employee business expenses (after a percentage reduction for
>> meals and entertainment)

Itemized deductions include, but are not limited to, the expenses listed in Exhibit 3–3. See Chapter 10 for a detailed discussion of itemized deductions.

Nondeductible Expenditures. Many expenditures are not deductible and, therefore, provide no tax benefit. Examples include, but are not limited to, the following:

- Personal living expenses including any losses on the sale of personal use property.
- Hobby losses.
- Life insurance premiums.
- Expenses incident to jury duty.
- Gambling losses (in excess of gains).
- Child support payments.
- Fines and penalties.
- Political contributions.
- Certain passive losses.
- Funeral expenses.
- Expenses paid on another's behalf.
- Capital expenditures.

Most of these nondeductible items are discussed in Chapter 6. Passive loss limitations, however, are treated in Chapter 11.

Standard Deduction. The **standard deduction**, which is set by Congress, is a specified amount that depends on the filing status of the taxpayer. The effect of the standard deduction is to exempt part of a taxpayer's income from Federal income tax liability. In the past, Congress has attempted to set the tax-free amount represented by the standard deduction approximately equal to an estimated poverty level,[6] but it has not always been consistent in doing so.

The standard deduction is the sum of two components: the *basic* standard deduction and the *additional* standard deduction.[7] Table 3–1 lists the basic

---

[6] S.Rep. No. 92–437, 92nd Cong., 1st Sess., 1971, p. 54. Another purpose of the standard deduction was discussed in Chapter 1 under Influence of the Internal Revenue Service—Administrative Feasibility. The size of the standard deduction has a direct bearing on the number of taxpayers who are in a position to itemize deductions. Reducing the number of taxpayers who itemize also reduces the audit effort required from the IRS.

[7] § 63(c)(1).

TABLE 3–1	Basic Standard Deduction Amounts	

| | Standard Deduction Amount | |
Filing Status	2007	2008
Single	$ 5,350	$ 5,450
Married, filing jointly	10,700	10,900
Surviving spouse	10,700	10,900
Head of household	7,850	8,000
Married, filing separately	5,350	5,450

TABLE 3–2	Amount of Each Additional Standard Deduction	

Filing Status	2007	2008
Single	$1,300	$1,350
Married, filing jointly	1,050	1,050
Surviving spouse	1,050	1,050
Head of household	1,300	1,350
Married, filing separately	1,050	1,050

standard deduction allowed for taxpayers in each filing status. All taxpayers allowed a *full* standard deduction are entitled to the applicable amount listed in Table 3–1. The standard deduction amounts are subject to adjustment for inflation each year.

Certain taxpayers are not allowed to claim *any* standard deduction, and the standard deduction is *limited* for others. These provisions are discussed later in the chapter.

A taxpayer who is age 65 or over *or* blind qualifies for an *additional standard deduction* of $1,050 or $1,350, depending on filing status (see amounts in Table 3–2). Two additional standard deductions are allowed for a taxpayer who is age 65 or over *and* blind. The additional standard deduction provisions also apply for a qualifying spouse who is age 65 or over or blind, but a taxpayer may not claim an additional standard deduction for a dependent.

To determine whether to itemize, the taxpayer compares the *total* standard deduction (the sum of the basic standard deduction and any additional standard deductions) with total itemized deductions. Taxpayers are allowed to deduct the *greater* of itemized deductions or the standard deduction. Taxpayers whose itemized deductions are less than the standard deduction compute their taxable income using the standard deduction rather than itemizing. Approximately 70 percent of individual taxpayers choose the standard deduction option.

EXAMPLE 6	Sara, who is single, is 66 years old. She had total itemized deductions of $6,200 during 2008. Her total standard deduction is $6,800 ($5,450 basic standard deduction plus $1,350 additional standard deduction). Sara should compute her taxable income for 2008 using the standard deduction ($6,800), since it exceeds her itemized deductions ($6,200). ∎

Personal and Dependency Exemptions. Exemptions are allowed for the taxpayer, the taxpayer's spouse, and each dependent of the taxpayer. The exemption amount is $3,400 in 2007 and $3,500 in 2008.

Application of the Tax Formula

The tax formula shown in Figure 3–1 is illustrated in Example 7.

EXAMPLE 7

Grace, age 25, is single and has no dependents. She is a high school teacher and earned a $40,000 salary in 2008. Her other income consisted of a $1,000 prize won in a sweepstakes contest and $500 interest on municipal bonds that she had received as a graduation gift in 2005. During 2008, she sustained a deductible capital loss of $1,000. Her itemized deductions are $5,600. Grace's taxable income for the year is computed as follows:

Income (broadly conceived)	
Salary	$40,000
Prize	1,000
Interest on municipal bonds	500
	$41,500
Less: Exclusion—	
Interest on municipal bonds	(500)
Gross income	$41,000
Less: Deduction *for* adjusted gross income—	
Capital loss	(1,000)
Adjusted gross income	$40,000
Less: The greater of total itemized deductions ($5,600) *or*	
the standard deduction ($5,450)	(5,600)
Personal and dependency exemptions	
(1 × $3,500)	(3,500)
Taxable income	$30,900

∎

The structure of the individual income tax return (Form 1040, 1040A, or 1040EZ) parallels the tax formula in Figure 3–1. Like the formula, the tax return places major emphasis on the adjusted gross income (AGI) and taxable income (TI) subtotals. In arriving at AGI, however, most exclusions are not reported on the tax return.

Individuals Not Eligible for the Standard Deduction

The following individual taxpayers are ineligible to use the standard deduction and must therefore itemize:[8]

- A married individual filing a separate return where either spouse itemizes deductions.
- A nonresident alien.
- An individual filing a return for a period of less than 12 months because of a change in the annual accounting period.

Special Limitations for Individuals Who Can Be Claimed as Dependents

Special rules apply to the standard deduction and personal exemption of an individual who can be claimed as a dependent on another person's tax return.

---

[8]§ 63(c)(6).

When filing his or her own tax return, a *dependent's* basic standard deduction in 2008 is limited to the greater of $900 or the sum of the individual's earned income for the year plus $300.[9] However, if the sum of the individual's earned income plus $300 exceeds the normal standard deduction, the standard deduction is limited to the appropriate amount shown in Table 3–1. These limitations apply only to the basic standard deduction. A dependent who is 65 or over or blind or both is also allowed the additional standard deduction amount on his or her own return (refer to Table 3–2). These provisions are illustrated in Examples 8 through 11.

EXAMPLE 8	Susan, who is 17 years old and single, is claimed as a dependent on her parents' tax return. During 2008, she received $1,200 interest (unearned income) on a savings account. She also earned $400 from a part-time job. When Susan files her own tax return, her standard deduction is $900 (the greater of $900 or the sum of earned income of $400 plus $300). ∎

EXAMPLE 9	Assume the same facts as in Example 8, except that Susan is 67 years old and is claimed as a dependent on her son's tax return. In this case, when Susan files her own tax return, her standard deduction is $2,250 [$900 (the greater of $900 or the sum of earned income of $400 plus $350) + $1,350 (the additional standard deduction allowed because Susan is 65 or over)]. ∎

EXAMPLE 10	Peggy, who is 16 years old and single, earned $700 from a summer job and had no unearned income during 2008. She is claimed as a dependent on her parents' tax return. Her standard deduction is $1,000 (the greater of $900 or the sum of $700 earned income plus $300). ∎

EXAMPLE 11	Jack, who is a 20-year-old, single, full-time college student, is claimed as a dependent on his parents' tax return. He worked as a musician during the summer of 2008, earning $5,900. Jack's standard deduction is $5,450 (the greater of $900 or the sum of $5,900 earned income plus $300, but limited to the $5,450 standard deduction for a single taxpayer). ∎

Personal Exemptions

LO.2

Apply the rules for arriving at personal exemptions.

The use of exemptions in the tax system is based in part on the idea that a taxpayer with a small amount of income should be exempt from income taxation. An exemption frees a specified amount of income from tax ($3,400 in 2007 and $3,500 in 2008). The exemption amount is indexed (adjusted) annually for inflation.

Exemptions that are allowed for the taxpayer and spouse are designated as **personal exemptions**. Those exemptions allowed for the care and maintenance of other persons are called dependency exemptions and are discussed in the next section.

An individual cannot claim a personal exemption if he or she is claimed as a dependent by another.

EXAMPLE 12	Assume the same facts as in Example 11. On his own income tax return,[10] Jack's taxable income is determined as follows:

Gross income	$ 5,900
Less: Standard deduction	(5,450)
Personal exemption	(–0–)
Taxable income	$ 450

---

[9]§ 63(c)(5). Both the $900 amount and the $300 amount are subject to adjustment for inflation each year. The $900 amount was raised from $850 in 2007, but the $300 amount was unchanged.

[10]As noted on page 3–25, Jack's situation is such that he will be required to file an income tax return.

TABLE 3–3	Marital Status for Exemption Purposes

	Marital Status for 2008
• Walt is the widower of Helen who died on January 3, 2008.	Walt and Helen are considered to be married for purposes of filing the 2008 return.
• Bill and Jane entered into a divorce decree that is effective on December 31, 2008.	Bill and Jane are considered to be unmarried for purposes of filing the 2008 return.

Note that Jack is not allowed a personal exemption because he is claimed as a dependent by his parents. ■

When a husband and wife file a joint return, they may claim two personal exemptions. However, when separate returns are filed, a married taxpayer cannot claim an exemption for his or her spouse *unless* the spouse has no gross income and is not claimed as the dependent of another taxpayer.[11]

The determination of marital status generally is made at the end of the taxable year, except when a spouse dies during the year. Spouses who enter into a legal separation under a decree of divorce or separate maintenance before the end of the year are considered to be unmarried at the end of the taxable year. Table 3–3 illustrates the effect of death or divorce upon marital status.

For *Federal* tax purposes, the law does not recognize same-sex marriages. By virtue of the Defense of Marriage Act (Pub. L. No. 104–199), a marriage means a legal union only between a man and a woman as husband and wife.

The amount of the exemption is not reduced due to the taxpayer's death. For example, refer to the case of Helen in Table 3–3. Although she lived for only three days in 2008, the full personal exemption of $3,500 is allowed for the tax year. The same rule applies to dependency exemptions. As long as an individual qualified as a dependent at the time of death, the full amount of the exemption can be claimed.

Dependency Exemptions

LO.3

Apply the rules for determining dependency exemptions.

As is the case with personal exemptions, a taxpayer is permitted to claim an exemption of $3,500 in 2008 ($3,400 in 2007) for each person who qualifies as a dependent. A **dependency exemption** is available for either a qualifying child or a qualifying relative and must not run afoul of certain other rules (i.e., joint return, nonresident alien prohibitions).

Qualifying Child

One of the objectives of the Working Families Tax Relief Act of 2004 was to establish a uniform definition of qualifying child. The qualifying child definition applies to the following tax provisions:

- Dependency exemption.
- Head-of-household filing status.
- Earned income tax credit.

[11]§ 151(b).

- Child tax credit.
- Credit for child and dependent care expenses.

A **qualifying child** must meet the relationship, abode, age, and support tests.[12] For dependency exemption purposes, a qualifying child must also satisfy the joint return test and the citizenship or residency test.

Relationship Test. The relationship test includes a taxpayer's child (son, daughter), adopted child, stepchild, eligible foster child, brother, sister, half brother, half sister, stepbrother, stepsister, or a *descendant* of any of these parties (e.g., grandchild, nephew, niece). Note that *ancestors* of any of these parties (e.g., uncles and aunts) and in-laws (e.g., son-in-law, brother-in-law) *are not included.*

An adopted child includes a child lawfully placed with the taxpayer for legal adoption even though the adoption is not final. An eligible foster child is one who is placed with the taxpayer by an authorized placement agency or by a judgment decree or other order of any court of competent jurisdiction.

EXAMPLE 13

Maureen's household includes her mother, grandson, stepbrother, stepbrother's daughter, uncle, and sister. All meet the relationship test for a qualifying child except the mother and uncle. ∎

Abode Test. A qualifying child must live with the taxpayer for more than half of the year. For this purpose, temporary absences (e.g., school, vacation, medical care, military service, detention in a juvenile facility) are disregarded. Special rules apply in the case of certain kidnapped children.[13]

Age Test. A qualifying child must be under age 19 or under age 24 in the case of a student. A student is a child who, during any part of five months of the year, is enrolled full time at a school or government-sponsored on-farm training course.[14] The age test does not apply to a child who is disabled during any part of the year.[15]

Support Test. In order to be a qualifying child, the individual must not be self-supporting (i.e., provide more than one-half of his or her own support). In the case of a child who is a full-time student, scholarships are not considered to be support.[16]

EXAMPLE 14

Shawn, age 23, is a full-time student and lives with his parents and an older cousin. During 2008, Shawn receives his support from the following sources: 30% from a part-time job, 30% from a scholarship, 20% from his parents, and 20% from the cousin. Shawn is not self-supporting and can be claimed by his parents as a dependent. (Note: Shawn cannot be a qualifying child as to his cousin due to the relationship test.) ∎

Tiebreaker Rules. In some situations, a child may be a qualifying child to more than one person. In this event, the tax law specifies which person has priority in claiming the dependency exemption.[17] Called "tiebreaker rules," these rules are summarized in Table 3–4 and are illustrated in the examples that follow.

EXAMPLE 15

Tim, age 15, lives in the same household with his mother and grandmother. As the parent (see Table 3–4), the mother has priority as to the dependency exemption. ∎

[12]§ 152(c).
[13]§ 152(f)(6).
[14]§ 152(f)(2).
[15]Within the meaning of § 22(e)(3). See the discussion of the credit for the elderly or disabled in Chapter 13.
[16]§ 152(f)(5).
[17]§ 152(c)(4).

TABLE 3–4	Tiebreaker Rules for Claiming Qualified Child

Persons Eligible to Claim Exemption	Person Prevailing
One of the persons is the parent.	Parent
Both persons are the parents, and the child lives longer with one parent.	Parent with the longer period of residence
Both persons are the parents, and the child lives with each the same period of time.	Parent with the higher adjusted gross income (AGI)
None of the persons is the parent.	Person with highest AGI

EXAMPLE 16

Jennifer, age 17, lives in the same household with her parents during the entire year. If her parents file separate returns, the one with the higher AGI has priority as to the dependency exemption. ■

EXAMPLE 17

Assume the same facts as in Example 16, except that the father moves into an apartment in November (Jennifer remains with her mother). The mother has priority as to the dependency exemption. ■

EXAMPLE 18

Carlos, age 12, lives in the same household with his two aunts. The aunt with the higher AGI has priority as to the dependency exemption. ■

Resorting to the tiebreaker rules in Table 3–4 is not necessary if the person who would prevail does not claim the exemption. Thus, in Example 15, the mother can allow the grandmother to claim Tim as a dependent by not claiming him on her own return.

ETHICAL and EQUITABLE *Considerations* — WHOSE QUALIFYING CHILD IS HE?

The Rands are successful professionals and have combined AGI of approximately $400,000. Their household includes two children: Henry (age 16) and Belinda (age 22). Belinda is not a student and has a job where she earns $15,000. After a short family meeting in early April 2008, the parties decide that Belinda should claim Henry as her qualifying child. As a result, Belinda is able to deduct a full dependency exemption and claim a child tax credit and an earned income tax credit for a tax saving of more than $3,000. Had the Rands claimed Henry on their joint return, only a partial dependency exemption would have been allowed, and no child tax credit or earned income tax credit would have been available. As noted in Chapter 13, these credits are phased out for higher-bracket taxpayers.

Has the Rand family acted properly?

Qualifying Relative

Besides establishing the concept of a qualifying child, the Working Families Tax Relief Act of 2004 also provided for a second category of dependency exemption designated as the **qualifying relative**. The rules involved largely carried over then-existing law to post-2004 years.

A qualifying relative must meet the relationship, gross income, and support tests.[18] As in the case of the qualifying child category, qualifying relative status also requires that the joint return and nonresident alien restrictions be avoided (see Other Rules for Dependency Exemptions below).

Relationship Test. The relationship test for a qualifying relative is more expansive than for a qualifying child. Also included are the following relatives:

- Lineal ascendants (e.g., parents, grandparents).
- Collateral ascendants (e.g., uncles, aunts).
- Certain in-laws (e.g., son-, daughter-, father-, mother-, brother-, and sister-in-law).[19]

Children who do not satisfy the qualifying child definition may meet the qualifying relative criteria.

EXAMPLE 19

Inez provides more than half of the support of her son, age 20, who is neither disabled nor a full-time student. The son is not a qualifying child due to the age test but would be a qualifying relative (if the gross income test is met). Consequently, Inez may claim a dependency exemption for her son. ■

The relationship test also includes unrelated parties who live with the taxpayer (i.e., are members of the household). Member-of-the-household status is not available for anyone whose relationship with the taxpayer violates local law or anyone who was a spouse during any part of the year.[20] However, an ex-spouse can qualify as a member of the household in a year following that of the divorce.

As the relationship test indicates, the category designation of "qualifying relative" is somewhat misleading. As just noted, persons other than relatives can qualify as dependents. Furthermore, not all relatives will qualify—notice the absence of the "cousin" grouping.

EXAMPLE 20

Charles provides more than half of the support of a family friend who lives with him and a cousin who lives in another city. Presuming the gross income test is met, the family friend is a qualifying relative, but the cousin is not. ■

Gross Income Test. A dependent's gross income must be *less* than the exemption amount—$3,400 in 2007 and $3,500 in 2008. Gross income is determined by the income that is taxable. In the case of scholarships, for example, include the taxable portion (e.g., amounts received for room and board) and exclude the nontaxable portion (e.g., amounts received for books and tuition).

EXAMPLE 21

Elsie provides more than half of the support of her son, Tom, who does not live with her. Tom, age 26, is a full-time student in medical school, earns $3,000 from a part-time job, and receives a $12,000 scholarship covering his tuition. Elsie may claim Tom as a dependent since he meets the gross income test and is a qualifying relative. (Note: Tom is not a qualifying child due to either the abode or the age test.) ■

EXAMPLE 22

Aaron provides more than half of the support of his widowed aunt, Myrtle, who does not live with him. Myrtle's income for the year is as follows: dividend income of $1,100, earnings from pet sitting of $1,200, Social Security benefits of $6,000, and interest from City of Milwaukee

---

[18]§ 152(d).

[19]Once established by marriage, in-law status continues to exist and survives divorce.

[20]§§ 152(d)(2)(H) and (f)(3).

bonds of $8,000. Since Myrtle's gross income is only $2,300 ($1,100 + $1,200), she meets the gross income test and can be claimed as Aaron's dependent. ■

Support Test.   Over one-half of the support of the qualifying relative must be furnished by the taxpayer. Support includes food, shelter, clothing, toys, medical and dental care, education, and the like. However, a scholarship (both taxable and nontaxable portions) received by a student is not included for purposes of computing whether the taxpayer furnished more than half of the child's support.

EXAMPLE 23

Hal contributed $3,400 (consisting of food, clothing, and medical care) toward the support of his nephew, Sam, who lives with him. Sam earned $1,500 from a part-time job and received a $2,000 scholarship to attend a local university. Assuming that the other dependency tests are met, Hal can claim Sam as a dependent since he has contributed more than half of Sam's support. The $2,000 scholarship is not included as support for purposes of this test. ■

If the individual does not spend funds that have been received from any source, the unexpended amounts are not counted for purposes of the support test.

EXAMPLE 24

Emily contributed $3,000 to her father's support during the year. In addition, her father received $2,400 in Social Security benefits, $200 of interest, and wages of $600. Her father deposited the Social Security benefits, interest, and wages in his own savings account and did not use any of the funds for his support. Thus, the Social Security benefits, interest, and wages are not considered as support provided by Emily's father. Emily may claim her father as a dependent if the other tests are met. ■

An individual's own funds, however, must be taken into account if applied toward support. In this regard, the source of the funds so used is immaterial.

EXAMPLE 25

Frank contributes $8,000 toward his parents' total support of $20,000. The parents, who do not live with Frank, obtain the other $12,000 from savings and a home equity loan on their residence. Although the parents have no income, their use of savings and borrowed funds are counted as part of their support. Because Frank does not satisfy the support test, he cannot claim his parents as dependents. ■

Capital expenditures for items such as furniture, appliances, and automobiles are included in total support if the item does, in fact, constitute support.

EXAMPLE 26

Norm purchased a television set costing $650 and gave it to his mother who lives with him. The television set was placed in the mother's bedroom and was used exclusively by her. Norm should include the cost of the television set in determining the support of his mother. ■

Multiple Support Agreements.   An exception to the support test involves a **multiple support agreement**. A multiple support agreement permits one of a group of taxpayers who furnish support for a qualifying relative to claim a dependency exemption for that individual even if no one person provides more than 50 percent of the support.[21] The group together must provide more than 50 percent of the support. Any person who contributed *more than 10 percent* of the support is entitled to claim the exemption if each person in the group who contributed more than 10 percent files a written consent. This provision frequently enables one of the children of aged dependent parents to claim an exemption when none of the children meets the 50 percent support test.

---

[21]§ 152(d)(3).

Each person who is a party to the multiple support agreement must meet all other requirements (except the support requirement) for claiming the exemption. A person who does not meet the relationship or member-of-the-household requirement, for instance, cannot claim the dependency exemption under a multiple support agreement. It does not matter if he or she contributes more than 10 percent of the individual's support.

| | EXAMPLE 27 | | Wanda, who resides with her son, Adam, received $12,000 from various sources during the year. This constituted her entire support for the year. She received support from the following: |

	Amount	Percentage of Total
Adam, a son	$ 5,760	48
Bob, a son	1,200	10
Carol, a daughter	3,600	30
Diane, a friend	1,440	12
	$12,000	100

If Adam and Carol file a multiple support agreement, either may claim the dependency exemption for Wanda. Bob may not claim Wanda because he did not contribute more than 10% of her support. Bob's consent is not required in order for Adam and Carol to file a multiple support agreement. Diane does not meet the relationship or member-of-the-household test and cannot be a party to the agreement. The decision as to who claims Wanda rests with Adam and Carol. It is possible for Carol to claim Wanda, even though Adam furnished more of Wanda's support. ■

Each person who qualifies under the more-than-10 percent rule (except for the person claiming the exemption) must complete Form 2120 (Multiple Support Declaration) waiving the exemption. The person claiming the exemption must attach all Forms 2120 to his or her own return.

ETHICAL and EQUITABLE *Considerations*

DISCOVERING LOST DEPENDENCY EXEMPTIONS

For the six years prior to his death in late 2008, Jesse lived with his daughter, Hannah. Because he had no source of income, Jesse was supported by equal contributions from Hannah and his two sons, Bill and Bob. At Jesse's funeral, his surviving children are amazed to discover that none of them has been claiming Jesse as a dependent. Upon the advice of the director of the funeral home, they decide to divide, among themselves, the dependency exemptions for the past six years. Multiple Forms 2120 are executed, and each of the three children files amended returns for different past years. As Jesse died before the end of the current year, no deduction is planned for 2008.

Comment on the tax expectations of the parties involved.

Children of Divorced or Separated Parents. Another exception to the support test applies when parents with children are divorced or separated under a decree of separate maintenance. For unmarried parents, living apart (for the last six months of the year) will suffice. Special rules apply if the parents meet the following conditions:

- They would have been entitled to the dependency exemption(s) had they been married and filed a joint return.
- They have custody (either jointly or singly) of the child (or children) for more than half of the year.

Under the general rule, the parent having custody of the child (children) for the greater part of the year (i.e., the custodial parent) is entitled to the dependency exemption(s).[22] The general rule does not apply if a multiple support agreement is in effect.[23] It also does not apply if the custodial parent issues a waiver in favor of the noncustodial parent.[24]

The waiver, Form 8332 (Release of Claim to Exemption of Child of Divorced or Separated Parents), can apply to a single year, a number of specified years, or all future years. The noncustodial parent must attach a copy of Form 8332 to his or her return. Under certain conditions, a copy of the divorce decree awarding the dependency exemptions to the noncustodial parent can be substituted for Form 8332.[25]

Other Rules for Dependency Exemptions

In addition to fitting into either the qualifying child or the qualifying relative category, a dependent must meet the joint return and the citizenship or residency tests.

Joint Return Test. If a dependent is married, the supporting taxpayer (e.g., the parent of a married child) generally is not permitted a dependency exemption if the married individual files a joint return with his or her spouse.[26] The joint return rule does not apply, however, if the following conditions are met:

- The reason for filing is to claim a refund for tax withheld.
- No tax liability would exist for either spouse on separate returns.
- Neither spouse is required to file a return.

See Table 3–6 later in the chapter and the related discussion concerning income level requirements for filing a return.

EXAMPLE 28

Paul provides over half of the support of his son Quinn. He also provides over half of the support of Vera, who is Quinn's wife. During the year, both Quinn and Vera had part-time jobs. In order to recover the taxes withheld, they file a joint return. If Quinn and Vera are not required to file a return, Paul is allowed to claim both as dependents. ■

Citizenship or Residency Test. To be a dependent, the individual must be either a U.S. citizen, a U.S. resident, or a resident of Canada or Mexico for some part of the calendar year in which the taxpayer's tax year begins.[27]

Under an exception, an adopted child need not be a citizen or resident of the United States (or a contiguous country) as long as his or her principal abode is with a U.S. citizen.

EXAMPLE 29

Esther is a U.S. citizen who lives and works in Spain. She has adopted Benito, a four-year-old Italian national, who lives with her and is a member of her household. Although Benito does not meet the usual citizenship or residency test, he is covered by the exception. Benito is a qualifying child, and Esther can claim him as a dependent. ■

---

[22]Reg. § 1.152–4T.
[23]§ 152(e)(5).
[24]§ 152(e)(2).

[25]These conditions are set forth in *Your Federal Income Tax* (IRS Publication 17), Chapter 3, page 34.
[26]§ 152(b)(2).
[27]§ 152(b)(3).

Comparison of Categories for Dependency Exemptions

Concept Summary 3–1 sets forth the tests for the two categories of dependency exemptions. In contrasting the two categories, the following observations are in order:

- As to the relationship tests, the qualifying relative category is considerably more expansive. Besides including those prescribed under the qualifying child grouping, other relatives are added. Nonrelated persons who are members of the household are also included.
- The support tests are entirely different. In the case of a qualifying child, support is not necessary. What is required is that the child not be self-supporting.
- The qualifying child category has no gross income limitation, whereas the qualifying relative category has no age restriction.

Phaseout of Exemptions

Several provisions of the tax law are intended to increase the tax liability of more affluent taxpayers who might otherwise enjoy some benefit from having some of their taxable income subject to the lower income tax brackets (e.g., 10 percent, 15 percent, 25 percent). One such provision phases out certain itemized deductions and is discussed in Chapter 10. Another provision phases out personal and dependency exemptions and is considered below.[28] In 2001, however, Congress decided that both of these provisions imposed an unfair burden on high-income individual taxpayers and decided on their repeal. To avoid an immediate revenue loss, the repeal was postponed until 2006. Furthermore, to spread the impact of the revenue loss, the repeal is taking place in two stages and will not be complete until 2010. The personal and dependency exemption phaseout remained at two-thirds for 2006 and 2007 and is at one-third for 2008 and 2009.

The phaseout of exemptions occurs as AGI exceeds specified threshold amounts (indexed annually for inflation). For 2007 and 2008, the phaseout *begins* when AGI exceeds the following:

	2007	2008
Joint returns/surviving spouse	$234,600	$239,950
Head of household	195,500	199,950
Single	156,400	159,950
Married, filing separately	117,300	119,975

Exemptions are phased out by 2 percent for each $2,500 (or fraction thereof) by which the taxpayer's AGI exceeds the threshold amounts. For a married taxpayer filing separately, the phaseout is 2 percent for each $1,250 or fraction thereof. Then, the amount of the phaseout is multiplied by $\frac{1}{3}$ (the reduction-of-phaseout fraction) for tax years 2008 and 2009.

The allowable exemption amount can be determined with the following steps:

1. AGI − threshold amount = excess amount
2. Excess amount ÷ $2,500 = reduction factor [rounded up to the next whole increment (e.g., 18.1 = 19)] × 2 = phaseout percentage

[28]§ 151(d)(3).

CONCEPT SUMMARY   3–1

Tests for Dependency Exemption

Category	
Qualifying Child	**Qualifying Relative**[1]
Relationship[2]	Support
Abode[3]	Relationship[4] or member of household[3]
Age	Gross income
Support	Joint return[5]
Joint return[5]	Citizenship or residency[6]
Citizenship or residency[6]	

[1] These rules are largely the same as those applicable to pre-2005 years.
[2] Children and their descendants, and siblings and stepsiblings and their descendants.
[3] The rules for abode are the same as for member of the household.
[4] Children and their descendants, siblings and their children, parents and their ascendants, uncles and aunts, stepparents and stepsiblings, and certain in-laws.
[5] The joint return rules are the same for each category.
[6] The citizenship or residency rules are the same for each category.

3. Phaseout percentage (from step 2) × exemption amount = amount of exemptions phased out
4. Amount of exemptions phased out × reduction-of-phaseout fraction = phaseout amount
5. Exemption amount − phaseout amount = allowable exemption deduction

---

EXAMPLE 30

Frederico is married but files a separate return in 2008. His AGI is $139,975. He is entitled to one personal exemption.

1. $139,975 − $119,975 = $20,000 excess amount
2. [($20,000 ÷ $1,250) × 2] = 32% (phaseout percentage)
3. 32% × $3,500 = $1,120 amount of exemption phased out
4. $1,120 × $\frac{1}{3}$* = $373 phaseout amount
5. $3,500 − $373 = $3,127 allowable exemption deduction

   * On its Deduction for Exemptions Worksheet, the IRS divides the amount in Step 4 by 3 rather than multiplying by $\frac{1}{3}$. Both approaches yield the same result. ■

In no event can the phaseout of personal and dependency exemptions result in a *reduction of* more than $1,167 ($\frac{1}{3}$ × $3,500) for 2008 [or $2,267 ($\frac{2}{3}$ × $3,400) for 2007] per exemption. Consequently, regardless of the amount of an individual's AGI, each exemption is *at least* $2,333 for 2008 ($1,133 for 2007).

The elimination of the phaseout of exemptions, as well as the phaseout of certain itemized deductions, will ultimately add much needed simplicity to the tax law. Unfortunately, reaching this objective by means of a gradual reduction of the phaseout (i.e., a phaseout of a phaseout) unduly adds further complexity to the existing rules.

Child Tax Credit

In addition to providing a dependency exemption, a child of the taxpayer may also generate a tax credit. Called the **child tax credit**, the amount allowed is $1,000 through 2009 for each dependent child (including stepchildren and eligible foster

TAX *in the News*	HOW TO SUBTLY PLUCK THE CHICKEN

No government likes to admit that it is enacting new taxes or even raising the rates on existing taxes. Needless to say, this is particularly true of the U.S. Congress. But there are more subtle ways to raise revenue (or to curtail revenue loss). The most popular way is to use a so-called *stealth tax*. A stealth tax is not really a tax at all. Instead, it is a means of depriving higher-income taxpayers of the benefits of certain tax provisions thought to be available to all.

The heart and soul of the stealth tax is the phaseout approach. Thus, as income increases, the tax benefit thought to be derived from a particular relief provision decreases.

Since the phaseout is gradual and not drastic, many affected taxpayers are unaware of what has happened. Although the tax law is rampant with phaseouts, the two most prominent limit the deductibility of personal and dependency exemptions and itemized deductions. (The itemized deduction phaseout is discussed in Chapter 10.)

As noted in the text, however, Congress has had some misgivings about the stealth tax imposed on personal and dependency exemptions. Consequently, this stealth tax is being removed in stages with final revocation scheduled for year 2010.

children) under the age of 17.[29] For a more complete discussion of the child tax credit, see Chapter 13.

<table>
<tr><td>**LO.4**</td></tr>
<tr><td>Use the proper method for determining the tax liability.</td></tr>
</table>

Tax Determination

Tax Table Method

The tax liability is computed using either the Tax Table method or the Tax Rate Schedule method. Most taxpayers compute their tax using the **Tax Table**. Eligible taxpayers compute taxable income (as shown in Figure 3–1) and *must* determine their tax by reference to the Tax Table. The following taxpayers, however, may not use the Tax Table method:

- An individual who files a short period return (see Chapter 18).
- Individuals whose taxable income exceeds the maximum (ceiling) amount in the Tax Table. The 2007 Tax Table applies to taxable income below $100,000 for Form 1040.
- An estate or trust.

The IRS does not release the Tax Tables until late in the year to which they apply. The Tax Rate Schedules, however, are released at the end of the year preceding their applicability. To illustrate, the Tax Table for 2008 will be available at the end of 2008. The Tax Rate Schedules for 2008, however, were released at the end of 2007.[30] For purposes of estimating tax liability and making quarterly prepayments, the Tax Rate Schedules will usually need to be consulted. Based on its availability, the 2007 Tax Table will be used to illustrate the tax computation using the Tax Table method.

Although the Tax Table is derived by using the Tax Rate Schedules (discussed below), the tax calculated using the two methods may vary slightly. This variation occurs because the tax for a particular income range in the Tax Table is based on the midpoint amount.

EXAMPLE 31

Linda is single and has taxable income of $30,000 for calendar year 2007. To determine Linda's tax using the Tax Table (see Appendix A), find the $30,000 to $30,050 income line. The tax of $4,113 is actually the tax the Tax Rate Schedule would yield on taxable income of $30,025 (i.e., the midpoint amount between $30,000 and $30,050). ■

---

[29]§ 24(a).

[30]The 2008 Tax Table was not available from the IRS at the date of publication of this text. The Tax Table for 2007 and the Tax Rate Schedules for 2007 and 2008 are reproduced in Appendix A. For quick reference, the rate schedules are also reproduced inside the front cover of this text.

TABLE 3–5	2008 Tax Rate Schedule for Single Taxpayers

If Taxable Income Is		The Tax Is:	Of the Amount Over
Over	**But Not Over**		
$ –0–	$ 8,025	10%	$ –0–
8,025	32,550	$ 802.50 + 15%	8,025
32,550	78,850	4,481.25 + 25%	32,550
78,850	164,550	16,056.25 + 28%	78,850
164,550	357,700	40,052.25 + 33%	164,550
357,700		103,791.75 + 35%	357,700

Tax Rate Schedule Method

Prior to 2001 tax legislation, the **Tax Rate Schedules** contained rates of 15, 28, 31, 36, and 39.6 percent. These rates were scheduled to be reduced to 10, 15, 25, 28, 33, and 35 percent by year 2006. JGTRRA of 2003, however, accelerated the phase-in and made the new rates effective as of January 1, 2003.[31] A sunset provision reinstates the original rates (pre-2001) after 2010.

The 2008 rate schedule for single taxpayers is reproduced in Table 3–5. This schedule is used to illustrate the tax computations in Examples 32 and 33.

Pat is single and had $5,870 of taxable income in 2008. His tax is $587 ($5,870 × 10%). ■

EXAMPLE 32

Several terms are used to describe tax rates. The rates in the Tax Rate Schedules are often referred to as *statutory* (or nominal) rates. The *marginal* rate is the highest rate that is applied in the tax computation for a particular taxpayer. In Example 32, the statutory rate and the marginal rate are both 10 percent.

Chris is single and had taxable income of $80,000 in 2008. Her tax is $16,378.25 [$16,056.25 + 28%($80,000 − $78,850)]. ■

EXAMPLE 33

The *average* rate is equal to the tax liability divided by taxable income. In Example 33, Chris has statutory rates of 10 percent, 15 percent, 25 percent, and 28 percent, and a marginal rate of 28 percent. Chris's average rate is 20 percent ($16,378.25 tax liability ÷ $80,000 taxable income).

A tax is *progressive* (or graduated) if a higher rate of tax applies as the tax base increases. The progressive nature of the Federal income tax on individuals is illustrated by computing the tax in Example 33 utilizing each rate bracket.

Tax on first $8,025 at 10%	$ 802.50
Tax on $32,550 − $8,025 at 15%	3,678.75
Tax on $78,850 − $32,550 at 25%	11,575.00
Tax on $80,000 − $78,850 at 28%	322.00
Total tax on taxable income of $80,000	$16,378.25

A special computation limits the effective tax rate on qualified dividends (see Chapter 4) and net long-term capital gain (see Chapter 16).

---

[31]§ 1(i).

Computation of Net Taxes Payable or Refund Due

The pay-as-you-go feature of the Federal income tax system requires payment of all or part of the taxpayer's income tax liability during the year. These payments take the form of Federal income tax withheld by employers or estimated tax paid by the taxpayer or both.[32] The payments are applied against the tax from the Tax Table or Tax Rate Schedules to determine whether the taxpayer will get a refund or pay additional tax.

Employers are required to withhold income tax on compensation paid to their employees and to pay this tax over to the government. The employer notifies the employee of the amount of income tax withheld on Form W–2 (Wage and Tax Statement). The employee should receive this form by January 31 after the year in which the income tax is withheld.

If taxpayers receive income that is not subject to withholding or income from which not enough tax is withheld, they may have to pay estimated tax. These individuals must file Form 1040–ES (Estimated Tax for Individuals) and pay in quarterly installments the income tax and self-employment tax estimated to be due (see Chapter 13 for a thorough discussion).

The income tax from the Tax Table or the Tax Rate Schedules is reduced first by the individual's tax credits. There is an important distinction between tax credits and tax deductions. Tax credits reduce the tax liability dollar-for-dollar. Tax deductions reduce taxable income on which the tax liability is based.

EXAMPLE 34

Gail is a taxpayer in the 25% tax bracket. As a result of incurring $1,000 in child care expenses (see Chapter 13 for details), she is entitled to a $200 child care credit ($1,000 child care expenses × 20% credit rate). She also contributed $1,000 to the American Cancer Society and included this amount in her itemized deductions. The child care credit results in a $200 reduction of Gail's tax liability for the year. The contribution to the American Cancer Society reduces taxable income by $1,000 and results in a $250 reduction in Gail's tax liability ($1,000 reduction in taxable income × 25% tax rate). ■

Tax credits are discussed in Chapter 13. The following are several of the more common credits:

- Earned income credit.
- Credit for child and dependent care expenses.
- Credit for the elderly.
- Foreign tax credit.
- Child tax credit.

EXAMPLE 35

Kelly, age 30, is a head of household with a disabled and dependent mother living with him. During 2008, Kelly had the following: taxable income, $30,000; income tax withheld, $3,250; estimated tax payments, $600; and credit for dependent care expenses, $200. Kelly's net tax payable is computed as follows:

Income tax (from 2008 Tax Rate Schedule, Appendix A)		$ 3,928
Less: Tax credits and prepayments—		
Credit for dependent care expenses	$ 200	
Income tax withheld	3,250	
Estimated tax payments	600	(4,050)
Net taxes payable or (refund due if negative)		$ (122) ■

[32]§ 3402 for withholding; § 6654 for estimated payments.

Unearned Income of Children under Age 19 Taxed at Parents' Rate

LO.5

Identify and report kiddie tax situations.

At one time, a dependent child could claim an exemption on his or her own return even if claimed as a dependent by the parents. This enabled a parent to shift investment income (such as interest and dividends) to a child by transferring ownership of the assets producing the income. The child would pay no tax on the income to the extent that it was sheltered by the child's exemption and standard deduction amounts.

Also, an additional tax motivation existed for shifting income from parents to children. Although a child's unearned income in excess of the exemption and standard deduction amounts was subject to tax, it was taxed at the child's rate, rather than the parents' rate.

To reduce the tax savings that result from shifting income from parents to children, the net **unearned income** (commonly called investment income) of certain children is taxed as if it were the parents' income. Unearned income includes such income as taxable interest, dividends, capital gains, rents, royalties, pension and annuity income, and income (other than earned income) received as the beneficiary of a trust. This provision, commonly referred to as the **kiddie tax**, applies to any child who is under age 19 (or under age 24 if a full-time student) and has unearned income of more than $1,800.[33] The kiddie tax does not apply if the child has earned income that exceeds half of his or her support, if the child is married and files a joint return, or if both parents are deceased.

Net Unearned Income. Net unearned income of a dependent child is computed as follows:

Unearned income
Less: $900
Less: The greater of
- $900 of the standard deduction *or*
- The amount of allowable itemized deductions directly connected with the production of the unearned income

Equals: Net unearned income

If net unearned income is zero (or negative), the child's tax is computed without using the parents' rate. If the amount of net unearned income (regardless of source) is positive, the net unearned income is taxed at the parents' rate. The $900 amounts in the preceding formula are subject to adjustment for inflation each year (these amounts were $850 for 2007).

Tax Determination. If a child is subject to the kiddie tax, there are two options for computing the tax on the income. A separate return may be filed for the child, or the parents may elect to report the child's income on their own return. If a separate return is filed for the child, the tax on net unearned income (referred to as the *allocable parental tax*) is computed as though the income had been included on the parents' return. Form 8615 is used to compute the tax. The steps required in this computation are illustrated below.

EXAMPLE 36

Olaf and Olga have a child, Hans (age 10). In 2008, Hans received $2,900 of interest income and paid investment-related fees of $200. Olaf and Olga had $70,000 of taxable income, not including their child's investment income. The parents have no qualified dividends or capital gains. Olaf and Olga do not make the parental election.

---

[33]§ 1(g)(2). Prior to 2008, the child had to be *under age 18* for the kiddie tax to apply.

1. **Determine Hans's net unearned income**

Gross income (unearned)	$ 2,900
Less: $900	(900)
Less: The greater of	
• $900 or	
• Investment expense ($200)	(900)
Equals: Net unearned income	$ 1,100

2. **Determine allocable parental tax**

Parents' taxable income	$ 70,000
Plus: Hans's net unearned income	1,100
Equals: Revised taxable income	$ 71,100
Tax on revised taxable income	$ 10,463
Less: Tax on parents' taxable income	(10,188)
Allocable parental tax	$ 275

3. **Determine Hans's nonparental source tax**

Hans's AGI	$ 2,900
Less: Standard deduction	(900)
Less: Personal exemption	(–0–)
Equals: Taxable income	$ 2,000
Less: Net unearned income	(1,100)
Nonparental source taxable income	$ 900
Equals: Tax ($900 × 10% rate)	$ 90

4. **Determine Hans's total tax liability**

Nonparental source tax (step 3)	$ 90
Allocable parental tax (step 2)	275
Total tax	$ 365

Election to Claim Certain Unearned Income on Parent's Return. If a child who is subject to the kiddie tax is required to file a tax return and meets all of the following requirements, the parent may elect to report the child's unearned income that exceeds $1,800 on the parent's own tax return:

- Gross income is from interest and dividends only.
- Gross income is more than $900 but less than $9,000.
- No estimated tax has been paid in the name and Social Security number of the child, and the child is not subject to backup withholding (see Chapter 13).

If the parental election is made, the child is treated as having no gross income and then is not required to file a tax return. The parental election is made by completing and filing Form 8814 (Parents' Election to Report Child's Interest and Dividends).

The parent(s) must also pay an additional tax equal to the smaller of $90 or 10 percent of the child's gross income over $900. Parents who have substantial itemized deductions based on AGI (see Chapter 10) may find that making the parental election increases total taxes for the family unit. Taxes should be calculated both with the parental election and without it to determine the appropriate choice.

Other Provisions. If parents have more than one child subject to the tax on net unearned income, the tax for the children is computed as shown in Example 36 and then allocated to the children based on their relative amounts of income. For children of divorced parents, the taxable income of the custodial parent is used to determine the allocable parental tax. This parent is the one who may elect to report the child's unearned income. For married individuals filing separate returns, the individual with the greater taxable income is the applicable parent.

Filing Considerations

Under the category of filing considerations, the following questions need to be resolved:

- Is the taxpayer required to file an income tax return?
- If so, which form should be used?
- When and how should the return be filed?
- In computing the tax liability, which column of the Tax Table or which Tax Rate Schedule should be used?

The first three questions are discussed under Filing Requirements, and the last is treated under Filing Status.

Filing Requirements

General Rules. An individual must file a tax return if certain minimum amounts of gross income have been received. The general rule is that a tax return is required for every individual who has gross income that equals or exceeds the sum of the exemption amount plus the applicable standard deduction.[34] For example, a single taxpayer under age 65 must file a tax return in 2008 if gross income equals or exceeds $8,950 ($3,500 exemption plus $5,450 standard deduction). Table 3–6 lists the income levels[35] that require tax returns under the general rule and under certain special rules.

The additional standard deduction for being age 65 or older is considered in determining the gross income filing requirements. For example, note in Table 3–6 that the 2008 filing requirement for a single taxpayer age 65 or older is $10,300 ($5,450 basic standard deduction + $1,350 additional standard deduction + $3,500 exemption). However, the additional standard deduction for blindness is not taken into account. The 2008 filing requirement for a single taxpayer under age 65 and blind is $8,950 ($5,450 basic standard deduction + $3,500 exemption).

A self-employed individual with net earnings of $400 or more from a business or profession must file a tax return regardless of the amount of gross income.

Even though an individual has gross income below the filing level amounts and therefore does not owe any tax, he or she must file a return to obtain a tax refund of amounts withheld. A return is also necessary to obtain the benefits of the earned income credit allowed to taxpayers with little or no tax liability. Chapter 13 discusses the earned income credit.

Filing Requirements for Dependents. Computation of the gross income filing requirement for an individual who can be claimed as a dependent on another person's tax return is subject to more complex rules. Such an individual must file a return if he or she has *any* of the following:

- Earned income only and gross income that is more than the total standard deduction (including any additional standard deduction) that the individual is allowed for the year.
- Unearned income only and gross income of more than $900 plus any additional standard deduction that the individual is allowed for the year.

---

[34]The gross income amounts for determining whether a tax return must be filed are adjusted for inflation each year.

[35]§ 6012(a)(1).

TABLE 3–6	Filing Levels		
Filing Status		**2007 Gross Income**	**2008 Gross Income**
Single			
Under 65 and not blind		$ 8,750	$ 8,950
Under 65 and blind		8,750	8,950
65 or older		10,050	10,300
Married, filing joint return			
Both spouses under 65 and neither blind		$17,500	$17,900
Both spouses under 65 and one or both spouses blind		17,500	17,900
One spouse 65 or older		18,550	18,950
Both spouses 65 or older		19,600	20,000
Married, filing separate return			
All—whether 65 or older or blind		$ 3,400	$ 3,500
Head of household			
Under 65 and not blind		$11,250	$11,500
Under 65 and blind		11,250	11,500
65 or older		12,550	12,850
Qualifying widow(er)			
Under 65 and not blind		$14,100	$14,400
Under 65 and blind		14,100	14,400
65 or older		15,150	15,450

- Both earned and unearned income and gross income of more than the larger of $900 or the sum of earned income plus $300 (but limited to the applicable basic standard deduction), plus any additional standard deduction that the individual is allowed for the year.

Thus, the filing requirement for a dependent who has no unearned income is the total of the *basic* standard deduction plus any *additional* standard deduction, which includes both the additional deduction for blindness and the deduction for being age 65 or older. For example, the 2008 filing requirement for a single dependent who is under age 65 and not blind is $5,450, the amount of the basic standard deduction for 2008. The filing requirement for a single dependent under age 65 and blind is $6,800 ($5,450 basic standard deduction + $1,350 additional standard deduction).

Selecting the Proper Form. The 2008 tax forms had not been released at the date of publication of this text. The following comments apply to the 2007 forms. It is possible that some provisions will change for the 2008 forms.

Although a variety of forms are available to individual taxpayers, the use of some of these forms is restricted. For example, Form 1040EZ cannot be used if:

- Taxpayer claims any dependents;
- Taxpayer (or spouse) is 65 or older or blind; or
- Taxable income is $100,000 or more.

Taxpayers who desire to itemize deductions *from* AGI cannot use Form 1040A, but must file Form 1040 (the long form).

The E-File Approach. In addition to traditional paper returns, the **e-file** program is an increasingly popular alternative. Here, the required tax information is

TAX *in the News*   **IRS VERSUS USCIS**

Foreign persons who earn income within the United States may need to file a Federal income tax return, but may not have a Social Security number for filing purposes. If not, they can use a nine-digit Individual Tax Identification Number (ITIN) instead. The IRS issues ITINs upon the submission of an application and proof of identification (e.g., a driver's license). As the IRS does not require an applicant to show that he or she is in the United States legally, the ITINs are freely available to undocumented persons (i.e., illegal immigrants). The use of an ITIN also can enable the holder to carry out other financial transactions (e.g., establish a bank account, secure a credit card, obtain a loan).

Through its lax procedures in issuing ITINs, is the IRS indirectly encouraging, or at least condoning, the status of undocumented persons? Along this line, should the IRS require proof of legal presence in the United States before issuing an ITIN? Since the IRS and USCIS (U.S. Citizenship and Immigration Services) do not collaborate on the issuance of ITINs, is this another example of one Federal agency not cooperating with another?

The position of the IRS is that the current ITIN procedure brings in revenue that otherwise would not be forthcoming. Some undocumented workers want to comply with the law and pay the income taxes they owe. This practice should not be discouraged as the tax law applies with equal force to legal and illegal residents of the United States. Although a breakdown between legal and illegal residents is not available, the tax liability of ITIN filers from 1996 to 2003 was $50 billion.

transmitted to the IRS electronically either directly from the taxpayer (i.e., an "e-file online return") or indirectly through an electronic return originator (ERO). EROs are tax professionals who have been accepted into the electronic filing program by the IRS. Such parties hold themselves out to the general public as "authorized IRS e-file providers." Providers often are also the preparers of the return.

Through prearrangement with the IRS, some providers offer free e-filing services. Generally, such services are available only to lower-income taxpayers (e.g., below $52,000) and if other specified conditions are satisfied. A list of these providers and their eligibility requirements can be obtained through the IRS Web site.

For direct online e-filing, a taxpayer must have a personal computer and tax preparation software with the capability of conveying the information via modem to an electronic return transmitter. Otherwise a taxpayer must use an authorized provider who makes the e-file transmission. Except as previously noted, the provider charges a fee for the e-filing service.

All taxpayers and tax return preparers must attest to the returns they file. For most taxpayers, this attesting can be done through an electronic return signature using a personal identification number (a Self-Select PIN). Information on establishing a Self-Select PIN can be found in the instructions to Form 1040, Form 1040A, or Form 1040EZ, or at **http://www.irs.gov/efile**. If certain paper documents must be submitted, a one-page form must be completed and filed when the return is e-filed. Form 8453 (U.S. Individual Income Tax Declaration for an IRS *e-file* Return) is the version required when a provider is used. A direct e-file online return requires the use of Form 8453–OL, which must be signed and filed by the taxpayer after the e-file return is accepted by the IRS.

The e-file approach has two major advantages. First, compliance with the format required by the IRS eliminates many errors that would otherwise occur. Second, the time required for processing a refund usually is reduced to three weeks or less.

When and Where to File.
Tax returns of individuals are due on or before the fifteenth day of the fourth month following the close of the tax year. For the calendar year taxpayer, the usual filing date is on or before April 15 of the following year.[36] When the due date falls on a Saturday, Sunday, or legal holiday, the last day for filing falls on the next business day. If the return is mailed to the proper

---

[36] § 6072(a).

TAX *in the News*   SPECIAL RULES FOR CERTAIN MILITARY PERSONNEL

The Military Family Tax Relief Act of 2003 allows certain members of the military more time to file their Federal income tax return. If they are outside the United States and Puerto Rico *but not* in a combat zone, the filing date is extended to June 15. If additional taxes are due, however, interest still begins to accrue after April 15. For those deployed in a designated combat zone, the filing date is postponed until 180 days after the last day of combat service. Furthermore, in such cases, interest *does not* accrue during the deferral period. These filing dates are equally applicable when the military person is married and files a joint return.

---

address with sufficient postage and is postmarked on or before the due date, it is deemed timely filed. The Code enables the IRS to prescribe rules governing the filing of returns using various private parcel delivery services (e.g., DHL, FedEx, UPS).[37]

If a taxpayer is unable to file the return by the specified due date, a six-month extension of time can be obtained by filing Form 4868 (Application for Automatic Extension of Time to File U.S. Individual Income Tax Return).[38]

Although obtaining an extension excuses a taxpayer from a penalty for failure to file, it does not insulate against the penalty for failure to pay. If more tax is owed, the filing of Form 4868 should be accompanied by an additional remittance to cover the balance due. The failure to file and failure to pay penalties are discussed in Chapter 1.

The return should be sent or delivered to the Regional Service Center listed in the instructions for each type of return or contained in software applications.[39] Because of an IRS reorganization that began in October 2000 and is still ongoing, some taxpayers may be required to file at a different Service Center than in the past.

If an individual taxpayer needs to file an amended return (e.g., because of a failure to report income or to claim a deduction or tax credit), Form 1040X is filed. The form generally must be filed within three years of the filing date of the original return or within two years from the time the tax was paid, whichever is later.

Mode of Payment. Usually, payment is made by check. In that event, the check should be made out to "United States Treasury."

The IRS has approved the use of MasterCard, American Express, Discover, and Visa to pay Federal taxes. The use of a credit card to pay taxes will result in a charge against the cardholder by the credit card company.

Filing Status

The amount of tax will vary considerably depending on which Tax Rate Schedule is used. This is illustrated in the following example.

EXAMPLE 37

The following amounts of tax are computed using the 2008 Tax Rate Schedules for a taxpayer (or taxpayers in the case of a joint return) with $60,000 of taxable income (see Appendix A).

Filing Status	Amount of Tax
Single	$11,344
Married, filing joint return	8,198
Married, filing separate return	11,344
Head of household	10,063

---

[37]§ 7502(f).
[38]Reg. § 1.6081–4.

[39]The Regional Service Centers and the geographic area each covers can also be found at **http://www.irs.gov/file** or in tax forms packages.

TAX *in the News*   **"CHARGE IT"—CONVENIENT BUT NOT CHEAP!**

When a consumer uses a credit card to buy goods, the merchant pays a fee to the credit card company. When a credit card is used to pay income taxes, however, the law prevents the IRS from paying any such fee. Instead, the credit card company charges the user a "convenience fee" equal to 2.5 percent of the tax paid. The fee must be paid even if the user pays the credit card bill in full when it arrives. If, for example, John uses his Visa card to pay the $10,000 in taxes that he owes, he will be charged $250 (2.5% × $10,000) as a convenience fee. John will have to pay the $250 fee even if he pays Visa the $10,000 when billed. Furthermore, regular credit card interest (usually 15 percent or more) will be charged on extended time payments.

Clearly, then, using credit cards to pay income taxes, though convenient, is not without cost!

Rates for Single Taxpayers. A taxpayer who is unmarried or separated from his or her spouse by a decree of divorce or separate maintenance and does not qualify for another filing status must use the rates for single taxpayers. Marital status is determined as of the last day of the tax year, except when a spouse dies during the year. In that case, marital status is determined as of the date of death. State law governs whether a taxpayer is considered married, divorced, or legally separated.

Under a special relief provision, however, married persons who live apart may be able to qualify as single. Married taxpayers who are considered single under the *abandoned spouse rules* are allowed to use the head-of-household rates. See the discussion of this filing status under Abandoned Spouse Rules later in the chapter.

Rates for Married Individuals. The joint return [Tax Rate Schedule Y, Code § 1(a)] was originally enacted in 1948 to establish equity between married taxpayers in common law states and those in community property states. Before the joint return rates were enacted, taxpayers in community property states were in an advantageous position relative to taxpayers in common law states because they could split their income. For instance, if one spouse earned $100,000 and the other spouse was not employed, each spouse could report $50,000 of income. Splitting the income in this manner caused the total income to be subject to lower marginal tax rates. Each spouse would start at the bottom of the rate structure.

Taxpayers in common law states did not have this income-splitting option, so their taxable income was subject to higher marginal rates. This inconsistency in treatment was remedied by the joint return provisions. The progressive rates in the joint return Tax Rate Schedule are constructed based on the assumption that income is earned equally by the two spouses.

If married individuals elect to file separate returns, each reports only his or her own income, exemptions, deductions, and credits, and each must use the Tax Rate Schedule applicable to married taxpayers filing separately. It is generally advantageous for married individuals to file a joint return, since the combined amount of tax is lower. However, special circumstances (e.g., significant medical expenses incurred by one spouse subject to the 7.5 percent limitation) may warrant the election to file separate returns. It may be necessary to compute the tax under both assumptions to determine the most advantageous filing status.

When Congress enacted the rate structure available to those filing joint returns, it generally favored married taxpayers. In certain situations, however, the parties would incur less tax if they were not married and filed separate returns. The additional tax that a joint return caused, commonly called the **marriage penalty**, usually developed when *both* spouses had large taxable incomes. Long aware of the inequity of the marriage penalty, Congress reduced the effect of the problem in JGTRRA of 2003. Beginning in 2003, the standard deduction available to married filers increased to 200 percent of that applicable to single persons. Furthermore

GLOBAL
Tax Issues

FILING A JOINT RETURN

John Garth is a U.S. citizen and resident, but he spends a lot of time in London where his employer sends him on frequent assignments. John is married to Victoria, a citizen and resident of the United Kingdom.

Can John and Victoria file a joint return for U.S. Federal income tax purposes? Although § 6013(a)(1) specifically precludes the filing of a joint return if one spouse is a nonresident alien, another Code provision permits an exception. Under § 6013(g), the parties can elect to treat the nonqualifying spouse as a "resident" of the United States. This election would allow John and Victoria to file jointly.

But should John and Victoria make this election? If Victoria has considerable income of her own (from non-U.S. sources), the election could be ill-advised. As a nonresident alien, Victoria's non-U.S. source income *would not* be subject to the U.S. income tax. If she is treated as a U.S. resident, however, her non-U.S. source income *will be subject to U.S. tax.* Under the U.S. global approach to taxation, all income (regardless of where earned) of anyone who is a *resident* or *citizen* of the United States is subject to tax.

and also beginning in 2003, the 15 percent bracket for joint filers increased to 200 percent of the size of that applicable to single filers.

Although changes in the tax rates and the standard deduction have reduced the marriage penalty, the Code places some limitations on married persons who file separate returns. Some examples of these limitations are listed below.

- If either spouse itemizes deductions, the other spouse must also itemize.
- The earned income credit and the credit for child and dependent care expenses cannot be claimed (see Chapter 13).
- No deduction is allowed for interest paid on qualified education loans (see Chapter 10).
- Only $1,500 of excess capital losses can be claimed (see Chapter 16).

In such cases, being single would be preferable to being married and filing separately.

The joint return rates also apply for two years following the death of one spouse, if the surviving spouse maintains a household for a dependent child. The child must be a son, stepson, daughter, or stepdaughter who qualifies as a dependent of the taxpayer. This is referred to as **surviving spouse** status.[40]

EXAMPLE 38

Fred dies in 2007 leaving Ethel with a dependent child. For the year of Fred's death (2007), Ethel files a joint return with Fred (presuming the consent of Fred's executor is obtained). For the next two years (2008 and 2009), Ethel, as a surviving spouse, may use the joint return rates. In subsequent years, Ethel may use the head-of-household rates if she continues to maintain a household as her home that is the domicile of the child. ■

Keep in mind, however, that for the year of death, the surviving spouse is treated as being married. Thus, a joint return can be filed if the deceased spouse's executor agrees. If not, the surviving spouse is forced into the status of married filing separately.

Rates for Heads of Household. Unmarried individuals who maintain a household for a dependent (or dependents) are generally entitled to use the

---

[40]§ 2(a). The IRS label for surviving spouse status is "Qualifying Widow(er) with Dependent Child."

head-of-household rates.[41] The tax liability using the head-of-household rates falls between the liability using the joint return Tax Rate Schedule and the liability using the Tax Rate Schedule for single taxpayers.

To qualify for head-of-household rates, a taxpayer must pay more than half the cost of maintaining a household as his or her home. The household must also be the principal home of a dependent. Except for temporary absences (e.g., school, hospitalization), the dependent must live in the taxpayer's household for over half the year.

A dependent must be either a qualifying child or a qualifying relative who meets the relationship test.[42]

EXAMPLE 39

Dylan is single and maintains a household in which he and his cousin live. Even though the cousin may qualify as a dependent (under the member-of-the-household test), Dylan cannot claim head-of-household filing status. A cousin does not meet the relationship test. ■

EXAMPLE 40

Emma, a widow, maintains a household in which she and her aunt live. If the aunt qualifies as a dependent, Emma may file as head of household. Note that an aunt meets the relationship test. ■

EXAMPLE 41

Nancy maintains a household in which she and her daughter, Bernice, live. Bernice, age 27, is single and earns $9,000 from a part-time job. Nancy does not qualify for head-of-household filing status as she cannot claim Bernice as a dependent (due to the gross income test).[43] ■

A special rule allows taxpayers to avoid having to live with their parents. Head-of-household status still may be claimed if the taxpayer maintains a *separate home* for his or her *parent or parents* if at least one parent qualifies as a dependent of the taxpayer.[44]

EXAMPLE 42

Rick, an unmarried individual, lives in New York City and maintains a household in Detroit for his dependent parents. Rick may use the head-of-household rates even though his parents do not reside in his New York home. ■

Head-of-household status is not changed during the year by the death of the dependent. As long as the taxpayer provided more than half of the cost of maintaining the household prior to the dependent's death, head-of-household status is preserved.

Abandoned Spouse Rules. When married persons file separate returns, several unfavorable tax consequences result. For example, the taxpayer must use the Tax Rate Schedule for married taxpayers filing separately. To mitigate such harsh treatment for some taxpayers, Congress enacted provisions commonly referred to as the **abandoned spouse** rules. These rules allow a married taxpayer to file as a head of household if all of the following conditions are satisfied:[45]

- The taxpayer does not file a joint return.
- The taxpayer paid more than one-half the cost of maintaining his or her home for the tax year.
- The taxpayer's spouse did not live in the home during the last six months of the tax year.

---

[41]§ 2(b).

[42]§ 2(b)(3)(B).

[43]Can Bernice be a dependent under the qualifying child rules? Even though the gross income test is inapplicable for a qualifying child, Bernice does not meet the age test.

[44]§ 2(b)(1)(B).

[45]§ 7703(b).

• The home was the principal residence of the taxpayer's son, daughter, step-son, stepdaughter, foster child, or adopted child for more than half the year, and the child can be claimed as a dependent.[46]

LO.7
Possess an overview of property transactions.

Gains and Losses from Property Transactions—In General

Gains and losses from property transactions are discussed in detail in Chapters 14 through 17. Because of their importance in the tax system, however, they are introduced briefly at this point.

When property is sold or otherwise disposed of, gain or loss may result. Such gain or loss has an effect on the income tax position of the party making the sale or other disposition when the *realized* gain or loss is *recognized* for tax purposes. Without realized gain or loss, there generally can be no recognized gain or loss. The concept of realized gain or loss is expressed as follows:

$$\begin{matrix} \text{Amount realized} \\ \text{from the sale} \end{matrix} - \begin{matrix} \text{Adjusted basis of} \\ \text{the property} \end{matrix} = \begin{matrix} \text{Realized gain} \\ \text{(or loss)} \end{matrix}$$

The amount realized is the selling price of the property less any costs of disposition (e.g., brokerage commissions) incurred by the seller. The adjusted basis of the property is determined as follows:

Cost (or other original basis) at date of acquisition[47]

Add: Capital additions

Subtract: Depreciation (if appropriate) and other capital recoveries
            (see Chapter 8)

Equals: Adjusted basis at date of sale or other disposition

All realized gains are recognized (taxable) unless some specific part of the tax law provides otherwise (see Chapter 15 dealing with certain nontaxable exchanges). Realized losses may or may not be recognized (deductible) for tax purposes, depending on the circumstances involved. Generally, losses realized from the disposition of personal use property (property neither held for investment nor used in a trade or business) are not recognized.

EXAMPLE 43	During the current year, Ted sells his sailboat (adjusted basis of $4,000) for $5,500. Ted also sells one of his personal automobiles (adjusted basis of $8,000) for $5,000. Ted's realized gain of $1,500 from the sale of the sailboat is recognized. On the other hand, the $3,000 realized loss on the sale of the automobile is not recognized and will not provide Ted with any deductible tax benefit. ∎

Once it has been determined that the disposition of property results in a recognized gain or loss, the next step is to classify the gain or loss as capital or ordinary. Although ordinary gain is fully taxable and ordinary loss is fully deductible, the same may not hold true for capital gains and capital losses.

---

[46]§ 152(f)(1). The dependency requirement does not apply, however, if the taxpayer could have claimed a dependency exemption except for the fact that the exemption was claimed by the noncustodial parent under a written agreement.

[47]Cost usually means purchase price plus expenses related to the acquisition of the property and incurred by the purchaser (e.g., brokerage commissions). For the basis of property acquired by gift or inheritance and other basis rules, see Chapter 14.

Gains and Losses from Property Transactions—Capital Gains and Losses

To obtain a good perspective on how the Federal income tax functions, some overview of property transactions is needed. This is particularly the case with capital gains and losses, which can generate unique tax consequences. For in-depth treatment of property transactions (including capital gains and losses), refer to Chapters 14 through 17. For now, the overview appearing below should suffice.

Definition of a Capital Asset

Capital assets are defined in the Code as any property held by the taxpayer *other than* property listed in § 1221. The list in § 1221 includes inventory, accounts receivable, and depreciable property or real estate used in a business. Thus, the sale or exchange of assets in these categories usually results in ordinary income or loss treatment (see Chapter 17).

EXAMPLE 44

Kelly owns a pizza parlor. During the current year, he sells two automobiles. The first automobile, which had been used as a pizza delivery car for three years, was sold at a loss of $1,000. Because this automobile is an asset used in his business, Kelly has an ordinary loss deduction of $1,000, rather than a capital loss deduction. The second automobile, which Kelly had owned for two years, was his personal use car. It was sold for a gain of $800. The personal use car is a capital asset. Therefore, Kelly has a capital gain of $800. ■

The principal capital assets held by an individual taxpayer include assets held for personal (rather than business) use, such as a personal residence or an automobile, and assets held for investment purposes (e.g., corporate securities and land). Capital assets generally include collectibles, which are subject to somewhat unique tax treatment. **Collectibles** include art, antiques, gems, metals, stamps, some coins and bullion, and alcoholic beverages that are held as investments.

Taxation of Net Capital Gain

Net capital gains are classified and taxed as follows:

Classification	Maximum Rate
Short-term gains (held for one year or less)	35%
Long-term gains (held for more than one year)—	
Collectibles	28%
Certain depreciable property used in a trade or business (known as unrecaptured § 1250 gain and discussed in Chapter 17)	25%
All other long-term capital gains	15%, 5%, or 0%

The special tax rate applicable to long-term capital gains is called the alternative tax computation. It is to be used only if the taxpayer's regular tax rate *exceeds* the applicable alternative tax rate. The 5 percent and 0 percent rates, noted above, apply only if the taxpayer's regular tax bracket is 15 percent or less. If so and the sale or exchange took place prior to 2008, the rate is 5 percent. If the transaction takes place after 2007 and before 2011, the rate is 0 percent.[48]

---

[48]§ 1(h)(1) as amended by JGTRRA of 2003 and further amended by TIPRA of 2005. For recognized gains prior to May 6, 2003, the maximum rates were 20% and 10%.

EXAMPLE 45

During 2007, Polly is in the 15% tax bracket and has the following capital gains for the year:

Robin Corporation stock (held for 6 months)	$1,000
Crow Corporation stock (held for 13 months)	1,000

Polly's tax on these transactions is $150 ($1,000 × 15%) as to Robin and $50 ($1,000 × 5%) as to Crow. ■

EXAMPLE 46

Assume the same facts as in Example 45, except that the year involved is 2008. Polly's tax on these transactions is $150 ($1,000 × 15%) as to Robin and $0 ($1,000 × 0%) as to Crow. ■

EXAMPLE 47

Assume the same facts as in Examples 45 and 46, except that Polly's regular tax bracket for the year is 33% (not 15%). Polly's tax on these transactions now becomes $330 ($1,000 × 33%) as to Robin and $150 ($1,000 × 15%) as to Crow. ■

Determination of Net Capital Gain

In order to arrive at a net capital gain, capital losses must be taken into account. The capital losses are aggregated by holding period (short term and long term) and applied against the gains in that category. If excess losses result, they are then shifted to the category carrying the *highest* tax rate. A *net capital gain* will occur if the net long-term capital gain (NLTCG) exceeds the net short-term capital loss (NSTCL).

EXAMPLE 48

In the current year, Colin is in the 35% tax bracket and has the following capital transactions:

Penguin Corporation stock (held for 8 months)	$ 1,000
Owl Corporation stock (held for 10 months)	(3,000)
Stamp collection (held for 5 years)	2,000
Land (held as an investment for 3 years)	4,000

The Penguin Corporation short-term capital gain (STCG) of $1,000 is offset by the Owl Corporation short-term capital loss (STCL) of $3,000. The net STCL of $2,000 is then applied against the collectible gain of $2,000. The end result is a net long-term capital gain of $4,000 from the land sale. Colin's net capital gain is taxed at a 15% rate. Note that the stamp collection gain would have been taxed at a higher 28% rate had it not been offset by the excess short-term capital loss. ■

Treatment of Net Capital Loss

For individual taxpayers, net capital loss can be used to offset ordinary income of up to $3,000 ($1,500 for married persons filing separate returns). If a taxpayer has both short- and long-term capital losses, the short-term category is used first to arrive at the $3,000. Any remaining net capital loss is carried over indefinitely until exhausted. When carried over, the excess capital loss retains its classification as short or long term.

EXAMPLE 49

In 2008, Tina has a short-term capital loss of $2,000, a long-term capital loss of $2,500, and no capital gains. She can deduct $3,000 ($2,000 short-term + $1,000 long-term) of this amount as an ordinary loss. The remaining $1,500 is carried over to 2009 as a long-term capital loss. ■

Maximizing the Use of the Standard Deduction

LO.8

Identify tax planning opportunities associated with the individual tax formula.

In most cases, the choice between using the standard deduction and itemizing deductions *from* AGI is a simple matter—pick whichever yields the larger tax benefit. Families in the initial stages of home ownership, for example, will invariably make the itemization choice due to the substantial mortgage interest and property tax payments involved. Older taxpayers, however, have paid for their homes and are enjoying senior citizen property tax exemptions. For them, the more attractive benefit is the additional standard deduction that can accompany the standard deduction choice.

TAX PLANNING
Considerations

In some cases, the difference between the standard deduction and itemizing may not be a significant amount. Here, taxes might be saved by alternating between the two options. The taxpayer does this by using the cash method to concentrate multiple years' deductions in a single year. Then, the standard deduction is used in alternate years.

The Chengs, ages 59 and 60, are married and file a joint return. Their usual AGI is $90,000, and their itemized annual expenses approximate $9,800 comprised as follows: $4,000 (state income tax), $3,600 (property taxes on personal residence), and $2,200 (yearly church pledge). For tax years 2007 and 2008, the Chengs make no changes and follow their usual payment procedure. As a result, they claim the standard deduction for each year for a total deduction of $21,600 ($10,700 for 2007 + $10,900 for 2008). ∎	**EXAMPLE 50**

Assume the same facts as in Example 50, except that the Chengs do the following in 2008: In January, they pay their property taxes[49] for 2007. During the year, they pay their 2008 church pledge, and in December they pay the property taxes for 2008 and their church pledge for 2009. Their total itemized deductions for 2008 become $15,600 [$4,000 (state income tax for 2007) + $7,200 (property taxes for 2007 and 2008) + $4,400 (church pledge for 2008 and 2009)]. If they claim the standard deduction for 2007, the two-year total is $26,300 ($10,700 + $15,600). Comparing this result with that reached in Example 50 reflects additional deductions of $4,700 ($26,300 − $21,600). Presuming a tax bracket of 25%, the procedure followed in Example 51 saves the Chengs $1,175 in taxes. ∎	**EXAMPLE 51**

The shifting of deductions between years through the timing of payments can be effective with certain other itemized deductions besides property taxes and charitable contributions. For a further discussion of this possibility, see Chapter 10.

Dependency Exemptions

The Joint Return Test. A married person can be claimed as a dependent only if that individual does not file a joint return with his or her spouse. If a joint return has been filed, the damage may be undone if separate returns are substituted on a timely basis (on or before the due date of the return).

While preparing a client's 2007 income tax return on April 4, 2008, the tax practitioner discovered that the client's daughter filed a joint return with her husband in late January of 2008. Presuming the daughter otherwise qualifies as the client's dependent, the exemption is not lost if she and her husband file separate returns on or before April 15, 2008. ∎	**EXAMPLE 52**

An initial election to file a joint return must be considered carefully in any situation in which the taxpayers might later decide to amend their return and file separately.

---

[49]In some taxing jurisdictions, it may be impossible to delay payment on ad valorem property taxes without incurring some penalty. If the delay is minimal, however, the penalty is apt to be mild.

As indicated above, separate returns may be substituted for a joint return only if the amended returns are filed on or before the normal due date of the return. If the taxpayers in Example 52 attempt to file separate returns after April 15, 2008, the returns will not be accepted, and the joint return election is binding.[50]

Keep in mind that the filing of a joint return is not fatal to the dependency exemption if the parties are filing solely to recover all income tax withholdings, they are not required to file a return, and no tax liability would exist on separate returns.

Support Considerations. The support of a qualifying child becomes relevant only if the child is self-supporting. In cases where the child has an independent source of funds, planning could help prevent an undesirable result. When a qualifying relative is involved, meeting the support test is essential, as the dependency exemption is not otherwise available.

EXAMPLE 53	In 2008, Imogene maintains a household that she shares with her son and mother. The son, Barry, is 23 years of age and a full-time student in law school. The mother, Gladys, is 68 years of age and active in charitable causes. Barry works part-time for a local law firm, while Gladys has income from investments. In resolving the support issue (or self-support in the case of Barry), compare Imogene's contribution with that made by Barry and Gladys.[51] In this connection, what Barry and Gladys do with their funds becomes crucial. The funds that are used for nonsupport purposes (e.g., purchase of investments) or not used at all (e.g., deposited in a bank) should not be considered. To the extent possible, control how much Barry and Gladys contribute to their own support. Records should be maintained showing the amount of support and its source. ∎

Example 53 does not mention the possible application of the gross income test. Presuming Barry is a qualifying child, the amount he earns does not matter, as the gross income test does not apply. Gladys, however, comes under the qualifying relative category, where the gross income test applies. Therefore, for her to be claimed as a dependent, her income that is taxable will have to be less than $3,500.

Community Property Ramifications. In certain cases, state law can have an effect on the availability of a dependency exemption.

EXAMPLE 54	In 2008, Mitch provides more than half of the support of his son, Ross, and daughter-in-law, Connie, who live with him. Ross, age 22, is a full-time student, while Connie earns $4,000 from a part-time job. Ross and Connie do not file a joint return. All parties live in New York, a common law state. Mitch can claim Ross as a dependent, as he is a qualifying child. Connie is not a dependent because she does not meet the gross income test under the qualifying relative category. ∎

EXAMPLE 55	Assume the same facts as in Example 54, except that all parties live in Arizona, a community property state. Now, Connie also qualifies as a dependent. Since Connie's gross income is only $2,000 (one-half of the community income), she satisfies the gross income test. ∎

Relationship to the Deduction for Medical Expenses. Generally, medical expenses are deductible only if they are paid on behalf of the taxpayer, his or her spouse, and their dependents. Since deductibility may rest on dependency status, planning is important in arranging multiple support agreements.

---

[50]Reg. § 1.6013–1(a)(1).

[51]As part of her support contribution to Barry and Gladys, Imogene can count the fair market value of the meals and lodging she provides.

During the year, Zelda will be supported by her two sons (Vern and Vito) and her daughter (Maria). Each will furnish approximately one-third of the required support. If the parties decide that the dependency exemption should be claimed by the daughter under a multiple support agreement, any medical expenses incurred by Zelda should be paid by Maria. ∎

In planning a multiple support agreement, take into account which of the parties is most likely to exceed the 7.5 percent limitation (see Chapter 10). In Example 56, for instance, Maria might be a poor choice if she and her family do not expect to incur many medical and drug expenses of their own.

One exception permits the deduction of medical expenses paid on behalf of someone who is not a spouse or a dependent. If the person could be claimed as a dependent *except* for the gross income or joint return test, the medical expenses are, nevertheless, deductible. For additional discussion, see Chapter 10.

ETHICAL and EQUITABLE *Considerations*   A TAX BENEFIT FROM NONDEPENDENTS

During 2008, Kristen provides more than half of the support of her parents who do not live with her. She cannot claim them as dependents, however, because they have too much gross income and file a joint return. She pays $20,000 for her mother's dental implants and $12,000 for her father's knee replacement. From a tax standpoint, has Kristen acted wisely?

Taking Advantage of Tax Rate Differentials

It is natural for taxpayers to be concerned about the tax rates they are paying. How does a tax practitioner communicate information about rates to clients? There are several possibilities.

The marginal rate (refer to Examples 32 and 33) provides information that can help a taxpayer evaluate a particular course of action or structure a transaction in the most advantageous manner. For example, a taxpayer who is in the 15 percent bracket this year and expects to be in the 28 percent bracket next year should, if possible, defer payment of deductible expenses until next year to maximize the tax benefit of the deduction.

A note of caution is in order with respect to shifting income and expenses between years. Congress has recognized the tax planning possibilities of such shifting and has enacted many provisions to limit a taxpayer's ability to do so. Some of these limitations on the shifting of income are discussed in Chapters 4, 5, and 18. Limitations that affect a taxpayer's ability to shift deductions are discussed in Chapters 6 through 11 and in Chapter 18.

A taxpayer's *effective rate* can be an informative measure of the effectiveness of tax planning. The effective rate is computed by dividing the taxpayer's tax liability by the total amount of income. A low effective rate can be considered an indication of effective tax planning.

One way of lowering the effective rate is to exclude income from the tax base. For example, a taxpayer might consider investing in tax-free municipal bonds rather than taxable corporate bonds. Although pre-tax income from corporate bonds is usually higher, after-tax income may be higher if the taxpayer invests in tax-free municipals.

Another way of lowering the effective rate is to make sure that the taxpayer's expenses and losses are deductible. For example, losses on investments in passive activities may not be deductible (see Chapter 11). Therefore, a taxpayer who plans to invest in an activity that will produce a loss in the early years should take steps to ensure that the business is treated as active rather than passive. Active losses are deductible while passive losses are not.

Income of Certain Children

Taxpayers can use several strategies to avoid or minimize the effect of the rules that tax the unearned income of certain children at the parents' rate. With the recent increase in the cutoff age from 18 to 19 (under 24 for full-time students), more minors will be vulnerable to the application of the kiddie tax.[52] Parents should consider giving a younger child assets that defer taxable income until the child reaches a nonvulnerable age. For example, U.S. government Series EE savings bonds can be used to defer income until the bonds are cashed in (see Chapter 4).

Growth stocks typically pay little in the way of dividends. However, the profit on an astute investment may more than offset the lack of dividends. The child can hold the stock until he or she reaches a safe age. If the stock is sold then at a profit, the profit is taxed at the child's low rates.

Taxpayers in a position to do so can employ their children in their business and pay them a reasonable wage for the work they actually perform (e.g., light office help, such as filing). The child's earned income is sheltered by the standard deduction, and the parents' business is allowed a deduction for the wages. The kiddie tax rules have no effect on earned income, even if it is earned from the parents' business.

KEY TERMS

Abandoned spouse, 3–31	Itemized deductions, 3–6	Qualifying relative, 3–13
Child tax credit, 3–19	Kiddie tax, 3–23	Standard deduction, 3–7
Collectibles, 3–33	Marriage penalty, 3–29	Surviving spouse, 3–30
Dependency exemption, 3–11	Multiple support agreement, 3–15	Tax Rate Schedules, 3–21
E-file, 3–26	Personal exemptions, 3–10	Tax Table, 3–20
Head-of-household, 3–31	Qualifying child, 3–12	Unearned income, 3–23

PROBLEM MATERIALS

DISCUSSION QUESTIONS

1. Rearrange the following items to show the correct formula for arriving at *taxable income* of individuals under the Federal income tax:
   a. Taxable income.
   b. Income (broadly conceived).
   c. Adjusted gross income.
   d. Deductions *for* AGI.
   e. The greater of the standard deduction or itemized deductions.
   f. Personal and dependency exemptions.

---

[52]See footnote 33 earlier in the chapter.

g.   Income tax withheld from wages.

h.   Gross income.

i.   Exclusions.

2.   During the year, Becky is involved in the following transactions: **Issue ID**

   • Won a new car in a raffle sponsored by her church.

   • Collected on a loan she had made several years ago to a college friend.

   • Sold a houseboat and a camper on eBay. Both were personal use items, and the gain from one offset the loss from the other.

   • Got married. Her first husband died several years ago.

   • One of her sons celebrated his nineteenth birthday.

   • Paid off the mortgage on her personal residence.

      What are the possible income tax ramifications of these transactions?

3.   Which of the following items are *inclusions* in gross income?

   a.   Funds the taxpayer embezzled from her employer.

   b.   A damage deposit the taxpayer recovered when he vacated the apartment he had rented.

   c.   Interest received by the taxpayer on an investment in bonds issued by Ford Motor Company.

   d.   Gratuities left by customers—the taxpayer is a bartender.

   e.   Amounts received by the taxpayer, a baseball "Hall of Famer," for autographing sports equipment (e.g., balls, gloves).

   f.   As her employer's leading salesperson, the taxpayer is awarded an all-expenses-paid trip to Spain.

   g.   Jury duty fees received.

4.   Which of the following items are *exclusions* from gross income?

   a.   Insurance proceeds paid to the taxpayer on the death of her uncle—she was the designated beneficiary under the policy.

   b.   Damages award paid to the taxpayer—one-third of the amount was for personal injury and the balance was for punitive damages.

   c.   Interest income on State of Delaware bonds.

   d.   Scholarship award that covers the taxpayer's college tuition as well as room and board.

   e.   Reward paid by the IRS for information provided that led to the conviction of the taxpayer's former employer for tax evasion.

   f.   A box store refund of $200 that the taxpayer received when she discovered an overcharge on the purchase of home appliances.

   g.   An envelope containing $8,000 found (and unclaimed) by the taxpayer in a bus station.

5.   Does a U.S. citizen who works abroad run the risk of "double taxation"? Why or why not?

6.   In late 2008, the Polks come to you for tax advice. They are considering selling some   **Decision Making**
     stock investments for a loss and making a contribution to a traditional IRA. In reviewing their situation, you note that they have large medical expenses and a casualty loss, with neither being covered by insurance. What advice would you give to the Polks?

7.   The Andersons retain you to compute their tax liability for 2008. They are expecting to   **Issue ID**
     pay less tax than usual for several reasons. First, both became 65 during the year. Second, they paid significant medical and dental bills that were not covered by insurance. Are the Andersons' expectations correct? Explain.

8.   Mel, age 76 and a widower, is being claimed as a dependent by his daughter. How does this situation affect the following?

   a.   Mel's own individual filing requirement.

   b.   Mel's personal exemption.

   c.   The standard deduction allowed to Mel.

   d.   The availability of any additional standard deduction.

Issue ID

9. Marie is married but files a separate return.
   a. Under what circumstances can she claim a personal exemption for her husband?
   b. Would it matter if the parties reside in a community property state?

Issue ID

10. Kimberly has two daughters over age 19 whom she claims as her dependents. One daughter is a qualifying child, and the other daughter is a qualifying relative. Explain.

11. Heather, age 12, lives in the same household with her mother, grandmother, and uncle.
    a. Who can qualify for the dependency exemption?
    b. Who takes preference?
    c. Suppose that Heather's father, who lives elsewhere and files a separate return, also wants to claim her. Can he do so?

12. Under what circumstances, if any, can a taxpayer claim an ex-spouse as a dependent? What about claiming the ex-spouse's relatives as dependents?

13. Margo and her two brothers equally provide more than half of their parents' support. Margo tells her brothers to decide which one of them will claim the parents as dependents because the exemptions will not save her any income taxes. What is Margo's reason for her position?

Issue ID

14. Roberto, who is single, is a U.S. citizen and resident. He provides almost all of the support of his parents and two aunts, who are citizens and residents of Guatemala. Roberto's parents and aunts are seriously considering moving to and becoming residents of Mexico. Would such a move have any impact on Roberto? Why or why not?

15. In determining his income tax liability for the year, Aaron finds that he would pay slightly less using the Tax Rate Schedules than under the Tax Tables.
    a. Why could this be the case?
    b. Does Aaron have freedom of choice in this matter? Explain.

16. In connection with the kiddie tax, comment on the following:
    a. Justification for the tax.
    b. Earned income versus unearned income.
    c. Age exception.
    d. Other exceptions to the kiddie tax.
    e. Effect of parental election.

Issue ID

17. Jack and Joyce, who are married, had itemized deductions of $7,500 and $500, respectively, during 2008. Jack suggests that they file separately—he will itemize his deductions *from* AGI, and she will claim the standard deduction.
    a. Evaluate Jack's suggestion.
    b. What should they do?

Issue ID

18. Oliver is a U.S. citizen employed by a multinational corporation at its London office. Oliver is married to Regina, a British citizen, and they reside in England. Regina receives substantial rent income from real estate she owns in western Europe.
    a. Must Oliver file a U.S. income tax return?
    b. Under what circumstances might Regina be considered a resident of the United States? Would such a classification be advantageous? Disadvantageous?

19. Comment on the availability of head-of-household filing status for 2008 in each of the following situations:
    a. Taxpayer lives alone but maintains the household of his parents, only one of whom qualifies as his dependent.
    b. Taxpayer, a single parent, maintains a home in which she and her unmarried son live. The son, age 18, earns $4,000 from a part-time job.
    c. Assume the same facts as in (b) except that the son is age 20, not 18.
    d. Taxpayer lives alone but maintains the household where her dependent daughter lives.

20. Florence's husband died in 2005. During 2008, Florence maintains a household in which she and her son, Derrick, live. Determine Florence's filing status for 2008 based on the following independent variables:

a.   Derrick is single and does not qualify as Florence's dependent.

b.   Derrick is married and does not qualify as Florence's dependent.

c.   Derrick is married and does qualify as Florence's dependent.

d.   Would any of the previous answers change if Florence's husband died in 2006 (not 2005)? Explain.

21. Several years ago, after a particularly fierce argument, Fran's husband moved out and has not been heard from or seen since. Because Fran cannot locate her husband, she has been using "married, filing separate" status when filing her income tax return. Comment on Fran's status.

Issue ID

22. During the year, Hernando has the following transactions:

- Gain on the sale of stock held as an investment for 10 months.
- Gain on the sale of land held as an investment for 4 years.
- Gain on the sale of a houseboat owned for 2 years and used for family vacations.
- Loss on the sale of a reconditioned motorcycle owned for 3 years and used for recreational purposes.

   How should Hernando treat these transactions for income tax purposes?

23. In December 2007, Hailey wants to sell a stock investment at a gain. Her broker, however, advises her to wait several days and make the sale in 2008. What could be a good tax reason for the broker's advice?

Issue ID

24. Several years ago, Milton and Arlene inherited equal shares of their father's coin collection. When they sold the collection this year, Milton paid a tax based on 28% on his profit while Arlene's tax rate was only 25%. Presuming each had the same amount of gain, explain the difference in result.

Issue ID

25. During the year, Brandi had the following transactions: a long-term capital gain from the sale of land; a short-term capital loss from the sale of stock; and a long-term capital gain from the sale of a gun collection.

a.   How are these transactions treated for income tax purposes?

b.   Does this treatment favor the taxpayer or the IRS? Explain.

26. Marcie is divorced, and her married son, Jamie (age 25), and his wife, Audry (age 18), live with her. During the year, Jamie earned $3,600 from a part-time job and filed a joint return with Audry to recover his withholdings. Audry has no income. Marcie can prove that she provided more than 50% of Jamie and Audry's support. Marcie does not plan to claim Jamie as a dependent because he has too much gross income. She does not plan to claim Audry as a dependent because Audry signed the joint return with Jamie. In fact, Marcie plans to use single filing status as none of the persons living in her household qualifies as her dependent. Comment on Marcie's intentions based on the following assumptions:

Issue ID

a.   All parties live in Indiana (a common law state).

b.   All parties live in California (a community property state).

27. Erica Hill and her two brothers, Ted and Rick Lamb, equally furnish all of the support of their mother. Erica is married and has four children. Her brothers are single and claim the standard deduction. Erica's mother, Donna Lamb, is not in good health. What suggestions can you make regarding the tax position of the parties?

Decision Making

PROBLEMS

28. Compute the taxable income for 2008 in each of the following independent situations:

a.   Sidney and Cora, ages 39 and 37, are married and file a joint return. In addition to two dependent children, they have AGI of $55,000 and itemized deductions of $8,300.

b.   Giselle, age 40, is single and supports her dependent parents who live with her and also supports her grandparents (mother's parents) who are in a nursing home. She has AGI of $80,000 and itemized deductions of $7,000.

c. Marco, age 42, is an abandoned spouse. His household includes three unmarried stepsons who qualify as his dependents. He has AGI of $75,000 and itemized deductions of $9,000.

d. Angel, age 33, is a surviving spouse and maintains a household for her four dependent children. She has AGI of $48,000 and itemized deductions of $8,200.

e. Dale, age 42, is divorced but maintains the home in which he and his daughter, Jill, live. Jill is single and qualifies as Dale's dependent. Dale has AGI of $54,000 and itemized deductions of $6,900.

Note: Problems 29 and 30 can be solved by referring to Figure 3–1, Exhibits 3–1 through 3–3, Tables 3–1 and 3–2, and the discussion under Deductions for Adjusted Gross Income in this chapter.

29. Compute the taxable income for 2008 for Irving on the basis of the following information. His filing status is single.

Salary	$70,000
Interest income from bonds issued by City of Phoenix	1,800
Alimony payments made	6,000
Contribution to traditional IRA	5,000
Gift from grandparents	30,000
Capital loss from stock investment	5,000
Amount won in football office pool (sports gambling is against the law where Irving lives)	1,500
Number of dependents (uncle and aunt, who live in another state)	2
Age	46

30. Compute the taxable income for 2008 for Marilyn on the basis of the following information. Marilyn is married but has not seen or heard from her husband since 2006.

Salary	$ 80,000
Interest on bonds issued by General Motors Corporation	3,000
Interest on CD issued by Wells Fargo Bank	2,800
Cash dividend received on GE common stock	3,300
Life insurance proceeds paid on death of aunt (Marilyn was the designated beneficiary of the policy)	100,000
Inheritance received on death of aunt	200,000
Carlton (a cousin) repaid a loan Marilyn made to him in 2005 (no interest was provided for)	6,000
Itemized deductions (state income tax, property taxes on residence, interest on home mortgage, charitable contributions)	7,900
Number of dependents (children, ages 13, 14, and 15)	3
Age	40

31. Determine the amount of the standard deduction allowed for 2008 in the following independent situations. In each case, assume the taxpayer is claimed as another person's dependent.

a. Edward, age 18, has income as follows: $600 interest from a certificate of deposit and $5,200 from repairing cars.

b. Sarah, age 18, has income as follows: $400 cash dividends from a stock investment and $3,600 from handling a paper route.

c. Colin, age 16, has income as follows: $900 interest on a bank savings account and $700 for painting a neighbor's fence.

d. Kara, age 15, has income as follows: $300 cash dividends from a stock investment and $500 from grooming pets.

e. Kay, age 67 and a widow, has income as follows: $1,200 from a bank savings account and $2,000 from baby-sitting.

32. Using the legend provided on the next page, classify each statement as to the taxpayer for dependency exemption purposes.

	Legend	
QC =	Could be a qualifying child	
QR =	Could be a qualifying relative	
B =	Could satisfy the definition of *both* a qualifying child and a qualifying relative	
N =	Could not satisfy the definition of *either* a qualifying child or a qualifying relative	

a. Taxpayer's son has gross income of $6,000.
b. Taxpayer's niece has gross income of $3,000.
c. Taxpayer's mother lives with him.
d. Taxpayer's daughter is age 25 and disabled.
e. Taxpayer's daughter is age 18 but does not live with him.
f. Taxpayer's cousin lives with her.
g. Taxpayer's brother does not live with her.
h. Taxpayer's sister lives with him.
i. Taxpayer's nephew is age 20 and a full-time student.
j. Taxpayer's grandson does not live with her and has gross income of $3,000.

33. For tax year 2008, determine the number of personal and dependency exemptions in each of the following independent situations:
   a. Leo and Amanda (ages 48 and 46) are husband and wife and furnish more than 50% of the support of their two children, Elton (age 18) and Trista (age 24). During the year, Elton earns $4,500 providing transportation for elderly persons with disabilities, and Trista receives a $5,000 scholarship for tuition at the law school she attends.
   b. Audry (age 65) is divorced and lives alone. She maintains a household in which her ex-husband, Clint, and his mother, Olive, live and furnishes more than 50% of their support. Olive is age 82 and blind.
   c. Jacque (age 52) furnishes more than 50% of the support of his married daughter, Carin, and her husband, Pierce, who live with him. Both Carin and Pierce are age 18. During the year, Pierce earned $4,000 from a part-time job. All parties live in New York (a common law state).
   d. Assume the same facts as in (c), except that all parties live in Nevada (a community property state).

34. Compute the number of personal and dependency exemptions in each of the following independent situations:
   a. Alberto, a U.S. citizen and resident, contributes 100% of the support of his parents who are citizens of Mexico and live there.
   b. Pablo, a U.S. citizen and resident, contributes 100% of the support of his parents who are citizens of Guatemala. Pablo's father is a resident of Guatemala, and his mother is a legal resident of the United States.
   c. Marlena, a U.S. citizen and resident, contributes 100% of the support of her parents who are also U.S. citizens but are residents of Germany.
   d. Elena is a U.S. citizen and a resident of Italy. Her household includes Mario, a four-year-old adopted son who is a citizen of Spain.

35. Determine how many dependency exemptions would be available in each of the following independent situations. Specify whether any such exemptions would come under the qualifying child or the qualifying relative category.
   a. Andy maintains a household that includes a cousin (age 12), a niece (age 18), and a son (age 26). All are full-time students. Andy furnishes all of their support.
   b. Minerva provides all of the support of a family friend's son (age 18) who lives with her. She also furnishes most of the support of her stepmother who does not live with her.
   c. Raul, a U.S. citizen, lives in Costa Rica. Raul's household includes an adopted daughter, Helena, who is age 9 and a citizen of Costa Rica. Raul provides all of Helena's support.
   d. Karen maintains a household that includes her ex-husband, her mother-in-law, and her brother-in-law (age 23 and not a full-time student). Karen provides more than half of all of their support. Karen is single and was divorced in the current year.

36. In 2008, Billy, age 10, lives in a household with his mother, aunt, and grandfather. The household is maintained by the grandfather. The parties, all of whom file separate returns, have AGI as follows: $18,000 (mother), $50,000 (aunt), and $60,000 (grandfather).
    a.   Who is eligible to claim Billy as a dependent?
    b.   Who has preference as to the exemption?

37. Determine the number of personal and dependency exemptions for 2008 in each of the following independent situations:
    a.   Marcus (age 68) and Alice (age 65 and blind) file a joint return. They furnish more than 50% of the support of a niece, Ida, who lives with them. Ida (age 20) is a full-time student and earns $4,000 during the year tutoring special needs children.
    b.   Penny (age 45) is single and maintains a household in which she and her cousin, Clint, live. Clint (age 18) earns $3,900 from doing yard work, but receives more than 50% of his support from Penny.
    c.   Trent (age 38) is single and lives alone. He provides more than 50% of the support of his parents (ages 69 and 70) who are in a nursing home.
    d.   Jack and Carol were divorced in 2006, and Carol has custody of their three children (ages 5, 7, and 9). Jack furnished more than half of their support, and the divorce decree awards the dependency exemptions to him. Carol does not sign a Form 8332.

38. Buddy and Heloise (ages 86 and 85) live in an assisted care facility and for years 2007 and 2008 received their support from the following sources:

	Percentage of Support
Social Security benefits	17%
Son	10
Daughter	27
Cousin	11
Brother	24
Family friend (not related)	11

    a.   Which persons are eligible to claim the dependency exemptions under a multiple support agreement?
    b.   Must Buddy and Heloise be claimed by the same person(s) for both 2007 and 2008?
    c.   Who, if anyone, can claim their medical expenses?

39. Jake and Georgia Heaton are married and file a joint return. Their four children and all four parents qualify as dependents. If the Heatons have AGI of $280,000, what is their allowable deduction for personal and dependency exemptions for 2008?

40. Jocelyn, age 17, is claimed as a dependent by her parents. For 2008, she has income as follows: $3,200 wages from a summer job, $1,800 interest from a certificate of deposit, and $800 interest from State of Maryland bonds.
    a.   What is Jocelyn's taxable income for 2008?
    b.   If Jocelyn's parents file a joint return for 2008 reflecting taxable income of $110,000 (no dividends or capital gain), determine Jocelyn's tax liability.

Issue ID

Decision Making

41. Walter and Nancy provide 60% of the support of their daughter (age 18) and son-in-law (age 22). The son-in-law (John) is a full-time student at a local university, while the daughter (Irene) holds various part-time jobs from which she earns $11,000. Walter and Nancy engage you to prepare their tax return for 2008. During a meeting with them in late March of 2009, you learn that John and Irene have filed a joint return. What tax advice would you give based on the following assumptions:
    a.   All parties live in Louisiana (a community property state).
    b.   All parties live in New Jersey (a common law state).

42. Using the Tax Rate Schedules, compute the 2008 tax liability for each taxpayer:
    a.   Miles (age 42) is a surviving spouse and provides all of the support of his four minor children who live with him. He also maintains the household in which his parents live and furnished 60% of their support. Besides interest on City of Dallas bonds in the amount of $1,500, Miles's father received $2,400 from a part-time job. Miles has

a salary of $80,000, a short-term capital loss of $4,000, a cash prize of $1,000 from a church raffle, and itemized deductions of $9,500.

b. Morgan (age 45) is single and provides more than 50% of the support of Rosalyn (a family friend), Flo (a niece, age 18), and Jerold (a nephew, age 18). Both Rosalyn and Flo live with Morgan, but Jerold (a French citizen) lives in Canada. Morgan earns a salary of $85,000, contributes $5,000 to a traditional IRA, and receives sales proceeds of $15,000 for an RV that cost $60,000 and was used for vacations. She has $8,200 in itemized deductions.

43. Terri, age 17, is claimed as a dependent on her parents' 2008 return, on which they report taxable income of $100,000 (no qualified dividends or capital gains). Terri earned $1,900 pet sitting and $2,400 in interest on a savings account. What are Terri's taxable income and tax liability for 2008?

44. Rhett, age 17, is claimed as a dependent on his parents' 2008 return. During the year, Rhett earned $3,200 in interest income and $1,400 from part-time jobs.
    a. What is Rhett's taxable income?
    b. How much of Rhett's income is taxed at his rate? At his parents' rate?
    c. Can the parental election be made? Why or why not?

45. Which of the following individuals are required to file a tax return for 2008? Should any of these individuals file a return even if filing is not required? Why?
    a. Sam is married and files a joint return with his spouse, Lana. Both Sam and Lana are 67 years old. Their combined gross income was $20,200.
    b. Ronald is a dependent child under age 19 who received $5,400 in wages from a part-time job.
    c. Mike is single and is 67 years old. His gross income from wages was $10,100.
    d. Patricia, age 19, is a self-employed single individual with gross income of $4,500 from an unincorporated business. Business expenses amounted to $4,000.

46. Which of the following taxpayers must file a Federal income tax return for 2008?
    a. Ben, age 19, is a full-time college student. He is claimed as a dependent by his parents. He earned $5,400 wages during the year.
    b. Anita, age 12, is claimed as a dependent by her parents. She earned interest income of $1,200 during the year.
    c. Earl, age 16, is claimed as a dependent by his parents. He earned wages of $2,700 and interest of $1,100 during the year.
    d. Pat, age 17, is claimed as a dependent by her parents. She earned interest of $300 during the year. In addition, she earned $550 during the summer operating her own business at the beach, where she painted caricatures of her customers.

47. In each of the following independent situations, provide the requested information.

    Decision Making

    a. Spencer and Ava are engaged and plan to get married in either late December 2008 or early January 2009. *Each* has taxable income for 2008 of $70,000 [$78,950 (salary) − $3,500 (personal exemption) − $5,450 (standard deduction)]. Contrast their total income tax liability *for 2008* if they marry in December or if they wait until January 2009.
    b. Corey and Addison are engaged and plan to get married. During 2008, Corey is a full-time student and earns $2,000 from a part-time job. With this income, student loans, savings, and nontaxable scholarships, he is self-supporting. For the year, Addison is employed and has taxable income of $50,000 [$58,950 (wages) − $3,500 (personal exemption) − $5,450 (standard deduction)]. How much income tax, if any, can Addison save if she and Corey marry in 2008 and file a joint return?

48. In each of the following *independent* situations, determine Winston's filing status for 2008. Winston is not married.
    a. Winston maintains a household in which he and his unmarried son, Ward, live. Ward does not qualify as Winston's dependent.
    b. Same as (a), except that Ward is married.
    c. Winston lives alone, but he maintains a household in which his parents live. The mother qualifies as Winston's dependent, but the father does not.
    d. Winston lives alone but maintains a household in which his married daughter, Karin, lives. Both Karin and her husband (Winston's son-in-law) qualify as Winston's dependents.

49. Nadia died in 2007 and is survived by her husband, Jerold, and her 18-year-old daughter, Macy. Jerold is the executor of Nadia's estate. Jerold maintains the household in which he and Macy live and furnishes more than 50% of her support. Macy had earnings from part-time employment as follows: $4,000 in 2007; $5,000 in 2008; and $6,000 in 2009. She is a full-time student for 2009 (but not for 2007 and 2008). What is Jerold's filing status for:
    a. 2007?
    b. 2008?
    c. 2009?

50. Perry died in 2007 and is survived by his wife, Rosalyn (age 39), his married daughter, Sue (age 18), and his son-in-law, Peyton (age 22). Rosalyn is the executor of her husband's estate. She also maintains the household where she, Sue, and Peyton live and furnishes more than 50% of their support. During 2007 and 2008, Peyton is a full-time student, while Sue earns $16,000 ($8,000 each year) conducting aerobics classes. Sue and Peyton do not file joint returns. For years 2007 and 2008, what is Rosalyn's filing status, and how many exemptions can she claim based on each of the following assumptions?
    a. All parties live in Pennsylvania (a common law state).
    b. All parties live in Texas (a community property state).

51. During the year, Olivia had the following transactions involving capital assets:

Gain on the sale of unimproved land (held as an investment for 4 years)	$4,000
Loss on the sale of a camper (purchased 2 years ago and used for family vacations)	(5,000)
Loss on the sale of IBM stock (purchased 9 months ago as an investment)	(1,000)
Gain on the sale of a fishing boat and trailer (acquired 11 months ago at an auction and used for recreational purposes)	2,000

    a. If Olivia is in the 33% bracket, how much income tax results?
    b. If Olivia is in the 15% bracket and 2008 is the year when these sales occurred?
    c. If Olivia is in the 15% bracket and 2007 is the year when these sales occurred?

52. During the year, Brayden had the following transactions involving capital assets:

Gain on the sale of an arrowhead collection (acquired as an investment at different times but all pieces have been held for more than one year)	$5,000
Loss on the sale of ADM Corporation stock (purchased 11 months ago as an investment)	(4,000)
Gain on the sale of a city lot (acquired 5 years ago as an investment)	2,000

    a. If Brayden is in the 35% bracket, how much income tax results?
    b. If Brayden is in the 15% bracket and 2008 is the year involved?
    c. If Brayden is in the 15% bracket and 2007 is the year involved?

Decision Making

53. Each year, the Hundleys normally have itemized deductions of $9,500, including a $3,600 pledge payment to their church. Upon the advice of a friend, they do the following: in early January 2008, they pay their pledge for 2007; during 2008, they pay the pledge for 2008; and in late December 2008, they prepay their pledge for 2009.
    a. Explain what the Hundleys are trying to accomplish.
    b. What will be the tax saving if their marginal tax bracket is 25% for all three years? (Assume the standard deduction amounts for 2008 and 2009 are the same.)

CUMULATIVE PROBLEMS

Tax Return Problem

54. John C. and Paula S. Inman live at 1382 Tarpon Springs Road, Haines City, FL 33844. John is the manager of the local outlet of a national fast-food franchise, while Paula is employed as a dental hygienist by a dental clinic.
    For tax year 2007, the Inmans had the following receipts:

Salaries (John, $48,000; Paula, $42,000)		$90,000
Interest income—		
Interest on CD at Orlando National Bank	$ 850	
Interest on City of Sarasota bonds	410	1,260
Payment received from Larry Inman		5,500
Gift from Paula's parents		24,000
Property transactions—		
Garage sale	$1,100	
Sale of city lot	9,000	10,100

Several years ago, John loaned his brother, Larry, $5,000. Although no rate was specified, John expected interest to be included as part of the arrangement. In late 2007, Larry repaid the loan and included interest of $500.

The garage sale involved personal items (e.g., clothing, books, furniture, appliances) that the Inmans had accumulated over the years. Although the Inmans do not have all of the receipts, they estimate the total cost of the items sold to be $5,000.

The lot in Haines City was purchased by Paula 3 years ago for $11,000. As her investment seemed to be declining (not increasing) in value, she decided to curtail any further loss and sold the property in 2007.

Not listed above is an ATV John won at his church's annual raffle. Under the rules of the drawing, John had a choice between $3,500 in cash or the ATV—he chose the ATV. The church treasurer told John that the results of the raffle are not reported to the IRS.

The Inmans had the following expenditures in 2007:

Contributions to traditional IRAs (John, $4,000; Paula, $4,000)—neither is covered by an employer pension plan		$8,000
Medical expenses (no insurance coverage)		9,500
Taxes—		
State sales taxes (supported by receipts)	$3,100	
Property tax on residence	3,700	6,800
Interest on home mortgage		4,200
Charitable contributions (supported by receipts)		2,400

The Inman household includes their two children, Robert (age 17) and Helen (age 18), and John's niece, Elizabeth (age 18). Robert is a full-time student, while Helen and Elizabeth work at various jobs. During the year, Helen earned $12,500 and Elizabeth earned $14,000, all of which was placed in savings accounts for college. In addition to furnishing all of the support of their children and niece, the Inmans provide one-third of the support of John's mother, Cecelia Inman. John's sister, Mary Graham, and brother, Larry Inman, provide the remainder of Cecelia's support. They have sent John a signed Form 2120 awarding him the dependency exemption for Cecelia.

Federal income tax withheld from the Inmans' salaries was $3,500 (John) and $3,000 (Paula). The appropriate amount of FICA taxes were withheld.

Relevant Social Security numbers are as follows:

John C. Inman	589–26–4591	Elizabeth Inman	591–84–7154
Paula Inman	589–37–6157	Cecelia Inman	594–72–4296
Robert Inman	590–41–7522	Larry Inman	593–94–6105
Helen Inman	595–62–9604	Mary Graham	592–44–3314

Compute the Inmans' Federal income tax for 2007. They do not wish to contribute to the Presidential Election Campaign Fund. If an overpayment results, it is to be refunded to them. Suggested Software: TaxCut.

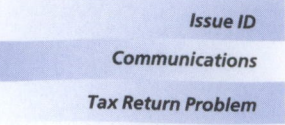

55. Betty N. Russo (age 53) lives at 1426 Bunting Drive, Fort Collins, CO 80525. Her household includes her daughters, Amy (age 27) and Emma (age 26), and her son, Jordan (age 24). None of Betty's children is disabled, and all are college graduates. Also residing with Betty is her widower father, Alan Rice (age 75). Betty lost her late husband, Donald, in December 2006 as a result of a ski-lift accident. Betty is employed as a paralegal with a local law firm at an annual salary of $59,000. No one else in the household has any income except Alan, who receives modest Social Security benefits.

Betty's receipts for 2007 are summarized below:

Salary		$ 59,000
Interest—		
City of Denver bonds	$7,000	
General Electric bonds	1,800	
Wachovia Bank certificate of deposit	3,100	11,900
Life insurance proceeds		200,000
Ski-lift settlement		250,000
Inheritance		185,000

The insurance proceeds were paid to Betty as beneficiary of a policy she held on Donald's life. The inheritance represents what was left of Donald's estate after all debts and administration expenses were paid. Because Betty believed that the ski lift that led to Donald's death was not being operated properly, she threatened to file suit against the owner. In a settlement with the owner's insurance carrier, Betty signed a release of all claims in return for $250,000. The payment was designated as being for the "personal injuries suffered by Donald Russo." Betty served as her own attorney.

Betty's expenses for 2007 are as follows:

Medical and dental (including insurance premiums and net of reimbursements)		$5,200
Taxes—		
State income tax (including withholdings)	$1,600	
State and local sales taxes	3,200	
Property tax on personal residence	1,900	6,700
Interest on home mortgage		4,200
Contributions to charity (substantiated)		1,100

The medical expenses include $3,300 for surgery to repair Alan's hernia, which Betty paid. Because Betty had planned on making major purchases during 2007 (e.g., auto, furniture, large appliances), she expected to choose the sales tax deduction over the state income tax option. Consequently, she has kept all of her sales tax receipts.

Relevant Social Security numbers are as follows:

Betty Russo	650–24–4596
Amy Russo	651–83–2965
Emma Russo	651–42–8311
Jordan Russo	653–76–5264
Alan Rice	650–18–5183

The appropriate amount of FICA taxes were withheld.

Part 1—Tax Computation

Determine Betty's Federal income tax liability for 2007. In addition to the income taxes of $4,400 withheld from her wages, she applied her 2006 overpayment of $400 toward her 2007 tax liability. As was true in the past, she wants any 2007 overpayment applied to next year's tax. She does not wish to contribute to the Presidential Election Campaign Fund. Suggested Software: TaxCut.

Part 2—Follow-up Advice
In early 2008, the following events take place:

- In January, Betty pays off the mortgage on her personal residence. Because the mortgage company is a client of her employer and the interest rate is low, she is able to do so without incurring a prepayment penalty.
- Both Amy and Emma accept jobs in Chicago. They move there in February and will share an apartment.
- Jordon marries a woman from Baltimore and moves there in March to work for her father.
- To be in a milder climate, Alan moves to Phoenix in April to live with his son (i.e., Betty's brother).

Betty is concerned about the effect these events will have on her income tax position in 2008 and requests your advice.

Write a letter to Betty telling her of the changes that will occur and include an estimate of the additional taxes that will result. Because Betty is a paralegal and prepared her own Federal income tax return for 2007, you can presume she has some understanding of basic income tax rules. Assume her salary will be the same. Also, her investment income remains constant as she has used any additional funds received (i.e., insurance proceeds, personal injury settlement) to pay off her mortgage and to invest in undeveloped land.

RESEARCH PROBLEMS

Note: Solutions to Research Problems can be prepared by using the **RIA Checkpoint®** **Student Edition** online research product, which is available to accompany this text. It is also possible to prepare solutions to the Research Problems by using tax research materials found in a standard tax library.

Research Problem 1.   Pat and Cathy McKeever are husband and wife and file a joint return. During 2008, they maintain a household that includes Cathy's parents (Barry and Mary Kilpatrick), a son (Tim), and a daughter (Eileen). The parents live in an apartment over the McKeevers' garage. The parents are retired with an annual income of $18,000, all from nontaxable sources (e.g., pensions and interest on state and local bonds). They pay the McKeevers $600 a month ($7,200 per year) for their room and board and place the remainder of their income in a money market account. (A competent appraiser finds the rental value of the furnished garage apartment to be $300 per month.)

The McKeevers' children, Tim and Eileen, live in the main house. Tim, age 24, is an army veteran and a full-time student. He receives $3,200 from the GI bill and $900 from a part-time job, all of which he spends on his education and support. Tim's parents, Pat and Cathy, contribute an additional $4,000 (which includes room and board) toward his support. Eileen, age 18, also is a full-time student, but has no income for the year.

Other relevant information about the McKeevers and their expenditures during 2008 is summarized below.

- The McKeevers spent $9,000 on groceries to provide meals for all six persons in the family.
- Cathy paid a $600 premium on her father's life insurance. The policy is owned by the father and designates Mary as the beneficiary.
- Cathy paid her parents' annual church pledge of $400.
- Cathy paid $300 to have her mother's hearing aid repaired.
- Eileen, tired of begging for the use of the family SUV, purchased a sports car for $22,000. Eileen paid for the car with savings and has the title registered in her name. (Eileen's savings account originated from funds she inherited from her uncle.)

a.   How many dependency exemptions will the McKeevers be entitled to claim on their Federal income tax return for 2008? Explain your answer.

b.   From a planning standpoint, how might the McKeevers have improved their tax result for 2008?

Partial list of research aids:
Reg. §§ 1.152–1(a) and 1(c).
Rev.Rul. 58–67, 1958–1 C.B. 62.
Your Federal Income Tax (IRS Pub. 17, 2007), Ch. 3.

Research Problem 2. Jeff and Suzy are the biological parents of Monique, born in 1993. The parents never married, and shortly after the birth, Suzy left the household and took Monique with her. In 1994, Jeff had Suzy sign a Form 8332 in which she waived the dependency exemption as to Monique for 1994 "and all years thereafter." Although Jeff contributes nothing toward the support of Monique, he has been claiming her as a dependent every year since 1994. Starting in 2003, Suzy has also been claiming Monique as a dependent.

Needless to say, the IRS is not likely to permit a dependent to be claimed twice! In the event of audit, should Jeff or Suzy be allowed the deduction for Monique? Why?

Partial list of research aids:
§§ 151(e)(1) and (2).
Jeffrey R. King, 121 T.C. 245 (2003).

Communications

Research Problem 3. Sophia Durbin maintains a household in which she, her son (Ryan), and her widowed mother-in-law (Isabella) live. Since 2006, she also has provided more than half of their support. Sophia's husband, Karl, left for parts unknown in April 2006 and, except for one postcard, has not been heard from since. The postcard (no return address included) was received by Sophia in March 2007 and announced that he planned to claim both Ryan and Isabella as dependents on his own tax return.

Ryan (age 19 in December 2006) graduated from high school on May 6, 2006, and plans to start college in 2008. Until then, he is working as much as possible to save for college expenses. He earned $8,000 in 2006 and $17,000 in 2007. Isabella's income is negligible and originates from nontaxable sources (e.g., Social Security benefits, interest on municipal bonds).

For tax year 2006, Sophia filed her Federal income tax return as married filing separately and claimed no exemptions for dependents. She has not yet filed for 2007. Being somewhat perplexed with her situation, she comes to you for advice in early March 2008.

a. Write a letter to Sophia Durbin addressing her concerns. She lives at 1310 Ash Street, Kearney, NE 68849.
b. Prepare a memo for your firm's client files that lists and discusses the legal basis for the advice rendered.

Research Problem 4. Bart and Arlene Keating are husband and wife and live in Mineola, Oregon. They have been married for 18 years and have four children, all of whom are teenagers. After the birth of her last child, Arlene took a job as a city clerk and, over the years, has become city treasurer. Since graduating from high school, Bart has worked as a dispatcher for the city fire and ambulance departments. As Arlene has some college training in finance and accounting, she handles the family's financial affairs, including reconciling the bank account, paying bills, and preparing all tax returns. She also takes care of major purchases (e.g., autos, furniture) and servicing of debt (e.g., home mortgage, auto loans, charge accounts).

The Keatings themselves maintain a modest lifestyle, but Arlene is quite generous with the children. All are well-dressed, attend summer camp, and have their own cars. Bart believes Arlene obtains any additional funds for the children's support through credit card financing and bank loans.

The Keatings filed joint returns for 2004 and 2005 that reflected their salary income. Arlene prepared the returns, and Bart signed them without reviewing them first. The returns did not show the $90,000 Arlene had embezzled from her employer over this two-year period.

The City of Mineola discovers the theft, and Arlene is tried and convicted of grand larceny. Due to the adverse publicity generated by these events, the Keatings are divorced, and Arlene moves to another state.

In 2008, the IRS assesses a deficiency against Bart for the income taxes that would have resulted if the embezzled amounts had been reported as income.

What are the rights of the parties?

Partial list of research aids:
§§ 6013(d)(3) and 6015.
Kathryn Cheshire, 115 T.C. 183 (2000).
Evelyn M. Martin, 80 TCM 665, T.C.Memo. 2000–346.

Use the tax resources of the Internet to address the following questions. Do not restrict your search to the World Wide Web, but include a review of newsgroups and general reference materials, practitioner sites and resources, primary sources of the tax law, chat rooms and discussion groups, and other opportunities.

Internet
Activity

Research Problem 5. Find and print a Form 2120, Multiple Support Declaration. Fill in the form and use it to illustrate one of your recommendations for Discussion Question 27.

Research Problem 6. What purpose is served by IRS Form 8857? In this regard, see IRS Publication 971.

Research Problem 7. A nonresident alien earns money in the United States that is subject to Federal income tax. What guidance does the IRS provide on what tax form needs to be used and on when it should be filed? In terms of the proper filing date, does it matter whether the earnings were subject to income tax withholding?

PART 2

Gross Income

Part II presents the income component of the basic tax model. Included in this presentation are the determination of what is income and the statutory exclusions that are permitted in calculating gross income. Because the taxpayer's accounting method and accounting period affect when income is reported, an introductory discussion of these topics is also included.

CHAPTER 4
Gross Income: Concepts and Inclusions

CHAPTER 5
Gross Income: Exclusions

CHAPTER 4

Gross Income: Concepts and Inclusions

LEARNING OBJECTIVES

After completing Chapter 4, you should be able to:

LO.1

Explain the concepts of gross income and realization and distinguish between the economic, accounting, and tax concepts of gross income.

LO.2

Describe the cash and accrual methods of accounting and the related effects of the choice of taxable year.

LO.3

Identify who should pay the tax on a particular item of income in various situations.

LO.4

Apply the Internal Revenue Code provisions on alimony, loans made at below-market interest rates, annuities, prizes and awards, group term life insurance, unemployment compensation, and Social Security benefits.

LO.5

Identify tax planning strategies for minimizing gross income.

OUTLINE

Gross Income—What Is It?, 4–2
  Definition, 4–2
  Economic and Accounting Concepts, 4–3
  Comparison of the Accounting and Tax
    Concepts of Income, 4–5
  Form of Receipt, 4–6
  Recovery of Capital Doctrine, 4–6
Year of Inclusion, 4–7
  Taxable Year, 4–7
  Accounting Methods, 4–7
  Exceptions Applicable to Cash Basis Taxpayers, 4–10
  Exceptions Applicable to Accrual Basis
    Taxpayers, 4–13
Income Sources, 4–14
  Personal Services, 4–14
  Income from Property, 4–15
  Income Received by an Agent, 4–17

Income from Partnerships, S Corporations,
    Trusts, and Estates, 4–17
  Income in Community Property States, 4–18
Items Specifically Included in Gross Income, 4–20
  Alimony and Separate Maintenance Payments, 4–20
  Imputed Interest on Below-Market Loans, 4–23
  Income from Annuities, 4–27
  Prizes and Awards, 4–31
  Group Term Life Insurance, 4–31
  Unemployment Compensation, 4–32
  Social Security Benefits, 4–33
Tax Planning Considerations, 4–34
  Nontaxable Economic Benefits, 4–34
  Tax Deferral, 4–34
  Shifting Income to Relatives, 4–36
  Accounting for Community Property, 4–37
  Alimony, 4–37

Mr. Zarin lost over $2.5 million of his own money gambling. The casino then allowed him to gamble on credit. After several months, his liability to the casino totaled more than $3.4 million. Following protracted negotiations, the casino agreed to settle its claim against Mr. Zarin for a mere $500,000. Although Mr. Zarin had paid for gambling losses of $3 million, the IRS had the audacity to ask him to pay tax on $2.9 million, that is, the amount the casino marked down his account.[1] Mr. Zarin undoubtedly had difficulty understanding how he could be deemed to have income in this situation.

Given an understanding of the income tax formula, though, one can see how the "free" gambling Mr. Zarin enjoyed could constitute income. The starting point in the formula is the determination of gross income rather than "net income." Once gross income is determined, the next step is to determine the allowable deductions. In Mr. Zarin's way of thinking, these steps were collapsed.

This chapter is concerned with the first step in the computation of taxable income—the determination of gross income. Questions that are addressed include the following:

- What: What is income?
- When: In which tax period is the income recognized?
- Who: Who must include the item of income in gross income?

The Code provides an all-inclusive definition of gross income in § 61. Chapter 5 presents items of income that are specifically excluded from gross income (exclusions).

LO.1

Explain the concepts of gross income and realization and distinguish between the economic, accounting, and tax concepts of gross income.

Gross Income—What Is It?

Definition

Section 61(a) of the Internal Revenue Code defines the term **gross income** as follows:

> Except as otherwise provided in this subtitle, gross income means all income from whatever source derived.

---

[1] *Zarin v. Comm.*, 90–2 USTC ¶50,530, 66 AFTR2d 90–5679, 916 F.2d 110 (CA–3, 1990).

FROM "ALL SOURCES" IS A BROAD DEFINITION

When § 61 refers to "income from whatever source derived," the taxing authorities are reaching far beyond the borders of the United States. Although one interpretation of "source" in this context is type of income (wages, interest, etc.), a broader interpretation revolves around the place where the income is generated. In this context, citizens and residents of the United States are subject to taxation on income earned from sources both inside and outside the country. This "worldwide income" tax base can cause potential double taxation problems, with other countries also taxing income earned within their borders, but mechanisms such as the foreign tax credit can alleviate these tax burdens.

Recently, some U.S. corporations have relocated to other countries to avoid the higher U.S. tax rates on income earned abroad. Congress is considering ways of stopping this "flight of capital." The American Jobs Creation Act of 2004 (AJCA) provided an incentive for companies to bring profits and production back into the United States. Some economists and politicians, however, have questioned how well this incentive has worked and how many jobs it has created.

GLOBAL *Tax Issues*

This definition is derived from the language of the Sixteenth Amendment to the Constitution.

Supreme Court decisions have made it clear that all sources of income are subject to tax unless Congress specifically excludes the type of income received:

> The starting point in all cases dealing with the question of the scope of what is included in "gross income" begins with the basic premise that the purpose of Congress was to use the full measure of its taxing power.[2]

Although at this point we know that *income* is to be broadly construed, we still do not have a satisfactory definition of the term *income*. Congress left it to the judicial and administrative branches to thrash out the meaning of income. Early in the development of the income tax law, a choice was made between two competing models: economic income and accounting income.

Economic and Accounting Concepts

The term **income** is used in the Code but is not separately defined. Thus, early in the history of our tax laws, the courts were required to interpret "the commonly understood meaning of the term which must have been in the minds of the people when they adopted the Sixteenth Amendment to the Constitution."[3] In determining the definition of income, the Supreme Court rejected the economic concept of income.

Economists measure income (**economic income**) by first determining the fair market value of the individual's net assets (assets minus liabilities) at the beginning and end of the year (change in net worth). Then, to arrive at economic income, this change in net worth is added to the goods and services that person actually consumed during the period. Economic income also includes imputed values for such items as the rental value of an owner-occupied home and the value of food a taxpayer might grow for personal consumption.[4]

---

[2]*James v. U.S.*, 61–1 USTC ¶9449, 7 AFTR2d 1361, 81 S.Ct. 1052 (USSC, 1961).

[3]*Merchants Loan and Trust Co. v. Smietanka*, 1 USTC ¶42, 3 AFTR 3102, 41 S.Ct. 386 (USSC, 1921).

[4]See Henry C. Simons, *Personal Income Taxation* (University of Chicago Press, Chicago: 1933), Chapters 2–3.

TAX *in the News*   **THE TAX GAP**

The "tax gap" is an estimate of the difference between what taxpayers should pay and what they actually pay in Federal income taxes each year. It is one of the yardsticks used to measure the effectiveness of the Federal income tax system. According to Treasury Department estimates, the tax gap is more than $300 billion per year. Some of the gap is due to deliberate actions by taxpayers, but much of the gap occurs because taxpayers do not understand the tax law. For example, in a recent survey H&R Block found that 60 percent of the respondents said they would not report as gross income the amounts they won betting on the NCAA basketball tournament. Only 35 percent were actually aware that their winnings were taxable.

Source: *Adapted from Sandra Block, "If You Gambled and Won, Don't Forget to Give Uncle Sam His Cut in Taxes," USA Today, March 27, 2007, p. B3.*

EXAMPLE 1

Helen's economic income is calculated as follows:

Fair market value of Helen's assets on December 31, 2008	$220,000	
Less liabilities on December 31, 2008	(40,000)	
Net worth on December 31, 2008		$ 180,000
Fair market value of Helen's assets on January 1, 2008	$200,000	
Less liabilities on January 1, 2008	(80,000)	
Net worth on January 1, 2008		(120,000)
Increase in net worth		$ 60,000
Consumption		
Food, clothing, and other personal expenditures		25,000
Imputed rental value of the home Helen owns and occupies		12,000
Economic income		$ 97,000

The need to value assets annually would make compliance with the tax law burdensome and would cause numerous controversies between the taxpayer and the IRS over valuation. In addition, using market values to determine income for tax purposes could result in liquidity problems. The taxpayer's assets may increase in value even though they are not readily convertible into the cash needed to pay the tax (e.g., commercial real estate). Thus, the IRS, Congress, and the courts have rejected the economic concept of income as impractical.

In contrast, the accounting concept of income is founded on the realization principle.[5] According to this principle, income (**accounting income**) is not recognized until it is realized. For realization to occur, (1) an exchange of goods or services must take place between the accounting entity and some independent, external group, and (2) in the exchange the accounting entity must receive assets that are capable of being objectively valued. Thus, the mere appreciation in the market value of assets before a sale or other disposition is not sufficient to warrant income recognition. In addition, the imputed savings that arise when individuals create assets for their own use (e.g., feed grown for a farmer's own livestock) are not income because no exchange has occurred. The courts and the IRS have ruled, however, that embezzlement proceeds and buried treasures found satisfy the realization requirement and, therefore, must be recognized as income.[6]

---

[5]See the American Accounting Association Committee Report on the "Realization Concept," *The Accounting Review* (April 1965): 312–322.

[6]*Rutkin v. U.S.*, 52–1 USTC ¶9260, 41 AFTR2d 596, 72 S.Ct. 571 (USSC, 1952); Rev.Rul. 61, 1953–1 C.B. 17.

The Supreme Court expressed an inclination toward the accounting concept of income when it adopted the realization requirement in *Eisner v. Macomber*:

> Income may be defined as the gain derived from capital, from labor, or from both combined, provided it is understood to include profit gained through a sale or conversion of capital assets. . . . Here we have the essential matter: not a gain accruing to capital; not a *growth* or *increment* of value *in* investment; but a gain, a profit, something of exchangeable value, *proceeding from* the property, *severed from* the capital however invested or employed, and *coming in*, being "*derived*"—that is, *received* or *drawn by* the recipient for his separate use, benefit and disposal—*that is*, income derived from the property.[7]

In summary, *income* represents an increase in wealth recognized for tax purposes only upon realization.

Comparison of the Accounting and Tax Concepts of Income

Although income tax rules frequently parallel financial accounting measurement concepts, differences do exist. Of major significance, for example, is the fact that unearned (prepaid) income received by an accrual basis taxpayer often is taxed in the year of receipt. For financial accounting purposes, such prepayments are not treated as income until earned.[8] Because of this and other differences, many corporations report financial accounting income that is substantially different from the amounts reported for tax purposes (see Reconciliation of Corporate Taxable Income and Accounting Income in Chapter 20).

The Supreme Court provided an explanation for some of the variations between accounting and taxable income in a decision involving inventory and bad debt adjustments:

> The primary goal of financial accounting is to provide useful information to management, shareholders, creditors, and others properly interested; the major responsibility of the accountant is to protect these parties from being misled. The primary goal of the income tax system, in contrast, is the equitable collection of revenue. . . . Consistently with its goals and responsibilities, financial accounting has as its foundation the principle of conservatism, with its corollary that 'possible errors in measurement [should] be in the direction of understatement rather than overstatement of net income and net assets.' In view of the Treasury's markedly different goals and responsibilities, understatement of income is not destined to be its guiding light.
>
> . . . Financial accounting, in short, is hospitable to estimates, probabilities, and reasonable certainties; the tax law, with its mandate to preserve the revenue, can give no quarter to uncertainty.[9]

---

[7]1 USTC ¶32, 3 AFTR 3020, 40 S.Ct. 189 (USSC, 1920).

[8]Similar differences exist in the deduction area.

[9]*Thor Power Tool Co. v. Comm.*, 79–1 USTC ¶9139, 43 AFTR2d 79–362, 99 S.Ct. 773 (USSC, 1979).

TAX *in the News*	BARRY BONDS MADE MATT MURPHY AND THE FEDERAL GOVERNMENT RICHER

Matt Murphy caught Barry Bonds's 756th home run ball. In an interview, Murphy commented, "Part of me wants to keep it. It's the greatest American sports accomplishment in history.... Part of me might want to sell it, but I really am leaning toward keeping it. It's just too valuable, sentimental."

A few days later Murphy said that several people had told him he would be taxed on his valuable souvenir, even if he did not sell it. Estimates were that the ball was worth $500,000, which meant Murphy would need almost $175,000 to pay the tax on his newfound wealth. So Murphy put the ball up for auction, where it brought more than $750,000. Commenting on his decision to sell the ball, Murphy said, "It wasn't hard. It was simple math. I'm upset by the decision I had to make. I wanted to keep it. I'm young. I don't have the bank account.... It would have cost me a lot more to keep it."

Source: *Adapted from "No. 756 Is Going to Auction," Associated Press, August 21, 2007.*

Form of Receipt

Gross income is not limited to cash received. "It includes income realized in any form, whether in money, property, or services. Income may be realized [and recognized], therefore, in the form of services, meals, accommodations, stock or other property, as well as in cash."[10]

EXAMPLE 2

Ostrich Corporation allows Bill, an employee, to use a company car for his vacation. Bill realizes income equal to the rental value of the car for the time and mileage. ∎

EXAMPLE 3

Terry owes $10,000 on a mortgage. The creditor accepts $8,000 in full satisfaction of the debt. Terry realizes income of $2,000 from retiring the debt.[11] ∎

EXAMPLE 4

Martha is an attorney. She agrees to draft a will for Tom, a neighbor, who is a carpenter. In exchange, Tom repairs her back porch. Martha and Tom both have gross income equal to the fair market value of the services they provide. ∎

Recovery of Capital Doctrine

The Constitution grants Congress the power to tax income but does not define the term. Because the Constitution does not define income, it would seem that Congress could simply tax gross receipts. Although Congress does allow certain deductions, none are constitutionally required. However, the Supreme Court has held that there is no income subject to tax until the taxpayer has recovered the capital invested.[12] This concept is known as the **recovery of capital doctrine**.

In its simplest application, this doctrine means that sellers can reduce their gross receipts (selling price) by the adjusted basis of the property sold.[13] This net amount, in the language of the Code, is gross income.

EXAMPLE 5

Dave sold common stock for $15,000. He had purchased the stock for $12,000. Dave's gross receipts are $15,000. This amount consists of a $12,000 recovery of capital and $3,000 of gross income. ∎

---

[10]Reg. § 1.61–1(a).

[11]Reg. § 1.61–12. See *U.S. v. Kirby Lumber Co.*, 2 USTC ¶814, 10 AFTR 458, 52 S.Ct. 4 (USSC, 1931). Exceptions to this general rule are discussed in Chapter 5.

[12]*Doyle v. Mitchell Bros. Co.*, 1 USTC ¶17, 3 AFTR 2979, 38 S.Ct. 467 (USSC, 1916).

[13]For a definition of "adjusted basis," see the Glossary of Tax Terms in Appendix C.

Collections on annuity contracts and installment payments received from sales of property must be allocated between recovery of capital and income. Annuities are discussed in this chapter, and installment sales are discussed in Chapter 18.

ETHICAL and EQUITABLE *Considerations*   **A BUSINESS MADE POSSIBLE BY eBAY**

Each Saturday morning Ted makes the rounds of the local yard sales. He has developed a keen eye for bargains, but he cannot use all the items he thinks are "real bargains." Ted has found a way to share the benefits of his talent with others. If Ted spots something priced at $40 that he knows is worth $100, for example, he will buy it and list it on eBay for $70. Ted does not include his gain in his gross income because he reasons that he is performing a valuable service for others (both the original sellers and the future buyers) and sacrificing profit he could receive. "Besides," according to Ted, "the IRS does not know about these transactions." Should Ted's ethical standards depend on his perception of his own generosity and the risk that his income-producing activities will be discovered by the IRS? Discuss.

Year of Inclusion

Taxable Year

The annual accounting period or **taxable year** is a basic component of our tax system.[14] Generally, an entity must use the *calendar year* to report its income. However, a *fiscal year* (a period of 12 months ending on the last day of any month other than December) can be elected if the taxpayer maintains adequate books and records. This fiscal year option generally is not available to partnerships, S corporations, and personal service corporations, as discussed in Chapter 18.[15]

Determining the particular year in which the income will be taxed is important for determining when the tax must be paid. But the year each item of income is subject to tax can also affect the total tax liability over the entity's lifetime. This is true for the following reasons:

- With a progressive rate system, a taxpayer's marginal tax rate can change from year to year.
- Congress may change the tax rates.
- The relevant rates may change because of a change in the entity's status (e.g., a person may marry or a business may be incorporated).
- Several provisions in the Code are dependent on the taxpayer's gross income for the year (e.g., whether the person can be claimed as a dependent, as discussed in Chapter 3).

> **LO.2**
> Describe the cash and accrual methods of accounting and the related effects of the choice of taxable year.

Accounting Methods

The year an item of income is subject to tax often depends upon which acceptable **accounting method** the taxpayer regularly employs.[16] The three primary methods of accounting are (1) the cash receipts and disbursements method, (2) the accrual method, and (3) the hybrid method. Most individuals use the cash receipts and disbursements method of accounting, whereas most corporations use the accrual method. The Regulations require the accrual method for determining purchases

---

[14]See Accounting Periods in Chapter 18.
[15]§§ 441(a) and (d).

[16]See Accounting Methods in Chapter 18.

and sales when inventory is an income-producing factor.[17] Some businesses employ a hybrid method that is a combination of the cash and accrual methods of accounting.

In addition to these overall accounting methods, a taxpayer may choose to spread the gain from an installment sale of property over the collection periods by using the *installment method* of income recognition. Contractors may either spread profits from contracts over the periods in which the work is done (the *percentage of completion method*) or defer all profit until the year in which the project is completed (the *completed contract method*, which can be used only in limited circumstances).[18]

The IRS has the power to prescribe the accounting method to be used by the taxpayer. Section 446(b) grants the IRS broad powers to determine if the accounting method used *clearly reflects income*:

> If no method of accounting has been regularly used by the taxpayer, or *if the method used does not clearly reflect income, the computation of taxable income shall be made under such method as, in the opinion of the Secretary . . . does clearly reflect income.*

A change in the method of accounting requires the consent of the IRS.[19]

Cash Receipts Method.

Cash Receipts Method. Under the **cash receipts method**, property or services received are included in the taxpayer's gross income in the year of actual or constructive receipt by the taxpayer or agent, regardless of whether the income was earned in that year.[20] The income received need not be reduced to cash in the same year. All that is necessary for income recognition is that property or services received have a fair market value—a cash equivalent.[21] Thus, a cash basis taxpayer who receives a note in payment for services has income in the year of receipt equal to the fair market value of the note. However, a creditor's mere promise to pay (e.g., an account receivable), with no supporting note, usually is not considered to have a fair market value.[22] Thus, the cash basis taxpayer defers income recognition until the account receivable is collected.

EXAMPLE 6

Dana, an accountant, reports her income by the cash method. In 2008, she performed an audit for Orange Corporation and billed the client for $5,000, which was collected in 2009. In 2008, Dana also performed an audit for Blue Corporation. Because of Blue's precarious financial position, Dana required Blue to issue an $8,000 secured negotiable note in payment of the fee. The note had a fair market value of $6,000. Dana collected $8,000 on the note in 2009. Dana's gross income for the two years is as follows:

	2008	2009
Fair market value of note received from Blue	$6,000	
Cash received		
From Orange on account receivable		$ 5,000
From Blue on note receivable		8,000
Less: Recovery of capital		(6,000)
Total gross income	$6,000	$ 7,000

■

Generally, a check received is considered a cash equivalent. Thus, a cash basis taxpayer must recognize the income when the check is received. This is true even if

---

[17]Reg. § 1.446–1(c)(2)(i). Other circumstances in which the accrual method must be used are presented in Chapter 18. For the small business exception to the inventory requirement, see Rev.Proc. 2002–28, 2002–1 C.B. 815.

[18]§§ 453 and 460. See Chapter 18 for limitations on the use of the installment method and the completed contract method.

[19]§ 446(e). See Chapter 18.

[20]*Julia A. Strauss*, 2 B.T.A. 598 (1925). See the Glossary of Tax Terms in Appendix C for a discussion of the terms "cash equivalent doctrine" and "constructive receipt."

[21]Reg. §§ 1.446–1(a)(3) and (c)(1)(i).

[22]*Bedell v. Comm.*, 1 USTC ¶359, 7 AFTR 8469, 30 F.2d 622 (CA–2, 1929).

the taxpayer receives the check after banking hours. An exception to this rule is that if the person paying with the check requests that the check not be cashed until a subsequent date, the cash basis income is deferred until the date the check can be cashed.[23]

<table>
<tr><td>**ETHICAL and EQUITABLE** *Considerations*</td><td>**THE CPAs' ACCOUNTING METHOD**</td></tr>
</table>

Accounting students understand that the accrual method of accounting is superior to the cash method for measuring the income and expenses from an ongoing business for financial reporting purposes. Thus, CPAs advise their clients to use the accrual method of accounting. Yet CPA firms generally use the cash method to prepare their tax returns. Are the CPAs being hypocritical?

Accrual Method. Under the **accrual method**, an item is generally included in the gross income for the year in which it is earned, regardless of when the income is collected. The income is earned when (1) all the events have occurred that fix the right to receive such income and (2) the amount to be received can be determined with reasonable accuracy.[24]

Generally, the taxpayer's rights to the income accrue when title to property passes to the buyer or the services are performed for the customer or client.[25] If the rights to the income have accrued but are subject to a potential refund claim (e.g., under a product warranty), the income is reported in the year of sale, and a deduction is allowed in subsequent years when actual claims accrue.[26]

Where the taxpayer's rights to the income are being contested (e.g., when a contractor fails to meet specifications), the year in which the income is subject to tax depends upon whether payment has been received. If payment has not been received, no income is recognized until the claim is settled. Only then is the right to the income established.[27] However, if the payment is received before the dispute is settled, the court-made **claim of right doctrine** requires the taxpayer to recognize the income in the year of receipt.[28]

EXAMPLE 7

A contractor completed a building in 2008 and presented a bill to the customer. The customer refused to pay the bill and claimed that the contractor had not met specifications. A settlement with the customer was not reached until 2009. No income accrues to the contractor until 2009. If the customer paid for the work and then filed suit for damages, the contractor cannot defer the income (the income is taxable in 2008). ∎

The measure of accrual basis income is generally the amount the taxpayer has a right to receive. Unlike the cash basis, the fair market value of the customer's obligation is irrelevant in measuring accrual basis income.

EXAMPLE 8

Assume the same facts as in Example 6, except that Dana is an accrual basis taxpayer. Dana must recognize $13,000 ($8,000 + $5,000) gross income in 2008, the year her rights to the income accrued. ∎

---

[23]*Charles F. Kahler*, 18 T.C. 31 (1952); *Bright v. U.S.*, 91–1 USTC ¶50,142, 67 AFTR2d 91–673, 926 F.2d 383 (CA–5, 1991).
[24]Reg. § 1.451–1(a).
[25]*Lucas v. North Texas Lumber Co.*, 2 USTC ¶484, 8 AFTR 10276, 50 S.Ct. 184 (USSC, 1930).

[26]*Brown v. Helvering*, 4 USTC ¶1222, 13 AFTR 851, 54 S.Ct. 356 (USSC, 1933).
[27]*Burnet v. Sanford and Brooks*, 2 USTC ¶636, 9 AFTR 603, 51 S.Ct. 150 (USSC, 1931).
[28]*North American Oil Consolidated Co. v. Burnet*, 3 USTC ¶943, 11 AFTR 16, 52 S.Ct. 613 (USSC, 1932).

Hybrid Method. The **hybrid method** is a combination of the accrual method and the cash method. Generally, when the hybrid method is used, inventory is an income-producing factor. Therefore, the Regulations require that the accrual method be used for determining sales and cost of goods sold. In this circumstance, to simplify record keeping, the taxpayer accounts for inventory using the accrual method and uses the cash method for all other income and expense items (e.g., dividend and interest income). The hybrid method is primarily used by small businesses.

Exceptions Applicable to Cash Basis Taxpayers

Constructive Receipt. Income that has not actually been received by the taxpayer is taxed as though it had been received—the income is constructively received—under the following conditions:

- The amount is made readily available to the taxpayer.
- The taxpayer's actual receipt is not subject to substantial limitations or restrictions.[29]

The rationale for the **constructive receipt** doctrine is that if the income is available, the taxpayer should not be allowed to postpone the income recognition. For instance, a taxpayer is not permitted to defer income for December services by refusing to accept payment until January. However, determining whether the income is *readily available* and whether *substantial limitations or restrictions exist* necessitates a factual inquiry that leads to a judgment call.[30] The following are some examples of the application of the constructive receipt doctrine.

EXAMPLE 9	Ted is a member of a barter club. In 2008, Ted performed services for other club members and earned 1,000 points. Each point entitles him to $1 in goods and services sold by other members of the club; the points can be used at any time. In 2009, Ted exchanged his points for a new high-definition TV. Ted must recognize $1,000 gross income in 2008 when the 1,000 points were credited to his account.[31] ∎

EXAMPLE 10	On December 31, an employer issued a bonus check to an employee but asked her to hold it for a few days until the company could make deposits to cover the check. The income was not constructively received on December 31 since the issuer did not have sufficient funds in its account to pay the debt.[32] ∎

EXAMPLE 11	Rick owns interest coupons that mature on December 31. The coupons can be converted to cash at any bank at maturity. Thus, the income is constructively received by Rick on December 31, even though Rick failed to cash in the coupons until the following year.[33] Dove Company mails a dividend check to Rick on December 31, 2008. Rick does not receive the check until January 2009. Rick does not realize gross income until 2009.[34] ∎

The constructive receipt doctrine does not reach income that the taxpayer is not yet entitled to receive even though the taxpayer could have contracted to receive the income at an earlier date.

---

[29]Reg. § 1.451–2(a).

[30]*Baxter v. Comm.*, 87–1 USTC ¶9315, 59 AFTR2d 87–1068, 816 F.2d 493 (CA–9, 1987).

[31]Rev.Rul. 80–52, 1980–1 C.B. 100.

[32]*L. M. Fischer*, 14 T.C. 792 (1950).

[33]Reg. § 1.451–2(b).

[34]Reg. § 1.451–2(b).

EXAMPLE 12

Sara offers to pay Ivan $100,000 for land in December 2008. Ivan refuses but offers to sell the land to Sara on January 1, 2009, when he will be in a lower tax bracket. If Sara accepts Ivan's offer, the gain is taxed to Ivan in 2009 when the sale is completed.[35] ■

Income set apart or made available is not constructively received if its actual receipt is subject to *substantial restrictions*. The life insurance industry has used substantial restrictions as a cornerstone for designing life insurance contracts with favorable tax features. Ordinary life insurance policies provide (1) current protection—an amount payable in the event of death—and (2) a savings feature—a cash surrender value payable to the policyholder if the policy is terminated during the policyholder's life. The annual increase in cash surrender value is not taxable because the policyholder must cancel the policy to actually receive the increase in value. Because the cancellation requirement is a substantial restriction, the policyholder does not constructively receive the annual increase in cash surrender value.[36] Employees often receive from their employers property subject to substantial restrictions. Generally, no income is recognized until the restrictions lapse.[37]

EXAMPLE 13

Carlos is a key employee of Red, Inc. The corporation gives stock with a value of $10,000 to Carlos. The stock cannot be sold, however, for five years. Carlos is not required to recognize income until the restrictions lapse at the end of five years. ■

Original Issue Discount. Lenders frequently make loans that require a payment at maturity of more than the amount of the original loan. The difference between the amount due at maturity and the amount of the original loan is actually interest but is referred to as **original issue discount**. Under the general rules of tax accounting, the cash basis lender would not report the original issue discount as interest income until the year the amount is collected, although an accrual basis borrower would deduct the interest as it is earned. However, the Code puts the lender and borrower on parity by requiring that the original issue discount be reported when it is earned, regardless of the taxpayer's accounting method.[38] The interest "earned" is calculated by the effective interest rate method.

EXAMPLE 14

On January 1, 2008, Mark, a cash basis taxpayer, pays $82,645 for a 24-month certificate. The certificate is priced to yield 10% (the effective interest rate) with interest compounded annually. No interest is paid until maturity, when Mark receives $100,000. Thus, Mark's gross income from the certificate is $17,355 ($100,000 − $82,645). Mark's income earned each year is calculated as follows:

2008 (.10 × $82,645) =	$ 8,264
2009 [.10 × ($82,645 + $8,264)] =	9,091
	$17,355

■

The original issue discount rules do not apply to U.S. savings bonds (discussed in the following paragraphs) or to obligations with a maturity date of one year or less from the date of issue.[39] See Chapter 16 for additional discussion of the tax treatment of original issue discount.

---

[35]*Cowden v. Comm.*, 61–1 USTC ¶9382, 7 AFTR2d 1160, 289 F.2d 20 (CA–5, 1961).

[36]*Theodore H. Cohen*, 39 T.C. 1055 (1963).

[37]§ 83(a). See also the discussion of Restricted Property Plans in Chapter 19.

[38]§§ 1272(a)(3) and 1273(a).

[39]§ 1272(a)(2).

GLOBAL
Tax Issues

TAX CREDIT NEUTRALIZES FOREIGN INCOME TAXES

When a U.S. taxpayer invests in a foreign country, that investment income is subject to tax in the United States and may also be subject to tax in the foreign country. However, the taxpayer is allowed a credit on his or her U.S. Federal income tax return for income taxes paid to the foreign country. The credit system allows the taxpayer to treat the taxes paid to the foreign country as though they were paid to the United States. If the foreign taxes paid are less than the U.S. tax on the income, the foreign taxes have cost the taxpayer nothing. On the other hand, if the foreign taxes are greater than the U.S. tax on the income, the credit is limited to the amount of the U.S. tax on the income. In this case, the taxes paid by the taxpayer will exceed what they would have been if the income had been earned in the United States.

Series E and Series EE Bonds. Certain U.S. government savings bonds (Series E before 1980 and Series EE after 1979) are issued at a discount and are redeemable for fixed amounts that increase at stated intervals. No interest payments are actually made. The difference between the purchase price and the amount received on redemption is the bondholder's interest income from the investment.

The income from these savings bonds is generally deferred until the bonds are redeemed or mature. Furthermore, Series E bonds previously could be exchanged within one year of their maturity date for Series HH bonds, and the interest on the Series E bonds could be further deferred until maturity of the Series HH bonds.[40] Thus, U.S. savings bonds have attractive income deferral features not available with corporate bonds and certificates of deposit issued by financial institutions.

Of course, the deferral feature of government bonds issued at a discount is not an advantage if the investor has insufficient income to be subject to tax as the income accrues. In fact, the deferral may work to the investor's disadvantage if the investor has other income in the year the bonds mature or the bunching of the bond interest into one tax year creates a tax liability. Fortunately, U.S. government bonds have a provision for these investors. A cash basis taxpayer can elect to include in gross income the annual increment in redemption value.[41]

EXAMPLE 15

Kate purchases Series EE U.S. savings bonds for $500 (face value of $1,000) on January 2 of the current year. If the bonds are redeemed during the first six months, no interest is paid. At December 31, the redemption value is $519.60.

If Kate elects to report the interest income annually, she must report interest income of $19.60 for the current year. If she does not make the election, she will report no interest income for the current year. ∎

When a taxpayer elects to report the income from the bonds on an annual basis, the election applies to all such bonds the taxpayer owns at the time of the election and to all such securities acquired subsequent to the election. A change in the method of reporting the income from the bonds requires permission from the IRS.

Amounts Received under an Obligation to Repay. The receipt of funds with an obligation to repay that amount in the future is the essence of borrowing. Because the taxpayer's assets and liabilities increase by the same amount, no income is realized when the borrowed funds are received. Because amounts paid to the taxpayer by mistake and customer deposits are often classified as borrowed funds, receipt of these funds is not a taxable event.

---

[40]Treas. Dept. Circulars No. 1–80 and No. 2–80, 1980–1 C.B. 714, 715. Note that interest is paid at semiannual intervals on the Series HH bonds and must be included in income as received. Refer to Chapter 5 for a discussion

of the savings bond interest exclusion. This exchange opportunity applied through August 31, 2004.

[41]§ 454(a).

E X A M P L E   16

A landlord receives a damage deposit from a tenant. The landlord does not recognize income until the deposit is forfeited because the landlord has an obligation to repay the deposit if no damage occurs.[42] However, if the deposit is in fact a prepayment of rent, it is taxed in the year of receipt. ■

Exceptions Applicable to Accrual Basis Taxpayers

Prepaid Income. For financial reporting purposes, advance payments received from customers are reflected as prepaid income and as a liability of the seller. However, for tax purposes, the prepaid income often is taxed in the year of receipt.

E X A M P L E   17

In December 2008, a tenant pays his January 2009 rent of $1,000. The accrual basis landlord must include the $1,000 in her 2008 gross income for tax purposes, although the unearned rent income is reported as a liability on the landlord's December 31, 2008 balance sheet. ■

Taxpayers have repeatedly argued that deferral of income until it is actually earned properly matches revenues and expenses. Moreover, a proper matching of income with the expenses of earning the income is necessary to clearly reflect income, as required by the Code. The IRS responds that § 446(b) grants it broad powers to determine whether an accounting method clearly reflects income. The IRS further argues that generally accepted financial accounting principles should not dictate tax accounting for prepaid income because of the practical problems of collecting Federal revenues. Collection of the tax is simplest in the year the taxpayer receives the cash from the customer or client.

After a number of years of continual disputes between the IRS and taxpayers, in 1971 the IRS relented and modified its rules on the prepaid income issue in some situations, as explained below.

Deferral of Advance Payments for Goods. Generally, a taxpayer can elect to defer recognition of income from *advance payments for goods* if the method of accounting for the sale is the same for tax and financial reporting purposes.[43]

E X A M P L E   18

Brown Company will ship goods only after payment for the goods has been received. In December 2008, Brown received $10,000 for goods that were not shipped until January 2009. Brown can elect to report the income for tax purposes in 2009, assuming the company reports the income in 2009 for financial reporting purposes. ■

Deferral of Advance Payments for Services. Revenue Procedure 2004–34[44] permits an accrual basis taxpayer to defer recognition of income for *advance payments for services* to be performed after the end of the tax year of receipt. The portion of the advance payment that relates to services performed in the tax year of receipt is included in gross income in the tax year of receipt. The portion of the advance payment that relates to services to be performed after the tax year of receipt is included in gross income in the *tax year following the tax year of receipt* of the advance payment.

E X A M P L E   19

Yellow Corporation, an accrual basis calendar year taxpayer, sells its services under 12-month, 24-month, and 36-month contracts. The corporation provides services to each customer every month. On May 1, 2008, Yellow Corporation sold the following customer contracts:

---

[42]*John Mantell,* 17 T.C. 1143 (1952).

[43]Reg. § 1.451–5(b). See Reg. § 1.451–5(c) for exceptions to this deferral opportunity. The financial accounting conformity requirement is not applicable to contractors who use the completed contract method.

[44]2004–1 C.B. 991.

Length of Contract	Total Proceeds
12 months	$3,000
24 months	4,800
36 months	7,200

Yellow may defer until 2009 all of the income that will be earned after 2008.

Length of Contract	Income Recorded in 2008	Income Recorded in 2009
12 months	$2,000 ($3,000 × 8/12)	$1,000 ($3,000 × 4/12)
24 months	1,600 ($4,800 × 8/24)	3,200 ($4,800 × 16/24)
36 months	1,600 ($7,200 × 8/36)	5,600 ($7,200 × 28/36)

Revenue Procedure 2004–34 does not apply to prepaid rent or prepaid interest. Advance payments for these items are always taxed in the year of receipt.

Income Sources

LO.3

Identify who should pay the tax on a particular item of income in various situations.

Personal Services

It is a well-established principle of taxation that income from personal services must be included in the gross income of the person who performs the services. This principle was first established in a Supreme Court decision, *Lucas v. Earl*.[45] Mr. Earl entered into a binding agreement with his wife under which Mrs. Earl was to receive one-half of Mr. Earl's salary. Justice Holmes used the celebrated **fruit and tree metaphor** to explain that the fruit (income) must be attributed to the tree from which it came (Mr. Earl's services). A mere **assignment of income** does not shift the liability for the tax.

Services of an Employee. Services performed by an employee for the employer's customers are considered performed by the employer. Thus, the employer is taxed on the income from the services provided to the customer, and the employee is taxed on any compensation received from the employer.[46]

EXAMPLE 20

Dr. Shontelle incorporates her medical practice and enters into a contract to work for the corporation for a salary. All patients contract to receive their services from the corporation, and those services are provided through the corporation's employee, Dr. Shontelle. The corporation must include the patients' fees in its gross income. Dr. Shontelle must include her salary in her gross income. The corporation is allowed a deduction for the reasonable salary paid to Dr. Shontelle (see the discussion of unreasonable compensation in Chapter 6). ∎

Services of a Child. In the case of a child, the Code specifically provides that amounts earned from personal services must be included in the child's gross income. This result applies even though the income is paid to other persons (e.g., the parents).[47]

---

[45]2 USTC ¶496, 8 AFTR 10287, 50 S.Ct. 241 (USSC, 1930).
[46]*Sargent v. Comm.*, 91–1 USTC ¶50,168, 67 AFTR2d 91–718, 929 F.2d 1252 (CA–8, 1991).

[47]§ 73. For circumstances in which the child's unearned income is taxed at the parents' rate, see Unearned Income of Children under Age 19 Taxed at Parents' Rate in Chapter 3.

Income from Property

Income from property (interest, dividends, rent) must be included in the gross income of the *owner* of the property. If a father clips interest coupons from bonds shortly before the interest payment date and gives the coupons to his son, the interest will still be taxed to the father. A father who assigns rents from rental property to his daughter will be taxed on the rent since he retains ownership of the property.[48]

Often income-producing property is transferred after income from the property has accrued, but before the income is recognized under the transferor's method of accounting. The IRS and the courts have developed rules to allocate the income between the transferor and the transferee.

Interest. According to the IRS, interest accrues daily. Therefore, the interest for the period that includes the date of the transfer is allocated between the transferor and transferee based on the number of days during the period that each owned the property.

EXAMPLE 21

Floyd, a cash basis taxpayer, gave his son, Seth, bonds with a face amount of $10,000 and an 8% stated annual interest rate. The gift was made on January 31, 2008, and the interest was paid on December 31, 2008. Floyd must recognize $68 in interest income (8% × $10,000 × $31/_{366}$). Seth will recognize $732 in interest income ($800 − $68). ■

When the transferor must recognize the income from the property depends upon the method of accounting and the manner in which the property was transferred. In the case of a gift of income-producing property, the donor must recognize his or her share of the accrued income at the time it would have been recognized had the donor continued to own the property.[49] However, if the transfer is a sale, the transferor must recognize the accrued income at the time of the sale. This results because the accrued interest will be included in the sales proceeds.

EXAMPLE 22

Assume the same facts as in Example 21, except that the interest that was payable as of December 31 was not actually or constructively received by the bondholders until January 3, 2009. As a cash basis taxpayer, Floyd generally does not recognize interest income until it is received. If Floyd had continued to own the bonds, the interest would have been included in his 2009 gross income, the year it would have been received. Therefore, Floyd must include the $68 accrued income in his gross income as of January 3, 2009.

Further assume that Floyd sold identical bonds on the date of the gift. The bonds sold for $9,900, including accrued interest. On January 31, 2008, Floyd must recognize the accrued interest of $68 on the bonds sold. Thus, the selling price of the bonds is $9,832 ($9,900 − $68). ■

Dividends. A corporation is taxed on its earnings, and the shareholders are taxed on the dividends paid to them from the corporation's after-tax earnings. The dividend can take the form of an actual dividend or a constructive dividend (e.g., shareholder use of corporate assets).

Partial relief from the double taxation of dividends has been provided in the Jobs and Growth Tax Relief Reconciliation Act of 2003 and extended by the Tax Increase Prevention Act of 2005 (TIPRA). Generally, dividends received in taxable years beginning after 2002 are taxed at the same marginal rate that is applicable to a net capital gain.[50] Thus, individuals otherwise subject to the 10 or 15 percent marginal tax rate pay only a 5 percent tax on qualified dividends received in 2007 and a

---

[48]*Galt v. Comm.*, 54–2 USTC ¶9457, 46 AFTR 633, 216 F.2d 41 (CA–7, 1954); *Helvering v. Horst*, 40–2 USTC ¶9787, 24 AFTR 1058, 61 S.Ct. 144 (USSC, 1940).

[49]Rev.Rul. 72–312, 1972–1 C.B. 22.

[50]§ 1(h)(11).

0 percent tax on qualified dividends received in 2008. Individuals subject to the 25, 28, 33, or 35 percent marginal tax rate pay a 15 percent tax on qualified dividends received. Thus, dividends receive favorable treatment as compared to interest income.

Note that qualified dividends are not treated as capital gains in the gains and losses netting process; thus, they are *not* reduced by capital losses. Qualified dividend income is merely taxed at the rates that would apply to the taxpayer if he or she had an excess of net long-term capital gain over net short-term capital loss.

Because the beneficial tax rate is intended to mitigate double taxation, only certain dividends are eligible for the beneficial treatment. Excluded are certain dividends from foreign corporations, dividends from tax-exempt entities, and dividends that do not satisfy the holding period requirement.

A dividend from a foreign corporation is eligible for qualified dividend status only if one of the following requirements is met: (1) the foreign corporation's stock is traded on an established U.S. securities market, or (2) the foreign corporation is eligible for the benefits of a comprehensive income tax treaty between its country of incorporation and the United States.

To satisfy the holding period requirement, the stock on which the dividend is paid must have been held for more than 60 days during the 121-day period beginning 60 days before the ex-dividend date.[51] The purpose of this requirement is to prevent the taxpayer from buying the stock shortly before the dividend is paid, receiving the dividend, and then selling the stock at a loss (a capital loss) after the stock goes ex-dividend. A stock's price often declines after the stock goes ex-dividend.

EXAMPLE 23

In June 2008, Green Corporation pays a dividend of $1.50 on each share of its common stock. Madison and Daniel, two unrelated shareholders, each own 1,000 shares of the stock. Consequently, each receives $1,500 (1,000 shares × $1.50). Assume Daniel satisfies the 60/121-day holding period rule, but Madison does not. The $1,500 Daniel receives is subject to preferential 15%/0% treatment in 2008 (15%/5% if the dividend had been paid in 2007). The $1,500 Madison receives, however, is not. Because Madison did not comply with the holding period rule, her dividend is not a *qualified dividend* and is taxed at ordinary income rates. ■

EXAMPLE 24

Assume that both Madison and Daniel in Example 23 are in the 35% tax bracket. Consequently, Madison pays a tax of $525 (35% × $1,500) on her dividend, while Daniel pays a tax of $225 (15% × $1,500) on his. The $300 saving that Daniel enjoys underscores the advantages of a qualified dividend. ■

Unlike interest, dividends do not accrue on a daily basis because the declaration of a dividend is at the discretion of the corporation's board of directors. Generally, dividends are taxed to the person who is entitled to receive them—the shareholder of record as of the corporation's record date.[52] Thus, if a taxpayer sells stock after a dividend has been declared but before the record date, the dividend generally will be taxed to the purchaser.

If a donor makes a gift of stock to someone (e.g., a family member) after the declaration date but before the record date, the Tax Court has held that the donor does not shift the dividend income to the donee. The *fruit* has sufficiently ripened as of the declaration date to tax the dividend income to the donor of the stock.[53] In a similar set of facts, the Fifth Circuit Court of Appeals concluded that the dividend income should be included in the gross income of the donee (the owner at the

---

[51]The ex-dividend date is the date following the record date on which the corporation finalizes the list of shareholders who will receive the dividends.

[52]Reg. § 1.61–9(c). The record date is the cutoff for determining the shareholders who are entitled to receive the dividend.

[53]*M. G. Anton*, 34 T.C. 842 (1960).

record date). In this case, the taxpayer gave stock to a qualified charity (a charitable contribution) after the declaration date and before the record date.[54]

EXAMPLE 25

On June 20, the board of directors of Black Corporation declares a $10 per share dividend. The dividend is payable on June 30, to shareholders of record on June 25. As of June 20, Maria owned 200 shares of Black Corporation's stock. On June 21, Maria sold 100 of the shares to Norm for their fair market value and gave 100 of the shares to Sam (her son). Both Norm and Sam are shareholders of record as of June 25. Norm (the purchaser) will be taxed on $1,000 since he is entitled to receive the dividend. However, Maria (the donor) will be taxed on the $1,000 received by Sam (the donee) because the gift was made after the declaration date of the dividend. ◾

ETHICAL and EQUITABLE *Considerations*   ENHANCING LOTTERY WINNINGS

Some family members have net losses from gambling, which can be used only to reduce gambling gains. Another family member has a substantial gain from winning the lottery. Suppose that the winner gives the winning ticket to the family members with gambling losses, thereby creating what is tantamount to tax-exempt income. Evaluate this proposal.

Income Received by an Agent

Income received by the taxpayer's agent is considered to be received by the taxpayer. A cash basis principal must recognize the income at the time it is received by the agent.[55]

EXAMPLE 26

Jack, a cash basis taxpayer, delivered cattle to the auction barn in late December. The auctioneer, acting as the farmer's agent, sold the cattle and collected the proceeds in December. The auctioneer did not pay Jack until the following January. Jack must include the sales proceeds in his gross income for the year the auctioneer received the funds. ◾

Income from Partnerships, S Corporations, Trusts, and Estates

A **partnership** is not a separate taxable entity. Rather, the partnership merely files an information return (Form 1065), which serves to provide the data necessary for determining the character and amount of each partner's distributive share of the partnership's income and deductions. Each partner must then report his or her distributive share of the partnership's income and deductions for the partnership's tax year ending within or with the partner's tax year. The income must be reported by each partner in the year it is earned, even if such amounts are not actually distributed to the partners. Because a partner pays tax on income as the partnership earns it, a distribution by the partnership to the partner is treated under the recovery of capital rules.[56]

EXAMPLE 27

Tara owns a one-half interest in the capital and profits of T & S Company (a calendar year partnership). For tax year 2008, the partnership earned revenue of $150,000 and had operating expenses of $80,000. During the year, Tara withdrew from her capital account $2,500 per month (for a total of $30,000). For 2008, Tara must report $35,000 as her share of the partnership's profits [½ × ($150,000 − $80,000)] even though she received distributions of only $30,000. ◾

[54]*Caruth Corp. v. U.S.*, 89–1 USTC ¶9172, 63 AFTR2d 89–716, 865 F.2d 644 (CA-5, 1989).
[55]Rev.Rul. 79–379, 1979–2 C.B. 204.
[56]§ 706(a) and Reg. § 1.706–1(a)(1). For further discussion, see Chapter 20.

Contrary to the general provision that a corporation must pay tax on its income, a *small business corporation* may elect to be taxed similarly to a partnership. Thus, the shareholders, rather than the corporation, pay the tax on the corporation's income.[57] The electing corporation is referred to as an **S corporation**. Generally, the shareholders report their proportionate shares of the corporation's income and deductions for the year, whether or not the corporation actually makes any distributions to the shareholders.

The *beneficiaries of estates and trusts* generally are taxed on the income earned by the estates or trusts that is actually distributed or required to be distributed to them.[58] Any income not taxed to the beneficiaries is taxable to the estate or trust.

Income in Community Property States

General. State law in Louisiana, Texas, New Mexico, Arizona, California, Washington, Idaho, Nevada, and Wisconsin is based upon a community property system. In Alaska, spouses can choose to have the community property rules apply. All other states have a common law property system. The basic difference between common law and community property systems centers around the property rights of married persons. Questions about community property income most frequently arise when the husband and wife file separate returns.

Under a **community property** system, all property is deemed either to be separately owned by the spouse or to belong to the marital community. Property may be held separately by a spouse if it was acquired before marriage or received by gift or inheritance following marriage. Otherwise, any property is deemed to be community property. For Federal tax purposes, each spouse is taxed on one-half of the income from property belonging to the community.

The laws of Texas, Louisiana, Wisconsin, and Idaho distinguish between separate property and the income it produces. In these states, the income from separate property belongs to the community. Accordingly, for Federal income tax purposes, each spouse is taxed on one-half of the income. In the remaining community property states, separate property produces separate income that the owner-spouse must report on his or her Federal income tax return.

What appears to be income, however, may really represent a recovery of capital. A recovery of capital and gain realized on separate property retain their identity as

---

[57]§§ 1361(a) and 1366. For further discussion, see Chapter 20.

[58]§§ 652(a) and 662(a). For further discussion of the taxation of income from partnerships, S corporations, trusts, and estates, see *South-Western Federal*

Taxation: Corporations, Partnerships, Estates, and Trusts, Chapters 10, 11, 12, and 19.

separate property. Items such as nontaxable stock dividends, royalties from mineral interests, and gains and losses from the sale of property take on the same classification as the assets to which they relate.

Bob and Jane are husband and wife and reside in California. Among other transactions during the year, the following occurred:

- Nontaxable stock dividend received by Jane on stock that was given to her after her marriage by her mother.
- Gain of $10,000 on the sale of unimproved land purchased by Bob before his marriage.
- Oil royalties of $15,000 from a lease Jane acquired after marriage with her separate funds.

Since the stock dividend was distributed on stock held by Jane as separate property, it also is her separate property. The same result occurs for the oil royalties Jane receives. All of the proceeds from the sale of the unimproved land (including the gain of $10,000) are Bob's separate property. ∎

EXAMPLE 28

In all community property states, income from personal services (e.g., salaries, wages, income from a professional partnership) is generally treated as if one-half is earned by each spouse.

Fred and Wilma are married but file separate returns. Fred received $25,000 salary and $300 taxable interest on a savings account he established in his name. The deposits to the savings account were made from Fred's salary that he earned since the marriage. Wilma collected $2,000 taxable dividends on stock she inherited from her father. Wilma's gross income is computed as follows under three assumptions as to the state of residency of the couple:

EXAMPLE 29

	California	Texas	Common Law States
Dividends	$ 2,000	$ 1,000	$2,000
Salary	12,500	12,500	–0–
Interest	150	150	–0–
	$14,650	$13,650	$2,000

∎

Community Property Spouses Living Apart.
The general rules for taxing the income from services performed by residents of community property states can create complications and even inequities for spouses who are living apart.

Cole and Debra were married but living apart for the first nine months of 2008 and were divorced as of October 1, 2008. In December 2008, Cole married Emily, who was married but living apart from Frank before their divorce in June 2008. Cole and Frank had no income from personal services in 2008.

Cole brought into his marriage to Emily a tax liability on one-half of Debra's earnings for the first nine months of the year. However, Emily left with Frank a tax liability on one-half of her earnings for the first six months of 2008. ∎

EXAMPLE 30

Congress has developed a simple solution to the many tax problems of community property spouses living apart. A spouse (or former spouse) is taxed only on his or her actual earnings from personal services if the following conditions are met:[59]

- The individuals live apart for the entire year.
- They do not file a joint return with each other.
- No portion of the earned income is transferred between the individuals.

---

[59]§ 66.

EXAMPLE 31

Jim and Lori reside in a community property state, and both are gainfully employed. On July 1, 2008, they separated, and on June 30, 2009, they were divorced. Assuming their only source of income is wages, one-half of such income for each year is earned by June 30, and they did not file a joint return for 2008, each should report the following gross income:

	Jim's Separate Return	Lori's Separate Return
2008	One-half of Jim's wages	One-half of Jim's wages
	One-half of Lori's wages	One-half of Lori's wages
2009	All of Jim's wages	All of Lori's wages

The results would be the same if Jim or Lori married another person in 2009, except that the newlyweds would probably file a joint return. ∎

The IRS may absolve from liability an *innocent spouse* who does not live apart for the entire year and files a separate return but omits his or her share of the community income received by the other spouse. To qualify for the innocent spouse relief, the taxpayer must not know or must have no reason to know of the omitted community income. Even if all of these requirements cannot be satisfied, the IRS has additional statutory authority to absolve the innocent spouse from tax liability. If, under the facts and circumstances, it is inequitable to hold the spouse liable for any unpaid tax, the IRS can absolve the spouse from tax liability.

LO.4

Apply the Internal Revenue Code provisions on alimony, loans made at below-market interest rates, annuities, prizes and awards, group term life insurance, unemployment compensation, and Social Security benefits.

Items Specifically Included in Gross Income

The general principles of gross income determination (discussed in the previous sections) as applied by the IRS and the courts have on occasion yielded results Congress found unacceptable. Consequently, Congress has provided more specific rules for determining the gross income from certain sources. Some of these special rules appear in §§ 71–90 of the Code.

Alimony and Separate Maintenance Payments

When a married couple divorce or become legally separated, state law generally requires a division of the property accumulated during the marriage. In addition, one spouse may have a legal obligation to support the other spouse. The Code distinguishes between the support payments (alimony or separate maintenance) and the property division in terms of the tax consequences.

Alimony and separate maintenance payments are *deductible* by the party making the payments and are *includible* in the gross income of the party receiving the payments.[60] Thus, income is shifted from the income earner to the income beneficiary, who is better able to pay the tax on the amount received.

EXAMPLE 32

Pete and Tina are divorced, and Pete is required to pay Tina $15,000 of alimony each year. Pete earns $31,000 a year. The tax law presumes that because Tina receives the $15,000, she is better able than Pete to pay the tax on that amount. Therefore, Tina must include the $15,000 in her gross income, and Pete is allowed to deduct $15,000 from his gross income. ∎

A transfer of property *other than cash* to a former spouse under a divorce decree or agreement is not a taxable event. The transferor is not entitled to a deduction

[60]§§ 71 and 215.

and does not recognize gain or loss on the transfer. The transferee does not recognize income and has a cost basis equal to the transferor's basis.[61]

Paul transfers stock to Rosa as part of a 2008 divorce settlement. The cost of the stock to Paul is $12,000, and the stock's value at the time of the transfer is $15,000. Rosa later sells the stock for $16,000. Paul is not required to recognize gain from the transfer of the stock to Rosa, and Rosa has a realized and recognized gain of $4,000 ($16,000 − $12,000) when she sells the stock. ■

In the case of *cash payments*, however, it is often difficult to distinguish payments under a support obligation (alimony) and payments for the other spouse's property (property settlement). In 1984, Congress developed objective rules to classify the payments.

Post-1984 Agreements and Decrees.

Payments made under post-1984 agreements and decrees are *classified as alimony* only if the following conditions are satisfied:

1. The payments are in cash.
2. The agreement or decree does not specify that the payments are not alimony.
3. The payor and payee are not members of the same household at the time the payments are made.
4. There is no liability to make the payments for any period after the death of the payee.[62]

Requirement 1 simplifies the law by clearly distinguishing alimony from a property division; that is, if the payment is not in cash, it must be a property division. Requirement 2 allows the parties to determine by agreement whether or not the payments will be alimony. The prohibition on cohabitation—requirement 3—is aimed at assuring the alimony payments are associated with duplicative living expenses (maintaining two households).[63] Requirement 4 is an attempt to prevent alimony treatment from being applied to what is, in fact, a payment for property rather than a support obligation. That is, a seller's estate generally will receive payments for property due after the seller's death. Such payments after the death of the payee could not be for the payee's support.

Front-Loading.

As a further safeguard against a property settlement being disguised as alimony, special rules apply to post-1986 agreements if payments in the first or second year exceed $15,000. If the change in the amount of the payments exceeds statutory limits, **alimony recapture** results to the extent of the excess alimony payments. In the *third* year, the payor must include the excess alimony payments for the first and second years in gross income, and the payee is allowed a deduction for these excess alimony payments. The recaptured amount is computed as follows:[64]

$$R = D + E$$
$$D = B - (C + \$15,000)$$
$$E = A - \left(\frac{B - D + C}{2} + \$15,000\right)$$

R = amount recaptured in Year 3 tax return
D = recapture from Year 2
E = recapture from Year 1
A, B, C = payments in the first (A), second (B), and third (C) calendar years of the agreement or decree, where $D \geq 0$, $E \geq 0$

---

[61]§ 1041, added to the Code in 1984 to repeal the rule of *U.S. v. Davis*, 62–2 USTC ¶9509, 9 AFTR2d 1625, 82 S.Ct. 1190 (USSC, 1962). Under the *Davis* rule, which applied to pre-1985 divorces, a property transfer incident to divorce was a taxable event.

[62]§ 71(b)(1). This set of alimony rules can also apply to pre-1985 agreements and decrees if both parties agree in writing. The rules applicable to pre-1985 agreements and decrees are not discussed in this text.

[63]*Alexander Washington*, 77 T.C. 601 (1981) at 604.

[64]§ 71(f).

CONCEPT SUMMARY 4-1

Tax Treatment of Payments and Transfers Pursuant to Post-1984 Divorce Agreements and Decrees

	Payor	Recipient
Alimony	Deduction from gross income.	Included in gross income.
Alimony recapture	Included in gross income of the third year.	Deducted from gross income of the third year.
Child support	Not deductible.	Not includible in gross income.
Property settlement	No income or deduction.	No income or deduction; basis for the property is the same as the transferor's basis.

The recapture formula provides an objective technique for determining alimony recapture. Thus, at the time of the divorce, the taxpayers can ascertain the tax consequences. The general concept is that if the alimony payments decrease by more than $15,000 between years in the first three years, there will be alimony recapture with respect to the decrease in excess of $15,000 each year. This rule is applied for the change between Year 2 and Year 3 (D in the above formula). However, rather than making the same calculation for Year 2 payments versus Year 1 payments, the Code requires that the *average* of the payments in Years 2 and 3 be compared with the Year 1 payments (E in the above formula). For this purpose, revised alimony for Year 2 (alimony deducted for Year 2 minus the alimony recapture for Year 2) is used.

EXAMPLE 34

Wes and Rita are divorced in 2008. Under the agreement, Rita is to receive $50,000 in 2008, $20,000 in 2009, and nothing thereafter. The payments are to cease upon Rita's death or remarriage. In 2010, Wes must include an additional $32,500 in gross income for alimony recapture, and Rita is allowed a deduction for the same amount.

$$D = \$20,000 - (\$0 + \$15,000) = \$5,000$$

$$E = \$50,000 - \left(\frac{\$20,000 - \$5,000 + \$0}{2} + \$15,000\right) = \$27,500$$

$$R = \$5,000 + \$27,500 = \$32,500$$

Note that for 2008 Wes deducts alimony of $50,000, and Rita includes $50,000 in her gross income. For 2009, the amount of the alimony deduction for Wes is $20,000, and Rita's gross income from the alimony is $20,000.

If instead Wes paid $50,000 of alimony in 2008 and nothing for the following years, $35,000 would be recaptured in 2010.

$$D = \$0 - (\$0 + \$15,000) = -\$15,000, \text{ but D must be} \geq \$0$$

$$E = \$50,000 - \left(\frac{\$0 - \$0 + \$0}{2} + \$15,000\right) = \$35,000$$

$$R = \$0 + \$35,000 = \$35,000$$

Alimony recapture does not apply if the decrease in payments is due to the death of either spouse or the remarriage of the payee.[65] Recapture is not applicable because these events typically terminate alimony under state laws. In addition, the recapture rules do not apply to payments where the amount is contingent (e.g., a percentage of income from certain property or a percentage of the payor spouse's compensation), the payments are to be made over a period of three years or longer (unless death, remarriage, or other contingency occurs), and the contingencies are beyond the payor's control.[66]

---

[65]§ 71(f)(5)(A).   [66]§ 71(f)(5)(C).

E X A M P L E   35

Under a 2008 divorce agreement, Ed is to receive an amount equal to one-half of Nina's income from certain rental properties for 2008–2011. Payments are to cease upon the death of Ed or Nina or upon the remarriage of Ed. Ed receives $50,000 in 2008 and $50,000 in 2009; in 2010, however, the property is vacant, and Ed receives nothing. Nina, who deducted alimony in 2008 and 2009, is not required to recapture any alimony in 2010 because the payments were contingent. ■

ETHICAL and EQUITABLE Considerations

AVOIDING FRONT-LOADING WITH EQUAL PAYMENTS

Ike and Tina accumulated substantial assets during their marriage. In the divorce negotiations, Tina is willing to allow Ike to take title to some of the jointly owned assets, but she expects a cash payment in exchange. Ike is concerned that under the front-loading rules for alimony, a lump-sum cash payment will result in gross income to him in the third year. He proposes to make equal annual cash payments over the next four years to Tina, rather than a lump-sum payment now. However, Tina does not want the amount she is entitled to receive to be subject to the risk that Ike will not be able to make future payments. Therefore, Ike proposes that he will place the lump-sum amount in an escrow account to be held by his attorney, and Tina will be permitted to withdraw an equal amount each year for the next four years (plus interest). Will Ike's plan achieve the tax avoidance he desires? Is the plan ethical?

Child Support. A taxpayer does not realize income from the receipt of child support payments made by his or her former spouse. This result occurs because the money is received subject to the duty to use the money for the child's benefit. The payor is not allowed to deduct the child support payments because the payments are made to satisfy the payor's legal obligation to support the child.

In many cases, it is difficult to determine whether an amount received is alimony or child support. If the amount of the payments would be reduced upon the happening of a contingency related to a child (e.g., the child attains age 21 or dies), the amount of the future reduction in the payment is deemed child support.[67]

E X A M P L E   36

A divorce agreement provides that Matt is required to make periodic alimony payments of $500 per month to Grace. However, when Matt and Grace's child reaches age 21, marries, or dies (whichever occurs first), the payments will be reduced to $300 per month. Grace has custody of the child. Since the required contingency is the cause for the reduction in the payments, from $500 to $300, child support payments are $200 per month, and alimony is $300 per month. ■

Imputed Interest on Below-Market Loans

As discussed earlier in the chapter, generally no income is recognized unless it is realized. Realization generally occurs when the taxpayer performs services or sells goods and thus becomes entitled to a payment from the other party. It follows that no income is realized if the goods or services are provided at no charge. Under this interpretation of the realization requirement, before 1984, interest-free loans were used to shift income between taxpayers.

E X A M P L E   37

Veneia (daughter) is in the 20% (combined Federal and state rates) tax bracket and has no investment income. Kareem (father) is in the 50% (combined Federal and state rates) tax bracket and has $400,000 in a money market account earning 5% interest. Kareem would

---

[67]§ 71(c)(2).

like Veneia to receive and pay tax on the income earned on the $400,000. Because Kareem would also like to have access to the $400,000 should he need the money, he does not want to make an outright gift of the money, nor does he want to commit the money to a trust.

Before 1984, Kareem could achieve his goals as follows. He could transfer the money market account to Veneia in exchange for her $400,000 non-interest-bearing note, payable on Kareem's demand. As a result, Veneia would receive the income, and the family's taxes would be decreased by $6,000.

Decrease in Kareem's tax—	
(.05 × $400,000).50 =	($10,000)
Increase in Veneia's tax—	
(.05 × $400,000).20 =	4,000
Decrease in the family's taxes	($ 6,000)

Under the 1984 amendments to the Code, Kareem in Example 37 is required to recognize **imputed interest** income.[68] Veneia is deemed to have incurred interest expense equal to Kareem's imputed interest income. Veneia's interest may be deductible on her return as investment interest if she itemizes deductions (see Chapter 10). To complete the fictitious series of transactions, Kareem is then deemed to have given Veneia the amount of the imputed interest she did not pay. The gift received by Veneia is not subject to income tax (see Chapter 5), although Kareem may be subject to the gift tax (unified transfer tax) on the amount deemed given to Veneia (refer to Chapter 1).

Imputed interest is calculated using the rate the Federal government pays on new borrowings and is compounded semiannually. This Federal rate is adjusted monthly and is published by the IRS.[69] Actually, there are three Federal rates: short-term (not over three years and including demand loans), mid-term (over three years but not over nine years), and long-term (over nine years).[70]

EXAMPLE 38

Assume the Federal rate applicable to the loan in Example 37 is 3.5% through June 30 and 4% from July 1 through December 31. Kareem made the loan on January 1, and the loan is still outstanding on December 31. Kareem must recognize interest income of $15,140, and Veneia has interest expense of $15,140. Kareem is deemed to have made a gift of $15,140 to Veneia.

Interest calculations:	
January 1–June 30—	
.035($400,000)(½ year)	$ 7,000
July 1–December 31—	
.04($400,000 + $7,000)(½ year)	8,140
	$15,140

If interest is charged on the loan but is less than the Federal rate, the imputed interest is the difference between the amount that would have been charged at the Federal rate and the amount actually charged.

EXAMPLE 39

Assume the same facts as in Example 38, except that Kareem charged 3% interest, compounded annually.

Interest at the Federal rate	$ 15,140
Less interest charged (.03 × $400,000)	(12,000)
Imputed interest	$ 3,140

---

[68]§ 7872(a)(1).
[69]§§ 7872(b)(2) and (f)(2).
[70]§ 1274 (d).

CONCEPT SUMMARY 4–2

Effect of Certain Below-Market Loans on the Lender and Borrower

Type of Loan		Lender	Borrower
Gift	Step 1	Interest income	Interest expense
	Step 2	Gift made	Gift received
Compensation-related	Step 1	Interest income	Interest expense
	Step 2	Compensation expense	Compensation income
Corporation to shareholder	Step 1	Interest income	Interest expense
	Step 2	Dividend paid	Dividend income

The imputed interest rules apply to the following *types* of below-market loans:[71]

1. Gift loans (made out of love, affection, or generosity, as in Example 37).
2. Compensation-related loans (employer loans to employees).
3. Corporation-shareholder loans (a corporation's loans to its shareholders).
4. Tax avoidance loans and other loans that significantly affect the borrower's or lender's Federal tax liability (discussed in the following paragraphs).

The effects of the first three types of loans on the borrower and lender are summarized in Concept Summary 4–2.

Tax Avoidance and Other Below-Market Loans. In addition to the three specific types of loans that are subject to the imputed interest rules, the Code includes a catchall provision for *tax avoidance loans* and other arrangements that have a significant effect on the tax liability of the borrower or lender. The Conference Report provides the following example of an arrangement that might be subject to the imputed interest rules.[72]

EXAMPLE 40

Annual dues for the Good Health Club are $400. In lieu of paying dues, a member can make a $4,000 deposit, refundable at the end of one year. The club can earn $400 interest on the deposit.

If interest were not imputed, an individual with $4,000 could, in effect, earn tax-exempt income on the deposit. That is, rather than invest the $4,000, earn $400 in interest, pay tax on the interest, and then pay $400 in dues, the individual could avoid tax on the interest by making the deposit. Thus, income and expenses are imputed as follows: interest income and nondeductible health club fees for the club member; income from fees and interest expense for the club. ■

Many commercially motivated transactions could be swept into this other below-market loans category. However, the Temporary Regulations have carved out a frequently encountered exception for customer prepayments. If the prepayments are included in the recipient's income under the recipient's method of accounting, the payments are not considered loans and, thus, are not subject to the imputed interest rules.[73]

Exceptions and Limitations. No interest is imputed on total outstanding *gift loans* of $10,000 or less between individuals, unless the loan proceeds are used to

---

[71]§ 7872(c).
[72]H. Rep. No. 98–861, 98th Cong., 2d Sess., 1984, p. 1023.

[73]Prop.Reg. § 1.7872–2(b)(1)(i).

TAX *in the News*   LOANS TO EXECUTIVES PROHIBITED

Interest-free loans have become a popular form of compensation for executives. Several examples of multimillion-dollar loans have come to light as a result of recent bankruptcies by large corporations. The board of directors often justifies the loans as necessary to enable the executive to purchase a residence or to buy stock in the company.

Loans by publicly held corporations to their executives are now generally prohibited by Federal law. The Sarbanes-Oxley Act of 2002 (Public Law No. 107–294) places a general prohibition on loans by corporations to their executives. However, an exception permits corporate loans to finance the acquisition of a personal residence for an executive.

---

purchase income-producing property.[74] This exemption eliminates from these complex provisions immaterial amounts that do not result in apparent shifts of income. However, if the proceeds of such a loan are used to purchase income-producing property, the limitations discussed in the following paragraphs apply instead.

On loans of $100,000 or less between individuals, the imputed interest cannot exceed the borrower's net investment income for the year (gross income from all investments less the related expenses).[75] As discussed above, one of the purposes of the imputed interest rules is to prevent high-income taxpayers from shifting income to relatives in a lower marginal bracket. This shifting of investment income is considered to occur only to the extent the borrower has net investment income. Thus, the income imputed to the lender is limited to the borrower's net investment income. As a further limitation, or exemption, if the borrower's net investment income for the year does not exceed $1,000, no interest is imputed on loans of $100,000 or less. However, these limitations for loans of $100,000 or less do not apply if a principal purpose of a loan is tax avoidance. In such a case, interest is imputed, and the imputed interest is not limited to the borrower's net investment income.[76]

EXAMPLE 41

Vicki made interest-free gift loans as follows:

Borrower	Amount	Borrower's Net Investment Income	Purpose
Susan	$ 8,000	$ –0–	Education
Dan	9,000	500	Purchase of stock
Bonnie	25,000	–0–	Purchase of a business
Megan	90,000	15,000	Purchase of a residence
Olaf	120,000	–0–	Purchase of a residence

Assume that tax avoidance is not a principal purpose of any of the loans. The loan to Susan is not subject to the imputed interest rules because the $10,000 exception applies. The $10,000 exception does not apply to the loan to Dan because the proceeds were used to purchase income-producing assets. However, under the $100,000 exception, the imputed interest is limited to Dan's investment income ($500). Since the $1,000 exception also applies to this loan, no interest is imputed.

No interest is imputed on the loan to Bonnie because the $100,000 exception applies. Interest is imputed on the loan to Megan based on the lesser of (1) the borrower's $15,000 net investment income or (2) the interest as calculated by applying the Federal rate to the outstanding loan. None of the exceptions apply to the loan to Olaf because the loan was for more than $100,000.

---

[74]§ 7872(c)(2).

[75]§ 7872(d).

[76]*Deficit Reduction Tax Bill of 1984: Explanation of the Senate Finance Committee* (April 2, 1984), p. 484.

CONCEPT SUMMARY 4–3

Exceptions to the Imputed Interest Rules for Below-Market Loans

Exception	Eligible Loans	Ineligible Loans and Limitations
De minimis—aggregate loans of $10,000 or less	Gift loans	Proceeds used to purchase income-producing assets.
	Employer-employee	Principal purpose is tax avoidance.
	Corporation-shareholder	Principal purpose is tax avoidance.
Aggregate loans of $100,000 or less	Between individuals	Principal purpose is tax avoidance. For all other loans, interest is imputed to the extent of the borrower's net investment income if that income exceeds $1,000.

Assume the relevant Federal rate is 10% and the loans were outstanding for the entire year. Vicki would recognize interest income, compounded semiannually, as follows:

Loan to Megan:

First 6 months (.10 × $90,000 × ½ year)	$ 4,500
Second 6 months (.10 × $94,500 × ½ year)	4,725
	$ 9,225

Loan to Olaf:

First 6 months (.10 × $120,000 × ½ year)	$ 6,000
Second 6 months (.10 × $126,000 × ½ year)	6,300
	$12,300
Total imputed interest ($9,225 + $12,300)	$21,525

As with gift loans, there is a $10,000 exemption for *compensation-related loans* and *corporation-shareholder loans*. However, the $10,000 exception does not apply if tax avoidance is one of the principal purposes of a loan.[77] This vague tax avoidance standard makes practically all compensation-related and corporation-shareholder loans suspect. Nevertheless, the $10,000 exception should apply when an employee's borrowing was necessitated by personal needs (e.g., to meet unexpected expenses) rather than tax considerations.

These exceptions to the imputed interest rules are summarized in Concept Summary 4–3.

Income from Annuities

Annuity contracts generally require the purchaser (the annuitant) to pay a fixed amount for the right to receive a future stream of payments. Typically, the issuer of the contract is an insurance company and will pay the annuitant a cash value if the annuitant cancels the contract. The insurance company invests the amounts received from the annuitant, and the income earned serves to increase the cash value of the policy. No income is recognized by the annuitant at the time the cash value of the annuity increases because the taxpayer has not actually received any income. The income is not constructively received because, generally, the taxpayer must cancel the policy to receive the increase in value (the increase in value is subject to substantial restrictions).

---

[77]§ 7872(c)(3).

EXAMPLE 42

Jean, age 50, pays $30,000 for an annuity contract that is to pay her $500 per month beginning when she reaches age 65 and continuing until her death. If Jean should cancel the policy after one year, she would receive $30,200. The $200 increase in value is not includible in Jean's gross income as long as she does not actually receive the $200. ■

The tax accounting problem associated with receiving payments under an annuity contract is one of apportioning the amounts received between recovery of capital and income.

EXAMPLE 43

In 2008, Tom purchased for $15,000 an annuity intended as a source of retirement income. In 2010, when the cash value of the annuity is $17,000, Tom collects $1,000 on the contract. Is the $1,000 gross income, recovery of capital, or a combination of recovery of capital and income? ■

The statutory solution to this problem depends upon whether the payments began before or after the annuity starting date and upon when the policy was acquired.

Collections before the Annuity Starting Date.

Generally, an annuity contract specifies a date on which monthly or annual payments will begin—the annuity starting date. Often the contract will also allow the annuitant to collect a limited amount before the starting date. The amount collected may be characterized as either an actual withdrawal of the increase in cash value or a loan on the policy. In 1982, Congress changed the rules applicable to these withdrawals and loans.

Collections (including loans) equal to or less than the post-August 13, 1982 increases in cash value must be included in gross income. Amounts received in excess of post-August 13, 1982 increases in cash value are treated as a recovery of capital until the taxpayer's cost has been entirely recovered. Additional amounts are included in gross income.[78]

The taxpayer may also be subject to a penalty on early distributions of 10 percent of the income recognized. The penalty generally applies if the amount is received before the taxpayer reaches age 59½ or is disabled.[79] The early distribution penalty is deemed necessary to prevent taxpayers from using annuities as a way of avoiding the original issue discount rules. That is, the investment in the annuity earns a return that is not taxed until it is collected under the annuity rules, whereas the interest on a certificate of deposit is taxed each year as the income accrues. Thus, the annuity offers a tax advantage (deferral of income) that Congress does not want exploited.

EXAMPLE 44

Jack, age 50, purchased an annuity policy for $30,000 in 2006. In 2008, when the cash value of the policy has increased to $33,000, Jack withdraws $4,000. He must recognize $3,000 of income ($33,000 cash value − $30,000 cost) and must pay a penalty of $300 ($3,000 × 10%). The remaining $1,000 is a recovery of capital and reduces Jack's basis in the annuity policy. ■

Collections on and after the Annuity Starting Date.

The annuitant can exclude from income (as a recovery of capital) the proportion of each payment that the investment in the contract bears to the expected return under the contract. The *exclusion amount* is calculated as follows:

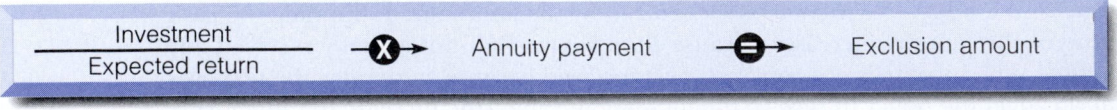

$$\frac{\text{Investment}}{\text{Expected return}} \quad \bigotimes \quad \text{Annuity payment} \quad \bigominus \quad \text{Exclusion amount}$$

---

[78]§ 72(e)(3); Reg. § 1.72–9.   [79]§ 72(q).

TABLE 4–1	Ordinary Life Annuities: One Life—Expected Return Multiples

Age	Multiple	Age	Multiple	Age	Multiple
5	76.6	42	40.6	79	10.0
6	75.6	43	39.6	80	9.5
7	74.7	44	38.7	81	8.9
8	73.7	45	37.7	82	8.4
9	72.7	46	36.8	83	7.9
10	71.7	47	35.9	84	7.4
11	70.7	48	34.9	85	6.9
12	69.7	49	34.0	86	6.5
13	68.8	50	33.1	87	6.1
14	67.8	51	32.2	88	5.7
15	66.8	52	31.3	89	5.3
16	65.8	53	30.4	90	5.0
17	64.8	54	29.5	91	4.7
18	63.9	55	28.6	92	4.4
19	62.9	56	27.7	93	4.1
20	61.9	57	26.8	94	3.9
21	60.9	58	25.9	95	3.7
22	59.9	59	25.0	96	3.4
23	59.0	60	24.2	97	3.2
24	58.0	61	23.3	98	3.0
25	57.0	62	22.5	99	2.8
26	56.0	63	21.6	100	2.7
27	55.1	64	20.8	101	2.5
28	54.1	65	20.0	102	2.3
29	53.1	66	19.2	103	2.1
30	52.2	67	18.4	104	1.9
31	51.2	68	17.6	105	1.8
32	50.2	69	16.8	106	1.6
33	49.3	70	16.0	107	1.4
34	48.3	71	15.3	108	1.3
35	47.3	72	14.6	109	1.1
36	46.4	73	13.9	110	1.0
37	45.4	74	13.2	111	.9
38	44.4	75	12.5	112	.8
39	43.5	76	11.9	113	.7
40	42.5	77	11.2	114	.6
41	41.5	78	10.6	115	.5

The *expected return* is the annual amount to be paid to the annuitant multiplied by the number of years the payments will be received. The payment period may be fixed (a *term certain*) or for the life of one or more individuals. When payments are for life, the taxpayer generally must use the annuity table published by the IRS to determine the expected return (see Table 4–1). This is an actuarial table that contains life expectancies.[80] The expected return is calculated by multiplying the appropriate multiple (life expectancy) by the annual payment.

[80]The life expectancies in Table 4–1 apply for annuity investments made on or after July 1, 1986. See *General Rules for Pensions and Annuities*, IRS Publication 939 (Rev. April 2003), p. 25. See also *Pension and Annuity Income*, IRS Publication 575 (Rev. Feb. 2006).

TABLE 4–2	Number of Anticipated Monthly Annuity Payments under the Simplified Method	

Age	Number of Anticipated Monthly Payments
55 and under	360
56–60	310
61–65	260
66–70	210
71 and over	160

EXAMPLE 45

The taxpayer, age 54, purchases an annuity from an insurance company for $90,000. She is to receive $500 per month for life. Her life expectancy (from Table 4–1) is 29.5 years from the annuity starting date. Thus, her expected return is $500 × 12 × 29.5 = $177,000, and the exclusion amount is $3,051 [($90,000 investment/$177,000 expected return) × $6,000 annual payment]. The $3,051 is a nontaxable return of capital, and $2,949 is included in gross income. ■

The *exclusion ratio* (investment ÷ expected return) applies until the annuitant has recovered his or her investment in the contract. Once the investment is recovered, the entire amount of subsequent payments is taxable. If the annuitant dies before recovering the investment, the unrecovered cost (adjusted basis) is deductible in the year the payments cease (usually the year of death).[81]

EXAMPLE 46

Assume the taxpayer in Example 45 receives annuity payments for 30.5 years (366 months). For the last 12 months [366 − (12 × 29.5) = 12], the taxpayer will include $500 each month in gross income. If instead the taxpayer dies after 36 months, she is eligible for an $80,847 deduction on her final tax return.

Cost of the contract	$90,000
Cost previously recovered $90,000/$177,000 × 36($500) =	(9,153)
Deduction	$80,847

■

Simplified Method for Annuity Distributions from Qualified Retirement Plans. A simplified method is required for allocating basis to the annuity payments received under a qualified retirement plan. The portion of each annuity payment that is excluded as a return of capital is the employee's investment in the contract divided by the number of anticipated monthly payments determined in accordance with Table 4–2.[82]

EXAMPLE 47

Andrea, age 62, receives an annuity distribution of $500 per month for life from her qualified retirement plan beginning in January 2008. Her investment in the contract is $100,100. The excludible amount of each payment is $385 ($100,100 investment/260 monthly payments). Thus, $115 ($500 − $385) of each annuity payment is included in Andrea's gross income. ■

The rules for annuity payments received after the basis has been recovered by the annuitant and for the annuitant who dies before the basis is recovered are the same as under the exclusion ratio method discussed earlier.

[81]§ 72(b).   [82]§ 72(d).

Prizes and Awards

The fair market value of prizes and awards (other than scholarships exempted under § 117, to be discussed subsequently) must be included in gross income.[83] Therefore, TV giveaway prizes, magazine publisher prizes, door prizes, and awards from an employer to an employee in recognition of performance are fully taxable to the recipient.

A narrow exception permits a prize or award to be excluded from gross income if *all* of the following requirements are satisfied:

- The prize or award is received in recognition of religious, charitable, scientific, educational, artistic, literary, or civic achievement (e.g., Nobel Prize, Pulitzer Prize, faculty teaching award).
- The recipient transfers the prize or award to a qualified governmental unit or nonprofit organization.
- The recipient was selected without any action on his or her part to enter the contest or proceeding.
- The recipient is not required to render substantial future services as a condition for receiving the prize or award.[84]

Because the transfer of the property to a qualified governmental unit or nonprofit organization ordinarily would be a charitable contribution (an itemized deduction as presented in Chapter 10), the exclusion produces beneficial tax consequences in the following situations:

- The taxpayer does not itemize deductions and thus would receive no tax benefit from the charitable contribution.
- The taxpayer's charitable contributions exceed the annual statutory ceiling on the deduction.
- Including the prize or award in gross income would reduce the amount of deductions the taxpayer otherwise would qualify for because of gross income limitations (e.g., the gross income test for a dependency exemption, the adjusted gross income limitation in calculating the medical expense deduction).

Another exception is provided for certain *employee achievement awards* in the form of tangible personal property (e.g., a gold watch). The awards must be made in recognition of length of service or safety achievement. Generally, the ceiling on the excludible amount for an employee is $400 per taxable year. However, if the award is a qualified plan award, the ceiling on the exclusion is $1,600 per taxable year.[85]

Group Term Life Insurance

For many years, the IRS did not attempt to tax the value of life insurance protection provided to an employee by the employer. Some companies took undue advantage of the exclusion by providing large amounts of insurance protection for executives. Therefore, Congress enacted § 79, which created a limited exclusion for **group term life insurance**. The premiums on the first $50,000 of group term life insurance protection are excludible from the employee's gross income.

The benefits of this exclusion are available only to employees. Proprietors and partners are not considered employees. The Regulations generally require broadscale coverage of employees to satisfy the *group* requirement (e.g., shareholder-employees would not constitute a qualified group). The exclusion applies only to term insurance (protection for a period of time but with no cash surrender value)

---

[83]§ 74.
[84]§ 74(b).

[85]§§ 74(c) and 274(j).

TABLE 4–3	Uniform Premiums for $1,000 of Group Term Life Insurance Protection

Attained Age on Last Day of Employee's Tax Year	Cost per $1,000 of Protection for One-Month Period*
Under 25	$ .05
25–29	.06
30–34	.08
35–39	.09
40–44	.10
45–49	.15
50–54	.23
55–59	.43
60–64	.66
65–69	1.27
70 and above	2.06

*Reg. § 1.79–3, effective for coverage after June 30, 1999.

and not to ordinary life insurance (lifetime protection plus a cash surrender value that can be drawn upon before death).

As mentioned, the exclusion applies to the first $50,000 of group term life insurance protection. For each $1,000 of coverage in excess of $50,000, the employee must include the amounts indicated in Table 4–3 in gross income.[86]

EXAMPLE 48

Finch Corporation has a group term life insurance policy with coverage equal to the employee's annual salary. Keith, age 52, is president of the corporation and receives an annual salary of $75,000. Keith must include $69 in gross income from the insurance protection for the year.

$$\frac{\$75,000 - \$50,000}{\$1,000} \times .23 \times 12 \, \text{months} = \$69$$

■

Generally, the amount that must be included in gross income, computed from Table 4–3, is much less than the price an individual would pay an insurance company for the same amount of protection. Thus, even the excess coverage provides some tax-favored income for employees when group term life insurance coverage in excess of $50,000 is desirable.

If the plan discriminates in favor of certain key employees (e.g., officers), the key employees are not eligible for the exclusion. In such a case, the key employees must include in gross income the *greater* of actual premiums paid by the employer or the amount calculated from the Uniform Premiums in Table 4–3. The other employees are still eligible for the $50,000 exclusion and continue to use the Uniform Premiums table to compute the income from excess insurance protection.[87]

Unemployment Compensation

The unemployment compensation program is sponsored and operated by the states and Federal government to provide a source of income for people who have been employed and are temporarily (hopefully) out of work. In a series of rulings over a period of 40 years, the IRS exempted unemployment benefits from tax. These payments were considered social benefit programs for the promotion of the

[86]Reg. § 1.79–3(d)(2).   [87]§ 79(d).

TAX *in the News* — **A TAXPAYER LEARNS ABOUT THE "QUIRKY" SOCIAL SECURITY BENEFITS TAXATION FORMULA**

The "base amount" used in the formula to compute taxable Social Security benefits generally enables low-income individuals to exclude all Social Security benefits received from gross income. But in a Tax Court case [*Thomas W. McAdams*, 118 T.C. 373 (2002)], a taxpayer discovered that the base amount can become zero for married couples who file separate returns. If a married couple file a joint return, the base amount is $32,000 (and the adjusted base amount is $44,000).

The law provides, however, that if a married couple live together at any time during the tax year and file separate returns, the base amount (and adjusted base amount) is zero. In the Tax Court case, the couple lived apart for 11 months of the year, but lived in separate portions of the same house for the remaining month. One month under the same roof with his wife caused part of the taxpayer's $12,000 in Social Security benefits to be included in his gross income.

---

general welfare. After experiencing dissatisfaction with the IRS's treatment of unemployment compensation, Congress amended the Code to provide that the benefits are taxable.[88]

Social Security Benefits

If a taxpayer's income exceeds a specified base amount, as much as 85 percent of Social Security retirement benefits must be included in gross income. The taxable amount of benefits is determined through the application of one of two formulas that utilize a unique measure of income—*modified adjusted gross income* (*MAGI*).[89] MAGI is, generally, the taxpayer's adjusted gross income from all sources (other than Social Security) plus the foreign earned income exclusion and any tax-exempt interest income.

In the formulas, two sets of base amounts are established. The first set is as follows:

- $32,000 for married taxpayers who file a joint return.
- $0 for married taxpayers who do not live apart for the entire year but file separate returns.
- $25,000 for all other taxpayers.

The second set of base amounts is as follows:

- $44,000 for married taxpayers who file a joint return.
- $0 for married taxpayers who do not live apart for the entire year but file separate returns.
- $34,000 for all other taxpayers.

If MAGI plus one-half of Social Security benefits exceeds the first set of base amounts, but not the second set, the taxable amount of Social Security benefits is the *lesser* of the following:

- .50(Social Security benefits).
- .50[MAGI + .50(Social Security benefits) − first base amount].

EXAMPLE 49

A married couple with adjusted gross income of $30,000, no tax-exempt interest, and $11,000 of Social Security benefits who file jointly must include $1,750 of the benefits in gross income. This works out as the lesser of the following:

1. .50($11,000) = $5,500.
2. .50[$30,000 + .50($11,000) − $32,000] = .50($3,500) = $1,750.

---

[88]§ 85.

[89]§ 86. The rationale for taxing 85% of the Social Security benefits is as follows: For the average Social Security recipient, 15% of the amount received is a re-

covery of amounts that the individual paid into the program, and the remainder of the benefits is financed by the employer's contribution and interest earned by the Social Security fund.

If instead the couple had adjusted gross income of $15,000 and their Social Security benefits totaled $5,000, none of the benefits would be taxable, since .50[$15,000 + .50($5,000) − $32,000] is not a positive number. ■

If MAGI plus one-half of Social Security benefits exceeds the second set of base amounts, the taxable amount of Social Security benefits is the *lesser* of 1 or 2 below:

1. .85 (Social Security benefits).
2. Sum of:
   a. .85 [MAGI + .50(Social Security benefits) − second base amount], and
   b. Lesser of:
      - Amount included through application of the first formula.
      - $4,500 ($6,000 for married filing jointly).

EXAMPLE 50

A married couple who file jointly have adjusted gross income of $72,000, no tax-exempt interest, and $12,000 of Social Security benefits. Their includible Social Security benefits will be $10,200.

Include the lesser of the following:

1. .85($12,000) = $10,200.
2. Sum of:
   a. .85[$72,000 + .50($12,000) − $44,000] = $28,900, and
   b. Lesser of:
      - Amount calculated by the first formula, which is the lesser of:
        - .50($12,000) = $6,000.
        - .50[$72,000 + .50($12,000) − $32,000] = $23,000.
      - $6,000.

The sum equals $34,900 ($28,900 + $6,000). Since 85% of the Social Security benefits received is less than this amount, $10,200 is included in the couple's gross income. ■

LO.5

Identify tax planning strategies for minimizing gross income.

The materials in this chapter have focused on the following questions:

- What is income?
- When is the income recognized?
- Who is the taxpayer?

TAX PLANNING *Considerations*

Planning strategies suggested by these materials include the following:

- Maximize economic benefits that are not included in gross income.
- Defer the recognition of income.
- Shift income to taxpayers who are in a lower marginal tax bracket.

Some specific techniques for accomplishing these strategies are discussed in the following paragraphs.

Nontaxable Economic Benefits

Home ownership is the prime example of economic income from capital that is not subject to tax. If the taxpayer uses his or her capital to purchase investments, but pays rent on a personal residence, the taxpayer would pay the rent from after-tax income. However, if the taxpayer purchases a personal residence instead of the investments, he or she would give up gross income from the forgone investments in exchange for the rent savings. The savings in rent enjoyed as a result of owning the home are not subject to tax. Thus, the homeowner will have substituted nontaxable for taxable income.

Tax Deferral

General. Since deferred taxes are tantamount to interest-free loans from the government, the deferral of taxes is a worthy goal of the tax planner. However, the tax planner must also consider the tax rates for the years the income is shifted from and to. For example, a one-year deferral of income from a year in which the taxpayer's tax rate was 28 percent to a year in which the tax rate will be 35 percent would not be advisable if the taxpayer expects to earn less than a 7 percent after-tax return on the deferred tax dollars.

The taxpayer can often defer the recognition of income from appreciated property by postponing the event triggering realization (the final closing on a sale or exchange of property). If the taxpayer needs cash, obtaining a loan by using the appreciated property as collateral may be the least costly alternative. When the taxpayer anticipates reinvesting the proceeds, a sale may be inadvisable.

EXAMPLE 51

Ira owns 100 shares of Pigeon Company common stock with a cost of $20,000 and a fair market value of $50,000. Although the stock's value has increased substantially in the past three years, Ira thinks the growth days are over. If he sells the Pigeon stock, Ira will invest the proceeds from the sale in other common stock. Assuming Ira's marginal tax rate on the sale is 15%, he will have only $45,500 [$50,000 − .15($50,000 − $20,000)] to reinvest. The alternative investment must substantially outperform Pigeon in the future in order for the sale to be beneficial. ■

Selection of Investments. Because no tax is due until a gain has been recognized, the law favors investments that yield appreciation rather than annual income.

EXAMPLE 52

Vera can buy a corporate bond or an acre of land for $10,000. The bond pays $1,000 of interest (10%) each year, and Vera expects the land to increase in value 10% each year for the next 10 years. She is in the 40% (combined Federal and state) tax bracket for ordinary income and 26% for qualifying capital gains. Assuming the bond would mature or the land would be sold in 10 years and Vera would reinvest the interest at a 10% before-tax return, she would accumulate the following amount at the end of 10 years.

		Bond	Land
Original investment		$10,000	$10,000
Annual income	$ 1,000		
Less tax	(400)		
	$ 600		
Compound amount reinvested for			
10 years at 6% after-tax	×13.18	7,908	
		$17,908	
Compound amount, 10 years at 10%			× 2.59
			$25,900
Less tax on sale:			
26%($25,900 − $10,000)			(4,134)
			$21,766

Therefore, the value of the deferral that results from investing in the land rather than in the bond is $3,858 ($21,766 − $17,908). ■

Series EE bonds can also be purchased for long-term deferrals of income. In situations where the taxpayer's goal is merely to shift income one year into the future, bank certificates of deposit are useful tools. If the maturity period is one year or less, all interest is reported in the year of maturity. Time certificates are especially useful for a taxpayer who realizes an unusually large gain from the sale of property in one year (and thus is in a high tax bracket) but expects his or her gross income to be less the following year.

Cash Basis. The timing of income from services can often be controlled through the use of the cash method of accounting. Although taxpayers are somewhat constrained by the constructive receipt doctrine (they cannot turn their backs on income), seldom will customers and clients offer to pay before they are asked. The usual lag between billings and collections (e.g., December's billings collected in January) will result in a continuous deferring of some income until the last year of operations. A salaried individual approaching retirement may contract with the employer before the services are rendered to receive a portion of compensation in the lower tax bracket retirement years.

Prepaid Income. For the accrual basis taxpayer who receives advance payments from customers, the transactions should be structured to avoid payment of tax on income before the time the income is actually earned. Revenue Procedure 2004–34 provides the guidelines for deferring the tax on prepayments for services, and Regulation § 1.451–5 provides the guidelines for deferrals on sales of goods. In addition, both cash and accrual basis taxpayers can sometimes defer income by stipulating that the payments are deposits rather than prepaid income. For example, a landlord should require an equivalent damage deposit rather than prepayment of the last month's rent under the lease.

Shifting Income to Relatives

The tax liability of a family can be minimized by shifting income from higher- to lower-bracket family members. This can be accomplished through gifts of income-producing property. Furthermore, in many cases, income can be shifted with no negative effect on the family's investment plans.

E X A M P L E 53	Adam, who is in the 28% tax bracket, would like to save for his children's education. All of the children are under 19 years of age and are dependents of Adam. Adam could transfer income-producing properties to the children, and the children could each receive up to $900 of income each year (refer to Chapter 3) with no tax liability. The next $900 would be taxed at the child's tax rate. After a child has more than $1,800 income, there is no tax advantage to shifting more income to the child (because the income will be taxed at the parents' rate) until the child is 19 years old (or age 24 if a full-time student), when all income will be taxed according to the child's tax rate. ∎

The Uniform Gifts to Minors Act, a model law adopted by all states (but with some variations among the states), facilitates income shifting. Under the Act, a gift of intangibles (e.g., bank accounts, stocks, bonds, life insurance contracts) can be made to a minor but with an adult serving as custodian. Usually, a parent who makes the gift is also named as custodian. The state laws allow the custodian to sell or redeem and reinvest the principal and to accumulate or distribute the income, practically at the custodian's discretion provided there is no commingling of the child's income with the parent's property. Thus, the parent can give appreciated securities to the child, and the donor custodian can then sell the securities and reinvest the proceeds, thereby shifting both the gain and the annual income to the child. Such planning is limited by the tax liability calculation provision for a child under the age of 19 (or age 24 if a full-time student) (refer to Chapter 3).

U.S. government bonds (Series EE) can be purchased by parents for their children. When this is done, the children generally should file a return and elect to report the income on the accrual basis.

E X A M P L E 54	Abby pays $7,500 for Series EE bonds in 2008 and immediately gives them to Wade (her son), who will enter college the year of original maturity of the bonds. The bonds have a maturity value of $10,000. Wade elects to report the annual increment in redemption

value as income for each year the bonds are held. The first year the increase is $250, and Wade includes that amount in his gross income. If Wade has no other income, no tax will be due on the $250 bond interest, since such an amount will be more than offset by his available standard deduction. The following year, the increment is $260, and Wade includes this amount in income. Thus, over the life of the bonds, Wade will include $2,500 in income ($10,000 − $7,500), none of which will result in a tax liability, assuming he has no other income. However, if the election had not been made, Wade would be required to include $2,500 in income on the bonds in the year of original maturity, if they were redeemed as planned. This amount of income might result in a tax liability. ■

In some cases, it may be advantageous for the child not to make the accrual election. For example, a child under age 19 (or age 24 if a full-time student) with investment income of more than $1,800 each year and parents in the 25, 28, 33, or 35 percent tax bracket would probably benefit from deferring the tax on the savings bond interest. The child would also benefit from the use of the usually lower tax rate (rather than subjecting the income to the parents' tax rate) if the bonds mature after the child is age 19 or older (or age 24 or older if a full-time student).

Accounting for Community Property

The classification of income as community or separate property becomes important when either of two events occurs:

- Husband and wife, married taxpayers, file separate income tax returns for the year.
- Husband and wife obtain a divorce and therefore have to file separate returns for the year (refer to Chapter 3).

For planning purposes, it behooves married persons to keep track of the source of income (community or separate). To be in a position to do this effectively when income-producing assets are involved, it may be necessary to distinguish between separate and community property.[90]

Alimony

The person making the alimony payments favors a divorce settlement that includes a provision for deductible alimony payments. On the other hand, the recipient prefers that the payments do not qualify as alimony. If the payor is in a higher tax bracket than the recipient, both parties may benefit by increasing the payments and structuring them so that they qualify as alimony.

EXAMPLE 55

Carl and Polly are negotiating a divorce settlement. Carl has offered to pay Polly $10,000 each year for 10 years, but payments would cease upon Polly's death. Polly is willing to accept the offer, if the agreement will specify that the cash payments are not alimony. Carl is in the 35% tax bracket, and Polly's marginal rate is 15%.

If Carl and Polly agree that Carl will pay Polly $12,000 of alimony each year, both will have improved after-tax cash flows.

---

[90]Being able to distinguish between separate and community property is crucial to the determination of a property settlement incident to a divorce. It also is vital in the estate tax area (refer to Chapter 1) since the surviving wife's or husband's share of the community property is not included in the gross estate of the deceased spouse.

	Annual Cash Flows	
	Carl	Polly
Nonalimony payments	($10,000)	$10,000
Alimony payments	($12,000)	$12,000
Tax effects		
.35 ($12,000)	4,200	
.15 ($12,000)		(1,800)
After-tax cash flows	($ 7,800)	$10,200
Benefit of alimony option	$ 2,200	$ 200

Both parties benefit at the government's expense if the $12,000 alimony option is used. ■

KEY TERMS

Accounting income, 4–4

Accounting method, 4–7

Accrual method, 4–9

Alimony and separate maintenance payments, 4–20

Alimony recapture, 4–21

Annuity, 4–27

Assignment of income, 4–14

Cash receipts method, 4–8

Claim of right doctrine, 4–9

Community property, 4–18

Constructive receipt, 4–10

Economic income, 4–3

Fruit and tree metaphor, 4–14

Gross income, 4–2

Group term life insurance, 4–31

Hybrid method, 4–10

Imputed interest, 4–24

Income, 4–3

Original issue discount, 4–11

Partnership, 4–17

Recovery of capital doctrine, 4–6

S corporation, 4–18

Taxable year, 4–7

PROBLEM MATERIALS

DISCUSSION QUESTIONS

1. Financial accounting rules used to measure income and expenses are sometimes based on the principle of conservatism. Should the conservatism principle be applicable in measuring taxable income?

2. In each of the following, determine the taxpayer's "income" for the current year as computed by an economist and as computed for tax purposes. Explain any differences.
   a. A cash basis taxpayer overcharged a customer by billing her twice for the same item in 2007. The taxpayer notified the customer of the mistake in December 2007 and refunded the overcharge in January 2008.
   b. In the previous year, the taxpayer purchased stock for $4,000. By the end of the year, the stock had declined in value to $3,000. In the current year, the taxpayer sold the stock for $6,500.
   c. The taxpayer, a carpenter, purchased a house for investment for $100,000. He renovated the house. The taxpayer spent $14,000 on materials, and he estimates that the value of his time spent on the work (what he would have charged a customer for the same work) was $20,000. He sold the property the following year for $140,000.
   d. The sole shareholder in a corporation purchased property from the corporation for $10,000. The fair market value of the property was $15,000.

Issue ID

3. Charley visits Reno, Nevada, once each year to gamble. This year his gambling loss was $15,000. He commented to you, "At least I didn't have to pay for my airfare and hotel

room. The casino paid that because I am such a good customer. That was worth at least $2,500." What are the relevant tax issues for Charley?

4. Reno paid $2,000 for an automobile that needed substantial repairs. He paid $1,400 for parts and worked nights and weekends to restore the car. Reno used the car as his personal automobile after it was restored. Reno's neighbor, Tom, worked overtime to obtain the funds to purchase a car similar to Reno's for $7,000. Tom also used his car for personal purposes. Reno and Tom are in the 25% marginal tax bracket. Who did the tax law a favor—Reno or Tom?

5. Cecil buys wrecked cars and stores them on his property. Recently, he purchased a 1990 Ford Taurus for $250. If he can sell all of the usable parts, his total proceeds from the Taurus would be over $2,000. As of the end of the year, he has sold only the radio for $50, and he does not know how many, if any, of the remaining parts will ever be sold. What are Cecil's income recognition issues?

Issue ID

6. On December 31, 2008, an employee received a $6,000 check from her employer's client. The check was payable to the employer, but the employee did not receive it until after the bank had closed. The employee did not remit the funds to the employer until January 2, 2009. When is the cash basis employer required to include the $6,000 in gross income?

7. Jared, a self-employed insect exterminator, uses the cash method of accounting to report his income. In December 2008, Jared received a check for $400 from a client. Jared deposited the check near the end of December. In early January 2009, the bank notified him that the check did not clear because of insufficient funds in the customer's account. The bank sent the check through a second time, and it cleared in January 2009. Jared computes his income using his deposit records. Therefore, he included the $400 in his 2008 gross income.
   a. In what year should Jared report the $400 of income?
   b. Why does it matter to Jared whether he reports the income in 2008 or 2009, as long as he actually reports it?

8. In 2008, Albert found dinosaur bones on a tract of land that he had owned for several years. When Albert bought the property, he was unaware that the bones were there. An appraiser told him the bones were worth $25,000. In 2009, Albert sold the bones to a museum for $26,000.
   a. What is Albert's gross income in 2008 from the discovery of the bones?
   b. What is Albert's gross income in 2009 from the sale of the bones?

9. Allyson, a cash basis taxpayer, pays $889 for a 4% certificate of deposit (CD) that is to pay her $1,000 at maturity. She purchases the certificate on July 1, 2008, and it will mature on June 30, 2011. Allyson holds the CD until maturity.
   a. Under the original issue discount (OID) rules, for which years does the CD affect Allyson's gross income?
   b. Do you think that the OID rules were enacted for equitable reasons, out of concern for the taxpayer's burden in complying with the law, or for other reasons?

10. A Series EE U.S. government savings bond accrues 3.5% interest each year. The bond matures in three years, at which time the principal and interest will be paid. The bank will pay the taxpayer at a 3.5% interest rate each year if he agrees to leave money on deposit for three years. What tax advantage does the Series EE bond offer that is not available with the bank deposit?

11. Parchment, Inc., is an accrual basis taxpayer. Under its present terms of sale, Parchment's customers have 30 days to return the goods. Payment is not due until after the customer has had possession of the goods for 30 days. Parchment is considering changing the sales contracts so that the customers can simply try the product for 30 days before purchasing the goods. If Parchment changes its terms of sale, how will this affect when the company recognizes gross income?

12. Rex paid $4,000 for an automobile that needed substantial repairs. He worked nights and weekends to restore the car and spent $1,200 on parts for it. He knows he can sell the car for $9,000. His daughter's college tuition is due in a few days. Would it matter,

after taxes, whether Rex sells the car and pays the tuition, or whether he gives the car to his daughter and she sells it for $9,000 and pays her tuition?

13. Sarah, a cash basis taxpayer, sued her former employer for wage discrimination. Her attorney agreed to pursue the case on a contingent fee basis—the attorney would receive one-third of any settlement or court award. The parties reached a settlement, and the attorney for Sarah's former employer wrote a check payable to Sarah for $200,000 and a check payable to her attorney for $100,000. Sarah reasons that she and the attorney were partners in the lawsuit who shared profits two-thirds and one-third. Therefore, she includes $200,000 in her gross income. Is Sarah's analysis correct? Explain.

14. Tom is a partner with a 50% interest in the partnership profits. In 2008, the partnership generated $300,000 of taxable income, but Tom could not withdraw any of the funds for this year because the partnership did not have any excess cash to distribute. In 2009, the partnership had $800,000 of taxable income, and Tom was able to withdraw $550,000. What is Tom's gross income from the partnership in 2008 and 2009?

Issue ID

15. Mike and Debbie were residents of California. In 2008, Debbie left Mike, and he has been unable to find her even though he hired a private investigator to do so. Mike and Debbie are still married at year-end. Both Debbie and Mike were employed, and each had substantial investments. They did not have any children. How will Debbie's absence complicate Mike's 2008 income tax return?

16. What is the purpose of the alimony recapture rules?

Decision Making

17. Sam and Jean are negotiating their divorce agreement, which requires the division of their jointly owned property. Sam has proposed that he receive the couple's house (basis of $60,000 and fair market value of $100,000) while Jean would receive (a) securities (basis of $115,000 and fair market value of $100,000) or (b) five annual payments of $23,739 each, which is equivalent to a $100,000 loan at 6% interest. Jean will probably sell the securities if she receives them. Jean has too many unhappy memories about the house and does not want to live in it or own it. Which option should she accept?

Issue ID

18. William and Abigail, who live in San Francisco, have been experiencing problems with their marriage. They have a three-year-old daughter, April, who stays with William's parents during the day since both William and Abigail are employed. Abigail worked to support William while he attended medical school, and now she has been accepted by a medical school in Mexico. Abigail has decided to divorce William and attend medical school. April will stay in San Francisco because of her strong attachment to her grandparents and because they can provide her with excellent day care. Abigail knows that William will expect her to contribute to the cost of raising April. Abigail also feels that, to finance her education, she must receive cash for her share of the property they accumulated during their marriage. In addition, she feels she should receive some reimbursement for her contribution to William's support while he was in medical school. She expects the divorce proceedings will take several months. Identify the relevant tax issues for Abigail.

Decision Making

19. David and Mary are planning to divorce. David has offered to pay Mary $12,000 each year for 10 years, until their daughter reaches age 21, or to transfer to her common stock he owns with a fair market value of $100,000 in satisfaction of Mary's share of the marital property. What factors should Mary and David consider in deciding between these two options?

20. In the case of a below-market loan between relatives, the tax law requires one party to recognize interest income and the other member of the family to recognize interest expense; thus, the total taxable income of the two family members does not change as a result of the loan. Why does the tax law require this treatment?

21. Rose Corporation made a $1 million interest-free loan to its new chief executive officer on July 1, 2008, so that he could acquire a personal residence. The Federal rate is 6%. What are the tax consequences of the loan to the CEO and to Rose?

Issue ID

22. Brad is the president of the Yellow Corporation. He and other members of his family control the corporation. Brad has a temporary need for $50,000, and the corporation has excess cash. He could borrow the money from a bank at 9%, and Yellow is earning

6% on its temporary investments. Yellow has made loans to other employees on several occasions. Therefore, Brad is considering borrowing $50,000 from the corporation. He will repay the loan principal in two years plus interest at 5%. Identify the relevant tax issues for Brad and the Yellow Corporation.

23. When Betty was 67 years old, she purchased an annuity contract for $84,000. The contract was to pay her $8,000 per year over her remaining life. How much of the annuity payments that she collects in the twentieth year must Betty include in gross income?

24. Given the broad concept of gross income contained in the Internal Revenue Code, does § 79 applicable to group term life insurance assure that some premiums can be excluded from gross income, or does it assure that some of the premiums in certain circumstances will be included in gross income?

25. Evelyn is age 66 and unmarried. She receives $14,000 a year in Social Security benefits and $16,000 from a taxable pension. She is in the 15% marginal tax bracket on her Federal income tax return. She claims the standard deduction. She is considering selling stock she has held for more than one year. Her cost of the stock is $5,000, and its fair market value is $13,000. She has no other gains or losses for the year. She has asked you to estimate the tax consequences of selling the stock.

Issue ID

PROBLEMS

26. Determine the taxpayer's current-year (1) economic income and (2) gross income for tax purposes from the following events:
    a. An executive was paid $1 million to terminate her long-term employment contract.
    b. A high school student received $800 for babysitting.
    c. The taxpayer borrowed $10,000 to purchase securities, which cost $10,000 on December 31, 2008. In 2008, he sold the securities for $12,000, but he did not repay the loan.
    d. The taxpayer owned land that increased in value by $200,000 when a national retailer announced plans to build a store on the adjoining property.
    e. The taxpayer's employer allowed the employee to use the company automobile for her vacation. The rental value of the automobile for the vacation period was $1,500.
    f. The taxpayer raised vegetables for use by his family. He spent $800 raising vegetables that would have sold for $2,000.

27. Amos recently completed medical school and is beginning his medical practice. Most of his patients are covered by health insurance with a co-pay requirement (e.g., the patient pays $10, and the insurance company is billed for the remainder). It takes approximately two months to collect from the health insurance plan. What advice can you provide Amos regarding the selection of a tax accounting method?

Issue ID

28. A taxpayer is considering three alternative investments of $10,000. Assume the taxpayer is in the 28% marginal tax bracket for ordinary income and 15% for qualifying capital gains and dividends in all tax years. The selected investment will be liquidated at the end of five years. The alternatives are:

Decision Making

- A taxable corporate bond yielding 6% before tax, and the interest can be reinvested at 6% before tax.
- A Series EE bond that will have a maturity value of $13,070 (a 5.5% before-tax rate of return).
- Land that will increase in value.

The gain on the land will be classified and taxed as a long-term capital gain. The income from the bonds is taxed as ordinary income. How much must the land increase in value to yield a greater after-tax return than either of the bonds?

Given: Compound amount of $1 and compound value of annuity payments at the end of five years:

Interest Rate	$1 Compounded for 5 Years	$1 Annuity Compounded for 5 Years
6%	$1.34	$5.64
5.50%	1.31	5.58
4.32%	1.24	5.45

29. Determine the taxpayer's gross income for tax purposes in each of the following situations:

    a. Olga, a cash basis taxpayer, sold a corporate bond with accrued interest of $300 for $10,800. Olga's cost of the bond was $10,000.

    b. Olga needed $10,000 to make a down payment on her house. She instructed her broker to sell some stock to raise the $10,000. Olga's cost of the stock was $3,000. Based on her broker's advice, instead of selling the stock, she borrowed the $10,000 using the stock as collateral for the debt.

    c. Olga owned a vacant lot that was zoned for residential housing. She spent $900 in attorney fees to get the property rezoned as commercial. The property's value increased by $10,000 as a result of the rezoning.

30. Determine Amos Seagull's gross income in each of the following cases:

    a. In the current year, Seagull Corporation purchased an automobile for $25,000. The company was to receive a $1,500 rebate from the manufacturer. However, the corporation directed that the rebate be paid to Amos, the corporation's sole shareholder.

    b. Amos sold his corporation. In addition to the selling price of the stock, he received $50,000 for a covenant not to compete—an agreement that he will not compete with his former business for five years.

    c. Amos and his neighbor got into an argument over Amos's dog. The neighbor built a fence to keep the dog out of his yard. The fence added $1,500 to the value of Amos's property.

31. Al is an attorney who conducts his practice as a sole proprietor. During 2008, he received cash of $150,000 for legal services. Of the amount collected, $25,000 was for services provided in 2007. At the end of 2008, Al had accounts receivable of $60,000, all for services rendered in 2008. At the end of the year, Al received $8,000 as a deposit on property a client was in the process of selling. Compute Al's gross income for 2008:

Decision Making

    a. Using the cash basis of accounting.

    b. Using the accrual basis of accounting.

    c. Advise Al on which method of accounting he should use.

32. Selma operates a contractor's supply store. She maintains her books using the cash method. At the end of the year, her accountant computes her accrual basis income that is used on her tax return. For 2008, Selma had cash receipts of $1.5 million, which included $200,000 collected on accounts receivable from 2007 sales. It also included the proceeds of a $100,000 bank loan. At the end of 2008, she had $400,000 in accounts receivable from customers, all from 2008 sales.

    a. Compute Selma's accrual basis gross receipts for 2008.

    b. Selma paid cash for all of the purchases. The total amount paid for merchandise in 2008 was $1.2 million. At the end of 2007, she had merchandise on hand with a cost of $100,000. At end of 2008, the cost of merchandise on hand was $300,000. Compute Selma's gross income from merchandise sales for 2008.

33. Your client is a new partnership, Aspen Associates, which is an engineering consulting firm. Generally, Aspen bills clients for services at the end of each month. Client billings are about $50,000 each month. On average, it takes 45 days to collect the receivables. Aspen's expenses are primarily for salary and rent. Salaries are paid on the last day of each month, and rent is paid on the first day of each month. The partnership has a line of credit with a bank, which requires monthly financial statements. These must be prepared using the accrual method. Aspen's managing partner, Amanda Sims, has suggested that the firm should also use the accrual method for tax purposes and thus reduce accounting fees by $600. Assume the partners are in the 35% (combined Federal and state) marginal tax bracket. Write a letter to your client explaining why you believe it would be worthwhile for Aspen to file its tax return on the cash basis even though its

Decision Making

Communications

financial statements are prepared on the accrual basis. Aspen's address is 100 James Tower, Denver, CO 80208.

34. Color Paint Shop, Inc. (459 Ellis Avenue, Harrisburg, PA 17111), is an accrual basis taxpayer that paints automobiles. During the year, the company painted Samuel's car and was to receive a $1,000 payment from his insurance company. Samuel was not satisfied with the work, however, and the insurance company refused to pay. In December 2008, Color and Samuel agreed that Color would receive $800 for the work, subject to final approval by the insurance company. In the past, Color had come to terms with customers only to have the insurance company negotiate an even lesser amount. In May 2009, the insurance company reviewed the claim and paid the $800 to Color. An IRS agent thinks that Color, as an accrual basis taxpayer, should report $1,000 of income in 2008, when the work was done, and then deduct a $200 loss in 2009. Prepare a memo to Susan Apple, a tax partner for whom you are working, with the recommended treatment for the disputed income.

Communications

35. Determine the effects of the following on a cash basis taxpayer's gross income for 2008 and 2009.
    a. On the morning of December 31, 2008, the taxpayer received an $800 check from a customer. The taxpayer did not cash the check until January 3, 2009.
    b. The same as part (a), except the check was not received until after the bank had closed on December 31, 2008.
    c. The same as part (a), except the customer asked the taxpayer not to cash the check until January 3, 2009, after the customer's salary check could be deposited.

36. Morris is not one to take a lot of risks. All of his investments are in Series EE U.S. government savings bonds and bank CDs. Determine the tax consequences from his investments for 2008.
    a. On June 30, 2008, he cashed in Series EE bonds that he had purchased in 1998. His cost of the bonds was $6,439, and the maturity value was $10,000. This is an effective before-tax yield of 4.5% per year. Morris did not elect to take the annual increments in value into income each year.
    b. On September 30, 2008, Morris redeemed a two-year CD, interest rate of 4.5%, that he had purchased from the local bank on October 1, 2006. He paid $9,157 for the CD and received $10,000 at maturity. He immediately invested the $10,000 in a one-year CD, interest rate of 5%, with a maturity value of $10,500.

37. Swan Appliance Company, an accrual basis taxpayer, sells home appliances and service contracts. Determine the effect of each of the following transactions on the company's 2008 gross income assuming that the company uses any available options to defer its taxes.
    a. In December 2007, the company received a $1,200 advance payment from a customer for an appliance that Swan special ordered from the manufacturer. The appliance did not arrive from the manufacturer until January 2008, and Swan immediately delivered it to the customer. The sale was reported in 2008 for financial accounting purposes.
    b. In June 2008, the company sold a 12-month service contract for $240. The company also sold a 24-month service contract for $480 in December 2008.
    c. On December 31, 2008, the company sold an appliance for $1,200. The company received $500 cash and a note from the customer for $700 and $260 interest, to be paid at the rate of $40 a month for 24 months. Because of the customer's poor credit record, the fair market value of the note was only $600. The cost of the appliance was $750.

38. Freda is a cash basis taxpayer. In 2008, she negotiated her salary for 2009. Her employer offered to pay her $20,000 each month—a total of $240,000 for the year. Freda countered that she would accept $20,000 each month for the first nine months of the year and the remaining $60,000 in January 2010. The employer accepted Freda's terms for 2009 and 2010.
    a. Did Freda actually or constructively receive $240,000 in 2009?
    b. What could explain Freda's willingness to spread her salary over a longer period of time?

39. The Bonhaus Apartments is a new development and is in the process of structuring its lease agreements. The company would like to set the damage deposits high enough that tenants will keep the apartments in good condition. The company is actually more concerned about damage than about tenants not paying their rent.
    a. Discuss the tax effects of the following alternatives:
        • $400 damage deposit and $400 rent for the final month of the lease.

Decision Making

- $800 rent for the final two months of the lease and no damage deposit.
- $800 damage deposit with no rent prepayment.

b.   Which option do you recommend?

40. Gus has been experiencing serious financial problems. His annual salary was $100,000, but a creditor garnished his salary for $20,000, so the employer paid the creditor (rather than Gus) the $20,000. To prevent creditors from attaching his investments, Gus gave his investments to his 21-year-old daughter, Rebecca. Rebecca received $5,000 in dividends and interest from the investments during the year. Gus transferred some cash to a Swiss bank account that paid him $3,000 interest during the year. Gus did not withdraw the interest from the Swiss bank account. Gus also hid some of his assets in his wholly owned corporation that received $150,000 rent income but had $160,000 in related expenses, including a $15,000 salary paid to Gus. Gus reasons that his gross income should be computed as follows:

Salary received	$80,000
Loss from rental property ($150,000 – $160,000)	(10,000)
Gross income	$70,000

Compute Gus's correct gross income for the year, and explain any differences between your calculation and Gus's.

41. Tracy, a cash basis taxpayer, is employed by Eagle Corporation, also a cash basis taxpayer. Tracy is a full-time employee of the corporation and receives a salary of $60,000 per year. He also receives a bonus equal to 10% of all collections from clients he serviced during the year. Determine the tax consequences of the following events to the corporation and to Tracy:

a.   On December 31, 2008, Tracy was visiting a customer. The customer gave Tracy a $3,000 check payable to the corporation for appraisal services Tracy performed during 2008. Tracy did not deliver the check to the corporation until January 2009.

b.   The facts are the same as in (a), except that the corporation is an accrual basis taxpayer and Tracy deposited the check on December 31, but the bank did not add the deposit to the corporation's account until January 2009.

c.   The facts are the same as in (a), except that the customer told Tracy to hold the check until January 2009 when the customer could make a bank deposit that would cover the check.

42. Fran, Gary, and Heidi each have a one-third interest in the capital and profits of the FGH Partnership. Each partner had a capital account of $50,000 at the beginning of the tax year. The partnership profits for the tax year were $210,000. Changes in their capital accounts during the tax year were as follows:

	Fran	Gary	Heidi	Total
Beginning balance	$ 50,000	$ 50,000	$ 50,000	$150,000
Withdrawals	(25,000)	(20,000)	(10,000)	(55,000)
Additional contributions	–0–	–0–	5,000	5,000
Allocation of profits	70,000	70,000	70,000	210,000
Ending balance	$ 95,000	$100,000	$115,000	$310,000

In arriving at the $210,000 of partnership profits, the partnership deducted $1,800 ($600 for each partner) in premiums paid for group term life insurance on the partners. Fran and Gary are 39 years old, and Heidi is 35 years old. Other employees are also eligible for group term life insurance equal to their annual salary. These premiums of $10,000 have been deducted in calculating the partnership profits of $210,000. Compute each partner's gross income from the partnership for the tax year.

43. In 2008, Alva received dividends on her stocks as follows:

Amur Corporation (a French corporation whose stock is traded on an established U.S. securities market)	$55,000
Blaze, Inc., a Delaware corporation	25,000
Grape, Inc., a Virginia corporation	12,000

a.   Alva purchased the Grape stock four years ago, and she purchased the Amur stock two years ago. She purchased the Blaze stock 15 days before it went ex-dividend and sold it 20 days later at a $22,000 loss. Alva had no other capital gains and losses for the year. She is in the 35% marginal tax bracket. Compute Alva's tax on her dividend income for 2008.

b.   Alva's daughter, who is not Alva's dependent, had taxable income of $6,000, which included $1,000 of dividends on Grape, Inc. stock. The daughter had purchased the stock two years ago. Compute the daughter's tax liability on the dividends.

c.   Alva can earn 5% before-tax interest on a corporate bond or a 4% dividend on a preferred stock. Assuming the appreciation in value is the same, which investment produces the greater after-tax income?

d.   The same as part (c), except Alva's daughter is to make the investment.

44. Liz and Doug were divorced on July 1 of the current year after 10 years of marriage. Their current year's income received before the divorce was as follows:

Doug's salary	$41,000
Liz's salary	55,000
Rent on apartments purchased by Liz 15 years ago	8,000
Dividends on stock Doug inherited from his mother 4 years ago	1,900
Interest on a savings account in Liz's name funded with her salary	2,400

Allocate the income to Liz and Doug assuming they live in:

a.   California.

b.   Texas.

45. Nell and Kirby are in the process of negotiating their divorce agreement. What should be the tax consequences to Nell and Kirby if the following, considered individually, became part of the agreement?

a.   In consideration for her one-half interest in their personal residence, Kirby will transfer to Nell stock with a value of $200,000. Kirby's cost of the stock was $150,000, and the value of the personal residence is $400,000. They purchased the residence three years ago for $300,000.

b.   Nell will receive $1,000 per month for the lesser of 120 months or the number of months she lives after the divorce becomes final.

c.   Nell is to have custody of their 12-year-old son, Bobby. She is to receive $900 per month until Bobby (1) dies or (2) attains age 21 (whichever occurs first). After either of these events occurs, Nell will receive only $600 per month for the remainder of her life.

46. Karen and Al are in the process of negotiating a divorce agreement. Al believes that Karen should pay him at least $30,000 per year, but he would like to get as much in the first two years in cash as the tax law will permit to be treated as alimony. He is willing to surrender his one-half interest in some stock in exchange for more cash. Karen and Al own stock worth $120,000 that originally cost $80,000. Al is aware that Karen is very concerned about the tax consequences of the divorce agreement. What would be the tax consequences of the following alternative agreements?

a.   Al receives $30,000 per year for life and one-half of the jointly owned stock.

b.   Al receives $50,000 per year in Years 1, 2, and 3 and $30,000 per year for the remainder of his life. He does not receive any of the stock.

c.   Al receives $80,000 in Year 1 and $30,000 per year for the remainder of his life.

47. Under the terms of their divorce agreement, Barry is to transfer common stock (cost of $25,000, market value of $60,000) to Sandra. Barry and Sandra have a 14-year-old child. Sandra will have custody of the child, and Barry is to pay $300 per month as child support. In addition, Sandra is to receive $1,000 per month for 10 years, or until her death if earlier. However, the payments will be reduced to $750 per month when their child reaches age 21. In the first year under the agreement, Sandra receives the common stock and the correct cash payments for six months. How will the terms of the agreement affect Sandra's gross income?

48. Roy decides to buy a personal residence and goes to the bank for a $150,000 loan. The bank tells him he can borrow the funds at 7% if his father will guarantee the debt. Roy's

Decision Making

father, Hal, owns CDs currently yielding 6%. The Federal rate is 5%. Hal is willing to do either of the following:

- Cash in the CDs and lend Roy the funds at 6% interest.
- Guarantee the loan for Roy.

Hal will consider lending the funds to Roy at an even lower interest rate, depending on the tax consequences. Hal is in the 35% marginal tax bracket. Roy, whose only source of income is his salary, is in the 15% marginal tax bracket. The interest Roy pays on the mortgage will be deductible by him. Considering only the tax consequences, which option will maximize the family's after-tax wealth?

49. On June 30, 2008, Ridge borrowed $62,000 from his employer. On July 1, 2008, Ridge used the money as follows:

Interest-free loan to Ridge's controlled corporation (operated by Ridge on a part-time basis)	$31,000
Interest-free loan to Tab (Ridge's son)	11,000
National Bank of Grundy 6% CD ($14,840 due at maturity, June 30, 2009)	14,000
National Bank of Grundy 6.25% CD ($6,773 due at maturity, June 30, 2010)	6,000
	$62,000

Ridge's employer did not charge him interest. The applicable Federal rate was 7% throughout the relevant period. Tab had investment income of $800 for the year, and he used the loan proceeds to pay medical school tuition. There were no other outstanding loans between Ridge and Tab. What are the effects of the preceding transactions on Ridge's taxable income for 2008?

50. Indicate whether the imputed interest rules should apply in the following situations. Assume all the loans were made at the beginning of the tax year unless otherwise indicated.
    a. Mike loaned his sister $90,000 to buy a new home. Mike did not charge interest on the loan. The Federal rate was 5%. Mike's sister had $900 of investment income for the year.
    b. Sam's employer maintains an emergency loan fund for its employees. During the year, Sam's wife was very ill, and he incurred unusually large medical expenses. He borrowed $8,500 from his employer's emergency loan fund for six months. The Federal rate was 5.5%. Sam and his wife had no investment income for the year.
    c. Jody borrowed $25,000 from her controlled corporation for six months. She used the funds to pay her daughter's college tuition. The corporation charged Jody 4% interest. The Federal rate was 5%. Jody had $3,500 of investment income for the year.
    d. Kait loaned her son, Jake, $60,000 for six months. Jake used the $60,000 to pay off college loans. The Federal rate was 5%, and Kait did not charge Jake any interest. Jake had dividend and interest income of $2,100 for the tax year.

51. Vito is the sole shareholder of Vito, Inc. He is also employed by the corporation. On June 30, 2008, Vito borrowed $8,000 from Vito, Inc., and on July 1, 2009, he borrowed an additional $4,000. Both loans were due on demand. No interest was charged on the loans, and the Federal rate was 8% for all relevant dates. Vito used the money to purchase a boat, and he had $1,100 of investment income. Determine the tax consequences to Vito and Vito, Inc., in each of the following situations:
    a. The loans are considered employer-employee loans.
    b. The loans are considered corporation-shareholder loans.

52. Thelma retires after 30 years of service with her employer. She is 66 years old and has contributed $20,000 to her employer's qualified pension fund. She elects to receive her retirement benefits as an annuity of $2,000 per month for the remainder of her life.
    a. Assume that Thelma retires in June 2008 and collects six annuity payments this year. What is her gross income from the annuity payments in the first year?
    b. Assume that Thelma lives 30 years after retiring. What is her gross income from the annuity payments in the twenty-ninth year?

c. Assume that Thelma dies after collecting 180 payments. She collected six payments in the year of her death. What are Thelma's gross income and deductions from the annuity contract in the year of her death?

53. For each of the following, determine the amount that should be included in gross income:
    a. Manny was selected as the most valuable player in the World Series. In recognition of this, he was awarded a sports car worth $60,000 and $100,000 in cash.
    b. Wanda won the Mrs. America beauty contest. She received various prizes valued at $100,000. None of the $100,000 was for a scholarship or travel expenses.
    c. Jacob was awarded the Nobel Prize in Medicine. He donated the $900,000 check he received to City University, his alma mater.

54. The LMN Partnership has a group term life insurance plan. Each partner has $150,000 protection, and each employee has protection equal to twice his or her annual salary. Employee Alice (age 36) has $85,000 of insurance under the plan, and partner Kay (age 54) has $150,000 of coverage. Because the plan is a "group plan," it is impossible to determine the cost of coverage for an individual employee or partner.
    a. Assuming the plan is nondiscriminatory, how much must Alice and Kay each include in gross income as a result of the partnership paying the insurance premiums?
    b. Assume that the partnership is incorporated. Kay becomes a shareholder and an employee who receives a $75,000 annual salary. The corporation provides Kay with $150,000 of group term life insurance coverage under a nondiscriminatory plan. What is Kay's gross income as a result of the corporation paying the insurance premiums?

55. Herbert was employed for the first six months of the year and earned $90,000 in salary. During the next six months, he collected $6,800 of unemployment compensation, borrowed $12,000 (using his personal residence as collateral), and withdrew $2,000 from his savings account (including $60 interest). He received dividends of $550. His luck was not all bad, for in December he won $1,500 in the lottery on a $5 ticket. Calculate Herbert's gross income.

56. Linda and Don are married and file a joint return. In 2008, they received $9,000 in Social Security benefits and $35,000 in taxable pension benefits and interest. *Decision Making*
    a. Compute the couple's adjusted gross income on a joint return.
    b. Don would like to know whether they should sell for $100,000 (at no gain or loss) a corporate bond that pays 8% in interest each year and use the proceeds to buy a $100,000 nontaxable State of Virginia bond that will pay $6,000 in interest each year.
    c. If Linda in (a) works part-time and earns $30,000, how much would Linda and Don's adjusted gross income increase?

57. Melissa, who is 62 years old, is unmarried and has no dependents. Her annual income consists of a taxable pension of $20,000, $12,000 in Social Security benefits, and $3,000 of interest income. She does not itemize her deductions. She is in the 15% marginal income tax bracket. She is considering getting a part-time job that would pay her $10,000 a year.
    a. What would be Melissa's after-tax income from the part-time job, considering Social Security and Medicare tax (7.65%) as well as Federal income tax on the earnings of $10,000?
    b. What would be the effective tax rate (increase in tax/increase in income) on the additional income from the part-time job?
    c. Assume instead that Melissa's only income is a taxable pension of $18,000 and $12,000 in Social Security benefits. She is considering selling land for $10,000 that she purchased as an investment in 2004 for $3,000. Her marginal tax rate on ordinary income is 15%. What would be the effective tax rate on the gain from the sale of the land?

58. Donna does not think she has an income tax problem but would like to discuss her situation with you just to make sure she will not get hit with an unexpected tax liability. Base your suggestions on the following relevant financial information:
    a. Donna's share of the SAT Partnership income is $70,000, but none of the income can be distributed because the partnership needs the cash for operations.

b.   Donna's Social Security benefits totaled $8,400, but Donna loaned the cash received to her nephew.

c.   Donna assigned to a creditor the right to collect $1,200 interest on some bonds she owned.

d.   Donna and her husband lived together in California until September, when they separated. Donna has heard rumors that her husband had substantial gambling winnings since they separated.

CUMULATIVE PROBLEMS

Tax Return Problem

Decision Making

Communications

59.   Daniel B. Butler and Freida C. Butler, husband and wife, file a joint return. The Butlers live at 625 Oak Street in Corbin, KY 27521. Dan's Social Security number is 482–61–1231, and Freida's is 162–79–1245. Dan was born on January 15, 1961, and Freida was born on August 20, 1961.

During 2007, Dan and Freida furnished over half of the total support of each of the following individuals, all of whom still live at home:

a.   Gina, their daughter, age 22, a full-time student, who married on December 21, 2007, has no income of her own, and for 2007 did not file a joint return with her husband, Casey, who earned $10,600 during 2007. Gina's Social Security number is 336–62–3760.

b.   Sam, their son, age 20, who had gross income of $6,300 in 2007. Sam dropped out of college in October 2007. He had graduated from high school in May 2007. Sam's Social Security number is 223–33–8906.

c.   Ben, their oldest son, age 27, who is a full-time graduate student with gross income of $5,200. Ben's Social Security number is 905–19–1760.

Dan was employed as a manager by WJJJ, Inc. (employer identification number 38–7766723, 604 Franklin Street, Corbin, KY 27521), and Freida was employed as a salesperson for Corbin Realty, Inc. (employer identification number 38–8455227, 899 Central Street, Corbin, Ky 27521). Information from the W–2 Forms provided by the employers is presented below. Dan and Freida use the cash method.

Line	Description	Dan	Freida
1	Wages, tips, other compensation	$86,000	$45,000
2	Federal income tax withheld	$12,000	$7,500
3	Social Security wages	$86,000	$45,000
4	Social Security tax withheld	$5,332	$2,790
5	Medicare wages and tips	$86,000	$45,000
6	Medicare tax withheld	$1,247	$653
15	State	Kentucky	Kentucky
16	State wages, tips, etc.	$86,000	$45,000
17	State income tax withheld	$2,700	$2,250

Freida sold a house on December 30, 2007, and will be paid a commission of $3,100 (not included in the $45,000 reported on the W–2) on the January 10, 2008 closing date.

Other income (as reported on 1099 Forms) for 2007 consisted of the following:

Dividends on CSX stock (qualified)	$3,000
Interest on savings at Second Bank	1,300
Interest on City of Corbin bonds	900
Interest on First Bank CD	383

The $383 from First Bank was original issue discount. Dan and Freida collected $15,000 on the First Bank CD that matured on September 30, 2007. The CD was purchased on October 1, 2005, for $14,000, and the yield to maturity was 3.5%.

Dan received a Schedule K–1 from the Falcon Partnership, which showed his distributive share as $11,000. In addition to the above information, Dan and Freida's itemized deductions included the following:

Paid on 2006 Kentucky income tax	$ 300
Personal property tax paid	600
Real estate taxes paid	1,800
Interest on home mortgage (Corbin S&L)	4,900
Cash contributions to the Boy Scouts	975

Sales tax from the sales tax table is $1,198. Dan and Freida made Federal estimated tax payments of $4,000.

Part 1—Tax Computation
Compute Dan and Freida's 2007 Federal income tax payable (or refund due). If you use tax forms for your computations, you will need Form 1040 and Schedules A, B, and E. Suggested software: Tax Cut.

Part 2—Tax Planning
Dan plans to reduce his work schedule and work only halftime for WJJJ in 2008. He has been writing songs for several years and wants to devote more time to developing a career as a songwriter. Because of the uncertainty in the music business, however, he would like you to make all computations assuming he will have no income from songwriting in 2008. To make up for the loss of income, Freida plans to increase the amount of time she spends selling real estate. She estimates she will be able to earn $70,000 in 2008. Assume all other income and expense items will be approximately the same as they were in 2007. Assume Sam will be enrolled in college as a full-time student for the summer and fall semesters. Will the Butlers have more or less disposable income (after Federal income tax) in 2008? Write a letter to the Butlers that contains your advice and prepare a memo for the tax files.

60. Cecil C. Seymour is a 66-year-old widower. He had income for 2008 as follows:

Tax Computation Problem

Pension from former employer	$32,000
Interest income from Alto National Bank	5,500
Interest income on City of Alto bonds	2,700
Dividends received from IBM	2,000
Collections on annuity contract he purchased from Great Life Insurance	5,400
Social Security benefits	12,000
Rent income on townhouse	7,600

The cost of the annuity was $54,000, and Cecil was expected to receive a total of 240 monthly payments of $450. Cecil has received 22 payments through 2008.

Cecil's 40-year-old daughter, Sarah C. Seymour, borrowed $40,000 from Cecil on January 2, 2008. She used the money to start a new business. Cecil does not charge her interest because she could not afford to pay it, but he does expect to eventually collect the principal. Sarah is living with Cecil until the business becomes profitable. Except for housing, Sarah provides her own support from her business and $1,600 in dividends on stocks that she inherited from her mother.

Other relevant information is presented below:

- Cecil's Social Security number: 259–83–4444
- Address: 3840 Springfield Blvd., Alto, GA 30754
- Sarah's Social Security number: 257–49–8862
- Expenses on rental townhouse:

Utilities	$1,500
Maintenance	1,000
Depreciation	2,000
Real estate taxes	750
Insurance	500

- State income taxes paid: $3,300
- County personal property taxes paid: $2,100
- Payments on estimated 2008 Federal income tax: $5,900
- Charitable contributions of cash to Alto Baptist Church: $6,400

• Federal interest rate: 6%
• Sales taxes paid: $912

Compute Cecil's 2008 Federal income tax payable (or refund due).

RESEARCH PROBLEMS

Note: Solutions to Research Problems can be prepared by using the **RIA Checkpoint®** **Student Edition** online research product, which is available to accompany this text. It is also possible to prepare solutions to the Research Problems by using tax research materials found in a standard tax library.

Communications

Research Problem 1. Tranquility Funeral Home, Inc., your client, is an accrual basis taxpayer that sells pre-need funeral contracts. Under these contracts, the customer pays in advance for goods and services to be provided at the contract beneficiary's death. These payments are refundable at the contract purchaser's request, pursuant to state law, at any time until the goods and services are furnished. Tranquility, consistent with its financial accounting reporting, includes the payments in income for the year the funeral service is provided. The IRS agent insists that the payments are prepaid income subject to tax in the year of receipt. Your client believes the amounts involved are customer deposits. Write a letter to Tranquility that contains your advice about how the issue should be resolved. The client's address is 400 Rock Street, Memphis, TN 38152.

Research Problem 2. Paul purchased a new automobile and was satisfied with the price he paid for the car. A few days after he purchased the car, however, the manufacturer sent him a $1,500 check. Unknown to Paul at the time of the purchase, he was eligible for a $1,500 rebate from the manufacturer. Paul considers this to be "money that blew in the window," since he purchased the car for what he believed it was worth and the rebate came as a complete surprise to him. Is Paul required to include the $1,500 in gross income for the year he received it?

Research Problem 3. The Cheyenne Golf and Tennis Club requires its members to purchase stock in the corporation and to make a deposit of $10,000. The deposit is to be repaid in 30 years, and no interest is charged. Is the deposit subject to the imputed interest rules for below-market loans?

Partial list of research aids:
TAM 9735002.

Research Problem 4. Jan was divorced in California, a community property state. Her former husband, William, was still working but had accumulated substantial pension benefits. Jan was entitled to one-half of the pension benefits. The California court, however, required William to make payments to Jan before his retirement. Otherwise, the court reasoned, the former husband could deny Jan her share of the pension simply by continuing to work. The payments did not meet the definition of alimony because, if Jan died, they could continue to her estate. William chose to reduce his gross income by the amount of the payments on the theory that the court had in effect ruled that the income earned by him but payable to his former wife under the California community property law should be included in her gross income. Jan is concerned that the IRS will require her to include the payments in her gross income. Can you relieve her concerns?

Internet *Activity*

Use the tax resources of the Internet to address the following questions. Do not restrict your search to the World Wide Web, but include a review of newsgroups and general reference materials, practitioner sites and resources, primary sources of the tax law, chat rooms and discussion groups, and other opportunities.

Research Problem 5. Determine the applicable Federal rate for purposes of below-market loans. Use this figure to complete Problem 49 for this chapter.

Communications

Research Problem 6. Go to the Web page of a consulting firm that offers counseling services to individuals as they negotiate the terms of a divorce. What specific tax-related services do these firms offer? Send an e-mail message to one of these firms suggesting that it add a specific service or revise its Web page to emphasize other tax-related services for its clients.

CHAPTER 5

Gross Income: Exclusions

LEARNING OBJECTIVES

After completing Chapter 5, you should be able to:

LO.1

Understand that statutory authority is required to exclude an item from gross income.

LO.2

Identify the circumstances under which various items are excludible from gross income.

LO.3

Determine the extent to which receipts can be excluded under the tax benefit rule.

LO.4

Describe the circumstances under which income must be reported from the discharge of indebtedness.

LO.5

Identify tax planning strategies for obtaining the maximum benefit from allowable exclusions.

OUTLINE

Items Specifically Excluded from Gross Income, 5–2
Statutory Authority, 5–4
Gifts and Inheritances, 5–4
    General, 5–5
    Gifts to Employees, 5–5
    Employee Death Benefits, 5–6
Life Insurance Proceeds, 5–6
    General Rule, 5–6
    Accelerated Death Benefits, 5–7
    Transfer for Valuable Consideration, 5–8
Scholarships, 5–9
    General Information, 5–9
    Timing Issues, 5–10
    Disguised Compensation, 5–10
    Qualified Tuition Reduction Plans, 5–10
Compensation for Injuries and Sickness, 5–11
    Damages, 5–11
    Workers' Compensation, 5–13
    Accident and Health Insurance Benefits, 5–13
Employer-Sponsored Accident and Health Plans, 5–13
    Medical Reimbursement Plans, 5–14
    Long-Term Care Insurance Benefits, 5–15

Meals and Lodging, 5–15
    Furnished for the Convenience of the Employer, 5–15
    Other Housing Exclusions, 5–17
Other Employee Fringe Benefits, 5–18
    Specific Benefits, 5–18
    Cafeteria Plans, 5–19
    Flexible Spending Plans, 5–20
    General Classes of Excluded Benefits, 5–20
    Taxable Fringe Benefits, 5–24
Foreign Earned Income, 5–25
Interest on Certain State and Local Government Obligations, 5–28
Dividends, 5–29
    General Information, 5–29
    Stock Dividends, 5–30
Educational Savings Bonds, 5–30
Qualified Tuition Programs (§ 529 Plans), 5–31
Tax Benefit Rule, 5–32
Income from Discharge of Indebtedness, 5–33
Tax Planning Considerations, 5–34
    Life Insurance, 5–34
    Employee Benefits, 5–34
    Investment Income, 5–35

Items Specifically Excluded from Gross Income

Chapter 4 discussed the concepts and judicial doctrines that affect the determination of gross income. If an income item is within the all-inclusive definition of gross income, the item can be excluded only if the taxpayer can locate specific authority for doing so. Chapter 5 focuses on the exclusions Congress has authorized. These exclusions are listed in Exhibit 5–1.

Tax advisers spend countless hours trying to develop techniques to achieve tax-exempt status for income. Employee benefits planning is greatly influenced by the availability of certain types of exclusions. Taxes play an important role in employee benefits, as well as in other situations, because attaining an exclusion is another means of enhancing after-tax income. For example, for a person whose combined Federal and state marginal tax rate is 40 percent, $1.00 of tax-exempt income is equivalent to $1.67 [$1 ÷ (1 − .4)] in income subject to taxation. The tax adviser's ideal is to attach the right labels or provide the right wording to render income nontaxable without affecting the economics of the transaction.

Consider the case of an employee who is in the 28 percent marginal tax bracket and is paying $3,000 a year for health insurance. If the employer provided this protection in a manner that qualified for exclusion treatment but reduced the employee's salary by $3,000, the employee's after-tax and after-insurance income would increase at no additional cost to the employer.

EXHIBIT 5–1	Summary of Principal Exclusions from Gross Income

1. Donative items
   Gifts, bequests, and inheritances (§ 102)
   Life insurance proceeds paid by reason of death (§ 101)
   Accelerated death benefits [§ 101(g)]
   Survivor benefits for public safety officer killed in the line of duty [§ 101(h)]
   Scholarships (§ 117)
2. Personal and welfare items
   Injury or sickness payments (§ 104)
   Public assistance payments (Rev.Rul. 71–425, 1971–2 C.B. 76)
   Amounts received under insurance contracts for certain living expenses (§ 123)
   Reimbursement for the costs of caring for a foster child (§ 131)
   Disaster relief payments (§ 139)
3. Wage and salary supplements
   a. Fringe benefits
      Accident and health benefits (§§ 105 and 106)
      Health Savings Accounts [§ 106(d)]
      Lodging and meals furnished for the convenience of the employer (§ 119)
      Rental value of parsonages (§ 107)
      Employee achievement awards [§ 74(c)]
      Employer contributions to employee group term life insurance (§ 79)
      Cafeteria plans (§ 125)
      Educational assistance payments (§ 127)
      Child or dependent care (§ 129)
      Services provided to employees at no additional cost to the employer (§ 132)
      Employee discounts (§ 132)
      Working condition and de minimis fringes (§ 132)
      Athletic facilities provided to employees (§ 132)
      Qualified transportation fringe (§ 132)
      Qualified moving expense reimbursement (§ 132)
      Qualified retirement planning services (§ 132)
      Tuition reductions granted to employees of educational institutions (§ 117)
      Child adoption expenses (§ 137)
      Long-term care insurance (§ 7702B)
   b. Military benefits
      Combat pay (§ 112)
      Housing, uniforms, and other benefits (§ 134)
   c. Foreign earned income (§ 911)
4. Investor items
   Interest on state and local government obligations (§ 103)
   Improvements by tenant to landlord's property (§ 109)
   Fifty percent exclusion for gain from sale of certain small business stock (§ 1202)
5. Benefits for the elderly
   Social Security benefits (except in the case of certain higher-income taxpayers) (§ 86)
6. Other benefits
   Income from discharge of indebtedness (§ 108)
   Recovery of a prior year's deduction that yielded no tax benefit (§ 111)
   Gain from the sale of personal residence (§ 121)
   Educational savings bonds (§ 135)
   Qualified tuition program (§ 529)
   Coverdell Education Savings Account (§ 530)
   Lessee construction allowances for short-term leases (§ 110)

Salary received to use to purchase health insurance	$ 3,000
Less: Taxes ($3,000 × 28%)	(840)
Cash available to purchase health insurance	$ 2,160
Less: Cost of health insurance	(3,000)
Excess of cost of health insurance over cash available	$ 840

Thus, the employee in this case is $840 better off with a salary reduction of $3,000 and employer-provided health insurance. The employee may still decide that the $3,000 salary is preferable if, for example, the employee has access to health insurance through a spouse's employer. Understanding the tax influence, however, does enable the employee to make a more informed choice.

Statutory Authority

LO.1

Understand that statutory authority is required to exclude an item from gross income.

Sections 101 through 150 provide the authority for excluding specific items from gross income. In addition, other exclusions are scattered throughout the Code. Each exclusion has its own legislative history and reason for enactment. Certain exclusions are intended as a form of indirect welfare payments. Other exclusions prevent double taxation of income or provide incentives for socially desirable activities (e.g., nontaxable interest on certain U.S. government bonds where the owner uses the funds for educational expenses).

In some cases, Congress has enacted exclusions to rectify the effects of judicial decisions. For example, the Supreme Court held that the fair market value of improvements (not made in lieu of rent) made by a tenant to the landlord's property should be included in the landlord's gross income upon termination of the lease.[1] The landlord was required to include the value of the improvements in gross income even though the property had not been sold or otherwise disposed of. Congress provided relief in this situation by enacting § 109, which defers taxing the value of the improvements until the property is sold.[2]

At times Congress responds to specific events. For example, in 2001 Congress enacted § 139 to ensure that victims of a *qualified disaster* (disaster resulting from a terrorist attack, presidentially declared disaster, common carrier accident of a catastrophic nature) would not be required to include payments received for living expenses, funeral expenses, and property damage resulting from the disaster in gross income.

Gifts and Inheritances

LO.2

Identify the circumstances under which various items are excludible from gross income.

General

Beginning with the Income Tax Act of 1913 and continuing to the present, Congress has allowed the recipient of a gift to exclude the value of the property from

---

[1] *Helvering v. Bruun*, 40–1 USTC ¶9337, 24 AFTR 652, 60 S.Ct. 631 (USSC, 1940).

[2] If the tenant made the improvements in lieu of rent, the value of the improvements is not eligible for exclusion.

TAX *in the News*   BEGGING AS A TAX-DISFAVORED OCCUPATION

In five recent decisions, the Tax Court ruled that amounts received from begging are nontaxable gifts. In a reversal of the normal roles, the beggars contended that the amounts received were earned income while the IRS argued that the taxpayers had merely received gifts. The beggars wanted the fruit of their efforts to be treated as earned income in order to qualify them for the earned income credit.

---

gross income. The exclusion applies to gifts made during the life of the donor (*inter vivos* gifts) and transfers that take effect upon the death of the donor (bequests and inheritances).[3] However, as discussed in Chapter 4, the recipient of a gift of income-producing property is subject to tax on the income subsequently earned from the property. Also, as discussed in Chapter 1, the donor or the decedent's estate may be subject to gift or estate taxes on the transfer.

In numerous cases, gifts are made in a business setting. For example, a salesperson gives a purchasing agent free samples; an employee receives cash from his or her employer on retirement; a corporation makes payments to employees who were victims of a natural disaster; a corporation makes a cash payment to a deceased employee's spouse. In these and similar instances, it is frequently unclear whether the payment was a gift or represents compensation for past, present, or future services.

The courts have defined a **gift** as "a voluntary transfer of property by one to another without adequate [valuable] consideration or compensation therefrom."[4] If the payment is intended to be for services rendered, it is not a gift, even though the payment is made without legal or moral obligation and the payor receives no economic benefit from the transfer. To qualify as a gift, the payment must be made "out of affection, respect, admiration, charity or like impulses."[5] Thus, the cases on this issue have been decided on the basis of the donor's intent.

In a landmark case, *Comm. v. Duberstein*,[6] the taxpayer (Duberstein) received a Cadillac from a business acquaintance. Duberstein had supplied the businessman with the names of potential customers with no expectation of compensation. The Supreme Court concluded:

> . . . despite the characterization of the transfer of the Cadillac by the parties [as a gift] and the absence of any obligation, even of a moral nature, to make it, it was at the bottom a recompense for Duberstein's past service, or an inducement for him to be of further service in the future.

Duberstein was therefore required to include the fair market value of the automobile in gross income.

Gifts to Employees

In the case of cash or other property *received by an employee* from his or her employer, Congress has eliminated any ambiguity. Transfers from an employer to an employee cannot be excluded as a gift.[7] However, victims of a qualified disaster who are reimbursed by their employers for living expenses, funeral expenses, and property damage can exclude the payments from gross income under § 139, as previously discussed.

---

[3]§ 102.

[4]*Estate of D. R. Daly*, 3 B.T.A. 1042 (1926).

[5]*Robertson v. U.S.*, 52–1 USTC ¶9343, 41 AFTR 1053, 72 S.Ct. 994 (USSC, 1952).

[6]60–2 USTC ¶9515, 5 AFTR2d 1626, 80 S.Ct. 1190 (USSC, 1960).

[7]§ 102(c).

TAX *in the News*   FREQUENT-FLYER MILES WILL NOT BE TAXED

IRS officials believe that when a taxpayer receives frequent-flyer miles in connection with business travel, the taxpayer has received income. This is clearly true if the taxpayer has deducted the cost of the airline ticket. Under the tax benefit rule, the frequent-flyer miles should be included in gross income as a recovery of a prior deduction. If the employer pays for the business travel but the employee is awarded the frequent-flyer miles, the employee has obviously received additional compensation.

Nevertheless, the IRS has announced (Announcement 2002–18) that it will not attempt to tax frequent-flyer miles. The major consideration in creating this nonstatutory exemption was the complexity that would result from attempting to tax the miles. Distinguishing the miles awarded for personal travel (nontaxable reduction in the cost of ticket) from the business miles would be difficult. Furthermore, the valuation issues would be horrendous.

Employee Death Benefits

Frequently, an employer makes payments (**death benefits**) to a deceased employee's surviving spouse, children, or other beneficiaries. If the decedent had a non-forfeitable right to the payments (e.g., the decedent's accrued salary), the amounts are generally taxable to the recipient just the same as if the employee had lived and collected the payments. But when the employer makes voluntary payments, the gift issue arises. Generally, the IRS considers such payments to be compensation for prior services rendered by the deceased employee.[8] However, some courts have held that payments to an employee's surviving spouse or other beneficiaries are gifts if the following are true:[9]

- The payments were made to the surviving spouse and children rather than to the employee's estate.
- The employer derived no benefit from the payments.
- The surviving spouse and children performed no services for the employer.
- The decedent had been fully compensated for services rendered.
- Payments were made pursuant to a board of directors' resolution that followed a general company policy of providing payments for families of deceased employees (but not exclusively for families of shareholder-employees).

When all of the above conditions are satisfied, the payment is presumed to have been made *as an act of affection or charity.* When one or more of these conditions is not satisfied, the surviving spouse and children may still be deemed the recipients of a gift if the payment is made in light of the survivors' financial needs.[10]

Life Insurance Proceeds

General Rule

Life insurance proceeds paid to the beneficiary because of the death of the insured are exempt from income tax.[11]

---

[8]Rev.Rul. 62–102, 1962–2 C.B. 37.

[9]*Estate of Sydney J. Carter v. Comm.*, 72–1 USTC ¶9129, 29 AFTR2d 332, 453 F.2d 61 (CA–2, 1972), and the cases cited there.

[10]*Simpson v. U.S.*, 58–2 USTC ¶9923, 2 AFTR2d 6036, 261 F.2d 497 (CA–7, 1958), *cert. denied* 79 S.Ct. 724 (USSC, 1958).

[11]§ 101(a).

EXAMPLE 1

Mark purchases an insurance policy on his life and names his wife, Linda, as the beneficiary. Mark pays $45,000 in premiums. When he dies, Linda collects the insurance proceeds of $200,000. The $200,000 is exempt from Federal income tax. ■

Congress chose to exempt life insurance proceeds for the following reasons:

- For family members, life insurance proceeds serve much the same purpose as a nontaxable inheritance.
- In a business context (as well as in a family situation), life insurance proceeds replace an economic loss suffered by the beneficiary.

EXAMPLE 2

Gold Corporation purchases a life insurance policy to cover its key employee. If the proceeds were taxable, the corporation would require more insurance coverage to pay the tax as well as to cover the economic loss of the employee. ■

Thus, in general, Congress concluded that making life insurance proceeds exempt from income tax was a good policy.

Accelerated Death Benefits

Generally, if the owner of a life insurance policy cancels the policy and receives the cash surrender value, the taxpayer must recognize gain equal to the excess of the amount received over premiums paid on the policy (a loss is not deductible). The gain is recognized because the general exclusion provision for life insurance proceeds applies only to life insurance proceeds paid upon the death of the insured. If the taxpayer cancels the policy and receives the cash surrender value, the life insurance policy is treated as an investment by the insured.

In a limited circumstance, however, the insured is permitted to receive the benefits of the life insurance contract without having to include the gain in gross income. Under the **accelerated death benefits** provisions, exclusion treatment is available for insured taxpayers who are either terminally ill or chronically ill.[12] A terminally ill taxpayer can collect the cash surrender value of the policy from the insurance company or assign the policy proceeds to a qualified third party. The resultant gain, if any, is excluded from the insured's gross income. A *terminally ill* individual is one whom a medical doctor certifies as having an illness that is reasonably expected to cause death within 24 months.

In the case of a chronically ill patient, no gain is recognized if the proceeds of the policy are used for the long-term care of the insured. A person is *chronically ill* if he or she is certified as being unable to perform without assistance certain activities of daily living. These exclusions for the terminally ill and the chronically ill are available only to the insured. Thus, a person who purchases a life insurance policy from the insured does not qualify.

EXAMPLE 3

Tom owned a term life insurance policy at the time he was diagnosed as having a terminal illness. After paying $5,200 in premiums, he sold the policy to Amber Benefits, Inc., a company that is authorized by the State of Virginia to purchase such policies. Amber paid Tom $50,000. When Tom died six months later, Amber collected the face amount of the policy, $75,000. Tom is not required to include the $44,800 gain ($50,000 − $5,200) on the sale of the policy in his gross income. Assume Amber pays additional premiums of $4,000 during the six-month period. When Amber collects the life insurance proceeds of $75,000, it must include the $21,000 gain ($75,000 proceeds − $50,000 cost − $4,000 additional premiums paid) in gross income. ■

---

[12]§ 101(g).

ETHICAL and EQUITABLE *Considerations*

SHOULD THE TERMINALLY ILL PAY SOCIAL SECURITY TAXES?

The rationale for excluding accelerated death benefits from the gross income of the terminally ill is that they often use the funds to pay medical expenses and other costs associated with dying and do not have the ability to pay tax on the gain from the accelerated receipt of the life insurance proceeds. Yet the wages of a terminally ill person who is employed (or profits of a self-employed person) are subject to Social Security taxes. The Social Security taxes are intended to pay for retirement benefits, but a terminally ill person is unlikely to collect any Social Security benefits.

Several bills have been introduced in Congress to exempt the terminally ill from the Social Security tax. Evaluate the equity of the current tax treatment versus that in the proposed legislation.

Transfer for Valuable Consideration

A life insurance policy (other than one associated with accelerated death benefits) may be transferred after it is issued by the insurance company. If the policy is *transferred for valuable consideration*, the insurance proceeds are includible in the gross income of the transferee to the extent the proceeds received exceed the amount paid for the policy by the transferee plus any subsequent premiums paid.

EXAMPLE 4

Adam pays premiums of $4,000 for an insurance policy in the face amount of $10,000 upon the life of Beth and subsequently transfers the policy to Carol for $6,000. On Beth's death, Carol receives the proceeds of $10,000. The amount that Carol can exclude from gross income is limited to $6,000 plus any premiums she paid subsequent to the transfer. ■

The Code, however, provides four exceptions to the rule illustrated in the preceding example. These exceptions permit exclusion treatment for transfers to the following:

1. A partner of the insured.
2. A partnership in which the insured is a partner.
3. A corporation in which the insured is an officer or shareholder.
4. A transferee whose basis in the policy is determined by reference to the transferor's basis.

The first three exceptions facilitate the use of insurance contracts to fund buy-sell agreements.

EXAMPLE 5

Rick and Sam are equal partners who have an agreement that allows either partner to purchase the interest of a deceased partner for $50,000. Neither partner has sufficient cash to actually buy the other partner's interest, but each has a life insurance policy on his own life in the amount of $50,000. Rick and Sam could exchange their policies (usually at little or no taxable gain), and upon the death of either partner, the surviving partner could collect tax-free insurance proceeds. The proceeds could then be used to purchase the decedent's interest in the partnership. ■

The fourth exception applies to policies that were transferred pursuant to a tax-free exchange or were received by gift.[13]

Investment earnings arising from the reinvestment of life insurance proceeds are generally subject to income tax. Often the beneficiary will elect to collect the

---

[13]See the discussion of gifts in Chapter 14 and tax-free exchanges in Chapters 15 and 20.

insurance proceeds in installments. The annuity rules (discussed in Chapter 4) are used to apportion the installment payment between the principal element (excludible) and the interest element (includible).[14]

Scholarships

General Information

Payments or benefits received by a student at an educational institution may be (1) compensation for services, (2) a gift, or (3) a scholarship. If the payments or benefits are received as compensation for services (past or present), the fact that the recipient is a student generally does not render the amounts received nontaxable.[15]

EXAMPLE 6

State University waives tuition for all graduate teaching assistants. The tuition waived is intended as compensation for services and is therefore included in the graduate assistant's gross income. ∎

As discussed earlier, gifts are not includible in gross income.

The **scholarship** rules are intended to provide exclusion treatment for education-related benefits that cannot qualify as gifts but are not compensation for services. According to the Regulations, "a scholarship is an amount paid or allowed to, or for the benefit of, an individual to aid such individual in the pursuit of study or research."[16] The recipient must be a candidate for a degree at an educational institution.[17]

EXAMPLE 7

Terry enters a contest sponsored by a local newspaper. Each contestant is required to submit an essay on local environmental issues. The prize is one year's tuition at State University. Terry wins the contest. The newspaper has a legal obligation to Terry (as contest winner). Thus, the benefits are not a gift. However, since the tuition payment aids Terry in pursuing her studies, the payment is a scholarship. ∎

A scholarship recipient may exclude from gross income the amount used for tuition and related expenses (fees, books, supplies, and equipment required for courses), provided the conditions of the grant do not require that the funds be used for other purposes.[18] Amounts received for room and board are *not* excludible and are treated as earned income for purposes of calculating the standard deduction for a taxpayer who is another taxpayer's dependent.[19]

EXAMPLE 8

Kelly receives a scholarship of $9,500 from State University to be used to pursue a bachelor's degree. She spends $4,000 on tuition, $3,000 on books and supplies, and $2,500 for room and board. Kelly may exclude $7,000 ($4,000 + $3,000) from gross income. The $2,500 spent for room and board is includible in Kelly's gross income.

The scholarship is Kelly's only source of income. Her parents provide more than 50% of Kelly's support and claim her as a dependent. Kelly's standard deduction of $2,800 ($2,500 + $300) exceeds her $2,500 gross income. Thus, she has no taxable income. ∎

---

[14]Reg. §§ 1.72–7(c)(1) and 1.101–7T.

[15]Reg. § 1.117–2(a). See *C. P. Bhalla*, 35 T.C. 13 (1960), for a discussion of the distinction between a scholarship and compensation. See also *Bingler v. Johnson*, 69–1 USTC ¶9348, 23 AFTR2d 1212, 89 S.Ct. 1439 (USSC, 1969). For potential exclusion treatment, see the subsequent discussion of qualified tuition reductions.

[16]Prop.Reg. § 1.117–6(c)(3)(i).

[17]§ 117(a).

[18]§ 117(b).

[19]Prop.Reg. § 1.117–6(h).

Timing Issues

Frequently, the scholarship recipient is a cash basis taxpayer who receives the money in one tax year but pays the educational expenses in a subsequent year. The amount eligible for exclusion may not be known at the time the money is received. In that case, the transaction is held *open* until the educational expenses are paid.[20]

EXAMPLE 9

In August 2008, Sanjay received $10,000 as a scholarship for the academic year 2008–2009. Sanjay's expenditures for tuition, books, and supplies were as follows:

August–December 2008	$3,000
January–May 2009	4,500
	$7,500

Sanjay's gross income for 2009 includes $2,500 ($10,000 − $7,500) that is not excludible as a scholarship. None of the scholarship is included in his gross income in 2008. ■

Disguised Compensation

Some employers make scholarships available solely to the children of key employees. The tax objective of these plans is to provide a nontaxable fringe benefit to the executives by making the payment to the child in the form of an excludible scholarship. However, the IRS has ruled that the payments are generally includible in the gross income of the parent-employee.[21]

Qualified Tuition Reduction Plans

Employees (including retired and disabled former employees) of nonprofit educational institutions are allowed to exclude a tuition waiver from gross income if the waiver is pursuant to a **qualified tuition reduction plan**.[22] The plan may not discriminate in favor of highly compensated employees. The exclusion applies to the employee, the employee's spouse, and the employee's dependent children. The exclusion also extends to tuition reductions granted by any nonprofit educational institution to employees of any other nonprofit educational institution (reciprocal agreements).

EXAMPLE 10

ABC University allows the dependent children of XYZ University employees to attend ABC University with no tuition charge. XYZ University grants reciprocal benefits to the children of ABC University employees. The dependent children can also attend tuition-free the university where their parents are employed. Employees who take advantage of these benefits are not required to recognize gross income. ■

Generally, the exclusion is limited to *undergraduate* tuition waivers. However, in the case of teaching or research assistants, graduate tuition waivers may also qualify for exclusion treatment. According to the Proposed Regulations, the exclusion is limited to the value of the benefit in excess of the employee's reasonable compensation.[23] Thus, a tuition reduction that is a substitute for cash compensation cannot be excluded.

EXAMPLE 11

Susan is a graduate research assistant. She receives a $5,000 salary for 500 hours of service over a nine-month period. This pay, $10 per hour, is reasonable compensation for Susan's services. In addition, Susan receives a waiver of $6,000 for tuition. Susan may exclude the tuition waiver from gross income. ■

---

[20]Prop.Reg. § 1.117–6(b)(2).
[21]Rev.Rul. 75–448, 1975–2 C.B. 55. *Richard T. Armantrout*, 67 T.C. 996 (1977).
[22]§ 117(d).
[23]Prop.Reg. § 1.117–6(d).

When an employer retaliated against a whistle-blowing employee who had reported various alleged infractions, the employee was awarded compensatory damages for emotional distress and damage to her professional reputation. In *Murphy v. IRS*, the U.S. Court of Appeals for the D.C. Circuit recently held that the award was not includible in gross income, but rather was a recovery of capital. The court concluded that Congress exceeded the bounds of its constitutional authority when it enacted a statute that taxes as income damages received for nonphysical injury. Most com-

mentators thought that the Supreme Court would reverse the decision because the taxpayer had no capital invested in the emotions that gave rise to the damages award.

Rather than filing a Writ of Certiorari with the Supreme Court, the government petitioned the Court of Appeals for the D.C. Circuit to rehear the case. In the rehearing, the court changed its mind. It rejected all of "Murphy's arguments in all aspects." So the full amount of the award Murphy received must be included in gross income.

Compensation for Injuries and Sickness

Damages

A person who suffers harm caused by another is often entitled to compensatory damages. The tax consequences of the receipt of damages depend on the type of harm the taxpayer has experienced. The taxpayer may seek recovery for (1) a loss of income, (2) expenses incurred, (3) property destroyed, or (4) personal injury.

Generally, reimbursement for a loss of income is taxed the same as the income replaced (see the exception under Personal Injury below). The recovery of an expense is not income, unless the expense was deducted. Damages that are a recovery of the taxpayer's previously deducted expenses are generally taxable under the tax benefit rule, discussed later in this chapter.

A payment for damaged or destroyed property is treated as an amount received in a sale or exchange of the property. Thus, the taxpayer has a realized gain if the damage payments received exceed the property's basis. Damages for personal injuries receive special treatment under the Code.

Personal Injury. The legal theory of personal injury damages is that the amount received is intended "to make the plaintiff [the injured party] whole as before the injury."[24] It follows that if the damage payments received were subject to tax, the after-tax amount received would be less than the actual damages incurred and the injured party would not be "whole as before the injury."

In terms of personal injury damages, a distinction is made between compensatory damages and punitive damages. Under specified circumstances, compensatory damages may be excluded from gross income. Under no circumstances may punitive damages be excluded from gross income.

Compensatory damages are intended to compensate the taxpayer for the damages incurred. Only those compensatory damages received on account of *physical personal injury or physical sickness* can be excluded from gross income.[25] Such exclusion treatment includes amounts received for loss of income associated with the physical personal injury or physical sickness. Compensatory damages awarded on account of emotional distress are not received on account of physical injury or physical sickness and thus cannot be excluded (except to the extent of any amount received for medical care) from gross income. Likewise, any amounts received for age discrimination or injury to one's reputation cannot be excluded.

Punitive damages are amounts the person who caused the harm must pay to the victim as punishment for outrageous conduct. Punitive damages are not

[24]*C. A. Hawkins*, 6 B.T.A. 1023 (1928).   [25]§ 104(a)(2).

CONCEPT SUMMARY 5–1

Taxation of Damages

Type of Claim	Taxation of Award or Settlement
Breach of contract (generally loss of income)	Taxable.
Property damages	Recovery of cost; gain to the extent of the excess over basis. A loss is deductible for business property and investment property to the extent of basis over the amount realized. A loss may be deductible for personal use property (see discussion of casualty losses in Chapter 7).
Personal injury	
Physical	All compensatory amounts are excluded unless previously deducted (e.g., medical expenses). Amounts received as punitive damages are included in gross income.
Nonphysical	Compensatory damages and punitive damages are included in gross income.

intended to compensate the victim, but rather to punish the party who caused the harm. Thus, it follows that amounts received as punitive damages may actually place the victim in a better economic position than before the harm was experienced. Logically, punitive damages are thus included in gross income.

EXAMPLE 12

Tom, a television announcer, was dissatisfied with the manner in which Ron, an attorney, was defending the television station in a libel case. Tom stated on the air that Ron was botching the case. Ron sued Tom for slander, claiming damages for loss of income from clients and potential clients who heard Tom's statement. Ron's claim is for damages to his business reputation, and the amounts received are taxable.

Ron collected on the suit against Tom and was on his way to a party to celebrate his victory when a negligent driver, Norm, drove a truck into Ron's automobile, injuring Ron. Ron filed suit for the physical personal injuries and claimed as damages the loss of income for the period he was unable to work as a result of the injuries. Ron also collected punitive damages that were awarded because of Norm's extremely negligent behavior. Ron's wife also collected damages for the emotional distress she experienced as a result of the accident. Ron may exclude the amounts he received for damages, except the punitive damages. Ron's wife must include the amounts she received for damages in gross income because the amounts were not received because of physical personal injuries or sickness. ■

ETHICAL and EQUITABLE *Considerations*

NEGOTIATING A DAMAGES AWARD

The taxpayer was shot in a hunting accident. The person who shot the taxpayer has admitted to being grossly negligent. The taxpayer estimates that he should receive $40,000 for the personal injury and $60,000 as punitive damages. The defendant has offered to pay $80,000 and sign a settlement agreement specifying that all of the payment is for the physical injury, with no mention of the punitive damages. The defendant argues that since the taxpayer is in the 35 percent marginal tax bracket, the $80,000 will yield a greater after-tax award than a $100,000 award with $60,000 specified as being for punitive damages. Should the taxpayer let the Federal income tax influence the negotiations and the characterization of the damages?

Workers' Compensation

State workers' compensation laws require the employer to pay fixed amounts for specific job-related injuries. The state laws were enacted so that the employee will not have to go through the ordeal of a lawsuit (and possibly not collect damages because of some defense available to the employer) to recover the damages. Although the payments are intended, in part, to compensate for a loss of future income, Congress has specifically exempted workers' compensation benefits from inclusion in gross income.[26]

Accident and Health Insurance Benefits

The income tax treatment of accident and health insurance benefits depends on whether the policy providing the benefits was purchased by the taxpayer or the taxpayer's employer. Benefits collected under an accident and health insurance policy *purchased by the taxpayer* are excludible. In this case, benefits collected under the taxpayer's insurance policy are excluded even though the payments are a substitute for income.[27]

EXAMPLE 13

Bonnie purchases a medical and disability insurance policy. The insurance company pays Bonnie $1,000 per week to replace wages she loses while in the hospital. Although the payments serve as a substitute for income, the amounts received are tax-exempt benefits collected under Bonnie's insurance policy. ■

EXAMPLE 14

Joe's injury results in a partial paralysis of his left foot. He receives $20,000 for the injury from his accident insurance company under a policy he had purchased. The $20,000 accident insurance proceeds are tax-exempt. ■

A different set of rules applies if the accident and health insurance protection was *purchased by the individual's employer*, as discussed in the following section.

Employer-Sponsored Accident and Health Plans

Congress encourages employers to provide employees, retired former employees, and their dependents with **accident and health benefits**, disability insurance, and long-term care plans. The *premiums* are deductible by the employer and excluded from the employee's income.[28] Although § 105(a) provides the general rule that the employee has includible income when he or she collects the insurance *benefits*, two exceptions are provided.

Section 105(b) generally excludes payments received for medical care of the employee, spouse, and dependents. However, if the payments are for expenses that do not meet the Code's definition of medical care,[29] the amount received must be included in gross income. In addition, the taxpayer must include in gross income any amounts received for medical expenses that were deducted by the taxpayer on a prior return.

EXAMPLE 15

In 2008, Tab's employer-sponsored health insurance plan pays $4,000 for hair transplants that do not meet the Code's definition of medical care. Tab must include the $4,000 in his gross income for 2008. ■

Section 105(c) excludes payments for the permanent loss or the loss of the use of a member or function of the body or the permanent disfigurement of the

---

[26]§ 104(a)(1).
[27]§ 104(a)(3).

[28]§ 106, Reg. § 1.106–1, and Rev.Rul. 82–196, 1982–1 C.B. 106.
[29]See the discussion of medical care in Chapter 10.

WHEN JOBS LEAVE THE COUNTRY, SO DO THE HEALTH INSURANCE BENEFITS

Firms in the textile industry generally provided health insurance coverage for their employees. As textile mills in the United States close and production is moved to foreign countries, often the U.S. employees lose their health insurance as well as their jobs. If and when the former textile worker finds new employment, the new employer may not provide health insurance. In addition, the pay on the new job is often so low that the worker cannot afford to purchase health insurance, which may cost over $500 per month.

Among the factors contributing to increased foreign competition for the domestic textile industry are the North American Free Trade Agreement of 1993, the Caribbean Basin Initiative of 2000, and the opening up of trade with China.

employee, spouse, or a dependent. Payments that are a substitute for salary (e.g., related to the period of time absent) are includible.

EXAMPLE 16

Jill loses an eye in an automobile accident unrelated to her work. As a result of the accident, Jill incurs $2,000 of medical expenses, which she deducts on her return. She collects $10,000 from an accident insurance policy carried by her employer. The benefits are paid according to a schedule of amounts that vary with the part of the body injured (e.g., $10,000 for loss of an eye, $20,000 for loss of a hand). Because the payment is for loss of a *member or function of the body*, the $10,000 is excluded from gross income. Jill is absent from work for a week as a result of the accident. Her employer provides her with insurance for the loss of income due to illness or injury. Jill collects $500, which is includible in gross income. ■

Medical Reimbursement Plans

In lieu of providing the employee with insurance coverage for hospital and medical expenses, the employer may agree to reimburse the employee for these expenses. The amounts received through the insurance coverage (insured plan benefits) are excluded from income under § 105 (as previously discussed). Unfortunately in terms of cost considerations, the insurance companies that issue this type of policy usually require a broad coverage of employees. An alternative is to have a plan that is not funded with insurance (a self-insured arrangement). The benefits received under a self-insured plan can be excluded from the employee's income if the plan does not discriminate in favor of highly compensated employees.[30]

Legislation enacted in 2003 provides an alternative means of accomplishing a medical reimbursement plan. The employer can purchase a medical insurance plan with a high deductible (e.g., the employee is responsible for the first $2,100 of medical expenses) and then make contributions to the employee's **Health Savings Account (HSA)**.[31] The employer can make contributions each month up to the maximum contribution of 100 percent of the deductible amount. The monthly deductible amount is limited to the *lesser* of one-twelfth of the annual deductible under a high-deductible plan or $2,900 for self-only coverage. An individual who has family coverage is limited to the *lesser* of one-twelfth of the annual deductible under a high-deductible plan or $5,800. Withdrawals from the HSA must be used to reimburse the employee for the medical expenses paid by the employee that are not covered under the high-deductible plan. The employee is not taxed on the employer's contributions to the HSA, the earnings on the funds in the account, or the withdrawals made for medical expenses.[32]

[30]§ 105(h).

[31]§§ 106(d) and 223. See additional coverage in Chapter 10.

[32]§§ 106(d), 223(b), and 223(d). The amounts for 2007 were $2,850 and $5,650.

Long-Term Care Insurance Benefits

Generally, **long-term care insurance**, which covers expenses such as the cost of care in a nursing home, is treated the same as accident and health insurance benefits. Thus, the employee does not recognize income when the employer pays the premiums. This exclusion is subject to annual limits as follows:

Insured's Age before Close of Tax Year	2007	2008
40 or less	$ 290	$ 310
41 to 50	550	580
51 to 60	1,110	1,150
61 to 70	2,950	3,080
More than 70	3,680	3,850

When benefits are received from the policy, whether the employer or the individual purchased the policy, the exclusion from gross income is limited to the greater of the following amounts:

- $270 in 2008 (indexed amount for 2007 was $260) for each day the patient receives the long-term care.
- The actual cost of the care.

The above amount is reduced by any amounts received from other third parties (e.g., damages received).[33]

Hazel, who suffers from Alzheimer's disease, is a patient in a nursing home for the last 30 days of 2008. While in the nursing home, she incurs total costs of $7,600. Medicare pays $3,200 of the costs. Hazel receives $5,100 from her long-term care insurance policy (which pays $170 per day while she is in the facility).

The amount that Hazel may exclude is calculated as follows:

Greater of:		
Daily statutory amount of $270 ($270 × 30 days)	$8,100	
Actual cost of the care	7,600	$ 8,100
Less: Amount received from Medicare		(3,200)
Amount of exclusion		$ 4,900

E X A M P L E   17

Therefore, Hazel must include $200 ($5,100 − $4,900) of the long-term care benefits received in her gross income. ■

The exclusion for long-term care insurance is not available if it is provided as part of a cafeteria plan or a flexible spending plan.

Meals and Lodging

Furnished for the Convenience of the Employer

As discussed in Chapter 4, income can take any form, including meals and lodging. However, § 119 excludes from income the value of meals and lodging provided to the employee and the employee's spouse and dependents under the following conditions:[34]

---

[33]§§ 7702B and § 213(d)(10).

[34]§ 119(a). The meals and lodging are also excluded from FICA and FUTA tax. *Rowan Companies, Inc. v. U.S.*, 81–1 USTC ¶9479, 48 AFTR2d 81–5115, 101 S.Ct. 2288 (USSC, 1981).

- The meals and/or lodging are *furnished* by the employer, on the employer's *business premises*, for the *convenience of the employer*.
- In the case of lodging, the *employee is required* to accept the lodging as a condition of employment.

The courts have construed both of these requirements strictly.

Furnished by the Employer. The following two questions have been raised with regard to the *furnished by the employer* requirement:

- Who is considered an *employee?*
- What is meant by *furnished?*

The IRS and some courts have reasoned that because a partner is not an employee, the exclusion does not apply to a partner. However, the Tax Court and the Fifth Circuit Court of Appeals have ruled in favor of the taxpayer on this issue.[35]

The Supreme Court held that a cash meal allowance was ineligible for the exclusion because the employer did not actually furnish the meals.[36] Similarly, one court denied the exclusion where the employer paid for the food and supplied the cooking facilities but the employee prepared the meal.[37]

On the Employer's Business Premises. The *on the employer's business premises* requirement, applicable to both meals and lodging, has resulted in much litigation. The Regulations define business premises as simply "the place of employment of the employee."[38] Thus, the Sixth Circuit Court of Appeals held that a residence, owned by the employer and occupied by an employee, two blocks from the motel that the employee managed was not part of the business premises.[39] However, the Tax Court considered an employer-owned house across the street from the hotel that was managed by the taxpayer to be on the business premises of the employer.[40] Apparently, the closer the lodging to the business operations, the more likely the convenience of the employer is served.

For the Convenience of the Employer. The *convenience of the employer* test is intended to focus on the employer's motivation for furnishing the meals and lodging rather than on the benefits received by the employee. If the employer furnishes the meals and lodging primarily to enable the employee to perform his or her duties properly, it does not matter that the employee considers these benefits to be a part of his or her compensation.

The Regulations give the following examples in which the tests for excluding meals are satisfied:[41]

- A restaurant requires its service staff to eat their meals on the premises during the busy lunch and breakfast hours.
- A bank furnishes meals on the premises for its tellers to limit the time the employees are away from their booths during the busy hours.
- A worker is employed at a construction site in a remote part of Alaska. The employer must furnish meals and lodging due to the inaccessibility of other facilities.

If more than half of the employees to whom meals are furnished receive their meals for the convenience of the employer, then all such employee meals are

[35]Rev.Rul. 80, 1953–1 C.B. 62; *Comm. v. Doak,* 56–2 USTC ¶9708, 49 AFTR 1491, 234 F.2d 704 (CA–4, 1956); but see *G. A. Papineau,* 16 T.C. 130 (1951); *Armstrong v. Phinney,* 68–1 USTC ¶9355, 21 AFTR2d 1260, 394 F.2d 661 (CA–5, 1968).

[36]*Comm. v. Kowalski,* 77–2 USTC ¶9748, 40 AFTR2d 6128, 98 S.Ct. 315 (USSC, 1977).

[37]*Tougher v. Comm.,* 71–1 USTC ¶9398, 27 AFTR2d 1301, 441 F.2d 1148 (CA–9, 1971).

[38]Reg. § 1.119–1(c)(1).

[39]*Comm. v. Anderson,* 67–1 USTC ¶9136, 19 AFTR2d 318, 371 F.2d 59 (CA–6, 1966).

[40]*J. B. Lindeman,* 60 T.C. 609 (1973).

[41]Reg. § 1.119–1(f).

treated as provided for the convenience of the employer.[42] Thus, in this situation, all employees are treated the same (either all of the employees are allowed exclusion treatment, or none of the employees can exclude the meals from gross income).

E X A M P L E   18

Allison's Restaurant has a restaurant area and a bar. Nine employees work in the restaurant and three work in the bar. All of the employees are provided one meal per day. In the case of the restaurant workers, the meals are provided for the convenience of the employer. The meals provided to the bar employees do not satisfy the convenience of the employer requirement. Because more than half of the employees receive their meal for the convenience of the employer, all 12 employees qualify for exclusion treatment. ∎

Required as a Condition of Employment.
The *employee is required to accept* test applies only to lodging. If the employee's use of the housing would serve the convenience of the employer, but the employee is not required to use the housing, the exclusion is not available.

E X A M P L E   19

VEP, a utilities company, has all of its service personnel on 24-hour call for emergencies. The company encourages its employees to live near the plant so that the employees can respond quickly to emergency calls. Company-owned housing is available rent-free. Only 10 of the employees live in the company housing because it is not suitable for families.

Although the company-provided housing serves the convenience of the employer, it is not required. Therefore, the employees who live in the company housing cannot exclude its value from gross income. ∎

In addition, if the employee has the *option* of cash or lodging, the *required* test is not satisfied.

E X A M P L E   20

Khalid is the manager of a large apartment complex. The employer gives Khalid the option of rent-free housing (value of $6,000 per year) or an additional $5,000 per year. Khalid selects the housing option. Therefore, he must include $6,000 in gross income. ∎

Other Housing Exclusions

Employees of Educational Institutions.
An employee of an educational institution may be able to exclude the value of campus housing provided by the employer. Generally, the employee does not recognize income if he or she pays annual rents equal to or greater than 5 percent of the appraised value of the facility. If the rent payments are less than 5 percent of the value of the facility, the deficiency must be included in gross income.[43]

E X A M P L E   21

Swan University provides on-campus housing for its full-time faculty during the first three years of employment. The housing is not provided for the convenience of the employer. Professor Edith pays $3,000 annual rent for the use of a residence with an appraised value of $100,000 and an annual rental value of $12,000. Edith must recognize $2,000 gross income [.05($100,000) − $3,000 = $2,000] for the value of the housing provided to her. ∎

Ministers of the Gospel.
Ministers of the gospel can exclude (1) the rental value of a home furnished as compensation; (2) a rental allowance paid to them as compensation, to the extent the allowance is used to rent or provide a home; or (3) the rental value of a home owned by the minister.[44] The housing or

---

[42]§ 119(b)(4).
[43]§ 119(d).

[44]§ 107 and Reg. § 1.107–1.

housing allowance must be provided as compensation for the conduct of religious worship, the administration and maintenance of religious organizations, or the performance of teaching and administrative duties at theological seminaries.

EXAMPLE 22

Pastor Bill is allowed to live rent-free in a house owned by the congregation. The annual rental value of the house is $6,000 and is provided as part of the pastor's compensation for ministerial services. Assistant Pastor Olga is paid a $4,500 cash housing allowance. She uses the $4,500 to pay rent and utilities on a home she and her family occupy. Neither Pastor Bill nor Assistant Pastor Olga is required to recognize gross income associated with the housing or housing allowance. ■

Military Personnel. Military personnel are allowed housing exclusions under various circumstances. Authority for these exclusions generally is found in Federal laws that are not part of the Internal Revenue Code.[45]

Other Employee Fringe Benefits

Specific Benefits

Congress has enacted exclusions to encourage employers to (1) finance and make available child care facilities, (2) provide athletic facilities for employees, (3) finance certain employees' education, and (4) pay or reimburse child adoption expenses. These provisions are summarized as follows:

- The employee does not have to include in gross income the value of child and dependent care services paid for by the employer and incurred to enable the employee to work. The exclusion cannot exceed $5,000 per year ($2,500 if married and filing separately). For a married couple, the annual exclusion cannot exceed the earned income of the spouse who has the lesser amount of earned income. For an unmarried taxpayer, the exclusion cannot exceed the taxpayer's earned income.[46]
- The value of the use of a gymnasium or other athletic facilities by employees, their spouses, and their dependent children may be excluded from an employee's gross income. The facilities must be on the employer's premises, and substantially all of the use of the facilities must be by employees and their family members.[47]
- Qualified employer-provided educational assistance (tuition, fees, books, and supplies) at the undergraduate and graduate level is excludible from gross income. The exclusion does not cover meals, lodging, and transportation costs. In addition, it does not cover educational payments for courses involving sports, games, or hobbies. The exclusion is subject to an annual employee statutory ceiling of $5,250.[48]
- The employee can exclude from gross income up to $11,650 of expenses incurred to adopt a child where the adoption expenses are paid or reimbursed by the employer under a qualified adoption assistance program.[49] The limit on the exclusion is the same even if the child has special needs (is not physically or mentally capable of caring for himself or herself). However, for a child with special needs, the $11,650 exclusion from gross income applies even if the actual adoption expenses are less than that amount. The exclusion is phased out as adjusted gross income increases from $174,730 to $214,730.

[45]H. Rep. No. 99–841, 99th Cong., 2d Sess., p. 548 (1986). See also § 134.

[46]§ 129. The exclusion applies to the same types of expenses that, if they were paid by the employee (and not reimbursed by the employer), would be eligible for the credit for child and dependent care expense discussed in Chapter 13.

[47]§ 132(j)(4).

[48]§ 127.

[49]§ 137.

TAX *in the News* EMPLOYEE TUITION ASSISTANCE OFFERS BENEFITS TO EMPLOYERS TOO

Some employers are reluctant to provide college tuition assistance to employees because they fear that the employees may use the benefits to enhance their qualifications so that they can find a job with another employer. Recent studies, however, have consistently shown that tuition assistance programs tend to attract higher-quality employees who stay on the job longer with that employer.

Large employers are more likely to provide educational assistance. According to academic research, 85 per-cent of 1,000 surveyed large employers offered some form of tuition assistance. The employers see these programs as both a recruitment tool and a retention tool. More education enables the employees to enjoy upward mobility within the company, and retaining highly trained employees is becoming more important as the baby boomers start to retire and the labor market becomes more competitive.

Source: *Adapted from Erin White, "Corporate Tuition Aid Appears to Keep Workers Loyal,"* Wall Street Journal, *May 21, 2007, p. B4.*

Cafeteria Plans

Generally, if an employee is offered a choice between cash and some other form of compensation, the employee is deemed to have constructively received the cash even when the noncash option is elected. Thus, the employee has gross income regardless of the option chosen.

An exception to this constructive receipt treatment is provided under the **cafeteria plan** rules. Under such a plan, the employee is permitted to choose between cash and nontaxable benefits (e.g., group term life insurance, health and accident protection, and child care). If the employee chooses the otherwise nontaxable benefits, the cafeteria plan rules enable the benefits to remain nontaxable.[50] Cafeteria plans provide tremendous flexibility in tailoring the employee pay package to fit individual needs. Some employees (usually the younger group) prefer cash, while others (usually the older group) will opt for the fringe benefit program. However, Congress excluded long-term care insurance from the excludible benefits that can be provided under a cafeteria plan.[51] Thus, the employer must provide these benefits separate from the cafeteria plan.

EXAMPLE 23

Hawk Corporation offers its employees (on a nondiscriminatory basis) a choice of any one or all of the following benefits:

Benefit	Cost
Group term life insurance	$ 200
Hospitalization insurance for family members	2,400
Child care payments	1,800
	$4,400

If a benefit is not selected, the employee receives cash equal to the cost of the benefit. Kay, an employee, has a spouse who works for another employer that provides hospitalization insurance but no child care payments. Kay elects to receive the group term life insurance, the child care payments, and $2,400 of cash. Only the $2,400 must be included in Kay's gross income. ∎

---

[50]§ 125. [51]§ 125(f).

Flexible Spending Plans

Flexible spending plans (often referred to as flexible benefit plans) operate much like cafeteria plans. Under these plans, the employee accepts lower cash compensation in return for the employer agreeing to pay certain costs that the employer can pay without the employee recognizing gross income. For example, assume the employer's health insurance policy does not cover dental expenses. The employee could estimate his or her dental expenses for the upcoming year and agree to a salary reduction equal to the estimated dental expenses. The employer then pays or reimburses the employee for the actual dental expenses incurred, with a ceiling of the amount of the salary reduction. If the employee's actual dental expenses are less than the reduction in cash compensation, the employee cannot recover the difference. Hence, these plans are often referred to as *use or lose* plans. As is the case for cafeteria plans, flexible spending plans cannot be used to pay long-term care insurance premiums.

Under recently issued IRS rules for these *use or lose* plans, the taxpayer has until the fifteenth day of the third month after the end of the plan year to use the funds for qualified expenses (a two and one-half month grace period). Employers have generally amended their plans to provide that payments made during the grace period will be taken first from the balance in the flexible spending account at the beginning of the plan year.

General Classes of Excluded Benefits

An employer can confer numerous forms and types of economic benefits on employees. Under the all-inclusive concept of income, the benefits are taxable unless one of the provisions previously discussed specifically excludes the item from gross income. The amount of the income is the fair market value of the benefit. This reasoning can lead to results that Congress considers unacceptable, as illustrated in the following example.

EXAMPLE 24

Vern is employed in New York as a ticket clerk for Trans National Airlines. He has a sick mother in Miami, Florida, but has no money for plane tickets. Trans National has daily flights from New York to Miami that often leave with empty seats. The cost of a round-trip ticket is $400, and Vern is in the 25% tax bracket. If Trans National allows Vern to fly without charge to Miami, under the general gross income rules, Vern has income equal to the value of a ticket. Therefore, Vern must pay $100 tax (.25 × $400) on a trip to Miami. Because Vern does not have $100, he cannot visit his mother, and the airplane flies with another empty seat. ∎

If Trans National in Example 24 will allow employees to use resources that would otherwise be wasted, why should the tax laws interfere with the employee's decision to take advantage of the available benefit? Thus, to avoid the undesirable results that occur in Example 24 and in similar situations, as well as to create uniform rules for fringe benefits, Congress established seven broad classes of nontaxable employee benefits:[52]

- No-additional-cost services.
- Qualified employee discounts.
- Working condition fringes.
- *De minimis* fringes.
- Qualified transportation fringes.
- Qualified moving expense reimbursements.
- Qualified retirement planning services.

---

[52]See, generally, § 132.

No-Additional-Cost Services. Example 24 illustrates the **no-additional-cost service** type of fringe benefit. The services will be nontaxable if all of the following conditions are satisfied:

- The employee receives services, as opposed to property.
- The employer does not incur substantial additional cost, including forgone revenue, in providing the services to the employee.
- The services are offered to customers in the ordinary course of the business in which the employee works.[53]

EXAMPLE 25

Assume that Vern in Example 24 can fly without charge only if the airline cannot fill the seats with paying customers. That is, Vern must fly on standby. Although the airplane may burn slightly more fuel because Vern is on the airplane and Vern may receive the same meal or snacks as paying customers, the additional costs would not be substantial. Thus, the trip could qualify as a no-additional-cost service.

On the other hand, assume that Vern is given a reserved seat on a flight that is frequently full. The employer would be forgoing revenue to allow Vern to fly. This forgone revenue would be a substantial additional cost, and thus the benefit would be taxable. ∎

Note that if Vern were employed in a hotel owned by Trans National, the receipt of the airline ticket would be taxable because Vern did not work in that line of business. However, the Code allows the exclusion for reciprocal benefits offered by employers in the same line of business.

EXAMPLE 26

Grace is employed as a desk clerk for Plush Hotels, Inc. The company and Chain Hotels, Inc., have an agreement that allows any of their employees to stay without charge in either company's resort hotels during the off-season. If Grace takes advantage of the plan by staying in a Chain Hotel, she is not required to recognize income. ∎

The no-additional-cost exclusion extends to the employee's spouse and dependent children and to retired and disabled former employees. In the Regulations, the IRS has conceded that partners who perform services for the partnership are employees for purposes of the exclusion.[54] (As discussed earlier in the chapter, the IRS's position is that partners are not employees for purposes of the § 119 meals and lodging exclusion.) However, the exclusion is not allowed to highly compensated employees unless the benefit is available on a nondiscriminatory basis.

Qualified Employee Discounts. When the employer sells goods or services (other than no-additional-cost benefits just discussed) to the employee for a price that is less than the price charged regular customers, the employee realizes income equal to the discount. However, the discount, referred to as a **qualified employee discount**, can be excluded from the gross income of the employee, subject to the following conditions and limitations:

- The exclusion is not available for real property (e.g., a house) or for personal property of the type commonly held for investment (e.g., common stocks).
- The property or services must be from the same line of business in which the employee works.
- In the case of *property*, the exclusion is limited to the *gross profit component* of the price to customers.
- In the case of *services*, the exclusion is limited to 20 percent of the customer price.[55]

---

[53]Reg. § 1.132–2.
[54]Reg. § 1.132–1(b).

[55]§ 132(c).

| EXAMPLE 27 | Silver Corporation, which operates a department store, sells a television set to a store employee for $300. The regular customer price is $500, and the gross profit rate is 25%. The corporation also sells the employee a service contract for $120. The regular customer price for the contract is $150. The employee must include $75 in gross income. |

Customer price for property	$ 500
Less: Gross profit (25%)	(125)
	$ 375
Employee price	(300)
Income	$ 75
Customer price for service	$ 150
Less: 20 percent	(30)
	$ 120
Employee price	(120)
Income	$ –0–

EXAMPLE 28

Assume the same facts as in Example 27, except that the employee is a clerk in a hotel operated by Silver Corporation. Because the line of business requirement is not met, the employee must recognize $200 income ($500 − $300) from the purchase of the television and $30 income ($150 − $120) from the service contract. ■

As in the case of no-additional-cost benefits, the exclusion applies to employees (including service partners), employees' spouses and dependent children, and retired and disabled former employees. However, the exclusion does not apply to highly compensated individuals unless the discount is available on a nondiscriminatory basis.

Working Condition Fringes. Generally, an employee is not required to include in gross income the cost of property or services provided by the employer if the employee could deduct the cost of those items if he or she had actually paid for them.[56] These benefits are called **working condition fringes**.

EXAMPLE 29

Mitch is a CPA employed by an accounting firm. The employer pays Mitch's annual dues to professional organizations. Mitch is not required to include the payment of the dues in gross income because if he had paid the dues, he would have been allowed to deduct the amount as an employee business expense (as discussed in Chapter 9). ■

In many cases, this exclusion merely avoids reporting income and an offsetting deduction. However, in two specific situations, the working condition fringe benefit rules allow an exclusion where the expense would not be deductible if paid by the employee:

- Automobile salespeople are allowed to exclude the value of certain personal use of company demonstrators (e.g., commuting to and from work).[57]
- The employee business expense would be eliminated by the 2 percent floor on miscellaneous deductions under § 67 (see Chapter 10).

Unlike the other fringe benefits discussed previously, working condition fringes can be made available on a discriminatory basis and still qualify for the exclusion.

---

[56]§ 132(d).
[57]§ 132(j)(3).

De Minimis **Fringes.** As the term suggests, *de minimis fringe* benefits are so small that accounting for them is impractical.[58] The House Report contains the following examples of *de minimis* fringes:

- The typing of a personal letter by a company secretary, occasional personal use of a company copying machine, occasional company cocktail parties or picnics for employees, occasional supper money or taxi fare for employees because of overtime work, and certain holiday gifts of property with a low fair market value are excluded.
- Subsidized eating facilities (e.g., an employees' cafeteria) operated by the employer are excluded if located on or near the employer's business premises, if revenue equals or exceeds direct operating costs, and if nondiscrimination requirements are met.

When taxpayers venture beyond the specific examples contained in the House Report and the Regulations, there is obviously much room for disagreement as to what is *de minimis*. However, note that except in the case of subsidized eating facilities, the *de minimis* fringe benefits can be granted in a manner that favors highly compensated employees.

Qualified Transportation Fringes. The intent of the exclusion for **qualified transportation fringes** is to encourage the use of mass transit for commuting to and from work. Qualified transportation fringes encompass the following transportation benefits provided by the employer to the employee:[59]

1. Transportation in a commuter highway vehicle between the employee's residence and the place of employment.
2. A transit pass.
3. Qualified parking.

Statutory dollar limits are placed on the amount of the exclusion. Categories (1) and (2) above are combined for purposes of applying the limit. In this case, the limit on the exclusion for 2008 is $115 per month ($110 in 2007). Category (3) has a separate limit. For qualified parking, the limit on the exclusion for 2008 is $220 per month ($215 in 2007). Both of these dollar limits are indexed annually for inflation.

A *commuter highway vehicle* is any highway vehicle with a seating capacity of at least six adults (excluding the driver). In addition, at least 80 percent of the vehicle's use must be for transporting employees between their residences and place of employment.

Qualified parking includes the following:

- Parking provided to an employee on or near the employer's business premises.
- Parking provided to an employee on or near a location from which the employee commutes to work via mass transit, in a commuter highway vehicle, or in a carpool.

Qualified transportation fringes may be provided directly by the employer or may be in the form of cash reimbursements.

EXAMPLE 30

Gray Corporation's offices are located in the center of a large city. The company pays for parking spaces to be used by the company officers. Steve, a vice president, receives $250 of such benefits each month. The parking space rental qualifies as a qualified transportation fringe. Of the $250 benefit received each month by Steve, $220 is excludible from gross income. The balance of $30 is included in his gross income. The same result would occur if Steve paid for the parking and was reimbursed by his employer. ■

---

[58]§ 132(e).   [59]§ 132(f).

Qualified Moving Expense Reimbursements. Qualified moving expenses that are reimbursed or paid by the employer are excludible from gross income. A qualified moving expense is one that would be deductible under § 217. See the discussion of moving expenses in Chapter 9.

Qualified Retirement Planning Services. Qualified retirement planning services include any retirement planning advice or information that an employer who maintains a qualified retirement plan provides to an employee or the employee's spouse.[60] Congress decided to exclude the value of such services from gross income because they are a key part of retirement income planning. Such an exclusion should motivate more employers to provide retirement planning services to their employees.

Nondiscrimination Provisions. For no-additional-cost services, qualified employee discounts, and qualified retirement planning services, if the plan is discriminatory in favor of highly compensated employees, these key employees are denied exclusion treatment. However, the non-highly compensated employees who receive benefits from the plan can still enjoy exclusion treatment for the no-additional-cost services, qualified employee discounts, and qualified retirement planning services.[61]

EXAMPLE 31

Dove Company's officers are allowed to purchase goods from the company at a 25% discount. Other employees are allowed only a 15% discount. The company's gross profit margin on these goods is 30%.

Peggy, an officer in the company, purchased goods from the company for $750 when the price charged to customers was $1,000. Peggy must include $250 in gross income because the plan is discriminatory.

Leo, an employee of the company who is not an officer, purchased goods for $850 when the customer price was $1,000. Leo is not required to recognize gross income because he received a qualified employee discount. ■

De minimis (except in the case of subsidized eating facilities) and working condition fringe benefits can be provided on a discriminatory basis. The *de minimis* benefits are not subject to tax because the accounting problems that would be created are out of proportion to the amount of additional tax that would result. A nondiscrimination test would simply add to the compliance problems. In the case of working condition fringes, the types of services required vary with the job. Therefore, a nondiscrimination test probably could not be satisfied, although usually there is no deliberate plan to benefit a chosen few. Likewise, the qualified transportation fringe and the qualified moving expense reimbursement can be provided on a discriminatory basis.

Taxable Fringe Benefits

If the fringe benefits cannot qualify for any of the specific exclusions or do not fit into any of the general classes of excluded benefits, the taxpayer must recognize gross income equal to the fair market value of the benefits. Obviously, problems are frequently encountered in determining values. The IRS has issued extensive Regulations addressing the valuation of personal use of an employer's automobiles and meals provided at an employer-operated eating facility.[62]

If a fringe benefit plan discriminates in favor of highly compensated employees, generally those employees are not allowed to exclude the benefits they receive that other employees do not enjoy. However, the highly compensated employees,

[60]§§ 132(a)(7) and (m).
[61]§§ 132(j)(1) and 132(m)(2).
[62]Reg. § 1.61–21(d). Generally, the income from the personal use of the employer's automobile is based on the lease value of the automobile (what it would have cost the employee to lease the automobile). Meals are valued at 150% of the employer's direct costs (e.g., food and labor) of preparing the meals.

as well as the other employees, are generally allowed to exclude the nondiscriminatory benefits.[63]

EXAMPLE 32

MED Company has a medical reimbursement plan that reimburses officers for 100% of their medical expenses, but reimburses all other employees for only 80% of their medical expenses. Cliff, the president of the company, was reimbursed $1,000 during the year for medical expenses. Cliff must include $200 in gross income [$(1 - .80) \times \$1,000 = \$200$]. Mike, an employee who is not an officer, received $800 (80% of his actual medical expenses) under the medical reimbursement plan. None of the $800 is includible in his gross income. ■

Foreign Earned Income

A U.S. citizen is generally subject to U.S. tax on his or her income regardless of the income's geographic origin. The income may also be subject to tax in the foreign country, and thus the taxpayer must carry a double tax burden. Out of a sense of fairness and to encourage U.S. citizens to work abroad (so that exports might be increased), Congress has provided alternative forms of relief from taxes on foreign earned income. The taxpayer can elect *either* (1) to include the foreign income in his or her taxable income and then claim a credit for foreign taxes paid or (2) to exclude the foreign earnings from his or her U.S. gross income (the **foreign earned income exclusion**).[64] The foreign tax credit option is discussed in Chapter 13, but as is apparent from the following discussion, most taxpayers will choose the exclusion.

Foreign earned income consists of the earnings from the individual's personal services rendered in a foreign country (other than as an employee of the U.S. government). To qualify for the exclusion, the taxpayer must be either of the following:

• A bona fide resident of the foreign country (or countries).
• Present in a foreign country (or countries) for at least 330 days during any 12 consecutive months.[65]

EXAMPLE 33

Sandra's trips to and from a foreign country in connection with her work were as follows:

Arrived in Foreign Country	Arrived in United States
March 10, 2007	February 1, 2008
March 7, 2008	June 1, 2008

During the 12 consecutive months ending on March 10, 2008, Sandra was present in the foreign country for at least 330 days (366 days less 29 days in February and 7 days in March 2008). Therefore, all income earned in the foreign country through March 10, 2008, is eligible for the exclusion. The income earned from March 11, 2008, through May 31, 2008, is also eligible for the exclusion because Sandra was present in the foreign country for 330 days during the 12 consecutive months ending on May 31, 2008. ■

The exclusion is *limited* to an indexed amount of $87,600 for 2008 ($85,700 in 2007). For married persons, both of whom have foreign earned income, the exclusion is computed separately for each spouse. Community property rules do not apply (the community property spouse is not deemed to have earned one-half of

---

[63]§§ 79(d), 105(h), 127(b)(2), and 132(j)(1). See the discussion of the term "highly compensated employee" in Chapter 19.
[64]§ 911(a).

[65]§ 911(d). For the definition of resident, see Reg. § 1.871–2(b). Under the Regulations, a taxpayer is not a resident if he or she is there for a definite period (e.g., until completion of a construction contract).

CONCEPT SUMMARY 5–2

General Classes of Excluded Benefits

Benefit	Description and Examples	Coverage Allowed	Effect of Discrimination
1. No-additional-cost services	The employee takes advantage of the employer's excess capacity (e.g., free passes for airline employees).	Current, retired, and disabled employees; their spouses and dependent children; spouses of deceased employees. Partners are treated as employees.	No exclusion for highly compensated employees.
2. Qualified discounts on goods	The employee is allowed to purchase the employer's merchandise at a price that is not less than the employer's cost.	Same as (1) above.	Same as (1) above.
3. Qualified discounts on services	The employee is allowed a discount (maximum of 20%) on services the employer offers to customers.	Same as (1) above.	Same as (1) above.
4. Working condition fringes	Expenses paid by the employer that would be deductible if paid by the employee (e.g., a mechanic's tools). Also, includes auto salesperson's use of a car held for sale.	Current employees, partners, directors, and independent contractors.	No effect.
5. De minimis items	Expenses so immaterial that accounting for them is not warranted (e.g., occasional supper money, personal use of the copy machine).	Any recipient of a fringe benefit.	No effect.
6. Qualified transportation fringes	Transportation benefits provided by the employer to employees including commuting in a commuter highway vehicle, a transit pass, and qualified parking.	Current employees.	No effect.
7. Qualified moving expense reimbursements	Qualified moving expenses that are paid or reimbursed by the employer. A qualified moving expense is one that would be deductible under § 217.	Current employees.	No effect.
8. Qualified retirement planning services	Qualified retirement planning services that are provided by the employer.	Current employees and spouses.	Same as (1) above.

U.S. TAXPAYERS ABROAD ARE GONE BUT NOT FORGOTTEN

U.S. citizens and residents working and living abroad create unique compliance issues for the IRS. These individuals are potentially liable for U.S. taxes and must file U.S. tax returns, even if they earn less than the § 911 foreign earned income exclusion amount. However, in practical terms, many of these individuals are outside the enforcement net of the IRS. In recent years, the IRS has taken several steps to improve compliance, including taxpayer education, simplification of the filing burden, and increased enforcement efforts.

GLOBAL
Tax Issues

the other spouse's foreign earned income). If all the days in the tax year are not qualifying days, then the taxpayer must compute the maximum exclusion on a daily basis ($87,600 divided by the number of days in the entire year and multiplied by the number of qualifying days).

EXAMPLE 34

Keith qualifies for the foreign earned income exclusion. He was present in France for all of 2008. Keith's salary for 2008 is $90,000. Since all of the days in 2008 are qualifying days, Keith can exclude $87,600 of his $90,000 salary.

Assume instead that only 335 days were qualifying days. Then, Keith's exclusion is limited to $80,180, computed as follows:

$$\$87,600 \times \frac{335 \text{ days in foreign country}}{366 \text{ days in the year}} = \$80,180 \quad \blacksquare$$

ETHICAL and EQUITABLE *Considerations*

WHO SHOULD BENEFIT FROM THE FOREIGN EARNED INCOME EXCLUSION?

Perhaps the tax law should be changed so that when an employer transfers an employee to a foreign country for a period sufficient to qualify for the foreign earned income exclusion, the benefits of the exclusion could be allocated to the employee, the employer, or both. The purpose of the tax law in this area is to increase exports; therefore, a case can be made that all of the tax benefits should be assigned to the employer.

One way of accomplishing this would be to ensure that the employer's after-tax cost for compensation paid to an employee is the same whether the employee works in the United States or in a foreign country. However, employees may not be willing to work abroad unless they receive some of the tax benefit. Evaluate the equity of a change in the tax law that would assign some or all of the tax benefit to the employer.

In addition to the exclusion for foreign earnings, the *reasonable housing costs* incurred by the taxpayer and the taxpayer's family in a foreign country in excess of a base amount may be excluded from gross income. The base amount is 16 percent of the statutory amount (indexed amount for 2008 is $87,600) assuming all of the days are qualifying days for the foreign earned income exclusion. The housing costs exclusion is limited to 30 percent of the statutory amount (as indexed) for the foreign earned income exclusion.[66]

As previously mentioned, the taxpayer may elect to include the foreign earned income in gross income and claim a credit (an offset against U.S. tax) for the foreign tax paid. The credit alternative may be advantageous if the individual's foreign earned income far exceeds the excludible amount so that the

---

[66]§ 911(c).

TAX *in the News*	TO QUALIFY FOR THE FOREIGN EARNED INCOME EXCLUSION, YOU MUST WORK IN A "COUNTRY"

Mr. Arnett found out that to qualify for the foreign earned income exclusion, it is not sufficient that where you work is "foreign"—you must also work in a country. Mr. Arnett worked in Antarctica for the requisite period of time, but the court concluded that the term "foreign country" means a territory under the sovereignty of a government other than that of the United States. Under various treaties, Antarctica is not under the sovereignty of any government. Therefore, Mr. Arnett did not qualify for the foreign earned income exclusion. Apparently, the exclusion would also be denied to a person working in outer space (i.e., at the International Space Station).

Source: *Arnett v. Comm.*, 99 AFTR2d 2007–492, 473 F.3d 790 (CA–7, 2007).

foreign taxes paid exceed the U.S. tax on the amount excluded. However, once an election is made, it applies to all subsequent years unless affirmatively revoked. A revocation is effective for the year of the change and the four subsequent years.

Interest on Certain State and Local Government Obligations

At the time the Sixteenth Amendment was ratified by the states, there was some question as to whether the Federal government possessed the constitutional authority to tax interest on state and local government obligations. Taxing such interest was thought to violate the doctrine of intergovernmental immunity in that the tax would impair the state and local governments' ability to finance their operations.[67] Thus, interest on state and local government obligations was specifically exempted from Federal income taxation.[68] However, the Supreme Court has concluded that there is no constitutional prohibition against levying a nondiscriminatory Federal income tax on state and local government obligations.[69] Nevertheless, currently the statutory exclusion still exists.

Obviously, the exclusion of the interest reduces the cost of borrowing for state and local governments. A taxpayer in the 35 percent tax bracket requires only a 5.2 percent yield on a tax-exempt bond to obtain the same after-tax income as a taxable bond paying 8 percent interest [$5.2\% \div (1 - .35) = 8\%$].

The current exempt status applies solely to state and local government bonds. Thus, income received from the accrual of interest on a condemnation award or an overpayment of state income tax is fully taxable.[70] Nor does the exemption apply to gains on the sale of tax-exempt securities.

EXAMPLE 35

Megan purchases State of Virginia bonds for $10,000 on July 1, 2007. The bonds pay $400 interest each June 30th and December 31st. On March 31, 2008, Megan sells the bonds for $10,500 plus $200 accrued interest. Megan must recognize a $500 gain ($10,500 − $10,000), but the $200 accrued interest is exempt from taxation. ■

Although the Internal Revenue Code excludes from Federal gross income the interest on state and local government bonds, the interest on U.S.

---

[67] *Pollock v. Farmer's Loan & Trust Co.*, 3 AFTR 2602, 15 S.Ct. 912 (USSC, 1895).

[68] § 103(a).

[69] *South Carolina v. Baker III*, 88–1 USTC ¶9284, 61 AFTR2d 88–995, 108 S.Ct. 1355 (USSC, 1988).

[70] *Kieselbach v. Comm.*, 43–1 USTC ¶9220, 30 AFTR 370, 63 S.Ct. 303 (USSC, 1943); *U.S. Trust Co. of New York v. Anderson*, 3 USTC ¶1125, 12 AFTR 836, 65 F.2d 575 (CA–2, 1933).

government bonds is not excluded from the Federal tax base. Congress has decided, however, that if the Federal government is not to tax state and local bond interest, the state and local governments are prohibited from taxing interest on U.S. government bonds.[71] While this parity between the Federal and state and local governments exists in regard to taxing each others' obligations, the states are free to tax one another's obligations. Thus, some states exempt the interest on the bonds they issue, but tax the interest on bonds issued by other states.[72]

EXAMPLE 36

Aaron is a resident of Virginia. He owns U.S. government bonds that paid him $800 interest during the current year. He also invests in American States Bond Fund, which reports to Aaron that his share of Virginia interest income is $300 and his share of interest income from other states is $600. Aaron must include the $800 in his Federal gross income. Virginia exempts from Virginia taxation the interest on the Virginia bonds, but taxes the interest on bonds issued by other states. Therefore, Aaron must include $600 of interest from other states in his Virginia gross income. ∎

Dividends

General Information

A *dividend* is a payment to a shareholder with respect to his or her stock (see Chapter 4). Dividends to shareholders are taxable only to the extent the payments are made from *either* the corporation's *current earnings and profits* (similar to net income per books) or its *accumulated earnings and profits* (similar to retained earnings per books).[73] Distributions that exceed earnings and profits are treated as a nontaxable recovery of capital and reduce the shareholder's basis in the stock. Once the shareholder's basis is reduced to zero, any subsequent distributions are taxed as capital gains (see Chapter 14).[74]

Some payments are frequently referred to as dividends but are not considered dividends for tax purposes:

- Dividends received on deposits with savings and loan associations, credit unions, and banks are actually interest (a contractual rate paid for the use of money).
- Patronage dividends paid by cooperatives (e.g., for farmers) are rebates made to the users and are considered reductions in the cost of items purchased from the association. The rebates are usually made after year-end (after the cooperative has determined whether it has met its expenses) and are apportioned among members on the basis of their purchases.
- Mutual insurance companies pay dividends on unmatured life insurance policies that are considered rebates of premiums.
- Shareholders in a mutual investment fund are allowed to report as capital gains their proportionate share of the fund's gains realized and distributed. The capital gain and ordinary income portions are reported on the Form 1099 that the fund supplies its shareholders each year.

---

[71]31 U.S.C.A. § 742.

[72]The practice of a state exempting interest on its bonds from tax but taxing the interest on bonds issued by other states is currently being challenged in the Supreme Court as a violation of the commerce clause of the U.S. Constitution. *Kentucky v. Davis*, 197 S.W.2d 557 (Ky. Ct. App., 2006), *cert. granted*, 127 S.Ct. 2451 (2007).

[73]§ 316(a). Refer to the discussion of the beneficial tax rates for qualified dividends in Chapter 4.

[74]§ 301(c). See Chapter 5, *South-Western Federal Taxation: Corporations, Partnerships, Estates, and Trusts*, for a detailed discussion of corporate distributions.

ETHICAL and EQUITABLE *Considerations*

BENEFICIARIES AND VICTIMS OF CHANGES IN DIVIDEND TAXATION

Beginning in 2003, the tax rate on dividends was reduced to the rate applied to long-term capital gains. Such a rate reduction should have caused the market prices of dividend-paying stocks to increase and the market prices of bonds to decrease as funds were diverted to investments in stock. Thus, taxpayers who were heavily invested in dividend-paying stocks at the time of the rate reduction were beneficiaries of the change while those individuals who were primarily invested in bonds were victims. When Congress enacts new laws, should it consider the economic consequences of the change on taxpayers who made investment decisions under a prior law? Would a "grandfather" provision help?

Stock Dividends

When a corporation issues a simple stock dividend (e.g., common stock issued to common shareholders), the shareholder has merely received additional shares that represent the same total investment. Thus, the shareholder does not realize income.[75] However, if the shareholder has the *option* of receiving either cash or stock in the corporation, the individual realizes gross income whether he or she receives stock or cash.[76] A taxpayer who elects to receive the stock could be deemed to be in constructive receipt of the cash he or she has rejected.[77] However, the amount of the income in this case is the value of the stock received, rather than the cash the shareholder has rejected. See Chapter 14 for a detailed discussion of stock dividends.

Educational Savings Bonds

The cost of a college education has risen dramatically during the past 15 years. According to U.S. Department of Education estimates, the cost of attending a publicly supported university for four years now commonly exceeds $60,000. For a private university, the cost often exceeds $200,000. Consequently, Congress has attempted to assist low- to middle-income parents in saving for their children's college education.

The assistance is in the form of an interest income exclusion on **educational savings bonds**.[78] The interest on Series EE U.S. government savings bonds may be excluded from gross income if the bond proceeds are used to pay qualified higher education expenses. The exclusion applies only if both of the following requirements are satisfied:

- The savings bonds are issued after December 31, 1989.
- The savings bonds are issued to an individual who is at least 24 years old at the time of issuance.

The exclusion is not available for a married couple who file separate returns.

The redemption proceeds must be used to pay qualified higher education expenses. *Qualified higher education expenses* consist of tuition and fees paid to an eligible educational institution for the taxpayer, spouse, or dependent. In calculating qualified higher education expenses, the tuition and fees paid are reduced by excludible scholarships and veterans' benefits received. If the redemption proceeds (both principal and interest) exceed the qualified higher education expenses, only a pro rata portion of the interest will qualify for exclusion treatment.

---

[75]*Eisner v. Macomber*, 1 USTC ¶32, 3 AFTR 3020, 40 S.Ct. 189 (USSC, 1920); § 305(a).

[76]§ 305(b).

[77]Refer to the discussion of constructive receipt in Chapter 4.

[78]§ 135.

EXAMPLE 37

Tracy's redemption proceeds from qualified savings bonds during the taxable year are $6,000 (principal of $4,000 and interest of $2,000). Tracy's qualified higher education expenses are $5,000. Since the redemption proceeds exceed the qualified higher education expenses, only $1,667 [($5,000/$6,000) × $2,000] of the interest is excludible. ■

The exclusion is limited by the application of the wherewithal to pay concept. That is, once the modified adjusted gross income exceeds a threshold amount, the phaseout of the exclusion begins. *Modified adjusted gross income (MAGI)* is adjusted gross income prior to the § 911 foreign earned income exclusion and the educational savings bond exclusion. The threshold amounts are adjusted for inflation each year. For 2008, the phaseout begins at $67,100 ($100,650 on a joint return).[79] The phaseout is completed when MAGI exceeds the threshold amount by more than $15,000 ($30,000 on a joint return). The otherwise excludible interest is reduced by the amount calculated as follows:

$$\frac{\text{MAGI} - \$67,100}{\$15,000} \times \frac{\text{Excludible interest}}{\text{before phaseout}} = \frac{\text{Reduction in}}{\text{excludible interest}}$$

On a joint return, $100,650 is substituted for $67,100 (in 2008), and $30,000 is substituted for $15,000.

EXAMPLE 38

Assume the same facts as in Example 37, except that Tracy's MAGI for 2008 is $70,000. The phaseout results in Tracy's interest exclusion being reduced by $322 { [($70,000 − $67,100)/ $15,000] × $1,667 }. Therefore, Tracy's exclusion is $1,345 ($1,667 − $322). ■

Qualified Tuition Programs (§ 529 Plans)

Nearly all, if not all, states have created programs whereby parents can in effect prepay their child's college tuition. The prepayment serves as a hedge against future increases in tuition. Generally, if the child does not attend college, the parents are refunded their payments plus interest. Upon first impression, these prepaid tuition programs resemble the below-market loans discussed in Chapter 4. That is, assuming the tuition increases, the parent receives a reduction in the child's tuition in exchange for the use of the funds. However, Congress has created an exclusion provision for these programs.[80]

Under a **qualified tuition program (§ 529 plan)**, the amounts contributed must be used for qualified higher education expenses. These expenses include tuition, fees, books, supplies, room and board, and equipment required for enrollment or attendance at a college, university, or certain vocational schools. Qualified higher education expenses also include the expenses for special needs services that are incurred in connection with the enrollment and attendance of special needs students.

The earnings of the contributed funds, including the discount on tuition charged to participants, are not included in Federal gross income provided that the contributions and earnings are used for qualified higher education expenses. Some states also exclude these educational benefits from state gross income.

EXAMPLE 39

Agnes paid $20,000 into a qualified tuition program to be used for her son's college tuition. When her son graduated from high school, the fund balance had increased to $30,000 as a result of interest credited to the account. The interest was not included in Agnes's gross

---

[79]The indexed amounts for 2007 were $65,600 and $98,400.

[80]§ 529. For another way to beneficially fund educational costs, see the discussion of Coverdell Education Savings Accounts (CESAs) in Chapter 19 (§ 530).

income. During the current year, $7,500 of the balance in the fund was used to pay the son's tuition and fees. None of this amount is included in either Agnes's or the son's gross income. ■

If the parent receives a refund (e.g., child does not attend college), the excess of the amount refunded over the amount contributed by the parent is included in the parent's gross income.

Qualified tuition programs have been expanded to apply to private educational institutions as well as public educational institutions. Distributions made after December 31, 2003, from such a plan maintained by an entity other than the state for qualified higher education expenses are eligible for exclusion from gross income.

LO.3
Determine the extent to which receipts can be excluded under the tax benefit rule.

Tax Benefit Rule

Generally, if a taxpayer obtains a deduction for an item in one year and in a later year recovers all or a portion of the prior deduction, the recovery is included in gross income in the year received.[81]

EXAMPLE 40

A taxpayer deducted as a loss a $1,000 receivable from a customer when it appeared the amount would never be collected. The following year, the customer paid $800 on the receivable. The taxpayer must report the $800 as gross income in the year it is received. ■

However, the § 111 **tax benefit rule** provides that no income is recognized upon the recovery of a deduction, or the portion of a deduction, that did not yield a tax benefit in the year it was taken. If the taxpayer in Example 40 had no tax liability in the year of the deduction (e.g., itemized deductions and personal exemptions exceeded adjusted gross income), the recovery would be partially or totally excluded from gross income in the year of the recovery.[82]

EXAMPLE 41

Before deducting a $1,000 loss from an uncollectible business receivable, Ali had taxable income of $200, computed as follows:

Adjusted gross income	$ 13,300
Itemized deductions and personal exemptions	(13,100)
Taxable income	$ 200

The business bad debt deduction yields only a $200 tax benefit. That is, taxable income is reduced by only $200 (to zero) as a result of the bad debt deduction. Therefore, if the customer makes a payment on the previously deducted receivable in a subsequent year, only the first $200 is a recovery of a prior deduction and thus is taxable. Any additional amount collected is nontaxable because only $200 of the loss yielded a reduction in taxable income. ■

---

[81]§ 111(a).   [82]Itemized deductions are discussed in Chapter 10.

Income from Discharge of Indebtedness

LO.4

Describe the circumstances under which income must be reported from the discharge of indebtedness.

A transfer of appreciated property (fair market value is greater than adjusted basis) in satisfaction of a debt is an event that triggers the realization of income. The transaction is treated as a sale of the appreciated property followed by payment of the debt.[83] Foreclosure by a creditor is also treated as a sale or exchange of the property.[84]

EXAMPLE 42

Juan owes State Bank $100,000 on an unsecured note. He satisfies the note by transferring to the bank common stock with a basis of $60,000 and a fair market value of $100,000. Juan must recognize a $40,000 gain on the transfer. Juan also owes the bank $50,000 on a note secured by land. When Juan's basis in the land is $20,000 and the land's fair market value is $50,000, the bank forecloses on the loan and takes title to the land. Juan must recognize a $30,000 gain on the foreclosure. ■

In some cases, creditors will not exercise their right of foreclosure and will even forgive a portion of the debt to assure the vitality of the debtor. In such cases, the debtor realizes income from discharge of indebtedness.

EXAMPLE 43

Brown Corporation is unable to meet the mortgage payments on its factory building. Both the corporation and the mortgage holder are aware of the depressed market for industrial property in the area. Foreclosure would only result in the creditor's obtaining unsalable property. To improve Brown Corporation's financial position and thus improve Brown's chances of obtaining the additional credit necessary for survival from other lenders, the creditor agrees to forgive all amounts past due and to reduce the principal amount of the mortgage. ■

Generally, the income realized by the debtor from the forgiveness of a debt is taxable.[85] A similar debt discharge (produced by a different creditor motivation) associated with personal use property is illustrated in Example 44.

EXAMPLE 44

In 2003, Joyce borrowed $60,000 from National Bank to purchase her personal residence. Joyce agreed to make monthly principal and interest payments for 15 years. The interest rate on the note was 7%. In 2008, when the balance on the note has been reduced through monthly payments to $48,000, the bank offers to accept $45,000 in full settlement of the note. The bank makes the offer because interest rates have increased to 11%. Joyce accepts the bank's offer. As a result, Joyce must recognize $3,000 ($48,000 − $45,000) of gross income.[86] ■

The following discharge of indebtedness situations are subject to special treatment:[87]

1. Creditors' gifts.
2. Discharges under Federal bankruptcy law.
3. Discharges that occur when the debtor is insolvent.
4. Discharge of the farm debt of a solvent taxpayer.
5. Discharge of **qualified real property business indebtedness**.
6. A seller's cancellation of the buyer's indebtedness.
7. A shareholder's cancellation of the corporation's indebtedness.
8. Forgiveness of certain loans to students.
9. Discharge of indebtedness on the taxpayer's principal residence that occurs between January 1, 2007 and January 1, 2010, and is the result of the financial condition of the debtor.

---

[83]Reg. § 1.1001–2(a).

[84]*Estate of Delman v. Comm.*, 73 T.C. 15 (1979).

[85]*U.S. v. Kirby Lumber Co.*, 2 USTC ¶814, 10 AFTR 458, 52 S.Ct. 4 (USSC, 1931), codified in § 61(a)(12).

[86]Rev.Rul. 82–202, 1982–1 C.B. 35.

[87]§§ 108 and 1017.

If the creditor reduces the debt as an act of *love, affection,* or *generosity,* the debtor has simply received a nontaxable gift (situation 1). Rarely will a gift be found to have occurred in a business context. A businessperson may settle a debt for less than the amount due, but as a matter of business expediency (e.g., high collection costs or disputes as to contract terms) rather than generosity.[88]

In situations 2, 3, 4, 5, and 9, the Code allows the debtor to reduce his or her basis in the assets by the realized gain from the discharge.[89] Thus, the realized gain is merely deferred until the assets are sold (or depreciated). Similarly, in situation 6 (a price reduction), the debtor reduces the basis in the specific assets financed by the seller.[90]

A shareholder's cancellation of the corporation's indebtedness to him or her (situation 7) usually is considered a contribution of capital to the corporation by the shareholder. Thus, the corporation's paid-in capital is increased, and its liabilities are decreased by the same amount.[91]

Many states make loans to students on the condition that the loan will be forgiven if the student practices a profession in the state upon completing his or her studies. The amount of the loan that is forgiven (situation 8) is excluded from gross income.[92]

LO.5

Identify tax planning strategies for obtaining the maximum benefit from allowable exclusions.

TAX PLANNING
Considerations

The present law excludes certain types of economic gains from taxation. Therefore, taxpayers may find tax planning techniques helpful in obtaining the maximum benefits from the exclusion of such gains. Following are some of the tax planning opportunities made available by the exclusions described in this chapter.

Life Insurance

Life insurance offers several favorable tax attributes. As discussed in Chapter 4, the annual increase in the cash surrender value of the policy is not taxable (because no income has been actually or constructively received). By borrowing on the policy's cash surrender value, the owner can actually receive the policy's increase in value in cash but without recognizing income.

Employee Benefits

Generally, employees view accident and health insurance, as well as life insurance, as necessities. Employees can obtain group coverage at much lower rates than individuals would have to pay for the same protection. Premiums paid by the employer

---

[88] *Comm. v. Jacobson,* 49–1 USTC ¶9133, 37 AFTR 516, 69 S.Ct. 358 (USSC, 1949).

[89] §§ 108(a), (c), (e), and (g). Note that § 108(b) provides that other tax attributes (e.g., net operating loss) will be reduced by the realized gain from the debt discharge prior to the basis adjustment unless the taxpayer elects to apply the basis adjustment first.

[90] § 108(e)(5).

[91] § 108(e)(6).

[92] § 108(f).

can be excluded from the employees' gross income. Because of the exclusion, employees will have a greater after-tax and after-insurance income if the employer pays a lower salary but also pays the insurance premiums.

EXAMPLE 45

Pat receives a salary of $30,000. The company has group insurance benefits, but Pat is required to pay his own premiums as follows:

Hospitalization and medical insurance	$1,400
Term life insurance ($30,000 coverage)	200
Disability insurance	400
	$2,000

To simplify the analysis, assume Pat's tax rate on income is 25%. After paying taxes of $7,500 (.25 × $30,000) and $2,000 for insurance, Pat has $20,500 ($30,000 − $7,500 − $2,000) for his other living needs.

    If Pat's employer reduced Pat's salary by $2,000 (to $28,000) but paid his insurance premiums, Pat's tax liability would be only $7,000 ($28,000 × .25). Thus, Pat would have $21,000 ($28,000 − $7,000) to meet his other living needs. The change in the compensation plan would save Pat $500 ($21,000 − $20,500). ∎

Similarly, employees must often incur expenses for child care and parking. The employee can have more income for other uses if the employer pays these costs for the employee but reduces the employee's salary by the cost of the benefits.

    The use of cafeteria plans has increased dramatically in recent years. These plans allow employees to tailor their benefits to meet their individual situations. Thus, where both spouses in a married couple are working, duplications of benefits can be avoided, and other needed benefits can often be added. If less than all of the employee's allowance is spent, the employee can receive cash.

    The meals and lodging exclusion enables employees to receive from their employer what they ordinarily must purchase with after-tax dollars. Although the requirements that the employee live and take his or her meals on the employer's premises limit the tax planning opportunities, the exclusion is an important factor in the employee's compensation in certain situations (e.g., hotels, motels, restaurants, farms, and ranches).

    The employees' discount provision is especially important for manufacturers and wholesalers. Employees of manufacturers can avoid tax on the manufacturer's, wholesaler's, and retailer's markups. The wholesaler's employees can avoid tax on an amount equal to the wholesale and retail markups.

    It should be recognized that the exclusion of benefits is generally available only to employees. Proprietors and partners must pay tax on the same benefits their employees receive tax-free. By incorporating and becoming an employee of the corporation, the former proprietor or partner can also receive these tax-exempt benefits. Thus, the availability of employee benefits is a consideration in the decision to incorporate.

Investment Income

Tax-exempt state and local government bonds are almost irresistible investments for many high-income taxpayers. To realize the maximum benefit from the exemption, the investor can purchase zero-coupon bonds. Like Series EE U.S. government savings bonds, these investments pay interest only at maturity. The advantage of the zero-coupon feature for a tax-exempt bond is that the investor can earn tax-exempt interest on the accumulated principal and interest. If the investor purchases a bond that pays the interest each year, the interest received may be such a small amount that an additional tax-exempt investment cannot be made. In addition, reinvesting the interest may entail transaction costs (broker's fees). The zero-coupon feature avoids these problems.

Series EE U.S. government savings bonds can earn tax-exempt interest if the bond proceeds are used for qualified higher education expenses. Many taxpayers can foresee these expenditures being made for their children's educations. In deciding whether to invest in the bonds, however, the investor must take into account the income limitations for excluding the interest from gross income.

KEY TERMS

Accelerated death benefits, 5–7	Foreign earned income exclusion, 5–25	Qualified real property business indebtedness, 5–33
Accident and health benefits, 5–13	Gift, 5–5	Qualified transportation fringes, 5–23
Cafeteria plan, 5–19	Health Savings Account (HSA), 5–14	Qualified tuition program (§ 529 plan), 5–31
Compensatory damages, 5–11	Life insurance proceeds, 5–6	Qualified tuition reduction plan, 5–10
De minimis fringe, 5–23	Long-term care insurance, 5–15	
Death benefits, 5–6	No-additional-cost service, 5–21	Scholarship, 5–9
Educational savings bonds, 5–30	Punitive damages, 5–11	Tax benefit rule, 5–32
Flexible spending plans, 5–20	Qualified employee discount, 5–21	Working condition fringes, 5–22

PROBLEM MATERIALS

DISCUSSION QUESTIONS

1. Uncle John promised Tom, "Come and take care of me and I will leave you the farm when I die." Tom took care of Uncle John for the five years preceding his death. When Uncle John died, in accordance with his will, Tom received the farm. Can Tom exclude the value of the farm from his gross income as a gift or inheritance, or has he received compensation income?

2. Albert was the beneficiary of Hattie's life insurance policy. Hattie had paid $16,000 in premiums. Hattie died in January, and Albert did not collect the proceeds until November. The insurance company paid Albert $52,000, the face amount of the policy of $50,000 plus $2,000 interest. What is Albert's gross income from the receipt of $52,000?

Issue ID

3. Pearl Lumber Company is located in an isolated area that is sometimes referred to as "Tornado Alley." Most of the people who live in the area are employed by Pearl. The company created a nonprofit foundation to assist tornado victims. The majority of the beneficiaries are Pearl's employees. What are the relevant issues regarding the payments made by the nonprofit foundation to tornado victims?

4. Hanna was a cash basis taxpayer. At the time of her death, she was owed $50,000 in accrued salary. She also owned several thousand shares of stock in her corporate employer. Her cost of the stock was $40,000. Her employer was required to purchase the stock on Hanna's death for $200,000. To fund the agreement, the employer had purchased an insurance policy on Hanna's life that cost $60,000. The insurance

company paid the employer the life insurance proceeds of $200,000. Wade, as the sole beneficiary of Hanna's estate, received the $250,000 from Hanna's estate, which included Hanna's $50,000 of accrued salary. What are the employer's and Wade's gross income from these transactions?

5. Matt is a waiter in a restaurant. His usual tip is 20% of the price of the meal. A customer, whose meal cost $5, left a $100 bill as a tip. Matt is sure the customer thought he had left a $1 bill. Nevertheless, Matt believes he can exclude the entire amount (or at least $99) from his gross income because it was received as a gift rather than as compensation for services rendered. Is Matt correct?

6. Ted is age 92 and is suffering from a terminal illness. He owes $50,000 in legal bills he incurred from an unsuccessful lawsuit. Ted does not have $50,000 in cash, but he does have a life insurance policy with a cash surrender value of $50,000. Ted has paid $32,000 in premiums on the policy. What are the tax consequences if Ted transfers the policy to the attorney in satisfaction of the debt to the attorney?

7. Amber Finance Company requires its customers to purchase a credit life insurance policy. Amber is the beneficiary of the policy to the extent of the remaining balance on the loan at the time of the customer's death. In 2007, Amber wrote off as uncollectible a $5,000 account receivable from Aly. When Aly died in 2008, the life insurance policy was still in force, and Amber received $5,000. Is the $5,000 of life insurance proceeds received by Amber included in its gross income?

8. Ed paid $39,000 of life insurance premiums before cashing in his life insurance policy for the $45,000 cash surrender value. He decided he could invest the money and earn a higher rate of return. Sarah, who has a terminal illness, cashed in her life insurance policy (cost of $39,000 and proceeds of $45,000) to go on an around-the-world cruise. Determine the amounts that Ed and Sarah should include in their gross income.

9. Joe is a graduate student who works as a resident adviser (RA) in the college dormitory. As compensation for serving as an RA, he is not charged the $3,000 other students pay for their dormitory rooms. He is also paid $1,500 per year for being available to dormitory residents at all hours. Joe also has a scholarship that pays his annual tuition of $12,000. What is Joe's gross income?

10. Sarah's automobile was struck by a corporate truck that was driven by a drunk employee of the corporation. The company has admitted liability, and Sarah is negotiating a settlement. Sarah has asked for $100,000 for the loss of income she suffered from the injury, $50,000 in medical bills (which she has not deducted), and $80,000 in punitive damages. The company has made the following counteroffer: it will pay her $50,000 for medical expenses and $160,000 for lost wages, but no punitive damages because punitive damages create complications with its insurance company. Assuming that Sarah is in the 33% marginal tax bracket, should she accept the company's offer?

Decision Making

11. Wes was a major league baseball pitcher before a career-ending injury caused by a negligent driver. Wes sued the driver and collected $15 million as compensation for lost estimated future income as a pitcher and $10 million as punitive damages. Sam was also a major league baseball pitcher and earned $25 million for pitching. Do the amounts that Wes and Sam receive have the same effect on their gross income? Explain.

12. Holly was injured while working in a factory and received $12,000 as workers' compensation while she was unable to work because of the injury. Jill was laid off by the same factory and collected $12,000 in unemployment compensation. Since neither Holly nor Jill actually worked for the amounts received, should they each include the $12,000 in gross income?

13. Under a Health Savings Account (HSA), how is the employee expected to pay the high deductible associated with the high-deductible health insurance policy?

14. Paul is in the 15% marginal tax bracket, and Betty is in the 35% marginal tax bracket. Their employer is experiencing financial difficulties and cannot continue to pay for the company's health insurance plan. The annual premiums are approximately $6,000 per employee. The employer has proposed to either (1) require the employee to pay the premium or (2) reduce each employee's pay by $7,500 per year with the employer

Decision Making

paying the premium. Which option is less objectionable to Paul, and which is less objectionable to Betty?

15. What is the difference between a "cafeteria plan" and an employee "flexible spending plan"?

16. Ted works for Sage Motors, an automobile dealership. All employees can buy a car at the company's cost plus 2%. The company does not charge employees the $175 transfer service fee that nonemployees must pay. Ted purchased an automobile for $24,480 ($24,000 + $480). The company's cost was $24,000. The price for a nonemployee would have been $27,775 ($27,600 + $175 transfer service fee). What is Ted's gross income from the purchase of the automobile?

17. Zack has been offered a job where his salary would be $50,000 and he would also receive health insurance. Another potential employer has offered to match the first offer but would not provide any health insurance coverage. Zack can purchase such health insurance for $6,000 per year. Assume that Zack is in the 25% marginal tax bracket and does not itemize his deductions. How much salary must the second potential employer pay so that Zack's financial status will be the same under both offers?

18. Eagle Life Insurance Company pays its employees $.30 per mile for driving their personal automobiles to and from work. The company reimburses each employee who rides the bus $100 a month for the cost of a pass. Tom collected $100 for his automobile mileage, and Ted received $100 as reimbursement for the cost of a bus pass.
    a. What are the effects of the above on Tom's and Ted's gross income?
    b. Assume that Tom and Ted are in the 28% marginal tax bracket and the actual before-tax cost for Tom to drive to and from work is $.30 per mile. What are Tom's and Ted's after-tax costs of commuting to and from work?

Issue ID

19. Several of Egret Company's employees have asked the company to create a hiking trail that employees could use during their lunch hours. The company owns vacant land that is being held for future expansion but would have to spend approximately $50,000 if it were to make a trail. Nonemployees would be allowed to use the facility as part of the company's effort to build strong community support. What are the relevant tax issues for the employees?

20. The Azure Company has found that it can attract and retain high-quality employees by providing a variety of fringe benefits to all employees. Among these benefits are family counseling services, group legal services, and retirement planning. Which of these benefits are excluded from gross income?

21. Marla, a U.S. citizen, has been working on a construction project in a foreign country for the past nine months. The project will be completed in a few weeks. She has an offer to work on another three-month project in that same foreign country. Alternatively, she could return to the United States and seek employment. How does the tax law affect Marla's decision?

Decision Making

22. Tedra, a resident of Virginia, is considering purchasing a corporate bond that yields 7% before tax. She is in the 35% Federal marginal tax bracket and the 5% marginal state tax bracket. She is aware that State of Virginia bonds of comparable risk are yielding 4.5%, and State of Maryland bonds are yielding 4.6%. Which of the three options will yield the greatest after-tax return to Tedra?

23. In 2007, Sam paid the property tax of $2,800 on a vacant lot where he planned to build his personal residence. In 2008, he protested the valuation and was refunded $500 of the 2007 property tax. Under what circumstance would Sam be required to include the $500 in his 2008 gross income?

24. Arthur paid $50,000 to the Virginia Qualified Tuition Program: $25,000 for his son, Robert, and $25,000 for his daughter, Peggy. Only Peggy went to college. The $25,000 in the account for her was accepted in full payment of four years of tuition, which otherwise would have been $40,000. Since Robert did not attend college, $31,100 ($25,000 plus $6,100 interest) was refunded to Arthur. What are the tax consequences to Arthur, to Peggy, and to Robert?

25. Mary is a cash basis taxpayer. In 2008, she earned only $5,400, which was less than her standard deduction and personal exemption. In January 2009, Mary's employer determined that he had miscalculated her December 2008 bonus and that she should have received an additional $1,000 of compensation in 2008. The employer paid Mary the $1,000 in 2009. If Mary had received the $1,000 in 2008, it would not have resulted in any tax liability because her gross income would still have been less than her standard deduction and personal exemption. In 2009, Mary had over $30,000 in taxable income. Does the tax benefit rule apply to Mary's situation? Explain.

26. Harry was experiencing financial difficulties and could not make the mortgage payments on his home. The mortgage holder agreed to reduce the debt principal by $50,000 because the real estate market was depressed. Assuming that Harry is not bankrupt or insolvent, would the tax consequences differ under the following circumstances?

    - The mortgage is held by the person who sold him the property.
    - The mortgage is held by the financial institution that made the loan for the purchase of his residence.

27. Harry has experienced financial difficulties as a result of his struggling business. He has been behind on his mortgage payments for the last six months. The mortgage holder, who is a friend of Harry's, has offered to accept $80,000 in full payment of the $100,000 owed on the mortgage and payable over the next 10 years. The interest rate of the mortgage is 7%, and the market rate is now 8%. What tax issues are raised by the creditor's offer?

Issue ID

PROBLEMS

28. Ed, an employee of the Natural Color Company, suffered from a rare disease that was very expensive to treat. The local media ran several stories about Ed's problems, and the family received more than $10,000 in gifts from individuals to help pay the medical bills. Ed's employer provided hospital and medical insurance for its employees, but the policy did not cover Ed's illness. Shortly before Ed's death his employer paid $50,000 of Ed's accumulated medical bills. After Ed's death his former employer paid Ed's widow $12,000 in "her time of need." Ed's widow also collected $25,000 on a group term life insurance policy paid for by Ed's employer. What are Ed's and his widow's gross income?

29. Determine the gross income to the beneficiaries in each of the following cases:
    a. When José died, his daughter collected $4,000 in accrued salary and $2,500 in accrued vacation pay from his employer.
    b. Josh was unable to work for several months because of an illness. His employer made Josh's car payments of $1,500 while Josh was ill.
    c. Jay died after purchasing a $50,000 life insurance policy that was pledged to pay the $40,000 mortgage on his home, with the remaining proceeds of $10,000 paid to his wife.
    d. Lavender, Inc., was the beneficiary of a $100,000 life insurance policy it had purchased on the life of its chief executive officer who died during the year.
    e. Jackson purchased a $75,000 life insurance policy (face value) on the life of his brother Rex from his brother for $45,000. Jackson named himself as beneficiary. Rex needed the funds to pay medical costs associated with his wife who has cancer. The treatments his wife is receiving are deemed experimental (and not a covered procedure) by Rex's health insurance policy. Rex had paid premiums of $20,000 on the life insurance policy.

30. Laura was recently diagnosed with cancer and has begun chemotherapy treatments. A cancer specialist has stated that Laura has less than one year to live. She has incurred a lot of medical bills and other general living expenses and is in need of cash. Therefore, she is considering selling stock that cost $35,000 and has a fair market value of $50,000.

Decision Making

This amount would be sufficient to pay her medical bills. However, she has read about a company (the Vital Benefits Company) that would purchase her life insurance policy for $50,000. She has paid $30,000 in premiums on the policy.

a. Considering only the tax effects, would selling the stock or selling the life insurance policy result in more beneficial tax treatment?

b. Assume that Laura is a dependent child and that her mother owns the stock and the life insurance policy, which is on the mother's life. Which of the alternative means of raising the cash would result in more beneficial tax treatment?

31. Kara is a chambermaid in a hotel. She received $8,000 of tips during the year. When her home was damaged by a flood, her employer allowed her to stay rent-free at the hotel for three months. The hotel's normal charge for the room for the three months was $9,000. The President declared that Kara's home was located in a "qualified disaster area." This entitled Kara to collect $1,500 from the Federal government for living expenses while her home was being repaired. What is Kara's gross income?

32. Donald was killed in an accident while he was on the job. His employer provided him with group term life insurance of $180,000 (twice his annual salary), which was payable to his widow, Darlene. Premiums on this policy totaling $1,800 have been included in Donald's gross income under § 79. Darlene also received $80,000 under workers' compensation associated with the accident. In addition, Donald had purchased a $100,000 life insurance policy that paid $200,000 in the case of an accidental death. The proceeds were payable to Darlene, who elected to receive payments of $28,000 each year for a 10-year period. What is Darlene's gross income from the above in 2008?

33. Fay and Edward are partners in an accounting firm. The partners have entered into an arm's length agreement requiring Fay to purchase Edward's partnership interest from Edward's estate if he dies before Fay. The price is set at 150% of the book value of Edward's partnership interest at the time of his death. Fay purchased an insurance policy on Edward's life to fund this agreement. After Fay had paid $45,000 in premiums, Edward was killed in an automobile accident, and Fay collected $1.75 million of life insurance proceeds. Fay used the life insurance proceeds to purchase Edward's partnership interest.

a. What amount should Fay include in her gross income from receiving the life insurance proceeds?

b. The insurance company paid Fay $20,000 interest on the life insurance proceeds during the period Edward's estate was in administration. During this period, Fay had left the insurance proceeds with the insurance company. Is this interest taxable?

c. When Fay paid $1.75 million for Edward's partnership interest, priced as specified in the agreement, the fair market value of Edward's interest was $2 million. How much should Fay include in her gross income from this bargain purchase?

34. Sally was an all-state soccer player during her junior and senior years in high school. She accepted an athletic scholarship from State University. The scholarship provided the following:

Tuition and fees	$15,000
Housing and meals	7,500
Books and supplies	2,000

a. Determine the effect of the scholarship on Sally's gross income.

b. Sally's brother, Willy, was not a gifted athlete, but he received $17,000 from their father's employer as a scholarship during the year. The employer grants the children of all executives a scholarship equal to annual tuition, fees, books, and supplies. Determine the effect of the scholarship on Willy's and his father's gross income.

35. Alejandro was awarded an academic scholarship to State University for the 2008–2009 academic year. He received $5,000 in August and $6,000 in December 2008. Alejandro had enough personal savings to pay all expenses as they came due. Alejandro's expenditures for the relevant period were as follows:

Tuition, August 2008	$3,300
Tuition, December 2008	3,400
Room and board	
August–December 2008	3,000
January–May 2009	2,400
Books and educational supplies	
August–December 2008	1,000
January–May 2009	1,200

Determine the effect on Alejandro's gross income for 2008 and 2009.

36. Leigh sued an overzealous bill collector and received the following settlement:

Damage to her automobile the collector attempted to repossess	$ 1,000
Physical damage to her arm caused by the collector	15,000
Loss of income while her arm was healing	8,000
Punitive damages	50,000

   a.   What effect does the settlement have on Leigh's gross income?

   b.   Assume Leigh also collected $40,000 of damages for slander to her personal reputation caused by the bill collector misrepresenting the facts to Leigh's employer and other creditors. Is this $40,000 included in Leigh's gross income?

37. Determine the effect on gross income in each of the following cases:

   a.   Eloise received $150,000 in settlement of a sex discrimination case against her former employer.

   b.   Nell received $10,000 for damages to her personal reputation. She also received $40,000 in punitive damages.

   c.   Orange Corporation, an accrual basis taxpayer, received $50,000 from a lawsuit filed against its auditor who overcharged for services rendered in a previous year.

   d.   Beth received $10,000 in compensatory damages and $30,000 in punitive damages in a lawsuit she filed against a tanning parlor for severe burns she received from using its tanning equipment.

   e.   Joanne received compensatory damages of $75,000 and punitive damages of $300,000 from a cosmetic surgeon who botched her nose job.

38. Rex, age 45, is an officer of Blue Company, which provides him with the following nondiscriminatory fringe benefits in 2008:

- Hospitalization insurance premiums for Rex and his dependents. The cost of the coverage for Rex is $2,700 per year, and the additional cost for his dependents is $3,600 per year. The plan has a $2,000 deductible, but his employer contributed $1,500 to Rex's Health Savings Account. Rex withdrew only $800 from the HSA, and the account earned $50 interest during the year.

- Long-term care insurance premiums for Rex, at a cost of $3,600 per year.

- Insurance premiums of $840 for salary continuation payments. Under the plan, Rex will receive his regular salary in the event he is unable to work due to illness. Rex collected $4,500 on the policy to replace lost wages while he was ill during the year.

- Rex is a part-time student working on his bachelor's degree in engineering. His employer reimbursed his $5,200 tuition under a plan available to all full-time employees.

Determine the amount Rex must include in gross income.

39. The UVW Union and HON Corporation are negotiating contract terms. Assume the union members are in the 28% marginal tax bracket and all benefits are provided on a nondiscriminatory basis. Write a letter to the UVW Union members explaining the tax consequences of the options discussed below. The union's address is 905 Spruce Street, Washington, D.C. 20227.

   Communications

   a.   The company would impose a $100 deductible on medical insurance benefits. Most employees incur more than $100 each year in medical expenses.

   b.   Employees would get an additional paid holiday with the same annual income (the same pay but less work).

c.   An employee who did not need health insurance (because the employee's spouse works and receives family coverage) would be allowed to receive the cash value of the coverage.

Decision Making

40. Mauve Corporation has a group hospitalization insurance plan that has a $200 deductible amount for hospital visits and a $15 deductible for doctor visits and prescriptions. The deductible portion paid by employees who have children has become substantial for some employees. The company is considering adopting a medical reimbursement plan or a flexible benefits plan to cover the deductible amounts. Either of these plans can be tailored to meet the needs of the employees. What are the cost considerations to the employer that should be considered in choosing between these plans?

41. Bertha spent the last 60 days of 2008 in a nursing home. The cost of the services provided to her was $12,000. Medicare paid $7,200 toward the cost of her stay. Bertha also received $9,800 of benefits under a long-term care insurance policy she purchased. What is the effect on Bertha's gross income?

42. Tim is the vice president of western operations for Maroon Oil Company and is stationed in San Francisco. He is required to live in an employer-owned home, which is three blocks from his company office. The company-provided home is equipped with high-speed Internet access and several telephone lines. Tim receives telephone calls and e-mails that require immediate attention any time of day or night because the company's business is spread all over the world. A full-time administrative assistant resides in the house to assist Tim with the urgent business matters. Tim often uses the home for entertaining customers, suppliers, and employees. The fair market value of comparable housing is $9,000 per month. Tim is also provided with free parking at his company's office. The value of the parking is $350 per month. Calculate the amount associated with the company-provided housing and free parking that Tim must include in his gross income.

43. Does the taxpayer recognize gross income in the following situations?
a.   Ann is a filing clerk at a large insurance company. She is permitted to leave the premises for her lunch, but she always eats in the company's cafeteria because doing so is much less expensive than purchasing a comparable meal at a nearby restaurant. On average she pays $3 for a lunch that would cost $8 at a restaurant.
b.   Ira is a resident adviser (RA) in a college dormitory and is provided with lodging in the dormitory. He is not required to pay the $250 per month that a room costs other students. In addition, he is paid $200 per month.
c.   Seth recently moved to accept a job. For the first six months on the new job, Seth was searching for a home to purchase or rent. During this time, his employer allowed Seth to live in an apartment the company has available for customers and employees.

Decision Making

44. Betty is considering taking an early retirement offered by her employer. She would receive $2,000 per month, indexed for inflation. However, she would no longer be able to use the company's health facilities, and she would be required to pay her hospitalization insurance of $7,800 each year. Betty and her husband will file a joint return and take the standard deduction. She currently receives a salary of $40,000 a year, and her employer pays for all of her hospitalization insurance. If she retires, Betty would not be able to use her former employer's exercise facilities because of the commuting distance. She would like to continue to exercise, however, and will therefore join a health club at a cost of $50 per month. Betty and her husband have other sources of income and are in and will remain in the 25% marginal tax bracket. She currently pays Social Security taxes of 7.65% on her salary, but her retirement pay would not be subject to this tax. She will earn about $11,000 a year from a part-time job. Betty would like to know whether she should accept the early retirement offer.

Communications

45. Finch Construction Company provides the carpenters it employs with all of the required tools. However, the company believes that this practice has led to some employees not taking care of the tools and to the mysterious disappearance of some tools. The company is considering requiring all of its employees to provide their own tools. Each employee's salary would be increased by $1,500 to compensate for the additional cost.

Write a letter to Finch's management explaining the tax consequences of this plan to the carpenters. Finch's address is 300 Harbor Drive, Vermillion, SD 57069.

46. Redbird, Inc., does not provide its employees with any tax-exempt fringe benefits. The company is considering adopting a hospital and medical benefits insurance plan that will cost approximately $7,000 per employee. In order to adopt this plan, the company may have to reduce salaries and/or lower future salary increases. Redbird is in the 35% (combined Federal and state rates) bracket. Redbird is also responsible for matching the Social Security and Medicare taxes withheld on employees' salaries. The benefits insurance plan will not be subject to the Social Security and Medicare taxes. The employees generally fall into three marginal tax rate groups:

Income Tax	Social Security and Medicare Tax	Total
.15	.0765	.2265
.25	.0765	.3265
.35	.0145	.3645

The company has asked you to assist in its financial planning for the benefits insurance plan by computing the following:
   a. How much taxable compensation is the equivalent of $7,000 exempt compensation for each of the three classes of employees?
   b. What is the company's after-tax cost of the taxable compensation computed in (a) above?
   c. What is the company's after-tax cost of the exempt compensation?
   d. Briefly explain your conclusions from the above analysis.

47. Rosa's employer has instituted a flexible benefits program. Rosa will use the plan to pay for her daughter's dental expenses and other medical expenses that are not covered by health insurance. Rosa is in the 25% marginal tax bracket and estimates that the medical and dental expenses not covered by health insurance will be within the range of $3,000 to $5,000. Her employer's plan permits her to set aside as much as $5,000 in the flexible benefits account. Rosa does not itemize her deductions.

Decision Making

   a. Rosa puts $3,000 into her flexible benefits account, and her actual expenses are $5,000. What is her cost of underestimating the expenses?
   b. Rosa puts $5,000 into her flexible benefits account, and her actual expenses are only $3,000. What is her cost of overestimating her expenses?
   c. What is Rosa's cost of underfunding as compared to the cost of overfunding the flexible benefits account?
   d. Does your answer in part (c) suggest that Rosa should fund the account closer to the low end or to the high end of her estimates?

48. Canary Corporation would like you to review its employee fringe benefits program with regard to the tax consequences of the plan for the company's president (Polly), who is also the majority shareholder:
   a. The company has a qualified retirement plan. The company pays the cost of employees attending a retirement planning seminar. The employee must be within 10 years of retirement, and the cost of the seminar is $1,500 per attendee.
   b. The company owns a parking garage that is used by customers, employees, and the general public. Only the general public is required to pay for parking. The charge to the general public for Polly's parking for the year would have been $2,700 (a $225 monthly rate).
   c. All employees are allowed to use the company's fixed charge long-distance telephone services, as long as the privilege is not abused. Although no one has kept track of the actual calls, Polly's use of the telephone had a value (what she would have paid on her personal telephone) of approximately $600.
   d. The company owns a condominium at the beach, which it uses to entertain customers. Employees are allowed to use the facility without charge when the company has no scheduled events. Polly used the facility 10 days during the year. Her use had a rental value of $1,000.

   e.   The company is in the household moving business. Employees are allowed to ship goods without charge whenever there is excess space on a truck. Polly purchased a dining room suite for her daughter. Company trucks delivered the furniture to the daughter. Normal freight charges would have been $750.

   f.   The company has a storage facility for household goods. Officers are allowed a 20% discount on charges for storing their goods. All other employees are allowed a 10% discount. Polly's discounts for the year totaled $900.

49.   George is a U.S. citizen who is employed by Hawk Enterprises, a global company. Beginning on June 1, 2008, George began working in London. He worked there until January 31, 2009, when he transferred to Paris. He worked in Paris the remainder of 2009. His salary for the first five months of 2008 was $95,000, and it was earned in the United States. His salary for the remainder of 2008 was $135,000, and it was earned in London. George's 2009 salary from Hawk was $275,000, with part being earned in London and part being earned in Paris. What is George's gross income in 2008 and 2009 (assume the 2009 indexed amount is the same as the 2008 indexed amount)?

50.   Determine Hazel's gross income from the following receipts for the year:

Gain on sale of Augusta County bonds	$ 600
Interest on U.S. government savings bonds	300
Interest on state income tax refund	150
Interest on Augusta County bonds	900
Patronage dividend from Potato Growers Cooperative	1,600

The patronage dividend was received in March of the current year for amounts paid and deducted in the previous year as expenses of Hazel's profitable cash basis farming business.

51.   Ezra purchased 1,000 shares of Golden Gate Utility Fund for $15,000 in 2008. At the end of 2008, he received an additional 50 fund shares in lieu of receiving $700 in cash dividends. At the end of the year, the value of Ezra's Golden Gate Utility Fund shares was $14,500.

   a.   What is Ezra's 2008 gross income from the Golden Gate Utility Fund shares?

   b.   Ezra also received 100 shares of Giant, Inc. stock when the company declared a two-for-one stock dividend. At the time of the stock dividend, the shares were trading for $90 a share. Ezra did not have the option of receiving cash in lieu of the Giant stock. What are the tax consequences of Ezra's receipt of the additional shares of Giant stock?

Decision Making

52.   Tonya inherited a $10,000 State of Virginia bond in 2008. Her marginal Federal tax rate is 15%, and her marginal state tax rate is 5%. The Virginia bond pays 4% interest, which is not subject to Virginia income tax. She can purchase a corporate bond of comparable risk that will yield 6.5% or a U.S. government bond that pays 6% interest. Tonya does not itemize her deductions. Which investment will provide the greatest after-tax yield?

Decision Making

Communications

53.   Lynn Swartz's husband died three years ago. Her parents have an income of over $200,000 a year and want to assure that funds will be available for the education of Lynn's 8-year-old son, Eric. Lynn is currently earning $45,000 a year. Lynn's parents have suggested that they start a savings account for Eric. They have calculated that if they invest $4,000 a year for the next 8 years, at the end of 10 years sufficient funds will be available for Eric's college expenses. Lynn realizes that the tax treatment of the investments could significantly affect the amount of funds available for Eric's education. She asked you to write a letter to her advising her about options available to her parents and to her for Eric's college education. Lynn's address is 100 Myrtle Cove, Fairfield, CT 06432.

54.   Starting in 1999, Chuck and Luane have been purchasing Series EE bonds in their name to use for the higher education of their daughter (Susie who currently is age 18). During the year, they cash in $12,000 of the bonds to use for freshman year tuition, fees, and room and board. Of this amount, $5,000 represents interest. Of the $12,000, $8,000 is used for tuition and fees, and $4,000 is used for room and board. Their AGI, before the educational savings bond exclusion, is $103,000.

a. Determine the tax consequences for Chuck and Luane, who will file a joint return, and for Susie.

b. Assume that Chuck and Luane purchased the bonds in Susie's name. Determine the tax consequences for Chuck and Luane and for Susie.

c. How would your answer for (a) change if Chuck and Luane file separate returns?

55. Carlos is considering investing $4,000 in a qualified tuition program for the benefit of his son. He estimates that in eight years, when his son enters college, the cost of tuition will have increased by 50%. His son will go to school full-time and should be in the 15% marginal tax bracket as a result of his part-time work. Alternatively, Carlos can invest the $4,000 in a corporate bond fund, which is expected to yield 7% each year. Carlos expects to be in the 33% marginal tax bracket in all relevant years. Which alternative appears preferable? The compound amount of $1 at 4.69% in eight years is 1.44.

56. How does the tax benefit rule apply in the following cases?

a. In 2006, the Lemon Furniture Store, an accrual method taxpayer, sold furniture on credit for $1,000 to Sammy. The cost of the furniture was $600. In 2007, Lemon took a bad debt deduction for the $1,000. Lemon had over $300,000 in taxable income. In 2008, Sammy inherited some money and paid Lemon the $1,000.

b. In 2007, Marvin, a cash basis taxpayer, took a $6,000 itemized deduction for state income taxes paid. This increased his itemized deductions to a total that was $4,000 more than the standard deduction. In 2008, Marvin received a $4,200 refund when he filed his 2007 state income tax return.

c. In 2007, Barb, a cash basis taxpayer, was in an accident and incurred $7,000 in medical expenses, which she claimed as an itemized deduction for medical expenses. Because of the 7.5% of AGI reduction, the expense reduced her taxable income by only $5,000. In 2008, Barb collected $15,000 from the person who caused the accident that resulted in her personal injury.

57. Fran, who is in the 35% tax bracket, recently collected $100,000 on a life insurance policy she carried on her father. She currently owes $120,000 on her personal residence and $120,000 on business property. National Bank holds the mortgage on both pieces of property and has agreed to accept $100,000 in complete satisfaction of either mortgage. The interest rate on the mortgages is 8%, and both mortgages are payable over 10 years. What would be the tax consequences of each of the following alternatives, assuming Fran currently deducts the mortgage interest on her tax return?

Decision Making

a. Retire the mortgage on the residence.

b. Retire the mortgage on the business property.

Which alternative should Fran select?

58. Robin, who was experiencing financial difficulties, was able to adjust his debts as follows:

a. His father agreed to cancel a $10,000 debt to help him out in his time of need. Robin's father told him, "I am not going to treat you any better than I treat your brothers and sister; therefore, the $10,000 is coming out of your inheritance from me."

b. Robin's controlled corporation canceled a $6,000 debt he owed to the company.

c. The Trust Land Company, which had sold Robin land, reduced the mortgage on the land by $12,000 and forgave him from paying $4,000 in accrued interest. Robin had deducted the interest on the previous year's tax return.

CUMULATIVE PROBLEMS

59. Alfred E. Old and Beulah A. Crane, each age 42, married on September 7, 2007. Alfred and Beulah will file a joint return for 2007. Alfred's Social Security number is 262–60–3815. Beulah's Social Security number is 259–68–4285, and she will adopt "Old" as her married name. They live at 211 Brickstone Drive, Atlanta, GA 30304.

Tax Return Problem

Alfred was divorced from Sarah Old in March 2006. Under the divorce agreement, Alfred is to pay Sarah $1,000 per month for the next 10 years or until Sarah's death, whichever occurs first. Alfred pays Sarah $12,000 in 2007. In addition, in January 2007, Alfred pays Sarah $50,000, which is designated as being for her share of the marital property. Also, Alfred is responsible for all prior years' income taxes. Sarah's Social Security number is 444–10–2211.

Alfred's salary for 2007 is $100,000, and his employer, Cherry, Inc. (Federal I.D. No. 59–7766723), provides him with group term life insurance equal to twice his annual salary. His employer withheld $14,400 for Federal income taxes and $3,400 for state income taxes. The following amounts were withheld for FICA taxes: $6,045 ($97,500 × 6.2%) for Social Security and $1,450 ($100,000 × 1.45%) for Medicare.

Beulah recently graduated from law school and is employed by Legal Aid Society, Inc. (Federal I.D. No. 59–9472635), as a public defender. She receives a salary of $40,000 in 2007. Her employer withheld $6,500 for Federal income taxes and $2,300 for state income taxes. The following amounts were withheld for FICA taxes: $2,480 ($40,000 × 6.2%) for Social Security and $580 ($40,000 × 1.45%) for Medicare.

Beulah has $1,500 in dividends on Yellow Corporation stock she inherited. Beulah receives a $950 refund of 2006 state income taxes. She used the standard deduction on her 2006 Federal income tax return. Alfred receives a $1,600 refund on his 2006 state income taxes. He itemized deductions on his 2006 Federal income tax return. Alfred and Beulah pay $4,800 interest and $1,450 property taxes on their personal residence in 2007. Their charitable contributions total $1,200 (all to their church). They paid sales taxes of $1,400 for which they maintain the receipts.

Compute the Olds' net tax payable (or refund due) for 2007. If you use tax forms for your solution, you will need Form 1040 and Schedules A and B. Suggested software: Tax Cut.

Tax Computation Problem

Decision Making

Communications

60. Martin S. Albert (Social Security number 363–22–1141) is 39 years old and is married to Michele R. Albert (Social Security number 259–05–8242). The Alberts live at 512 Ferry Road, Newport News, VA 23601. They file a joint return and have two dependent children (Charlene, age 17, and Jordan, age 18). Charlene's Social Security number is 260–12–1234, and Jordan's Social Security number is 263–23–4321. In 2008, Martin and Michele had the following transactions:

a. Martin received $108,000 in salary from Red Steel Corporation, where he is a construction engineer. Withholding for Federal income tax was $9,500. The amounts withheld for FICA tax were as follows: $6,324 ($102,000 × 6.2%) for Social Security and $1,566 ($108,000 × 1.45%) for Medicare. Martin worked in Mexico from January 1, 2007, until February 15, 2008. His $108,000 salary for 2008 includes $16,000 he earned for January and one-half of February 2008 while working in Mexico.

b. Martin and Michele received $800 in dividends on Green, Inc. stock and $400 interest on Montgomery County (Virginia) school bonds.

c. Martin received $2,300 interest from a Bahamian bank account.

d. Michele received 50 shares of Applegate Corporation common stock as a stock dividend. The shares had a fair market value of $2,000 at the time Michele received them, and she did not have the option of receiving cash.

e. Martin and Michele received a $900 refund on their 2007 Virginia income taxes. Their itemized deductions in 2007 totaled $12,500.

f. Martin paid $6,000 alimony to his former wife, Rose T. Morgan (Social Security number 262–55–4813).

g. Martin and Michele kept the receipts for their sales taxes paid of $1,100.

h. Martin and Michele's itemized deductions were as follows:

- State income tax paid and withheld totaled $5,100.
- Real estate taxes on their principal residence were $3,400.
- Mortgage interest on their principal residence was $2,500.
- Cash contributions to the church totaled $2,800.

Part 1—Tax Computation
Compute the Alberts' net tax payable (or refund due) for 2008.

Part 2—Tax Planning
The Alberts are considering buying another house. Their house mortgage payments would increase by $500 (to $1,500) per month, which includes a $250 increase in interest and a $100 increase in property tax. The Alberts would like to know how much the mortgage payments would increase net of any change in their income tax. Write a letter to the Alberts that contains your advice.

RESEARCH PROBLEMS

Note: Solutions to Research Problems can be prepared by using the **RIA Checkpoint®** **Student Edition** online research product, which is available to accompany this text. It is also possible to prepare solutions to the Research Problems by using tax research materials found in a standard tax library.

Research Problem 1. Murray reported to the Environmental Protection Agency that his employer was illegally dumping chemicals into a river. His charges were true, and Murray's employer was fined. In retaliation, Murray's employer fired him and made deliberate efforts to prevent Murray from obtaining other employment. Murray sued the employer claiming that his reputation had been damaged. Murray won his lawsuit and received an award as "damages to his personal and professional reputation and for his mental suffering." Now he would like to know whether the award is taxable. He argues that he was awarded damages as a recovery of his human capital and a recovery of capital is not income. Therefore, the Federal government does not have the power to tax the award.

Communications

Research Problem 2. Sam received a MegaBank credit card in 2002 and charged items costing over $3,000. He moved to a new location, misplaced the card, and forgot that he owed the money. In 2006, MegaBank decided that Sam's account would never be collected. MegaBank sent him a Form 1099–C, indicating that he had $3,000 of income from discharge of the debt in 2006. The IRS is trying to collect tax on the $3,000. Sam contends that he still owes the money to MegaBank, that he intends to repay it, and that he informed MegaBank of this after the IRS informed him that he had income from the discharge of the debt. Sam is neither bankrupt nor insolvent. Is Sam required to recognize income in 2006 from the discharge of the indebtedness?

Research Problem 3. Sales personnel employed by Ivory Sales, Inc., accumulate substantial frequent-flyer miles traveling for the company. Since Ivory Sales reimburses its employees for travel expenses incurred, the company, rather than the employee, is entitled to the frequent-flyer miles. The company is considering a change in policy that would permit the employees to retain the miles for their personal use. Ivory Sales would like to know the income tax implications to the employees of the proposed change in policy.

Research Problem 4. Aubrey Brown is a decorated veteran of the Vietnam War. As a result of his exposure to Agent Orange during the war, Aubrey developed lung cancer and is unable to work. He received $12,000 of Social Security disability payments in the current year. He reasons that the payments should be excluded from his gross income because the payments are compensation for the physical injury he suffered as a result of his service in the armed forces. Is Aubrey correct?

Partial list of research aids:
Rev.Rul. 77–318, 1977–2 C.B. 45.
Reimels v. Comm., 2006–1 USTC ¶50,147, 97 AFTR2d 2006–820, 436 F.3d 344 (CA–2, 2006).

Use the tax resources of the Internet to address the following questions. Do not restrict your search to the World Wide Web, but include a review of newsgroups and general reference materials, practitioner sites and resources, primary sources of the tax law, chat rooms and discussion groups, and other opportunities.

Internet *Activity*

Research Problem 5. Go to the IRS site on the Internet and download instructions and regulations relative to educational savings bonds and qualified tuition programs. Summarize one of the key provisions in these materials in outline format.

Communications

Research Problem 6. Employers often use the Internet as a means of attracting applications from potential employees. Locate an Internet site offering employment opportunities, ideally one provided by a well-known corporation. How does the employer promote its fringe benefit and cafeteria plan packages? Compare and contrast several such sites.

PART 3

Deductions

Part III presents the deduction component of the basic tax model. Deductions are classified as business versus nonbusiness, "for" versus "from," employee versus employer, active versus passive, and reimbursed versus unreimbursed. The effect of each of these classifications is analyzed. The presentation includes not only the deductions that are permitted, but also limitations and disallowances associated with deductions. Because deductions can exceed gross income, the treatment of losses is also included.

CHAPTER 6
Deductions and Losses: In General

CHAPTER 7
Deductions and Losses: Certain Business Expenses and Losses

CHAPTER 8
Depreciation, Cost Recovery, Amortization, and Depletion

CHAPTER 9
Deductions: Employee and Self-Employed-Related Expenses

CHAPTER 10
Deductions and Losses: Certain Itemized Deductions

CHAPTER 11
Investor Losses

CHAPTER 6

Deductions and Losses: In General

After completing Chapter 6, you should be able to:

LO.1

Differentiate between deductions *for* and *from* adjusted gross income and understand the relevance of the differentiation.

LO.2

Describe the cash and accrual methods of accounting.

LO.3

Apply the Internal Revenue Code deduction disallowance provisions associated with the following: public policy limitations, political activities, excessive executive compensation, investigation of business opportunities, hobby losses, vacation home rentals, payment of others' expenses, personal expenditures, capital expenditures, related-party transactions, and expenses related to tax-exempt income.

LO.4

Identify tax planning opportunities for maximizing deductions and minimizing the disallowance of deductions.

OUTLINE

Classification of Deductible Expenses, 6–2
Deductions for Adjusted Gross Income, 6–3
Itemized Deductions, 6–4
Trade or Business Expenses and Production
   of Income Expenses, 6–5
Business and Nonbusiness Losses, 6–7
Reporting Procedures, 6–7
**Deductions and Losses—Timing of Expense
Recognition, 6–8**
Importance of Taxpayer's Method of Accounting, 6–8
Cash Method Requirements, 6–9
Accrual Method Requirements, 6–10
Disallowance Possibilities, 6–11
Public Policy Limitation, 6–11
Political Contributions and Lobbying Activities, 6–13
Excessive Executive Compensation, 6–14
Investigation of a Business, 6–15
Hobby Losses, 6–16

Rental of Vacation Homes, 6–19
Expenditures Incurred for Taxpayer's Benefit
   or Taxpayer's Obligation, 6–22
Disallowance of Personal Expenditures, 6–24
Disallowance of Deductions for Capital
   Expenditures, 6–24
Transactions between Related Parties, 6–26
Substantiation Requirements, 6–27
Expenses and Interest Relating
   to Tax-Exempt Income, 6–28
Tax Planning Considerations, 6–29
Time Value of Tax Deductions, 6–29
Unreasonable Compensation, 6–29
Excessive Executive Compensation, 6–29
Shifting Deductions, 6–31
Hobby Losses, 6–31
Capital Expenditures, 6–32

LO.1

Differentiate between deductions *for* and *from* adjusted gross income and understand the relevance of the differentiation.

Classification of Deductible Expenses

The tax law has an all-inclusive definition of income; that is, income from whatever source derived is includible in gross income. Income cannot be excluded unless there is a specific statement to that effect in the Internal Revenue Code.

Similarly, deductions are disallowed unless a specific provision in the tax law permits them. The inclusive definition of income and the exclusive definition of deductions may not seem fair to taxpayers, but it is the structure of the tax law.

The courts have held that whether and to what extent deductions are allowed depends on legislative grace.[1] In other words, any exclusions from income and all deductions are gifts from Congress!

It is important to classify deductible expenses as **deductions for adjusted gross income** (AGI) or **deductions from adjusted gross income**. Deductions *for* AGI can be claimed whether or not the taxpayer itemizes. Deductions *from* AGI result in a tax benefit only if they exceed the taxpayer's standard deduction. If itemized deductions (*from* AGI) are less than the standard deduction, they provide no tax benefit.

E X A M P L E   1

Steve is a self-employed CPA. Ralph is one of Steve's employees. During the year, Steve and Ralph incur the following expenses:

	Steve	Ralph
Dues to American Institute of CPAs and State Society of CPAs	$ 400	$ 300
Subscriptions to professional journals	500	200
Registration fees for tax conferences	800	800
	$1,700	$1,300

---

[1] *New Colonial Ice Co. v. Helvering,* 4 USTC ¶1292, 13 AFTR 1180, 54 S.Ct. 788
(USSC, 1934).

TAX *in the News* | **PROPER TREATMENT OF YOUR VOICE**

Almost all people use their voice in their work. What do you do if it does not function the way that you want it to? An increasing number of people are deciding that their voice is too high pitched, too monotone, too nasal, or too much like the opposite sex. Women are often concerned that they sound too shrill, too Valley girl, or too faint, whereas men worry about being too gravelly or too weak.

Help in achieving the desired vocal results, often referred to as cosmetic voice changing, is available from personal voice trainers. Such treatments are not cheap. Sandra McKnight, a voice coach in Santa Fe who offers voice training over the phone, charges $640 for a typical treatment program consisting of four 75-minute sessions. In-person sessions with a speech pathologist can cost much more.

Are such treatments deductible for tax purposes? One possible approach might be to deduct the cost as a medical expense (assuming the reasons for the treatment are not merely cosmetic). The disadvantage here is the 7.5 percent floor on medical expenses. Another possibility might be to deduct the cost as a § 162 trade or business expense. Unfortunately, such an approach is more likely to be successful for an entertainer than for a business executive.

Source: *Adapted from Jennifer Saranow, "A Personal Trainer for Your Voice,"* Wall Street Journal, *February 17, 2005, p. D1.*

Steve does not reimburse any of his employees for dues, subscriptions, or educational programs.

Steve's expenses are classified as a deduction *for* AGI. Therefore, he can deduct the $1,700 on his Federal income tax return. Ralph's expenses are classified as deductions *from* AGI. Ralph will be able to benefit from the $1,300 of expenses on his Federal income tax return only if he itemizes deductions. If he takes the standard deduction instead, the $1,300 of expenses will have no effect on the calculation of his taxable income. Even if Ralph does itemize deductions, he must reduce the $1,300 of expenses, which are classified as miscellaneous itemized deductions, by 2% of his AGI. As this example illustrates, whether a deduction is classified as *for* AGI or *from* AGI can affect the benefit the taxpayer receives from the deduction. ■

See Concept Summary 6–3 later in the chapter for the classification of deductions as deductions *for* AGI or as deductions *from* AGI.

Deductions *for* AGI are also important in determining the *amount* of itemized deductions because many itemized deductions are limited to amounts in excess of specified percentages of AGI. Examples of itemized deductions that are limited by AGI are medical expenses and personal casualty losses. Itemized deductions that are deductible only to the extent that they exceed a specified percentage of AGI are increased when AGI is decreased. Likewise, when AGI is increased, these itemized deductions are decreased.

EXAMPLE 2

Tina earns a salary of $20,000 and has no other income. She itemizes deductions during the current year. Medical expenses for the year are $1,800. Since medical expenses are deductible only to the extent they exceed 7.5% of AGI, Tina's medical expense deduction is $300 [$1,800 − (7.5% × $20,000)]. If Tina had a $2,000 deduction *for* AGI, her medical expense deduction would be $450 [$1,800 − (7.5% × $18,000)], or $150 more. If the $2,000 deduction was *from* AGI, her medical expense deduction would remain $300 since AGI is unchanged. ■

Deductions for Adjusted Gross Income

To understand how deductions of individual taxpayers are classified, it is necessary to examine the role of § 62. The purpose of § 62 is to classify various deductions as deductions *for* AGI. It does not provide the statutory authority for taking the deduction. For example, § 212 allows individuals to deduct expenses attributable to income-producing property. Section 212 expenses that are attributable to rents or royalties are classified as deductions *for* AGI. Likewise, a deduction for trade or business expenses is allowed by § 162. These expenses are classified as deductions *for* AGI.

If a deduction is not listed in § 62, it is an itemized deduction, not a deduction *for* AGI. Following is a *partial* list of the items classified as deductions *for* AGI by § 62:

- Expenses attributable to a trade or business carried on by the taxpayer. A trade or business does not include the performance of services by the taxpayer as an employee.
- Expenses incurred by a taxpayer in connection with the performance of services as an employee if the expenses are reimbursed and other conditions are satisfied.
- Deductions that result from losses on the sale or exchange of property by the taxpayer.
- Deductions attributable to property held for the production of rents and royalties.
- The deduction for payment of alimony.
- The deduction for one-half of the self-employment tax paid by a self-employed taxpayer.
- The deduction for the medical insurance premiums paid by a self-employed taxpayer for coverage of the taxpayer, spouse, and any dependents.
- Certain contributions to pension, profit sharing, and annuity plans of self-employed individuals.
- The deduction for certain retirement savings allowed by § 219 (e.g., traditional IRAs).
- The penalty imposed on premature withdrawal of funds from time savings accounts or deposits.
- The deduction for moving expenses.
- The deduction for interest paid on student loans.
- The deduction for qualified tuition and related expenses under § 222 (refer to Chapter 9).
- The deduction for up to $250 for teacher supplies for elementary and secondary school teachers (refer to Chapter 9).

These items are covered in detail in various chapters in the text.

Itemized Deductions

The Code defines itemized deductions as the deductions allowed other than "the deductions allowable in arriving at adjusted gross income."[2] Thus, if a deduction is not properly classified as a deduction *for* AGI, then it is classified as an itemized deduction.

Section 212 Expenses.

Section 212 allows deductions for ordinary and necessary expenses paid or incurred for the following:

- The production or collection of income.
- The management, conservation, or maintenance of property held for the production of income.
- Expenses paid in connection with the determination, collection, or refund of any tax.

Section 212 expenses related to rent and royalty income are deductions *for* AGI.[3] Expenses paid in connection with the determination, collection, or refund of taxes related to the income of sole proprietorships, rents and royalties, or farming operations are deductions *for* AGI. All other § 212 expenses are itemized deductions (deductions *from* AGI). For example, investment-related expenses (e.g., safe deposit box rentals) are deductible as itemized deductions attributable to the production of investment income.[4]

---

[2] § 63(d).
[3] § 62(a)(4).

[4] Reg. § 1.212–1(g).

Deductible Personal Expenses. Taxpayers are allowed to deduct certain expenses that are primarily personal in nature. These expenses, which generally are not related to the production of income, are deductions *from* AGI (itemized deductions). Some of the more frequently encountered deductions in this category include the following:

- Contributions to qualified charitable organizations (not to exceed a specified percentage of AGI).
- Medical expenses (in excess of 7.5 percent of AGI).
- Certain state and local taxes (e.g., real estate taxes and state and local income or sales taxes).
- Personal casualty losses (in excess of an aggregate floor of 10 percent of AGI and a $100 floor per casualty).
- Certain personal interest (e.g., mortgage interest on a personal residence).

Itemized deductions are discussed in detail in Chapter 10.

Trade or Business Expenses and Production of Income Expenses

Section 162(a) permits a deduction for all ordinary and necessary expenses paid or incurred in carrying on a trade or business. These include reasonable salaries paid for services, expenses for the use of business property, and one-half of self-employment taxes paid (see Chapter 13). Such expenses are deducted *for* AGI.

It is sometimes difficult to determine whether an expenditure is deductible as a trade or business expense. The term "trade or business" is not defined in the Code or Regulations, and the courts have not provided a satisfactory definition. It is usually necessary to ask one or more of the following questions to determine whether an item qualifies as a trade or business expense:

- Was the use of the particular item related to a business activity? For example, if funds are borrowed for use in a business, the interest is deductible as a business expense.
- Was the expenditure incurred with the intent to realize a profit or to produce income? For example, expenses in excess of the income from raising horses are not deductible if the activity is classified as a personal hobby rather than a trade or business.
- Were the taxpayer's operation and management activities extensive enough to indicate the carrying on of a trade or business?

Section 162 *excludes* the following items from classification as trade or business expenses:

- Charitable contributions or gifts.
- Illegal bribes and kickbacks and certain treble damage payments.
- Fines and penalties.

A bribe paid to a domestic official is not deductible if it is illegal under the laws of the United States. Foreign bribes are deductible unless they are unlawful under the Foreign Corrupt Practices Act of 1977.[5]

Ordinary and Necessary Requirement. The terms **ordinary and necessary** are found in both §§ 162 and 212. To be deductible, any trade or business expense must be "ordinary and necessary." In addition, compensation for services must be "reasonable" in amount.

Many expenses that are necessary are *not* ordinary. Neither "ordinary" nor "necessary" is defined in the Code or Regulations. The courts have held that

---

[5] § 162(c)(1).

an expense is *necessary* if a prudent businessperson would incur the same expense and the expense is expected to be appropriate and helpful in the taxpayer's business.[6]

EXAMPLE 3

Pat purchased a manufacturing concern that had just been adjudged bankrupt. Because the business had a poor financial rating, Pat satisfied some of the obligations to employees and outside salespeople incurred by the former owners. Pat had no legal obligation to pay these debts, but felt this was the only way to keep salespeople and employees. The Second Circuit Court of Appeals found that the payments were necessary in that they were both appropriate and helpful.[7] However, the court held that the payments were *not* ordinary but were in the nature of capital expenditures to build a reputation. Therefore, no deduction was allowed. ■

An expense is *ordinary* if it is normal, usual, or customary in the type of business conducted by the taxpayer and is not capital in nature.[8] However, an expense need not be recurring to be deductible as ordinary.

EXAMPLE 4

Albert engaged in a mail-order business. The post office judged that his advertisements were false and misleading. Under a fraud order, the post office stamped "fraudulent" on all letters addressed to Albert's business and returned them to the senders. Albert spent $30,000 on legal fees in an unsuccessful attempt to force the post office to stop. The legal fees (though not recurring) were ordinary business expenses because they were normal, usual, or customary in the circumstances.[9] ■

For § 212 deductions, the law requires that expenses bear a reasonable and proximate relationship to (1) the production or collection of income or to (2) the management, conservation, or maintenance of property held for the production of income.[10]

EXAMPLE 5

Wendy owns a small portfolio of investments, including 10 shares of Hawk, Inc. common stock worth $1,000. She incurred $350 in travel expenses to attend the annual shareholders' meeting where she voted her 10 shares against the current management group. No deduction is permitted because a 10-share investment is insignificant in value in relation to the travel expenses incurred.[11] ■

Reasonableness Requirement. The Code refers to **reasonableness** solely with respect to salaries and other compensation for services.[12] But the courts have held that for any business expense to be ordinary and necessary, it must also be reasonable in amount.[13]

What constitutes reasonableness is a question of fact. If an expense is unreasonable, the excess amount is not allowed as a deduction. The question of reasonableness generally arises with respect to closely held corporations where there is no separation of ownership and management.

Transactions between the shareholders and the closely held company may result in the disallowance of deductions for excessive salaries and rent expense paid by the corporation to the shareholders. The courts will view an unusually large salary in light of all relevant circumstances and may find that the salary is reasonable despite its size.[14] If excessive payments for salaries and rents are closely related to

---

[6]*Welch v. Helvering*, 3 USTC ¶1164, 12 AFTR 1456, 54 S.Ct. 8 (USSC, 1933).

[7]*Dunn and McCarthy, Inc. v. Comm.*, 43–2 USTC ¶9688, 31 AFTR 1043, 139 F.2d 242 (CA–2, 1943).

[8]*Deputy v. DuPont*, 40–1 USTC ¶9161, 23 AFTR 808, 60 S.Ct. 363 (USSC, 1940).

[9]*Comm. v. Heininger*, 44–1 USTC ¶9109, 31 AFTR 783, 64 S.Ct. 249 (USSC, 1943).

[10]Reg. § 1.212–1(d).

[11]*J. Raymond Dyer*, 36 T.C. 456 (1961).

[12]§ 162(a)(1).

[13]*Comm. v. Lincoln Electric Co.*, 49–2 USTC ¶9388, 38 AFTR 411, 176 F.2d 815 (CA–6, 1949).

[14]*Kennedy, Jr. v. Comm.*, 82–1 USTC ¶9186, 49 AFTR2d 82–628, 671 F.2d 167 (CA–6, 1982), *rev'g* 72 T.C. 793 (1979).

the percentage of stock owned by the recipients, the payments are generally treated as dividends.[15] Since dividends are not deductible by the corporation, the disallowance results in an increase in the corporate taxable income. Deductions for reasonable salaries will not be disallowed *solely* because the corporation has paid insubstantial portions of its earnings as dividends to its shareholders.

EXAMPLE 6

Sparrow Corporation, a closely held corporation, is owned equally by Lupe, Carlos, and Ramon. The company has been highly profitable for several years and has not paid dividends. Lupe, Carlos, and Ramon are key officers of the company, and each receives a salary of $200,000. Salaries for similar positions in comparable companies average only $100,000. Amounts paid the owners in excess of $100,000 may be deemed unreasonable, and, if so, a total of $300,000 in salary deductions by Sparrow is disallowed. The disallowed amounts are treated as dividends rather than salary income to Lupe, Carlos, and Ramon because the payments are proportional to stock ownership. Salaries are deductible by the corporation, but dividends are not. ■

Business and Nonbusiness Losses

Section 165 provides for a deduction for losses not compensated for by insurance. As a general rule, deductible losses of individual taxpayers are limited to those incurred in a trade or business or in a transaction entered into for profit. Individuals are also allowed to deduct losses that are the result of a casualty. Casualty losses include, but are not limited to, those caused by fire, storm, shipwreck, and theft. See Chapter 7 for a further discussion of this topic. Deductible personal casualty losses are reduced by $100 per casualty, and the aggregate of all personal casualty losses is reduced by 10 percent of AGI. A personal casualty loss is an itemized deduction. See Concept Summary 6–3 near the end of the chapter for the classification of expenses.

Reporting Procedures

All deductions *for* and *from* AGI wind up on pages 1 and 2 of Form 1040. All deductions *for* AGI are reported on page 1. The last line on page 1 is adjusted gross income.

The first item on page 2 is also adjusted gross income. Itemized deductions are entered next, followed by the deduction for personal and dependency exemptions. The result is taxable income.

Most of the deductions *for* AGI on page 1 originate on supporting schedules. Examples include business expenses (Schedule C); rent, royalty, partnership, and fiduciary deductions (Schedule E); and farming expenses (Schedule F). Other deductions *for* AGI, such as traditional IRAs, Keogh retirement plans, and alimony, are entered directly on page 1 of Form 1040.

All itemized deductions on page 2 are carried over from Schedule A. Some Schedule A deductions originate on other forms. Examples include investment interest, noncash charitable contributions in excess of $500, casualty losses, and unreimbursed employee expenses.

Form 1040 becomes a summary of the detailed information entered on the other schedules and forms. See Figure 6–1.

See Concept Summary 6–3 later in the chapter for the classification of deductions as deductions *for* AGI or as deductions *from* AGI.

---

[15]Reg. § 1.162–8.

FIGURE 6–1   Format of Form 1040

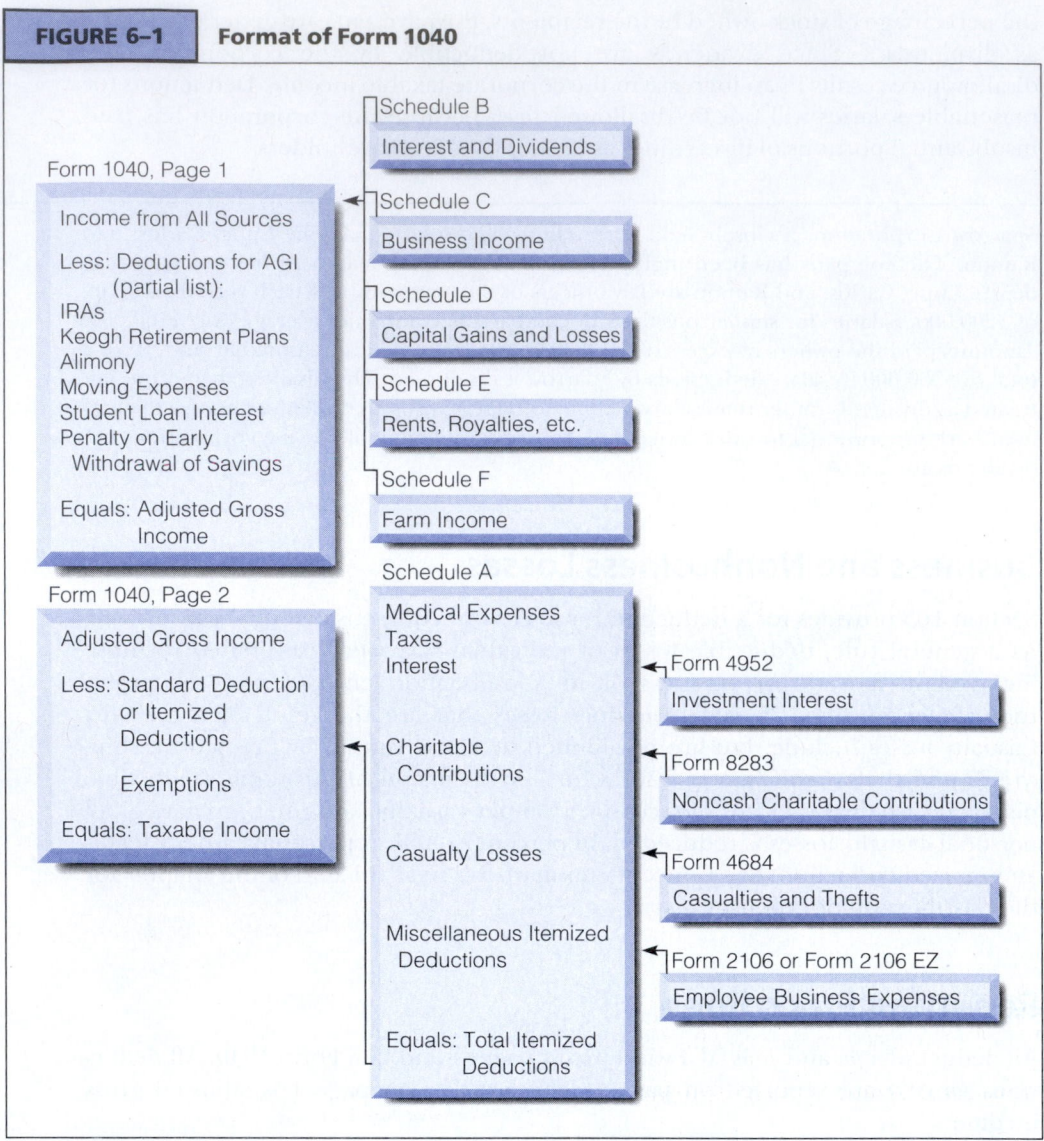

Deductions and Losses—Timing of Expense Recognition

LO.2

Describe the cash and accrual methods of accounting.

Importance of Taxpayer's Method of Accounting

A taxpayer's **accounting method** is a major factor in determining taxable income. The method used determines when an item is includible in income and when an item is deductible on the tax return. Usually, the taxpayer's regular method of record keeping is used for income tax purposes.[16] The taxing authorities do not require uniformity among all taxpayers. They do require that the method used clearly reflect income and that items be handled consistently.[17] The most common methods of accounting are the cash method and the accrual method. If a taxpayer owns multiple businesses, it may be possible to use the cash method for some and the accrual method for others.

[16]§ 446(a).   [17]§§ 446(b) and (e); Reg. § 1.446–1(a)(2).

Throughout the portions of the Code dealing with deductions, the phrase "paid or incurred" is used. *Paid* refers to the cash basis taxpayer who gets a deduction only in the year of payment. *Incurred* concerns the accrual basis taxpayer who obtains the deduction in the year in which the liability for the expense becomes certain (refer to Chapter 4).

Cash Method Requirements

The expenses of cash basis taxpayers are deductible only when they are actually paid with cash or other property. Promising to pay or issuing a note does not satisfy the actually paid requirement.[18] However, the payment can be made with borrowed funds. At the time taxpayers charge expenses on their credit cards, they are allowed to claim the deduction. They are deemed to have simultaneously borrowed money from the credit card issuer and constructively paid the expenses.[19]

Although the cash basis taxpayer must have actually or constructively paid the expense, payment does not assure a current deduction. Cash basis and accrual basis taxpayers cannot take a current deduction for capital expenditures except through amortization, depletion, or depreciation over the life (actual or statutory) of the asset. The Regulations set forth the general rule that an expenditure that creates an asset having a useful life that extends substantially beyond the end of the tax year must be capitalized.[20]

EXAMPLE 7

John, a calendar year and cash basis taxpayer, rents property from Carl. On July 1, 2008, John pays $24,000 rent for the 24 months ending June 30, 2010. The prepaid rent extends 18 months after the close of the tax year—substantially beyond the year of payment. Therefore, John must capitalize the prepaid rent and amortize the expense on a monthly basis. His deduction for 2008 is $6,000. ■

The Tax Court and the IRS took the position that an asset that will expire or be consumed by the end of the tax year following the year of payment must be prorated. The Ninth Circuit Court of Appeals held that such expenditures are currently deductible, however, and the Supreme Court apparently concurs (the one-year rule for prepaid expenses).[21]

EXAMPLE 8

Assume the same facts as in Example 7 except that John is required to pay only 12 months' rent in 2008. He pays $12,000 on July 1, 2008. The entire $12,000 is deductible in 2008. ■

The payment must be required, not a voluntary prepayment, to obtain the current deduction under the one-year rule.[22] The taxpayer must also demonstrate that allowing the current deduction will not result in a material distortion of income. Generally, the deduction will be allowed if the item is recurring or was made for a business purpose rather than to manipulate income.[23]

As Chapter 18 explains, not all taxpayers are allowed to use the cash method.[24] For example, in most cases the taxpayer is required to use the accrual method for sales and cost of goods sold if inventories are an income-producing factor of the business.

---

[18]*Page v. Rhode Island Trust Co., Exr.*, 37–1 USTC ¶9138, 19 AFTR 105, 88 F.2d 192 (CA–1, 1937).

[19]Rev.Rul. 78–39, 1978–1 C.B. 73. See also Rev.Rul. 80–335, 1980–2 C.B. 170, which applies to pay-by-phone arrangements.

[20]Reg. § 1.461–1(a).

[21]*Zaninovich v. Comm.*, 80–1 USTC ¶9342, 45 AFTR2d 80–1442, 616 F.2d 429 (CA–9, 1980), *rev'g* 69 T.C. 605 (1978). Cited by the Supreme Court in

Hillsboro National Bank v. Comm., 83–1 USTC ¶9229, 51 AFTR2d 83–874, 103 S.Ct. 1134 (USSC, 1983).

[22]*Bonaire Development Co. v. Comm.*, 82–2 USTC ¶9428, 50 AFTR2d 82–5167, 679 F.2d 159 (CA–9, 1982).

[23]*Keller v. Comm.*, 84–1 USTC ¶9194, 53 AFTR2d 84–663, 725 F.2d 1173 (CA–8, 1984), *aff'g* 79 T.C. 7 (1982).

[24]§ 448.

Accrual Method Requirements

The period in which an accrual basis taxpayer can deduct an expense is determined by applying the *all events test* and the *economic performance test*. A deduction cannot be claimed until (1) all the events have occurred to create the taxpayer's liability and (2) the amount of the liability can be determined with reasonable accuracy. Once these requirements are satisfied, the deduction is permitted only if economic performance has occurred. The economic performance test is met only when the service, property, or use of property giving rise to the liability is actually performed for, provided to, or used by the taxpayer.[25]

EXAMPLE 9

On December 22, 2008, Chris's entertainment business sponsored a jazz festival in a rented auditorium at a local college. His business is responsible for cleaning up the auditorium after the festival and for reinstalling seats that were removed so more people could attend the festival. Since the college is closed over the Christmas holidays, the company hired by Chris to perform the work did not begin these activities until January 2, 2009. The cost to Chris is $1,200. Chris cannot deduct the $1,200 until 2009, when the services are performed. ■

An exception to the economic performance requirements allows certain *recurring items* to be deducted if the following conditions are met:

- The item is recurring in nature and is treated consistently by the taxpayer.
- Either the accrued item is not material, or accruing it results in better matching of income and expenses.
- All the events have occurred that determine the fact of the liability, and the amount of the liability can be determined with reasonable accuracy.
- Economic performance occurs within a reasonable period (but not later than 8½ months after the close of the taxable year).[26]

EXAMPLE 10

Rick, an accrual basis, calendar year taxpayer, entered into a monthly maintenance contract during the year. He makes a monthly accrual at the end of every month for this service and pays the fee sometime between the first and fifteenth of the following month when services are performed. The amount involved is immaterial, and all the other tests are met. The December 2008 accrual is deductible in 2008 even though the service is performed on January 12, 2009. ■

EXAMPLE 11

Rita, an accrual basis, calendar year taxpayer, shipped merchandise sold on December 30, 2008, via Greyhound Van Lines on January 2, 2009, and paid the freight charges at that time. Since Rita reported the sale of the merchandise in 2008, the shipping charge should also be deductible in 2008. This procedure results in a better matching of income and expenses. ■

Reserves for estimated expenses (frequently employed for financial accounting purposes) generally are not allowed for tax purposes because the economic performance test cannot be satisfied.

EXAMPLE 12

Blackbird Airlines is required by Federal law to test its engines after 3,000 flying hours. Aircraft cannot return to flight until the tests have been conducted. An unrelated aircraft maintenance company does all of the company's tests for $1,500 per engine. For financial reporting purposes, the company accrues an expense based upon $.50 per hour of flight and credits an allowance account. The actual amounts paid for maintenance are offset against the allowance account. For tax purposes, the economic performance test is not satisfied until the work has been done. Therefore, the reserve method cannot be used for tax purposes. ■

---

[25]§ 461(h).   [26]§ 461(h)(3)(A).

Disallowance Possibilities

LO.3

Apply the Internal Revenue Code deduction disallowance provisions associated with the following: public policy limitations, political activities, excessive executive compensation, investigation of business opportunities, hobby losses, vacation home rentals, payment of others' expenses, personal expenditures, capital expenditures, related-party transactions, and expenses related to tax-exempt income.

The tax law provides for the disallowance of certain types of expenses. Without specific restrictions in the tax law, taxpayers might attempt to deduct certain items that in reality are personal expenditures. For example, specific tax rules are provided to determine whether an expenditure is for trade or business purposes or related to a personal hobby.

Certain disallowance provisions are a codification or extension of prior court decisions. After the courts denied deductions for payments considered to be in violation of public policy, the tax law was changed to provide specific authority for the disallowance of these deductions. Discussions of specific disallowance provisions in the tax law follow.

Public Policy Limitation

Justification for Denying Deductions.
The courts developed the principle that a payment that is in violation of public policy is not a necessary expense and is not deductible.[27] Although a bribe or fine may be appropriate, helpful, and even contribute to the profitability of an activity, the courts held that to allow such expenses would frustrate clearly defined public policy. A deduction would dilute the effect of the penalty since the government would be indirectly subsidizing a taxpayer's wrongdoing.

Accordingly, the IRS was free to restrict deductions if, in its view, the expenses were contrary to public policy. But since the law did not explain which actions violated public policy, taxpayers often had to go to court to determine whether or not their expense fell into this category.

Furthermore, the public policy doctrine could be arbitrarily applied in cases where no clear definition had emerged. To solve these problems, Congress enacted legislation that attempts to limit the use of the doctrine. Under the legislation, deductions are disallowed for certain specific types of expenditures that are considered contrary to public policy:

- Bribes and kickbacks, including those associated with Medicare or Medicaid (in the case of foreign bribes and kickbacks, only if the payments violate the U.S. Foreign Corrupt Practices Act of 1977).
- Fines and penalties paid to a government for violation of law.

EXAMPLE 13

Brown Corporation, a moving company, consistently loads its trucks with weights in excess of the limits allowed by state law. The additional revenue more than offsets the fines levied. The fines are for a violation of public policy and are not deductible. ■

- Two-thirds of the treble damage payments made to claimants resulting from violation of the antitrust law.[28]

To be disallowed, the bribe or kickback must be illegal under either Federal or state law and must also subject the payor to a criminal penalty or the loss of a license or privilege to engage in a trade or business. For a bribe or kickback that is illegal under state law, a deduction is denied only if the state law is generally enforced.

EXAMPLE 14

During the year, Keith, an insurance salesman, paid $5,000 to Karen, a real estate broker. The payment represented 20% of the commissions Keith earned from customers referred by Karen. Under state law, the splitting of commissions by an insurance salesperson is an act of misconduct that could warrant a revocation of the salesperson's license. Keith's $5,000 payments to Karen are not deductible provided the state law is generally enforced. ■

---

[27]*Tank Truck Rentals, Inc. v. Comm.*, 58–1 USTC ¶9366, 1 AFTR2d 1154, 78 S.Ct. 507 (USSC, 1958).

[28]§§ 162(c), (f), and (g).

ETHICAL and EQUITABLE *Considerations*   **KNOWING THE RIGHT PEOPLE**

Abner, a real estate developer, has a contract with a major retailer to handle its land acquisitions in the southeastern part of the state. One of Abner's major responsibilities is to secure the requisite zoning to enable the retailer to build and operate its outlets. Typically, obtaining proper zoning is not a difficult matter.

Abner has identified a site that his client would like to acquire. It is located in a small community of historic repute and is surrounded by two counties with large populations. Unfortunately, the community has very restrictive zoning rules for commercial properties, and obtaining zoning variances will be challenging.

Abner's normal strategy in such a situation is to hire the leading law firm in the community to represent him in purchasing the property and securing the desired zoning. In this instance, however, the senior partner in the leading law firm is also the mayor. To avoid an obvious conflict of interest, Abner hires another law firm to carry out the acquisition. To avoid antagonizing the mayor, he pays a $25,000 retainer to the mayor's law firm to serve as his legal representative on any other real estate acquisitions during the coming year in the two adjoining counties. Abner is successful in securing the zoning variances and acquires the site for the retailer. During the following 12-month period, Abner does not utilize the services of the mayor's law firm. Abner deducts the $25,000 payment as an ordinary and necessary business expense.

What is Abner trying to achieve, and will he be successful?

Legal Expenses Incurred in Defense of Civil or Criminal Penalties. To deduct legal expenses, the taxpayer must be able to show that the origin and character of the claim are directly related to a trade or business, an income-producing activity, or the determination, collection, or refund of a tax. Personal legal expenses are not deductible. Thus, legal fees incurred in connection with a criminal defense are deductible only if the crime is associated with the taxpayer's trade or business or income-producing activity.[29]

EXAMPLE 15

Debra, a financial officer of Blue Corporation, incurs legal expenses in connection with her defense in a criminal indictment for evasion of Blue's income taxes. Debra may deduct her legal expenses because she is deemed to be in the trade or business of being an executive. The legal action impairs her ability to conduct this business activity.[30] ■

Deductible legal expenses associated with the following are deductible *for* AGI:

- Ordinary and necessary expenses incurred in connection with a trade or business.
- Ordinary and necessary expenses incurred in conjunction with rental or royalty property held for the production of income.

All other deductible legal expenses are deductible *from* AGI. For example, legal expenses generally are deductible *from* AGI if they are for fees for tax advice relative to the preparation of an individual's income tax return. Contrast this with the deduction *for* classification of legal fees for tax advice relative to the preparation of the portion of the tax return for a sole proprietor's trade or business (Schedule C) or an individual's rental or royalty income (Schedule E).

Expenses Relating to an Illegal Business. The usual expenses of operating an illegal business (e.g., a numbers racket) are deductible.[31] However, § 162 disallows a deduction for fines, bribes to public officials, illegal kickbacks, and other illegal payments.

---

[29]*Comm. v. Tellier*, 66–1 USTC ¶9319, 17 AFTR2d 633, 86 S.Ct. 1118 (USSC, 1966).

[30]Rev.Rul. 68–662, 1968–2 C.B. 69.

[31]*Comm. v. Sullivan*, 58–1 USTC ¶9368, 1 AFTR2d 1158, 78 S.Ct. 512 (USSC, 1958).

DISALLOWANCE OF DEDUCTION FOR BRIBES IN OTHER COUNTRIES

GLOBAL *Tax Issues*

Japan has enacted legislation that denies a tax deduction for bribes paid to foreign public officials. Japan is one of the 36 nations that have ratified and implemented a 1997 treaty that outlawed bribery of foreign public officials in international business transactions (Organization for Economic Cooperation and Development [OECD] Convention on Combating the Bribery of Foreign Public Officials in International Business).

In 2006, the OECD praised Japan for complying with the treaty by enacting the nondeductibility legislation. At the same time, however, the OECD encouraged Japan to take a more active role in discovering such bribes by conducting tax audits and then following up with prosecutions that lead to convictions for corruption.

EXAMPLE 16

Sam owns and operates an illegal gambling establishment. In connection with this activity, he has the following expenses during the year:

Rent	$ 60,000
Payoffs to the police	40,000
Depreciation on equipment	100,000
Wages	140,000
Interest	30,000
Criminal fines	50,000
Illegal kickbacks	10,000
Total	$430,000

All of the usual expenses (rent, depreciation, wages, and interest) are deductible; payoffs, fines, and kickbacks are not deductible. Of the $430,000 spent, $330,000 is deductible and $100,000 is not. ∎

An exception applies to expenses incurred in illegal trafficking in drugs.[32] *Drug dealers* are not allowed a deduction for ordinary and necessary business expenses incurred in their business. In arriving at gross income from the business, however, dealers may reduce total sales by the cost of goods sold.[33] In this regard, no distinction is made between legal and illegal businesses in calculating gross income. Treating cost of goods sold as a negative income item rather than as a deduction item produces the unseemly result that a drug dealer's taxable income is reduced by cost of goods sold.

Political Contributions and Lobbying Activities

Political Contributions. Generally, no business deduction is permitted for direct or indirect payments for political purposes.[34] Historically, the government has been reluctant to accord favorable tax treatment to business expenditures for political purposes. Allowing deductions might encourage abuses and enable businesses to have undue influence upon the political process.

Lobbying Expenditures. Lobbying expenses incurred in attempting to influence state or Federal legislation or the actions of certain high-ranking public officials (e.g., the President, Vice President, cabinet-level officials, and the two most

---

[32]§ 280E.

[33]Reg. § 1.61–3(a). Gross income is defined as sales minus cost of goods sold. Thus, while § 280E prohibits any deductions for drug dealers, it does not modify the normal definition of gross income.

[34]§ 276.

senior officials in each agency of the executive branch) are not deductible.[35] The disallowance also applies to a pro rata portion of the membership dues of trade associations and other groups that are used for lobbying activities.

EXAMPLE 17

Egret Company pays a $10,000 annual membership fee to the Free Trade Group, a trade association for plumbing wholesalers. The trade association estimates that 70% of its dues are allocated to lobbying activities. Thus, Egret Company's deduction is limited to $3,000 ($10,000 × 30%). ■

There are three exceptions to the disallowance of lobbying expenses. An exception is provided for influencing local legislation (e.g., city and county governments). Second, the disallowance provision does not apply to activities devoted solely to monitoring legislation. Third, a *de minimis* exception is provided for annual in-house expenditures (lobbying expenses other than those paid to professional lobbyists or any portion of dues used by associations for lobbying) if such expenditures do not exceed $2,000. If the in-house expenditures exceed $2,000, none of the in-house expenditures can be deducted.

Excessive Executive Compensation

The deduction of executive compensation is subject to two limitations. As discussed earlier in this chapter, the compensation of shareholder-employees of closely held corporations is subject to the reasonableness requirement. The second limitation, the so-called millionaires' provision, applies to publicly held corporations (a corporation that has at least one class of stock registered under the Securities Exchange Act of 1934).[36]

The millionaires' provision does not limit the amount of compensation that can be paid to an employee. Instead, it limits the amount the employer can deduct for the compensation of a covered executive to $1 million annually. Covered employees include the chief executive officer and the four other most highly compensated officers.

Employee compensation *excludes* the following:

- Commissions based on individual performance.
- Certain performance-based compensation based on company performance according to a formula approved by a board of directors compensation

---

[35]§ 162(e).

[36]§ 162(m).

committee (comprised solely of two or more outside directors) and by share-holder vote. The performance attainment must be certified by this compensation committee.
- Payments to tax-qualified retirement plans.
- Payments that are excludible from the employee's gross income (e.g., certain fringe benefits).

Investigation of a Business

Investigation expenses are expenses paid or incurred to determine the feasibility of entering a new business or expanding an existing business. They include such costs as travel, engineering and architectural surveys, marketing reports, and various legal and accounting services. How such expenses are treated for tax purposes depends on a number of variables, including the following:

- The current business, if any, of the taxpayer.
- The nature of the business being investigated.
- The extent to which the investigation has proceeded.
- Whether or not the acquisition actually takes place.

If the taxpayer is in a business the *same as or similar to* that being investigated, all investigation expenses are deductible in the year paid or incurred. The tax result is the same whether or not the taxpayer acquires the business being investigated.[37]

EXAMPLE 18

Terry, an accrual basis sole proprietor, owns and operates three motels in Georgia. In the current year, Terry incurs expenses of $8,500 in investigating the possibility of acquiring several additional motels located in South Carolina. The $8,500 is deductible in the current year whether or not Terry acquires the motels in South Carolina. ■

When the taxpayer is *not* in a business that is the same as or similar to the one being investigated, the tax result depends on whether the new business is acquired. If the business is not acquired, all investigation expenses generally are nondeductible.[38]

EXAMPLE 19

Lynn, a retired merchant, incurs expenses in traveling from Rochester, New York, to California to investigate the feasibility of acquiring several auto care centers. If no acquisition takes place, none of the expenses are deductible. ■

If the taxpayer is *not* in a business that is the same as or similar to the one being investigated and actually acquires the new business, the expenses must be capitalized as startup expenses. At the election of the taxpayer, the first $5,000 of the expenses can be immediately deducted. Any excess expenses can be amortized over a period of 180 months (15 years). In arriving at the $5,000 immediate deduction allowed, a dollar-for-dollar reduction must be made for those expenses in excess of $50,000.[39]

EXAMPLE 20

Tina owns and operates 10 restaurants located in various cities throughout the Southeast. She travels to Atlanta to discuss the acquisition of an auto dealership. In addition, she incurs legal and accounting costs associated with the potential acquisition. After incurring total investigation costs of $52,000, she acquires the auto dealership on October 1, 2008.

---

[37]§ 195. *York v. Comm.*, 58–2 USTC ¶9952, 2 AFTR2d 6178, 261 F.2d 421 (CA–4, 1958).
[38]Rev.Rul. 57–418, 1957–2 C.B. 143; *Morton Frank*, 20 T.C. 511 (1953); and *Dwight A. Ward*, 20 T.C. 332 (1953).
[39]§ 195(b).

CONCEPT SUMMARY 6–1

Costs of Investigating a Business

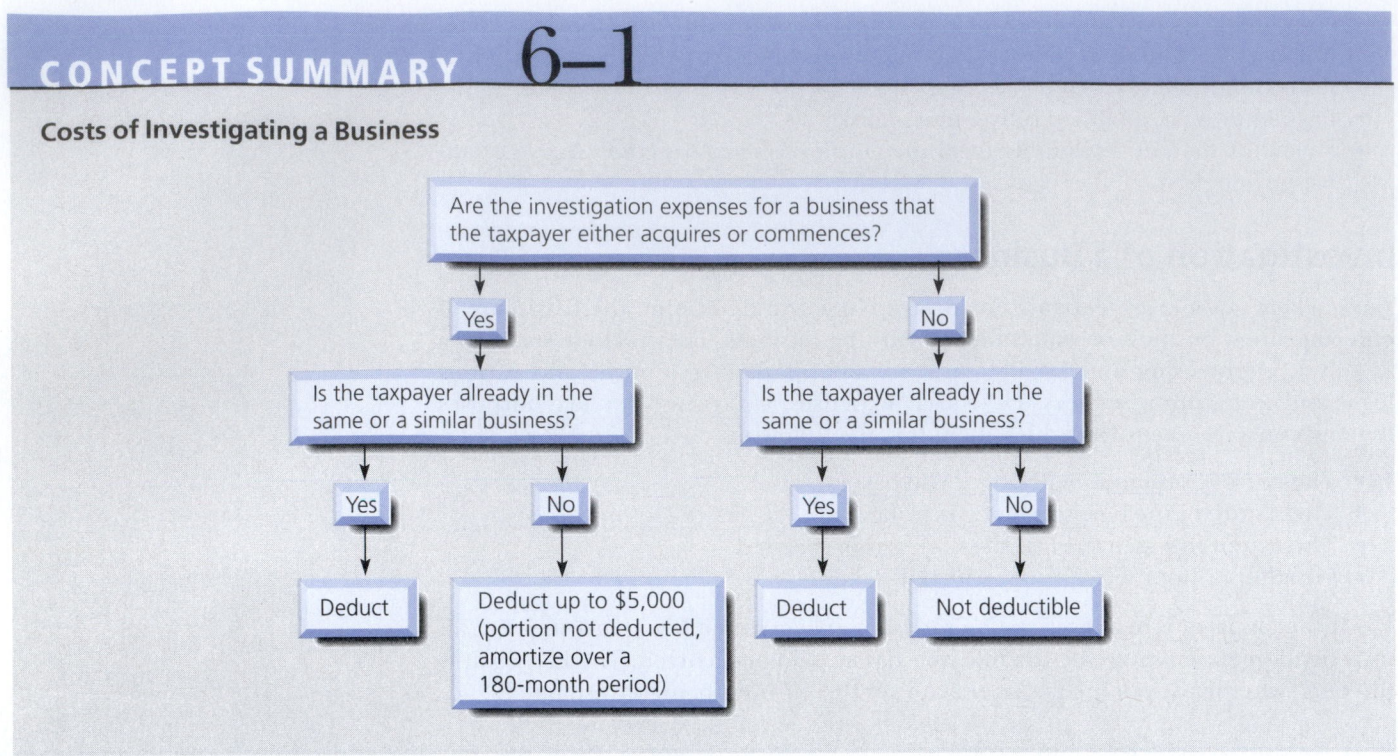

Tina may immediately deduct $3,000 [$5,000 − ($52,000 − $50,000)] and amortize the balance of $49,000 ($52,000 − $3,000) over a period of 180 months. For calendar year 2008, therefore, Tina can deduct $3,817 [$3,000 + ($49,000 × 3/180)]. ∎

Hobby Losses

Business or investment expenses are deductible only if the taxpayer can show that the activity was entered into for the purpose of making a profit. Certain activities may have either profit-seeking or personal attributes, depending upon individual circumstances. Examples include raising horses and operating a farm used as a weekend residence. While personal losses are not deductible, losses attributable to profit-seeking activities may be deducted and used to offset a taxpayer's other income. For this reason, the tax law limits the deductibility of **hobby losses**.

General Rules. If an individual can show that an activity has been conducted with the intent to earn a profit, losses from the activity are fully deductible. The hobby loss rules apply only if the activity is not engaged in for profit. Hobby expenses are deductible only to the extent of hobby income.[40]

The Regulations stipulate that the following nine factors should be considered in determining whether an activity is profit seeking or a hobby:[41]

- Whether the activity is conducted in a businesslike manner.
- The expertise of the taxpayers or their advisers.
- The time and effort expended.
- The expectation that the assets of the activity will appreciate in value.
- The taxpayer's previous success in conducting similar activities.
- The history of income or losses from the activity.
- The relationship of profits earned to losses incurred.

---

[40]§ 183(b)(2).   [41]Reg. §§ 1.183–2(b)(1) through (9).

| TAX *in the News* | IRS DOING POORLY IN POLICING HOBBY LOSS DEDUCTIONS |

The Treasury Inspector General for Tax Administration (TIGTA) has issued a report on the number of taxpayers who file Schedule C of Form 1040 showing losses over several consecutive years. Many of the returns examined reported substantial income from other sources, and the majority of the individuals involved had their tax returns prepared by tax practitioners. By claiming the Schedule C losses, approximately 1.2 million taxpayers were able to save $2.8 billion in taxes for tax year 2005.

Because of the subjective nature of the hobby loss rules (i.e., whether or not a profit motive exists), these Schedule C losses can be controlled only through thorough policing by the IRS. Unfortunately, the IRS has neither the time nor the resources to carry out the audit efforts required. The TIGTA report, therefore, suggests that § 183 be changed by legislation to establish a clear standard for determining whether an activity is a business or a hobby.

Source: *"Significant Challenges Exist in Determining Whether Taxpayers with Schedule C Losses Are Engaged in Tax Abuse,"* Treasury Inspector General for Tax Administration, *September 7, 2007 (Reference No. 2007-30-173).*

- The financial status of the taxpayer (e.g., if the taxpayer does not have substantial amounts of other income, this may indicate that the activity is engaged in for profit).
- Elements of personal pleasure or recreation in the activity.

The presence or absence of a factor is not by itself determinative of whether the activity is profit seeking or a hobby. Rather, the decision is a subjective one that is based on an analysis of the facts and circumstances.

Presumptive Rule of § 183.

The Code provides a rebuttable presumption that an activity is profit seeking if the activity shows a profit in at least three of any five prior consecutive years.[42] If the activity involves horses, a profit in at least two of seven consecutive years meets the presumptive rule. If these profitability tests are met, the activity is presumed to be a trade or business rather than a personal hobby. In this situation, the IRS bears the burden of proving that the activity is personal rather than trade or business related.

EXAMPLE 21

Camille, an executive for a large corporation, is paid a salary of $200,000. Her husband is a collector of antiques. Several years ago, he opened an antique shop in a local shopping center and spends most of his time buying and selling antiques. He occasionally earns a small profit from this activity but more frequently incurs substantial losses. If the losses are business related, they are fully deductible against Camille's salary income on a joint return. In resolving this issue, consider the following:

- Initially determine whether the antique activity has met the three-out-of-five years profit test.
- If the presumption is not met, the activity may nevertheless qualify as a business if the taxpayer can show that the intent is to engage in a profit-seeking activity. It is not necessary to show actual profits.
- Attempt to fit the operation within the nine criteria prescribed in the Regulations and listed above. These criteria are the factors considered in trying to rebut the § 183 presumption. ■

Determining the Amount of the Deduction.

If an activity is deemed to be a hobby, the expenses are deductible only to the extent of the gross income from the hobby. These expenses must be deducted in the following order:

---

[42]§ 183(d).

- Amounts deductible under other Code sections without regard to the nature of the activity, such as property taxes and home mortgage interest.
- Amounts deductible under other Code sections if the activity had been engaged in for profit, but only if those amounts do not affect adjusted basis. Examples include maintenance, utilities, and supplies.
- Amounts that affect adjusted basis and would be deductible under other Code sections if the activity had been engaged in for profit.[43] Examples include depreciation, amortization, and depletion.

These deductions are deductible *from* AGI as itemized deductions to the extent they exceed 2 percent of AGI.[44] If the taxpayer uses the standard deduction rather than itemizing, all hobby loss deductions are wasted.

EXAMPLE 22

Jim, the vice president of an oil company, has AGI of $80,000. He decides to pursue painting in his spare time. He uses a home studio, comprising 10% of the home's square footage. During the current year, Jim incurs the following expenses:

Frames	$ 350
Art supplies	300
Fees paid to models	1,000
Home studio expenses:	
Total property taxes	900
Total home mortgage interest	10,000
Depreciation on 10% of home	500
Total home maintenance and utilities	3,600

During the year, Jim sold paintings for a total of $3,200. If the activity is held to be a hobby, Jim is allowed deductions as follows:

Gross income		$ 3,200
Deduct: Taxes and interest (10% of $10,900)		(1,090)
Remainder		$ 2,110
Deduct: Frames	$ 350	
Art supplies	300	
Models' fees	1,000	
Maintenance and utilities (10%)	360	(2,010)
Remainder		$ 100
Deduct: Depreciation ($500, but limited to $100)		(100)
Net income		$ –0–

Jim includes the $3,200 of income in AGI, making his AGI $83,200. The taxes and interest are itemized deductions, deductible in full. The remaining $2,110 of expenses are reduced by 2% of his AGI ($1,664), so the net deduction is $446. Since the property taxes and home mortgage interest are deductible anyway, the net effect is a $2,754 ($3,200 less $446) increase in taxable income. ■

EXAMPLE 23

Assume that Jim's activity in Example 22 is held to be a business. The business is located in a small office building he owns. Expenses are property taxes of $90, mortgage interest of $1,000, frames of $350, art supplies of $300, models' fees of $1,000, maintenance and utilities of $360, and depreciation of $500. Under these circumstances, Jim could deduct expenses totaling $3,600. All these expenses would be trade or business expenses deductible *for* AGI. His reduction in AGI would be as follows:

---

[43]Reg. § 1.183–1(b)(1).   [44]Reg. § 1.67–1T(a)(1)(iv) and Rev.Rul. 75–14, 1975–1 C.B. 90.

Gross income		$ 3,200
Less: Taxes and interest	$1,090	
Other business expenses	2,010	
Depreciation	500	(3,600)
Reduction in AGI		($ 400)

Rental of Vacation Homes

Restrictions on the deductions allowed for part-year rentals of personal **vacation homes** were written into the law to prevent taxpayers from deducting essentially personal expenses as rental losses. Many taxpayers who owned vacation homes had formerly treated the homes as rental property and generated rental losses as deductions *for* AGI. For example, a summer cabin would be rented for 2 months per year, used for vacationing for 1 month, and left vacant the rest of the year. The taxpayer would then deduct 11 months' depreciation, utilities, maintenance, etc., as rental expenses, resulting in a rental loss. Section 280A eliminates this treatment by allowing deductions on residences used primarily for personal purposes only to the extent of the income generated. Only a break-even situation is allowed; no losses can be deducted.

There are three possible tax treatments for residences used for both personal and rental purposes. The treatment depends upon the *relative time* the residence is used for personal purposes versus rental use.

Primarily Personal Use. If the residence is *rented* for *fewer than 15 days* in a year, it is treated as a personal residence. The rent income is excluded from gross income, and mortgage interest and real estate taxes are allowed as itemized deductions, as with any personal residence.[45] No other expenses (e.g., depreciation, utilities, maintenance) are deductible. Although this provision exists primarily for administrative convenience, several bills have been introduced in Congress that would have repealed this exclusion from gross income.

EXAMPLE 24

Dixie owns a vacation cottage on the lake. During the current year, she rented it for $1,600 for two weeks, lived in it two months, and left it vacant the remainder of the year. The year's expenses amounted to $6,000 mortgage interest expense, $500 property taxes, $1,500 utilities and maintenance, and $2,400 depreciation. Since the property was not rented for at least

---

[45]§ 280A(g).

15 days, the income is excluded, the mortgage interest and property tax expenses are itemized deductions, and the remaining expenses are nondeductible personal expenses. ∎

Primarily Rental Use. If the residence is *rented* for 15 days or more in a year and is *not used* for personal purposes for more than the greater of (1) 14 days or (2) 10 percent of the total days rented, the residence is treated as rental property.[46] The expenses must be allocated between personal and rental days if there are any personal use days during the year. The deduction of the expenses allocated to rental days can exceed rent income and result in a rental loss. The loss may be deductible under the passive activity loss rules (discussed in Chapter 11).

EXAMPLE 25

Assume instead that Dixie in Example 24 used the cottage for 12 days and rented it for 48 days for $4,800. Since she rented the cottage for 15 days or more but did not use it for more than 14 days, the cottage is treated as rental property. The expenses must be allocated between personal and rental days.

| | Percentage of Use | |
	Rental 80%	Personal 20%
Income	$ 4,800	$ –0–
Expenses		
Mortgage interest ($6,000)	($ 4,800)	($1,200)
Property taxes ($500)	(400)	(100)
Utilities and maintenance ($1,500)	(1,200)	(300)
Depreciation ($2,400)	(1,920)	(480)
Total expenses	($ 8,320)	($2,080)
Rental loss	($ 3,520)	$ –0–

Dixie deducts the $3,520 rental loss *for* AGI (assuming she meets the passive activity loss rules, discussed in Chapter 11). She also has an itemized deduction for property taxes of $100 associated with the personal use. The mortgage interest of $1,200 associated with the personal use is not deductible as an itemized deduction because the cottage is not a qualified residence (qualified residence interest) for this purpose (see Chapter 10). The portion of utilities and maintenance and depreciation attributable to personal use is not deductible. ∎

EXAMPLE 26

Assume instead that Dixie in Example 24 rented the cottage for 200 days and lived in it for 19 days. The cottage is primarily rental use since she rented it for 15 days or more and did not use it for personal purposes for more than 20 days (10% of the rental days). The expenses must be allocated between personal and rental days as illustrated in Example 25. ∎

Personal/Rental Use. If the residence is rented for 15 days or more in a year *and* is used for personal purposes for more than the greater of (1) 14 days or (2) 10 percent of the total days rented, it is treated as a personal/rental use residence. The expenses must be allocated between personal days and rental days. Expenses are allowed only to the extent of rent income.

EXAMPLE 27

Assume instead that Dixie in Example 24 rented the property for 30 days and lived in it for 30 days. The residence is classified as personal/rental use property since she used it more than 14 days and rented it for 15 days or more. The expenses must be allocated between rental use and personal use, and the rental expenses are allowed only to the extent of rent income. ∎

---

[46]§ 280A(d) and Prop.Reg. § 1.280A–3(c).

If a residence is classified as personal/rental use property, the expenses that are deductible anyway (e.g., real estate taxes and mortgage interest) must be deducted first. If a positive net income results, otherwise nondeductible expenses that do not affect adjusted basis (e.g., maintenance, utilities, insurance) are allowed next. Finally, if any positive balance remains, depreciation is allowed. Any disallowed expenses allocable to rental use are carried forward and used in future years subject to the same limitations.

Expenses must be allocated between personal and rental days before the limits are applied. The courts have held that real estate taxes and mortgage interest, which accrue ratably over the year, are allocated on the basis of 365 days.[47] The IRS, however, disagrees and allocates real estate taxes and mortgage interest on the basis of total days of use.[48] Other expenses (utilities, maintenance, depreciation, etc.) are allocated on the basis of total days used.

EXAMPLE 28

Jason rents his vacation home for 60 days and lives in the home for 30 days. The limitations on personal/rental use residences apply. Jason's gross rent income is $10,000. For the entire year (not a leap year), the real estate taxes are $2,190; his mortgage interest expense is $10,220; utilities and maintenance expense equals $2,400; and depreciation is $9,000. Using the IRS approach, these amounts are deductible in this specific order:

Gross income	$10,000
Deduct: Taxes and interest ($^{60}/_{90}$ × $12,410)	(8,273)
Remainder to apply to rental operating expenses and depreciation	$ 1,727
Deduct: Utilities and maintenance ($^{60}/_{90}$ × $2,400)	(1,600)
Balance	$ 127
Deduct: Depreciation ($^{60}/_{90}$ × $9,000 = $6,000 but limited to above balance)	(127)
Net rent income	$ –0–

The nonrental use portion of real estate taxes and mortgage interest ($4,137 in this case) is deductible if the taxpayer elects to itemize (see Chapter 10). The personal use portion of utilities, maintenance, and depreciation is not deductible in any case. Jason has a carryover of $5,873 ($6,000 − $127) of the unused depreciation. Also note that the basis of the property is not reduced by the $5,873 depreciation not allowed because of the above limitation. (See Chapter 14 for a discussion of the reduction in basis for depreciation allowed or allowable.) ∎

EXAMPLE 29

Using the court's approach in allocating real estate taxes and mortgage interest, Jason, in Example 28, would have this result:

Gross income	$10,000
Deduct: Taxes and interest ($^{60}/_{365}$ × $12,410)	(2,040)
Remainder to apply to rental operating expenses and depreciation	$ 7,960
Deduct: Utilities and maintenance ($^{60}/_{90}$ × $2,400)	(1,600)
Balance	$ 6,360
Deduct: Depreciation ($^{60}/_{90}$ × $9,000, but limited to $6,360)	(6,000)
Net rent income	$ 360

Jason can deduct $10,370 ($12,410 paid − $2,040 deducted as expense in computing net rent income) of personal use mortgage interest and real estate taxes as itemized deductions. ∎

---

[47]*Bolton v. Comm.*, 82–2 USTC ¶9699, 51 AFTR2d 83–305, 694 F.2d 556 (CA–9, 1982).

[48]Prop.Reg. § 1.280A–3(d)(4).

Note the contrasting results in Examples 28 and 29. The IRS's approach (Example 28) results in no rental gain or loss and an itemized deduction for real estate taxes and mortgage interest of $4,137. In Example 29, Jason has net rent income of $360 and $10,370 of itemized deductions. The court's approach decreases his taxable income by $10,010 ($10,370 itemized deductions less $360 net rent income). The IRS's approach reduces his taxable income by only $4,137.

EXAMPLE 30

Assume instead that Jason in Example 28 had not lived in the home at all during the year. The house is rental property. The rental loss is calculated as follows:

Gross income	$10,000
Expenses	
Taxes and interest	($12,410)
Utilities and maintenance	(2,400)
Depreciation	(9,000)
Total expenses	($23,810)
Rental loss	($13,810)

Whether any of the rental loss would be deductible depends upon whether Jason actively participated in the rental activity and met the other requirements for passive activity losses (discussed in Chapter 11). ∎

Conversion to Rental Property. A related issue is whether or not a taxpayer's *primary residence* is subject to the preceding rules if it is converted to rental property. If the vacation home rules apply, a taxpayer who converts a personal residence to rental property during the tax year, without any tax avoidance motive, could have the allowable deductions limited to the rent income. This would occur if the personal use exceeded the greater of 14 days or 10 percent of rental days test (a likely situation). The Code, however, provides that during a *qualified rental period*, any personal use days are not counted as personal use days in terms of classifying the use of the residence as *personal/rental use* rather than as *primarily rental use.*[49] In effect, the deduction for expenses of the property incurred during a qualified rental period is not subject to the personal use test of the vacation home rules. A qualified rental period is a consecutive period of 12 or more months. The period begins or ends in the taxable year in which the residence is rented or held for rental at a fair price. The residence must not be rented to a related party. If the property is sold before the 12-month period expires, the qualified rental period is the actual time rented.

EXAMPLE 31

Rhonda converts her residence to rental property on May 1 and rents it for the remainder of 2008 for $5,600 and for all of 2009 for $8,400. The house would be classified as personal/rental use property (personal use days during 2008 are greater than both 14 days and 10% of rental days) except that this is a qualified rental period. Therefore, Rhonda's deduction for rental expenses is not limited to the gross income of $5,600 in 2008. ∎

See Concept Summary 6–2 for a summary of the vacation home rules.

Expenditures Incurred for Taxpayer's Benefit or Taxpayer's Obligation

An expense must be incurred for the taxpayer's benefit or arise from the taxpayer's obligation. An individual cannot claim a tax deduction for the payment of the expenses of another individual.

---

[49]§ 280A(d).

CONCEPT SUMMARY 6–2

Vacation/Rental Home

Was the residence rented for 15 or more days during the year?

→ No → Treat as a second home. Income is excludible. Itemize taxes and interest.

→ Yes

Were personal use days more than the greater of 14 days or 10% of the total rental days?

→ No → Property is a rental activity.

→ Allocate expenses to personal use. Taxes are itemized deductions.

→ Remaining expenses and income are from rental activity subject to at-risk and passive activity loss rules.

→ Yes

Does rental portion of taxes and interest expenses* exceed rent income?

→ Yes → Deduct interest and taxes only to extent of income. Other expenses are nondeductible. Remainder of taxes and interest are itemized deductions.

→ No

Does rental portion of all other expenses** except depreciation exceed remaining net income?

→ Yes → Deduct only to extent of remaining net income. Itemize personal part of interest and taxes. Remainder is nondeductible.

→ No

Does rental portion of depreciation** exceed remaining net income?

→ Yes → Deduct only to extent of remaining net income. Itemize personal part of interest and taxes. Remainder is nondeductible.

→ No

Remaining net income is passive rental activity subject to at-risk and passive activity loss rules.

→ Report on Schedule E.

*Allocated on the basis of 365 (366 in a leap year) days (court) or total days of use (IRS).
**Allocated on the basis of total days of use.

EXAMPLE 32

During the current year, Fred pays the property taxes on his son Vern's home. Neither Fred nor Vern can take a deduction for the amount paid for Vern's property taxes. Fred is not entitled to a deduction because the property taxes are not his obligation. Vern cannot claim a deduction because he did not pay the property taxes. The tax result would have been more favorable had Fred made a cash gift to Vern and let him pay the property taxes. Then Vern could have deducted the property taxes. Fred likely would not be liable for any gift taxes depending upon the amount involved due to the annual exclusion (see Chapter 1). A deduction would have been created with no cash difference to the family. ∎

One exception to this disallowance rule is the payment of medical expenses for a dependent. Such expenses are deductible by the payor subject to the normal rules that limit the deductibility of medical expenses (see Chapter 10).[50]

---

[50]§ 213(a).

| TAX *in the News* | NASCAR AND ANOTHER TAXPAYER'S OBLIGATIONS |

Dale Earnhardt Jr. is one of NASCAR's most popular and most visible drivers. At a race at Darlington Raceway, he was docked 100 points in the "Chase for the Cup" for allegedly having an illegal part on his car (i.e., an illegal modification of the rear wing). In addition, NASCAR levied a fine of $100,000 and a six-race suspension against crew chief Tony Eury (Dale's cousin).

Dale Earnhardt, Inc. (DEI), the race team for which Dale Jr. currently drives, will appeal the suspension. In addition, Dale Jr. has announced that he will pay the $100,000 fine for Tony Eury if the appeal is not successful.

The payment of the fine raises two tax issues. First, it appears to be a legitimate trade or business expense under § 162(a). Section 162(f) on fines and penalties does not apply because the NASCAR fine is "not paid to the government for the violation of any law." Instead it is paid to NASCAR for a violation of its rules.

Whether the fine is deductible then depends on who pays it. If Dale Jr. pays it directly, the $100,000 payment will not be deductible because he will be satisfying another taxpayer's obligation. A better way to structure the payment would be for Dale Jr. to make a $100,000 gift to Tony who would then pay the fine. In this situation, Tony would be able to deduct the $100,000 on Schedule A of Form 1040 as a trade or business expense (as an employee, he will be subject to the 2 percent-of-AGI floor on miscellaneous deductions—see Chapter 10).

Source: *Adapted from Jenna Fryer (Associated Press), "Junior's Points Docked,"* Newport News Daily Press, *May 16, 2007, p. C1.*

Disallowance of Personal Expenditures

Section 262 states that "except as otherwise expressly provided in this chapter, no deduction shall be allowed for personal, living, or family expenses." To justify a deduction, an individual must be able to identify a particular section of the Code that sanctions the deduction (e.g., charitable contributions, medical expenses). Sometimes the character of a particular expenditure is not easily determined.

EXAMPLE 33

During the current year, Howard pays $2,500 in legal fees and court costs to obtain a divorce from his wife, Vera. Included in the divorce action is a property settlement concerning the disposition of income-producing property owned by Howard. In a similar situation, the Tax Court held that the taxpayer could not deduct any such costs.[51] "Although fees primarily related to property division concerning his income-producing property, they weren't ordinary and necessary expenses paid for conservation or maintenance of property held for production of income. Legal fees incurred in defending against claims that arise from a taxpayer's marital relationship aren't deductible expenses regardless of possible consequences on taxpayer's income-producing property." ■

The IRS has clarified the issue of the deduction of legal fees incurred in connection with a divorce.[52] To be deductible, an expense must relate solely to tax advice in a divorce proceeding. For example, legal fees attributable to the determination of dependency exemptions of children are deductible if the fees are distinguishable from the general legal fees incurred in obtaining a divorce. Other examples are the costs of creating a trust to make periodic alimony payments and the determination of the tax consequences of a property settlement. Therefore, it is advisable to request an itemization of attorney's fees to substantiate a deduction for the tax-related amounts.

Disallowance of Deductions for Capital Expenditures

The Code specifically disallows a deduction for "any amount paid out for new buildings or for permanent improvements or betterments made to increase the value of any property or estate."[53] The Regulations further define capital expenditures to

[51] *Harry H. Goldberg*, 29 TCM 74, T.C.Memo. 1970–27.
[52] Rev.Rul. 72–545, 1972–2 C.B. 179.
[53] § 263(a)(1).

include those expenditures that add to the value or prolong the life of property or adapt the property to a new or different use.[54] Incidental repairs and maintenance of the property are not capital expenditures and can be deducted as ordinary and necessary business expenses. Repairing a roof is a deductible expense, but replacing a roof is a capital expenditure subject to depreciation deductions over its useful life. The tune-up of a delivery truck is an expense; a complete overhaul probably is a capital expenditure.

Capitalization versus Expense. When an expenditure is capitalized rather than expensed, the deduction is at best deferred and at worst lost forever. Although an immediate tax benefit for a large cash expenditure is lost, the cost may be deductible in increments over a longer period of time.

If the expenditure is for a tangible asset that has an ascertainable life, it is capitalized and may be deducted as depreciation (or cost recovery) over the life of the asset (for depreciation) or over a statutory period (for cost recovery under either ACRS or MACRS).[55] Land is not subject to depreciation (or cost recovery) since it does not have an ascertainable life.

EXAMPLE 34

Stan purchased a prime piece of land located in an apartment-zoned area. Stan paid $500,000 for the property, which had an old but usable apartment building on it. He immediately had the building demolished at a cost of $100,000. The $500,000 purchase price and the $100,000 demolition costs must be capitalized, and the basis of the land is $600,000. Since land is a nondepreciable asset, no deduction is allowed.

Assume instead that Stan intended to rent the apartment building. However, several months after he acquires the building, the city passes an ordinance that outlaws street parking in the area. Since the building is no longer functional without a built-in garage for tenants and visitors, Stan demolishes the building. Under these circumstances, Stan should be able to allocate a substantial portion of the original purchase price of the property to the building (a depreciable asset). When the building is demolished, the adjusted basis can be deducted as an ordinary (§ 1231) loss. (See Chapter 17 for a discussion of the treatment of § 1231 assets.) ■

If the expenditure is for an intangible asset (e.g., copyright, patent, covenant not to compete, goodwill), the capitalized expenditure can be amortized, regardless of whether or not the intangible asset has an ascertainable life. Intangible assets, referred to as § 197 intangibles, are amortized over a 15-year statutory period using the straight-line method. See Chapter 8 for additional discussion of the amortization of intangibles.

ETHICAL and EQUITABLE *Considerations*

EXPENSING TOO EARLY: A PROBLEM FOR SELF-CONSTRUCTED BUILDINGS

Albert owns a business that manufactures coolers for convenience stores. In preparation for a public offering of the company's stock, Albert hires you to audit the financial statements and to prepare the income tax return for the current year.

You discover that three of the four factory buildings were self-constructed by Albert's company. You also determine that the costs of these self-constructed buildings were expensed by his bookkeeping service. The purchased building was properly capitalized and depreciated.

You revise the financial statements to reflect the capitalization of the costs of these buildings and the related depreciation. From a tax perspective, the statute of limitations has expired on the income tax returns involved. However, Albert insists that this capitalization and related depreciation should also apply for income tax purposes so that the financial statements and the income tax returns will be consistent. How do you respond to Albert's demand as you prepare the current-year income tax return?

---

[54]Reg. § 1.263(a)–1(b).

[55]See Chapter 8 for the discussion of depreciation and cost recovery.

Transactions between Related Parties

The Code places restrictions on the recognition of gains and losses from **related-party transactions**. Without these restrictions, relationships created by birth, marriage, and business would provide endless possibilities for engaging in financial transactions that produce tax savings with no real economic substance or change. For example, to create an artificial loss, a wife could sell investment property to her husband at a loss and deduct the loss on their joint return. Her husband could then hold the asset indefinitely, and the family would sustain no real economic loss. A complex set of laws has been designed to eliminate such possibilities.

Losses. The Code provides for the disallowance of any "losses from sales or exchanges of property ... directly or indirectly" between related parties.[56] When the property is subsequently sold to a nonrelated party, any gain recognized is reduced by the loss previously disallowed. Any disallowed loss not used by the related-party buyer to offset the recognized gain on a subsequent sale or exchange to an unrelated party is permanently lost.

| EXAMPLE 35 | Freida sells common stock with a basis of $1,000 to her son, Bill, for $800. Bill sells the stock several years later for $1,100. Freida's $200 loss is disallowed upon the sale to Bill, and only $100 of gain ($1,100 selling price − $800 basis − $200 disallowed loss) is taxable to him upon the subsequent sale. ∎ |

| EXAMPLE 36 | George sells common stock with a basis of $1,050 to his son, Ray, for $800. Ray sells the stock eight months later to an unrelated party for $900. Ray's gain of $100 ($900 selling price − $800 basis) is not recognized because of George's previously disallowed loss of $250. Note that the offset may result in only partial tax benefit upon the subsequent sale (as in this case). If the property had not been transferred to Ray, George could have recognized a $150 loss upon the subsequent sale to the unrelated party ($1,050 basis − $900 selling price). ∎ |

| EXAMPLE 37 | Pete sells common stock with a basis of $1,000 to an unrelated third party for $800. Pete's son repurchased the same stock in the market on the same day for $800. The $200 loss is not allowed because the transaction is an indirect sale between related parties.[57] ∎ |

Unpaid Expenses and Interest. The law prevents related taxpayers from engaging in tax avoidance schemes where one related taxpayer uses the accrual method of accounting and the other uses the cash basis. An accrual basis, closely held corporation, for example, could borrow funds from a cash basis individual shareholder. At the end of the year, the corporation would accrue and deduct the interest, but the cash basis lender would not recognize interest income since no interest had been paid. Section 267 specifically defers the deduction of the accruing taxpayer until the recipient taxpayer must include it in income; that is, when it is actually paid to the cash basis taxpayer. This *matching* provision applies to interest as well as other expenses, such as salaries and bonuses.

This deduction deferral provision does not apply if both of the related taxpayers use the accrual method or both use the cash method. Likewise, it does not apply if the related party reporting income uses the accrual method and the related party taking the deduction uses the cash method.

Relationships and Constructive Ownership. Section 267 operates to disallow losses and defer deductions only between related parties. Losses or deductions

---

[56] § 267(a)(1).
[57] *McWilliams v. Comm.*, 47–1 USTC ¶9289, 35 AFTR 1184, 67 S.Ct. 1477 (USSC, 1947).

generated by similar transactions with an unrelated party are allowed. *Related parties* include the following:

- Brothers and sisters (whether whole, half, or adopted), spouse, ancestors (parents, grandparents), and lineal descendants (children, grandchildren) of the taxpayer.
- A corporation owned more than 50 percent (directly or indirectly) by the taxpayer.
- Two corporations that are members of a controlled group.
- A series of other complex relationships between trusts, corporations, and individual taxpayers.

Constructive ownership provisions are applied to determine whether the taxpayers are related. Under these provisions, stock owned by certain relatives or related entities is *deemed* to be owned by the taxpayer for purposes of applying the loss and expense deduction disallowance provisions. A taxpayer is deemed to own not only his or her stock but also the stock owned by lineal descendants, ancestors, brothers and sisters or half-brothers and half-sisters, and spouse. The taxpayer is also deemed to own his or her proportionate share of stock owned by any partnership, corporation, estate, or trust of which the taxpayer is a member. An individual is deemed to own any stock owned, directly or indirectly, by his or her partner. However, constructive ownership by an individual of the partnership's and the other partner's shares does not extend to the individual's spouse or other relatives (no double attribution).

EXAMPLE 38

The stock of Sparrow Corporation is owned 20% by Ted, 30% by Ted's father, 30% by Ted's mother, and 20% by Ted's sister. On July 1 of the current year, Ted loaned $10,000 to Sparrow Corporation at 8% annual interest, principal and interest payable on demand. For tax purposes, Sparrow uses the accrual basis, and Ted uses the cash basis. Both are on a calendar year. Since Ted is deemed to own the 80% owned by his parents and sister, he constructively owns 100% of Sparrow Corporation. If the corporation accrues the interest within the taxable year, no deduction can be taken until payment is made to Ted. ■

Substantiation Requirements

The tax law is built on a voluntary system. Taxpayers file their tax returns, report income and take deductions to which they are entitled, and pay their taxes through withholding or estimated tax payments during the year. The taxpayer has the burden of proof for substantiating expenses deducted on the returns and must retain adequate records. Upon audit, the IRS will disallow any undocumented or unsubstantiated deductions. These requirements have resulted in numerous conflicts between taxpayers and the IRS.

In the case of charitable contributions, Congress has enacted stringent substantiation requirements. All cash contributions, for example, must be supported by receipts (e.g., cancelled checks).[58] Single donations of $250 or more of both cash and property require an acknowledgment from the charity. Substantial donations of property (i.e., $500 or more) necessitate the filing of Form 8283 and may have to be supported by appraisals—see Chapter 10 for further details.

Specific and *more stringent* rules for deducting travel, entertainment, and gift expenses are discussed in Chapter 9. Certain mixed-use (both personal and business use) and listed property are also subject to the adequate records requirement (discussed in Chapter 8).

---

[58]Rev.Proc. 92–71, 1992–2 C.B. 437, addresses circumstances where checks are not returned by a financial institution or where electronic transfers are made.

Expenses and Interest Relating to Tax-Exempt Income

Certain income, such as interest on municipal bonds, is tax-exempt.[59] The law also allows the taxpayer to deduct expenses incurred for the production of income.[60] Deduction disallowance provisions, however, make it impossible to make money at the expense of the government by excluding interest income and deducting interest expense.[61]

EXAMPLE 39

Sandy, a taxpayer in the 35% bracket, purchased $100,000 of 6% municipal bonds. At the same time, she used the bonds as collateral on a bank loan of $100,000 at 8% interest. A positive cash flow would result from the tax benefit as follows:

Cash paid out on loan	($8,000)
Cash received from bonds	6,000
Tax savings from deducting interest expense (35% of $8,000 interest expense)	2,800
Net positive cash flow	$ 800

To eliminate the possibility illustrated in Example 39, the Code specifically disallows as a deduction the expenses of producing tax-exempt income. Interest on any indebtedness incurred or continued to purchase or carry tax-exempt obligations also is disallowed.

Judicial Interpretations. It is often difficult to show a direct relationship between borrowings and investment in tax-exempt securities. Suppose, for example, that a taxpayer borrows money, adds it to existing funds, buys inventory and stocks, then later sells the inventory and buys municipal bonds. A series of transactions such as these can completely obscure any connection between the loan and the tax-exempt investment. One solution would be to disallow interest on any debt to the extent that the taxpayer holds any tax-exempt securities. This approach would preclude individuals from deducting part of their home mortgage interest if they owned any municipal bonds. The law was not intended to go to such extremes. As a result, judicial interpretations have tried to be reasonable in disallowing interest deductions.

In one case, a company used municipal bonds as collateral on short-term loans to meet seasonal liquidity needs.[62] The court disallowed the interest deduction on the grounds that the company could predict its seasonal liquidity needs. The company could anticipate the need to borrow the money to continue to carry the tax-exempt securities. The same company *was* allowed an interest deduction on a building mortgage, even though tax-exempt securities it owned could have been sold to pay off the mortgage. The court reasoned that short-term liquidity needs would have been impaired if the tax-exempt securities were sold. Furthermore, the court ruled that carrying the tax-exempt securities bore no relationship to the long-term financing of a construction project.

EXAMPLE 40

In January of the current year, Alan borrowed $100,000 at 8% interest. He used the loan proceeds to purchase 5,000 shares of stock in White Corporation. In July, he sold the stock for $120,000 and reinvested the proceeds in City of Denver bonds, the income from which is tax-

---

[59]§ 103.
[60]§ 212.
[61]§ 265.

[62]*The Wisconsin Cheeseman, Inc. v. U.S.*, 68–1 USTC ¶9145, 21 AFTR2d 383, 388 F.2d 420 (CA–7, 1968).

exempt. Assuming the $100,000 loan remained outstanding throughout the entire year, Alan cannot deduct the interest attributable to the period in which he held the bonds. ∎

Time Value of Tax Deductions

Cash basis taxpayers often have the ability to make early payments for their expenses at the end of the tax year. This may permit the payments to be deducted currently instead of in the following tax year. In view of the time value of money, a tax deduction this year may be worth more than the same deduction next year. Before employing this strategy, the taxpayer must consider next year's expected income and tax rates and whether a cash-flow problem may develop from early payments. Thus, the time value of money as well as tax rate changes must be considered when an expense can be paid and deducted in either of two years.

> **LO.4**
>
> Identify tax planning opportunities for maximizing deductions and minimizing the disallowance of deductions.

TAX PLANNING
Considerations

E X A M P L E   41

Jena pledged $5,000 to her church's special building fund. She can make the contribution in December 2008 or January 2009. Jena is in the 35% tax bracket in 2008, and in the 28% bracket in 2009. She itemizes in both years. Assume Jena's discount rate is 8%. If she takes the deduction in 2008, she saves $454 ($1,750 − $1,296), due to the decrease in the tax rates and the time value of money.

	2008	2009
Contribution	$5,000	$5,000
Tax bracket	.35	.28
Tax savings	$1,750	$1,400
Discounted @ 8%	1.0	.926
Savings in present value	$1,750	$1,296

∎

Unreasonable Compensation

In substantiating the reasonableness of a shareholder-employee's compensation, an internal comparison test is sometimes useful. If it can be shown that nonshareholder-employees and shareholder-employees in comparable positions receive comparable compensation, it is indicative that compensation is not unreasonable.

Another possibility is to demonstrate that the shareholder-employee has been underpaid in prior years. For example, the shareholder-employee may have agreed to take a less-than-adequate salary during the unprofitable formative years of the business. The expectation is that the "postponed" compensation would be paid in later, more profitable years. The agreement should be documented, if possible, in the corporate minutes.

Keep in mind that in testing for reasonableness, the *total* pay package must be considered. Look at all fringe benefits or perquisites, such as contributions by the corporation to a qualified pension plan. Even though those amounts are not immediately available to the covered shareholder-employee, they must be taken into account.

Excessive Executive Compensation

With the $1 million limit on the deduction of compensation of covered employees, many corporations and their executives must engage in additional tax planning. Previously, concerns over the deductibility of compensation related primarily to closely held corporations. The $1 million limit applies specifically to publicly held corporations. In many instances, it is now necessary for these corporations to restructure the compensation packages of their top executives in order

CONCEPT SUMMARY   6–3

Classification of Expenses

Expense Item	Deductible		Not Deductible	Applicable Code §
	For AGI	From AGI		
Investment expenses				
Rent and royalty	X			§ 62(a)(4)
All other investments		X[4]		§ 212
Employee expenses				
Commuting expenses			X	§ 262
Travel and transportation[1]		X[4,5]		§ 162(a)(2)
Reimbursed expenses[1]	X			§ 62(a)(2)(A)
Moving expenses	X			§ 62(a)(15)
Entertainment[1]		X[4,5]		§ 162(a)
Teacher supplies	X[11]	X[4]		§ 62(a)(2)(D)
All other employee expenses[1]		X[4,5]		§ 162(a)
Certain expenses of performing artists	X			§ 62(a)(2)(B)
Trade or business expenses	X			§§ 162 and 62(a)(1)
Casualty losses				
Business	X			§ 165(c)(1)
Personal		X[6]		§ 165(c)(3)
Tax determination				
Collection or refund expenses	X[8]	X		§§ 212 and 62(a)(1) or (4)
Bad debts	X			§§ 166 and 62(a)(1) or (3)
Medical expenses		X[7]		§ 213
Charitable contributions		X		§ 170
Taxes				
Trade or business	X			§§ 162, 164, and 62(a)(1)
Personal taxes				
Real property		X		§ 164(a)(1)
Personal property		X		§ 164(a)(2)
State and local income *or* sales		X		§§ 164(a)(3) and (b)(5)
Investigation of a business[2]	X			§§ 162 and 62(a)(1)
Interest				
Business	X			§§ 162, 163, and 62(a)(1)
Personal	X[9]	X[3]	X[10]	§§ 163(a), (d), and (h)
Qualified tuition and related expenses	X			§§ 62(a)(18) and 222
All other personal expenses			X	§ 262

[1] Deduction for AGI if reimbursed, an adequate accounting is made, and employee is required to repay excess reimbursements.

[2] Provided certain criteria are met.

[3] Subject to the excess investment interest and the qualified residence interest provisions.

[4] Subject (in the aggregate) to a 2%-of-AGI floor imposed by § 67.

[5] Only 50% of meals and entertainment are deductible.

[6] Subject to a $100 floor per event and a 10%-of-AGI floor per tax year.

[7] Subject to a 7.5%-of-AGI floor.

[8] Only the portion relating to business, rental, or royalty income or losses.

[9] Only the portion relating to student loans.

[10] Other personal interest is disallowed.

[11] Subject to a statutory limit of $250.

to deduct payments in excess of $1 million. Opportunities include compensation payable on a commission basis, certain other performance-based compensation, payments to qualified retirement plans, and payments that are excludible fringe benefits.

Shifting Deductions

Taxpayers should manage their obligations to avoid the loss of a deduction. Deductions can be shifted among family members, depending upon which member makes the payment. For example, a father buys a condo for his daughter and puts the title in both names. The taxpayer who makes the payment gets the deduction for the property taxes. If the condo is owned by the daughter only and her father makes the payment, neither is entitled to a deduction. In this case, the father should make a cash gift to the daughter who then makes the payment to the taxing authority.

Hobby Losses

To demonstrate that an activity has been entered into for the purpose of making a profit, a taxpayer should treat the activity as a business. The business should engage in advertising, use business letterhead stationery, and maintain a business phone.

If a taxpayer's activity earns a profit in three out of five consecutive years, the presumption is that the activity is engaged in for profit. It may be possible for a cash basis taxpayer to meet these requirements by timing the payment of expenses or the receipt of revenues. The payment of certain expenses incurred before the end of the year might be made in the following year. The billing of year-end sales might be delayed so that collections are received in the following year.

Keep in mind that the three-out-of-five-years rule under § 183 is not absolute. All it does is shift the presumption. If a profit is not made in three out of five years, the losses may still be allowed if the taxpayer can show that they are due to the nature of the business. For example, success in artistic or literary endeavors can take a long time. Also, depending on the state of the economy, even full-time farmers and ranchers are often unable to show a profit. How can one expect a part-time farmer or rancher to do so?

Merely satisfying the three-out-of-five-years rule does not guarantee that a taxpayer is automatically home free. If the three years of profits are insignificant relative to the losses of other years, or if the profits are not from the ordinary operation of the business, the taxpayer is vulnerable. The IRS may still be able to establish that the taxpayer is not engaged in an activity for profit.

EXAMPLE 42

Ashley had the following gains and losses in an artistic endeavor:

2004	($50,000)
2005	(65,000)
2006	400
2007	200
2008	125

Under these circumstances, the IRS might try to overcome the presumption. ∎

If Ashley in Example 42 could show conformity with the factors enumerated in the Regulations or could show evidence of business hardships (e.g., injury, death, or illness), the government cannot override the presumption.[63]

---

[63]*Faulconer, Sr. v. Comm.*, 84–2 USTC ¶9955, 55 AFTR2d 85–302, 748 F.2d 890 (CA–4, 1984), *rev'g* 45 TCM 1084, T.C.Memo. 1983–165.

Capital Expenditures

On the sale of a sole proprietorship where the sales price exceeds the fair market value of the tangible assets and stated intangible assets, a planning opportunity may exist for both the seller and the buyer. The seller's preference is for the excess amount to be allocated to goodwill. Goodwill is a capital asset, whereas a covenant not to compete produces ordinary income treatment (see Chapter 16).

Because both a covenant and goodwill are amortized over a statutory 15-year period, the tax results of a covenant and goodwill are the same for the buyer. However, the buyer should recognize that an allocation to goodwill rather than a covenant may provide a tax benefit to the seller. Therefore, the seller and buyer, in negotiating the sales price, should factor in the tax benefit to the seller of having the excess amount labeled goodwill rather than a covenant not to compete. Of course, if the noncompetition aspects of a covenant are important to the buyer, part of the excess amount can be assigned to a covenant.

KEY TERMS

Accounting method, 6–8

Deductions for adjusted gross income, 6–2

Deductions from adjusted gross income, 6–2

Hobby losses, 6–16

Ordinary and necessary, 6–5

Reasonableness, 6–6

Related-party transactions, 6–26

Vacation homes, 6–19

PROBLEM MATERIALS

DISCUSSION QUESTIONS

1. "All income must be reported and all deductions are allowed unless specifically disallowed in the Code." Discuss.

2. Discuss the difference in the tax treatment of deductions *for* and deductions *from* AGI.

3. Does an expenditure that is classified as a deduction *from* AGI produce the same tax benefit as an expenditure that is classified as a deduction *for* AGI? Explain.

4. Classify each of the following expenditures as a deduction *for* AGI, a deduction *from* AGI, or not deductible:
   a. Allison pays qualified moving expenses of $7,000.
   b. Emalie gives $1,000 to the Girl Scouts.
   c. Amos pays alimony of $2,500 per month to his former spouse.
   d. Arnold pays $1,900 for real estate taxes levied by the county on his personal residence.
   e. April pays $1,200 for insurance on her personal residence.

5. Classify each of the following expenditures as a deduction *for* AGI, a deduction *from* AGI, or not deductible:
   a. Amos contributes $500 to his H.R. 10 plan (i.e., a retirement plan for a self-employed individual).
   b. Keith pays $500 of child support to his former wife, Renee, for the support of their son, Chris.
   c. Judy pays $500 for professional dues that are reimbursed by her employer.
   d. Ted pays $500 as the monthly mortgage payment on his personal residence. Of this amount, $100 represents a payment on principal, and $400 represents an interest payment.

    e.   Lynn pays $500 to a moving company for moving her household goods to Detroit where she is starting a new job. She is not reimbursed by her employer.

    f.   Ralph pays property taxes of $1,500 on his personal residence.

6. Larry and Susan each invest $10,000 in separate investment activities. They each incur deductible expenses of $800 associated with their respective investments. Explain why Larry's expenses are properly classified as deductions *from* AGI (itemized deductions) and Susan's expenses are appropriately classified as deductions *for* AGI.

7. Define and contrast the "ordinary" and "necessary" tests for business expenses.

8. Mabel, a machinist employed by Silver Airlines, owns 100 shares of Silver Airlines stock. Silver has 900,000 shares of stock outstanding. Mabel spends $1,500 to travel to Denver for Silver's annual meeting. Her expenses would have been $750 more, but she was permitted to fly free on Silver. She attended both days of the shareholders' meeting and actively participated. What are the tax consequences of the trip for Mabel?

9. Sid and Vienne are the owners of a corporation. To reduce the corporation's taxable income, they pay a $3,000 salary each month to their eight-year-old daughter, Paula. Why is this salary disallowed as a deduction?

10. Which of the following losses are deductible?
    a.   Loss on the sale of an office building used in a trade or business.
    b.   Loss on the sale of an SUV held for personal use.
    c.   Loss from the destruction by a hurricane of a warehouse used in a trade or business.
    d.   Loss on the destruction by fire of the taxpayer's residence.
    e.   Loss on the sale of Lavender Corporation bonds held as an investment.

11. Mary Kate owns a building that she leases to an individual who operates a grocery store. Rent income is $10,000 and rental expenses are $6,000. On what Form 1040 schedule or schedules are the income and expenses reported?

12. Distinguish between the timing for the recording of a deduction under the cash method versus the accrual method. Discuss any exceptions.

13. Aubry, a cash basis and calendar year taxpayer, decides to reduce his taxable income for 2008 by buying $30,000 worth of supplies on December 24, 2008. The supplies will be used up in 2009.
    a.   Can Aubry deduct the expenditure for 2008?
    b.   Would your answer in part (a) change if Aubry bought the supplies because the seller was going out of business and offered a significant discount on the price?

14. What is the significance of the all events and economic performance tests?

15. Pelican, an accrual method taxpayer, provides a one-year warranty on the vacuum cleaners it manufactures. Claims under the warranty typically amount to 2% of sales. Can Pelican use the reserve method to account for the warranty expense?

16. Explain why certain deductions are disallowed as violations of public policy.

Issue ID

17. Ted is an agent for an airline manufacturer and is negotiating a sale with a representative of the U.S. government and with a representative of a developing country. Ted's company has sufficient capacity to handle only one of the orders. Both orders will have the same contract price. Ted believes that if his employer will authorize a $500,000 payment to the representative of the foreign country, he can guarantee the sale. He is not sure that he can obtain the same result with the U.S. government. Identify the relevant tax issues for Ted.

18. Stuart, an insurance salesman, is arrested for allegedly robbing a convenience store. He hires an attorney who is successful in getting the charges dropped. Is the attorney's fee deductible?

19. Linda operates a drug-running operation. Which of the following expenses she incurs can reduce taxable income?
    a.   Bribes paid to border guards.
    b.   Salaries to employees.
    c.   Price paid for drugs purchased for resale.

    d. Kickbacks to police.

    e. Rent on an office.

    f. Depreciation on office furniture and equipment.

    g. Tenant's casualty insurance.

20. Gordon anticipates that being positively perceived by the individual who is elected mayor will be beneficial for his business. Therefore, he contributes to the campaigns of both the Democratic and the Republican candidates. The Republican candidate is elected mayor. Can Gordon deduct any of the political contributions he made?

21. Carmine, Inc., a tobacco manufacturer, incurs certain expenditures associated with political contributions and lobbying activities. Which of these expenditures can be deducted?

Payments to Washington, D.C. law firm to lobby members of Congress	$800,000
Payments to Washington, D.C. law firm to lobby the head of the FDA	25,000
Payments to Richmond law firm to lobby members of the state legislature	50,000
Payments to Lexington law firm to lobby members of the Lexington City Council	5,000
Political contribution to Committee to Reelect the Mayor of Lexington	6,000

22. Agnes, an executive of a large corporation, receives a salary of $1.5 million. Taylor, who is an executive of another large corporation, receives a salary of $1.3 million. Agnes's corporation is permitted to deduct all of her salary while Taylor's corporation is permitted to deduct only part of his. Assuming both salaries are reasonable, explain the result.

23. Ralph is the owner of a restaurant in Worcester and is considering expanding to Cambridge. He can purchase either an existing restaurant or an economy hotel (that does not offer food services). What are the tax consequences to Ralph as to the costs incurred in investigating each of these businesses?

24. An individual operates an activity at a loss. What is the tax effect of the loss if the activity is classified as:

    a. A hobby?

    b. A business?

25. Classify each of the following as primarily personal, primarily rental, or personal/rental:

    a. Judy rented her vacation cottage for 15 days, lived in it for 18 days, and left it vacant for the remainder of the year.

    b. Marshall rented his vacation cottage for 160 days, lived in it for two weeks, and left it vacant for the remainder of the year.

    c. Libby rented her vacation cottage for two weeks, lived in it for nine weeks, and left it vacant for the remainder of the year.

26. Under what circumstances may a taxpayer deduct a rental loss associated with a vacation home?

Issue ID

27. Karen and Andy own a beach house. They have an agreement with a rental agent to rent it up to 200 days per year. For the past three years, the agent has been successful in renting it for 200 days. Karen and Andy use the beach house for one week during the summer and one week during Thanksgiving. Their daughter, Sarah, a college student, has asked if she and some friends can use the beach house for the week of spring break. Advise Karen and Andy how they should respond and identify any relevant tax issues.

28. Hank was transferred from Phoenix to North Dakota on March 1 of the current year. He immediately put his home in Phoenix up for rent. The home was rented May 1 to November 30 and was vacant during the month of December. It was rented again on January 1 for six months. What expenses, if any, can Hank deduct on his return? Which deductions are *for* AGI and which ones are *from* AGI?

Decision Making

29. Erika would like to help Hillary and James, her daughter and son-in-law, with their short-term financial problems. To help them avoid foreclosure, she proposes to make the monthly mortgage payments on their home for the past six months. Erika's preference is to make the payments directly to the mortgage company. However, she is willing to give the money to Hillary and James who would then make the payments. Advise Erika on which option, if either, offers preferential tax treatment to her.

30. Isiah repaired the roof on his apartment building at a cost of $9,200. During the same year, Rachel replaced the roof on her rental house for $9,200. Both taxpayers are on the cash basis. Are their expenditures treated the same on their tax returns? Why or why not?

31. a. Which of the following are related parties under § 267?

    - Father
    - Brother
    - Niece
    - Uncle
    - Cousin
    - Grandson
    - Corporation and a shareholder who owns 52% of the stock

    b. What negative tax consequences can result from being classified as a related party?

32. Jake owns City of Charleston bonds with an adjusted basis of $100,000. During the year, he receives interest payments of $4,000. Jake partially financed the purchase of the bonds by borrowing $70,000 at 6% interest. Jake's interest payments on the loan this year are $4,100, and his principal payments are $1,000.
    a. Should Jake report any interest income this year?
    b. Can Jake deduct any interest expense this year?

PROBLEMS

33. Sandra is an attorney. She incurs the following expenses when she and her employee, Fred, attend the American Bar Association convention in San Francisco:

Conference registration:
Sandra	$800
Fred	800

Airline tickets from Pittsburgh to San Francisco:
Sandra	900
Fred	400

Lodging in San Francisco:
Sandra	650
Fred	350

Rental car in San Francisco:
Sandra	325
Fred	–0–

Calculate the effect of these expenses on Sandra's AGI.

34. Mac received the following income and incurred and paid the following expenses during 2008:

Salary income	$82,000
Dividend income	5,000
Interest income	3,000
Contributions to First Church	3,100
Real estate taxes on personal residence	1,900
Alimony paid to former spouse	12,000
Contribution to traditional IRA	5,000
Mortgage interest on personal residence	6,000
State income taxes	3,700
Loss on the sale of stock	900
State sales tax	1,150

Mac is not yet eligible to participate in his employer's retirement plan.

a. Calculate Mac's AGI.

b. Should Mac itemize deductions *from* AGI or take the standard deduction?

35. Julie is a student and earns $8,200 working part-time at the college ice cream shop in 2008. She has no other income. Her medical expenses for the year totaled $2,700. During the year, she suffered a casualty loss of $2,900 when her apartment burned. Julie contributed $1,450 to her church. On the advice of her parents, Julie is trying to decide whether to contribute $500 to the traditional IRA her parents have set up for her. What effect would the IRA contribution have on Julie's itemized deductions?

36. Drew and his wife Cassie own all of the stock of Thrush. Cassie is the president and Drew is the vice president. Cassie and Drew are paid salaries of $400,000 and $300,000, respectively, each year. They consider the salaries to be reasonable based on a comparison with salaries paid for comparable positions in comparable companies. They project Thrush's taxable income for next year, before their salaries, to be $800,000. They decide to place their four teenage children on the payroll and to pay them total salaries of $100,000. The children will each work about five hours per week for Thrush.

a. What are Drew and Cassie trying to achieve by hiring the children?

b. Calculate the tax consequences of hiring the children on Thrush, and on Drew and Cassie's family.

37. Mary incurs the following losses during the current tax year:

Sale of bedroom suite	$ 1,200
Sale of personal use car	9,000
Sale of personal residence	14,000
Sale of Green Corporation stock	3,000
Sale of City of York bonds	4,500
Theft of uninsured business use notebook computer	2,000

Calculate Mary's deductible losses.

38. The income statement for Monroe's business shows the following revenues and expenses for 2008, the initial year of operations:

Sales revenue (including $19,000 credit sales uncollected at year-end)	$95,000
Wage expenses (including $3,000 unpaid at year-end)	29,000
Office expenses (supplies, copying, etc.)	2,000
Bad debt expense (of the $4,000 reserve established, $500 was written off as being currently uncollectible)	4,000
Utilities and telephone expense*	5,400
Insurance expense*	4,000
Rent expense (January 1, 2008–January 31, 2009)	9,750

* Amount incurred is the same as the amount paid.

a. Calculate Monroe's AGI using the accrual method.

b. Calculate Monroe's AGI using the cash method.

39. Doris, a calendar year taxpayer, is the owner of a sole proprietorship that uses the cash method. On September 1, 2008, she leases an office building to use in her business for $90,000 for an 18-month period. In order to obtain this favorable lease rate, she pays the $90,000 at the inception of the lease. How much rent expense may Doris deduct on her 2008 tax return?

40. Duck, an accrual basis corporation, sponsored a rock concert on December 29, 2008. Gross receipts were $300,000. The following expenses were incurred and paid as indicated:

Expense		Payment Date
Rental of coliseum	$ 25,000	December 21, 2008
Cost of goods sold:		
Food	30,000	December 30, 2008
Souvenirs	60,000	December 30, 2008
Performers	100,000	January 5, 2009
Cleaning of coliseum	10,000	February 1, 2009

Since the coliseum was not scheduled to be used again until January 15, the company with which Duck had contracted did not actually perform the cleanup until January 8–10, 2009.

Calculate Duck's net income from the concert for tax purposes for 2008.

41. Mercedes, an attorney with a leading Miami law firm, is convicted of failing to file Federal income tax returns for 2003–2005. Her justification for failing to do so was the pressures of her profession (80- to 90-hour workweeks). She is assessed taxes, interest, and penalties of $112,000 by the IRS. In addition, she incurs related legal fees of $75,000. Determine the amount that Mercedes can deduct, and classify it as a deduction *for* or a deduction *from* AGI.

42. Darby runs an illegal numbers racket. His gross revenues are $550,000, and he incurs the following expenses:

Illegal kickbacks	$20,000
Salaries	80,000
Rent	24,000
Utilities and telephone	9,000
Bribes to police	25,000
Interest	6,000
Medical insurance premiums for employees	4,000
Depreciation on equipment	12,000

  a. What is Darby's net income from this business that is includible in taxable income?

  b. If the business was an illegal drug operation and cost of goods sold was $100,000, how would your answer in part (a) differ?

43. Edward, an attorney, is hired by a major accounting firm to represent it and clients in dealing with members of the U.S. Congress. The accounting firm is supporting liability reform that would limit the "joint and several" liability of professionals such as attorneys and CPAs. Edward is paid a retainer of $40,000, $50,000 for chargeable time, and reimbursement of $12,500 for meal and entertainment expenses incurred in meeting with members of Congress and their staffs. Which of these payments to Edward can the firm deduct?

44. Amber, a publicly held corporation, currently pays its president an annual salary of $900,000. In addition, it contributes $20,000 annually to a defined contribution pension plan for him. As a means of increasing company profitability, the board of directors decides to increase the president's compensation. Two proposals are being considered. Under the first proposal, the salary and pension contribution for the president would be increased by 30%. Under the second proposal, Amber would implement a performance-based compensation program that is projected to provide about the same amount of additional compensation and pension contribution for the president.

Decision Making

Communications

  a. Evaluate the alternatives from the perspective of Amber, Inc.

  b. Prepare a letter to Amber's board of directors that contains your recommendations. Address the letter to the board chairperson, Agnes Riddle, whose address is 100 James Tower, Cleveland, OH 44106.

45. Vermillion, Inc., a publicly held corporation, pays the following salaries to its executives:

	Salary	Bonus	Retirement Plan Contribution
CEO	$2,000,000	$100,000	$80,000
Executive vice president	1,800,000	90,000	72,000
Treasurer	1,600,000	–0–	64,000
Marketing vice president	1,500,000	75,000	60,000
Operations vice president	1,400,000	70,000	56,000
Distribution vice president	1,200,000	60,000	48,000
Research vice president	1,100,000	–0–	44,000
Controller	800,000	–0–	32,000

Vermillion normally does not pay bonuses, but after reviewing the results of operations for the year, the board of directors decided to pay a 5% bonus to selected executives. What is the amount of these payments that Vermillion may deduct?

46. Joanne, the owner of a very successful restaurant chain, is exploring the possibility of expanding the chain into a city in the neighboring state. She incurs $32,000 of expenses associated with this investigation. Based on the regulatory environment for restaurants in the city, she decides not to expand. During the year, she also investigates opening a hotel that will be part of a national hotel chain. Her expenses for this are $54,000. The hotel begins operations on November 1. Determine the amount that Joanne can deduct in the current year for investigating these two businesses.

47. Tim traveled to a neighboring state to investigate the purchase of two restaurants. His expenses included travel, legal, accounting, and miscellaneous expenses. The total was $30,000. He incurred the expenses in June and July 2008.
    a. What can Tim deduct in 2008 if he was in the restaurant business and did not acquire the two restaurants?
    b. What can Tim deduct in 2008 if he was in the restaurant business and acquired the two restaurants and began operating them on October 1, 2008?
    c. What can Tim deduct in 2008 if he did not acquire the two restaurants and was not in the restaurant business?
    d. What can he deduct in 2008 if he acquired the two restaurants, but was not in the restaurant business when he acquired them? Operations began on September 1, 2008.

48. Hank is single and a doctor in a west Texas community. He owns and operates a cattle ranch, which has been profitable in only one of the last 10 years. He believes that he satisfies one-third of the nine factors that the IRS uses to determine whether an activity is profit seeking or a hobby. Without regard to this activity, Hank's AGI is $225,000. His only other itemized deductions are $4,000 of property taxes on his residence and $3,500 of charitable contributions. The ranch produces the following revenues and expenses in 2008:

Revenues	$31,000
Mortgage interest on barn	9,000
Property taxes on barn and land	7,500
Cattle feed	14,000
Hay	4,725
Maintenance on barn	3,000
Depreciation on barn	2,950

    a. Is Hank's cattle ranch profit seeking or a hobby? Explain the probabilities.
    b. Determine Hank's taxable income if the ranch is a hobby.
    c. Determine his taxable income if the ranch is a business.

49. Sandra, an orthodontist, is single and has net earnings of $90,000 from her practice. In addition, she collects antique books that she buys and sells at antique shows. She participates in six to eight weekend shows per year. Her income and expenses for the current year are as follows:

Revenue from sale of antique books	$22,000
Expenses	
Cost of goods sold	12,000
Show registration costs	3,000
Advertising	1,000
Dealer's license—annual fee	500
Insurance	900
Depreciation of display cases	1,200

Sandra has no other items that would affect her AGI. Itemized deductions consisting of taxes, interest, and charitable contributions are $19,000. Calculate Sandra's taxable income if the antique book activity is classified as:

a. A hobby.
b. A business.

50. Adelene, who lives in a winter resort area, rented her personal residence for 14 days while she was visiting Brussels. Rent income was $5,000. Related expenses for the year were as follows:

Real property taxes	$ 3,800
Mortgage interest	7,500
Utilities	3,700
Insurance	2,500
Repairs	2,100
Depreciation	15,000

Determine the effect on Adelene's AGI.

51. During the year (not a leap year), Anna rented her vacation home for 45 days, used it personally for 20 days, and left it vacant for 300 days. She had the following income and expenses:

Rent income	$ 7,000
Expenses	
Real estate taxes	2,500
Interest on mortgage	9,000
Utilities	2,400
Repairs	1,000
Roof replacement (a capital expenditure)	12,000
Depreciation	7,000

a. Compute Anna's net rent income or loss and the amounts she can itemize on her tax return, using the court's approach to allocating property taxes and interest.
b. How would your answer in part (a) differ using the IRS's method of allocating property taxes and interest?

52. How would your answer in Problem 51 differ if Anna had rented the house for 87 days and had used it personally for 13 days?

53. Chee, single, age 40, had the following income and expenses during the year (not a leap year):

Income	
Salary	$43,000
Rental of vacation home (rented 60 days, used personally 60 days, vacant 245 days)	4,000
Municipal bond interest	2,000
Dividend from General Electric	400
Expenses	
Interest	
On home mortgage	8,400
On vacation home	4,758
On loan used to buy municipal bonds	3,100

Taxes

Property tax on home	$2,200
Property tax on vacation home	1,098
State income tax	3,300
State sales tax	900
Charitable contributions	1,100
Tax return preparation fee	300
Utilities and maintenance on vacation home	2,600
Depreciation on rental 50% of vacation home	3,500

Calculate Chee's taxable income for the year before personal exemptions.

Decision Making

54. Velma and Clyde operate a retail sports memorabilia shop. For the current year, sales revenue is $50,000 and expenses are as follows:

Cost of goods sold	$19,000
Advertising	1,000
Utilities	2,000
Rent	4,000
Insurance	1,500
Wages to Boyd	7,000

Velma and Clyde pay $7,000 in wages to Boyd, a part-time employee. Since this amount is $1,000 below the minimum wage, Boyd threatens to file a complaint with the appropriate Federal agency. Although Velma and Clyde pay no attention to Boyd's threat, Chelsie (Velma's mother) gives Boyd a check for $1,000 for the disputed wages. Both Velma and Clyde ridicule Chelsie for wasting money when they learn what she has done. The retail shop is the only source of income for Velma and Clyde.
a. Calculate Velma and Clyde's AGI.
b. Can Chelsie deduct the $1,000 payment on her tax return?
c. How could the tax position of the parties be improved?

55. Calvin is purchasing a business from Loriann. The amount being paid exceeds the fair market value of the identifiable assets of the business by $625,000. Advise Calvin on the tax consequences of the $625,000 being allocated to goodwill versus it being allocated to an 8-year covenant not to compete.

Decision Making

56. Jay's sole proprietorship has the following assets:

	Basis	Fair Market Value
Cash	$ 10,000	$ 10,000
Accounts receivable	18,000	18,000
Inventory	25,000	30,000
Patent	22,000	40,000
Land	50,000	75,000
	$125,000	$173,000

The building in which Jay's business is located is leased. The lease expires at the end of the year.

Jay is age 70 and would like to retire. He expects to be in the 35% tax bracket. Jay is negotiating the sale of the business with Lois, a key employee. They have agreed on the fair market value of the assets, as indicated above, and agree the total purchase price should be about $200,000.
a. Advise Jay regarding how the sale should be structured.
b. Advise Lois regarding how the purchase should be structured.
c. What might they do to achieve an acceptable compromise?

Decision Making

Communications

57. Eleanor Saxon sold stock (basis of $65,000) to her brother, Ridge, for $60,000, the fair market value.
a. What are the tax consequences to Eleanor?

    b.   What are the tax consequences to Ridge if he later sells the stock for $75,000? For $52,000? For $64,000?

    c.   Write a letter to Eleanor in which you inform her of the tax consequences if she sells the stock to Ridge for $60,000 and explain how a sales transaction could be structured that would produce better tax consequences for her. Eleanor's address is 32 Country Lane, Lawrence, KS 66045.

58. The Robin Corporation is owned as follows:

Isabelle	26%
Peter, Isabelle's husband	19%
Sonya, Isabelle's mother	15%
Reggie, Isabelle's father	25%
Quinn, an unrelated party	15%

Robin is on the accrual basis, and Isabelle and Peter are on the cash basis. Isabelle and Peter each loaned the Robin Corporation $40,000 out of their separate funds. On December 31, 2008, Robin accrued interest at 7% on both loans. The interest was paid on February 4, 2009. What is the tax treatment of this interest expense/income to Isabelle, Peter, and Robin?

59. What is Karla's constructive ownership of Wren Corporation, given the following information?

Shares owned by Karla	900
Shares owned by Sam, Karla's uncle	600
Shares owned by Barbara, Karla's partner	30
Shares owned by Vera, Karla's granddaughter	670
Shares owned by unrelated parties	800

60. Chris has a brokerage account and buys on the margin, which resulted in an interest expense of $15,000 during the year. Income generated through the brokerage account was as follows:

Municipal interest	$ 40,000
Taxable dividends and interest	160,000

How much investment interest can Chris deduct?

61. Lee incurred the following expenses in the current tax year. Indicate, in the spaces provided, whether each expenditure is deductible *for* AGI, *from* AGI, or not deductible.

		Deductible		
Expense Item		For AGI	From AGI	Not Deductible
a.	Lee's personal medical expenses	____	____	____
b.	Lee's dependent daughter's medical expenses	____	____	____
c.	Real estate taxes on Lee's rental property	____	____	____
d.	Real estate taxes on Lee's personal residence	____	____	____
e.	Real estate taxes on daughter's personal residence	____	____	____
f.	Lee's state income taxes	____	____	____
g.	Interest on Lee's rental property mortgage	____	____	____
h.	Interest on Lee's personal residence mortgage	____	____	____
i.	Interest on daughter's personal residence mortgage	____	____	____
j.	Interest on Lee's business loans	____	____	____
k.	Lee's charitable contributions	____	____	____
l.	Depreciation on Lee's rental property	____	____	____
m.	Depreciation on auto used in Lee's business	____	____	____
n.	Depreciation on Lee's personal use auto	____	____	____
o.	Depreciation on daughter's personal use auto	____	____	____

CUMULATIVE PROBLEMS

62. Helen Archer, age 38, is single and lives at 120 Sanborne Avenue, Springfield, IL 60740. Her Social Security number is 648–11–9981. Helen has been divorced from her former husband, Albert, for three years. She has a son, Jason, who is age 17, and a daughter, June, who is age 18. Jason's Social Security number is 648–98–3471 and June's is 658–40–1234. Helen does not wish to contribute $3 to the Presidential Election Campaign Fund.

Helen, an advertising executive, earned a salary of $66,000 in 2007. Her employer withheld $7,700 in Federal income tax, $3,100 in state income tax, and the appropriate amount of FICA tax: $4,092 for Social Security tax and $957 for Medicare tax.

Helen has legal custody of Jason and June. The divorce decree provides that Helen is to receive the dependency deductions for the children. Jason lives with his father during summer vacation. Albert indicates that his expenses for Jason are $11,000. Helen can document that she spent $5,500 for Jason's support during 2007. In prior years, Helen gave a signed Form 8332 to Albert regarding Jason. For 2007, she has decided not to do so. Helen provides all of June's support.

Helen's mother died on January 7, 2007. Helen inherited assets worth $400,000 from her mother. As the sole beneficiary of her mother's life insurance policy, Helen received insurance proceeds of $250,000. Her mother's cost basis for the life insurance policy was $70,000. Helen's favorite aunt gave her $12,000 for her birthday in October.

On November 8, 2007, Helen sells for $19,000 Amber stock that she had purchased for $23,000 from her first cousin, Walt, on December 5, 2002. Walt's cost basis for the stock was $26,000, and the stock was worth $23,000 on December 5, 2002. On December 1, 2007, Helen sold Falcon stock for $12,000. She had acquired the stock on July 2, 2005, for $7,000.

An examination of Helen's records reveals that she received the following:

- Interest income of $1,800 from First Savings Bank.
- Groceries valued at $500 from a local grocery store for being the 100,000th customer.
- Qualified dividend income of $600 from Amber.
- Interest income of $3,500 on City of Springfield school bonds.
- Alimony of $12,000 from Albert.
- Distribution of $4,200 from ST Partnership. Her distributive share of the partnership passive taxable income was $4,800.

From her checkbook records, she determines that she made the following payments during 2007:

- Charitable contributions of $2,100 to First Presbyterian Church and $1,000 to the American Red Cross (proper receipts obtained).
- Mortgage interest on her residence of $6,500.
- Property taxes of $3,100 on her residence and $900 on her car.
- Estimated Federal income taxes of $3,300 and estimated state income taxes of $1,000.
- Medical expenses of $5,000 for her and $800 for Jason. In December her medical insurance policy reimbursed $1,200 of her medical expenses.
- A $1,000 ticket for parking in a handicapped space.
- Attorney's fees of $250 associated with unsuccessfully contesting the parking ticket.
- Contribution of $200 to the campaign of a candidate for governor.
- Since she did not maintain records of the sales tax she paid, she calculates the amount from the sales tax table to be $994.

Calculate Helen's net tax payable or refund due for 2007. If you use tax forms, you will need Form 1040 and Schedules A, B, D, and E. Suggested software: TaxCut.

63. John and Mary Jane Sanders are married, filing jointly. Their address is 204 Shoe Lane, Blacksburg, VA 24061. They are expecting their first two children (twins) in early 2009. John's salary in 2008 was $94,000, from which $19,200 of Federal income tax and $4,700 of state income tax were withheld. Mary Jane made $45,000 and had $3,000 of Federal income tax and $2,025 of state income tax withheld. The appropriate amount of FICA

tax was withheld for John and for Mary Jane: for John, Social Security tax of $5,828 and Medicare tax of $1,363; for Mary Jane, Social Security tax of $2,790 and Medicare tax of $653. John's Social Security number is 648–11–8899, and Mary Jane's Social Security number is 648–22–7788.

John and Mary Jane are both covered by their employer's medical insurance policies with three-fourths of the premiums being paid by the employers. The total premiums were $4,500 for John and $3,300 for Mary Jane. Mary Jane received medical benefits of $6,800 under the plan. John was not ill during 2008.

John makes child support payments of $12,000 for his son, Rod, who lives with June, John's former spouse, except for two months in the summer when he visits John and Mary Jane. At the time of the divorce, John worked for a Fortune 500 company and received a salary of $250,000. As a result of corporate downsizing, he lost his job.

Mary Jane's father lived with them until his death in November. His only sources of income were salary of $1,900, unemployment compensation benefits of $3,500, and Social Security benefits of $3,200. Of this amount, he deposited $4,800 in a savings account. The remainder of his support of $8,000, which included funeral expenses of $5,100, was provided by John and Mary Jane.

Other income received by the Sanderses was as follows:

Interest on certificates of deposit	$4,700
Share of S corporation taxable income (distributions from the S corporation to Mary Jane were $600)	1,200
Award received by Mary Jane from employer for outstanding suggestion for cutting costs	2,000

John has always wanted to operate his own business. In October 2008, he incurred expenses of $12,000 in investigating the establishment of a retail computer franchise. With the birth of the twins expected next year, however, he decides to forgo self-employment for at least a couple of years.

John and Mary Jane made charitable contributions of $4,400 during the year and paid an additional $1,200 in state income taxes in 2008 upon filing their 2007 state income tax return. Their deductible home mortgage interest was $9,000, and their property taxes came to $3,900. They paid sales taxes of $1,700 for which they have receipts.

Part 1—Tax Computation
Calculate John and Mary Jane's tax (or refund) due for 2008.

Part 2—Tax Planning
Assume that the Sanderses come to you for advice in December 2008. John has learned that he will receive a $30,000 bonus. He wants to know if he should take it in December 2008 or in January 2009. Mary Jane will quit work on December 31 to stay home with the twins. Their itemized deductions will decrease by $2,025 because Mary Jane will not have state income taxes withheld. Mary Jane will not receive the employee award in 2009. She expects the medical benefits received to be $9,000. The Sanderses expect all of their other income items to remain the same in 2009. Write a letter to John and Mary Jane that contains your advice and prepare a memo for the tax files.

RESEARCH PROBLEMS

Note: Solutions to Research Problems can be prepared by using the **RIA Checkpoint®** **Student Edition** online research product, which is available to accompany this text. It is also possible to prepare solutions to the Research Problems by using tax research materials found in a standard tax library.

Research Problem 1. Amos is a computer consultant, and his office is located in Orange, California. He and his wife, Susan, used their Lear jet, which they had purchased for $2 million, to travel to their timber farm in Oregon (10 trips), to their Tahiti property (2 trips), to computer symposia (5 trips), and to Park City, Utah (8 trips). The timber farm is operated in a businesslike fashion. Amos and Susan have spent nearly $2 million remodeling the Tahiti house and related property. They travel to Tahiti twice a year and stay there for several weeks each time. They travel to Park City to go skiing. The annual costs of operating the Lear jet, including depreciation, are $700,000.

On their tax return, Amos and Susan deducted the $700,000 as a business expense under § 162. An IRS agent countered that this expense was not ordinary and necessary or that it was a personal expense. Therefore, she disallowed the deduction. Evaluate the positions taken by Amos and Susan and by the IRS agent with respect to the Lear jet deduction.

Communications

Research Problem 2. Gray Chemical Company manufactured pesticides that were toxic. Over the course of several years, the toxic waste contaminated the air and water around the company's plant. Several employees suffered toxic poisoning, and the Environmental Protection Agency cited the company for violations. In court, the judge found Gray guilty and imposed fines of $15 million. The company voluntarily set up a charitable fund for the purpose of bettering the environment and funded it with $8 million. The company incurred legal expenses in setting up the foundation and defending itself in court. The court reduced the fine from $15 million to $7 million.

Gray Chemical Company deducted the $8 million paid to the foundation and the legal expenses incurred. The IRS disallowed both deductions on the grounds that the payment was, in fact, a fine and in violation of public policy.

Gray's president, Ted Jones, has contacted you regarding the deductibility of the $7 million fine, the $8 million payment to the foundation, and the legal fees. Write a letter to Mr. Jones that contains your advice and prepare a memo for the tax files. Gray's address is 200 Lincoln Center, Omaha, NE 68182.

Partial list of research aids:
§§ 162(a) and (f).
Reg. § 1.162–21(b).

Research Problem 3. Rex and Agnes Harrell purchased a beach house at Duck, North Carolina, in early 2006. Although they intended to use the beach house occasionally for recreational purposes, they also planned to rent it through the realty agency that had handled the purchase in order to help pay the mortgage payments, property taxes, and maintenance costs. Rex is a surgeon, and Agnes is a counselor.

The beach house was in need of substantial repairs. Rather than hiring a contractor, Rex and Agnes decided they would make the repairs themselves. During both high school and college, Rex had worked summers in construction. In addition, he had taken an advanced course in woodworking and related subjects from a local community college several years ago.

During 2006, according to a log maintained by the Harrells, they occupied the beach house 38 days and rented it 49 days. The log also indicated that on 24 of the 38 days that they occupied the beach house, one or both of them were engaged in work on the beach house. Their two teenage children were with them on all of these days, but did not help with the work being done. On their 2006 income tax return, Rex and Agnes, who filed a joint return, treated the beach house as a rental property and deducted a pro rata share of the property taxes, mortgage interest, utilities, maintenance and repairs, and depreciation in determining their net loss from the beach home. An IRS agent has limited the deductions to the rent income. He contends that the 14-day personal use provision was exceeded and that many of the alleged repairs were capital expenditures. Advise the Harrells on how they should respond to the IRS.

Research Problem 4. As a result of a bitter divorce, Arlene found herself with no visible means of support. Drawing on her talents as an equestrian, she established a business (an LLC) that integrated equestrian activities with a home and barn design activity.

Arlene was an accomplished equestrian and competed frequently and successfully in horse shows. These shows enabled her to be recognized in the equestrian community as a skilled competitor and to make contact with potential clients. Since she felt direct contact and satisfied clients provided the necessary marketing for her business, she chose not to advertise in trade publications. All of her client relationships were developed in this manner.

Her barn designs factored in her knowledge of the idiosyncrasies of each of her client's horses. Because her clients are wealthy "horse people," the interior design of a client's home often required knowledge related to horses.

During a seven-year period, Arlene's equestrian activity produced annual losses, while the horse barn and home design activity produced profits. The loss on the equestrian activity would have been larger except for recognized gain on the occasional sale of one of her horses. On a combined basis, the two activities produced substantial profits in six of the seven years. For the loss year, the amount of the loss was small.

Arlene reported the revenue and expenses of the two activities on a single Schedule C. An IRS agent contends that the activities are separate. Although the horse barn and home design activity is a trade or business, the equestrian activity is a hobby. Thus, the losses from the equestrian activity cannot be used to offset the gains from the design activity. Which position is correct?

Research Problem 5. Professor Shelia Crane is a drama professor at Municipal University with an annual salary of $75,000. In addition, Professor Crane is a playwright. She normally writes two plays each year. Her revenues and expenses from the playwright activity are as follows:

	Revenues	Expenses
2003	$ –0–	$ 9,000
2004	–0–	7,000
2005	500	10,000
2006	4,000	8,500
2007	–0–	6,000

Professor Crane works diligently to get her plays produced. One of her plays has been read at Lincoln Center, and two have been performed by local theater groups. In 2003, she was awarded a sabbatical, and in 2006, she received a $2,000 summer research grant from the university.

The IRS audited Professor Crane's 2005 return and classified her playwright activity as a hobby. Professor Crane comes to you for advice.

Use the tax resources of the Internet to address the following questions. Do not restrict your search to the World Wide Web, but include a review of newsgroups and general reference materials, practitioner sites and resources, primary sources of the tax law, chat rooms and discussion groups, and other opportunities.

Internet *Activity*

Research Problem 6. Locate and read a recent judicial or administrative ruling regarding the deductibility of hobby losses. Look for rulings that deal with horse breeding, professional sports teams, or art collecting activities. Which criteria did the ruling emphasize in upholding or reversing the taxpayer's deduction for such losses?

Research Problem 7. The $1 million maximum compensation deduction does not seem to have deterred large corporations from remunerating their executives at very high levels. What techniques are being used to work around the millionaires' provision? Are executives taking pay cuts, or are their salaries being deferred or changed in nature due to § 162(m)?

CHAPTER 7

Deductions and Losses: Certain Business Expenses and Losses

LEARNING OBJECTIVES

After completing Chapter 7, you should be able to:

LO.1
Determine the amount, classification, and timing of the bad debt deduction.

LO.2
Understand the tax treatment of worthless securities including §1244 stock.

LO.3
Distinguish between deductible and nondeductible losses of individuals.

LO.4
Identify a casualty and determine the amount, classification, and timing of casualty and theft losses.

LO.5
Recognize and apply the alternative tax treatments for research and experimental expenditures.

LO.6
Calculate the domestic production activities deduction.

LO.7
Determine the amount of the net operating loss and recognize the impact of the carryback and carryover provisions.

LO.8
Identify tax planning opportunities in deducting certain business expenses, business losses, and personal losses.

OUTLINE

Bad Debts, 7–3
  Specific Charge-Off Method, 7–3
  Business versus Nonbusiness Bad Debts, 7–4
  Loans between Related Parties, 7–5
Worthless Securities, 7–6
  Small Business Stock, 7–6
Losses of Individuals, 7–8
  Events That Are Not Casualties, 7–8
  Theft Losses, 7–9
  When to Deduct Casualty Losses, 7–9
  Measuring the Amount of Loss, 7–10
  Statutory Framework for Deducting Losses
    of Individuals, 7–13
  Personal Casualty Gains and Losses, 7–13
Research and Experimental Expenditures, 7–15
  Expense Method, 7–15
  Deferral and Amortization Method, 7–16

Domestic Production Activities Deduction, 7–17
  Operational Rules, 7–17
  Eligible Taxpayers, 7–18
Net Operating Losses, 7–19
  Carryback and Carryover Periods, 7–20
  Computation of the Net Operating Loss, 7–21
  Recomputation of Tax Liability for Year to Which
    Net Operating Loss Is Carried, 7–23
  Calculation of the Remaining Net Operating Loss, 7–24
Tax Planning Considerations, 7–25
  Tax Consequences of the *Groetzinger* Case, 7–25
  Documentation of Related-Taxpayer Loans, Casualty
    Losses, and Theft Losses, 7–26
  Worthless Securities, 7–26
  Small Business Stock, 7–26
  Casualty Losses, 7–26
  Net Operating Losses, 7–27

Working with the tax formula for individuals requires the proper classification of items that are deductible *for* adjusted gross income (AGI) and items that are deductions *from* AGI (itemized deductions). Business expenses and losses, discussed in this chapter, are reductions of gross income to arrive at the taxpayer's AGI. Expenses and losses incurred in connection with a transaction entered into for profit and attributable to rents and royalties are deducted *for* AGI. All other expenses and losses incurred in connection with a transaction entered into for profit are deducted *from* AGI.

The situation of Robert P. Groetzinger provides an interesting insight into the importance of the proper classification for the individual taxpayer. Groetzinger terminated his employment with a private company and devoted virtually all of his working time to pari-mutuel wagering on dog races. He had no other profession or employment, and his only sources of income, apart from his gambling winnings, were interest, dividends, and sales from investments. During the tax year in question, he went to the track six days a week and devoted 60 to 80 hours per week to preparing and making wagers on his own account.

The tax question that this case presents is whether Groetzinger's gambling activities constitute a trade or business. If the gambling is a trade or business, his gambling losses are deductions *for* AGI. If the gambling activity is not a trade or business, the losses are itemized deductions, and Groetzinger's taxes increase by $2,142.[1]

Deductible losses on personal use property are deducted as an itemized deduction. Itemized deductions are deductions *from* AGI. While the general coverage of itemized deductions is in Chapter 10, casualty and theft losses on personal use property are discussed in this chapter.

In determining the amount and timing of the deduction for bad debts, proper classification is again important. A business bad debt is classified as a deduction *for* AGI, and a nonbusiness bad debt is classified as a short-term capital loss.

Other topics discussed in Chapter 7 are research and experimental expenditures, the domestic production activities deduction, and the net operating loss deduction.

---

[1] *Groetzinger v. Comm.*, 85–2 USTC ¶9622, 56 AFTR2d 85–5683, 771 F.2d 269 (CA–7, 1985).

Bad Debts

<table>
<tr><td>**LO.1**</td></tr>
<tr><td>Determine the amount, classification, and timing of the bad debt deduction.</td></tr>
</table>

If a taxpayer sells goods or provides services on credit and the account receivable subsequently becomes worthless, a **bad debt** deduction is permitted only if income arising from the creation of the account receivable was previously included in income.[2] No deduction is allowed, for example, for a bad debt arising from the sale of a product or service when the taxpayer is on the cash basis because no income is reported until the cash has been collected. Permitting a bad debt deduction for a cash basis taxpayer would amount to a double deduction because the expenses of the product or service rendered are deducted when payments are made to suppliers and to employees, or at the time of the sale.

EXAMPLE 1

Tracy, an individual engaged in the practice of accounting, performed accounting services for Pat for which she charged $8,000. Pat never paid the bill, and his whereabouts are unknown.

If Tracy is an accrual basis taxpayer, she includes the $8,000 in income when the services are performed. When she determines that Pat's account will not be collected, she deducts the $8,000 as a bad debt expense.

If Tracy is a cash basis taxpayer, she does not include the $8,000 in income until payment is received. When she determines that Pat's account will not be collected, she cannot deduct the $8,000 as a bad debt expense because it was never recognized as income. ■

A bad debt can also result from the nonrepayment of a loan made by the taxpayer or from purchased debt instruments.

ETHICAL and EQUITABLE *Considerations*   A BAD DEBT DEDUCTION?

Jake and Mary Snow are residents of the state of New York. They are cash basis taxpayers and file a joint return for the calendar year. Jake is a licensed master plumber. Two years ago, Jake entered into a contract with New York City to perform plumbing services. During the current year, Jake was declared to be in breach of the contract, and he ceased performing plumbing services. Jake received a Form W–2 that reported $50,000 for wages paid. He also maintains that the city has not paid him $35,000 for work he performed. Jake is considering claiming a $35,000 business bad debt on his tax return. Evaluate Jake's plan.

Specific Charge-Off Method

Taxpayers (other than certain financial institutions) may use only the **specific charge-off method** in accounting for bad debts. Certain financial institutions are allowed to use the **reserve method** for computing deductions for bad debts.

A taxpayer using the specific charge-off method may claim a deduction when a specific business debt becomes either partially or wholly worthless or when a specific nonbusiness debt becomes wholly worthless.[3] For the business debt, the taxpayer must satisfy the IRS that the debt is partially worthless and must demonstrate the amount of worthlessness.

If a business debt previously deducted as partially worthless becomes totally worthless in a future year, only the remainder not previously deducted can be deducted in the future year.

In the case of total worthlessness, a deduction is allowed for the entire amount in the year the debt becomes worthless. The amount of the deduction depends on the taxpayer's basis in the bad debt. If the debt arose from the sale of services or

---

[2]Reg. § 1.166–1(e).   [3]§ 166(a) and Reg. § 1.166.

CONCEPT SUMMARY 7-1

Specific Charge-Off Method

Expense deduction and account write-off	The expense arises and the write-off takes place when a specific business account becomes either partially or wholly worthless or when a specific nonbusiness account becomes wholly worthless.
Recovery of accounts previously written off	If the account recovered was written off during the current taxable year, the write-off entry is reversed. If the account recovered was written off during a previous taxable year, income is created subject to the tax benefit rule.

products and the face amount was previously included in income, that amount is deductible. If the taxpayer purchased the debt, the deduction is equal to the amount the taxpayer paid for the debt instrument.

One of the more difficult tasks is determining if and when a bad debt is worthless. The loss is deductible only in the year of partial or total worthlessness for business debts and only in the year of total worthlessness for nonbusiness debts. Legal proceedings need not be initiated against the debtor when the surrounding facts indicate that such action will not result in collection.

EXAMPLE 2

In 2006, Ross loaned $1,000 to Kay, who agreed to repay the loan in two years. In 2008, Kay disappeared after the note became delinquent. If a reasonable investigation by Ross indicates that he cannot find Kay or that a suit against Kay would not result in collection, Ross can deduct the $1,000 in 2008. ■

Bankruptcy is generally an indication of at least partial worthlessness of a debt. Bankruptcy may create worthlessness before the settlement date. If this is the case, the deduction may be taken in the year of worthlessness.

EXAMPLE 3

In Example 2, assume that Kay filed for personal bankruptcy in 2007 and that the debt is a business debt. At that time, Ross learned that unsecured creditors (including Ross) were ultimately expected to receive 20 cents on the dollar. In 2008, settlement is made and Ross receives only $150. He should deduct $800 ($1,000 loan − $200 expected settlement) in 2007 and $50 in 2008 ($200 balance − $150 proceeds). ■

If a receivable has been written off as uncollectible during the current tax year and is subsequently collected during the current tax year, the write-off entry is reversed. If a receivable has been written off as uncollectible, the collection of the receivable in a later tax year may result in income being recognized. Income will result if the deduction yielded a tax benefit in the year it was taken. See Examples 40 and 41 in Chapter 5.

Business versus Nonbusiness Bad Debts

A **nonbusiness bad debt** is a debt unrelated to the taxpayer's trade or business either when it was created or when it became worthless. The nature of a debt depends on whether the lender was engaged in the business of lending money or whether there is a proximate relationship between the creation of the debt and the lender's trade or business. The use to which the borrowed funds are put by the debtor is of no consequence. Loans to relatives or friends are the most common type of nonbusiness bad debt.

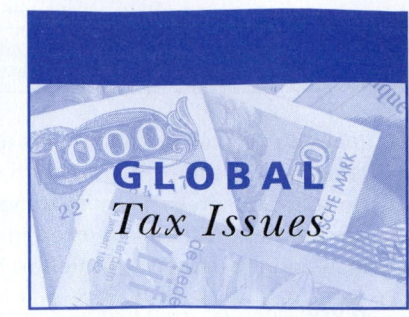

WRITING OFF BAD DEBTS IN AUSTRALIA

As of July, small businesses in Australia should review their accounts receivable for possible bad debt deductions. To obtain a bad debt deduction, it is not enough just to say that it is uncollectible. The business must have actively pursued the receivable and be able to show that it has done everything possible to collect the debt. For some businesses, it might be worth the cost to outsource all of their accounts receivable to a financial services company.

Source: *Adapted from David Potts, "An End-of-Year Guide to Putting the House in Order: Small Business Review," The Sun Herald (Sydney, Australia), May 20, 2007, Supplement, p. 6.*

GLOBAL *Tax Issues*

EXAMPLE 4

Jamil loaned his friend, Esther, $1,500. Esther used the money to start a business, which subsequently failed. Even though the proceeds of the loan were used in a business, the loan is a nonbusiness bad debt because the business was Esther's, not Jamil's. ■

The distinction between a business bad debt and a nonbusiness bad debt is important. A **business bad debt** is deductible as an ordinary loss in the year incurred, whereas a nonbusiness bad debt is always treated as a short-term capital loss. Thus, regardless of the age of a nonbusiness bad debt, the deduction may be of limited benefit due to the limitations on capital loss deductibility in any one year. The maximum amount of a net short-term capital loss that an individual can deduct against ordinary income in any one year is $3,000 (see Chapter 16 for a detailed discussion). Although no deduction is allowed when a nonbusiness bad debt is partially worthless, the taxpayer is entitled to deduct the net amount of the loss upon final settlement.

The following example is an illustration of business bad debts adapted from the Regulations.[4]

EXAMPLE 5

In 2007, Leif sold his business but retained a claim (note or account receivable) against Bob. The claim became worthless in 2008. Leif's loss is treated as a business bad debt because the debt was created in the conduct of his former trade or business. Leif is accorded business bad debt treatment even though he was holding the note as an investor and was no longer in a trade or business when the claim became worthless. ■

The nonbusiness bad debt provisions are *not* applicable to corporations. It is assumed that any loans made by a corporation are related to its trade or business. Therefore, any bad debts of a corporation are business bad debts.

Loans between Related Parties

Loans between related parties (especially family members) raise the issue of whether the transaction was a *bona fide* loan or a gift. The Regulations state that a bona fide debt arises from a debtor-creditor relationship based on a valid and enforceable obligation to pay a fixed or determinable sum of money. Thus, individual circumstances must be examined to determine whether advances between related parties are gifts or loans. Some considerations are these:

- Was a note properly executed?
- Was there a reasonable rate of interest?

---

[4]Reg. § 1.166–5(d).

TAX *in the News*   **HIGHER TAXES AND SMALL BUSINESS OWNERS?**

Small business owners and others are worried that with the Democrats' sweep of the midterm elections, the Democrat-controlled Congress may not extend President Bush's temporary tax cuts. Without an extension, taxes will increase for small business owners. In an effort to mitigate the negative cash flow associated with any increase in taxes, a small business should make all reasonable efforts to collect business debts as soon as possible. Then, if the attempt is unsuccessful, all or part of the uncollected debts should be deducted as bad debts.

Source: *Adapted from Cyndia Zwahlen, "Small-Business Report: Year-End Tax Planning Can Be Profitable," Los Angeles Times, November 15, 2006, Business, p. C7.*

- Was collateral provided?
- What collection efforts were made?
- What was the intent of the parties?

EXAMPLE 6

Lana loans $2,000 to her widowed mother for an operation. Lana's mother owns no property and is not employed, and her only income consists of Social Security benefits. No note is issued for the loan, no provision for interest is made, and no repayment date is mentioned. In the current year, Lana's mother dies, leaving no estate. Assuming the loan is not repaid, Lana cannot take a deduction for a nonbusiness bad debt because the facts indicate that no debtor-creditor relationship existed. ∎

LO.2

Understand the tax treatment of worthless securities including § 1244 stock.

Worthless Securities

A loss is allowed for securities that become *completely* worthless during the year (**worthless securities**).[5] Such securities are shares of stock, bonds, notes, or other evidence of indebtedness issued by a corporation or government. The losses generated are treated as capital losses deemed to have occurred on the *last day* of the taxable year. By treating the loss as having occurred on the last day of the taxable year, a loss that would otherwise have been classified as short term (if the date of worthlessness was used) may be classified as a long-term capital loss. Capital losses may be of limited benefit due to the $3,000 capital loss limitation.[6]

EXAMPLE 7

Ali, a calendar year taxpayer, owns stock in Owl Corporation (a publicly held company). The stock was acquired as an investment on May 31, 2007, at a cost of $5,000. On April 1, 2008, the stock became worthless. Since the stock is deemed to have become worthless as of December 31, 2008, Ali has a capital loss from an asset held for 19 months (a long-term capital loss). ∎

Small Business Stock

The general rule is that shareholders receive capital gain or loss treatment upon the sale or exchange of stock. However, it is possible to receive an ordinary loss deduction if the loss is sustained on **small business stock (§ 1244 stock)**. This loss could arise from a sale of the stock or from the stock becoming worthless. Only *individuals*[7] who acquired the stock *from* the corporation are eligible to receive ordinary

---

[5]§ 165(g).

[6]§ 1211(b).

[7]The term "individuals" for this purpose includes a partnership but not a trust or an estate.

CONCEPT SUMMARY 7–2

Bad Debt Deductions

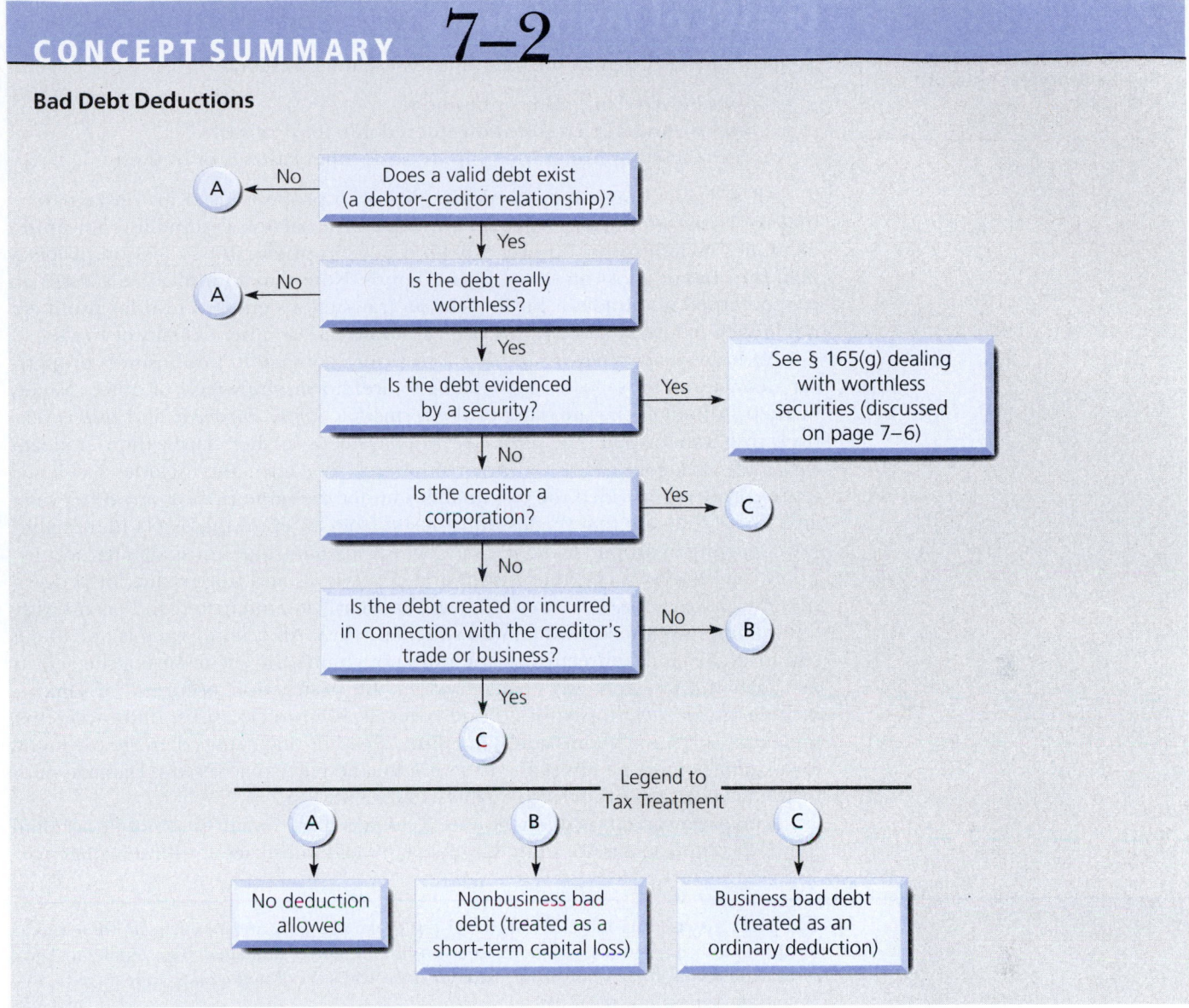

loss treatment under § 1244. The ordinary loss treatment is limited to $50,000 ($100,000 for married individuals filing jointly) per year. Losses on § 1244 stock in excess of the statutory limits receive capital loss treatment.

The corporation must meet certain requirements for the loss on § 1244 stock to be treated as an *ordinary*—rather than a capital—loss. The major requirement is that the total amount of money and other property received by the corporation for stock as a contribution to capital (or paid-in surplus) does not exceed $1 million. The $1 million test is made at the time the stock is issued. Section 1244 stock can be common or preferred stock. Section 1244 applies only to losses. If § 1244 stock is sold at a gain, the Section is not applicable, and the gain is capital gain.

EXAMPLE 8

On July 1, 2006, Iris, a single individual, purchased 100 shares of Eagle Corporation common stock for $100,000. The Eagle stock qualifies as § 1244 stock. On June 20, 2008, Iris sells all of the Eagle stock for $20,000. Because the Eagle stock is § 1244 stock, Iris has $50,000 of ordinary loss and $30,000 of long-term capital loss. ■

LO.3

Distinguish between deductible and nondeductible losses of individuals.

Losses of Individuals

An individual may deduct the following losses under § 165(c):

- Losses incurred in a trade or business.
- Losses incurred in a transaction entered into for profit.
- Losses caused by fire, storm, shipwreck, or other casualty or by theft.

An individual taxpayer may deduct losses to property used in the taxpayer's trade or business or losses to property used in a transaction entered into for profit. Examples include a loss on property used in a proprietorship, a loss on property held for rent, or a loss on stolen bearer bonds. Note that an individual's losses on property used in a trade or business or on transactions entered into for profit are not limited to losses caused by fire, storm, shipwreck, or other casualty or by theft.

An individual taxpayer suffering losses from damage to nonbusiness property can deduct only those losses attributable to fire, storm, shipwreck, or other casualty or theft. Although the meaning of the terms *fire, storm, shipwreck,* and *theft* is relatively free from dispute, the term *other casualty* needs further clarification. It means casualties analogous to fire, storm, or shipwreck. The term also includes accidental loss of property provided the loss qualifies under the same rules as any other casualty. These rules are that the loss must result from an event that is (1) identifiable; (2) damaging to property; and (3) sudden, unexpected, and unusual in nature.

A *sudden event* is one that is swift and precipitous and not gradual or progressive. An *unexpected event* is an event that is ordinarily unanticipated and occurs without the intent of the individual who suffers the loss. An *unusual event* is one that is extraordinary and nonrecurring and does not commonly occur during the activity in which the taxpayer was engaged when the destruction occurred.[8] Examples include hurricanes, tornadoes, floods, storms, shipwrecks, fires, auto accidents, mine cave-ins, sonic booms, and vandalism. Weather that causes damage (drought, for example) must be unusual and severe for the particular region. Damage must be to the taxpayer's property to qualify as a **casualty loss**.

A taxpayer can take a deduction for a casualty loss from an automobile accident only if the damage was not caused by the taxpayer's willful act or willful negligence.

EXAMPLE 9	Ted parks his car on a hill and fails to set the brake properly and to curb the wheels. As a result of Ted's negligence, the car rolls down the hill and is damaged. The repairs to Ted's car should qualify for casualty loss treatment since Ted's act of negligence appears to be simple rather than willful. ■

LO.4

Identify a casualty and determine the amount, classification, and timing of casualty and theft losses.

Events That Are Not Casualties

Not all acts of God are treated as casualty losses for income tax purposes. Because a casualty must be sudden, unexpected, and unusual, progressive deterioration (such as erosion due to wind or rain) is not a casualty because it does not meet the suddenness test.

Examples of nonsudden events that generally do not qualify as casualties include disease and insect damage. When the damage was caused by termites over a period of several years, some courts have disallowed a casualty loss deduction.[9] On the other hand, some courts have held that termite damage over periods of up to 15 months after infestation constituted a sudden event and was, therefore, deductible as a casualty loss.[10] Despite the existence of some judicial support for the

---

[8]Rev.Rul. 72–592, 1972–2 C.B. 101.

[9]*Fay v. Helvering,* 41–2 USTC ¶9494, 27 AFTR 432, 120 F.2d 253 (CA–2, 1941); *U.S. v. Rogers,* 41–1 USTC ¶9442, 27 AFTR 423, 120 F.2d 244 (CA–9, 1941).

[10]*Rosenberg v. Comm.,* 52–2 USTC ¶9377, 42 AFTR 303, 198 F.2d 46 (CA–8, 1952); *Shopmaker v. U.S.,* 54–1 USTC ¶9195, 45 AFTR 758, 119 F.Supp. 705 (D.Ct. Mo., 1953).

deductibility of termite damage as a casualty loss, the current position of the IRS is that termite damage is not deductible.[11]

Other examples of events that are not casualties are losses resulting from a decline in value rather than an actual loss of the property. No loss was allowed where the taxpayer's home declined in value as a result of a landslide that destroyed neighboring homes but did no actual damage to the taxpayer's home.[12] Similarly, a taxpayer was allowed a loss for the actual flood damage to his property but not for the decline in market value due to the property's being flood-prone.[13]

Theft Losses

Theft includes, but is not necessarily limited to, larceny, embezzlement, and robbery.[14] Theft does not include misplaced items.[15]

Theft losses are computed like other casualty losses (discussed in the following section), but the *timing* for recognition of the loss differs. A theft loss is deducted in the year of discovery, not the year of the theft (unless, of course, the discovery occurs in the same year as the theft). If, in the year of the discovery, a claim exists (e.g., against an insurance company) and there is a reasonable expectation of recovering the adjusted basis of the asset from the insurance company, no deduction is permitted.[16] If, in the year of settlement, the recovery is less than the asset's adjusted basis, a partial deduction may be available. If the recovery is greater than the asset's adjusted basis, gain may be recognized.

EXAMPLE 10

Keith's new sailboat, which he uses for personal purposes, was stolen from the storage marina in December 2007. He discovered the loss on June 3, 2008, and filed a claim with his insurance company that was settled on January 30, 2009. Assuming there is a reasonable expectation of full recovery, no deduction is allowed in 2008. A partial deduction may be available in 2009 if the actual insurance proceeds are less than the lower of the fair market value or the adjusted basis of the asset. (Loss measurement rules are discussed later in this chapter.) ■

When to Deduct Casualty Losses

General Rule. Generally, a casualty loss is deducted in the year the loss occurs. However, no casualty loss is permitted if a reimbursement claim with a *reasonable prospect of full recovery* exists.[17] If the taxpayer has a partial claim, only part of the loss can be claimed in the year of the casualty, and the remainder is deducted in the year the claim is settled.

EXAMPLE 11

Brian's new sailboat was completely destroyed by fire in 2008. Its cost and fair market value were $10,000. Brian's only claim against the insurance company was on a $7,000 policy and was not settled by year-end. The following year, 2009, Brian settled with the insurance company for $6,000. He is entitled to a $3,000 deduction in 2008 and a $1,000 deduction in 2009. If Brian held the sailboat for personal use, the $3,000 deduction in 2008 is reduced first by $100 and then by 10% of his 2008 AGI. The $1,000 deduction in 2009 is reduced by 10% of his 2009 AGI (see the following discussion on the $100 and 10% floors). ■

If a taxpayer receives reimbursement for a casualty loss sustained and deducted in a previous year, an amended return is not filed for that year. Instead, the taxpayer must include the reimbursement in gross income on the return for the year in which it is received to the extent that the previous deduction resulted in a tax benefit.

---

[11]Rev.Rul. 63–232, 1963–2 C.B. 97.
[12]*H. Pulvers v. Comm.*, 69–1 USTC ¶9222, 23 AFTR2d 69–678, 407 F.2d 838 (CA–9, 1969).
[13]*S. L. Solomon*, 39 TCM 1282, T.C.Memo. 1980–87.

[14]Reg. § 1.165–8(d).
[15]*Mary Francis Allen*, 16 T.C. 163 (1951).
[16]Reg. §§ 1.165–1(d)(2) and 1.165–8(a)(2).
[17]Reg. § 1.165–1(d)(2)(i).

Fran had a deductible casualty loss of $5,000 on her 2007 tax return. Fran's taxable income for 2007 was $60,000. In June 2008, Fran is reimbursed $3,000 for the prior year's casualty loss. Fran includes the entire $3,000 in gross income for 2008 because the deduction in 2007 produced a tax benefit. ■

Disaster Area Losses.

An exception to the general rule for the time of deduction is allowed for **disaster area losses**, which are casualties sustained in an area designated as a disaster area by the President of the United States.[18] In such cases, the taxpayer may *elect* to treat the loss as having occurred in the taxable year immediately *preceding* the taxable year in which the disaster actually occurred. The rationale for this exception is to provide immediate relief to disaster victims in the form of accelerated tax benefits.

If the due date, plus extensions, for the prior year's return has not passed, a taxpayer makes the election to claim the disaster area loss on the prior year's tax return. If the disaster occurs after the prior year's return has been filed, it is necessary to file either an amended return or a refund claim. In any case, the taxpayer must show clearly that such an election is being made.

Disaster loss treatment also applies in the case of a personal residence that has been rendered unsafe for use as a residence because of a disaster. This provision applies when, within 120 days after the President designates the area as a disaster area, the state or local government where the residence is located orders the taxpayer to demolish or relocate the residence.[19]

Janice owns a personal residence in Louisiana. On September 28, 2008, a hurricane severely damaged Janice's home. The amount of her uninsured loss was $50,000. Because of the extent of the damage in the area, the President of the United States designated the area a disaster area. Because Janice's loss is a disaster area loss, she may elect to file an amended return for 2007 and take the loss in that year. If Janice elects this course of action, the amount of the loss will be reduced first by $100 and then by 10% of her 2007 AGI. If Janice forgoes the election, she may take the loss on her 2008 income tax return. The amount of the loss will be reduced first by $100 and then by 10% of her 2008 AGI. ■

Measuring the Amount of Loss

Amount of Loss.

The rules for determining the amount of a loss depend in part on whether business use, income-producing use, or personal use property was involved. Another factor that must be considered is whether the property was partially or completely destroyed.

If business property or property held for the production of income (e.g., rental property) is *completely destroyed*, the loss is equal to the adjusted basis of the property at the time of destruction.

Vicki's automobile, which was used only for business purposes, was destroyed by fire. Vicki had unintentionally allowed her insurance coverage to expire. The fair market value of the automobile was $9,000 at the time of the fire, and its adjusted basis was $10,000. Vicki is allowed a loss deduction of $10,000 (the basis of the automobile). The $10,000 loss is a deduction *for* AGI. ■

A different measurement rule applies for *partial destruction* of business property and income-producing property and for *partial* or *complete destruction* of personal use property. In these situations, the loss is the *lesser* of the following:

- The adjusted basis of the property.
- The difference between the fair market value of the property before the event and the fair market value immediately after the event.

---

[18]§ 165(h).   [19]§ 165(k).

Kelly's uninsured automobile, which was used only for business purposes, was damaged in an accident. At the date of the accident, the fair market value of the automobile was $12,000, and its adjusted basis was $9,000. After the accident, the automobile was appraised at $4,000. Kelly's loss deduction is $8,000 (the lesser of the adjusted basis or the decrease in fair market value). The $8,000 loss is a deduction *for* AGI. ∎

The deduction for the loss of property that is part business and part personal must be computed separately for the business portion and the personal portion.

Any insurance recovery reduces the loss for business, production of income, and personal use losses. In fact, a taxpayer may realize a gain if the insurance proceeds exceed the amount of the loss. Chapter 17 discusses the treatment of net gains and losses on business property and income-producing property.

A taxpayer is not permitted to deduct a casualty loss for damage to insured personal use property unless a *timely insurance claim* is filed with respect to the damage to the property. This rule applies to the extent that any insurance policy provides for full or partial reimbursement for the loss.[20]

Generally, an appraisal before and after the casualty is needed to measure the amount of the loss. However, the *cost of repairs* to the damaged property is acceptable as a method of establishing the loss in value provided the following criteria are met:

- The repairs are necessary to restore the property to its condition immediately before the casualty.
- The amount spent for such repairs is not excessive.
- The repairs do not extend beyond the damage suffered.
- The value of the property after the repairs does not, as a result of the repairs, exceed the value of the property immediately before the casualty.[21]

Reduction for $100 and 10 Percent-of-AGI Floors.

The amount of the loss for personal use property must be further reduced by a $100 *per event* floor and a 10 percent-of-AGI *aggregate* floor.[22] The $100 floor applies separately to each casualty and applies to the entire loss from each casualty (e.g., if a storm damages both a taxpayer's residence and automobile, only $100 is subtracted from the total amount of the loss). The losses are then added together, and the total is reduced by 10 percent of the taxpayer's AGI. The resulting loss is the taxpayer's itemized deduction for casualty and theft losses.

Rocky, who had AGI of $30,000, was involved in a motorcycle accident. His motorcycle, which was used only for personal use and had a fair market value of $12,000 and an adjusted basis of $9,000, was completely destroyed. He received $5,000 from his insurance company. Rocky's casualty loss deduction is $900 [$9,000 basis − $5,000 insurance − $100 floor − $3,000 (.10 × $30,000 AGI)]. The $900 casualty loss is an itemized deduction (*from* AGI). ∎

When a nonbusiness casualty loss is spread between two taxable years because of the *reasonable prospect of recovery* doctrine, the loss in the second year is not reduced by the $100 floor. This result occurs because this floor is imposed per event and has already reduced the amount of the loss in the first year. However, the loss in the second year is still subject to the 10 percent floor based on the taxpayer's second-year AGI (refer to Example 11).

Taxpayers who suffer qualified disaster area losses can elect to deduct the losses in the year preceding the year of occurrence. The disaster loss is treated as having occurred in the preceding taxable year. Hence, the 10 percent-of-AGI floor is determined by using the AGI of the year for which the deduction is claimed.[23]

---

[20]§ 165(h)(4)(E).
[21]Reg. § 1.165–7(a)(2)(ii).

[22]§ 165(c)(3).
[23]§ 165(i).

Multiple Losses. The rules for computing loss deductions where multiple losses have occurred are explained in Examples 17 and 18.

EXAMPLE 17

During the year, Tim had the following casualty losses:

| | | Fair Market Value of Asset | | |
Asset	Adjusted Basis	Before the Casualty	After the Casualty	Insurance Recovery
A	$900	$600	$–0–	$400
B	300	800	250	100

Assets A and B were used in Tim's business at the time of the casualty. The following losses are allowed:

Asset A: $500. The complete destruction of a business asset results in a deduction of the adjusted basis of the property (reduced by any insurance recovery) regardless of the asset's fair market value.

Asset B: $200. The partial destruction of a business (or personal use) asset results in a deduction equal to the lesser of the adjusted basis ($300) or the decline in value ($550), reduced by any insurance recovery ($100).

Both the Asset A and Asset B losses are deductions *for* AGI. The $100 floor and the 10%-of-AGI floor do not apply because the assets are business assets. ■

EXAMPLE 18

During the year, Emily had AGI of $20,000 and the following casualty losses:

| | | Fair Market Value of Asset | | |
Asset	Adjusted Basis	Before the Casualty	After the Casualty	Insurance Recovery
A	$ 900	$ 600	$ –0–	$200
B	2,500	4,000	1,000	–0–
C	800	400	100	250

Assets A, B, and C were held for personal use, and the losses to these three assets are from three different casualties. The loss for each asset is computed as follows:

Asset A: $300. The lesser of the adjusted basis of $900 or the $600 decline in value, reduced by the insurance recovery of $200, minus the $100 floor.

Asset B: $2,400. The lesser of the adjusted basis of $2,500 or the $3,000 decline in value, minus the $100 floor.

Asset C: $0. The lesser of the adjusted basis of $800 or the $300 decline in value, reduced by the insurance recovery of $250, minus the $100 floor.

Emily's itemized casualty loss deduction for the year is $700:

Asset A loss	$ 300
Asset B loss	2,400
Asset C loss	–0–
Total loss	$ 2,700
Less: 10% of AGI (10% × $20,000)	(2,000)
Itemized casualty loss deduction	$ 700

■

Statutory Framework for Deducting Losses of Individuals

Casualty and theft losses incurred by an individual in connection with a trade or business are deductible *for* AGI.[24] These losses are not subject to the $100 per event and the 10 percent-of-AGI limitations.

Casualty and theft losses incurred by an individual in a transaction entered into for profit are not subject to the $100 per event and the 10 percent-of-AGI limitations. If these losses are attributable to rents or royalties, the deduction is *for* AGI.[25] However, if these losses are not connected with property held for the production of rents and royalties, they are deductions *from* AGI. More specifically, these losses are classified as other miscellaneous itemized deductions. An example of this type of loss would be the theft of a security. However, theft losses of investment property are not subject to the 2 percent-of-AGI floor on certain miscellaneous itemized deductions (explained in Chapter 9).

Casualty and theft losses attributable to personal use property are subject to the $100 per event and the 10 percent-of-AGI limitations. These losses are itemized deductions, but they are not subject to the 2 percent-of-AGI floor.[26]

Personal Casualty Gains and Losses

If a taxpayer has personal casualty and theft gains as well as losses, a special set of rules applies for determining the tax consequences. A **personal casualty gain** is the recognized gain from a casualty or theft of personal use property. A **personal casualty loss** for this purpose is a casualty or theft loss of personal use property after the application of the $100 floor. A taxpayer who has both gains and losses for the taxable year must first net (offset) the personal casualty gains and personal casualty losses. If the gains exceed the losses, the gains and losses are treated as gains and losses from the sale of capital assets. The capital gains and losses are short term or long term, depending on the period the taxpayer held each of the assets. In the netting process, personal casualty and theft gains and losses are not netted with the gains and losses on business and income-producing property.

EXAMPLE 19

During the year, Cliff had the following personal casualty gains and losses (after deducting the $100 floor):

Asset	Holding Period	Gain or (Loss)
A	Three months	($ 300)
B	Three years	(2,400)
C	Two years	3,200

Cliff computes the tax consequences as follows:

Personal casualty gain	$ 3,200
Personal casualty loss ($300 + $2,400)	(2,700)
Net personal casualty gain	$ 500

Cliff treats all of the gains and losses as capital gains and losses and has the following:

Short-term capital loss (Asset A)	$ 300
Long-term capital loss (Asset B)	2,400
Long-term capital gain (Asset C)	3,200

■

---

[24]§ 62(a)(1).   [26]§ 67(b)(3).
[25]§ 62(a)(4).

CONCEPT SUMMARY 7–3

Casualty Gains and Losses

	Business Use or Income-Producing Property	Personal Use Property
Event creating the loss	Any event.	Casualty or theft.
Amount	The lesser of the decline in fair market value or the adjusted basis, but always the adjusted basis if the property is totally destroyed.	The lesser of the decline in fair market value or the adjusted basis.
Insurance	Insurance proceeds received reduce the amount of the loss.	Insurance proceeds received (or for which there is an unfiled claim) reduce the amount of the loss.
$100 floor	Not applicable.	Applicable per event.
Gains and losses	Gains and losses are netted (see detailed discussion in Chapter 17).	Personal casualty and theft gains and losses are netted.
Gains exceeding losses		The gains and losses are treated as gains and losses from the sale of capital assets.
Losses exceeding gains		The gains—and the losses to the extent of gains—are treated as ordinary items in computing AGI. The losses in excess of gains, to the extent they exceed 10% of AGI, are itemized deductions.

If personal casualty losses exceed personal casualty gains, all gains and losses are treated as ordinary items. The gains—and the losses to the extent of gains—are treated as ordinary income and ordinary loss in computing AGI. Losses in excess of gains are deducted as itemized deductions to the extent the losses exceed 10 percent of AGI.[27]

EXAMPLE 20

During the year, Hazel had AGI of $20,000 and the following personal casualty gain and loss (after deducting the $100 floor):

Asset	Holding Period	Gain or (Loss)
A	Three years	($2,700)
B	Four months	200

Hazel computes the tax consequences as follows:

Personal casualty loss	($2,700)
Personal casualty gain	200
Net personal casualty loss	($2,500)

Hazel treats the gain and the loss as ordinary items. The $200 gain and $200 of the loss are included in computing AGI. Hazel's itemized deduction for casualty losses is computed as follows:

Casualty loss in excess of gain ($2,700 − $200)	$ 2,500
Less: 10% of AGI (10% × $20,000)	(2,000)
Itemized deduction	$ 500

---

[27]§ 165(h).

THE AMOUNT OF A CASUALTY LOSS

In the case of a casualty loss to personal use property, the loss is allowed only to the extent that it exceeds $100 and the net casualty loss for the tax year exceeds 10 percent of AGI. The amount of the loss allowed is the lesser of (1) the decline in the fair market value of the property as a result of the casualty or (2) the adjusted basis of the property.

Milt and his family sold their home, put their belongings in storage units, and rented a smaller residence. Abnormally wet weather during the year caused the storage units to leak badly. Among the items in storage was a large personal library that Milt's wife had inherited from her father many years ago. The collection included leather-bound, antebellum books and signed editions. Most of the books suffered water damage and were destroyed beyond repair. Following the damage, Milt had the books appraised. The appraiser calculated a replacement value of $35,000 for the books. Milt is considering claiming a loss deduction of $35,000 for the damage to the books. Evaluate Milt's plan.

Research and Experimental Expenditures

Section 174 covers the treatment of research and experimental expenditures. The Regulations define **research and experimental expenditures** as follows:

> all such costs incident to the development of an experimental or pilot model, a plant process, a product, a formula, an invention, or similar property, and the improvement of already existing property of the type mentioned. The term does not include expenditures such as those for the ordinary testing or inspection of materials or products for quality control or those for efficiency surveys, management studies, consumer surveys, advertising, or promotions.[28]

Expenses in connection with the acquisition or improvement of land or depreciable property are not research and experimental expenditures. Rather, they increase the basis of the land or depreciable property. However, depreciation on a building used for research may be a research and experimental expense. Only the depreciation that is a research and experimental expense (not the cost of the asset) is subject to the three alternatives discussed below.

The law permits the following *three alternatives* for the handling of research and experimental expenditures:

- Expensed in the year paid or incurred.
- Deferred and amortized.
- Capitalized.

If the costs are capitalized, a deduction is not available until the research project is abandoned or is deemed worthless. Since many products resulting from research projects do not have a definite and limited useful life, a taxpayer should ordinarily elect to write off the expenditures immediately or to defer and amortize them. It is generally preferable to elect an immediate write-off of the research expenditures because of the time value of the tax deduction.

The law also provides for a research activities credit. The credit amounts to 20 percent of certain research and experimental expenditures.[29] (The credit is discussed more fully in Chapter 13.)

Expense Method

A taxpayer can elect to expense all of the research and experimental expenditures incurred in the current year and all subsequent years. The consent of the IRS is not

---

[28]Reg. § 1.174–2(a)(1).

[29]§ 41. See the information in Chapter 13 on the termination date for the research activities credit.

required if the method is adopted for the first taxable year in which such expenditures were paid or incurred. Once the election is made, the taxpayer must continue to expense all qualifying expenditures unless a request for a change is made to, and approved by, the IRS. In certain instances, a taxpayer may incur research and experimental expenditures before actually engaging in any trade or business activity. In such instances, the Supreme Court has applied a liberal standard of deductibility and permitted a deduction in the year of incurrence.[30]

Deferral and Amortization Method

Alternatively, research and experimental expenditures may be deferred and amortized if the taxpayer makes an election.[31] Under the election, research and experimental expenditures are amortized ratably over a period of not less than 60 months. A deduction is allowed beginning with the month in which the taxpayer first realizes benefits from the experimental expenditure. The election is binding, and a change requires permission from the IRS.

EXAMPLE 21

Gold Corporation decides to develop a new line of adhesives. The project begins in 2008. Gold incurs the following expenses in 2008 in connection with the project:

Salaries	$25,000
Materials	8,000
Depreciation on machinery	6,500

Gold incurs the following expenses in 2009 in connection with the project:

Salaries	$18,000
Materials	2,000
Depreciation on machinery	5,700

The benefits from the project will be realized starting in March 2010. If Gold Corporation elects a 60-month deferral and amortization period, there is no deduction prior to March 2010, the month benefits from the project begin to be realized. The deduction for 2010 is $10,867, computed as follows:

Salaries ($25,000 + $18,000)	$43,000
Materials ($8,000 + $2,000)	10,000
Depreciation ($6,500 + $5,700)	12,200
Total	$65,200
$65,200 × (10 months/60 months) =	$10,867

■

The option to treat research and experimental expenditures as deferred expense is usually employed when a company does not have sufficient income to offset the research and experimental expenses. Rather than create net operating loss carryovers that might not be utilized because of the 20-year limitation on such carryovers, the deferral and amortization method may be used. The deferral of research and experimental expenditures should also be considered if the taxpayer expects higher tax rates in the future.

---

[30]*Snow v. Comm.*, 74–1 USTC ¶9432, 33 AFTR2d 74–1251, 94 S.Ct. 1876 (USSC, 1974).   [31]§ 174(b)(2).

Domestic Production Activities Deduction

The American Jobs Creation Act of 2004 was enacted to replace certain tax provisions that our world trading partners regarded as allowing unfair advantage to U.S. exports. Among other changes, the Act created a new deduction based on the income from manufacturing activities (designated as *production activities*).[32] The new **domestic production activities deduction (DPAD)** is contained in § 199.

Operational Rules

Calculation of the Domestic Production Activities Deduction. For tax years beginning in 2007 to 2009, the DPAD is based on the following formula:[33]

$$6\% \times \text{Lesser of} \begin{cases} \text{Qualified production activities income (QPAI)} \\ \text{Taxable (or modified adjusted gross) income} \\ \text{or alternative minimum taxable income} \end{cases}$$

For tax years beginning in 2005 or 2006, the 6 percent factor was 3 percent. For tax years beginning in 2010 and thereafter, the factor is increased to 9 percent.

Taxable income is determined without regard to the DPAD. In the case of an individual (a sole proprietorship or an owner of a flow-through entity), **modified adjusted gross income** is substituted for taxable income.[34]

The taxable income limitation is determined after the application of any net operating loss (NOL) deduction for the tax year (NOLs are explained in detail later in the chapter). Thus, a company with an NOL carryforward for a tax year is ineligible for the DPAD if the carryforward eliminates current taxable income. Further, a taxpayer that has an NOL carryback may lose part or all of the DPAD benefit for that year. As taxable income is reduced by the NOL carryback, there is a corresponding reduction in the DPAD. If qualified production activities income (QPAI) cannot be used in a particular year due to the taxable income limitation (see the above formula), it is lost forever. (The calculation of QPAI is explained in the next section.)

EXAMPLE 22

Opal, Inc., manufactures and sells costume jewelry. It also sells costume jewelry purchased from other manufacturers. During 2008, Opal had a *profit* of $200,000 (QPAI) from the sale of its own manufactured jewelry and a *loss* of $50,000 from the sale of the purchased jewelry. Based on this information, Opal's QPAI is $200,000, and its taxable income is $150,000 ($200,000 − $50,000). Opal's DPAD becomes $9,000 [6% of the lesser of $200,000 (QPAI) or $150,000 (taxable income)]. ■

EXAMPLE 23

Assume the same facts as in Example 22, except that Opal also has an NOL carryover from 2007 of $300,000. As taxable income for 2008 is zero ($200,000 − $50,000 − $300,000), there is no DPAD. ■

Another important limitation is that the amount of the DPAD cannot exceed 50 percent of certain **W–2 wages** paid by the taxpayer during the tax year.[35] The purpose of this limitation is to preserve U.S. manufacturing jobs and to discourage their outsourcing. An employer's W–2 wages include the sum of the aggregate amount of wages and elective deferrals required to be included on the W–2 wage statements for certain employees during the employer's taxable year. Elective deferrals include those amounts deferred under § 457 plans and Roth contributions (see Chapter 19). An employer previously included wages paid to all workers

---

[32]Section 101 of the *American Jobs Creation Act of 2004*, Public Law No. 108-357 (October 22, 2004).
[33]§ 199(a).
[34]§ 199(d)(2). Generally, modified AGI is AGI prior to the effect of § 199.
[35]§ 199(b).

during a tax year and not just the wages of the employees engaged in qualified production activities. However, as a result of a recent statutory change, an employer is permitted to include only those W–2 wages paid to employees engaged in qualified production activities.

EXAMPLE 24

In 2008, Red, Inc., a calendar year taxpayer, has QPAI of $2 million and taxable income of $2.1 million. Since Red outsources much of its work to independent contractors, its W–2 wage base, which for Red is related entirely to production activities, is $80,000. Although Red's DPAD normally would be $120,000 [6% of the lesser of $2 million (QPAI) or $2.1 million (taxable income)], it is limited to $40,000 [50% of $80,000 (W–2 wages)]. ■

EXAMPLE 25

Assume the same facts as in Example 24, except that Red also pays salaries of $50,000 related to its *nonproduction* activities. Because these wages are not paid to employees engaged in production activities, the wage limitation on the DPAD remains at $40,000 [50% of $80,000 ($80,000 + $0)]. ■

Calculation of Qualified Production Activities Income. **Qualified production activities income (QPAI)** is the excess of **domestic production gross receipts (DPGR)** over the sum of:

- The cost of goods sold allocated to such receipts.
- Other deductions, expenses, or losses directly allocated to such receipts.
- The ratable portion of deductions, expenses, and losses not directly allocable to such receipts or another class of income.[36]

QPAI is determined on an item-by-item basis—not on a division-by-division or transaction-by-transaction basis. Because all items must be netted in the calculation, the final QPAI amount can be either positive or negative. The effect of the netting rule is to preclude taxpayers from selecting only profitable product lines or profitable transactions when calculating QPAI.

EXAMPLE 26

A taxpayer manufactures pants and shirts with the following QPAI results: $5 for one pair of pants and a negative $2 for one shirt. Because the two items are netted, the QPAI amount that controls is $3 ($5 − $2). ■

Five specific categories of DPGR qualify for the DPAD:[37]

- The lease, license, sale, exchange, or other disposition of qualified production property (QPP) that was manufactured, produced, grown, or extracted (MPGE) in the United States.
- Qualified films largely created in the United States.
- The production of electricity, natural gas, or potable water.
- Construction (but not self-construction) performed in the United States.
- Engineering and architectural services for domestic construction.

The sale of food and beverages prepared by a taxpayer at a retail establishment and the transmission or distribution of electricity, natural gas, or potable water are specifically excluded from the definition of DPGR.

Eligible Taxpayers

The deduction is available to a variety of taxpayers including individuals, partnerships, S corporations, C corporations, cooperatives, estates, and trusts. For a pass-

---

[36]§ 199(c).   [37]§ 199(c)(4).

through entity (e.g., partnerships, S corporations), the deduction flows through to the individual owners. In the case of a sole proprietor, a deduction *for* AGI results and is claimed on Form 1040, line 35 on page 1. A Form 8903 must be attached to support the deduction.

For additional information on the DPAD, see Chapter 3 in *South-Western Federal Taxation: Corporations, Partnerships, Estates, and Trusts.*

Net Operating Losses

The requirement that every taxpayer file an annual income tax return (whether on a calendar year or a fiscal year) may result in certain inequities for taxpayers who experience cyclical patterns of income or expense. Inequities result from the application of a progressive rate structure to taxable income determined on an annual basis. A **net operating loss (NOL)** in a particular tax year would produce no tax benefit if the Code did not provide for the carryback and carryforward of such losses to profitable years.

LO.7

Determine the amount of the net operating loss and recognize the impact of the carryback and carryover provisions.

EXAMPLE 27

Juanita has a business and realizes the following taxable income or loss over a five-year period: Year 1, $50,000; Year 2, ($30,000); Year 3, $100,000; Year 4, ($200,000); and Year 5, $380,000. She is married and files a joint return. Hubert also has a business and has a taxable income pattern of $60,000 every year. He, too, is married and files a joint return. Note that both Juanita and Hubert have total taxable income of $300,000 over the five-year period. Assume there is no provision for carryback or carryover of NOLs. Juanita and Hubert would have the following five-year tax bills:

Year	Juanita's Tax	Hubert's Tax
1	$ 6,698	$ 8,198
2	–0–	8,198
3	17,688	8,198
4	–0–	8,198
5	104,575	8,198
	$128,961	$40,990

The computation of tax is made without regard to any NOL benefit.
Rates applicable to 2008 are used to compute the tax.

Even though Juanita and Hubert realized the same total taxable income ($300,000) over the five-year period, Juanita had to pay taxes of $128,961, while Hubert paid taxes of only $40,990. ■

To provide partial relief from this inequitable tax treatment, a deduction is allowed for NOLs.[38] This provision permits NOLs for any one year to be offset against taxable income of other years. The NOL provision is intended as a form of relief for business income and losses. Thus, only losses from the operation of a trade or business (or profession), casualty and theft losses, or losses from the confiscation of a business by a foreign government can create an NOL. In other words, a salaried individual with itemized deductions and personal exemptions in excess of gross income is not permitted to deduct the excess amounts as an NOL. On the other hand, a personal casualty loss is treated as a business loss and can therefore create (or increase) an NOL for an individual.

---

[38]§ 172.

| **TAX** *in the News* | **TAX SAVINGS FROM NOLs** |

Delta Airlines reported earnings of $155 million from operations for the first quarter of 2007. This was the last full quarter before the airline emerged from Chapter 11 bankruptcy protection. CEO Gerald Grinstein estimated that pretax earnings would be $800 million for all 2007. Delta, however, has $10 billion in NOL carryforwards. The company projects that these loss carryforwards are sufficient to offset its estimated taxable income through 2010.

Source: *Adapted from David Bond, "Delta Posts $155 Million Operating Profit in Runup to Exit from Chapter 11,"* Aviation *Daily, April 24, 2007, News, p. 1.*

Carryback and Carryover Periods

General Rules. An NOL must be applied initially to the two taxable years preceding the year of the loss (unless an election is made not to carry the loss back at all). It is carried first to the second prior year, and then to the immediately preceding tax year (or until used up). If the loss is not fully used in the carryback period, it must be carried forward to the first year after the loss year, and then forward to the second, third, etc., year after the loss year. The carryover period is 20 years. A loss sustained in 2008 is used in this order: 2006, 2007, 2009 through 2028.

A three-year carryback period is available for any portion of an individual's NOL resulting from a casualty or theft loss. The three-year carryback rule also applies to NOLs that are attributable to presidentially declared disasters that are incurred by a small business. A small business is one whose average annual gross receipts for a three-year period are $5 million or less.

A 5-year carryback period and a 20-year carryover period are allowed for a farming loss. A taxpayer may elect to waive the special five-year carryback period. If this election is made, the general two-year carryback period applies. A farming loss is the amount of the NOL for the taxable year if only income and deductions attributable to the farming business are taken into account. However, the amount of the farming loss cannot exceed the amount of the taxpayer's NOL for the taxable year. To determine the amount of the carryback and carryover, a farming loss for any taxable year is treated as a separate NOL for such year and applied after the remaining portion of the NOL for the year is taken into account.

EXAMPLE 28

For the year 2008, taxpayer and spouse have an NOL of $50,000. The $50,000 NOL includes a $40,000 loss that is attributable to a farming business. Only the $40,000 loss attributable to the farming business can be carried back five years. The loss not attributable to the farming business can be carried back only two years. ∎

If the loss is being carried to a preceding year, an amended return is filed on Form 1040X, or a quick refund claim is filed on Form 1045. In either case, a refund of taxes previously paid is requested. Form 1045 is an application for a tentative refund. The IRS normally will process Form 1045 and pay the refund within 90 days of the date it is filed. When the loss is carried forward, the current return shows an NOL deduction for the prior year's loss.

Sequence of Use of NOLs. When the taxpayer has NOLs in two or more years, the rule is always to use the earliest year's loss first until it is completely absorbed. The later years' losses can then be used until they also are absorbed or lost. Thus, one year's return could show NOL carryovers from two or more years. Each loss is computed and applied separately.

GLOBAL
Tax Issues

NEW NOL INCENTIVES

Philippine senators are working on a bill that would change the fiscal incentives available to investors. One of the changes would be a new NOL carryover system. Export firms' losses created in the first 5 years of operation could be carried over to the next 10 years as tax deductions. For domestic firms, the carryover period would be only 5 years.

Source: *Adapted from Reagan D. Tan and Michelle Syonne M. Reyes, "Senate Leaders to Defy Malacanang on Revision of Incentives Package," Business World, October 9, 2006, p. S1/1.*

Election to Forgo Carryback. A taxpayer can *irrevocably elect* not to carry back an NOL to any of the prior years. In that case, the loss is available as a carryover for 20 years. The election is made if it is to the taxpayer's tax advantage. For example, a taxpayer might be in a low marginal tax bracket in the carryback years but expect to be in a high marginal tax bracket in future years. Therefore, it would be to the taxpayer's advantage to use the NOL to offset income in years when the tax rate is high rather than use it when the tax rate is relatively low.

For 2008, taxpayer and spouse have an NOL of $10,000. The NOL may be carried back and applied against taxable income first in 2006 and then in 2007. Any remaining NOL is carried forward to years 2009 through 2028. If, however, the taxpayer and spouse elect to forgo the carryback period, the NOL initially is carried to 2009 and then to years 2010 through 2028. ∎

EXAMPLE 29

Computation of the Net Operating Loss

Since the NOL provisions apply solely to business-related losses, certain adjustments must be made so that the loss more closely resembles the taxpayer's *economic* loss. The required adjustments for corporate taxpayers are usually insignificant because a corporation's tax loss is generally similar to its economic loss. However, in computing taxable income, individual taxpayers are allowed deductions for such items as personal and dependency exemptions and itemized deductions that do not reflect actual business-related economic losses.

To arrive at the NOL for an individual, taxable income must be adjusted by adding back the following items:[39]

1. No deduction is allowed for personal and dependency exemptions. These amounts do not reflect economic, or business, outlays and hence must be added back.
2. The NOL carryover or carryback from another year is not allowed in the computation of the current year's NOL.
3. Capital losses and nonbusiness deductions are limited in determining the current year's NOL. These limits are as follows:
   a. The excess of nonbusiness capital losses over nonbusiness capital gains must be added back.
   b. The excess of nonbusiness deductions over the sum of nonbusiness income and *net* nonbusiness capital gains must be added back. *Net*

---

[39] § 172(d); Reg. § 1.172–3(a).

nonbusiness capital gains are the excess of nonbusiness capital gains over nonbusiness capital losses. *Nonbusiness income* includes such passive items as dividends and interest. It does not include such items as salaries, alimony, rents, and gains and losses on the sale or exchange of business assets. *Nonbusiness deductions* are total itemized deductions less personal casualty and theft losses and losses incurred in a transaction entered into for profit.

A taxpayer who does not itemize deductions computes the excess of nonbusiness deductions over nonbusiness income by substituting the standard deduction for total itemized deductions.

c. The excess of business capital losses over the sum of business capital gains and the excess of nonbusiness income and net nonbusiness capital gains over nonbusiness deductions must be added back.

d. The add-back for net nonbusiness capital losses and excess business capital losses does not include net capital losses not included in the current-year computation of taxable income because of the capital loss limitation provisions (discussed in Chapter 16).

The capital loss and nonbusiness deduction limits are illustrated in Examples 30 through 33.

EXAMPLE 30

For 2008, taxpayer and spouse have $6,000 of nonbusiness capital losses and $4,000 of nonbusiness capital gains. They must add back $2,000 ($6,000 − $4,000) in determining the excess of nonbusiness capital losses over nonbusiness capital gains. ■

EXAMPLE 31

For 2008, taxpayer and spouse have $2,600 of nonbusiness capital gains, $1,000 of nonbusiness capital losses, $2,000 of interest income, and no itemized deductions. They must add back $7,300 {$10,900 standard deduction − [$2,000 interest income + $1,600 ($2,600 − $1,000) net nonbusiness capital gains]}. Note that, in this example, there is no excess of nonbusiness capital losses over nonbusiness capital gains. ■

EXAMPLE 32

For 2008, taxpayer and spouse have $2,600 of nonbusiness capital gains, $1,000 of nonbusiness capital losses, $12,000 of interest income, $11,500 of itemized deductions (none of which are personal casualty and theft losses), $4,000 of business capital losses, and $1,000 of business capital gains. They must add back $900 {$4,000 business capital losses − [$1,000 business capital gains + ($12,000 nonbusiness income + $1,600 net nonbusiness capital gains − $11,500 nonbusiness deductions)]}. Note that, in this example, there is no excess of nonbusiness capital losses over nonbusiness capital gains, nor is there an excess of nonbusiness deductions over the sum of nonbusiness income and net nonbusiness capital gains. ■

EXAMPLE 33

For 2008, taxpayer and spouse have $2,600 of nonbusiness capital gains, $3,000 of nonbusiness capital losses, $13,000 of interest income, $15,000 of itemized deductions (none of which are personal casualty and theft losses), $8,000 of business capital losses, and $4,000 of business capital gains. They must add back $2,000 ($15,000 − $13,000), the excess of nonbusiness deductions over nonbusiness income, and $3,000, the excess of combined capital losses. Because of the capital loss limitations, only $3,000 of the loss would have been used in computing taxable income for the year. ■

Example 34 illustrates the computation of an NOL.

EXAMPLE 34

James opened a retail store in 2007 and experienced an NOL of $185 for that year. James had no taxable income for 2005 or 2006. James is married, has no dependents, and files a joint return. For 2008, James and his wife have the following taxable income:

Gross income from the business	$ 67,000	
Less: Business expenses	(71,000)	($ 4,000)
Salary from a part-time job		875
Interest on savings account		525
Nonbusiness long-term capital gain		1,000
NOL carryover from 2007		(185)
Net loss on rental property		(100)
Adjusted gross income		($ 1,885)
Less: Itemized deductions		
Interest expense	$ 4,600	
Taxes	5,300	
Casualty loss	2,000	
Total itemized deductions		(11,900)
Exemptions (2 × $3,500)		(7,000)
Taxable income		($20,785)

James's NOL is computed as follows:

Taxable income			($20,785)	
Add:				
Net operating loss from 2007		$ 185		
Personal exemptions (2)		7,000		
Excess of nonbusiness				
deductions over				
nonbusiness income				
Total itemized deductions	$11,900			
Less: Casualty loss	(2,000)			
	$ 9,900			
Less: Interest	$ 525			
Less: Long-term capital gain	1,000	(1,525)	8,375	15,560
Net operating loss			($ 5,225)	

The NOL can be thought of as follows:

Business loss	($ 4,000)
Rental loss	(100)
Casualty loss	(2,000)
Salary income	875
Net operating loss	($ 5,225)

Recomputation of Tax Liability for Year to Which Net Operating Loss Is Carried

When an NOL is carried back to a nonloss year, the taxable income and income tax for the carryback year must be recomputed by including the NOL as a deduction *for* AGI. Several deductions (such as medical expenses and charitable contributions) are based on the amount of AGI. When an NOL is carried back, all such deductions *except* the charitable contributions deduction must be recomputed on the basis of the new AGI after the NOL has been applied. The deduction for charitable contributions is determined without regard to any NOL carryback but with regard to any other modification affecting AGI. Furthermore, any tax credits limited by or based upon the tax must be recomputed, based on the recomputed tax.

EXAMPLE 35

Peggy sustains an NOL of $11,000 in 2008. Because Peggy had no taxable income in 2006, the loss is carried back to 2007. For 2007, the joint income tax return of Peggy and her husband was as follows:

Salary income		$ 15,000
Dividends (not qualified dividends)		4,000
Net short-term capital gain		1,400
Adjusted gross income		$ 20,400
Itemized deductions		
Charitable contributions	$3,700	
Medical [$1,600 − ($20,400 × 7.5%)]	70	
Interest	5,700	
Taxes	2,420	(11,890)
Exemptions (2 × $3,400)		(6,800)
Taxable income		$ 1,710
Tax (married filing jointly)		$ 171

Peggy's new tax liability for the carryback year is computed as follows:

Adjusted gross income		$ 20,400
Less: Net operating loss		(11,000)
Recomputed adjusted gross income		$ 9,400
Itemized deductions		
Charitable contributions	$3,700	
Medical [$1,600 − ($9,400 × 7.5%)]	895	
Interest	5,700	
Taxes	2,420	(12,715)
Exemptions (2 × $3,400)		(6,800)
Recomputed taxable income		($ 10,115)
Tax		$ –0–
Tax originally paid and refund claim		$ 171

Calculation of the Remaining Net Operating Loss

After computing the amount of the refund claim for the initial carryback year, it is then necessary to determine the extent to which any NOL remains to carry over to future years. The amount of this carryover loss is the excess of the NOL over the taxable income of the year to which the loss is being applied. However, the taxable income of the year to which the loss is being applied must be determined with the following *modifications*:

- No deduction is allowed for excess capital losses over capital gains.
- No deduction is allowed for the NOL that is being carried back. However, deductions are allowed for NOLs occurring before the loss year.
- Any deductions claimed that are based on or limited by AGI must be determined after making the preceding adjustments. However, charitable contributions do not take into account any NOL carryback.
- No deduction is allowed for personal and dependency exemptions.

CONCEPT SUMMARY 7-4

Computation of Net Operating Loss

Taxable income shown on the return
Add back:

1. Personal and dependency exemptions.
2. Net operating loss carryover or carryback from another year.
3. The excess of nonbusiness capital losses over nonbusiness capital gains.
4. The excess of nonbusiness deductions over the sum of nonbusiness income plus *net* nonbusiness capital gains.

5. The excess of business capital losses over the sum of business capital gains plus the excess of nonbusiness income and *net* nonbusiness capital gains over nonbusiness deductions. The add-back from the total of items 3 and 5 will not exceed $3,000 because of the capital loss limitation rules.

Equals the net operating loss

EXAMPLE 36

Referring to the facts in Example 35, the NOL carryover from 2007 available for future years is ($2,490), computed as follows:

Salary income		$ 15,000
Dividends (not qualified dividends)		4,000
Net short-term capital gain		1,400
Adjusted gross income		$ 20,400
Itemized deductions		
Charitable contributions	$3,700	
Medical [$1,600 − ($20,400 × 7.5%)]	70	
Interest	5,700	
Taxes	2,420	(11,890)
Exemptions (not allowed)		–0–
Modified taxable income		$ 8,510
Net operating loss		($ 11,000)
Modified taxable income		8,510
Net operating loss to carry forward		($ 2,490)

Since the ending figure is negative, it represents the NOL remaining to carry over to 2009 or later years. ∎

Tax Consequences of the *Groetzinger* Case

LO.8

Identify tax planning opportunities in deducting certain business expenses, business losses, and personal losses.

In the *Groetzinger* case discussed earlier in the chapter, the court established that the appropriate tests for determining if gambling is a trade or business are whether an individual engages in gambling full-time in good faith, with regularity, and for the production of income as a livelihood, and not as a mere hobby. The court held that Robert Groetzinger satisfied the tests because of his constant and large-scale effort. Skill was required and was applied. He did what he did for a livelihood, though with less than successful results. His gambling was not a hobby, a passing fancy, or an occasional bet for amusement. Therefore, his gambling was a trade or business, and hence, he was able to deduct his gambling losses *for* AGI. If the court had ruled that Groetzinger's gambling was not a trade or business, his gambling losses would have been limited to his gambling winnings and would have been classified as itemized deductions.

TAX PLANNING
Considerations

Documentation of Related-Taxpayer Loans, Casualty Losses, and Theft Losses

Since non-bona fide loans between related taxpayers may be treated as gifts, adequate documentation is needed to substantiate a bad debt deduction if the loan subsequently becomes worthless. Documentation should include proper execution of the note (legal form) and the establishment of a bona fide purpose for the loan. In addition, it is desirable to stipulate a reasonable rate of interest and a fixed maturity date.

Since a theft loss is not permitted for misplaced items, a loss should be documented by a police report and evidence of the value of the property (e.g., appraisals, pictures of the property, newspaper clippings). Similar documentation of the value of property should be provided to support a casualty loss deduction because the amount of loss is measured, in part, by the decline in fair market value of the property.

Casualty loss deductions must be reported on Form 4684.

Worthless Securities

To be deductible, a security must be completely worthless. To obtain the deduction, the taxpayer must prove that the security was not worthless in a prior year and that the security was worthless in the year claimed. Because of the subjectivity associated with this burden of proof, the only safe practice is to claim a loss for the earliest year when it may possibly be allowed and to renew the claim in subsequent years if there is any reasonable chance that it will be applicable to the income for those years.[40] Fortunately, the statute of limitations for worthless securities is seven years.[41]

Small Business Stock

Because § 1244 limits the amount of loss classified as ordinary loss on a yearly basis, a taxpayer might maximize the benefits of § 1244 by selling the stock in more than one taxable year. The result could be that the losses in any one taxable year would not exceed the § 1244 limits on ordinary loss.

EXAMPLE 37

Mitch, a single individual, purchased small business stock in 2006 for $150,000 (150 shares at $1,000 per share). On December 20, 2008, the stock is worth $60,000 (150 shares at $400 per share). Mitch wants to sell the stock at this time. Mitch earns a salary of $80,000 a year, has no other capital transactions, and does not expect any in the future. If Mitch sells all of the small business stock in 2008, his recognized loss will be $90,000 ($60,000 − $150,000). The loss will be characterized as a $50,000 ordinary loss and a $40,000 long-term capital loss. In computing taxable income for 2008, Mitch could deduct the $50,000 ordinary loss but could deduct only $3,000 of the capital loss. The remainder of the capital loss could be carried over and used in future years subject to the $3,000 limitation if Mitch has no capital gains. If Mitch sells 82 shares in 2008, he will recognize an ordinary loss of $49,200 [82 × ($1,000 − $400)]. If Mitch then sells the remainder of the shares in 2009, he will recognize an ordinary loss of $40,800 [68 × ($1,000 − $400)]. Mitch could deduct the $49,200 ordinary loss in computing 2008 taxable income and the $40,800 ordinary loss in computing 2009 taxable income. ■

Casualty Losses

A special election is available for taxpayers who sustain casualty losses in an area designated by the President as a disaster area. This election affects only the timing,

---

40 *Young v. Comm.*, 41–2 USTC ¶9744, 28 AFTR 365, 123 F.2d 597 (CA–2, 1941).   41 § 6511(d)(1).

TAX *in the News*   WHEN IS A SECURITY WORTHLESS?

Usually, losses that have not been documented by the market-place cannot be deducted (i.e., unrealized losses). An exception exists for securities that are completely worthless. But proving complete worthlessness can sometimes be difficult. Just because a company declares bankruptcy does not necessarily prove that its stock is completely worthless because in some cases the stock can recover. Determining whether this can happen requires an analysis of the relevant facts and circumstances. Even though a stock may be selling for a fraction of a penny (i.e., has some value), some tax advisers argue that if the stock's selling price would be less than the broker's commission for selling the stock, a deduction can be taken at that time.

not the calculation, of the deduction. The deduction can be taken in the year before the year in which the loss occurred. Thus, for a loss occurring between January 1 and December 31, 2008, an individual can take the deduction on the 2007 return. The benefit, of course, is a faster refund (or reduction in tax). It will also be advantageous to carry the loss back if the taxpayer's tax rate in the carryback year is higher than the tax rate in the year of the loss.

To find out if an event qualifies as a disaster area loss, one can look in any of the major tax services, the Weekly Compilation of Presidential Documents, or the *Internal Revenue Bulletin.*

Net Operating Losses

In certain instances, it may be advisable for a taxpayer to elect not to carry back an NOL. For an individual, the benefits from the loss carryback could be scaled down or lost due to the economic adjustments that must be made to taxable income for the year to which the loss is carried. For example, a taxpayer should attempt to minimize the number of taxable years to which an NOL is carried. The more years to which the NOL is applied, the more benefits are lost from adjustments for items such as personal and dependency exemptions.

The election not to carry back the loss might also be advantageous if there is a disparity in marginal tax rates applicable to different tax years.

EXAMPLE 38

Abby sustained an NOL of $10,000 in Year 3. Her marginal tax bracket in Year 1 was 15%. In Year 4, however, she expects her bracket to be 35% due to a large profit she will make on a business deal. If Abby carries her loss back, her refund will be $1,500 (15% × $10,000). If she elects not to carry it back to Year 1 but chooses, instead, to carry it forward, her savings will be $3,500 (35% × $10,000). Even considering the time value of an immediate tax refund, Abby appears to be better off using the carryover approach. ■

KEY TERMS

Bad debt, 7–3	Net operating loss (NOL), 7–19	Section 1244 stock, 7–6
Business bad debt, 7–5	Nonbusiness bad debt, 7–4	Small business stock, 7–6
Casualty loss, 7–8	Personal casualty gain, 7–13	Specific charge-off method, 7–3
Disaster area losses, 7–10	Personal casualty loss, 7–13	Theft losses, 7–9
Domestic production activities deduction (DPAD), 7–17	Qualified production activities income (QPAI), 7–18	Worthless securities, 7–6
Domestic production gross receipts (DPGR), 7–18	Research and experimental expenditures, 7–15	W–2 wages, 7–17
Modified adjusted gross income, 7–17	Reserve method, 7–3	

PROBLEM MATERIALS

DISCUSSION QUESTIONS

1. Explain how a purchased debt instrument can give rise to a bad debt deduction.

2. Ron sells his business accounts receivable of $100,000 to Mike for $80,000 (80% of the actual accounts receivable). Mike later determines that he will be able to collect only $9,000 of a $10,000 receivable. Discuss the amount and classification of Mike's bad debt deduction.

3. Discuss whether legal proceedings are necessary to show that a debt is worthless.

4. During the past tax year, Mark identified $10,000 as a nonbusiness bad debt. In that tax year, Mark had $50,000 of taxable income, none of which consisted of capital gains. During the current tax year, Mark collected $5,000 of the amount he had previously identified as a bad debt. Discuss Mark's tax treatment of the $5,000 received in the current tax year.

5. Discuss the application of the business bad debt provisions to a business entity.

6. Discuss whether a bona fide loan can exist between related parties.

Issue ID

7. Jack's son Mike, while a student at the university, was employed part-time at a pet store. He continued to work in the business and became manager of the store. The owner of the store decided to sell the business. Since Mike had worked in the business for several years and was intimately acquainted with its customers and its merchandise, he decided to buy the business. To facilitate the purchase, Jack mortgaged his home through a local bank. He then loaned Mike the $60,000 proceeds from the mortgage. At the time of the loan, Mike executed in favor of Jack an unsecured promissory note in the amount of $60,000. Shortly after Mike purchased the business, serious competition arose in the pet store business. Mike could not compete with the larger businesses and became insolvent. The store was closed, and Mike filed for bankruptcy under Chapter 7 of the Bankruptcy Code. Jack filed a proof of claim in the bankruptcy proceeding, but no assets were available to unsecured creditors. When Mike defaulted on his loan from Jack, Jack was required to pay the bank the $60,000 he had borrowed. Identify the relevant tax issues for Jack.

8. Mary is in the business of buying and selling stocks and bonds. She has a bond of Velvet Corporation for which she paid $15,000. If the bond becomes worthless, what are the tax consequences of the bond being characterized as a worthless security? As a bad debt?

9. Discuss the ordinary loss limitations on the sale of § 1244 stock and the advantages of such a characterization.

10. Jim discovers that one of his business warehouses has extensive termite damage. Discuss whether he may take a deduction for the damage to the building.

11. Janice was involved in an automobile accident, and the police cited her for driving under the influence of alcohol. Discuss whether Janice may claim a casualty loss deduction for the damage to her car.

12. Discuss at what point in time a theft loss is recognized.

13. Mary's diamond ring was stolen last year. She originally paid $8,000 for the ring, but it was worth considerably more at the time of the theft. Mary filed an insurance claim for the stolen ring, but the claim was denied. Because the insurance claim was denied, Mary took a casualty loss for the stolen ring on last year's tax return. Last year, Mary had AGI of $32,000. In the current year, the insurance company had a "change of heart" and sent Mary a check for $5,000 for the stolen ring. Discuss the proper tax treatment of the $5,000 Mary received from the insurance company in the current year.

14. Discuss the measurement rule for partial or complete destruction of personal use property.

15. Discuss the tax consequences of not making an insurance claim when insured personal use property is subject to a loss.

16. Discuss the circumstances under which the cost of repairs to the damaged property can be used to measure the amount of a casualty loss.

17. Discuss the treatment of casualty losses associated with rental property.

18. Hazel sustained a loss on the theft of a painting. She had paid $20,000 for the painting, but it was worth $25,000 at the time of the theft. Evaluate the tax consequences of treating the painting as investment property or as personal use property.

19. When casualty losses exceed casualty gains, only the amount of the casualty loss in excess of casualty gains is subject to the 10%-of-AGI floor. Discuss the significance of netting losses against gains in this manner rather than having the entire casualty loss be subject to the 10%-of-AGI floor.

20. Kelly decided to invest in Lime, Inc. common stock after reviewing Lime's public disclosures, including recent financial statements and a number of press releases issued by Lime. On August 7, 2006, Kelly purchased 60,000 shares of Lime for $210,000. In May 2007, Lime entered into a joint venture with Cherry, Inc. In November 2007, the joint venture failed, and Lime's stock began to decline in value. In December 2007, Cherry filed a lawsuit against Lime for theft of corporate opportunity and breach of fiduciary responsibility. In February 2008, Lime filed a countersuit against Cherry for fraud and misappropriation of funds. At the end of December 2008, Kelly's stock in Lime was worth $15,000. Identify the relevant tax issues for Kelly.   *Issue ID*

21. Henry owned 1,000 acres of unimproved farmland. During the spring of the current year, shortly after Henry had tilled the ground, a storm blew away four inches of topsoil from 60% of his acreage. Identify the relevant tax issues for Henry.   *Issue ID*

22. Discuss whether depreciation can qualify as a research and experimental expenditure.

23. Discuss under what circumstances a company would elect to amortize research and experimental expenditures rather than use the expense method.

24. Amos began a business, Silver, Inc., on July 1, 2005. The business extracts and processes silver ore. During 2008, Amos becomes aware of the domestic production activities deduction (DPAD) and would like to take advantage of this deduction. Identify the relevant tax issues for Silver, Inc.   *Issue ID*

25. The DPAD is unlike other deductions and is designed to provide a tax benefit in a somewhat unique manner. Explain this statement.

26. Discuss the definition of W–2 wages for purposes of determining the DPAD for a calendar year taxpayer for 2008.

27. Discuss whether stolen bearer bonds can create an NOL for an individual taxpayer.

28. Discuss how the carryback period for a loss attributable to a farming business differs from the carryback period for a regular NOL.

29. Discuss whether an NOL carryover from a prior year can create an NOL for the current year.

30. Discuss the recomputation of the tax liability for the year to which an NOL is carried.

31. Thomas believes that he has an NOL for the current year and wants to carry it back to a previous year and receive a tax refund. In determining his NOL, Thomas offset his business income by alimony payments he made to his ex-wife, contributions he made to his traditional Individual Retirement Account (IRA), and moving expenses he incurred. His reason for using these items in the NOL computation is that each item is a deduction *for* AGI. Identify the relevant tax issues for Thomas.   *Issue ID*

PROBLEMS

Communications

32. Several years ago John Johnson, who is not in the lending business, loaned Sara $30,000 to purchase an automobile to be used for personal purposes. In August of the current year, Sara filed for bankruptcy, and John was notified that he could not expect to receive more than $4,000. As of the end of the current year, John has received $1,000. John has contacted you about the possibility of taking a bad debt deduction for the current year.

Write a letter to John that contains your advice as to whether he can claim a bad debt deduction for the current year. Also, prepare a memo for the tax files. John's address is 100 Tyler Lane, Erie, PA 16563.

33. Sue loaned her friend John $15,000 four years ago. John signed a note and made payments on the loan. Last year, when the remaining balance of the loan was $8,000, John filed for bankruptcy and notified Sue that he would be unable to repay the $8,000 balance remaining on the loan. Sue treated the $8,000 as a bad debt. Last year Sue had net long-term capital gains of $1,000 and taxable income of $41,000. Sue did not itemize her deductions last year. During the current year, John paid Sue $5,000 in satisfaction of the debt. Determine Sue's tax treatment for the $5,000 received in the current year.

34. Ron is in the business of purchasing accounts receivable. Last year, Ron purchased an account receivable with a face value of $100,000 for $72,000. During the current year, Ron was notified that he could not expect to collect more than 80 cents on the dollar with respect to the receivable. Determine the maximum amount of the bad debt deduction for Ron for the current year.

35. Mable and Jack file a joint return. For the current year, they had the following items:

Salaries	$180,000
Loss on sale of § 1244 stock acquired two years ago	105,000
Gain on sale of § 1244 stock acquired six months ago	20,000
Nonbusiness bad debt	19,000

Determine their AGI for the current year.

Decision Making

36. Mary, a single taxpayer, purchased 10,000 shares of § 1244 stock several years ago at a cost of $20 per share. In November of the current year, Mary received an offer to sell the stock for $12 per share. She has the option of either selling all of the stock now or selling half of the stock now and half of the stock in January of next year. Mary will receive a salary of $80,000 for the current year and $90,000 next year. Mary will have long-term capital gains of $8,000 for the current year and $10,000 next year. If Mary's goal is to minimize her AGI for the two years, determine whether she should sell all of her stock this year or half of her stock this year and half next year.

37. During the current year, someone broke into Jacob's personal residence and took the following items:

Asset	Adjusted Basis	FMV before	FMV after	Insurance Recovery
Business computer	$15,000	$10,000	–0–	$3,000
Bearer bonds	30,000	32,000	–0–	–0–
Silverware	7,000	10,000	–0–	2,000
Cash	8,000	8,000	–0–	–0–

Jacob's AGI for the year, before considering any of the above items, is $50,000. Determine the total deduction for the stolen items on Jacob's current-year tax return.

Decision Making

38. Olaf owns a 500-acre farm in Minnesota. A tornado hit the area and destroyed a farm building and some farm equipment and damaged a barn. Fortunately for Olaf, the tornado occurred after he had harvested his corn crop. Applicable information is as follows:

Item	Adjusted Basis	FMV before	FMV after	Insurance Proceeds
Building	$90,000	$ 70,000	$ –0–	$70,000
Equipment	40,000	50,000	–0–	25,000
Barn	90,000	120,000	70,000	25,000

Because of the extensive damage caused by the tornado, the President designated the area as a disaster area.

Olaf, who files a joint return with his wife, Anna, had $174,000 of taxable income last year. Their taxable income for the current year, excluding the loss from the tornado, is $250,000.

Determine the amount of Olaf and Anna's loss and the year in which they should take the loss.

39. Heather owns a two-story building. The building is used 60% for business use and 40% for personal use. During the current year, a fire caused major damage to the building and its contents. Heather purchased the building for $800,000 and has taken depreciation of $150,000 on the business portion. At the time of the fire, the building had a fair market value of $900,000. Immediately after the fire, the fair market value was $200,000. The insurance recovery on the building was $600,000. The contents of the building were insured for any loss at fair market value. The business assets had an adjusted basis of $220,000 and a fair market value of $175,000. These assets were totally destroyed. The personal use assets had an adjusted basis of $50,000 and a fair market value of $65,000. These assets were also totally destroyed. If Heather's AGI is $100,000 before considering the effects of the fire, determine her itemized deduction as a result of the fire. Also determine Heather's AGI.

40. On July 24 of the current year, Sam Smith was involved in an accident with his business use automobile. Sam had purchased the car for $30,000. The automobile had a fair market value of $20,000 before the accident and $8,000 immediately after the accident. Sam has taken $20,000 of depreciation on the car. The car is insured for the fair market value of any loss. Because of Sam's history, he is afraid that if he submits a claim, his policy will be canceled. Therefore, he is considering not filing a claim. Sam believes that the tax loss deduction will help mitigate the loss of the insurance reimbursement. Sam's current marginal tax rate is 35%.

Decision Making

Communications

Write a letter to Sam that contains your advice with respect to the tax and cash-flow consequences of filing versus not filing a claim for the insurance reimbursement for the damage to his car. Also, prepare a memo for the tax files. Sam's address is 450 Colonel's Way, Warrensburg, MO 64093.

41. Blue Corporation, a manufacturing company, decided to develop a new line of merchandise. The project began in 2008. Blue had the following expenses in connection with the project:

	2008	2009
Salaries	$300,000	$400,000
Materials	80,000	70,000
Insurance	10,000	15,000
Utilities	7,000	8,000
Cost of inspection of materials for quality control	4,000	4,000
Promotion expenses	10,000	7,000
Advertising	–0–	30,000
Equipment depreciation	10,000	12,000
Cost of market survey	8,000	–0–

The new product will be introduced for sale beginning in July 2010. Determine the amount of the deduction for research and experimental expenditures for 2008, 2009, and 2010 if:

    a.   Blue Corporation elects to expense the research and experimental expenditures.

    b.   Blue Corporation elects to amortize the research and experimental expenditures over 60 months.

42. In 2008, Purple, Inc., a C corporation, has QPAI of $100,000 and a marginal tax rate of 35%. Calculate the tax savings resulting from the DPAD.

43. Barbara, a calendar year taxpayer, owns and operates a company that manufactures toys. For 2008, she has modified AGI of $500,000 and QPAI of $550,000. Ignoring the W–2 wage limitation, calculate Barbara's DPAD.

44. Tan, Inc., has QPAI of $400,000 but has an overall NOL of $15,000 for the tax year. Calculate Tan's DPAD, if any, for 2008.

45. Green, Inc., manufactures skirts and blouses in the United States. The QPAI derived from the manufacture of one skirt is $7, and the QPAI from one blouse is a negative $3. What amount of QPAI is available to Green for calculating the DPAD?

Decision Making

46. In 2008, Rose, Inc., has QPAI of $4 million and taxable income of $3 million. Rose pays independent contractors $400,000. Rose's W–2 wages are $500,000, but only $300,000 of the wages are paid to employees engaged in qualified domestic production activities.

    a.   Calculate the DPAD for Rose, Inc., for 2008.

    b.   What suggestions could you make to enable Rose to increase its DPAD?

47. Sam, age 45, is single. For 2008, he has the following items:

Business income	$70,000
Business expenses	65,000
Alimony paid	12,000
Interest income	3,000
Itemized deductions	4,000

    a.   Determine Sam's taxable income for 2008.

    b.   Determine Sam's NOL for 2008.

48. Mary, a single taxpayer with two dependent children, has the following items of income and expense during 2008:

Gross receipts from business	$144,000
Business expenses	180,000
Alimony received	22,000
Interest income	40,000
Itemized deductions (no casualty or theft)	28,000

    a.   Determine Mary's taxable income for 2008.

    b.   Determine Mary's NOL for 2008.

49. Gus, who is married and files a joint return, owns a grocery store. In 2008, his gross sales were $276,000, and operating expenses were $320,000. Other items on his 2008 return were as follows:

Nonbusiness capital gains (short term)	$20,000
Nonbusiness capital losses (long term)	9,000
Itemized deductions (no casualty or theft)	18,000
Ordinary nonbusiness income	8,000
Salary from part-time job	10,000

During the year 2006, Gus had no taxable income. In 2007, Gus had taxable income of $22,300 computed as follows:

Net business income	$ 60,000
Interest income	2,000
Adjusted gross income	$ 62,000

Less: Itemized deductions

Charitable contributions of $40,000, limited to 50% of AGI	$31,000	
Medical expenses of $6,550, limited to the amount in excess of 7.5% of AGI ($6,550 − $4,650)	1,900	
Total itemized deductions		(32,900)
Exemptions (2 × $3,400)		(6,800)
Taxable income		$ 22,300

   a.   What is Gus's 2008 NOL?
   b.   Determine Gus's recomputed taxable income for 2007.
   c.   Determine the amount of Gus's 2008 NOL to be carried forward to 2009.

50. During 2008, Rick and his wife, Sara, had the following items of income and expense to report:

Gross receipts from farming business	$400,000
Farming expenses	525,000
Interest income from bank savings accounts	8,000
Sara's salary	50,000
Long-term capital gain on stock held as an investment	4,000
Itemized deductions (no casualty or theft)	15,000

   a.   Assuming Rick and Sara file a joint return, what is their taxable income for 2008?
   b.   What is the amount of Rick and Sara's farming loss for 2008?
   c.   What is the amount of Rick and Sara's NOL for 2008?
   d.   To what years can Rick and Sara's NOL be carried?

51. Assume that in addition to the information in Problem 50, Rick and Sara had no taxable income for the years 2003, 2004, 2005, and 2006 and $4,900 of taxable income for 2007 computed as follows:

Salary		$ 25,000
Capital loss		(1,000)
Adjusted gross income		$ 24,000
Less: Itemized deductions		
Charitable contributions of $20,000, limited to 50% of AGI	$12,000	
Medical expenses of $2,100, limited to the amount in excess of 7.5% of AGI ($2,100 − $1,800)	300	
Total itemized deductions		$(12,300)
Exemptions (2 × $3,400)		(6,800)
Taxable income		$ 4,900

   a.   Determine Rick and Sara's recomputed taxable income for 2007.
   b.   Determine the amount of Rick and Sara's 2008 NOL to be carried forward to 2009.

52. During 2008, Ron and his wife, Sue, had the following items of income and expense to report:

Farming income	$200,000
Farming expenses	240,000
Interest income	15,000
Medical expenses (after 7.5%-of-AGI reduction)	8,000
Casualty loss (after $100 reduction and 10%-of-AGI reduction)	20,000

   a.   Determine Ron and Sue's taxable income for 2008.
   b.   Determine Ron and Sue's NOL for 2008.
   c.   Determine Ron and Sue's farming loss for 2008.
   d.   To what years can Ron and Sue's NOL be carried?

53. Robert and Susan Reid had an NOL of $30,000 in 2008. They had no taxable income for the year 2006 and $15,450 of taxable income for 2007 computed as follows:

Communications

Salary		$ 50,000
Capital loss		(4,000)
Adjusted gross income		$ 46,000
Less: Itemized deductions		
Charitable contributions of $24,000, limited to 50% of AGI	$23,000	
Medical expenses of $4,200, limited to the amount in excess of 7.5% of AGI ($4,200 − $3,450)	750	
Total itemized deductions		(23,750)
Exemptions (2 × $3,400)		(6,800)
Taxable income		$ 15,450

Write a letter to Robert and Susan informing them of the amount of the remaining NOL to be carried forward if the loss is applied against the 2007 taxable income. Also, prepare a memo for the tax files. Their address is 201 Jerdone Avenue, Conway, SC 29526.

54. Pete and Polly are married and file a joint return. They had the following income and deductions for 2008:

Salary	$50,000
Interest from savings account	5,000
Itemized deductions	8,000
2007 NOL carried to 2008	60,000

   a. What is Pete and Polly's taxable income for 2008?
   b. What is Pete and Polly's NOL for 2008?
   c. What is Pete and Polly's NOL to be carried to 2009?

55. Soong, single and age 32, had the following items for the tax year 2008:

   • Salary of $30,000.
   • Interest income from U.S. government bonds of $2,000.
   • Dividends from a foreign corporation of $500.
   • Sale of small business § 1244 stock on October 20, 2008, for $20,000. The stock had been acquired two years earlier for $65,000.
   • Business bad debt of $4,000.
   • Nonbusiness bad debt of $5,000.
   • Sale of small business § 1244 stock on November 12, 2008, for $4,000. The stock had been acquired on June 5, 2008, for $800.
   • Sale of preferred stock on December 4, 2008, for $40,000. The stock was acquired four years ago for $18,000.
   • Total itemized deductions of $20,000 (no casualty or theft).

   a. Determine Soong's NOL for 2008.
   b. Assuming Soong has had taxable income for each of the last five years, determine the carryback year to which the 2008 NOL should be applied.

56. Nell, single and age 38, had the following income and expense items in 2008:

Nonbusiness bad debt	$ 6,000
Business bad debt	2,000
Nonbusiness long-term capital gain	4,000
Nonbusiness short-term capital loss	3,000
Salary	40,000
Interest income	1,000

   Determine Nell's AGI for 2008.

57. Assume that in addition to the information in Problem 56, Nell had the following items in 2008:

Personal casualty gain on an asset held for four months	$10,000
Personal casualty loss on an asset held for two years	1,000

   Determine Nell's AGI for 2008.

58. Assume that in addition to the information in Problems 56 and 57, Nell had the following items in 2008:

Personal casualty loss on an asset held for five years	$60,000
Interest expense on home mortgage	5,000

Determine Nell's taxable income and NOL for 2008.

59. Jed, age 55, is married with no children. During 2008, Jed had the following income and expense items:
   a. Three years ago, Jed loaned a friend $10,000 to help him purchase a new car. In June of the current year, Jed learned that his friend had been declared bankrupt and had left the country. There is no possibility that Jed will ever collect any of the $10,000.
   b. In April of last year, Jed purchased some stock for $5,000. In March of the current year, the company was declared bankrupt, and Jed was notified that his shares of stock were worthless.
   c. Several years ago, Jed purchased some § 1244 stock for $120,000. This year, he sold the stock for $30,000.
   d. In July of this year, Jed sold some land that he had held for two years for $60,000. He had originally paid $42,000 for the land.
   e. Jed received $40,000 of interest income from State of Minnesota bonds.
   f. In September, Jed's home was damaged by an earthquake. Jed's basis in his home was $430,000. The value of the home immediately before the quake was $610,000. After the quake, the home was worth $540,000. Because earthquake damage was an exclusion on Jed's homeowner's insurance policy, he received no insurance recovery.
   g. Jed received a salary of $80,000.
   h. Jed made a charitable contribution of $4,000.

   If Jed files a joint return for 2008, determine his NOL for the year.

CUMULATIVE PROBLEMS

60. Jane Smith, age 40, is single and has no dependents. She is employed as a legal secretary by Legal Services, Inc. She owns and operates Typing Services located near the campus of Florida Atlantic University at 1986 Campus Drive. Jane is a material participant in the business. She is a cash basis taxpayer. Jane lives at 2020 Oakcrest Road, Boca Raton, FL 33431. Jane's Social Security number is 123–89–6666. Jane indicates that she wishes to designate $3 to the Presidential Election Campaign Fund. During 2007, Jane had the following income and expense items:
   a. $50,000 salary from Legal Services, Inc.
   b. $20,000 gross receipts from her typing services business.
   c. $700 interest income from Acme National Bank.
   d. $1,000 Christmas bonus from Legal Services, Inc.
   e. $60,000 life insurance proceeds on the death of her sister.
   f. $5,000 check given to her by her wealthy aunt.
   g. $100 won in a bingo game.
   h. Expenses connected with the typing service:

Office rent	$7,000
Supplies	4,400
Utilities and telephone	4,680
Wages to part-time typists	5,000
Payroll taxes	500
Equipment rentals	3,000

   i. $8,346 interest expense on a home mortgage (paid to San Jose Savings and Loan).
   j. $5,000 fair market value of silverware stolen from her home by a burglar on October 12, 2007. Jane had paid $4,000 for the silverware on July 1, 1998. She was reimbursed $1,500 by her insurance company.

Tax Return Problem

Decision Making

Communications

k.   Jane had loaned $2,100 to a friend, Joan Jensen, on June 3, 2004. Joan declared bankruptcy on August 14, 2007, and was unable to repay the loan. Assume the loan is a bona fide debt.

l.   Legal Services, Inc., withheld Federal income tax of $7,500 and FICA tax of $3,551 {Social Security tax of $2,878 [($51,000 − $4,580) × 6.2%] + Medicare tax of $673 [($51,000 − $4,580) × 1.45%]}.

m.   Alimony of $10,000 received from her former husband, Ted Smith.

n.   Interest income of $800 on City of Boca Raton bonds.

o.   Jane made estimated Federal tax payments of $1,000.

p.   Sales taxes from the sales tax table of $654.

q.   Charitable contributions of $2,500.

Part 1—Tax Computation

Compute Jane Smith's 2007 Federal income tax payable (or refund due). If you use tax forms for your computations, you will need Forms 1040 and 4684 and Schedules A, C, and D. Suggested software: TaxCut.

Part 2—Tax Planning

In 2008, Jane plans to continue her job with Legal Services, Inc. Therefore, items a, d, and l will recur in 2008. Jane plans to continue her typing services business (refer to item b) and expects gross receipts of $26,000. She projects that all business expenses (refer to item h) will increase by 10%, except for office rent, which, under the terms of her lease, will remain the same as in 2007. Items e, f, g, j, and k will not recur in 2008. Items c, i, m, n, p, and q will be approximately the same as in 2007.

Jane would like you to compute the minimum amount of estimated tax she will have to pay for 2008 so that she will not have to pay any additional tax upon filing her 2008 Federal income tax return. Write a letter to Jane that contains your advice and prepare a memo for the tax files.

Tax Computation Problem

61.   Alan Rice, age 45, and his wife, Ruth, live at 230 Wood Lane, Salt Lake City, UT 84201. Alan's Social Security number is 885–33–3774. Ruth's Social Security number is 885–33–4985. Alan and Ruth are cash basis taxpayers and had the following items for the year 2008:

• Salary of $80,000.

• Business bad debt of $30,000 from uncollected rent.

• Sale of § 1244 stock resulting in a gain of $20,000. The stock was acquired nine months earlier.

• Rental income of $40,000.

• Rental expenses of $28,000.

• Casualty loss on rental property of $8,000.

• Personal casualty loss (from one event) of $23,000.

• Other itemized deductions of $15,000.

• NOL carryover from 2007 of $18,000.

• Federal income tax withheld of $8,000.

Compute Alan and Ruth's 2008 Federal income tax payable (or refund due).

RESEARCH PROBLEMS

Note: Solutions to Research Problems can be prepared by using the **RIA Checkpoint®Student Edition** online research product, which is available to accompany this text. It is also possible to prepare solutions to the Research Problems by using tax research materials found in a standard tax library.

Research Problem 1.   During 2008, John was the chief executive officer and a shareholder of Maze, Inc. He owned 60% of the outstanding stock of Maze. In 2005, John and Maze, as co-borrowers, obtained a $100,000 loan from United National Bank. This loan was secured by John's personal residence. Though Maze was listed as a co-borrower, John repaid the loan in full in 2008. On Maze's Form 1120 tax returns, no loans from shareholders were reported. Discuss whether John is entitled to a bad debt deduction for the amount of the payment on the loan.

Partial list of research aids:
U.S. v. Generes, 405 U.S. 93 (1972).
Dale H. Sundby, T.C.Memo. 2003–204.
Arrigoni v. Comm., 73 T.C. 792 (1980).
Estate of Herbert M. Rapoport, T.C.Memo. 1982–584.
Clifford L. Brody and Barbara J. DeClerk, T.C. Summary Opinion, 2004–149.

Research Problem 2.   Henry Hansen is a real estate developer. He was successful for many years. Three years ago, however, the real estate market crashed, and Henry reported losses for the two following tax years. The IRS disputed these losses and assessed tax deficiencies of $300,000 and $200,000 for the two years in question. In March of the current year, Henry offered to resolve all issues relating to those two years by paying the IRS $250,000 or $125,000 for each year. In April of the current year, the Commissioner accepted Henry's offer without discussion or negotiation. Henry now finds that he has an NOL for last year. If he carries the NOL back to the two years for which he has reached a settlement with the IRS, the stipulated tax deficiency will be eliminated. Discuss whether Henry will be allowed to carry his NOL back to the two prior years for which he has reached a settlement.

Research Problem 3.   Jeb Simmons operated an illegal gambling business out of his home. While executing a search warrant, the local sheriff seized gambling paraphernalia and $200,000 in cash. Subsequently, Jeb voluntarily consented to forfeit to the state the cash that had been seized in connection with the execution of the search warrant. Write a letter to Jeb advising him as to whether he can claim a loss under § 165 for the seized cash. Also, prepare a memo for the tax files. Jeb's address is 100 Honey Lane, Macon, GA 62108.

Communications

Research Problem 4.   Bill Baker was a partner with Buddy Jones. Last year Buddy prepared the U.S. Partnership Return (Form 1065) reporting $250,000 of ordinary income. The Schedule K–1 issued to Bill reported his distributive share as $125,000. Bill reported this amount on his personal income tax return. Bill never received his distributive share of $125,000. This year he learned that Buddy had stolen all of the partnership assets. Evaluate the possibility of Bill claiming a theft loss on his current year's Federal income tax return for his distributive share of the partnership income of $125,000.

Research Problem 5.   Rocky Sole, Inc., is in the business of designing, developing, manufacturing, and selling hiking boots. The company's design department activities relate to the design, development, modification, and improvement of Rocky Sole's hiking boots. The department produces drawings containing ideas for new products or improvements on existing products. When agreement is reached on a new design, the department evaluates the appropriate manufacturing process. The design department does no internal testing to determine how the hiking boots will perform. Evaluate the possibility of Rocky Sole, Inc., claiming all of the costs incurred by the design department as research and experimental expenditures under § 174.

Use the tax resources of the Internet to address the following questions. Do not restrict your search to the World Wide Web, but include a review of newsgroups and general reference materials, practitioner sites and resources, primary sources of the tax law, chat rooms and discussion groups, and other opportunities.

Internet
Activity

Research Problem 6.   Find a newspaper article that discusses tax planning for casualty losses when a disaster area designation is made. Does the article convey the pertinent tax rules correctly? Then list all of the locations identified by the President as Federal disaster areas in the last two years.

Research Problem 7.   Scan several publications that are read by owners of small businesses. Some of the articles in these publications address tax-related issues such as how to structure a new business. Do these articles do an adequate job of conveying the benefits of issuing § 1244 small business stock? Prepare a short memo explaining the use of § 1244 stock and post it to a newsgroup that is frequented by inventors, engineers, and others involved in startup corporations.

Communications

CHAPTER 8

Depreciation, Cost Recovery, Amortization, and Depletion

LEARNING OBJECTIVES

After completing Chapter 8, you should be able to:

LO.1
Understand the rationale for the cost consumption concept and identify the relevant time periods for depreciation, ACRS, and MACRS.

LO.2
Determine the amount of cost recovery under MACRS.

LO.3
Recognize when and how to make the § 179 expensing election, calculate the amount of the deduction, and apply the effect of the election in making the MACRS calculation.

LO.4
Identify listed property and apply the deduction limitations on listed property and on luxury automobiles.

LO.5
Determine when and how to use the alternative depreciation system (ADS).

LO.6
Be aware of the major characteristics of ACRS.

LO.7
Identify intangible assets that are eligible for amortization and calculate the amount of the deduction.

LO.8
Determine the amount of depletion expense including being able to apply the alternative tax treatments for intangible drilling and development costs.

LO.9
Perform the reporting procedures for cost recovery.

LO.10
Identify tax planning opportunities for cost recovery, amortization, and depletion.

OUTLINE

Overview, 8–2
   General, 8–2
   Concepts Relating to Depreciation, 8–3
Modified Accelerated Cost Recovery System (MACRS), 8–4
   Personalty: Recovery Periods and Methods, 8–5
   Realty: Recovery Periods and Methods, 8–10
   Straight-Line Election, 8–11
   Farm Property, 8–11
   Leasehold Improvement Property, 8–12
   Election to Expense Assets, 8–13
   Business and Personal Use of Automobiles and Other
      Listed Property, 8–15

   Alternative Depreciation System (ADS), 8–20
Accelerated Cost Recovery System (ACRS), 8–22
Amortization, 8–22
Depletion, 8–24
   Intangible Drilling and Development Costs (IDC), 8–25
   Depletion Methods, 8–25
Reporting Procedures, 8–28
Tax Planning Considerations, 8–31
   Cost Recovery, 8–31
   Amortization, 8–32
   Depletion, 8–32
Cost Recovery Tables, 8–33

L0.1

Understand the rationale for the cost consumption concept and identify the relevant time periods for depreciation, ACRS, and MACRS.

Overview

General

The Internal Revenue Code provides for a deduction for the consumption of the cost of an asset through depreciation, cost recovery, amortization, or depletion. These deductions are applications of the recovery of capital doctrine (discussed in Chapter 4). The concept of depreciation is based on the premise that the asset acquired (or improvement made) benefits more than one accounting period. Otherwise, the expenditure is deducted in the year incurred—see Chapter 6 and the discussion of capitalization versus expense.

Congress completely overhauled the **depreciation** rules in 1981 tax legislation by creating the accelerated **cost recovery** system (ACRS). Substantial modifications were made to ACRS in 1986 tax legislation (MACRS). These changes to the depreciation rules and the time frames involved are noted in Concept Summary 8–1. A knowledge of all of the depreciation and cost recovery rules may be needed as Example 1 illustrates for cost recovery.

EXAMPLE 1

The Brown Company owns a building purchased in 1986 that has a 19-year cost recovery life. In 2008, the business purchased a computer. To compute the cost recovery for 2008, Brown used the ACRS rules for the building and the MACRS rules for the computer. For 2008, there would be no additional cost recovery for the building because the basis of the building at the beginning of 2008 would be $0. ■

The statutory changes that have taken place since 1980 have widened the gap that exists between the accounting and tax versions of depreciation. The tax rules that existed prior to 1981 were much more compatible with generally accepted accounting principles.

This chapter initially focuses on the MACRS rules.[1] Because they cover more recent property acquisitions (i.e., after 1986), their use is more widespread. The ACRS rules, however, are reviewed in Concept Summary 8–5 and briefly discussed on page 8–20. The pre-1981 rules are covered in Appendix H. The chapter concludes with a discussion of the amortization of intangible property and startup expenditures and the depletion of natural resources.

---

[1]§ 168. The terms "depreciation" and "cost recovery" are used interchangeably in the text and in § 168.

CONCEPT SUMMARY 8–1

Depreciation and Cost Recovery: Relevant Time Periods

System	Date Property Is Placed in Service
Pre-1981 depreciation	Before January 1, 1981, and *certain* property placed in service after December 31, 1980.
Original accelerated cost recovery system (ACRS)	After December 31, 1980, and before January 1, 1987.
Modified accelerated cost recovery system (MACRS)	After December 31, 1986.

Taxpayers may write off the cost of certain assets that are used in a trade or business or held for the production of income. A write-off may take the form of depreciation (or cost recovery), depletion, or amortization. Tangible assets, other than natural resources, are *depreciated*. Natural resources, such as oil, gas, coal, and timber, are *depleted*. Intangible assets, such as copyrights and patents, are *amortized*. Generally, no write-off is allowed for an asset that does not have a determinable useful life.

Concepts Relating to Depreciation

Nature of Property. Property includes both realty (real property) and personalty (personal property). Realty generally includes land and buildings permanently affixed to the land. Personalty is defined as any asset that is not realty.[2] Personalty includes furniture, machinery, equipment, and many other types of assets. Do not confuse personalty (or personal property) with *personal use* property. Personal use property is any property (realty or personalty) that is held for personal use rather than for use in a trade or business or an income-producing activity. Write-offs are not allowed for personal use assets.

In summary, both realty and personalty can be either business use/income-producing property or personal use property. Examples include a residence (realty that is personal use), an office building (realty that is business use), a dump truck (personalty that is business use), and regular wearing apparel (personalty that is personal use). It is imperative that this distinction between the *classification* of an asset (realty or personalty) and the *use* to which the asset is put (business or personal) be understood.

Assets used in a trade or business or for the production of income are eligible for cost recovery if they are subject to wear and tear, decay or decline from natural causes, or obsolescence. Assets that do not decline in value on a predictable basis or that do not have a determinable useful life (e.g., land, stock, antiques) are not eligible for cost recovery.

Placed in Service Requirement. The key date for the commencement of depreciation is the date an asset is placed in service. This date, and not the purchase date of an asset, is the relevant date. This distinction is particularly important for an asset that is purchased near the end of the tax year, but not placed in service until after the beginning of the following tax year.

Cost Recovery Allowed or Allowable. The basis of cost recovery property must be reduced by the cost recovery allowed and by not less than the allowable

---

[2]Refer to Chapter 1 for a further discussion.

amount. The *allowed* cost recovery is the cost recovery actually taken, whereas the *allowable* cost recovery is the amount that could have been taken under the applicable cost recovery method. If the taxpayer does not claim any cost recovery on property during a particular year, the basis of the property must still be reduced by the amount of cost recovery that should have been deducted (the allowable cost recovery).

E X A M P L E   2

On March 15, Jack paid $10,000 for a copier to be used in his business. The copier is five-year property. Jack elected to use the straight-line method of cost recovery, but did not take cost recovery in years 3 or 4. Therefore, the allowed cost recovery (cost recovery actually deducted) and the allowable cost recovery are as follows:

	Cost Recovery Allowed	Cost Recovery Allowable
Year 1	$1,000	$1,000
Year 2	2,000	2,000
Year 3	–0–	2,000
Year 4	–0–	2,000
Year 5	2,000	2,000
Year 6	1,000	1,000

If Jack sold the copier for $800 in year 7, he would recognize an $800 gain ($800 amount realized − $0 adjusted basis) because the adjusted basis of the copier is zero. ∎

Cost Recovery Basis for Personal Use Assets Converted to Business or Income-Producing Use. If personal use assets are converted to business or income-producing use, the basis for cost recovery and for loss is the *lower* of the adjusted basis or the fair market value at the time the property was converted. As a result of this lower-of-basis rule, losses that occurred while the property was personal use property will not be recognized for tax purposes through the cost recovery of the property.

E X A M P L E   3

Hans acquires a personal residence for $120,000. Four years later, when the fair market value is only $100,000, he converts the property to rental use. The basis for cost recovery is $100,000, since the fair market value is less than the adjusted basis. The $20,000 decline in value is deemed to be personal (since it occurred while the property was held for personal use) and therefore nondeductible. ∎

LO.2

Determine the amount of cost recovery under MACRS.

Modified Accelerated Cost Recovery System (MACRS)

Under the **modified accelerated cost recovery system (MACRS)**, the cost of an asset is recovered over a predetermined period that is generally shorter than the useful life of the asset or the period the asset is used to produce income. The MACRS rules were designed to encourage investment, improve productivity, and simplify the law and its administration.

MACRS provides separate cost recovery tables for realty (real property) and personalty (personal property). Write-offs are not available for land because it does not have a determinable useful life. Cost recovery allowances for real property, other than land, are based on recovery lives specified in the law. The IRS provides tables that specify cost recovery allowances for personalty and for realty.

SIMPLIFIED DEPRECIATION FOR SMALL BUSINESS

Starting July 1, 2007, more small businesses in Australia qualify for a simplified tax system. One of the features of this system is the ability to immediately expense, rather than capitalize and depreciate, any asset that costs less than $1,000.

Source: *Adapted from David Potts, "An End-of-Year Guide to Putting the House in Order; Small Business Review," The Sun Herald (Sydney, Australia), May 20, 2007, Supplement p. 6.*

GLOBAL
Tax Issues

Personalty: Recovery Periods and Methods

Classification of Property. The general effect of TRA of 1986 was to lengthen asset lives compared to those used under ACRS. MACRS provides that the cost recovery basis of eligible personalty (and certain realty) is recovered over 3, 5, 7, 10, 15, or 20 years. Property is classified by recovery period under MACRS as follows (see Exhibit 8–1 for examples):[3]

3-year 200% class . . . . . . ADR midpoints of 4 years and less.[4] Excludes automobiles and light trucks. Includes racehorses more than 2 years old and other horses more than 12 years old.

5-year 200% class . . . . . . ADR midpoints of more than 4 years and less than 10 years, adding automobiles, light trucks, qualified technological equipment, renewable energy and biomass properties that are small power production facilities, research and experimentation property, semiconductor manufacturing equipment, and computer-based central office switching equipment.

7-year 200% class . . . . . . ADR midpoints of 10 years and more and less than 16 years, adding property with no ADR midpoint not classified elsewhere. Includes railroad track and office furniture, fixtures, and equipment.

10-year 200% class . . . . . ADR midpoints of 16 years and more and less than 20 years, adding single-purpose agricultural or horticultural structures, any tree or vine bearing fruits or nuts.

15-year 150% class . . . . . ADR midpoints of 20 years and more and less than 25 years, including sewage treatment plants, and telephone distribution plants and comparable equipment used for the two-way exchange of voice and data communications.

20-year 150% class . . . . . ADR midpoints of 25 years and more, other than real property with an ADR midpoint of 27.5 years and more, and including sewer pipes.

---

[3]§ 168(e).   [4]Rev.Proc. 87–56, 1987–2 C.B. 674 is the source for the ADR midpoint lives.

| | EXHIBIT 8–1 | Cost Recovery Periods: MACRS Personalty |

Class of Property	Examples
3-year	Tractor units for use over-the-road.
	Any horse that is not a racehorse and is more than 12 years old at the time it is placed in service.
	Any racehorse that is more than 2 years old at the time it is placed in service.
	Breeding hogs.
	Special tools used in the manufacturing of motor vehicles such as dies, fixtures, molds, and patterns.
5-year	Automobiles and taxis.
	Light and heavy general-purpose trucks.
	Buses.
	Trailers and trailer-mounted containers.
	Typewriters, calculators, and copiers.
	Computers and peripheral equipment.
	Breeding and dairy cattle.
	Rental appliances, furniture, carpets, etc.
7-year	Office furniture, fixtures, and equipment.
	Breeding and work horses.
	Agricultural machinery and equipment.
	Railroad track.
10-year	Vessels, barges, tugs, and similar water transportation equipment.
	Assets used for petroleum refining or for the manufacture of grain and grain mill products, sugar and sugar products, or vegetable oils and vegetable oil products.
	Single-purpose agricultural or horticultural structures.
15-year	Land improvements.
	Assets used for industrial steam and electric generation and/or distribution systems.
	Assets used in the manufacture of cement.
	Assets used in pipeline transportation.
	Electric utility nuclear production plant.
	Municipal wastewater treatment plant.
20-year	Farm buildings except single-purpose agricultural and horticultural structures.
	Gas utility distribution facilities.
	Water utilities.
	Municipal sewer.

Accelerated depreciation is allowed for these six MACRS classes of property. Two hundred percent declining-balance is used for the 3-, 5-, 7-, and 10-year classes, with a switchover to straight-line depreciation when it yields a larger amount. One hundred and fifty percent declining-balance is allowed for the 15- and 20-year classes, with an appropriate straight-line switchover.[5] The appropriate computation methods and conventions are built into the tables, so it is not necessary to calculate the appropriate percentages. To determine the amount of the cost recovery allowances, simply identify the asset by class and go to the appropriate table for the percentage. The MACRS percentages for personalty appear in Table 8–1 (*all tables are located at the end of the chapter prior to the Problem Materials*).

Taxpayers may *elect* the straight-line method to compute cost recovery allowances for each of these classes of property. Certain property is not eligible for accelerated cost recovery and must be depreciated under an alternative depreciation system (ADS). Both the straight-line election and ADS are discussed later in the chapter.

MACRS views property as placed in service in the middle of the first year (the **half-year convention**).[6] Thus, for example, the statutory recovery period for three-year property begins in the middle of the year an asset is placed in service and ends three years later. In practical terms, this means that taxpayers must wait an extra year to recover the cost of depreciable assets. That is, the actual write-off periods are 4, 6, 8, 11, 16, and 21 years. MACRS also allows for a half-year of cost recovery in the year of disposition or retirement.

EXAMPLE 4

Kareem acquires a five-year class asset on April 10, 2008, for $30,000 and elects not to take additional first-year depreciation (see subsequent discussion). Kareem's cost recovery deduction for 2008 is $6,000, computed as follows:

MACRS cost recovery
[$30,000 × .20 (Table 8–1)] $6,000   ∎

EXAMPLE 5

Assume the same facts as in Example 4 and that Kareem disposes of the asset on March 5, 2010. Kareem's cost recovery deduction for 2010 is $2,880 [$30,000 × ½ × .192 (Table 8–1)]. ∎

Additional First-Year Depreciation. The Economic Stimulus Act of 2008 provides for **additional first-year depreciation** on qualified property acquired after December 31, 2007, and before January 1, 2009, and placed in service before January 1, 2009. The provision allows for an additional 50 percent cost recovery in the year the asset is placed in service. The term *qualified property* includes most types of *new* property other than buildings. The term *new* means original or first use of the property. Property that is used but new to the taxpayer does not qualify.[7]

---

[5]§ 168(b).
[6]§ 168(d)(4)(A).

[7]§ 168(k).

The additional first-year depreciation is taken in the year in which the qualifying property is placed in service and may be claimed in addition to the otherwise available depreciation deduction. After calculating the additional first-year depreciation, the standard cost recovery allowance under MACRS is calculated by multiplying the cost recovery basis (original cost recovery basis less additional first-year depreciation) by the percentage that reflects the applicable cost recovery method and the applicable cost recovery convention.

EXAMPLE 6

Morgan acquires a five-year class asset on March 20, 2008, for $50,000. Morgan's cost recovery deduction for 2008 is $30,000, computed as follows:

50% additional first-year depreciation ($50,000 × .50)	$25,000
MACRS cost recovery [($50,000 − $25,000) × .20 (Table 8–1)]	5,000
Total cost recovery	$30,000 ∎

EXAMPLE 7

Assume the same facts as in Example 6 and that Morgan disposes of the asset on October 17, 2010. Morgan's cost recovery deduction for 2010 is $2,400[$25,000 × ½ × .192 (Table 8-1)]. ∎

A taxpayer may make an election to *not* take additional first-year depreciation. Electing out of taking additional first-year depreciation is an affirmative election, and it is made separately for each class of property that qualifies for the 50 percent rate. The likely position of the IRS is that taxpayers who fail to claim additional first-year depreciation without electing out will have to treat the forgone additional first-year depreciation as if it had been deducted before computing the regular MACRS cost recovery deduction.

Hence, in the absence of an election out, the forgone additional first-year depreciation will be "allowable" depreciation and will reduce the basis of the property.[8]

EXAMPLE 8

Andrew acquired the following new assets on June 4, 2008:

Class	Amount
5-year	$40,000
10-year	70,000

Andrew made an election to take no additional first-year depreciation on the five-year class assets. He made no election with respect to the 10-year class assets. Andrew's total cost recovery with respect to these assets, for the 2008 taxable year, is $46,500, computed as follows:

5-year class	
MACRS cost recovery [$40,000 × .20 (Table 8–1)]	$ 8,000
10-year class	
50% additional first-year depreciation ($70,000 × .50)	35,000
MACRS cost recovery [($70,000 − $35,000) × .10 (Table 8–1)]	3,500
Total cost recovery	$46,500 ∎

---

[8]See, for example, Rev. Proc. 2002–33, I.R.B. No. 20, 963 where this position was taken by the IRS associated with bonus depreciation that applied from 2001 through 2004.

Mid-Quarter Convention. If more than 40 percent of the value of property other than eligible real estate (see Realty: Recovery Periods and Methods for a discussion of eligible real estate) is placed in service during the last quarter of the year, a **mid-quarter convention** applies.[9] Under this convention, property acquisitions are grouped by the quarter they were acquired for cost recovery purposes. Acquisitions during the first quarter are allowed 10.5 months of cost recovery; the second quarter, 7.5 months; the third quarter, 4.5 months; and the fourth quarter, 1.5 months. The percentages are shown in Table 8–2.

EXAMPLE 9

Silver Corporation acquires the following five-year class property in 2008 and elects not to take additional first-year depreciation.

Property Acquisition Dates	Cost
February 15	$ 200,000
July 10	400,000
December 5	600,000
Total	$1,200,000

If Silver Corporation uses the statutory percentage method, the cost recovery allowances for the first two years are computed as indicated below. Since more than 40% ($600,000/$1,200,000 = 50%) of the acquisitions are in the last quarter, the mid-quarter convention applies.

2008

	Mid-Quarter Convention Depreciation	Total Depreciation
February 15	$200,000 × .35 (Table 8–2)	$ 70,000
July 10	$400,000 × .15	60,000
December 5	$600,000 × .05	30,000
		$160,000

2009

	Mid-Quarter Convention Depreciation	Total Depreciation
February 15	$200,000 × .26 (Table 8–2)	$ 52,000
July 10	$400,000 × .34	136,000
December 5	$600,000 × .38	228,000
		$416,000

When property to which the mid-quarter convention applies is disposed of, the property is treated as though it were disposed of at the midpoint of the quarter. Hence, in the quarter of disposition, cost recovery is allowed for one-half of the quarter.

---

[9]§ 168(d)(3).

CONCEPT SUMMARY 8–2

Statutory Percentage Method under MACRS

	Personal Property	Real Property*
Convention	Half-year or mid-quarter	Mid-month
Cost recovery deduction in the year of disposition	Half-year for year of disposition or half-quarter for quarter of disposition	Half-month for month of disposition

*Straight-line method must be used.

EXAMPLE 10

Assume the same facts as in Example 9, except that Silver Corporation sells the $400,000 asset on November 30 of 2009. The cost recovery allowance for 2009 is computed as follows:

February 15	$200,000 × .26 (Table 8–2)	$ 52,000
July 10	$400,000 × .34 × (3.5/4)	119,000
December 5	$600,000 × .38	228,000
Total		$399,000

■

Realty: Recovery Periods and Methods

Under MACRS, the cost recovery period for residential rental real estate is 27.5 years, and the straight-line method is used for computing the cost recovery allowance. **Residential rental real estate** includes property where 80 percent or more of the gross rental revenues are from nontransient dwelling units (e.g., an apartment building). Hotels, motels, and similar establishments are not residential rental property. Low-income housing is classified as residential rental real estate. Nonresidential real estate has a recovery period of 39 years (31.5 years for such property placed in service before May 13, 1993) and is also depreciated using the straight-line method.[10]

Some items of real property are not treated as real estate for purposes of MACRS. For example, single-purpose agricultural structures are in the 10-year MACRS class. Land improvements are in the 15-year MACRS class.

All eligible real estate is depreciated using the **mid-month convention**. Regardless of when during the month the property is placed in service, it is deemed to have been placed in service at the middle of the month. This allows for one-half month's cost recovery for the month the property is placed in service. If the property is disposed of before the end of the recovery period, one-half month's cost recovery is permitted for the month of disposition regardless of the specific date of disposition.

Cost recovery is computed by multiplying the applicable rate (Table 8–6) by the cost recovery basis.

EXAMPLE 11

Alec acquired a building on April 1, 1993, for $800,000. If the building is classified as residential rental real estate, the cost recovery deduction for 2008 is $29,088 (.03636 × $800,000). If the building is sold on October 7, 2008, the cost recovery deduction for 2008 is $23,028 [.03636 × (9.5/12) × $800,000]. (See Table 8–6 for percentage.) ■

---

[10]§§ 168(b), (c), and (e).

EXAMPLE 12

Jane acquired a building on March 2, 1993, for $1 million. If the building is classified as nonresidential real estate, the cost recovery deduction for 2008 is $31,750 (.03175 × $1,000,000). If the building is sold on January 5, 2008, the cost recovery deduction for 2008 is $1,323 [.03175 × (.5/12) × $1,000,000]. (See Table 8–6 for percentage.) ■

EXAMPLE 13

Mark acquired a building on November 19, 2008, for $1.2 million. If the building is classified as nonresidential real estate, the cost recovery deduction for 2008 is $3,852 [.00321 × $1,200,000 (Table 8–6)]. The cost recovery deduction for 2009 is $30,768 [.02564 × $1,200,000 (Table 8–6)]. If the building is sold on May 21, 2009, the cost recovery deduction for 2009 is $11,538 [.02564 × (4.5/12) × $1,200,000 (Table 8–6)]. ■

Straight-Line Election

Although MACRS requires straight-line depreciation for all eligible real estate as previously discussed, the taxpayer may *elect* to use the straight-line method for personal property.[11] The property is depreciated using the class life (recovery period) of the asset with a half-year convention or a mid-quarter convention, whichever is applicable. The election is available on a class-by-class and year-by-year basis. The percentages for the straight-line election with a half-year convention appear in Table 8–3.

EXAMPLE 14

Terry acquires a 10-year class asset on August 4, 2008, for $100,000 and elects not to take additional first-year depreciation. He elects the straight-line method of cost recovery. Terry's cost recovery deduction for 2008 is $5,000 ($100,000 × .050). His cost recovery deduction for 2009 is $10,000 ($100,000 × .100). (See Table 8–3 for percentages.) ■

EXAMPLE 15

Assume the same facts as in Example 14, except that Terry sells the asset on November 21, 2009. His cost recovery deduction for 2009 is $5,000 [$100,000 × .100 × (½) (Table 8–3)]. ■

Farm Property

When tangible personal property is used in a farming business, generally the cost of the asset is recovered under MACRS using the 150 percent declining-balance method.[12] However, the MACRS straight-line method is required for any tree or vine bearing fruits or nuts.[13] The cost of real property used in the farming business is recovered over the normal periods (27.5 years and 39 years) using the straight-line method. A farming business is defined as the trade or business of farming, which includes operating a nursery or sod farm and the raising or harvesting of trees bearing fruit, nuts, or other crops, or ornamental trees.[14] The applicable cost

---

[11]§ 168(b)(5).
[12]§ 168(b)(2)(B).

[13]§§ 168(b)(3)(E) and 168(e)(3)(D)(ii).
[14]§ 263A(e)(4).

EXHIBIT 8–2	Cost Recovery Periods for Farming Assets		

	Recovery Period in Years	
Assets	MACRS	ADS
Agricultural structures (single purpose)	10	15
Cattle (dairy or breeding)	5	7
Farm buildings	20	25
Farm machinery and equipment	7	10
Fences (agricultural)	7	10
Horticultural structures (single purpose)	10	15
Trees or vines bearing fruit or nuts	10	20
Truck (heavy duty, unloaded weight 13,000 pounds or more)	5	6
Truck (actual weight less than 13,000 pounds)	5	5

recovery method is also affected if the taxpayer elects to not have the uniform capitalization rules apply to the farming business.[15] Under the uniform capitalization rules, the costs of property produced or acquired for resale must be capitalized. When this election is made, the cost recovery method required is the alternative depreciation system (ADS) straight-line method (discussed further later in the chapter). This method must be applied to all assets placed in service in any taxable year during which the election is in effect. Even though this election is made and the straight-line method must be used, it does not prevent the taxpayer from electing to expense personalty under § 179.[16] Exhibit 8–2 shows examples of cost recovery periods for farming assets.

EXAMPLE 16

James purchased farm equipment on July 10, 2008, for $80,000 and elects not to take additional first-year depreciation. If James does not elect to expense any of the cost under § 179, his cost recovery deduction for 2008 is $8,568 [(.1071 × $80,000) (Table 8–4)]. ∎

EXAMPLE 17

Assume the same facts as in Example 16, except that James has made an election to not have the uniform capitalization rules apply. His 2008 cost recovery deduction is $4,000 [(.05 × $80,000) (Table 8–5)]. ∎

Leasehold Improvement Property

When the lessor is the owner of leasehold improvement property, the cost recovery period is the statutorily prescribed life. The recovery period for residential rental real estate is 27.5 years, and the recovery period for nonresidential real estate is 39 years. For these real property leasehold improvements, the straight-line method is used. If the improvement is tangible personal property, the shorter MACRS lives and accelerated methods are used.

When lessor-owned leasehold improvements are disposed of or abandoned by the lessor because of the termination of the lease, the property will be treated as disposed of by the lessor, and hence, a loss can be taken for the unrecovered basis.[17]

[15]§ 263A(d)(3)(A).
[16]Reg. § 1.263A–4(d)(4)(ii).

[17]§ 163(i)(8)(B).

E X A M P L E   18

On April 7, 2008, Mary signed a 10-year lease with John on a building to be used for her business. The lease period begins on May 1, 2008, and ends on April 30, 2018. Prior to the signing of the lease, John paid $300,000 to have a unique storefront added to the building. John's cost recovery deduction for 2008 for the addition is $4,815 [(.01605 × $300,000) (Table 8–6)]. ∎

E X A M P L E   19

Assume the same facts as in Example 18. John's cost recovery deduction for 2018 is $2,244 {[.02564 × (3.5/12) × $300,000] (Table 8–6)}. At the end of the lease, John has to remove the unique storefront, so he can lease the building to other tenants. John's loss as a result of the termination of the lease and the removal of the unique storefront is $223,713 computed as follows:

Cost	$300,000
Less: Cost recovery	
2008 (Example 18)	(4,815)
2009–2017 (.02564 × $300,000 × 9 years)	(69,228)
2018	(2,244)
Loss (unrecovered cost)	$223,713

∎

The costs of leasehold improvements made to leased property and owned by the lessee are recovered in accordance with the general cost recovery rules. This means that the cost recovery period is determined without regard to the lease term. Any unrecovered basis in the leasehold improvement property not retained by the lessee is deducted in the year the lease is terminated.

Election to Expense Assets

LO.3

Recognize when and how to make the § 179 expensing election, calculate the amount of the deduction, and apply the effect of the election in making the MACRS calculation.

Section 179 (Election to Expense Certain Depreciable Business Assets) permits the taxpayer to elect to write off up to $250,000 in 2008 ($125,000 in 2007) of the acquisition cost of *tangible personal property* used in a trade or business. Amounts that are expensed under § 179 may not be capitalized and depreciated. The **§ 179 expensing** election is an annual election and applies to the acquisition cost of property placed in service that year. The immediate expense election is not available for real property or for property used for the production of income.[18]

In addition, any elected § 179 expense is taken *before* the 50 percent additional first-year depreciation is computed. The base for calculating the standard MACRS deduction is net of the § 179 expense and the 50 percent additional first-year depreciation.

E X A M P L E   20

Kelly acquires machinery (five-year class asset) on February 1, 2008, at a cost of $275,000 and elects to expense $250,000 under § 179. Kelley also takes the 50% additional first-year depreciation and the statutory percentage cost recovery (see Table 8–1 for percentage) for 2008. As a result, the total deduction for the year is calculated as follows:

§ 179 expense	$250,000
50% additional first-year depreciation [($275,000 − $250,000) × .50]	12,500
Standard MACRS calculation [($275,000 − $250,000 − $12,500) × .20]	2,500
	$265,000

∎

---

[18]§§ 179(b) and (d). The § 179 amount allowed is per taxpayer, per year. On a joint return, the statutory amount applies to the couple. If the taxpayers are married and file separate returns, each spouse is eligible for 50% of the statutory amount.

CONCEPT SUMMARY 8–3

Straight-Line Election under MACRS

	Personal Property	Real Property*
Convention	Half-year or mid-quarter	Mid-month
Cost recovery deduction in the year of disposition	Half-year for year of disposition or half-quarter for quarter of disposition	Half-month for month of disposition
Elective or mandatory	Elective	Mandatory
Breadth of election	Class by class	

*Straight-line method must be used.

Annual Limitations. Two additional limitations apply to the amount deductible under § 179. First, the ceiling amount on the deduction is reduced dollar-for-dollar when property (other than eligible real estate) placed in service during the taxable year exceeds $800,000 in 2008 ($500,000 in 2007).[19] Second, the amount expensed under § 179 cannot exceed the aggregate amount of taxable income derived from the conduct of any trade or business by the taxpayer. Taxable income of a trade or business is computed without regard to the amount expensed under § 179. Any § 179 expensed amount in excess of taxable income is carried forward to future taxable years and added to other amounts eligible for expensing. The § 179 amount eligible for expensing in a carryforward year is limited to the *lesser* of (1) the statutory dollar amount ($250,000 in 2008) reduced by the cost of § 179 property placed in service in excess of $800,000 in the carryforward year or (2) the business income limitation in the carryforward year.

EXAMPLE 21

Jill owns a computer service and operates it as a sole proprietorship. In 2008, she will net $11,000 before considering any § 179 deduction. If Jill spends $825,000 on new equipment, her § 179 expense deduction is computed as follows:

§ 179 deduction before adjustment	$250,000
Less: Dollar limitation reduction ($825,000 − $800,000)	(25,000)
Remaining § 179 deduction	$225,000
Business income limitation	$ 11,000
§ 179 deduction allowed	$ 11,000
§ 179 deduction carryforward ($225,000 − $11,000)	$214,000

Effect on Basis. The basis of the property for cost recovery purposes is reduced by the § 179 amount after it is adjusted for property placed in service in excess of $800,000. This adjusted amount does not reflect any business income limitation.

EXAMPLE 22

Assume the same facts as in Example 21 and that the new equipment is five-year class property. Jill elects not to take additional first-year depreciation. After considering the § 179

---

[19]The $250,000 and $800,000 amounts apply to tax years beginning in 2008. The $250,000 amount replaces the indexed amount of $128,000 that was to apply to 2008. The $800,000 amount replaces the indexed amount of $510,000 that was to apply to 2008.

deduction, Jill's cost recovery deduction for 2008 (see Table 8–1 for percentage) is calculated as follows:

Standard MACRS calculation
[($825,000 − $225,000) × .20] $120,000

Conversion to Personal Use.
Conversion of the expensed property to personal use at any time results in recapture income (see Chapter 17). A property is converted to personal use if it is not used predominantly in a trade or business. Regulations provide for the mechanics of the recapture.[20]

Business and Personal Use of Automobiles and Other Listed Property

> **LO.4**
>
> Identify listed property and apply the deduction limitations on listed property and on luxury automobiles.

Limits exist on MACRS deductions for automobiles and other listed property that are used for both personal and business purposes.[21] If the listed property is *predominantly used* for business, the taxpayer is allowed to use the *statutory percentage method* to recover the cost. In cases where the property is *not predominantly used* for business, the cost is recovered using the *straight-line method*.

Listed property includes the following:

- Any passenger automobile.
- Any other property used as a means of transportation.
- Any property of a type generally used for purposes of entertainment, recreation, or amusement.
- Any computer or peripheral equipment, with the exception of equipment used exclusively at a regular business establishment, including a qualifying home office.
- Any cellular telephone or other similar telecommunications equipment.
- Any other property specified in the Regulations.

Automobiles and Other Listed Property Used Predominantly in Business.
For listed property to be considered as *predominantly used in business*, its *business usage* must exceed 50 percent.[22] The use of listed property for production of income does not qualify as business use for purposes of the more-than-50 percent test. However, both production of income and business use percentages are used to compute the cost recovery deduction.

EXAMPLE 23

On September 1, 2008, Emma places in service listed five-year recovery property. The property cost $10,000. She elects not to take additional first-year depreciation. If Emma uses the property 40% for business and 25% for the production of income, the property is not considered as predominantly used for business. The cost is recovered using straight-line cost recovery. Emma's cost recovery allowance for the year is $650 ($10,000 × 10% × 65%). If, however, Emma uses the property 60% for business and 25% for the production of income, the property is considered as used predominantly for business. Therefore, she may use the statutory percentage method. Emma's cost recovery allowance for the year is $1,700 ($10,000 × .200 × 85%). ■

The method for determining the percentage of business usage for listed property is specified in the Regulations. The Regulations provide that for automobiles a mileage-based percentage is to be used. Other listed property is to use the most appropriate unit of time (e.g., hours) the property is actually used (rather than available for use).[23]

---

[20]Reg. § 1.179–1(e).
[21]§ 280F.
[22]§ 280F(b)(3).
[23]Reg. § 1.280F–6T(e).

Limits on Cost Recovery for Automobiles. The law places special limitations on the cost recovery deduction for passenger automobiles. These statutory dollar limits were imposed on passenger automobiles because of the belief that the tax system was being used to underwrite automobiles whose cost and luxury far exceeded what was needed for their business use.

A *passenger automobile* is any four-wheeled vehicle manufactured for use on public streets, roads, and highways with an unloaded gross vehicle weight (GVW) rating of 6,000 pounds or less.[24] This definition specifically excludes vehicles used directly in the business of transporting people or property for compensation such as taxicabs, ambulances, hearses, and trucks and vans as prescribed by the Regulations.

The following limits apply to the cost recovery deductions for passenger automobiles for 2007:[25]

Year	Recovery Limitation*
1	$3,060
2	4,900
3	2,850
Succeeding years until the cost is recovered	1,775

* The indexed amounts for 2008 were not available at the time of this writing.

In the event that a passenger automobile used predominantly for business qualifies for 50 percent additional first-year depreciation (i.e., new property), the first-year recovery limitation is increased by $8,000. Therefore, for acquisitions made in 2008, the initial-year cost recovery limitation increases from $3,060 to $11,060 ($3,060 + $8,000).[26]

For an automobile placed in service in 2007, the limitation for subsequent years' cost recovery will be based on the limits for the year the automobile was placed in service. Hence, the limit for the third year's cost recovery for an automobile placed in service in 2007 is $2,850 and not a limit published in 2009.[27]

There are also separate cost recovery limitations for trucks and vans and for electric automobiles. Because these limitations are applied in the same manner as those imposed on passenger automobiles, these additional limitations are not discussed further in this chapter.

The limits are imposed before any percentage reduction for personal use. In addition, the limitation in the first year includes any amount the taxpayer elects to expense under § 179.[28] If the passenger automobile is used partly for personal use, the personal use percentage is ignored for the purpose of determining the unrecovered cost available for deduction in later years.

EXAMPLE 24

On July 1, 2008, Dan places in service a new automobile that cost $40,000. He does not elect § 179 expensing. The car is always used 80% for business and 20% for personal. Dan chooses the MACRS 200% declining-balance method of cost recovery (see the 5-year column in Table 8–1). The depreciation computation for 2008–2013 is summarized below:

---

[24]§ 280F(d)(5).

[25]§ 280F(a)(1). Since the 2008 indexed amounts were not available at the time of this writing, the 2007 amounts are used in the Examples and in the Problem Materials.

[26]§ 168(k)(2)(F)(i).

[27]Cost recovery limitations for prior years can be found in IRS Publication 463.

[28]§ 280F(d)(1).

Year	MACRS Amount	Recovery Limitation	Depreciation Allowed
2008	$19,200	$8,848	$8,848
	{[($40,000 × 50%) + ($20,000 × 20%)] × 80%}	($11,060 × 80%)	
2009	$5,120	$3,920	$3,920
	($20,000 × 32% × 80%)	($4,900 × 80%)	
2010	$3,072	$2,280	$2,280
	($20,000 × 19.2% × 80%)	($2,850 × 80%)	
2011	$1,843	$1,420	$1,420
	($20,000 × 11.52% × 80%)	($1,775 × 80%)	
2012	$1,843	$1,420	$1,420
	($20,000 × 11.52% × 80%)	($1,775 × 80%)	
2013	$922	$1,420	$ 922
	($20,000 × 5.76% × 80%)	($1,775 × 80%)	

The cost recovery allowed is the lesser of the MACRS amount or the recovery limitation. If Dan continues to use the car after 2013, his cost recovery is limited to the lesser of the recoverable basis or the recovery limitation (i.e., $1,775 × business use percentage). For this purpose, the recoverable basis is computed as if the full recovery limitation was allowed even if it was not. Thus, the recoverable basis as of January 1, 2014, is $15,865 ($40,000 − $11,060 − $4,900 − $2,850 − $1,775 − $1,775 − $1,775). ■

The cost recovery limitations are maximum amounts. If the regular calculation produces a lesser amount of cost recovery, the lesser amount is used.

On April 2, 2008, Gail places in service a used automobile that cost $10,000. The car is always used 70% for business and 30% for personal use. Therefore, the cost recovery allowance for 2008 is $1,400 ($10,000 × 20% × 70%), which is less than $7,742 ($11,060 × 70%). ■

Note that the cost recovery limitations apply *only* to passenger automobiles and not to other listed property.

Special Limitation. The American Jobs Creation Act of 2004 (AJCA) placed a limit on the § 179 deduction for certain vehicles not subject to the statutory dollar limits on cost recovery deductions that are imposed on passenger automobiles. This new limit is $25,000. The limit applies to sport utility vehicles with an unloaded GVW rating of more than 6,000 pounds and not more than 14,000 pounds.[29]

During 2008, Jay acquires and places in service a sport utility vehicle that cost $70,000 and has a GVW of 8,000 pounds. Jay uses the vehicle 100% of the time for business use. The total deduction for 2008 with respect to the SUV is $34,000, computed as follows:

§ 179 expense	$25,000
50% additional first-year depreciation [($70,000 − $25,000) × .50]	22,500
Standard MACRS calculation [($70,000 − $25,000 − $22,500) × .20 (Table 8–1)]	4,500
	$52,000 ■

Automobiles and Other Listed Property Not Used Predominantly in Business. The cost of listed property that does not pass the more-than-50 percent

---

[29]§ 179(b)(6).

business usage test in the year the property is placed in service must be recovered using the straight-line method.[30] In addition, such property does not qualify for the 50 percent additional first-year depreciation. The straight-line method to be used is that required under the alternative depreciation system (explained later in the chapter). This system requires a straight-line recovery period of five years for automobiles. However, even though the straight-line method is used, the cost recovery allowance for passenger automobiles cannot exceed the dollar limitations.

EXAMPLE 27

On July 27, 2008, Fred places in service an automobile that cost $20,000. The auto is used 40% for business and 60% for personal use. The cost recovery allowance for 2008 is $800 [$20,000 × 10% (Table 8–5) × 40%]. ∎

EXAMPLE 28

Assume the same facts as in Example 27, except that the automobile cost $50,000. The cost recovery allowance for 2008 is $1,224 [$50,000 × 10% (Table 8–5) = $5,000 (limited to $3,060) × 40%]. ∎

If the listed property fails the more-than-50 percent business usage test, the straight-line method must be used for the remainder of the property's life. This applies even if at some later date the business usage of the property increases to more than 50 percent. Even though the straight-line method must continue to be used, however, the amount of cost recovery will reflect the increase in business usage.

EXAMPLE 29

Assume the same facts as in Example 28, except that in 2009, Fred uses the automobile 70% for business and 30% for personal use. Fred's cost recovery allowance for 2009 is $2,800 [$20,000 × 20% (Table 8–5) × 70%], which is less than 70% of the second-year limit. ∎

Change from Predominantly Business Use.

If the business use percentage of listed property falls to 50 percent or lower after the year the property is placed in service, the property is subject to *cost recovery recapture*. The amount required to be recaptured and included in the taxpayer's return as ordinary income is the excess cost recovery.

Excess cost recovery is the excess of the cost recovery deduction taken in prior years using the statutory percentage method over the amount that would have been allowed if the straight-line method had been used since the property was placed in service.[31]

EXAMPLE 30

Seth purchased a car on January 22, 2008, at a cost of $20,000. Business usage was 80% in 2008, 70% in 2009, 40% in 2010, and 60% in 2011. Seth's excess cost recovery to be recaptured as ordinary income in 2010 is computed as follows:

2008	
MACRS {[($20,000 × .50) + ($10,000 × .20)] × .80	
(limited to $11,060) × .80}	$ 8,848
Straight-line [($20,000 × .10 × .80)	
(limited to $3,060) × .80]	(1,600)
Excess	$ 7,248
2009	
MACRS [($10,000 × .32 × .70)	
(limited to $4,900) × .70]	$ 2,240
Straight-line [($20,000 × .20 × .70)	
(limited to $4,900) × .70]	(2,800)
Excess	$ (560)

---

[30]§ 280F(b)(1).

[31]§ 280F(b)(2).

2010	
2008 excess	$7,248
2009 excess	(560)
Ordinary income recapture	$6,688

■

After the business usage of the listed property drops below the more-than-50 percent level, the straight-line method must be used for the remaining life of the property.

EXAMPLE 31

Assume the same facts as in Example 30. Seth's cost recovery allowance for the years 2010 and 2011 would be $1,140 and $1,065, computed as follows:

2010—$1,140   [($20,000 × 20% × .40) limited to $2,850 × 40%]
2011—$1,065   [($20,000 × 20% × .60) limited to $1,775 × 60%]

■

Leased Automobiles. A taxpayer who leases a passenger automobile must report an *inclusion amount* in gross income. The inclusion amount is computed from an IRS table for each taxable year for which the taxpayer leases the automobile. The purpose of this provision is to prevent taxpayers from circumventing the cost recovery dollar limitations by leasing, instead of purchasing, an automobile.

The dollar amount of the inclusion is based on the fair market value of the automobile and is prorated for the number of days the auto is used during the taxable year. The prorated dollar amount is then multiplied by the business and income-producing usage percentage to determine the amount to be included in gross income.[32] The taxpayer deducts the lease payments, multiplied by the business and income-producing usage percentage. The net effect is that the annual deduction for the lease payment is reduced by the inclusion amount.

EXAMPLE 32

On April 1, 2008, Jim leases and places in service a passenger automobile worth $40,000. The lease is to be for a period of five years. During the taxable years 2008 and 2009, Jim uses the automobile 70% for business and 30% for personal use. Assuming the dollar amounts from the IRS table for 2008 and 2009 are $166 and $363, Jim must include $87 in gross income for 2008 and $254 for 2009, computed as follows:

2008 $166 × (275/366) × 70% = $87
2009 $363 × (365/365) × 70% = $254

In addition, Jim can deduct 70% of the lease payments each year because this is the business use percentage. ■

Substantiation Requirements. Listed property is now subject to the substantiation requirements of § 274. This means that the taxpayer must prove the business usage as to the amount of expense or use, the time and place of use, the business purpose for the use, and the business relationship to the taxpayer of persons using the property. Substantiation requires adequate records or sufficient evidence corroborating the taxpayer's statement. However, these substantiation requirements do not apply to vehicles that, by reason of their nature, are not likely to be used more than a *de minimis* amount for personal purposes.[33]

[32]Reg. § 1.280F–7(a).   [33]§§ 274(d) and (i).

ETHICAL and EQUITABLE Considerations   SUBSTANTIATION REQUIREMENTS

Aaron is employed as an outside sales representative by a company that provides payroll services to businesses. Aaron drives his car to visit existing and potential customers in his sales territory, which consists of New Hampshire and Vermont. His home is 70 miles round trip from the company office. Aaron estimates that he uses his car 70 percent for business and 30 percent for personal use. He is planning on calculating his business mileage expense by reviewing the odometer of his automobile and taking 70 percent of the miles driven during the year as business miles. Evaluate the appropriateness of Aaron's plan.

LO.5

Determine when and how to use the alternative depreciation system (ADS).

Alternative Depreciation System (ADS)

The **alternative depreciation system (ADS)** must be used for the following:[34]

- To calculate the portion of depreciation treated as an alternative minimum tax (AMT) adjustment for purposes of the corporate and individual AMT (see Chapters 12 and 20).[35]
- To compute depreciation allowances for property for which any of the following is true:
  - Used predominantly outside the United States.
  - Leased or otherwise used by a tax-exempt entity.
  - Financed with the proceeds of tax-exempt bonds.
  - Imported from foreign countries that maintain discriminatory trade practices or otherwise engage in discriminatory acts.
- To compute depreciation allowances for earnings and profits purposes (see Chapter 20).

In general, ADS depreciation is computed using straight-line recovery without regard to salvage value. However, for purposes of the AMT, depreciation of personal property is computed using the 150 percent declining-balance method with an appropriate switch to the straight-line method.

The taxpayer must use the half-year or the mid-quarter convention, whichever is applicable, for all property other than eligible real estate. The mid-month convention is used for eligible real estate. The applicable ADS rates are found in Tables 8–4, 8–5, and 8–7.

The recovery periods under ADS are as follows:[36]

- The ADR midpoint life for property that does not fall into any of the following listed categories.
- Five years for qualified technological equipment, automobiles, and light-duty trucks.
- Twelve years for personal property with no class life.
- Forty years for all residential rental property and all nonresidential real property.

Taxpayers may *elect* to use the 150 percent declining-balance method to compute the regular income tax rather than the 200 percent declining-balance method that is available for personal property. Hence, if the election is made, there will be

---

[34]§ 168(g).

[35]This AMT adjustment applies for real and personal property placed in service before January 1, 1999. However, it will continue to apply for personal property placed in service after December 31, 1998, if the taxpayer uses the

200% declining-balance method for regular income tax purposes. See Chapter 12.

[36]The class life for certain properties described in § 168(e)(3) is specially determined under § 168(g)(3)(B).

CONCEPT SUMMARY 8–4

Listed Property Cost Recovery

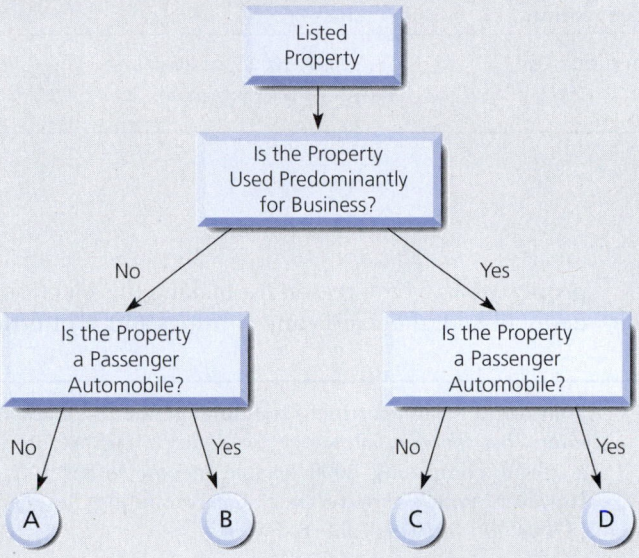

Legend to Tax Treatment

A Straight-line cost recovery reduced by the personal use percentage.
B Straight-line cost recovery subject to the recovery limitations ($3,060, $4,900, $2,850, $1,775) and reduced by the personal use percentage.
C Statutory percentage cost recovery reduced by the personal use percentage.
D Statutory percentage cost recovery subject to the recovery limitations ($11,060 or $3,060, $4,900, $2,850, $1,775) and reduced by the personal use percentage.

no difference between the cost recovery for computing the regular income tax and the AMT.[37]

EXAMPLE 33

On March 1, 2008, Abby purchases computer-based telephone central office switching equipment for $80,000. If Abby uses statutory percentage cost recovery and elects not to take additional first-year depreciation (assuming no § 179 election), the cost recovery allowance for 2008 is $16,000 [$80,000 × 20% (Table 8–1, five-year class property)]. If Abby elects to use ADS 150% declining-balance cost recovery for the regular income tax (assuming no § 179 election), the cost recovery allowance for 2008 is $12,000 [$80,000 × 15% (Table 8–4, five-year class property)]. ■

If the taxpayer takes the 50 percent additional first-year depreciation, there is no AMT adjustment associated with the additional depreciation for the entire recovery period of the property.[38]

In lieu of depreciation under the regular MACRS method, taxpayers may *elect* straight-line under ADS for property that qualifies for the regular MACRS method. The election is available on a class-by-class and year-by-year basis for property other than eligible real estate. The election for eligible real estate is on a property-by-

---

[37]For personal property placed in service before January 1, 1999, taxpayers making the election are required to use the ADS recovery periods in com-

puting cost recovery for the regular income tax. The ADS recovery periods generally are longer than the regular recovery periods under MACRS.
[38]§ 168(k)(2)(G).

CONCEPT SUMMARY 8–5

Characteristics of ACRS

Property	Accounting Convention	Life	Method
Personalty	Half-year or mid-quarter	3, 5, 7, 10, 15, or 20 years	Accelerated or straight-line
Realty	Mid-month	15, 18, or 19 years	Accelerated or straight-line

property basis. One reason for making this election is to avoid a difference between deductible depreciation and earnings and profits depreciation.

EXAMPLE 34

Polly acquires an apartment building on March 17, 2008, for $700,000. She takes the maximum cost recovery allowance for determining taxable income. Polly's cost recovery allowance for computing 2008 taxable income is $20,153 [$700,000 × .02879 (Table 8–6)]. However, Polly's cost recovery for computing her earnings and profits is only $13,853 [$700,000 × .01979 (Table 8–7)]. ■

LO.6

Be aware of the major characteristics of ACRS.

Accelerated Cost Recovery System (ACRS)

The major characteristics of the **accelerated cost recovery system (ACRS)** are listed in Concept Summary 8–5. Note that for personalty, except for 20-year property, the recovery period expired (all of the cost recovery basis has been recovered) prior to 2005. For 20-year property, the recovery period expired during 2005. For realty, the recovery period also expired during 2005.

LO.7

Identify intangible assets that are eligible for amortization and calculate the amount of the deduction.

Amortization

Taxpayers can claim an **amortization** deduction on intangible assets called "amortizable § 197 intangibles." The amount of the deduction is determined by amortizing the adjusted basis of such intangibles ratably over a 15-year period beginning in the month in which the intangible is acquired.[39]

An *amortizable § 197 intangible* is any § 197 intangible acquired after August 10, 1993, and held in connection with the conduct of a trade or business or for the production of income. Section 197 intangibles include goodwill and going-concern value, franchises, trademarks, and trade names. Covenants not to compete, copyrights, and patents are also included if they are acquired in connection with the acquisition of a business. Generally, self-created intangibles are not § 197 intangibles. The 15-year amortization period applies regardless of the actual useful life of an amortizable § 197 intangible. No other depreciation or amortization deduction is permitted with respect to any amortizable § 197 intangible except those permitted under the 15-year amortization rules.

EXAMPLE 35

On June 1, 2008, Neil purchased and began operating the Falcon Café. Of the purchase price, $90,000 is correctly allocated to goodwill. The deduction for amortization for 2008 is $3,500 [($90,000/15) × (7/12)]. ■

[39]§ 197(a).

ETHICAL and EQUITABLE Considerations

ALLOCATION OF PURCHASE PRICE TO COVENANT NOT TO COMPETE

Red Corporation and Bernie Jones, an officer of the corporation, signed an agreement that called for $400,000 to be paid to Bernie for the redemption of his stock in Red Corporation and for a covenant not to compete. When Bernie and the corporation negotiated the agreement, neither side called for the $400,000 to be allocated between the stock and the covenant not to compete. The agreement itself specifically stated that the amount to be paid was for the purchase of Bernie's stock. Nothing in the agreement allocated a portion of the payment to the covenant not to compete. Now that the transaction has been completed, Red Corporation is considering unilaterally allocating a portion of the payment to the covenant not to compete so that the allocated amount can be capitalized and amortized under § 197. Evaluate the appropriateness of Red Corporation's plan.

Startup expenditures are also partially amortizable under § 195. This treatment is available only by election.[40] A taxpayer must make this election no later than the time prescribed by law for filing the return for the taxable year in which the trade or business begins.[41] If no election is made, the startup expenditures must be capitalized.[42]

The elective treatment for startup expenditures allows the taxpayer to deduct the lesser of (1) the amount of startup expenditures with respect to the trade or business or (2) $5,000, reduced, but not below zero, by the amount by which the startup expenditures exceed $50,000. Any startup expenditures not deducted may be amortized ratably over a 180-month period beginning in the month in which the trade or business begins.[43]

EXAMPLE 36

Green Corporation begins business on August 1, 2008. The corporation has startup expenditures of $47,000. If Green Corporation elects § 195, the total amount of startup expenditures that Green Corporation may deduct in 2008 is $6,167, computed as follows:

Deductible amount	$5,000
Amortizable amount {[($47,000 − $5,000)/180] × 5 months}	1,167
Total deduction	$6,167 ∎

EXAMPLE 37

Assume the same facts as in Example 36, except that the startup expenditures are $53,000. The total deduction for the year 2008 is $3,417, computed as follows:

Deductible amount [$5,000 − ($53,000 − $50,000)]	$2,000
Amortizable amount {[($53,000 − $2,000)/180] × 5 months}	1,417
Total deduction	$3,417 ∎

Expenditures that are subject to capitalization and elective amortization under § 195 as startup expenditures generally must satisfy two requirements.[44] First, the expenditures must be paid or incurred in connection with any one of the following:

- The creation of an active trade or business.
- The investigation of the creation or acquisition of an active trade or business.
- Any activity engaged in for profit in anticipation of such activity becoming an active trade or business.

---

[40] § 195(b).
[41] § 195(d).
[42] § 195(a).

[43] § 195(b)(1)(A) and (B).
[44] § 195(c)(1)(A) and (B).

Second, such costs must be the kinds of costs that would be currently deductible if paid or incurred in connection with the operation of an existing trade or business in the same field as that entered into by the taxpayer.

The costs of creating a new active trade or business could include advertising; salaries and wages; travel and other expenses incurred in lining up prospective distributors, suppliers, or customers; and salaries and fees for executives, consultants, and professional services. Costs that relate to either created or acquired businesses could include expenses incurred for the analysis or survey of potential markets, products, labor supply, transportation facilities, and the like. Startup expenditures do not include any amount with respect to which a deduction is allowable under § 163(a) (interest), § 164 (taxes), and § 174 (research and experimental expenditures).[45]

Other assets that could be subject to amortization include research and experimental expenditures under § 174 (see Chapter 7) and organization expenses under § 248 (see Chapter 20).

Depletion

LO.8

Determine the amount of depletion expense including being able to apply the alternative tax treatments for intangible drilling and development costs.

Natural resources (e.g., oil, gas, coal, gravel, timber) are subject to **depletion**, which is simply a form of depreciation applicable to natural resources. Land generally cannot be depleted.

The owner of an interest in the natural resource is entitled to deduct depletion. An owner is one who has an economic interest in the property.[46] An economic interest requires the acquisition of an interest in the resource in place and the receipt of income from the extraction or severance of that resource. Like depreciation, depletion is a deduction *for* adjusted gross income.

Although all natural resources are subject to depletion, oil and gas wells are used as an example in the following paragraphs to illustrate the related costs and issues.

In developing an oil or gas well, the producer must make four types of expenditures:

- Natural resource costs.
- Intangible drilling and development costs.
- Tangible asset costs.
- Operating costs.

Natural resources are physically limited, and the costs to acquire them (e.g., oil under the ground) are, therefore, recovered through depletion. Costs incurred in making the property ready for drilling such as the cost of labor in clearing the property, erecting derricks, and drilling the hole are **intangible drilling and development costs (IDC)**. These costs generally have no salvage value and are a lost cost if the well is dry. Costs for tangible assets such as tools, pipes, and engines are capital in nature. These costs must be capitalized and recovered through depreciation (cost recovery). Costs incurred after the well is producing are operating costs. These costs would include expenditures for such items as labor, fuel, and supplies. Operating costs are deductible when incurred (on the accrual basis) or when paid (on the cash basis).

The expenditures for depreciable assets and operating costs pose no unusual problems for producers of natural resources. The tax treatment of depletable costs and intangible drilling and development costs is quite a different matter.

---

[45]§ 195(c).   [46]Reg. § 1.611–1(b).

TAX *in the News*	DEPLETION OF LANDFILL SITES

Landfill operators are allowed a depletion allowance, which is a deduction in computing Federal taxable income. The depletion deduction is the value of the air space that is being filled up. The value of the air space is the product of some of the goodwill costs, some of the land costs, and all of the engineering, siting, and construction costs.

Intangible Drilling and Development Costs (IDC)

Intangible drilling and development costs can be handled in one of two ways at the option of the taxpayer. They can be *either* charged off as an expense in the year in which they are incurred *or* capitalized and written off through depletion. The taxpayer makes the election in the first year such expenditures are incurred either by taking a deduction on the return or by adding them to the depletable basis. No formal statement of intent is required. Once made, the election is binding on both the taxpayer and the IRS for all such expenditures in the future. If the taxpayer fails to make the election to expense IDC on the original timely filed return the first year such expenditures are incurred, an automatic election to capitalize them has been made and is irrevocable.

As a general rule, it is more advantageous to expense IDC. The obvious benefit of an immediate write-off (as opposed to a deferred write-off through depletion) is not the only advantage. Since a taxpayer can use percentage depletion, which is calculated without reference to basis (see Example 41), the IDC may be completely lost as a deduction if they are capitalized.

Depletion Methods

There are two methods of calculating depletion: cost and percentage. Cost depletion can be used on any wasting asset (and is the only method allowed for timber). Percentage depletion is subject to a number of limitations, particularly for oil and gas deposits. Depletion should be calculated both ways, and generally the method that results in the *larger* deduction is used. The choice between cost and percentage depletion is an annual election.

Cost Depletion. **Cost depletion** is determined by using the adjusted basis of the asset.[47] The basis is divided by the estimated recoverable units of the asset (e.g., barrels, tons) to arrive at the depletion per unit. The depletion per unit then is multiplied by the number of units sold (*not* the units produced) during the year to arrive at the cost depletion allowed. Cost depletion, therefore, resembles the units-of-production method of calculating depreciation.

EXAMPLE 38

On January 1, 2008, Pablo purchases the rights to a mineral interest for $1 million. At that time, the remaining recoverable units in the mineral interest are estimated to be 200,000. The depletion per unit is $5 [$1,000,000 (adjusted basis) ÷ 200,000 (estimated recoverable units)]. If during the year 60,000 units are mined and 25,000 are sold, the cost depletion is $125,000 [$5 (depletion per unit) × 25,000 (units sold)]. ■

If the taxpayer later discovers that the original estimate was incorrect, the depletion per unit for future calculations must be redetermined based on the revised estimate.[48]

---

[47]§ 612.   [48]§ 611(a).

| EXHIBIT 8–3 | Sample of Percentage Depletion Rates |

22% Depletion

Cobalt	Sulfur
Lead	Tin
Nickel	Uranium
Platinum	Zinc

15% Depletion

Copper	Oil and gas
Gold	Oil shale
Iron	Silver

14% Depletion

Borax	Magnesium carbonates
Calcium carbonates	Marble
Granite	Potash
Limestone	Slate

10% Depletion

Coal	Perlite
Lignite	Sodium chloride

5% Depletion

Gravel	Pumice
Peat	Sand

EXAMPLE 39

Assume the same facts as in Example 38. In 2009, Pablo realizes that an incorrect estimate was made. The remaining recoverable units now are determined to be 400,000. Based on this new information, the revised depletion per unit is $2.1875 [$875,000 (adjusted basis) ÷ 400,000 (estimated recoverable units)]. Note that the adjusted basis is the original cost ($1,000,000) reduced by the depletion claimed in 2008 ($125,000). If 30,000 units are sold in 2009, the depletion for the year is $65,625 [$2.1875 (depletion per unit) × 30,000 (units sold)]. ∎

Percentage Depletion. **Percentage depletion** (also referred to as statutory depletion) is a specified percentage provided for in the Code. The percentage varies according to the type of mineral interest involved. A sample of these percentages is shown in Exhibit 8–3. The rate is applied to the gross income from the property, but in no event may percentage depletion exceed 50 percent of the taxable income from the property before the allowance for depletion.[49]

EXAMPLE 40

Assuming gross income of $100,000, a depletion rate of 22%, and other expenses relating to the property of $60,000, the depletion allowance is determined as follows:

---

[49]§ 613(a). Special rules apply for certain oil and gas wells under § 613A (e.g., the 50% ceiling is replaced with a 100% ceiling, and the percentage depletion may not exceed 65% of the taxpayer's taxable income from all sources before the allowance for depletion).

TAX *in the News*	DEPLETION FOR MARGINAL OIL AND GAS WELLS

The Energy Advancement and Investment Act of 2007, under consideration by the Senate Finance Committee, would extend for two years (through December 31, 2009) the sus-pension on the taxable income limit for purposes of depleting a marginal oil or gas well.

Source: *Adapted from "Senator Charles Grassley: Energy Tax Package,"* States News Service, *June 14, 2007.*

Gross income	$100,000
Less: Other expenses	(60,000)
Taxable income before depletion	$ 40,000
Depletion allowance [the lesser of $22,000 (22% × $100,000) or $20,000 (50% × $40,000)]	(20,000)
Taxable income after depletion	$ 20,000

The adjusted basis of the property is reduced by $20,000, the depletion allowed. If the other expenses had been only $55,000, the full $22,000 could have been deducted, and the adjusted basis would have been reduced by $22,000. ■

Note that percentage depletion is based on a percentage of the gross income from the property and makes no reference to cost. Thus, when percentage depletion is used, it is possible to deduct more than the original cost of the property. If percentage depletion is used, however, the adjusted basis of the property (for computing cost depletion) must be reduced by the amount of percentage depletion taken until the adjusted basis reaches zero.

Effect of Intangible Drilling Costs on Depletion.

The treatment of IDC has an effect on the depletion deduction in two ways. If the costs are capitalized, the basis for cost depletion is increased. As a consequence, the cost depletion is increased. If IDC are expensed, they reduce the taxable income from the property. This reduction may result in application of the provision that limits depletion to 50 percent (100 percent for certain oil and gas wells) of taxable income before deducting depletion.

EXAMPLE 41

Iris purchased the rights to an oil interest for $1 million. The recoverable barrels were estimated to be 200,000. During the year, 50,000 barrels were sold for $2 million. Regular expenses amounted to $800,000, and IDC were $650,000. If the IDC are capitalized, the depletion per unit is $8.25 ($1,000,000 + $650,000 ÷ 200,000 barrels), and the following taxable income results:

Gross income	$2,000,000
Less: Expenses	(800,000)
Taxable income before depletion	$1,200,000
Cost depletion ($8.25 × 50,000) = $412,500	
Percentage depletion (15% × $2,000,000) = $300,000	
Greater of cost or percentage depletion	(412,500)
Taxable income	$ 787,500

If the IDC are expensed, the taxable income is $250,000, calculated as follows:

Gross income	$ 2,000,000
Less: Expenses, including IDC	(1,450,000)
Taxable income before depletion	$ 550,000
Cost depletion [($1,000,000 ÷ 200,000 barrels) × 50,000 barrels] = $250,000	
Percentage depletion (15% of $2,000,000 = $300,000, limited to 100% of $550,000 taxable income before depletion) = $300,000	
Greater of cost or percentage depletion	(300,000)
Taxable income	$ 250,000

For further restrictions on the use or availability of the percentage depletion method, see § 613.

LO.9

Perform the reporting procedures for cost recovery.

Reporting Procedures

Sole proprietors engaged in a business should file a Schedule C, Profit or Loss from Business, to accompany Form 1040. Schedule C for 2007 is presented because the 2008 form was not yet available.

The top part of page 1 requests certain key information about the taxpayer (e.g., name, address, Social Security number, principal business activity, and the accounting method used). Part I provides for the reporting of items of income. If the business requires the use of inventories and the computation of cost of goods sold (see Chapter 18 for when this is necessary), Part III must be completed and the cost of goods sold amount transferred to line 4 of Part I.

Part II allows for the reporting of deductions. Some of the deductions discussed in this chapter and their location on the form are depletion (line 12) and depreciation (line 13). Other expenses (line 27) include those items not already covered (see lines 8–26). An example would be research and experimental expenditures.

If depreciation is claimed, it should be supported by completing Form 4562. Form 4562 for 2007 is presented because the 2008 form was not yet available. The amount listed on line 22 of Form 4562 is then transferred to line 13 of Part II of Schedule C.

EXAMPLE 42

Thomas Andrews, Social Security number 123–45–6789, was employed as an accountant until May 2007, when he opened his own practice. His address is 279 Mountain View, Ogden, UT 84201. Andrews keeps his books on the cash basis and had the following revenue and business expenses in 2007:

a.   Revenue from accounting practice, $192,000.
b.   Insurance, $5,000.
c.   Office supplies, $4,000.
d.   Office rent, $16,000.
e.   Copier lease payments, $3,000.
f.   Licenses, $2,000.
g.   New furniture and fixtures were acquired on May 10, for $142,000. Thomas elects § 179 expensing and uses the statutory percentage cost recovery method.

Andrews would report the above information on Schedule C and Form 4562 as illustrated on the following pages. ■

Form **4562**	**Depreciation and Amortization**	OMB No. 1545-0172
Department of the Treasury Internal Revenue Service	**(Including Information on Listed Property)** " See separate instructions. " Attach to your tax return.	**20**07 Attachment Sequence No. **67**

Name(s) shown on return	Business or activity to which this form relates	Identifying number
Thomas Andrews	*Accounting services*	*123 45 6789*

Part I **Election To Expense Certain Property Under Section 179**
Note: *If you have any listed property, complete Part V before you complete Part I.*

1	Maximum amount. See the instructions for a higher limit for certain businesses	**1**	*$125,000*
2	Total cost of section 179 property placed in service (see instructions)	**2**	*142,000*
3	Threshold cost of section 179 property before reduction in limitation	**3**	*$500,000*
4	Reduction in limitation. Subtract line 3 from line 2. If zero or less, enter -0-	**4**	*-0-*
5	Dollar limitation for tax year. Subtract line 4 from line 1. If zero or less, enter -0-. If married filing separately, see instructions	**5**	*125,000*

(a) Description of property	(b) Cost (business use only)	(c) Elected cost	
6 *Furniture and Fixtures*	*142,000*	*125,000*	

7	Listed property. Enter the amount from line 29 . . . . **7**		
8	Total elected cost of section 179 property. Add amounts in column (c), lines 6 and 7 . . .	**8**	*125,000*
9	Tentative deduction. Enter the **smaller** of line 5 or line 8.	**9**	*125,000*
10	Carryover of disallowed deduction from line 13 of your 2006 Form 4562	**10**	*-0-*
11	Business income limitation. Enter the smaller of business income (not less than zero) or line 5 (see instructions)	**11**	*125,000*
12	Section 179 expense deduction. Add lines 9 and 10, but do not enter more than line 11 . .	**12**	*125,000*
13	Carryover of disallowed deduction to 2008. Add lines 9 and 10, less line 12 " **13**		

Note: *Do not use Part II or Part III below for listed property. Instead, use Part V.*

Part II **Special Depreciation Allowance and Other Depreciation (Do not** include listed property.**)** (See instructions.)

14	Special allowance for qualified New York Liberty or Gulf Opportunity Zone property (other than listed property) and cellulosic biomass ethanol plant property placed in service during the tax year (see instructions)	**14**	
15	Property subject to section 168(f)(1) election	**15**	
16	Other depreciation (including ACRS)	**16**	

Part III **MACRS Depreciation (Do not** include listed property.**)** (See instructions.)

Section A

17	MACRS deductions for assets placed in service in tax years beginning before 2007 . . .	**17**	
18	If you are electing to group any assets placed in service during the tax year into one or more general asset accounts, check here . . . . " ☐		

Section B—Assets Placed in Service During 2007 Tax Year Using the General Depreciation System

(a) Classification of property	(b) Month and year placed in service	(c) Basis for depreciation (business/investment use only—see instructions)	(d) Recovery period	(e) Convention	(f) Method	(g) Depreciation deduction
19a 3-year property						
b 5-year property		*17,000*	*7- year*	*HY*	*200DB*	*2,429*
c 7-year property						
d 10-year property						
e 15-year property						
f 20-year property						
g 25-year property			25 yrs.		S/L	
h Residential rental property			27.5 yrs.	MM	S/L	
			27.5 yrs.	MM	S/L	
i Nonresidential real property			39 yrs.	MM	S/L	
				MM	S/L	

Section C—Assets Placed in Service During 2007 Tax Year Using the Alternative Depreciation System

20a Class life					S/L	
b 12-year			12 yrs.		S/L	
c 40-year			40 yrs.	MM	S/L	

Part IV **Summary** (see instructions)

21	Listed property. Enter amount from line 28	**21**	
22	**Total.** Add amounts from line 12, lines 14 through 17, lines 19 and 20 in column (g), and line 21. Enter here and on the appropriate lines of your return. Partnerships and S corporations—see instr.	**22**	*127,429*
23	For assets shown above and placed in service during the current year, enter the portion of the basis attributable to section 263A costs . **23**		

For Paperwork Reduction Act Notice, see separate instructions.   Cat. No. 12906N   Form **4562** (2007)

SCHEDULE C
(Form 1040)

Department of the Treasury
Internal Revenue Service   (99)

Profit or Loss From Business
(Sole Proprietorship)

▶ **Partnerships, joint ventures, etc., must file Form 1065 or 1065-B.**

▶ **Attach to Form 1040, 1040NR, or 1041.**   ▶ **See Instructions for Schedule C (Form 1040).**

OMB No. 1545-0074

2007

Attachment
Sequence No. **09**

Name of proprietor	Social security number (SSN)
Thomas Andrews	123 45 6789

A Principal business or profession, including product or service (see page C-2 of the instructions)

B Enter code from pages C-8, 9, & 10
▶

C Business name. If no separate business name, leave blank.
Andrews Accounting Services

D Employer ID number (EIN), if any

E Business address (including suite or room no.) ▶ *279 Mountain View*
City, town or post office, state, and ZIP code   *Ogden, UT 84201*

F Accounting method: **(1)** ☒ Cash   **(2)** ☐ Accrual   **(3)** ☐ Other (specify) ▶ ....

G Did you "materially participate" in the operation of this business during 2007? If "No," see page C-3 for limit on losses   ☒ **Yes**   ☐ **No**

H If you started or acquired this business during 2007, check here . . . . ▶ ☐

Part I   Income

1	Gross receipts or sales. **Caution.** If this income was reported to you on Form W-2 and the "Statutory employee" box on that form was checked, see page C-3 and check here ▶ ☐	1	192,000
2	Returns and allowances	2	
3	Subtract line 2 from line 1	3	192,000
4	Cost of goods sold (from line 42 on page 2)	4	
5	**Gross profit.** Subtract line 4 from line 3	5	192,000
6	Other income, including federal and state gasoline or fuel tax credit or refund (see page C-3)	6	
7	**Gross income.** Add lines 5 and 6 ▶	7	192,000

Part II   Expenses. Enter expenses for business use of your home **only** on line 30.

8	Advertising	8	18	Office expense	4,000
9	Car and truck expenses (see page C-4)	9	19	Pension and profit-sharing plans	
10	Commissions and fees	10	20	Rent or lease (see page C-5):	
11	Contract labor (see page C-4)	11	20a	**a** Vehicles, machinery, and equipment	3,000
12	Depletion	12	20b	**b** Other business property	16,000
13	Depreciation and section 179 expense deduction (not included in Part III) (see page C-4)	13 127,429	21	Repairs and maintenance	
			22	Supplies (not included in Part III)	
			23	Taxes and licenses	2,000
14	Employee benefit programs (other than on line 19)	14	24	Travel, meals, and entertainment:	
			24a	**a** Travel	
15	Insurance (other than health)	15 5,000	24b	**b** Deductible meals and entertainment (see page C-6)	
16	Interest:		25	Utilities	
a	Mortgage (paid to banks, etc.)	16a	26	Wages (less employment credits)	
b	Other	16b	27	Other expenses (from line 48 on page 2)	
17	Legal and professional services	17			

28	**Total expenses** before expenses for business use of home. Add lines 8 through 27 in columns ▶	28	157,429
29	Tentative profit (loss). Subtract line 28 from line 7	29	34,571
30	Expenses for business use of your home. Attach **Form 8829**	30	
31	**Net profit or (loss).** Subtract line 30 from line 29. • If a profit, enter on both **Form 1040, line 12,** and **Schedule SE, line 2,** or on **Form 1040NR, line 13** (statutory employees, see page C-7). Estates and trusts, enter on Form 1041, line 3. • If a loss, you **must** go to line 32.	31	34,571

32 If you have a loss, check the box that describes your investment in this activity (see page C-7).

• If you checked 32a, enter the loss on both **Form 1040, line 12,** and **Schedule SE, line 2,** or on **Form 1040NR, line 13** (statutory employees, see page C-7). Estates and trusts, enter on Form 1041, line 3.

• If you checked 32b, you **must** attach **Form 6198.** Your loss may be limited.

32a ☐ All investment is at risk.
32b ☐ Some investment is not at risk.

For Paperwork Reduction Act Notice, see page C-8 of the instructions.	Cat. No. 11334P	Schedule C (Form 1040) 2007

Cost Recovery

Cost recovery schedules should be reviewed annually for possible retirements, abandonments, and obsolescence.

EXAMPLE 43

An examination of the cost recovery schedule of Eagle Company reveals the following:

- Asset A was abandoned when it was discovered that the cost of repairs would be in excess of the cost of replacement. Asset A had an adjusted basis of $3,000.
- Asset J became obsolete this year, at which point, its adjusted basis was $8,000.

Assets A and J should be written off for an additional expense of $11,000 ($3,000 + $8,000). ■

Because of the deductions for cost recovery, interest, and ad valorem property taxes, investments in real estate can be highly attractive. In figuring the economics of such investments, one should be sure to take into account any tax savings that result.

> **LO.10**
>
> Identify tax planning opportunities for cost recovery, amortization, and depletion.

EXAMPLE 44

In early January 2007, Vern purchased residential rental property for $170,000 (of which $20,000 was allocated to the land and $150,000 to the building). Vern made a down payment of $25,000 and assumed the seller's mortgage for the balance. Under the mortgage agreement, monthly payments of $1,000 are required and are applied toward interest, taxes, insurance, and principal. Since the property was already occupied, Vern continued to receive rent of $1,200 per month from the tenant. Vern actively participates in this activity and hence comes under the special rule for a rental real estate activity with respect to the limitation on passive activity losses (refer to Chapter 11). Vern is in the 33% tax bracket.

During 2008, Vern's expenses were as follows:

Interest	$10,000
Taxes	800
Insurance	1,000
Repairs and maintenance	2,200
Depreciation ($150,000 × .03636)	5,454
Total	$19,454

The deductible loss from the rental property is computed as follows:

Rent income ($1,200 × 12 months)	$ 14,400
Less expenses (see above)	(19,454)
Net loss	($ 5,054)

But what is Vern's overall position for the year when the tax benefit of the loss is taken into account? Considering just the cash intake and outlay, it is summarized below:

Intake—		
Rent income	$14,400	
Tax savings [33% (income tax bracket) × $5,054 (loss from the property)]	1,668	$ 16,068
Outlay—		
Mortgage payments ($1,000 × 12 months)	$12,000	
Repairs and maintenance	2,200	(14,200)
Net cash benefit		$ 1,868

■

It should be noted, however, that should Vern cease being an active participant in the rental activity, the passive activity loss rules would apply, and Vern could lose the current period benefit of the loss.

Another consideration when making decisions with respect to cost recovery is whether fast or slow cost recovery will be more beneficial for the taxpayer. If the taxpayer's goal is to recover the cost of fixed assets as quickly as possible, the following strategies should be used:

- When constructing a facility, try to avoid "fixture" classification. Refer to the discussion in Chapter 1 on page 1–6.
- When electing § 179 expensing, choose assets with longer lives.
- Choose accelerated cost recovery methods where available.

If a taxpayer has a new business with little income or a business with a net operating loss carryover, the taxpayer's goal may be to slow down cost recovery. In such a situation, the taxpayer should:

- Choose the straight-line cost recovery method.
- Make no election under § 179.
- Defer placing assets in service in the current tax year or postpone capital outlays until future tax years.

Amortization

When a business is purchased, goodwill and covenants not to compete are both subject to a statutory amortization period of 15 years. Therefore, the purchaser does not derive any tax benefits when part of the purchase price is assigned to a covenant rather than to goodwill.

Thus, from the purchaser's perspective, bargaining for a covenant should be based on legal rather than tax reasons. Note, however, that from the seller's perspective, goodwill is a capital asset and the covenant is an ordinary income asset.

Since the amortization period for both goodwill and a covenant is 15 years, the purchaser may want to attempt to minimize these amounts if the purchase price can be assigned to assets with shorter lives (e.g., inventory, receivables, and personalty). Conversely, the purchaser may want to attempt to maximize these amounts if part of the purchase price will otherwise be assigned to assets with longer recovery periods (e.g., realty) or to assets not eligible for cost recovery (e.g., land).

Depletion

Since the election to use the cost or percentage depletion method is an annual election, a taxpayer can use cost depletion (if higher) until the basis is exhausted and then switch to percentage depletion in the following years.

EXAMPLE 45

Assume the following facts for Melissa:

Remaining depletable basis	$ 11,000
Gross income (10,000 units)	100,000
Expenses (other than depletion)	30,000

Since cost depletion is limited to the basis of $11,000 and if the percentage depletion is $22,000 (assume a 22% rate), Melissa would choose the latter. Her basis is then reduced to zero. In future years, however, she can continue to take percentage depletion since percentage depletion is taken without reference to the remaining basis. ■

The election to expense intangible drilling and development costs is a onetime election. Once the election is made to either expense or capitalize the IDC, it is binding on all future expenditures. The permanent nature of the election makes it extremely important for the taxpayer to determine which treatment will provide the greater tax advantage. (Refer to Example 41 for an illustration of the effect of using the two different alternatives for a given set of facts.)

Cost Recovery Tables

Summary of Tables

Table 8–1	Modified ACRS statutory percentage table for personalty.
	Applicable depreciation methods: 200 or 150 percent declining-balance switching to straight-line.
	Applicable recovery periods: 3, 5, 7, 10, 15, 20 years.
	Applicable convention: half-year.
Table 8–2	Modified ACRS statutory percentage table for personalty.
	Applicable depreciation method: 200 percent declining-balance switching to straight-line.
	Applicable recovery periods: 3, 5, 7 years.
	Applicable convention: mid-quarter.
Table 8–3	Modified ACRS optional straight-line table for personalty.
	Applicable depreciation method: straight-line.
	Applicable recovery periods: 3, 5, 7, 10, 15, 20 years.
	Applicable convention: half-year.
Table 8–4	Alternative minimum tax declining-balance table for personalty.
	Applicable depreciation method: 150 percent declining-balance switching to straight-line.
	Applicable recovery periods: 3, 5, 7, 9.5, 10, 12 years.
	Applicable convention: half-year.
Table 8–5	Alternative depreciation system straight-line table for personalty.
	Applicable depreciation method: straight-line.
	Applicable recovery periods: 5, 10, 12 years.
	Applicable convention: half-year.
Table 8–6	Modified ACRS straight-line table for realty.
	Applicable depreciation method: straight-line.
	Applicable recovery periods: 27.5, 31.5, 39 years.
	Applicable convention: mid-month.
Table 8–7	Alternative depreciation system straight-line table for realty.
	Applicable depreciation method: straight-line.
	Applicable recovery period: 40 years.
	Applicable convention: mid-month.

| TABLE 8–1 | **MACRS Accelerated Depreciation for Personal Property Assuming Half-Year Convention** |

For Property Placed in Service after December 31, 1986

Recovery Year	3-Year (200% DB)	5-Year (200% DB)	7-Year (200% DB)	10-Year (200% DB)	15-Year (150% DB)	20-Year (150% DB)
1	33.33	20.00	14.29	10.00	5.00	3.750
2	44.45	32.00	24.49	18.00	9.50	7.219
3	14.81*	19.20	17.49	14.40	8.55	6.677
4	7.41	11.52*	12.49	11.52	7.70	6.177
5		11.52	8.93*	9.22	6.93	5.713
6		5.76	8.92	7.37	6.23	5.285
7			8.93	6.55*	5.90*	4.888
8			4.46	6.55	5.90	4.522
9				6.56	5.91	4.462*
10				6.55	5.90	4.461
11				3.28	5.91	4.462
12					5.90	4.461
13					5.91	4.462
14					5.90	4.461
15					5.91	4.462
16					2.95	4.461
17						4.462
18						4.461
19						4.462
20						4.461
21						2.231

* Switchover to straight-line depreciation.

| TABLE 8–2 | **MACRS Accelerated Depreciation for Personal Property Assuming Mid-Quarter Convention** |

For Property Placed in Service after December 31, 1986 (Partial Table*)

Recovery Year	First Quarter	3-Year Second Quarter	Third Quarter	Fourth Quarter
1	58.33	41.67	25.00	8.33
2	27.78	38.89	50.00	61.11

Recovery Year	First Quarter	5-Year Second Quarter	Third Quarter	Fourth Quarter
1	35.00	25.00	15.00	5.00
2	26.00	30.00	34.00	38.00

Recovery Year	First Quarter	7-Year Second Quarter	Third Quarter	Fourth Quarter
1	25.00	17.85	10.71	3.57
2	21.43	23.47	25.51	27.55

* The figures in this table are taken from the official tables that appear in Rev.Proc. 87–57, 1987–2 C.B. 687. Because of their length, the complete tables are not presented.

TABLE 8–3	**MACRS Straight-Line Depreciation for Personal Property Assuming Half-Year Convention***

For Property Placed in Service after December 31, 1986

MACRS Class	% First Recovery Year	Other Recovery Years Years	Other Recovery Years %	Last Recovery Year Year	Last Recovery Year %
3-year	16.67	2–3	33.33	4	16.67
5-year	10.00	2–5	20.00	6	10.00
7-year	7.14	2–7	14.29	8	7.14
10-year	5.00	2–10	10.00	11	5.00
15-year	3.33	2–15	6.67	16	3.33
20-year	2.50	2–20	5.00	21	2.50

*The official table contains a separate row for each year. For ease of presentation, certain years are grouped in this table. In some instances, this will produce a difference of .01 for the last digit when compared with the official table.

TABLE 8–4	**Alternative Minimum Tax: 150% Declining-Balance Assuming Half-Year Convention**

For Property Placed in Service after December 31, 1986 (Partial Table*)

Recovery Year	3-Year 150%	5-Year 150%	7-Year 150%	9.5-Year 150%	10-Year 150%	12-Year 150%
1	25.00	15.00	10.71	7.89	7.50	6.25
2	37.50	25.50	19.13	14.54	13.88	11.72
3	25.00**	17.85	15.03	12.25	11.79	10.25
4	12.50	16.66**	12.25**	10.31	10.02	8.97
5		16.66	12.25	9.17**	8.74**	7.85
6		8.33	12.25	9.17	8.74	7.33**
7			12.25	9.17	8.74	7.33
8			6.13	9.17	8.74	7.33
9				9.17	8.74	7.33
10				9.16	8.74	7.33
11					4.37	7.32
12						7.33
13						3.66

*The figures in this table are taken from the official table that appears in Rev.Proc. 87–57, 1987–2 C.B. 687. Because of its length, the complete table is not presented.
**Switchover to straight-line depreciation.

TABLE 8–5	ADS Straight-Line for Personal Property Assuming Half-Year Convention

For Property Placed in Service after December 31, 1986 (Partial Table)*

Recovery Year	5-Year Class	10-Year Class	12-Year Class
1	10.00	5.00	4.17
2	20.00	10.00	8.33
3	20.00	10.00	8.33
4	20.00	10.00	8.33
5	20.00	10.00	8.33
6	10.00	10.00	8.33
7		10.00	8.34
8		10.00	8.33
9		10.00	8.34
10		10.00	8.33
11		5.00	8.34
12			8.33
13			4.17

*The figures in this table are taken from the official table that appears in Rev.Proc. 87–57, 1987–2 C.B. 687. Because of its length, the complete table is not presented. The tables for the mid-quarter convention also appear in Rev.Proc. 87–57.

TABLE 8–6	MACRS Straight-Line Depreciation for Real Property Assuming Mid-Month Convention*

For Property Placed in Service after December 31, 1986: 27.5-Year Residential Real Property

Recovery Year(s)	The Applicable Percentage Is (Use the Column for the Month in the First Year the Property Is Placed in Service):											
	1	2	3	4	5	6	7	8	9	10	11	12
1	3.485	3.182	2.879	2.576	2.273	1.970	1.667	1.364	1.061	0.758	0.455	0.152
2–18	3.636	3.636	3.636	3.636	3.636	3.636	3.636	3.636	3.636	3.636	3.636	3.636
19–27	3.637	3.637	3.637	3.637	3.637	3.637	3.637	3.637	3.637	3.637	3.637	3.637
28	1.970	2.273	2.576	2.879	3.182	3.485	3.636	3.636	3.636	3.636	3.636	3.636
29	0.000	0.000	0.000	0.000	0.000	0.000	0.152	0.455	0.758	1.061	1.364	1.667

For Property Placed in Service after December 31, 1986, and before May 13, 1993: 31.5-Year Nonresidential Real Property

Recovery Year(s)	The Applicable Percentage Is (Use the Column for the Month in the First Year the Property Is Placed in Service):											
	1	2	3	4	5	6	7	8	9	10	11	12
1	3.042	2.778	2.513	2.249	1.984	1.720	1.455	1.190	0.926	0.661	0.397	0.132
2–19	3.175	3.175	3.175	3.175	3.175	3.175	3.175	3.175	3.175	3.175	3.175	3.175
20–31	3.174	3.174	3.174	3.174	3.174	3.174	3.174	3.174	3.174	3.174	3.174	3.174
32	1.720	1.984	2.249	2.513	2.778	3.042	3.175	3.175	3.175	3.175	3.175	3.175
33	0.000	0.000	0.000	0.000	0.000	0.000	0.132	0.397	0.661	0.926	1.190	1.455

For Property Placed in Service after May 12, 1993: 39-Year Nonresidential Real Property

Recovery Year(s)	The Applicable Percentage Is (Use the Column for the Month in the First Year the Property Is Placed in Service):											
	1	2	3	4	5	6	7	8	9	10	11	12
1	2.461	2.247	2.033	1.819	1.605	1.391	1.177	0.963	0.749	0.535	0.321	0.107
2–39	2.564	2.564	2.564	2.564	2.564	2.564	2.564	2.564	2.564	2.564	2.564	2.564
40	0.107	0.321	0.535	0.749	0.963	1.177	1.391	1.605	1.819	2.033	2.247	2.461

* The official tables contain a separate row for each year. For ease of presentation, certain years are grouped in these tables. In some instances, this will produce a difference of .001 for the last digit when compared with the official tables.

TABLE 8–7	ADS Straight-Line for Real Property Assuming Mid-Month Convention

For Property Placed in Service after December 31, 1986

Recovery Year	Month Placed in Service											
	1	**2**	**3**	**4**	**5**	**6**	**7**	**8**	**9**	**10**	**11**	**12**
1	2.396	2.188	1.979	1.771	1.563	1.354	1.146	0.938	0.729	0.521	0.313	0.104
2–40	2.500	2.500	2.500	2.500	2.500	2.500	2.500	2.500	2.500	2.500	2.500	2.500
41	0.104	0.312	0.521	0.729	0.937	1.146	1.354	1.562	1.771	1.979	2.187	2.396

KEY TERMS

Accelerated cost recovery system (ACRS), 8–22

Additional first-year depreciation, 8-7

Alternative depreciation system (ADS), 8–20

Amortization, 8–22

Cost depletion, 8–25

Cost recovery, 8–2

Depletion, 8–24

Depreciation, 8–2

Half-year convention, 8–7

Intangible drilling and development costs (IDC), 8–24

Listed property, 8–15

Mid-month convention, 8–10

Mid-quarter convention, 8–9

Modified accelerated cost recovery system (MACRS), 8–4

Percentage depletion, 8–26

Residential rental real estate, 8–10

Section 179 expensing, 8–13

Startup expenditures, 8–23

PROBLEM MATERIALS

DISCUSSION QUESTIONS

1. Discuss the differences between depreciation and cost recovery.

2. If a taxpayer does not take any cost recovery on an asset during the year, what will be the impact on the basis of the asset?

3. Discuss why land is not eligible for cost recovery.

4. At the beginning of the current year, Henry purchased a ski resort for $10 million. Henry does not own the land on which the resort is located. The Federal government owns the land, and Henry has the right to operate the resort on the land pursuant to Special Use Permits, which are terminable at will by the Federal government, and Term Special Use Permits, which allow the land to be used for a fixed number of years. In preparing the income tax return for the current year, Henry properly allocated $2 million of the purchase price to the costs of constructing mountain roads, slopes, and trails. Since the acquisition, Henry has spent an additional $1 million on maintaining the mountain roads, slopes, and trails. Identify the relevant tax issues for Henry.

Issue ID

5. Discuss whether the purchase date of an asset is important in determining whether the mid-quarter convention applies for personalty.

6. Discuss the computation of cost recovery in the year an asset is placed in service when the half-year convention is used.

7. Discuss the computation of cost recovery in the year of sale of an asset when the half-year convention is being used.

8. Discuss whether the acquisition of real property affects the 40% test to determine whether the mid-quarter convention must be used.

9. Discuss the computation of cost recovery in the year of sale of an asset when the mid-quarter convention is being used.

10. Discuss the mid-month convention.

11. Discuss whether the mid-quarter convention applies if a taxpayer makes a straight-line election under MACRS.

12. Discuss the general cost recovery method for farming assets.

13. Discuss the cost recovery method for farming assets if an election is made to not have the uniform capitalization rules apply.

Issue ID

14. Jim owns a very large ranch. A large part of his business is the production and raising of breeding cattle. Jim understands that under MACRS he is entitled to cost recovery on breeding cattle. Identify the relevant tax issues for Jim with respect to taking cost recovery on his self-produced breeding cattle.

15. Discuss the cost recovery periods and methods to be used on leasehold improvement property owned by the lessor.

16. Discuss the cost recovery periods and methods to be used on leasehold improvement property owned by the lessee.

17. Discuss the tax treatment for the unrecovered basis in leasehold property owned by the lessee when the lease terminates.

18. Discuss whether § 179 expensing may be taken on an asset that a taxpayer acquires to help with her personal investments.

19. Explain how the § 179 limited expensing deduction affects the computation of MACRS cost recovery.

20. Discuss the treatment of a § 179 expensing carryforward.

21. Discuss the definition of *taxable income* as it is used in limiting the § 179 expensing amount.

Issue ID

22. Ana owns a motor home sales and rental business. During the current year, her rental fleet had a total of 33 motor homes, including a new Gulfstream Motor Home. The Gulfstream was purchased for $80,000 in July of the current year. The usual terms of the motor home rentals are much like those for car rentals—a daily or weekly fee, a daily mileage allowance of 100 miles, and a mileage charge of $.50 for each additional mile. Most renters use the motor homes for fewer than 30 days. Although the motor homes are rented out, they are also listed for sale. As such, any motor home can be sold at any time. Identify the relevant tax issues for Ana with respect to the new Gulfstream Motor Home.

23. Discuss the implications of an automobile used in a trade or business having a gross vehicle weight (GVW) exceeding 6,000 pounds.

24. Discuss how the limits on cost recovery for passenger automobiles apply to taxicabs.

25. Discuss the purpose of the lease inclusion amount and explain how it is determined with respect to leased passenger automobiles.

26. Explain the amortization period of a § 197 intangible if the actual useful life is less than 15 years.

Issue ID

27. Harold and Bart own 75% of the stock of Orange Motors. The other 25% of the stock is owned by Jeb. Orange Motors entered into an agreement with Harold and Bart to acquire all of their stock in Orange Motors. In addition, Harold and Bart signed a noncompete agreement with Orange Motors. Under the terms of the noncompete agreement, Orange will pay Harold and Bart $15,000 each per year for four years. Identify the relevant tax issues for Orange Motors.

28. Discuss the amortization of startup expenditures.

Issue ID

29. In May 2008, George began searching for a trade or business to acquire. In anticipation of finding a suitable aquisition, George hired an investment banker to evaluate three potential businesses. He also hired a law firm to begin drafting regulatory approval

documents for a target company. Eventually, George decided to purchase all the assets of Blue Corporation. Blue Corporation and George entered into an acquisition agreement on December 1, 2008. Identify the relevant tax issues for George.

30. Discuss how the cost of mineral rights enters into the calculation of percentage depletion.

PROBLEMS

31. On November 4, 2006, Blue Company acquired an asset (27.5-year residential real property) for $100,000 for use in its business. In 2006 and 2007, respectively, Blue took $321 and $2,564 of cost recovery. These amounts were incorrect because Blue applied the wrong percentages (i.e., those for 39-year rather than 27.5-year). Blue should have taken $455 and $3,636 cost recovery in 2006 and 2007. On January 1, 2008, the asset was sold for $98,000. Calculate the gain or loss on the sale of the asset in 2008.

32. José purchased a house for $175,000 in 2005. He used the house as his personal residence. In March 2008, when the fair market value of the house was $255,000, he converted the house to rental property. What is José's cost recovery for 2008?

33. Blue Corporation acquired new office furniture on August 15, 2008, for $150,000. Blue did not elect immediate expensing under § 179. Determine Blue's cost recovery for 2008.

34. Weston acquires a used office machine (seven-year class asset) on November 2, 2008, for $75,000. This is the only asset acquired by Weston during the year. He does not elect immediate expensing under § 179. On September 15, 2009, Weston sells the machine.
    a. Determine Weston's cost recovery for 2008.
    b. Determine Weston's cost recovery for 2009.

35. Juan acquires a new five-year class asset on March 14, 2008, for $200,000. This is the only asset acquired by Juan during the year. He does not elect immediate expensing under § 179. On July 15, 2009, Juan sells the asset.
    a. Determine Juan's cost recovery for 2008.
    b. Determine Juan's cost recovery for 2009.

36. Debra acquired the following new assets during the current year:

Date	Asset	Cost
April 11	Furniture	$50,000
July 28	Trucks	30,000
November 3	Computers	60,000

Determine the cost recovery for the current year. Debra does not elect immediate expensing under § 179.

37. On August 2, 2008, Wendy purchased a new office building for $2.7 million. On October 1, 2008, she began to rent out office space in the building. On April 15, 2012, Wendy sold the office building.
    a. Determine Wendy's cost recovery for 2008.
    b. Determine Wendy's cost recovery for 2012.

38. On April 3, 2008, Terry purchased and placed in service a building. The building cost $2 million. An appraisal determined that 25% of the total cost was attributed to the value of the land. The bottom floor of the building is leased to a retail business for $32,000. The other floors of the building are rental apartments with an annual rent of $160,000. Determine Terry's cost recovery for 2008.

39. On February 5, 2008, Christy purchased and placed in service a hotel. The hotel cost $1.8 million. Calculate Christy's cost recovery for 2008. For 2018.

40. Janice acquired an apartment building on June 4, 2008, for $1.4 million. The value of the land is $200,000. Janice sold the apartment building on November 29, 2014.

a.   Determine Janice's cost recovery for 2008.

b.   Determine Janice's cost recovery for 2014.

41. On April 20, 2008, Ralph purchased a new heavy-duty truck to be used in his farming business. The cost of the truck is $80,000. Ralph does not elect immediate expensing under § 179; nor does he elect to not have the uniform capitalization rules apply. Compute Ralph's cost recovery for 2008.

42. During the month of March 2008, Sam constructed agricultural fences on his farm. The cost of the fencing was $70,000. Sam does not elect immediate expensing under § 179, but an election to not have the uniform capitalization rules apply is in effect. Compute Sam's cost recovery for 2008.

43. As a condition of leasing a warehouse, Martha had to make capital improvements to the building to accommodate the lessee. These improvements cost Martha $250,000. The improvements were completed and the 10-year lease commenced on October 28, 2008. Determine Martha's cost recovery for 2008 with respect to the leasehold improvement.

44. On January 1, 2001, Jim leased a building to be used in his business as an office building. The lease will terminate on December 31, 2008. On February 2, 2002, Jim made a capital improvement to the building. The cost of the leasehold improvement to Jim was $80,000. Jim has no legal rights in the capital improvement after the termination of the lease. Determine Jim's loss in 2008, if any, with respect to the leasehold improvement as a result of the termination of the lease.

Decision Making   45. Lori, who is single, purchased a new copier (five-year class property) for $50,000 and new furniture (seven-year class property) for $216,000 on May 20, 2008. Lori expects the taxable income derived from her business (without regard to the amount expensed under § 179) to be about $300,000. Lori wants to elect immediate § 179 expensing, but she doesn't know which asset she should expense under § 179.

a.   Determine Lori's total deduction if the § 179 expense is first taken with respect to the copier.

b.   Determine Lori's total deduction if the § 179 expense is first taken with respect to the furniture.

c.   What is your advice to Lori?

46. Olga is the proprietor of a small business. In 2008, the business income, before consideration of any cost recovery or § 179 deduction, is $250,000. Olga spends $550,000 on new seven-year class assets and elects to take the § 179 deduction on them. Olga elects not to take additional first-year depreciation. Olga's cost recovery deduction for 2008, except for the cost recovery with respect to the new seven-year assets, is $95,000. Determine Olga's total cost recovery for 2008 with respect to the seven-year class assets and the amount of any § 179 carryforward.

Decision Making   47. On March 10, 2008, Yoon purchased three-year class property for $20,000. On December 15, 2008, Yoon purchased five-year class property for $340,000. He has net business income of $500,000 before consideration of any § 179 deduction.

a.   Calculate Yoon's cost recovery for 2008, assuming he does not make the § 179 election or use straight-line cost recovery. He elects not to take additional first-year depreciation.

b.   Calculate Yoon's cost recovery for 2008, assuming he does elect to use § 179 and does not elect to use straight-line cost recovery. He elects not to take additional first-year depreciation.

c.   Assuming Yoon's marginal tax rate is 33%, determine his tax benefit from electing § 179.

Communications   48. John Johnson is considering acquiring an automobile at the beginning of 2008 that he will use 100% of the time as a taxi. The purchase price of the automobile is $35,000. John has heard of cost recovery limits on automobiles and wants to know how much of the $35,000 he can deduct in the first year. Write a letter to John in which you present your calculations. Also, prepare a memo for the tax files. John's address is 100 Morningside, Clinton, MS 39058.

49. On October 15, 2008, Jon purchased and placed in service a new car. The purchase price was $30,000. This was the only business use asset Jon acquired in 2008. He used the car 80% of the time for business and 20% for personal use. Jon used the statutory percentage method of cost recovery. He elects not to take additional first-year depreciation. Calculate the total deduction Jon may take for 2008 with respect to the car.

50. On June 5, 2008, Leo purchased and placed in service a new car that cost $20,000. The business use percentage for the car is always 100%. Compute Leo's cost recovery deduction in 2008 and 2009.

51. On March 15, 2008, Helen purchased and placed in service a new Ford Excursion. The purchase price was $60,000, and the vehicle had a rating of 6,500 GVW. The vehicle was used 100% for business. Calculate the maximum total deduction Helen may take with respect to the vehicle in 2008.

52. On May 28, 2008, Mary purchased and placed in service a new $40,000 car. The car was used 60% for business, 20% for production of income, and 20% for personal use in 2008. In 2009, the usage changed to 40% for business, 30% for production of income, and 30% for personal use. Mary did not elect immediate expensing under § 179. Compute the cost recovery and any cost recovery recapture in 2009.

53. Sally purchased a new computer (five-year property) on June 1, 2008, for $4,000. Sally could use the computer 100% of the time in her business, or she could allow her family to also use the computer. Sally estimates that if her family uses the computer, the business use will be 45% and the personal use will be 55%. Determine the tax cost to Sally, in the year of acquisition, of allowing her family to use the computer. Assume that Sally would not elect § 179 limited expensing, elected not to take additional first-year depreciation, and that her marginal tax rate is 28%.

Decision Making

54. Dennis Harding is considering acquiring a new automobile that he will use 100% for business. The purchase price of the automobile would be $35,000. If Dennis leased the car for five years, the lease payments would be $375 per month. Dennis will acquire the car on January 1, 2008. The inclusion dollar amounts from the IRS table for the next five years are $131, $288, $430, $515, and $593. Dennis desires to know the effect on his adjusted gross income of purchasing versus leasing the car for the next five years. Write a letter to Dennis and present your calculations. Also, prepare a memo for the tax files. His address is 150 Avenue I, Memphis, TN 38112.

Decision Making

Communications

55. In 2008, Muhammad purchased a new computer for $14,000. The computer is used 100% for business. Muhammad did not make a § 179 election with respect to the computer. He elected not to take additional first-year depreciation. If Muhammad uses the statutory percentage method, determine his cost recovery deduction for 2008 for computing taxable income and for computing his alternative minimum tax.

56. Jamie purchased $100,000 of new office furniture for her business in June of the current year. Jamie understands that if she elects to use ADS to compute her regular income tax, there will be no difference between the cost recovery for computing the regular income tax and the AMT. Jamie wants to know the *regular* income tax cost, after three years, of using ADS rather than MACRS. Assume that Jamie does not elect § 179 limited expensing and that her marginal tax rate is 28%. She elected not to take additional first-year depreciation.

Decision Making

57. Mike Saxon is negotiating the purchase of a business. The final purchase price has been agreed upon, but the allocation of the purchase price to the assets is still being discussed. Appraisals on a warehouse range from $1.2 million to $1.5 million. If a value of $1.2 million is used for the warehouse, the remainder of the purchase price, $800,000, will be allocated to goodwill. If $1.5 million is allocated to the warehouse, goodwill will be $500,000. Mike wants to know what effect each alternative will have on cost recovery and amortization during the first year. Under the agreement, Mike will take over the business on January 1 of next year. Write a letter to Mike in which you present your calculations and recommendation. Also, prepare a memo for the tax files. Mike's address is 200 Rolling Hills Drive, Shavertown, PA 18708.

Decision Making

Communications

58. Oleander Corporation, a calendar year entity, begins business on March 1, 2008. The corporation has startup expenditures of $58,000. If Oleander elects § 195 treatment, determine the total amount of startup expenditures that it may deduct in 2008.

59. Martha was considering starting a new business. During her preliminary investigations, she incurred the following expenditures:

Salaries	$20,000
Travel	18,000
Interest on short-term note	2,000
Professional fees	13,000

Martha begins the business on June 1 of the current year. If Martha elects § 195 treatment, determine her startup expenditure deduction for the current year.

60. Wes acquired a mineral interest during the year for $10 million. A geological survey estimated that 250,000 tons of the mineral remained in the deposit. During the year, 80,000 tons were mined, and 45,000 tons were sold for $12 million. Other expenses amounted to $5 million. Assuming the mineral depletion rate is 22%, calculate Wes's lowest taxable income.

Decision Making

61. Chris purchased an oil interest for $2 million. Recoverable barrels were estimated to be 500,000. During the year, 120,000 barrels were sold for $3.84 million, regular expenses (including cost recovery) were $1.24 million, and IDC were $1 million. Calculate Chris's taxable income under the expensing and capitalization methods of handling IDC.

CUMULATIVE PROBLEMS

Tax Return Problem

62. Janice Morgan, age 32, is single and has no dependents. She is a freelance writer. In January 2007, Janice opened her own office located at 2751 Waldham Road, Pleasantville, NM 17196. She called her business Writers Anonymous. Janice is a cash basis taxpayer. She lives at 132 Stone Avenue, Pleasantville, NM 17196. Her Social Security number is 189–57–6691. Janice desires to contribute to the Presidential Election Campaign Fund.

During 2007, Janice had the following income and expense items connected with her business:

Income from sale of articles	$105,000
Rent	16,500
Utilities	7,900
Supplies	1,800
Insurance	5,000
Travel (including meals of $1,200)	3,500

Janice purchased and placed in service the following fixed assets for her business:

- Furniture and fixtures (new) costing $17,000 on January 10, 2007.
- Computer equipment (new) costing $40,000 on July 28, 2007.

Janice did not elect immediate expensing under § 179.

Janice's itemized deductions are as follows:

State income tax	$3,000
Home mortgage interest paid to First Bank	6,000
Property taxes on home	1,500
Charitable contributions	1,200

Janice did not keep a record of the sales tax she paid. The amount from the sales tax table is $437.

Janice has interest income of $5,000 on certificates of deposit at Second Bank. Janice makes estimated tax payments of $17,000 for 2007.

Compute Janice Morgan's 2007 Federal income tax payable (or refund due). If you use tax forms for your computations, you will need Form(s) 1040 and 4562 and Schedules A, B, C, and SE. Suggested software: TaxCut.

Tax Computation Problem

Decision Making

Communications

63. John Smith, age 31, is single and has no dependents. At the beginning of 2008, John started his own excavation business and named it Earth Movers. John lives at 1045 Center Street, Lindon, UT, and his business is located at 381 State Street, Lindon, UT. The zip code for both addresses is 84059. John's Social Security number is 321–09–6456, and the business identification number is 98–1234567. John is a cash basis taxpayer. During 2008, John had the following items in connection with his business:

Fees for services	$912,000
Building rental expense	36,000
Office furniture and equipment rental expense	9,000
Office supplies	2,500
Utilities	4,000
Salary for secretary	34,000
Salary for equipment operators	42,000
Payroll taxes	7,000
Fuel and oil for the equipment	21,000
Purchase of three new front-end loaders on January 15, 2008, for $390,000. John made the election under § 179.	390,000
Purchase of a new dump truck on January 18, 2008	65,000

During 2008, John had the following additional items:

Interest income from First National Bank	$ 10,000
Dividends from ExxonMobil	9,500
Quarterly estimated tax payments	11,500

On October 8, 2008, John inherited IBM stock from his Aunt Mildred. John had been her favorite nephew. According to the data provided by the executor of Aunt Mildred's estate, the stock was valued for estate tax purposes at $110,000. John is considering selling the IBM stock for $115,000 on December 29, 2008, and using $75,000 of the proceeds to purchase an Acura NSX. He would use the car 100% for business. John wants to know what effect these transactions would have on his 2008 adjusted gross income.

Write a letter to John in which you present your calculations. Also, prepare a memo for the tax files.

RESEARCH PROBLEMS

Note: Solutions to Research Problems can be prepared by using the **RIA Checkpoint®** **Student Edition** online research product, which is available to accompany this text. It is also possible to prepare solutions to the Research Problems by using tax research materials found in a standard tax library.

Communications

Research Problem 1. Harry Pickart, one of your clients, operates a business that rents aircraft parts to motion picture studios for use in film production. Harry purchased most of the aircraft parts at auctions held throughout the United States. At those auctions, Harry usually acquired the parts in large quantities because he speculated that he would be able to use at least some of them in his rental business. After the conclusion of a film production, the movie studio returns the aircraft parts it rented from Harry. The parts are often returned in damaged condition or with pieces missing. Harry sometimes attempts to repair a damaged part so that it can be rented again. After being subjected to wear and tear from use, however, a part deteriorates over time, which varies depending on the particular part and its treatment by the studios during rental. Harry believes that all of the aircraft parts have a useful life of less than four years and, therefore, are entitled to be classed as three-year property. Write a letter to Harry that contains your advice on whether the aircraft parts can be depreciated over three years. Also, prepare a memo for the tax files. Harry's mailing address is P.O. Box 100, Sun River, OR 97600.

Research Problem 2. United Bank is a federally chartered banking institution engaged in the business of issuing credit cards to customers. United also regularly purchases credit card receivables and/or cardholders' accounts from other financial institutions. Thereafter, United may or may not extend additional credit to the customers on these accounts. In connection with its credit card business, United derives interest income, fees, and interchange income. United wants to know whether costs incurred in connection with the acquisition of credit card receivables must be capitalized under § 263 or whether they can be amortized under § 195.

Research Problem 3.   Royal Hotel has recently replaced the mechanical key locks on its interior guest room doors with a new magnetic stripe keycard locking system. Royal wants to know whether the new magnetic stripe keycard locking system is classified as nonresidential real property or tangible personal property.

Research Problem 4.   Juan owns a business that acquires exotic automobiles that are high-technology, state-of-the-art vehicles with unique design features or equipment. The exotic automobiles are not licensed or set up to be used on the road. Rather, the cars are used exclusively for car shows or related promotional photography. Juan would like to know whether he can take a cost recovery deduction with respect to the exotic automobiles on his Federal income tax return.

Partial list of research aids:
Bruce Selig, 70 TCM 1125, T.C.Memo. 1995–519.

Research Problem 5.   George Black operates a winery and vineyards. In the process of growing grapes, trellis systems are used to support the grape vines. The primary structural components that affix the trellis to the earth are the end and in-line posts, which are rammed 2 to 3 feet into the ground and secured by metal stakes and/or mechanically screwed-in anchors. George would like to know how the trellis system will be classified for purposes of computing cost recovery.

Internet
Activity

Use the tax resources of the Internet to address the following questions. Do not restrict your search to the World Wide Web, but include a review of newsgroups and general reference materials, practitioner sites and resources, primary sources of the tax law, chat rooms and discussion groups, and other opportunities.

Research Problem 6.   Locate a financial calculator program that assesses the wisdom of buying versus leasing a new car. Install the program on your computer and become familiar with it. Use the program to work through Problem 54 in this chapter.

Communications

Research Problem 7.   Changes to depreciation systems often are discussed by policy makers and observers of the tax system. Outline the terms and policy objectives of one of the changes currently proposed by the Treasury, a member of Congress, or a tax policy think tank.

CHAPTER 9

Deductions: Employee and Self-Employed-Related Expenses

LEARNING OBJECTIVES

After completing Chapter 9, you should be able to:

LO.1
Distinguish between employee and self-employed status.

LO.2
Recognize deductible transportation expenses.

LO.3
Know how travel expenses are treated.

LO.4
Determine the moving expense deduction.

LO.5
Differentiate between deductible and nondeductible education expenses.

LO.6
Understand how entertainment expenses are treated.

LO.7
Identify other employee expenses.

LO.8
Become familiar with various deductions for contributions to retirement accounts.

LO.9
Appreciate the difference between accountable and nonaccountable employee plans.

LO.10
Work with the limitations on miscellaneous itemized deductions.

LO.11
Develop tax planning ideas related to employee business expenses.

OUTLINE

Employee versus Self-Employed, 9–2

Employee Expenses—In General, 9–4

Transportation Expenses, 9–4
Qualified Expenditures, 9–4
Computation of Automobile Expenses, 9–6

Travel Expenses, 9–7
Definition of Travel Expenses, 9–7
Away-from-Home Requirement, 9–7
Restrictions on Travel Expenses, 9–8
Combined Business and Pleasure Travel, 9–9

Moving Expenses, 9–11
Distance Test, 9–11
Time Test, 9–11
Treatment of Moving Expenses, 9–12

Education Expenses, 9–13
General Requirements, 9–13
Requirements Imposed by Law or by the Employer
   for Retention of Employment, 9–14
Maintaining or Improving Existing Skills, 9–14
Classification of Specific Items, 9–14
A Limited Deduction Approach, 9–15
Other Provisions Dealing with Education, 9–16

Entertainment Expenses, 9–17
Cutback Adjustment, 9–18
Classification of Expenses, 9–19
Restrictions upon Deductibility, 9–19

Other Employee Expenses, 9–21
Office in the Home, 9–21
Miscellaneous Employee Expenses, 9–23

Contributions to Retirement Accounts, 9–25
Employee IRAs, 9–25
Self-Employed Keogh (H.R. 10) Plans, 9–25

Classification of Employee Expenses, 9–25
Accountable Plans, 9–26
Nonaccountable Plans, 9–27
Reporting Procedures, 9–27

Limitations on Itemized Deductions, 9–28
Miscellaneous Itemized Deductions Subject to the
   2 Percent Floor, 9–28
Miscellaneous Itemized Deductions Not Subject to the
   2 Percent Floor, 9–29

Tax Planning Considerations, 9–29
Self-Employed Individuals, 9–29
Shifting Deductions between Employer and
   Employee, 9–30
Transportation and Travel Expenses, 9–31
Moving Expenses, 9–31
Education Expenses, 9–31
Entertainment Expenses, 9–32
Unreimbursed Employee Business Expenses, 9–33

Considering the large number of taxpayers affected, the tax treatment of job-related expenses is unusually complex. To resolve this matter in a systematic fashion, a number of key questions must be asked:

- Is the taxpayer an *employee* or *self-employed?*
- If an employee, what expenses *qualify* as deductions?
- How are the expenses that qualify *classified* for tax purposes?
- To the extent the expenses are classified as deductions *from* AGI, are they subject to any *limitation?*

Once these questions have been posed and answered, the chapter considers various planning procedures available to maximize the deductibility of employee expenses.

LO.1

Distinguish between employee and self-employed status.

Employee versus Self-Employed

When one person performs services for another, the person performing the service is either an employee or self-employed (an **independent contractor**). Failure to recognize employee status can have serious consequences. Tax deficiencies as well as interest and penalties may result.

The problem is likely to intensify since businesses are increasingly relying on the services of self-employed persons for numerous reasons. Unlike employees, self-employed persons do not have to be included in various fringe benefit programs (e.g., group term life insurance) and retirement plans. Since they are not covered by FICA and FUTA (see Chapter 1), these payroll costs are avoided. The IRS is very much aware of the tendency of businesses to wrongly classify workers as self-employed rather than as employees.

In terms of tax consequences, employment status also makes a great deal of difference to the persons who perform the services. Expenses of self-employed taxpayers, to the extent allowable, are classified as deductions *for* AGI and are reported on Schedule C (Profit or Loss From Business) of Form 1040.[1] With the exception of reimbursement under an accountable plan (see later in the chapter), expenses of employees are deductions *from* AGI. They are reported on Form 2106 (Employee Business Expenses) and Schedule A (Itemized Deductions) of Form 1040.[2]

Most persons classified as employees are common law employees. The common law employee classification originated in judicial case law and is summarized in various IRS pronouncements.[3] Revenue Ruling 87–41, for example, lists 20 factors that can be used in determining whether a worker is a common law employee or an independent contractor (and, thus, self-employed).[4]

But when does a common law employee-employer relationship exist? Such a relationship exists when the employer has the right to specify the end result and the ways and means by which that result is to be attained.[5] An employee is subject to the will and control of the employer with respect not only to what shall be done but also to how it shall be done. If the individual is subject to the direction or control of another only to the extent of the end result but not as to the means of accomplishment, an employee-employer relationship does not exist.

Certain factors indicate an employee-employer relationship. These include the performance of the following by the employer:

- Furnishing of tools or equipment and a place to work.
- Providing support services including the hiring of assistants to help do the work.
- Making training available to provide needed job skills.
- Allowing participation in various workplace fringe benefits (e.g., accident and health plans, group life insurance, retirement plans).
- Paying for services based on time rather than the task performed.

For their part, independent contractors are more likely than employees to have unreimbursed business expenses, a significant investment in tools and work facilities, and less permanency in their business relationships. Independent contractors, moreover, anticipate a profit from their work, make their services available to the relevant marketplace, and are paid a flat fee on a per-job basis. Although the right to discharge may depend on any contractual arrangement between the parties, employees generally are easier to terminate than independent contractors.

In resolving employment status, each case must be tested on its own merits. Keep in mind, however, that the right to control the means and methods of accomplishment is the definitive test that leads to a common law employee result.

EXAMPLE 1

Arnold is a lawyer whose major client accounts for 60% of his billings. He does the routine legal work and income tax returns at the client's request. He is paid a monthly retainer in addition to amounts charged for extra work. Arnold is a self-employed individual. Even though most of his income comes from one client, he still has the right to determine how the end result of his work is attained. ■

EXAMPLE 2

Ellen is a lawyer hired by Arnold to assist him in the performance of services for the client mentioned in Example 1. Ellen is under Arnold's supervision; he reviews her work and pays her an hourly fee. Ellen is an employee of Arnold. ■

---

[1]Under certain conditions, a Schedule C–EZ can be substituted. Also, a Schedule SE (Self-Employment Tax) must be filed.

[2]In certain cases, a Form 2106–EZ (Unreimbursed Employee Business Expenses) can be substituted.

[3]See, for example, *Employer's Supplemental Tax Guide* (IRS Publication 15-A).

[4]1987–1 C.B. 296.

[5]Reg. § 31.3401(c)–(1)(b).

When one taxpayer holds multiple jobs, it is possible to have dual status as both an employee and an independent contractor (i.e., self-employed).

| EXAMPLE 3 | Dr. Davis, DDS, is a full-time employee at the Robin University Health Center. In the evenings and on weekends, he shares a practice with another dentist who works the Monday through Friday daytime shifts. Dr. Davis is both employed and self-employed. ∎ |

Certain workers who *are not* common law employees are treated as employees for employment tax purposes. Known as **statutory employees**, this group includes certain drivers (e.g., nondairy beverage distributors, laundry and dry cleaning pickup service), life insurance sales agents, home workers, and other sales persons. These employees are allowed to claim their business-related expenses as deductions *for* AGI by using Schedule C. The wages or commissions paid to statutory employees are not subject to Federal income tax withholding but are subject to Social Security tax.[6]

If a taxpayer wants clarification as to whether employee or independent contractor status exists, a ruling from the IRS can be obtained by filing Form SS–8 (Determination of Worker Status for Purposes of Federal Employment Taxes and Income Tax Withholding). An adverse ruling is appealable to the U.S. Tax Court.[7]

Employee Expenses—In General

Once the employment relationship is established, employee expenses fall into one of the following categories:

- Transportation.
- Travel.
- Moving.
- Education.
- Entertainment.
- Other.

These expenses are discussed below in the order presented.

Keep in mind, however, that these expenses are not necessarily limited to employees. A deduction for business transportation, for example, is equally available to taxpayers who are self-employed.

Transportation Expenses

LO.2

Recognize deductible transportation expenses.

Qualified Expenditures

An employee may deduct unreimbursed employment-related transportation expenses as an itemized deduction *from* AGI. **Transportation expenses** include only the cost of transporting the employee from one place to another in the course of employment when the employee is *not* away from home *in travel status*. Such costs include taxi fares, automobile expenses, tolls, and parking.

Commuting Expenses. Commuting between home and one's place of employment is a personal, nondeductible expense. The fact that one employee drives 30 miles to work and another employee walks six blocks is of no significance.

| EXAMPLE 4 | Geraldo is employed by Sparrow Corporation. He drives 22 miles each way to work. The 44 miles he drives each workday are nondeductible commuting expenses. ∎ |

---

[6]§ 3121(d)(3). See Circular E, *Employer's Tax Guide* (IRS Publication 15), for further discussion of statutory employees.   [7]§ 7436.

The rule that disallows a deduction for commuting expenses has several exceptions. An employee who uses an automobile to transport heavy tools to work and who otherwise would not drive to work is allowed a deduction, but only for the additional costs incurred to transport the work implements. Additional costs are those exceeding the cost of commuting by the same mode of transportation without the tools. For example, the rental of a trailer for transporting tools is deductible, but the expenses of operating the automobile generally are not deductible. The Supreme Court has held that a deduction is permitted only when the taxpayer can show that the automobile would not have been used without the necessity to transport tools or equipment.[8]

Another exception is provided for an employee who has a second job. The expenses of getting from one job to another are deductible. If the employee goes home between jobs, the deduction is based on the distance between jobs.

EXAMPLE 5

In the current year, Cynthia holds two jobs, a full-time job with Blue Corporation and a part-time job with Wren Corporation. During the 250 days that she works (adjusted for weekends, vacation, and holidays), Cynthia customarily leaves home at 7:30 A.M. and drives 30 miles to the Blue Corporation plant, where she works until 5:00 P.M. After dinner at a nearby café, Cynthia drives 20 miles to Wren Corporation and works from 7:00 to 11:00 P.M. The distance from the second job to Cynthia's home is 40 miles. Her deduction is based on 20 miles (the distance between jobs). ∎

If the taxpayer is required to incur a transportation expense to travel between work stations, that expense is deductible.

EXAMPLE 6

Norman is the local manager for a national chain of fast-food outlets. Each workday he drives from his home to his office to handle administrative matters. Most of his day, however, is then spent making the rounds of the retail outlets, after which he drives home. The costs incurred in driving to his office and driving home from the last outlet are nondeductible commuting expenses. The other transportation costs are deductible. ∎

Likewise, the commuting costs from home to a temporary work station and from the temporary work station to home are deductible.

EXAMPLE 7

Vivian works for a firm in downtown Denver and commutes to work. She occasionally works in a customer's office. On one such occasion, Vivian drove directly to the customer's office, a round-trip distance from her home of 40 miles. She did not go into her office, which is a 52-mile round-trip. Her mileage for going to and from the temporary work station is deductible. ∎

Also deductible is the reasonable travel cost between the general working area and a temporary work station outside that area.

EXAMPLE 8

Sam, a building inspector in Minneapolis, regularly inspects buildings for building code violations for his employer, a general contractor. During one busy season, the St. Paul inspector became ill, and Sam was required to inspect several buildings in St. Paul. The expenses for transportation for the trips to St. Paul are deductible. ∎

What constitutes the general working area depends on the facts and circumstances of each situation. Furthermore, if an employee customarily works on several temporary assignments in a localized area, that localized area becomes the regular place of employment. Transportation from home to these locations becomes a personal, nondeductible commuting expense.

---

[8]*Fausner v. Comm.*, 73–2 USTC ¶9515, 32 AFTR2d 73–5202, 93 S.Ct. 2820 (USSC, 1973).

Computation of Automobile Expenses

A taxpayer has two choices in determining automobile expenses: the automatic mileage method and the actual cost method. If a mixed-use automobile is involved, only the expenses attributable to the business use are deductible. The percentage of business use is usually arrived at by comparing the business mileage with total mileage—both business and personal.

Automatic Mileage Method. Also called the standard mileage method, the **automatic mileage method** is convenient in that it simplifies record keeping. The rate allowed per mile takes into account average operating expenses (such as gas and oil, repairs, and depreciation). Consequently, the taxpayer only has to multiply the automatic mileage rate by the miles driven to compute the deduction for business transportation.

For 2008, the deduction is based on 50.5 cents per mile for business miles.[9] The mileage rate for 2007 was 48.5 cents per mile. Parking fees and tolls are allowed in addition to expenses computed using the automatic mileage method.

Generally, a taxpayer may elect either method for any particular year. However, the following restrictions apply:

- The vehicle must be owned or leased by the taxpayer.
- The vehicle is not used for hire (e.g., taxicab).
- If five or more vehicles are in use (for business purposes) at the *same* time (not alternately), a taxpayer may not use the automatic mileage method.
- A basis adjustment is required if the taxpayer changes from the automatic mileage method to the actual operating cost method. Depreciation is considered allowed for the business miles in accordance with the following schedule for the most recent five years:

Year	Rate per Mile
2008	21 cents
2007	19 cents
2006	17 cents
2005	17 cents
2004	16 cents

EXAMPLE 9

Tim purchased his automobile in 2005 for $36,000. It is used 90% for business purposes. Tim drove the automobile for 10,000 business miles in 2007; 8,500 business miles in 2006; and 6,000 business miles in 2005. At the beginning of 2008, the basis of the business portion is $28,035.

Depreciable basis ($36,000 × 90%)	$32,400
Less depreciation:	
2007 (10,000 miles × 19 cents)	(1,900)
2006 (8,500 miles × 17 cents)	(1,445)
2005 (6,000 miles × 17 cents)	(1,020)
Adjusted business basis 1/1/2008	$28,035

- Use of the automatic mileage method in the first year the auto is placed in service is considered an election to exclude the auto from the MACRS method of depreciation (discussed in Chapter 8).
- A taxpayer may not switch to the automatic mileage method if the MACRS statutory percentage method or the election to expense under § 179 has been used.

---

[9]Rev.Proc. 2007–70, I.R.B. No. 50, 1158.

Actual Cost Method. Under this method, the actual cost of operating the automobile is used to compute the deduction. Actual costs include the following expenses:

- Gas and oil, lubrication.
- Depreciation (or lease payments).
- Insurance.
- Dues to auto clubs.
- Repairs.
- Tires and other parts.
- Licenses and registration fees.
- Parking and tolls.

As noted in Chapter 8, the allowance for depreciation (or lease payments) is subject to limitations when mixed-use vehicles are involved (see Example 21 on page 8–15). Interest on car loans is not deductible if the taxpayer is an employee, but it can qualify as a business expense if the taxpayer is self-employed.[10] Sales taxes paid on the purchase of a car are added to the cost of the car and recovered by means of the depreciation deduction. In mixed-use situations, the portion of the sales tax attributable to personal use may, in some cases, be claimed as a deduction *from* AGI (see Chapter 10 and the choice required between state and local income and sales taxes).

Except for parking and tolls, none of the expenses noted above can be separately claimed under the automatic mileage method. A deduction for parking tickets and other traffic violations is not allowed under either method due to the public policy limitation (see Chapter 6).

Travel Expenses

LO.3

Know how travel expenses are treated.

Definition of Travel Expenses

An itemized deduction is allowed for unreimbursed travel expenses related to a taxpayer's employment. **Travel expenses** are more broadly defined in the Code than are transportation expenses. Travel expenses include transportation expenses and meals and lodging while away from home in the pursuit of a trade or business. Meals cannot be lavish or extravagant under the circumstances. Transportation expenses (as previously discussed) are deductible even though the taxpayer is not away from home. A deduction for travel expenses is available only if the taxpayer is away from his or her tax home. Travel expenses also include reasonable laundry and incidental expenses.

Away-from-Home Requirement

The crucial test for the deductibility of travel expenses is whether the employee is away from home overnight. "Overnight" need not be a 24-hour period, but it must be a period substantially longer than an ordinary day's work and must require rest, sleep, or a relief-from-work period.[11] A one-day business trip is not travel status, and meals and lodging for such a trip are not deductible.

Temporary Assignments. The employee must be away from home for a temporary period. If the taxpayer-employee is reassigned to a new post for an indefinite period of time, that new post becomes his or her tax home. *Temporary* indicates that the assignment's termination is expected within a reasonably short period of time. The position of the IRS is that the tax home is the business location, post, or station of the taxpayer. Thus, travel expenses are not deductible if a taxpayer is reassigned for an indefinite period and does not move his or her place of residence to the new location.

---

[10]An interest deduction could be available if the purchase of the auto was financed with a home equity loan. See the discussion of itemized deductions in Chapter 10.

[11]*U.S. v. Correll,* 68–1 USTC ¶9101, 20 AFTR2d 5845, 88 S.Ct. 445 (USSC, 1967); Rev.Rul. 75–168, 1975–1 C.B. 58.

EXAMPLE 10

Malcolm's employer opened a branch office in San Diego. Malcolm was assigned to the new office for three months to train a new manager and to assist in setting up the new office. He tried commuting from his home in Los Angeles for a week and decided that he could not continue driving several hours a day. He rented an apartment in San Diego, where he lived during the week. He spent weekends with his wife and children at their home in Los Angeles. Malcolm's rent, meals, laundry, incidentals, and automobile expenses in San Diego are deductible. To the extent that Malcolm's transportation expense related to his weekend trips home exceeds what his cost of meals and lodging would have been, the excess is personal and nondeductible. ■

EXAMPLE 11

Assume that Malcolm in Example 10 was transferred to the new location to become the new manager permanently. His wife and children continued to live in Los Angeles until the end of the school year. Malcolm is no longer "away from home" because the assignment is not temporary. His travel expenses are not deductible. ■

To curtail controversy in this area, the Code specifies that a taxpayer "*shall not be treated as temporarily away from home during any period of employment if such period exceeds 1 year.*"[12]

Determining the Tax Home.

Under ordinary circumstances, determining the location of a taxpayer's tax home does not present a problem. The tax home is the area in which the taxpayer derives his or her principal source of income. When the taxpayer has more than one place of employment, the tax home is based on the amount of time spent in each area.

It is possible for a taxpayer never to be away from his or her tax home. In other words, the tax home follows the taxpayer. Thus, all meals and lodging remain personal and are not deductible. The reason for this result is that there is no duplication of expenses.[13]

EXAMPLE 12

Jim is single and lives with his parents. Although he is employed full-time as a long-haul truck driver, he contributes nothing toward the cost of maintaining his parents' household. The meals and lodging expenses Jim incurs while on the road are not deductible. ■

Restrictions on Travel Expenses

The possibility always exists that taxpayers will attempt to treat vacation or pleasure travel as deductible business travel. To prevent such practices, the law contains restrictions on certain travel expenses.

Conventions.

For travel expenses to be deductible, a convention must be directly related to the taxpayer's trade or business.[14]

EXAMPLE 13

Dr. Hill, a pathologist who works for a hospital in Ohio, travels to Las Vegas to attend a two-day session on recent developments in estate planning. No deduction is allowed for Dr. Hill's travel expenses. ■

EXAMPLE 14

Assume the same facts as in Example 13, except that the convention deals entirely with recent developments in forensic medicine. Under these circumstances, a travel deduction is allowed. ■

If the proceedings of the convention are videotaped, the taxpayer must attend convention sessions to view the videotaped materials along with other participants.

---

[12]§ 162(a).

[13]Rev.Rul. 73–539, 1973–2 C.B. 37 and *James O. Henderson*, 70 TCM 1407, T.C.Memo. 1995–559, *aff'd* by 98–1 USTC ¶50,375, 81 AFTR2d 98–1748, 143 F.3d 497 (CA–9, 1998).

[14]§ 274(h)(1).

This requirement does not disallow deductions for costs (other than travel, meals, and entertainment) of renting or using videotaped materials related to business.

EXAMPLE 15

A CPA is unable to attend a convention at which current developments in taxation are discussed. She pays $200 for videotapes of the lectures and views them at home later. The $200 is an itemized deduction if the CPA is an employee. If she is self-employed, the $200 is a deduction *for* AGI. ∎

The Code places stringent restrictions on the deductibility of travel expenses of the taxpayer's spouse or dependent.[15] Generally, the accompaniment by the spouse or dependent must serve a bona fide business purpose, and the expenses must be otherwise deductible.

EXAMPLE 16

Assume the same facts as in Example 14 with the additional fact that Dr. Hill is accompanied by Mrs. Hill. Mrs. Hill is not employed, but possesses secretarial skills and takes notes during the proceedings. No deduction is allowed for Mrs. Hill's travel expenses. ∎

EXAMPLE 17

Modify the facts in Example 16 to make Mrs. Hill a nurse trained in pathology, who is employed by Dr. Hill as his assistant. Now, Mrs. Hill's travel expenses qualify as deductions. ∎

Education. Travel as a form of education is not deductible.[16] If, however, the education qualifies as a deduction, the travel involved is allowed.

EXAMPLE 18

Greta, a German teacher, travels to Germany to maintain general familiarity with the language and culture. No travel expense deduction is allowed. ∎

EXAMPLE 19

Jean-Claude, a scholar of French literature, travels to Paris to do specific library research that cannot be done elsewhere and to take courses that are offered only at the Sorbonne. The travel costs are deductible, assuming that the other requirements for deducting education expenses (discussed later in the chapter) are met. ∎

Combined Business and Pleasure Travel

To be deductible, travel expenses need not be incurred in the performance of specific job functions. Travel expenses incurred in attending a professional convention are deductible by an employee if attendance is connected with services as an employee. For example, an employee of a law firm can deduct travel expenses incurred in attending a meeting of the American Bar Association.

Domestic Travel. Travel deductions have been used in the past by persons who claimed a tax deduction for what was essentially a personal vacation. As a result, several provisions have been enacted to govern deductions associated with combined business and pleasure trips. If the business/pleasure trip is from one point in the United States to another point in the United States, the transportation expenses are deductible only if the trip is *primarily for business*.[17] If the trip is primarily for pleasure, no transportation expenses qualify as a deduction. Meals, lodging, and other expenses are allocated between business and personal days.

EXAMPLE 20

In the current year, Hana travels from Seattle to New York primarily for business. She spends five days conducting business and three days sightseeing and attending shows. Her plane and taxi fare amounts to $560. Her meals amount to $100 per day, and lodging and incidental

---

[15]§ 274(m)(3).
[16]§ 274(m)(2).

[17]Reg. § 1.162–2(b)(1).

GLOBAL *Tax Issues*

CONVENTIONS IN FARAWAY LANDS

Certain restrictions are imposed on the deductibility of expenses paid or incurred to attend conventions located outside the North American area. The expenses are disallowed unless it is established that the meeting is directly related to a trade or business of the taxpayer. Disallowance also occurs unless the taxpayer shows that it is as reasonable for the meeting to be held in a foreign location as within the North American area.

The stringent restrictions applicable to conventions in foreign countries do not apply to those held in the North American area. Here, the regular rules governing domestic (U.S.) conventions apply. The North American area is broadly defined to include, among others, such locales as Antigua, Aruba, the Bahamas, Barbados, Bermuda, Canada, Costa Rica, the Dominican Republic, Grenada, Honduras, Jamaica, Mexico, Puerto Rico, and Trinidad and Tobago. It also includes certain U.S. possessions in the Pacific area, such as Guam, Midway, the Mariana Islands, and Wake Island.

Sources: Travel, Entertainment, Gift and Car Expenses *(IRS Publication 463) Ch. 2, and Rev.Rul. 2007–28 (I.R.B. No. 18, 1039).*

expenses are $150 per day. She can deduct the transportation charges of $560, since the trip is primarily for business (five days of business versus three days of sightseeing). Meals are limited to five days and are subject to the 50% cutback (discussed later in the chapter) for a total of $250 [5 days × ($100 × 50%)], and other expenses are limited to $750 (5 days × $150). If Hana is an employee, the unreimbursed travel expenses are miscellaneous itemized deductions. ∎

EXAMPLE 21

Assume Hana goes to New York for a two-week vacation. While there, she spends several hours renewing acquaintances with people in her company's New York office. Her transportation expenses are not deductible. ∎

Foreign Travel. When the trip is *outside the United States*, special rules apply. Transportation expenses must be allocated between business and personal unless (1) the taxpayer is away from home for seven days or less *or* (2) less than 25 percent of the time was for personal purposes. No allocation is required if the taxpayer has no substantial control over arrangements for the trip or the desire for a vacation is not a major factor in taking the trip. If the trip is primarily for pleasure, no transportation charges are deductible. Days devoted to travel are considered business days. Weekends, legal holidays, and intervening days are considered business days, provided that both the preceding and succeeding days were business days.[18]

EXAMPLE 22

In the current year, Robert takes a trip from New York to Japan primarily for business purposes. He is away from home from June 10 through June 19. He spends three days vacationing and seven days conducting business (including two travel days). His airfare is $2,500, his meals amount to $100 per day, and lodging and incidental expenses are $160 per day. Since Robert is away from home for more than seven days and more than 25% of his time is devoted to personal purposes, only 70% (7 days business/10 days total) of the transportation is deductible. His deductions are as follows:

Transportation (70% × $2,500)		$1,750
Lodging ($160 × 7)		1,120
Meals ($100 × 7)	$ 700	
Less: 50% cutback (discussed later)	(350)	350
Total		$3,220

∎

---

[18]§ 274(c) and Reg. § 1.274–4. For purposes of the seven-days-or-less exception, the departure travel day is not counted.

EXAMPLE 23

Assume the same facts as in Example 22. Robert is gone the same period of time but spends only two days (rather than three) vacationing. Now no allocation of transportation is required. Since the pleasure portion of the trip is less than 25% of the total, all of the airfare qualifies for the travel deduction. ∎

Moving Expenses

LO.4

Determine the moving expense deduction.

Moving expenses are deductible for moves in connection with the commencement of work at a new principal place of work.[19] Both employees and self-employed individuals can deduct these expenses. To be eligible for a moving expense deduction, a taxpayer must meet two basic tests: distance and time.

Distance Test

To meet the distance test, the taxpayer's new job location must be at least 50 miles farther from the taxpayer's old residence than the old residence was from the former place of employment. In this regard, the location of the new residence is not relevant. This eliminates a moving deduction for taxpayers who purchase a new home in the same general area without changing their place of employment. Those who accept a new job in the same general area as the old job location are also eliminated.

EXAMPLE 24

Harry is permanently transferred to a new job location. The distance from Harry's former home to his new job (80 miles) exceeds the distance from his former home to his old job (30 miles) by at least 50 miles. Harry has met the distance test for a moving expense deduction. (See the following diagram.)

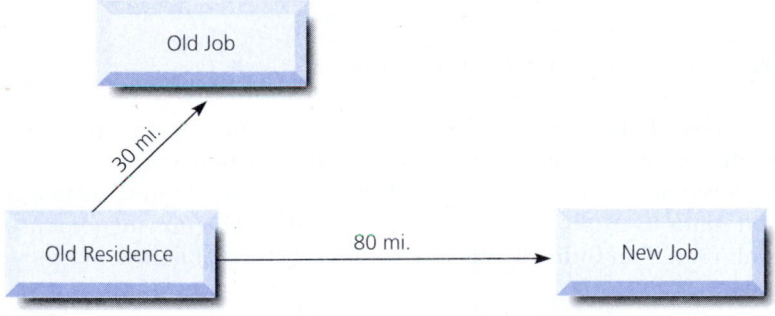

If Harry is not employed before the move, his new job must be at least 50 miles from his former residence. In this instance, Harry has met the distance test if he was not previously employed. ∎

Time Test

To meet the time test, an employee must be employed on a full-time basis at the new location for 39 weeks in the 12-month period following the move. If the taxpayer is a self-employed individual, he or she must work in the new location for 78 weeks during the next two years. The first 39 weeks must be in the first 12 months. The time test is disregarded if the taxpayer dies, becomes disabled, or is discharged (other than for willful misconduct) or transferred by the new employer.

A taxpayer might not be able to meet the 39-week test by the due date of the tax return for the year of the move. For this reason, two alternatives are allowed. The taxpayer can take the deduction in the year the expenses are incurred, even though

---

[19]§ 217(a).

the 39-week test has not been met. If the taxpayer later fails to meet the test, either (1) the income of the following year is increased by an amount equal to the deduction previously claimed for moving expenses, or (2) an amended return is filed for the year of the move. The second alternative is to wait until the test is met and then file an amended tax return for the year of the move.

Treatment of Moving Expenses

What Is Included. "Qualified" moving expenses include *reasonable* expenses of:

- Moving household goods and personal effects.
- Traveling from the former residence to the new place of residence.

For this purpose, *traveling* includes lodging, but not meals, for the taxpayer and members of the household.[20] The taxpayer can elect to use actual auto expenses (no depreciation is allowed) or the automatic mileage method. In this case, moving expense mileage is limited in 2008 to 19 cents per mile for each car. The automatic mileage rate for 2007 was 20 cents per mile. These expenses are also limited by the reasonableness standard. For example, if one moves from Texas to Florida via Maine and takes six weeks to do so, the transportation and lodging must be allocated between personal and moving expenses.

E X A M P L E   25

Jill is transferred by her employer from the Atlanta office to the San Francisco office. In this connection, she spends the following amounts:

Cost of moving furniture	$4,800
Transportation	700
Meals	450
Lodging	600

Jill's total qualified moving expense is $6,100 ($4,800 + $700 + $600). ∎

The moving expense deduction is allowed regardless of whether the employee is transferred by the existing employer or is employed by a new employer. It is allowed if the employee moves to a new area and obtains employment or switches from self-employed status to employee status (and vice versa). The moving expense deduction is also allowed if an individual is unemployed before obtaining employment in a new area.

What Is Not Included. In addition to meals while en route, the moving expense deduction does *not* include the following costs:

- New car tags and driver's licenses.
- Loss on the sale of a residence or penalty for breaking a lease.
- Forfeiture of security deposits and loss from disposing of club memberships.
- Pre-move house-hunting expenses.
- Temporary living expenses.

Also not deductible are the costs of moving servants and others who are not members of the household.

How Treated. Qualified moving expenses that are paid (or reimbursed) by the employer are not reported as part of the gross income of the employee.[21] Moving expenses that are paid (or reimbursed) by the employer and are not qualified moving expenses are included in the employee's gross income and are not deductible.

---

[20]§ 217(b).

[21]§§ 132(a)(6) and (g).

GLOBAL *Tax Issues*

EXPATRIATES AND THE MOVING EXPENSE DEDUCTION

Expatriates, U.S. persons who accept work assignments overseas, enjoy several favorable tax advantages regarding foreign moves. First, the cost of storing household goods qualifies as a moving expense. This could lead to a major tax saving since expatriates do not ship most of their household effects to the foreign location. Furthermore, the cost of storage, particularly in a climate-controlled facility, is not insignificant.

The second advantage expatriates could enjoy is an exemption from the time test. Those who return to the United States to retire are absolved from the 39-week or 78-week work requirement. Thus, the return home expenses are treated as qualified moving expenses.

The employer is responsible for allocating the reimbursement between the qualified and nonqualified moving expenses. Reimbursed qualified moving expenses are separately stated on the Form W–2 given to the employee for the year involved. Qualified moving expenses that are not reimbursed and those of self-employed taxpayers are deductions *for* AGI.[22]

Form 3903 is used to report the details of the moving expense deduction if the employee is not reimbursed or a self-employed person is involved.

ETHICAL and EQUITABLE *Considerations*   **MANIPULATING THE REAL ESTATE MARKET**

Ingrid is a key employee of Robin Corporation, an auto parts manufacturer located in Detroit. Robin would like to establish a presence in Tennessee and wants Ingrid to be in charge of the regional operation. Ingrid is reluctant to make the move because she fears that she will have to sell her residence in Detroit at a loss. Robin buys the house from Ingrid for $620,000, its cost to her. One year later, Robin sells the property for $550,000. Nothing regarding the sale of the residence is ever reflected on Ingrid's income tax return. Robin Corporation pays for all of Ingrid's other moving expenses. Do you have any qualms as to the way these matters have been handled for income tax purposes?

Education Expenses

General Requirements

LO.5

Differentiate between deductible and nondeductible education expenses.

An employee can deduct expenses incurred for education (**education expenses**) as ordinary and necessary business expenses provided the expenses are incurred for either of two reasons:

- To maintain or improve existing skills required in the present job.
- To meet the express requirements of the employer or the requirements imposed by law to retain his or her employment status.

Education expenses are *not* deductible if the education is for either of the following purposes (except as discussed below under A Limited Deduction Approach):

- To meet the minimum educational standards for qualification in the taxpayer's existing job.
- To qualify the taxpayer for a new trade or business.[23]

---

[22]§ 62(a)(15).   [23]Reg. §§ 1.162–5(b)(2) and (3).

Fees incurred for professional qualification exams (the bar exam, for example) and fees for review courses (such as a CPA review course) are not deductible.[24] If the education incidentally results in a promotion or raise, the deduction still can be taken as long as the education maintained and improved existing skills and did not qualify a person for a new trade or business. A change in duties is not always fatal to the deduction if the new duties involve the same general work. For example, the IRS has ruled that a practicing dentist's education expenses incurred to become an orthodontist are deductible.[25]

Requirements Imposed by Law or by the Employer for Retention of Employment

Taxpayers are permitted to deduct education expenses if additional courses are required by the employer or are imposed by law. Many states require a minimum of a bachelor's degree and a specified number of additional courses to retain a teaching job. In addition, some public school systems have imposed a master's degree requirement and require teachers to make satisfactory progress toward a master's degree in order to keep their positions. If the required education is the minimum degree required for the job, no deduction is allowed.

A taxpayer classified as a staff accountant who went back to school to obtain a bachelor's degree in accounting was not allowed to deduct the expenses. Although some courses tended to maintain and improve his existing skills in his entry-level position, the degree was the minimum requirement for his job.[26]

Expenses incurred for education required by law for various professions will also qualify for deduction.

EXAMPLE 26	In order to satisfy the State Board of Public Accountancy rules for maintaining her CPA license, Nancy takes an auditing course sponsored by a local college. The cost of the education is deductible. ∎

Maintaining or Improving Existing Skills

The "maintaining or improving existing skills" requirement in the Code has been difficult for both taxpayers and the courts to interpret. For example, a business executive may be permitted to deduct the costs of obtaining an MBA on the grounds that the advanced management education is undertaken to maintain and improve existing management skills. The executive is eligible to deduct the costs of specialized, nondegree management courses that are taken for continuing education or to maintain or improve existing skills. Expenses incurred by the executive to obtain a law degree are not deductible, however, because the education constitutes training for a new trade or business. The Regulations deny a self-employed accountant a deduction for expenses relating to law school.[27]

Classification of Specific Items

Education expenses include books, tuition, typing, and transportation (e.g., from the office to night school) and travel (e.g., meals and lodging while away from home at summer school).

---

[24]Reg. § 1.212–1(f) and Rev.Rul. 69–292, 1969–1 C.B. 84.

[25]Rev.Rul. 74–78, 1974–1 C.B. 44.

[26]Reg. § 1.162–5(b)(2)(iii) Example (2); *Collin J. Davidson*, 43 TCM 743, T.C.Memo. 1982–119. But see the subsequent discussion of § 222 (i.e., the deduction for higher education qualified tuition and related expenses).

[27]Reg. § 1.162–5(b)(3)(ii) Example (1).

TAX *in the News*   IS AN MBA DEGREE DEDUCTIBLE?

Education that maintains or improves existing skills is deductible, but education that qualifies a taxpayer for a new field is not. But how do these basic rules apply to a conventional (i.e., nonspecialized) MBA degree? Does being a manager or a consultant require an MBA degree? Generally, the answer has always been that it does not. In this regard, therefore, the education does not create a new skill, so its cost should be deductible.

Several recent holdings, however, have found that an MBA degree can lead to qualifying for a new trade or business.

But these holdings involved situations where the education resulted in a job change and satisfied different minimum requirements set by the employer. In one case, for example, the taxpayer moved from the position of investment analyst to become an investment banker, and the latter position required an MBA degree. Under these circumstances, the cost of the education was held to be nondeductible.

But barring a change to a job where the degree is required, the cost of an MBA degree should be deductible as merely improving existing managerial skills.

EXAMPLE 27

Bill, who holds a bachelor of education degree, is a secondary education teacher in the Los Angeles school system. The school board recently raised its minimum education requirement for new teachers from four years of college training to five. A grandfather clause allows teachers with only four years of college to continue to qualify if they show satisfactory progress toward a graduate degree. Bill enrolls at the University of California and takes three graduate courses. His unreimbursed expenses for this purpose are as follows:

Books and tuition	$3,600
Lodging while in travel status (June–August)	2,150
Meals while in travel status	1,100
Laundry while in travel status	220
Transportation	900

Bill has an itemized deduction as follows:

Books and tuition	$3,600
Lodging	2,150
Meals less 50% cutback (see below)	550
Laundry	220
Transportation	900
	$7,420

■

A Limited Deduction Approach

One of the major shortcomings of the education deduction, previously discussed, is that it is unavailable for taxpayers obtaining a basic skill. Thus, a taxpayer working for an accounting firm cannot deduct the cost of earning a bachelor's degree in accounting. Under 2001 tax legislation, this shortcoming has been partly resolved with the **deduction for qualified tuition and related expenses**.

A deduction *for* AGI is allowed for qualified tuition and related expenses involving higher education (i.e., postsecondary). The maximum amount of the deduction varies depending on the year involved. Further, the deduction is unavailable if the taxpayer's MAGI exceeds a prescribed amount.[28] The limitations are summarized in Table 9–1.[29]

---

[28]MAGI is modified adjusted gross income as defined in § 222(b)(2)(C), Examples of some of these modifications include the adding back to regular AGI of the foreign earned income exclusion and the domestic production activities deduction. See *Tax Benefits for Education* (IRS Publication 970).

[29]This provision expired at the end of 2007, but is expected to be extended by Congress.

TABLE 9–1	Rules for Qualified Tuition Deduction

Tax Years Involved	Filing Status	MAGI Limit	Maximum Deduction Allowed
2004–2007	Single	65,000	4,000
	Married	130,000	
	Single	65,001 to 80,000*	2,000
	Married	130,001 to 160,000*	2,000

*No deduction at all is available if MAGI exceeds this amount.

Various aspects of the higher education tuition deduction are summarized below:

- Qualified tuition and related expenses include whatever is required for enrollment at the institution. Usually, student activity fees, books, and room and board are not included.[30]
- The expense need not be employment related, although it can be.
- The deduction is available for a taxpayer's spouse or anyone who can be claimed as a dependent and is an eligible student.
- The deduction is not available for married persons who file separate returns.
- To avoid a "double benefit," the deduction must be coordinated with other education provisions (e.g., HOPE and lifetime learning credits). Along this same line, no deduction is allowed for a taxpayer who qualifies as another's dependent.[31]
- The deduction *for* AGI classification avoids the 2 percent-of-AGI floor on miscellaneous itemized deductions. As noted later in the chapter, this is the fate suffered by other education-related employee expenses.

EXAMPLE 28

Tina is single and a full-time employee of a CPA firm. During 2007, she attends law school at night and incurs the following expenses: $4,200 for tuition and $340 for books and supplies. Presuming she satisfies the MAGI limitation (see Table 9–1), she can claim $4,000 as a deduction *for* AGI. If she itemizes her deductions for the year, can she claim the $540 not allowed under § 222 ($200 tuition in excess of $4,000 + $340 for books and supplies) as an education expense eligible for itemized deduction treatment? No, because obtaining a law degree leads to a new trade or business.[32] ∎

The deduction for qualified tuition and related expenses can be determined by completing Form 8917 (Tuition and Fees Deduction). The form should be attached to Form 1040 (or Form 1040–A).

Other Provisions Dealing with Education

Although this chapter deals with employment-related expenses, mention should be made of various other tax provisions that deal with education. Because the encouragement of education is a desirable social goal, Congress has not been hesitant in

---

[30]Section 222(d) refers to § 25A(f), which deals with the HOPE and lifetime learning credits (see Chapter 13). Student activity fees and prescribed course-related books could be allowed if they are a condition for enrollment.

[31]§ 222(c).

[32]*Steven Galligan*, 83 TCM 1859, T.C.Memo. 2002–150.

enacting laws that provide tax incentives. The incentives come in the form of income exclusions, deductions (both *for* AGI and *from* AGI), and various credits. The paragraphs that follow summarize these benefits and note where they are discussed in the text.

Similar to the § 222 deduction for qualified tuition and related expenses just discussed is a deduction for interest on student loans.[33] Also treated as a deduction *for* AGI, a maximum of up to $2,500 per year is allowed. As noted in Chapter 10 in the discussion of Interest, the deduction is phased out for taxpayers with higher MAGI.

In the area of exclusions from gross income are Coverdell Education Savings Accounts (CESAs).[34] The maximum annual contribution to a CESA is $2,000. Although no deduction is allowed for contributions, earnings on these funds accumulate free of tax. Distributions also are nontaxable if used for tuition and related expenses. CESAs are further explained in Chapter 19 in the discussion of Individual Retirement Accounts (IRAs).

Qualified tuition programs (commonly referred to as "§ 529 plans") have the same objective as CESAs—to help pay for a beneficiary's (usually a dependent family member) education. The tax consequences are also similar, with no deduction allowed for any contribution to the plan and no tax imposed on income accumulations.[35] Distributions result in income only to the extent they are not applied toward educational purposes. There is no limit on the amount that can be contributed to a § 529 plan. Since the plan must be sponsored by a state or a private university, the terms and conditions set forth in the plan will vary accordingly. Section 529 plans are discussed in Chapter 5 under the heading Qualified Tuition Programs.

Another exclusion from gross income comes in the form of education assistance programs.[36] Sponsored by employers, such programs cover up to $5,250 per year of an employee's education costs (e.g., tuition, fees, books, supplies), which can be at the undergraduate or graduate level. Education assistance programs are discussed in Chapter 5 under the heading Other Employee Fringe Benefits.

Last but not least in the area of exclusions are certain scholarship awards.[37] As noted in Chapter 5, exclusion treatment is available for scholarships covering tuition and related expenses but not for those providing room and board.

In the area of tax credits, taxpayers benefit significantly from two provisions: the HOPE scholarship and the lifetime learning credits.[38] Both cover tuition and related expenses but not room and board and book costs. The HOPE credit allows no more than $1,800 per year for the first two years of college, while the lifetime credit permits up to $2,000 (20 percent of qualifying costs up to $10,000) per year with no time constraints. As noted in Chapter 13 in the discussion of Education Tax Credits, the credits are phased out for taxpayers with higher MAGI.

Entertainment Expenses

LO.6

Understand how entertainment expenses are treated.

Many taxpayers attempt to deduct personal entertainment expenses as business expenses. For this reason, the tax law restricts the deductibility of entertainment expenses. The Code contains strict record-keeping requirements and provides restrictive tests for the deduction of certain types of **entertainment expenses**.

---

[33]§ 221.

[34]§ 530.

[35]The major advantage of one of the two types of § 529 plans is protection against increasing tuition cost. The plan freezes the tuition that will be charged to the current amount.

[36]§ 127.

[37]§ 117.

[38]§ 25A.

Cutback Adjustment

During the administration of Jimmy Carter, considerable controversy arose regarding the "three martini" business lunch. By virtue of allowing a tax deduction, should the tax law be subsidizing a practice that contained a significant element of personal pleasure? One possible remedy for the situation was to disallow any deduction for business entertainment, but this option was regarded as being too harsh. Instead the *cutback* rule was instituted. Rather than disallowing *all* of the deduction, allow only a certain percentage, and the rest of the expenditure would be cut back. Currently, only 50 percent of meal and entertainment expenses are allowed as a deduction.[39] The limitation applies in the context of both employment and self-employment status. Although the 50 percent cutback can apply to either the employer or the employee, it will not apply twice. The cutback applies to the one who really pays (economically) for the meals or entertainment.

EXAMPLE 29

Jane, an employee of Pato Corporation, entertains one of her clients. If Pato Corporation does not reimburse Jane, she is subject to the cutback adjustment. If, however, Pato Corporation reimburses Jane (or pays for the entertainment directly), Pato suffers the cutback. ■

In certain situations, however, a full 50 percent cutback seems unfair. If, for example, the hours of service are regulated (by the U.S. Department of Transportation) and away-from-home meals are frequent and necessary, the "three martini" business lunch type of abuse is unlikely. Consequently, the cutback rule is mitigated for the following types of employees:

- Certain air transportation employees, such as flight crews, dispatchers, mechanics, and control tower operators.
- Interstate truck and bus drivers.
- Certain railroad employees, such as train crews and dispatchers.
- Certain merchant mariners.

Starting in 1998, the cutback for these types of employees has been reduced by 5 percent at two-year intervals until it reached 20 percent in year 2008 and thereafter. Thus, 80 percent of the cost of meals now is allowed as a deduction. For 2006–2007, 75 percent was allowed.

What Is Covered. Transportation expenses are not affected by the cutback rule—only meals and entertainment. The cutback also applies to taxes and tips relating to meals and entertainment. Cover charges, parking fees at an entertainment location, and room rental fees for a meal or cocktail party are also subject to the 50 percent rule.

EXAMPLE 30

Joe pays a $30 cab fare to meet his client for dinner. The meal costs $120, and Joe leaves a $20 tip. His deduction is $100 [($120 + $20) × 50% + $30 cab fare]. ■

What Is Not Covered. The cutback rule has a number of exceptions. One exception covers the case where the full value of the meals or entertainment is included in the compensation of the employee (or independent contractor).

EXAMPLE 31

Myrtle wins an all-expense-paid trip to Europe for selling the most insurance for her company during the year. Her employer treats this trip as additional compensation to Myrtle. The cutback adjustment does not apply to the employer. ■

---

[39]§ 274(n).

Another exception applies to meals and entertainment in a subsidized eating facility or where the *de minimis* fringe benefit rule is met (see Chapter 5).

General Hospital has an employee cafeteria on the premises for its doctors, nurses, and other employees. The cafeteria operates at cost. The cutback rule does not apply to General Hospital. ∎

Canary Corporation gives a ham, a fruitcake, and a bottle of wine to each employee at year-end. Since the *de minimis* fringe benefit exclusion applies to business gifts of packaged foods and beverages, their *full* cost is deductible by Canary. ∎

A similar exception applies to employer-paid recreational activities for employees (e.g., the annual Christmas party or spring picnic).[40]

Classification of Expenses

Entertainment expenses are categorized as follows: those *directly related* to business and those *associated with* business.[41] Directly related expenses are related to an actual business meeting or discussion. These expenses are distinguished from entertainment expenses that are incurred to promote goodwill, such as maintaining existing customer relations. To obtain a deduction for directly related entertainment, it is not necessary to show that actual benefit resulted from the expenditure as long as there was a reasonable expectation of benefit. To qualify as directly related, the expense should be incurred in a clear business setting. If there is little possibility of engaging in the active conduct of a trade or business due to the nature of the social facility, it is difficult to qualify the expenditure as directly related to business.

Expenses associated with, rather than directly related to, business entertainment must serve a specific business purpose, such as obtaining new business or continuing existing business. These expenditures qualify only if the expenses directly precede or follow a bona fide business discussion. Entertainment occurring on the same day as the business discussion meets the test.

Restrictions upon Deductibility

Business Meals. Any business meal is deductible only if the following are true:[42]

- The meal is directly related to or associated with the active conduct of a trade or business.
- The expense is not lavish or extravagant under the circumstances.
- The taxpayer (or an employee) is present at the meal.

A business meal with a business associate or customer is not deductible unless business is discussed before, during, or after the meal. This requirement is not intended to disallow the deduction for a meal consumed while away from home on business.

Lacy travels to San Francisco for a business convention. She pays for dinner with three colleagues and is not reimbursed by her employer. They do not discuss business. She can deduct 50% of the cost of her meal. However, she cannot deduct the cost of her colleagues' meals. ∎

---

[40]§ 274(e)(4).
[41]§ 274(a)(1)(A).

[42]§ 274(k).

To encourage future patronage, most casinos reward favored customers with complimentary goods and services (called "comps"). For example, an active member of a casino's "slot club" might receive comps in the form of free meals, lodging, and other gifts (e.g., fruit baskets, flowers, boxes of candy). The type and amount of comps awarded depend on the patron's gambling activity. (Using various procedures, most casinos are able to track the level of play of regular patrons.) Of course, patrons are well aware that the more they gamble, the bigger and better the comps they may receive.

Should these comps be subject to the limitations on deductibility imposed by the general rule of § 274(a)? For example, should the cutback adjustment apply to meals and entertainment, and should the deductibility of gifts be limited to $25? The casinos contend that comps fall under an exception of § 274(e)(7) that exempts goods and services made available to the general public for *promotional purposes*. The IRS questions whether a casino is promoting its facilities to the general public when only the heavy gamblers receive comps.

To save time and effort, however, the IRS has instructed its field agents not to raise the issue on audit as long as the comp programs continue to be followed in the same manner as in the past. In the interest of administrative convenience, therefore, it appears that the IRS grants special treatment to casinos.

Source: *IRS Memorandum for Industry Director Directive on Deductibility of Casino Comps*, LMSB-04-0706-990, *July 31, 2006*.

The *clear business purpose* test requires that meals be directly related to or associated with the active conduct of a business. A meal is not deductible if it serves no business purpose.

The taxpayer or an employee must be present at the business meal for the meal to be deductible. An independent contractor who renders significant services to the taxpayer is treated as an employee.

EXAMPLE 35

Lance, a party to a contract negotiation, buys dinner for other parties to the negotiation but does not attend the dinner. No deduction is allowed. ■

ETHICAL and EQUITABLE *Considerations*   **YOUR TURN OR MINE?**

Jordan, an attorney, Corey, a banker, Courtney, a CPA, and Kelly, an insurance broker, maintain private practices in the same business community. During the year, they get together for lunch every two weeks. They take turns paying for the group's lunch. Since they all do business with each other, each claims an entertainment expense deduction for the amount he or she paid for the lunches. Evaluate this practice.

Club Dues. The Code provides: "No deduction shall be allowed . . . for amounts paid or incurred for membership in any club organized for business, pleasure, recreation, or other social purpose."[43] Although this prohibition seems quite broad, the IRS does allow a deduction for dues to clubs whose primary purpose is public service and community volunteerism (e.g., Kiwanis, Lions, Rotary).

Even though dues are not deductible, actual entertainment at a club may qualify.

[43]§ 274(a)(3).

EXAMPLE 36

During the current year, Vincent spent $1,400 on business lunches at the Lakeside Country Club. The annual membership fee was $6,000, and Vincent used the facility 60% of the time for business. Presuming the lunches meet the business meal test, Vincent may claim $700 (50% × $1,400) as a deduction. None of the club dues are deductible. ■

Ticket Purchases for Entertainment. A deduction for the cost of a ticket for an entertainment activity is limited to the face value of the ticket.[44] This limitation is applied before the 50 percent rule. The face value of a ticket includes any tax. Under this rule, the excess payment to a scalper for a ticket is not deductible. Similarly, the fee to a ticket agency for the purchase of a ticket is not deductible.

Expenditures for the rental or use of a luxury skybox at a sports arena in excess of the face value of regular tickets are disallowed as deductions. If a luxury skybox is used for entertainment that is directly related to or associated with business, the deduction is limited to the face value of nonluxury box seats. All seats in the luxury skybox are counted, even when some seats are unoccupied.

The taxpayer may also deduct stated charges for food and beverages under the general rules for business entertainment. The deduction for skybox seats, food, and beverages is limited to 50 percent of cost.

EXAMPLE 37

In the current year, Jay Company pays $12,000 to rent a 10-seat skybox at City Stadium for three football games. Nonluxury box seats at each event range in cost from $55 to $95 a seat. In September, a Jay representative and five clients use the skybox for the first game. The entertainment follows a bona fide business discussion, and Jay spends $290 for food and beverages during the game. The deduction for the first sports event is as follows:

Food and beverages	$ 290
Deduction for seats ($95 × 10 seats)	950
Total entertainment expense	$1,240
50% limitation	× .50
Deduction	$ 620

■

Business Gifts. Business gifts are deductible to the extent of $25 per donee per year.[45] An exception is made for gifts costing $4 or less (e.g., pens with the employee's or company's name on them) or promotional materials. Such items are not treated as business gifts subject to the $25 limitation. In addition, incidental costs such as engraving of jewelry and nominal charges for gift-wrapping, mailing, and delivery are not included in the cost of the gift in applying the limitation. Gifts to superiors and employers are not deductible.

The $25 limitation on business gifts cannot be circumvented by having the donor's spouse join in the gift or by making multiple gifts that include the customer's family.

Records must be maintained to substantiate business gifts.

Other Employee Expenses

LO.7

Identify other employee expenses.

Office in the Home

Employees and self-employed individuals are not allowed a deduction for **office in the home expenses** unless a portion of the residence is used *exclusively* on a *regular basis* as either of the following:

- The principal place of business for any trade or business of the taxpayer.
- A place of business used by clients, patients, or customers.

---

[44]§ 274(l).

[45]§ 274(b)(1).

Employees must meet an additional test: The use must be for the *convenience of the employer* rather than merely being "appropriate and helpful."[46]

The precise meaning of "principal place of business" has been the subject of considerable controversy.[47] Congress ultimately resolved the issue by amending the Code.[48] The term "principal place of business" now includes a place of business that satisfies the following requirements:

- The office is used by the taxpayer to conduct administrative or management activities of a trade or business.
- There is no other fixed location of the trade or business where the taxpayer conducts these activities.

EXAMPLE 38

Dr. Smith is a self-employed anesthesiologist. During the year, he spends 30 to 35 hours per week administering anesthesia and postoperative care to patients in three hospitals, none of which provides him with an office. He also spends two or three hours per day in a room in his home that he uses exclusively as an office. He does not meet patients there, but he performs a variety of tasks related to his medical practice (e.g., contacting surgeons, bookkeeping, reading medical journals). A deduction will be allowed since Dr. Smith uses the office in the home to conduct administrative or management activities of his trade or business, and there is no other fixed location where these activities can be carried out. ■

The exclusive use requirement means that part of the home must be used solely for business purposes. An exception allows mixed use (both business and personal) of the home if a licensed day-care business is involved.

EXAMPLE 39

Troy is self-employed and maintains an office in his home for business purposes. The office is also used by his wife to pay the family bills and by his children to do homework assignments. Troy does not satisfy the exclusive use requirement, and no office in the home deduction is allowed. ■

EXAMPLE 40

Morgan operates a licensed day-care center in her home. The children use the living room as a play area during the day, and Morgan and her family use it for personal purposes in the evening and on weekends. The mixed use of the living room does not disqualify Morgan from an office in the home deduction. ■

In arriving at the office in the home deduction, relevant expenses are categorized as direct or indirect. Direct expenses benefit only the business part of the home (e.g., the office is repainted) and are deducted in full. Indirect expenses are for maintaining and operating the home. Since they benefit both business and personal use, an allocation between the two is necessary. The allocation is made based on the floor space involved—divide the business area by the total home area to arrive at the business percentage.

The allowable home office expenses cannot exceed the gross income from the business less all other business expenses attributable to the activity. Furthermore, the home office expenses that are allowed as itemized deductions anyway (e.g., mortgage interest and real estate taxes) must be deducted first. All home office expenses of an employee are miscellaneous itemized deductions, except those (such as interest and taxes) that qualify as other personal itemized deductions. Home office expenses of a self-employed individual are trade or business expenses and are deductible *for* AGI.

---

[46]§ 280A(c)(1).

[47]See the restrictive interpretation arrived at in *Comm. v. Soliman*, 93–1 USTC ¶50,014, 71 AFTR2d 93–463, 113 S.Ct. 701 (USSC, 1993).

[48]§ 280A(c)(1) as modified by the Tax Reform Act of 1997.

CHAPTER 9 Deductions: Employee and Self-Employed-Related Expenses   9

Any disallowed home office expenses are *carried forward* and used in future years subject to the same limitations.

EXAMPLE 41

Rick is a certified public accountant employed by a regional CPA firm as a tax manager. He operates a separate business in which he refinishes furniture in his home. For this business, he uses two rooms in the basement of his home exclusively and regularly. The floor space of the two rooms constitutes 10% of the floor space of his residence. Gross income from the business totals $8,000. Expenses of the business (other than home office expenses) are $6,500. Rick incurs the following home office expenses:

Real property taxes on residence	$ 4,000
Interest expense on residence	7,500
Operating expenses of residence	2,000
Depreciation on residence (based on 10% business use)	250

Rick's deductions are determined as follows:

Business income		$ 8,000
Less: Other business expenses		(6,500)
		$ 1,500
Less: Allocable taxes ($4,000 × 10%)	$400	
Allocable interest ($7,500 × 10%)	750	(1,150)
		$ 350
Allocable operating expenses of the residence ($2,000 × 10%)		(200)
		$ 150
Allocable depreciation ($250, limited to remaining income)		(150)
		$ –0–

Rick has a carryover of $100 (the unused excess depreciation). Because he is self-employed, the allocable taxes and interest ($1,150), the other deductible office expenses ($200 + $150), and $6,500 of other business expenses are deductible *for* AGI. ∎

To claim the office in the home deduction, use Form 8829 (Expenses for Business Use of Your Home). For further information on the deduction, see the instructions for Form 8829 and *Business Use of Your Home* (Publication 587) issued by the IRS.

Miscellaneous Employee Expenses

Miscellaneous employee expenses include those costs that are job related and are not otherwise covered elsewhere. As the focus here is on their deductibility, this discussion presumes that such expenses have not been reimbursed by the employer under an accountable plan arrangement (discussed later in the chapter).

Expenses related to maintaining job status make up a significant category of miscellaneous expenses. They include such costs as union dues, membership dues to professional organizations, subscriptions to trade publications and professional journals, and various license fees paid to government agencies and other regulatory bodies.

Special Clothing. To be deductible, special clothing must be both specifically required as a condition of employment and not adaptable for regular wear. For example, a police officer's uniform must be worn when "on duty" but is not suitable for "off-duty" activities. Its cost, therefore, is deductible. When special clothing qualifies for deductibility, so does the cost of its maintenance (i.e., alterations, laundry, dry cleaning).

Encouraging employees to maintain an office in the home normally will produce savings for the employer. When employees work at home, the employer can avoid the cost of office space (rent, furnishings) and incidental benefits (parking, technical support). Besides cost savings for the employer, telecommuting can provide significant benefits to employees. Not only do they save time by avoiding a commute, but those who normally would drive will save on fuel consumption. With the escalating price of gasoline, the cost saving by working at home can be significant. The cost factor plus the increased flexibility in work scheduling that comes with telecommuting is adding to the popularity of maintaining an office in the home.

Whether the out-of-pocket cost of military uniforms is deductible depends on the duty status of the taxpayer. If a member of the National Guard (or reserves) is not on active duty, then the cost of the uniform qualifies for deductibility. For those on active duty, the cost of regular uniforms does not qualify because the uniforms are suitable for ordinary street wear. Even for those on active duty, some apparel, such as ceremonial attire (dress blues) or combat gear, will qualify because it is not adaptable for regular wear.

The cost of clothing possessing *safety* features to prevent workplace injuries will qualify. This includes such items as safety glasses, shoes (e.g., "steel-toed"), special gloves, lab coats, and "hard hats." The tolerance of the IRS in the area of safety clothing is partially attributable to its lack of suitability for personal use.

Job Hunting. The expenses incurred in seeking employment can be deductible under certain conditions. The search must involve the same trade or business as the taxpayer's current position. No deduction is allowed for the cost of obtaining the first job. An unemployed person, however, can qualify for the deduction if there has not been a significant time lapse since the last job. In terms of deductibility, it does not matter whether the job search is successful. Nor does a change in jobs have to result. Costs that qualify include job counseling, compilation and distribution of biographical data (such as work history), and unreimbursed travel for job interviews.

Educator Expenses. Many teachers purchase school supplies for classroom use and are not reimbursed by their employer. These out-of-pocket expenses can be deducted only if the teacher itemizes his or her deductions *from* AGI, and even then they are subject to the 2 percent-of-AGI floor (see later in this chapter). Thus, these restrictions can reduce or eliminate any tax benefit available to the teacher. Recent legislation provides *modest* relief for such out-of-pocket expenses by allowing elementary and secondary school teachers to claim up to $250 for school supplies as a deduction *for* AGI.[49] Eligible educators must work at least 900 hours during a school year as a teacher, instructor, counselor, principal, or aide at either public or private elementary and secondary schools. Covered costs include unreimbursed expenses for books, supplies, computer and other equipment, and supplementary materials used in the classroom.

EXAMPLE 42

Hortense is a full-time teacher at Hoover Elementary. During 2007, she spends $1,200 for school supplies for her fourth grade class. Under an accountable plan (see later in the chapter), Hoover reimburses her for $400 of these supplies. As to the $800 balance, Hortense may claim $250 as a deduction *for* AGI and $550 as a miscellaneous itemized deduction (subject to the 2%-of-AGI floor). ■

---

[49]§ 62(a)(2)(D). This provision expired at the end of 2007, but is expected to be extended by Congress.

Although the educator expense provision expired at the end of 2007, there is good reason to believe that Congress will extend it.

Contributions to Retirement Accounts

LO.8

Become familiar with various deductions for contributions to retirement accounts.

Pension considerations are an essential feature of any compensation arrangement. As noted in Chapter 1, providing retirement security for employees can be justified on both economic and social grounds. Because the public sector (i.e., Social Security) will not provide sufficient retirement security for recipients, the private sector must fill the need. Congress has given the private sector the necessary incentive by enacting various measures that provide significant tax advantages for retirement plans. These plans fall into two major classifications: those available to employees and those available to self-employed persons.

Employee IRAs

Pension plans covering employees follow one of two income tax approaches. Most plans allow an *exclusion* for the contributions the employee makes to the plan. The employee's income tax return shows nothing regarding the contribution—no income, exclusion, or deduction. This is the case even if the contribution is funded entirely (or partially) by means of a salary reduction.[50]

The other income tax approach is followed by the **traditional IRA**. Here, the contributing employee is allowed a deduction *for* AGI. The amount, a maximum of $5,000 for 2008, is reported as a deduction on Form 1040.[51] As with the exclusion variety of pension plan, nothing is taxed to the employee-participant until distributions from the traditional IRA occur. Consequently, all of these types of retirement plans carry the advantage of deferring the taxation of income. As described in Chapter 19, all retirement plans are subject to various rules regarding coverage requirements, degree of vesting, excessive contributions, and premature distributions. Generally, these rules are less stringent for traditional IRAs.

The traditional IRA is to be distinguished from the **Roth IRA**, which takes a radically different tax approach. No tax benefit (i.e., exclusion or deduction) results from the initial contribution to a Roth IRA. Instead, later distributions (including postcontribution earnings) are recovered tax-free.[52]

Self-Employed Keogh (H.R. 10) Plans

Self-employed taxpayers can also participate in retirement plans with tax-favored benefits. Known as Keogh (or H.R. 10) plans, these arrangements follow the deduction approach of traditional IRAs.[53] The amount contributed under a plan is a deduction *for* AGI and is reported as a deduction on Form 1040. The plan established by a self-employed taxpayer who has employees must meet stringent requirements to ensure that it provides similar retirement benefits for the group. The law is structured to ensure that employees share an owner-employer's ability to defer taxes.

The operational rules governing Keogh (H.R. 10) plans are covered in Chapter 19.

Classification of Employee Expenses

LO.9

Appreciate the difference between accountable and nonaccountable employee plans.

The classification of employee expenses depends on whether they are reimbursed by the employer under an accountable plan. If so, then they are not reported by the employee at all. In effect, therefore, this result is equivalent to treating the

---

[50]See, for example, §§ 401(k), 403(b), and 457.

[51]§§ 219 and 408.

[52]§ 408A.

[53]§ 401(c).

expenses as deductions *for* AGI.[54] If the expenses are reimbursed under a nonaccountable plan or are not reimbursed at all, then they are classified as deductions *from* AGI and can be claimed only if the employee-taxpayer itemizes. An exception is made for moving expenses and the employment-related expenses of a qualified performing artist.[55] Here, deduction *for* AGI classification is allowed.

For classification purposes, therefore, the difference between accountable and nonaccountable plans is significant.

Accountable Plans

In General. An **accountable plan** requires the employee to satisfy these two requirements:

- Adequately account for (substantiate) the expenses. An employee renders an *adequate accounting* by submitting a record, with receipts and other substantiation, to the employer.[56]
- Return any excess reimbursement or allowance. An "excess reimbursement or allowance" is any amount that the employee does not adequately account for as an ordinary and necessary business expense.

Substantiation. The law provides that no deduction is allowed for any travel, entertainment, business gift, or listed property (automobiles, computers) expenditure unless properly substantiated by adequate records. The records should contain the following information:[57]

- The amount of the expense.
- The time and place of travel or entertainment (or date of gift).
- The business purpose of the expense.
- The business relationship of the taxpayer to the person entertained (or receiving the gift).

This means the taxpayer must maintain an account book or diary in which the above information is recorded at the time of the expenditure. Documentary evidence, such as itemized receipts, is required to support any expenditure for lodging while traveling away from home and for any other expenditure of $75 or more. If a taxpayer fails to keep adequate records, each expense must be established by a written or oral statement of the exact details of the expense and by other corroborating evidence.[58]

EXAMPLE 43

Bertha has travel expenses substantiated only by canceled checks. The checks establish the date, place, and amount of the expenditure. Because neither the business relationship nor the business purpose is established, the deduction is disallowed.[59] ∎

EXAMPLE 44

Dwight has travel and entertainment expenses substantiated by a diary showing the time, place, and amount of the expenditure. His oral testimony provides the business relationship and business purpose. However, since he has no receipts, any expenditures of $75 or more are disallowed.[60] ∎

Deemed Substantiation. In lieu of reimbursing actual expenses for travel away from home, many employers reduce their paperwork by adopting a policy of

---

[54]§ 62(a)(2).
[55]As defined in § 62(b).
[56]Reg. § 1.162–17(b)(4).
[57]§ 274(d).

[58]Reg. § 1.274–5T(c)(3).
[59]*William T. Whitaker*, 56 TCM 47, T.C.Memo. 1988–418.
[60]*W. David Tyler*, 43 TCM 927, T.C.Memo. 1982–160.

reimbursing employees with a *per diem* allowance, a flat dollar amount per day of business travel. Of the substantiation requirements listed previously, the *amount* of the expense is proved, or *deemed substantiated*, by using such a per diem allowance or reimbursement procedure. The amount of expenses that is deemed substantiated is equal to the lesser of the per diem allowance or the amount of the Federal per diem rate.

The regular Federal per diem rate is the highest amount that the Federal government will pay to its employees for lodging, meals, and incidental expenses[61] while in travel status away from home in a particular area. The rates are different for different locations.[62]

The use of the standard Federal per diem rates for meals and incidental expenses constitutes an adequate accounting. Employees and self-employed persons can use these standard allowances instead of deducting the actual cost of daily meals and incidental expenses, even if not reimbursed. There is no standard lodging allowance, however.

Only the amount of the expense is considered substantiated under the deemed substantiated method. The other substantiation requirements must be provided: place, date, business purpose of the expense, and the business relationship of the parties involved.

Nonaccountable Plans

A **nonaccountable plan** is one in which an adequate accounting or return of excess amounts, or both, is not required. All reimbursements of expenses are reported in full as wages on the employee's Form W–2. Any allowable expenses are deductible in the same manner as are unreimbursed expenses.

Unreimbursed Employee Expenses.
Unreimbursed employee expenses are treated in a straightforward manner. Meals and entertainment expenses are subject to the 50 percent limit. Total unreimbursed employee business expenses are usually reported as miscellaneous itemized deductions subject to the 2 percent-of-AGI floor (see below). If the employee could have received, but did not seek, reimbursement for whatever reason, none of the employment-related expenses are deductible.

Failure to Comply with Accountable Plan Requirements.
An employer may have an accountable plan and require employees to return excess reimbursements or allowances, but an employee may fail to follow the rules of the plan. In that case, the expenses and reimbursements are subject to nonaccountable plan treatment.

Reporting Procedures

The reporting requirements range from no reporting at all (accountable plans when all requirements are met) to the use of some or all of the following forms: Form W–2 (Wage and Tax Statement), Form 2106 (Employee Business Expenses) or Form 2106–EZ (Unreimbursed Employee Business Expenses), and Schedule A (Itemized Deductions) for nonaccountable plans and unreimbursed employee expenses.

Reimbursed employee expenses that are adequately accounted for under an accountable plan are deductible *for* AGI on Form 2106. Allowed excess expenses, expenses reimbursed under a nonaccountable plan, and unreimbursed expenses are deductible *from* AGI on Schedule A, subject to the 2 percent-of-AGI floor.

When a reimbursement under an accountable plan is paid in separate amounts relating to designated expenses such as meals or entertainment, no problem arises.

---

[61]Incidental expenses include tips and fees to porters, bellhops, hotel maids, etc. For travel away from home after 2002, the term does *not* include expenses for laundry and dry cleaning of clothing, lodging taxes, and telephone calls.

[62]*Per Diem Rates* (IRS Publication 1542) contains the list and amounts for the year. This publication is available only on the Internet at **http://www.irs.gov**. A print edition is no longer published. Links to per diem rates can also be found at **http://www.gsa.gov**.

The reimbursements and expenses are reported as such on the appropriate forms. If the reimbursement is made in a single amount, an allocation must be made to determine the appropriate portion of the reimbursement that applies to meals and entertainment and to other employee expenses.

EXAMPLE 45

Elizabeth, who is employed by Green Company, had AGI of $42,000. During the year, she incurred $2,000 of transportation and lodging expense and $1,000 of meals and entertainment expense, all fully substantiated. Elizabeth received $1,800 reimbursement under an accountable plan. The reimbursement rate that applies to meals and entertainment is 33.33% ($1,000 meals and entertainment expense/$3,000 total expenses). Thus, $600 ($1,800 × 33.33%) of the reimbursement applies to meals and entertainment, and $1,200 ($1,800 − $600) applies to transportation and lodging. Elizabeth's itemized deduction consists of the $800 ($2,000 total − $1,200 reimbursement) of unreimbursed transportation and lodging expenses and $400 ($1,000 − $600) of unreimbursed meal and entertainment expenses as follows:

Transportation and lodging	$ 800
Meals and entertainment ($400 × 50%)	200
Total (reported on Form 2106)	$1,000
Less: 2% of $42,000 AGI (see limitation discussed below)	(840)
Deduction (reported on Schedule A)	$ 160

In summary, Elizabeth reports $3,000 of expenses and the $1,800 reimbursement on Form 2106 and $160 as a miscellaneous itemized deduction on Schedule A. ∎

ETHICAL and EQUITABLE *Considerations*   A SANITIZED EXPENSE ACCOUNT

Donald is a star traveling salesperson for Cardinal Supply, a nationwide wholesaler of sporting goods equipment. He also has a reputation with management of being very conservative in his use of company funds. Because of these traits—salesmanship and frugality—Donald has received frequent promotions and bonuses.

Unknown to the company, Donald is quite generous when entertaining customers. He feels that his high level of "wine and dine" is largely responsible for his outstanding

sales record. In the expense account he submits to the company, Donald omits the excessive portion. He is not sure that the company would reimburse him for the extra costs, and he wants to maintain his reputation for frugality. On his own tax return, however, Donald deducts the portion of the expenses that were not included in his expense account.

What difficulties, if any, do you anticipate with what Donald is doing?

LO.10

Work with the limitations on miscellaneous itemized deductions.

Limitations on Itemized Deductions

Many itemized deductions, such as medical expenses and charitable contributions, are subject to limitations expressed as a percentage of AGI. These limitations may be expressed as floors or ceilings and are discussed in Chapter 10.

Miscellaneous Itemized Deductions Subject to the 2 Percent Floor

Certain miscellaneous itemized deductions, including most *unreimbursed employee business expenses*, are aggregated and then reduced by 2 percent of AGI.[63] Expenses subject to the 2 percent floor include the following:

---

[63]§ 67.

- All § 212 expenses, except expenses of producing rent and royalty income (refer to Chapter 6).
- All unreimbursed employee expenses (after the 50 percent reduction, if applicable) except moving.
- Professional dues and subscriptions.
- Union dues and work uniforms.
- Employment-related education expenses (except for § 222 qualified tuition and related expenses).
- Malpractice insurance premiums.
- Expenses of job hunting (including employment agency fees and résumé-writing expenses).
- Home office expenses of an employee or outside salesperson.
- Legal, accounting, and tax return preparation fees.
- Hobby expenses (up to hobby income).
- Investment expenses, including investment counsel fees, subscriptions, and safe deposit box rental.
- Custodial fees relating to income-producing property or a traditional IRA or a Keogh plan.
- Any fees paid to collect interest or dividends.
- Appraisal fees establishing a casualty loss or charitable contribution.

Miscellaneous Itemized Deductions Not Subject to the 2 Percent Floor

Certain miscellaneous itemized deductions, including the following, are not subject to the 2 percent floor:

- Impairment-related work expenses of handicapped individuals.
- Gambling losses to the extent of gambling winnings.
- Certain terminated annuity payments.

EXAMPLE 46

Ted, who has AGI of $40,000, has the following miscellaneous itemized deductions:

Gambling losses (to extent of gains)	$2,200
Tax return preparation fees	500
Unreimbursed employee transportation	600
Professional dues and subscriptions	360
Safe deposit box rental	90

Ted's itemized deductions are as follows:

Deduction not subject to 2% floor (gambling losses)		$2,200
Deductions subject to 2% floor ($500 + $600 + $360 + $90)	$1,550	
Less 2% of AGI	(800)	750
Total miscellaneous itemized deductions		$2,950

If instead Ted's AGI is $80,000, the floor is $1,600 (2% of $80,000), and he cannot deduct any expenses subject to the 2% floor. ∎

LO.11

Develop tax planning ideas related to employee business expenses.

Self-Employed Individuals

Some taxpayers have the flexibility to be classified as either employees or self-employed individuals. Examples include real estate agents and direct sellers. These taxpayers should carefully consider all factors and not automatically assume that self-employed status is preferable.

TAX PLANNING
Considerations

It is advantageous to deduct one's business expenses *for* AGI and avoid the 2 percent floor. However, a self-employed individual may have higher expenses, such as local gross receipts taxes, license fees, franchise fees, personal property taxes, and occupation taxes. In addition, the record-keeping and filing requirements can be quite burdensome.

One of the most expensive considerations is the Social Security tax versus the self-employment tax. For an employee in 2008, for example, the Social Security tax applies at a rate of 6.2 percent on a base amount of wages of $102,000, and the Medicare tax applies at a rate of 1.45 percent with no limit on the base amount. For self-employed persons, the rate, but not the base amount, for each tax doubles. Even though a deduction *for* AGI is allowed for one-half of the self-employment tax paid, an employee and a self-employed individual are not in the same tax position on equal amounts of earnings. The self-employment tax is explained in Chapter 13. For the applicability of these taxes to employees, see Chapter 1.

If a taxpayer misclassifies workers as self-employed, rather than employees, one of the penalties for being wrong is the liability for the employment taxes that should have been paid. But this penalty for misclassifying workers will be avoided if *all* three of the following requirements are met:

- The employer has a reasonable basis for *not* treating the workers as employees. Reasonable basis means reliance on any of the following—
  - A judicial precedent, published ruling, or technical advice.
  - A past IRS audit that resulted in no employment tax assessment.
  - A longstanding practice of independent contractor status in the same industry.
- The employer has consistently treated the workers as independent contractors.
- The employer has filed Form 1099 MISC (Miscellaneous Income) for each worker (when such filing was required).

Satisfaction of these requirements will help an employer avoid disputes with the IRS over workers' employment status.[64]

Shifting Deductions between Employer and Employee

An employee can avoid the 2 percent floor for employee business expenses. Typically, an employee incurs travel and entertainment expenses in the course of employment. The employer gets the deduction if it reimburses the employee, and the employee gets the deduction *for* AGI. An adequate accounting must be made, and excess reimbursements cannot be kept by the employee.

[64]This safe harbor for withholding purposes originated in § 530 of the Revenue Act of 1978. See IRS *Headliner* vol. 152 (March 27, 2006).

Transportation and Travel Expenses

Adequate detailed records of all transportation and travel expenses should be kept. Since the regular mileage allowance often is modest in amount, a new, expensive automobile used primarily for business may generate a higher expense based on actual cost. In using the actual cost method, include the business portion of depreciation, repairs and maintenance, automobile club dues, insurance, gasoline and oil, and other related costs. The cost of gasoline, when coupled with the poor mileage performance of some vehicles, can be a significant factor. If the taxpayer is located in a metropolitan area, automobile insurance is more expensive. For the self-employed taxpayer, the business portion of finance charges (i.e., interest on car loans) can be included.

Once a method is chosen, a later change may be possible. Conversion from the automatic mileage method to the actual cost method is allowed if a basis adjustment is made for depreciation deemed taken (see Example 9). Conversion from the actual cost method to the automatic mileage method is possible only if the taxpayer has not used the MACRS statutory percentage method or claimed § 179 limited expensing.

If a taxpayer wishes to sightsee or vacation on a business trip, it would be beneficial to schedule business on both a Friday and a Monday to turn the weekend into business days for allocation purposes. It is especially crucial to schedule appropriate business days when foreign travel is involved.

Moving Expenses

Persons who retire and move to a new location incur personal nondeductible moving expenses. If the retired person accepts a full-time job in the new location, the moving expenses are deductible.

EXAMPLE 47

At the time of his retirement from the national office of a major accounting firm, Gordon had an annual salary of $420,000. He moves from New York City to Seattle to retire. To qualify for the moving expense deduction, Gordon accepts a full-time teaching position at a Seattle junior college at an annual salary of $15,000. If Gordon satisfies the 39-week test, his moving expenses are deductible. The disparity between the two salaries (previous and current) is of no consequence. ■

Education Expenses

Education expenses are treated as nondeductible personal items unless the individual is employed or is engaged in a trade or business. A temporary leave of absence for further education is one way to reasonably assure that the taxpayer is still qualified, even if a full-time student. An individual was permitted to deduct education expenses even though he resigned from his job, returned to school full-time for two years, and accepted another job in the same field upon graduation. The court held that the student had merely suspended active participation in his field.[65]

If the time out of the field is too long, educational expense deductions will be disallowed. For example, a teacher who left the field for four years to raise her child and curtailed her employment searches and writing activities was denied a deduction. She was not actively engaged in the trade or business of being an educator.[66]

To secure the deduction, an individual should arrange his or her work situation to preserve employee or business status.

The deduction for qualified tuition and related expenses provides some relief from the current restrictions on the deduction of education expenses by employees.

---

[65]*Stephen G. Sherman*, 36 TCM 1191, T.C.Memo. 1977–301.

[66]*Brian C. Mulherin*, 42 TCM 834, T.C.Memo. 1981–454; *George A. Baist*, 56 TCM 778, T.C.Memo. 1988–554.

Somewhat concerned about the way it was handling the moving expenses of new employees and existing employees who were relocated, the Smithsonian Institution underwent an audit by its Inspector General Division. The results of the audit revealed weak controls and inconsistent practices. Many of the payments were made to third-party providers of services (e.g., hotels, restaurants) while other payments were direct reimbursements to employees. Expenses reimbursed included temporary living expenses, closing costs on the purchase of a new home, and tuition deposits for the children of new hires—all of which are clearly income to the recipients. Whether such reimbursements were ever subject to income tax is problematical, as some ($200,000 out of $1.4 million) were never included in the W–2 forms issued to the employees involved.

After learning of the audit results, the Smithsonian announced that it would establish new payroll procedures to correct the problems. Until this is done, any such disbursements will be labeled and reported as "recruitment payments."

When a prestigious organization like the Smithsonian is having difficulty properly accounting for the treatment of moving expense reimbursements, one has to wonder how prevalent the problem might be. For example, how many nonqualifying reimbursements escape income recognition because they are misclassified (or not reported) by the employer—either deliberately or inadvertently. (See the *Ethical and Equitable Considerations* on page 9–13 of this chapter.)

Source: *Audit Report of the Office of Inspector General of the Smithsonian Institution,* Administration of Relocation and Recruitment Payments, *September 28, 2007.*

First, the education expense does not have to be work related. Second, it is a deduction *for* (not *from*) AGI. Unfortunately, the deduction possesses severe shortcomings: not only is the annual amount allowed quite modest, but it may be unavailable to certain taxpayers. It is not available, for example, to those who exceed an AGI ceiling or to someone who can be claimed as a dependent of another.

Before selecting the § 222 deduction approach, however, consider the possible availability of the HOPE credit or the lifetime learning credit under § 25A.[67] As credits provide a dollar-for-dollar reduction of tax liability, these provisions could yield a greater tax benefit than deductions *for* AGI. But these credits may not be available to higher-income taxpayers. Although both § 222 deductions and § 25A credits are subject to MAGI limitations, the credits begin phasing out at $48,000 ($96,000 on a joint return) and are eliminated by $58,000 ($116,000 on a joint return). Moreover, the MAGI limitations extend to $80,000 ($160,000 on a joint return) for § 222. Thus, a married couple with MAGI in excess of $116,000 (but not more than $160,000) would have to use the § 222 deduction for tuition expenses, as the § 25A credits are not available.

Entertainment Expenses

Proper documentation of expenditures is essential because of the strict record-keeping requirements and the restrictive tests that must be met. For example, documentation that consists solely of credit card receipts and canceled checks may be inadequate to substantiate the business purpose and business relationship.[68] Taxpayers should maintain detailed records of amounts, time, place, business purpose, and business relationships. A credit card receipt details the place, date, and amount of the expense. A notation made on the receipt of the names of the person(s) attending, the business relationship, and the topic of discussion should constitute proper documentation.

Associated with or goodwill entertainment is not deductible unless a business discussion is conducted immediately before or after the entertainment. Furthermore, a

---

[67]The HOPE and lifetime learning credits are briefly mentioned on page 9–17 in this chapter and are discussed at greater length in Chapter 13.

[68]*Kenneth W. Guenther*, 54 TCM 382, T.C.Memo. 1987–440.

business purpose must exist for the entertainment. Taxpayers should arrange for a business discussion before or after such entertainment. They must provide documentation of the business purpose, such as obtaining new business from a prospective customer.

Unreimbursed meals and entertainment are subject to the 50 percent cutback rule in addition to the 2 percent floor. Consequently, the procedure of negotiating a salary reduction, as discussed in the next section, is even more valuable to the taxpayer.

Unreimbursed Employee Business Expenses

The 2 percent floor for unreimbursed employee business expenses offers a tax planning opportunity for married couples. If one spouse has high miscellaneous expenses subject to the floor, it may be beneficial for the couple to file separate returns. If they file jointly, the 2 percent floor is based on the incomes of both. Filing separately lowers the reduction to 2 percent of only one spouse's income.

Other provisions of the law should be considered, however. For example, filing separately could cost a couple losses of up to $25,000 from self-managed rental units under the passive activity loss rules (discussed in Chapter 11).

Another possibility is to negotiate a salary reduction with one's employer in exchange for the 100 percent reimbursement of employee expenses. The employee is better off because the 2 percent floor does not apply. The employer is better off because certain expense reimbursements are not subject to Social Security and other payroll taxes.

KEY TERMS

Accountable plan, 9–26

Automatic mileage method, 9–6

Deduction for qualified tuition and related expenses, 9–15

Education expenses, 9–13

Entertainment expenses, 9–17

Independent contractor, 9–2

Moving expenses, 9–11

Nonaccountable plan, 9–27

Office in the home expenses, 9–21

Roth IRA, 9–25

Statutory employees, 9–4

Traditional IRA, 9–25

Transportation expenses, 9–4

Travel expenses, 9–7

PROBLEM MATERIALS

DISCUSSION QUESTIONS

1. John and Mary are married and file joint returns for 2007 and 2008. The 2007 return includes a Schedule C and a Form 2106 for John and a Form 2106 for Mary. The 2008 return includes only a Schedule C for John.
   a. Comment on the job status (i.e., employed or self-employed) of the parties for 2007.
   b. What are some possible reasons why no Form 2106 is included with the return filed for 2008?

Issue ID

2. Bill performs services for Bob. In ascertaining whether Bill is an employee or an independent contractor, discuss the relevance of each of the separate factors appearing below:
   a. The work is performed at Bob's business location.
   b. Bill has his own helpers to assist him in his work.
   c. Bill makes his services available to others.

d.   As to job skills, Bill provided for his own training.
e.   Bill charges a flat fee that is based on an hourly rate.
f.   Bill reports his income and expenses on Form 2106.
g.   Bill has unreimbursed job-related expenses.
h.   Bill has to file a Schedule SE with his Form 1040.

Decision Making

3. Bernard operates a hair styling salon as a sole proprietor. Because his shop has several extra work stations that are not being used, he is considering renting these to other stylists, but he wants to avoid any employer-employee relationship with them. Advise Bernard on the type of working arrangement he should set up to ensure that any new stylists will be classified as independent contractors and not as employees.

4. What are statutory employees? How are they treated for:
    a.   Federal income tax purposes?
    b.   Federal employment tax purposes?

Decision Making

5. Kristen has just purchased a new automobile that she plans to use about 70% of the time for business. As to the difference between the actual cost method and the automatic mileage method, advise Kristen on the tax treatment of the following items:
    a.   State and local sales tax on the purchase of the auto.
    b.   Business parking.
    c.   Interest on auto loan.
    d.   Depreciation.
    e.   Auto insurance and automobile club dues.
    f.   Toll charges while on family vacation trip.
    g.   Periodic oil changes and rotation of tires.
    h.   Fines for traffic violations incurred during business use.

Issue ID

6. In 2006, Emma purchased an automobile, which she uses for both business and personal purposes. Although Emma does not keep records as to operating expenses (e.g., gas, oil, repairs), she can prove the percentage of business use and the miles driven each year. In March 2008, Emma seeks your advice as to what income tax benefit, if any, she can derive from the use of her automobile. What would you suggest?

7. Tyler, a member of a St. Louis law firm, travels to Chicago for business conferences on Friday and Monday. During the intervening weekend, he attends a Cubs baseball game and visits various museums. Discuss the deductibility of Tyler's expenses for the trip.

Issue ID

8. Dr. Werner is a full-time professor of accounting at Pelican University. During the year, he teaches continuing education programs for CPA groups in several cities. He also serves as an expert witness in numerous lawsuits involving accounting fraud. Comment on the possible tax treatment of Dr. Werner's job-related expenses.

9. Under what circumstances might a taxpayer never be away from home for income tax purposes?
    a.   What are the tax consequences of such a status?
    b.   What is the principal consideration in avoiding this result?

10. Dr. and Mrs. Hampton attend a two-day seminar in Baltimore on current developments in orthopedic surgery. Dr. Hampton owns and operates a bone and joint clinic in Charleston, West Virginia. Mrs. Hampton is the office manager and accountant for the clinic and also schedules all the surgeries performed. Comment on the deductibility of the Hamptons' expenses in attending the seminar.

11. Dr. Mendoza is a professor of Romance languages at State University. In order to prepare a paper to be delivered at an academic symposium, he travels to Spain to conduct research on the life of Cervantes. Comment on the tax treatment of Dr. Mendoza's trip expenses based on the following assumptions:
    a.   He spends two days doing research and three days sightseeing.
    b.   He spends three weeks doing research and two weeks sightseeing.
    c.   He spends four weeks doing research and one week sightseeing.

Decision Making

12. Marge is scheduled to go to Paris on business. While there, she would like to do some sightseeing. When she mentions this to a friend, the friend suggests that she plan her weekends wisely. What does the friend's suggestion mean from a tax perspective?

13. In October 2008, Stefanie moved from Tampa to Dallas to accept a new job with Green Corporation. In July 2009, she left her job with Green Corporation and returned to Tampa. Stefanie's moving expenses from Tampa to Dallas are not paid for or reimbursed by Green Corporation.

Issue ID

   a. Discuss the deductibility of these moving expenses.
   b. To resolve Stefanie's tax status, make a list of any additional information that is needed.
   c. Would it matter if Stefanie always claims the standard deduction and never itemizes her deductions *from* AGI when she files her tax returns?

14. For the convenience of her employer, Ashley is transferred from the Manhattan office to the Los Angeles office. In addition to the usual moving expenses, she incurs the following costs: penalty for breaking the old apartment lease, forfeiture of health club deposit, and cost of driver training course. Comment on the tax treatment of Ashley's moving expenses based on the following assumptions:

   a. The employer reimburses Ashley for *all* expenses.
   b. The employer pays for *all* expenses directly.

15. During 2008, Noah incurs deductible travel expenses for education purposes (out-of-town weekend MBA program) and to move to a new job.

Issue ID

   a. Contrast the travel expenses allowed as a deduction for education with those allowed for moving.
   b. If Noah uses his personal automobile for both purposes, how is the automatic mileage deduction determined?

16. During the current year, Kaitlyn incurs both deductible and nondeductible education expenses. Some of the deductible expenses are deductions *for* AGI, while the rest are deductions *from* AGI. Provide examples of Kaitlyn's expenses that could be:

Issue ID

   a. Nondeductible.
   b. Deductible as deductions *for* AGI.
   c. Deductible as deductions *from* AGI.

17. In connection with § 222 (deduction for qualified tuition and related expenses), comment on the relevance of the following:

   a. A chemical engineer enrolls in law school.
   b. The standard deduction is claimed.
   c. Enrollment at a college requires the payment of a student activity fee.
   d. The lifetime learning credit is claimed.
   e. Taxpayer is married and has MAGI of $131,000.
   f. Miscellaneous itemized deductions do not exceed 2% of AGI.
   g. A qualified child pays her own tuition out of savings.

18. The Federal income tax contains many provisions that encourage education. In this regard, give examples of various benefits available in the form of:

   a. Exclusions from gross income.
   b. Deductions.
   c. Credits.

19. What was the original justification for the cutback adjustment?

   a. Does the cutback adjustment completely solve the problem it was intended to correct?
   b. Are any exceptions made to the cutback adjustment? Why?

20. In each of the following situations, indicate whether there is a cutback adjustment and, if so, to whom it applies (i.e., employer or employee):

   a. The employer expects certain employees to entertain their key customers. The employer does not reimburse the employees for these costs.
   b. Same as (a) except that the employees are reimbursed for these costs.
   c. Each year the employer awards its top salesperson an expense-paid trip to the Cayman Islands.
   d. The employer has a cafeteria for its employees where meals are furnished at cost.
   e. The employer sponsors an annual Fourth of July picnic for its employees.
   f. Every Christmas, the employer gives each employee a turkey.

21. At the last minute, a law firm purchases 10 tickets to the Super Bowl in order to entertain certain key clients. Comment on some possible tax ramifications of this situation.

Issue ID

22. In connection with the office in the home deduction, comment on the following:
    a. When justified if the taxpayer is an employee.
    b. The exclusive use requirement.
    c. The distinction between *direct* and *indirect* expenses.
    d. Taxpayer is a statutory employee and claims the standard deduction.
    e. Taxpayer is a common law employee and claims the standard deduction.

23. In 2007, Myrna, a full-time fifth grade teacher, spent $1,400 on supplies for her classes. The school district, upon the rendition of an adequate accounting, reimbursed her for $400 of these expenses. How should Myrna handle this matter for income tax purposes?

Issue ID

24. Trent, a resident of Florida, attends Vanderbilt University. After graduation, he moves to Dallas where he begins a job search. Shortly thereafter, he accepts a position with a local radio station as an announcer. Trent's college degree is in management. Presuming no reimbursement, what employment-related expenses might Trent be eligible to deduct?

25. Regarding the tax implications of various retirement plans, comment on the following:
    a. The difference between Keogh (H.R. 10) and traditional deductible IRA plans.
    b. The difference between traditional IRA and Roth IRA plans.

26. What tax return reporting procedures must be followed by an employee under the following circumstances?
    a. Expenses and reimbursements are equal under an accountable plan.
    b. Reimbursements at the appropriate Federal per diem rate exceed expenses, and an adequate accounting is made to the employer.
    c. Expenses exceed reimbursements under a nonaccountable plan.

Issue ID

27. Olivia, a recent graduate from law school, is employed by a law firm as an attorney. In order to specialize, she would like to continue her education and earn a graduate degree in tax law. She is hesitant to quit her job and go back to school full-time, however, as that might jeopardize her deduction for education expenses. Furthermore, she is concerned that developing a tax specialty could be treated as acquiring skills for a new trade or business. Comment on Olivia's concerns and provide constructive planning advice.

Decision Making

28. Kim has just graduated from college and is interviewing for a position in marketing. Crane Corporation has offered her a job as a sales representative that will require extensive travel and entertainment but provide valuable experience. Under the offer, she has two options: a salary of $48,000 and she absorbs all expenses; a salary of $35,000 and Crane reimburses for all expenses. Crane assures Kim that the $13,000 difference in the two options will be adequate to cover the expenses incurred. What issues should have an impact on Kim's choice?

Issue ID

Decision Making

29. Harriet plans to retire and move to Arizona. In connection with the move, she will incur considerable expense. Do you have any tax advice for Harriet?

30. Comment on the deductibility of each of the following items:
    a. Gambling losses in excess of gambling gains. Taxpayer is not a professional gambler.
    b. Expenses incurred in applying for the job of police chief of Birmingham, Alabama. Taxpayer, an FBI agent, did not get the job.
    c. Annual dues paid to belong to Rotary Club. Taxpayer is a life insurance broker and is active in Rotary's various civic projects.
    d. Cost of visual aids prepared by a college professor for use in a graduate seminar.
    e. Cost of dry cleaning uniforms (including alterations by a tailor). Taxpayer is the doorman at a New York City hotel.
    f. Cost of safety glasses. Taxpayer is a self-employed chimney sweep.
    g. Cost of noncredit bar exam review program. Taxpayer just graduated from law school and is employed by a law firm.
    h. Office in the home expenses that exceed the income from taxpayer's trade or business.
    i. Expenses incurred by taxpayer, a member of the Vermont National Guard, to participate in a two-day training session conducted in Pennsylvania.

PROBLEMS

31. During the year, Courtney holds two jobs. After an eight-hour day at the first job, she works three hours at the second job. On Mondays and Fridays of each week, she returns home for dinner before going to the second job. On the midweek days (Tuesday through Thursday), she goes directly from the first job to the second job, stopping along the way for a meal. The mileage involved is as follows:

Home to first job	15
First job to second job	20
Home to second job	25

    a. Assuming Courtney works 49 weeks during the year, how much of her mileage is deductible?

    b. Can Courtney deduct the midweek meals she purchased? Why or why not?

32. Becky is the regional sales manager for a donut retail chain. She starts her working day by driving from home to the regional office, works there for several hours, and then visits the three sales outlets in her region. Relevant mileage is as follows:

Home to regional office	10
Regional office to sales outlet #1	12
Sales outlet #1 to sales outlet #2	11
Sales outlet #2 to sales outlet #3	14
Sales outlet #3 to home	15

If Becky uses the automatic mileage method and works on 245 days in 2008, what is her deduction for the year?

33. On July 1, 2006, Jeb purchased a new automobile for $40,000. Miles driven are as follows: 16,000 in 2006; 21,000 in 2007; and 19,000 in 2008. If Jeb uses the auto 80% for business and 20% for personal use, determine its basis as of January 1, 2009, based on the following assumptions:

    a. Jeb uses the automatic mileage method.

    b. Jeb uses the actual cost method. (Assume that *no* § 179 expensing is claimed and that 200% declining-balance with the half-year convention is used—see Chapter 8.)

34. Brittany went from Seattle to Rome (Georgia) on business. Her time was spent as follows:

Tuesday	Travel
Wednesday	Business
Thursday	Sightseeing
Friday	Business
Saturday and Sunday	Sightseeing
Monday	Business
Tuesday	Travel

Brittany's expenses are summarized below:

Airfare	$2,600
Lodging (Tuesday through Monday at $140 per day)	980
Meals (Wednesday through Monday at $130 per day)	780

Brittany is a self-employed real estate consultant who specializes in assisted-living housing projects.

    a. How much can Brittany deduct for the trip?

    b. Assume instead that the destination of Brittany's business trip is Rome, Italy (not Rome, Georgia). How much can she deduct?

    c. How will any deductions in (a) and (b) be classified?

35. Roy, the regional manager for a national retail drug chain, is based in Detroit. During March and April of this year, he has to replace temporarily the district manager in Cleveland. During this period, Roy flies to Cleveland on Sunday night, spends the week

at the district office, and returns home to Detroit on Friday afternoon. The cost of returning home is $560, while the cost of spending the weekend in Cleveland would have been $420.

a. Presuming no reimbursement by his employer, how much, if any, of these weekend expenses may Roy deduct?

b. Would your answer in (a) change if the amounts involved are reversed (i.e., the trip home cost $420; staying in Cleveland would have been $560)?

36. In June of this year, Dr. and Mrs. Alvin Lord traveled to Memphis to attend a three-day conference sponsored by the American Society of Implant Dentistry. Alvin, a practicing oral surgeon, participated in scheduled technical sessions dealing with the latest developments in surgical procedures. On two days, Mrs. Lord attended group meetings where various aspects of family tax planning were discussed. On the other day, she went sightseeing. Mrs. Lord does not work for her husband, but she does their tax returns and handles the family investments. Expenses incurred in connection with the conference are summarized below:

Airfare (two tickets)	$1,040
Lodging (single and double occupancy are the same rate—$220 each day)	660
Meals ($200 × 3 days)*	600
Conference registration fee (includes $120 for Family Tax Planning sessions)	520
Car rental	240

* Split equally between Dr. and Mrs. Lord.

How much, if any, of these expenses can the Lords deduct?

37. On Thursday, Justin flies from Baltimore (his home office) to Cadiz (Spain). He conducts business on Friday and Tuesday; vacations on Saturday, Sunday, and Monday (a legal holiday in Spain); and returns to Baltimore on Thursday. Justin was scheduled to return home on Wednesday, but all flights were canceled due to bad weather. Therefore, he spent Wednesday watching floor shows at a local casino.

a. For tax purposes, what portion of Justin's trip is regarded as being for business?

b. Suppose Monday had not been a legal holiday. Would this change your answer in (a)?

c. Under either (a) or (b), how much of Justin's airfare qualifies as a deductible business expense?

Decision Making

38. Monica travels from her office in Boston to Lisbon, Portugal, on business. Her absence of 13 days was spent as follows:

Thursday	Depart for and arrive at Lisbon
Friday	Business transacted
Saturday and Sunday	Vacationing
Monday through Friday	Business transacted
Saturday and Sunday	Vacationing
Monday	Business transacted
Tuesday	Depart Lisbon and return to office in Boston

a. For tax purposes, how many days has Monica spent on business?

b. What difference does it make?

c. Could Monica have spent more time than she did vacationing on the trip without loss of existing tax benefits? Explain.

39. Marlo, a financial planner, decides to quit his job with an investment bank in Columbia, South Carolina, and establish a private practice in Albuquerque, New Mexico. In connection with the move, he incurs the following expenses:

Moving van charge	$4,300
Lodging during move	520
Meals during move	360
Loss on sale of residence in Columbia	4,000
Mileage for personal autos	3,400 miles

How much of these expenses, if any, can Marlo deduct?

40. Crissa is employed as a full-time high school teacher. The school district where she works recently instituted a policy requiring all of its teachers to start working on a master's degree. Pursuant to this new rule, Crissa spent most of the summer of 2008 taking graduate courses at an out-of-town university. Her expenses are as follows:

Tuition	$4,200
Books and course materials	850
Lodging	1,100
Meals	1,800
Laundry and dry cleaning	120
Campus parking	200

In addition, Crissa drove her personal automobile 1,600 miles in connection with the education. She uses the automatic mileage method.
   a. How much, if any, of these expenses might qualify as deductions *for* AGI?
   b. How much, if any, of these expenses might qualify as deductions *from* AGI?

41. In each of the following independent situations, determine how much, if any, qualifies as a deduction *for* AGI under § 222 (qualified tuition and related expenses):
   a. Ruby is single and is employed as a nurse practitioner. During 2007, she spends $4,200 in tuition to attend law school at night. Her AGI is $64,000.
   b. Jacque is single and is employed as a pharmacist. During 2007, he spends $2,100 ($1,900 for tuition and $200 for books) to take a course in herbal supplements at a local university. His AGI is $70,000.
   c. How much, if any, of the above amounts *not allowed under* § 222 might otherwise qualify as a deduction *from* AGI?

42. Kinsey is a licensed commercial pilot who works for Bluegrass Charter Jet Service. Typically, Kinsey, who lives near the airport, flies a charter out of Winchester, Kentucky, to either Las Vegas or Reno, spends several nights there, and then returns home with the same group. Bluegrass provides Kinsey with a travel allowance of $1,500 per month but requires no accountability. For calendar year 2008, Kinsey had the following job-related expenses:

Meals	$ 6,900
Lodging	10,000
Transportation (taxis, limos)	480
Uniforms	1,250
Dry cleaning of uniforms	280
Annual physical exam	820

The uniforms are required to be worn on the job. The Federal Aviation Administration requires the annual physical exam for the maintenance of a commercial pilot's license. How may Kinsey treat these expenses for Federal income tax purposes?

43. Brown Associates paid $50,000 for a 20-seat skybox at Memorial Stadium for eight professional football games. Regular seats to these games range from $60 to $120 each. At one game, an employee of Brown entertained 19 clients. Brown furnished food and beverages for the event at a cost of $750. The game was preceded by a bona fide business discussion, and all expenses are adequately substantiated.
   a. How much may Brown deduct for this event?
   b. Would your answer in (a) change if only 18 (not 19) clients participated—one of the seats was not occupied?

44. During the current year, Paul, the vice president of a bank, made gifts in the following amounts:

To Sarah (Paul's personal assistant) at Christmas	$36
To Darryl (a key client)—$3 was for gift wrapping	53
To Darryl's wife (a homemaker) on her birthday	20
To Veronica (Paul's boss) at Christmas	30

In addition, on professional assistants' day, Paul takes Sarah to lunch at a cost of $82. Presuming Paul has adequate substantiation and is not reimbursed, how much can he deduct?

45. Christine is employed full-time as an accountant for a national hardware chain. She also has a private consulting practice, which provides tax advice and financial planning to the general public. For this purpose, she maintains an office in her home. Expenses relating to her home are as follows:

Real property taxes	$3,900
Interest on home mortgage	4,000
Operating expenses of home	1,100
Depreciation allocated to 20% business use	1,600

Christine's income from consulting is $16,000, and the related expenses are $5,000.
   a. What is Christine's office in the home deduction?
   b. Suppose that Christine also spent $3,000 to repaint and replace the carpet in the office. How do these additional costs change the answer to part (a)?
   c. Suppose that Christine's income from consulting is only $8,000 (not $16,000). How does this change the answer to part (a)?

46. Jake has AGI of $89,000 during the year and the following expenses related to his employment:

Lodging while in travel status	$3,600
Meals during travel	3,300
Business transportation	5,400
Entertainment of clients	3,200
Professional dues and subscriptions	1,100

Jake is reimbursed $12,000 under his employer's accountable plan. What are his deductions *for* and *from* AGI?

Decision Making

47. During the year, Brenda had the following expenses related to her employment:

Airfare	$8,500
Meals	4,000
Lodging	4,900
Transportation while in travel status (taxis, limos)	940
Entertainment of clients	8,000

Although Brenda renders an adequate accounting to her employer, she is reimbursed for only $12,000 of the above expenses. What are Brenda's tax consequences based on the following assumptions?
   a. The $12,000 reimbursement does not designate which expenses are covered.
   b. The reimbursement specifically covers *only* the meals and entertainment expenses.
   c. The reimbursement covers any of the expenses *other than* meals and entertainment.
   d. If Brenda has a choice of reimbursement procedures [parts (a), (b), or (c) above], which should she select and why?

48. Audry, age 38 and single, earned a salary of $59,000. She had interest income of $1,600 and had a $2,000 long-term capital loss from the sale of a stock investment. Audry incurred the following employment-related expenses during the year:

Transportation	$5,500
Meals	2,800
Lodging	4,200
Entertaining clients	2,200
Professional dues and subscriptions	300

Under an accountable plan, Audry receives reimbursements of $4,500 from her employer. Calculate her AGI and itemized employee business expenses.

49. B. J. and Carolyn Grace are full-time employees. B. J. is a junior college teacher, and Carolyn is a registered nurse at a hospital. During 2008, they incur the following employment-related expenses:

School supplies for use in the classroom	$1,400
Emergency room uniforms	800
Union dues (teachers association)	200
Job hunting expenses (Carolyn obtained another nursing position but decided not to change jobs)	1,300
Continuing education correspondence courses (required to maintain nursing license)	380
Professional dues and subscriptions	1,100

None of these expenses are reimbursed by the employers.

For the year, the Graces file a joint return reflecting AGI of $94,000. They have other itemized deductions (i.e., interest on home mortgage, property taxes on personal residence, state income taxes, charitable contributions) of $14,500. Determine the total amount of itemized deductions allowed to the Graces for tax year 2008.

CUMULATIVE PROBLEMS

50. Frank B. and Lucy B. Rose have no dependents and are both under age 65. Frank is a statutory employee of Green Valley, a wholesaler of recyclable materials (business code is 421930); his Social Security number is 589–64–2896. Lucy is a manager with Freight-Rite, a trucking company, and her Social Security number is 592–31–4694. The Roses live at 482 Devon Drive, Clearwater, FL 33758. They do not contribute to the Presidential Election Campaign fund.

Tax Return Problem

Decision Making

Communications

In 2007, Frank earned $65,200 in commissions. His employer withheld FICA taxes of $4,988 [($65,200 × 6.2%) + ($65,200 × 1.45%)] but does not withhold income taxes. Frank paid $6,000 in estimated taxes. Lucy earned $69,000 from which her employer withheld FICA taxes of $5,279 [($69,000 × 6.2%) + ($69,000 × 1.45%)] and Federal income taxes of $6,700. Neither Frank nor Lucy received any expense reimbursements.

Frank uses his automobile in his employment, and during 2007, his business mileage is 27,000 miles. Parking and tolls in connection with business use are $520 and $190, respectively. Fines paid for traffic violations (during business use) total $600. In deducting business use of his automobile, Frank always uses the automatic mileage method. His other employment-related expenses for the year are as follows:

Airfare	$3,050
Meals	3,500
Lodging	2,800
Entertainment	1,600
Business gifts	1,320

The business gifts consist of 30 fruit baskets Frank sent to key customers during the Christmas season. Each basket cost $40 (not including $4 for wrapping and shipping).

During the year, Lucy enrolled in a weekend MBA program at a local university. In this regard, she spent the following amounts: $3,400 (tuition), $610 (books and computer supplies), $205 (meals while on campus), and $220 (bus fare to and from campus). Lucy took her secretary to lunch on two occasions ($91 and $86) and her boss on one occasion ($110). She spent $340 on professional dues and $120 on trade journals.

Neither Frank nor Lucy is covered under an employer-sponsored retirement plan. However, each contributes $4,000 (for a total of $8,000) to a traditional IRA.

In addition to their salaries, the Roses received the amounts listed below during the year:

Interest on certificate of deposit issued by Tampa State Bank	$ 1,800
Inheritance from Albert	50,000
Distribution from Cardinal Life	100,600

The distribution from Cardinal Life represents the maturity value ($100,000) plus interest ($600) of an insurance policy on Albert's life. Albert was Frank's uncle and had designated Frank as the beneficiary of the policy. Because Albert died overseas, the insurance company had delayed in making the distribution to Frank.

The Roses had other expenditures as follows:

Charitable contributions (cash)	$2,400
Medical and dental expenses	8,900
Real property taxes on residence	4,800
Sales taxes—actual amount (receipts available)	2,000
Home mortgage interest	6,600
Tax return preparation fee	600

Part 1—Tax Computation

Compute the Roses' Federal income tax payable or refund due, assuming they file a joint income tax return, for 2007. If they have overpaid, they want the amount refunded. You will need Forms 1040 and 2106 and Schedules A, B, and C. Suggested software: TaxCut.

Part 2—Tax Planning

The Roses request your help in deciding where to invest the extra $150,000 (life insurance and inheritance) they received in 2007. They are considering two alternatives:

- Municipal bonds that yield 4.5%.
- Common stock that regularly pays cash dividends (and appreciates) at the rate of 7%.
  a. Calculate the better alternative for next year. Assume that Lucy and Frank will have the same income and deductions in 2008, except for the income from the investment they choose.
  b. Write a memo to the Roses, explaining their alternatives.

Tax Computation Problem

51. Tracy S. Kent, single and age 36, lives at 4321 Laurel Drive, Duquesne, PA 15110. She is employed as a regional sales manager by Fashion Stride, Ltd., a national retail chain of women's shoes. Tracy is paid an annual salary of $69,000, which *does not include* a separate travel and entertainment allowance of $15,000 and an annual performance bonus. Fashion Stride treats the travel and entertainment allowance as additional compensation and does not require any accounting by the employee.

- Pursuant to company policy, an employee's performance bonus is not paid until February of the following year. Tracy's bonus for 2007 (received in 2008) is $4,000, while her bonus for 2008 (received in 2009) is $7,000.
- Tracy began maintaining an office in her home in May 2007 when Fashion Stride closed its Pittsburgh facility. Her office takes up 18% of the total floor space of her residence, which was acquired four years ago at a cost of $300,000 (not including cost of land). As of January 1, 2008, the residence has a fair market value of $350,000 (not including land). Tracy has based past depreciation on MACRS, using straight-line depreciation over 39 years (see Table 8–6 in Chapter 8). Other relevant expenses as to the residence for 2008 include utilities of $4,100; homeowners' insurance of $1,800; and interest and taxes (see below). In early December 2008, Tracy had the office repainted at a cost of $480.
- Tracy uses her personal automobile partly for business, for which she claims the automatic mileage method. Her records for 2008 reflect the following mileage: 11,000 business and 9,000 personal. Business parking and toll charges are $280.
- Tracy's job-related expenses for 2008 are listed below:

Airfare	$5,200
Lodging	2,800
Meals	3,300
Entertainment	2,500
Transportation (taxis, airport limos)	710
Business gifts	336
Professional journals	170

Tracy's business trips involve visits to the retail outlets in her region. Store managers and their key employees are the parties entertained. The business gifts were boxes of candy costing $28 ($23 cost + $5 wrapping and shipping) and sent to 12 store managers as Christmas presents.

- Tracy's other expenses for 2008 are as follows:

Contribution to traditional IRA (Fashion Stride has no retirement plan)	$5,000
Contribution to § 529 plan (on behalf of a favorite nephew)	500
Dental bills (not covered by Fashion Stride's employee medical plan)	1,200
Additional state income tax paid in 2008 on 2007 liability	150
Property taxes on personal residence	4,200
Interest on home mortgage	3,600

- Besides the job income already noted, Tracy had the following receipts for 2008:

Interest on CD with Keystone State Bank	$ 840
Interest on City of Reading general purpose bonds	600
Settlement from Eagle Casualty company	6,000

In late December 2007, a fire in Tracy's basement caused $7,000 in property damage. The $6,000 received from Eagle Casualty in February represents the amount due under Tracy's homeowners' policy. None of the loss was deducted as a casualty for income tax purposes.

Tracy (Social Security number 162–48–4956) made no estimated tax payments during the year. Fashion Stride withheld $9,000 for Federal income tax and $2,700 for state income tax. Using the Tax Rate Schedules, determine Tracy's Federal income tax payable or refund due for 2008.

RESEARCH PROBLEMS

Note: Solutions to Research Problems can be prepared by using the **RIA Checkpoint®** **Student Edition** online research product, which is available to accompany this text. It is also possible to prepare solutions to the Research Problems by using tax research materials found in a standard tax library.

Research Problem 1. Richard Harding is the sheriff of Howard County, Indiana. In addition to the usual law enforcement duties, the sheriff has the responsibility of maintaining the detention facility (i.e., county jail). Further, he must furnish meals for all prisoners in accordance with certain nutritional standards prescribed by the state. Although the sheriff must absorb the cost of the meals, the county provides a personal allowance.

During the year, Sheriff Harding received a salary of $35,000 (as reported on a Form W–2 issued by Howard County). He spent $90,000 on prisoner meals and received meal allowances of $110,000. On his income tax return, he reported the salary as employee income, but listed the allowances and meals on a Schedule C. Thus, he treated himself as self-employed by claiming the cost of the meals as a deduction *for* AGI.

Upon audit, the IRS determined that the Schedule C treatment was improper. Harding was not in a separate trade or business of providing meals, but was merely carrying out his employment-related duties. The costs of the meals are employee business expenses deductible only as miscellaneous itemized deductions on Schedule A. As such, they are subject to the 2%-of-AGI floor.

Is Sheriff Harding or the IRS correct? Why?

Research Problem 2. In which, if either, of the following independent situations is the taxpayer "away from home" so as to permit a deduction for the cost of meals obtained during the trip?

Case A. Ryan is the sales representative for a national greeting card company. As he has a rather extensive sales territory, Ryan makes his rounds using a company-owned car over a 16- to 19-hour period. During these one-day business trips, Ryan will pull over to a roadside park at least once and take a short nap in the backseat of his auto.

Case B. Matthew is the captain of a ferryboat that carries several hundred tourists on round trips from Seattle to Victoria and back. Each voyage lasts from 15 to 17 hours and provides for a 6- to 7-hour layover in Victoria, enabling the passengers to shop and sightsee. During the layover, Matthew usually takes a 4-hour nap on a cot located in the pilothouse of the ferryboat.

Partial list of research aids:
§ 162(a)(2).
Rev.Rul. 61–221, 1961–2 C.B. 34
Frederick J. Barry, 54 T.C. 1210 (1970), aff'd in 71–USTC ¶9126, 27 AFTR2d 71–334, 435 F.2d 1290 (CA–1, 1970).
Marc G. Bissonnette, 127 T.C. 124 (2006).

Research Problem 3.   Al Hardee has been employed as a salesman by Robin Chevrolet at its Milwaukee dealership. In early May, Al and the general manager of the office had a serious dispute over job procedures. When it became clear that the two could no longer work together amicably, Al contacted Robin's CEO regarding a possible solution. As the general manager planned to retire in five months, it was decided that Al would spend this period working at the Green Bay branch. After the manager's retirement, Al was to rejoin the Milwaukee office.

Al's residence is only a few blocks from the Milwaukee office, but it is 96 miles (one-way) from the Green Bay worksite. During the next five months (i.e., May to October), Al made 120 trips driving from his home in Milwaukee to the Green Bay job. His only records of his trips are a wall calendar with the workdays circled and the credit card receipts he received from gasoline purchases. The employee records of the Green Bay dealership can, however, support Al's on-the-job presence.

Upon termination of the five-month assignment and after the retirement of the general manager, Al requested a transfer back to the Milwaukee office. The CEO turned down the request on the grounds that Al was no longer needed in Milwaukee. During his absence and unknown to Al, his job position in Milwaukee had been eliminated. However, the CEO offered to make the Green Bay assignment permanent. Hurt and disgusted, Al quit and took a job with a competing Milwaukee car dealership.

On his Federal income tax return, Al claimed a deduction for employee transportation expenses, computed as follows: 120 (number of trips) × 192 (round-trip mileage) × automatic mileage rate for the year. The IRS disallowed the deduction on two grounds. First, Al's job status in Green Bay was *permanent*, not *temporary*. Thus, his tax home had changed from Milwaukee to Green Bay. This, in turn, made his transportation expenses nondeductible commuting expenses. Second, even if the transportation was warranted, the expenses were not properly substantiated. Consequently, the lack of substantiation precludes any deduction.

Should Al be allowed a deduction for his transportation expenses? Explain.

Partial list of research aids:
Reg. § 1.162–2(e).
Reg. § 1.274–5T(c)(3).
Rev.Rul. 99–7, 1999–1 C.B. 363.
Teresita T. Diaz, 84 TCM 148, T.C.Memo. 2002–192.
Richard M. Brockman, 85 TCM 733, T.C.Memo. 2003–3.

Communications

Research Problem 4.   Rick Beam has been an independent sales representative for various textile manufacturers for many years. His products consist of soft goods, such as tablecloths, curtains, and drapes. Rick's customers are clothing store chains, department stores, and smaller specialty stores. The employees of these companies who are responsible for purchasing merchandise are known as buyers. These companies generally prohibit their buyers from accepting gifts from manufacturers' sales representatives.

Each year Rick gives cash gifts (never more than $25) to most of the buyers who are his customers. Generally, he cashes a large check in November and gives the money personally to the buyers around Christmas. Rick says, "This is one of the ways that I maintain my relationship with my buyers." He maintains adequate substantiation of all the gifts.

Rick's deductions for these gifts have been disallowed by the IRS, based on § 162(c)(2). Rick is confused and comes to you, a CPA, for advice.

a. Write a letter to Rick concerning his tax position on this issue. Rick's address is 948 Octavia Street, Baton Rouge, LA 70821.

b. Prepare a memo for your files supporting the advice you have given.

Use the tax resources of the Internet to address the following questions. Do not restrict your search to the World Wide Web, but include a review of newsgroups and general reference materials, practitioner sites and resources, primary sources of the tax law, chat rooms and discussion groups, and other opportunities.

Internet
Activity

Research Problem 5.   What are the guidelines regarding the deductibility of conventions held outside the North American area? Refer to Chapter 1 of IRS Publication No. 463.

Research Problem 6.   In reporting the transactions of a self-employed taxpayer, when can a Schedule C–EZ be used instead of the regular Schedule C of Form 1040?

Research Problem 7.   Determine whether your city qualifies for the "high-cost" travel per diem allowances provided by the IRS.

Research Problem 8.   In 2006, the IRS modified Form 8829 to add a new line 18. Why was this line added, and what purpose does it serve?

Research Problem 9.   Retrieve Form 8919 from the IRS Web site and answer the following questions:

a. Who should file the form?

b. Will any tax consequences result from filing the form?

CHAPTER 10

Deductions and Losses: Certain Itemized Deductions

LEARNING OBJECTIVES

After completing Chapter 10, you should be able to:

LO.1
Distinguish between deductible and nondeductible personal expenses.

LO.2
Define medical expenses and compute the medical expense deduction.

LO.3
Contrast deductible taxes with nondeductible fees, licenses, and other charges.

LO.4
Understand the Federal income tax treatment of state and local income taxes and sales taxes.

LO.5
Distinguish between deductible and nondeductible interest and apply the appropriate limitations to deductible interest.

LO.6
Understand charitable contributions and their related measurement problems and percentage limitations.

LO.7
List the business and personal expenditures that are deductible either as miscellaneous itemized deductions or as other itemized deductions.

LO.8
Recognize the limitation on certain itemized deductions applicable to high-income taxpayers.

LO.9
Identify tax planning strategies that can maximize the benefit of itemized deductions.

OUTLINE

General Classification of Expenses, 10–2
Medical Expenses, 10–2
   General Requirements, 10–2
   Medical Expenses Defined, 10–3
   Capital Expenditures for Medical Purposes, 10–5
   Medical Expenses Incurred for Spouse
      and Dependents, 10–6
   Transportation, Meal, and Lodging Expenses
      for Medical Treatment, 10–6
   Amounts Paid for Medical Insurance Premiums, 10–7
   Year of Deduction, 10–8
   Reimbursements, 10–8
   Health Savings Accounts, 10–9
Taxes, 10–11
   Deductibility as a Tax, 10–11
   Property Taxes, 10–11
   State and Local Income Taxes and Sales Taxes, 10–13
Interest, 10–14
   Allowed and Disallowed Items, 10–14
   Restrictions on Deductibility and Timing
      Considerations, 10–17
   Classification of Interest Expense, 10–18

Charitable Contributions, 10–18
   Criteria for a Gift, 10–19
   Qualified Organizations, 10–20
   Time of Deduction, 10–20
   Record-Keeping and Valuation Requirements, 10–21
   Limitations on Charitable Contribution Deduction, 10–22
Miscellaneous Itemized Deductions, 10–27
Other Miscellaneous Deductions, 10–28
Comprehensive Example of Schedule A, 10–28
Overall Limitation on Certain
Itemized Deductions, 10–28
Tax Planning Considerations, 10–32
   Effective Utilization of Itemized Deductions, 10–32
   Utilization of Medical Deductions, 10–32
   Timing the Payment of Deductible Taxes, 10–33
   Protecting the Interest Deduction, 10–33
   Assuring the Charitable Contribution Deduction, 10–34

LO.1

Distinguish between deductible and nondeductible personal expenses.

General Classification of Expenses

As a general rule, the deduction of personal expenditures is disallowed by § 262 of the Code. However, Congress has chosen to allow certain personal expenditures to be deducted as itemized deductions. Personal expenditures that are deductible as itemized deductions include medical expenses, certain taxes, mortgage interest, investment interest, and charitable contributions. These expenditures and other personal expenditures that are allowed as itemized deductions are covered in this chapter. Any personal expenditures not specifically allowed as itemized deductions by the tax law are nondeductible.

Allowable itemized deductions are deductible *from* AGI in arriving at taxable income if the taxpayer elects to itemize. The election to itemize is appropriate when total itemized deductions exceed the standard deduction based on the taxpayer's filing status.[1]

LO.2

Define medical expenses and compute the medical expense deduction.

Medical Expenses

General Requirements

Medical expenses paid for the care of the taxpayer, spouse, and dependents are allowed as an itemized deduction to the extent the expenses are not reimbursed. The **medical expense** deduction is limited to the amount by which such expenses *exceed* 7.5 percent of the taxpayer's AGI.

EXAMPLE 1

During the year, Iris had medical expenses of $4,800, of which $1,000 was reimbursed by her insurance company. If her AGI for the year is $40,000, the itemized deduction for medical expenses is limited to $800 [($4,800 − $1,000) − (7.5% × $40,000)]. ∎

---

[1]The total standard deduction is the sum of the basic standard deduction and the additional standard deduction (refer to Chapter 3).

TAX *in the News*

THE PRESIDENT AND VICE PRESIDENT ITEMIZE

Approximately two-thirds of all individual taxpayers take the standard deduction each year rather than itemize. President George W. Bush and Vice President Richard B. Cheney are among the one-third who itemize. The President, who files a joint return with his wife, released their 2006 tax return to the public. The itemized deductions, along with certain other information from the Bush tax return, are shown in the column to the right.

Vice President Cheney, who did not release Schedule A–Itemized Deductions, reported gross income of $1,809,296 and itemized deductions of $184,210.

Gross income	$765,801
Adjusted gross income	$765,801
Itemized deductions:	
Medical expenses	$ –0–
Taxes	27,474
Interest	–0–
Charitable contributions	78,100
Job expenses and other miscellaneous deductions	27,428
Total itemized deductions	$133,002

Medical Expenses Defined

The term *medical care* includes expenditures incurred for the "diagnosis, cure, mitigation, treatment, or prevention of disease, or for the purpose of affecting any structure or function of the body."[2] A *partial* list of deductible and nondeductible medical items appears in Exhibit 10–1.

A medical expense does not have to relate to a particular ailment to be deductible. Since the definition of medical care is broad enough to cover preventive measures, the cost of periodic physical and dental exams qualifies even for a taxpayer in good health.

Amounts paid for unnecessary *cosmetic surgery* are not deductible medical expenses. However, if cosmetic surgery is deemed necessary, it is deductible as a medical expense. Cosmetic surgery is necessary when it ameliorates (1) a deformity arising from a congenital abnormality, (2) a personal injury, or (3) a disfiguring disease.

EXAMPLE 2

Art, a calendar year taxpayer, paid $11,000 to a plastic surgeon for a face lift. Art, age 75, merely wanted to improve his appearance. The $11,000 does not qualify as a medical expense since the surgery was unnecessary. ■

EXAMPLE 3

As a result of a serious automobile accident, Marge's face is disfigured. The cost of restorative cosmetic surgery is deductible as a medical expense. ■

The cost of care in a *nursing home or home for the aged*, including meals and lodging, can be included in deductible medical expenses if the primary reason for being in the home is to get medical care. If the primary reason for being there is personal, any costs for medical or nursing care can be included in deductible medical expenses, but the cost of meals and lodging must be excluded.[3]

EXAMPLE 4

Norman has a chronic heart ailment. In October, his family decides to place Norman in a nursing home equipped to provide medical and nursing care facilities. Total nursing home expenses amount to $15,000 during the year. Of this amount, $4,500 is directly attributable to medical and nursing care. Since Norman is in need of significant medical and nursing

---

[2]§ 213(d)(1)(A).   [3]Reg. § 1.213–1(e)(1)(v).

EXHIBIT 10–1	Examples of Deductible and Nondeductible Medical Expenses

Deductible	Nondeductible
Medical (including dental, mental, and hospital) care	Funeral, burial, or cremation expenses
Prescription drugs	Nonprescription drugs (except insulin)
Special equipment	Bottled water
Wheelchairs	Toiletries, cosmetics
Crutches	Diaper service, maternity clothes
Artificial limbs	Programs for the *general* improvement of health
Eyeglasses (including contact lenses)	Weight reduction
Hearing aids	Health spas
Transportation for medical care	Social activities (e.g., dancing and swimming lessons)
Medical and hospital insurance premiums	Unnecessary cosmetic surgery
Long-term care insurance premiums (subject to limitations)	
Cost of alcohol and drug rehabilitation	
Certain costs to stop smoking	
Weight reduction programs related to obesity	

care and is placed in the facility primarily for this purpose, all $15,000 of the nursing home costs are deductible (subject to the 7.5% floor). ∎

Tuition expenses of a dependent at a special school may be deductible as a medical expense. The cost of medical care can include the expenses of a special school for a mentally or physically handicapped individual. The deduction is allowed if a principal reason for sending the individual to the school is the school's special resources for alleviating the infirmities. In this case, the cost of meals and lodging, in addition to the tuition, is a proper medical expense deduction.[4]

EXAMPLE 5

Jason's daughter Marcia attended public school through the seventh grade. Because Marcia was a poor student, she was examined by a psychiatrist who diagnosed a problem that created a learning disability. Upon the recommendation of the psychiatrist, Marcia is enrolled in a private school so that she can receive individual attention. The school has no special program for students with learning disabilities and does not provide special medical treatment. The expense related to Marcia's attendance is not deductible as a medical expense. The cost of any psychiatric care, however, qualifies as a medical expense. ∎

Example 5 shows that the recommendation of a physician does not automatically make the expenditure deductible.

---

[4]*Donald R. Pfeifer*, 37 TCM 816, T.C.Memo. 1978–189. Also see Rev.Rul. 78–340, 1978–2 C.B. 124.

ETHICAL and EQUITABLE *Considerations*
PIGGING OUT TO GET A DEDUCTION

Michael has always been overweight, and now he has decided to do something about it. He recently read in a news story that the IRS allows a medical expense deduction for the cost of weight reduction programs. He scheduled an appointment with his doctor to discuss enrolling in the clinic's weight reduction program and mentioned that he was happy that he would be able to deduct the cost. His doctor, who was familiar with the IRS's position, informed Michael that he was 10 pounds below the weight considered obese under the IRS guidelines and would not be able to take the medical expense deduction. Michael scheduled another appointment and proceeded to eat much more than usual for the next month. He returned 20 pounds heavier than at the first appointment and joked with the doctor that he now qualified for the medical expense deduction. Discuss whether Michael is justified in deducting the cost of the weight reduction program.

Capital Expenditures for Medical Purposes

Some examples of *capital expenditures* for medical purposes are swimming pools if the taxpayer does not have access to a neighborhood pool and air conditioners if they do not become permanent improvements (e.g., window units).[5] Other examples include dust elimination systems,[6] elevators,[7] and a room built to house an iron lung. These expenditures are medical in nature if they are incurred as a medical necessity upon the advice of a physician, the facility is used primarily by the patient alone, and the expense is reasonable.

Capital expenditures normally are adjustments to basis and are not deductible. However, both a capital expenditure for a permanent improvement and expenditures made for the operation or maintenance of the improvement may qualify as medical expenses. If a capital expenditure qualifies as a medical expense, the allowable cost is deductible in the year incurred. Although depreciation is required for most other capital expenditures, it is not required for capital expenditures for medical purposes.

A capital improvement that ordinarily would not have a medical purpose qualifies as a medical expense if it is directly related to prescribed medical care and is deductible to the extent that the expenditure *exceeds* the increase in value of the related property. Appraisal costs related to capital improvements are also deductible, but not as medical expenses. These costs are expenses incurred in the determination of the taxpayer's tax liability.[8]

EXAMPLE 6

Fred is afflicted with heart disease. His physician advises him to install an elevator in his residence so he will not be required to climb the stairs. The cost of installing the elevator is $3,000, and the increase in the value of the residence is determined to be only $1,700. Therefore, $1,300 ($3,000 − $1,700) is deductible as a medical expense. Additional utility costs to operate the elevator and maintenance costs are deductible as medical expenses as long as the medical reason for the capital expenditure continues to exist. ■

The full cost of certain home-related capital expenditures incurred to enable a *physically handicapped* individual to live independently and productively qualifies as a medical expense. Qualifying costs include expenditures for constructing entrance and exit ramps to the residence, widening hallways and doorways to accommodate wheelchairs, installing support bars and railings in bathrooms and other rooms, and

[5]Reg. § 1.213–1(e)(1)(iii).
[6]Ltr.Rul. 7948029.
[7]*Riach v. Frank*, 62–1 USTC ¶9419, 9 AFTR2d 1263, 302 F.2d 374 (CA–9, 1962).
[8]§ 212(3).

adjusting electrical outlets and fixtures.[9] These expenditures are subject to the 7.5 percent floor only, and the increase in the home's value is deemed to be zero.

Medical Expenses Incurred for Spouse and Dependents

In computing the medical expense deduction, a taxpayer may include medical expenses for a spouse and for a person who was a dependent at the time the expenses were paid or incurred. Of the requirements that normally apply in determining dependency status,[10] neither the gross income nor the joint return test applies in determining dependency status for medical expense deduction purposes.

| EXAMPLE 7 | Ernie (age 22) is married and a full-time student at a university. During the year, Ernie incurred medical expenses that were paid by Matilda (Ernie's mother). She provided more than half of Ernie's support for the year. Even if Ernie files a joint return with his wife, Matilda may claim the medical expenses she paid for him. Matilda would combine Ernie's expenses with her own before applying the 7.5% floor. ■ |

For *divorced persons* with children, a special rule applies to the noncustodial parent. The noncustodial parent may claim any medical expenses he or she pays even though the custodial parent claims the children as dependents. This rule applies if the dependency exemptions could have been shifted to the noncustodial parent by the custodial parent's waiver (refer to Chapter 3).

| EXAMPLE 8 | Irv and Joan were divorced last year, and Joan was awarded custody of their child, Keith. During the current year, Irv makes the following payments to Joan: $3,600 for child support and $2,500 for Keith's medical bills. Together, Irv and Joan provide more than half of Keith's support. Even though Joan claims Keith as a dependent, Irv can combine the $2,500 of medical expenses that he pays for Keith with his own when calculating his medical expense deduction. ■ |

Transportation, Meal, and Lodging Expenses for Medical Treatment

Payments for transportation to and from a point of treatment for medical care are deductible as medical expenses (subject to the 7.5 percent floor). Transportation expenses for medical care include bus, taxi, train, or plane fare, charges for ambulance service, and out-of-pocket expenses for the use of an automobile. A mileage allowance of 19 cents per mile[11] for 2008 may be used instead of actual out-of-pocket automobile expenses. Whether the taxpayer chooses to claim out-of-pocket automobile expenses or the 19 cents per mile automatic mileage option, related parking fees and tolls can also be deducted. The cost of meals while en route to obtain medical care is not deductible.

A deduction is also allowed for the transportation expenses of a parent who must accompany a child who is receiving medical care or for a nurse or other person giving assistance to a person who is traveling to get medical care and cannot travel alone.

A deduction is allowed for lodging while away from home for medical care if the following requirements are met:[12]

- The lodging is primarily for and essential to medical care.
- Medical care is provided by a doctor in a licensed hospital or a similar medical facility (e.g., a clinic).

[9]For a complete list of the items that qualify, see Rev.Rul. 87–106, 1987–2 C.B. 67.

[10]Refer to Chapter 3 for discussion of these requirements.

[11]This amount is adjusted periodically. The allowance was 20 cents for 2007.

[12]§ 213(d)(2).

- The lodging is not lavish or extravagant under the circumstances.
- There is no significant element of personal pleasure, recreation, or vacation in the travel away from home.

The deduction for lodging expenses included as medical expenses cannot exceed $50 *per* night for *each* person. The deduction is allowed not only for the patient but also for a person who must travel with the patient (e.g., a parent traveling with a child who is receiving medical care).

EXAMPLE 9

Herman, a resident of Winchester, Kentucky, is advised by his family physician that Martha, Herman's dependent and disabled mother, needs specialized treatment for her heart condition. Consequently, Herman and Martha fly to Cleveland, Ohio, where Martha receives the therapy at a heart clinic on an outpatient basis. Expenses in connection with the trip are as follows:

Round-trip airfare ($250 each)	$500
Lodging in Cleveland for two nights ($60 each per night)	240

Herman's medical expense deduction for transportation is $500, and his medical expense deduction for lodging is $200 ($50 per night per person). Because Martha is disabled, it is assumed that his accompanying her is justified. ■

No deduction is allowed for the cost of meals unless they are part of the medical care and are furnished at a medical facility. When allowable, such meals are not subject to the 50 percent limit applicable to business meals.

Amounts Paid for Medical Insurance Premiums

Medical insurance premiums are included with other medical expenses subject to the 7.5 percent floor. Premiums paid by the taxpayer under a group plan or an individual plan are included as medical expenses. If an employer pays all or part of the taxpayer's medical insurance premiums, the amount paid by the employer is not included in gross income by the employee. Likewise, the premium is not included in the employee's medical expenses.

If a taxpayer is *self-employed*, insurance premiums paid for medical coverage are deductible as a *business* expense (*for* AGI).[13] The deduction *for* AGI is allowed for premiums paid on behalf of the taxpayer, the taxpayer's spouse, and dependents of the taxpayer. The deduction is not allowed to any taxpayer who is eligible to participate in a subsidized health plan maintained by any employer of the taxpayer or of the taxpayer's spouse. Premiums paid for medical insurance coverage of *employees* are deductible as business expenses.

EXAMPLE 10

Ellen, a sole proprietor of a restaurant, has two dependent children. During the year, she paid health insurance premiums of $8,400 for her own coverage and $7,000 for coverage of her two children. Ellen can deduct $15,400 as a business deduction (*for* AGI) in computing her taxable income. ■

Taxpayers may also include premiums paid on qualified long-term care insurance contracts in medical expenses, subject to limitations based on the age of the insured. For 2008, the per-person limits range from $310 for taxpayers age 40 and under to $3,850 for taxpayers over age 70. See IRS Publication 502 for details relating to requirements for deducting qualified long-term care insurance contracts.[14]

---

[13]§ 162(l).

[14]The amounts for 2007 were $290 for taxpayers age 40 and under and $3,680 for taxpayers over age 70.

Year of Deduction

Regardless of a taxpayer's method of accounting, medical expenses are deductible only in the year *paid*. In effect, this places all individual taxpayers on a cash basis as far as the medical expense deduction is concerned. One exception, however, is allowed for deceased taxpayers. If the medical expenses are paid within one year from the day following the day of death, they can be treated as being paid at the time they were *incurred*. Thus, such expenses may be reported on the final income tax return of the decedent or on earlier returns if incurred before the year of death.

No current deduction is allowed for payment for medical care to be rendered in the future unless the taxpayer is under an obligation to make the payment. Whether an obligation to make the payment exists depends upon the policy of the physician or the institution furnishing the medical care.

EXAMPLE 11	Upon the recommendation of his regular dentist, in late December 2008 Gary consults Dr. Smith, a prosthodontist, who specializes in crown and bridge work. Dr. Smith tells Gary that he can do the restorative work for $12,000. To cover his lab bill, however, Dr. Smith requires that 40% of this amount be prepaid. Accordingly, Gary pays $4,800 in December 2008. The balance of $7,200 is paid when the work is completed in July 2009. Under these circumstances, the qualifying medical expenses are $4,800 for 2008 and $7,200 in 2009. The result would be the same even if Gary prepaid the full $12,000 in 2008. ∎

Reimbursements

If medical expenses are reimbursed in the same year as paid, no problem arises. The reimbursement merely reduces the amount that would otherwise qualify for the medical expense deduction. But what happens if the reimbursement occurs in a later year than the expenditure? In computing casualty losses, any reasonable prospect of recovery must be considered (refer to Chapter 7). For medical expenses, however, any expected reimbursement is disregarded in measuring the amount of the deduction. Instead, the reimbursement is accounted for separately in the year in which it occurs.

Under the *tax benefit rule*, a taxpayer who receives an insurance reimbursement for medical expenses deducted in a previous year might have to include the reimbursement in gross income in the year of receipt. However, a taxpayer who did not itemize deductions in the year the expenses were paid did not receive a tax benefit and is *not* required to include a reimbursement in gross income.

The tax benefit rule applies to reimbursements if the taxpayer itemized deductions in the previous year. In this case, the taxpayer may be required to report some or all of the medical expense reimbursement in income in the year the reimbursement is received. Under the tax benefit rule, the taxpayer must include the reimbursement in income up to the amount of the deductions that decreased taxable income in the earlier year.

EXAMPLE 12	Homer had AGI of $60,000 for 2008. He was injured in a car accident and paid $4,300 for hospital expenses and $700 for doctor bills. Homer also incurred medical expenses of $600 for his dependent child. In 2009, Homer was reimbursed $650 by his insurance company for the medical expenses attributable to the car accident. His deduction for medical expenses in 2008 is computed as follows:

Hospitalization	$ 4,300
Bills for doctor's services	700
Medical expenses for dependent	600
Total	$ 5,600
Less: 7.5% of $60,000	(4,500)
Medical expense deduction (assuming Homer itemizes his deductions)	$ 1,100

TAX *in the News*   **PROMOTERS' ENTHUSIASM FOR HSAs IS TEMPERED BY USERS' DISSATISFACTION**

The old saying "all that glitters is not gold" may apply to Health Savings Accounts (HSAs), at least according to the taxpayers who have chosen not to participate. Since late 2003 when HSAs first became available, many employers have pushed these "consumer-directed plans" involving high-deductible medical insurance policies and savings accounts as a way to control rapidly increasing health costs. The plans typically provide a much lower health insurance premium but shift much of the responsibility for health care spending to the consumer.

More taxpayers than ever are contributing to HSAs, but recent growth in participation has been sluggish. Many consumers participate only because their employers offer no other medical benefit options. Some taxpayers are dissatis-fied because they are confused about how the plans are supposed to work, and they feel that the plans have not saved them any money. Others are frustrated by the difficulty of having to shop for their health care. Think about the prospect of shopping around the medical community to get the "best deal" on needed heart bypass surgery.

According to a recent survey conducted by the Kaiser Family Foundation, only 19 percent of employees who were offered a choice in health plan options chose to participate in HSAs. In reaction to this low acceptance rate, one industry expert commented, "If I were a product manager in any other industry and saw scores this low in customer satisfaction and understanding, I'd be thinking of pulling that product from the shelves or retooling it."

Source: *Adapted from Vanessa Furhmans, "Health Savings Plans Start to Falter,"* Wall Street Journal, *June 12, 2007, pp. D1 and D6.*

Assume that Homer would have elected to itemize his deductions even if he had no medical expenses in 2008. If the reimbursement for medical care had occurred in 2008, the medical expense deduction would have been only $450 [$5,600 (total medical expenses) − $650 (reimbursement) − $4,500 (floor)], and Homer would have paid more income tax.

Since the reimbursement was made in a subsequent year, Homer will include $650 in gross income for 2009. If Homer had not itemized in 2008, he would *not* include the $650 reimbursement in 2009 gross income because he would have received no tax benefit in 2008. ■

Health Savings Accounts

Qualifying individuals may make deductible contributions to a **Health Savings Account (HSA)**. An HSA is a qualified trust or custodial account administered by a qualified HSA trustee, which can be a bank, insurance company, or other IRS-approved trustee. The HSA funds are used to pay for the individual's medical expenses in excess of the deductible amount under a high-deductible policy.[15]

A taxpayer can use an HSA in conjunction with a high-deductible medical insurance policy to help reduce the overall cost of medical coverage. Converting from a low-deductible to a high-deductible plan can generally save an individual 20 to 40 percent in premiums. The high-deductible policy provides coverage for extraordinary medical expenses (in excess of the deductible), and expenses not covered by the policy can be paid with funds withdrawn tax-free from the HSA.

E X A M P L E   1 3

Sanchez, who is married and has three dependent children, carries a high-deductible medical insurance policy with a deductible of $4,400. He establishes an HSA and contributes the maximum allowable amount to the HSA in 2008. During 2008, the Sanchez family incurs medical expenses of $7,000. The high-deductible policy covers $2,600 of the expenses ($7,000 expenses − $4,400 deductible). Sanchez may withdraw $4,400 from the HSA to pay the medical expenses not covered by the high-deductible policy. ■

High-Deductible Plans. High-deductible policies are less expensive than low-deductible policies, so taxpayers with low medical costs can benefit from the lower premiums and use funds from the HSA to pay costs not covered by the high-deductible policy. A plan must meet two requirements to qualify as a high-deductible plan.[16]

---

[15]§ 223.   [16]§ 223(c)(2).

1. The annual deductible is not less than $1,100 for self-only coverage ($2,200 for family coverage).
2. The annual limit on total out-of-pocket costs (excluding premiums) under the plan does not exceed $5,600 for self-only coverage ($11,200 for family coverage).

Tax Treatment of HSA Contributions and Distributions. To establish an HSA, a taxpayer contributes funds to a tax-exempt trust.[17] As illustrated in the preceding example, funds can be withdrawn from an HSA to pay medical expenses that are not covered by the high-deductible policy. The following general tax rules apply to HSAs:

1. Contributions made by the taxpayer to an HSA are deductible from gross income to arrive at AGI (deduction *for* AGI). Thus, the taxpayer does not need to itemize in order to take the deduction.
2. Earnings on HSAs are not subject to taxation unless distributed, in which case taxability depends on the way the funds are used.[18]

   • Distributions from HSAs are excluded from gross income if they are used to pay for medical expenses not covered by the high-deductible policy.
   • Distributions that are not used to pay for medical expenses are included in gross income and are subject to an additional 10 percent penalty if made before age 65, death, or disability. Such distributions made by reason of death or disability and distributions made after the HSA beneficiary becomes eligible for Medicare are taxed but not penalized.

HSAs have at least two other attractive features. First, an HSA is portable. Taxpayers who switch jobs can take their HSAs with them. Second, more people than ever before can qualify to set up an HSA. Generally, anyone under age 65 who has a high-deductible plan and is not covered by another policy that is not a high-deductible plan can establish an HSA.

Deductible Amount. The annual deduction for contributions to an HSA is limited to the sum of the monthly limitations. The monthly limitation is calculated for each month that the individual is an eligible individual. The monthly deduction is not allowed after the individual becomes eligible for Medicare coverage.

The amount of the monthly limitation for an individual who has self-only coverage in 2008 is the *lesser* of one-twelfth of the annual deductible under the high-deductible plan or $2,900. An individual who has family coverage in 2008 is limited to the *lesser* of one-twelfth of the annual deductible under the high-deductible plan or $5,800. These amounts are subject to annual cost-of-living adjustments.[19] For an eligible taxpayer who has attained age 55 by the end of the tax year, the limit on annual contributions in 2008 is increased by $900 ($1,000 after 2008). This additional amount is referred to as a *catchup* contribution.

EXAMPLE 14

Liu, who is married and self-employed, carries a high-deductible medical insurance policy with an annual deductible of $4,000. In addition, he has established an HSA. Liu's maximum annual contribution to the HSA is $4,000 (the lesser of $5,800 or the annual deductible). ∎

EXAMPLE 15

During 2008, Adam, who is self-employed, made 12 monthly payments of $700 for an HSA contract that provides medical insurance coverage with a $3,600 deductible. The plan covers Adam, his wife, and two children. Of the $700 monthly fee, $400 was for the high-deductible policy and $300 was deposited into an HSA. The deductible monthly contribution to the HSA is calculated as follows:

---

[17]§ 223(d).
[18]§ 223(f).

[19]§ 223(b)(2). The limits were $2,850 and $5,650 in 2007.

Amount of the annual deductible under the plan	$3,600
Maximum annual deduction for family coverage	$5,800
Monthly limitation (1/12 of $3,600)	$ 300

Because Adam is self-employed, he can deduct $4,800 of the amount paid for the high-deductible policy ($400 per month × 12 months) as a deduction *for* AGI (refer to Example 10). In addition, he can deduct the $3,600 ($300 × 12) paid to the HSA as a deduction *for* AGI. ■

Taxes

A deduction is allowed for certain state and local taxes paid or accrued by a tax-payer.[20] The deduction was created to relieve the burden of multiple taxes upon the same source of revenue.

> **LO.3**
>
> Contrast deductible taxes with nondeductible fees, licenses, and other charges.

Deductibility as a Tax

A distinction must be made between a tax and a fee, since fees are not deductible unless incurred as an ordinary and necessary business expense or as an expense in the production of income. The IRS has defined a tax as follows:

> A tax is an enforced contribution exacted pursuant to legislative authority in the exercise of taxing power, and imposed and collected for the purpose of raising revenue to be used for public or governmental purposes, and not as payment for some special privilege granted or service rendered. Taxes are, therefore, distinguished from various other contributions and charges imposed for particular purposes under particular powers or functions of the government. In view of such distinctions, the question whether a particular contribution or charge is to be regarded as a tax depends upon its real nature.[21]

Accordingly, fees for dog licenses, automobile inspection, automobile titles and registration, hunting and fishing licenses, bridge and highway tolls, drivers' licenses, parking meter deposits, and postage are not deductible if personal in nature. These items, however, could be deductible if incurred as a business expense or for the production of income. Deductible and nondeductible taxes are summarized in Exhibit 10–2.

Property Taxes

State, local, and foreign taxes on real property are generally deductible only by the person upon whom the tax is imposed. Deductible personal property taxes must be *ad valorem* (assessed in relation to the value of the property). Therefore, a motor vehicle tax based on weight, model, year, and horsepower is not an ad valorem tax. However, a tax based on value and other criteria may qualify in part.

EXAMPLE 16

A state imposes a motor vehicle registration tax on 4% of the value of the vehicle plus 40 cents per hundredweight. Belle, a resident of the state, owns a car having a value of $4,000 and weighing 3,000 pounds. Belle pays an annual registration fee of $172. Of this amount, $160 (4% of $4,000) is deductible as a personal property tax. The remaining $12, based on the weight of the car, is not deductible. ■

Assessments for Local Benefits. As a general rule, real property taxes do not include taxes assessed for local benefits because such assessments tend to increase the value of the property (e.g., special assessments for streets, sidewalks, curbing, and other similar improvements). A taxpayer was denied a deduction for the cost

---

[20]Most deductible taxes are listed in § 164, while nondeductible items are included in § 275.

[21]Rev.Rul. 57–345, 1957–2 C.B. 132, and Rev.Rul. 70–622, 1970–2 C.B. 41.

EXHIBIT 10–2	Deductible and Nondeductible Taxes

Deductible	Nondeductible
State, local, and foreign real property taxes	Federal income taxes
	FICA taxes imposed on employees
State and local personal property taxes	Employer FICA taxes paid on domestic household workers
State and local income taxes *or* sales/use taxes	Estate, inheritance, and gift taxes
	Federal, state, and local excise taxes (e.g., gasoline, tobacco, spirits)
Foreign income taxes	Foreign income taxes if the taxpayer chooses the foreign tax credit option
	Taxes on real property to the extent such taxes are to be apportioned and treated as imposed on another taxpayer

of a new sidewalk (relative to a personal residence), even though the construction was required by the city and the sidewalk may have provided an incidental benefit to the public welfare.[22] Such assessments are added to the adjusted basis of the taxpayer's property.

Apportionment of Real Property Taxes between Seller and Purchaser.

Real estate taxes for the entire year are apportioned between the buyer and seller on the basis of the number of days the property was held by each during the real property tax year. This apportionment is required whether the tax is paid by the buyer or the seller or is prorated according to the purchase agreement. It is the apportionment that determines who is entitled to deduct the real estate taxes in the year of sale. The required apportionment prevents the shifting of the deduction for real estate taxes from the buyer to the seller, or vice versa. In making the apportionment, the assessment date and the lien date are disregarded.[23]

EXAMPLE 17

A county's real property tax year runs from January 1 to December 31. Susan, the owner on January 1 of real property located in the county, sells the real property to Bob on June 30 (assume this year is not a leap year). Bob owns the real property from June 30 through December 31. The tax for the real property tax year, January 1 through December 31, is $3,650. The portion of the real property tax treated as imposed upon Susan, the seller, is $1,800 [(180/365) × $3,650, January 1 through June 29], and $1,850 [(185/365) × $3,650, June 30 through December 31] of the tax is treated as imposed upon Bob, the purchaser. ■

If the actual real estate taxes are not prorated between the buyer and seller as part of the purchase agreement, adjustments are required. The adjustments are necessary to determine the amount realized by the seller and the adjusted basis of the property to the buyer. If the buyer pays the entire amount of the tax, he or she has, in effect, paid the seller's portion of the real estate tax and has therefore paid more for the property than the actual purchase price. Thus, the amount of real estate tax that is apportioned to the seller (for Federal income tax purposes) and

---

[22]*Erie H. Rose*, 31 TCM 142, T.C.Memo. 1972–39; Reg. § 1.164–4(a).

[23]For most years, the apportionment is based on a 365-day year. However, in a leap year (i.e., a year that is evenly divisible by 4), the taxes are prorated over 366 days. In making the apportionment, the date of sale counts as a day the property is owned by the buyer.

DEDUCTIBILITY OF FOREIGN TAXES

Josef, a citizen of the United States who works primarily in New York, also works several months each year in Austria. He owns a residence in Austria and pays income taxes to Austria on the income he earns there. Both the property tax he pays on his Austrian residence and the income tax he pays on his Austrian income are deductible in computing U.S. taxable income. However, if Josef deducts the Austrian income tax, he may not claim the foreign tax credit with respect to this tax (see Chapter 13).

GLOBAL *Tax Issues*

paid by the buyer is added to the buyer's adjusted basis. The seller must increase the amount realized on the sale by the same amount.

EXAMPLE 18

Seth sells real estate on October 3 for $100,000. The buyer, Wilma, pays the real estate taxes of $3,650 for the calendar year, which is the real estate property tax year. Assuming this is not a leap year, $2,750 (for 275 days) of the real estate taxes is apportioned to and is deductible by the seller, Seth, and $900 (for 90 days) of the taxes is deductible by Wilma. The buyer has, in effect, paid Seth's real estate taxes of $2,750 and has therefore paid $102,750 for the property. Wilma's basis is increased to $102,750, and the amount realized by Seth from the sale is increased to $102,750. ■

The opposite result occurs if the seller (rather than the buyer) pays the real estate taxes. In this case, the seller reduces the amount realized from the sale by the amount that has been apportioned to the buyer. The buyer is required to reduce his or her adjusted basis by a corresponding amount.

EXAMPLE 19

Ruth sells real estate to Butch for $100,000 on October 3. While Ruth held the property, she paid the real estate taxes of $3,650 for the calendar year, which is the real estate property tax year. Although Ruth paid the entire $3,650 of real estate taxes, $900 of that amount is apportioned to Butch, based on the number of days he owned the property, and is therefore deductible by him. The effect is that the buyer, Butch, has paid only $99,100 ($100,000 − $900) for the property. The amount realized by Ruth, the seller, is reduced by $900, and Butch reduces his basis in the property to $99,100. ■

State and Local Income Taxes and Sales Taxes

LO.4

Understand the Federal income tax treatment of state and local income taxes and sales taxes.

The position of the IRS is that state and local income taxes imposed upon an individual are deductible only as itemized deductions, even if the taxpayer's sole source of income is from a business, rents, or royalties.

Cash basis taxpayers are entitled to deduct state income taxes withheld by the employer in the year the taxes are withheld. In addition, estimated state income tax payments are deductible in the year the payment is made by cash basis taxpayers even if the payments relate to a prior or subsequent year.[24] If the taxpayer overpays state income taxes because of excessive withholdings or estimated tax payments, the refund received is included in gross income of the following year to the extent that the deduction reduced taxable income in the prior year.

EXAMPLE 20

Leona, a cash basis, unmarried taxpayer, had $800 of state income tax withheld during 2008. Additionally in 2008, Leona paid $100 that was due when she filed her 2007 state income tax return and made estimated payments of $300 on her 2008 state income tax. When Leona

[24]Rev.Rul. 71–190, 1971–1 C.B. 70. See also Rev.Rul. 82–208, 1982–2 C.B. 58, where a deduction is not allowed when the taxpayer cannot, in good faith, reasonably determine that there is additional state income tax liability.

files her 2008 Federal income tax return in April 2009, she elects to itemize deductions, which amount to $7,500, including the $1,200 of state income tax payments and withholdings, all of which reduce her taxable income.

As a result of overpaying her 2008 state income tax, Leona receives a refund of $200 early in 2009. She will include this amount in her 2009 gross income in computing her Federal income tax. It does not matter whether Leona received a check from the state for $200 or applied the $200 toward her 2009 state income tax. ∎

Itemized Deduction for Sales Taxes Paid. Individuals can elect to deduct either their state and local income taxes *or* their sales/use taxes paid as an itemized deduction on Schedule A of Form 1040. The annual election can reflect actual sales/use tax payments *or* an amount from an IRS table (see Appendix A). The amount from the table may be increased by sales tax paid on the purchase of motor vehicles, boats, and other specified items. Most likely, the sales tax deduction will be elected by those living in states with no individual income tax. At the time of this writing, this deduction alternative is available only through 2007. However, the general consensus is that Congress will extend this provision for 2008.

Interest

LO.5

Distinguish between deductible and nondeductible interest and apply the appropriate limitations to deductible interest.

A deduction for interest has been allowed since the income tax law was enacted in 1913. Despite its long history of congressional acceptance, the interest deduction has been one of the most controversial areas in the tax law. The controversy centered around the propriety of allowing the deduction of interest charges for the purchase of consumer goods and services and interest on borrowings used to acquire investments (investment interest). Personal (consumer) interest is not deductible. This includes credit card interest, interest on car loans, and any other interest that is not interest on qualified student loans, investment interest, home mortgage interest, or business interest. Interest on qualified student loans, investment interest, and **qualified residence** (home mortgage) **interest** continue to be deductible, subject to the limits discussed on the following pages.

Allowed and Disallowed Items

The Supreme Court has defined *interest* as compensation for the use or forbearance of money.[25] The general rule permits a deduction for interest paid or accrued within the taxable year on indebtedness.

Interest on Qualified Student Loans. Taxpayers who pay interest on a qualified student loan may be able to deduct the interest as a deduction *for* AGI. The deduction is allowable only to the extent that the proceeds of the loan are used to pay qualified education expenses. Such payments must be made to qualified educational institutions. See IRS Publication 970, *Tax Benefits for Education*, for details.

The maximum deduction for qualified student loan interest is $2,500. However, the deduction is phased out for taxpayers with modified AGI (MAGI) between $55,000 and $70,000 ($115,000 and $145,000 on joint returns). The deduction is not allowed for taxpayers who are claimed as dependents or for married taxpayers filing separately.[26]

The numerator in the phaseout computation is equal to MAGI minus the floor of the phaseout range (i.e., $55,000 or $115,000, depending on filing status). The

---

[25] *Old Colony Railroad Co. v. Comm.,* 3 USTC ¶880, 10 AFTR 786, 52 S.Ct. 211 (USSC, 1932).

[26] § 221. See § 221(b)(2)(C) for the definition of MAGI. The phaseout amounts are subject to adjustments for inflation. The phaseout amounts apply to tax returns for 2008. For 2007, the amounts were $55,000 and $70,000 ($110,000 and $140,000 on joint returns).

denominator is equal to the amount in the phaseout range (e.g., $145,000 − $115,000 = $30,000 for married taxpayers filing jointly).

In 2008 Curt and Rita, who are married and file a joint return, paid $3,000 interest on a qualified student loan. Their MAGI was $130,000. Their maximum potential deduction for qualified student interest is $2,500, but it must be reduced by $1,250 as the result of the phaseout rules.

$$\$2,500 \text{ interest} \times (\$130,000 \text{ MAGI} - \$115,000 \text{ phaseout floor})/\$30,000$$
$$\text{phaseout range} = \$1,250 \text{ reduction}$$

Curt and Rita would be allowed a student loan interest deduction of $1,250 ($2,500 maximum deduction − $1,250 reduction = $1,250 deduction *for* AGI). ■

Investment Interest. Taxpayers frequently borrow funds that they use to acquire investment assets. Congress, however, has limited the deductibility of interest on funds borrowed for the purpose of purchasing or continuing to hold investment property. Under this limitation, the deduction for investment interest expense may not exceed the net investment income for the year. A complete discussion of investment interest occurs in Chapter 11 in the context of the limitations that taxpayers face when dealing with assets held for investment purposes.

Qualified Residence Interest. *Qualified residence interest* is interest paid or accrued during the taxable year on indebtedness (subject to limitations) *secured* by any property that is a qualified residence of the taxpayer. Qualified residence interest falls into two categories: (1) interest on acquisition indebtedness and (2) interest on home equity loans. Before discussing each of these categories, however, the term *qualified residence* must be defined.

A *qualified residence* includes the taxpayer's principal residence and one other residence of the taxpayer or spouse. The *principal residence* is one that meets the requirement for nonrecognition of gain upon sale under § 121 (see Chapter 15). The *one other residence*, or second residence, refers to one that is used as a residence if not rented or, if rented, meets the requirements for a personal residence under the rental of vacation home rules (refer to Chapter 6). A taxpayer who has more than one second residence can make the selection each year of which one is the qualified second residence. A residence includes, in addition to a house in the ordinary sense, cooperative apartments, condominiums, and mobile homes and boats that have living quarters (sleeping accommodations and toilet and cooking facilities).

Although in most cases interest paid on a home mortgage is fully deductible, there are limitations.[27] Interest paid or accrued during the tax year on aggregate **acquisition indebtedness** of $1 million or less ($500,000 for married persons filing separate returns) is deductible as qualified residence interest. *Acquisition indebtedness* refers to amounts incurred in acquiring, constructing, or substantially improving a qualified residence of the taxpayer.

Qualified residence interest also includes interest on **home equity loans**. These loans utilize the personal residence of the taxpayer as security. Because the funds from home equity loans can be used for personal purposes (e.g., auto purchases, medical expenses), what would otherwise have been nondeductible consumer interest becomes deductible qualified residence interest.

However, interest is deductible only on the portion of a home equity loan that does not exceed the *lesser of*:

- The fair market value of the residence, reduced by the acquisition indebtedness, *or*
- $100,000 ($50,000 for married persons filing separate returns).

---

[27]§ 163(h)(3).

EXAMPLE 22

Larry owns a personal residence with a fair market value of $450,000 and an outstanding first mortgage of $420,000. Therefore, his equity in his home is $30,000 ($450,000 − $420,000). Larry issues a lien on the residence and in return borrows $15,000 to purchase a new family automobile. All interest on the $435,000 of debt is treated as qualified residence interest. ■

EXAMPLE 23

Leon and Pearl, married taxpayers, took out a mortgage on their home for $290,000 in 1991. In March of the current year, when the home has a fair market value of $400,000 and they owe $195,000 on the mortgage, Leon and Pearl take out a home equity loan for $120,000. They use the funds to purchase a boat to be used for recreational purposes. The boat, which does not have living quarters, does not qualify as a personal residence. On a joint return, Leon and Pearl can deduct all of the interest on the first mortgage since it is acquisition indebtedness. Of the $120,000 home equity loan, only the interest on the first $100,000 is deductible. The interest on the remaining $20,000 is not deductible because it exceeds the statutory ceiling of $100,000. ■

Interest Paid for Services. Mortgage loan companies commonly charge a fee for finding, placing, or processing a mortgage loan. Such fees are often called **points** and are expressed as a percentage of the loan amount. Borrowers often have to pay points to obtain the necessary financing. To qualify as deductible interest, the points must be considered compensation to a lender solely for the use or forbearance of money. The points cannot be a form of service charge or payment for specific services if they are to qualify as deductible interest.[28]

Points must be capitalized and are amortized and deductible ratably over the life of the loan. A special exception, however, permits the purchaser of a principal residence to deduct qualifying points in the year of payment.[29] The exception also covers points paid to obtain funds for home improvements.

Points paid to *refinance* an existing home mortgage cannot be immediately expensed, but must be capitalized and amortized as interest expense over the life of the new loan.[30]

EXAMPLE 24

Sandra purchased her residence several years ago, obtaining a 30-year mortgage at an annual interest rate of 9%. In the current year, Sandra refinances the mortgage in order to reduce the interest rate to 6%. To obtain the refinancing, she has to pay points of $2,600. The $2,600 paid comes under the usual rule applicable to points. The $2,600 must be capitalized and amortized over the life of the mortgage. ■

Points paid by the seller for a buyer are, in effect, treated as an adjustment to the price of the residence, and the buyer is treated as having used cash to pay the points that were paid by the seller. A buyer may deduct seller-paid points in the tax year in which they are paid if several conditions are met. Refer to Revenue Procedure 94–27 for a complete list of these conditions.[31]

Mortgage Insurance Payments. Mortgage insurance is an additional cost that some taxpayers incur when purchasing a home. To protect their interests, mortgage lenders may require this coverage if the homebuyer cannot afford to make a down payment of at least 20 percent. The borrower pays the premiums on the policy, but the lender is the beneficiary who receives reimbursement in the event of foreclosure. Beginning in 2007, mortgage insurance premiums are deductible as interest if they relate to a qualified residence of the taxpayer. However, the deduction begins to phase out for taxpayers with AGI in excess of $100,000 ($50,000 for married taxpayers filing separately). This provision which was scheduled to expire at the end of 2007 has been extended through 2010.[32]

---

[28]Rev.Rul. 67–297, 1967–2 C.B. 87.
[29]§ 461(g)(2).
[30]Rev.Rul. 87–22, 1987–1 C.B. 146.

[31]Rev.Proc. 94–27, 1994–1 C.B. 613.
[32]§ 163(h)(3)(E)(i). The deduction is fully phased out when AGI exceeds $109,000 ($54,500 for married taxpayers filing separately).

Prepayment Penalty. When a mortgage or loan is paid off in full in a lump sum before its term (early), the lending institution may require an additional payment of a certain percentage applied to the unpaid amount at the time of prepayment. This is known as a prepayment penalty and is considered to be interest (e.g., personal, qualified residence, investment) in the year paid. The general rules for deductibility of interest also apply to prepayment penalties.

Interest Paid to Related Parties. Nothing prevents the deduction of interest paid to a related party as long as the payment actually took place and the interest meets the requirements for deductibility. Recall from Chapter 6 that a special rule for related taxpayers applies when the debtor uses the accrual basis and the related creditor is on the cash basis. If this rule is applicable, interest that has been accrued but not paid at the end of the debtor's tax year is not deductible until payment is made and the income is reportable by the cash basis recipient.

Tax-Exempt Securities. The tax law provides that no deduction is allowed for interest on debt incurred to purchase or carry tax-exempt securities.[33] A major problem for the courts has been to determine what is meant by the words *to purchase or carry*. Refer to Chapter 6 for a detailed discussion of these issues.

Restrictions on Deductibility and Timing Considerations

Taxpayer's Obligation. Allowed interest is deductible if the related debt represents a bona fide obligation for which the taxpayer is liable.[34] Thus, for interest to be deductible, both the debtor and the creditor must intend for the loan to be repaid. Intent of the parties can be especially crucial between related parties such as a shareholder and a closely held corporation. In addition, an individual may not deduct interest paid on behalf of another taxpayer. For example, a shareholder may not deduct interest paid by the corporation on his or her behalf.[35] Likewise, a husband may not deduct interest paid on his wife's property if he files a separate return, except in the case of qualified residence interest. If both husband and wife consent in writing, either the husband or the wife may deduct the allowed interest on the principal residence and one other residence.

Time of Deduction. Generally, interest must be paid to secure a deduction unless the taxpayer uses the accrual method of accounting. Under the accrual method, interest is deductible ratably over the life of the loan.

On November 1, 2008, Ramon borrows $1,000 to purchase appliances for a rental house. The loan is payable in 90 days at 12% interest. On the due date in January 2009, Ramon pays the $1,000 note and interest amounting to $30. Ramon can deduct the accrued portion ($2/3 \times$ $30 = $20) of the interest in 2008 only if he is an accrual basis taxpayer. Otherwise, the entire amount of interest ($30) is deductible in 2009. ∎

E X A M P L E   2 5

Prepaid Interest. Accrual method reporting is imposed on cash basis taxpayers for interest prepayments that extend beyond the end of the taxable year.[36] Such payments must be allocated to the tax years to which the interest payments relate.

---

[33]§ 265(a)(2).

[34]*Arcade Realty Co.*, 35 T.C. 256 (1960).

[35]*Continental Trust Co.*, 7 B.T.A. 539 (1927).

[36]§ 461(g)(1).

CONCEPT SUMMARY 10–1

Deductibility of Personal, Student Loan, Investment, and Mortgage Interest

Type	Deductible	Comments
Personal (consumer) interest	No	Includes any interest that is not home mortgage interest, qualified student loan interest, investment interest, or business interest. Examples include interest on car loans and credit card debt.
Qualified student loan interest	Yes	Deduction *for* AGI; subject to limitations.
Investment interest (*not* related to rental or royalty property)	Yes	Itemized deduction; limited to net investment income for the year; disallowed interest can be carried over to future years. See Chapter 11 for a complete discussion of investment interest.
Investment interest (related to rental or royalty property)	Yes	Deduction *for* AGI; limited to net investment income for the year; disallowed interest can be carried over to future years. See Chapter 11 for a complete discussion of investment interest.
Qualified residence interest on acquisition indebtedness	Yes	Deductible as an itemized deduction; limited to indebtedness of $1 million.
Qualified residence interest on home equity indebtedness	Yes	Deductible as an itemized deduction; limited to indebtedness equal to lesser of $100,000 or FMV of residence minus acquisition indebtedness.

These provisions are intended to prevent cash basis taxpayers from *manufacturing* tax deductions before the end of the year by prepaying interest.

Classification of Interest Expense

Whether interest is deductible *for* AGI or as an itemized deduction (*from* AGI) depends on whether the indebtedness has a business, investment, or personal purpose. If the indebtedness is incurred in relation to a business (other than performing services as an employee) or for the production of rent or royalty income, the interest is deductible *for* AGI. If the indebtedness is incurred for personal use, such as qualified residence interest, any deduction allowed is taken *from* AGI and is reported on Schedule A of Form 1040 if the taxpayer elects to itemize. Note, however, that interest on a student loan is a deduction *for* AGI. If the taxpayer is an employee who incurs debt in relation to his or her employment, the interest is considered to be personal, or consumer, interest. Business expenses appear on Schedule C of Form 1040, and expenses related to rents or royalties are reported on Schedule E.

If a taxpayer deposits money in a certificate of deposit (CD) that has a term of one year or less and the interest cannot be withdrawn without penalty, the full amount of the interest must still be included in income, even though part of the interest is forfeited due to an early withdrawal. However, the taxpayer will be allowed a deduction *for* AGI as to the forfeited amount.

LO.6

Understand charitable contributions and their related measurement problems and percentage limitations.

Charitable Contributions

Section 170 allows individuals and corporations to deduct contributions made to qualified *domestic* organizations. Contributions to qualified charitable organizations serve certain social welfare needs and thus relieve the government of the cost of providing these needed services to the community.

The **charitable contribution** provisions are among the most complex in the tax law. To determine the amount deductible as a charitable contribution, several important questions must be answered:

- What constitutes a charitable contribution?
- Was the contribution made to a qualified organization?
- When is the contribution deductible?
- What record-keeping and reporting requirements apply to charitable contributions?
- How is the value of donated property determined?
- What special rules apply to contributions of property that has increased in value?
- What percentage limitations apply to the charitable contribution deduction?
- What rules apply to amounts in excess of percentage limitations (carryovers)?

These questions are addressed in the sections that follow.

Criteria for a Gift

A *charitable contribution* is defined as a gift made to a qualified organization.[37] The major elements needed to qualify a contribution as a gift are a donative intent, the absence of consideration, and acceptance by the donee. Consequently, the taxpayer has the burden of establishing that the transfer was made from motives of *disinterested generosity* as established by the courts.[38] This test is quite subjective and has led to problems of interpretation (refer to the discussion of gifts in Chapter 5).

Benefit Received Rule. When a donor derives a tangible benefit from a contribution, he or she cannot deduct the value of the benefit.

EXAMPLE 26

Ralph purchases a ticket at $100 for a special performance of the local symphony (a qualified charity). If the price of a ticket to a symphony concert is normally $35, Ralph is allowed only $65 as a charitable contribution. ■

An exception to this benefit rule provides for the deduction of an automatic percentage of the amount paid for the right to purchase athletic tickets from colleges and universities.[39] Under this exception, 80 percent of the amount paid to or for the benefit of the institution qualifies as a charitable contribution deduction.

EXAMPLE 27

Janet donates $500 to State University's athletic department. The payment guarantees that she will have preferred seating on the 50-yard line at football games. Subsequently, Janet buys four $35 game tickets. Under the exception to the benefit rule, she is allowed a $400 (80% of $500) charitable contribution deduction for the taxable year.

If, however, Janet's $500 donation includes four $35 tickets, that portion [$140 ($35 × 4)] and the remaining portion of $360 ($500 − $140) are treated as separate amounts. Thus, Janet is allowed a charitable contribution deduction of $288 (80% of $360). ■

Contribution of Services. No deduction is allowed for a contribution of one's services to a qualified charitable organization. However, unreimbursed expenses related to the services rendered may be deductible. For example, the cost of a uniform (without general utility) that is required to be worn while performing services

---

[37]§ 170(c).

[38]*Comm. v. Duberstein*, 60–2 USTC ¶9515, 5 AFTR2d 1626, 80 S.Ct. 1190 (USSC, 1960).

[39]§ 170(l).

may be deductible, as are certain out-of-pocket transportation costs incurred for the benefit of the charity. In lieu of these out-of-pocket costs for an automobile, a standard mileage rate of 14 cents per mile is allowed.[40] Deductions are permitted for transportation, reasonable expenses for lodging, and the cost of meals while away from home incurred in performing the donated services. The travel expenses are not deductible if the travel involves a significant element of personal pleasure, recreation, or vacation.[41]

EXAMPLE 28

Grace, a delegate representing her church in Miami, Florida, travels to a two-day national meeting in Denver, Colorado, in February. After the meeting, Grace spends two weeks at a nearby ski resort. Under these circumstances, none of the transportation, meals, or lodging is deductible because the travel involved a significant element of personal pleasure, recreation, or vacation. ■

Nondeductible Items. In addition to the benefit received rule and the restrictions placed on contribution of services, the following items may *not* be deducted as charitable contributions:

- Dues, fees, or bills paid to country clubs, lodges, fraternal orders, or similar groups.
- Cost of raffle, bingo, or lottery tickets.
- Cost of tuition.
- Value of blood given to a blood bank.
- Donations to homeowners associations.
- Gifts to individuals.
- Rental value of property used by a qualified charity.

Qualified Organizations

To be deductible, a contribution must be made to one of the following organizations:[42]

- A state or possession of the United States or any subdivisions thereof.
- A corporation, trust, community chest, fund, or foundation that is situated in the United States and is organized and operated exclusively for religious, charitable, scientific, literary, or educational purposes or for the prevention of cruelty to children or animals.
- A veterans' organization.
- A fraternal organization operating under the lodge system.
- A cemetery company.

The IRS publishes a list of organizations that have applied for and received tax-exempt status under § 501 of the Code.[43] This publication is updated frequently and may be helpful in determining if a gift has been made to a qualifying charitable organization.

Because gifts made to needy individuals are not deductible, a deduction will not be permitted if a gift is received by a donee in an individual capacity rather than as a representative of a qualifying organization.

Time of Deduction

A charitable contribution generally is deducted in the year the payment is made. This rule applies to both cash and accrual basis individuals. A contribution is

---

[40]§ 170(i).

[41]§ 170(j).

[42]§ 170(c).

[43]Although this *Cumulative List of Organizations*, IRS Publication 78, may be helpful, qualified organizations are not required to be listed. Not all organizations that qualify are listed in this publication. The list is available on the Web at **http://www.irs.gov**.

CHOOSE THE CHARITY WISELY

Ibrahim, a U.S. citizen of Turkish descent, was distressed by the damage caused by a major earthquake in Turkey. He donated $100,000 to the Earthquake Victims' Relief Fund, a Turkish charitable organization that was set up to help victims of the earthquake. Ahmed, also a U.S. citizen of Turkish descent, donated $200,000 to help with the relief effort. However, Ahmed's contribution went to his mosque, which sent the proceeds of a fund drive to the Earthquake Victims' Relief Fund in Turkey. Ibrahim's contribution is not deductible, but Ahmed's is. Why? Contributions to charitable organizations are not deductible unless the organization is a U.S. charity.

ordinarily deemed to have been made on the delivery of the property to the donee. For example, if a gift of securities (properly endorsed) is made to a qualified charitable organization, the gift is considered complete on the day of delivery or mailing. However, if the donor delivers the certificate to his or her bank or broker or to the issuing corporation, the gift is considered complete on the date the stock is transferred on the books of the corporation.

A contribution made by check is considered delivered on the date of mailing. Thus, a check mailed on December 31, 2008, is deductible on the taxpayer's 2008 tax return. If the contribution is charged on a credit card, the date the charge is made determines the year of deduction.

Record-Keeping and Valuation Requirements

Record-Keeping Requirements. No deduction is allowed for contributions of $250 or more unless the taxpayer obtains *written substantiation* of the contribution from the charitable organization. The substantiation must specify the amount of cash and a description (but not value) of any property other than cash contributed. The substantiation must be obtained before the earlier of (1) the due date (including extensions) of the return for the year the contribution is claimed or (2) the date such return is filed. See the Tax in the News on page 10–23 for additional substantiation requirements.

Additional information is required if the value of the donated property is over $500 but not over $5,000. The taxpayer provides this by filing Section A of Form 8283 (Noncash Charitable Contributions) for such contributions.

For noncash contributions with a claimed value in excess of $5,000 ($10,000 in the case of nonpublicly traded stock), the taxpayer must obtain a qualified appraisal and must file Section B of Form 8283. This schedule must show a summary of the appraisal and must be attached to the taxpayer's return. Failure to comply with these reporting rules may result in disallowance of the charitable contribution deduction. Additionally, significant overvaluation exposes the taxpayer to rather stringent penalties.[44]

Valuation Requirements. Property donated to a charity is generally valued at fair market value at the time the gift is made. The Code and Regulations give very little guidance on the measurement of the fair market value except to say, "The fair market value is the price at which the property would change hands between a willing buyer and a willing seller, neither being under any compulsion to buy or sell and both having reasonable knowledge of relevant facts."

---

[44]The amounts discussed in this section ($250, $500, $5,000, and $10,000) and other details as to the documentation required are provided in §§ 170(f)(8) and (11).

Generally, charitable organizations do not attest to the fair market value of the donated property. Nevertheless, the taxpayer must maintain reliable written evidence of the following information concerning the donation:

- The fair market value of the property and how that value was determined.
- The amount of the reduction in the value of the property (if required) for certain appreciated property and how that reduction was determined.
- Terms of any agreement with the charitable organization dealing with the use of the property and potential sale or other disposition of the property by the organization.
- A signed copy of the appraisal if the value of the property was determined by appraisal. For a contribution of art with an aggregate value of $20,000 or more, a copy of the appraisal itself must be attached to the taxpayer's return.

ETHICAL and EQUITABLE *Considerations*

A SECOND APPRAISAL

Ken donated a painting to the Hamilton City Art Museum. He acquired the painting 20 years ago at a cost of $10,000. Ken had the painting appraised by the owner of a Hamilton art store, a qualified art appraiser, who estimated its value at $50,000. Ken believed the painting was worth more than $50,000, so he had it appraised by an art dealer from Chicago.

The Chicago art dealer, also a qualified art appraiser, appraised the painting at a value of $120,000. Ken itemized deductions and took a charitable contribution deduction of $120,000. Was Ken justified in taking a deduction based on the higher appraisal?

Limitations on Charitable Contribution Deduction

In General. The potential charitable contribution deduction is the total of all donations, both money and property, that qualify for the deduction. After this determination is made, the actual amount of the charitable contribution deduction that is allowed for individuals for the tax year is limited as follows:

- If the qualifying contributions for the year total 20 percent or less of AGI, they are fully deductible.
- If the qualifying contributions are more than 20 percent of AGI, the deductible amount may be limited to either 20 percent, 30 percent, or 50 percent of AGI, depending on the type of property given and the type of organization to which the donation is made.
- In any case, the maximum charitable contribution deduction may not exceed 50 percent of AGI for the tax year.

To understand the complex rules for computing the amount of a charitable contribution deduction, it is necessary to understand the distinction between capital gain property and ordinary income property. In addition, it is necessary to understand when the 50 percent, 30 percent, and 20 percent limitations apply. If a taxpayer's contributions for the year exceed the applicable percentage limitations, the excess contributions may be carried forward and deducted during a five-year carryover period. These topics are discussed in the sections that follow.

Ordinary Income Property. **Ordinary income property** is any property that, if sold, will result in the recognition of ordinary income. The term includes inventory for sale in the taxpayer's trade or business, a work of art created by the donor, and a manuscript prepared by the donor. It also includes, *for purposes of the charitable*

TAX *in the News*	**CONGRESS CHALLENGES QUESTIONABLE CONTRIBUTION DEDUCTIONS**

Taxpayers are generally allowed to take a deduction equal to the fair market value of capital gain property contributed to charity. Certain charities formerly attempted to exploit this provision by soliciting donations of used cars and claiming that the donor could deduct the fair market value of the vehicle. Congress suspected that some donors were basing their deductions on inflated fair market values and changed the law to counter this behavior. As a result, the deduction for donations of used cars now is generally limited to the amount the charity receives on the sale of the car.

Congress continued to challenge questionable contribution deductions in the Pension Protection Act of 2006, which contains more stringent requirements for substantiation of cash donations. For a number of years, taxpayers contributing $250 or more have been required to obtain a written acknowledgment from the charity to secure the deduction. But beginning in 2007, cash contributions of *less than* $250 must be supported by a bank record (e.g., a canceled check) or written documentation from the charity. This rule applies to any contribution, regardless of how small it may be. Therefore, the days of claiming a deduction for the loose change one drops into a red Salvation Army kettle seem to be a thing of the past.

Contributions of used clothing and household items now are also subject to stricter substantiation requirements, including a detailed statement from the charity. In addition, the items must be in "good used condition or better." The IRS has not defined this term.

contribution calculation, a capital asset held by the donor for less than the required holding period for long-term capital gain treatment (long term is a period longer than one year). To the extent that disposition of property results in the recognition of ordinary income due to the recapture of depreciation, it is ordinary income property.[45]

If ordinary income property is contributed, the deduction is equal to the fair market value of the property less the amount of ordinary income that would have been reported if the property were sold. In most instances, the deduction is limited to the adjusted basis of the property to the donor.

EXAMPLE 29

Tim donates stock in White Corporation to a university on May 1, 2008. Tim had purchased the stock for $2,500 on March 3, 2008, and the stock had a value of $3,600 when he made the donation. Since he had not held the property long enough to meet the long-term capital gain requirement, Tim would have recognized a short-term capital gain of $1,100 if he had sold the property. Since short-term capital gain property is treated as ordinary income property for charitable contribution purposes, Tim's charitable contribution deduction is limited to the property's adjusted basis of $2,500 ($3,600 − $1,100). ∎

In Example 29, suppose the stock had a fair market value of $2,300 (rather than $3,600) when it was donated to charity. Because the fair market value now is less than the adjusted basis, the charitable contribution deduction is $2,300.

Capital Gain Property. **Capital gain property** is any property that would have resulted in the recognition of long-term capital gain or § 1231 gain if the property had been sold by the donor.[46] As a general rule, the deduction for a contribution of capital gain property is equal to the fair market value of the property.

Three major exceptions disallow the deductibility of the appreciation on long-term capital gain property. One exception concerns certain private foundations. Private foundations are organizations that traditionally do not receive their funding from the general public (e.g., the Ford Foundation). Generally, foundations fall into two categories: operating and nonoperating. A private *operating* foundation is one that spends substantially all of its income in the active conduct of the charitable

[45]For a more complete discussion of the difference between ordinary income and capital gain property, see Chapter 16.

[46]See General Scheme of Taxation in Chapter 16 for a discussion of holding periods.

undertaking for which it was established. Other private foundations are *nonoperating* foundations. However, if a private nonoperating foundation distributes the contributions it receives according to special rules within two and one-half months following the year of the contribution, the organization is treated the same as public charities and private operating foundations. Often, only the private foundation knows its status (operating or nonoperating) for sure, and the status can change from year to year.

If capital gain property is contributed to a private *nonoperating* foundation, the taxpayer must reduce the contribution by the long-term capital gain that would have been recognized if the property had been sold at its fair market value. The effect of this provision is to limit the deduction to the property's adjusted basis.[47]

| EXAMPLE 30 | Walter purchased land for $8,000 on January 1, 1986, and has held it as an investment since then. This year, when the land is worth $20,000, he donates it to a private nonoperating foundation. Walter's charitable contribution is $8,000 ($20,000 − $12,000), the land's basis. ∎ |

If, in Example 30, Walter had donated the land to either a public charity or a private operating foundation, his charitable contribution would be $20,000, the fair market value of the land.

A second exception applying to capital gain property relates to *tangible personalty*. Tangible personalty is all property that is not realty (land and buildings) and does not include intangible property such as stock or securities. If tangible personalty is contributed to a public charity such as a museum, church, or university, the charitable deduction may have to be reduced. The amount of the reduction is the long-term capital gain that would have been recognized if the property had been sold for its fair market value. The reduction is required in either of the following situations:

- The property is put to an *unrelated use*. The term *unrelated use* means a use that is unrelated to the exempt purpose or function of the charitable organization. For example, a piece of artwork donated to the American Red Cross is unlikely to be put to a related use. Instead, the Red Cross would likely sell the art to generate funds that would then be used to support its mission of providing assistance to individuals who have been struck by disasters.
- The property, for which a deduction of more than $5,000 is claimed, is sold, exchanged, or otherwise disposed of by the donee before the close of the tax year unless the donee certifies that it put the property to a related use or intended to put the property to a related use.

This reduction generally will not apply if the property is, in fact, not put to an unrelated use or if, at the time of the contribution, it was reasonable to anticipate that the property would not be put to an unrelated use by the donee.[48]

| EXAMPLE 31 | Myrtle contributes a Picasso painting, for which she paid $20,000, to a local museum. She had owned the painting for four years. It had a value of $30,000 at the time of the donation. The museum displays the painting for five years and subsequently sells it for $50,000. The charitable contribution is $30,000. It is not reduced by the unrealized appreciation since the painting is not put to an unrelated use even though it is later sold by the museum. ∎ |

---

[47]§ 170(e)(1)(B)(ii). However, § 170(e)(5) provides that taxpayers who donate *qualified appreciated stock* to private nonoperating foundations may deduct the fair market value of the stock. Qualified appreciated stock is stock for which market quotations are readily available on an established securities market.

[48]§ 170(e)(1)(B)(i) and Reg. § 1.170A–4(b)(3)(ii)(b). In certain situations, if the donee disposes of the property within three years of the contribution, the donor is required to recapture the appreciation element of the deduction unless the donee certifies that it put the property to a related use or intended to put the property to a related use.

A third exception applying to capital gain property disallows a deduction for the appreciation on several types of intellectual property. Patents, certain copyrights, trademarks, trade names, trade secrets, know-how, and some software are subject to this rule, which limits the contribution to the lesser of the taxpayer's basis in the property or the property's fair market value. As a consequence of this exception, if many of these types of intellectual property are donated by their creator, the charitable contribution deduction will be relatively small because the creator usually has a low basis for them.

Fifty Percent Ceiling. Contributions made to public charities may not exceed 50 percent of an individual's AGI for the year. Excess contributions may be carried over to the next five years. The 50 percent ceiling on contributions applies to the following types of public charities:

- A church or a convention or association of churches.
- An educational organization that maintains a regular faculty and curriculum.
- A hospital or medical school.
- An organization supported by the government that holds property or investments for the benefit of a college or university.
- A Federal, state, or local governmental unit.
- An organization normally receiving a substantial part of its support from the public or a governmental unit.

In the remaining discussion of charitable contributions, public charities and private foundations (both operating and nonoperating) that qualify for the 50 percent ceiling will be referred to as *50 percent organizations*.

The 50 percent ceiling also applies to contributions to the following organizations:

- All private operating foundations.
- Certain private nonoperating foundations that distribute the contributions they receive to public charities and private operating foundations within two and one-half months following the year they receive the contribution.
- Certain private nonoperating foundations in which the contributions are pooled in a common fund and the income and principal sum are paid to public charities.

Thirty Percent Ceiling. A 30 percent ceiling applies to contributions of cash and ordinary income property to private nonoperating foundations that are not 50 percent organizations. The 30 percent ceiling also applies to contributions of appreciated capital gain property to 50 percent organizations unless the taxpayer makes a special election (see below).

In the event the contributions for any one tax year involve both 50 percent and 30 percent property, the allowable deduction comes first from the 50 percent property.

E X A M P L E   32

During the year, Lisa makes the following donations to her church: cash of $2,000 and unimproved land worth $30,000. Lisa had purchased the land four years ago for $22,000 and held it as an investment. Therefore, it is long-term capital gain property. Lisa's AGI for the year is $60,000. Disregarding percentage limitations, Lisa's potential deduction is $32,000 [$2,000 (cash) + $30,000 (fair market value of land)].

In applying the percentage limitations, however, the *current* deduction for the land is limited to $18,000 [30% (limitation applicable to long-term capital gain property) × $60,000 (AGI)]. Thus, the total current deduction is $20,000 ($2,000 cash + $18,000 land). Note that the total deduction does not exceed $30,000, which is 50% of Lisa's AGI. ■

Under a special election, a taxpayer may choose to forgo a deduction of the appreciation on capital gain property. Referred to as the *reduced deduction election*, this enables the taxpayer to move from the 30 percent limitation to the 50 percent limitation.

CONCEPT SUMMARY 10–2

Determining the Deduction for Contributions of Appreciated Property by Individuals

If the Type of Property Contributed Is:	And the Property Is Contributed to:	The Contribution Is Measured by:	But the Deduction Is Limited to:
1. Capital gain property	A 50% organization	Fair market value of the property	30% of AGI
2. Ordinary income property	A 50% organization	The basis of the property*	50% of AGI
3. Capital gain property (and the property is tangible personal property put to an unrelated use by the donee)	A 50% organization	The basis of the property*	50% of AGI
4. Capital gain property (and the reduced deduction is elected)	A 50% organization	The basis of the property	50% of AGI
5. Capital gain property	A private nonoperating foundation that is not a 50% organization	The basis of the property*	The lesser of: 1. 20% of AGI 2. 50% of AGI minus other contributions to 50% organizations

*If the fair market value of the property is less than the adjusted basis (i.e., the property has declined in value instead of appreciating), the fair market value is used.

EXAMPLE 33

Assume the same facts as in Example 32, except that Lisa makes the reduced deduction election. Now the deduction becomes $24,000 [$2,000 (cash) + $22,000 (basis in land)] because both donations fall under the 50% limitation. Thus, by making the election, Lisa has increased her current charitable contribution deduction by $4,000 [$24,000 − $20,000 (Example 32)]. ∎

Although the reduced deduction election appears attractive, it should be considered carefully. The election sacrifices a deduction for the appreciation on long-term capital gain property that might eventually be allowed. Note that in Example 32, the potential deduction was $32,000, yet in Example 33 only $24,000 is allowed. The reason the potential deduction is decreased by $8,000 ($32,000 − $24,000) is that no carryover is allowed for the amount sacrificed by the election.

Twenty Percent Ceiling. A 20 percent ceiling applies to contributions of appreciated long-term capital gain property to private nonoperating foundations that are not 50 percent organizations.

Contribution Carryovers. Contributions that exceed the percentage limitations for the current year can be carried over for five years. In the carryover process, such contributions do not lose their identity for limitation purposes. Thus, if the contribution originally involved 30 percent property, the carryover will continue to be classified as 30 percent property in the carryover year.

EXAMPLE 34

Assume the same facts as in Example 32. Because only $18,000 of the $30,000 value of the land is deducted in the current year, the balance of $12,000 may be carried over to the following year. But the carryover will still be treated as long-term capital gain property and is subject to the 30%-of-AGI limitation. ∎

In applying the percentage limitations, current charitable contributions must be claimed first before any carryovers can be considered. If carryovers involve more than one year, they are utilized in a first-in, first-out order.

Miscellaneous Itemized Deductions

No deduction is allowed for personal, living, or family expenses.[49] However, a taxpayer may incur a number of expenditures related to employment. If an employee or outside salesperson incurs unreimbursed business expenses or expenses that are reimbursed under a nonaccountable plan, including travel and transportation, the expenses are deductible as **miscellaneous itemized deductions**.[50] Certain other expenses also fall into the special category of miscellaneous itemized deductions. Some are deductible only if, in total, they exceed 2 percent of the taxpayer's AGI. These miscellaneous itemized deductions include (but are not limited to) the following:

LO.7
List the business and personal expenditures that are deductible either as miscellaneous itemized deductions or as other itemized deductions.

- Professional dues to membership organizations.
- Uniforms or other clothing that cannot be used for normal wear.
- Fees incurred for the preparation of one's tax return or fees incurred for tax litigation before the IRS or the courts.
- Job-hunting costs.
- Fee paid for a safe deposit box used to store papers and documents relating to taxable income-producing investments.
- Investment expenses that are deductible under § 212 as discussed in Chapter 6.
- Appraisal fees to determine the amount of a casualty loss or the fair market value of donated property.
- Hobby losses up to the amount of hobby income (refer to Chapter 6).
- Unreimbursed employee expenses (refer to Chapter 9).

Certain employee business expenses that are reimbursed are not itemized deductions, but are deducted *for* AGI. Employee business expenses are discussed in depth in Chapter 9.

ETHICAL and EQUITABLE *Considerations*

JOB HUNTING IN SKI COUNTRY: A DEDUCTIBLE EXPENSE?

George, an avid skier, manages the ski department of a sporting goods store in St. Louis. He has been taking ski vacations in Lake Tahoe for several years and is considering finding a job in Lake Tahoe and moving there. George recently learned that he can deduct job-hunting expenses on his Federal income tax return. One of his customers, who is a CPA, told George that transportation costs can be deducted if the primary purpose of the trip is to hunt for a job. According to the CPA, other travel costs must be allocated between job-hunting days and personal days. George

plans to fly to Reno on Sunday, have job interviews each morning from Monday through Thursday, and ski each afternoon after the job interviews are concluded. He plans to ski all day Friday and Saturday and fly back to St. Louis on Saturday night. Is George justified in taking a deduction for job-hunting expenses this year? Will he be justified in taking future deductions if he is unable to find a job this year and continues his job-hunting trips each year for the next several years?

---

[49]§ 262.

[50]Actors and performing artists who meet certain requirements are not subject to this rule. See § 62(a)(2)(B).

Other Miscellaneous Deductions

Certain expenses and losses do not fall into any category of itemized deductions already discussed but are nonetheless deductible. The following expenses and losses are deductible on line 28 of Schedule A as Other Miscellaneous Deductions.

- Gambling losses up to the amount of gambling winnings.
- Impairment-related work expenses of a handicapped person.
- Federal estate tax on income in respect of a decedent.
- Deduction for repayment of amounts under a claim of right if more than $3,000 (discussed in Chapter 18).
- The unrecovered investment in an annuity contract when the annuity ceases by reason of death, discussed in Chapter 4.

Unlike the expenses and losses discussed previously under Miscellaneous Itemized Deductions, the above expenses and losses are not subject to the 2 percent-of-AGI floor.

Comprehensive Example of Schedule A

Harry and Jean Brown, married filing jointly, had the following transactions for 2007:

Medicines that required a prescription	$ 430
Doctor and dentist bills paid and not reimbursed	2,120
Medical insurance premium payments	1,200
Contact lenses	170
Transportation for medical purposes (280 miles × 20 cents/mile + $6.60 parking)	63
State income tax withheld	1,900
Real estate taxes	1,580
Interest paid on qualified residence mortgage	2,340
Qualifying charitable contributions paid by check	860
Transportation in performing charitable services (800 miles × 14 cents/mile + $7.00 parking and tolls)	119
Unreimbursed employee expenses (from Form 2106)	870
Tax return preparation	150
Safe deposit box (used for keeping investment documents and tax records)	170

The Browns' AGI is $40,000. Their completed 2007 Schedule A on the following page reports itemized deductions totaling $8,172. Schedule A for 2007 is used for illustration purposes because the 2008 form was not available at the date of this printing.

LO.8

Recognize the limitation on certain itemized deductions applicable to high-income taxpayers.

Overall Limitation on Certain Itemized Deductions

Congress has enacted several provisions limiting tax benefits for high-income taxpayers. These limitations include the exemption phaseout (refer to Chapter 3) and a phaseout of itemized deductions. For 2008, the phaseout of itemized deductions (also referred to as a *cutback adjustment*) applies to taxpayers whose AGI exceeds

SCHEDULES A&B (Form 1040) Department of the Treasury Internal Revenue Service	**Schedule A—Itemized Deductions** (Schedule B is on back) ▶ Attach to Form 1040. ▶ See Instructions for Schedules A&B (Form 1040).		OMB No. 1545-0074 **2007** Attachment Sequence No. **07**	

Name(s) shown on Form 1040   *Harry and Jean Brown*   **Your social security number**   *371 | 30 | 3987*

Medical and Dental Expenses	**1** **2** **3** **4**	**Caution.** Do not include expenses reimbursed or paid by others. Medical and dental expenses (see page A-1) Enter amount from Form 1040, line 38 [**2**	*40,000*] Multiply line 2 by 7.5% (.075). Subtract line 3 from line 1. If line 3 is more than line 1, enter -0-	**1** *3,983* **3** *3,000*	**4** *983*
Taxes You Paid (See page A-2.)	**5** **6** **7** **8** **9**	State and local (**check only one box**): **a** ☒ Income taxes, **or** **b** ☐ General sales taxes Real estate taxes (see page A-5) Personal property taxes Other taxes. List type and amount ▶ _____ Add lines 5 through 8	**5** *1,900* **6** *1,580* **7** **8**	**9** *3,480*
Interest You Paid (See page A-5.) **Note.** Personal interest is not deductible.	**10** **11** **12** **13** **14** **15**	Home mortgage interest and points reported to you on Form 1098 Home mortgage interest not reported to you on Form 1098. If paid to the person from whom you bought the home, see page A-6 and show that person's name, identifying no., and address ▶ _____ Points not reported to you on Form 1098. See page A-6 for special rules Qualified mortgage insurance premiums (See page A-7) Investment interest. Attach Form 4952 if required. (See page A-7.) Add lines 10 through 14	**10** *2,340* **11** **12** **13** **14**	**15** *2,340*
Gifts to Charity If you made a gift and got a benefit for it, see page A-8.	**16** **17** **18** **19**	Gifts by cash or check. If you made any gift of $250 or more, see page A-8 Other than by cash or check. If any gift of $250 or more, see page A-8. You **must** attach Form 8283 if over $500 Carryover from prior year Add lines 16 through 18	**16** *860* **17** *119* **18**	**19** *979*
Casualty and Theft Losses	**20**	Casualty or theft loss(es). Attach Form 4684. (See page A-9.)	**20**	
Job Expenses and Certain Miscellaneous Deductions (See page A-9.)	**21** **22** **23** **24** **25** **26** **27**	Unreimbursed employee expenses—job travel, union dues, job education, etc. Attach Form 2106 or 2106-EZ if required. (See page A-9.) ▶ _____ Tax preparation fees. Other expenses—investment, safe deposit box, etc. List type and amount ▶ ___ *Safe deposit box* ___ Add lines 21 through 23 Enter amount from Form 1040, line 38 [**25**	*40,000*] Multiply line 25 by 2% (.02) Subtract line 26 from line 24. If line 26 is more than line 24, enter -0-	**21** *870* **22** *150* **23** *170* **24** *1,190* **26** *800*	**27** *390*
Other Miscellaneous Deductions	**28**	Other—from list on page A-10. List type and amount ▶ _____		**28**
Total Itemized Deductions	**29** **30**	Is Form 1040, line 38, over $156,400 (over $78,200 if married filing separately)? ☒ **No.** Your deduction is not limited. Add the amounts in the far right column for lines 4 through 28. Also, enter this amount on Form 1040, line 40. ☐ **Yes.** Your deduction may be limited. See page A-10 for the amount to enter. If you elect to itemize deductions even though they are less than your standard deduction, check here ▶ ☐	**29**	**29** *8,172*

For Paperwork Reduction Act Notice, see Form 1040 instructions.   Cat. No. 11330X   **Schedule A (Form 1040) 2007**

$159,950 ($79,975 for married taxpayers filing separately).[51] The limitation applies to the following frequently encountered itemized deductions:[52]

- Taxes.
- Home mortgage interest, including points.
- Charitable contributions.
- Unreimbursed employee expenses subject to the 2 percent-of-AGI floor.
- All other expenses subject to the 2 percent-of-AGI floor.

The following deductions are *not* subject to the limitation on itemized deductions:

- Medical and dental expenses.
- Investment interest expense.
- Nonbusiness casualty and theft losses.
- Gambling losses.

The overall limitation applicable to itemized deductions is being phased out over a four-year period, beginning in 2006. Therefore, taxpayers subject to the limitation must use a two-step computation to determine the reduction required by the overall limitation.

Step 1

Calculate the lesser of :

- 3 percent of the amount by which AGI exceeds $159,950 ($79,975 if married filing separately).
- 80 percent of itemized deductions that are affected by the limit.

Step 2

Multiply the amount computed in Step 1 by the fraction that applies to the tax year involved. For 2006 and 2007, the phaseout was equal to two-thirds of the Step 1 amount. For 2008 and 2009, the phaseout is equal to one-third of the Step 1 amount. The overall limitation will no longer exist for taxable years beginning after 2009.

The overall limitation is applied after applying all other limitations to itemized deductions that are affected by the overall limitation. For example, as discussed, other limitations apply to charitable contributions, certain meals and entertainment expenses, and certain miscellaneous itemized deductions.

EXAMPLE 35

Herman, who is single, had AGI of $200,000 for 2008. He incurred the following expenses and losses during the year:

Medical expenses before 7.5%-of-AGI limitation	$16,000
State and local income taxes	3,200
Real estate taxes	2,800
Home mortgage interest	7,200
Charitable contributions	2,000
Casualty loss before 10% limitation (after $100 floor)	21,500
Unreimbursed employee expenses subject to 2%-of-AGI limitation	4,300
Gambling losses (Herman had $3,000 gambling income)	7,000

---

[51]§ 68. For 2007, the limitation applied if AGI exceeded $156,400 ($78,200 for married taxpayers filing separately).

[52]Other deductions subject to the limitation include Federal estate tax on income in respect of a decedent, certain amortizable bond premiums, the deduction for repayment of certain amounts, certain unrecovered investments in an annuity, and impairment-related work expenses.

TAX *in the News*

THE FIRST FAMILY AND ITEMIZED DEDUCTION PHASEOUTS

President George W. and Laura Bush itemized deductions on their 2006 tax return (refer to Tax in the News, page 10–3). Because of their income level, their itemized deductions were reduced, as shown in the column to the right.

The top marginal rate of 35 percent applied to President and Mrs. Bush's taxable income in 2006. Therefore, the phaseout of itemized deductions cost them $4,307 in additional Federal income tax ($12,306 reduction × 35% marginal tax rate).

Itemized Deductions	
Medical expenses	$ –0–
Taxes	27,474
Interest	–0–
Charitable contributions	78,100
Job expenses and most other miscellaneous deductions	27,428
Total itemized deductions	$133,002
Reduction due to phaseout [($765,801 AGI – $150,500) × .03 × ⅔]	(12,306)
Itemized deductions allowed	$120,696

Herman's itemized deductions *before* the overall limitation are computed as follows:

Medical expenses [$16,000 – (7.5% × $200,000)]	$ 1,000
State and local income taxes	3,200
Real estate taxes	2,800
Home mortgage interest	7,200
Charitable contributions	2,000
Casualty loss [$21,500 – (10% × $200,000)]	1,500
Unreimbursed employee expenses [$4,300 – (2% × $200,000)]	300
Gambling losses ($7,000 loss limited to $3,000 of gambling income)	3,000
Total itemized deductions before overall limitation	$21,000

Herman's itemized deductions subject to the overall limitation are as follows:

State and local income taxes	$ 3,200
Real estate taxes	2,800
Home mortgage interest	7,200
Charitable contributions	2,000
Unreimbursed employee expenses	300
Total	$15,500

Step 1

Calculate the lesser of :

• 3%($200,000 AGI – $159,950)	$ 1,202
• 80% of itemized deductions subject to limitation ($15,500 × .80)	12,400

Step 2

Multiply the Step 1 amount by one-third ($1,202 × ⅓)	$401

Therefore, the amount of the reduction is $401, and Herman has $20,599 of deductible itemized deductions, computed as follows:

ETHICAL and EQUITABLE *Considerations*

BETWEEN A ROCK AND A HARD PLACE

Robert Ryan, a candidate for governor, has released his tax return to the public. As Ryan's former tax adviser, you examine the return closely and realize that a considerable amount of his income was not reported on the return. You confide to a friend in the tabloid newspaper business that you are aware that a candidate for a high public office has filed a fraudulent tax return. Your friend assures you that you will

be able to sell your story for at least $25,000 to a tabloid and still remain anonymous. Another friend, a CPA, argues that you should inform Ryan and give him an opportunity to correct the problem. You tell your friend that you are concerned that Ryan will be very vindictive if you approach him about the issue. Which course of action will you choose?

Deductible itemized deductions subject to overall limitation ($15,500 − $401)	$15,099
Itemized deductions not subject to overall limitation:	
Medical expenses	1,000
Casualty loss	1,500
Gambling losses	3,000
Deductible itemized deductions	$20,599

LO.9

Identify tax planning strategies that can maximize the benefit of itemized deductions.

TAX PLANNING *Considerations*

Effective Utilization of Itemized Deductions

Since an individual may use the standard deduction in one year and itemize deductions in another year, it is frequently possible to obtain maximum benefit by shifting itemized deductions from one year to another. For example, if a taxpayer's itemized deductions and the standard deduction are approximately the same for each year of a two-year period, the taxpayer should use the standard deduction in one year and shift itemized deductions (to the extent permitted by law) to the other year. The individual could, for example, prepay a church pledge for a particular year to shift the deduction to the current year or avoid paying end-of-the-year medical expenses to shift the deduction to the following year.

Utilization of Medical Deductions

When a taxpayer anticipates that medical expenses will approximate the percentage floor, much might be done to generate a deductible excess. Any of the following procedures can help build a deduction by the end of the year:

- Incur the obligation for needed dental work or have needed work carried out.[53] Orthodontic treatment, for example, may have been recommended for a member of the taxpayer's family.
- Have elective remedial surgery that may have been postponed from prior years (e.g., tonsillectomies, vasectomies, correction of hernias, hysterectomies).
- Incur the obligation for capital improvements to the taxpayer's personal residence recommended by a physician (e.g., an air filtration system to alleviate a respiratory disorder).

---

[53]Prepayment of medical expenses does not generate a current deduction unless the taxpayer is under an obligation to make the payment.

As an aid to taxpayers who may experience temporary cash-flow problems at the end of the year, the use of credit cards is deemed to be payment for purposes of timing the deductibility of charitable and medical expenses.

E X A M P L E   36

On December 13, 2008, Marge (a calendar year taxpayer) purchases two pairs of prescription contact lenses and one pair of prescribed orthopedic shoes for a total of $450. These purchases are separately charged to Marge's credit card. On January 6, 2009, Marge receives her statement containing these charges and makes payment shortly thereafter. The purchases are deductible as medical expenses in the year charged (2008) and not in the year the account is settled (2009). ∎

Recognizing which expenditures qualify for the medical deduction also may be crucial to exceeding the percentage limitations.

E X A M P L E   37

Mortimer employs Lana (an unrelated party) to care for his incapacitated and dependent mother. Lana is not a trained nurse but spends approximately one-half of the time performing nursing duties (e.g., administering injections and providing physical therapy) and the rest of the time doing household chores. An allocable portion of Lana's wages that Mortimer pays (including the employer's portion of FICA taxes) qualifies as a medical expense. ∎

Timing the Payment of Deductible Taxes

It is sometimes possible to defer or accelerate the payment of certain deductible taxes, such as state income tax, real property tax, and personal property tax. For instance, the final installment of estimated state income tax is generally due after the end of a given tax year. Accelerating the payment of the final installment could result in larger itemized deductions for the current year.

E X A M P L E   38

Jenny, who is single, expects to have itemized deductions of $5,000 in 2008 and $2,500 in 2009. She plans to pay $900 as the final installment on her 2008 estimated state income tax, which is due on January 15, 2009. The standard deduction for 2008 is $5,450 for single taxpayers. If Jenny does not pay the final installment until 2009, she will not itemize in either 2008 or 2009. However, if she pays the final installment in December 2008, her itemized deductions will be $5,900 ($5,000 + $900) in 2008, and she will benefit from itemizing. ∎

Protecting the Interest Deduction

Although the deductibility of prepaid interest by a cash basis taxpayer has been severely restricted, a notable exception allows a deduction for points paid by the buyer to obtain financing for the purchase or improvement of a principal residence in the year of payment. However, such points must actually be paid by the taxpayer obtaining the loan and must represent a charge for the use of money. It has been held that points paid from the mortgage proceeds do not satisfy the payment requirement.[54] Also, the portion of the points attributable to service charges does not represent deductible interest.[55] Taxpayers financing home purchases or improvements usually should direct their planning toward avoiding these two hurdles to immediate deductibility.

In rare instances, a taxpayer may find it desirable to forgo the immediate expensing of points in the year paid. Instead, it could prove beneficial to capitalize the points and write them off as interest expense over the life of the mortgage.

---

[54]*Alan A. Rubnitz*, 67 T.C. 621 (1977). Seller-paid points may also be deductible by the buyer under the provisions of Rev.Proc. 94–27, cited in footnote 31.

[55]*Donald L. Wilkerson*, 70 T.C. 240 (1978).

EXAMPLE 39

Gerald purchases a home on December 15, 2008, for $380,000 with $120,000 cash and a 15-year mortgage of $260,000 financed by the Greater Metropolis National Bank. Gerald pays two points in addition to interest allocated to the period from December 15 until December 31, 2008, at an annual rate of 6%. Since Gerald does not have enough itemized deductions to exceed the standard deduction for 2008, he should elect to capitalize the points and amortize them over 15 years. In this instance, Gerald would deduct $346.67 for 2009, as part of his qualified residence interest expense [$5,200 (two points) divided by 15 years], if he elects to itemize that year. ∎

Because personal (consumer) interest is not deductible, taxpayers should consider making use of home equity loans. Recall that these loans utilize the personal residence of the taxpayer as security. The funds from these loans can be used for personal purposes (e.g., auto loans, vacations). By making use of home equity loans, therefore, what would have been nondeductible consumer interest becomes deductible qualified residence interest.

Assuring the Charitable Contribution Deduction

For a charitable contribution deduction to be available, the recipient must be a qualified charitable organization. Sometimes the mechanics of how the contribution is carried out can determine whether a deduction results.

EXAMPLE 40

Fumiko wants to donate $5,000 to her church's mission in Kobe, Japan. In this regard, she considers three alternatives:

1. Send the money directly to the mission.
2. Give the money to her church with the understanding that it is to be passed on to the mission.
3. Give the money directly to the missionary in charge of the mission who is currently in the United States on a fund-raising trip.

If Fumiko wants to obtain a deduction for the contribution, she should choose alternative 2. A direct donation to the mission (alternative 1) is not deductible because the mission is a foreign charity. A direct gift to the missionary (alternative 3) does not comply since an individual cannot be a qualified charity for income tax purposes.[56] ∎

When making noncash donations, the type of property chosen can have decided implications in determining the amount, if any, of the deduction.

EXAMPLE 41

Sam wants to give $60,000 in value to his church in some form other than cash. In this connection, he considers four alternatives:

1. Stock held for two years as an investment with a basis of $100,000 and a fair market value of $60,000.
2. Stock held for five years as an investment with a basis of $10,000 and a fair market value of $60,000.
3. The rent-free use for a year of a building that normally leases for $5,000 a month.
4. A valuable stamp collection held as an investment and owned for 10 years with a basis of $10,000 and a fair market value of $60,000. The church plans to sell the collection if and when it is donated.

Alternative 1 is ill-advised as the subject of the gift. Even though Sam would obtain a deduction of $60,000, he would forgo the potential loss of $40,000 that would be recognized if the property were sold.[57] Alternative 2 makes good sense since the deduction still is $60,000 and none of the $50,000 of appreciation that has occurred must be recognized as income. Alternative 3 yields no deduction at all and is not a wise choice. Alternative 4 involves tangible

[56]*Thomas E. Lesslie*, 36 TCM 495, T.C.Memo. 1977–111.   [57]*LaVar M. Withers*, 69 T.C. 900 (1978).

personalty that the recipient does not plan to use. As a result, the amount of the deduction is limited to $10,000, the stamp collection's basis.[58] ■

For property transfers (particularly real estate), the ceiling limitations on the amount of the deduction allowed in any one year (50 percent, 30 percent, or 20 percent of AGI, as the case may be) could be a factor to take into account. With proper planning, donations can be controlled to stay within the limitations and therefore avoid the need for a carryover of unused charitable contributions.

EXAMPLE 42

Andrew wants to donate a tract of unimproved land held as an investment to Eastern University (a qualified charitable organization). The land has been held for six years and has a current fair market value of $300,000 and a basis to Andrew of $50,000. Andrew's AGI for the current year is estimated to be $200,000, and he expects much the same for the next few years. In the current year, he deeds (transfers) an undivided one-fifth interest in the real estate to the university. ■

What has Andrew in Example 42 accomplished for income tax purposes? In the current year, he will be allowed a charitable contribution deduction of $60,000 ($\frac{1}{5}$ × $300,000), which will be within the applicable limitation of AGI (30% × $200,000). Presuming no other charitable contributions for the year, Andrew has avoided the possibility of a carryover. In future years, Andrew can arrange donations of undivided interests in the real estate to stay within the bounds of the percentage limitations. The only difficulty with this approach is the need to revalue the real estate each year before the donation, since the amount of the deduction is based on the fair market value of the interest contributed at the time of the contribution.

EXAMPLE 43

Tiffany dies in October 2008. In completing her final income tax return for 2008, Tiffany's executor determines the following information: AGI of $104,000 and a donation by Tiffany to her church of stock worth $60,000. Tiffany had purchased the stock two years ago for $50,000 and held it as an investment. Tiffany's executor makes the reduced deduction election and, as a consequence, claims a charitable contribution deduction of $50,000. With the election, the potential charitable contribution deduction of $50,000 ($60,000 − $10,000) is less than the 50% ceiling of $52,000 ($104,000 × 50%). If the executor had not made the election, the potential charitable contribution deduction of $60,000 would have been reduced by the 30% ceiling to $31,200 ($104,000 × 30%). No carryover of the $28,800 ($60,000 − $31,200) would have been available. ■

KEY TERMS

Acquisition indebtedness, 10–15

Capital gain property, 10–23

Charitable contribution, 10–19

Health Savings Account (HSA), 10–9

Home equity loans, 10–15

Medical expense, 10–2

Miscellaneous itemized deductions, 10–27

Ordinary income property, 10–22

Points, 10–16

Qualified residence interest, 10–14

---

[58]No reduction of appreciation is necessary in alternative 2 since stock is intangible property and not tangible personalty.

PROBLEM MATERIALS

DISCUSSION QUESTIONS

1. Dan, a self-employed individual taxpayer, prepared his own income tax return for the past year and has asked you to check it for accuracy. Your review indicates that Dan failed to claim certain business entertainment expenses.
   a. Will the correction of this omission affect the amount of medical expenses Dan can deduct? Explain.
   b. Would it matter if Dan were employed rather than self-employed?

2. Barbara incurred the following expenses during the year: $840 dues at a health club she joined at the suggestion of her physician to improve her general physical condition; $240 for multiple vitamins and antioxidant vitamins; $500 for a smoking cessation program; $240 for nonprescription nicotine gum; $600 for insulin; and $7,200 for funeral expenses for her mother who passed away in June. Which of these expenses may be included in computing the medical expense deduction?

3. Joe was in an accident and required cosmetic surgery for injuries to his nose. He also had the doctor do additional surgery to reshape his chin, which had not been injured. Will the cosmetic surgery to Joe's nose qualify as a medical expense? Will the cosmetic surgery to Joe's chin qualify as a medical expense? Explain.

4. Jerry and Ernie are comparing their tax situations. Both are paying all of the nursing home expenses of their parents. Jerry may include the expenses in computing his medical expense deduction, but Ernie may not. Can you offer any explanation for the difference?

Issue ID 5. Brittany incurred $8,700 of medical expenses in November 2008. On December 5, the clinic where she was treated mailed her the insurance claim form it had prepared for her with a suggestion that she sign and return the form immediately in order to receive her reimbursement from the insurance company by December 31. What tax issues should Brittany consider in deciding whether to sign and return the form in December 2008 or January 2009?

Issue ID 6. During the current year, Maria and her three dependent children had annual physical exams, which cost $750, and dental checkups for all four of them, which cost $420. In addition, Maria paid $800 for medically supervised treatments to enable her to stop smoking. After she stopped smoking, she began to gain weight and incurred $1,200 in costs for a medically supervised weight loss program. Which of these expenses qualify for the medical expense deduction?

7. In 2008, David, a sole proprietor of a bookstore, pays a $7,500 premium for medical insurance for himself and his family. Joan, an employee of a small firm that doesn't provide her with medical insurance, pays medical insurance premiums of $8,000 for herself. How does the tax treatment differ for David and Joan?

8. Arturo, a calendar year taxpayer, paid $16,000 in medical expenses and sustained a $20,000 casualty loss in 2008. He expects $12,000 of the medical expenses and $14,000 of the casualty loss to be reimbursed by insurance companies in 2009. Before considering any limitations on these deductions, how much can Arturo include in determining his itemized deductions for 2008?

9. Hubert, a self-employed taxpayer, is married and has two children. He has asked you to explain the tax and nontax advantages of establishing a Health Savings Account (HSA) for himself and his family.

Issue ID 10. A local ophthalmologist's advertising campaign included a certificate for free LASIK eye surgery for the lucky winner of a drawing. Ahmad held the winning ticket, which was drawn in December 2007. Ahmad had no vision problems and was uncertain what he should do with the prize. In February 2008, Ahmad's daughter, who lives with his former wife, was diagnosed with a vision problem that could be treated with either prescription glasses or LASIK surgery. The divorce decree requires that Ahmad pay for all medical expenses incurred for his daughter. Identify the relevant tax issues for Ahmad.

11. Diego sold his personal residence to Dinah on July 1, 2008. He had paid real property taxes on March 1, 2008, the due date for property taxes for 2008.

    Issue ID

    a. How will Diego's payment affect his deduction for property taxes in 2008?
    b. Will Diego's payment of the taxes have any effect on Dinah's itemized deductions for 2008?
    c. What other tax or financial effects will Diego's payment of the taxes have on either party?

12. In 2008, a state issued checks to homeowners as a rebate of property taxes. Funds for the rebate were available because of unexpectedly high state tax revenues due to a new law that legalized gambling in the state. In December 2008, Edward received a $290 rebate check from the state. In January 2009, he returned the check to the governor because he thought it was improper for the state to spend the money in this manner. Edward, a dedicated opponent of gambling and other "games of chance," attached a letter to the governor indicating his desire to have the $290 spent on a campaign to educate youth about the financial and nonfinancial dangers of gambling. List some of the tax issues relevant to Edward's situation.

    Issue ID

13. Julia owns a principal residence in California, a condo in New York City, and a houseboat in Florida. All of the properties have mortgages on which Julia pays interest. What are the limitations on Julia's mortgage interest deduction? What strategy should Julia consider to maximize her mortgage interest deduction?

    Decision Making

14. Jimmy Wolf's car was destroyed by a tornado. Unfortunately, his insurance had lapsed two days before he incurred the loss. Jimmy uses his car for both business and personal use. Jimmy, who is self-employed, does not have adequate savings to replace the car and must borrow money to purchase a new car. He is considering taking out a home equity loan, at a 4% interest rate, to obtain funds for the purchase. Sherry, his wife, would prefer not to do so because they paid off their mortgage recently and she does not want to incur any obligations related to their home. She would prefer to sell some of their stock in Bluebird, Inc., to raise funds to purchase the new car. Jimmy does not want to sell the stock because it has declined in value since they purchased it and he is convinced that its price will increase within the next two years. Jimmy has suggested that they obtain conventional financing for the purchase from their bank, which charges 7% interest on car loans. Identify the tax issues related to each of the three alternatives Jimmy and Sherry are considering.

    Issue ID

15. Jerry purchased a personal residence from Kim. In order to sell the residence, Kim agreed to pay $3,000 in points related to Jerry's mortgage. Discuss the deductibility of the points.

16. Central Bank has initiated an advertising campaign that encourages customers to take out home equity loans to pay for purchases of automobiles. Are there any tax advantages related to this type of borrowing? Explain.

17. The city of Ogden was devastated by a tornado in April of this year, leaving many families in need of food, clothing, shelter, and other necessities. Betty contributed $500 to a family whose home was completely destroyed by the tornado. Jack contributed $700 to the family's church, which gave the money to the family. Discuss the deductibility of these contributions.

18. Mike purchased four $100 tickets to a fund-raising dinner and dance sponsored by the public library, a qualified charitable organization. In its advertising for the event, the library indicated that the cost of the tickets would be deductible for Federal income tax purposes. Comment on the library's assertion.

19. Nancy, who is a professor at State University, does some of her writing and class preparation at home at night. Her department provides faculty members with a $1,500 allowance for a desktop computer for use at school, but does not ordinarily provide computers for use at home. In order to have a computer for use at school and at home,

    Issue ID

Nancy has asked the department to provide her with a notebook computer that costs $2,500. The head of her department is willing to provide the standard $1,500 allowance and will permit Nancy to purchase the $2,500 notebook computer if she makes a donation of $1,000 to the department. If she acquires the notebook computer, Nancy's home use of the computer will be approximately 60% for business and 40% for personal use not related to her job. Discuss the tax issues that Nancy should consider in deciding whether to acquire the notebook computer under these conditions.

20. Jean traveled to New York City during the year to do volunteer work for one week for the Salvation Army. She normally receives $1,000 salary per week at her job and is planning to deduct the $1,000 as a charitable contribution. In addition, Jean incurred the following costs in connection with the trip: $300 for transportation, $1,300 for lodging, and $250 for meals. What is Jean's deduction associated with this charitable activity?

Issue ID

21. Zina decided to have a garage sale to get rid of a number of items that she no longer needed, including books, old stereo equipment, clothing, bicycles, and furniture. She scheduled the sale for Friday and Saturday, but was forced to close at noon Friday because of a torrential downpour. She had collected $500 for the items she sold before closing. The heavy rains continued through the weekend, and Zina was unable to continue the sale. She had not enjoyed dealing with the people who came to the sale on Friday morning, so she donated the remaining items to several local organizations. Zina has asked your advice on how she should treat these events on her tax return. List some of the tax issues you would discuss with her.

Issue ID

22. William, a high school teacher, earns about $40,000 each year. In December 2008, he won $1 million in the state lottery. William plans to donate $100,000 to his church. He has asked you, his tax adviser, whether he should donate the $100,000 in 2008 or 2009. Identify the tax issues related to William's decision.

Decision Making

23. Colin had AGI of $180,000 in 2008. He contributed stock in White, Inc. (a publicly traded corporation), to the United Way, a qualified charitable organization. The stock was worth $105,000 on the date it was contributed. Colin had acquired it as an investment two years ago at a cost of $84,000.
    a. What is the total amount that Colin can deduct as a charitable contribution, assuming he carries over any disallowed contribution from 2008 to future years?
    b. What is the maximum amount that Colin can deduct as a charitable contribution in 2008?
    c. What factors should Colin consider in deciding how to treat the contribution for Federal income tax purposes?
    d. Assume Colin dies in December 2008. What advice would you give the executor of his estate with regard to possible elections that can be made relative to the contribution?

PROBLEMS

Communications

24. Emma Doyle is employed as a corporate attorney. For calendar year 2008, she had AGI of $100,000 and paid the following medical expenses:

Medical insurance premiums	$3,700
Doctor and dentist bills for Bob and April (Emma's parents)	6,800
Doctor and dentist bills for Emma	5,200
Prescription medicines for Emma	400
Nonprescription insulin for Emma	350

Bob and April would qualify as Emma's dependents except that they file a joint return. Emma's medical insurance policy does not cover them. Emma filed a claim for reimbursement of $2,800 of her own expenses with her insurance company in December 2008 and received the reimbursement in January 2009. What is Emma's maximum allowable medical expense deduction for 2008? Prepare a memo for your firm's tax files where you document your conclusions.

25. Reba, who is single, does a lot of business entertaining at home. Lawrence, Reba's 84-year-old dependent grandfather, lived with Reba until this year when he moved to Lakeside Nursing Home because he needs medical and nursing care. During the year, Reba made the following payments on behalf of Lawrence:

Room at Lakeside	$11,000
Meals for Lawrence at Lakeside	2,200
Doctor and nurse fees at Lakeside	1,700
Cable TV service for Lawrence's room at Lakeside	380
Total	$15,280

Lakeside has medical staff in residence. Disregarding the 7.5% floor, how much, if any, of these expenses qualifies for a medical expense deduction by Reba?

26. Roberto suffers from emphysema and severe allergies and, upon the recommendation of his physician, has a dust elimination system installed in his personal residence. In connection with the system, Roberto incurs and pays the following amounts during the current year:

Doctor and hospital bills	$1,600
Dust elimination system	8,800
Increase in utility bills due to the system	350
Cost of certified appraisal	220
Prescribed medicines	750

The system has an estimated useful life of 15 years. The appraisal was to determine the value of Roberto's residence with and without the system. The appraisal states that his residence was worth $125,000 before the system was installed and $127,500 after the installation. Roberto's AGI for the year was $50,000. How much qualifies for the medical expense deduction in the current year?

27. For calendar year 2008, Jean was a self-employed consultant with no employees. She had $80,000 net profit from consulting and paid $7,000 in medical insurance premiums on a policy covering 2008. How much of these premiums may Jean deduct as a deduction *for* AGI, and how much may she deduct as an itemized deduction (subject to the 7.5% floor)?

28. During the current year, Susan incurred and paid the following expenses for Beth (her daughter), Ed (her father), and herself:

Surgery for Beth	$7,200
Red River Academy charges for Beth:	
Tuition	4,400
Room, board, and other expenses	4,100
Psychiatric treatment	4,500
Doctor bills for Ed	1,800
Prescription drugs for Susan, Beth, and Ed	890
Insulin for Ed	430
Nonprescription drugs for Susan, Beth, and Ed	570
Charges at Heartland Nursing Home for Ed:	
Medical care	4,000
Lodging	3,700
Meals	2,650

Beth qualifies as Susan's dependent, and Ed would also qualify except that he receives $8,500 of taxable retirement benefits from his former employer. Beth's psychiatrist recommended Red River Academy because of its small classes and specialized psychiatric treatment program that is needed to treat Beth's illness. Ed, who is a paraplegic and diabetic, entered Heartland in October. Heartland offers the type of care that he requires.

Upon the recommendation of a physician, Susan has an air filtration system installed in her personal residence. She suffers from severe allergies. In connection with this equipment, Susan incurs and pays the following amounts during the year:

Filtration system and cost of installation	$6,500
Increase in utility bills due to the system	400
Cost of certified appraisal	275

The system has an estimated useful life of 10 years. The appraisal was to determine the value of Susan's residence with and without the system. The appraisal states that the system increased the value of Susan's residence by $2,200. Ignoring the 7.5% floor, what is the total of Susan's expenses that qualifies for the medical expense deduction?

Issue ID

29. In May, Rebecca's daughter, Susan, sustained a serious injury that made it impossible for her to continue living alone. Susan, who is a novelist, moved back into Rebecca's home after the accident. Susan has begun writing a new novel based on her recent experiences. To accommodate Susan, Rebecca incurred significant remodeling expenses (widening hallways, building a separate bedroom and bathroom, making kitchen appliances accessible to Susan). In addition, Rebecca had an indoor swimming pool constructed so Susan could do rehabilitation exercises prescribed by her physician.

In September, Susan underwent major reconstructive surgery in Denver. The surgery was performed by Dr. Rama Patel, who specializes in treating injuries of the type sustained by Susan. Rebecca drove Susan from Champaign, Illinois, to Denver, a total of 1,100 miles, in Susan's specially equipped van. They left Champaign on Tuesday morning and arrived in Denver on Thursday afternoon. Rebecca incurred expenses for gasoline, highway tolls, meals, and lodging while traveling to Denver. Rebecca stayed in a motel near the clinic for eight days while Susan was hospitalized. Identify the relevant tax issues based on this information and prepare a list of questions that you would need to ask Rebecca and Susan in order to advise them as to the resolution of any issues you have identified.

30. In 2008, Vaughn pays a $3,000 premium for high-deductible medical insurance for himself and his family. In addition, he contributes $2,600 to a Health Savings Account.
    a. How much may Vaughn deduct if he is self-employed? Is the deduction *for* AGI or *from* AGI?
    b. How much may Vaughn deduct if he is an employee? Is the deduction *for* AGI or *from* AGI?

31. Alicia sold her personal residence to Rick on June 30 for $300,000. Before the sale, Alicia paid the real estate taxes of $4,380 for the calendar year. For income tax purposes, the deduction is apportioned as follows: $2,160 to Alicia and $2,220 to Rick. What is Rick's basis in the residence?

32. Dorian, who uses the cash method of accounting, lives in a state that imposes an income tax. In April 2008, she files her state income tax return for 2007 and pays an additional $1,000 in state income taxes. During 2008, her withholdings for state income tax purposes amount to $7,400, and she pays estimated state income tax of $700. In April 2009, she files her state income tax return for 2008 claiming a refund of $1,800. Dorian receives the refund in August 2009.
    a. Assuming Dorian itemized deductions in 2008, how much may she claim as a deduction for state income taxes on her Federal return for calendar year 2008 (filed in April 2009)?
    b. Assuming Dorian itemized deductions in 2008, how will the refund of $1,800 that she received in 2009 be treated for Federal income tax purposes?
    c. Assume that Dorian itemized deductions in 2008 and that she elects to have the $1,800 refund applied toward her 2009 state income tax liability. How will the $1,800 be treated for Federal income tax purposes?
    d. Assuming Dorian did not itemize deductions in 2008, how will the refund of $1,800 received in 2009 be treated for Federal income tax purposes?

33. In 1998, Stephen, who is single, purchased a personal residence for $400,000 and took out a mortgage of $250,000 on the property. In May of the current year, when the residence had a fair market value of $640,000 and Stephen owed $220,000 on the mortgage, he took out a home equity loan for $260,000. He used the funds to purchase

a recreational vehicle, which he uses 100% for personal use. What is the maximum amount on which Stephen can deduct home equity interest?

34. Joe owns 60% and Bill owns 40% of Magpie Corporation. On July 1, 2008, each lends the corporation $30,000 at an annual interest rate of 10%. Joe and Bill are not related. Both shareholders are on the cash method of accounting, and Magpie Corporation is on the accrual method. All parties use the calendar year for tax purposes. On June 30, 2009, Magpie repays the loans of $60,000 together with the specified interest of $6,000.
    a.   How much of the interest can Magpie Corporation deduct in 2008? In 2009?
    b.   When is the interest included in Joe and Bill's gross income?

35. Nadia donates $4,000 to Eastern University's athletic department. The payment guarantees that Nadia will have preferred seating near the 50-yard line.
    a.   Assume Nadia subsequently buys four $100 game tickets. How much can she deduct as a charitable contribution to the university's athletic department?
    b.   Assume that Nadia's $4,000 donation includes four $100 tickets. How much can she deduct as a charitable contribution to the university's athletic department?

36. Becky had AGI of $100,000 in 2008. She donated Amber Corporation stock with a basis of $13,000 to a qualified charitable organization on July 5, 2008.
    a.   What is the amount of Becky's deduction, assuming that she purchased the stock on December 4, 2007, and the stock had a fair market value of $23,000 when she made the donation?
    b.   Assume the same facts as in (a), except that Becky purchased the stock on July 1, 2005.
    c.   Assume the same facts as in (a), except that the stock had a fair market value of $7,500 (rather than $23,000) when Becky donated it to the charity.

37. Pedro contributes a painting to an art museum in October of this year. He has owned the painting for 12 years, and it is worth $130,000 at the time of the donation. Pedro's adjusted basis for the painting is $90,000, and his AGI for the year is $250,000. Pedro has asked you whether he should make the reduced deduction election for this contribution. Write a letter to Pedro Valdez at 1289 Greenway Avenue, Foster City, CA 94404 and advise him on this matter.

Decision Making

Communications

38. During the year, Ricardo made the following contributions to a qualified public charity:

Cash	$110,000
Stock in Seagull, Inc. (a publicly traded corporation)	140,000

Ricardo acquired the stock in Seagull, Inc., as an investment six years ago at a cost of $60,000. Ricardo's AGI is $420,000.
    a.   What is Ricardo's charitable contribution deduction (before application of the overall limitation on certain itemized deductions)?
    b.   How are excess amounts, if any, treated?

39. Russell, who has AGI of $200,000 in 2008, contributes stock in Blue Corporation (a publicly traded corporation) to City College, a qualified charitable organization. The stock is worth $118,000, and Russell acquired it as an investment two years ago at a cost of $88,000.
    a.   What amount can Russell deduct as a charitable contribution, assuming he carries over any disallowed contribution from 2008 to future years?
    b.   What is the maximum amount that Russell can deduct as a charitable contribution in 2008?
    c.   What factors should Russell consider in deciding how to treat the contribution for Federal income tax purposes?
    d.   Assume Russell dies in December 2008. What advice would you give the executor of his estate with regard to possible elections that can be made relative to the contribution?

Decision Making

40. On December 30, 2008, Roberta purchased four tickets to a charity ball sponsored by the city of San Diego for the benefit of underprivileged children. Each ticket cost $200 and had a fair market value of $35. On the same day as the purchase, Roberta gave the tickets to the minister of her church for personal use by his family. At the time of the gift

of the tickets, Roberta pledged $4,000 to the building fund of her church. The pledge was satisfied by a check dated December 31, 2008, but not mailed until January 3, 2009.

   a.   Presuming Roberta is a cash basis and calendar year taxpayer, how much can she deduct as a charitable contribution for 2008?

   b.   Would the amount of the deduction be any different if Roberta is an accrual basis taxpayer? Explain.

Decision Making

Communications

41. In December each year, Alice Young contributes 10% of her gross income to the United Way (a 50% organization). Alice, who is in the 35% marginal tax bracket, is considering the following alternatives for satisfying the contribution.

	Fair Market Value
(1) Cash donation	$21,000
(2) Unimproved land held for six years ($3,000 basis)	21,000
(3) Blue Corporation stock held for eight months ($3,000 basis)	21,000
(4) Gold Corporation stock held for two years ($26,000 basis)	21,000

Alice has asked you to help her decide which of the potential contributions listed above will be most advantageous taxwise. Evaluate the four alternatives and write a letter to Alice to communicate your advice to her. Her address is 2622 Bayshore Drive, Berkeley, CA 94709.

Decision Making

Communications

42. Bart and Tara Parker, both age 47, are married and have no dependents. They have asked you to advise them whether they should file jointly or separately in 2008. They present you with the following information:

	Bart	Tara	Joint
Salary	$40,000		
Business net income		$100,000	
Interest income	400	1,200	$2,200
Deductions *for* AGI	2,000	13,000	
Medical expenses	9,500	600	
State income tax	800	2,000	
Real estate tax			3,400
Mortgage interest			5,200
Unreimbursed employee expenses	1,100		

If they file separately, Bart and Tara will split the real estate tax and mortgage interest deductions equally. Write Bart and Tara a letter in which you make and explain a recommendation on filing status for 2008. Bart and Tara reside at 2003 Highland Drive, Durham, NC 27707.

43. For calendar year 2008, Jon and Betty Hansen file a joint return reflecting AGI of $240,000. Their itemized deductions are as follows:

Medical expenses	$23,000
Casualty loss (not covered by insurance)	26,000
Interest on home mortgage	10,000
Property taxes on home	13,000
Charitable contributions	17,000
State income tax	15,000

After all necessary adjustments are made, what is the amount of itemized deductions the Hansens may claim?

44. Jose and Juanita Garza are married, have two dependents, and file a joint return for 2008. Information for the year includes the following:

AGI	$237,300
State and local income taxes	5,600

Real estate taxes	$7,900
Home mortgage interest	8,400
Charitable contributions	7,300
Gambling losses (gambling income of $4,200 was included in AGI)	6,600

Compute allowable itemized deductions for 2008 for the Garzas.

45. Phil, who is single, had AGI of $355,900 during 2008. He incurred the following expenses and losses during the year:

Medical expenses before 7.5%-of-AGI limitation	$36,443
State and local income taxes	5,636
State sales tax	1,140
Real estate taxes	4,950
Home mortgage interest	5,849
Charitable contributions	5,265
Casualty loss before 10% limitation (after $100 floor)	44,589
Unreimbursed employee expenses subject to 2%-of-AGI limitation	8,318
Gambling losses (Phil had $6,800 of gambling income)	7,900

Compute Phil's itemized deductions before and after the overall limitation.

46. For calendar year 2008, Roger and Sue Peterson file a joint return reflecting AGI of $269,900. Their itemized deductions are as follows:

Medical expenses	$25,890
Casualty loss (not covered by insurance)	29,190
Interest on home mortgage	10,150
Interest on credit cards	670
Property taxes on home	14,800
Charitable contributions	19,050
State income tax	16,500
Tax return filing fees	1,800

After all necessary adjustments are made, what is the amount of itemized deductions the Petersons may claim?

CUMULATIVE PROBLEMS

47. Alice J. and Bruce M. Byrd are married taxpayers who file a joint return. Their Social Security numbers are 034–48–4382 and 016–50–9556, respectively. Alice's birthday is September 21, 1960, and Bruce's is June 27, 1959. They live at 473 Revere Avenue, Ames, MA 01850. Alice is the office manager for Ames Dental Clinic, 433 Broad Street, Ames, MA 01850 (employer identification number 37–4000456). Bruce is the manager of a Super Burgers fast-food outlet owned and operated by Plymouth Corporation, 1247 Central Avenue, Hauppauge, NY 11788 (employer identification number 37–6000987).

Tax Return Problem

Decision Making

The following information is shown on their Wage and Tax Statements (Form W–2) for 2007.

Line	Description	Alice	Bruce
1	Wages, tips, other compensation	$58,000	$62,100
2	Federal income tax withheld	4,500	6,300
3	Social Security wages	58,000	62,100
4	Social Security tax withheld	3,596	3,850

Line	Description	Alice	Bruce
5	Medicare wages and tips	$58,000	$62,100
6	Medicare tax withheld	841	900
15	State	Massachusetts	Massachusetts
16	State wages, tips, etc.	58,000	62,100
17	State income tax withheld	2,950	3,100

The Byrds provide over half of the support of their two children, Cynthia (born January 25, 1983, Social Security number 017–44–9126) and John (born February 7, 1987, Social Security number 017–27–4148). Both children are full-time students and live with the Byrds except when they are away at college. Cynthia earned $4,200 from a summer internship in 2007, and John earned $3,800 from a part-time job.

During 2007, the Byrds furnished 60% of the total support of Bruce's widower father, Sam Byrd (born March 6, 1931, Social Security number 034–82–8583). Sam lived alone and covered the rest of his support with his Social Security benefits. Sam died in November, and Bruce, the beneficiary of a policy on Sam's life, received life insurance proceeds of $800,000 on December 28.

The Byrds had the following expenses relating to their personal residence during 2007:

Property taxes	$5,000
Interest on home mortgage	8,800
Repairs to roof	5,750
Utilities	4,100
Fire and theft insurance	1,900

The following facts relate to medical expenses for 2007:

Medical insurance premiums	$4,500
Doctor bill for Sam incurred in 2006 and not paid until 2007	7,600
Operation for Sam	8,500
Prescription medicines for Sam	900
Hospital expenses for Sam	3,500
Reimbursement from insurance company, received in 2007	3,600

The medical expenses for Sam represent most of the 60% Bruce contributed toward his father's support.

Other relevant information follows:

- When they filed their 2006 state return in 2007, the Byrds paid additional state income tax of $900.
- During 2007, Alice and Bruce attended a dinner dance sponsored by the Ames Police Disability Association (a qualified charitable organization). The Byrds paid $300 for the tickets. The cost of comparable entertainment would normally be $50.
- The Byrds contributed $5,000 to Ames Presbyterian Church and gave used clothing (cost of $1,200 and fair market value of $350) to the Salvation Army. All donations are supported by receipts and are in very good condition.
- In 2007, the Byrds received interest income of $2,750, which was reported on a Form 1099–INT from Second National Bank.
- Alice's employer requires that all employees wear uniforms to work. During 2007, Alice spent $450 on new uniforms and $225 on laundry charges.
- Bruce paid $400 for an annual subscription to the *Journal of Franchise Management*.
- Neither Alice's nor Bruce's employer reimburses for employee expenses.
- The Byrds do not keep the receipts for the sales taxes they paid and had no major purchases subject to sales tax.
- Alice and Bruce paid no estimated Federal income tax. Neither Alice nor Bruce wishes to designate $3 to the Presidential Election Campaign Fund.

Part 1—Tax Computation

Compute net tax payable or refund due for Alice and Bruce Byrd for 2007. If they have overpaid, they want the amount to be refunded to them. If you use tax forms for your computations, you will need Forms 1040 and 2106 and Schedules A and B. Suggested software: TaxCut.

Part 2—Tax Planning

Alice and Bruce are planning some significant changes for 2008. They have provided you with the following information and asked you to project their taxable income and tax liability for 2008.

The Byrds will invest the $800,000 of life insurance proceeds in short-term certificates of deposit (CDs) and use the interest for living expenses during 2008. They expect to earn total interest of $32,000 on the CDs.

Bruce has been promoted to regional manager, and his salary for 2008 will be $88,000. He estimates that state income tax withheld will increase by $4,000.

Alice, who has been diagnosed with a serious illness, will take a leave of absence from work during 2008. The estimated cost for her medical treatment is $15,400, of which $4,700 will be reimbursed by their insurance company in 2008. Their medical insurance premiums will increase to $5,000.

John will graduate from college in December 2007 and will take a job in New York City in January 2008. His starting salary will be $46,000.

Assume all the information reported in 2007 will be the same in 2008 unless other information has been presented above.

48. Paul and Donna Decker are married taxpayers, ages 44 and 42, who file a joint return for 2008. The Deckers live at 1121 College Avenue, Carmel, IN 46032. Paul is an assistant manager at Carmel Motor Inn, and Donna is a teacher at Carmel Elementary School. They present you with W–2 forms that reflect the following information:

Tax Computation Problem

	Paul	Donna
Salary	$58,000	$56,000
Federal tax withheld	6,770	6,630
State income tax withheld	900	800
FICA (Social Security and Medicare) withheld	4,437	4,284
Social Security numbers	222–11–4567	333–11–9872

Donna is the custodial parent of two children from a previous marriage who reside with the Deckers through the school year. The children, Larry and Jane Parker, reside with their father, Bob, during the summer. Relevant information for the children follows:

	Larry	Jane
Age	17	18
Social Security numbers	305–11–4567	303–11–9872
Months spent with Deckers	9	9

Under the divorce decree, Bob pays child support of $150 per month per child during the nine months the children live with the Deckers. Bob says he spends $200 per month per child during the three summer months they reside with him. Donna and Paul can document that they provide $2,000 support per child per year. The divorce decree is silent as to which parent can claim the exemption for the children.

In August, Paul and Donna added a suite to their home to provide more comfortable accommodations for Hannah Snyder (263–33–4738), Donna's mother, who had moved in with them in February 2007 after the death of Donna's father. Not wanting to borrow money for this addition, Paul sold 300 shares of Acme Corporation stock for $50 per share on May 3, 2008, and used the proceeds of $15,000 to cover construction costs. The Deckers had purchased the stock on April 29, 2003, for $25 per share. They received dividends of $750 on the jointly owned stock a month before the sale.

Hannah, who is 66 years old, received $7,500 in Social Security benefits during the year, of which she gave the Deckers $2,000 to use toward household expenses and deposited the remainder in her personal savings account. The Deckers determine that they have spent $2,500 of their own money for food, clothing, medical expenses, and other items for Hannah. They do not know what the rental value of Hannah's suite would be, but they estimate it would be at least $300 per month.

Interest paid during the year included the following:

Home mortgage interest (paid to Carmel Federal Savings & Loan)	$7,890
Interest on an automobile loan (paid to Carmel National Bank)	1,660
Interest on Citibank Visa card	620

In July, Paul hit a submerged rock while boating. Fortunately, he was thrown from the boat, landed in deep water, and was uninjured. However, the boat, which was uninsured, was destroyed. Paul had paid $25,000 for the boat in June 2007, and its value was appraised at $18,000 on the date of the accident.

The Deckers paid doctor and hospital bills of $8,700 and were reimbursed $2,000 by their insurance company. They spent $640 for prescription drugs and medicines and $2,810 for premiums on their health insurance policy. They have filed additional claims of $1,200 with their insurance company and have been told they will receive payment for that amount in January 2009. Included in the amounts paid for doctor and hospital bills were payments of $380 for Hannah and $850 for the children.

Additional information of potential tax consequence follows:

Real estate taxes paid	$3,850
Sales taxes paid (per table)	1,379
Contributions to church	1,950
Appraised value of books donated to public library	740
Paul's unreimbursed employee expenses to attend hotel management convention:	
Airfare	340
Hotel	170
Meals	95
Registration fee	340
Refund of state income tax for 2007 (the Deckers itemized on their 2007 Federal tax return)	1,520

Compute net tax payable or refund due for the Deckers for 2008. Ignore the child tax credit in your computations. If they have overpaid, the amount is to be credited toward their taxes for 2009.

RESEARCH PROBLEMS

THOMSON
RIA

Communications

Note: Solutions to Research Problems can be prepared by using the **RIA Checkpoint®** **Student Edition** online research product, which is available to accompany this text. It is also possible to prepare solutions to the Research Problems by using tax research materials found in a standard tax library.

Research Problem 1.   After several years of a difficult marriage, Donald and Marla agreed to a divorce. As part of the property settlement, Marla transferred to Donald corporate stock, a commercial building, and a personal residence. Donald transferred other property to Marla, but the fair market value of the property was $600,000 less than the fair market value of the property Marla had transferred to him. To make the settlement equal, Donald agreed to pay Marla $600,000, payable over 10 years at 8% interest. For several years, Donald deducted the interest on his Federal income tax return as investment interest. Upon audit, the IRS disallowed the interest deduction, classifying it as nondeductible personal interest. Donald believes the interest is deductible and has asked you to find support for the deduction. Write a letter indicating your findings to Donald Jansen, 104 South Fourth Street, Dalton, GA 30720.

Partial list of research aids:
U.S. v. Gilmore, 63–1 USTC ¶9285, 11 AFTR2d 758, 83 S.Ct. 623 (USSC, 1963).
John L. Seymour, 109 T.C. 279 (1997).

Research Problem 2.   Jane suffers from a degenerative spinal disorder. Her physician said that swimming could help prevent the onset of permanent paralysis and recommended the installation of a swimming pool at her residence for her use. Jane's residence had a market value of approximately $500,000 before the swimming pool was installed. The swimming pool was built, and an appraiser estimated that the value of Jane's home increased by $98,000 because of the addition.

   The pool cost $194,000, and Jane claimed a medical expense deduction of $96,000 ($194,000 − $98,000) on her tax return. Upon audit of the return, the IRS determined that an adequate pool should have cost $70,000 and would increase the value of her home by only $31,000. Thus, the IRS claims that Jane is entitled to a deduction of only $39,000 ($70,000 − $31,000).

a.   Is there any ceiling limitation on the amount deductible as a medical expense?
b.   Can capital expenditures be deducted as medical expenses?
c.   What is the significance of a "minimum adequate facility"? Should aesthetic or architectural qualities be considered in this determination?

Research Problem 3.   The city of Cincinnati wished to establish a scenic corridor along portions of Interstate 75 but did not have the funds to purchase all of the land involved and to make the necessary improvements (e.g., terracing and other landscaping). Likewise, the city was fearful of any personal liability that might result from the operation of the scenic corridor. If, however, state funding could be obtained to cover the improvements and liability costs, the project would be carried out. State funding was possible but not probable.

   In 2006, all but one of the property owners affected by the project donated the necessary land to the city. The city purchased the land of the one owner who refused to make a donation. The city agreed to return the land to the donors in the event the project was not carried out. By 2008, it became certain that state funding would not be forthcoming. Therefore, the city returned the land to the donors, except for the parcel it had purchased.

   William Baird, one of the donors, claimed a charitable deduction for the fair market value of the land transferred in 2006. Upon audit of William's 2006 income tax return, the IRS disallowed the deduction and assessed the penalty for overvaluation. Is the IRS correct?

a.   Write a letter to William that contains your tax advice. His address is 405 Westwood, Cincinnati, OH 45999.
b.   Prepare a memo for your firm's tax files.

Partial list of research aids:
§ 6662(b)(3).
Reg. § 1.170A–1(e).
Ronald W. McCrary, 92 T.C. 827 (1989).

Research Problem 4.   Tom and Mary Smith, whose son was found murdered in a parking garage, offered a $100,000 reward for the city police to use to obtain information leading to the arrest and conviction of the murderer. As a result of the reward, a person who had overheard the murderer telling a friend about the crime reported the conversation to the police. The murderer was arrested and convicted, and the Smiths contributed the money to the police department, which gave the reward to the informant. Can the Smiths treat the payment as an itemized deduction?

Research Problem 5.   Marcia, a shareholder in a corporation with stores in five states, donated stock with a basis of $10,000 to a qualified charitable organization in 2007. Although the stock of the corporation was not traded on a public stock exchange, many shares had been sold over the past several years. Based on the average selling price for the stock in 2007, Marcia deducted $95,000 on her 2007 tax return. Marcia received a notice from the IRS that the $95,000 deduction had been reduced to $10,000 because she had not obtained a qualified appraisal or attached a summary of her appraisal to her tax

Communications

Communications

return. Marcia has asked you to advise her on this matter. Write a letter containing your conclusions to Ms. Marcia Meyer, 1311 Santos Court, San Bruno, CA 94066.

Partial list of research aids:
Reg. § 1.170A–13(c)(2).

Internet Activity

Use the tax resources of the Internet to address the following questions. Do not restrict your search to the World Wide Web, but include a review of newsgroups and general reference materials, practitioner sites and resources, primary sources of the tax law, chat rooms and discussion groups, and other opportunities.

Research Problem 6.   Find the IRS Web site and print a copy of Schedule A. If the 2008 Schedule A is available, compare it with the 2007 Schedule A in the text (page 10–29) and discuss any changes.

Research Problem 7.   Search the Internet for stories about major charitable contributions by individuals, including Bill Gates, Warren Buffett, and at least one other individual. Briefly discuss any tax issues that are related to the contributions.

CHAPTER 11

Investor Losses

LEARNING OBJECTIVES

After completing Chapter 11, you should be able to:

LO.1
Discuss tax shelters and the reasons for at-risk and passive loss limitations.

LO.2
Explain the at-risk limitation.

LO.3
Describe how the passive loss rules limit deductions for losses, and identify the taxpayers subject to these restrictions.

LO.4
Discuss the definition of passive activities and the rules for identifying an activity.

LO.5
Analyze and apply the tests for material participation.

LO.6
Understand the nature of rental activities under the passive loss rules.

LO.7
Recognize the relationship between the at-risk and passive activity limitations.

LO.8
Discuss the special treatment available to real estate activities.

LO.9
Determine the proper tax treatment upon the disposition of a passive activity.

LO.10
Identify restrictions placed on the deductibility of other investor losses and deductions, including those that apply to investment interest.

LO.11
Suggest tax planning strategies to minimize the effect of the passive loss limitations.

OUTLINE

The Tax Shelter Problem, 11–2
At-Risk Limits, 11–4
Passive Loss Limits, 11–5
   Classification and Impact of Passive Income
     and Losses, 11–5
   Taxpayers Subject to the Passive Loss Rules, 11–8
   Passive Activities Defined, 11–10
   Interaction of the At-Risk and Passive Activity
     Limits, 11–18

Special Passive Activity Rules for Real Estate
   Activities, 11–19
Dispositions of Passive Interests, 11–22
Investment Interest, 11–24
Other Investment Losses, 11–26
Tax Planning Considerations, 11–27
   Utilizing Passive Losses, 11–27

As discussed in Chapter 6, a tax deduction for an expense or a loss is not allowed unless specifically provided for by Congress. For example, losses can be recognized and deducted in the case of certain unprofitable investments only because the Code so provides. Such losses can arise from the operation of an activity or upon its ultimate disposition. For most individual taxpayers, deductible investor losses come within the scope of § 165(c)(2) relating to transactions entered into for profit.[1] In many situations, the tax law limits the *amount* or *timing* of a deduction or loss, or even changes its *nature* (i.e., ordinary rather than capital). Thus, for various reasons, Congress has imposed restrictions on the deductibility of investor losses. This, in turn, may affect the viability of the investment itself.

LO.1

Discuss tax shelters and the reasons for at-risk and passive loss limitations.

The Tax Shelter Problem

Before Congress enacted legislation to reduce their effectiveness, **tax shelters** provided a popular way to avoid or defer taxes, as they could generate deductions and other benefits to offset income from other sources. Because of the tax avoidance potential of many tax shelters, they were attractive to wealthy taxpayers in high income tax brackets. Many tax shelters merely provided an opportunity for "investors" to buy deductions and credits in ventures that were not expected to generate a profit, even in the long run.

Although it may seem odd that a taxpayer would intentionally invest in an activity that was designed to produce losses, there is a logical explanation. The typical tax shelter operated as a partnership and relied heavily on nonrecourse financing.[2] Accelerated depreciation and interest expense deductions generated large losses in the early years of the activity. At the very least, the tax shelter deductions deferred the recognition of any net income from the venture until the activity was sold. In the best of situations, the investor could realize additional tax savings by offsetting other income (e.g., salary, interest, and dividends) with deductions flowing from the tax shelter. Ultimately, the sale of the investment would result in capital gain. The following examples illustrate what was possible *before* Congress enacted legislation to curb tax shelter abuses.

EXAMPLE 1

Bob, who earned a salary of $400,000 as a business executive and dividend income of $15,000, invested $20,000 for a 10% interest in a cattle-breeding tax shelter. Through the use of $800,000 of nonrecourse financing and available cash of $200,000, the partnership acquired a herd of an exotic breed of cattle costing $1 million. Depreciation, interest, and

---

[1] If the losses are incurred in connection with a trade or business, § 165(c)(1) applies.

[2] Nonrecourse debt is an obligation for which the borrower is not personally liable. An example of nonrecourse debt is a liability on real estate acquired

by a partnership without the partnership or any of the partners assuming any liability for the mortgage. The acquired property generally is pledged as collateral for the loan.

other deductions related to the activity resulted in a loss of $400,000, of which Bob's share was $40,000. Bob was allowed to deduct the $40,000 loss, even though he had invested and stood to lose only $20,000 if the investment became worthless. The net effect of the $40,000 deduction from the partnership was that a portion of Bob's salary and dividend income was "sheltered," and as a result, he was required to calculate his tax liability on only $375,000 of income [$415,000 (salary and dividends) − $40,000 (deduction)] rather than $415,000. If this deduction were available under current law and if Bob was in a combined Federal and state income tax bracket of 40%, this deduction would generate a tax savings of $16,000 ($40,000 × 40%) in the first year alone! ■

A review of Example 1 shows that the taxpayer took a *two-for-one* write-off ($40,000 deduction, $20,000 investment). In the heyday of tax shelters, promoters often promised *multiple* write-offs for the investor.

The first major provision aimed at tax shelters was the **at-risk limitation**. Its objective is to limit a taxpayer's deductions to the amount "at risk," which is the amount the taxpayer stands to lose if the investment becomes worthless.

EXAMPLE 2

Returning to the facts of Example 1, under the current at-risk rules Bob would be allowed to deduct $20,000 (i.e., the amount that he could lose if the business failed). This deduction would reduce his other income, and as a result, Bob would have to report only $395,000 of income ($415,000 − $20,000). The remaining nondeductible $20,000 loss and any future losses flowing from the partnership would be suspended under the at-risk rules and would be deductible in the future only as his at-risk amount increased. ■

The second major attack on tax shelters came with the passage of the passive activity loss rules. These rules are intended to halt an investor's ability to benefit from the mismatching of an entity's expenses and income that often occurs in the early years of the business. Congress observed that despite the at-risk limitations, investors could still deduct losses flowing from an entity and thereby defer their tax liability on other income. In effect, the passive activity rules have, to a great degree, limited the tax benefits arising from such investments. Now ventures where investors are not involved in the day-to-day operations of the business are generally referred to as passive investments, or *passive activities*, rather than tax shelters.

The **passive loss** rules require the taxpayer to segregate all income and losses into three categories: active, passive, and portfolio. In general, the passive loss limits disallow the deduction of passive losses against active or portfolio income, even when the taxpayer is at risk to the extent of the loss. In general, passive losses can only offset passive income.

EXAMPLE 3

Returning to the facts of Example 1, the passive activity loss rules further restrict Bob's ability to claim the $20,000 tax deduction shown in Example 2. Because Bob is a passive investor and does not materially participate in any meaningful way in the activities of the cattle-breeding operation, the $20,000 loss allowed under the at-risk rules is disallowed under the passive loss rules. The passive loss is disallowed because Bob does not generate any passive income that could absorb his passive loss. Further, his salary (active income) and dividends (portfolio income) cannot be used to absorb any of the passive loss. Consequently, Bob's current-year taxable income must reflect his nonpassive income of $415,000, and he receives no current benefit from his share of the partnership loss. However, all is not lost because Bob's share of the entity's loss is *suspended*; it is carried forward and can be deducted in the future when he has passive income or sells his interest in the activity. ■

The nature of the at-risk limits and the passive activity loss rules and their impact on investors are discussed in the pages that follow. An interesting consequence of these rules is that now investors evaluating potential investments must consider mainly the economics of the venture instead of the tax benefits or tax avoidance possibilities that an investment may generate.

At-Risk Limits

LO.2

Explain the at-risk limitation.

The at-risk provisions limit the deductibility of losses from business and income-producing activities. These provisions, which apply to individuals and closely held corporations, are designed to prevent taxpayers from deducting losses in excess of their actual economic investment in an activity. In the case of an S corporation or a partnership, the at-risk limits apply at the owner level. Under the at-risk rules, a taxpayer's deductible loss from an activity for any taxable year is limited to the amount the taxpayer has at risk at the end of the taxable year (the amount the taxpayer could actually lose in the activity).

While the amount at risk generally vacillates over time, the initial amount considered at risk consists of the following:[3]

- The amount of cash and the adjusted basis of property contributed to the activity by the taxpayer.
- Amounts borrowed for use in the activity for which the taxpayer is personally liable or has pledged as security property not used in the activity.

This amount generally is increased each year by the taxpayer's share of income and is decreased by the taxpayer's share of losses and withdrawals from the activity. In addition, because general partners are jointly and severally liable for recourse debts of the partnership, their at-risk amounts are increased when the partnership increases its debt and are decreased when the partnership reduces its debt. However, a taxpayer generally is not considered at risk with respect to borrowed amounts if either of the following is true:

- The taxpayer is not personally liable for repayment of the debt (e.g., nonrecourse debt).
- The lender has an interest (other than as a creditor) in the activity.

An important exception provides that in the case of an activity involving the holding of real property, a taxpayer is considered at risk for his or her share of any *qualified nonrecourse financing* that is secured by real property used in the activity.[4]

Subject to the passive activity rules discussed later in the chapter, a taxpayer may deduct a loss as long as the at-risk amount is positive. However, once the at-risk amount is exhausted, any remaining loss cannot be deducted until a later year. Any losses disallowed for any given taxable year by the at-risk rules may be deducted in the first succeeding year in which the rules do not prevent the deduction—that is, when there is, and to the extent of, a positive at-risk amount.

EXAMPLE 4

In 2008, Sue invests $40,000 in an oil partnership that, by the use of nonrecourse loans, spends $60,000 on deductible intangible drilling costs applicable to her interest. Assume Sue's interest in the partnership is subject to the at-risk limits but is not subject to the passive loss limits. Since Sue has only $40,000 of capital at risk, she cannot deduct more than $40,000 against her other income and must reduce her at-risk amount to zero ($40,000 at-risk amount − $40,000 loss deducted). The nondeductible loss of $20,000 ($60,000 loss generated − $40,000 loss allowed) can be carried over to 2009. ■

EXAMPLE 5

In 2009, Sue has taxable income of $15,000 from the oil partnership and invests an additional $10,000 in the venture. Her at-risk amount is now $25,000 ($0 beginning balance + $15,000 taxable income + $10,000 additional investment). This enables Sue to deduct the carryover loss and requires her to reduce her at-risk amount to $5,000 ($25,000 at-risk amount − $20,000 carryover loss allowed). ■

---

[3]§ 465(b)(1).   [4]Section 465(b)(6) defines qualified nonrecourse financing.

CONCEPT SUMMARY   11–1

Calculation of At-Risk Amount

Increases to a taxpayer's at-risk amount:

- Cash and the adjusted basis of property contributed to the activity.
- Amounts borrowed for use in the activity for which the taxpayer is personally liable or has pledged as security property not used in the activity.
- Taxpayer's share of amounts borrowed for use in the activity that are qualified nonrecourse financing.
- Taxpayer's share of the activity's income.

Decreases to a taxpayer's at-risk amount:

- Withdrawals from the activity.
- Taxpayer's share of the activity's loss.
- Taxpayer's share of any reductions of debt for which recourse against the taxpayer exists or reductions of qualified nonrecourse debt.

An additional complicating factor is that previously allowed losses must be recaptured to the extent the at-risk amount is reduced below zero.[5] That is, previous losses that were allowed must be offset by the recognition of enough income to bring the at-risk amount up to zero. This rule applies in such situations as when the amount at risk is reduced below zero by distributions to the taxpayer or when the status of indebtedness changes from recourse to nonrecourse.

Passive Loss Limits

Classification and Impact of Passive Income and Losses

Classification. The passive loss rules require income and losses to be classified into one of three categories: active, passive, or portfolio. **Active income** includes the following:

- Wages, salary, commissions, bonuses, and other payments for services rendered by the taxpayer.
- Profit from a trade or business in which the taxpayer is a material participant.
- Gain on the sale or other disposition of assets used in an active trade or business.
- Income from intangible property if the taxpayer's personal efforts significantly contributed to the creation of the property.

   Portfolio income includes the following:

- Interest, dividends, annuities, and royalties not derived in the ordinary course of a trade or business.
- Gain or loss from the disposition of property that produces portfolio income or is held for investment purposes.

   Section 469 provides that income or loss from the following activities is treated as *passive*:

- Any trade or business or income-producing activity in which the taxpayer does not materially participate.
- Subject to certain exceptions, all rental activities, whether the taxpayer materially participates or not.

> **LO.3**
>
> Describe how the passive loss rules limit deductions for losses, and identify the taxpayers subject to these restrictions.

---

[5]§ 465(e).

Although the Code defines rental activities as passive activities, several exceptions allow losses from certain real estate rental activities to offset nonpassive (active or portfolio) income. These exceptions are discussed under Special Passive Activity Rules for Real Estate Activities later in the chapter.

General Impact. Losses or expenses generated by passive activities can be deducted only to the extent of income from all of the taxpayer's passive activities. Any excess may not be used to offset income from active sources or portfolio income. Instead, any unused passive losses are suspended and carried forward to future years to offset passive income generated in those years. Otherwise, suspended losses may be used only when a taxpayer disposes of his or her entire interest in an activity. In that event, all current and suspended losses related to the activity may offset active and portfolio income.

EXAMPLE 6

Kim, a physician, earns $150,000 from her full-time practice. She also receives $10,000 in dividends and interest from various portfolio investments, and her share of loss from a passive investment not limited by the at-risk rules is $60,000. Because the loss is a passive loss, it is not deductible against her other income. The loss is suspended and is carried over to the future. If Kim has passive income from this investment or from other passive investments in the future, she can offset the suspended loss against that passive income. If she does not have passive income to offset this suspended loss in the future, she will be allowed to offset the loss against other types of income when she eventually disposes of the passive activity. ∎

Impact of Suspended Losses. When a taxpayer disposes of his or her entire interest in a passive activity, the actual economic gain or loss from the investment, including any suspended losses, can finally be determined. As a result, under the passive loss rules, upon a fully taxable disposition, any overall loss realized from the activity by the taxpayer is recognized and can be offset against any income.

A fully taxable disposition generally involves a sale of the property to a third party at arm's length and thus, presumably, for a price equal to the property's fair market value. Gain recognized upon a transfer of an interest in a passive activity generally is treated as passive and is first offset by the suspended losses from that activity.

EXAMPLE 7

Rex sells an apartment building, a passive activity, with an adjusted basis of $100,000 for $180,000. In addition, he has suspended losses of $60,000 associated with the building. His total gain, $80,000, and his taxable gain, $20,000, are calculated as follows:

Net sales price	$ 180,000
Less: Adjusted basis	(100,000)
Total gain	$ 80,000
Less: Suspended losses	(60,000)
Taxable gain (passive)	$ 20,000

∎

If current and suspended losses of the passive activity exceed the gain realized or if the sale results in a realized loss, the amount of

- any loss from the activity for the tax year (including losses suspended in the activity disposed of)

in excess of

- net income or gain for the tax year from all passive activities (without regard to the activity disposed of) is treated as a loss that is not from a passive activity. In computing the loss from the activity for the year of disposition, any gain or loss recognized is included.

Dean sells an apartment building, a passive activity, with an adjusted basis of $100,000 for $150,000. In addition, he has current and suspended losses of $60,000 associated with the building and has no other passive activities. His total gain of $50,000 and his deductible loss of $10,000 are calculated as follows:

Net sales price	$ 150,000
Less: Adjusted basis	(100,000)
Total gain	$ 50,000
Less: Suspended losses	(60,000)
Deductible loss (not passive)	($ 10,000)

The $10,000 deductible loss is offset against Dean's active and portfolio income. ∎

Carryovers of Suspended Losses. In the above examples, it was assumed that the taxpayer had an interest in only one passive activity, and as a result, the suspended loss was related exclusively to the activity that was disposed of. Taxpayers often own interests in more than one activity, however, and in that case, any suspended losses must be allocated among the activities in which the taxpayer has an interest. The allocation to an activity is made by multiplying the disallowed passive activity loss from all activities by the following fraction:

$$\frac{\text{Loss from activity}}{\text{Sum of losses for taxable year from all activities having losses}}$$

Diego has investments in three passive activities with the following income and losses for 2007:

Activity A	($ 30,000)
Activity B	(20,000)
Activity C	25,000
Net passive loss	($ 25,000)
Net passive loss allocated to:	
Activity A ($25,000 × $30,000/$50,000)	($ 15,000)
Activity B ($25,000 × $20,000/$50,000)	(10,000)
Total suspended losses	($ 25,000)

∎

Suspended losses are carried over indefinitely and are offset in the future against any passive income from the activities to which they relate.[6]

Assume the same facts as in Example 9 and that Activity A produces $10,000 of income in 2008. Of the suspended loss of $15,000 from 2007 for Activity A, $10,000 is offset against the income from this activity. If Diego sells Activity A in early 2009, then the remaining $5,000 suspended loss is used in determining his taxable gain or loss. ∎

Passive Credits. Credits arising from passive activities are limited in much the same way as passive losses. Passive credits can be utilized only against regular tax attributable to passive income,[7] which is calculated by comparing the tax on all income (including passive income) with the tax on income excluding passive income.

---

[6]§ 469(b).   [7]§ 469(d)(2).

EXAMPLE 11

Sam owes $50,000 of tax, disregarding net passive income, and $80,000 of tax, considering both net passive and other taxable income (disregarding the credits in both cases). The amount of tax attributable to the passive income is $30,000. ∎

Sam in the preceding example can claim a maximum of $30,000 of passive activity credits; the excess credits are carried over. These passive activity credits (such as the low-income housing credit and rehabilitation credit—discussed in Chapter 13) can be used only against the *regular* tax attributable to passive income. If a taxpayer has a net loss from passive activities during a given year, no credits can be used.

Carryovers of Passive Credits. Tax credits attributable to passive activities can be carried forward indefinitely much like suspended passive losses. Unlike passive losses, however, passive credits are lost forever when the activity is disposed of in a taxable transaction where loss is recognized. Credits are allowed on dispositions only when there is sufficient tax on passive income to absorb them.

EXAMPLE 12

Alicia sells a passive activity for a gain of $10,000. The activity had suspended losses of $40,000 and suspended credits of $15,000. The $10,000 gain is offset by $10,000 of the suspended losses, and the remaining $30,000 of suspended losses is deductible against Alicia's active and portfolio income. The suspended credits are lost forever because the sale of the activity did not generate any tax. This is true even if Alicia has positive taxable income or is subject to the alternative minimum tax (discussed in Chapter 12). ∎

EXAMPLE 13

If Alicia in Example 12 had realized a $100,000 gain on the sale of the passive activity, the suspended credits could have been used to the extent of the regular tax attributable to the net passive income.

Gain on sale	$100,000
Less: Suspended losses	(40,000)
Taxable gain	$ 60,000

If the tax attributable to the taxable gain of $60,000 is $15,000 or more, the entire $15,000 of suspended credits can be used. If the tax attributable to the gain is less than $15,000, the excess of the suspended credits over the tax attributable to the gain is lost forever. ∎

When a taxpayer has sufficient regular tax liability from passive activities to trigger the use of suspended credits, the credits lose their character as passive credits. They are reclassified as regular tax credits and made subject to the same limits as other credits (discussed in Chapter 13).

Passive Activity Changes to Active. If a formerly passive activity becomes an active one, suspended losses are allowed to the extent of income from the now active business.[8] If any of the suspended loss remains, it continues to be treated as a loss from a passive activity. The excess suspended loss can be deducted from passive income or carried over to the next tax year and deducted to the extent of income from the now active business in the succeeding year(s). The activity must continue to be the same activity.

Taxpayers Subject to the Passive Loss Rules

The passive loss rules apply to individuals, estates, trusts, personal service corporations, and closely held C corporations.[9] Passive income or loss from investments in

---

[8]§ 469(f).   [9]§ 469(a).

TAX *in the News*	BEWARE OF PASSIVE LOSS RESTRICTIONS THAT APPLY TO INVESTMENTS IN PUBLICLY TRADED PARTNERSHIPS

Under the general passive activity loss rules, expenses and losses arising from a passive activity can be deducted against income generated by a taxpayer's other passive activities. Therefore, the losses of one passive activity can shelter the income from other passive activities. However, passive investments in publicly traded partnerships (PTPs) are subject to more restrictive rules.

Like corporate stock, interests in PTPs are publicly traded. PTPs are taxed either as corporations or, if certain conditions are met, as partnerships. For the PTPs taxed as partnerships, the limited partners (i.e., private investors) are taxed on income generated by the PTP. Any losses, however, are limited by a special set of passive loss rules. The PTP losses may not offset passive income from *other* passive activities. Losses can only offset passive income from the *same* PTP. Thus, they can produce a tax benefit in a subsequent year when the PTP generates a profit or when the partner sells the PTP interest.

S corporations or partnerships (see Chapter 20) flows through to the owners, and the passive loss rules are applied at the owner level.

Personal Service Corporations.

Application of the passive loss limitations to **personal service corporations** is intended to prevent taxpayers from sheltering personal service income by creating personal service corporations and acquiring passive activities at the corporate level.

EXAMPLE 14

Two tax accountants, who earn an aggregate of $200,000 a year in their individual practices, agree to work together in a newly formed personal service corporation. Shortly after its formation, the corporation invests in a passive activity that produces a $200,000 loss during the year. Because the passive loss rules apply to personal service corporations, the corporation may not deduct the $200,000 loss against the $200,000 of active income. ∎

Determination of whether a corporation is a *personal service corporation* is based on rather broad definitions. A personal service corporation is a corporation that meets *both* of the following conditions:

- The principal activity is the performance of personal services.
- Such services are substantially performed by employee-owners.

Generally, personal service corporations include those in the fields of health, law, engineering, architecture, accounting, actuarial science, performing arts, and consulting.[10] A corporation is treated as a personal service corporation if more than 10 percent of the stock (by value) is held by employee-owners.[11] An employee is treated as an employee-owner if he or she owns stock on *any day* during the taxable year.[12] For these purposes, shareholder status and employee status do not even have to occur on the same day.

Closely Held C Corporations.

Application of the passive loss rules to closely held (non-personal service) C corporations is also intended to prevent individuals from incorporating to avoid the passive loss limitations. A corporation is classified as a **closely held corporation** if at any time during the taxable year more than 50 percent of the value of its outstanding stock is owned, directly or indirectly, by or for five or fewer individuals. Closely held C corporations (other than personal service corporations) may use passive losses to offset *active* income, but not portfolio income.

---

[10]§ 448(d)(2)(A).
[11]§ 469(j)(2).
[12]§ 269A(b)(2).

EXAMPLE 15

Silver Corporation, a closely held (non-personal service) C corporation, has $500,000 of passive losses from a rental activity, $400,000 of active income, and $100,000 of portfolio income. The corporation may offset $400,000 of the $500,000 passive loss against the $400,000 of active business income, but may not offset the remainder against the $100,000 of portfolio income. Thus, $100,000 of the passive loss is suspended ($500,000 passive loss − $400,000 offset against active income). ■

Application of the passive loss limitations to closely held C corporations prevents taxpayers from transferring their portfolio investments to such corporations in order to offset passive losses against portfolio income.

LO.4

Discuss the definition of passive activities and the rules for identifying an activity.

Passive Activities Defined

Section 469 specifies that the following types of activities are to be treated as passive:

- Any trade or business or income-producing activity in which the taxpayer does not materially participate.
- Subject to certain exceptions, all rental activities.

To understand the meaning of the term *passive activity* and the impact of the rules, one must address the following issues, each of which is the subject of statutory or administrative guidance:

- What constitutes an activity?
- What is meant by material participation?
- When is an activity a rental activity?

Even though guidance is available to help the taxpayer deal with these issues, their resolution is anything but simple.

Identification of an Activity.
Identifying what constitutes an activity is a necessary first step in applying the passive loss limitations. Taxpayers who are involved in complex business operations need to determine whether a given segment of their overall business operations constitutes a separate activity or is to be treated as part of a single activity. Proper treatment is necessary in order to determine whether income or loss from an activity is active or passive.

EXAMPLE 16

Ben owns a business with two separate departments. Department A generates net income of $120,000, and Department B generates a net loss of $95,000. Ben participates for 700 hours in the operations of Department A and for 100 hours in Department B. If Ben is allowed to treat the departments as components of a single activity, he can offset the $95,000 loss from Department B against the $120,000 of income from Department A. ■

EXAMPLE 17

Assume the same facts as in the previous example. If Ben is required to treat each department as a separate activity, the tax result is not as favorable. Because he is a material participant in Department A (having devoted 700 hours to it), the $120,000 profit is active income. However, he is not considered a material participant in Department B (100 hours), and the $95,000 loss is a passive loss. Therefore, Ben cannot offset the $95,000 passive loss from Department B against the $120,000 of active income from Department A. (A complete discussion of the material participation rules follows.) ■

Recall that on the disposition of a passive activity, a taxpayer is allowed to offset suspended losses from the activity against other types of income. Therefore, identifying what constitutes an activity is of crucial importance for this purpose too.

EXAMPLE 18

Linda owns a business with two departments. Department A has a net loss of $125,000 in the current year, and Department B has a $70,000 net loss. She disposes of Department B at the end of the year. Assuming Linda is allowed to treat the two departments as separate passive activities, she can offset the passive loss from Department B against other types of income in the following order: gain from disposition of the passive activity, other passive income, and nonpassive income. This treatment leaves her with a suspended loss of $125,000 from Department A. If Departments A and B are treated as components of the same activity, however, on the disposal of Department B, its $70,000 net loss would be suspended along with the other $125,000 of suspended loss of the activity. ■

The rules used to delineate what constitutes an activity for purposes of the passive loss limitations are provided in the Regulations.[13] These guidelines state that, in general, a taxpayer can treat one or more trade or business activities or rental activities as a single activity if those activities form an *appropriate economic unit* for measuring gain or loss. To determine what ventures form an appropriate economic unit, all of the relevant facts and circumstances must be considered. Taxpayers may use any reasonable method in applying the facts and circumstances. The following example, adapted from the Regulations, illustrates the application of the general rules for grouping activities.[14]

EXAMPLE 19

George owns a men's clothing store and a video game parlor in Chicago. He also owns a men's clothing store and a video game parlor in Milwaukee. Reasonable methods of applying the facts and circumstances test may result in any of the following groupings:

- All four activities may be grouped into a single activity because of common ownership and control.
- The clothing stores may be grouped into an activity, and the video game parlors may be grouped into a separate activity.
- The Chicago activities may be grouped into an activity, and the Milwaukee activities may be grouped into a separate activity.
- Each of the four activities may be treated as a separate activity.   ■

Regrouping of Activities. Taxpayers should carefully consider all tax factors in deciding how to group their activities. Once activities have been grouped, they cannot be regrouped unless the original grouping was clearly inappropriate or there has been a material change in the facts and circumstances. The Regulations also grant the IRS the right to regroup activities when both of the following conditions exist:[15]

- The taxpayer's grouping fails to reflect one or more appropriate economic units.
- One of the primary purposes of the taxpayer's grouping is to avoid the passive loss limitations.

Special Grouping Rules for Rental Activities. Two rules deal specifically with the grouping of rental activities. These provisions are designed to prevent taxpayers from grouping rental activities, which are generally passive, with other businesses in a way that would result in a tax advantage.

First, a rental activity may be grouped with a trade or business activity only if one activity is insubstantial in relation to the other. That is, the rental activity must be insubstantial in relation to the trade or business activity, or the trade or business activity must be insubstantial in relation to the rental activity. The Regulations provide no clear guidelines as to the meaning of "insubstantial."[16]

---

[13]Reg. § 1.469–4.
[14]Reg. § 1.469–4(c)(3).

[15]Reg. § 1.469–4(f).
[16]Reg. § 1.469–4(d).

EXAMPLE 20

Schemers, a firm of CPAs, owns a building in downtown Washington, D.C., in which they conduct their public accounting practice. The firm also rents space on the street level of the building to several retail establishments. Of the total revenue generated by the firm, 95% is associated with the public accounting practice, and 5% is related to the rental operation. It is likely that the rental activity would be considered insubstantial relative to the accounting practice and the two ventures could be grouped as one nonrental activity. This grouping could be advantageous to the firm, particularly if the rental operation generates a loss! Alternatively, treating the rental operation as a *separate* activity may be advantageous if this operation produces (passive) income. The passive income could then be used to absorb otherwise nondeductible passive losses. ■

Second, taxpayers generally may not treat an activity involving the rental of real property and an activity involving the rental of personal property as a single activity.

LO.5

Analyze and apply the tests for material participation.

Material Participation. If an individual taxpayer materially participates in a nonrental trade or business activity, any loss from that activity is treated as an active loss that can offset active or portfolio income. If a taxpayer does not materially participate, however, the loss is treated as a passive loss, which can only offset passive income. Therefore, controlling whether a particular activity is treated as active or passive is an important part of the tax strategy of a taxpayer who owns an interest in one or more businesses. Consider the following examples.

EXAMPLE 21

Dewayne, a corporate executive, earns a salary of $600,000 per year. In addition, he owns a separate business in which he participates. The business produces a loss of $100,000 during the year. If Dewayne materially participates in the business, the $100,000 loss is an active loss that may offset his active income from his corporate employer. If he does not materially participate, the loss is passive and is suspended. Dewayne may use the suspended loss in the future only when he has passive income or disposes of the activity. ■

EXAMPLE 22

Kay, an attorney, earns $350,000 a year in her law practice. She owns interests in two activities, A and B, in which she participates. Activity A, in which she does *not* materially participate, produces a loss of $50,000. Kay has not yet met the material participation standard for Activity B, which produces income of $80,000. However, she can meet the material participation standard if she spends an additional 50 hours in Activity B during the year. Should Kay attempt to meet the material participation standard for Activity B? If she continues working in Activity B and becomes a material participant, the $80,000 of income from the activity is *active*, and the $50,000 passive loss from Activity A must be suspended. A more favorable tax strategy is for Kay to *not meet* the material participation standard for Activity B, thus making the income from that activity passive. This enables her to offset the $50,000 passive loss from Activity A against the passive income from Activity B. ■

It is possible to devise numerous scenarios in which the taxpayer could control the tax outcome by increasing or decreasing his or her participation in different activities. Examples 21 and 22 demonstrate some of the possibilities. The conclusion reached in most analyses of this type is that taxpayers will benefit by having profitable activities classified as passive so that any passive losses can be used to offset that passive income. If the activity produces a loss, however, the taxpayer will benefit if it is classified as active so that the loss is not subject to the passive loss limitations.

As discussed previously, a nonrental trade or business in which a taxpayer owns an interest must be treated as a passive activity unless the taxpayer materially participates. As the Staff of the Joint Committee on Taxation explained, a material participant is one who has "a significant nontax economic profit motive" for taking on activities and selects them for their economic value. In contrast, a passive investor mainly seeks a return from a capital investment (including a possible reduction in taxes) as a supplement to an ongoing source of livelihood.[17] Even if the concept or the implication of being a material participant is clear, the precise meaning of the term **material participation** can be vague. As enacted, § 469 requires a taxpayer to participate on a *regular, continuous, and substantial* basis in order to be a material participant. In many situations, however, it is difficult or impossible to gain any assurance that this nebulous standard is met.

In response to this dilemma, Temporary Regulations[18] provide seven tests that are intended to help taxpayers cope with these issues. Material participation is achieved by meeting any *one* of the tests. These tests can be divided into three categories:

- Tests based on current participation.
- Tests based on prior participation.
- Test based on facts and circumstances.

Tests Based on Current Participation. The first four tests are quantitative tests that require measurement, in hours, of the taxpayer's participation in the activity during the year.

1. *Does the individual participate in the activity for more than 500 hours during the year?*

The purpose of the 500-hour requirement is to restrict deductions from the types of trade or business activities Congress intended to treat as passive activities. The 500-hour standard for material participation was adopted for the following reasons:[19]

- Few investors in traditional tax shelters devote more than 500 hours a year to such an investment.
- The IRS believes that income from an activity in which the taxpayer participates for more than 500 hours a year should not be treated as passive.

2. *Does the individual's participation in the activity for the taxable year constitute substantially all of the participation in the activity of all individuals (including nonowner employees) for the year?*

EXAMPLE 23

Ned, a physician, operates a separate business in which he participates for 80 hours during the year. He is the only participant and has no employees in the separate business. Ned meets the material participation standard of Test 2. If he had employees, it could be difficult to apply Test 2, because the Temporary Regulations do not define the term *substantially all.* ■

3. *Does the individual participate in the activity for more than 100 hours during the year, and is the individual's participation in the activity for the year not less than the participation of any other individual (including nonowner employees) for the year?*

EXAMPLE 24

Adam, a college professor, owns a separate business in which he participates 110 hours during the year. He has an employee who works 90 hours during the year. Adam meets the material participation standard under Test 3, but probably does not meet it under Test 2 because his participation is only 55% of the total participation. It is unlikely that 55% would meet the *substantially all* requirement of Test 2. ■

Tests 2 and 3 are included because the IRS recognizes that the operation of some activities does not require more than 500 hours of participation during the year.

---

[17]*General Explanation of the Tax Reform Act of 1986* ("Blue Book"), prepared by The Staff of the Joint Committee on Taxation, May 4, 1987, H.R. 3838, 99th Cong., p. 212.

[18]Temp.Reg. § 1.469–5T(a). The Temporary Regulations are also Proposed Regulations. Temporary Regulations have the same effect as final Regulations. Refer to Chapter 2 for a discussion of the different categories of Regulations.

[19]T.D. 8175, 1988–1 C.B. 191.

4. *Is the activity a significant participation activity for the taxable year, and does the individual's aggregate participation in all significant participation activities during the year exceed 500 hours?*

A **significant participation activity** is a trade or business in which the individual's participation exceeds 100 hours during the year. This test treats taxpayers as material participants if their aggregate participation in several significant participation activities exceeds 500 hours. Test 4 thus accords the same treatment to an individual who devotes an aggregate of more than 500 hours to several significant participation activities as to an individual who devotes more than 500 hours to a single activity.

EXAMPLE 25

Mike owns five different businesses. He participates in each activity during the year as follows:

Activity	Hours of Participation
A	110
B	140
C	120
D	150
E	100

Activities A, B, C, and D are significant participation activities, and Mike's aggregate participation in those activities is 520 hours. Therefore, Activities A, B, C, and D are not treated as passive activities. Activity E is not a significant participation activity (not more than 100 hours), so it is not included in applying the 500-hour test. Activity E is treated as a passive activity, unless Mike meets one of the other material participation tests for that activity. ■

EXAMPLE 26

Assume the same facts as in the previous example, except that Activity A does not exist. All of the activities are now treated as passive. Activity E is not counted in applying the more-than-500-hour test, so Mike's aggregate participation in significant participation activities is 410 hours (140 in Activity B + 120 in Activity C + 150 in Activity D). He could meet the significant participation test for Activity E by participating for one more hour in the activity. This would cause Activities B, C, D, and E to be treated as nonpassive activities. However, before deciding whether to participate for at least one more hour in Activity E, Mike should assess how the participation would affect his overall tax liability. ■

Tests Based on Prior Participation. Tests 5 and 6 are based on material participation in prior years. Under these tests, a taxpayer who is no longer a participant in an activity can continue to be *classified* as a material participant. The IRS takes the position that material participation in a trade or business for a long period of time is likely to indicate that the activity represents the individual's principal livelihood, rather than a passive investment. Consequently, withdrawal from the activity, or reduction of participation to the point where it is not material, does not change the classification of the activity from active to passive.

5. *Did the individual materially participate in the activity for any 5 taxable years (whether consecutive or not) during the 10 taxable years that immediately precede the taxable year?*

EXAMPLE 27

Dawn, who owns a 50% interest in a restaurant, was a material participant in the operations of the restaurant from 2002 through 2006. She retired at the end of 2006 and is no longer involved in the restaurant except as an investor. Dawn will be treated as a material participant in the restaurant in 2007. Even if she does not become involved in the restaurant as a material participant again, she will continue to be treated as a material participant in 2008, 2009, 2010, and 2011. In 2012 and later years, Dawn's share of income or loss from the restaurant will be classified as passive unless she materially participates in those years. ∎

6. *Is the activity a personal service activity, and did the individual materially participate in the activity for any three preceding taxable years (whether consecutive or not)?*

As indicated above, the material participation standards differ for personal service activities and other businesses. An individual who was a material participant in a personal service activity for *any three years* prior to the taxable year continues to be treated as a material participant after withdrawal from the activity.

EXAMPLE 28

Evan, a CPA, retires from the EFG Partnership after working full-time in the partnership for 30 years. As a retired partner, he will continue to receive a share of the profits of the firm for the next 10 years, even though he will not participate in the firm's operations. Evan also owns an interest in a passive activity that produces a loss for the year. Because he continues to be treated as a material participant in the EFG Partnership, his income from the partnership is active income. Therefore, he is not allowed to offset the loss from his passive investment against the income from the EFG Partnership. ∎

Test Based on Facts and Circumstances. Test 7 assesses the facts and circumstances to determine whether the taxpayer has materially participated.

7. *Based on all the facts and circumstances, did the individual participate in the activity on a regular, continuous, and substantial basis during the year?*

Unfortunately, the Temporary Regulations provide little guidance as to the meaning of regular, continuous, and substantial participation.[20] However, a part of the Temporary Regulations has been reserved for further development of this test. For the time being, taxpayers should rely on Tests 1 through 6 in determining whether the material participation standards have been met.

Participation Defined. Participation generally includes any work done by an individual in an activity that he or she owns. Participation does not include work if it is of a type not customarily done by owners *and* if one of its principal purposes is to avoid the disallowance of passive losses or credits. Also, work done in an individual's capacity as an investor (e.g., reviewing financial reports in a nonmanagerial capacity) is not counted in applying the material participation tests. However, participation by an owner's spouse counts as participation by the owner.[21]

EXAMPLE 29

Tom, who is a partner in a CPA firm, owns a computer store that has operated at a loss during the year. In order to offset this loss against the income from his CPA practice, Tom would like to avoid having the computer business classified as a passive activity. Through December 15, he has worked 400 hours in the business in management and selling activities. During the last two weeks of December, he works 80 hours in management and selling activities and 30 hours doing janitorial chores. Also during the last two weeks in December, Tom's wife participates 40 hours as a salesperson. She has worked as a salesperson in the computer store in prior years, but has not done so during the current year. If any of Tom's work is of a type not customarily done by owners *and* if one of its principal purposes is to avoid the disallowance of passive losses or credits, it is not counted in applying the material participation tests. It is likely that Tom's 480 hours of participation in management and selling activities will count as participation, but the 30 hours spent doing janitorial chores will not. However, the 40 hours of participation by his wife will count,

---

[20]Temp.Reg. § 1.469–5T(b)(2).   [21]Temp.Reg. § 1.469–5T(f)(3).

and as a result, Tom will qualify as a material participant under the more-than-500-hour rule (480 + 40 = 520). ■

Limited Partners. A *limited* partner is one whose liability to third-party creditors of the partnership is limited to the amount the partner has invested in the partnership. Such a partnership must have at least one *general* partner, who is fully liable in an individual capacity for the debts of the partnership to third parties. Generally, a *limited partner* is not considered a material participant unless he or she qualifies under Test 1, 5, or 6 in the above list. However, a *general partner* may qualify as a material participant by meeting any of the seven tests. If a general partner also owns a limited interest in the same limited partnership, all interests are treated as a general interest.[22]

LO.6
Understand the nature of rental activities under the passive loss rules.

Rental Activities Defined. Subject to certain exceptions, all rental activities are to be treated as passive activities.[23] A **rental activity** is defined as any activity where payments are received principally for the use of tangible (real or personal) property.[24] Importantly, an activity that is classified as a rental activity is subject to the passive activity loss rules, even if the taxpayer involved is a material participant.

EXAMPLE 30

Sarah owns an apartment building and spends an average of 60 hours a week in its operation. Assuming that the apartment building operation is classified as a rental activity, it is automatically subject to the passive activity rules, even though Sarah spends more than 500 hours a year in its operation. ■

Temporary Regulations, however, provide exceptions for certain situations where activities involving rentals of real and personal property are *not* to be *treated* as rental activities.[25]

EXAMPLE 31

Dan owns a DVD rental business. Because the average period of customer use is seven days or less, Dan's DVD business is not treated as a rental activity. ■

The fact that Dan's DVD business in the previous example is not treated as a rental activity does not necessarily mean that it is classified as a nonpassive activity. Instead, the DVD business is treated as a trade or business activity subject to the material participation standards. If Dan is a material participant, the business is treated as active. If he is not a material participant, it is treated as a passive activity.

Thus, activities covered by any of the following six exceptions provided by the Temporary Regulations are not *automatically* treated as nonpassive activities merely because they would not be classified as rental activities. Instead, the activities are subject to the material participation tests.

1. *The average period of customer use of the property is seven days or less.*

Under this exception, activities involving the short-term use of tangible property such as automobiles, DVDs, tuxedos, tools, and other such property are not treated as rental activities. The provision also applies to short-term rentals of hotel or motel rooms.

This exception is based on the presumption that a person who rents property for seven days or less is generally required to provide *significant services* to the customer. Providing such services supports a conclusion that the person is engaged in a service business rather than a rental business.

2. *The average period of customer use of the property is 30 days or less, and the owner of the property provides significant personal services.*

---

[22]Temp.Reg. § 1.469–5T(e)(3)(ii).
[23]§ 469(c)(2).

[24]§ 469(j)(8).
[25]Temp.Reg. § 1.469–1T(e)(3)(ii).

For longer-term rentals, the presumption that significant services are provided is not automatic, as it is in the case of the seven-day exception. Instead, the taxpayer must be able to *prove* that significant personal services are rendered in connection with the activity. Relevant facts and circumstances include the frequency with which such services are provided, the type and amount of labor required to perform the services, and the value of the services relative to the amount charged for the use of the property. Significant personal services include only services provided by *individuals*.[26]

3. *The owner of the property provides extraordinary personal services. The average period of customer use is of no consequence in applying this test.*

Extraordinary personal services are services provided by individuals where the customers' use of the property is incidental to their receipt of the services. For example, a patient's use of a hospital bed is incidental to his or her receipt of medical services. Another example is the use of a boarding school's dormitory, which is incidental to the scholastic services received.

4. *The rental of the property is treated as incidental to a nonrental activity of the taxpayer.*

Rentals of real property incidental to a nonrental activity are not considered a passive activity. The Temporary Regulations provide that the following rentals are not passive activities:[27]

- *Property held primarily for investment.* This occurs where the principal purpose for holding the property is the expectation of gain from the appreciation of the property and the gross rent income is less than 2 percent of the lesser of (1) the unadjusted basis or (2) the fair market value of the property.

EXAMPLE 32

Ramon invests in vacant land for the purpose of realizing a profit on its appreciation. He leases the land during the period it is held. The land's unadjusted basis is $250,000, and the fair market value is $350,000. The lease payments are $4,000 per year. Because gross rent income is less than 2% of $250,000, the activity is not a rental activity. ∎

- *Property used in a trade or business.* This occurs where the property is owned by a taxpayer who is an owner of the trade or business using the rental property. The property must also have been used in the trade or business during the year or during at least two of the five preceding taxable years. The 2 percent test above also applies in this situation.

EXAMPLE 33

A farmer owns land with an unadjusted basis of $250,000 and a fair market value of $350,000. He used it for farming purposes in 2006 and 2007. In 2008, he leases the land to another farmer for $4,000. The activity is not a rental activity. ∎

- *Lodging rented for the convenience of an employer.* If an employer provides lodging for an employee incidental to the employee's performance of services in the employer's trade or business, no rental activity exists.

These rules were written to prevent taxpayers from converting active or portfolio income into passive income for the purpose of offsetting other passive losses.

5. *The taxpayer customarily makes the property available during defined business hours for nonexclusive use by various customers.*

EXAMPLE 34

Pat is the owner-operator of a public golf course. Some customers pay daily greens fees each time they use the course, while others purchase weekly, monthly, or annual passes. The golf

---

[26]Temp.Reg. § 1.469–1T(e)(3)(iv).   [27]Temp.Regs. §§ 1.469–1T(e)(3)(vi)(B) through (D).

course is open every day from sunrise to sunset, except on certain holidays and on days when the course is closed due to inclement weather conditions. Pat is not engaged in a rental activity, regardless of the average period customers use the course. ■

6. *The property is provided for use in an activity conducted by a partnership, S corporation, or joint venture in which the taxpayer owns an interest.*

EXAMPLE 35

Joe, a partner in the Skyview Partnership, contributes the use of a building to the partnership. The partnership has net income of $30,000 during the year, of which Joe's share is $10,000. Unless the partnership is engaged in a rental activity, none of Joe's income from the partnership is income from a rental activity. ■

LO.7

Recognize the relationship between the at-risk and passive activity limitations.

Interaction of the At-Risk and Passive Activity Limits

The determination of whether a loss is suspended under the passive loss rules is made *after* application of the at-risk rules, as well as other provisions relating to the measurement of taxable income. A loss that is not allowed for the year because the taxpayer is not at risk with respect to it is suspended under the at-risk provision and not under the passive loss rules. Further, a taxpayer's basis is reduced by deductions (e.g., depreciation) even if the deductions are not currently usable because of the passive loss rules.

EXAMPLE 36

Jack's adjusted basis in a passive activity is $10,000 at the beginning of 2007. His loss from the activity in 2007 is $4,000. Since Jack has no passive activity income, the $4,000 cannot be deducted. At year-end, Jack has an adjusted basis and an at-risk amount of $6,000 in the activity and a suspended passive loss of $4,000. ■

EXAMPLE 37

Jack in Example 36 has a loss of $9,000 in the activity in 2008. Since the $9,000 exceeds his at-risk amount ($6,000) by $3,000, that $3,000 loss is disallowed by the at-risk rules. If Jack has no passive activity income, the remaining $6,000 is suspended under the passive activity rules. At year-end, he has:

- A $3,000 loss suspended under the at-risk rules.
- $10,000 of suspended passive losses.
- An adjusted basis and an at-risk amount in the activity of zero. ■

EXAMPLE 38

Jack in Example 37 realizes $1,000 of passive income from the activity in 2009. Because the $1,000 increases his at-risk amount, $1,000 of the $3,000 unused loss is reclassified as a passive loss. If he has no other passive income, the $1,000 income is offset by $1,000 of suspended passive losses. At the end of 2009, Jack has:

- No taxable passive income.
- $2,000 ($3,000 − $1,000) of unused losses under the at-risk rules.
- $10,000 of (reclassified) suspended passive losses ($10,000 + $1,000 of reclassified unused at-risk losses − $1,000 of passive losses offset against passive income).
- An adjusted basis and an at-risk amount in the activity of zero. ■

EXAMPLE 39

In 2010, Jack has no gain or loss from the activity in Example 38. He contributes $5,000 more to the passive activity. Because the $5,000 increases his at-risk amount, the $2,000 of losses suspended under the at-risk rules is reclassified as passive. Jack gets no passive loss deduction in 2010. At year-end, he has:

- No suspended losses under the at-risk rules.
- $12,000 of suspended passive losses ($10,000 + $2,000 of reclassified suspended at-risk losses).

TAX *in the News*	NEWLY DEVELOPED TAX SHELTER STRATEGIES NOW PROTECTED BY PATENTS—BUT FOR HOW LONG?

A patent is generally thought of as an intangible asset that protects the intellectual property underlying a new drug, manufacturing process, or consumer item. In such cases, the U.S. Patent and Trademark Office grants a patent that legally protects the holder's exclusive right to the invention. Now, tax and financial planners are patenting their newest tax shelters and strategies to prevent competitors from using them. Some of the patented strategies involve making mixed gifts of art to charities and family or transferring appreciated assets to heirs with minimal tax consequences.

The applicant for a patent should be aware, however, that acquiring such legal protection can be costly. Furthermore, even if the Patent and Trademark Office grants a so-called business method patent, there is no assurance that the IRS will approve of the technique. In fact, then IRS Commissioner Mark Everson testified before a congressional panel that "the grant of a patent for a tax strategy has absolutely no impact on the IRS's determination of the effectiveness or legitimacy of the strategy." Nonetheless, taxpayers have obtained 51 patents related to tax strategies since 1998, and another 83 have been submitted to the Patent and Trademark Office for review.

Not only has the IRS cautioned against relying too heavily on a patented tax strategy, but others have questioned the wisdom of even allowing such patents. The AICPA has pressed Congress to enact legislation restricting the procedure. As of the date of this writing, the House has passed a bill that would make tax planning techniques unpatentable.

- An adjusted basis and an at-risk amount of $3,000 ($5,000 additional investment − $2,000 of reclassified losses). ■

Special Passive Activity Rules for Real Estate Activities

LO.8

Discuss the special treatment available to real estate activities.

The passive loss limits contain two exceptions related to real estate activities. These exceptions allow all or part of real estate rental losses to offset active or portfolio income, even though the activity otherwise is defined as a passive activity.

Material Participation in a Real Property Trade or Business.

Losses from real estate rental activities are *not* treated as passive losses for certain real estate professionals.[28] To qualify for nonpassive treatment, a taxpayer must satisfy both of the following requirements:

- More than half of the personal services that the taxpayer performs in trades or businesses are performed in real property trades or businesses in which the taxpayer materially participates.
- The taxpayer performs more than 750 hours of services in these real property trades or businesses as a material participant.

Taxpayers who do not satisfy the above requirements must continue to treat losses from real estate rental activities as passive losses.

EXAMPLE 40

During the current year, Della performs personal service activities as follows: 900 hours as a personal financial planner, 550 hours in a real estate development business, and 600 hours in a real estate rental activity. Any loss Della incurs in the real estate rental activity will *not* be subject to the passive loss rules, since more than 50% of her personal services are devoted to real property trades or businesses, and her material participation in those real estate activities exceeds 750 hours. Thus, any loss from the real estate rental activity can offset active and portfolio sources of income. ■

As discussed earlier, a spouse's work is taken into consideration in satisfying the material participation requirement. However, the hours worked by a spouse are *not* taken into account when ascertaining whether a taxpayer has worked for more than 750 hours in real property trades or businesses during a year.[29] Services performed

---

[28]§ 469(c)(7).

[29]§ 469(c)(7)(B) and Reg. § 1.469–9.

TAX *in the News*   RECORD KEEPING INVOLVES CREATIVE WRITING FOR SOME!

One exception to the passive loss rules allows real estate professionals to treat rental losses as active if they arise from a business that is an active endeavor as opposed to one that is more passive oriented. To receive this preferential treatment, however, Temp.Reg. § 1.469–5T(f)(4) requires a real estate professional to show "by any reasonable means" that more than half of his or her personal services rendered during a year were devoted to real estate trades or businesses. Although contemporaneous records may be the best way to accumulate the necessary proof of involvement, many taxpayers wait to build their case "after the fact." This approach can result in the taxpayers providing nothing more than "ballpark guesstimates!"

The Lee brothers, one a doctor and professor and the other a full-time IRS employee, apparently found themselves in just such a predicament (*Kai H. and Susanna Lee; Ulysses K. and Jane Lee,* 92 TCM 263, T.C.Memo. 2006–193). After they deducted significant rental losses on their returns as real estate professionals, the IRS asked for documentation of their hours. Not only did the claims that the Lees presented in court more than double the time of the first logs submitted to the IRS but some of their log entries strained credibility. For example, one brother claimed that he spent "24 hours to replace four miniblinds in one of the apartments, 42 hours to paint another, and 56 hours to install a new toilet in a third." Such seemingly inflated hours devoted to their real estate ventures were accompanied by unrealistically low assessments of the hours spent at their full-time jobs. Needless to say, the court concluded that the logs were not credible and, therefore, the Lees were not real estate professionals.

---

by an employee are not treated as being related to a real estate trade or business unless the employee performing the services owns more than a 5 percent interest in the employer. Additionally, a closely held C corporation may also qualify for the passive loss relief if more than 50 percent of its gross receipts for the year are derived from real property trades or businesses in which it materially participates.

Real Estate Rental Activities.

The second exception is more significant in that it is not restricted to real estate professionals. This exception allows individuals to deduct up to $25,000 of losses from real estate rental activities against active and portfolio income.[30] The potential annual $25,000 deduction is reduced by 50 percent of the taxpayer's AGI in excess of $100,000. Thus, the entire deduction is phased out at $150,000 of AGI. If married individuals file separately, the $25,000 deduction is reduced to zero unless they lived apart for the entire year. If they lived apart for the entire year, the loss amount is $12,500 each, and the phaseout begins at $50,000. AGI for purposes of the phaseout is calculated without regard to IRA deductions, Social Security benefits, interest deductions on education loans, and net losses from passive activities.

To qualify for the $25,000 exception, a taxpayer must meet the following requirements:[31]

- Actively participate in the real estate rental activity.
- Own 10 percent or more (in value) of all interests in the activity during the entire taxable year (or shorter period during which the taxpayer held an interest in the activity).

The difference between *active participation* and *material participation* is that the former can be satisfied without regular, continuous, and substantial involvement in operations as long as the taxpayer participates in making management decisions in a significant and bona fide sense. In this context, relevant management decisions include such decisions as approving new tenants, deciding on rental terms, and approving capital or repair expenditures.

The $25,000 allowance is available after all active participation rental losses and gains are netted and applied to other passive income. If a taxpayer has a real estate rental loss in excess of the amount that can be deducted under the real estate rental exception, that excess is treated as a passive loss.

---

[30]§ 469(i).   [31]§ 469(i)(6).

Brad, who has $90,000 of AGI before considering rental activities, has $85,000 of losses from a real estate rental activity in which he actively participates. He also actively participates in another real estate rental activity from which he has $25,000 of income. He has other passive income of $36,000. Of the net rental loss of $60,000, $36,000 is absorbed by the passive income, leaving $24,000 that can be deducted against active or portfolio income because of the availability of the $25,000 allowance. ■

The $25,000 offset allowance is an aggregate of both deductions and credits in deduction equivalents. The deduction equivalent of a passive activity credit is the amount of deductions that reduces the tax liability for the taxable year by an amount equal to the credit.[32] A taxpayer with $5,000 of credits and a tax bracket of 25 percent would have a deduction equivalent of $20,000 ($5,000 ÷ 25%).

If the total deduction and deduction equivalent exceed $25,000, the taxpayer must allocate the allowance on a pro rata basis, first among the losses (including real estate rental activity losses suspended in prior years) and then to credits in the following order: (1) credits other than rehabilitation and low-income housing credits, (2) rehabilitation credits, and (3) low-income housing credits.

Kevin is an active participant in a real estate rental activity that produces $8,000 of income, $26,000 of deductions, and $1,500 of credits. Kevin, who is in the 25% tax bracket, may deduct the net passive loss of $18,000 ($8,000 − $26,000). After deducting the loss, he has an available deduction equivalent of $7,000 ($25,000 − $18,000 passive loss). Therefore, the maximum amount of credits that he may claim is $1,750 ($7,000 × 25%). Since the actual credits are less than this amount, Kevin may claim the entire $1,500 credit. ■

Kelly, who is in the 25% tax bracket, is an active participant in three separate real estate rental activities. The relevant tax results for each activity are as follows:

- Activity A: $20,000 of losses.
- Activity B: $10,000 of losses.
- Activity C: $4,200 of credits.

Kelly's deduction equivalent from the credits is $16,800 ($4,200 ÷ 25%). Therefore, the total passive deductions and deduction equivalents are $46,800 ($20,000 + $10,000 + $16,800), which exceeds the maximum allowable amount of $25,000. Consequently, Kelly must allocate pro rata first from among losses and then from among credits. Deductions from losses are limited as follows:

- Activity A {$25,000 × [$20,000 ÷ ($20,000 + $10,000)]} = $16,667.
- Activity B {$25,000 × [$10,000 ÷ ($20,000 + $10,000)]} = $8,333.

Since the amount of passive deductions exceeds the $25,000 maximum, the deduction balance of $5,000 and passive credits of $4,200 must be carried forward. Kelly's suspended losses and credits by activity are as follows:

	Total	Activity A	Activity B	Activity C
Allocated losses	$ 30,000	$ 20,000	$10,000	$ –0–
Allocated credits	4,200	–0–	–0–	4,200
Utilized losses	(25,000)	(16,667)	(8,333)	–0–
Suspended losses	5,000	3,333	1,667	–0–
Suspended credits	4,200	–0–	–0–	4,200

■

---

[32]§ 469(j)(5).

ETHICAL and EQUITABLE Considerations   PUNCHING THE TIME CLOCK AT YEAR-END

As the end of the tax year approaches, Ralph, a successful full-time real estate developer and investor, recognizes that his income tax situation for the year could be bleak. Unless he and his wife are able to generate more hours of participation in one of his rental activities, they will not reach the material participation threshold. Consequently, the tax losses from the venture will not be deductible. To ensure deductibility, he suggests the following plan:

- Ralph will document the time he spends "thinking" about his rental activities.
- During the week, his wife will visit the apartment building to oversee (in a management role) the operations of the rentals.

- On weekends, Ralph *and* his wife will visit the same units to further evaluate the operations.
- Also, on the weekends, they will drive around the community looking for other rental properties to buy. Ralph plans to count both his and his wife's weekend hours toward the tally of total participation.

Ralph contends that the law clearly allows the efforts of one's spouse to count for purposes of the material participation tests. Likewise, nothing in the tax law requires taxpayers to be efficient in their hours of participation. How do you react?

LO.9

Determine the proper tax treatment upon the disposition of a passive activity.

Dispositions of Passive Interests

Recall from an earlier discussion that if a taxpayer disposes of an entire interest in a passive activity, any suspended losses (and in certain cases, suspended credits) may be utilized when calculating the final economic gain or loss on the investment. In addition, if a loss ultimately results, that loss can offset other types of income. However, the consequences may differ if the activity is disposed of in a transaction that is other than a fully taxable transaction. The following discusses the treatment of suspended passive losses in other types of dispositions.

Disposition of a Passive Activity at Death. A transfer of a taxpayer's interest in an activity by reason of the taxpayer's death results in suspended losses being allowed (to the decedent) to the extent they exceed the amount, if any, of the step-up in basis allowed.[33] Suspended losses are lost to the extent of the amount of the basis increase. The losses allowed generally are reported on the final return of the deceased taxpayer.

EXAMPLE 44

A taxpayer dies with passive activity property having an adjusted basis of $40,000, suspended losses of $10,000, and a fair market value at the date of the decedent's death of $75,000. The increase (i.e., step-up) in basis (see Chapter 14) is $35,000 (fair market value at date of death in excess of adjusted basis). None of the $10,000 suspended loss is deductible by either the decedent or the beneficiary. The suspended losses ($10,000) are lost because they do not exceed the step-up in basis ($35,000). ∎

EXAMPLE 45

A taxpayer dies with passive activity property having an adjusted basis of $40,000, suspended losses of $10,000, and a fair market value at the date of the decedent's death of $47,000. Since the step-up in basis is only $7,000 ($47,000 − $40,000), the suspended losses allowed are limited to $3,000 ($10,000 suspended loss at time of death − $7,000 increase in basis). The $3,000 loss available to the decedent is reported on the decedent's final income tax return. ∎

---

[33]§ 469(g)(2).

ETHICAL and EQUITABLE *Considerations*

HOW MUCH LATITUDE CAN A TAXPAYER TAKE IN SETTING FAIR MARKET VALUE?

Lucien dies in the current year holding an interest in a limited partnership that owns and operates an apartment complex. Lucien's interest includes a $10,000 suspended passive activity loss that he had not been able to claim. Ron, the executor of Lucien's estate, is not aware of any recent qualified appraisals or sales that would help determine the fair market value of the limited partnership interest. Ron decides not to hire a qualified appraiser to determine this value because Lucien's estate is not large enough to be subject to the Fed-

eral estate tax. Lucien's records reflect a predeath basis in the interest of $65,000.

The partnership's bookkeeper has a "gut feeling" that the partnership interest is worth anywhere between $65,000 and $80,000. This is good news to Ron, and based on her "guesstimate," Ron sets the value at $65,000.

What is Ron trying to accomplish in arriving at this valuation? What ethical and equitable issues arise?

Disposition of a Passive Activity by Gift. In a disposition of a taxpayer's interest in a passive activity by gift, the suspended losses are added to the basis of the property.[34]

EXAMPLE 46

A taxpayer makes a gift of passive activity property having an adjusted basis of $40,000, suspended losses of $10,000, and a fair market value at the date of the gift of $100,000. The taxpayer cannot deduct the suspended losses in the year of the disposition. However, the suspended losses transfer with the property and are added to the adjusted basis of the property in the hands of the donee. ■

When a passive activity is transferred by gift, the suspended losses become permanently nondeductible to both the donor and the donee. Nonetheless, a tax *benefit* may be available to the donee for another reason. Due to the increase in the property's basis, greater depreciation deductions can result, and there will be less gain (or more loss) on a subsequent sale of the property. The side benefits of increased basis do not materialize if the recipient is a charity, as such organizations generally are not subject to income taxation.

Installment Sale of a Passive Activity. An installment sale of a taxpayer's entire interest in a passive activity triggers the recognition of the suspended losses.[35] The losses are allowed in each year of the installment obligation in the ratio that the gain recognized in each year bears to the total gain on the sale.

EXAMPLE 47

Stan sells his entire interest in a passive activity for $100,000. His adjusted basis in the property is $60,000. If he uses the installment method, his gross profit ratio is 40% ($40,000/ $100,000). If Stan receives a $20,000 down payment, he will recognize a gain of $8,000 (40% of $20,000). If the activity has a suspended loss of $25,000, Stan will deduct $5,000 [($8,000 ÷ $40,000) × $25,000] of the suspended loss in the first year. ■

Nontaxable Exchange of a Passive Activity. In a nontaxable exchange of a passive investment, the taxpayer keeps the suspended losses, which generally become deductible when the acquired property is sold. If the activity of the old and the new property is the same, suspended losses can be used before the activity's disposition.

---

[34]§ 469(j)(6).   [35]§ 469(g)(3).

CONCEPT SUMMARY   11–2

Passive Activity Loss Rules: General Concepts

What is the fundamental passive activity rule?	Passive activity losses may be deducted only against passive activity income and gains. Losses not allowed are suspended and used in future years.
Who is subject to the passive activity rules?	Individuals. Estates. Trusts. Personal service corporations. Closely held C corporations.
What is a passive activity?	Trade or business or income-producing activity in which the taxpayer does not materially participate during the year, or rental activities, subject to certain exceptions, regardless of the taxpayer's level of participation.
What is an activity?	One or more trade or business or rental activities that comprise an appropriate economic unit.
How is an appropriate economic unit determined?	Based on a reasonable application of the relevant facts and circumstances.
What is material participation?	In general, the taxpayer participates on a regular, continuous, and substantial basis. More specifically, when the taxpayer meets the conditions of one of the seven tests provided in the Regulations.
What is a rental activity?	In general, an activity where payments are received for the use of tangible property. More specifically, a rental activity that does *not* meet one of the six exceptions provided in the Regulations. Special rules apply to rental real estate.

E X A M P L E   4 8

A taxpayer exchanges a duplex for a limited partnership interest in a § 721 nonrecognition transaction (see Chapter 20 for details). The suspended losses from the duplex are not deductible until the limited partnership interest is sold. Two different activities exist: a real estate rental activity and a limited partnership activity. If the taxpayer had continued to own the duplex and the duplex had future taxable income, the suspended losses would have become deductible before the time of disposition. ■

E X A M P L E   4 9

In a § 1031 nontaxable exchange (see Chapter 15 for details), a taxpayer exchanges a duplex for an apartment building. The suspended losses from the duplex are deductible against future taxable income of the apartment building, because the same activity exists. ■

LO.10

Identify restrictions placed on the deductibility of other investor losses and deductions, including those that apply to investment interest.

Investment Interest

Taxpayers frequently borrow funds that they use to acquire investment assets. When the interest expense is large relative to the income from the investments, substantial tax benefits could result. Congress has therefore limited the deductibility of interest on funds borrowed for the purpose of purchasing or continuing to hold investment property. **Investment interest** expense is *now* limited to net investment income for the year.

Investment income is gross income from interest, dividends (see below), annuities, and royalties not derived in the ordinary course of a trade or business. However, income from a passive activity and income from a real estate activity in which the taxpayer actively participates are not included in investment income.

The following types of income are not included in investment income unless the taxpayer *elects* to do so.

- Net capital gain attributable to the disposition of (1) property producing the types of income just enumerated or (2) property held for investment purposes.
- Qualified dividends that are taxed at the same marginal rate that is applicable to a net capital gain.

A taxpayer may include net capital gain and qualifying dividends as investment income by electing to do so on Form 4952. The election is available only if the taxpayer agrees to reduce amounts qualifying for the 15 percent (0 percent for low-income taxpayers) rates that otherwise apply to net capital gain (see Chapter 16) and qualifying dividends (refer to Chapter 4) by an equivalent amount.

EXAMPLE 50

Terry incurred $13,000 of interest expense related to her investments during the year. Her investment income included $4,000 of interest, $2,000 of qualifying dividends, and a $5,000 net capital gain on the sale of investment securities. If Terry does not make the election to include the net capital gain and qualified dividends in investment income, her investment income for purposes of computing the investment income limitation is $4,000 (interest income). If she does make the election, her investment income is $11,000 ($4,000 interest + $2,000 qualifying dividends + $5,000 net capital gain). ■

Net investment income is the excess of investment income over investment expenses. Investment expenses are those deductible expenses directly connected with the production of investment income. Investment expenses *do not* include interest expense. When investment expenses fall into the category of miscellaneous itemized deductions that are subject to the 2 percent-of-AGI floor (refer to Chapter 10), some may not enter into the calculation of net investment income because of the floor.

EXAMPLE 51

Gina has AGI of $80,000, which includes qualified dividends of $15,000 and interest income of $3,000. Besides investment interest expense, she paid $3,000 of city ad valorem property tax on stocks and bonds and had the following miscellaneous itemized expenses:

Safe deposit box rental (to hold investment securities)	$ 120
Investment counsel fee	1,200
Unreimbursed business travel	850
Uniforms	600
Total miscellaneous itemized expenses	$2,770

Before Gina can determine her investment expenses for purposes of calculating net investment income, those miscellaneous expenses that are not investment expenses are disallowed before any investment expenses are disallowed under the 2%-of-AGI floor. This is accomplished by selecting the *lesser* of the following:

1. The amount of investment expenses included in the total of miscellaneous itemized deductions subject to the 2%-of-AGI floor.
2. The amount of miscellaneous expenses deductible after the 2%-of-AGI rule is applied.

The amount under item 1 is $1,320 [$120 (safe deposit box rental) + $1,200 (investment counsel fee)]. The item 2 amount is $1,170 [$2,770 (total of miscellaneous expenses) − $1,600 (2% of $80,000 AGI)].

Then, Gina's investment expenses are calculated as follows:

Deductible miscellaneous deductions investment expense (the lesser of item 1 or item 2)	$1,170
Plus: Ad valorem tax on investment property	3,000
Total investment expenses	$4,170

| TAX *in the News* | **PROVING REAL ESTATE PROFESSIONAL STATUS CAN BE A BIG DEAL** |

If a taxpayer fits the definition of a "real estate professional," rental losses are not limited by the passive loss rules. This provision can have a huge impact because it enables the current deduction of losses that otherwise would not be allowed. Furthermore, the tax saving resulting from an immediate deduction can boost the taxpayer's financial return from the activity. Just because a taxpayer looks, acts, and walks like a real estate professional, however, does not necessarily mean that the IRS will readily accept the characterization.

The IRS apparently is devoting more time to examining real estate activities because this is an area where taxpayers are regularly underreporting income (and overstating deductions). Consequently, some real estate professionals believe they are mistakenly being targeted by the IRS in its effort to expose investors who are posing as real estate professionals. To be prepared for this possibility, therefore, wise real estate professionals should be ready to fully document that the real estate business is their livelihood rather than an investment activity pursued on the side.

Source: *Adapted from Kemba J. Dunham, "Real-Estate Professionals Say IRS Snares Them by Mistake," Wall Street Journal, February 28, 2007, p. B4.*

Gina elects to include the qualified dividends in investment income. Gina's net investment income is $13,830 ($18,000 investment income − $4,170 investment expenses). ■

After net investment income is determined, deductible investment interest expense can be calculated.

EXAMPLE 52

Adam is an attorney employed by a law firm. His investment activities for the year are as follows:

Net investment income	$30,000
Investment interest expense	44,000

Adam's investment interest deduction is $30,000. ■

The amount of investment interest disallowed is carried over to future years. In Example 52, therefore, the amount that is carried over to the following year is $14,000 ($44,000 investment interest expense − $30,000 allowed). No limit is placed on the length of the carryover period. The investment interest expense deduction is determined by completing Form 4952.

Other Investment Losses

The investment activities summarized below are discussed elsewhere in this text (see the references provided).

- Sales of securities held as investments for less than basis yield capital losses. These losses can offset capital gains. In the case of individual taxpayers, excess losses are applied against ordinary income up to $3,000 (§ 1211). Any remaining excess capital losses are carried over for use in future years (§ 1212). See Chapter 16 for additional discussion.
- Securities held as an investment that become worthless produce capital losses. The losses are usually long term since they are treated as occurring on the last day of the year in which the securities become worthless [(§ 165(g)(1)]. Because the securities must be completely worthless, determining the year when this takes place often is difficult. See Chapter 7 for additional discussion.
- Losses on small business stock (i.e., stock that qualifies under § 1244) are treated as ordinary losses up to a maximum of $100,000. Thus, the limitations

placed on capital losses (see above) are avoided. See Chapter 7 for additional discussion.

- As discussed in Chapter 6, vacation homes that are rented for part of the year may generate investment losses depending on the extent of the rental period as compared to time devoted to personal use (§ 280A). If sufficient rental activity takes place, the facility may be treated as rental property. As such, any losses could be subject to the passive loss rules. See the discussion earlier in this chapter.

- When an activity is classified as a hobby, any losses resulting are limited to the income from the activity [§ 183(b)(2)]. If the activity is not a hobby (i.e., a profit motive controls), however, full deduction of the losses is allowed [§§ 162 and 212(2)]. See the relevant discussion of hobby losses in Chapter 6.

Utilizing Passive Losses

Perhaps the biggest challenge individuals face with the passive loss rules is to recognize the potential impact of the rules and then to structure their affairs to minimize this impact. Taxpayers who have passive activity losses (PALs) should adopt a strategy of generating passive activity income that can be sheltered by existing passive losses. One approach is to buy an interest in a passive activity that is generating income (referred to as passive income generators, or PIGs). Then the PAL can offset income from the PIG. From a tax perspective, it would be foolish to buy a loss-generating passive activity unless one has other passive income to shelter or the activity is rental real estate that can qualify for the $25,000 exception or the exception available to real estate professionals.

If a taxpayer does invest in an activity that produces losses subject to the passive loss rules, the following strategies may help to minimize the loss of current deductions:

- If money is borrowed to finance the purchase of a passive activity, the associated interest expense is generally treated as part of any passive loss. Consequently, by increasing the amount of cash used to purchase the passive investment, the investor will need less debt and will incur less interest expense. By incurring less interest expense, a possible suspended passive loss deduction is reduced.

- If the investor does not have sufficient cash readily available for the larger down payment, it can be obtained by borrowing against the equity in his or her personal residence. The interest expense on such debt will be deductible under the qualified residence interest provisions (see Chapter 10) and will not be subject to the passive loss limitations. Thus, the taxpayer avoids the passive loss limitation and secures a currently deductible interest expense.

Often unusable passive losses accumulate and provide no current tax benefit because the taxpayer has no passive income. When the taxpayer disposes of the entire interest in a passive activity, however, any suspended losses from that activity are used to reduce the taxable gain. If any taxable gain still remains, it can be offset by losses from other passive activities. As a result, the taxpayer should carefully select the year in which a passive activity is disposed of. It is to the taxpayer's advantage to wait until sufficient passive losses have accumulated to offset any gain recognized on the asset's disposition.

LO.11

Suggest tax planning strategies to minimize the effect of the passive loss limitations.

TAX PLANNING
Considerations

EXAMPLE 53

Bill, a calendar year taxpayer, owns interests in two passive activities: Activity A, which he plans to sell in December of this year at a gain of $100,000; and Activity B, which he plans to keep indefinitely. Current and suspended losses associated with Activity B total $60,000, and Bill expects losses from the activity to be $40,000 next year. If Bill sells Activity A this year, the $100,000 gain can be offset by the current and suspended losses of $60,000 from Activity B, producing a net taxable gain of $40,000. However, if Bill delays the sale of Activity A until January of next year, the $100,000 gain will be fully offset by the $100,000 of losses generated by Activity B ($60,000 current and prior losses + $40,000 next year's loss). Consequently, by postponing the sale by one month, he could avoid recognizing $40,000 of gain that would otherwise result. ■

Taxpayers with passive losses should consider the level of their involvement in all other trades or businesses in which they have an interest. If they show that they do not materially participate in a profitable activity, the activity becomes a passive activity. Any income generated by the profitable business then could be sheltered by current and suspended passive losses. Family partnerships in which certain members do not materially participate would qualify. The silent partner in any general partnership engaged in a trade or business would also qualify.

EXAMPLE 54

Gail has an investment in a limited partnership that produces annual passive losses of approximately $25,000. She also owns a newly acquired interest in a convenience store where she works. Her share of the store's income is $35,000. If she works enough to be classified as a material participant, her $35,000 share of income is treated as active income. This results in $35,000 being subject to tax every year, while her $25,000 loss is suspended. However, if Gail reduces her involvement at the store so that she is not a material participant, the $35,000 of income receives passive treatment. Consequently, the $35,000 of income can be offset by the $25,000 passive loss, resulting in only $10,000 being subject to tax. Thus, by reducing her involvement, Gail ensures that the income from the profitable trade or business receives passive treatment and can then be used to absorb passive losses from other passive activities. ■

As this chapter has shown, the passive loss rules can have a dramatic effect on a taxpayer's ability to claim passive losses currently. As a result, it is important to keep accurate records of all sources of income and losses, particularly any suspended passive losses and credits and the activities to which they relate, so that their potential tax benefit will not be lost.

Finally, because of the restrictive nature of the passive activity loss rules, it may be advantageous for a taxpayer to use a vacation home enough to convert it to a second residence. This would enable all of the qualified interest and real estate taxes to be deducted without limitation. However, this strategy would lead to the loss of other deductions, such as repairs, maintenance, and insurance. See Examples 24 and 27 and the related discussion in Chapter 6.

KEY TERMS

Active income, 11–5	Investment interest, 11–24	Portfolio income, 11–5
At-risk limitation, 11–3	Material participation, 11–13	Rental activity, 11–16
Closely held corporation, 11–9	Net investment income, 11–25	Significant participation activity, 11–14
Extraordinary personal services, 11–17	Passive loss, 11–3	Tax shelters, 11–2
Investment income, 11–24	Personal service corporations, 11–9	

PROBLEM MATERIALS

DISCUSSION QUESTIONS

1. Identify two provisions designed to limit the tax benefits that a taxpayer may obtain from a tax shelter investment. Describe, in general, how these rules reduce or defer the recognition of tax losses.

2. Alice invested $100,000 for a 25% interest in a partnership in which she is not a material participant. The partnership borrowed $200,000 from a bank on a recourse loan and used the proceeds to acquire a building. What is Alice's at-risk amount?

3. List some events that increase and decrease an investor's at-risk amount. What are some strategies that a taxpayer can employ to increase the at-risk amount in order to claim a higher deduction for losses?

4. Roberto invested $18,000 in a chicken-production operation. Using nonrecourse notes, the business purchases $120,000 worth of grain to feed the chickens. If Roberto's share of the expense is $26,000, how much can he deduct?

5. Explain the meaning of the terms *active income, portfolio income,* and *passive income.*

6. Manuel owns an interest in an activity that produces a $100,000 loss during the year. Would he generally prefer to have the activity classified as active or passive? Discuss.

7. Kim owns an interest in an activity that produces $100,000 of income during the year. Would Kim prefer to have the activity classified as active or passive? Discuss.

8. Felicia owns a passive activity acquired several years ago that has incurred losses since its acquisition. This is the only passive activity she has ever owned. How will these passive losses affect Felicia's tax when she disposes of the activity?

9. Upon a taxable disposition of a passive activity, the taxpayer can utilize any suspended losses and credits related to that activity. Do you agree? Explain.

10. Discuss whether the passive loss rules apply to the following: individuals, closely held C corporations, S corporations, partnerships, and personal service corporations.

11. New-Tech Services, Inc., is owned by four engineers, all of whom work full-time for the corporation. The corporation has eight other full-time employees, all on the clerical staff. New-Tech provides consulting services to inventors. The corporation has invested in a passive activity that produces a $60,000 loss this year. Can New-Tech deduct the loss in the current year? Explain.

12. Gray Corporation has $100,000 of active income and a $55,000 passive loss. Under what circumstances is Gray prohibited from deducting the loss? Allowed to deduct the loss?

13. Discuss what constitutes a passive activity.

14. Under what circumstances may the IRS regroup activities in a different way than the taxpayer?

15. What is the significance of the term *material participation?* Why is the extent of a taxpayer's participation in an activity important in determining whether a loss from the activity is deductible or nondeductible?

16. Why did the IRS adopt the more-than-500-hour standard for material participation?

17. Keith, a physician, operates a separate business that he acquired nine years ago. If he participates 90 hours in the business and it incurs a loss of $20,000, under what circumstances can Keith claim an active loss?

18. Suzanne owns interests in a bagel shop, a lawn and garden store, and a convenience store. Several full-time employees work at each of the enterprises. As of the end of November of the current year, Suzanne has worked 150 hours in the bagel shop,

Decision Making

250 hours at the lawn and garden store, and 70 hours at the convenience store. In reviewing her financial records, you learn that she has no passive investments that are generating income and that she expects these three ventures collectively to produce a loss. What recommendation would you offer Suzanne as she plans her activities for the remainder of the year?

Issue ID

19. Rita retired from public accounting after a long and successful career of 45 years. As part of her retirement package, she continues to share in the profits and losses of the firm, albeit at a lower rate than when she was working full-time. Because Rita wants to stay busy during her retirement years, she has invested and works in a local hardware business, operated as a partnership. Unfortunately, the business has recently gone through a slump and has not been generating profits. Identify relevant tax issues for Rita.

20. Some types of work are counted in applying the material participation standards, and some types are not counted. Discuss and give examples of each type.

Issue ID

21. Last year, Alan's accountant informed him that he could not claim any of his passive activity losses on his income tax return because of his lack of material participation. To circumvent the tax problem this year, Alan tells his wife that she may have to put in some time at the various businesses. Identify the tax issues that Alan faces.

22. Kevin, a limited partner in Zelcova Gardens, is informed that his portion of the entity's current loss is $10,000. As a limited partner, can Kevin assume that his share of the partnership loss is a passive loss?

23. What are *significant personal services*, and what role do they play in determining whether a rental activity is treated as a passive activity?

24. How is *passive activity* defined in the Code, and what aspects of the definition have been clarified by final or Temporary Regulations?

25. What are *extraordinary personal services*, and why are they important in determining whether a rental activity is treated as a passive activity?

26. Hilda incurs a loss of $60,000 on a real estate rental activity during the current year. Under what circumstances can Hilda treat the entire loss as nonpassive?

Issue ID

27. Since his college days, Charles has developed an entrepreneurial streak. After working in his family's grocery business, he has decided to start several ventures on his own. Even though Charles is independently wealthy, he is looking forward to working in each of the ventures. He plans to "drop in" on the businesses from time to time between personal trips to Europe, the Caribbean, and the South Pacific. As of the end of the year, he has established computer software stores in Dayton, Austin, and Seattle; bagel bakeries in Albany, Athens (Georgia), and Tallahassee; and mountain bike and ski rental shops in small towns in Vermont, West Virginia, Colorado, and California. Identify the tax issues facing Charles.

Issue ID

28. In the current year, David and Debbie Wayland, both successful physicians, made a cash investment for a limited partnership interest in a California berry farm. In addition to the cash obtained from the investors, management borrowed a substantial sum to purchase assets necessary for the farm's operation. The Waylands' investment adviser told them that their share of the tax loss in the first year alone would be in excess of their initial cash investment. This would be followed by several more years of losses. They feel confident that their interest in the berry farm is a sound investment. Identify the tax issues facing the Waylands.

29. Elizabeth owns an interest in a dress shop that has three full-time employees; during the year, she works 450 hours in the shop. Elizabeth also owns an apartment building with no employees in which she works 1,200 hours. Is either activity a passive activity? Explain.

30. Matt owns a small apartment building that generates a loss during the year. Under what circumstances can Matt deduct a loss from the rental activity, and what limitations apply?

31. In connection with passive activities, what is a *deduction equivalent*, and how is it computed?

32. Betty and Steve plan to use some of an inheritance for a beach-related investment. They identify two possibilities that seem worthwhile. First, they would purchase a beach cottage and use it for both personal and rental purposes. Second, they would pool their money with Steve's brother and purchase several cottages. One of the cottages would be held for personal use, while the others would be held for rental use. Identify the tax issues facing Betty and Steve.

Issue ID

PROBLEMS

33. In 2007, Fred invested $50,000 in a general partnership. Fred's interest is not considered to be a passive activity. If his share of the partnership losses is $35,000 in 2007 and $25,000 in 2008, how much can he deduct in each year?

34. In the current year, Bill Parker (54 Oak Drive, St. Paul, MN 55162) is considering making an investment of $60,000 in Best Choice Partnership. The prospectus provided by Bill's broker indicates that the partnership investment is not a passive activity and that Bill's share of the entity's loss in the current year will likely be $40,000, while his share of the partnership loss next year will probably be $25,000. Write a letter to Bill in which you indicate how the losses would be treated for tax purposes in the current and next years.

Communications

35. Amanda wishes to invest $40,000 in a relatively safe venture and has discovered two alternatives that would produce the following reportable ordinary income and loss over the next three years:

Decision Making

Year	Alternative 1 Income (Loss)	Alternative 2 Income (Loss)
1	($ 24,000)	($48,000)
2	(24,000)	32,000
3	72,000	40,000

She is interested in the after-tax effects of these alternatives over a three-year horizon. Assume that Amanda's investment portfolio produces sufficient passive income to offset any potential passive loss that may arise from these alternatives, that her cost of capital is 8% (the present value factors are 0.92593, 0.85734, and 0.79383), that she is in the 25% tax bracket, that each investment alternative possesses equal growth potential, and that each alternative exposes her to comparable financial risk. In addition, assume that in the loss years for each alternative, there is no cash flow from or to the investment (i.e., the loss is due to depreciation), while in those years when the income is positive, cash flows to Amanda equal the amount of the income. Based on these facts, compute the present value of these two investment alternatives and determine which option Amanda should choose.

36. Dorothy acquired passive Activity A in January 2003 and Activity B in September 2004. Through 2006, Activity A was profitable, but it produced losses of $200,000 in 2007 and $100,000 in 2008. Dorothy has passive income from Activity B of $20,000 in 2007 and $40,000 in 2008. After offsetting passive income, how much of the net losses may she deduct?

37. A number of years ago, Kay acquired an interest in a partnership in which she is not a material participant. Kay's basis in her partnership interest at the beginning of 2007 is $40,000. Kay's share of the partnership loss is $35,000 in 2007, while her share of the partnership income is $15,000 in 2008. How much can Kay deduct in 2007 and 2008?

38. Bob, an attorney, earns $200,000 from his law practice in the current year. He receives $45,000 in dividends and interest during the year. In addition, he incurs a loss of $50,000 from an investment in a passive activity acquired three years ago. What is Bob's net income for the current year after considering the passive investment?

39. Emily has $100,000 that she wishes to invest and is considering the following two options:

Decision Making

- Option A: Investment in Redbird Mutual Fund, which is expected to produce interest income of $8,000 per year.
- Option B: Investment in Cardinal Limited Partnership (buys, sells, and operates wine vineyards). Emily's share of the partnership's ordinary income and loss over the next three years would be:

Year	Income (Loss)
1	($ 8,000)
2	(2,000)
3	34,000

Emily is interested in the after-tax effects of these alternatives over a three-year horizon. Assume that Emily's investment portfolio produces ample passive income to offset any passive losses that may be generated. Her cost of capital is 8% (the present value factors are 0.92593, 0.85734, and 0.79383), and she is in the 28% tax bracket. The two investment alternatives possess equal growth potential and comparable financial risk. Based on these facts, compute the present value of these two investment alternatives and determine which option Emily should choose.

40. Ray acquired an activity several years ago, and in the current year, it generated a loss of $50,000. Ray has AGI of $140,000 before considering the loss from the activity. If the activity is a bakery and Ray is not a material participant, what is his AGI?

Decision Making

41. Wade owns two passive investments, Activity A and Activity B. He plans to dispose of Activity A, either in the current year or next year. Celene has offered to buy Activity A this year for an amount that would produce a taxable passive gain to Wade of $100,000. However, if the sale, for whatever reason, is not made to Celene, Wade feels that he could find a buyer who would pay about $5,000 less than Celene. Passive losses and gains generated (and expected to be generated) by Activity B follow:

Two years ago	($35,000)
Last year	(35,000)
This year	(5,000)
Next year	(20,000)
Future years	Minimal profits

All of Activity B's losses are suspended. Should Wade close the sale of Activity A with Celene this year, or should he wait until next year and sell to another buyer? Wade is in the 35% tax bracket.

42. Saundra has investments in four passive activity partnerships purchased several years ago. Last year, the income and losses were as follows:

Activity	Income (Loss)
A	$ 30,000
B	(30,000)
C	(15,000)
D	(5,000)

In the current year, she sold her interest in Activity D for a $10,000 gain. Activity D, which had been profitable until last year, had a current loss of $1,500. How will the sale of Activity D affect Saundra's taxable income in the current year?

43. Leon sells his interest in a passive activity for $100,000. Determine the tax effect of the sale based on each of the following independent facts:
   a. Adjusted basis in this investment is $35,000. Losses from prior years that were not deductible due to the passive loss restrictions total $40,000.
   b. Adjusted basis in this investment is $75,000. Losses from prior years that were not deductible due to the passive loss restrictions total $40,000.

c.   Adjusted basis in this investment is $75,000. Losses from prior years that were not deductible due to the passive loss restrictions total $40,000. In addition, suspended credits total $10,000.

44. In the current year, White, Inc., earns $400,000 from operations and receives $36,000 in dividends and interest on various portfolio investments. White also pays $150,000 to acquire a 20% interest in a passive activity that produces a $200,000 loss.
   a.   Assuming White is a personal service corporation, how will these transactions affect its taxable income?
   b.   Same as (a), except that White is closely held but not a personal service corporation.

45. Green Corporation is closely held and not a personal service corporation. It earns active income of $50,000 and dividend income of $60,000 in the current year. In addition, Green incurs a loss of $80,000 from an investment in a passive activity acquired last year. What is Green's taxable income for the current year after considering the passive investment?

46. Carol Schneider (123 Baskerville Mill Road, Jamison, PA 18929) is trying to decide how to invest a $50,000 inheritance. One option is to make an additional $50,000 investment in Rocky Road Adventures in which she has an at-risk basis of $0, suspended losses under the at-risk rules of $28,000, and suspended passive losses of $2,000. If Carol makes this investment, her share of the expected profits this year would be $30,000. If her investment stays the same, her share of profits from Rocky Road Adventures would be $4,000. Another option is to invest $50,000 as a limited partner in the Ragged Mountain Berry Farm; this investment would produce passive income of $33,000. Write a letter to Carol to review the tax consequences of each alternative. Carol is in the 35% tax bracket.

Decision Making

Communications

47. Last year, Juan, a real estate developer, purchased 25 acres of farmland on the outskirts of town for $100,000. He expects that the land's value will appreciate rapidly as the town expands in that direction. Since the property was recently reappraised at $115,000, some of the appreciation has already taken place. To enhance his return from the investment, Juan decides he will begin renting the land to a local farmer. He has determined that a fair rent would be at least $1,500 but no more than $3,500 per year. Juan also has an interest in a passive activity that generates a $2,800 loss annually. How do the passive loss rules affect Juan's decision on how much rent to charge for the farmland?

Decision Making

48. The end of the year is approaching, and Maxine has begun to focus on ways of minimizing her income tax liability. Several years ago, she purchased an investment in Teal Limited Partnership, which is subject to both the at-risk and the passive activity loss rules. (Last year, Maxine sold a different investment that was subject to these rules but produced passive income.) She believes that her investment in Teal has good long-term economic prospects. However, it has been generating tax losses for several years in a row. In fact, when she was discussing last year's income tax return with her tax accountant, he said that unless "things change" with respect to her investments, she would not be able to deduct losses this year.
   a.   What was the accountant referring to in his comment?
   b.   You learn that Maxine's current at-risk basis in her investment is $1,000 and her share of the current loss is expected to be $13,000. Based on these facts, how will her loss be treated?
   c.   After reviewing her situation, Maxine's financial adviser suggests that she invest at least an additional $12,000 in Teal in order to ensure a full loss deduction in the current year. How do you react to his suggestion?
   d.   What would you suggest Maxine consider as she attempts to maximize her current-year deductible loss?

Decision Making

49. A number of years ago, Lee acquired a 20% interest in the BlueSky Partnership for $60,000. The partnership was profitable through 2007, and Lee's amount at risk in the partnership interest was $120,000 at the beginning of 2008. BlueSky incurred a loss of $400,000 in 2008 and reported income of $200,000 in 2009. Assuming Lee is not a material participant, how much of his loss from BlueSky Partnership is deductible in 2008 and 2009?

50. Ann acquired an activity four years ago. The loss from the activity is $50,000 in the current year (at-risk basis of $40,000 as of the beginning of the year). Without considering the loss from the activity, she has AGI of $140,000. If the activity is a convenience store and Ann is a material participant, what is her AGI after considering this activity?

51. Jonathan, a physician, earns $200,000 from his practice. He also receives $18,000 in dividends and interest on various portfolio investments. During the year, he pays $45,000 to acquire a 20% interest in a partnership that produces a $300,000 loss. Compute Jonathan's AGI, assuming that:
    a. He does not participate in the operations of the partnership.
    b. He is a material participant in the operations of the partnership.

52. Five years ago, Gerald invested $150,000 in a passive activity, his sole investment venture. On January 1, 2007, his amount at risk in the activity was $30,000. His shares of the income and losses were as follows:

Year	Income (Loss)
2007	($ 40,000)
2008	(30,000)
2009	50,000

    How much can Gerald deduct in 2007 and 2008? What is his taxable income from the activity in 2009? Consider the at-risk rules as well as the passive loss rules.

Communications

53. Several years ago, Benny Jackson (125 Hill Street, Charleston, WV 25301) acquired an apartment building that currently generates a loss of $60,000. Benny's AGI is $130,000 before considering the loss. The apartment building is in an exclusive part of the city, and Benny is an active participant. Write a letter to Benny explaining what effect the loss will have on his AGI.

54. Several years ago, Rachel acquired an apartment building that currently generates a loss of $35,000. She has AGI of $120,000 before considering the loss. If Rachel is not an active participant in the activity, what is the effect of the loss on her AGI?

Decision Making

55. Bonnie and Adam are married with no dependents and live in New Hampshire (not a community property state). Since Adam has large medical expenses, they seek your advice about filing separately to save taxes. Their income and expenses for 2008 are as follows:

Bonnie's salary	$ 42,500
Adam's salary	26,000
Interest income (joint)	1,900
Rental loss from actively managed rental property	(22,000)
Adam's unreimbursed medical expenses	8,500
All other itemized deductions:*	
Bonnie	9,000
Adam	3,400

    *None subject to limitations

    Determine whether Bonnie and Adam should file jointly or separately for 2008.

Decision Making

56. Mary and Charles have owned a beach cottage on the New Jersey shore for several years and have always used it as a family retreat. When they acquired the property, they had no intentions of renting it. Because family circumstances have changed, they are considering using the cottage for only two weeks a year and renting it for the remainder of the year. Their AGI approximates $80,000 per year, and they are in the 30% tax bracket (combined Federal and state). Interest and real estate taxes total $8,000 per year and are expected to continue at this level in the foreseeable future. If Mary and Charles rent the property, their *incremental* revenue and expenses are projected to be:

Rent income	$ 20,000
Rental commissions	(3,000)
Maintenance expenses	(8,000)
Depreciation expense	(10,000)

If the cottage is converted to rental property, they plan to be actively involved in key rental and maintenance decisions. Given the tax effects of converting the property to rental use, would the cash flow from renting the property be enough to meet the $12,000 annual mortgage payment?

57. During the current year, Gene performs services as follows: 1,800 hours as a CPA in his tax practice and 50 hours in an apartment leasing operation in which he has a 15% interest. Because of his oversight duties, Gene is considered to be an active participant. He expects that his share of the loss realized from the apartment leasing operation will be $30,000 while his tax practice will show a profit of approximately $80,000. Gene is single and has no other income besides that stated above. Discuss the character of the income and losses generated by these activities.

58. Ida, who has AGI of $80,000 before considering rental activities, is active in three separate real estate rental activities and is in the 28% tax bracket. She has $12,000 of losses from Activity A, $18,000 of losses from Activity B, and income of $10,000 from Activity C. She also has $2,100 of tax credits from Activity A. Calculate her deductions and credits allowed and the suspended losses and credits.

59. Ella has $105,000 of losses from a real estate rental activity in which she actively participates. She has other rental income of $25,000 and other passive income of $32,000. How much rental loss can Ella deduct against active and portfolio income (ignoring the at-risk rules)? Does she have any suspended losses to carry over?

60. At death, Lucile owns an interest in a passive activity property (adjusted basis of $160,000, suspended losses of $16,000, and fair market value of $170,000). What can be deducted on Lucile's final income tax return?

61. In the current year, Abe gives an interest in a passive activity to his daughter, Andrea. The value of the interest at the date of the gift is $25,000, and its adjusted basis to Abe is $13,000. During the time that Abe owned the investment, losses of $3,000 could not be deducted because of the passive loss limitations. What is the tax treatment of the suspended passive activity losses to Abe and Andrea?

62. Tonya sells a passive activity in the current year for $150,000. Her adjusted basis in the activity is $50,000, and she uses the installment method of reporting the gain. The activity has suspended losses of $12,000. Tonya receives $60,000 in the year of sale. What is her gain? How much of the suspended losses can she deduct?

63. In 2008, Irina Gray incurs $29,250 of interest expense related to her investments. Her investment income includes $7,000 of interest, $5,500 of qualified dividends, and a $12,750 net capital gain on the sale of securities. Irina asks you to compute the amount of her deduction for investment interest, taking into consideration any options she might have. In addition, she wants your suggestions as to any tax planning alternatives that are available. Write a letter to her that contains your advice. Irina lives at 432 Clinton Circle, Rochester, NY 14604.

Decision Making

Communications

64. Helen borrowed $300,000 to acquire a parcel of land to be held for investment purposes. During 2008, she paid interest of $30,000 on the loan. She had AGI of $75,000 for the year. Other items related to Helen's investments include the following:

Investment income	$21,150
Long-term capital gain on sale of stock	8,250
Investment counsel fees	2,250

Helen is unmarried and elects to itemize her deductions. She has no miscellaneous itemized deductions other than the investment counsel fees.
a.   Determine Helen's investment interest deduction for 2008.
b.   Discuss the treatment of the portion of Helen's investment interest that is disallowed in 2008.

RESEARCH PROBLEMS

Note: Solutions to Research Problems can be prepared by using the **RIA Checkpoint®
Student Edition** online research product, which is available to accompany this text. It is
also possible to prepare solutions to the Research Problems by using tax research materials found in a standard tax library.

Research Problem 1.   George and Judy Cash own a 30-foot yacht that is moored at Oregon
Inlet on the Outer Banks of North Carolina. The yacht is offered for rent to tourists
during March through November every year. George and Judy live too far away to be
involved in the yacht's routine operation and maintenance. They are, however, able to
perform certain periodic tasks, such as cleaning and winterizing it. Routine daily
management, operating, and chartering responsibilities have been contracted to
"Captain Mac." George and Judy are able to document spending 120 hours on the yacht
chartering activities during the year. Determine how any losses resulting from the activity
are treated under the passive activity loss rules.

Research Problem 2.   Carol is a successful physician who owns 100% of her incorporated
medical practice. She and her husband, Dick, are considering the purchase of a
commercial office building located near the local community hospital. If they purchase the
building, Carol would move her medical practice to the new location. The practice would
rent the building for an arm's length price. The rent income that results will be available to
absorb passive losses generated by other passive activities. The net effect of absorbing the
passive losses is a reduction in their income tax liability. Will Carol and Dick's plan work?

Communications

Research Problem 3.   David Drayer (2632 Holkham Drive, Lewisburg, PA 17837) is the lead
partner in a local accounting firm whose practice consists of tax consulting and compliance.
The firm also serves clients by providing write-up and payroll processing services. As his firm
has grown, David has developed various ways to build its business prospects.

David and his wife, Judy, created DJ Partnership to purchase an office building
where David moved his practice. Because the building is larger than what the practice
currently needs, space is rented to other tax practitioners. In addition to providing office
space, the partnership offers professional and administrative services on an exclusive
basis to the tenants. These services include secretarial support, telephone answering
service, tax professionals available for special projects, access to a tax research library,
computer hardware technology, and miscellaneous administrative support. DJ
Partnership considers its primary activity to be providing professional and
administrative services to its tenants rather than being a lessor.

Because of the attractiveness of the services offered to its tenants, the building is fully
leased. In the first year, Judy works full-time at the partnership, and David commits about
550 hours to its affairs. For the first year, the partnership incurs a tax loss of $60,000.
Without considering the impact of the loss, David and Judy's AGI is $175,000. Write a
letter to David in which you provide advice on the deductibility of the $60,000 loss for
Federal income tax purposes. Because David is a professional, feel free to make use of
technical language in your letter.

Partial list of research aids:
Reg. § 1.469–1T(e)(3)(ii).

Research Problem 4.   Ida Ross has decided to purchase a new home in a retirement
community for $400,000. She has $50,000 in cash for the down payment, but needs to
borrow the remaining $350,000 to finance the purchase. Her financial adviser, Marc,
suggests that rather than seeking a conventional mortgage, she should borrow the funds
from State Bank using her portfolio of appreciated securities as collateral. Selling the
securities to generate $350,000 in cash would lead to a substantial tax on the capital gain
recognized. Therefore, a better strategy would be to borrow against her securities and
then claim a deduction for the interest paid on the loan. How do you react to the
financial adviser's strategy?

Partial list of research aids:
Temp.Reg. § 1.163–8T(c).

Use the tax resources of the Internet to address the following questions. Do not restrict your search to the World Wide Web, but include a review of newsgroups and general reference materials, practitioner sites and resources, primary sources of the tax law, chat rooms and discussion groups, and other opportunities.

Internet *Activity*

Research Problem 5. Oil and gas ventures operating as publicly traded partnerships typically attract sophisticated investors who purchase limited partnership interests. Investments in these types of publicly traded partnerships are subject to a restrictive set of passive loss rules. Identify three oil and gas publicly traded partnerships that are currently marketed to new investors, and describe the benefits the promoters claim will result from such investments.

Research Problem 6. Download and print a copy of Form 8582 and its instructions. Use these materials to complete the requirements of Problem 53.

Research Problem 7. Code § 199 (i.e., the domestic production activities deduction) makes reference to § 469. In what context?

PART 4

Special Tax Computation Methods, Payment Procedures, and Tax Credits

Part IV presents several topics that relate to the theme of tax liability determination. The taxpayer must calculate the tax liability in accordance with the basic tax formula and also in accordance with the tax formula for the alternative minimum tax (AMT). The basic tax formula was presented in Part I, and the AMT formula is covered in Part IV. Tax credits reduce the amount of the calculated tax liability. The specific procedures for the timing of the payment of the tax liability are also discussed.

CHAPTER 12
Alternative Minimum Tax

CHAPTER 13
Tax Credits and Payment Procedures

CHAPTER 12

Alternative Minimum Tax

LEARNING OBJECTIVES

After completing Chapter 12, you should be able to:

LO.1
Explain the rationale for the alternative minimum tax (AMT).

LO.2
Understand the formula for computing the AMT for individuals.

LO.3
Identify the adjustments made in calculating the AMT.

LO.4
Identify the tax preferences that are included in calculating the AMT.

LO.5
Apply the formula for computing the AMT and illustrate Form 6251.

LO.6
Describe the role of the AMT credit in the alternative minimum tax structure.

LO.7
Understand the basic features of the corporate AMT.

LO.8
Identify tax planning opportunities to minimize the AMT.

OUTLINE

Individual Alternative Minimum Tax, 12–2
  AMT Formula for Alternative Minimum Taxable
    Income (AMTI), 12–2
  AMT Formula: Other Components, 12–6
  AMT Adjustments, 12–8
  AMT Preferences, 12–20
  Illustration of the AMT Computation, 12–23
  AMT Credit, 12–24
Corporate Alternative Minimum Tax, 12–26
  Repeal of AMT for Small Corporations, 12–26
  AMT Adjustments, 12–27

  Tax Preferences, 12–29
  Exemption Amount, 12–29
  Other Aspects of the AMT, 12–29
Tax Planning Considerations, 12–30
  Responding to Bob and Carol, 12–30
  Avoiding Preferences and Adjustments, 12–30
  Controlling the Timing of Preferences
    and Adjustments, 12–30
  Taking Advantage of the AMT/Regular Tax Rate
    Differential, 12–30

LO.1

Explain the rationale for the alternative minimum tax (AMT).

Bob and Carol are unmarried individuals who work for the same employer and have the same amount of gross income and the same amount of deductions. Bob's tax return is prepared by Adam, and Carol's tax return is prepared by Eve. While discussing their tax liability one day at lunch, Carol is dismayed to learn that she paid $15,000 more in Federal income taxes than Bob did for the tax year. Carol meets with Eve that evening. Eve reviews Carol's tax return and assures her that her tax liability was properly calculated.

The above events raise a number of interesting questions for Bob and Carol that can be answered after completing this chapter. Why didn't Bob and Carol have the same tax liability? Were both tax returns properly prepared? Should Carol consider replacing her tax return preparer Eve with Adam? Is it possible and/or desirable for Carol to file an amended return? Should Bob do anything?

The tax law contains many incentives that are intended to influence the economic and social behavior of taxpayers (refer to Chapter 1). Some taxpayers have been able to take advantage of enough of these incentives to avoid or minimize any liability for Federal income tax. Although these taxpayers were reducing taxes legally, Congress became concerned about the inequity that results when taxpayers with substantial economic incomes can avoid paying any income tax. Such inequity undermines respect for the entire tax system.[1] To attempt to alleviate this inequity, the **alternative minimum tax (AMT)** was enacted as a backup to the regular income tax.

The individual AMT is discussed in the first part of this chapter. The corporate AMT is similar to the individual AMT, but differs in several important ways. Details of the corporate AMT are presented in the last part of the chapter.

Individual Alternative Minimum Tax

LO.2

Understand the formula for computing the AMT for individuals.

AMT Formula for Alternative Minimum Taxable Income (AMTI)

The AMT is separate from, but parallel to, the regular income tax system.[2] Most income and expense items are treated the same way for both regular income tax and AMT purposes. For example, a taxpayer's salary is included in computing taxable income and is also included in alternative minimum taxable income (AMTI). Alimony paid is allowed as a deduction *for* AGI for both regular income tax and AMT purposes. Certain itemized deductions, such as charitable contributions and gambling losses, are allowed for both regular income tax and AMT purposes.

---

[1] *General Explanation of the Tax Reform Act of 1986 ("Blue Book"),* prepared by The Staff of the Joint Committee on Taxation, May 4, 1987, H.R. 3838, 99th Cong., pp. 432–433.

[2] § 55.

TAX *in the News* — THE GROWING TENTACLES OF THE AMT

The AMT exists because of congressional reaction to a report in 1969 that 155 taxpayers who made more than $200,000 did not pay any Federal income tax. As such, it was intended as a tax that would be levied only on the rich. However, times are changing.

As it now stands, even with annual Band-Aid fixes by Congress (increases in the exemption amount), the AMT continues to catch more and more taxpayers.

Congress, late in December, enacted a one-year fix for 2007 that keeps the number of AMT taxpayers at the 2006 level.

For 2008, if Congress does nothing, more than 70 percent of taxpayers who file tax returns with incomes between $100,000 and $200,000 will be subject to the AMT. So will more than one-third of those with incomes between $75,000 and $100,000.

	AMT Taxpayers
1990	.1 million
1996	.7 million
2001	1.3 million
2002	1.9 million
2003	2.4 million
2004	3.1 million
2005	3.5 million
2006	4 million
2007 (projected if no fix)	25 million
2010 (projected if no fix)	33 million

Source: *Adapted from Tom Herman, "The ABCs of Dealing with the AMT," Wall Street Journal, April 18, 2007, p. D1.*

On the other hand, some income and expense items are treated differently for regular income tax and AMT purposes. For example, interest income on bonds issued by state, county, or local governments is *excluded* in computing taxable income. However, interest on such bonds is *included* in computing AMTI if the bonds are private activity bonds. The deduction for personal and dependency exemptions is *allowed* for regular income tax purposes, but is *disallowed* for AMT purposes.

In other cases, certain items are considered in both the regular income tax and AMT computations, but the amounts are different. For example, the completed contract method can be used to report income from some long-term contracts for regular income tax purposes, but the percentage of completion method is required for AMT purposes. Thus, the amount of income included in taxable income will differ from the amount included in AMTI. Depreciation is allowed as a deduction for both regular income tax and AMT purposes, but the *amount* of the regular income tax deduction may be different from the amount of the AMT deduction. Medical expenses are deductible in calculating both taxable income and AMTI, but the floor on the deduction is different.

The parallel but separate nature of the AMT means that AMTI will differ from taxable income. It is possible to compute AMTI by direct application of the AMT provisions, using the following formula:

Gross income computed by applying the AMT rules
Minus: Deductions computed by applying the AMT rules
Equals: AMTI before tax preferences
Plus: Tax preferences
Equals: Alternative minimum taxable income

While the direct approach for computing AMTI appears quite logical, both the tax law and the tax forms provide a very different approach. Both of these use taxable income (for Form 6251, taxable income *before* the deduction for personal exemptions and dependency deductions) as the starting point for computing AMTI, as shown in Figure 12–1. This indirect approach for computing AMTI is analogous to the indirect approach used in calculating a net operating loss.

FIGURE 12–1	Alternative Minimum Taxable Income (AMTI) Formula

Taxable income
Plus: Positive AMT adjustments
Minus: Negative AMT adjustments
Equals: Taxable income after AMT adjustments
Plus: Tax preferences
Equals: Alternative minimum taxable income

The purpose of the AMT formula is to *reconcile* taxable income to AMTI. This reconciliation is similar to a bank reconciliation, which reconciles a checkbook balance to a bank balance by considering differences between the depositor's records and the bank's records. The reconciliation of taxable income to AMTI is accomplished by entering reconciling items to account for differences between regular income tax provisions and AMT provisions. These reconciling items are referred to as **AMT adjustments** or **tax preferences**. *Adjustments* can be either positive or negative, as shown in the formula in Figure 12–1. Tax preferences are always positive.

Adjustments. Most adjustments relate to *timing differences* that arise because of *separate* regular income tax and AMT treatments. Adjustments that are caused by timing differences will eventually *reverse*; that is, positive adjustments will be offset by negative adjustments in the future, and vice versa.[3]

For example, **circulation expenditures** can give rise to a timing difference that requires an AMT adjustment. For regular income tax purposes, circulation expenditures can be deducted in the year incurred. For AMT purposes, however, circulation expenditures must be deducted over a three-year period. This difference in treatment will be used to illustrate the role of adjustments in the formula for computing AMTI.

EXAMPLE 1

Bob had taxable income of $100,000 in 2008. In computing taxable income, he deducted $30,000 of circulation expenditures incurred in 2008. Bob's allowable deduction for AMT purposes was only $10,000. Therefore, an AMT adjustment was required in 2008 as follows:

Taxable income		$100,000
+AMT adjustment:		
Circulation expenditures deducted for regular income tax purposes	$ 30,000	
Circulation expenditures allowed for AMT purposes	(10,000)	
Positive adjustment		20,000
=AMTI before tax preferences		$120,000
+Tax preferences		–0–
AMTI		$120,000

Analysis of this computation shows that the allowable AMT deduction is $20,000 less than the allowable regular income tax deduction. Therefore, AMTI is $20,000 greater than taxable income. This is accomplished by entering a positive AMT adjustment of $20,000. ■

EXAMPLE 2

Assume that Bob from Example 1 has taxable income of $95,000 in 2009. He is allowed to deduct $10,000 of circulation expenditures for AMT purposes, but is not allowed a deduction for regular income tax purposes because all $30,000 was deducted in 2008. Therefore, a *negative* AMT adjustment is required.

---

[3]§ 56.

Taxable income		$ 95,000
−AMT adjustment:		
Circulation expenditures deducted for regular income tax purposes	$ –0–	
Circulation expenditures allowed for AMT purposes	(10,000)	
Negative adjustment		(10,000)
=AMTI before tax preferences		$ 85,000
+Tax preferences		–0–
AMTI		$ 85,000

Analysis of this computation shows that the allowable AMT deduction is $10,000 more than the allowable regular income tax deduction. Therefore, AMTI is $10,000 less than taxable income. This is accomplished by entering a negative AMT adjustment of $10,000. ■

As noted previously, timing differences eventually reverse. Therefore, total positive adjustments will be offset by total negative adjustments with respect to a particular item.

Refer to Examples 1 and 2. The difference in regular income tax and AMT treatments of circulation expenditures will result in AMT adjustments over a three-year period.

EXAMPLE 3

Year	Regular Income Tax Deduction	AMT Deduction	AMT Adjustment
2008	$30,000	$10,000	+$20,000
2009	–0–	10,000	−10,000
2010	–0–	10,000	−10,000
Total	$30,000	$30,000	$ –0–

As the last column illustrates, if positive and negative AMT adjustments with respect to a particular item are caused by a timing difference, they will eventually net to zero. ■

The adjustments for circulation expenditures and other items are discussed in detail under AMT Adjustments.

Although most adjustments relate to timing differences, there are exceptions. See the subsequent discussion of such items under Itemized Deductions. Adjustments that do not relate to timing differences result in a permanent difference between taxable income and AMTI.

Tax Preferences. Some deductions and exclusions allowed to taxpayers for regular income tax purposes provide extraordinary tax savings. Congress has chosen to single out these items, which are referred to as tax preferences.[4] The AMT is designed to take back all or part of the tax benefits derived through the use of preferences in the computation of taxable income for regular income tax purposes. This is why taxable income, which is the starting point in computing AMTI, is increased by tax preference items. The effect of adding these preference items is to disallow for *AMT purposes* those preferences that were allowed in the regular income tax computation. Tax preferences include the following items, which are discussed in detail under AMT Preferences:

- Percentage depletion in excess of the property's adjusted basis.
- Excess intangible drilling costs reduced by 65 percent of the net income from oil, gas, and geothermal properties.

[4]§ 57.

FIGURE 12–2	Alternative Minimum Tax Formula

Regular taxable income
Plus or minus: Adjustments
Equals: Taxable income after AMT adjustments
Plus: Tax preferences
Equals: Alternative minimum taxable income
Minus: Exemption
Equals: Alternative minimum tax base
Times: 26% or 28% rate
Equals: Tentative minimum tax before foreign tax credit
Minus: Alternative minimum tax foreign tax credit
Equals: Tentative minimum tax
Minus: Regular tax liability*
Equals: Alternative minimum tax (if amount is positive)

*This is the regular tax liability for the year reduced by any allowable foreign tax credit.

- Interest on certain private activity bonds.
- Excess of accelerated over straight-line depreciation on real property placed in service before 1987.
- Excess of accelerated over straight-line depreciation on *leased* personal property placed in service before 1987.
- Excess of amortization allowance over depreciation on pre-1987 certified pollution control facilities.
- Seven percent of the exclusion from gross income associated with gains on the sale of certain small business stock under § 1202.

AMT Formula: Other Components

To convert AMTI to AMT, other formula components including the exemption, rates, credit, and regular tax liability must be considered. The impact of each of these components is depicted in the AMT formula in Figure 12–2.

The relationship between the regular tax liability and the tentative AMT is key to the AMT formula. If the regular tax liability exceeds tentative AMT, then the AMT is zero. If the tentative AMT exceeds the regular tax liability, the amount of the excess is the AMT. In essence, the taxpayer will pay whichever tax liability is greater—that calculated using the regular income tax rules or that calculated using the AMT rules. However, both the tax law and Form 6251 adopt this excess approach with the taxpayer paying the regular tax liability plus any AMT.

EXAMPLE 4

Anna, an unmarried individual, has regular taxable income of $100,000. She has positive adjustments of $40,000 and tax preferences of $25,000. Calculate her AMT for 2008. Anna's regular tax liability is $21,978. Her AMT is calculated as follows:

Taxable income (TI)	$100,000
Plus: Adjustments	40,000
Equals: TI after AMT adjustments	$140,000
Plus: Tax preferences	25,000
Equals: AMTI	$165,000
Minus: AMT exemption ($44,350 − $13,125)	(31,225)*
Equals: AMT base	$133,775
Times: AMT rate	× 26%

Equals: Tentative AMT		$ 34,782
Minus: Regular tax liability		(21,978)
Equals: AMT		$ 12,804

*Discussed under Exemption Amount.

Anna will pay the IRS a total of $34,782, consisting of her regular tax liability of $21,978 plus her AMT of $12,804. ■

Exemption Amount. The exemption amount can be thought of as a materiality provision. As such, it enables a taxpayer with a small amount of positive adjustments and tax preferences to avoid being subject to the burden of the AMT.

The *initial* exemption amount in 2008 is $66,250 for married taxpayers filing joint returns, $44,350 for single taxpayers, and $33,125 for married taxpayers filing separate returns.[5] However, the exemption is *phased out* at a rate of 25 cents on the dollar when AMTI exceeds these levels:

- $112,500 for single taxpayers.
- $150,000 for married taxpayers filing jointly.
- $75,000 for married taxpayers filing separately.

The phaseout of the exemption amount is an application of the wherewithal to pay concept. As the income level increases, so does the taxpayer's ability to pay income taxes.

The following example explains the calculation of the phaseout of the AMT exemption.

EXAMPLE 5

Hugh, who is single, has AMTI of $192,500 for the year. His $44,350 initial exemption amount is reduced by $20,000 [($192,500 − $112,500) × 25% phaseout rate]. Hugh's AMT exemption is $24,350 ($44,350 exemption − $20,000 reduction). ■

The following table shows the beginning and end of the AMT exemption phaseout range for each filing status.

		Phaseout	
Status	Exemption	Begins at	Ends at
Married, joint	$66,250*	$150,000	$415,000
Single or head of household	44,350*	112,500	289,900
Married, separate	33,125*	75,000	207,500

*See footnote 5.

AMT Rate Schedule. A graduated, two-tier AMT rate schedule applies to non-corporate taxpayers. A 26 percent rate applies to the first $175,000 of the AMT base ($87,500 for married, filing separately), and a 28 percent rate applies to the AMT base in excess of $175,000 ($87,500 for married, filing separately).[6] Any net capital gain and qualified dividend income included in the AMT base are taxed at the favorable alternative tax rates for capital gains (15 percent or 0 percent [5 percent prior to 2008]) rather than at the AMT statutory rates. See the discussion of the alternative tax on capital gains in Chapter 16.

---

[5]§ 55(d). For tax years beginning in 2008 and thereafter, the exemption amount is scheduled to be reduced to $45,000 for married taxpayers filing jointly, $33,750 for single or head-of-household taxpayers, and $22,500 for married taxpayers filing separately. However, the general consensus is that

Congress is highly likely to extend the increased exemption amounts for 2008. Thus, these increased amounts (2007 exemption amounts) are used in all AMT calculations in this chapter.
[6]§ 55(b)(1).

ETHICAL and EQUITABLE *Considerations*

THE CASE OF THE DISAPPEARING INFLATION ADJUSTMENTS

Many areas of the regular income tax (e.g., rates, standard deductions, personal and dependency exemptions) are indexed annually for the effect of inflation. The alternative minimum tax (AMT), however, is not.

The AMT is defined as the excess of the tentative AMT over the regular income tax liability. Thus, the AMT results only if there is such an excess. Due to the absence of indexing for the AMT, a taxpayer's AMT can increase from one year to the next even though no other changes occur in the taxpayer's situation.

Suppose, for example, that for 2007 a taxpayer's regular income tax liability is $98,000 and the tentative AMT is

$106,000. Consequently, the AMT is $8,000. Further assume that for 2008 the taxpayer's financial information is identical to 2007. Because of indexing, however, the regular income tax liability is only $91,000, so the AMT becomes $15,000 ($106,000 − $91,000). Thus, the relief that indexation provides for regular income tax purposes is taken away by the AMT.

Is the tax law properly structured when it provides a hedge against inflation for some taxpayers (those not subject to the AMT) but not for others (those subject to the AMT)?

Regular Tax Liability. The AMT is equal to the tentative minimum tax minus the *regular tax liability*. In most cases, the regular tax liability is equal to the amount of tax from the Tax Table or Tax Rate Schedules decreased by any foreign tax credit allowable for regular income tax purposes. The foreign tax credit is allowed as a reduction of the tentative minimum tax.

In an AMT year, the taxpayer's total tax liability is equal to the tentative minimum tax (refer to Figure 12–2). The tentative minimum tax consists of two potential components: the regular tax liability and the AMT. The disallowance of credits does not affect a taxpayer's total liability in an AMT year. However, it does decrease the amount of the AMT and, as a consequence, reduces the minimum tax credit (discussed subsequently) available to be carried forward.

It is also possible that taxpayers who have adjustments and preferences but *do not pay* AMT will lose the benefit of some or all of their nonrefundable credits. This result occurs because a taxpayer may claim many nonrefundable credits only to the extent that his or her regular tax liability exceeds the tentative minimum tax.

EXAMPLE 6

Vern has total nonrefundable *business* credits of $10,000, regular tax liability of $33,000, and tentative minimum tax of $25,000. He can claim only $8,000 of the nonrefundable credits in the current year ($33,000 − $8,000 = $25,000). The disallowed $2,000 credit is eligible for carryback and carryover. ∎

For tax years 2000–2007, all nonrefundable personal credits can offset both the regular income tax (less foreign tax credit) and the AMT. For tax years after 2007, only *certain* nonrefundable personal tax credits (i.e., child tax credit, adoption expenses credit, and credit for elective deferrals and IRA contributions) can offset both the regular income tax (less any foreign tax credit) and the AMT in full after all other nonrefundable personal tax credits have been utilized.[7]

LO.3

Identify the adjustments made in calculating the AMT.

AMT Adjustments

Direction of Adjustments. It is necessary to determine not only the amount of an adjustment, but also whether the adjustment is positive or negative. Careful study of Example 3 reveals the following pattern with regard to *deductions:*

[7]§ 26(a)(2).

- If the deduction allowed for regular income tax purposes exceeds the deduction allowed for AMT purposes, the difference is a positive adjustment.
- If the deduction allowed for AMT purposes exceeds the deduction allowed for regular income tax purposes, the difference is a negative adjustment.

Conversely, the direction of an adjustment attributable to an *income* item can be determined as follows:

- If the income reported for regular income tax purposes exceeds the income reported for AMT purposes, the difference is a negative adjustment.
- If the income reported for AMT purposes exceeds the income reported for regular income tax purposes, the difference is a positive adjustment.

Circulation Expenditures. For regular income tax purposes, circulation expenditures, other than those the taxpayer elects to charge to a capital account, may be expensed in the year incurred.[8] These expenditures include expenses incurred to establish, maintain, or increase the circulation of a newspaper, magazine, or other periodical.

Circulation expenditures are not deductible in the year incurred for AMT purposes. In computing AMTI, these expenditures must be capitalized and amortized ratably over the three-year period beginning with the year in which the expenditures were made.[9]

The AMT adjustment for circulation expenditures is the amount expensed for regular income tax purposes minus the amount that can be amortized for AMT purposes. The adjustment can be either positive or negative (refer to Examples 1, 2, and 3). A taxpayer can avoid the AMT adjustments for circulation expenditures by electing to write off the expenditures over a three-year period for regular income tax purposes.[10]

Depreciation of Post-1986 Real Property. The AMT depreciation adjustment for real property applies only to real property placed in service before January 1, 1999. Real property placed in service after December 31, 1998, uses the same MACRS recovery periods (see Table 8–6) for calculating the AMT as for calculating the regular income tax. Therefore, for such property, the AMT conforms to the regular income tax.

For real property placed in service after 1986 (MACRS property) and before January 1, 1999, AMT depreciation is computed under the alternative depreciation system (ADS), which uses the straight-line method over a 40-year life. The depreciation lives for regular income tax purposes are 27.5 years for residential rental property and 39 years for all other real property.[11] The difference between AMT depreciation and regular income tax depreciation is treated as an adjustment in computing the AMT. The differences will be positive during the regular income tax life of the asset because the cost is written off over a shorter period for regular income tax purposes. For example, during the 27.5-year income tax life of residential real property, the regular income tax depreciation will exceed the AMT depreciation because AMT depreciation is computed over a 40-year period.

Table 8–6 is used to compute regular income tax depreciation on real property placed in service after 1986. For AMT purposes, depreciation on real property placed in service after 1986 and before January 1, 1999, is computed under the ADS (refer to Table 8–7).

---

[8]§ 173(a).
[9]§ 56(b)(2)(A)(i).
[10]§ 59(e)(2)(A).

[11]The 39-year life generally applies to nonresidential real property placed in service on or after May 13, 1993.

EXAMPLE 7

In January 1998, Sara placed in service a residential building that cost $100,000. Regular income tax depreciation, AMT depreciation, and the AMT adjustment are as follows:

	Depreciation		
Year	Regular Income Tax	AMT	AMT Adjustment
1998	$ 3,485[a]	$ 2,396[b]	$ 1,089
1999	3,636[c]	2,500[d]	1,136
2000	3,636	2,500	1,136
2001	3,636	2,500	1,136
2002	3,636	2,500	1,136
2003	3,636	2,500	1,136
2004	3,636	2,500	1,136
2005	3,636	2,500	1,136
2006	3,636	2,500	1,136
2007	3,636	2,500	1,136
2008	3,636	2,500	1,136
Total	$39,845	$27,396	$12,449

[a]$100,000 cost × 3.485% (Table 8–6) = $3,485.
[b]$100,000 cost × 2.396% (Table 8–7) = $2,396.
[c]$100,000 cost × 3.636% (Table 8–6) = $3,636.
[d]$100,000 cost × 2.500% (Table 8–7) = $2,500.

Note that if the building had been placed in service in 1999 or thereafter, there would have been no AMT depreciation adjustment for the tax year it was placed in service or for subsequent years. The depreciation for the tax year the building was placed in service would have been $3,485 ($100,000 × 3.485%) for both regular income tax purposes and AMT purposes. ∎

After real property placed in service before January 1, 1999, has been held for the entire depreciation period for regular income tax purposes, the asset will be fully depreciated. However, the depreciation period under the ADS is 41 years due to application of the half-year convention, so depreciation will continue for AMT purposes. This causes negative adjustments after the property has been fully depreciated for regular income tax purposes.

EXAMPLE 8

Assume the same facts as in the previous example for the building placed in service in 1998, and compute the AMT adjustment for 2026 (the twenty-ninth year of the asset's life). Regular income tax depreciation is zero (refer to Table 8–6). AMT depreciation is $2,500 ($100,000 cost × 2.500% from Table 8–7). Therefore, Sara has a negative AMT adjustment of $2,500 ($0 regular income tax depreciation − $2,500 AMT depreciation). ∎

After real property is fully depreciated for both regular income tax and AMT purposes, the positive and negative adjustments that have been made for AMT purposes will net to zero.

Depreciation of Post-1986 Personal Property.
For most personal property placed in service after 1986 (MACRS property), the MACRS deduction for regular income tax purposes is based on the 200 percent declining-balance method with a switch to straight-line when that method produces a larger depreciation deduction for the asset. Refer to Table 8–1 for computing regular income tax depreciation.

For AMT purposes, the taxpayer must use the ADS for such property placed in service before January 1, 1999. This method is based on the 150 percent declining-balance method with a similar switch to straight-line for all personal property.[12] Refer to Table 8–4 for percentages to be used in computing AMT depreciation.

All personal property placed in service after 1986 may be taken into consideration in computing one net adjustment. Using this netting process, the AMT adjustment for a tax year is the difference between the total MACRS depreciation for all personal property computed for regular income tax purposes and the total ADS depreciation computed for AMT purposes. When the total of MACRS deductions exceeds the total of ADS deductions, the amount of the adjustment is positive. When the total of ADS deductions exceeds the total of MACRS deductions, the adjustment for AMTI is negative.

The MACRS deduction for personal property is larger than the ADS deduction in the early years of an asset's life. However, the ADS deduction is larger in the later years. This is so because ADS lives (based on class life) are longer than MACRS lives (based on recovery period).[13] Over the ADS life of the asset, the same amount of depreciation is deducted for both regular income tax and AMT purposes. In the same manner as other timing adjustments, the AMT adjustments for depreciation will net to zero over the ADS life of the asset.

The taxpayer may elect to use the ADS for regular income tax purposes. If this election is made, no AMT adjustment is required because the depreciation deduction is the same for regular income tax and for the AMT. The election eliminates the burden of maintaining two sets of tax depreciation records.

Tax legislation enacted in 1997 either reduced or eliminated the AMT adjustment for the depreciation of personal property. Prior to the effective date of this legislation, the difference between regular income tax depreciation and AMT depreciation was caused by longer recovery periods for the AMT (class life versus MACRS recovery periods) and more accelerated depreciation methods for the regular income tax (200 percent declining balance rather than 150 percent declining balance). The statute now provides that the MACRS recovery periods are to be used in calculating AMT depreciation. Thus, if the taxpayer elects to use the 150 percent declining-balance method for regular income tax purposes, there are no AMT adjustments. Conversely, if the taxpayer uses the 200 percent declining-balance method for regular income tax purposes, there is an AMT adjustment for depreciation. Note, however, that this AMT recovery period conformity provision applies only to property placed in service after December 31, 1998. Thus, the adjustment continues to apply for personal property placed in service before January 1, 1999.

Pollution Control Facilities. For regular income tax purposes, the cost of certified pollution control facilities may be amortized over a period of 60 months. For AMT purposes, the cost of these facilities placed in service after 1986 and before January 1, 1999, must be depreciated under the ADS over the appropriate class life, determined as explained above for depreciation of post-1986 property.[14] The required adjustment for AMTI is equal to the difference between the amortization deduction allowed for regular income tax purposes and the depreciation deduction computed under the ADS. The adjustment may be positive or negative.

Tax legislation enacted in 1997 reduced the AMT adjustment for pollution control facilities for property placed in service after December 31, 1998. This reduction is achieved by providing conformity in the recovery periods used for regular income tax purposes and AMT purposes (MACRS recovery periods).

---

[12] § 56(a)(1).

[13] Class lives and recovery periods are established for all assets in Rev.Proc. 87–56, 1987–2 C.B. 674.

[14] § 56(a)(5).

Expenditures Requiring 10-Year Write-off for AMT Purposes. Certain expenditures that may be deducted in the year incurred for regular income tax purposes must be written off over a 10-year period for AMT purposes. These rules apply to (1) mining exploration and development costs and (2) research and experimental expenditures.

In computing taxable income, taxpayers are allowed to deduct certain mining exploration and development expenditures. The deduction is allowed for expenditures paid or incurred during the taxable year for exploration (ascertaining the existence, location, extent, or quality of a deposit or mineral) and for development of a mine or other natural deposit, other than an oil or gas well.[15] Mining development expenditures are expenses paid or incurred after the existence of ores and minerals in commercially marketable quantities has been disclosed.

For AMT purposes, however, mining exploration and development costs must be capitalized and amortized ratably over a 10-year period.[16] The AMT adjustment for mining exploration and development costs that are expensed is equal to the amount expensed minus the allowable expense if the costs had been capitalized and amortized ratably over a 10-year period. This provision does not apply to costs relating to an oil or gas well.

E X A M P L E 9	In 2008, Audrey incurs $150,000 of mining exploration expenditures and deducts this amount for regular income tax purposes. For AMT purposes, these mining exploration expenditures must be amortized over a 10-year period. Audrey must make a positive adjustment for AMTI of $135,000 ($150,000 allowed for regular income tax − $15,000 for AMT) for 2008, the first year. In each of the next nine years for AMT purposes, Audrey is required to make a negative adjustment of $15,000 ($0 allowed for regular income tax − $15,000 for AMT). ∎

To avoid the AMT adjustments for mining exploration and development costs, a taxpayer may elect to write off the expenditures over a 10-year period for regular income tax purposes.[17]

Similar rules apply to the computation of the adjustment for research and experimental expenditures.

Use of Completed Contract Method of Accounting. For a long-term contract, taxpayers are required to use the percentage of completion method for AMT purposes.[18] However, in limited circumstances, taxpayers can use the completed contract method for regular income tax purposes.[19] Thus, a taxpayer recognizes a different amount of income for regular income tax purposes than for AMT purposes. The resulting AMT adjustment is equal to the difference between income reported under the percentage of completion method and the amount reported using the completed contract method. The adjustment can be either positive or negative, depending on the amount of income recognized under the different methods.

A taxpayer can avoid an AMT adjustment on long-term contracts by using the percentage of completion method for regular income tax purposes rather than the completed contract method.

Incentive Stock Options. Incentive stock options (ISOs) are granted by employers to help attract new personnel and retain those already employed. At the time an ISO is granted, the employer corporation sets an option price for the corporate stock. If the value of the stock increases during the option period, the employee can obtain stock at a favorable price by exercising the option. Employees are generally restricted as to when they can dispose of stock acquired under an ISO (e.g., a certain length of employment may be required). Therefore, the stock may

---

[15]§§ 617(a) and 616(a).
[16]§ 56(a)(2).
[17]§§ 59(e)(2)(D) and (E).

[18]§ 56(a)(3).
[19]See Chapter 18 for a detailed discussion of the completed contract and percentage of completion methods of accounting.

not be freely transferable until some specified period has passed. See Chapter 19 for details regarding ISOs.

The exercise of an ISO does not increase regular taxable income.[20] However, for AMT purposes, the excess of the fair market value of the stock over the exercise price (the *spread*) is treated as an adjustment in the first taxable year in which the rights in the stock are freely transferable or are not subject to a substantial risk of forfeiture.[21]

EXAMPLE 10

In 2006, Manuel exercised an ISO that had been granted by his employer, Gold Corporation. Manuel acquired 1,000 shares of Gold stock for the option price of $20 per share. The stock became freely transferable in 2008. The fair market value of the stock at the date of exercise was $50 per share. For AMT purposes, Manuel has a positive adjustment of $30,000 ($50,000 fair market value − $20,000 option price) for 2008. The transaction does not affect regular taxable income in 2006 or 2008. ∎

No adjustment is required if the taxpayer exercises the option and disposes of the stock in the same tax year because the bargain element gain is reported for both regular income tax and AMT purposes in the same tax year.

The regular income tax basis of stock acquired through exercise of ISOs is different from the AMT basis. The regular income tax basis of the stock is equal to its cost, whereas the AMT basis is equal to the fair market value on the date the options are exercised. Consequently, the gain or loss upon disposition of the stock is different for regular income tax purposes and AMT purposes.

EXAMPLE 11

Assume the same facts as in the previous example and that Manuel sells the stock for $60,000 in 2010. His gain for regular income tax purposes is $40,000 ($60,000 amount realized − $20,000 regular income tax basis). For AMT purposes, the gain is $10,000 ($60,000 amount realized − $50,000 AMT basis). Therefore, Manuel has a $30,000 negative adjustment in computing AMT in 2010 ($40,000 regular income tax gain − $10,000 AMT gain). Note that the $30,000 negative adjustment upon disposition in 2010 offsets the $30,000 positive adjustment when the stock became freely transferable in 2008. ∎

Adjusted Gain or Loss. When property is sold during the year or a casualty occurs to business or income-producing property, gain or loss reported for regular income tax may be different than gain or loss determined for the AMT. This difference occurs because the adjusted basis of the property for AMT purposes must reflect any current and prior AMT adjustments for the following:[22]

- Depreciation.
- Circulation expenditures.
- Research and experimental expenditures.
- Mining exploration and development costs.
- Amortization of certified pollution control facilities.

A negative gain or loss adjustment is required if:

- the gain for AMT purposes is less than the gain for regular income tax purposes;
- the loss for AMT purposes is more than the loss for regular income tax purposes; or
- a loss is computed for AMT purposes and a gain is computed for regular income tax purposes.

Otherwise, the AMT gain or loss adjustment is positive.

---

[20]§ 421(a).
[21]§ 56(b)(3).

[22]§ 56(a)(6).

EXAMPLE 12

Assume the same facts as in Example 7, except that Sara sells the building on December 20, 2008, for $105,000. When Sara sells the building, she has two tax consequences. She must determine her depreciation adjustment for 2008 and the gain (or loss) resulting from the sale.

As to the depreciation adjustment for 2008, the regular income tax depreciation for 2008 is $3,485 [($100,000 cost × 3.636% from Table 8–6) × (11.5/12)]. AMT depreciation for 2008 is $2,396 [($100,000 × 2.500% from Table 8–7) × (11.5/12)]. Sara's positive AMT adjustment for 2008 is $1,089 ($3,485 regular income tax depreciation − $2,396 AMT depreciation).

In computing gain (or loss), the adjusted basis of the building is different for regular income tax purposes than for AMT purposes. For regular income tax purposes, the adjusted basis is $60,306 [$100,000 (cost) − $36,209 (depreciation claimed for 1998–2007, see Example 7) − $3,485 (depreciation claimed for 2008, see above)]. For AMT purposes, the adjusted basis is $72,708 [$100,000 (cost) − $24,896 (depreciation claimed for 1998–2007, see Example 7) − $2,396 (depreciation for 2008, see above)].

The regular income tax gain is $44,694, and the AMT gain is $32,292.

	Regular Income Tax	AMT
Amount realized	$105,000	$105,000
Adjusted basis	(60,306)	(72,708)
Recognized gain	$ 44,694	$ 32,292

Because the regular income tax and AMT gain on the sale of the building differ, Sara must make a negative AMT adjustment of $12,402 ($44,694 regular income tax gain − $32,292 AMT gain). Note that this negative adjustment offsets the $12,402 total of the 11 positive adjustments for depreciation. ■

Passive Activity Losses. Losses on passive activities are not deductible in computing either the regular income tax or the AMT. This does not, however, eliminate the possibility of adjustments attributable to passive activities.

The rules for computing taxable income differ from the rules for computing AMTI. It follows, then, that the rules for computing a loss for regular income tax purposes differ from the AMT rules for computing a loss. Therefore, any *passive loss* computed for regular income tax purposes may differ from the passive loss computed for AMT purposes.[23]

EXAMPLE 13

Soong acquired two passive activities in 2008. He received net passive income of $10,000 from Activity A and had no AMT adjustments or preferences in connection with the activity. Activity B had gross income of $27,000 and operating expenses (not affected by AMT adjustments or preferences) of $19,000. Soong claimed MACRS depreciation of $20,000 for Activity B; depreciation under the ADS would have been $15,000. In addition, Soong deducted $10,000 of percentage depletion in excess of basis. The following comparison illustrates the differences in the computation of the passive loss for regular income tax and AMT purposes for Activity B.

	Regular Income Tax	AMT
Gross income	$ 27,000	$ 27,000
Deductions:		
Operating expenses	($ 19,000)	($ 19,000)
Depreciation	(20,000)	(15,000)
Depletion	(10,000)	–0–
Total deductions	($ 49,000)	($ 34,000)
Passive loss	($ 22,000)	($ 7,000)

[23]See Chapter 11.

Because the adjustment for depreciation ($5,000) applies and the preference for depletion ($10,000) is not taken into account in computing AMTI, the regular income tax passive activity loss of $22,000 for Activity B is reduced by these amounts, resulting in a passive activity loss of $7,000 for AMT purposes. ∎

For regular income tax purposes, Soong would offset the $10,000 of net passive income from Activity A with $10,000 of the passive loss from Activity B. For AMT purposes, he would offset the $10,000 of net passive income from Activity A with the $7,000 passive activity loss allowed from Activity B, resulting in passive activity income of $3,000. Thus, in computing AMTI, Soong makes a positive passive loss adjustment of $3,000 [$10,000 (passive activity loss allowed for regular income tax) − $7,000 (passive activity loss allowed for the AMT)]. To avoid duplication, the AMT adjustment for depreciation and the preference for depletion are *not* reported separately. They are accounted for in determining the AMT passive loss adjustment.

EXAMPLE 14

Assume the same facts as in the previous example. For regular income tax purposes, Soong has a suspended passive loss of $12,000 [$22,000 (amount of loss) − $10,000 (used in 2008)]. This suspended passive loss can offset passive income in the future or can offset active or portfolio income when Soong disposes of the loss activity (refer to Chapter 11). For AMT purposes, Soong's suspended passive loss is $0 [$7,000 (amount of loss) − $7,000 (amount used in 2008)]. ∎

Alternative Tax Net Operating Loss Deduction. In computing taxable income, taxpayers are allowed to deduct net operating loss (NOL) carryovers and carrybacks (refer to Chapter 7). The regular income tax NOL must be modified, however, in computing AMTI. The starting point in computing the **alternative tax NOL deduction (ATNOLD)** is the NOL computed for regular income tax purposes. The regular income tax NOL is then modified for AMT adjustments and tax preferences with the result being the ATNOLD. Thus, preferences and adjustment items that have benefited the taxpayer in computing the regular income tax NOL are added back, thereby reducing or eliminating the ATNOLD.[24]

EXAMPLE 15

In 2008, Max incurred an NOL of $100,000. Max had no AMT adjustments, but his deductions included tax preferences of $18,000. His ATNOLD carryback to 2006 is $82,000 ($100,000 regular income tax NOL − $18,000 tax preferences deducted in computing the NOL). ∎

In Example 15, if the adjustment was not made to the regular income tax NOL, the $18,000 in tax preference items deducted in 2008 would have the effect of reducing AMTI in the year (or years) the 2008 NOL is utilized. This would weaken the entire concept of the AMT.

A ceiling exists on the amount of the ATNOLD that can be deducted in the carryback or carryforward year. The deduction is limited to 90 percent of AMTI (before the ATNOLD) for the carryback or carryforward year.

EXAMPLE 16

Assume the same facts as in the previous example. Max's AMTI (before the ATNOLD) in 2006 is $90,000. Therefore, of the $82,000 ATNOLD carried back to 2006 from 2008, only $81,000 ($90,000 × 90%) can be used in recalculating the 2006 AMT. The unused $1,000 of 2008 ATNOLD is now carried to 2007 for use in recalculating the 2007 AMT. ∎

A taxpayer who has an ATNOLD that is carried back or over to another year must use the ATNOLD against AMTI in the carryback or carryforward year even if the regular income tax, rather than the AMT, applies.

---

[24]§ 56(a)(4).

EXAMPLE 17

Emily's ATNOLD for 2009 (carried over from 2008) is $10,000. AMTI before considering the ATNOLD is $25,000. If Emily's regular income tax exceeds the AMT, the AMT does not apply. Nevertheless, Emily's ATNOLD of $10,000 is "used up" in 2009 and is not available for carryover to a later year. ■

For regular income tax purposes, the NOL generally can be carried back 2 years and forward 20 years. However, the taxpayer may elect to forgo the 2-year carryback. These rules generally apply to the ATNOLD as well, except that the election to forgo the 2-year carryback is available for the ATNOLD only if the taxpayer elected it for the regular income tax NOL.

Itemized Deductions. Most of the itemized deductions that are allowed for regular income tax purposes are allowed for AMT purposes. Itemized deductions that are allowed for AMT purposes include the following:

- Casualty losses.
- Gambling losses.
- Charitable contributions.
- Medical expenses in excess of 10 percent of AGI.
- Estate tax on income in respect of a decedent.
- Qualified interest.

Taxes (state, local, and foreign income taxes, sales taxes, and property taxes) and miscellaneous itemized deductions that are subject to the 2 percent-of-AGI floor are not allowed in computing AMT.[25] A positive AMT adjustment in the total amount of the regular income tax deduction for each is required.

If the taxpayer's gross income includes the recovery of any tax deducted as an itemized deduction for regular income tax purposes, a negative AMT adjustment in the amount of the recovery is allowed for AMTI purposes.[26] For example, state, local, and foreign income taxes can be deducted for regular income tax purposes, but cannot be deducted in computing AMTI. Because of this, any refund of such taxes from a prior year is not included in AMTI. Therefore, in calculating AMTI, the taxpayer must make a negative adjustment for an income tax refund that has been included in computing regular taxable income. Under the tax benefit rule, a tax refund is included in regular taxable income to the extent that the taxpayer obtained a tax benefit by deducting the tax in a prior year.

Cutback Adjustment. The 3 percent cutback adjustment that applies to regular income tax itemized deductions of certain high-income taxpayers (refer to Chapter 10) does not apply in computing AMT.[27] The effect of the 3 percent cutback adjustment is to disallow a portion of the taxpayer's itemized deductions for regular income tax purposes. Because this cutback adjustment does not apply for AMT purposes, taxable income, which is the starting point for computing AMTI, must be reduced by the amount of the disallowed deductions. This reduction is a negative AMT adjustment.

Medical Expenses. The rules for determining the AMT deductions for medical expenses are sufficiently complex to require further explanation. For regular income tax purposes, medical expenses are deductible to the extent they exceed 7.5 percent of AGI. However, for AMT purposes, medical expenses are deductible only to the extent they exceed 10 percent of AGI.[28]

---

[25]§ 56(b)(1)(A).
[26]§ 56(b)(1)(D).

[27]§ 56(b)(1)(F).
[28]§ 56(b)(1)(B).

TAX *in the News* — WHO PAYS THE AMT?

The percentage of taxpayers who pay the AMT is not spread evenly among the states. The top five states are as follows:

State	Percentage of Returns with AMT
New Jersey	7.56%
New York	7.37%
Connecticut	6.31%
California	5.84%
Maryland	5.23%

If the District of Columbia were included, it would be fifth with 5.81 percent.

The bottom five states include the following:

State	Percentage of Returns with AMT
Alaska	0.87%
South Dakota	0.87%
Tennessee	1.06%
North Dakota	1.08%
Mississippi	1.16%

A major contributing factor among the top five is the imposition of heavy state and local income and property taxes. With the exception of Maryland, these states are in the top 12 with respect to the combined state and local tax burden. While such taxes are deductible in calculating the regular income tax, they cannot be deducted in calculating the AMT.

Sources: *Adapted from "More Taxpayers Feel Alternative Minimum Tax Bite,"* Wall Street Journal, *April 15, 2007, p. D3; and "Democrats and the AMT,"* Wall Street Journal, *April 14, 2007, p. A8.*

EXAMPLE 18

Joann incurred medical expenses of $16,000 in 2008. She had AGI of $100,000 for the year. Her AMT adjustment for medical expenses is computed as follows:

	Regular Income Tax	AMT
Medical expenses incurred	$16,000	$ 16,000
Less reduction:		
$100,000 AGI × 7.5%	(7,500)	
$100,000 AGI × 10%		(10,000)
Medical expense deduction	$ 8,500	$ 6,000

Joann's AMT adjustment for medical expenses is $2,500 ($8,500 regular income tax deduction − $6,000 AMT deduction). ■

Interest in General. The AMT itemized deduction allowed for interest expense includes only qualified housing interest and investment interest to the extent of net investment income that is included in the determination of AMTI.[29] Any interest that is deducted in calculating the regular income tax that is not permitted in calculating the AMT is treated as a positive adjustment.

In computing regular taxable income, taxpayers who itemize can deduct the following types of interest (refer to Chapter 10):

- Qualified residence interest.
- Investment interest, subject to the investment interest limitations (discussed under Investment Interest below).
- Qualified interest on student loans.

---

[29]§ 56(b)(1)(C).

Housing Interest. Under current regular income tax rules, taxpayers who itemize can deduct *qualified residence interest* on up to two residences. The deduction is limited to interest on acquisition indebtedness up to $1 million and home equity indebtedness up to $100,000. Acquisition indebtedness is debt that is incurred in acquiring, constructing, or substantially improving a qualified residence of the taxpayer and is secured by the residence. Home equity indebtedness is indebtedness secured by a qualified residence of the taxpayer, but does not include acquisition indebtedness.

EXAMPLE 19

Gail, who used the proceeds of a mortgage to acquire a personal residence, paid mortgage interest of $112,000 in 2008. Of this amount, $14,000 is attributable to acquisition indebtedness in excess of $1 million. For regular income tax purposes, Gail may deduct mortgage interest of $98,000 ($112,000 total − $14,000 disallowed). ∎

The mortgage interest deduction for AMT purposes is limited to *qualified housing interest*, rather than *qualified residence interest*. Qualified housing interest includes only interest incurred to acquire, construct, or substantially improve the taxpayer's principal residence and such interest on one other qualified dwelling used for personal purposes. A home equity loan qualifies only if it meets the definition of qualified housing interest, which frequently is not the case. When additional mortgage interest is incurred (e.g., a mortgage refinancing), interest paid is deductible as qualified housing interest for AMT purposes only if:

- The proceeds are used to acquire or substantially improve a qualified residence.
- Interest on the prior loan was qualified housing interest.
- The amount of the loan was not increased.

A positive AMT adjustment is required in the amount of the difference between qualified *residence* interest allowed as an itemized deduction for regular income tax purposes and qualified *housing* interest allowed in the determination of AMTI.

Investment Interest. Investment interest is deductible for regular income tax purposes and for AMT purposes to the extent of qualified net investment income.

EXAMPLE 20

For the year, Dan had net investment income of $16,000 before deducting investment interest. He incurred investment interest expense of $30,000 during the year. His investment interest deduction is $16,000. ∎

Even though investment interest is deductible for both regular income tax and AMT purposes, an adjustment is required if the amount of investment interest deductible for regular income tax purposes differs from the amount deductible for AMT purposes. For example, an adjustment will arise if proceeds from a home equity loan are used to purchase investments. Interest on a home equity loan is deductible as qualified residence interest for regular income tax purposes, but is not deductible for AMT purposes unless the proceeds are used to acquire or substantially improve a qualified residence. For AMT purposes, however, interest on a home equity loan is deductible as investment interest expense if proceeds from the loan are used for investment purposes.

To determine the AMT adjustment for investment interest expense, it is necessary to compute the investment interest deduction for both regular income tax and AMT purposes. This computation is illustrated in the following example.

EXAMPLE 21

Tom had $20,000 interest income from corporate bonds and $5,000 dividends from preferred stock. He reported the following amounts of investment income for regular income tax and AMT purposes:

	Regular Income Tax	AMT
Corporate bond interest	$20,000	$20,000
Preferred stock dividends	5,000	5,000
Net investment income	$25,000	$25,000

Tom incurred investment interest expense of $10,000 related to the corporate bonds. He also incurred $4,000 interest on a home equity loan and used the proceeds of the loan to purchase preferred stock. For regular income tax purposes, this $4,000 is deductible as qualified residence interest. His *investment* interest expense for regular income tax and AMT purposes is computed below:

	Regular Income Tax	AMT
To carry corporate bonds	$10,000	$10,000
On home equity loan to carry preferred stock	–0–	4,000
Total investment interest expense	$10,000	$14,000

Investment interest expense is deductible to the extent of net investment income. Because the amount deductible for regular income tax purposes ($10,000) differs from the amount deductible for AMT purposes ($14,000), an AMT adjustment is required. The adjustment is computed as follows:

AMT deduction for investment interest expense	$ 14,000
Regular income tax deduction for investment interest expense	(10,000)
Negative AMT adjustment	$ 4,000 ∎

As discussed subsequently under AMT Preferences, the interest on private activity bonds is a tax preference for AMT purposes. Such interest can also affect the calculation of the AMT investment interest deduction in that it is included in the calculation of net investment income.

Other Adjustments. The standard deduction and the personal and dependency exemption also give rise to AMT adjustments.[30] The standard deduction is not allowed as a deduction in computing AMTI. Although a person who does not itemize is rarely subject to the AMT, it is possible. In such a case, the taxpayer is required to enter a positive adjustment for the standard deduction in computing the AMT.

The personal and dependency exemption amount deducted for regular income tax purposes is not allowed in computing AMT. Therefore, taxpayers must enter a positive AMT adjustment for the personal and dependency exemption amount claimed in computing the regular income tax. A separate exemption (see Exemption Amount) is allowed for AMT purposes. To allow both the regular income tax exemption amount and the AMT exemption amount would result in extra benefits for taxpayers.

EXAMPLE 22

Eli, who is single, has no dependents and does not itemize deductions. He earned a salary of $108,950 in 2008. Based on this information, Eli's taxable income for 2008 is $100,000 ($108,950 – $5,450 standard deduction – $3,500 exemption). ∎

---

[30]§ 56(b)(1)(E).

EXAMPLE 23

Assume the same facts as in Example 22. In addition, assume Eli's tax preferences for the year totaled $150,000. Eli's AMTI is $258,950 ($100,000 taxable income + $5,450 adjustment for standard deduction + $3,500 adjustment for exemption + $150,000 tax preferences). ■

LO.4

Identify the tax preferences that are included in calculating the AMT.

AMT Preferences

Percentage Depletion. Congress originally enacted the percentage depletion rules to provide taxpayers with incentives to invest in the development of specified natural resources. Percentage depletion is computed by multiplying a rate specified in the Code times the gross income from the property (refer to Chapter 8).[31] The percentage rate is based on the type of mineral involved. The basis of the property is reduced by the amount of depletion taken until the basis reaches zero. However, once the basis of the property reaches zero, taxpayers are allowed to continue taking percentage depletion deductions. Thus, over the life of the property, depletion deductions may greatly exceed the cost of the property.

The percentage depletion preference is equal to the excess of the regular income tax deduction for percentage depletion over the adjusted basis of the property at the end of the taxable year.[32] Basis is determined without regard to the depletion deduction for the taxable year. This preference item is figured separately for each piece of property for which the taxpayer is claiming depletion.

EXAMPLE 24

Kim owns a mineral property that qualifies for a 22% depletion rate. The basis of the property at the beginning of the year is $10,000. Gross income from the property for the year is $100,000. For regular income tax purposes, Kim's percentage depletion deduction (assume it is not limited by taxable income from the property) is $22,000. For AMT purposes, Kim has a tax preference of $12,000 ($22,000 − $10,000). ■

Intangible Drilling Costs. In computing the regular income tax, taxpayers are allowed to deduct certain intangible drilling and development costs in the year incurred, although such costs are normally capital in nature (refer to Chapter 8). The deduction is allowed for costs incurred in connection with oil and gas wells and geothermal wells.

For AMT purposes, excess intangible drilling costs (IDC) for the year are treated as a preference.[33] The preference for excess IDC is computed as follows:

IDC expensed in the year incurred
Minus: Deduction if IDC were capitalized and amortized over 10 years
Equals: Excess of IDC expense over amortization
Minus: 65% of net oil and gas and geothermal income
Equals: Tax preference item

EXAMPLE 25

Ben, who incurred IDC of $50,000 during the year, elected to expense that amount. His net oil and gas income for the year was $60,000. Ben's tax preference for IDC is $6,000 [($50,000 IDC − $5,000 amortization) − (65% × $60,000 income)]. ■

A taxpayer can avoid the preference for IDC by electing to write off the expenditures over a 10-year period for regular income tax purposes.

Interest on Private Activity Bonds. Income from private activity bonds is not included in taxable income, and expenses related to carrying such bonds are not deductible for regular income tax purposes. However, interest on private activity bonds is included as a preference in computing AMTI. Therefore, expenses incurred in carrying the bonds are offset against the interest income in computing the tax preference.[34]

---

[31] § 613(a).

[32] § 57(a)(1). Note that the preference label does not apply to percentage depletion on oil and gas wells for independent producers and royalty owners as defined in § 613A(c).

[33] § 57(a)(2).

[34] § 57(a)(5).

TAX *in the News* | TAX-FREE MUNICIPAL BONDS: MARKET REACTION TO BEING TAXED

Municipal bonds are not subject to Federal income tax. Therefore, assuming equal risk, the market assigns a lower interest rate to municipal bonds than it does to taxable bonds.

Generally, municipal bonds are not subject to the AMT. However, an exception exists for such bonds that are classified as private activity bonds. These bonds are used to finance projects such as airports, housing developments, wastewater treatment plants, and athletic stadiums. As more and more taxpayers become subject to the AMT each year, the vulnerability of some municipal bond interest becomes a cause for concern when devising an investment strategy.

When investing in individual bonds issued by a particular municipality, it is easy to discern which are private activity bonds. Many investors, however, choose bond mutual funds rather than purchasing particular issues. According to the Securities and Exchange Commission's rules, tax-exempt mutual funds can have as much as one-fifth of their holdings in private activity bonds, creating a potential tax pitfall for investors.

A number of companies that offer mutual funds have responded by creating funds that are both AMT-free and regular income tax-free. These funds invest only in tax-exempts that are not private activity bonds. Companies offering these funds include Fidelity Investments, Charles Schwab, Eaton Vance, Pioneer Investments, Putman Investments, Oppenheimer Funds, Vanguard Group, and T. Rowe Price Group.

Of course, as with any investment, the taxpayer should consider the after-tax yield of these AMT-free municipal bond funds.

Sources: *Adapted from Jane J. Kim, "Do You Need an 'AMT' Free Fund?"* Wall Street Journal, *April 21, 2007, p. B1; and Michael A. Pollock, "AMT Strikes in Unlikely Spot: Tax-Free Muni-Bond Funds,"* Wall Street Journal, *March 5, 2007, p. R1.*

The Code contains a lengthy, complex definition of private activity bonds.[35] In general, **private activity bonds** are bonds issued by states or municipalities with more than 10 percent of the proceeds being used for private business use. For example, a bond issued by a city whose proceeds are used to construct a factory that is leased to a private business at a favorable rate is a private activity bond.

Depreciation. For real property and leased personal property placed in service before 1987, there is an AMT preference for the excess of accelerated depreciation over straight-line depreciation.[36] However, examination of the cost recovery tables for pre-1987 real property (refer to Chapter 8) reveals that from the eighth year on, accelerated depreciation will not exceed straight-line depreciation. Consequently, taxpayers no longer have preferences attributable to pre-1987 real property.

Accelerated depreciation on pre-1987 leased personal property was computed using specified ACRS percentages. AMT depreciation was based on the straight-line method, which was computed using the half-year convention, no salvage value, and a longer recovery period.[37] As a result, in the early years of the life of the asset, the cost recovery allowance used in computing the regular income tax was greater than the straight-line depreciation deduction allowed in computing AMT. The excess depreciation was treated as a tax preference item. For all leased personal property placed in service before 1987 (3-year, 5-year, 10-year, and 15-year public utility property), the cost recovery period has expired. Since there is no excess depreciation, there is no tax preference for AMT purposes.

The preference item for excess depreciation on leased personal property is figured separately for each piece of property. No preference is reported in the year the taxpayer disposes of the property.

Fifty Percent Exclusion for Certain Small Business Stock. Fifty percent of the gain on the sale of certain small business stock is excludible from gross income

---

[35]§ 141.
[36]§ 57(a)(6).

[37]The specified lives for AMT purposes are 5 years for 3-year property, 8 years for 5-year property, 15 years for 10-year property, and 22 years for 15-year property.

CONCEPT SUMMARY 12–1

AMT Adjustments and Preferences for Individuals

Adjustments	Positive	Negative	Both*
Circulation expenditures			X
Depreciation of post-1986 real property			X
Depreciation of post-1986 personal property			X
Pollution control facilities			X
Mining exploration and development costs			X
Research and experimental expenditures			X
Completed contract method			X
Incentive stock options	X**		
Adjusted gain or loss			X
Passive activity losses			X
Alternative tax NOL deduction			X
Itemized deductions:			
Medical expenses	X		
State income tax or sales tax	X		
Property tax on realty	X		
Property tax on personalty	X		
Miscellaneous itemized deductions	X		
Tax benefit rule for state income tax refund		X	
Cutback adjustment		X	
Qualified interest on student loans	X		
Qualified residence interest that is not qualified housing interest	X		
Qualified residence interest that is AMT investment interest	X	X	
Private activity bond interest that is AMT investment interest		X	
Standard deduction	X		
Personal exemptions and dependency deductions	X		

Preferences

	Positive	Negative	Both*
Percentage depletion in excess of adjusted basis	X		
Intangible drilling costs	X		
Private activity bond interest income	X		
Depreciation on pre-1987 leased personal property	X		
§ 1202 exclusion for certain small business stock	X		

*Timing differences.

**While the adjustment is a positive adjustment, the AMT basis for the stock is increased by the amount of the positive adjustment.

for regular income tax purposes. Seven percent of the excluded amount is a tax preference for AMT purposes.[38]

The adjustments and preferences to taxable income in arriving at AMTI are set forth in Concept Summary 12–1.

[38]§ 57(a)(7).

Illustration of the AMT Computation

The computation of the AMT is illustrated in the following example.

LO.5

Apply the formula for computing the AMT and illustrate Form 6251.

E X A M P L E   26

Hans Sims, who is single, had taxable income for 2008 as follows:

Salary		$ 92,000
Interest		8,000
Adjusted gross income		$100,000
Less itemized deductions:		
Medical expenses		
($17,500 − 7.5% of $100,000 AGI)[a]	$10,000	
State income taxes	4,000	
Interest[b]		
Home mortgage (for qualified		
housing)	20,000*	
Investment interest	3,300*	
Contributions (cash)	5,000*	
Casualty losses ($14,000 − 10% of		
$100,000 AGI)	4,000*	(46,300)
		$ 53,700
Less personal exemption		(3,500)
Taxable income		$ 50,200

[a] Total medical expenses were $17,500, reduced by 7.5% of AGI, resulting in an itemized deduction of $10,000. However, for AMT purposes, the reduction is 10%, which leaves an AMT itemized deduction of $7,500 ($17,500 − 10% of $100,000 AGI). Therefore, an adjustment of $2,500 ($10,000 − $7,500) is required for medical expenses disallowed for AMT purposes.

[b] In this illustration, all interest is deductible in computing AMTI. Qualified housing interest is deductible. Investment interest ($3,300) is deductible to the extent of net investment income included in the minimum tax base. For this purpose, the $8,000 of interest income is treated as net investment income.

Deductions marked by an asterisk are allowed as *alternative minimum tax itemized deductions,* and AMT adjustments are required for the other itemized deductions. Thus, adjustments are required for state income taxes and for medical expenses to the extent the medical expenses deductible for regular income tax purposes are not deductible in computing AMT (see note [a]). In addition to the items that affected taxable income, Hans had $35,000 interest on private activity bonds (an exclusion tax preference). AMTI is computed as follows:

Taxable income	$ 50,200
Plus: Adjustments	
State income taxes	4,000
Medical expenses (see note [a])	2,500
Personal exemption	3,500
Plus: Tax preference (interest on private activity bonds)	35,000
Equals: AMTI	$ 95,200
Minus: AMT exemption	(44,350)
Equals: Minimum tax base	$ 50,850
Times: AMT rate	× 26%
Equals: Tentative AMT	$ 13,221
Minus: Regular income tax on taxable income	(8,894)
Equals: AMT	$ 4,327

The solution to Example 26 is also presented on Form 6251. Though this example is for 2008, 2007 tax forms are used because the 2008 tax forms were not available at the time of this writing.

Note that the $3,500 personal exemption amount is a positive adjustment in the Example 26 solution, but does not appear as an adjustment in Form 6251. This difference occurs because line 1 of Form 6251 includes the amount from line 41 of Form 1040. Line 41 of Form 1040 is taxable income before the deduction for personal and dependency exemptions.

AMT Credit

LO.6

Describe the role of the AMT credit in the alternative minimum tax structure.

As discussed previously, timing differences give rise to adjustments to the minimum tax base. In later years, the timing differences reverse, as was illustrated in several of the preceding examples. To provide equity for the taxpayer when timing differences reverse, the regular income tax liability may be reduced by a tax credit for prior years' minimum tax liability attributable to timing differences. The **alternative minimum tax credit** may be carried over indefinitely. Therefore, there is no need to keep track of when the minimum tax credit arose.[39]

EXAMPLE 27

Assume the same facts as in Example 3. Also assume that in 2008, Bob paid AMT as a result of the $20,000 positive adjustment arising from the circulation expenditures. In 2009, $10,000 of the timing difference reverses, resulting in regular taxable income that is $10,000 greater than AMTI. Because Bob has already paid AMT as a result of the write-off of circulation expenditures, he is allowed an AMT credit in 2009. The AMT credit can offset Bob's regular income tax liability in 2009 to the extent that his regular income tax liability exceeds his tentative AMT. ■

The AMT credit is applicable only for the AMT that results from timing differences. It is not available in connection with **AMT exclusions**, which represent permanent differences rather than timing differences between the regular income tax liability and the AMT. These AMT exclusions include the following:

- The standard deduction.
- Personal exemptions.
- Medical expenses, to the extent deductible for regular income tax purposes but not deductible in computing AMT.
- Other itemized deductions not allowable for AMT purposes, including miscellaneous itemized deductions, taxes, and interest expense.
- Excess percentage depletion.
- Tax-exempt interest on specified private activity bonds.

EXAMPLE 28

Don, who is single, has zero taxable income for 2008. He also has positive timing adjustments of $300,000 and AMT exclusions of $100,000. His AMT base is $400,000 because his AMT exemption is phased out completely due to the level of AMTI. Don's tentative AMT is $108,500 [($175,000 × 26% AMT rate) + ($225,000 × 28% AMT rate)]. ■

To determine the amount of AMT credit to carry over, the AMT must be recomputed reflecting only the AMT exclusions and the AMT exemption amount.

EXAMPLE 29

Assume the same facts as in the previous example. If there had been no positive timing adjustments for the year, Don's tentative AMT would have been $14,469 [($100,000 AMT exclusions − $44,350 exemption) × 26% AMT rate]. Don may carry over an AMT credit of $94,031 ($108,500 AMT − $14,469 related to AMT exclusions) to 2009 and subsequent years. ■

---

[39]§ 53.

Form **6251**	**Alternative Minimum Tax—Individuals**	OMB No. 1545-0074
Department of the Treasury Internal Revenue Service (99)	▶ See separate instructions. ▶ Attach to Form 1040 or Form 1040NR.	**2007** Attachment Sequence No. **32**

Name(s) shown on Form 1040 or Form 1040NR

Hans Sims

Your social security number

Part I Alternative Minimum Taxable Income (See instructions for how to complete each line.)

1	If filing Schedule A (Form 1040), enter the amount from Form 1040, line 41, and go to line 2. Otherwise, enter the amount from Form 1040, line 38, and go to line 7. (If less than zero, enter as a negative amount.)	**1**	*53,700*
2	Medical and dental. Enter the **smaller** of Schedule A (Form 1040), line 4, **or** 2.5% (.025) of Form 1040, line 38. If zero or less, enter -0-	**2**	*2,500*
3	Taxes from Schedule A (Form 1040), line 9	**3**	*4,000*
4	Enter the home mortgage interest adjustment, if any, from line 6 of the worksheet on page 2 of the instructions	**4**	
5	Miscellaneous deductions from Schedule A (Form 1040), line 27	**5**	
6	If Form 1040, line 38, is over $156,400 (over $78,200 if married filing separately), enter the amount from line 11 of the **Itemized Deductions Worksheet** on page A-10 of the instructions for Schedule A (Form 1040)	**6**	( )
7	Tax refund from Form 1040, line 10 or line 21	**7**	( )
8	Investment interest expense (difference between regular tax and AMT)	**8**	
9	Depletion (difference between regular tax and AMT)	**9**	
10	Net operating loss deduction from Form 1040, line 21. Enter as a positive amount	**10**	
11	Interest from specified private activity bonds exempt from the regular tax	**11**	*35,000*
12	Qualified small business stock (7% of gain excluded under section 1202)	**12**	
13	Exercise of incentive stock options (excess of AMT income over regular tax income)	**13**	
14	Estates and trusts (amount from Schedule K-1 (Form 1041), box 12, code A)	**14**	
15	Electing large partnerships (amount from Schedule K-1 (Form 1065-B), box 6)	**15**	
16	Disposition of property (difference between AMT and regular tax gain or loss)	**16**	
17	Depreciation on assets placed in service after 1986 (difference between regular tax and AMT)	**17**	
18	Passive activities (difference between AMT and regular tax income or loss)	**18**	
19	Loss limitations (difference between AMT and regular tax income or loss)	**19**	
20	Circulation costs (difference between regular tax and AMT)	**20**	
21	Long-term contracts (difference between AMT and regular tax income)	**21**	
22	Mining costs (difference between regular tax and AMT)	**22**	
23	Research and experimental costs (difference between regular tax and AMT)	**23**	
24	Income from certain installment sales before January 1, 1987	**24**	( )
25	Intangible drilling costs preference	**25**	
26	Other adjustments, including income-based related adjustments	**26**	
27	Alternative tax net operating loss deduction	**27**	( )
28	**Alternative minimum taxable income.** Combine lines 1 through 27. (If married filing separately and line 28 is more than $207,500, see page 7 of the instructions.)	**28**	*95,200*

Part II Alternative Minimum Tax

29	Exemption. (If this form is for a child under age 18, see page 7 of the instructions.)		

IF your filing status is . . .	**AND line 28 is not over . . .**	**THEN enter on line 29 . . .**		
Single or head of household	$112,500	$44,350		
Married filing jointly or qualifying widow(er)	150,000	66,250	**29**	*44,350*
Married filing separately	75,000	33,125		

	If line 28 is **over** the amount shown above for your filing status, see page 7 of the instructions.		
30	Subtract line 29 from line 28. If more than zero, go to line 31. If zero or less, enter -0- here and on lines 33 and 35 and skip the rest of Part II	**30**	*50,850*
31	• If you are filing Form 2555 or 2555-EZ, see page 8 of the instructions for the amount to enter. • If you reported capital gain distributions directly on Form 1040, line 13; you reported qualified dividends on Form 1040, line 9b; **or** you had a gain on both lines 15 and 16 of Schedule D (Form 1040) (as refigured for the AMT, if necessary), complete Part III on the back and enter the amount from line 55 here. • All others: If line 30 is $175,000 or less ($87,500 or less if married filing separately), multiply line 30 by 26% (.26). Otherwise, multiply line 30 by 28% (.28) and subtract $3,500 ($1,750 if married filing separately) from the result.	**31**	*13,221*
32	Alternative minimum tax foreign tax credit (see page 8 of the instructions)	**32**	
33	Tentative minimum tax. Subtract line 32 from line 31	**33**	*13,221*
34	Tax from Form 1040, line 44 (minus any tax from Form 4972 and any foreign tax credit from Form 1040, line 51). If you used Schedule J to figure your tax, the amount from line 44 of Form 1040 must be refigured without using Schedule J (see page 9 of the instructions)	**34**	*8,894*
35	**Alternative minimum tax.** Subtract line 34 from line 33. If zero or less, enter -0-. Enter here and on Form 1040, line 45	**35**	*4,327*

For Paperwork Reduction Act Notice, see page 10 of the instructions.   Cat. No. 13600G   Form **6251** (2007)

FIGURE 12–3	AMT Formula for Corporations

Taxable income
Plus: Income tax NOL deduction
Plus or minus: AMT adjustments
Plus: Tax preferences
Equals: AMTI before ATNOLD
Minus: ATNOLD (limited to 90% of AMTI before ATNOLD)
Equals: AMTI
Minus: Exemption
Equals: AMT base
Times: 20% rate
Equals: Tentative minimum tax before AMT foreign tax credit
Minus: AMT foreign tax credit
Equals: Tentative minimum tax
Minus: Regular tax liability before credits minus regular foreign tax credit
Equals: AMT if positive

LO.7

Understand the basic features of the corporate AMT.

Corporate Alternative Minimum Tax

The AMT applicable to corporations is similar to that applicable to noncorporate taxpayers. However, there are several important differences:

- The corporate AMT rate is 20 percent versus a top rate of 28 percent for noncorporate taxpayers.[40]
- The AMT exemption for corporations is $40,000 reduced by 25 percent of the amount by which AMTI exceeds $150,000.[41]
- Tax preferences applicable to noncorporate taxpayers are also applicable to corporate taxpayers, but some adjustments differ (shown later in the chapter).

Although there are computational differences, the corporate AMT and the noncorporate AMT have the identical objective: to force taxpayers who are more profitable than their taxable income reflects to pay additional tax. The formula for determining the corporate AMT appears in Figure 12–3.

Repeal of AMT for Small Corporations

Tax legislation enacted in 1997 repealed the AMT for small corporations for tax years beginning after December 31, 1997. For this purpose, a corporation is classified as a small corporation if it had average annual gross receipts of not more than $5 million for the three-year period beginning after December 1993. A corporation will continue to be classified as a small corporation if its average annual gross receipts for the three-year period preceding the current tax year and any intervening three-year periods do not exceed $7.5 million. However, if a corporation ever fails the gross receipts test, it is ineligible for small corporation classification in future tax years.[42]

Tax legislation enacted in 1998 provided an additional opportunity for a corporation to be classified as a small corporation. A corporation will automatically be classified as a small corporation in the first tax year of existence.[43]

---

[40]§ 55(b)(1)(B).
[41]§§ 55(d)(2) and (3).

[42]§§ 55(e)(1)(A) and (B). An estimated 3 million corporations (95% of incorporated businesses) qualify for this exemption.
[43]§ 55(e)(1)(C).

ETHICAL and EQUITABLE *Considerations*   **A SMALL CORPORATION ELECTS S STATUS**

Victor created Clear, Inc., in 2003 by incorporating his sole proprietorship. For 2004, 2005, 2006, and 2007, Clear satisfied the small corporation exception and thus was able to avoid the AMT. As a result of a large increase in gross receipts in 2007 (a one-year windfall that will not recur), it appears that Clear will not meet the small corporation exception in 2008.

Victor elects S corporation status for 2008. Therefore, Clear's AMT preferences and adjustments are passed through to him on the Schedule K-1 he receives. Although this results in a small amount of AMT for 2008, there will be no AMT in 2009 or 2010. Victor plans to revoke the S corporation election for 2011. Based on the gross receipts for 2008–2010, Clear will again be eligible for the small corporation exception.

Has Victor acted appropriately in temporarily electing S status for Clear, Inc.?

AMT Adjustments

Adjustments Applicable to Individuals and Corporations.
The following adjustments that were discussed in connection with the individual AMT also apply to the corporate AMT:

- Excess of MACRS over ADS depreciation on real and personal property placed in service after 1986.
- Pollution control facilities placed in service after 1986 (AMT requires ADS depreciation over the asset's ADR life if placed in service before January 1, 1999, and over the MACRS recovery period if placed in service after December 31, 1998; 60-month amortization is allowed for regular income tax purposes).
- Mining and exploration expenditures (AMT requires amortization over 10 years versus immediate expensing allowed for regular income tax purposes).
- Income on long-term contracts (AMT requires percentage of completion method; completed contract method is allowed in limited circumstances for regular income tax purposes).
- Dispositions of assets (if gain or loss for AMT purposes differs from gain or loss for regular income tax purposes).
- Allowable ATNOLD (which cannot exceed 90 percent of AMTI before deduction for ATNOLD).

Adjustment Applicable Only to Corporations.
An AMT adjustment applicable only to corporations is the adjusted current earnings (ACE) adjustment.[44] The **ACE adjustment** generally applies to all corporations[45] and has a significant impact on both tax and financial accounting.

Corporations are subject to an AMT adjustment equal to 75 percent of the excess of ACE over AMTI before the ACE adjustment.[46] Historically, the government has not required conformity between tax accounting and financial accounting. For many years, the only *direct* conformity requirement was that a corporation that used the LIFO method for tax accounting also had to use LIFO for financial accounting.[47] Through the ACE adjustment, Congress is *indirectly* imposing a conformity requirement on corporations. Though a corporation may still choose to use different methods for tax and financial accounting purposes, it may no longer be able to do so without incurring AMT as a result of the ACE adjustment. Thus, a corporation may incur AMT not only because of specifically targeted adjustments and preferences, but also as a result of any methods that cause ACE to exceed AMTI before the ACE adjustment.

---

[44]§ 56(c).
[45]The ACE adjustment does not apply to S corporations. § 56(g)(6).

[46]§ 56(g).
[47]§ 472(c).

CONCEPT SUMMARY   12–2

Determining the ACE Adjustment*

```
                          Calculate Taxable Income

                    Calculate AMTI by adjusting Taxable
                    Income as required by § 56 and § 58
                     and increasing Taxable Income by
                          § 57 tax preference items

                    Calculate Adjusted Current Earnings
                     by adjusting AMTI as required (many
                      of the adjustments based on earnings
                           and profits adjustments)

                                    Is
                            Adjusted Current
                                Earnings
              Yes           greater than pre-          No
                                adjustment
                                  AMTI?

     Increase AMTI by 75% of the excess of      Decrease AMTI by 75% of the excess of
       Adjusted Current Earnings over AMTI       AMTI (pre-adjustment) over Adjusted
              (pre-adjustment)                   Current Earnings to extent of net
                                                        previous increases
```

*Reprinted with permission from *Oil and Gas Tax Quarterly*. Copyright 1989 Matthew Bender & Company, Inc., a member of the LexisNexis Group. All Rights Reserved.

The ACE adjustment can be either a positive or a negative amount. AMTI is increased by 75 percent of the excess of ACE over unadjusted AMTI. Or AMTI is reduced by 75 percent of the excess of unadjusted AMTI over ACE. The negative adjustment is limited to the aggregate of the positive adjustments under ACE for prior years, reduced by the previously claimed negative adjustments. See Concept Summary 12–2. Thus, the ordering of the timing differences is crucial because any lost negative adjustment is permanent. Unadjusted AMTI is AMTI without the ACE adjustment or the ATNOLD.[48]

EXAMPLE 30

A calendar year corporation has the following data:

	2007	2008	2009
Pre-adjusted AMTI	$3,000	$3,000	$3,100
Adjusted current earnings	4,000	3,000	2,000

In 2007, because ACE exceeds unadjusted AMTI by $1,000, $750 (75% × $1,000) is included as a positive adjustment to AMTI. No adjustment is necessary for 2008. As unadjusted AMTI exceeds ACE by $1,100 in 2009, there is a potential negative adjustment to AMTI of $825 ($1,100 × 75%). Since the total increases to AMTI for prior years equal $750 and there are no previously claimed negative adjustments, only $750 of the potential negative adjustment reduces AMTI for 2009. Further, $75 of the negative amount is lost forever. ■

---

[48]§§ 56(g)(1) and (2).

ACE should not be confused with current earnings and profits. Although many items are treated in the same manner, certain variations exist. For example, Federal income taxes, deductible in computing earnings and profits, are not deductible in determining ACE.

The starting point for computing ACE is AMTI, which is defined as regular taxable income after AMT adjustments (other than the ATNOLD and ACE adjustments) and tax preferences. The resulting figure is adjusted for several items in order to arrive at ACE.[49]

Tax Preferences

AMTI includes designated tax preference items. In some cases, this has the effect of subjecting nontaxable income to the AMT. Tax preference items that apply to individuals also apply to corporations.

EXAMPLE 31

The following information applies to Brown Corporation (a calendar year taxpayer) for 2008:

Taxable income	$4,000,000
Mining exploration costs	500,000
Percentage depletion claimed (the property has a zero adjusted basis)	1,700,000
Interest on City of Elmira (Michigan) private activity bonds	900,000

Brown Corporation's AMTI for 2008 is determined as follows:

Taxable income		$4,000,000
Adjustments:		
Excess mining exploration costs [$500,000 (amount expensed) − $50,000 (amount allowed over a 10-year amortization period)]		450,000
Tax preferences:		
Excess depletion	$1,700,000	
Interest on private activity bonds	900,000	2,600,000
AMTI		$7,050,000	■

Exemption Amount

The tentative AMT is 20 percent of AMTI that exceeds the corporation's exemption amount. The exemption amount for a corporation is $40,000 reduced by 25 percent of the amount by which AMTI exceeds $150,000.

EXAMPLE 32

Blue Corporation has AMTI of $180,000. The exemption amount is reduced by $7,500 [25% × ($180,000 − $150,000)], and the amount remaining is $32,500 ($40,000 − $7,500). Thus, Blue Corporation's AMT base (refer to Figure 12–3) is $147,500 ($180,000 − $32,500). ■

Note that the exemption amount phases out entirely when AMTI reaches $310,000.

Other Aspects of the AMT

All of a corporation's AMT is available for carryover as a minimum tax credit. This is so regardless of whether the adjustments and preferences originate from timing differences or AMT exclusions.

---

[49]For additional coverage of the calculation of ACE, refer to Chapter 3 in *South-Western Federal Taxation: Corporations, Partnerships, Estates, and Trusts.*

EXAMPLE 33

In Example 31, the AMTI exceeds $310,000, so no exemption is allowed. The tentative minimum tax is $1,410,000 (20% of $7,050,000). Assume the regular income tax liability is $1,360,000, and the AMT liability is $50,000 ($1,410,000 − $1,360,000). The amount of the minimum tax credit carryover is $50,000, which is all of the current year's AMT. ■

LO.8

Identify tax planning opportunities to minimize the AMT.

TAX PLANNING
Considerations

Responding to Bob and Carol

The chapter began with a set of circumstances involving Bob and Carol that raised a number of interesting questions. By now, the student should have arrived at a logical reason for the difference in Bob and Carol's tax liabilities and expect the following to happen to Bob.

Bob contacts Adam, his tax return preparer, and explains in an excited voice that he has received a bill from the IRS for $15,000 plus interest associated with the underpayment of his tax liability. Adam has Bob fax him a copy of the IRS deficiency notice. He checks Bob's tax file and then calls Bob to explain that Bob does owe the IRS the $15,000 plus interest. Somehow Bob's tax return was prepared without including a Form 6251 (the alternative minimum tax). Adam suggests that Bob stop by his office later that afternoon to discuss the disposition of the matter further.

Avoiding Preferences and Adjustments

Several strategies and elections are available to help taxpayers avoid having preferences and adjustments.

- A taxpayer who is in danger of incurring AMT liability should not invest in tax-exempt private activity bonds unless doing so makes good investment sense. Any AMT triggered by interest on private activity bonds reduces the yield on an investment in the bonds. Other tax-exempt bonds or taxable corporate bonds might yield a better after-tax return.
- A taxpayer may elect to expense certain costs in the year incurred or to capitalize and amortize the costs over some specified period. The decision should be based on the present discounted value of after-tax cash flows under the available alternatives. Costs subject to elective treatment include circulation expenditures, mining exploration and development costs, and research and experimental expenditures.

Controlling the Timing of Preferences and Adjustments

The AMT exemption often keeps items of tax preference from being subject to the AMT. To use the AMT exemption effectively, taxpayers should avoid bunching preferences and positive adjustments in any one year. To avoid this bunching, taxpayers should attempt to control the timing of such items when possible.

Taking Advantage of the AMT/Regular Tax Rate Differential

A taxpayer who cannot avoid triggering the AMT in a given year can usually save taxes by taking advantage of the rate differential between the AMT and the regular income tax.

EXAMPLE 34

Peter, a real estate dealer who expects to be in the 35% regular income tax bracket in 2009, is subject to the AMT in 2008 at the 26% rate. He is considering the sale of a parcel of land (inventory) at a gain of $100,000. If he sells the land in 2009, he will have to pay tax of $35,000 ($100,000 gain × 35% regular income tax rate). However, if he sells the land in 2008, he will pay tax of $26,000 ($100,000 gain × 26% AMT rate). Thus, accelerating the sale into 2008 will save Peter $9,000 ($35,000 − $26,000) in tax. ■

EXAMPLE 35

Cora, who expects to be in the 35% tax bracket in 2009, is subject to the AMT in 2008 at the 26% rate. She is going to contribute $10,000 in cash to her alma mater, State University. If Cora makes the contribution in 2009, she will save tax of $3,500 ($10,000 contribution × 35% regular income tax rate). However, if she makes the contribution in 2008, she will save tax of $2,600 ($10,000 contribution × 26% AMT rate). Thus, deferring the contribution until 2009 will save Cora $900 ($3,500 − $2,600) in tax. ■

This deferral/acceleration strategy should be considered for any income or expenses where the taxpayer can control the timing. This strategy applies to corporations as well as to individuals.

KEY TERMS

ACE adjustment, 12–27

Alternative minimum tax (AMT), 12–2

Alternative minimum tax credit, 12–24

Alternative tax NOL deduction (ATNOLD), 12–15

AMT adjustments, 12–4

AMT exclusions, 12–24

Circulation expenditures, 12–4

Incentive stock options (ISOs), 12–12

Private activity bonds, 12–21

Tax preferences, 12–4

PROBLEM MATERIALS

DISCUSSION QUESTIONS

1. Since there is a regular income tax, why is there a need for an AMT?

2. Distinguish between the *direct* and *indirect* methods of calculating the AMT.

3. What is the difference between AMT adjustments and tax preferences?

4. Identify which of the following are tax preferences:
   a. Seven percent of the exclusion associated with gains on the sale of certain small business stock.
   b. Exclusion on the receipt of property by gift or by inheritance.
   c. Exclusion associated with payment of premiums by the employer on group term life insurance for coverage not in excess of $50,000.
   d. Percentage depletion in excess of the property's adjusted basis.
   e. Tax-exempt interest on certain private activity bonds.
   f. Exclusion of life insurance proceeds received as the result of death.
   g. Exclusion to the employee on the employer's payments of health insurance premiums for employees.

5. Identify which of the following are tax preferences:
   a. Exclusion for qualified employee discount provided by employer.
   b. Exclusion to employee on the employer's contribution to the employee's pension plan.
   c. Excess of deduction for circulation expenditures for regular income tax purposes over the deduction for AMT purposes.
   d. Excess of amortization allowance over depreciation on pre-1987 certified pollution control facilities.
   e. Excess of accelerated over straight-line depreciation on real property placed in service before 1987.

6. Describe the tax formula for the AMT.

7. If the regular income tax liability is greater than the tentative AMT, there is no AMT liability, and the total income tax liability is equal to the regular income tax liability. Evaluate the correctness of this statement.

8. For the exemption amount, indicate the following:
   a. Purpose of the exemption.
   b. Amount of the exemption in 2008.
   c. Reason for the phaseout of the exemption.
   d. Amount at which the phaseout of the exemption begins.
   e. Amount at which the phaseout of the exemption is complete.

9. What are the AMT rates for an individual taxpayer? To what levels of income do the rates apply?

10. How do nonrefundable tax credits affect the calculation of the AMT?

11. Tony, who owns and operates a business, made improvements to land which were placed in service in June 1998. The improvements are 15-year property. Does Tony need to make an AMT adjustment in 1998 and in 2008 for the depreciation on the land improvements? Explain.

12. How can an individual taxpayer avoid having an AMT adjustment for circulation expenditures?

Issue ID

13. Rick, who is single, incurs mining exploration and development costs associated with his energy company. He would expense the costs in the current year in order to reduce his regular income tax but is aware that this would create a positive adjustment for AMT purposes. His AGI is large enough to reduce the AMT exemption amount to zero. Therefore, he is considering electing to amortize the mining exploration and development costs over 10 years to avoid having to pay any AMT. Advise Rick.

14. Both Janice and April own and operate construction companies. Janice uses the completed contract method, while April uses the percentage of completion method. Why does Janice have to be concerned with the AMT, while April does not?

15. Rocky acquired stock under an incentive stock option plan in 2005. After all conditions of employment were satisfied in 2007, the stock became freely transferable. Rocky sold the stock in 2008. Discuss the possible effects on taxable income and AMTI in each of the three years involved (i.e., 2005, 2007, 2008).

16. Two years ago, Lucy acquired a machine (seven-year property) for $30,000. She depreciated it using an accelerated method under MACRS. When she sells the machine at a gain this year, will her recognized gain for regular income tax and AMT purposes be the same? Explain.

Issue ID

17. Celine is going to be subject to the AMT in 2008. She owns an investment building and is considering disposing of it and investing in other realty. Based on an appraisal of the building's value, the realized gain would be $85,000. Ed has offered to purchase the building from Celine with the closing date being December 29, 2008. Ed wants to close the transaction in 2008 because certain beneficial tax consequences will result only if the transaction is closed prior to the beginning of 2009. Abby has offered to purchase the building with the closing date being January 2, 2009. The building has a $95,000 greater AMT adjusted basis. For regular income tax purposes, Celine expects to be in the 25% tax bracket in 2008 and the 28% tax bracket in 2009. What are the relevant tax issues that Celine faces in making her decision?

18. Passive activity losses are not deductible in computing either taxable income or AMTI. Explain why an adjustment for passive activity losses may be required for AMT purposes.

19. What effect do adjustments and preferences have on the calculation of the ATNOLD?

20. The following itemized deductions are allowed for regular income tax purposes: medical expenses, state and local income taxes or sales tax, real estate taxes, personal property taxes, home mortgage interest, investment interest, charitable contributions of cash, charitable contributions of property, casualty and theft losses, unreimbursed

employee business expenses, and gambling losses. Which of these itemized deductions can result in an AMT adjustment?

21. Matt, who is single, has always elected to itemize deductions rather than take the standard deduction. In prior years, his itemized deductions always exceeded the standard deduction by a substantial amount. As a result of paying off the mortgage on his residence, he projects that his itemized deductions for 2008 will exceed the standard deduction by only $500. Matt anticipates that the amount of his itemized deductions will remain about the same in the foreseeable future. Matt's AGI is $150,000. He is investing the amount of his former mortgage payment each month in tax-exempt bonds. A friend recommends that Matt buy a beach house in order to increase his itemized deductions with the mortgage interest deduction. What are the relevant tax issues for Matt?

Issue ID

22. Willy's 3% cutback adjustment for regular income tax purposes reduces his itemized deductions from $34,000 to $28,000. What effect will this have in calculating Willy's AMTI?

23. In computing the AMT itemized deduction for interest, it is possible that some interest allowed for regular income tax purposes will not be allowed. Explain.

24. Could computation of the AMT ever require an adjustment for the standard deduction or personal and dependency exemptions? Explain.

25. Karl owns a mineral deposit that qualifies for percentage depletion. In 2008, he deducts $30,000 for regular income tax purposes. Cost depletion for the year would have been $18,000.
    a. Does the fact that percentage depletion exceeds cost depletion produce an AMT preference?
    b. Under what circumstances would Karl have an AMT preference for depletion?

26. Erika receives $4,200 of interest on private activity bonds and has related expenses of $400.
    a. What is the effect on Erika's taxable income?
    b. What is the effect on her AMTI?
    c. Could there be a related beneficial effect in calculating AMTI?

Decision Making

27. What is the purpose of the AMT credit? Briefly describe how the credit is computed.

28. Gray was incorporated in 1998, while Char was incorporated in 2008.
    a. Under what circumstances is Gray exempt from the AMT?
    b. Under what circumstances is Char exempt from the AMT?

29. What is the ACE adjustment? Does it apply to both individual and corporate taxpayers?

30. Lee is an equipment dealer who will be subject to the AMT in 2008. He has an opportunity to make a sale of equipment at a substantial gain in either December 2008 or January 2009. Discuss tax planning strategies Lee should consider in connection with the sale.

Issue ID

PROBLEMS

31. Use the following data to calculate Reba's AMT base in 2008:

Taxable income	$190,000
Positive AMT adjustments	75,000
Negative AMT adjustments	70,000
AMT preferences	30,000

Reba will file as a single tax payer.

32. Arthur Wesson, an unmarried individual who is age 68, has taxable income of $157,000. He has AMT positive adjustments of $43,000 and tax preferences of $40,000.
    a. What is Arthur's AMT?
    b. What is the total amount of Arthur's tax liability?
    c. Draft a letter to Arthur explaining why he must pay more than the regular income tax liability. Arthur's address is 100 Colonel's Way, Conway, SC 29526.

Communications

33. Calculate the AMT for the following cases in 2008. The taxpayer has regular taxable income of $475,000 and does not have any credits.

| | Tentative AMT | |
Filing Status	Case 1	Case 2
Single	$190,000	$175,000
Married, filing jointly	190,000	175,000

34. Calculate the exemption amount for the following cases in 2008 for a single taxpayer, a married taxpayer filing jointly, and a married taxpayer filing separately.

Case	AMTI
1	$150,000
2	260,000
3	500,000

35. Leona has nonrefundable credits of $65,000 for 2008. None of these nonrefundable credits are personal credits that qualify for special treatment. Her regular income tax liability before credits is $135,000, and her tentative AMT is $78,000.
    a.   What is the amount of Leona's AMT?
    b.   What is the amount of Leona's regular income tax liability after credits?

Decision Making

36. Angela, who is single, incurs circulation expenditures of $153,000 during 2008. She is in the process of deciding whether to expense the $153,000 or to capitalize it and elect to deduct it over a three-year period. Angela already knows that she will be subject to the AMT for 2008 at both the 26% and the 28% rates. Angela is in the 28% bracket for regular income tax purposes this year (has regular taxable income of $153,000 before considering the circulation expenses) and expects to be in the 28% bracket in 2009 and 2010. Advise Angela on whether she should elect the three-year write-off rather than expensing the $153,000 in 2008.

37. Vito owns and operates a news agency (as a sole proprietorship). During 2008, he incurred expenses of $150,000 to increase circulation of newspapers and magazines that his agency distributes. For regular income tax purposes, he elected to expense the $150,000 in 2008. In addition, he incurred $90,000 in circulation expenditures in 2009 and again elected expense treatment. What AMT adjustments will be required in 2008 and 2009 as a result of the circulation expenditures?

38. Ted acquires an apartment building for $900,000 in March with $700,000 being allocated to the building and $200,000 to the land. Determine the amount of the AMT cost recovery adjustment for 2008 if the apartment building is purchased and placed in service in:
    a.   1998.
    b.   2008.

Decision Making

Communications

39. In March 2008, Helen Carlon acquired used equipment for her business at a cost of $300,000. The equipment is five-year class property for regular income tax purposes and for AMT purposes.
    a.   If Helen depreciates the equipment using the method that will produce the greatest deduction for 2008 for regular income tax purposes, what is the amount of the AMT adjustment? Helen does not elect § 179 limited expensing.
    b.   How can Helen reduce the AMT adjustment to $0? What circumstances would motivate her to do so?
    c.   Draft a letter to Helen regarding the choice of depreciation methods. Helen's address is 500 Monticello Avenue, Glendale, AZ 85306.

Decision Making

40. In 2008, Geoff incurred $800,000 of mining and exploration expenditures. He elects to deduct the expenditures as quickly as the tax law allows for regular income tax purposes.

a. How will Geoff's treatment of mining and exploration expenditures affect his regular income tax and AMT computations for 2008?

b. How can Geoff avoid having AMT adjustments related to the mining and exploration expenditures?

c. What factors should Geoff consider in deciding whether to deduct the expenditures in the year incurred?

41. Josepi's construction company uses the completed contract method. During the three-year period 2008–2010, Josepi recognized the following income on his two construction contracts:

Year	Contract 1	Contract 2
2008	$600,000*	$ –0–
2009	–0–	–0–
2010	–0–	700,000**

  * Construction completed in 2008.

**Construction completed in 2010.

If Josepi had used the percentage of completion method, he would have recognized the following income:

Year	Contract 1	Contract 2
2008	$40,000	$175,000
2009	–0–	225,000
2010	–0–	300,000

Calculate the AMT adjustment for 2008, 2009, and 2010.

42. Burt, the CFO of Amber, Inc., is granted stock options in 2008 that qualify as incentive stock options. In 2013, the rights in the stock become freely transferable and not subject to a substantial risk of forfeiture. Burt exercises the stock options in 2012 when the option price is $70,000 and the fair market value of the stock is $100,000. He sells the stock in 2016 for $150,000. What are the regular income tax consequences and the AMT consequences for Burt in:

a. 2008?

b. 2012?

c. 2013?

d. 2016?

43. On June 1, 2007, Len, the CFO of Beige, Inc., received options to purchase 1,000 shares of stock at $20 per share. The stock options qualify as ISOs. On the issue date, the stock was selling for $15 per share. Len exercised all of the options on May 15, 2008, when the stock was selling for $26 per share. There are no limitations on Len's ability to sell the stock. Len sold the 1,000 shares of stock on July 12, 2009, for $38,000.

a. Determine the regular income tax consequences for Len in 2007, 2008, and 2009.

b. Calculate the AMT consequences for Len in 2007, 2008, and 2009.

44. Buford sells an apartment building for $720,000. His adjusted basis is $406,000 for regular income tax purposes and $450,000 for AMT purposes. Calculate Buford's:

a. Gain for regular income tax purposes.

b. Gain for AMT purposes.

c. AMT adjustment, if any.

45. Freda acquired a passive activity in 2008 for $870,000. Gross income from operations of the activity was $160,000. Operating expenses, not including depreciation, were $122,000. Regular income tax depreciation of $49,750 was computed under MACRS. AMT depreciation, computed under ADS, was $41,000. Compute Freda's passive loss deduction and passive loss suspended for regular income tax purposes and for AMT purposes.

46. Wally and Gloria incur and pay medical expenses in excess of insurance reimbursements during the year as follows:

For Wally	$11,000
For Gloria (spouse)	4,000
For Chuck (son)	1,500
For Carter (Gloria's father)	13,000

Wally and Gloria's AGI is $200,000. They file a joint return. Chuck and Carter are Wally and Gloria's dependents.
a.   What is Wally and Gloria's medical expense deduction for regular income tax purposes?
b.   What is Wally and Gloria's medical expense deduction for AMT purposes?
c.   What is the amount of the AMT adjustment for medical expenses?

47. Wolfgang's AGI is $140,000. He has the following itemized deductions for 2008:

Medical expenses [$12,000 – (7.5% × $140,000)]	$ 1,500
State income taxes	4,200
Charitable contributions	5,000
Home mortgage interest on his personal residence	6,500
Casualty loss (after $100 and 10% reductions)	1,800
Miscellaneous itemized deductions [$3,500 – 2%($140,000)]	700
	$19,700

a.   Calculate Wolfgang's itemized deductions for AMT purposes.
b.   What is the amount of the AMT adjustment?

48. Tom, who is single, owns a personal residence in the city. He also owns a cabin near a ski resort in the mountains. He uses the cabin as a vacation home. In February 2008, he borrowed $75,000 on a home equity loan and used the proceeds to reduce credit card obligations and other debt. During 2008, he paid the following amounts of interest:

On his personal residence	$12,000
On the cabin	6,000
On the home equity loan	4,500
On credit card obligations	1,200

What amount, if any, must Tom recognize as an AMT adjustment in 2008?

49. Gail pays investment interest of $52,000. She has interest income of $21,000 on taxable bonds, $12,000 on tax-exempt private activity bonds, and $14,000 on regular tax-exempt bonds. Her other investment expenses are $4,000, none of which relates to the tax-exempt bonds.
a.   What is Gail's deduction for investment interest for regular income tax purposes?
b.   What is the amount of her investment interest carryover for regular income tax purposes?
c.   What is the amount of the adjustment for AMT purposes?

50. Bill, who is single with no dependents, had AGI of $100,000 in 2008. His AGI included net investment income of $15,000 and gambling income of $1,100. Bill incurred the following itemized deductions for income tax purposes:

Medical expenses (before 7.5%-of-AGI floor)	$11,000
State income taxes	3,200
Personal property tax	2,000
Real estate tax	8,400
Interest on personal residence	12,200
Interest on home (never rented to others)	3,800
Interest on home equity loan (proceeds were used to buy a new automobile)	2,700
Investment interest expense	3,300
Charitable contribution	5,000
Casualty loss (after $100 floor, before 10%-of-AGI floor)	13,000
Unreimbursed employee expenses (before 2%-of-AGI floor)	2,400
Gambling losses	900

What is the amount of Bill's AMT adjustment for itemized deductions and is it positive or negative?

51. Peggy is single and has no dependents. She has taxable income of $125,000 and tax preferences of $50,500 in 2008. She does not itemize deductions for regular income tax purposes. Compute Peggy's AMT exemption and AMTI for 2008.

52. Hector purchased a silver mine several years ago for $800,000. His adjusted basis at the beginning of the year is $350,000. For the year, he deducts depletion of $500,000 (greater of cost depletion of $230,000 or percentage depletion of $500,000) for regular income tax purposes. Calculate Hector's:
    a. AMT adjustment.
    b. Adjusted basis for regular income tax purposes.
    c. Adjusted basis for AMT purposes.

53. Amos incurred and expensed intangible drilling costs (IDC) of $70,000. His net oil and gas income was $60,000. What is the amount of Amos's tax preference item for IDC?

54. Jack, who is single with no dependents and does not itemize, provides you with the following information for 2008:

Short-term capital loss	$ 5,000
Long-term capital gain	25,000
Municipal bond interest received on private activity bonds acquired in 1997	9,000
Dividends from Citigroup	1,500
Excess of FMV over cost of ISOs (the rights became freely transferable and not subject to a substantial risk of forfeiture in 2008)	35,000

What is the total amount of Jack's tax preference items and AMT adjustments for 2008?

55. Pat, who is single with no dependents, received a salary of $90,000 in 2008. She had interest income of $1,000, dividend income of $5,000, gambling income of $4,000, and interest income from private activity bonds of $40,000. The dividends are not qualified dividends. The following additional information is relevant:

Medical expenses (before 7.5%-of-AGI floor)	$12,000
State income taxes	4,100
Real estate taxes	2,800
Mortgage interest on residence	3,100
Investment interest expense	1,800
Gambling losses	5,100

Compute Pat's tentative minimum tax for 2008.

56. Renee and Sanjeev, who are married, had taxable income of $273,000 for 2008. They had positive AMT adjustments of $38,000, negative AMT adjustments of $14,000, and tax preference items of $67,500.
    a. Compute their AMTI.
    b. Compute their tentative minimum tax.

57. Farr, who is single, has no dependents and does not itemize. She has the following items relative to her tax return for 2008:

Bargain element from the exercise of an ISO (no restrictions apply to the stock)	$ 45,000
MACRS depreciation on shopping mall building acquired after 1986 and before 1999 (ADS depreciation would have yielded $26,000)	49,000
Percentage depletion in excess of property's adjusted basis	50,000
Taxable income for regular income tax purposes	121,000

    a. Determine Farr's AMT adjustments and preferences for 2008.
    b. Calculate the AMT (if any) for 2008.

58. Hal and Wilma have no dependents and file a joint return for 2008. Based on the information below, compute their AMT for the year.

Income:

Hal's salary	$100,000
Dividend income (jointly owned stock)	5,500
Wilma's business income	70,000

Expenditures:

State income taxes	1,500
Real estate taxes	4,800
Mortgage (qualified housing) interest	8,600
Investment interest	7,000
Charitable contributions	28,000

Additional information:

- Wilma's business income comes from a news agency she owns and operates as a sole proprietorship. During 2008, Wilma incurred expenses of $30,000 to increase circulation of the newspapers and magazines her agency distributes. She elects to expense these items for regular income tax purposes.
- Hal and Wilma earn $12,000 interest on State of New York bonds they acquired in 2004. These bonds are classified as private activity bonds.

59. Bonnie, who is single, has taxable income of $0 in 2008. She has positive timing adjustments of $200,000 and AMT exclusion items of $100,000 for the year. What is the amount of Bonnie's AMT credit for carryover to 2009?

60. Aqua, Inc., a calendar year corporation, has the following gross receipts and taxable income for 2001–2008:

Year	Gross Receipts	Taxable Income
2001	$6,000,000	$1,450,000
2002	6,200,000	1,375,000
2003	6,100,000	1,425,000
2004	8,000,000	1,400,000
2005	7,000,000	1,312,000
2006	7,500,000	985,000
2007	7,200,000	1,002,000
2008	7,100,000	1,010,000

a. When is Aqua first exempt from the AMT as a small corporation?
b. Is Aqua subject to the AMT for 2008?

61. Gray Corporation (a calendar year corporation) reports the following information for the years listed below:

	2007	2008	2009
Unadjusted AMTI	$3,000	$2,000	$5,000
Adjusted current earnings	4,000	3,000	2,000

Compute the ACE adjustment for each year.

62. In each of the following independent situations, determine the tentative AMT:

	AMTI (before the exemption amount)
Quincy Corporation	$150,000
Redland Corporation	160,000
Tanzen Corporation	320,000

63. Amber, Inc., has taxable income of $200,000. During the year, Amber paid dividends of $30,000. The corporation had $20,000 of positive AMT adjustments and $25,000 of tax preferences.
    a.   Calculate Amber's regular income tax liability.
    b.   Calculate Amber's AMTI and AMT.

CUMULATIVE PROBLEMS

64. Robert M. and Jane R. Armstrong live at 1802 College Avenue, Carmel, IN 46302. They are married and file a joint return for 2007. The Armstrongs have two dependent children, Ellen J. and Sean M., who are 10-year-old twins. Ellen's Social Security number is 333–42–3368, and Sean's is 333–42–3369. Robert pays child support of $12,000 for Amy, his 17-year-old daughter from his previous marriage. Amy's Social Security number is 111–22–4300. According to the divorce decree, Margaret, Robert's former wife, has legal custody of Amy. Margaret provides the balance of Amy's support (about $6,000).

   Robert (224–36–9987) is a factory foreman, and Jane (443–56–3421) is a computer systems analyst. The Armstrongs' W–2 Forms for 2007 reflect the following information:

Tax Return Problem

Communications

	Robert	Jane
Salary (Indiana Foundry, Inc.)	$91,000	
Salary (Carmel Computer Associates)		$104,000
Federal income tax withheld	22,750	26,000
Social Security wages	91,000	97,500
Social Security tax withheld	5,642	6,045
Medicare wages	91,000	104,000
Medicare tax withheld	1,320	1,508
State wages	91,000	104,000
State income tax withheld	3,970	4,710

In addition to their salaries, the Armstrongs had the following income items in 2007:

Interest income (Carmel Sanitation District Bonds)	$20,500
Interest income (Carmel National Bank)	3,100
Qualified dividend income (Able Computer Corporation)	14,000
Gambling income	4,200
Gift from Uncle Raymond to Robert	5,000

Jane inherited $600,000 from her grandfather in January and invested the money in the Carmel Sanitation District Bonds, which are private activity bonds. Jane was selected as the "Citizen of the Year" and received an award of $6,000. She used the $6,000 to pay credit card debt.

   The Armstrongs incurred the following expenses during 2007:

Medical expenses (doctor and hospital bills)	$19,000
Real property tax on personal residence	4,900
Mortgage interest on personal residence (reported on Form 1098)	6,400
Investment interest expense	2,300
Contributions	9,000
Gambling losses	4,800
Sales taxes (from sales tax table)	1,851

On March 1, Robert and Jane contributed Ace stock to the Carmel Salvation Army, a public charity. They had acquired the stock on February 9, 1996, for $5,200. The stock was listed on the New York Stock Exchange at a value of $6,500 on the date of the contribution. In addition, Robert and Jane contributed $2,500 during the year to Second Church.

Robert sold five acres of land to a real estate developer on October 12, 2007, for $95,000. He had acquired the land on May 15, 2003, for $77,000.

Use Forms 1040, 4952, 6251, and 8283 and Schedules A, B, and D to compute the tax liability (including AMT) for Robert and Jane Armstrong for 2007. Suggested software: TaxCut. Write a letter to the Armstrongs indicating whether they have a refund or balance due for 2007, and suggest possible tax planning strategies for 2008.

Tax Computation Problem

65. Ron T. Freeman, age 38, is single and has no dependents. Ron's Social Security number is 444–11–2222. His address is 201 Front Street, Missoula, MT 59812. He is independently wealthy as a result of having inherited sizable holdings in real estate and corporate stocks and bonds. Ron is a minister at First Methodist Church, but he accepts no salary from the church. However, he does reside in the church's parsonage free of charge. The fair rental value of the parsonage is $2,500 a month. The church also provides him a cash grocery allowance of $250 a week. Examination of Ron's financial records provides the following information for 2008:

a. On January 16, 2008, Ron sold 2,000 shares of stock for a gain of $29,000. The stock was acquired nine months ago.

b. He received $40,000 of interest on private activity bonds. He also received $20,000 of interest on tax-exempt bonds that are not private activity bonds.

c. He received gross rent income of $178,000 from an apartment complex he owns. He qualifies as an active participant.

d. Expenses related to the apartment complex, which he acquired in 1986, were $217,000.

e. Ron's interest income (on CDs) totaled $15,000. Since he invests only in growth stocks, he has no dividend income.

f. He won $6,000 on the lottery.

g. On October 9, 2005, Ron exercised his rights under Egret Corporation's incentive stock option plan. For an option price of $30,000, he acquired stock worth $65,000. The stock became freely transferable in 2008. At the date the stocks became freely transferable, the fair market value was $90,000.

h. Ron was the beneficiary of an $800,000 life insurance policy on his Uncle Jake. He received the proceeds in October.

i. Ron had the following potential itemized deductions *from* AGI:

- $4,600 fair market value of stock contributed to Methodist Church (basis of stock was $3,000). He had owned the stock for two years.
- $3,800 interest on consumer purchases.
- $4,200 state and local income tax.
- $5,500 medical expenses (before 7.5% floor) for himself. He also paid $10,000 of medical expenses for a parishioner who died.
- $300 for a safe deposit box that is used to store investments and related legal documents.
- $4,500 paid for lottery tickets associated with playing the state lottery. Ron contributed his net winnings of $1,500 to the church.
- $4,000 contribution to his traditional IRA.
- Since Ron lived in Montana, he had no sales tax.
- $500 contribution to the campaign of the Democratic candidate for governor.

Compute Ron's tax liability, including AMT if applicable, before prepayments or credits, for 2008.

RESEARCH PROBLEMS

Note: Solutions to Research Problems can be prepared by using the **RIA Checkpoint®** **Student Edition** online research product, which is available to accompany this text. It is also possible to prepare solutions to the Research Problems by using tax research materials found in a standard tax library.

Research Problem 1. Samuel had worked for Pearl, Inc., for 35 years when he was discharged and his position filled by a much younger person. He filed and pursued a suit for age discrimination and received an award of $1.5 million. Under the contingent fee arrangement with his attorney, one-third of the award was paid directly to the attorney with the balance going to Samuel. Samuel reported the $1 million on his income tax return but did not include the $500,000 paid to the attorney.

The IRS audited Samuel's return and included the $500,000 contingency fee in his gross income. Additionally, Samuel was allowed a miscellaneous itemized deduction (subject to the 2% floor) for the fee paid to the attorney. The IRS adjustment caused a tax deficiency to be assessed for both the regular income tax and the AMT.

Evaluate the result reached.

Research Problem 2. In filing his tax return for 2007, Rayford Giles includes a Form 6251 for the AMT. In making the AMT calculation, he included itemized deductions that were allowable for AMT purposes of $20,000. In calculating his regular income tax liability, he used the standard deduction of $5,000 because his itemized deductions were completely phased out under § 68. By using the itemized deductions in calculating his AMT, Rayford was able to reduce his AMT liability. As support for his position, Rayford cites § 56(b)(1)(F), which provides that the itemized deduction phaseout (applicable in calculating the regular income tax) does not apply in calculating the AMT.

Will Rayford's position withstand IRS scrutiny?

Research Problem 3. Masha Quigly filed her return for 2006 and reported taxable income of $48,700. This consisted of the following:

AGI (includes $2,000 state income tax refund previously deducted with a tax benefit)	$80,000
Personal exemption	(3,300)
Miscellaneous itemized deductions in excess of 2% of AGI	(28,000)
Taxable income	$48,700

Although Masha had state and local tax expense of $9,000, she chose not to deduct them in calculating taxable income. Masha believed that if she claimed the state and local taxes, she would be subject to the AMT. As a result, she reported a tax liability of $8,739.

Upon audit of the return, the IRS concluded that Masha should have included the $9,000 of state and local taxes in her itemized deductions. Thus, her decision to not deduct the state and local taxes did not relieve her from being subject to the AMT.

Who is right?

Research Problem 4. On his 2007 Federal income tax return, Walter deducted state income taxes of $8,000 for amounts withheld and estimated tax payments made in 2007. When he filed his 2007 state income tax return in April 2008, he discovered that he had overpaid his state income taxes by $1,500. Rather than having the $1,500 refunded to him, he treated it as a 2008 estimated tax payment. The year 2007 was not an AMT year for Walter.

In preparing his 2008 Federal income tax return, Walter is confused about how he should treat the $1,500 in calculating his Federal income tax liability. He knows that under the § 111 tax benefit rule, he should include the $1,500 in gross income in calculating his regular taxable income. However, since he is going to be subject to the AMT, he is uncertain as to how he should treat the $1,500 in calculating AMT. He thinks that the amount could be treated as a negative adjustment in converting taxable income to AMTI if 2007 had been an AMT year. Since it was not, Walter is unsure of the treatment.

Advise Walter on the appropriate treatment of the $1,500 in calculating his 2008 Federal income tax liability.

Use the tax resources of the Internet to address the following questions. Do not restrict your search to the World Wide Web, but include a review of newsgroups and general reference materials, practitioner sites and resources, primary sources of the tax law, chat rooms and discussion groups, and other opportunities.

 **Internet** *Activity*

Research Problem 5. Locate a current proposal to modify the structure or scope of the AMT for individuals. Describe the proposal, the entity making the proposal, and potential motivations for submitting the modification to Congress.

Research Problem 6.   Go to one of the tax newsgroups and post a short note on one of the following items relative to individuals who are subject to the AMT:

a. Interest deductions on vacation homes.
b. Charitable contributions of appreciated securities.
c. Tax preparation fees.
d. Adequacy of the exemption amount.
e. Indexing of AMT rates.

Research Problem 7.   Ascertain if your state's income tax has an AMT component. If your state does not levy an income tax, choose a contiguous state that does.

CHAPTER **13**

Tax Credits and Payment Procedures

LEARNING OBJECTIVES

After completing Chapter 13, you should be able to:

LO.1
Explain how tax credits are used as a tool of Federal tax policy.

LO.2
Distinguish between refundable and nonrefundable credits and understand the order in which they can be used by taxpayers.

LO.3
Describe various business-related tax credits.

LO.4
Describe various tax credits that are available primarily to individual taxpayers.

LO.5
Understand the tax withholding and payment procedures applicable to employers.

LO.6
Understand the payment procedures applicable to self-employed persons.

LO.7
Identify tax planning opportunities related to tax credits and payment procedures.

OUTLINE

Tax Policy Considerations, 13–3
Overview and Priority of Credits, 13–4
   Refundable versus Nonrefundable Credits, 13–4
   General Business Credit, 13–5
   Treatment of Unused General Business Credits, 13–6
Specific Business-Related Tax Credit Provisions, 13–7
   Tax Credit for Rehabilitation Expenditures, 13–7
   Work Opportunity Tax Credit, 13–9
   Research Activities Credit, 13–10
   Low-Income Housing Credit, 13–13
   Disabled Access Credit, 13–13
   Credit for Small Employer Pension Plan Startup Costs, 13–14
   Credit for Employer-Provided Child Care, 13–14
Other Tax Credits, 13–15
   Earned Income Credit, 13–15

Tax Credit for Elderly or Disabled Taxpayers, 13–17
Foreign Tax Credit, 13–18
Adoption Expenses Credit, 13–20
Child Tax Credit, 13–21
Credit for Child and Dependent Care Expenses, 13–21
Education Tax Credits, 13–24
Credit for Certain Retirement Plan Contributions, 13–25
Recovery Rebate Credit, 13–26
Payment Procedures, 13–26
   Procedures Applicable to Employers, 13–26
   Procedures Applicable to Self-Employed Persons, 13–38
Tax Planning Considerations, 13–42
   Foreign Tax Credit, 13–42
   Credit for Child and Dependent Care Expenses, 13–42
   Adjustments to Increase Withholding, 13–44
   Adjustments to Avoid Overwithholding, 13–44

As explained in Chapter 1, Federal tax law often serves purposes besides merely raising revenue for the government. Evidence of equity, social, and economic considerations, among others, is found throughout the tax law. These considerations also bear heavily in the area of **tax credits**. Consider the following examples:

EXAMPLE 1

Paul and Peggy, husband and wife, are both employed outside the home. Their combined salaries are $50,000. However, after paying for child care expenses of $2,000 on behalf of their daughter, Polly, the net economic benefit from both spouses working is $48,000. The child care expenses are, in a sense, business related since they would not have been incurred if both spouses did not work outside the home. If no tax benefits are associated with the child care expenditures, $50,000 is subject to tax.

Another couple, Alicia and Diego, also have a child, John. Diego stays at home to care for John (the value of those services is $2,000) while Alicia earns a $48,000 salary. Because the value of Diego's services rendered is not subject to tax, only Alicia's earnings of $48,000 are subject to tax. ■

The credit for child and dependent care expenses mitigates the inequity felt by working taxpayers who must pay for child care services in order to work outside the home.

EXAMPLE 2

Graham, age 66, is a retired taxpayer who receives $17,000 of Social Security benefits as his only source of income in 2008. His Social Security benefits are excluded from gross income. Therefore, Graham's income tax is $0. In 2008, Olga, a single taxpayer 66 years of age, has, as her sole source of income, $17,000 from a pension plan funded by her former employer. Assuming Olga has no itemized deductions or deductions *for* AGI, her income tax for 2008 (before credits) is $670, based on the following computation:

Pension plan benefits	$17,000
Less: Basic standard deduction	(5,450)
Additional standard deduction	(1,350)
Personal exemption	(3,500)
Taxable income	$ 6,700
Income tax (at 10%)	$ 670

The tax credit for elderly or disabled taxpayers was enacted to mitigate this inequity.

EXAMPLE 3

Jane is a single parent who depends on the government's "safety net" for survival—she receives benefits under the Temporary Assistance to Needy Families program in the amount of $15,000 per year. However, she very much wishes to work. Jane has located a job that will pay $15,500 per year and has found an individual to care for her child at no cost. But, with the $1,185.75 ($15,500 × 7.65%) withholding for Social Security and Medicare taxes, the economic benefit from working is less than remaining reliant on the government ($14,314.25 as compared to $15,000). ∎

To help offset the effect of Social Security and Medicare taxes on wages of the working poor and to provide an incentive to work, the earned income credit is used to increase the after-tax earnings of qualified individuals. In addition, the earned income credit helps offset the regressive nature of certain taxes, such as the Social Security and Medicare taxes, which impose a relatively larger burden on low-income taxpayers than on more affluent taxpayers.

These tax credits and many of the other important tax credits available to individuals and other types of taxpayers are a major focus of this chapter. The chapter begins by discussing important tax policy considerations relevant to tax credits. Tax credits are categorized as being either refundable or nonrefundable. The distinction between refundable and nonrefundable credits is important because it may affect the taxpayer's ability to enjoy a tax benefit from a particular credit.

Next, an overview of the priority of tax credits is presented. The chapter continues with a discussion of the credits available to businesses and to individual taxpayers and the ways in which credits enter into the calculation of the tax liability.

The Federal tax system has long been based on the pay-as-you-go concept. That is, taxpayers or their employers are required to make regular deposits with the Federal government during the year as payment toward the tax liability that will be determined at the end of the tax year. These deposits are in effect refundable credits. The chapter concludes with a discussion of procedures used in calculating tax deposits, special problems encountered by self-employed persons when estimating their tax payments, and penalties imposed on underpayments.

Tax Policy Considerations

LO.1

Explain how tax credits are used as a tool of Federal tax policy.

Congress has generally used tax credits to achieve social or economic objectives or to promote equity among different types of taxpayers. For example, the disabled access credit was enacted to accomplish a social objective: to encourage taxpayers to renovate older buildings so they would be in compliance with the Americans with Disabilities Act. This Act requires businesses and institutions to make their facilities more accessible to persons with various types of disabilities. As another example, the foreign tax credit, which has been a part of the law for decades, has as its purpose the economic and equity objectives of mitigating the burden of multiple taxation on a single stream of income.

A tax credit should not be confused with an income tax deduction. Certain expenditures of individuals (e.g., business expenses) are permitted as deductions from gross income in arriving at adjusted gross income (AGI). Additionally, individuals are allowed to deduct certain nonbusiness and investment-related expenses *from* AGI. While the tax benefit received from a tax deduction depends on the tax rate, a tax credit is not affected by the tax rate of the taxpayer.

EXAMPLE 4

Assume Congress wishes to encourage a certain type of expenditure. One way to accomplish this objective is to allow a tax credit of 25% for such expenditures. Another way is to allow an itemized deduction for the expenditures. Assume that Abby's tax rate is 15%, while Bill's tax rate is 35%, and that each itemizes deductions. In addition, assume that Carmen does not

---

TAX *in the News*   FEDERAL TAX LAW IS A KEY COMPONENT OF U.S. ENERGY POLICY

To help stem the increasing dependence of the United States on foreign sources of energy, Congress enacted the Energy Tax Incentives Act of 2005. The legislation provides numerous tax breaks for power producers as well as for consumers, many of which take the form of tax credits. The primary goals of the tax provisions are to improve energy-related infrastructure, provide more incentives for traditional fossil fuel production, and encourage higher levels of energy conservation.

Some of the more widely applicable provisions include credits for:

- Builders who construct energy-efficient homes.
- Individuals who make energy-saving improvements to their residences.
- Manufacturers that make energy-efficient appliances.

- Businesses that buy fuel cell and microturbine power plants.
- Taxpayers who purchase alternative power motor vehicles and refueling property.

Like many other tax credits, the energy credits have been designed to modify taxpayer behavior. More specifically, in this case, Congress's intention is that these credits will lead to greater conservation and more efficient use of energy. At the bill-signing ceremony, President Bush remarked that the legislation is "not a bill for today or necessarily a bill for tomorrow, but it's a bill for the future." Only time will tell whether Congress's intentions and President Bush's prediction of greater energy independence for the United States will prove to be true.

---

incur enough qualifying expenditures to itemize deductions. The following tax benefits are available to each taxpayer for a $1,000 expenditure:

	Abby	Bill	Carmen
Tax benefit if a 25% credit is allowed	$250	$250	$250
Tax benefit if an itemized deduction is allowed	150	350	–0–

As these results indicate, tax credits provide benefits on a more equitable basis than do tax deductions. Equally apparent is that the deduction approach in this case benefits only taxpayers who itemize deductions, while the credit approach benefits all taxpayers who make the specified expenditure. ■

For many years, Congress has used the tax credit provisions of the Code liberally in implementing tax policy. Although budget constraints and economic considerations often have dictated the repeal of some credits, other credits, such as those applicable to expenses incurred for child and dependent care, have been kept to respond to important social policy considerations. Still other credits, such as the one available to low-income workers, have been retained based on economic and equity considerations. Finally, as the myriad of tax proposals so frequently pending before Congress makes clear, the use of tax credits as a tax policy tool continues to evolve as economic and political circumstances change.

LO.2

Distinguish between refundable and nonrefundable credits and understand the order in which they can be used by taxpayers.

Overview and Priority of Credits

Refundable versus Nonrefundable Credits

As illustrated in Exhibit 13–1, certain credits are refundable while others are nonrefundable. **Refundable credits** are paid to the taxpayer even if the amount of the credit (or credits) exceeds the taxpayer's tax liability.

EXAMPLE 5

Ted, who is single, had taxable income of $21,000 in 2008. His income tax from the 2008 Tax Rate Schedule is $2,749. During 2008, Ted's employer withheld income tax of $3,200. Ted is entitled to a refund of $451 because the credit for tax withheld on wages is a refundable credit. ■

EXHIBIT 13–1	Partial Listing of Refundable and Nonrefundable Credits

Refundable Credits

Taxes withheld on wages

Earned income credit

Nonrefundable Credits

Credit for child and dependent care expenses

Credit for elderly or disabled

Adoption expenses credit

Child tax credit*

Education tax credits

Credit for certain retirement plan contributions

Foreign tax credit

General business credit, which includes the following:

- Tax credit for rehabilitation expenditures
- Work opportunity tax credit
- Research activities credit
- Low-income housing credit
- Disabled access credit
- Credit for small employer pension plan startup costs
- Credit for employer-provided child care

* The credit is refundable to the extent of 15 percent of the taxpayer's earned income in excess of $12,050 for 2008 (indexed for inflation). Parents with three or more qualifying children may compute the refundable portion using an alternative method.

Nonrefundable credits are not paid if they exceed the taxpayer's tax liability.

EXAMPLE 6

Tina is single, age 67, and retired. Her taxable income for 2008 is $1,320, and the tax on this amount is $132. Tina's tax credit for the elderly is $225. This credit can be used to reduce her net tax liability to zero, but it will not result in a refund, even though the credit ($225) exceeds Tina's tax liability ($132). This result occurs because the tax credit for the elderly is a nonrefundable credit. ∎

Some nonrefundable credits, such as the foreign tax credit, are subject to carryover provisions if they exceed the amount allowable as a credit in a given year. Other nonrefundable credits, such as the tax credit for the elderly (refer to Example 6), are lost if they exceed the limitations. Because some credits are refundable and others are not and because some credits are subject to carryover provisions while others are not, the order in which credits are offset against the tax liability can be important.[1]

General Business Credit

As shown in Exhibit 13–1, the **general business credit** is composed of a number of other credits, each of which is computed separately under its own set of rules. The

---

[1] With the passage of the Tax Relief Reconciliation Act of 2001, the ordering rules and limitations applied when offsetting tax credits against both the regular income tax liability and the alternative minimum tax liability have become increasingly complex. In addition, different variations of these rules will apply over time as this legislation is fully implemented. Further discussion of the intricacies of these rules is beyond the scope of this chapter.

general business credit combines these credits into one amount to limit the amount of business credits that can be used to offset a taxpayer's income tax liability. The idea behind combining the credits is to prevent a taxpayer from completely avoiding an income tax liability in any one year by offsetting it with business credits that would otherwise be available.

Two special rules apply to the general business credit. First, any unused credit must be carried back 1 year, then forward 20 years. Second, for any tax year, the general business credit is limited to the taxpayer's *net income tax* reduced by the greater of:[2]

- The *tentative minimum tax.*
- 25 percent of *net regular tax liability* that exceeds $25,000.[3]

In order to understand the general business credit limitation, several terms need defining:

- *Net income tax* is the sum of the regular tax liability and the alternative minimum tax reduced by certain nonrefundable tax credits.
- *Tentative minimum tax* for this purpose is reduced by the foreign tax credit allowed.
- *Regular tax liability* is determined from the appropriate tax table or tax rate schedule, based on taxable income. However, the regular tax liability does not include certain taxes (e.g., alternative minimum tax).
- *Net regular tax liability* is the regular tax liability reduced by certain nonrefundable credits (e.g., credit for child and dependent care expenses, foreign tax credit).

EXAMPLE 7	Floyd's general business credit for the current year is $70,000. His net income tax is $150,000, tentative minimum tax is $130,000, and net regular tax liability is $150,000. He has no other tax credits. Floyd's general business credit allowed for the tax year is computed as follows:

Net income tax	$ 150,000
Less: The greater of	
$130,000 (tentative minimum tax)	
$31,250 [25% × ($150,000 − $25,000)]	(130,000)
Amount of general business credit allowed for tax year	$ 20,000

Floyd then has $50,000 ($70,000 − $20,000) of unused general business credits that may be carried back or forward as discussed below. ■

Treatment of Unused General Business Credits

Unused general business credits are initially carried back one year and are applied to reduce the tax liability during that year. Thus, the taxpayer may receive a tax refund as a result of the carryback. Any remaining unused credits are then carried forward 20 years.[4]

A FIFO method is applied to the carrybacks, carryovers, and utilization of credits earned during a particular year. The oldest credits are used first in determining the amount of the general business credit. The FIFO method minimizes the potential for loss of a general business credit benefit due to the expiration of credit carryovers, since the earliest years are used before the current credit for the taxable year.

---

[2]§ 38(c).

[3]This amount is $12,500 for married taxpayers filing separately unless one of the spouses is not entitled to the general business credit.

[4]§ 39(a)(1).

This example illustrates the use of general business credit carryovers.

General business credit carryovers		
2005	$ 4,000	
2006	6,000	
2007	2,000	
Total carryovers	$12,000	
2008 general business credit		$ 40,000
Total credit allowed in 2008 (based on tax liability)	$50,000	
Less: Utilization of carryovers		
2005	(4,000)	
2006	(6,000)	
2007	(2,000)	
Remaining credit allowed in 2008	$38,000	
Applied against		
2008 general business credit		(38,000)
2008 unused amount carried forward to 2009		$ 2,000 ∎

Specific Business-Related Tax Credit Provisions

Each component of the general business credit is determined separately under its own set of rules. Some of the more important credits that make up the general business credit are explained here in the order listed in Exhibit 13–1.

Tax Credit for Rehabilitation Expenditures

Taxpayers are allowed a tax credit for expenditures incurred to rehabilitate industrial and commercial buildings and certified historic structures. The **rehabilitation expenditures credit** is intended to discourage businesses from moving from older, economically distressed areas (e.g., inner cities) to newer locations and to encourage the preservation of historic structures. The current operating features of this credit follow:[5]

Rate of the Credit for Rehabilitation Expenses	Nature of the Property
10%	Nonresidential buildings and residential rental property, other than certified historic structures, originally placed in service before 1936
20%	Nonresidential and residential certified historic structures

When taking the credit, the basis of a rehabilitated building must be reduced by the full rehabilitation credit allowed.[6]

Juan spent $60,000 to rehabilitate a building (adjusted basis of $40,000) that had originally been placed in service in 1932. He is allowed a $6,000 (10% × $60,000) credit for rehabilitation expenditures. Juan then increases the basis of the building by $54,000 [$60,000 (rehabilitation expenditures) − $6,000 (credit allowed)]. If the building were an historic structure, the credit

[5]§ 47.　　　　　　　　　　　　　　　[6]§ 50(c).

TABLE 13–1	Recapture Calculation for Rehabilitation Expenditures Credit
If the Property Is Held for	**The Recapture Percentage Is**
Less than 1 year	100
One year or more but less than 2 years	80
Two years or more but less than 3 years	60
Three years or more but less than 4 years	40
Four years or more but less than 5 years	20
Five years or more	0

allowed would be $12,000 (20% × $60,000), and the building's depreciable basis would increase by $48,000 [$60,000 (rehabilitation expenditures) − $12,000 (credit allowed)]. ∎

To qualify for the credit, buildings must be substantially rehabilitated. A building has been *substantially rehabilitated* if qualified rehabilitation expenditures exceed the greater of:

- The adjusted basis of the property before the rehabilitation expenditures, or
- $5,000.

Qualified rehabilitation expenditures do not include the cost of acquiring a building, the cost of facilities related to a building (such as a parking lot), and the cost of enlarging an existing building.

Recapture of Tax Credit for Rehabilitation Expenditures. The rehabilitation credit taken must be recaptured if the rehabilitated property is disposed of prematurely or if it ceases to be qualifying property. The **rehabilitation expenditures credit recapture** is based on a holding period requirement of five years and is added to the taxpayer's regular tax liability in the recapture year. The recapture amount is also *added* to the adjusted basis of the rehabilitation expenditures for purposes of determining the amount of gain or loss realized on the property's disposition.

The portion of the credit recaptured is a specified percentage of the credit that was taken by the taxpayer. This percentage is based on the period the property was held by the taxpayer, as shown in Table 13–1.

EXAMPLE 10

On March 15, 2005, Rashad placed in service $30,000 of rehabilitation expenditures on a building qualifying for the 10% credit. A credit of $3,000 ($30,000 × 10%) was allowed, and the basis of the building was increased by $27,000 ($30,000 − $3,000). The building was sold on December 15, 2008. Rashad must recapture a portion of the rehabilitation credit based on the schedule in Table 13–1. Because he held the rehabilitated property for more than three years but less than four, 40% of the credit, or $1,200, is added to his 2008 tax liability. Also, the adjusted basis of the rehabilitation expenditures is increased by the $1,200 recapture amount. ∎

ETHICAL and EQUITABLE *Considerations*

THE REHABILITATION TAX CREDIT

Your brother—who buys, modernizes, and sells buildings in a large metropolitan city—has come to you for advice. Given the recent credit market conditions, business has been tough, and he has sold only a few buildings. One of your brother's buildings is a certified historic structure that would qualify for the 20 percent rehabilitation tax credit. Based on several recent appraisals, the building is currently worth $400,000. The expenditures needed to rehabilitate the building would be about $250,000, all of which would qualify for the rehabilitation tax credit. Your brother has been approached by an individual who is interested in buying the building. The customer has offered to pay your brother $300,000 for the build-

ing and $350,000 for the rehabilitation work. This approach would provide the customer with a larger tax credit ($350,000 × 20% versus $250,000 × 20%) and provide a needed sale for your brother's business. How do you respond?

Work Opportunity Tax Credit

The **work opportunity tax credit** was enacted to encourage employers to hire individuals from one or more of a number of targeted and economically disadvantaged groups.[7] Examples of such targeted persons include qualified ex-felons, high-risk youths, food stamp recipients, veterans, summer youth employees, and long-term family assistance recipients.

Computation of the Work Opportunity Tax Credit: General.
The credit is generally equal to 40 percent of the first $6,000 of wages (per eligible employee) for the first 12 months of employment. Thus, the credit is not available for any wages paid to an employee after the *first year* of employment. If the employee's first year overlaps two of the employer's tax years, however, the employer may take the credit over two tax years. If the credit is taken, the employer's tax deduction for wages is reduced by the amount of the credit.

For an employer to qualify for the 40 percent credit, the employee must (1) be certified by a designated local agency as being a member of one of the targeted groups and (2) have completed at least 400 hours of service to the employer. If an employee meets the first condition but not the second, the credit rate is reduced to 25 percent provided the employee has completed a minimum of 120 hours of service to the employer.

EXAMPLE 11

In January 2008, Green Company hires four individuals who are certified to be members of a qualifying targeted group. Each employee works 800 hours and is paid wages of $8,000 during the year. Green Company's work opportunity credit is $9,600 [($6,000 × 40%) × 4 employees]. If the tax credit is taken, Green must reduce its deduction for wages paid by $9,600. No credit is available for wages paid to these employees after their first year of employment. ■

EXAMPLE 12

On June 1, 2008, Maria, a calendar year taxpayer, hires Joe, a certified member of a targeted group. During the last seven months of 2008, Joe is paid $3,500 for 500 hours of work. Maria is allowed a credit of $1,400 ($3,500 × 40%) for 2008. Joe continues to work for Maria in 2009 and is paid $7,000 through May 31, 2009. Because up to $6,000 of first-year wages are eligible for the credit, Maria is allowed a 40% credit on $2,500 [$6,000 − $3,500 (wages paid in 2008)] of wages paid in 2009, or $1,000 ($2,500 × 40%). None of Joe's wages paid after May 31, the end of the first year of employment, is eligible for the credit. ■

Computation of the Work Opportunity Tax Credit: Qualified Summer Youth Employees.
The credit for qualified summer youth employees is allowed on wages for services during any 90-day period between May 1 and September 15. The maximum wages eligible for the credit are $3,000 per summer youth employee. The credit rate is the same as the general work opportunity tax credit rate.

---

[7]§ 51. The credit is available only if qualifying employees start work by August 31, 2011.

If the employee continues employment after the 90-day period as a member of another targeted group, the amount of the wages eligible for the general work opportunity tax credit as a member of the new target group is reduced by the wages paid to the employee as a qualified summer youth employee.

A *qualified summer youth employee* must be age 16 or 17 on the hiring date. In addition, the individual's principal place of abode must be within an empowerment zone, enterprise community, or renewal community.

Computation of the Work Opportunity Tax Credit: Long-Term Family Assistance Recipient.
The credit[8] is available to employers hiring individuals who have been long-term recipients of family assistance welfare benefits. In general, *long-term recipients* are those individuals who are certified by a designated local agency as being a member of a family receiving assistance under a public aid program for at least an 18-month period ending on the hiring date. Unlike the work opportunity credit for other targeted groups, which applies only to first-year wages paid to qualified individuals, the credit is available for qualified wages paid in the *first two years* of employment if the employee is a long-term family assistance recipient. If an employee's first and second work years overlap two or more of the employer's tax years, the employer may take the credit during the applicable tax years.

The credit is equal to 40 percent of the first $10,000 of qualified wages paid to an employee in the first year of employment, plus 50 percent of the first $10,000 of qualified wages paid in the second year of employment, resulting in a maximum credit per qualified employee of $9,000 [$4,000 (year 1) + $5,000 (year 2)]. The credit rate is higher for second-year wages to encourage employers to retain qualified individuals, thereby promoting the overall welfare-to-work goal.

EXAMPLE 13

In April 2008, Blue Company hired three individuals who are certified as long-term family assistance recipients. Each employee is paid $12,000 during 2008. Two of the three individuals continue to work for Blue Company in 2009, earning $9,000 each during the year. Blue Company's work opportunity tax credit is $12,000 [(40% × $10,000) × 3 employees] for 2008 and $9,000 [(50% × $9,000) × 2 employees] for 2009. In each year, Blue must reduce its deduction for wages paid by the amount of the credit for that year. ∎

Research Activities Credit

To encourage research and experimentation, usually described as research and development (R&D), a credit is allowed for certain qualifying expenditures paid or incurred by a taxpayer. The **research activities credit** is the *sum* of three components: an incremental research activities credit, a basic research credit, and an energy research credit.[9]

Incremental Research Activities Credit.
The incremental research activities credit is equal to 20 percent of the *excess* of qualified research expenses for the taxable year over the base amount.[10]

In general, *research expenditures* qualify if the research relates to discovering technological information that is intended for use in the development of a new or

---

[8]Prior to 2007, this component of the work opportunity tax credit was the welfare-to-work credit, which was provided for under § 51A. Under current law, long-term family assistance recipients are a designated targeted group under the work opportunity tax credit (§ 51(d)(1)(I)), and the maximum credit is now slightly more generous than under prior law.

[9]§ 41. Each component of the research credit is available only if qualifying expenditures are paid or incurred by December 31, 2007. However, it is

likely that Congress will extend this credit. Therefore, Chapter 13 examples and problems assume its continuing availability for qualifying expenditures paid or incurred after December 31, 2007.

[10]In lieu of determining the incremental research credit as described here, a taxpayer may elect to calculate the credit using an alternative incremental credit regime or an alternative simplified credit procedure. See §§ 41(c)(4) and (5).

improved business component of the taxpayer. Such expenses qualify fully if the research is performed in-house (by the taxpayer or employees). If the research is conducted by persons outside the taxpayer's business (under contract), only 65 percent of the amount paid qualifies for the credit.[11]

EXAMPLE 14

George incurs the following research expenditures:

In-house wages, supplies, computer time	$50,000
Paid to Cutting Edge Scientific Foundation for research	30,000

George's qualified research expenditures are $69,500 [$50,000 + ($30,000 × 65%)]. ∎

Beyond the general guidelines described above, the Code does not give specific examples of qualifying research. However, the credit is *not* allowed for research that falls into certain categories, including the following:[12]

- Research conducted after the beginning of commercial production of the business component.
- Surveys and studies such as market research, testing, or routine data collection.
- Research conducted *outside* the United States (other than research undertaken in Puerto Rico or possessions of the United States).
- Research in the social sciences, arts, or humanities.

Determining the *base amount* involves a relatively complex series of computations, meant to approximate recent historical levels of research activity by the taxpayer. Thus, the credit is allowed only for increases in research expenses. A discussion of these computations is beyond the scope of this presentation.

EXAMPLE 15

Jack, a calendar year taxpayer, incurs qualifying research expenditures of $200,000 at the beginning of the year. Assuming the base amount is $100,000, the incremental research activities credit is $20,000 [($200,000 − $100,000) × 20%]. ∎

Qualified research and experimentation expenditures are not only eligible for the 20 percent credit, but can also be *deducted* in the year incurred.[13] In this regard, a taxpayer has two choices:[14]

- Use the full credit and reduce the expense deduction for research expenses by 100 percent of the credit.
- Retain the full expense deduction and reduce the credit by the product of 100 percent of the credit times the maximum corporate tax rate (35 percent).

As an alternative to the expense deduction, the taxpayer may *capitalize* the research expenses and *amortize* them over 60 months or more. In this case, the amount capitalized and subject to amortization is reduced by the full amount of the credit *only* if the credit exceeds the amount allowable as a deduction.

EXAMPLE 16

Assume the same facts as in Example 15, which shows that the potential incremental research activities credit is $20,000. In the current year, the expense that the taxpayer can deduct and the credit amount are as follows:

---

[11]In the case of payments to a qualified research consortium, § 41(b)(3)(A) provides that 75% of the amount paid qualifies for the credit. In contrast, for amounts paid to an energy research consortium, § 41(b)(3)(D) allows the full amount to qualify for the credit.

[12]§ 41(d). See also Reg. §§ 1.41–1 through 1.41–7.

[13]§ 174. Also refer to the discussion of rules for deducting research and experimental expenditures in Chapter 7.

[14]§ 280C(c).

	Credit Amount	Deduction Amount
Full credit and reduced deduction		
$20,000 − $0	$20,000	
$200,000 − $20,000		$180,000
Reduced credit and full deduction		
$20,000 − [(100% × $20,000) × 35%]	13,000	
$200,000 − $0		200,000
Full credit and capitalize and elect to amortize costs over 60 months		
$20,000 − $0	20,000	
($200,000/60) × 12		40,000

Basic Research Credit. Corporations (other than S corporations or personal service corporations) are allowed an additional 20 percent credit for basic research payments made in *excess* of a base amount. This credit is not available to individual taxpayers. *Basic research payments* are defined as amounts paid in cash to a qualified basic research organization, such as a college or university or a tax-exempt organization operated primarily to conduct scientific research.

Basic research is defined generally as any original investigation for the advancement of scientific knowledge not having a specific commercial objective. The definition excludes basic research conducted outside the United States and basic research in the social sciences, arts, or humanities. This reflects the intent of Congress to encourage high-tech research in the United States.

The calculation of this additional credit for basic research expenditures is complex and is based on expenditures in excess of a specially defined base amount. The portion of the basic research expenditures not in excess of the base amount is treated as a part of the qualifying expenditures for purposes of the regular credit for incremental research activities.

EXAMPLE 17

Orange Corporation, a qualifying corporation, pays $75,000 to a university for basic research. Assume that Orange's base amount for the basic research credit is $50,000. The basic research activities credit allowed is $5,000 [($75,000 − $50,000) × 20%]. The $50,000 of basic research expenditures that equal the base amount are treated as research expenses for purposes of the regular incremental research activities credit. ■

Energy Research Credit. This component of the research credit is intended to stimulate additional energy research. The calculation of the credit is relatively straightforward and is equal to 20 percent of the amounts paid or incurred by a taxpayer to an energy research consortium for energy research.

ETHICAL and EQUITABLE *Considerations*

WHEN DOES "RESEARCH" QUALIFY AS R&D?

The research activities credit is designed to encourage taxpayers to engage in research relating to the discovery of technological information that is intended for use in the development of a new or improved business component of the taxpayer.

You are employed as a staff accountant for a privately held corporation that manufactures medical equipment. During the current year, the corporation purchases new communications software and related document-management systems with the goal of enhancing employee efficiency and productivity. To familiarize employees with these new systems, an outside firm is hired to conduct numerous software training seminars during the first six months the new systems are in place. Substantial costs are incurred in connection with these training seminars. Not surprisingly, various inefficiencies are also encountered until the employees have had sufficient training and time to use the new systems.

The corporation's new president, ever mindful of the company's profitability and tax position, urges you to claim the research activities credit with respect to the software training costs. The president justifies this position on the grounds that the employees were "researching" the new software and its use. How do you respond?

Low-Income Housing Credit

To encourage building owners to make affordable housing available for low-income individuals, Congress has made a credit available to owners of qualified low-income housing projects.[15]

More than any other, the **low-income housing credit** is influenced by nontax factors. For example, certification of the property by the appropriate state or local agency authorized to provide low-income housing credits is required. These credits are issued based on a nationwide allocation.

The amount of the credit is based on the qualified basis of the property. The qualified basis depends on the number of units rented to low-income tenants. Tenants are low-income tenants if their income does not exceed a specified percentage of the area median gross income. The amount of the credit is determined by multiplying the qualified basis by a credit rate.[16] The credit is allowed over a 10-year period if the property continues to meet the required conditions.

EXAMPLE 18

Sarah spends $1 million to build a qualified low-income housing project completed January 1 of the current year. The entire project is rented to low-income families. Assume the credit rate for property placed in service during January is 7.93%. Sarah may claim a credit of $79,300 ($1,000,000 × 7.93%) in the current year and in each of the following nine years. Generally, first-year credits are prorated based on the date the project is placed in service. A full year's credit is taken in each of the next nine years, and any remaining first-year credit is claimed in the eleventh year. ∎

Recapture of a portion of the credit may be required if the number of units set aside for low-income tenants falls below a minimum threshold, if the taxpayer disposes of the property or the interest in it, or if the taxpayer's amount at risk decreases.

Disabled Access Credit

The **disabled access credit** is designed to encourage small businesses to make their facilities more accessible to disabled individuals. The credit is available for any eligible access expenditures paid or incurred by an eligible small business. The credit is calculated at the rate of 50 percent of the eligible expenditures that exceed $250 but do not exceed $10,250. Thus, the maximum amount for the credit is $5,000 ($10,000 × 50%).[17]

An *eligible small business* is one that during the previous year either had gross receipts of $1 million or less or had no more than 30 full-time employees. An eligible business can include a sole proprietorship, partnership, regular corporation, or S corporation.

Eligible access expenditures are generally any reasonable and necessary amounts that are paid or incurred to make certain changes to facilities. These changes must involve the removal of architectural, communication, physical, or transportation barriers that would otherwise make a business inaccessible to disabled and handicapped

---

[15]§ 42.   [17]§ 44.
[16]The rate is subject to adjustment every month by the IRS.

individuals. Examples of qualifying projects include installing ramps, widening door-ways, and adding raised markings on elevator control buttons. However, eligible expenditures do *not* include amounts that are paid or incurred in connection with any facility that has been placed in service after the enactment of the credit (i.e., November 5, 1990).

To the extent a disabled access credit is available, no deduction or credit is allowed under any other provision of the tax law. The adjusted basis for deprecia-tion is reduced by the amount of the credit.

EXAMPLE 19

This year Red, Inc., an eligible business, makes $11,000 of capital improvements to business realty that had been placed in service in June 1990. The expenditures are intended to make Red's business more accessible to the disabled and are considered eligible expenditures for purposes of the disabled access credit. The amount of the credit is $5,000 [($10,250 − $250) × 50%]. Although $11,000 of eligible expenditures are incurred, only the excess of $10,250 over $250 qualifies for the credit. Further, the depreciable basis of the capital improvement is $6,000 because the basis must be reduced by the amount of the credit [$11,000 (cost) − $5,000 (amount of the credit)]. ■

Credit for Small Employer Pension Plan Startup Costs

Small businesses are entitled to a nonrefundable credit for administrative costs associated with establishing and maintaining certain qualified retirement plans.[18] While such costs (e.g., payroll system changes, consulting fees) generally are deductible as ordinary and necessary business expenses, the credit is intended to lower the after-tax cost of establishing a qualified retirement program and thereby encourage qualifying businesses to offer retirement plans for their employees. The **credit for small employer pension plan startup costs** is available for eligible employ-ers at the rate of 50 percent of qualified startup costs. An eligible employer is one with fewer than 100 employees who have earned at least $5,000 of compensation. Qualified startup costs include ordinary and necessary expenses incurred in con-nection with establishing or maintaining an employer pension plan and retirement-related education costs.[19] The maximum credit is $500 (based on a maximum $1,000 of qualifying expenses), and the deduction for the startup costs incurred is reduced by the amount of the credit. The credit can be claimed for qualifying costs incurred in each of the three years beginning with the tax year in which the retirement plan becomes effective (maximum total credit over three years of $1,500).

EXAMPLE 20

Maple Company decides to establish a qualified retirement plan for its employees. In the process, it pays consulting fees of $1,200 to a firm that will provide educational seminars to Maple's employees and will assist the payroll department in making necessary changes to the payroll system. Maple may claim a credit for the pension plan startup costs of $500 ($1,200 of qualifying costs, limited to $1,000 × 50%), and its deduction for these expenses is reduced to $700 ($1,200 − $500). ■

Credit for Employer-Provided Child Care

The scope of § 162 trade or business expenses includes an employer's expenditures incurred to provide for the care of children of employees as ordinary and necessary business expenses. Alternatively, employers may claim a credit for qualifying expen-ditures incurred while providing child care facilities to their employees during nor-mal working hours.[20] The **credit for employer-provided child care**, limited annually to $150,000, is composed of the aggregate of two components: 25 percent

---

[18]§ 45E. Currently, this credit is scheduled to expire for years after December 31, 2010.

[19]§§ 45E(c)(1) and (d)(1).

[20]§ 45F. Currently, this credit is scheduled to expire for years after December 31, 2010.

of qualified child care expenses and 10 percent of qualified child care resource and referral services. *Qualified child care expenses* include the costs of acquiring, constructing, rehabilitating, expanding, and operating a child care facility. *Child care resource and referral services* include amounts paid or incurred under a contract to provide child care resource and referral services to an employee. Any qualifying expenses otherwise deductible by the taxpayer must be reduced by the amount of the credit. In addition, the taxpayer's basis for any property acquired or constructed and used for qualifying purposes is reduced by the amount of the credit. If within 10 years of being placed in service, a child care facility ceases to be used for a qualified use, the taxpayer will be required to recapture a portion of the credit previously claimed.[21]

During the year, Tan Company constructed a child care facility for $400,000 to be used by its employees who have preschool-aged children in need of child care services while their parents are at work. In addition, Tan incurred salaries for child care workers and other administrative costs associated with the facility of $100,000. As a result, Tan's credit for employer-provided child care is $125,000 [($400,000 + $100,000) × 25%]. Correspondingly, the basis of the facility is reduced to $300,000 ($400,000 − $100,000), and the deduction for salaries and administrative costs is reduced to $75,000 ($100,000 − $25,000). ∎

Other Tax Credits

Earned Income Credit

LO.4

Describe various tax credits that are available primarily to individual taxpayers.

The **earned income credit**, which has been a part of the law for many years, consistently has been justified as a means of providing tax equity to the working poor. In addition, the credit has been designed to help offset regressive taxes that are a part of our tax system, such as the gasoline tax. Further, the credit is intended to encourage economically disadvantaged individuals to become contributing members of the workforce.[22]

In 2008, the earned income credit is determined by multiplying a maximum amount of earned income by the appropriate credit percentage (see Table 13–2). Generally, earned income includes employee compensation and net earnings from self-employment but excludes items such as interest, dividends, pension benefits, nontaxable employee compensation, and alimony. If a taxpayer has children, the credit percentage used in the calculation depends on the number of qualifying children. Thus, in 2008, the maximum earned income credit for a taxpayer with one qualifying child is $2,917 ($8,580 × 34%) and $4,824 ($12,060 × 40%) for a taxpayer with two or more qualifying children. However, the maximum earned income credit is phased out completely if the taxpayer's earned income or AGI exceeds certain thresholds as shown in Table 13–2.[23] To the extent that the greater of earned income or AGI exceeds $18,740 in 2008 for married taxpayers filing a joint return ($15,740 for other taxpayers), the difference, multiplied by the appropriate phaseout percentage, is subtracted from the maximum earned income credit.

In 2008, Grace Brown, who is married, files a joint return and otherwise qualifies for the earned income credit. Grace receives wages of $25,000, and she and her husband have no other income. The Browns have one qualifying child. The current earned income credit is $2,917 ($8,580 × 34%) reduced by $1,000 [($25,000 − $18,740) × 15.98%]. Thus, the earned income credit is $1,917. If the Browns have two or more qualifying children, the

---

[21]§ 45F(d).

[22]§ 32. The earned income credit is not available if the taxpayer's unearned income (e.g., interest, dividends) exceeds $2,950 in 2008 ($2,900 in 2007). See § 32(i).

[23]§ 32(a)(2)(B).

TABLE 13–2	Earned Income Credit and Phaseout Percentages

Tax Year	Number of Qualifying Children	Maximum Earned Income	Credit Percentage	Maximum Credit	Phaseout Begins	Phaseout Percentage	Phaseout Ends
2008	*Married, Filing Jointly:*						
	One child	$ 8,580	34.00	$2,917	$18,740	15.98	$36,995
	Two or more children	12,060	40.00	4,824	18,740	21.06	41,646
	No qualifying children	5,720	7.65	438	10,160	7.65	15,880
	Other Taxpayers:						
	One child	$ 8,580	34.00	$2,917	$15,740	15.98	$33,995
	Two or more children	12,060	40.00	4,824	15,740	21.06	38,646
	No qualifying children	5,720	7.65	438	7,160	7.65	12,880
2007	*Married, Filing Jointly:*						
	One child	$ 8,390	34.00	$2,853	$17,390	15.98	$35,241
	Two or more children	11,790	40.00	4,716	17,390	21.06	39,783
	No qualifying children	5,590	7.65	428	9,000	7.65	14,590
	Other Taxpayers:						
	One child	$ 8,390	34.00	$2,853	$15,390	15.98	$33,241
	Two or more children	11,790	40.00	4,716	15,390	21.06	37,783
	No qualifying children	5,590	7.65	428	7,000	7.65	12,590

calculation produces a credit of $4,824 ($12,060 × 40%) reduced by $1,318 [($25,000 − $18,740) × 21.06%]. Thus, the Brown's earned income credit is $3,506 if they have two or more children. ■

Earned Income Credit Table. It is not necessary to compute the credit as shown in Example 22. To simplify the compliance process, the IRS issues an Earned Income Credit Table for the determination of the appropriate amount of the credit. This table and a worksheet are included in the instructions available to individual taxpayers.

Eligibility Requirements. Eligibility for the credit depends not only on the taxpayer meeting the earned income and AGI thresholds, but also on whether he or she has a qualifying child. The term *qualifying child* generally has the same meaning here as it does for purposes of determining who qualifies as a dependent (see Chapter 3).

In addition to being available for taxpayers with qualifying children, the earned income credit is also available to certain *workers without children*. However, this provision is available only to taxpayers aged 25 through 64 who cannot be claimed as a dependent on another taxpayer's return. As shown in Table 13–2, the credit for 2008 is calculated on a maximum earned income of $5,720 times 7.65 percent and reduced by 7.65 percent of earned income over $10,160 for married taxpayers filing a joint return ($7,160 for other taxpayers).

EXAMPLE 23	Walt, who is single, 28 years of age, and is not claimed as a dependent on anyone else's return, earns $7,500 during 2008. Even though he does not have any qualifying children, he qualifies for the earned income credit. His credit is $438 ($5,720 × 7.65%) reduced by $26 [($7,500 − $7,160) × 7.65%]. Thus, Walt's earned income credit is $412. If, instead, Walt's earned income is $6,000, his earned income credit is $438. In this situation, there is no phaseout of the maximum credit because his earned income is not in excess of $7,160. ■

Advance Payment. The earned income credit is a form of negative income tax (a refundable credit for taxpayers who do not have a tax liability). An eligible individual may elect to receive advance payments of the earned income credit from his or her employer (rather than receiving the credit from the IRS upon filing the tax return). The amount that can be received in advance is limited to 60 percent of the credit that is available to a taxpayer with only one qualifying child. If this election is made, the taxpayer must file a certificate of eligibility (Form W–5) with his or her employer and *must* file a tax return for the year the income is earned.[24]

Tax Credit for Elderly or Disabled Taxpayers

The credit for the elderly was originally enacted to provide tax relief on retirement income for individuals who were not receiving substantial benefits from tax-free Social Security payments.[25] Currently, the **tax credit for the elderly or disabled** applies to the following:

- Taxpayers age 65 or older.
- Taxpayers under age 65 who are retired with a **permanent and total disability** and who have disability income from a public or private employer on account of the disability. A person generally is considered permanently and totally disabled if he or she is unable to engage in any substantial gainful activity due to a physical or mental impairment for a period of at least 12 months (or lesser period if the disability results in death).

The *maximum* allowable credit is $1,125 (15% × $7,500 of qualifying income), but the credit will be less for a taxpayer who receives Social Security benefits or has AGI exceeding specified amounts. Under these circumstances, the qualifying income base amount used in the credit computation is reduced. Many taxpayers receive Social Security benefits or have AGI high enough to reduce the base for the credit to zero. In addition, because the credit is nonrefundable, the allowable credit cannot exceed the taxpayer's tax liablity.

The eligibility requirements and the tax computation are somewhat complicated. Consequently, an individual may elect to have the IRS compute his or her tax and the amount of the tax credit.

The credit generally is based on a qualifying income amount (referred to as the *base amount*) and the filing status of the taxpayer in accordance with Table 13–3. To

---

[24]§ 3507.

[25]§ 22. This credit is not subject to indexation.

TABLE 13–3	Base and Threshold Amounts for Tax Credit for Elderly or Disabled Taxpayers		
Status		**Base Amount**	**Threshold Amount**
Single, head of household, or surviving spouse		$5,000	$ 7,500
Married, joint return, only one spouse qualifies		5,000	10,000
Married, joint return, both spouses qualify		7,500	10,000
Married, separate returns, spouses live apart the entire year (amount for each spouse)		3,750	5,000

qualify for the credit, married taxpayers who live together must file a joint return. For taxpayers under age 65 who are retired on permanent and total disability, the base amounts could be less than those shown in Table 13–3 because these amounts are limited to taxable disability income.

This initial base amount is *reduced* by (1) Social Security, Railroad Retirement, and certain excluded pension benefits and (2) one-half of the taxpayer's AGI in excess of a threshold amount (see Table 13–3), which is a function of the taxpayer's filing status.

EXAMPLE 24

Paul and Peggy, husband and wife, are both over age 65 and receive Social Security benefits of $1,000 in the current year. On a joint return, they report AGI of $21,000.

Base amount (from Table 13–3)		$ 7,500
Less: Social Security benefits	$1,000	
One-half of excess of AGI over threshold amount (from Table 13–3) [($21,000 − $10,000) × ½]	5,500	
Total reductions		(6,500)
Remaining base amount		$ 1,000
Multiply remaining base amount by 15%—this is the tax credit allowed, subject to tax liability limitation		$ 150 ∎

Schedule R of Form 1040 is used to calculate and report the credit.

Foreign Tax Credit

Both individual taxpayers and corporations may claim a tax credit for foreign income tax paid on income earned and subject to tax in another country or a U.S. possession.[26] As an alternative, a taxpayer may claim a deduction instead of a credit.[27] In most instances, the **foreign tax credit (FTC)** is advantageous since it provides a direct offset against the tax liability.

The purpose of the FTC is to mitigate double taxation since income earned in a foreign country is subject to both U.S. and foreign taxes. However, the FTC is subject to an overall limitation. This limitation may result in some form of double taxation or taxation at rates in excess of U.S. rates when the foreign tax rates are higher than the U.S. rates. This is a distinct possibility because U.S. tax rates are lower than those of many foreign countries.

---

[26]Section 27 provides for the credit, but the qualifications and calculation procedure for the credit are contained in §§ 901–908.   [27]§ 164.

GLOBAL
Tax Issues

SOURCING INCOME IN CYBERSPACE—GETTING IT RIGHT WHEN CALCULATING THE FOREIGN TAX CREDIT

The overall limitation on the foreign tax credit (FTC) plays a critical role in restricting the amount of the credit available to a taxpayer. In the overall limitation formula, the taxpayer must characterize the year's taxable income as either earned (or sourced) inside the United States or earned from sources outside the United States. As a general rule, a relatively greater percentage of foreign-source income in the formula will lead to a larger FTC. Therefore, determining the source of various types of income is critical in the proper calculation of the credit. However, classifying income as either foreign or U.S. source is not always a simple matter.

For example, consumers and businesses are using the Internet to conduct more and more commerce involving both products and services. The problem is that the existing income-sourcing rules were developed long before the existence of the Internet, and taxing authorities are finding it challenging to apply these rules to Internet transactions. Where does a sale take place when the Web server is in Scotland, the seller is in India, and the customer is in Illinois? Where is a service performed when all activities take place over the Net? These questions and more will have to be answered by the United States and its trading partners as the Internet economy grows in size and importance.

Other special tax treatments applicable to taxpayers working outside the United States include the foreign earned income exclusion (see Chapter 5) and limitations on deducting expenses of employees working outside the United States (see Chapter 9). Recall from the earlier discussion that a taxpayer may not take advantage of *both* the FTC and the foreign earned income exclusion.

Computation. Taxpayers are required to compute the FTC based upon an overall limitation.[28] The FTC allowed is the *lesser* of the foreign taxes imposed or the *overall limitation* determined according to the following formula:

$$\frac{\text{Foreign-source taxable income}}{\text{Worldwide taxable income}} \times \text{U.S. tax before FTC}$$

For individual taxpayers, worldwide taxable income in the overall limitation formula is determined *before* personal and dependency exemptions are deducted.

EXAMPLE 25

In 2008, Carlos, a calendar year taxpayer, has $10,000 of income from Country Y, which imposes a 15% tax, and $20,000 from Country Z, which imposes a 50% tax. He has taxable income of $56,000 from within the United States, is married filing a joint return, and claims two dependency exemptions. Thus, although Carlos's taxable income for purposes of determining U.S. tax is $86,000, taxable income amounts used in the limitation formula are not reduced by personal and dependency exemptions. Thus, for this purpose, taxable income is $100,000 [$86,000 + (4 × $3,500)]. Assume that Carlos's U.S. tax before the credit is $17,688. Overall limitation:

$$\frac{\text{Foreign-source taxable income}}{\text{Worldwide taxable income}} = \frac{\$30,000}{\$100,000} \times \$17,688 = \$5,306$$

In this case, $5,306 is allowed as the FTC because this amount is less than the $11,500 of foreign taxes imposed [$1,500 (Country Y) + $10,000 (Country Z)]. ■

---

[28]§ 904.

TAX *in the News*   **IRS TARGETS FOREIGN TAX CREDIT GENERATORS**

In an attempt to identify aggressive corporate tax avoidance through a pooling of expertise, tax authorities in Australia, Canada, the United Kingdom, and the United States have set up an international task force, known as the Joint International Tax Shelter Information Centre. The tax authorities hope that the task force will enhance their ability to curb abusive tax avoidance schemes.

Among other things, the members of the task force are scrutinizing tax arbitrage schemes used by multinational corporations and are also examining the work of accountants, bankers, and lawyers who advise companies on tax avoidance

strategies. Recent work has focused on transactions by U.S. taxpayers with foreign counterparts to generate foreign tax credits. Former IRS Commissioner Mark Everson said that the task force helped the IRS to detect "things we either would never have picked up or would have picked up years down the road." He added that the task force is necessary because in contrast to previous tax avoidance schemes, when taxpayers would simply try to take advantage of the nation with the most favorable tax rate, "we are seeing now that entities are trying to structure transactions which result in the payment of no tax at all. That is clearly of concern."

Source: *Adapted from* Financial Times *(February 27, 2005) and "Tax Matters,"* Journal of Accountancy *(June 2007).*

Thus, the overall limitation may result in some of the foreign income being subjected to double taxation. Unused FTCs [e.g., the $6,194 ($11,500 − $5,306) from Example 25] can be carried back 1 year and forward 10 years.[29]

Only foreign income taxes, war profits taxes, and excess profits taxes (or taxes paid in lieu of such taxes) qualify for the credit.[30] In determining whether or not a tax is an income tax, U.S. criteria are applied. Thus, value added taxes (VAT), severance taxes, property taxes, and sales taxes do not qualify because they are not regarded as taxes on income. Such taxes may be deductible, however.

Adoption Expenses Credit

Adoption expenses paid or incurred by a taxpayer may give rise to the **adoption expenses credit**.[31] The provision is intended to assist taxpayers who incur nonrecurring costs directly associated with the adoption process, such as adoption fees, attorney fees, court costs, social service review costs, and transportation costs.

In 2008, up to $11,650 of costs incurred to adopt an eligible child qualify for the credit.[32] An eligible child is one who is:

- under 18 years of age at the time of the adoption or
- physically or mentally incapable of taking care of himself or herself.

A taxpayer may claim the credit in the year qualifying expenses were paid or incurred if they were paid or incurred *during or after* the tax year in which the adoption was finalized. For qualifying expenses paid or incurred in a tax year *prior* to the year when the adoption was finalized, the credit must be claimed in the tax year following the tax year during which the expenses are paid or incurred. A married couple must file a joint return.

E X A M P L E   2 6

In late 2007, Sam and Martha pay $4,000 in legal fees, adoption fees, and other expenses directly related to the adoption of an infant daughter, Susan. In 2008, the year in which the adoption becomes final, they pay an additional $8,000. Sam and Martha are eligible for an

---

[29]§ 904(c) and Reg. § 1.904–2(g), Example 1. This treatment of unused FTCs applies to tax years ending after October 22, 2004. Prior law provided a two-year carryback and a five-year carryforward.

[30]Reg. § 1.901–1(a)(3)(i).

[31]§ 23.

[32]§ 23(b)(1). In 2007, the maximum amount of eligible costs was $11,390. This ceiling is adjusted for inflation annually. Special rules are used in calculating the credit when adopting "a child with special needs." See § 23(d)(3).

$11,650 credit in 2008 (for expenses, limited by the $11,650 ceiling, paid in 2007 and 2008). ■

The amount of the credit that is otherwise available is phased out for taxpayers whose AGI (modified for this purpose) exceeds $174,730 in 2008, and the credit is completely eliminated when the AGI reaches $214,730. The resulting credit is calculated by reducing the allowable credit (determined without this reduction) by the allowable credit multiplied by the ratio of the excess of the taxpayer's AGI over $174,730 to $40,000.[33]

EXAMPLE 27

Assume the same facts as in the previous example, except that Sam and Martha's AGI is $199,730 in 2008. As a result, their available credit in 2008 is reduced from $11,650 to $4,369 {$11,650 − [$11,650 ($25,000/$40,000)]}. ■

The credit is nonrefundable and is available to taxpayers only in a year in which this credit and the other nonrefundable credits do not exceed the taxpayer's tax liability. However, any unused adoption expenses credit may be carried over for up to five years, being utilized on a first-in, first-out basis.

Child Tax Credit

The **child tax credit** provisions allow individual taxpayers to take a tax credit based solely on the *number* of their qualifying children. This credit is one of several "family-friendly" provisions that currently are part of our tax law. To be eligible for the credit, the child must be under age 17, a U.S. citizen, and claimed as a dependent on the taxpayer's return.

Maximum Credit and Phaseouts. Under current law, the maximum credit available is $1,000 per child.[34] The available credit is phased out for higher-income taxpayers beginning when AGI reaches $110,000 for joint filers ($55,000 for married taxpayers filing separately) and $75,000 for single taxpayers. The credit is phased out by $50 for each $1,000 (or part thereof) of AGI above the threshold amounts.[35] Since the maximum credit amount available to taxpayers depends on the number of qualifying children, the income level at which the credit is phased out completely also depends on the number of children qualifying for the credit.

EXAMPLE 28

Juanita and Alberto are married and file a joint tax return claiming their two children, ages six and eight, as dependents. Their AGI is $122,400. Juanita and Alberto's maximum child tax credit is $2,000 ($1,000 × 2 children). Since Juanita and Alberto's AGI is in excess of the $110,000 threshold, the maximum credit must be reduced by $50 for every $1,000 (or part thereof) above the threshold amount {$50 × [($122,400 − $110,000)/$1,000]}. Thus, the credit reduction equals $650 [$50 × 13 (rounded from 12.4)]. Therefore, Juanita and Alberto's child tax credit is $1,350. ■

Credit for Child and Dependent Care Expenses

A credit is allowed to taxpayers who incur employment-related expenses for child or dependent care.[36] The **credit for child and dependent care expenses** is a speci-

---

[33]§ 23(b)(2). The AGI threshold amount is indexed for inflation. In 2007, the phaseout of the credit began when AGI exceeded $170,820.

[34]§ 24. The maximum credit per child is scheduled to remain at $1,000 through 2010.

[35]AGI is modified for purposes of this calculation. The threshold amounts are *not* indexed for inflation. See §§ 24(a) and (b).

[36]§ 21.

fied percentage of expenses incurred to enable the taxpayer to work or to seek employment. Expenses on which the credit for child and dependent care expenses is based are subject to limitations.

Eligibility.

Eligibility. To be eligible for the credit, an individual must have either of the following:

- A dependent under age 13.
- A dependent or spouse who is physically or mentally incapacitated and who lives with the taxpayer for more than one-half of the year.

Generally, married taxpayers must file a joint return to obtain the credit.

Eligible Employment-Related Expenses. Eligible expenses include amounts paid for household services and care of a qualifying individual that are incurred to enable the taxpayer to be employed. Child and dependent care expenses include expenses incurred in the home, such as payments for a housekeeper. Out-of-the-home expenses incurred for the care of a dependent under the age of 13 also qualify for the credit. In addition, out-of-the-home expenses incurred for an older dependent or spouse who is physically or mentally incapacitated qualify for the credit if that person regularly spends at least eight hours each day in the taxpayer's household. This makes the credit available to taxpayers who keep handicapped older children and elderly relatives in the home instead of institutionalizing them. Out-of-the-home expenses incurred for services provided by a dependent care center will qualify only if the center complies with all applicable laws and regulations of a state or unit of local government.

Child care payments to a relative are eligible for the credit unless the relative is a child (under age 19) of the taxpayer.

EXAMPLE 29	Wilma is an employed mother of an eight-year-old child. She pays her mother, Rita, $1,500 per year to care for the child after school. Wilma pays her daughter Eleanor, age 17, $900 for the child's care during the summer. Of these amounts, only the $1,500 paid to Rita qualifies as employment-related child care expenses. ∎

Earned Income Ceiling. Qualifying employment-related expenses are limited to an individual's earned income. For married taxpayers, this limitation applies to the spouse with the *lesser* amount of earned income. Special rules are provided for taxpayers with nonworking spouses who are disabled or are full-time students. If a nonworking spouse is physically or mentally disabled or is a full-time student, he or she is *deemed* to have earned income for purposes of this limitation. The deemed amount is $250 per month if there is one qualifying individual in the household or $500 per month if there are two or more qualifying individuals in the household. In the case of a student-spouse, the student's income is *deemed* to be earned only for the months that the student is enrolled on a full-time basis at an educational institution.[37]

Calculation of the Credit. In general, the credit is equal to a percentage of *unreimbursed* employment-related expenses up to $3,000 for one qualifying individual and $6,000 for two or more individuals. The credit rate varies between 20 percent and 35 percent, depending on the taxpayer's AGI. The following chart shows the applicable percentage for taxpayers as AGI increases:

[37]§ 21(d).

Adjusted Gross Income

Over	But Not Over	Applicable Rate of Credit
$ 0	$15,000	35%
15,000	17,000	34%
17,000	19,000	33%
19,000	21,000	32%
21,000	23,000	31%
23,000	25,000	30%
25,000	27,000	29%
27,000	29,000	28%
29,000	31,000	27%
31,000	33,000	26%
33,000	35,000	25%
35,000	37,000	24%
37,000	39,000	23%
39,000	41,000	22%
41,000	43,000	21%
43,000	No limit	20%

EXAMPLE 30

Nancy, who has two children under age 13, worked full-time while her spouse, Ron, was attending college for 10 months during the year. Nancy earned $22,000 and incurred $6,200 of child care expenses. Ron is *deemed* to be fully employed and to have earned $500 for each of the 10 months (or a total of $5,000). Since Nancy and Ron have AGI of $22,000, they are allowed a credit rate of 31%. Nancy and Ron are limited to $5,000 in qualified child care expenses ($6,000 maximum expenses, limited to Ron's deemed earned income of $5,000). Therefore, they are entitled to a tax credit of $1,550 (31% × $5,000) for the year. ■

ETHICAL and EQUITABLE *Considerations*

USING THE CREDIT FOR CHILD AND DEPENDENT CARE EXPENSES

Your friends, Bob and Carol, have hired a child care provider to come into their home for three hours a day to care for their child while they both are at work. The child care provider, Delores, charges $2,400 for her services for the year. Bob and Carol have learned that up to $3,000 of qualifying expenditures will generate a credit for child and dependent care expenses and that qualifying expenditures can include payments for housecleaning services. As a result, they ask Delores whether she would be interested in working several hours more per week, after Bob returns from work, for the sole purpose of cleaning the house. Bob offers to pay Delores $600 for the additional work, and she seems interested. For Bob and Carol, the net cost of the additional services would be $480 [$600 − ($600 × 20%)] due to the availability of the credit for child and dependent care expenses.

You learn of Bob and Carol's opportunity, but think it is unfair. If you hired Delores to perform similar housecleaning services, your net cost would be $600, and not $480, because you do not qualify for the credit. You are not sure that Bob and Carol should "take advantage" of the system in this way. How do you suppose Bob and Carol will feel, or should feel, about this "abuse" if you approach them?

Dependent Care Assistance Program. Recall from Chapter 5 that a taxpayer is allowed an exclusion from gross income for a limited amount reimbursed for child or dependent care expenses. However, the taxpayer is not allowed both an exclusion from gross income and a child and dependent care credit on the same amount. The $3,000 and $6,000 ceilings for allowable child and dependent care expenses are reduced dollar for dollar by the amount of reimbursement.[38]

EXAMPLE 31

Assume the same facts as in Example 30, except that of the $6,200 paid for child care, Nancy was reimbursed $2,500 by her employer under a qualified dependent care assistance program. Under the employer's plan, the reimbursement reduces Nancy's taxable wages. Thus, Nancy and Ron have AGI of $19,500 ($22,000 − $2,500). The maximum amount of child care expenses for two or more dependents of $6,000 is reduced by the $2,500 reimbursement, resulting in a tax credit of $1,120 [32% × ($6,000 − $2,500)]. ■

Reporting Requirements. The credit is claimed by completing and filing Form 2441, Credit for Child and Dependent Care Expenses.

Education Tax Credits

Two credits, the **HOPE scholarship credit** and the **lifetime learning credit**,[39] are available to help qualifying low- and middle-income individuals defray the cost of higher education. The credits, both of which are nonrefundable, are available for qualifying tuition and related expenses incurred by students pursuing undergraduate or graduate degrees or vocational training. Room, board, and book costs are ineligible for the credits.

Maximum Credit. The HOPE scholarship credit permits a maximum credit of $1,800 per year (100 percent of the first $1,200 of tuition expenses plus 50 percent of the next $1,200 of tuition expenses) for the *first two years* of postsecondary education.[40] The lifetime learning credit permits a credit of 20 percent of qualifying expenses (up to $10,000 per year) incurred in a year in which the HOPE scholarship credit is not claimed with respect to a given student. Generally, the lifetime learning credit is used for individuals who are beyond the first two years of postsecondary education.

Eligible Individuals. Both education credits are available for qualified expenses incurred by a taxpayer, taxpayer's spouse, or taxpayer's dependent. The HOPE scholarship credit is available per eligible student, while the lifetime learning credit is calculated per taxpayer. To be eligible for the HOPE credit, a student must take at least one-half the full-time course load for at least one academic term at a qualifying educational institution. No comparable requirement exists for the lifetime learning credit. Therefore, taxpayers who are seeking new job skills or maintaining existing skills through graduate training or continuing education are eligible for the lifetime learning credit. Taxpayers who are married must file a joint return in order to claim either education credit.

Income Limitations. Both education credits are subject to income limitations and are combined for purposes of the limitation calculation. The allowable credit amount is phased out, beginning when the taxpayer's AGI (modified for this purpose) reaches $48,000 ($96,000 for married taxpayers filing jointly).[41] The reduction in 2008 is equal to the extent to which AGI exceeds $48,000 ($96,000 for married filing jointly) as a percentage of the $10,000 ($20,000 for married filing jointly) phaseout range. The credits are completely eliminated when AGI reaches $58,000 ($116,000 for married filing jointly).

---

[38]§ 21(c).
[39]§ 25A.

[40]The qualifying expense base for the HOPE scholarship credit is subject to inflation adjustment. The base was $1,100 in 2007 and 2006 and $1,000 for years prior to 2006.
[41]§ 25A(d). For 2007, the AGI bases were $47,000 and $94,000. § 25A(h)(2)(A).

Dean and Audry are married, file a joint tax return, have modified AGI under $96,000, and have two children, Raymond and Kelsey. During fall 2008, Raymond is beginning his freshman year at State University, and Kelsey is beginning her senior year. During the prior semester, Kelsey completed her junior year. Both Raymond and Kelsey are full-time students and may be claimed as dependents on their parents' tax return. Raymond's qualifying expenses total $4,300 for the fall semester while Kelsey's qualifying expenses total $10,200 for the prior and current semesters. For 2008, Dean and Audry may claim a $1,800 HOPE scholarship credit [(100% × $1,200) + (50% × $1,200)] relating to Raymond's expenses and a $2,000 lifetime learning credit (20% × $10,000) relating to Kelsey's expenses. Kelsey's tuition expenses are ineligible for the HOPE scholarship credit because she is beyond the first two years of postsecondary education. ■

Assume the same facts as in Example 32, except that Dean and Audry's modified AGI for 2008 is $108,000. Dean and Audry are eligible to claim $1,520 in total education credits for 2008. Their available credits totaling $3,800 ($1,800 HOPE scholarship credit + $2,000 lifetime learning credit) must be reduced because their AGI exceeds the $96,000 limit for married taxpayers. The percentage reduction is computed as the amount by which modified AGI exceeds the limit, expressed as a percentage of the phaseout range, or [($108,000 − $96,000)/$20,000)], resulting in a 60% reduction. Therefore, the maximum available credit for 2008 is $1,520 ($3,800 × 40% allowable portion). ■

Restrictions on Double Tax Benefit. Taxpayers are prohibited from receiving a double tax benefit associated with qualifying educational expenses. Therefore, taxpayers who claim an education credit may not deduct the expenses, nor may they claim the credit for amounts that are otherwise excluded from gross income (e.g., scholarships, employer-paid educational assistance). However, a taxpayer may claim an education tax credit and exclude from gross income amounts distributed from a Coverdell Education Savings Account as long as the distribution is not used for the same expenses for which the credit is claimed.

Credit for Certain Retirement Plan Contributions

Taxpayers may claim a nonrefundable **credit for certain retirement plan contributions** based on eligible contributions of up to $2,000 to certain qualified retirement plans, such as traditional and Roth IRAs and § 401(k) plans.[42] This credit, sometimes referred to as the "saver's credit," is intended to encourage lower- and middle-income taxpayers to contribute to qualified retirement plans. The benefit provided by this credit is in addition to any deduction or exclusion that otherwise is available due to the qualifying contribution. In calculating the credit, the qualifying contributions are reduced by taxable distributions from any of the qualifying plans received by the taxpayer and spouse during the tax year and the two previous tax years and during the period prior to the due date of the return.

The credit rate applied to the eligible expenses depends on the taxpayer's AGI[43] and filing status as shown in Table 13–4. However, the maximum credit allowed to an individual is $1,000 ($2,000 × 50%). As the taxpayer's AGI increases, the rate applied to contributions in calculating the credit is reduced, and once AGI exceeds the upper end of the applicable range, no credit is available. To qualify for the credit, the taxpayer must be at least 18 years of age and cannot be a dependent of another taxpayer or a full-time student.

---

[42]§ 25B.

[43]For years beginning after 2006, the AGI thresholds are indexed for inflation. The amounts shown in Table 13–4 are the relevant thresholds for 2008. For purposes of this credit, the AGI thresholds are modified to include certain excluded income items. See § 25B(e).

| TABLE 13-4 | "Saver's" Credit Rate and AGI Thresholds | | | | | | |

Joint Return		Head of Household		All Other Cases		Applicable Percentage
Over	Not Over	Over	Not Over	Over	Not Over	
$0	$32,000	$0	$24,000	$0	$16,000	50%
32,000	34,500	24,000	25,875	16,000	17,250	20%
34,500	53,000	25,875	39,750	17,250	26,500	10%
53,000		39,750		26,500		0%

EXAMPLE 34

Earl and Josephine, married taxpayers, each contribute $2,500 to their respective § 401(k) plans offered through their employers. The AGI reported on their joint return is $45,000. The maximum amount of contributions that may be taken into account in calculating the credit is limited to $2,000 for Earl and $2,000 for Josephine. As a result, they may claim a credit for their retirement plan contributions of $400 [($2,000 × 2) × 10%]. They would not qualify for the credit if their AGI had exceeded $53,000. ■

Recovery Rebate Credit

See Exhibit 13–2 for a discussion of the recovery rebate credit contained in the Economic Stimulus Act of 2008.

LO.5

Understand the tax withholding and payment procedures applicable to employers.

Payment Procedures

The tax law contains elaborate rules that require the prepayment of various Federal taxes. Consistent with the pay-as-you-go approach to the collection of taxes, these rules carry penalties for lack of compliance.[44] Prepayment procedures fall into two major categories: those applicable to employers and those applicable to self-employed persons. For employers, both payroll taxes (FICA and FUTA) and income taxes may be involved. With self-employed taxpayers, the focus is on the income tax and the self-employment tax.

Procedures Applicable to Employers

Employment taxes include FICA (Federal Insurance Contributions Act) and FUTA (Federal Unemployment Tax Act). The employer usually is responsible for withholding the employee's share of FICA (commonly referred to as Social Security tax) and appropriate amounts for income taxes. In addition, the employer must match the FICA portion withheld and fully absorb the cost of FUTA. The sum of the employment taxes and the income tax withholdings must be paid to the IRS at specified intervals.

The key to employer compliance in this area involves the resolution of the following points:

- Ascertaining which employees and wages are covered by employment taxes and are subject to withholding for income taxes.
- Arriving at the amount to be paid and/or withheld.
- Reporting and paying employment taxes and income taxes withheld to the IRS on a timely basis through the use of proper forms and procedures.

---

[44]See, for example, § 3403 (employer liable for any taxes withheld and not paid over to the IRS), § 6656 (penalty on amounts withheld and not paid over), and § 6654 (penalty for failure by an individual to pay estimated income taxes).

| **EXHIBIT 13–2** | **Recovery Rebate Credit** |

The Economic Stimulus Act of 2008 provides a refundable tax credit for certain taxpayers (§ 6428). The Treasury Department issued rebate checks (effectively, an advance payment of the credit) to taxpayers in the spring of 2008 to help stimulate the economy. The credit includes two components—a basic credit and a qualifying child credit.

Eligible individuals received a *basic credit* equal to the greater of:

1. The taxpayer's net income tax liability up to a maximum of $600 ($1,200 in the case of a joint return), or
2. $300 ($600 in the case of a joint return) if the individual had:

   (1) at least $3,000 of earned income (generally defined in the same manner as for the earned income tax credit but increased by all of the Social Security benefits received), or
   (2) net income tax liability of at least $1 and gross income greater than the sum of the applicable basic standard deduction amount and one personal exemption (two personal exemptions for a joint return).

If an individual is eligible for any amount of the basic credit, the individual also may have received a *qualifying child credit* of $300 for each qualifying child (defined in the same manner as for the child tax credit).

Rebate Credit Phaseout. The combined rebate credit phased out at a rate of 5 percent of adjusted gross income above $75,000 ($150,000 for joint returns). The *Rebate Rules Illustrated* section which follows provides a series of examples illustrating the rebate computation and phaseout.

Reconciliation on 2008 Tax Returns. The rebate checks issued by the Treasury Department were based on 2007 tax return information (as 2008 tax return information would not be available until the end of 2008). On their 2008 tax returns, taxpayers will reconcile the amount of the credit with the rebate received. If the rebate check is less than the computed credit, the difference will be claimed as a credit against the taxpayer's 2008 tax liability. If the rebate check is greater than the computed credit, the taxpayer will not have to repay the difference to the Treasury Department. If, for whatever reason, the Treasury Department failed to issue a rebate check to the taxpayer, the reconciliation process will allow a credit on the 2008 tax return.

Rebate Rules Illustrated. The following examples show the rebate amounts based on a taxpayer's 2007 tax return.

Example 1   A single taxpayer has $14,000 in Social Security income, no qualifying children, and no net tax liability prior to the application of refundable credits and the child credit. The taxpayer will receive a rebate of $300 for meeting the qualifying income test.

Example 2   A head of household taxpayer has $4,000 in earned income, one qualifying child, and no net tax liability prior to the application of refundable credits and the child credit. The taxpayer will receive a rebate of $600 ($300 for meeting the qualifying income test and $300 for the qualifying child).

Example 3   A married taxpayer filing jointly has $6,000 in earned income, one qualifying child, and no net tax liability prior to the application of refundable credits and the child credit. The taxpayer will receive a rebate of $900 ($600 for meeting the qualifying income test and $300 for the qualifying child).

Example 4   A married taxpayer filing jointly has $2,000 in earned income, one qualifying child, and $1,100 in net tax liability (resulting from other unearned income) prior to the application of refundable credits and the child credit (the taxpayer's actual liability after the child credit is $100). The qualifying income test is not met, but the taxpayer has net tax liability for purposes of determining the rebate of $1,100. The taxpayer will receive a rebate of $1,400 ($1,100 of net tax liability and $300 for the qualifying child).

Example 5   A married taxpayer filing jointly has $40,000 in earned income, two qualifying children, and a net tax liability of $1,573 prior to the application of refundable credits and child credits [the taxpayer's actual tax liability after the child credit is ($427)]. The taxpayer meets the qualifying income test and the net tax liability test. The taxpayer will receive a rebate of $1,800 [$1,200 (the greater of $600 or net tax liability not to exceed $1,200) and $300 for each qualifying child].

Example 6   A married taxpayer filing jointly has $175,000 in earned income, two qualifying children, and a net tax liability of $31,189 (the taxpayer's actual liability after the child credit also is $31,189 as the joint income is too high to qualify for the child credit). The taxpayer meets the qualifying income test and the net tax liability test. Before applying the rebate phaseout rules, the taxpayer qualifies for a rebate of $1,800 [$1,200 (the greater of $600 or net tax liability not to exceed $1,200) and $300 for each qualifying child]. The phaseout rules reduce the total rebate amount by 5 percent of the amount by which the taxpayer's adjusted gross income exceeds $150,000. Five percent of $25,000 ($175,000 − $150,000) equals $1,250. The taxpayer's rebate is $550 ($1,800 − $1,250).

CONCEPT SUMMARY   13–1

Tax Credits

Credit	Computation	Comments
Tax withheld on wages (§ 31)	Amount is reported to employee on Form W–2.	Refundable credit.
Earned income (§ 32)	Amount is determined by reference to Earned Income Credit Table published by IRS. Computations of underlying amounts in Earned Income Credit Table are illustrated in Example 22.	Refundable credit. A form of negative income tax to assist low-income taxpayers. Earned income and AGI must be less than certain threshold amounts. Generally, one or more qualifying children must reside with the taxpayer.
Child and dependent care (§ 21)	Rate ranges from 20% to 35% depending on AGI. Maximum base for credit is $3,000 for one qualifying individual, $6,000 for two or more.	Nonrefundable personal credit. No carryback or carryforward. Benefits taxpayers who incur employment-related child or dependent care expenses in order to work or seek employment. Eligible taxpayers must have a dependent under age 13 or a dependent (any age) or spouse who is physically or mentally incapacitated.
Elderly or disabled (§ 22)	15% of sum of base amount minus reductions for (1) Social Security and other nontaxable benefits and (2) excess AGI. Base amount is fixed by law (e.g., $5,000 for a single taxpayer).	Nonrefundable personal credit. No carryback or carryforward. Provides relief for taxpayers not receiving substantial tax-free retirement benefits.
Adoption expenses (§ 23)	Up to $11,650 of costs incurred to adopt an eligible child qualify for the credit. Taxpayer claims the credit in the year qualified expenses were paid or incurred if they were paid or incurred during or after year in which adoption was finalized. For expenses paid or incurred in a year prior to when adoption was finalized, credit must be claimed in tax year following the tax year during which the expenses are paid or incurred.	Nonrefundable credit. Unused credit may be carried forward five years. Purpose is to assist taxpayers who incur nonrecurring costs associated with the adoption process.
Child (§ 24)	Credit is based on *number* of qualifying children under age 17. Maximum credit is $1,000 per child. Credit is phased out for higher-income taxpayers.	Generally a nonrefundable credit. Refundable in certain cases. Purpose is to provide tax relief for low- to moderate-income families with children.
Education (§ 25A)	HOPE scholarship credit is available for qualifying education expenses of students in first two years of postsecondary education. Maximum credit is $1,800 per year per eligible student. Credit is phased out for higher-income taxpayers.	Nonrefundable credit. Credit is designed to help defray costs of first two years of higher education for low- to middle-income families.
	Lifetime learning credit permits a credit of 20% of qualifying expenses (up to $10,000 per year) provided HOPE scholarship credit is not claimed with respect to those expenses. Credit is calculated per taxpayer, not per student, and is phased out for higher-income taxpayers.	Nonrefundable credit. Credit is designed to help defray costs of higher education beyond first two years, and for costs incurred in maintaining or improving existing job skills, for low- to middle-income taxpayers.

Tax Credits—Continued

Credit	Computation	Comments
Credit for certain retirement plan contributions (§ 25B)	Calculation is based on amount of contribution multiplied by a percentage that depends on the taxpayer's filing status and AGI.	Nonrefundable credit. Purpose is to encourage contributions to qualified retirement plans by low- and middle-income taxpayers.
Foreign tax (§ 27)	Foreign taxable income/total worldwide taxable income × U.S. tax = overall limitation. Lesser of foreign taxes imposed or overall limitation.	Nonrefundable credit. Unused credits may be carried back 1 year and forward 10 years. Purpose is to prevent double taxation of foreign income.
General business (§ 38)	May not exceed net income tax minus the greater of tentative minimum tax or 25% of net regular tax liability that exceeds $25,000.	Nonrefundable credit. Components include tax credit for rehabilitation expenditures, work opportunity tax credit, research activities credit, low-income housing credit, disabled access credit, credit for small employer pension plan startup costs, and credit for employer-provided child care. Unused credit may be carried back 1 year and forward 20 years. FIFO method applies to carrybacks, carryovers, and credits earned during current year.
Rehabilitation expenditures (§ 47)	Qualifying investment times rehabilitation percentage, depending on type of property. Regular rehabilitation rate is 10%; rate for certified historic structures is 20%.	Nonrefundable credit. Part of general business credit and therefore subject to same carryback, carryover, and FIFO rules. Purpose is to discourage businesses from moving from economically distressed areas to newer locations.
Research activities (§ 41)	Incremental credit is 20% of excess of computation year expenditures over the base amount. Basic research credit is allowed to certain corporations for 20% of cash payments to qualified organizations that exceed a specially calculated base amount. An energy research credit is allowed for 20% of qualifying payments made to an energy research consortium.	Nonrefundable credit. Part of general business credit and therefore subject to same carryback, carryover, and FIFO rules. Purpose is to encourage high-tech and energy research in the United States.
Low-income housing (§ 42)	Appropriate rate times eligible basis (portion of project attributable to low-income units). Credit is available each year for 10 years. Recapture may apply.	Nonrefundable credit. Part of general business credit and therefore subject to same carryback, carryover, and FIFO rules. Purpose is to encourage construction of housing for low-income individuals.
Disabled access (§ 44)	Credit is 50% of eligible access expenditures that exceed $250 but do not exceed $10,250. Maximum credit is $5,000. Available only to eligible small businesses.	Nonrefundable credit. Part of general business credit and therefore subject to same carryback, carryover, and FIFO rules. Purpose is to encourage small businesses to become more accessible to disabled individuals.
Credit for small employer pension plan startup costs (§ 45E)	Credit equals 50% of qualified startup costs incurred by eligible employers. Maximum annual credit is $500. Deduction for related expenses is reduced by the amount of the credit.	Nonrefundable credit. Part of general business credit and therefore subject to same carryback, carryover, and FIFO rules. Purpose is to encourage small employers to establish qualified retirement plans for their employees.

Tax Credits—Continued

Credit	Computation	Comments
Credit for employer-provided child care (§ 45F)	Credit is equal to 25% of qualified child care expenses plus 10% of qualified expenses for child care resource and referral services. Maximum credit is $150,000. Deduction for related expenses or basis must be reduced by the amount of the credit.	Nonrefundable credit. Part of general business credit and therefore subject to same carryback, carryover, and FIFO rules. Purpose is to encourage employers to provide child care for their employees' children during normal working hours.
Work opportunity (§ 51)	Credit is limited to 40% of the first $6,000 of wages paid to each eligible employee. For long-term family assistance recipients, credit is limited to 40% of first $10,000 of wages paid to each eligible employee in first year of employment, plus 50% of first $10,000 of wages paid to each eligible employee in second year of employment.	Nonrefundable credit. Part of the general business credit and therefore subject to the same carryback, carryover, and FIFO rules. Purpose is to encourage employment of individuals in specified groups.

Coverage Requirements. Circular E, *Employer's Tax Guide* (Publication 15), issued by the IRS, contains a listing of which employees and which wages require withholdings for income taxes and employment taxes. Excerpts from Circular E appear in Exhibit 13–3. In working with Exhibit 13–3, consider the following observations:

- The designation "Exempt" in the income tax withholding column does not mean that the amount paid is nontaxable to the employee. It merely relieves the employer from having to withhold.

EXAMPLE 35

Lee works for Yellow Corporation and has the type of job where tips are not common but do occur. If Lee's total tips amount to less than $20 per month, Yellow Corporation need not withhold Federal income taxes on the tips (see Exhibit 13–3). Nevertheless, Lee must include the tips in his gross income. ∎

- In some cases, income tax withholding is not required but is voluntary. This is designated "Exempt (withhold if both employer and employee agree)."

EXAMPLE 36

Pat is employed as a gardener by a wealthy family. In the past, he has encountered difficulty in managing his finances so as to be in a position to pay the income tax due every April 15. To ease the cash-flow problem that develops in April, Pat asks his employer to withhold income taxes from his wages. ∎

- The Social Security and Medicare (FICA) column refers to the employer's share. The same is true of the Federal Unemployment (FUTA) column since the employee does not contribute to this tax.

Amount of FICA Taxes. The FICA tax has two components: Social Security tax (old age, survivors, and disability insurance) *and* Medicare tax (hospital insurance). The tax rates and wage base under FICA have increased substantially over the years. The base amount is adjusted each year for inflation. As Table 13–5 shows, the top base amount differs for the Medicare portion (now unlimited) and for the Social Security portion. Table 13–5 represents the employee's share of the tax. The employer must match the employee's portion.

EXHIBIT 13–3 | **Withholding Classifications**

Special Classes of Employment and Special Types of Payments	Treatment under Employment Taxes		
	Income Tax Withholding	Social Security and Medicare	Federal Unemployment
Employee business expense reimbursement:			
1. Accountable plan.			
a. Amounts not exceeding specified government rate for per diem or standard mileage.	Exempt	Exempt	Exempt
b. Amounts in excess of specified government rate for per diem or standard mileage.	Withhold	Taxable	Taxable
2. Nonaccountable plan.	Withhold	Taxable	Taxable
Family employees:			
1. Child employed by parent (or partnership in which each partner is a parent of the child).	Withhold	Exempt until age 18; age 21 for domestic service.	Exempt until age 21
2. Parent employed by child.	Withhold	Taxable if in course of the son's or daughter's business.	Exempt
3. Spouse employed by spouse.	Withhold	Taxable if in course of spouse's business.	Exempt
Household employees: Domestic service in private homes. Farmers see Publication 51(Circular A).	Exempt (withhold if both employer and employee agree).	Taxable if paid $1,600 or more in cash in 2008. Exempt if performed by an individual under age 18 during any portion of the calendar year and is not the principal occupation of the employee.	Taxable if employer paid total cash wages of $1,000 or more in any quarter in the current or preceding calendar year.
Interns working in hospitals.	Withhold	Taxable	Exempt
Newspaper carriers under age 18.	Exempt (withhold if both employer and employee agree).	Exempt	Exempt
Salespersons:			
1. Common law employees.	Withhold	Taxable	Taxable
2. Statutory employees.	Exempt	Taxable	Taxable, except for full-time life insurance sales agents.
Scholarships and fellowship grants: [includible in income under § 117(c)].	Withhold	Taxability depends on the nature of the employment and the status of the organization.	Taxability depends on the nature of the employment and the status of the organization.
Severance or dismissal pay.	Withhold	Taxable	Taxable
Tips, if less than $20 in a month.	Exempt	Exempt	Exempt
Worker's compensation.	Exempt	Exempt	Exempt

TABLE 13–5	FICA Rates and Base

	Social Security Tax			Medicare Tax			
	Percent	×	Base Amount	+	Percent	×	Base Amount	=	Maximum Tax
1991	6.20%	×	$53,400	+	1.45%	×	$125,000	=	$5,123.30
1992	6.20%	×	55,500	+	1.45%	×	130,200	=	5,328.90
1993	6.20%	×	57,600	+	1.45%	×	135,000	=	5,528.70
1994	6.20%	×	60,600	+	1.45%	×	Unlimited	=	Unlimited
1995	6.20%	×	61,200	+	1.45%	×	Unlimited	=	Unlimited
1996	6.20%	×	62,700	+	1.45%	×	Unlimited	=	Unlimited
1997	6.20%	×	65,400	+	1.45%	×	Unlimited	=	Unlimited
1998	6.20%	×	68,400	+	1.45%	×	Unlimited	=	Unlimited
1999	6.20%	×	72,600	+	1.45%	×	Unlimited	=	Unlimited
2000	6.20%	×	76,200	+	1.45%	×	Unlimited	=	Unlimited
2001	6.20%	×	80,400	+	1.45%	×	Unlimited	=	Unlimited
2002	6.20%	×	84,900	+	1.45%	×	Unlimited	=	Unlimited
2003	6.20%	×	87,000	+	1.45%	×	Unlimited	=	Unlimited
2004	6.20%	×	87,900	+	1.45%	×	Unlimited	=	Unlimited
2005	6.20%	×	90,000	+	1.45%	×	Unlimited	=	Unlimited
2006	6.20%	×	94,200	+	1.45%	×	Unlimited	=	Unlimited
2007	6.20%	×	97,500	+	1.45%	×	Unlimited	=	Unlimited
2008	6.20%	×	102,000	+	1.45%	×	Unlimited	=	Unlimited
2009 on	6.20%	×	*	+	1.45%	×	Unlimited	=	Unlimited

*Not yet determined.

Withholdings from employees must continue until the maximum base amount is reached. In 2008, for example, FICA withholding ceases for the Social Security portion (6.2 percent) once the employee has earned wages subject to FICA in the amount of $102,000. For the Medicare portion (1.45 percent), however, the employer is required to withhold on all wages without limit. This contrasts with years prior to 1994 when a maximum base existed for the Medicare portion also.

EXAMPLE 37

In 2008, Keshia earned a salary of $140,000 from her employer. Therefore, FICA taxes withheld from her salary are $6,324 ($102,000 × 6.2%) plus $2,030 ($140,000 × 1.45%) for a total of $8,354. In addition to paying the amount withheld from Keshia's salary to the government, her employer also has to pay $8,354. ■

In at least two situations, it is possible for an employee to have paid excess FICA taxes.

EXAMPLE 38

During 2008, Kevin changed employers in the middle of the year and earned $60,000 (all of which was subject to FICA) from each job. As a result, each employer withheld $4,590 [(6.2% × $60,000) + (1.45% × $60,000)] for a total of $9,180. Although each employer acted properly, Kevin's total FICA tax liability for the year is only $8,064 [(6.2% × $102,000) + (1.45% × $120,000)]. Thus, Kevin has overpaid his share of FICA taxes by $1,116 [$9,180 (amount paid) − $8,064 (amount of correct liability)]. He should claim this amount as a tax credit when filing his income tax return for 2008. The tax credit will reduce any income tax Kevin might owe or, possibly, generate a tax refund. ■

EXAMPLE 39

During 2008, Lori earned $94,000 from her regular job and $26,000 from a part-time job (all of which was subject to FICA). As a result, one employer withheld $7,191 [(6.2% × $94,000) +

TAX *in the News*   **WILL SOCIAL SECURITY BE THERE FOR YOU WHEN YOU NEED IT?**

With an estimated 77 million baby boomers becoming eligible for Social Security over the next decade or so, and with fewer employees paying into the system, a logical question for younger Americans who are just now entering the workforce is whether the Social Security system will be solvent when they reach their retirement years. This question often arises during political campaigns and is discussed in the news media as well as in hearings in Congress. Reality seems to suggest that with a burgeoning number of retirees drawing Social Security for a longer period of time because their life expectancies are increasing, the assets accumulated in the Social Security trust fund will be strained at some point in the future.

Things seem to be fine now, but beginning in about 2018, the Social Security Administration expects to be paying out more in benefits than it collects from the payroll tax. Interest income on the trust fund assets will help balance the books until about 2028 when the trust fund assets are expected to begin falling. Some suggest that by as early as 2042, the Social Security trust fund could run dry.

So, do we have a crisis on our hands? Will benefits be cut or will payroll taxes be increased? Will a "means test" be applied before retirees can receive their monthly checks? Will part or all of the Social Security contributions be "privatized"? The answers to these questions and the integrity of the system are issues that undoubtedly will take years to resolve.

$(1.45\% \times \$94,000)$] while the other employer withheld $1,989 [$(6.2\% \times \$26,000) + (1.45\% \times \$26,000)$] for a total of $9,180. Lori's total FICA tax liability for the year is only $8,064 [$(6.2\% \times \$102,000) + (1.45\% \times \$120,000)$]. Thus, Lori has overpaid her share of FICA taxes by $1,116 [$9,180 (amount paid) − $8,064 (amount of correct liability)]. She should claim this amount as a tax credit when filing her income tax return for 2008. ∎

In Examples 38 and 39, the employee is subject to overwithholding. In both cases, however, the employee was able to obtain a credit for the excess withheld. The same result does not materialize for the portion paid by the employer. Since this amount is not refundable, in some situations employers may pay more FICA taxes than the covered employees.

The mere fact that a husband and wife are both employed does not, by itself, result in overwithholding of FICA taxes.

EXAMPLE 40

During 2008, Jim and Betty (husband and wife) are both employed, and each earns wages subject to FICA of $60,000. Accordingly, each has $4,590 FICA withheld [$(6.2\% \times \$60,000) + (1.45\% \times \$60,000)$] for a total of $9,180. Since neither spouse paid FICA tax on wages in excess of $102,000 (Social Security tax) [see Table 13–5], there is no overwithholding. ∎

A spouse employed by another spouse is subject to FICA. However, children under the age of 18 who are employed in a parent's trade or business are exempted.

Amount of Income Tax Withholding. Arriving at the amount to be withheld for income tax purposes is not so simple. It involves three basic steps:[45]

- Have the employee complete Form W–4, Employee's Withholding Allowance Certificate.
- Determine the employee's payroll period.
- Compute the amount to be withheld, usually using either the wage-bracket tables or the percentage method.

Form W–4 reflects the employee's marital status and **withholding allowances**. Generally, it need not be filed with the IRS and is retained by the employer as part of the payroll records.

---

[45]The withholding provisions are contained in §§ 3401 and 3402. These Sections will not be referenced specifically in the discussion that follows.

The employer need not verify the number of exemptions claimed. Any misinformation on the form will be attributed to the employee. However, if the employer has reason to believe that the employee made a false statement, the IRS should be notified. In the meantime, the Form W–4 should be honored. Employees are subject to both civil and criminal penalties for filing false withholding statements.

On the current Form W–4, an employee may claim *withholding allowances* for the following: personal exemptions for self and spouse and dependency exemptions. One *special withholding allowance* may be claimed if the employee is single and has only one job, if the employee is married and has only one job and the spouse is not employed, or if wages from a second job or a spouse's wages (or both) are $1,000 or less. An additional allowance is available if the employee expects to file using the head-of-household status or if the employee expects to claim a credit for child and dependent care expenses on qualifying expenditures of at least $1,600. A taxpayer qualifying for the child tax credit may claim one or two additional allowances for each eligible child. An employee who plans to itemize deductions or claim adjustments to income (e.g., alimony, deductible IRA contributions) should use the worksheet provided on Form W–4 to determine the correct number of additional allowances.

To avoid having too little tax withheld, some employees may find it necessary to reduce their withholding allowances. This might be the case for an employee who has more than one job or who has other sources of income that are not subject to adequate withholding. Likewise, a married employee who has a working spouse or more than one job might wish to claim fewer allowances.

If both spouses of a married couple are employed, they may allocate their total allowances between themselves as they see fit. The same allocation procedure is required if a taxpayer has more than one job. In no event should the same allowance be claimed more than once at the same time. It is permissible to declare *fewer* allowances than the taxpayer is entitled to in order to increase the amount of withholding. Doing so, however, does not affect the number of personal and dependency exemptions allowable on the employee's income tax return. An employee is also permitted to have the employer withhold a certain dollar amount in addition to the required amount. This additional dollar amount can be arbitrary or calculated in accordance with a worksheet on Form W–4.

EXAMPLE 41

Carl, who earns $75,000, is married to Carol, who earns $85,000. They have three dependent children and will claim the standard deduction. Assume they do not qualify to claim the child tax credit. Together they should be entitled to five allowances [2 (for personal exemptions) + 3 (for dependency exemptions)]. The special withholding allowance is not available since both spouses earn more than $1,000. If Carl is the spouse first employed and his Form W–4 reflects five allowances, Carol's Form W–4 should report none. They could, however, reallocate their allowances between them as long as the total claimed does not exceed five. ∎

The period of service for which an employee is paid is known as the *payroll period*. Daily, weekly, biweekly, semimonthly, and monthly periods are the most common arrangements. If an employee has no regular payroll period, he or she is considered to be paid on a daily basis.

Once the allowances are known (as reflected on Form W–4) and the payroll period determined, the amount to be withheld for Federal income taxes can be computed. The computation usually is made by using the wage-bracket tables or the percentage method.

Wage-bracket tables are available for daily, weekly, biweekly, semimonthly, and monthly payroll periods for single (including heads of household) and married taxpayers. An extract of the tables dealing with married persons on a monthly payroll period is reproduced in Table 13–6. The data in Table 13–6 are for wages paid in 2008. Example 42 illustrates the use of withholding tables.

TABLE 13–6   Wage-Bracket Withholding Table

MARRIED Persons—MONTHLY Payroll Period
(For Wages Paid in 2008)

If the wages are—		And the number of withholding allowances claimed is—										
At least	But less than	0	1	2	3	4	5	6	7	8	9	10
		The amount of income tax to be withheld is—										
$3,240	$3,280	$324	$280	$237	$193	$149	$114	$84	$55	$26	$0	$0
3,280	3,320	330	286	243	199	155	118	88	59	30	1	0
3,320	3,360	336	292	249	205	161	122	92	63	34	5	0
3,360	3,400	342	298	255	211	167	126	96	67	38	9	0
3,400	3,440	348	304	261	217	173	130	100	71	42	13	0
3,440	3,480	354	310	267	223	179	135	104	75	46	17	0
3,480	3,520	360	316	273	229	185	141	108	79	50	21	0
3,520	3,560	366	322	279	235	191	147	112	83	54	25	0
3,560	3,600	372	328	285	241	197	153	116	87	58	29	0
3,600	3,640	378	334	291	247	203	159	120	91	62	33	4
3,640	3,680	384	340	297	253	209	165	124	95	66	37	8
3,680	3,720	390	346	303	259	215	171	128	99	70	41	12
3,720	3,760	396	352	309	265	221	177	134	103	74	45	16
3,760	3,800	402	358	315	271	227	183	140	107	78	49	20
3,800	3,840	408	364	321	277	233	189	146	111	82	53	24
3,840	3,880	414	370	327	283	239	195	152	115	86	57	28
3,880	3,920	420	376	333	289	245	201	158	119	90	61	32
3,920	3,960	426	382	339	295	251	207	164	123	94	65	36
3,960	4,000	432	388	345	301	257	213	170	127	98	69	40
4,000	4,040	438	394	351	307	263	219	176	132	102	73	44
4,040	4,080	444	400	357	313	269	225	182	138	106	77	48
4,080	4,120	450	406	363	319	275	231	188	144	110	81	52
4,120	4,160	456	412	369	325	281	237	194	150	114	85	56
4,160	4,200	462	418	375	331	287	243	200	156	118	89	60
4,200	4,240	468	424	381	337	293	249	206	162	122	93	64
4,240	4,280	474	430	387	343	299	255	212	168	126	97	68
4,280	4,320	480	436	393	349	305	261	218	174	130	101	72
4,320	4,360	486	442	399	355	311	267	224	180	136	105	76
4,360	4,400	492	448	405	361	317	273	230	186	142	109	80
4,400	4,440	498	454	411	367	323	279	236	192	148	113	84
4,440	4,480	504	460	417	373	329	285	242	198	154	117	88
4,480	4,520	510	466	423	379	335	291	248	204	160	121	92
4,520	4,560	516	472	429	385	341	297	254	210	166	125	96
4,560	4,600	522	478	435	391	347	303	260	216	172	129	100
4,600	4,640	528	484	441	397	353	309	266	222	178	134	104
4,640	4,680	534	490	447	403	359	315	272	228	184	140	108
4,680	4,720	540	496	453	409	365	321	278	234	190	146	112
4,720	4,760	546	502	459	415	371	327	284	240	196	152	116
4,760	4,800	552	508	465	421	377	333	290	246	202	158	120
4,800	4,840	558	514	471	427	383	339	296	252	208	164	124
4,840	4,880	564	520	477	433	389	345	302	258	214	170	128
4,880	4,920	570	526	483	439	395	351	308	264	220	176	133
4,920	4,960	576	532	489	445	401	357	314	270	226	182	139
4,960	5,000	582	538	495	451	407	363	320	276	232	188	145
5,000	5,040	588	544	501	457	413	369	326	282	238	194	151
5,040	5,080	594	550	507	463	419	375	332	288	244	200	157
5,080	5,120	600	556	513	469	425	381	338	294	250	206	163
5,120	5,160	606	562	519	475	431	387	344	300	256	212	169
5,160	5,200	612	568	525	481	437	393	350	306	262	218	175
5,200	5,240	618	574	531	487	443	399	356	312	268	224	181
5,240	5,280	624	580	537	493	449	405	362	318	274	230	187
5,280	5,320	630	586	543	499	455	411	368	324	280	236	193
5,320	5,360	636	592	549	505	461	417	374	330	286	242	199
5,360	5,400	642	598	555	511	467	423	380	336	292	248	205
5,400	5,440	648	604	561	517	473	429	386	342	298	254	211
5,440	5,480	654	610	567	523	479	435	392	348	304	260	217
5,480	5,520	660	616	573	529	485	441	398	354	310	266	223
5,520	5,560	666	622	579	535	491	447	404	360	316	272	229
5,560	5,600	672	628	585	541	497	453	410	366	322	278	235
5,600	5,640	678	634	591	547	503	459	416	372	328	284	241
5,640	5,680	684	640	597	553	509	465	422	378	334	290	247
5,680	5,720	690	646	603	559	515	471	428	384	340	296	253
5,720	5,760	696	652	609	565	521	477	434	390	346	302	259
5,760	5,800	702	658	615	571	527	483	440	396	352	308	265
5,800	5,840	708	664	621	577	533	489	446	402	358	314	271
5,840	5,880	714	670	627	583	539	495	452	408	364	320	277

$5,880 and over   Use Table 4(b) for a **MARRIED person**.

TABLE 13–7	Conversion Chart for 2008
Payroll Period	**Amount of One Allowance**
Daily	$ 13.46
Weekly	67.31
Biweekly	134.62
Semimonthly	145.83
Monthly	291.67
Quarterly	875.00
Semiannual	1,750.00
Annual	3,500.00

EXAMPLE 42

Tom is married and has three dependent children and no additional withholding allowances are available. In his job with Pink Corporation, he earns $4,500 in May 2008. Assuming Tom's wife has a part-time job for which she earns $5,000 for the year and all available allowances are claimed on his Form W–4, Pink should withhold $291 a month from his wages. This amount is taken from the five allowances column in the $4,480–$4,520 wage bracket. The five allowances result from personal exemptions (two) plus dependency exemptions (three). Note that an additional withholding allowance is not available for Tom's wife because she has a job for which she earned more than $1,000. ■

Although the wage-bracket table requires few, if any, calculations, the percentage method is equally acceptable. Its use may be necessary for payroll periods where no wage-bracket tables are available (quarterly, semiannual, and annual payroll periods) and where wages paid exceed the amount allowed for use of the wage-bracket tables. The percentage method is particularly useful when payroll computations are computerized. This method, however, requires the use of a conversion chart based on one withholding allowance. That is, the amount of one allowance is equal to the personal and dependency exemption amount divided by the number of payroll periods in a year. For example, the amount of one allowance for a taxpayer who is paid weekly is $67.31 ($3,500/52 payroll periods)—see Table 13–7.

To use the percentage method, proceed as follows:

Step 1. Multiply the amount of one allowance (as specified in the conversion chart in Table 13–7) by the employee's total allowances (taken from Form W–4).

Step 2. Subtract the product reached in step 1 from the employee's wages. The remainder is called "amount of wages."

Step 3. Using the result derived in step 2, compute the income tax withholding under the proper percentage-method table.

The table used in applying the percentage method for those with monthly payroll periods is reproduced in Table 13–8. An illustration of the percentage method follows.

EXAMPLE 43

Assume the same facts as in Example 42, except that Tom's income tax withholding is determined using the percentage method.

Step 1. $291.67 (amount of one allowance for a monthly payroll period) × 5 (total allowances) = $1,458.35.

Step 2. $4,500.00 (monthly salary) − $1,458.35 (step 1) = $3,041.65 (amount of wages).

Step 3. Referring to Table 13–8: $129.60 + 15% ($3,041.65 − $1,963.00) = $291.40. ■

| TABLE 13–8 | Table for Percentage Method of Withholding for Wages Paid through 2008 |

TABLE 4—MONTHLY Payroll Period

(a) SINGLE person (including head of household)—

If the amount of wages (after subtracting withholding allowances) is: The amount of income tax to withhold is:

Not over $221 . . . . $0

Over—	But not over—		of excess over—
$221	—$858	. . . 10%	—$221
$858	—$2,830	. . . $63.70 plus 15%	—$858
$2,830	—$6,644	. . . $359.50 plus 25%	—$2,830
$6,644	—$13,875	. . . $1,313.00 plus 28%	—$6,644
$13,875	—$29,971	. . . $3,337.68 plus 33%	—$13,875
$29,971	. . . .	$8,649.36 plus 35%	—$29,971

(b) MARRIED person—

If the amount of wages (after subtracting withholding allowances) is: The amount of income tax to withhold is:

Not over $667 . . . . $0

Over—	But not over—		of excess over—
$667	—$1,963	. . . 10%	—$667
$1,963	—$6,013	. . . $129.60 plus 15%	—$1,963
$6,013	—$11,488	. . . $737.10 plus 25%	—$6,013
$11,488	—$17,308	. . . $2,105.85 plus 28%	—$11,488
$17,308	—$30,425	. . . $3,735.45 plus 33%	—$17,308
$30,425	. . . .	$8,064.06 plus 35%	—$30,425

Note that the wage-bracket tables yield an amount for income tax withholding of $291 (refer to Example 42) while the percentage method results in $291.40 (refer to Example 43). The difference occurs because the wage-bracket table amounts are derived by computing the withholding on the median wage within each bracket and rounded to the nearest dollar.

Reporting and Payment Procedures. Proper handling of employment taxes and income tax withholdings requires considerable compliance efforts by the employer. Among the Federal forms that have to be filed are the following:

Tax Form	Title
SS–4	Application for Employer Identification Number
W–2	Wage and Tax Statement
W–3	Transmittal of Wage and Tax Statements
940 or 940 EZ	Employer's Annual Federal Unemployment (FUTA) Tax Return
941	Employer's Quarterly Federal Tax Return

Form SS–4 is the starting point since it provides the employer with an identification number that must be used on all of the other forms filed with the IRS and the Social Security Administration. The number issued consists of nine digits and is hyphenated between the second and third digits (e.g., 72–1987316).

Form W–2 furnishes essential information to employees concerning wages paid, FICA, and income tax withholdings. Copies of Form W–2 are distributed to several parties for various purposes: to enable the employee to complete his or her income tax return, to inform the Social Security Administration of the amount of FICA wages earned by the employee, and to serve as a permanent record for the employer and employee of the payroll information contained on the form. Form W–2 (reporting information for the previous calendar year) must be furnished to an employee not later than January 31. If an employee leaves a place of employment before the end of the year, Form W–2 can be given to him or her at any time after employment ends but no later than the following January 31. However, if the terminated employee asks for Form W–2, it must be given to him or her within 30 days after the request or the final wage payment, whichever is later.

GLOBAL
Tax Issues

FOREIGN "WITHHOLDING TAX" PERFORMS AN IMPORTANT ROLE

Taxpayers in the United States are accustomed to having their employer withhold a portion of their salary or wages and then forward the amounts to the government in payment of their income tax liabilities. As a rule, other types of income, such as dividends, interest, and annuities, are not subject to withholding because the IRS has adequate mechanisms in place to assure a high level of tax compliance. But for payments of U.S.-source income to foreign taxpayers, the IRS would not be as confident that it is getting its due were it not for the so-called withholding tax.

To ensure the collection of the income tax on amounts paid to nonresident aliens and foreign corporations, the person *paying* the income, rather than the recipient, is required to withhold and forward the appropriate payment to the government. Although the withholding rate is typically 30 percent, the rate can vary in certain situations. In some situations, this withholding mechanism will also prevent the taxpayer from having to file an income tax return with the U.S. government.

Form W–3 must accompany the copies of Forms W–2 filed by the employer with the Social Security Administration. Its basic purpose is to summarize and reconcile the amounts withheld for FICA and income taxes from *all* employees.

Form 940 (or Form 940 EZ) constitutes the employer's annual accounting for FUTA purposes. Generally, it must be filed on or before January 31 of the following year and must be accompanied by the payment of any undeposited FUTA due the Federal government.

Whether or not deposits[46] are required, most employers must settle their employment taxes every quarter. To do this, Form 941 must be filed on or before the last day of the month following the end of each calendar quarter.

Backup Withholding. Some types of payments made to individuals by banks or businesses are subject to backup withholding under certain conditions. Backup withholding is designed to ensure that income tax is collected on interest and other payments reported on a Form 1099. If backup withholding applies in 2008, the payer must withhold 28 percent of the gross amount. Backup withholding applies when the taxpayer does not give the business or bank his or her identification number in the required manner and in certain other situations.[47]

Procedures Applicable to Self-Employed Persons

LO.6

Understand the payment procedures applicable to self-employed persons.

Although the following discussion largely centers on self-employed taxpayers, some of the procedures may be applicable to employed persons. In many cases, for example, employed persons may be required to pay estimated tax if they have income other than wages that is not subject to withholding. An employee may conduct a second trade or business in a self-employment capacity. Depending on the circumstances, the second job may require the payment of a self-employment tax. In addition, taxpayers whose income consists primarily of rentals, dividends, or interest (this list is not all-inclusive) may be required to pay estimated tax.

Estimated Tax for Individuals. **Estimated tax** is the amount of tax (including alternative minimum tax and self-employment tax) an individual expects to owe for the year after subtracting tax credits and income tax withheld. Any individual who has estimated tax for the year of $1,000 or more *and* whose withholding does not

---

[46]Deposit requirements are specified in each current issue of Circular E, *Employer's Tax Guide*, IRS Publication 15. Under current rules, employers must make deposits on either a monthly or a semiweekly basis.

[47]§ 3406(a). The backup withholding rate is equal to the fourth lowest tax rate for single filers.

equal or exceed the required annual payment (discussed below) must make quarterly payments.[48] Otherwise, a penalty may be assessed. No quarterly payments are required (and no penalty will apply on an underpayment) if the taxpayer's estimated tax is under $1,000. No penalty will apply if the taxpayer had no tax liability for the preceding tax year *and* the preceding tax year was a taxable year of 12 months *and* the taxpayer was a citizen or resident for the entire preceding tax year. In this regard, having no tax liability is not the same as having no additional tax to pay.

The required annual payment must first be computed. This is the *smaller* of the following amounts:

- Ninety percent of the tax shown on the current year's return.
- One hundred percent of the tax shown on the preceding year's return (the return must cover the full 12 months of the preceding year). If the AGI on the preceding year's return exceeds $150,000 ($75,000 if married filing separately), the 100 percent requirement is increased to 110 percent.

In general, one-fourth of this required annual payment is due on April 15, June 15, and September 15 of the tax year and January 15 of the following year.

An equal part of withholding is deemed paid on each due date. Thus, the quarterly installment of the required annual payment reduced by the applicable withholding is the estimated tax to be paid. Payments are to be accompanied by the payment voucher for the appropriate date from Form 1040–ES.

Married taxpayers may make joint estimated tax payments even though a joint income tax return is not subsequently filed. In such event, the estimated tax payments may be applied against the separate return liability of the spouses as they see fit. If a husband and wife cannot agree on a division of the estimated tax payments, the Regulations provide that the payments are to be allocated in proportion to the tax liability on the separate returns.

Penalty on Underpayments. A nondeductible penalty is imposed on the amount of underpayment of estimated tax. The rate for this penalty is adjusted quarterly to reflect changes in the average prime rate.

An *underpayment* occurs when any installment (the sum of estimated tax paid and income tax withheld) is less than 25 percent of the required annual payment. The penalty is applied to the amount of the underpayment for the period of the underpayment.[49]

E X A M P L E   44

Marta made the following payments of estimated tax for 2008 and had no income tax withheld:

April 15, 2008	$1,400
June 16, 2008	2,300
September 15, 2008	1,500
January 15, 2009	1,800

Marta's actual tax for 2008 is $8,000, and her tax in 2007 was $10,000. Therefore, each installment should have been at least $1,800 [($8,000 × 90%) × 25%]. Of the payment on June 16, $400 will be credited to the unpaid balance of the first quarterly installment due on April 15,[50] thereby effectively stopping the underpayment penalty for the first quarterly period. Of the remaining $1,900 payment on June 16, $100 is credited to the September 15 payment, resulting in this third quarterly payment being $200 short. Then $200 of the January 15 payment is credited to the September 15 shortfall, ending the period of underpayment for that portion due. The January 15, 2009 installment is now underpaid by $200, and a penalty will

---

[48]§§ 6654(c)(1) and 6654(e)(1).
[49]§ 6654(b)(2).

[50]Payments are credited to unpaid installments in the order in which the installments are required to be paid. § 6654(b)(3).

TABLE 13–9	Self-Employment Tax: Social Security and Medicare Portions		
Year		Tax Rate	Ceiling Amount
2008	Social Security portion	12.4%	$102,000
	Medicare portion	2.9%	Unlimited
	Aggregate rate	15.3%	
2007	Social Security portion	12.4%	$97,500
	Medicare portion	2.9%	Unlimited
	Aggregate rate	15.3%	

apply from January 15, 2009, to April 15, 2009 (unless paid sooner). Marta's underpayments for the periods of underpayment are as follows:

1st installment due:	$400 from April 15 to June 16
2nd installment due:	Paid in full
3rd installment due:	$200 from September 15, 2008 to January 15, 2009
4th installment due:	$200 from January 15 to April 15, 2009 ∎

If a possible underpayment of estimated tax is indicated, Form 2210 should be filed to compute the penalty due or to justify that no penalty applies.

Self-Employment Tax. The tax on self-employment income is levied to provide Social Security and Medicare benefits (old age, survivors, and disability insurance and hospital insurance) for self-employed individuals. Individuals with net earnings of $400 or more from self-employment are subject to the **self-employment tax**.[51] For 2008, the self-employment tax is 15.3 percent of self-employment income up to $102,000 and 2.9 percent of self-employment income in excess of $102,000. In other words, for 2008 the self-employment tax is 12.4 percent of self-employment earnings up to $102,000 (for the Social Security portion) *plus* 2.9 percent of the total amount of self-employment earnings (for the Medicare portion)—see Table 13–9.

Currently, self-employed taxpayers are allowed a deduction from net earnings from self-employment, at one-half of the self-employment rate, for purposes of determining self-employment tax[52] *and* an income tax deduction for one-half the amount of self-employment tax paid.[53]

Determining the amount of self-employment tax to be paid for 2008 involves completing the steps in Figure 13–1. The result of step 3 or 4 is the amount of self-

FIGURE 13–1	2008 Self-Employment Tax Worksheet

1. Net earnings from self-employment.   _____
2. Multiply line 1 by 92.35%.   _____
3. If the amount on line 2 is $102,000 or less, multiply the line 2 amount by 15.3%. This is the self-employment tax.   _____
4. If the amount on line 2 is more than $102,000, multiply the excess of line 2 over $102,000 by 2.9% and add $15,606. This is the self-employment tax.   _____

[51]§ 6017.
[52]§ 1402(a)(12).
[53]§ 164(f).

employment tax to be paid. For *income tax purposes*, the amount to be reported is net earnings from self-employment before the deduction for one-half of the self-employment tax. Then the taxpayer is allowed a deduction *for* AGI of one-half of the self-employment tax.

EXAMPLE 45

Using the format in Figure 13–1, the self-employment tax is determined for two taxpayers with net earnings from self-employment for 2008 as follows: Ned, $55,000 and Terry, $120,000.

Ned's Self-Employment Tax Worksheet

1.	Net earnings from self-employment.	$ 55,000.00
2.	Multiply line 1 by 92.35%.	$ 50,792.50
3.	If the amount on line 2 is $102,000 or less, multiply the line 2 amount by 15.3%. This is the self-employment tax.	$ 7,771.25
4.	If the amount on line 2 is more than $102,000, multiply the excess of line 2 over $102,000 by 2.9% and add $15,606. This is the self-employment tax.	

Terry's Self-Employment Tax Worksheet

1.	Net earnings from self-employment.	$120,000.00
2.	Multiply line 1 by 92.35%.	$110,820.00
3.	If the amount on line 2 is $102,000 or less, multiply the line 2 amount by 15.3%. This is the self-employment tax.	
4.	If the amount on line 2 is more than $102,000, multiply the excess of line 2 over $102,000 by 2.9% and add $15,606. This is the self-employment tax.	$ 15,861.78

For income tax purposes, Ned has net earnings from self-employment of $55,000 and a deduction *for* AGI of $3,885.63 (one-half of $7,771.25). Terry has net earnings from self-employment of $120,000 and a deduction *for* AGI of $7,930.89 (one-half of $15,861.78). Both taxpayers benefit from the deduction for one-half of the self-employment tax paid. ∎

For 2007, the self-employment tax computations are similar to those for 2008. The only difference is that the tax base was lower for 2007 than it is for 2008 (see Table 13–9 and Figure 13–2).

If an individual also receives wages subject to FICA tax, the ceiling amount of the Social Security portion on which the self-employment tax is computed is reduced. Thus, the self-employment tax may be reduced if a self-employed individual also receives FICA wages in excess of the ceiling amount.

FIGURE 13–2 | **2007 Self-Employment Tax Worksheet**

1.	Net earnings from self-employment.	_____
2.	Multiply line 1 by 92.35%.	_____
3.	If the amount on line 2 is $97,500 or less, multiply the line 2 amount by 15.3%. This is the self-employment tax.	_____
4.	If the amount on line 2 is more than $97,500, multiply the excess of line 2 over $97,500 by 2.9% and add $14,917.50. This is the self-employment tax.	_____

EXAMPLE 46

In 2008, Kelly had $70,000 of net earnings from the conduct of a bookkeeping service (trade or business activity). She also received wages as an employee amounting to $40,000 during the year. The amount of Kelly's self-employment income subject to the Social Security portion (12.4%) is $62,000 ($102,000 − $40,000), producing a tax of $7,688 ($62,000 × 12.4%). All of Kelly's net self-employment earnings are subject to the Medicare portion of the self-employment tax of 2.9%. Therefore, the self-employment tax on this portion is $1,874.71 ($64,645 × 2.9%).

	Social Security Portion
Ceiling amount	$ 102,000
Less: FICA wages	(40,000)
Net ceiling	$ 62,000
Net self-employment income ($70,000 × 92.35%)	$ 64,645
Lesser of net ceiling or net self-employment income	$ 62,000

Net earnings from self-employment include gross income from a trade or business less allowable trade or business deductions, the distributive share of any partnership income or loss derived from a trade or business activity, and net income from rendering personal services as an independent contractor. Gain or loss from the disposition of property (including involuntary conversions) is excluded from the computation of self-employment income unless the property involved is inventory.

<table>
<tr><td>

LO.7

Identify tax planning opportunities related to tax credits and payment procedures.

</td></tr>
</table>

TAX PLANNING
Considerations

Foreign Tax Credit

A U.S. citizen or resident working abroad (commonly referred to as an *expatriate*) may elect to take either a foreign tax credit or the foreign earned income exclusion. In cases where the income tax of a foreign country is higher than the U.S. income tax, the credit choice usually is preferable. If the reverse is true, electing the foreign earned income exclusion probably reduces the overall tax burden.

Unfortunately, the choice between the credit and the earned income exclusion is not without some limitations. The election of the foreign earned income exclusion, once made, can be revoked for a later year. However, once revoked, the earned income exclusion will not be available for a period of five years unless the IRS consents to an earlier date. This will create a dilemma for expatriates whose job assignments over several years shift between low- and high-bracket countries.

EXAMPLE 47

In 2007, Ira, a calendar year taxpayer, is sent by his employer to Saudi Arabia (a low-tax country). For 2007, therefore, Ira elects the foreign earned income exclusion. In 2008, Ira's employer transfers him to France (a high-tax country). Accordingly, he revokes the foreign earned income exclusion election for 2008 and chooses instead to use the foreign tax credit. If Ira is transferred back to Saudi Arabia (or any other low-tax country) within five years, he may not utilize the foreign earned income exclusion. ■

Credit for Child and Dependent Care Expenses

A taxpayer may incur employment-related expenses that also qualify as medical expenses (e.g., a nurse is hired to provide in-the-home care for an ill and incapacitated dependent parent). Such expenses may be either deducted as medical expenses (subject to the 7.5 percent limitation) or utilized in determining the credit for child and dependent care expenses. If the credit for child and dependent care expenses is chosen and the employment-related expenses exceed the limitation ($3,000, $6,000, or earned income, as the case may be), the excess may be considered a medical expense. If, however, the taxpayer chooses to deduct qualified employment-related expenses as medical expenses, any portion that is not deductible because of the 7.5 percent limitation may not be used in computing the credit for child and dependent care expenses.

EXAMPLE 48

Alicia has the following tax position for 2008:

Adjusted gross income		$30,000
Potential itemized deductions *from* AGI—		
Other than medical expenses	$3,500	
Medical expenses	6,600	$10,100

All of Alicia's medical expenses were incurred to provide nursing care for her disabled father while she was working. The father lives with Alicia and qualifies as her dependent. ∎

What should Alicia do in this situation? One approach would be to use $3,000 of the nursing care expenses to obtain the maximum credit for child and dependent care expenses allowed of $810 (27% × $3,000). The balance of these expenses should be claimed as medical expenses. After a reduction of 7.5 percent of AGI, this would produce a medical expense deduction of $1,350 [$3,600 (remaining medical expenses) − (7.5% × $30,000)].

Another approach would be to claim the full $6,600 as a medical expense and forgo the credit for child and dependent care expenses. After the 7.5 percent adjustment of $2,250 (7.5% × $30,000), a deduction of $4,350 remains.

The choice, then, is between a credit of $810 plus a deduction of $1,350 or a credit of $0 plus a deduction of $4,350. Which is better, of course, depends on the relative tax savings involved, which in turn are dependent on the taxpayer's marginal tax bracket.

One of the traditional goals of *family tax planning* is to minimize the total tax burden within the family unit. With proper planning and implementation, the credit for child and dependent care expenses can be used to help achieve this goal. For example, payments to certain relatives for the care of qualifying dependents and children qualify for the credit if the care provider is *not* a child (under age 19) of the taxpayer. Thus, if the care provider is in a lower tax bracket than the taxpayer, the following benefits result:

• Income is shifted to a lower-bracket family member.
• The taxpayer qualifies for the credit for child and dependent care expenses.

In addition, the goal of minimizing the family income tax liability can be enhanced in some other situations, but only if the credit's limitations are recognized and avoided. For example, tax savings may still be enjoyed even if the qualifying expenditures incurred by a cash basis taxpayer have already reached the annual ceiling ($3,000 or $6,000). To the extent that any additional payments can be shifted into future tax years, the benefit from the credit may be preserved on these excess expenditures.

EXAMPLE 49

Andre, a calendar year and cash basis taxpayer, has spent $3,000 by December 1 on qualifying child care expenditures for his dependent 11-year-old son. The $250 that is due the care provider for child care services rendered in December does not generate a tax credit benefit if the amount is paid in the current year because the $3,000 ceiling has been reached. However, if the payment can be delayed until the next year, the total credit over the two-year period for which Andre is eligible may be increased. ∎

A similar shifting of expenditures to a subsequent year may be wise if the potential credit otherwise generated would exceed the tax liability available to absorb the credit.

Adjustments to Increase Withholding

The penalty for underpayment of estimated tax by individuals is computed for each quarter of the tax year. A taxpayer can play *catch-up* to a certain extent. Each quarterly payment is credited to the unpaid portion of any previous required installment. Thus, the penalty stops on that portion of the underpayment for the previous quarter. However, since income tax withheld is assumed to have been paid evenly throughout the year and is allocated equally among the four installments in computing any penalty, a taxpayer who would otherwise be subject to a penalty for underpayment should increase withholdings late in the year. This can be done by changing the number of allowances claimed on Form W–4 or by special arrangement with the employer to increase the amount withheld.

A similar way to avoid (or reduce) a penalty for underpayment is to have the employer continue Social Security withholding beyond the base amount.

EXAMPLE 50

Rose, a calendar year taxpayer, earns $125,000 from her job. In late October 2008, she realizes that she will be subject to a penalty for underpayment of estimated tax due to income from outside sources. Consequently, she instructs her employer to continue FICA withholdings for the rest of 2008. If this is done, an extra $23,000 [$125,000 (annual salary) − $102,000 (base amount of the Social Security portion for 2008)] will be subject to the 6.2% Social Security portion of the FICA tax [7.65% (total FICA rate) − 1.45% (Medicare portion of the FICA rate)]. Thus, Rose generates an additional $1,426 (6.2% × $23,000) that will be deemed withheld ratably during 2008. ■

Adjustments to Avoid Overwithholding

Publication 505, *Tax Withholding and Estimated Tax*, contains worksheets that taxpayers may use to take advantage of special provisions for avoiding overwithholding. Extra exemptions for withholding purposes are allowed if the taxpayer has unusually large itemized deductions, deductions *for* AGI, or tax credits. Net losses from Schedules C, D, E, and F may be considered in computing the number of extra withholding exemptions. Net operating loss carryovers may also be considered in the computation. A taxpayer who is entitled to extra withholding exemptions for any of these reasons should file a new Form W–4, Employee's Withholding Allowance Certificate, with his or her employer.

KEY TERMS

Adoption expenses credit, 13–20

Child tax credit, 13–21

Credit for certain retirement plan contributions, 13–25

Credit for child and dependent care expenses, 13–21

Credit for employer-provided child care, 13–14

Credit for small employer pension plan startup costs, 13–14

Disabled access credit, 13–13

Earned income credit, 13–15

Employment taxes, 13–26

Estimated tax, 13–38

Foreign tax credit (FTC), 13–18

General business credit, 13–5

HOPE scholarship credit, 13–24

Lifetime learning credit, 13–24

Low-income housing credit, 13–13

Nonrefundable credits, 13–5

Permanent and total disability, 13–17

Refundable credits, 13–4

Rehabilitation expenditures credit, 13–7

Rehabilitation expenditures credit recapture, 13–8

Research activities credit, 13–10

Self-employment tax, 13–40

Tax credit for the elderly or disabled, 13–17

Tax credits, 13–2

Withholding allowances, 13–33

Work opportunity tax credit, 13–9

P R O B L E M   M A T E R I A L S

DISCUSSION QUESTIONS

1. Would an individual taxpayer receive greater benefit from deducting an expenditure or from taking a credit equal to 25% of the expenditure? How would your response change if the item would only be deductible *from* AGI?

2. What is a refundable credit? Give examples. What is a nonrefundable credit? Give examples.

3. Tax credits are offset against the tax liability in a prescribed order. Explain why the order in which credits are utilized is important.

4. In determining the maximum amount of the general business credit allowed to an individual taxpayer during a tax year, a number of concepts are important. These include *net income tax, tentative minimum tax, regular tax liability*, and *net regular tax liability*.
   a. Define each term.
   b. Using these terms, state the general business credit limitation for an individual taxpayer for the current year.

5. Clint, a self-employed engineering consultant, is contemplating purchasing an old building for renovation. After the work is completed, Clint plans to rent out two-thirds of the floor space to businesses and to live and work in the remaining portion. Identify the relevant tax issues for Clint.   *Issue ID*

6. If property on which the tax credit for rehabilitation expenditures was claimed is prematurely disposed of or ceases to be qualified property, how is the tax liability affected in the year of the disposition or disqualification?

7. Discuss the purpose of the work opportunity tax credit. Who receives the tax benefits from the credit? Give examples of the types of individuals who, if hired, give rise to the credit.

8. Explain the alternatives a taxpayer has in claiming the deduction and credit for research and experimentation expenditures.

9. Explain the purpose of the disabled access credit and describe the general characteristics of its computation.

10. Is the earned income credit a form of negative income tax? Why or why not?

11. Briefly discuss the requirements that must be satisfied for a taxpayer to qualify for the earned income credit.

12. Individuals who receive substantial Social Security benefits are usually not eligible for the tax credit for the elderly or disabled because these benefits effectively eliminate the base upon which the credit is computed. Explain.

13. In general, when would an individual taxpayer find it more beneficial to use the foreign earned income exclusion rather than the foreign tax credit in computing his or her income tax liability?

14. Tara was recently called into the partner's office and offered a one-year assignment in her public accounting firm's London office. Realizing that Tara will face incremental expenses while in London, such as for foreign income taxes and rent, the firm will try to make her "whole" from a financial perspective by increasing her salary to help offset the expenses she will incur while living overseas. If Tara takes the assignment, she will likely rent her personal residence and sell several major tangible assets such as her personal automobile. Identify the relevant tax issues.   *Issue ID*

15. What purpose is served by the overall limitation on the foreign tax credit?

16. Discuss, in general, the calculation of the adoption expenses credit.

17. Distinguish between the child tax credit and the credit for child and dependent care expenses.

18. Sam and Rhonda are married and have a dependent child seven years of age. Sam earns $15,000 during the current year. Rhonda, a full-time student for the entire year, is not employed. Sam and Rhonda believe they are not entitled to the child and dependent care credit because Rhonda is not employed. Is this correct? Explain your answer.

Decision Making

19. Polly and her spouse, Leo, file a joint return and expect to report AGI of $70,000 in 2008. Polly's employer offers a child and dependent care reimbursement plan that allows up to $3,500 of qualifying expenses to be reimbursed in exchange for a $3,500 reduction in the employee's salary. Because Polly and Leo have one minor child requiring child care that costs $3,500 each year, she is wondering if she should sign up for the program instead of taking advantage of the credit for child and dependent care expenses. Assuming Polly and Leo are in the 25% tax bracket, analyze the effect of the two alternatives. How would your answer differ if Polly and Leo's AGI was $14,000 instead of $70,000? Assume in this case that their marginal tax rate is 10%.

Issue ID

20. Roger and Debra are approaching an exciting time in their lives as their oldest daughter, Samantha, graduates from high school and moves on to college. What are some of the tax issues Roger and Debra should consider as they think about paying for Samantha's college education?

21. Identify two tax credits enacted by Congress that are designed to encourage the establishment of or contributions to qualified retirement plans.

22. Discuss the rationale underlying the enactment of the following tax credits:
    a. Rehabilitation expenditures credit.
    b. Low-income housing credit.
    c. Research activities credit.
    d. Earned income credit.
    e. Foreign tax credit.

Issue ID

23. Elaborate rules exist that require employers to prepay various types of Federal taxes. Summarize the major issues that an employer must resolve if it is to comply with the requirements.

24. If an employer is not required to withhold income taxes on an item of income paid to an employee, does this mean that the item is nontaxable? Explain.

25. Keith, a sole proprietor, owns and operates a grocery store. Keith's wife and his 17-year-old son work in the business and are paid wages. Will the wife and son be subject to FICA? Explain.

26. Under what circumstances will the special withholding allowance be allowed for purposes of determining income tax withholding?

27. Describe the exposure (i.e., wage base and tax rate) that a self-employed individual has to the self-employment tax for 2008.

PROBLEMS

28. Earl has a tentative general business credit of $28,000 for the current year. His net regular tax liability before the general business credit is $95,000, and his tentative minimum tax is $80,000. Compute Earl's allowable general business credit for the year.

29. Oak Corporation has the following general business credit carryovers:

2004	$ 30,000
2005	70,000
2006	40,000
2007	50,000
Total carryovers	$190,000

If the general business credit generated by activities during 2008 equals $170,000 and the total credit allowed during the current year is $320,000 (based on tax liability), what amounts of the current general business credit and carryovers are utilized against the 2008 income tax liability? What is the amount of unused credit carried forward to 2009?

30. In the current year, Simon Cho (4588 Norris Avenue, St. Charles, IL 60174) acquires a qualifying historic structure for $250,000 (excluding the cost of the land) and plans to substantially rehabilitate the structure. He is planning to spend either $245,000 or $255,000 on rehabilitation expenditures. Write a letter to Simon and a memo for the tax files explaining, for the two alternative expenditures, (1) the computation that determines the rehabilitation expenditures tax credit available to Simon, (2) the impact of the credit on Simon's adjusted basis in the property, and (3) the cash-flow differences as a result of the tax consequences related to his expenditure choice.

Decision Making

Communications

31. Red Company hires six individuals on January 15, 2008, qualifying Red for the work opportunity tax credit (e.g., food stamp recipients). Three of these individuals receive wages of $7,000 each during 2008, with each working more than 400 hours during the year. The other three receive wages of $4,000 each in 2008, with each working 300 hours during the year.
    a. Calculate the amount of Red's work opportunity tax credit for 2008.
    b. Assume Red pays total wages of $120,000 to its employees during the year. How much of this amount is deductible in 2008 if the work opportunity tax credit is taken?

32. In March 2008, Wren Corporation hired three individuals, Trent, Bernice, and Benita, all of whom are certified as long-term family assistance recipients. Each employee is paid $11,000 during 2008. Only Bernice continued to work for Wren in 2009, earning $13,500.
    a. Compute Wren Corporation's work opportunity tax credit for 2008 and 2009.
    b. Assume Wren Corporation pays total wages of $325,000 to its employees during 2008 and $342,000 during 2009. How much may Wren claim as a wage deduction for 2008 and 2009 if the work opportunity tax credit is claimed in both years?

33. Michael, a calendar year taxpayer, informs you that during June 2008, he incurs expenditures of $50,000 that qualify for the incremental research activities credit. In addition, it is determined that his base amount for the year is $35,000.
    a. Determine Michael's incremental research activities credit for the year.
    b. Michael is in the 25% tax bracket. Determine which approach to the research expenditures and the research activities credit (other than capitalization and subsequent amortization) would provide the greater tax benefit to Michael.

Decision Making

34. Ahmed Zinna (16 Southside Drive, Charlotte, NC 28204), one of your clients, owns two restaurants in downtown Charlotte and has come to you seeking advice concerning the tax consequences of complying with the Americans with Disabilities Act. He understands that he needs to install various features at his businesses (e.g., ramps, doorways, and restrooms that are handicapped accessible) to make them more accessible to disabled individuals. He asks whether any tax credits will be available to help offset the cost of the necessary changes. He estimates the cost of the planned changes to his facilities as follows:

Communications

Location	Projected Cost
Calvin Street	$22,000
Stowe Avenue	8,500

He reminds you that the Calvin Street restaurant was constructed in 2001 while the Stowe Avenue restaurant is in a building that was constructed in 1986. Ahmed operates his business as a sole proprietorship and has approximately eight employees at each location. Write a letter to Ahmed in which you summarize your conclusions concerning the tax consequences of his proposed capital improvements.

35. Which of the following individuals qualify for the earned income credit for 2008?
    a. Kristy is single, 23 years of age, and has no children. She earns $8,000.

    b.   Kareem is single, 32 years of age, and has no children. He earns $6,000.

    c.   Carlos maintains a household for a dependent 13-year-old daughter and qualifies for the head-of-household filing status. Carlos's income consists of a $35,000 salary.

    d.   Floyd and Grace are married, file a joint return, and have two children. Their combined income consists of salary of $14,000 and interest income of $50.

36. Alex, a widower, lives in an apartment with his three minor children (ages 2, 4, and 5) whom he supports. Alex earns $19,500 during 2008. He contributes $500 to a traditional IRA and uses the standard deduction. Calculate the amount, if any, of Alex's earned income credit.

Decision Making

37. Joyce, a widow, lives in an apartment with her two minor children (ages 8 and 10) whom she supports. Joyce earns $32,000 during 2008. She uses the standard deduction.

    a.   Calculate the amount, if any, of Joyce's earned income credit.

    b.   During the year, Joyce is offered a new job that has greater future potential than her current job. If she accepts the job offer, her earnings for the year would be $38,000; however, she will not qualify for the earned income credit. Using after-tax cash-flow calculations, determine whether Joyce should accept the new job offer.

38. Robert, age 68, and Tanya, age 66, are married retirees who receive the following income and retirement benefits during the current year:

Fully taxable pension from Robert's former employer	$ 8,000
Dividends and interest	2,500
Social Security benefits	4,000
Total	$14,500

Assume Robert and Tanya file a joint tax return, have no deductions *for* AGI, and use the standard deduction. Are they eligible for the tax credit for the elderly? If so, calculate the amount of the credit, assuming the credit is not limited by their tax liability.

Decision Making

39. Kim, a U.S. citizen and resident, owns and operates a novelty goods business. During 2008, Kim has taxable income of $100,000, made up as follows: $50,000 from foreign sources and $50,000 from U.S. sources. In calculating taxable income, the standard deduction is used. The income from foreign sources is subject to foreign income taxes of $26,000. For 2008, Kim files a joint return claiming his three children as dependents.

    a.   Assuming Kim chooses to claim the foreign taxes as an income tax credit, what is his income tax liability for 2008?

    b.   Recently, Kim has become disenchanted with the location of his business and is considering moving his foreign operation to a different country. Based on his research, if he moves his business to his country of choice, all relevant revenues and costs would remain approximately the same except that the income taxes payable to that country would be only $8,000. Given that all of the foreign income taxes paid are available to offset the U.S. tax liability (whether he operates in a high-tax or a low-tax foreign jurisdiction), what impact will this have on his decision regarding the potential move?

40. Blue Horizons, Inc., a U.S. corporation, is a manufacturing concern that sells most of its products in the United States. It also does some business in the European Union through various branches. During the current year, Blue Horizons has taxable income of $500,000, of which $350,000 is U.S.-sourced and $150,000 is foreign-sourced. Foreign income taxes paid amounted to $45,000. Blue Horizons' U.S. income tax liability is $170,000. What is its U.S. income tax liability net of the allowable foreign tax credit?

41. Ann and Bill were on the list of a local adoption agency for several years seeking to adopt a child. Finally, in 2007, good news comes their way and an adoption seems imminent. They pay qualified adoption expenses of $4,000 in 2007 and $11,000 in 2008. Assume the adoption becomes final in 2008. Ann and Bill always file a joint income tax return.

    a.   Determine the amount of the adoption expenses credit available to Ann and Bill assuming their combined annual income is $100,000. What year(s) will they benefit from the credit?

    b.   Assuming Ann and Bill's modified AGI in 2007 and 2008 is $200,000, calculate the amount of the adoption expenses credit.

42. Durell and Earline are married, file a joint return, and claim dependency exemptions for their two children, ages 5 years and 6 months. They also claim Earline's son from a previous marriage, age 18, as a dependent. Durell and Earline's combined AGI is $68,000.
    a. Compute Durell and Earline's child tax credit.
    b. Assume the same facts, except that Durell and Earline's combined AGI is $122,000. Compute their child tax credit.

43. John and Jerri are husband and wife, and both are gainfully employed. They have three children under the age of 13. During the year, John earns $70,000, while Jerri earns $8,200. In order for them to work, they pay $7,000 to various unrelated parties to care for their children. Assuming John and Jerri file a joint return, what, if any, is their tax credit for child and dependent care expenses for the year?

44. Ralph and Jill are husband and wife and have two dependent children under the age of 13. They both are gainfully employed and during the current year earn salaries as follows: $24,000 (Ralph) and $4,500 (Jill). To care for their children while they work, they pay Megan (Ralph's mother) $5,000. Assuming Ralph and Jill file a joint return, what, if any, is their credit for child and dependent care expenses?

45. Bernadette, a longtime client of yours, is an architect and president of the local Rotary chapter. To keep up-to-date with the latest developments in her profession, she attends continuing education seminars offered by the architecture school at State University. During 2008, Bernadette spends $2,000 on course tuition to attend such seminars. She also spends another $400 on architecture books during the year. Bernadette's son is a senior majoring in engineering at the University of the Midwest. During the 2008 calendar year, Bernadette's son incurs the following expenses: $8,200 for tuition ($4,100 per semester) and $750 for books and supplies. Bernadette's son, whom she claims as a dependent, lives at home while attending school full-time. Bernadette is married, files a joint return, and has a combined AGI with her husband of $99,000.
    Communications
    a. Calculate Bernadette's education tax credit for 2008.
    b. In her capacity as president of the local Rotary chapter, Bernadette has asked you to make a 30–45 minute speech outlining the different ways the tax law helps defray (1) the cost of higher education and (2) the cost of continuing education once someone is in the workforce. Prepare an outline of possible topics for presentation. A tentative title for your presentation is "How Can the Tax Law Help Pay for College and Continuing Professional Education?"

46. Kathleen and Glenn decide that this is the year to begin getting serious about saving for their retirement by participating in their employers' § 401(k) plans. As a result, they each have $3,000 of their salary set aside in their qualified plans.
    a. Calculate the credit for certain retirement plan contributions available to Kathleen and Glenn if the AGI on their joint return is $33,000.
    b. Kathleen and Glenn persuade their dependent 15-year-old son, Joel, to put $500 of his part-time earnings into a Roth IRA during the year. What is the credit for certain retirement plan contributions available to Joel? His AGI is $7,000.

47. In each of the following independent situations, determine the amount of FICA that should be withheld from the employee's 2008 salary by the employer.
    a. Harry earns a $50,000 salary, files a joint return, and claims four withholding allowances.
    b. Hazel earns a $105,000 salary, files a joint return, and claims four withholding allowances.
    c. Tracy earns a $180,000 salary, files a joint return, and claims four withholding allowances.
    d. Alicia's 17-year-old son, Carlos, earns $10,000 at the family business.

48. During 2008, Greg Cruz (1401 Orangedale Road, Troy, MI 48084) works for Maple Corporation and Gray Company. He earns $60,000 at Maple Corporation where he is a full-time employee. Greg also works part-time for Gray Company for wages of $45,000.
    Communications
    a. Did Greg experience an overwithholding of FICA taxes? Write a letter to Greg and a memo for the tax files in which you explain your conclusion.
    b. Did Maple Corporation and Gray Company overpay the employer's portion of FICA? Explain.

49. In each of the following independent situations, determine the maximum withholding allowances permitted Eli (an employee) on Form W–4.
    a. Eli is single with no dependents.
    b. Eli is married to a nonemployed spouse, and they have no dependents.
    c. Eli is married to Vera, an employed spouse who earns $25,000, and they have three dependent children. Eli and Vera do not qualify for the child tax credit. On the Form W–4 that she filed with the employer, Vera claimed zero allowances.
    d. Assume the same facts as in (c), except that Eli and Vera fully support Eli's mother, who lives with them. The mother (age 70 and blind) qualifies as their dependent. (Refer to Chapter 3.)
    e. Eli is single with no dependents but works for two employers, one on a full-time basis and the other on a part-time basis. The Form W–4 filed with the first employer (the full-time job) reflects two withholding exemptions. The wages from each job exceed $1,000.
    f. Assume the same facts as in (e), except that Eli is married to a nonemployed spouse.

Decision Making

50. Jane, who is expecting to finish college in May 2008, is fortunate to have already arranged full-time employment for after graduation. She will begin work on July 1, 2008, as a staff accountant at a nearby professional services firm with a starting salary of $45,000 per year. Jane is married to Craig, who plans to be a full-time student throughout the year. They anticipate generating no income for the year other than the salary from her new position.
    a. How many withholding allowances would you expect Jane to claim on her Form W–4?
    b. Assuming Jane receives her salary on a monthly basis, what amount will be withheld if her employer uses the wage-bracket tables to calculate withholdings?
    c. Assuming Jane receives her salary on a monthly basis, what amount will be withheld if her employer uses the percentage method to calculate withholdings?
    d. Assuming Jane and Craig use the standard deduction, calculate the Federal income tax liability on their projected taxable income for 2008. What changes would you recommend Jane make to her W–4 to correct any over- or under-withholding for the current year?
    e. What further changes should she make to her W–4 at the beginning of 2009?

51. Norm is married to a nonemployed spouse and has four dependents. He is employed by Beige Corporation and is paid a monthly salary of $4,245 ($50,940 per year). Using these facts, determine the amount to be withheld by Beige Corporation for Federal income tax purposes under the wage-bracket tables and under the percentage method for 2008.

52. Julie, being self-employed, is required to make estimated payments of her tax liability for the year. Her tax liability for 2007 was $25,000, and her AGI was less than $150,000. For 2008, Julie ultimately determines that her income tax liability is $18,000. During the year, however, she made the following payments, totaling $13,000:

April 15, 2008	$ 4,500
June 16, 2008	2,800
September 15, 2008	4,100
January 15, 2009	1,600
	$13,000

Because she prepaid so little of her ultimate income tax liability, she now realizes that she may be subject to the penalty for underpayment of estimated tax.
    a. Determine Julie's exposure to the penalty for underpayment of estimated tax.
    b. The same as (a) except that Julie's tax liability for 2007 was $15,960.

53. In 2008, Maria has self-employed earnings of $125,000. Using the format illustrated in the text, compute Maria's self-employment tax liability and the allowable income tax deduction for the self-employment tax paid.

CUMULATIVE PROBLEMS

54. Janice A. French lives at 48122 Tangerine Road, Tucson, AZ 85704. She is a tax accountant with Tucson Industries, 844 Eastern Avenue, Tucson, AZ 85702 (employer identification number 38–7788214). She also writes computer software programs for tax practitioners and has a part-time tax practice. Janice is single and has no dependents. Janice's birthday is August 14, 1972, and her Social Security number is 148–57–1111. She wants to contribute $3 to the Presidential Election Campaign Fund.

Tax Return Problem

The following information is shown on Janice's Wage and Tax Statement (Form W–2) for 2007.

Line	Description	Amount
1	Wages, tips, other compensation	$63,000.00
2	Federal income tax withheld	11,000.00
3	Social Security wages	63,000.00
4	Social Security tax withheld	3,906.00
5	Medicare wages and tips	63,000.00
6	Medicare tax withheld	913.50
15	State	Arizona
16	State wages, tips, etc.	63,000.00
17	State income tax withheld	1,650.00

During 2007, Janice received interest of $1,500 from Arizona Federal Savings and Loan and $300 from Arizona State Bank. Each financial institution reported the interest income on a Form 1099–INT. She received qualified dividends of $500 from Blue Corporation, $400 from Green Corporation, and $2,000 from Orange Corporation. Each corporation reported Janice's dividend payments on a Form 1099–DIV.

Janice received a $1,600 income tax refund from the state of Arizona on April 29, 2007. On her 2006 Federal income tax return, she reported total itemized deductions of $7,900, which included $2,100 of state income tax withheld by her employer.

Fees earned from her part-time tax practice in 2007 totaled $4,200. She paid $700 to have the tax returns processed by a computerized tax return service.

On February 8, 2007, Janice bought 500 shares of Gray Corporation common stock for $17.60 a share. On September 12, Janice sold the stock for $14 a share.

Janice bought a used sports utility vehicle for $3,000 on June 5, 2007. She purchased the vehicle from her brother-in-law, who was unemployed and was in need of cash. On November 2, 2007, she sold the vehicle to a friend for $3,500.

On January 2, 2007, Janice acquired 100 shares of Blue Corporation common stock for $30 a share. She sold the stock on December 19, 2007, for $55 a share.

During 2007, Janice received royalties of $16,000 on a software program she had written. Janice incurred the following expenditures in connection with her software-writing activities:

Cost of personal computer (100% business use)	$6,000
Cost of printer (100% business use)	3,000
Furniture	2,500
Supplies	800
Fee paid to computer consultant	3,200

Janice elected to expense the maximum portion of the cost of the computer, printer, and furniture allowed under the provisions of § 179. This equipment and furniture were placed in service on January 15, 2007.

Although her employer suggested that Janice attend a convention on current developments in corporate taxation, Janice was not reimbursed for the travel expenses of $1,420 she incurred in attending the convention. The $1,420 included $200 for the cost of meals.

During 2007, Janice paid $500 for prescription medicines and $1,250 in doctor bills, hospital bills, and medical insurance premiums. Janice paid real property taxes of $2,482 on her home. Interest on her home mortgage was $4,220, and interest to credit card companies was $320. Janice contributed $20 each week to her church and $5 each week to the United Way. Professional dues and subscriptions totaled $300. Janice maintained her sales tax receipts. The total is $1,954.

Janice paid estimated taxes of $1,000.

Part 1—Tax Computation

Compute the net tax payable or refund due for Janice A. French for 2007. If you use tax forms for your solution, you will need Forms 1040, 2106–EZ, and 4562 and Schedules A, B, C, D, and SE. Suggested software: TaxCut.

Part 2—Tax Planning

Janice is anticipating significant changes in her life in 2008, and she has asked you to estimate her taxable income and tax liability for 2008. She just received word that she has been qualified to adopt a two-year-old daughter. Janice expects the adoption will be finalized in 2008 and that she will incur approximately $2,000 of adoption expenses. In addition, she expects to incur approximately $3,500 of child and dependent care expenses relating to the care of her new daughter, which will enable her to keep her job at Tucson Industries. However, with the additional demands on her time because of her daughter, she has decided to discontinue her two part-time jobs (i.e., the part-time tax practice and her software business) and she will cease making estimated income tax payments. In your computations, assume all other income and expenditures will remain at approximately the same levels as in 2007.

Tax Computation Problem

55. Tim and Sarah Lawrence are married and file a joint return. Tim's Social Security number is 222–33–1111, and Sarah's Social Security number is 111–22–5555. They reside at 100 Olive Lane, Covington, LA 70400. They have two dependent children, Sean and Debra, ages 12 and 16, respectively. Tim is a self-employed businessman (sole proprietor of an unincorporated business), and Sarah is a corporate executive. Tim has the following income and expenses from his business:

Gross income	$280,000
Business expenses	166,000

Records related to Sarah's employment provide the following information:

Salary	$130,000
Unreimbursed travel expenses (including $200 of meals)	1,100
Unreimbursed entertainment expenses	500

Other pertinent information relating to 2008 follows:

Proceeds from sale of stock acquired on July 15, 2008 (cost of $10,000), and sold on August 1, 2008	$ 8,500
Proceeds from sale of stock acquired on September 18, 2007 (cost of $6,000), and sold on October 5, 2008	3,800
Wages paid to full-time domestic worker for housekeeping and child supervision	9,000
Interest income received	8,000
Total itemized deductions (not including any potential deductions above)	26,900
Federal income tax withheld	29,000
Estimated payments of Federal income tax	32,000

Compute the net tax payable or refund due for Tim and Sarah Lawrence for 2008.

RESEARCH PROBLEMS

Note: Solutions to Research Problems can be prepared by using the **RIA Checkpoint®
Student Edition** online research product, which is available to accompany this text. It is
also possible to prepare solutions to the Research Problems by using tax research materials found in a standard tax library.

Research Problem 1.   Ashby and Curtis, a young professional couple, have a two-year-old son,
Jason. Curtis works full-time as an electrical engineer, but Ashby has not worked outside the
home since Jason was born. As Jason is getting older, Ashby feels that he would benefit from
attending nursery school several times a week, which would give her an opportunity to
reinvigorate her love of painting at a nearby art studio. Ashby thinks that if she is lucky, the
proceeds from the sale of her paintings will pay for the nursery school tuition. But, in
addition, she is planning to claim the credit for child and dependent care expenses because
the care provided Jason at the nursery school is required for her to pursue her art. Can
Ashby and Curtis claim the credit for child and dependent care expenses for the nursery
school expenditure?

Research Problem 2.   Sandy and John Via (12 Maple Avenue, Albany, NY 12205) are
married, file a joint Federal income tax return, and have a 12-year-old son and a 10-year-
old daughter. Sandy is currently in the U.S. Air Force and has been stationed in Germany
for the entire year. John and their children have remained in the United States where
John picks up work only on an irregular basis. In working on their Federal income tax
return for 2008, John wonders if they qualify for the earned income credit. Sandy's
income consists of salary of $25,000 (taxable) and food and lodging provided by the Air
Force, valued at $10,000 (not taxable), while John's earnings for the current year total
$8,000. John approaches you and asks your advice. Write a letter to Sandy and John that
contains your conclusion and prepare a memo for the tax files.

Communications

Research Problem 3.   You recently read an article in your school newspaper about Professor
Rodney Taylor, one of your favorite professors in the religious studies department. According
to the article, he and the university have been negotiating an early retirement package and
have reached a stumbling block. Under the agreement, Professor Taylor is to receive a lump-
sum payment equal to one year's salary in exchange for his retirement and the release of any
and all rights associated with his tenure status. While recognizing that the payment would be
subject to income tax, Taylor contends that the amount is not earned income and thus
should not be subject to the FICA tax. The university negotiators say that they are not aware
of any authority that supports Taylor's view. In fact, they have learned that other universities
in the state system have been withholding amounts for FICA for years in situations involving
early retirement buyout packages for high-level administrators. The university's position is
that lacking the authority to not withhold for FICA and given the precedent set in similar
early retirement packages at other universities, they are obligated to withhold FICA from the
payment. You want to come to the aid of Professor Taylor. Obviously, if the payments are
considered wages subject to the FICA tax, the value of the offer to Professor Taylor will be
significantly reduced. Can you find any authority for his position?

Research Problem 4.   George and Louise's dependent daughter, Jamie, is a full-time
university student who recently completed her first semester. The tuition expense for
Jamie's first semester was $11,000. George and Louise have read about various education
credits that are generally available to offset the cost of higher education, but they have
concluded that they do not qualify because their AGI is too high.

Decision Making

  Nonetheless, George asks you about a tax strategy that he recently overheard being
discussed. According to his recollection of the discussion, if he and Louise would forgo
claiming Jamie as a dependent on their joint income tax return, Jamie could claim the
HOPE scholarship credit on her income tax return. What do you tell George about this
strategy? Under what conditions should George and Louise take advantage of this
approach if it is available?

Partial list of research aids:
Reg. § 1.25A–1(f).

Internet
Activity

Use the tax resources of the Internet to address the following questions. Do not restrict your search to the World Wide Web, but include a review of newsgroups and general reference materials, practitioner sites and resources, primary sources of the tax law, chat rooms and discussion groups, and other opportunities.

Research Problem 5.   The IRS has unveiled a Web-based tool to help taxpayers determine whether they or their clients are eligible for the earned income credit. Locate this tool at the IRS Web site and then apply the facts related to a hypothetical taxpayer and determine if the earned income credit is available.

Research Problem 6.   Congress is considering ways to improve and simplify education tax incentives, which have become an important complement to direct assistance programs. Pell Grants (means-tested grants for higher education) and subsidized student loans have provided aid directly to needy students since 1972. More recently, the Internal Revenue Code has offered educational subsidies through the lifetime learning credit, the HOPE credit, and deductions for education expenses and interest on student loans. It also encourages taxpayers to save for college through several tax-free savings opportunities including Coverdell Eduction Savings Accounts and § 529 savings plans. Critics feel that the existing incentives are complicated and may not reach those most in need. Find several news stories, policy center studies, or government reports that discuss education tax incentives.

Research Problem 7.   Download a copy of Form W–4 and complete the accompanying worksheet. File the worksheet with your employer if you discover that you currently are being under- or overwithheld.

PART 5

Property Transactions

Part V presents the tax treatment of sales, exchanges, and other dispositions of property. Included are the determination of the realized gain or loss, recognized gain or loss, and the classification of the recognized gain or loss as capital or ordinary. The topic of basis is evaluated both in terms of its effect on the calculation of the gain or loss and in terms of the determination of the basis of any contemporaneous or related subsequent acquisitions of property.

CHAPTER 14
Property Transactions: Determination of Gain or Loss and Basis Considerations

CHAPTER 15
Property Transactions: Nontaxable Exchanges

CHAPTER 16
Property Transactions: Capital Gains and Losses

CHAPTER 17
Property Transactions: § 1231 and Recapture Provisions

CHAPTER 14

Property Transactions: Determination of Gain or Loss and Basis Considerations

LEARNING OBJECTIVES

After completing Chapter 14, you should be able to:

LO.1

Understand the computation of realized gain or loss on property dispositions.

LO.2

Distinguish between realized and recognized gain or loss.

LO.3

Apply the recovery of capital doctrine.

LO.4

Explain how basis is determined for various methods of asset acquisition.

LO.5

Describe various loss disallowance provisions.

LO.6

Identify tax planning opportunities related to selected property transactions.

OUTLINE

Determination of Gain or Loss, 14–3
  Realized Gain or Loss, 14–3
  Recognized Gain or Loss, 14–6
  Nonrecognition of Gain or Loss, 14–6
  Recovery of Capital Doctrine, 14–7
Basis Considerations, 14–8
  Determination of Cost Basis, 14–8
  Gift Basis, 14–11
  Property Acquired from a Decedent, 14–14
  Disallowed Losses, 14–16
  Conversion of Property from Personal Use to Business or
    Income-Producing Use, 14–19

Additional Complexities in Determining
    Realized Gain or Loss, 14–20
  Summary of Basis Adjustments, 14–22
Tax Planning Considerations, 14–22
  Tax Consequences of Alice's Proposed Transaction, 14–22
  Cost Identification and Documentation
    Considerations, 14–24
  Selection of Property for Making Gifts, 14–24
  Selection of Property for Making Bequests, 14–25
  Disallowed Losses, 14–25

This chapter and the following three chapters are concerned with the income tax consequences of property transactions (the sale or other disposition of property). The following questions are considered with respect to the sale or other disposition of property:

- Is there a realized gain or loss?
- If so, is the gain or loss recognized?
- If the gain or loss is recognized, is it ordinary or capital?
- What is the basis of any replacement property that is acquired?

EXAMPLE 1

Alice owns a house that she received from her mother seven months ago. Her mother's cost for the house was $75,000. Alice is considering selling the house to her favorite nephew, Dan, for $75,000. Alice anticipates she will have no gain or loss on the transaction. She comes to you for advice.

As Alice's tax adviser, you need answers to the following questions:

- You are aware that Alice's mother died around the time Alice indicates she received the house from her mother. Did Alice receive the house by gift prior to her mother's death? If so, what was the mother's adjusted basis? Did Alice instead inherit the house from her mother? If so, what was the fair market value of the house on the date of her mother's death?
- Has the house been Alice's principal residence during the period she has owned it? Was it her principal residence before she received it from her mother?
- How long did Alice's mother own the house?
- What is the fair market value of the house?
- Does Alice intend for the transaction with Dan to be a sale or part sale and part gift?
- What does Alice intend to do with the sale proceeds?

Once you have the answers to these questions, you can advise Alice on the tax consequences of the proposed transaction. ■

Chapters 14 and 15 discuss the determination of realized and recognized gain or loss and the basis of property. Chapters 16 and 17 cover the classification of the recognized gain or loss as ordinary or capital.

Determination of Gain or Loss

LO.1

Understand the computation of realized gain or loss on property dispositions.

Realized Gain or Loss

Realized gain or loss is the difference between the amount realized from the sale or other disposition of property and the property's adjusted basis on the date of disposition. If the amount realized exceeds the property's adjusted basis, the result is a **realized gain**. Conversely, if the property's adjusted basis exceeds the amount realized, the result is a **realized loss**.[1]

Tab sells Swan Corporation stock with an adjusted basis of $3,000 for $5,000. Tab's realized gain is $2,000. If Tab had sold the stock for $2,000, he would have had a realized loss of $1,000. ■

EXAMPLE 2

Sale or Other Disposition. The term *sale or other disposition* is defined broadly in the tax law and includes virtually any disposition of property. Thus, transactions such as trade-ins, casualties, condemnations, thefts, and bond retirements are treated as dispositions of property. The most common disposition of property is through a sale or exchange. Usually, the key factor in determining whether a disposition has taken place is whether an identifiable event has occurred[2] as opposed to a mere fluctuation in the value of the property.[3]

Lori owns Tan Corporation stock that cost $3,000. The stock has appreciated in value by $2,000 since Lori purchased it. Lori has no realized gain since mere fluctuation in value is not a disposition or identifiable event for tax purposes. Nor would Lori have a realized loss had the stock declined in value by $2,000. ■

EXAMPLE 3

Amount Realized. The **amount realized** from a sale or other disposition of property is the sum of any money received plus the fair market value of other property received. The amount realized also includes any real property taxes treated as imposed on the seller that are actually paid by the buyer.[4] The reason for including these taxes in the amount realized is that by paying the taxes, the purchaser is, in effect, paying an additional amount to the seller of the property.

The amount realized also includes any liability on the property disposed of, such as a mortgage debt, if the buyer assumes the mortgage or the property is sold subject to the mortgage.[5] The amount of the liability is included in the amount realized even if the debt is nonrecourse and the amount of the debt is greater than the fair market value of the mortgaged property.[6]

Barry sells property on which there is a mortgage of $20,000 to Cole for $50,000 cash. Barry's amount realized from the sale is $70,000 if Cole assumes the mortgage or takes the property subject to the mortgage. ■

EXAMPLE 4

The **fair market value** of property received in a sale or other disposition has been defined by the courts as the price at which property will change hands between a willing seller and a willing buyer when neither is compelled to sell or buy.[7] Fair market value is determined by considering the relevant factors in each case.[8] An expert appraiser is often required to evaluate these factors in arriving at

---

[1]§ 1001(a) and Reg. § 1.1001–1(a).
[2]Reg. § 1.1001–1(c)(1).
[3]*Lynch v. Turrish*, 1 USTC ¶18, 3 AFTR 2986, 38 S.Ct. 537 (USSC, 1918).
[4]§ 1001(b) and Reg. § 1.1001–1(b). Refer to Chapter 10 for a discussion of this subject.
[5]*Crane v. Comm.*, 47–1 USTC ¶9217, 35 AFTR 776, 67 S.Ct. 1047 (USSC, 1947). Although a legal distinction exists between the direct assumption of a

mortgage and taking property subject to a mortgage, the tax consequences in calculating the amount realized are the same.
[6]*Comm. v. Tufts*, 83–1 USTC ¶9328, 51 AFTR2d 83–1132, 103 S.Ct. 1826 (USSC, 1983).
[7]*Comm. v. Marshman*, 60–2 USTC ¶9484, 5 AFTR2d 1528, 279 F.2d 27 (CA–6, 1960).
[8]*O'Malley v. Ames*, 52–1 USTC ¶9361, 42 AFTR 19, 197 F.2d 256 (CA–8, 1952).

ETHICAL and EQUITABLE *Considerations*   WHOSE PROPERTY TAX BILL?

Martha sells her house to Sachin on November 1, 2008, for $480,000. On December 5, the property tax due date, Sachin pays property taxes of $800. Even though the property tax bill from the county is for $4,800, Sachin concludes that he owes only for the months of November and December and that the other $4,000 is Martha's liability. On Schedule A of Form 1040 for 2008, Sachin deducts the $800 of property tax he paid.

When Sachin tries to sell his house 18 months later, he discovers that the county has placed a lien on the property. In order to get a clear title, he pays the $4,000 of property taxes due. He subsequently sells his house for a recognized gain of $38,000.

Sachin deducts the $4,000 of property taxes that relate to the period Martha owned the house on his 2010 tax return.

Has Sachin acted properly?

---

fair market value. When the fair market value of the property received cannot be determined, the value of the property given up by the taxpayer may be used.[9]

In calculating the amount realized, selling expenses such as advertising, commissions, and legal fees relating to the disposition are deducted. The amount realized is the net amount that the taxpayer received directly or indirectly, in the form of cash or anything else of value, from the disposition of the property.

Adjusted Basis. The **adjusted basis** of property disposed of is the property's original basis adjusted to the date of disposition.[10] Original basis is the cost or other basis of the property on the date the property is acquired by the taxpayer. Considerations involving original basis are discussed later in this chapter. *Capital additions* increase and *recoveries of capital* decrease the original basis so that on the date of disposition the adjusted basis reflects the unrecovered cost or other basis of the property.[11] Adjusted basis is determined as follows:

Cost (or other adjusted basis) on date of acquisition

+ Capital additions

− Capital recoveries

= Adjusted basis on date of disposition

Capital Additions. Capital additions include the cost of capital improvements and betterments made to the property by the taxpayer. These expenditures are distinguishable from expenditures for the ordinary repair and maintenance of the property, which are neither capitalized nor added to the original basis (refer to Chapter 6). The latter expenditures are deductible in the current taxable year if they are related to business or income-producing property. Amounts representing real property taxes treated as imposed on the seller but paid or assumed by the buyer are part of the cost of the property.[12] Any liability on property that is assumed by the buyer is also included in the buyer's original basis of the property. The same rule applies if property is acquired subject to a liability. Amortization of the discount on bonds increases the adjusted basis of the bonds.[13]

Capital Recoveries. Capital recoveries decrease the adjusted basis of property. The following are examples of capital recoveries:

1. *Depreciation and cost recovery allowances.* The original basis of depreciable property is reduced by the annual depreciation charges (or cost recovery allowances)

---

[9]*U.S. v. Davis*, 62–2 USTC ¶9509, 9 AFTR2d 1625, 82 S.Ct. 1190 (USSC, 1962).

[10]§ 1011(a) and Reg. § 1.1011–1.

[11]§ 1016(a) and Reg. § 1.1016–1.

[12]Reg. §§ 1.1001–1(b)(2) and 1.1012–1(b). Refer to Chapter 10 for a discussion of this subject.

[13]See Chapter 16 for a discussion of bond discount and the related amortization.

while the property is held by the taxpayer. The amount of depreciation that is subtracted from the original basis is the greater of the *allowed* or *allowable* depreciation calculated on an annual basis.[14] In most circumstances, the allowed and allowable depreciation amounts are the same (refer to Chapter 8).

2. *Casualties and thefts.* A casualty or theft may result in the reduction of the adjusted basis of property.[15] The adjusted basis is reduced by the amount of the deductible loss. In addition, the adjusted basis is reduced by the amount of insurance proceeds received. However, the receipt of insurance proceeds may result in a recognized gain rather than a deductible loss. The gain increases the adjusted basis of the property.[16]

EXAMPLE 5

An insured truck used in a trade or business is destroyed in an accident. The adjusted basis is $8,000, and the fair market value is $6,500. Insurance proceeds of $6,500 are received. The amount of the casualty loss is $1,500 ($6,500 insurance proceeds − $8,000 adjusted basis). The adjusted basis is reduced by the $1,500 casualty loss and the $6,500 of insurance proceeds received. ∎

EXAMPLE 6

An insured truck used in a trade or business is destroyed in an accident. The adjusted basis is $6,500, and the fair market value is $8,000. Insurance proceeds of $8,000 are received. The amount of the casualty gain is $1,500 ($8,000 insurance proceeds − $6,500 adjusted basis). The adjusted basis is increased by the $1,500 casualty gain and is reduced by the $8,000 of insurance proceeds received ($6,500 basis before casualty + $1,500 casualty gain − $8,000 insurance proceeds = $0 basis). ∎

---

3. *Certain corporate distributions.* A corporate distribution to a shareholder that is not taxable is treated as a return of capital, and it reduces the basis of the shareholder's stock in the corporation.[17] For example, if a corporation makes a cash distribution to its shareholders and has no earnings and profits, the distributions are treated as a return of capital. Once the basis of the stock is reduced to zero, the amount of any subsequent distributions is a capital gain if the stock is a capital asset. These rules are illustrated in Example 23 of Chapter 20.

4. *Amortizable bond premium.* The basis in a bond purchased at a premium is reduced by the amortizable portion of the bond premium.[18] Investors in taxable bonds may *elect* to amortize the bond premium, but the premium on tax-exempt bonds *must be* amortized.[19] The amount of the amortized premium on taxable bonds is permitted as an interest deduction. Therefore, the election enables the taxpayer to take an annual interest deduction to offset ordinary income in exchange for a larger capital gain or smaller capital loss on the disposition of the bond. No such interest deduction is permitted for tax-exempt bonds.

   The amortization deduction is allowed for taxable bonds because the premium is viewed as a cost of earning the taxable interest from the bonds. The reason the basis of taxable bonds is reduced is that the amortization deduction is a recovery of the cost or basis of the bonds. The basis of tax-exempt bonds is reduced even though the amortization is not allowed as a deduction. No amortization deduction is permitted on tax-exempt bonds because the interest income is exempt from tax and the amortization of the bond premium merely represents an adjustment of the effective amount of such income.

EXAMPLE 7

Antonio purchases Eagle Corporation taxable bonds with a face value of $100,000 for $110,000, thus paying a premium of $10,000. The annual interest rate is 7%, and the bonds

---

[14]§ 1016(a)(2) and Reg. § 1.1016–3(a)(1)(i).
[15]Refer to Chapter 7 for the discussion of casualties and thefts.
[16]Reg. § 1.1016–6(a).
[17]§ 1016(a)(4) and Reg. § 1.1016–5(a).

[18]§ 1016(a)(5) and Reg. § 1.1016–5(b). The accounting treatment of bond premium amortization is the same as for tax purposes. The amortization results in a decrease in the bond investment account.
[19]§ 171(c).

CONCEPT SUMMARY 14–1

Recognized Gain or Loss

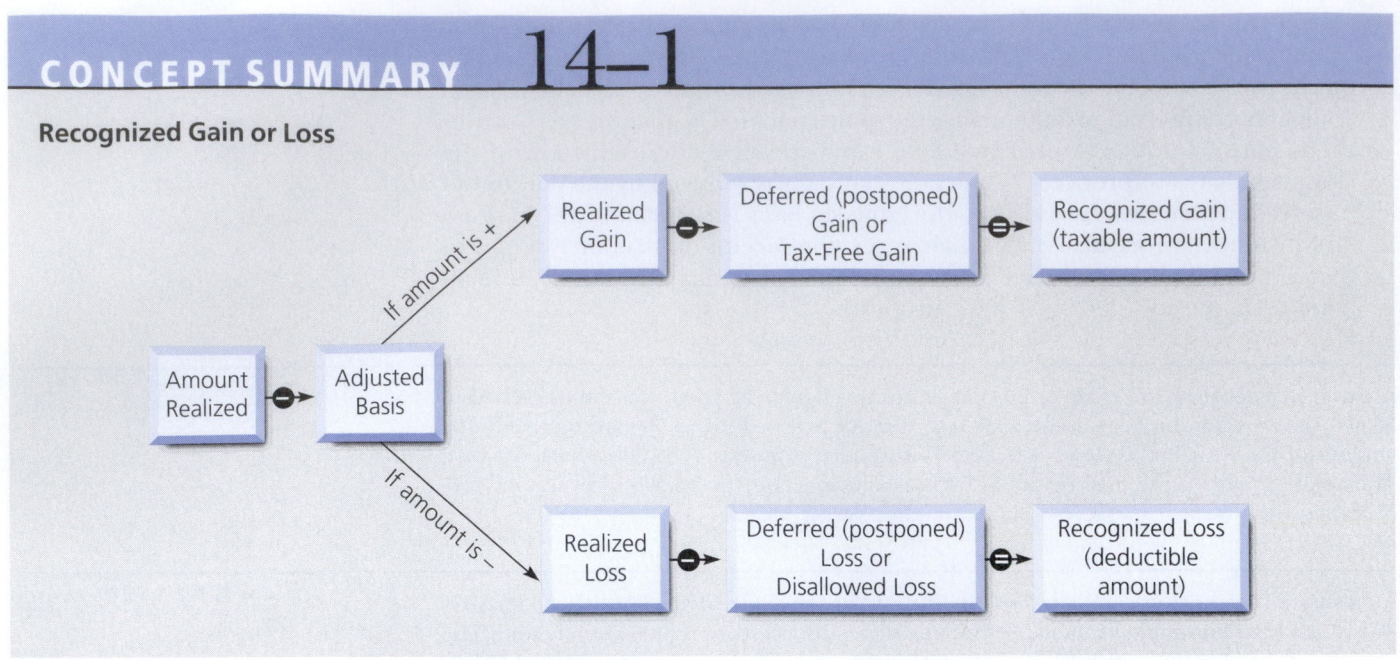

mature 10 years from the date of purchase. The annual interest income is $7,000 (7% × $100,000). If Antonio elects to amortize the bond premium, the $10,000 premium is deducted over the 10-year period. Antonio's basis for the bonds is reduced each year by the amount of the amortization deduction. Note that if the bonds were tax-exempt, amortization of the bond premium and the basis adjustment would be mandatory. However, no deduction would be allowed for the amortization. ∎

5. *Easements.* An easement is the legal right to use another's land for a special purpose. Historically, easements were commonly used to obtain rights-of-way for utility lines and roads. In recent years, grants of conservation easements have become a popular means of obtaining charitable contribution deductions and reducing the value of real estate for transfer tax (i.e., estate and gift) purposes. Likewise, scenic easements are used to reduce the value of land as assessed for ad valorem property tax purposes.

    If the taxpayer does not retain any right to the use of the land, all of the basis is assigned to the easement. However, if the use of the land is only partially restricted, an allocation of some of the basis to the easement is appropriate.

LO.2

Distinguish between realized and recognized gain or loss.

Recognized Gain or Loss

Recognized gain is the amount of the realized gain that is included in the taxpayer's gross income.[20] A **recognized loss**, on the other hand, is the amount of a realized loss that is deductible for tax purposes.[21] As a general rule, the entire amount of a realized gain or loss is recognized.[22]

Concept Summary 14–1 summarizes the realized gain or loss and recognized gain or loss concepts.

Nonrecognition of Gain or Loss

In certain cases, a realized gain or loss is not recognized upon the sale or other disposition of property. One such case involves nontaxable exchanges, which are covered in Chapter 15. Others include losses realized upon the sale,

[20]§ 61(a)(3) and Reg. § 1.61–6(a).
[21]§ 165(a) and Reg. § 1.165–1(a).

[22]§ 1001(c) and Reg. § 1.1002–1(a).

exchange, or condemnation of personal use assets (as opposed to business or income-producing property) and gains realized upon the sale of a residence (see Chapter 15). In addition, realized losses from the sale or exchange of business or income-producing property between certain related parties are not recognized.[23]

Sale, Exchange, or Condemnation of Personal Use Assets. A realized loss from the sale, exchange, or condemnation of personal use assets (e.g., a personal residence or an automobile not used at all for business or income-producing purposes) is not recognized for tax purposes. An exception exists for casualty or theft losses from personal use assets (see Chapter 7). In contrast, any gain realized from the sale or other disposition of personal use assets is, generally, fully taxable.

Freda sells an automobile, which she has held exclusively for personal use, for $6,000. The adjusted basis of the automobile is $5,000. Freda has a realized and recognized gain of $1,000. ∎

EXAMPLE 8

Freda sells the automobile in Example 8 for $4,000. She has a realized loss of $1,000, but the loss is not recognized. ∎

EXAMPLE 9

Recovery of Capital Doctrine

LO.3

Apply the recovery of capital doctrine.

Doctrine Defined. The **recovery of capital doctrine** pervades all the tax rules relating to property transactions. The doctrine derives its roots from the very essence of the income tax—a tax on income. Under the doctrine, as a general rule, a taxpayer is entitled to recover the cost or other original basis of property acquired and is not taxed on that amount.

The cost or other original basis of depreciable property is recovered through annual depreciation deductions. The basis is reduced as the cost is recovered over the period the property is held. Therefore, when property is sold or otherwise disposed of, it is the adjusted basis (unrecovered cost or other basis) that is compared with the amount realized from the disposition to determine realized gain or loss.

Relationship of the Recovery of Capital Doctrine to the Concepts of Realization and Recognition. If a sale or other disposition results in a realized gain, the taxpayer has recovered more than the adjusted basis of the property. Conversely, if a sale or other disposition results in a realized loss, the taxpayer has recovered less than the adjusted basis.

The general rules for the relationship between the recovery of capital doctrine and the realized and recognized gain and loss concepts are summarized as follows:

Rule 1. A realized gain that is *never recognized* results in the *permanent recovery* of more than the taxpayer's cost or other basis for tax purposes. For example, all or a portion of the realized gain on the sale of a personal residence can be excluded from gross income under § 121.

Rule 2. A realized gain on which *recognition is postponed* results in the *temporary recovery* of more than the taxpayer's cost or other basis for tax purposes. For example, an exchange of like-kind property under § 1031 and an involuntary conversion under § 1033 are both eligible for postponement treatment.

---

[23]§ 267(a)(1).

Rule 3. A realized loss that is *never recognized* results in the *permanent recovery* of less than the taxpayer's cost or other basis for tax purposes. For example, a loss on the sale of an automobile held for personal use is not deductible.

Rule 4. A realized loss on which *recognition is postponed* results in the *temporary recovery* of less than the taxpayer's cost or other basis for tax purposes. For example, the realized loss on the exchange of like-kind property under § 1031 is postponed.

These rules are illustrated in discussions to follow in this and the next chapter.

LO.4

Explain how basis is determined for various methods of asset acquisition.

Basis Considerations

Determination of Cost Basis

As noted earlier, the basis of property is generally the property's cost. Cost is the amount paid for the property in cash or other property.[24] This general rule follows logically from the recovery of capital doctrine; that is, the cost or other basis of property is to be recovered tax-free by the taxpayer.

A *bargain purchase* of property is an exception to the general rule for determining basis. A bargain purchase may result when an employer transfers property to an employee at less than the property's fair market value (as compensation for services) or when a corporation transfers property to a shareholder at less than the property's fair market value (a dividend). The amount included in income either as compensation for services or dividend income is the difference between the bargain purchase price and the property's fair market value. The basis of property acquired in a bargain purchase is the property's fair market value.[25] If the basis of the property were not increased by the bargain amount, the taxpayer would be taxed on this amount again at disposition.

EXAMPLE 10

Wade buys land from his employer for $10,000 on December 30. The fair market value of the land is $15,000. Wade must include the $5,000 difference between the cost and the fair market value of the land in gross income for the taxable year. The bargain element represents additional compensation to Wade. His basis for the land is $15,000, the land's fair market value. ■

Identification Problems. Cost identification problems are frequently encountered in securities transactions. For example, the Regulations require that the taxpayer adequately identify the particular stock that has been sold.[26] A problem arises when the taxpayer has purchased separate lots of stock on different dates or at different prices and cannot adequately identify the lot from which a particular sale takes place. In this case, the stock is presumed to come from the first lot or lots purchased (a FIFO presumption).[27] When securities are left in the custody of a broker, it may be necessary to provide specific instructions and receive written confirmation as to which securities are being sold.

EXAMPLE 11

Polly purchases 100 shares of Olive Corporation stock on July 1, 2006, for $5,000 ($50 a share) and another 100 shares of Olive stock on July 1, 2007, for $6,000 ($60 a share). She sells 50 shares of the stock on January 2, 2008. The cost of the stock sold, assuming Polly cannot adequately identify the shares, is $50 a share, or $2,500. This is the cost Polly will compare with the amount realized in determining the gain or loss from the sale. ■

---

[24]§ 1012 and Reg. § 1.1012–1(a).

[25]Reg. §§ 1.61–2(d)(2)(i) and 1.301–1(j). See the discussion in Chapter 5 of the circumstances under which what appears to be a taxable bargain purchase is an excludible qualified employee discount.

[26]Reg. § 1.1012–1(c)(1).

[27]*Kluger Associates, Inc.*, 69 T.C. 925 (1978).

TAX *in the News*	WHAT IS YOUR STOCK BASIS?

In calculating the recognized gain on the sale of stock, whether owned directly or through a mutual fund, the taxpayer needs to know the basis for the asset being sold. Complicating this determination are such factors as multiple purchases on different dates for different amounts, dividend reinvestments, stock splits, nontaxable stock dividends, and return of capital distributions. Given the high chance for error in this area, some experts believe that the government is losing billions in tax revenues each year as a result of basis overstatements and the related effect on the calculation of gain or loss on stock sales.

The IRS has proposed an obvious solution: let the brokers and mutual funds do it. Ultimately, under this proposal, the broker or fund would be responsible for reporting the basis of an investment to the investor and to the IRS.

Two proposals have been introduced in Congress to require brokers to report tax basis. The staff of the Senate Finance Committee has recommended such reporting, and Senators Evan Bayh of Indiana and Tom Coburn of Oklahoma have introduced legislation that would require it. The bill would generate an estimated $7 billion of revenue over the next decade.

Unfortunately, there is no perfect solution in this area. Even if the broker reporting proposal is enacted into law, the problem would not be entirely solved. One of the shortcomings of this solution is that in some situations the broker may not know the basis of the securities being sold. Furthermore, the compliance costs to the parties involved would be considerable.

Source: *Adapted from Rob Wells, "Plan to Collect Gains Taxes Relies on 'Basis' Reporting,"* Wall Street Journal, *May 26, 2007, p. B2.*

Allocation Problems. When a taxpayer acquires *multiple assets in a lump-sum purchase*, the total cost must be allocated among the individual assets.[28] Allocation is necessary for several reasons:

- Some of the assets acquired may be depreciable (e.g., buildings), while others may not be (e.g., land).
- Only a portion of the assets acquired may be sold.
- Some of the assets may be capital or § 1231 assets that receive special tax treatment upon subsequent sale or other disposition.

The lump-sum cost is allocated on the basis of the fair market values of the individual assets acquired.

EXAMPLE 12

Harry purchases a building and land for $800,000. Because of the depressed nature of the industry in which the seller was operating, Harry was able to negotiate a very favorable purchase price. Appraisals of the individual assets indicate that the fair market value of the building is $600,000 and that of the land is $400,000. Harry's basis for the building is $480,000 [($600,000/$1,000,000) × $800,000], and his basis for the land is $320,000 [($400,000/$1,000,000) × $800,000]. ■

If a business is purchased and **goodwill** is involved, a special allocation rule applies. Initially, the purchase price is assigned to the assets, excluding goodwill, to the extent of their total fair market value. This assigned amount is allocated among the assets on the basis of the fair market value of the individual assets acquired. Goodwill is then assigned the residual amount of the purchase price. The resultant allocation is applicable to both the buyer and the seller.[29]

EXAMPLE 13

Rocky sells his business to Paul. They agree that the values of the individual assets are as follows:

Inventory	$ 50,000
Building	500,000
Land	200,000
Goodwill	150,000

---

[28]Reg. § 1.61–6(a).   [29]§ 1060.

After negotiations, Rocky and Paul agree on a sales price of $1 million. Applying the residual method with respect to goodwill results in the following allocation of the $1 million purchase price:

Inventory	$ 50,000
Building	500,000
Land	200,000
Goodwill	250,000

The residual method requires that all of the excess of the purchase price over the fair market value of the assets ($1,000,000 − $900,000 = $100,000) be allocated to goodwill. Without this requirement, the purchaser could allocate the excess pro rata to all of the assets, including goodwill, based on their respective fair market values. This would have resulted in only $166,667 [$150,000 + ($150,000 ÷ $900,000 × $100,000)] being assigned to goodwill. ■

In the case of *nontaxable stock dividends*, the allocation depends on whether the dividend is a common stock dividend on common stock or a preferred stock dividend on common stock. If the dividend is common on common, the cost of the original common shares is allocated to the total shares owned after the dividend.[30]

E X A M P L E   1 4

Susan owns 100 shares of Sparrow Corporation common stock for which she paid $1,100. She receives a 10% common stock dividend, giving her a new total of 110 shares. Before the stock dividend, Susan's basis was $11 per share ($1,100 ÷ 100 shares). The basis of each share after the stock dividend is $10 ($1,100 ÷ 110 shares). ■

If the nontaxable stock dividend is preferred stock on common, the cost of the original common shares is allocated between the common and preferred shares on the basis of their relative fair market values on the date of distribution.[31]

E X A M P L E   1 5

Fran owns 100 shares of Cardinal Corporation common stock for which she paid $1,000. She receives a nontaxable stock dividend of 50 shares of preferred stock on her common stock. The fair market values on the date of distribution of the preferred stock dividend are $30 a share for common stock and $40 a share for preferred stock.

Fair market value of common ($30 × 100 shares)	$3,000
Fair market value of preferred ($40 × 50 shares)	2,000
	$5,000
Basis of common: 3/5 × $1,000	$ 600
Basis of preferred: 2/5 × $1,000	$ 400

The basis per share for the common stock is $6 ($600/100 shares). The basis per share for the preferred stock is $8 ($400/50 shares). ■

The holding period for a nontaxable stock dividend, whether received in the form of common stock or preferred stock, includes the holding period of the original shares.[32] The significance of the holding period for capital assets is discussed in Chapter 16.

In the case of *nontaxable stock rights*, the basis of the rights is zero unless the taxpayer elects or is required to allocate a portion of the cost of the stock already held to the newly received stock rights. If the fair market value of the rights is 15 percent or more of the fair market value of the stock, the taxpayer is required to allocate. If the value of the rights is less than 15 percent of the fair market value of the stock, the taxpayer may elect to allocate.[33] When allocation is required or elected, the cost

---

[30]§§ 305(a) and 307(a).
[31]Reg. § 1.307–1(a).

[32]§ 1223(5) and Reg. § 1.1223–1(e).
[33]§ 307(b).

TAX *in the News*	FREQUENT-FLYER MILES AND BASIS

There are many ways to get frequent-flyer miles. Perhaps the most logical is to fly on an airplane, but staying in a hotel, renting a car, and using your credit card can also generate frequent-flyer miles. A more novel approach is to buy shares in a mutual fund.

Always watch out for the tax consequences, though. In a letter ruling, the IRS held that taxpayers who receive frequent-flyer miles for buying mutual fund shares must reduce their mutual fund basis by the fair market value of the miles received. The mutual fund must notify its shareholders of the fair market value, which is based on the cost of buying frequent-flyer miles from the airlines.

of the stock on which the rights are received is allocated between the stock and the rights on the basis of their relative fair market values.

EXAMPLE 16

Donald receives nontaxable stock rights with a fair market value of $1,000. The fair market value of the stock on which the rights were received is $8,000 (cost $10,000). Donald does not elect to allocate. The basis of the rights is zero. If he exercises the rights, the basis of the new stock is the exercise (subscription) price. ∎

EXAMPLE 17

Assume the same facts as in Example 16, except the fair market value of the rights is $3,000. Donald must allocate because the value of the rights ($3,000) is 15% or more of the value of the stock ($3,000/$8,000 = 37.5%).

- The basis of the stock is $7,273 [($8,000/$11,000) × $10,000].
- The basis of the rights is $2,727 [($3,000/$11,000) × $10,000].

If Donald exercises the rights, the basis of the new stock is the exercise (subscription) price plus the basis of the rights. If he sells the rights, he recognizes gain or loss equal to the difference between the amount realized and the basis of the rights. This allocation rule applies only when the rights are exercised or sold. Therefore, if the rights are allowed to lapse (expire), they have no basis, and the basis of the original stock is the stock's cost, $10,000. ∎

The holding period of nontaxable stock rights includes the holding period of the stock on which the rights were distributed. However, if the rights are exercised, the holding period of the newly acquired stock begins with the date the rights are exercised.[34]

Gift Basis

When a taxpayer receives property as a gift, there is no cost to the donee (recipient). Thus, under the cost basis provision, the donee's basis would be zero. However, this would violate the statutory intent that gifts not be subject to the income tax.[35] With a zero basis, if the donee sold the property, all of the amount realized would be treated as realized gain. Therefore, a basis is assigned to the property received depending on the following:

- The date of the gift.
- The basis of the property to the donor.
- The amount of the gift tax paid.
- The fair market value of the property.

---

[34]§ 1223(5) and Reg. §§ 1.1223–1(e) and (f).   [35]§ 102(a).

Gift Basis Rules If No Gift Tax Is Paid. Property received by gift can be referred to as *dual basis* property; that is, the basis for gain and the basis for loss might not be the same amount. The present basis rules for gifts of property are as follows:

- If the donee disposes of gift property in a transaction that results in a gain, the basis to the donee is the same as the donor's adjusted basis.[36] The donee's basis in this case is referred to as the *gain basis*. Therefore, a *realized gain* results if the amount realized from the disposition exceeds the donee's gain basis.

| EXAMPLE 18 | Melissa purchased stock in 2007 for $10,000. She gave the stock to her son, Joe, in 2008, when the fair market value was $15,000. No gift tax is paid on the transfer, and Joe subsequently sells the property for $15,000. Joe's basis is $10,000, and he has a realized gain of $5,000. ∎ |

- If the donee disposes of gift property in a transaction that results in a loss, the basis to the donee is the *lower* of the donor's adjusted basis or the fair market value on the date of the gift. The donee's basis in this case is referred to as the *loss basis*. Therefore, a *realized loss* results if the amount realized from the disposition is less than the donee's loss basis.

| EXAMPLE 19 | Burt purchased stock in 2007 for $10,000. He gave the stock to his son, Cliff, in 2008, when the fair market value was $7,000. No gift tax is paid on the transfer. Cliff later sells the stock for $6,000. Cliff's basis is $7,000 (fair market value is less than donor's adjusted basis of $10,000), and the realized loss from the sale is $1,000 ($6,000 amount realized − $7,000 basis). ∎ |

The amount of the loss basis will *differ* from the amount of the gain basis only if, at the date of the gift, the adjusted basis of the property exceeds the property's fair market value. Note that the loss basis rule prevents the donee from receiving a tax benefit from a decline in value that occurred while the donor held the property. Therefore, in Example 19, Cliff has a loss of only $1,000 rather than a loss of $4,000. The $3,000 difference represents the decline in value that occurred while Burt held the property. Ironically, however, the gain basis rule may result in the donee being subject to income tax on the appreciation that occurred while the donor held the property, as illustrated in Example 18.

If the amount realized from a sale or other disposition is *between* the basis for loss and the basis for gain, no gain or loss is realized.

| EXAMPLE 20 | Assume the same facts as in Example 19, except that Cliff sells the stock for $8,000. Application of the gain basis rule produces a loss of $2,000 ($8,000 − $10,000). Application of the loss basis rule produces a gain of $1,000 ($8,000 − $7,000). Because the amount realized is between the gain basis and the loss basis, Cliff recognizes neither a gain nor a loss. ∎ |

Adjustment for Gift Tax. If gift taxes are paid by the donor, the donee's gain basis may exceed the adjusted basis of the property to the donor. This occurs only if the fair market value of the property at the date of the gift is greater than the donor's adjusted basis (the property has appreciated in value). The portion of the gift tax paid that is related to the appreciation is added to the donor's basis in calculating the donee's gain basis for the property. In this circumstance, the following formula is used for calculating the donee's gain basis:[37]

---

[36]§ 1015(a) and Reg. § 1.1015–1(a)(1). See Reg. § 1.1015–1(a)(3) for cases in which the facts necessary to determine the donor's adjusted basis are unknown. Refer to Example 24 for the effect of depreciation deductions by the donee.

[37]§ 1015(d)(6) and Reg. § 1.1015–5(c)(2).

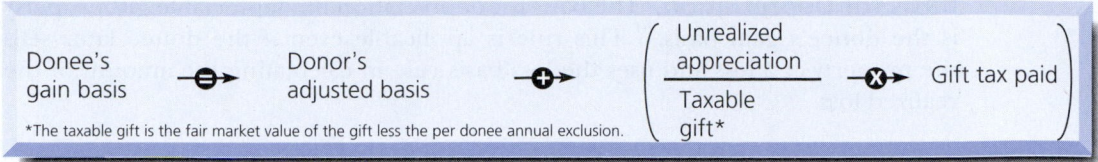

*The taxable gift is the fair market value of the gift less the per donee annual exclusion.

EXAMPLE 21

In 2008, Bonnie made a gift of stock (adjusted basis of $15,000) to Peggy. The stock had a fair market value of $50,000, and the transfer resulted in a gift tax of $4,000. The unrealized appreciation of the stock is $35,000 ($50,000 fair market value – $15,000 adjusted basis), and the taxable gift is $38,000 ($50,000 fair market value of gift – $12,000 annual exclusion). Peggy's basis in the stock is $18,680, determined as follows:

Donor's adjusted basis	$15,000
Gift tax attributable to appreciation—	
$35,000/$38,000 = 92% (rounded) × $4,000	3,680
Donee's gain basis	$18,680

■

EXAMPLE 22

Don made a gift of stock to Matt in 2008, when the fair market value of the stock was $50,000. Don paid gift tax of $4,000. Don had purchased the stock in 1988 for $65,000. Because there is no unrealized appreciation at the date of the gift, none of the gift tax paid is added to Don's basis in calculating Matt's gain basis. Therefore, Matt's gain basis is $65,000. ■

For *gifts made before 1977*, the full amount of the gift tax paid is added to the donor's basis. However, the ceiling on this total is the fair market value of the property at the date of the gift. Thus, in Example 21, if the gift had been made before 1977, the basis of the property would be $19,000 ($15,000 + $4,000). In Example 22, the gain basis would still be $65,000 ($65,000 + $0).

Holding Period. The **holding period** for property acquired by gift begins on the date the donor acquired the property if the gain basis rule applies.[38] The holding period starts on the date of the gift if the loss basis rule applies.[39] The significance of the holding period for capital assets is discussed in Chapter 16.

The following example summarizes the basis and holding period rules for gift property:

EXAMPLE 23

Jill acquired 100 shares of Wren Corporation stock on December 30, 1990, for $40,000. On January 3, 2008, when the stock has a fair market value of $38,000, Jill gives it to Dennis and pays gift tax of $4,000. The basis is not increased by a portion of the gift tax paid because the property has not appreciated in value at the time of the gift, Therefore, Dennis's gain basis is $40,000. Dennis's basis for determining loss is $38,000 (fair market value) because the fair market value on the date of the gift is less than the donor's adjusted basis.

- If Dennis sells the stock for $45,000, he has a recognized gain of $5,000. The holding period for determining whether the capital gain is short term or long term begins on December 30, 1990, the date Jill acquired the property.
- If Dennis sells the stock for $36,000, he has a recognized loss of $2,000. The holding period for determining whether the capital loss is short term or long term begins on January 3, 2008, the date of the gift.
- If Dennis sells the property for $39,000, there is no loss because the amount realized is less than the gain basis of $40,000 and more than the loss basis of $38,000. ■

---

[38]§ 1223(2) and Reg. § 1.1223–1(b).   [39]Rev.Rul. 59–86, 1959–1 C.B. 209.

Basis for Depreciation. The basis for depreciation on depreciable gift property is the donee's gain basis.[40] This rule is applicable even if the donee later sells the property at a loss and uses the loss basis rule in calculating the amount of the realized loss.

EXAMPLE 24

Vito gave a machine to Tina in 2008. At that time, the adjusted basis was $32,000 (cost of $40,000 − accumulated depreciation of $8,000), and the fair market value was $26,000. No gift tax was paid. Tina's gain basis at the date of the gift is $32,000, and her loss basis is $26,000. During 2008, Tina deducts depreciation (cost recovery) of $6,400 ($32,000 × 20%). (Refer to Chapter 8 for the cost recovery tables.) At the end of 2008, Tina's gain basis and loss basis are calculated as follows:

	Gain Basis	Loss Basis
Donor's basis or fair market value	$32,000	$26,000
Depreciation	(6,400)	(6,400)
	$25,600	$19,600

■

Property Acquired from a Decedent

General Rules. The basis of property acquired from a decedent is generally the property's fair market value at the date of death (referred to as the *primary valuation amount*).[41] The property's basis is the fair market value six months after the date of death if the executor or administrator of the estate *elects* the alternate valuation date for estate tax purposes. This amount is referred to as the *alternate valuation amount*.

EXAMPLE 25

Linda and various other family members inherited property from Linda's father, who died in 2008. At the date of death, her father's adjusted basis for the property Linda inherited was $35,000. The property's fair market value at the date of death was $50,000. The alternate valuation date was not elected. Linda's basis for income tax purposes is $50,000. This is commonly referred to as a *stepped-up basis*. ■

EXAMPLE 26

Assume the same facts as in Example 25, except the property's fair market value at the date of death was $20,000. Linda's basis for income tax purposes is $20,000. This is commonly referred to as a *stepped-down basis*. ■

No estate tax return must be filed for estates below a threshold amount. In such cases, the alternate valuation date and amount are not available. Even if an estate tax return is filed and the executor elects the alternate valuation date, the six months after death date is available only for property that the executor has not distributed before this date. For any property distributed or otherwise disposed of by the executor during the six-month period preceding the alternate valuation date, the adjusted basis to the beneficiary will equal the fair market value on the date of distribution or other disposition.[42]

The alternate valuation date can be *elected only* if, as a result of the election, both the value of the gross estate and the estate tax liability are lower than they would have been if the primary valuation date had been used. This provision prevents the alternate valuation election from being used to increase the basis of the property to the beneficiary for income tax purposes without simultaneously increasing the estate tax liability (because of estate tax deductions or credits).[43]

---

[40]§ 1011 and Reg. §§ 1.1011–1 and 1.167(g)–1.
[41]§ 1014(a).

[42]§ 2032(a)(1) and Rev.Rul. 56–60, 1956–1 C.B. 443.
[43]§ 2032(c).

Nancy inherited all the property of her father, who died in 2008. Her father's adjusted basis for the property at the date of death was $650,000. The property's fair market value was $2,750,000 at the date of death and $2,760,000 six months after death. The alternate valuation date cannot be elected because the value of the gross estate has increased during the six-month period. Nancy's basis for income tax purposes is $2,750,000. ■

Assume the same facts as in Example 27, except the property's fair market value six months after death was $2,745,000. If the executor elects the alternate valuation date, Nancy's basis for income tax purposes is $2,745,000. ■

Assume the same facts as in the previous example, except the property is distributed four months after the date of the decedent's death. At the distribution date, the property's fair market value is $2,747,500. Since the executor elected the alternate valuation date, Nancy's basis for income tax purposes is $2,747,500. ■

For inherited property, both unrealized appreciation and decline in value are taken into consideration in determining the basis of the property for income tax purposes. Contrast this with the carryover basis rules for property received by gift.

Deathbed Gifts. The Code contains a provision designed to eliminate a tax avoidance technique referred to as *deathbed gifts*. With this technique, a donor makes a gift of appreciated property to a dying person with the understanding that the donor (or the donor's spouse) will inherit the property on the donee's death. If the time period between the date of the gift and the date of the donee's death is not longer than one year, the usual basis rule (stepped-up basis) for inherited property may not apply. The adjusted basis of such property inherited by the donor or his or her spouse from the donee is the same as the decedent's adjusted basis for the property rather than the fair market value at the date of death or the alternate valuation date.[44]

Ned gives stock to his uncle, Vern, in 2008. Ned's basis for the stock is $100,000, and the fair market value is $900,000. No gift tax is paid. Eight months later, Ned inherits the stock from Vern. At the date of Vern's death, the fair market value of the stock is $980,000. Ned's adjusted basis for the stock is $100,000. ■

Survivor's Share of Property. Both the decedent's share and the survivor's share of *community property* have a basis equal to the fair market value on the date of the decedent's death.[45] This result applies to the decedent's share of the community property because the property flows to the surviving spouse from the estate (fair market value basis is assigned to inherited property). Likewise, the surviving spouse's share of the community property is deemed to be acquired by bequest, devise, or inheritance from the decedent. Therefore, it also has a basis equal to the fair market value.

Floyd and Vera reside in a community property state. They own as community property 200 shares of Crow stock acquired in 1984 for $100,000. Floyd dies in 2008, when the securities are valued at $300,000. One-half of the Crow stock is included in Floyd's estate. If Vera inherits Floyd's share of the community property, the basis for determining gain or loss is $300,000, determined as follows:

---

[44]§ 1014(e).

[45]§ 1014(b)(6). See the listing of community property states in Chapter 4.

TAX *in the News*

EFFECT OF 2001 TAX LEGISLATION ON THE BASIS OF INHERITED PROPERTY: BAD NEWS/GOOD NEWS!

The *bad news* is that the Tax Relief Reconciliation Act of 2001 repeals the current step-up or step-down (i.e., fair market value) rules for the beneficiary's basis in inherited property and replaces them with a modified carryover basis. By itself, this change significantly increases the complexity of the tax law. A potential decedent will need to maintain detailed records on the cost of his or her assets and have such data readily available for the executor. Otherwise, the executor will be unable to determine the cost of many assets included in the estate.

So what is the *good news*? First, the effective date for this new carryover basis provision is deferred to deaths occurring after December 31, 2009. Second, the carryover basis approach for inherited property has been tried before. The results were so unsuccessful that the legislation was repealed retroactively by Congress. Hopefully, if the new carryover basis ever becomes effective, history will repeat itself, and another retroactive repeal by Congress will occur.

Vera's one-half of the community property (stepped up from $50,000 to $150,000 due to Floyd's death)	$150,000
Floyd's one-half of the community property (stepped up from $50,000 to $150,000 due to inclusion in his gross estate)	150,000
Vera's new basis	$300,000 ∎

In a *common law* state, only one-half of jointly held property of spouses (tenants by the entirety or joint tenants with rights of survivorship) is included in the estate.[46] In such a case, no adjustment of the basis is permitted for the excluded property interest (the surviving spouse's share).

EXAMPLE 32

Assume the same facts as in the previous example, except that the property is jointly held by Floyd and Vera who reside in a common law state. Floyd purchased the property and made a gift of one-half of the property to Vera when the stock was acquired. No gift tax was paid. Only one-half of the Crow stock is included in Floyd's estate. Vera's basis for determining gain or loss in the excluded half is not adjusted upward for the increase in value to date of death. Therefore, Vera's basis is $200,000, determined as follows:

Vera's one-half of the jointly held property (carryover basis of $50,000)	$ 50,000
Floyd's one-half of the jointly held property (stepped up from $50,000 to $150,000 due to inclusion in his gross estate)	150,000
Vera's new basis	$200,000 ∎

Holding Period of Property Acquired from a Decedent. The holding period of property acquired from a decedent is *deemed to be long term* (held for the required long-term holding period). This provision applies regardless of whether the property is disposed of at a gain or at a loss.[47]

LO.5

Describe various loss disallowance provisions.

Disallowed Losses

Related Taxpayers. Section 267 provides that realized losses from sales or exchanges of property, directly or indirectly, between certain related parties are not recognized. This loss disallowance provision applies to several types of related-party transactions. The most common involve (1) members of a family and (2) an

---

[46]§ 2040(b).   [47]§ 1223(11).

individual and a corporation in which the individual owns, directly or indirectly, more than 50 percent in value of the corporation's outstanding stock. Section 707 provides a similar loss disallowance provision where the related parties are a partner and a partnership in which the partner owns, directly or indirectly, more than 50 percent of the capital interests or profits interests in the partnership. The rules governing the relationships covered by § 267 were discussed in Chapter 6. See Chapter 15 for the discussion of the special rules under § 1041 for property transfers between spouses or incident to divorce.

If income-producing or business property is transferred to a related taxpayer and a loss is disallowed, the basis of the property to the recipient is the property's cost to the transferee. However, if a subsequent sale or other disposition of the property by the original transferee results in a realized gain, the amount of gain is reduced by the loss that was previously disallowed.[48] This *right of offset* is not applicable if the original sale involved the sale of a personal use asset (e.g., the sale of a personal residence between related taxpayers). Furthermore, the right of offset is available only to the original transferee (the related-party buyer).

Pedro sells business property with an adjusted basis of $50,000 to his daughter, Josefina, for its fair market value of $40,000. Pedro's realized loss of $10,000 is not recognized.

- How much gain does Josefina recognize if she sells the property for $52,000? Josefina recognizes a $2,000 gain. Her realized gain is $12,000 ($52,000 less her basis of $40,000), but she can offset Pedro's $10,000 loss against the gain.
- How much gain does Josefina recognize if she sells the property for $48,000? Josefina recognizes no gain or loss. Her realized gain is $8,000 ($48,000 less her basis of $40,000), but she can offset $8,000 of Pedro's $10,000 loss against the gain. Note that Pedro's loss can only offset Josefina's gain. It cannot create a loss for Josefina.
- How much loss does Josefina recognize if she sells the property for $38,000? Josefina recognizes a $2,000 loss, the same as her realized loss ($38,000 less $40,000 basis). Pedro's loss does not increase Josefina's loss. His loss can be offset only against a gain. Since Josefina has no realized gain, Pedro's loss cannot be used and is never recognized. This part of the example assumes that the property is business or income-producing property to Josefina. If not, her $2,000 loss is personal and is not recognized. ∎

EXAMPLE 33

The loss disallowance rules are designed to achieve two objectives. First, the rules prevent a taxpayer from directly transferring an unrealized loss to a related taxpayer in a higher tax bracket who could receive a greater tax benefit from recognition of the loss. Second, the rules eliminate a substantial administrative burden on the Internal Revenue Service as to the appropriateness of the selling price (fair market value or not). The loss disallowance rules are applicable even where the selling price is equal to the fair market value and can be validated (e.g., listed stocks).

The holding period of the buyer for the property is not affected by the holding period of the seller. That is, the buyer's *holding period* includes only the period of time he or she has held the property.[49]

Wash Sales. Section 1091 stipulates that in certain cases, a realized loss on the sale or exchange of stock or securities is not recognized. Specifically, if a taxpayer sells or exchanges stock or securities and within 30 days before *or* after the date of the sale or exchange acquires substantially identical stock or securities, any loss realized from the sale or exchange is not recognized because the transaction is a **wash sale**.[50] The term *acquire* means acquire by purchase or in a taxable exchange and includes an option to purchase substantially identical securities. *Substantially identical* means the same in all important particulars. Corporate bonds and

---

[48]§ 267(d) and Reg. § 1.267(d)–1(a).
[49]§§ 267(d) and 1223(2) and Reg. § 1.267(d)–1(c)(3).
[50]§ 1091(a) and Reg. §§ 1.1091–1(a) and (f).

preferred stock are normally not considered substantially identical to the corporation's common stock. However, if the bonds and preferred stock are convertible into common stock, they may be considered substantially identical under certain circumstances.[51] Attempts to avoid the application of the wash sales rules by having a related taxpayer repurchase the securities have been unsuccessful.[52] The wash sales provisions do *not* apply to gains.

Recognition of the loss is disallowed because the taxpayer is considered to be in substantially the same economic position after the sale and repurchase as before the sale and repurchase. This disallowance rule does not apply to taxpayers engaged in the business of buying and selling securities.[53] Investors, however, are not allowed to create losses through wash sales to offset income for tax purposes.

Realized loss that is not recognized is added to the *basis* of the substantially identical stock or securities whose acquisition resulted in the nonrecognition of loss.[54] In other words, the basis of the replacement stock or securities is increased by the amount of the unrecognized loss. If the loss were not added to the basis of the newly acquired stock or securities, the taxpayer would never recover the entire basis of the old stock or securities.

The basis of the new stock or securities includes the unrecovered portion of the basis of the formerly held stock or securities. Therefore, the *holding period* of the new stock or securities begins on the date of acquisition of the old stock or securities.[55]

EXAMPLE 34

Bhaskar owns 100 shares of Green Corporation stock (adjusted basis of $20,000). He sells 50 shares for $8,000. Ten days later, he purchases 50 shares of the same stock for $7,000. Bhaskar's realized loss of $2,000 ($8,000 amount realized − $10,000 adjusted basis of 50 shares) is not recognized because it resulted from a wash sale. Bhaskar's basis in the newly acquired stock is $9,000 ($7,000 purchase price + $2,000 unrecognized loss from the wash sale). ■

A taxpayer may acquire fewer shares than the number sold in a wash sale. In this case, the loss from the sale is prorated between recognized and unrecognized loss on the basis of the ratio of the number of shares acquired to the number of shares sold.[56]

ETHICAL and EQUITABLE *Considerations*

DRYING OUT A WASH SALE

Webb owned 1,000 shares of Taupe, Inc. stock that he had purchased three years ago for $50,000. Due to financial problems, he sold the stock on October 5, 2008, for $48,000. Although the stock had declined in value, Webb viewed it as a good long-term investment. After he unexpectedly inherited $200,000 from an uncle, he reacquired 3,000 shares of Taupe stock on November 1, 2008, for $156,000.

In a conversation with a friend who is actively involved in day trading, Webb becomes aware of the wash sale rules. To avoid the disallowance of the $2,000 loss on the October 5 sale, on November 3, 2008, Webb sells 1,000 of the 3,000 shares purchased on November 1, 2008, for $53,000.

Webb intends to show a $2,000 ($48,000 – $50,000) capital loss and a $1,000 ($53,000 – $52,000) capital gain on his 2008 tax return. Evaluate Webb's treatment of these stock transactions.

[51]Rev.Rul. 56–406, 1956–2 C.B. 523.
[52]*McWilliams v. Comm.*, 47–1 USTC ¶9289, 35 AFTR 1184, 67 S.Ct. 1477 (USSC, 1947).
[53]Reg. § 1.1091–1(a).

[54]§ 1091(d) and Reg. § 1.1091–2(a).
[55]§ 1223(4) and Reg. § 1.1223–1(d).
[56]§ 1091(b) and Reg. § 1.1091–1(c).

Conversion of Property from Personal Use to Business or Income-Producing Use

As discussed previously, losses from the sale of personal use assets are not recognized for tax purposes, but losses from the sale of business and income-producing assets are deductible. Can a taxpayer convert a personal use asset that has declined in value to business or income-producing use and then sell the asset to recognize a business or income-producing loss? The tax law prevents this practice by specifying that the *original basis for loss* on personal use assets converted to business or income-producing use is the *lower* of the property's adjusted basis or fair market value on the date of conversion.[57] The *gain basis* for converted property is the property's adjusted basis on the date of conversion. The tax law is not concerned with gains on converted property because gains are recognized regardless of whether property is business, income-producing, or personal use.

EXAMPLE 35

Diane's personal residence has an adjusted basis of $175,000 and a fair market value of $160,000. Diane converts the personal residence to rental property. Her basis for loss is $160,000 (lower of $175,000 adjusted basis and fair market value of $160,000). The $15,000 decline in value is a personal loss and can never be recognized for tax purposes. Diane's basis for gain is $175,000. ■

The basis for loss is also the *basis for depreciating* the converted property.[58] This is an exception to the general rule that the basis for depreciation is the gain basis (e.g., property received by gift). This exception prevents the taxpayer from recovering a personal loss indirectly through depreciation of the higher original basis. After the property is converted, both its basis for loss and its basis for gain are adjusted for depreciation deductions from the date of conversion to the date of disposition. These rules apply only if a conversion from personal to business or income-producing use has actually occurred.

EXAMPLE 36

At a time when his personal residence (adjusted basis of $140,000) is worth $150,000, Keith converts one-half of it to rental use. Assume the property is not MACRS recovery property. At this point, the estimated useful life of the residence is 20 years, and there is no estimated salvage value. After renting the converted portion for five years, Keith sells the property for $144,000. All amounts relate only to the building; the land has been accounted for separately. Keith has a $2,000 realized gain from the sale of the personal use portion of the residence and a $19,500 realized gain from the sale of the rental portion. These gains are computed as follows:

	Personal Use	Rental
Original basis for gain and loss—adjusted basis on date of conversion (fair market value is greater than the adjusted basis)	$70,000	$70,000
Depreciation—five years	None	17,500
Adjusted basis—date of sale	$70,000	$52,500
Amount realized	72,000	72,000
Realized gain	$ 2,000	$19,500

■

As discussed in Chapter 15, Keith may be able to exclude the $2,000 realized gain from the sale of the personal use portion of the residence under § 121. If the

---

[57]Reg. § 1.165–9(b)(2).   [58]Reg. § 1.167(g)–1.

§ 121 exclusion applies, only $17,500 (equal to the depreciation deducted) of the $19,500 realized gain from the rental portion is recognized.

EXAMPLE 37

Assume the same facts as in the previous example, except that the fair market value on the date of conversion is $130,000 and the sales proceeds are $90,000. Keith has a $25,000 realized loss from the sale of the personal use portion of the residence and a $3,750 realized loss from the sale of the rental portion. These losses are computed as follows:

	Personal Use	Rental
Original basis for loss—fair market value on date of conversion (fair market value is less than the adjusted basis)	*	$65,000
Depreciation—five years	None	16,250
Adjusted basis—date of sale	$70,000	$48,750
Amount realized	45,000	45,000
Realized loss	($25,000)	($ 3,750)

*Not applicable.

The $25,000 loss from the sale of the personal use portion of the residence is not recognized. The $3,750 loss from the rental portion is recognized. ■

Additional Complexities in Determining Realized Gain or Loss

Amount Realized. The calculation of the amount realized may appear to be one of the least complex areas associated with property transactions. However, because numerous positive and negative adjustments may be required, this calculation can be complex and confusing. In addition, determining the fair market value of the items received by the taxpayer can be difficult. The following example provides insight into various items that can affect the amount realized.

EXAMPLE 38

Ridge sells an office building and the associated land on October 1, 2008. Under the terms of the sales contract, Ridge is to receive $600,000 in cash. The purchaser is to assume Ridge's mortgage of $300,000 on the property. To enable the purchaser to obtain adequate financing, Ridge is to pay the $15,000 in points charged by the lender. The broker's commission on the sale is $45,000. The purchaser agrees to pay the $12,000 in property taxes for the entire year. The amount realized by Ridge is calculated as follows:

Selling price		
Cash	$600,000	
Mortgage assumed by purchaser	300,000	
Seller's property taxes paid by purchaser ($12,000 × $^{9}/_{12}$)	9,000	$909,000
Less		
Broker's commission	$ 45,000	
Points paid by seller	15,000	(60,000)
Amount realized		$849,000

■

Adjusted Basis. Three types of issues tend to complicate the determination of adjusted basis. First, the applicable tax provisions for calculating the adjusted basis depend on how the property was acquired (e.g., purchase, taxable exchange,

---

TAX *in the News*   **WHERE TO INVEST: GROWTH STOCK VERSUS INCOME STOCK**

Prior to the effective date of the Jobs and Growth Tax Relief Reconciliation Act of 2003 (JGTRRA), there was a basic difference in the tax treatment of growth stock and income stock. Growth stock generated capital gains, which received beneficial tax rate treatment, whereas income stock generated dividends, which were classified as ordinary income and taxed at the taxpayer's marginal tax rate.

JGTRRA eliminated this difference. Qualified dividends are now eligible for the same beneficial rate treatment (i.e., 15%/0%) as capital gains.

This change has contributed to increased interest in stocks that pay dividends and has motivated corporate boards of directors to declare larger dividends than in the past. Since the JGTRRA dividend rate cut took effect, numerous S&P 500 companies have announced dividend increases with many companies paying dividends for the first time. Meanwhile, investments are increasing in equity-income mutual funds, which focus largely on owning stocks of dividend-paying companies.

---

nontaxable exchange, gift, inheritance). Second, if the asset is subject to depreciation, cost recovery, amortization, or depletion, adjustments must be made to the basis during the time period the asset is held by the taxpayer. Upon disposition of the asset, the taxpayer's records for both of these items may be deficient. For example, the donee does not know the amount of the donor's basis or the amount of gift tax paid by the donor, or the taxpayer does not know how much depreciation he or she has deducted. Third, the complex positive and negative adjustments encountered in calculating the amount realized are also involved in calculating the adjusted basis.

EXAMPLE 39

Jane purchased a personal residence in 1999. The purchase price and the related closing costs were as follows:

Purchase price	$125,000
Recording costs	140
Title fees and title insurance	815
Survey costs	115
Attorney's fees	750
Appraisal fee	60

Other relevant tax information for the house during the time Jane owned it is as follows:

- Constructed a swimming pool for medical reasons. The cost was $10,000, of which $3,000 was deducted as a medical expense.
- Added a solar heating system. The cost was $15,000.
- Deducted home office expenses of $6,000. Of this amount, $3,200 was for depreciation.

The adjusted basis for the house is calculated as follows:

Purchase price	$125,000
Recording costs	140
Title fees and title insurance	815
Survey costs	115
Attorney's fees	750
Appraisal fee	60
Swimming pool ($10,000 − $3,000)	7,000
Solar heating system	15,000
	$148,880
Less: Depreciation deducted on home office	(3,200)
Adjusted basis	$145,680

■

Summary of Basis Adjustments

Some of the more common items that either increase or decrease the basis of an asset appear in Concept Summary 14–2.

In discussing the topic of basis, a number of specific techniques for determining basis have been presented. Although the various techniques are responsive to and mandated by transactions occurring in the marketplace, they do possess enough common characteristics to be categorized as follows:

- The basis of the asset may be determined by reference to the asset's cost.
- The basis of the asset may be determined by reference to the basis of another asset.
- The basis of the asset may be determined by reference to the asset's fair market value.
- The basis of the asset may be determined by reference to the basis of the asset to another taxpayer.

Tax Consequences of Alice's Proposed Transaction

LO.6

Identify tax planning opportunities related to selected property transactions.

TAX PLANNING
Considerations

In Example 1 earlier in the chapter, Alice's tax adviser asked a number of questions in order to advise her on a proposed transaction. Alice provided the following answers:

- Alice inherited the house from her mother. The fair market value of the house at the date of her mother's death, based on the estate tax return, was $225,000. Based on an appraisal, the house is worth $230,000. Alice's mother lived in the house for 48 years. According to the mother's attorney, her adjusted basis for the house was $75,000.
- As a child, Alice lived in the house for 10 years. She has not lived there during the 35 years she has been married.
- The house has been vacant during the seven months that Alice has owned it. She has been trying to decide whether she should sell it for its fair market value or sell it to her nephew for $75,000. Alice has suggested a $75,000 price for the sale to Dan because she believes this is the amount at which she will have no gain or loss.
- Alice intends to invest the $75,000 in stock.

You advise Alice that her adjusted basis for the house is the $225,000 fair market value on the date of her mother's death. If Alice sells the house for $230,000 (assuming no selling expenses), she would have a recognized gain of $5,000 ($230,000 amount realized − $225,000 adjusted basis). The house is a capital asset, and Alice's holding period is long term since she inherited the house. Thus, the gain would be classified as a long-term capital gain. If, instead, Alice sells the house to her nephew for $75,000, she will have a part sale and part gift. The realized gain on the sale of $1,630 is recognized.

Amount realized	$ 75,000
Less: Adjusted basis	(73,370)*
Realized gain	$ 1,630
Recognized gain	$ 1,630

*[($75,000/$230,000) × $225,000] = $73,370.

The gain is classified as a long-term capital gain. Alice is then deemed to have made a gift to Dan of $155,000 ($230,000 − $75,000).

With this information, Alice can make an informed selection between the two options.

CONCEPT SUMMARY 14–2

Adjustments to Basis

Item	Effect	Refer to Chapter	Explanation
Amortization of bond discount.	Increase	16	Amortization is mandatory for certain taxable bonds and elective for tax-exempt bonds.
Amortization of bond premium.	Decrease	14	Amortization is mandatory for tax-exempt bonds and elective for taxable bonds.
Amortization of covenant not to compete.	Decrease	8	Covenant must be for a definite and limited time period. The amortization period is a statutory period of 15 years.
Amortization of intangibles.	Decrease	8	Intangibles are amortized over a 15-year period.
Assessment for local benefits.	Increase	10	To the extent not deductible as taxes (e.g., assessment for streets and sidewalks that increase the value of the property versus one for maintenance or repair or for meeting interest charges).
Bad debts.	Decrease	7	Only the specific charge-off method is permitted.
Capital additions.	Increase	14	Certain items, at the taxpayer's election, can be capitalized or deducted (e.g., selected medical expenses).
Casualty.	Decrease	7	For a casualty loss, the amount of the adjustment is the sum of the deductible loss and the insurance proceeds received. For a casualty gain, the amount of the adjustment is the insurance proceeds received reduced by the recognized gain.
Condemnation.	Decrease	15	See casualty explanation.
Cost recovery.	Decrease	8	§ 168 is applicable to tangible assets placed in service after 1980 whose useful life is expressed in terms of years.
Depletion.	Decrease	8	Use the greater of cost or percentage depletion. Percentage depletion can still be deducted when the basis is zero.
Depreciation.	Decrease	8	§ 167 is applicable to tangible assets placed in service before 1981 and to tangible assets not depreciated in terms of years.
Easement.	Decrease	14	If the taxpayer does not retain any use of the land, all of the basis is allocable to the easement transaction. However, if only part of the land is affected by the easement, only part of the basis is allocable to the easement transaction.
Improvements by lessee to lessor's property.	Increase	5	Adjustment occurs only if the lessor is required to include the fair market value of the improvements in gross income under § 109.
Imputed interest.	Decrease	18	Amount deducted is not part of the cost of the asset.
Inventory: lower of cost or market.	Decrease	18	Not available if the LIFO method is used.
Limited expensing under § 179.	Decrease	8	Occurs only if the taxpayer elects § 179 treatment.
Medical capital expenditure permitted as a medical expense.	Decrease	10	Adjustment is the amount of the deduction (the effect on basis is to increase it by the amount of the capital expenditure net of the deduction).

Adjustments to Basis—Continued

Item	Effect	Refer to Chapter	Explanation
Real estate taxes: apportionment between the buyer and seller.	Increase or decrease	10	To the extent the buyer pays the seller's pro rata share, the buyer's basis is increased. To the extent the seller pays the buyer's pro rata share, the buyer's basis is decreased.
Rebate from manufacturer.	Decrease		Since the rebate is treated as an adjustment to the purchase price, it is not included in the buyer's gross income.
Stock dividend.	Decrease	5	Adjustment occurs only if the stock dividend is nontaxable. While the basis per share decreases, the total stock basis does not change.
Stock rights.	Decrease	14	Adjustment to stock basis occurs only for nontaxable stock rights and only if the fair market value of the rights is at least 15% of the fair market value of the stock or, if less than 15%, the taxpayer elects to allocate the basis between the stock and the rights.
Theft.	Decrease	7	See casualty explanation.

Cost Identification and Documentation Considerations

When multiple assets are acquired in a single transaction, the contract price must be allocated for several reasons. First, some of the assets may be depreciable, while others are not. From the different viewpoints of the buyer and the seller, this may produce a tax conflict that needs to be resolved. That is, the seller prefers a high allocation for nondepreciable assets, whereas the purchaser prefers a high allocation for depreciable assets (see Chapters 16 and 17). Second, the seller needs to know the amount realized on the sale of the capital assets and the ordinary income assets so that the recognized gains and losses can be classified as capital or ordinary. For example, an allocation to goodwill or to a covenant not to compete (see Chapters 8, 16, and 17) produces different tax consequences to the seller. Third, the buyer needs the adjusted basis of each asset to calculate the realized gain or loss on a subsequent sale or other disposition of each asset.

Selection of Property for Making Gifts

A donor can achieve several tax advantages by making gifts of appreciated property. The donor avoids income tax on the unrealized gain that would have occurred had the donor sold the property. A portion of this amount can be permanently avoided because the donee's adjusted basis is increased by part or all of any gift tax paid by the donor. Even without this increase in basis, the income tax liability on the sale of the property by the donee can be less than the income tax liability that would have resulted from the donor's sale of the property, if the donee is in a lower tax bracket than the donor. In addition, any subsequent appreciation during the time the property is held by the lower tax bracket donee results in a tax savings on the sale or other disposition of the property. Such gifts of appreciated property can be an effective tool in family tax planning.

Taxpayers should generally not make gifts of depreciated property (property that, if sold, would produce a realized loss) because the donor does not receive an income tax deduction for the unrealized loss element. In addition, the donee receives no benefit from this unrealized loss upon the subsequent sale of the property because of the loss basis rule. The loss basis rule provides that the donee's basis is the lower of the donor's basis or the fair market value at the date of the gift. If the donor anticipates that the donee will sell the property upon receiving it, the donor should sell the property and take the loss deduction, assuming the loss is deductible. The donor can then give the proceeds from the sale to the donee.

Selection of Property for Making Bequests

A taxpayer should generally make bequests of appreciated property in his or her will. Doing so enables both the decedent and the heir to avoid income tax on the unrealized gain because the recipient takes the fair market value as his or her basis.

Taxpayers generally should not make bequests of depreciated property (property that, if sold, would produce a realized loss) because the decedent does not receive an income tax deduction for the unrealized loss element. In addition, the heir will receive no benefit from this unrealized loss upon the subsequent sale of the property.

E X A M P L E   40

On the date of her death, Marta owned land held for investment purposes. The land had an adjusted basis of $130,000 and a fair market value of $100,000. If Marta had sold the property before her death, the recognized loss would have been $30,000. If Roger inherits the property and later sells it for $90,000, the recognized loss is $10,000 (the decline in value since Marta's death). In addition, regardless of the period of time Roger holds the property, the holding period is long term (see Chapter 16). ∎

From an income tax perspective, it is preferable to transfer appreciated property as a bequest rather than as a gift. The reason is that inherited property receives a step-up in basis, whereas property received by gift has a carryover basis to the donee. However, in making this decision, the estate tax consequences of the bequest should also be weighed against the gift tax consequences of the gift.

Disallowed Losses

Section 267 Disallowed Losses.
Taxpayers should be aware of the desirability of avoiding transactions that activate the loss disallowance provisions for related parties. This is so even in light of the provision that permits the related-party buyer to offset his or her realized gain by the related-party seller's disallowed loss. Even with this offset, several inequities exist. First, the tax benefit associated with the disallowed loss ultimately is realized by the wrong party (the related-party buyer rather than the related-party seller). Second, the tax benefit of this offset to the related-party buyer does not occur until the buyer disposes of the property. Therefore, the longer the time period between the purchase and disposition of the property by the related-party buyer, the less the economic benefit. Third, if the property does not appreciate to at least its adjusted basis to the related-party seller during the time period the related-party buyer holds it, part or all of the disallowed loss is permanently lost. Fourth, since the right of offset is available only to the original transferee (the related-party buyer), all of the disallowed loss is permanently lost if the original transferee subsequently transfers the property by gift or bequest.

E X A M P L E   41

Tim sells property with an adjusted basis of $35,000 to Wes, his brother, for $25,000, the fair market value of the property. The $10,000 realized loss to Tim is disallowed by § 267. If Wes subsequently sells the property to an unrelated party for $37,000, he has a recognized gain of $2,000 (realized gain of $12,000 reduced by disallowed loss of $10,000). Therefore, from the perspective of the family unit, the original $10,000 realized loss ultimately is recognized. However, if Wes sells the property for $29,000, he has a recognized gain of $0 (realized gain of $4,000 reduced by disallowed loss of $4,000 necessary to offset the realized gain). From the perspective of the family unit, $6,000 of the realized loss of $10,000 is permanently wasted ($10,000 realized loss − $4,000 offset permitted). ■

Wash Sales. The wash sales provisions can be avoided if the security that was sold is replaced within the statutory time period with a similar rather than a substantially identical security. For example, a sale of Dell, Inc. common stock accompanied by a purchase of Hewlett-Packard common stock is not treated as a wash sale. Such a procedure can enable the taxpayer to use an unrealized capital loss to offset a recognized capital gain. The taxpayer can sell the security before the end of the taxable year, offset the recognized capital loss against the capital gain, and invest the sales proceeds in a similar security.

Because the wash sales provisions do not apply to gains, it may be desirable to engage in a wash sale before the end of the taxable year. The recognized capital gain may be used to offset capital losses or capital loss carryovers from prior years. Since the basis of the replacement stock or securities will be the purchase price, the taxpayer in effect has exchanged a capital gain for an increased basis for the stock or securities.

KEY TERMS

Adjusted basis, 14–4	Holding period, 14–13	Recognized loss, 14–6
Amount realized, 14–3	Realized gain, 14–3	Recovery of capital doctrine, 14–7
Fair market value, 14–3	Realized loss, 14–3	
Goodwill, 14–9	Recognized gain, 14–6	Wash sale, 14–17

PROBLEM   MATERIALS

DISCUSSION QUESTIONS

1. Upon the sale or other disposition of property, what four questions should be considered for income tax purposes?

2. Define each of the following terms:
    a. Amount realized.
    b. Realized gain.
    c. Realized loss.

3. Which of the following would be treated as a "sale or other disposition"?
    a. Sale for cash.
    b. Sale on credit.
    c. Exchange.
    d. Involuntary conversion.
    e. Bond retirement.
    f. Gift to nephew.

Decision Making

4. Ivan invests in land and Grace invests in taxable bonds. The land appreciates by $8,000 each year, and the bonds earn interest of $8,000 each year. After holding the land and bonds for five years, Ivan and Grace sell them. There is a $40,000 realized gain on the sale of the land and no realized gain or loss on the sale of the bonds. Are the tax consequences to Ivan and Grace the same for each of the five years? Explain.

5. Carol and Dave each purchase 100 shares of stock of Burgundy, Inc., a publicly owned corporation, in July for $10,000 each. Carol sells her stock on December 31 for $8,000. Since Burgundy's stock is listed on a national exchange, Dave is able to ascertain that his shares are worth $8,000 on December 31. Does the tax law treat the decline in value of the stock differently for Carol and Dave? Explain.

6. If a taxpayer sells property for cash, the amount realized consists of the net proceeds from the sale. For each of the following, indicate the effect on the amount realized:
   a. The property is sold on credit.
   b. A mortgage on the property is assumed by the buyer.
   c. A mortgage on the property is assumed by the seller.
   d. The buyer acquires the property subject to a mortgage of the seller.
   e. Stock that has a basis to the purchaser of $6,000 and a fair market value of $10,000 is received by the seller as part of the consideration.

7. If the buyer pays real property taxes that are treated as imposed on the seller, what are the effects on the seller's amount realized and the buyer's adjusted basis for the property? If the seller pays real property taxes that are treated as imposed on the buyer, what are the effects on the seller's amount realized and the buyer's adjusted basis for the property?

8. Tad is negotiating to buy some land. Under the first option, Tad will give Sandra $120,000 and assume her mortgage on the land for $80,000. Under the second option, Tad will give Sandra $200,000, and she will immediately pay off the mortgage. Tad wants his basis for the land to be as high as possible. Given this objective, which option should Tad select?

Decision Making

9. Eve purchases land from Gillen. Eve gives Gillen $100,000 in cash and agrees to pay Gillen an additional $400,000 one year later plus interest at 6%.
   a. What is Eve's adjusted basis for the land at the acquisition date?
   b. What is Eve's adjusted basis for the land one year later?

10. A taxpayer owns land and a building with an adjusted basis of $75,000 and a fair market value of $240,000. The property is subject to a mortgage of $360,000. Since the taxpayer is in arrears on the mortgage payments, the creditor is willing to accept the property in return for canceling the amount of the mortgage.
   a. How can the adjusted basis of the property be less than the amount of the mortgage?
   b. If the creditor's offer is accepted, what are the effects on the amount realized, the adjusted basis, and the realized gain or loss?
   c. Does it matter in (b) if the mortgage is recourse or nonrecourse?

11. Discuss the effect of capital additions and capital recoveries on adjusted basis.

12. On October 16, 2008, Tolly acquires land and a building for $800,000 to use in his sole proprietorship. Of the purchase price, $700,000 is allocated to the building, and $100,000 is allocated to the land. Cost recovery of $3,745 is deducted in 2008 for the building.
   a. What is the adjusted basis for the land and the building at the acquisition date?
   b. What is the adjusted basis for the land and the building at the end of 2008?

13. Abby owns stock in Orange Corporation and Blue Corporation. She receives a $1,000 distribution from both corporations. The instructions from Orange state that the $1,000 is a dividend. The instructions from Blue state that the $1,000 is not a dividend. What could cause the instructions to differ as to the tax consequences?

14. A taxpayer who acquires a taxable bond at a premium may elect to amortize the premium, whereas a taxpayer who acquires a tax-exempt bond at a premium must amortize the premium.
   a. Why would a taxpayer make the amortization election for taxable bonds?
   b. What effect does the mandatory amortization of tax-exempt bonds have on taxable income?

15. Rachel owns her personal use automobile, which has an adjusted basis of $26,000. Since she is interested in purchasing a newer model, she sells her car to Mason for $12,000.
   a. What is Rachel's realized and recognized loss resulting from this transaction?
   b. Could Rachel achieve better tax consequences if she traded her old car in for the newer model rather than selling it to Mason?

Decision Making

Issue ID

16. Ron sold his sailboat for a $5,000 loss in the current year because he was diagnosed as having skin cancer. His spouse wants him to sell his Harley Davidson motorcycle because her brother broke his leg while riding his motorcycle. Since Ron no longer has anyone to ride with, he is seriously considering accepting his wife's advice. Because the motorcycle is a classic, Ron has received two offers. Each offer would result in a $5,000 gain. Joe would like to purchase the motorcycle before Christmas, and Jeff would like to purchase it after New Year's. Identify the relevant tax issues Ron faces in making his decision.

17. Lee owns a life insurance policy that will pay $100,000 to Rita, his spouse, on his death. At the date of Lee's death, he had paid total premiums of $65,000 on the policy. In accordance with § 101(a)(1), Rita excludes the $100,000 of insurance proceeds. Discuss the relationship, if any, between the § 101 exclusion and the recovery of capital doctrine.

18. How is the basis of the property determined in a bargain purchase? Why is this method used?

19. When a business is purchased and goodwill is involved, why is the basis of goodwill determined by the residual method rather than by using the amount assigned under the purchase contract?

20. Distinguish between the procedures for determining the basis of stock received as a nontaxable stock dividend when the stock dividend is:
    a. Common stock on common stock.
    b. Preferred stock on common stock.

21. Marla bought a small sailboat for $13,000 in 2003. In January 2008, when the fair market value of the sailboat is $11,200, Marla makes a gift of it to Janine. No gift tax is due on the transfer. Six months later, Janine sells the boat for $9,500. What is Janine's:
    a. Adjusted basis in the sailboat?
    b. Recognized gain or loss on the sale?

Issue ID

22. In January, Agnes is diagnosed as having a terminal disease. Her nephew, Stan, will graduate from college in May, and she would like to give him $50,000 as a graduation present. She has stock worth $50,000 that she could either give him directly or sell and transfer the cash. Since she may not be alive in May, Agnes is considering making the gift now (four months prior to graduation). If Agnes should die before making the gift, her will stipulates that Stan will receive the stock. Identify the relevant tax issues that Agnes should consider in making her decision.

23. Howard receives a gift of appreciated land from Del who pays a gift tax on the transfer. What effect does the gift tax have on Howard's basis in the land if the gift was made:
    a. Before 1977?
    b. After 1976?

24. Immediately before his death in 2008, Karl sells securities (adjusted basis of $95,000) for their fair market value of $20,000. The sale was not to a related party. Karl is survived by his wife, Zoe, who inherits all of his property.
    a. Did Karl act wisely? Why or why not?
    b. Suppose the figures are reversed (sale for $95,000 of property with an adjusted basis of $20,000). Would the sale be wise? Why or why not?

25. Gary makes a gift of an appreciated building to Carmen. She dies three months later, and Gary inherits the building from her. During the period that Carmen held the building, she deducted depreciation and made a capital expenditure. What effect might these items have on Gary's basis for the inherited building?

26. Jo inherited property from Robert with a date of death value of $2,732,000 and a value of $2,745,000 six months later. Robert's adjusted basis for the property was $200,000. Jo wants the executor of Robert's estate to elect the alternate valuation date.
    a. Why does Jo want the election made?
    b. Can it be made?

27. On December 30, 2008, Ada sells 1,000 shares of Tan, Inc. stock for $60,000 and realizes a loss of $9,000. On January 23, 2009, Ada purchases 700 shares of Tan, Inc. stock for $44,000. What is her adjusted basis in the 700 shares?

28. What is the basis for depreciation of property that is converted from personal to business use? What is the justification for this rule?

PROBLEMS

29. Anne sold her home for $260,000 in 2008. Selling expenses were $15,000. She had purchased it in 2001 for $190,000. During the period of ownership, Anne had done the following:

   - Deducted $50,500 office-in-home expenses, which included $4,500 in depreciation. (Refer to Chapter 9.)
   - Deducted a casualty loss for residential trees destroyed by a hurricane. The total loss was $19,000 (after the $100 floor and the 10%-of-AGI floor), and Anne's insurance company reimbursed her for $13,500. (Refer to Chapter 7.)
   - Paid street paving assessment of $7,000 and added sidewalks for $11,000.
   - Installed an elevator for medical reasons. The total cost was $20,000, and Anne deducted $12,000 as medical expenses. (Refer to Chapter 10.)

   What is Anne's realized gain?

30. Kareem bought a rental house in October 2003 for $250,000, of which $50,000 is allocated to the land and $200,000 to the building. Early in 2005, he had a tennis court built in the backyard at a cost of $5,000. Kareem has deducted $30,900 for depreciation on the house and $1,300 for depreciation on the court. In January 2008, he sells the house and tennis court for $400,000 cash.
   a. What is Kareem's realized gain or loss?
   b. If an original mortgage of $75,000 is still outstanding and the buyer assumes the mortgage in addition to the cash payment, what is Kareem's realized gain or loss?
   c. If the buyer takes the property subject to the mortgage, rather than assuming it, what is Kareem's realized gain or loss?

31. Norm is negotiating the sale of a tract of his land to Pat. Use the following classification scheme to classify each of the items contained in the proposed sales contract:

Legend		
DARN	=	Decreases amount realized by Norm
IARN	=	Increases amount realized by Norm
DABN	=	Decreases adjusted basis to Norm
IABN	=	Increases adjusted basis to Norm
DABP	=	Decreases adjusted basis to Pat
IABP	=	Increases adjusted basis to Pat

   a. Norm is to receive cash of $50,000.
   b. Norm is to receive Pat's note payable for $25,000, payable in three years.
   c. Pat assumes Norm's mortgage of $5,000 on the land.
   d. Pat agrees to pay the realtor's sales commission of $8,000.
   e. Pat agrees to pay the property taxes on the land for the entire year. If each party paid his or her respective share, Norm's share would be $1,000, and Pat's share would be $3,000.
   f. Pat pays legal fees of $500.
   g. Norm pays legal fees of $750.

32. Gayla owns a building (adjusted basis of $375,000 on January 1, 2008) that she rents to Len who operates a restaurant in the building. The municipal health department closed the restaurant for two months during 2008 because of health code violations. Under MACRS, the cost recovery deduction for 2008 would be $24,000. However, Gayla deducted cost recovery only for the 10 months the restaurant was open since she waived the rent income during the two-month period the restaurant was closed.

a. What is the amount of the cost recovery deduction that Gayla should report on her 2008 income tax return?

b. Calculate the adjusted basis of the building at the end of 2008.

33. Melanie owns a personal use boat that has a fair market value of $32,500 and an adjusted basis of $45,000. Melanie's AGI is $90,000. Calculate the realized and recognized loss if:

a. Melanie sells the boat for $32,500.

b. Melanie exchanges the boat for another boat worth $32,500.

c. The boat is stolen and Melanie receives insurance proceeds of $32,500.

34. Alton owns stock in Dove Corporation. His adjusted basis for the stock is $85,000. During the year, he receives a distribution from the corporation of $65,000 that is labeled a return of capital (i.e., Dove has no earnings and profits).

a. Determine the tax consequences to Alton.

b. Assume instead that the amount of the distribution is $100,000. Determine the tax consequences to Alton.

c. Assume instead in (a) that the $65,000 distribution is labeled a taxable dividend (i.e., Dove has earnings and profits of at least $65,000).

35. Chee purchases Tan, Inc. bonds for $110,000 on January 2, 2008. The face value of the bonds is $100,000, the maturity date is December 31, 2012, and the annual interest rate is 8%. Chee will amortize the premium only if he is required to do so. Chee sells the bonds on July 1, 2010, for $109,000.

a. Determine the interest income Chee should report for 2008.

b. Calculate Chee's recognized gain or loss on the sale of the bonds in 2010.

36. Which of the following results in a recognized gain or loss?

a. Kay sells her vacation cabin (adjusted basis of $100,000) for $150,000.

b. Adam sells his personal residence (adjusted basis of $150,000) for $100,000.

c. Carl's personal residence (adjusted basis of $65,000) is condemned by the city. He receives condemnation proceeds of $55,000.

d. Olga's land is worth $40,000 at the end of the year. She had purchased the land six months earlier for $25,000.

e. Vera's personal vehicle (adjusted basis of $22,000) is stolen. She receives $23,000 from the insurance company and does not plan to replace the automobile.

f. Jerry sells used clothing (adjusted basis of $500) to a thrift store for $50.

37. Hubert's personal residence is condemned as part of an urban renewal project. His adjusted basis for the residence is $325,000. He receives condemnation proceeds of $300,000 and invests the proceeds in stock.

a. Calculate Hubert's realized and recognized gain or loss.

b. If the condemnation proceeds are $355,000, what are Hubert's realized and recognized gain or loss?

c. What are Hubert's realized and recognized gain or loss in (a) if the house was rental property?

Communications

38. Will Morris is a real estate agent for Presidential Estates, a residential real estate development. Because of his outstanding sales performance, Will is permitted to buy a lot that normally would sell for $350,000 for $305,000. Will is the only real estate agent for Presidential Estates who is permitted to do so.

a. Does Will have gross income from the transaction?

b. What is Will's adjusted basis for the land?

c. Write a letter to Will informing him of the tax consequences of his acquisition of the lot. His address is 100 Tower Road, San Diego, CA 92182.

39. Karen makes the following purchases and sales of stock:

Transaction	Date	Number of Shares	Company	Price per Share
Purchase	1–1–2006	300	MDG	$ 75
Purchase	6–1–2006	150	GRU	300
Purchase	11–1–2006	60	MDG	70
Sale	12–3–2006	180	MDG	70

Transaction	Date	Number of Shares	Company	Price per Share
Purchase	3–1–2007	120	GRU	375
Sale	8–1–2007	90	GRU	330
Sale	1–1–2008	150	MDG	90
Sale	2–1–2008	75	GRU	500

Assuming that Karen is unable to identify the particular lots that are sold with the original purchase, what is the recognized gain or loss on each type of stock as of the following dates:

a. 7–1–2006.
b. 12–31–2006.
c. 12–31–2007.
d. 7–1–2008.

40. Kevin purchases 1,000 shares of Bluebird Corporation stock on October 3, 2008, for $200,000. On December 12, 2008, Kevin purchases an additional 500 shares of Bluebird stock for $112,500. According to market quotations, Bluebird stock is selling for $240 per share on December 31, 2008. Kevin sells 400 shares of Bluebird stock on March 1, 2009, for $100,000.

a. What is the adjusted basis of Kevin's Bluebird stock on December 31, 2008?
b. What is Kevin's recognized gain or loss from the sale of Bluebird stock on March 1, 2009, assuming the shares sold are from the shares purchased on December 12, 2008?
c. What is Kevin's recognized gain or loss from the sale of Bluebird stock on March 1, 2009, assuming Kevin cannot adequately identify the shares sold?

41. Stella Simson purchases a business from Marco for $650,000. Marco paid a broker a sales commission of $30,000. The values assigned to the assets in the sales contract are as follows:

Communications

	Adjusted Basis	Fair Market Value
Production equipment	$ 62,000	$ 93,750
Packaging equipment	120,000	156,250
Distribution equipment	145,000	187,500
Building and land	100,000	125,000
Goodwill	–0–	62,500

a. What is Marco's recognized gain or loss?
b. What is Stella's adjusted basis for each of the assets?
c. Write a letter to Stella informing her of the tax consequences of the purchase. Her address is 300 Woodland Drive, Cincinnati, OH 45207.

42. Diane owns 1,000 shares of Robin, Inc. common stock with an adjusted basis of $100,000. During the year, she receives the following distributions associated with the stock:

- $3,000 taxable cash dividend in March.
- 2% stock dividend in the form of 20 shares of preferred stock in July. The fair market value of the common stock was $110,000, and the fair market value of the preferred stock was $2,000. Shareholders do not have the option to receive cash.
- 5% stock dividend in the form of 50 shares of common stock in November. The fair market value of the 1,000 shares of common stock was $115,000. Shareholders do not have the option to receive cash.

a. Determine the amount of gross income Diane must recognize.
b. Calculate Diane's adjusted basis for her 1,050 shares of common stock and her 20 shares of preferred stock.

43. Sherry owns 1,000 shares of Taupe Corporation stock with a basis of $15,000 and a fair market value of $20,000. She receives nontaxable stock rights to purchase additional shares. The rights have a fair market value of $2,000.

a. What are the basis of the stock and the basis of the stock rights?

b. What is the holding period for the stock rights?

c. What is the recognized gain or loss if the stock rights are sold for $2,000?

d. What is the recognized gain or loss if the stock rights are allowed to lapse?

44. Roberto has received various gifts over the years. He has decided to dispose of the following assets that he received as gifts:

a. In 1950, he received land worth $25,000. The donor's adjusted basis was $40,000. Roberto sells the land for $92,000 in 2008.

b. In 1955, he received stock in Gold Company. The donor's adjusted basis was $22,000. The fair market value on the date of the gift was $30,000. Roberto sells the stock for $40,000 in 2008.

c. In 1961, he received land worth $15,000. The donor's adjusted basis was $25,000. Roberto sells the land for $9,000 in 2008.

d. In 2002, he received stock worth $30,000. The donor's adjusted basis was $42,000. Roberto sells the stock for $35,000 in 2008.

What is the recognized gain or loss from each of the preceding transactions? Assume for each of the gift transactions that no gift tax was paid.

45. Beth receives a car from Sam as a gift. Sam paid $26,000 for the car. He had used it for business purposes and had deducted $12,000 for depreciation up to the time he gave the car to Beth. The fair market value of the car is $9,000.

a. Assuming Beth uses the car for business purposes, what is her basis for depreciation?

b. If the estimated useful life is two years (from the date of the gift), what is her depreciation deduction for each year? Assume Beth elects the straight-line method.

c. If Beth sells the car for $1,500 one year after receiving it, what is her gain or loss?

d. If Beth sells the car for $8,800 one year after receiving it, what is her gain or loss?

46. In 2008, Felix receives a gift of property with a fair market value of $111,000 (adjusted basis to the donor of $40,000). Assume the donor paid gift tax of $30,000 on the transfer.

a. What is Felix's basis for gain and loss and for depreciation?

b. If the gift occurred in 1975, what is Felix's basis for gain and loss and for depreciation?

47. Natalie receives an original Matisse painting as a gift from her aunt. At the date of the gift, the adjusted basis of the painting is $825,000, and its fair market value is $1,120,000. Her aunt paid gift tax of $392,000.

a. What is Natalie's adjusted basis in the painting?

b. If the fair market value of the painting at the date of the gift is $824,000 (not $1,120,000), what is Natalie's adjusted basis?

Decision Making

Communications

48. Ira Cook is planning to make a charitable contribution of Crystal, Inc. stock worth $20,000 to the Boy Scouts. The stock has an adjusted basis of $15,000. A friend has suggested that Ira sell the stock and contribute the $20,000 in proceeds rather than contribute the stock.

a. Should Ira follow the friend's advice? Why?

b. Assume the fair market value is only $13,000. In this case, should Ira follow the friend's advice? Why?

c. Rather than make a charitable contribution to the Boy Scouts, Ira is going to make a gift to Nancy, his niece. Advise Ira regarding (a) and (b).

d. Write a letter to Ira regarding whether in (a) he should sell the stock and contribute the cash or contribute the stock. He has informed you that he purchased the stock six years ago. Ira's address is 500 Ireland Avenue, De Kalb, IL 60115.

49. Catherine died in March 2008 leaving real estate (adjusted basis of $500,000) to her niece, Amanda. The fair market value of the real estate at the date of Catherine's death is $3,825,000. The executor of the estate does not distribute the real estate to Amanda until November 2008, when its fair market value is $3,813,000. The fair market value of the real estate six months after Catherine's death is $3,815,000.

a. What are the possibilities as to Amanda's adjusted basis in the real estate?

b. What purpose does the alternate valuation date serve?

c. Assume instead that the fair market value six months after Catherine's death is $3,860,000. What is Amanda's basis in the real estate?

50. The portion of Earl's estate distributed to Robert, one of Earl's beneficiaries, is valued as follows:

Asset	Earl's Adjusted Basis	FMV at Date of Death	FMV at Alternate Valuation Date
Cash	$10,000	$ 10,000	$ 10,000
Stock	40,000	125,000	60,000
Apartment building	60,000	300,000	325,000
Land	75,000	100,000	110,000

Although the fair market value of the stock six months after Earl's death turned out to be $60,000, the executor of the estate distributed it to Robert one month after Earl's death when it was worth $85,000. Determine Robert's basis for the assets if:

a. The primary valuation date applies.

b. The executor elects the alternate valuation date.

51. Emily makes a gift of 100 shares of appreciated stock to her uncle, George, on January 5, 2008. The basis of the stock is $3,150, and the fair market value is $5,250. George dies on October 8, 2008. During the period that George held the stock, he received a 5% nontaxable stock dividend. Under the provisions of George's will, Emily inherits 100 shares of the stock. The value of the stock for Federal estate tax purposes is $55 per share.

a. What is the basis of the inherited stock to Emily?

b. What would have been the basis of the inherited stock to Emily if she had given the stock to George on January 5, 2007?

52. Larry and Grace live in Arizona, a community property state. They own land (community property) that has an adjusted basis to them of $150,000. When Grace dies, Larry inherits her share of the land. At the date of Grace's death, the fair market value of the land is $200,000. Six months after Grace's death, the land is worth $220,000.

a. What is Larry's basis for the land?

b. What would Larry's basis for the land be if he and Grace lived in Kansas, a common law state, and Larry inherited Grace's share?

53. Jessie sold her business car (adjusted basis of $7,000; fair market value of $3,000) to Amy, her sister, for $3,000. Amy personally overhauled the engine with out-of-pocket costs of $2,000. She then sold the car to an unrelated party for $5,500.

a. What is Jessie's recognized gain or loss?

b. What is Amy's recognized gain or loss?

c. Assume instead that after overhauling the engine, Amy gives the car to Ted, her 21-year-old son. One week after receiving the car, Ted sells it for $5,500. What is Ted's recognized gain or loss?

54. TJ Partnership sells property (adjusted basis of $200,000) to Thad (a partner who owns a 60% capital and profits interest) for its fair market value of $165,000.

a. Calculate the realized and recognized loss to the partnership.

b. Calculate the basis of the property to Thad.

c. If Thad subsequently sells the property for $187,000, calculate his realized and recognized gain or loss.

d. If Thad gives the property to his daughter, Donna, who subsequently sells it for $187,000, calculate Donna's realized and recognized gain or loss. (Assume no gift tax is paid and the fair market value on the date of the gift is $180,000.)

e. Determine the tax consequences in (a) through (d) if Thad is a shareholder and TJ is a corporation.

55. Justin owns 1,000 shares of Oriole Corporation common stock (adjusted basis of $12,000). On April 27, 2008, he sells 400 of these shares for $4,000. On May 5, 2008, Justin purchases 300 shares of Oriole Corporation common stock for $3,300.

a. What is Justin's recognized gain or loss resulting from these transactions?

b. What is Justin's basis for the stock acquired on May 5?

Decision Making

c.   Could Justin have obtained different tax consequences in (a) and (b) if he had sold the 400 shares on December 27, 2008, and purchased the 300 shares on January 5, 2009?

Decision Making

56. Frank owns 1,000 shares of Amber, Inc. stock (adjusted basis of $10,000). On December 28, 2007, he sells 400 shares for $3,600. On January 19, 2008, he purchases 300 shares of Amber stock for $2,850.
a.   Calculate Frank's realized and recognized loss on the sale.
b.   Determine Frank's adjusted basis for the 300 shares purchased in 2008.
c.   Advise Frank on how he can avoid any negative tax consequences resulting in part (a).

57. Jeffrey leaves a public accounting firm to enter private practice. He had bought a home two years earlier for $300,000 (ignore land). When starting his business, he converts one-fourth of the home into an office. The fair market value of the home on the date of the conversion (January 1, 2003) is $350,000, while the adjusted basis remains at $300,000. Jeffrey lives and works in the home for six years and sells it at the end of the sixth year. He deducted $11,400 of cost recovery (using the statutory percentage method). How much gain or loss is recognized if Jeffrey sells the home for:
a. $280,000?
b. $400,000?

Decision Making

58. Surendra's personal residence originally cost $340,000 (ignore land). After living in the house for five years, he converts it to rental property. At the date of conversion, the fair market value of the house is $320,000. As to the rental property, calculate Surendra's basis for:
a.   Loss.
b.   Depreciation.
c.   Gain.
d.   Could Surendra have obtained better tax results if he had sold his personal residence for $320,000 and then purchased another house for $320,000 to hold as rental property?

Decision Making

59. Hun, age 93, has accumulated substantial assets during his life. Among his many assets are the following, which he is considering giving to Koji, his grandson.

Asset	Adjusted Basis	Fair Market Value
Red Corporation stock	$900,000	$700,000
Silver Corporation stock	70,000	71,000
Emerald Corporation stock	200,000	500,000

Hun has been in ill health for the past five years. His physician has informed him that he probably will not live for more than six months. Advise Hun on which of the stocks should be transferred as gifts and which as bequests.

CUMULATIVE PROBLEMS

Tax Return Problem

60. Albert Sims, age 67, is married and files a joint return with his wife, Carol, age 65. Albert and Carol are both retired, and during 2007, they received Social Security benefits of $10,000. Albert's Social Security number is 366–55–1111, and Carol's is 555–66–2222. They reside at 210 College Drive, Columbia, SC 29201.

Albert, who retired on January 1, 2007, receives benefits from a qualified pension plan of $800 a month for life. His total contributions to the plan (none of which were deductible) were $72,000. In January 2007, he received a bonus of $1,000 from his former employer for service performed in 2006. Although the former employer accrued the bonus in 2006, it was not paid until 2007.

Carol, who retired on December 31, 2006, started receiving benefits of $900 a month on January 1, 2007. Her contributions to the qualified pension plan (none of which were deductible) were $74,000.

Carol had casino winnings for the year of $5,500 and casino losses of $2,100 while Albert won $20,000 on a $1 lottery ticket.

On September 27, 2007, Albert and Carol received a 10% stock dividend on 60 shares of stock they owned. They had bought the stock on March 5, 2000, for $12 a share. On December 16, 2007, they sold the 6 dividend shares for $50 a share.

On October 10, 2007, Carol sold the car she had used in commuting to and from work for $12,000. She had paid $29,000 for the car in 2001.

On July 14, 1999, Albert and Carol received a gift of 800 shares of stock from their son, Thomas. Thomas's basis in the stock was $29 a share (fair market value at the date of gift was $25). No gift tax was paid on the transfer. Albert and Carol sold the stock on October 8, 2007, for $23 a share.

On May 1, 2007, Carol's mother died, and Carol inherited her personal residence. The residence had a fair market value of $210,000 and an adjusted basis to the mother of $160,000. Carol listed the house with a realtor who estimated it was worth $218,000 as of December 31, 2007.

Carol received rent income of $3,500 on a beach house she inherited three years ago from her Uncle Chuck. She had rented the property for one week during the July 4th weekend and one week during the Thanksgiving holidays. Uncle Chuck's adjusted basis in the beach house was $150,000, and its fair market value on the date of his death was $240,000. Carol and Albert used the beach house for personal purposes for 56 days during the year. Expenses associated with the house were $3,400 for utilities, maintenance, and repairs; $2,200 for property taxes; and $800 for insurance. There are no mortgages on the property.

Albert and Carol paid estimated Federal income tax of $3,100 and had itemized deductions of $6,600 (excluding any itemized deductions associated with the beach house and gambling). If they have overpaid their Federal income tax, they want the amount refunded. Both Albert and Carol wish to have $3 go to the Presidential Election Campaign Fund.

Compute their net tax payable or refund due for 2007. If you use tax forms for your computations, you will need Form 1040 and Schedule D. Suggested software: TaxCut.

61. John Custer, age 35, is single. His Social Security number is 443–11–2222, and he resides at 150 Highway 51, Tangipahoa, LA 70443.

Tax Computation Problem

Decision Making

Communications

John has a five-year-old child, Kendra, who lives with her mother, Katy. John pays alimony of $18,000 per year to Katy and child support of $12,000. The $12,000 of child support covers 70% of Katy's costs of rearing Kendra. Kendra's Social Security number is 432–60–1000, and Katy's is 444–00–1234. John expected to receive alimony of $12,000 during the year from his second wife, Debra. However, she died in November, and John received only $11,000.

John's mother, Sally, lived with him until her death in early September 2008. He incurred and paid medical expenses for her of $11,500 and other support payments of $9,000. Sally's only sources of income were $4,000 of interest income on certificates of deposit and $5,600 of Social Security benefits, which she spent on her medical expenses and helping to maintain John's household. Sally's Social Security number was 400–10–2000.

John is employed by the Highway Department of the State of Louisiana in an executive position. His salary is $90,000. The appropriate amounts of Social Security tax ($5,580) and Medicare tax ($1,305) were withheld. In addition, $12,000 was withheld for Federal income taxes, and $4,500 was withheld for state income taxes.

In addition to his salary, John's employer provides him with the following fringe benefits:

- Group term life insurance with a maturity value of $49,000. The cost of the premiums for the employer was $325.
- Group health insurance plan. John's employer paid premiums of $4,600 for his coverage. The plan paid $1,700 for John's medical expenses during the year.

Upon the death of his Aunt Josie in December 2007, John, her only recognized heir, inherited the following assets:

Asset	Josie's Adjusted Basis	FMV at Date of Death
Car	$ 22,000	$ 15,000
Land—300 acres	150,000	500,000
IBM stock	80,000	135,000
Cash	50,000	50,000

Six months prior to her death, Josie gave John a mountain cabin. Her adjusted basis for the mountain cabin was $270,000, and the fair market value was $350,000. She paid gift tax of $18,000.

During the year, John had the following transactions:

- On February 1, 2008, he sold for $45,000 Microsoft stock that he inherited from his father four years ago. His father's adjusted basis was $49,000, and the fair market value at the date of the father's death was $41,000.
- The car John inherited from Josie was destroyed in a wreck on October 1, 2008. He had loaned the car to Katy to use for a two-week period while the engine in her car was being replaced. Fortunately, neither Katy nor Kendra was injured. John received insurance proceeds of $12,500, the fair market value of the car on October 1.
- On October 30, 2008, John gambled away the $50,000 he inherited at a casino in Biloxi. He had hoped this activity would help with the bouts of depression he had been suffering since Sally's death.
- On December 28, 2008, John sold the 300 acres of land to his brother, James, for its fair market value of $475,000. James planned on using the land for his dairy farm.

Other sources of income for John were as follows:

Dividend income	$20,000
Interest income:	
Guaranty Bank	10,000
City of Kentwood water bonds	20,000
Award from State of Louisiana for outstanding	
suggestion for highway beautification	7,500

Potential itemized deductions for John, in addition to items already mentioned, were as follows:

Property taxes paid on his residence	$4,500
Property taxes paid on personalty	2,500
Estimated Federal income taxes paid	4,300
Estimated state income taxes paid	2,300
Charitable contributions	5,500
Mortgage interest on his residence	7,100
Orthodontic expenses for Kendra	4,000
Psychiatric expenses for John	3,500
Sales taxes paid	7,500

Part 1—Tax Computation
Compute John's net tax payable or refund due for 2008.

Part 2—Tax Planning
Assume that rather than selling the land to James, John is considering leasing it to him for $30,000 annually with the lease beginning on October 1, 2008. James would prepay the lease payments through December 31, 2008. Thereafter, he would make monthly lease payments at the beginning of each month. What effect would this have on John's

2008 tax liability? What potential problem might John encounter? Write a letter to John in which you advise him of the tax consequences of leasing versus selling. Also, prepare a memo for the tax files.

RESEARCH PROBLEMS

Note: Solutions to Research Problems can be prepared by using the **RIA Checkpoint**® **Student Edition** online research product, which is available to accompany this text. It is also possible to prepare solutions to the Research Problems by using tax research materials found in a standard tax library.

Research Problem 1. Mitchell died on April 13, 2005. The executor of his estate made the § 2032(a) election to use the alternate valuation date in filing Mitchell's estate tax return. Using the primary valuation date and amount, the estate assets would have been valued at $1.5 million. With the election, the estate assets were valued at $1.25 million.

A major asset of the estate consisted of shares of BFI Corporation. The shares of BFI were traded on an established securities market. Since the estate owned 2% of BFI's stock, the executor secured the services of a major brokerage firm to calculate the blockage discount on the BFI stock. Shortly before the estate tax return due date of January 13, 2006, the executor filed a Form 4768 (Application for Extension of Time To File a Return and/or Pay U.S. Estate Taxes) requesting an extension for filing to July 13, 2006. At this time, the estate paid estimated estate taxes of $400,000. In early June, a representative of the brokerage firm notified the executor that it would not be able to finish the valuation on time. Another firm was engaged, and it completed the valuation as of November 29, 2006. Mitchell's executor finally filed the return on January 19, 2008, and made the § 2032(a) election.

The IRS determined that a § 2032(a) election cannot be made unless the estate tax return is timely filed. A deficiency was assessed based on an asset valuation of $1.5 million rather than $1.25 million. Evaluate the position of the IRS.

Research Problem 2. Terry owns real estate with an adjusted basis of $600,000 and a fair market value of $1.1 million. The amount of the nonrecourse mortgage on the property is $2.5 million. Because of substantial past and projected future losses associated with the real estate development (occupancy rate of only 37% after three years), Terry deeds the property to the creditor.
a. What are the tax consequences to Terry?
b. Assume the data are the same, except the fair market value of the property is $2,525,000. Therefore, when Terry deeds the property to the creditor, she also receives $25,000 from the creditor. What are the tax consequences to Terry?

Research Problem 3. Abner gives stock worth $400,000 to Hattie. Abner's adjusted basis in the stock is $95,000, and the gift taxes generated as a result of the transfer are $122,400. As a condition for receiving the stock, Hattie agrees to pay the gift tax. The stock is transferred to Hattie on February 5, 2008.
a. What are the income tax consequences to Abner?
b. What are the income tax consequences to Abner if the gift was made on February 5, 1981?

Research Problem 4. Ruth Ames died on January 10, 2008. In filing the estate tax return, her executor, Melvin Sims, elects the primary valuation date and amount (fair market value on the date of death). On March 12, 2008, Melvin invests $30,000 of cash that Ruth had in her money market account in acquiring 1,000 shares of Orange, Inc. ($30 per share). On January 10, 2008, Orange was selling for $29 per share. The stock is distributed to a beneficiary, Annette Rust, on June 1, 2008, when it is selling for $33 per share. Melvin wants you to determine the amount at which the Orange shares should appear on the estate tax return and the amount of Annette's adjusted basis for the stock. Write a letter to Melvin in which you respond to his inquiry and prepare a memo for the tax files. His address is 100 Center Lane, Miami, FL 32124.

Communications

Research Problem 5.   Amanda purchased the following lots of stock of Pearl, Inc. (a pharmaceutical company) during 2005:

Date	Number of Shares	Cost per Share
February 1	100	$150
July 25	100	140
November 3	100	130

On December 20, 2007, Amanda sold the 300 shares for $145 each.

In early January 2008, the Food and Drug Administration granted approval for a new drug developed by Pearl. Expecting the stock to continue to increase in value, Amanda purchased 300 shares on January 5, 2008, for $175 per share.

Amanda calculated her recognized gain as $1,500 ($43,500 amount realized − $42,000 adjusted basis). The IRS contends that the transaction must be treated as the sale of three lots of stock because of the wash sale rules. As a result, the $500 realized gain on the sale of the second lot and the $1,500 realized gain on the sale of the third lot must be recognized, and the $500 realized loss on the sale of the first lot is disallowed under § 1091.

Who is correct?

Research Problem 6.   Cecelia owned 30% of the stock of Lime, Inc., a family corporation. Her basis for the stock was $280,000. As a result of a dispute with the majority shareholder regarding a projected expansion of the company, the corporation redeemed her stock for $900,000. Cecelia received $300,000 in cash plus a $600,000 interest-bearing promissory note. Cecelia had been the vice president of Lime, but after the redemption, she was no longer employed by the corporation.

The contract describing the stock redemption and the termination of employment included a three-year covenant not to compete by Cecelia in the citrus industry in Florida. The contract did not allocate any of the purchase price to the covenant. Cecelia was well known in the industry, highly respected among her associates, and had many business contacts.

The promissory note was payable in three installments over a three-year period. The note contained a provision that any breach of the covenant not to compete could result in a right of offset. This meant that future payments on the note could be offset against any damages caused by Cecelia's breach of the covenant.

Six months after the stock redemption, Cecelia's CPA informed her that there would have been tax benefits to Lime if part of the payment to her had been allocated to the covenant (i.e., § 197 amortization treatment). Otherwise, no deduction results when a corporation redeems its stock. Therefore, if Cecelia would renegotiate the agreement and accept such an allocation, she would receive additional payments or a reduction in the three-year noncompete period. Although meetings were held, no modification of the original agreement was made.

Cecelia reported all of the $900,000 of payments received as the amount realized from the stock redemption (i.e., eligible for the beneficial capital gains tax rate of 15%). Lime treated $400,000 of the payments as a § 197 intangible for the covenant and amortized it under § 197.

Not wishing to be whipsawed by these inconsistent positions, the IRS levied assessments against *both* Cecelia and Lime. For Cecelia, it disallowed part of her capital gain and treated it as ordinary income (i.e., proceeds from a covenant not to compete). For Lime, it disallowed the § 197 deduction and classified the payments as a nondeductible redemption of stock. Which party should prevail?

Internet Activity

Use the tax resources of the Internet to address the following question. Do not restrict your search to the World Wide Web, but include a review of newsgroups and general reference materials, practitioner sites and resources, primary sources of the tax law, chat rooms and discussion groups, and other opportunities.

Research Problem 7.   Many see the "step-up in basis at death" rule of § 1014 as an expensive tax loophole enjoyed by the wealthy. Find the latest estimates of the revenue loss to the Treasury that is attributable to this rule.

CHAPTER 15

Property Transactions: Nontaxable Exchanges

LEARNING OBJECTIVES

After completing Chapter 15, you should be able to:

LO.1
Understand the rationale for nonrecognition (postponement) of gain or loss in certain property transactions.

LO.2
Apply the nonrecognition provisions and basis determination rules for like-kind exchanges.

LO.3
Explain the nonrecognition provisions available on the involuntary conversion of property.

LO.4
Describe the provision for the permanent exclusion of gain on the sale of a personal residence.

LO.5
Identify other nonrecognition provisions contained in the Code.

LO.6
Identify tax planning opportunities related to the nonrecognition provisions discussed in the chapter.

OUTLINE

General Concept of a Nontaxable Exchange, 15–2
Like-Kind Exchanges—§ 1031, 15–3
  Like-Kind Property, 15–3
  Exchange Requirement, 15–6
  Boot, 15–7
  Basis and Holding Period of Property Received, 15–8
  Reporting Considerations, 15–11
Involuntary Conversions—§ 1033, 15–11
  Involuntary Conversion Defined, 15–11
  Computing the Amount Realized, 15–12
  Replacement Property, 15–12
  Time Limitation on Replacement, 15–13
  Nonrecognition of Gain, 15–14
  Involuntary Conversion of a Personal Residence, 15–15
  Reporting Considerations, 15–16
Sale of a Residence—§ 121, 15–16
  Requirements for Exclusion Treatment, 15–16
  Exceptions to the Two-Year Ownership Rule, 15–17
  Calculation of the Amount of the Exclusion, 15–19

  Principal Residence, 15–22
  Involuntary Conversion and Using §§ 121 and 1033, 15–22
Other Nonrecognition Provisions, 15–23
  Exchange of Stock for Property—§ 1032, 15–23
  Certain Exchanges of Insurance Policies—§ 1035, 15–23
  Exchange of Stock for Stock of the Same
    Corporation—§ 1036, 15–23
  Certain Reacquisitions of Real Property—§ 1038, 15–23
  Transfers of Property between Spouses or Incident
    to Divorce—§ 1041, 15–23
  Rollovers into Specialized Small Business Investment
    Companies—§ 1044, 15–24
  Rollover of Gain from Qualified Small Business Stock into
    Another Qualified Small Business Stock—§ 1045, 15–24
Tax Planning Considerations, 15–24
  Like-Kind Exchanges, 15–24
  Involuntary Conversions, 15–25
  Sale of a Principal Residence, 15–25

LO.1

Understand the rationale for nonrecognition (postponement) of gain or loss in certain property transactions.

General Concept of a Nontaxable Exchange

A taxpayer who is going to replace a productive asset (e.g., machinery) used in a trade or business may structure the transactions as a sale of the old asset and the purchase of a new asset. When this approach is used, any realized gain or loss on the asset sale is recognized. The basis of the new asset is its cost. Alternatively, the taxpayer may be able to trade the old asset for the new asset. This exchange of assets may produce beneficial tax consequences by qualifying for nontaxable exchange treatment.

The tax law recognizes that nontaxable exchanges result in a change in the *form* but not in the *substance* of the taxpayer's relative economic position. The replacement property received in the exchange is viewed as substantially a continuation of the old investment.[1] Additional justification for nontaxable exchange treatment is that this type of transaction does not provide the taxpayer with the wherewithal to pay the tax on any realized gain.

The nonrecognition provisions for nontaxable exchanges do not apply to realized losses from the sale or exchange of personal use assets. Such losses are not recognized (are disallowed) because they are personal in nature and not because of any nonrecognition provision.

In a **nontaxable exchange**, realized gains or losses are not recognized. However, the nonrecognition is usually temporary. The recognition of gain or loss is *postponed* (deferred) until the property received in the nontaxable exchange is subsequently disposed of in a taxable transaction. This is accomplished by assigning a carryover basis to the replacement property.

EXAMPLE 1

Debra exchanges property with an adjusted basis of $10,000 and a fair market value of $12,000 for property with a fair market value of $12,000. The transaction qualifies for nontaxable exchange treatment. Debra has a realized gain of $2,000 ($12,000 amount realized − $10,000 adjusted basis). Her recognized gain is $0. Her basis in the replacement property is a

---

[1]Reg. § 1.1002–1(c).

carryover basis of $10,000. Assume the replacement property is nondepreciable and Debra subsequently sells it for $12,000. Her realized and recognized gain will be the $2,000 gain that was postponed (deferred) in the nontaxable transaction. If the replacement property is depreciable, the carryover basis of $10,000 is used in calculating depreciation. ∎

In some nontaxable exchanges, only part of the property involved in the transaction qualifies for nonrecognition treatment. If the taxpayer receives cash or other nonqualifying property, part or all of the realized gain from the exchange is recognized. In these instances, gain is recognized because the taxpayer has changed or improved his or her relative economic position and has the wherewithal to pay income tax to the extent of cash or other property received.

It is important to distinguish between a nontaxable disposition, as the term is used in the statute, and a tax-free transaction. First, a direct exchange is not required in all circumstances (e.g., replacement of involuntarily converted property). Second, as previously mentioned, the term *nontaxable* refers to postponement of recognition via a carryover basis. In a *tax-free* transaction, the nonrecognition is permanent (e.g., see the discussion later in the chapter of the § 121 exclusion of realized gain on the sale of a personal residence). Therefore, the basis of any property acquired in a tax-free transaction does not depend on the basis of the property disposed of by the taxpayer.

Like-Kind Exchanges—§ 1031

LO.2

Apply the nonrecognition provisions and basis determination rules for like-kind exchanges.

Section 1031 provides for nontaxable exchange treatment if the following requirements are satisfied:[2]

- The form of the transaction is an exchange.
- Both the property transferred and the property received are held either for productive use in a trade or business or for investment.
- The property is like-kind property.

Like-kind exchanges include business for business, business for investment, investment for business, or investment for investment property. Property held for personal use, inventory, and partnership interests (both limited and general) do not qualify under the like-kind exchange provisions. Securities, even though held for investment, do not qualify for like-kind exchange treatment.

The nonrecognition provision for like-kind exchanges is *mandatory* rather than elective. A taxpayer who wants to recognize a realized gain or loss will have to structure the transaction in a form that does not satisfy the statutory requirements for a like-kind exchange. This topic is discussed further under Tax Planning Considerations.

Like-Kind Property

"The words 'like-kind' refer to the nature or character of the property and not to its grade or quality. One kind or class of property may not . . . be exchanged for property of a different kind or class."[3]

The term *like-kind* is intended to be interpreted very broadly. However, three categories of exchanges are not included. First, livestock of different sexes do not qualify as like-kind property. Second, real estate can be exchanged only for other real estate, and personalty can be exchanged only for other personalty. For example, the exchange of a machine (personalty) for an office building (realty) is not a like-kind exchange. *Real estate* (or realty) includes principally rental buildings, office and store buildings, manufacturing plants, warehouses, and land. It is immaterial whether real estate is improved or unimproved. Thus, unimproved land can be exchanged for an apartment house. Personalty includes principally machines,

---

[2]§ 1031(a) and Reg. § 1.1031(a)–1(a).   [3]Reg. § 1.1031(a)–1(b).

equipment, trucks, automobiles, furniture, and fixtures. Third, real property located in the United States exchanged for foreign real property (and vice versa) does not qualify as like-kind property.

EXAMPLE 2

Wade made the following exchanges during the taxable year:

a.   Inventory for a machine used in business.
b.   Land held for investment for a building used in business.
c.   Stock held for investment for equipment used in business.
d.   A business truck for a business truck.
e.   An automobile used for personal transportation for an automobile used in business.
f.   Livestock for livestock of a different sex.
g.   Land held for investment in New York for land held for investment in London.

Exchanges (b), investment real property for business real property, and (d), business personalty for business personalty, qualify as exchanges of like-kind property. Exchanges (a), inventory; (c), stock; (e), personal use automobile (not held for business or investment purposes); (f), livestock of different sexes; and (g), U.S. and foreign real estate do not qualify. ■

A special provision relates to the location where personal property is used. Personal property used predominantly within the United States and personal property used predominantly outside the United States are not like-kind property. The location of use for the personal property given up is its location during the two-year period ending on the date of disposition of the property. The location of use for the personal property received is its location during the two-year period beginning on the date of the acquisition.

EXAMPLE 3

In October 2007, Walter exchanges a machine used in his factory in Denver for a machine that qualifies as like-kind property. In January 2008, the factory, including the machine, is moved to Berlin, Germany. As of January 2008, the exchange is not an exchange of like-kind property. The predominant use of the original machine was in the United States, whereas the predominant use of the new machine is foreign. ■

Another special provision applies if the taxpayers involved in the exchange are *related parties* under § 267(b). To qualify for like-kind exchange treatment, the taxpayer and the related party must not dispose of the like-kind property received in the exchange within the two-year period following the date of the exchange. If such an early disposition does occur, the postponed gain is recognized as of the date of the early disposition. Dispositions due to death, involuntary conversions, and certain non-tax avoidance transactions are not treated as early dispositions.

ETHICAL and EQUITABLE *Considerations*

AN ASSUMPTION FOR A RELATED-PARTY EXCHANGE

Marcie owns a 10 percent interest in a shopping mall located in Portland, Maine. Her adjusted basis for her interest is $250,000, and its fair market value is $900,000. She exchanges it for undeveloped land in York, Pennsylvania, that is held by her sister, Sandra. Marcie is aware of the § 1031 related-party requirement that neither she nor Sandra dispose of the property received for a two-year period. Both Marcie and Sandra intend to hold the property as long-term investments. However, they agree to notify each other if a disposition does take place within two years of the exchange.

During the next six months, the land that Marcie received in the exchange continues to appreciate. Due to poor management, however, the value of Sandra's interest in the shopping mall declines to $700,000. As a result, Sandra is angry with Marcie and vows "never to speak to Marcie, her husband, or any of Marcie's children again."

As Marcie receives no communication from Sandra during the next 18 months, she assumes that her gain of $650,000 will continue to be deferred. Evaluate Marcie's assumption.

Regulations dealing with § 1031 like-kind exchange treatment provide that if the exchange transaction involves multiple assets of a business (e.g., a television station for another television station), the determination of whether the assets qualify as like-kind property will not be made at the business level.[4] Instead, the underlying assets must be evaluated.

The Regulations also provide for greater specificity in determining whether depreciable tangible personal property is of a like kind or class. Such property held for productive use in a business is of a like class only if the exchanged property is within the same *general business asset class* (as specified by the IRS in Revenue Procedure 87–57 or as subsequently modified) or the same *product class* (as specified by the Department of Commerce). Property included in a general business asset class is evaluated under this system rather than under the product class system.

The following are examples of general business asset classes:

- Office furniture, fixtures, and equipment.
- Information systems (computers and peripheral equipment).
- Airplanes.
- Automobiles and taxis.
- Buses.
- Light general-purpose trucks.
- Heavy general-purpose trucks.

These Regulations have made it more difficult for depreciable tangible personal property to qualify for § 1031 like-kind exchange treatment. For example, the exchange of office equipment for a computer does not qualify as an exchange of like-kind property. Even though both assets are depreciable tangible personal

---

[4]Reg. § 1.1031(j)–1.

TAX *in the News*   DOING A LIKE-KIND EXCHANGE TWICE

Section 1031 provides for tax-deferred treatment on the exchange of investment or productive use real estate. For this purpose, the definition of like-kind property is very broad. Almost any type of real estate qualifies.

However, there are several constraints, one of which involves related parties. If the two taxpayers involved in the exchange transaction are related parties, a two-year holding period requirement must be met. That is, if either party disposes of the like-kind property received within the two-year

period following the date of the exchange, the tax deferral ends. But does a "disposal" take place if a party engages in another like-kind exchange of the property?

A recent IRS ruling answers this question and amplifies the definition of "disposal." Another like-kind exchange of the property received within the two-year period is not regarded as a disposal and, therefore, will not terminate the deferral period.

---

property, they are not like-kind property because they are in different general business asset classes.

Exchange Requirement

The transaction must involve a direct exchange of property to qualify as a like-kind exchange. The sale of old property and the purchase of new property, even though like kind, is generally not an exchange. However, if the two transactions are mutually dependent, the IRS may treat them as a like-kind exchange. For example, if the taxpayer sells an old business machine to a dealer and purchases a new one from the same dealer, like-kind exchange treatment could result.[5]

The taxpayer may want to avoid nontaxable exchange treatment. Recognition of gain gives the taxpayer a higher basis for depreciation (see Example 33). To the extent that such gains would, if recognized, either receive favorable capital gain treatment or be passive activity income that could offset passive activity losses, it might be preferable to avoid the nonrecognition provisions through an indirect exchange transaction. For example, a taxpayer may sell property to one individual, recognize the gain, and subsequently purchase similar property from another individual. The taxpayer may also want to avoid nontaxable exchange treatment so that a realized loss can be recognized.

If the exchange is a delayed (nonsimultaneous) exchange, there are time limits on its completion. In a delayed like-kind exchange, one party fails to take immediate title to the new property because it has not yet been identified. The Code provides that the delayed swap will qualify as a like-kind exchange if the following requirements are satisfied:

- *Identification period.* The new property must be identified within 45 days of the date when the old property was transferred.
- *Exchange period.* The new property must be received by the earlier of the following:
  - Within 180 days of the date when the old property was transferred.
  - The due date (including extensions) for the tax return covering the year of the transfer.

Are these time limits firm, or can they be extended due to unforeseen circumstances? Indications are that the IRS will allow no deviation from either the identification period or the exchange period even when events outside the taxpayer's control preclude strict compliance.

---

[5]Rev.Rul. 61–119, 1961–1 C.B. 395.

TAX *in the News*   BE CAREFUL WHEN SELECTING A QUALIFIED INTERMEDIARY

In order to receive tax-deferred treatment in a nonsimultaneous § 1031 like-kind exchange, a qualified intermediary (QI) must be used. A nonsimultaneous § 1031 like-kind exchange occurs when one of the parties transfers qualified property to the other party but has not yet identified the property to be received in exchange. Such a taxpayer generally has 45 days to identify the property and 180 days to complete the transaction.

In effect, the QI serves as a middleman. The taxpayer who has transferred the title to his or her property must not have access to the cash transferred to acquire the like-kind property. Unfortunately, this part of the real estate industry is lightly regulated at best. Many QIs are banks or title insurance companies, but some are independent businesses that

charge for performing this function. During the period the QI holds the funds, there is little or no restriction on their use. Often the QIs attempt to profit from the spread between the amount they can earn on investments and the interest paid to clients.

In several recent and very visible cases, independent QIs became overly speculative with the funds they were holding for clients. The result was bankruptcy for the QIs and multimillion dollar losses for the clients.

Therefore, when engaging in a nonsimultaneous § 1031 like-kind exchange, the taxpayer should be careful in choosing a QI. Even better, require the QI to place the funds with a reputable escrow agent or an independent trustee.

Source: *Adapted from Peter Lattman and Kemba Dunham, "Tax Strategy for Real Estate Hits Rocky Turf," Wall Street Journal, May 26, 2007, p. B1.*

ETHICAL and EQUITABLE *Considerations*   A DELAYED § 1031 LIKE-KIND EXCHANGE: IDENTIFYING MORE THAN ONE PROPERTY

Roy owns an office building (adjusted basis of $250,000) that he has been renting to a group of physicians. Due to conflicts over repairs, maintenance, and rent increases, the physicians offer to purchase the building for $700,000. Roy accepts the offer with the stipulation that the sale be structured in part as a delayed § 1031 transaction. Consequently, the sales proceeds are paid to a qualified third-party intermediary on the closing date of September 30, 2008.

On October 2, 2008, Roy properly identifies an office building that he would like to acquire. Unfortunately, on

November 10, 2008, the property selected is withdrawn from the market. On the same day, however, Roy identifies another office building. The purchase of this property closes on December 15, 2008, and the title is transferred to Roy.

Roy treats the transaction as a § 1031 like-kind exchange. Even though the original office building identified was not acquired, Roy concludes that in substance he has satisfied the 45-day rule. He identified the acquired office building as soon as the negotiations ceased on his first choice. Should the IRS accept Roy's attempt to comply?

Boot

If the taxpayer in a like-kind exchange gives or receives some property that is not like-kind property, recognition may occur. Property that is not like-kind property, including cash, is referred to as **boot**. Although the term *boot* does not appear in the Code, tax practitioners commonly use it rather than saying "property that is not like-kind property."

The *receipt* of boot will trigger recognition of gain if there is realized gain. The amount of the recognized gain is the *lesser* of the boot received or the realized gain (realized gain serves as the ceiling on recognition).

EXAMPLE 4

Emily and Fran exchange machinery, and the exchange qualifies as like kind under § 1031. Since Emily's machinery (adjusted basis of $20,000) is worth $24,000 and Fran's machine has a fair market value of $19,000, Fran also gives Emily cash of $5,000. Emily's recognized gain is $4,000, the lesser of the realized gain ($24,000 amount realized − $20,000 adjusted basis = $4,000) or the fair market value of the boot received ($5,000). ∎

EXAMPLE 5

Assume the same facts as in the previous example, except that Fran's machine is worth $21,000 (not $19,000). Under these circumstances, Fran gives Emily cash of $3,000 to make up the difference. Emily's recognized gain is $3,000, the lesser of the realized gain of $4,000 ($24,000 amount realized − $20,000 adjusted basis) or the fair market value of the boot received of $3,000. ∎

The receipt of boot does not result in recognition if there is realized loss.

EXAMPLE 6

Assume the same facts as in Example 4, except that the adjusted basis of Emily's machine is $30,000. Emily's realized loss is $6,000 ($24,000 amount realized − $30,000 adjusted basis). The receipt of the boot of $5,000 does not trigger recognition. Therefore, the recognized loss is $0. ∎

The *giving* of boot usually does not trigger recognition. If the boot given is cash, no realized gain or loss is recognized.

EXAMPLE 7

Fred and Gary exchange equipment in a like-kind exchange. Fred receives equipment with a fair market value of $25,000 and transfers equipment worth $21,000 (adjusted basis of $15,000) and cash of $4,000. Fred's realized gain is $6,000 ($25,000 amount realized − $15,000 adjusted basis − $4,000 cash). However, none of the realized gain is recognized. ∎

If, however, the boot given is appreciated or depreciated property, gain or loss is recognized to the extent of the difference between the adjusted basis and the fair market value of the boot. For this purpose, *appreciated or depreciated property* is defined as property whose adjusted basis is not equal to the fair market value.

EXAMPLE 8

Assume the same facts as in the previous example, except that Fred transfers equipment worth $10,000 (adjusted basis of $12,000) and boot worth $15,000 (adjusted basis of $9,000). Fred's realized gain appears to be $4,000 ($25,000 amount realized − $21,000 adjusted basis). Since realization previously has served as a ceiling on recognition, it appears that the recognized gain is $4,000 (lower of realized gain of $4,000 or amount of appreciation on boot of $6,000). However, the recognized gain actually is $6,000 (full amount of the appreciation on the boot). In effect, Fred must calculate the like-kind and boot parts of the transaction separately. That is, the realized loss of $2,000 on the like-kind property is not recognized ($10,000 fair market value − $12,000 adjusted basis), and the $6,000 realized gain on the boot is recognized ($15,000 fair market value − $9,000 adjusted basis). ∎

Basis and Holding Period of Property Received

If an exchange does not qualify as nontaxable under § 1031, gain or loss is recognized, and the basis of property received in the exchange is the property's fair market value. If the exchange qualifies for nonrecognition, the basis of property received must be adjusted to reflect any postponed (deferred) gain or loss. The *basis of like-kind property* received in the exchange is the property's fair market value less postponed gain or plus postponed loss. If the exchange partially qualifies for nonrecognition (if recognition is associated with boot), the basis of like-kind property received in the exchange is the property's fair market value less postponed gain or plus postponed loss. The *basis* of any *boot* received is the boot's fair market value.

If there is a postponed loss, nonrecognition creates a situation in which the taxpayer has recovered *less* than the cost or other basis of the property exchanged in an amount equal to the unrecognized loss. If there is a postponed gain, the taxpayer has recovered *more* than the cost or other basis of the property exchanged in an amount equal to the unrecognized gain.

EXAMPLE 9

Jaime exchanges a building (used in his business) with an adjusted basis of $30,000 and a fair market value of $38,000 for land with a fair market value of $38,000. The land is to be held as an investment. The exchange qualifies as like kind (an exchange of business real property for investment real property). Thus, the basis of the land is $30,000 (the land's fair market value of $38,000 less the $8,000 postponed gain on the building). If the land is later sold for its fair market value of $38,000, the $8,000 postponed gain is recognized. ∎

EXAMPLE 10

Assume the same facts as in the previous example, except that the building has an adjusted basis of $48,000 and a fair market value of only $38,000. The basis in the newly acquired land is $48,000 (fair market value of $38,000 plus the $10,000 postponed loss on the building). If the land is later sold for its fair market value of $38,000, the $10,000 postponed loss is recognized. ∎

The Code provides an alternative approach for determining the basis of like-kind property received:

> Adjusted basis of like-kind property surrendered
> + Adjusted basis of boot given
> + Gain recognized
> − Fair market value of boot received
> − Loss recognized
> = *Basis of like-kind property received*

This approach is logical in terms of the recovery of capital doctrine. That is, the unrecovered cost or other basis is increased by additional cost (boot given) or decreased by cost recovered (boot received). Any gain recognized is included in the basis of the new property. The taxpayer has been taxed on this amount and is now entitled to recover it tax-free. Any loss recognized is deducted from the basis of the new property. The taxpayer has received a tax benefit on that amount.

The holding period of the property surrendered in the exchange carries over and *tacks on* to the holding period of the like-kind property received.[6] The holding period for boot received in a like-kind exchange begins with the date of the exchange. See Chapter 16 for a discussion of the relevance of the holding period.

Depreciation recapture potential carries over to the property received in a like-kind exchange.[7] See Chapter 17 for a discussion of this topic.

The following comprehensive example illustrates the like-kind exchange rules.

EXAMPLE 11

Vicki exchanged the following old machines for new machines in five independent like-kind exchanges:

Exchange	Adjusted Basis of Old Machine	Fair Market Value of New Machine	Adjusted Basis of Boot Given	Fair Market Value of Boot Received
1	$4,000	$9,000	$ –0–	$ –0–
2	4,000	9,000	3,000	–0–
3	4,000	9,000	6,000	–0–
4	4,000	9,000	–0–	3,000
5	4,000	3,500	–0–	300

---

[6]§ 1223(1) and Reg. § 1.1223–1(a). For this carryover holding period rule to apply to like-kind exchanges after March 1, 1954, the like-kind property surrendered must have been either a capital asset or § 1231 property. See Chapters 16 and 17 for the discussion of capital assets and § 1231 property.

[7]Reg. §§ 1.1245–2(a)(4) and 1.1250–2(d)(1).

Vicki's realized and recognized gains and losses and the basis of each of the like-kind properties received are as follows:

			New Basis Calculation									
Exchange	Realized Gain (Loss)	Recognized Gain (Loss)	Old Adj. Basis	+	Boot Given	+	Gain Recognized	–	Boot Received	=	New Basis
1	$ 5,000	$ –(0)–	$4,000	+	$ –0–	+	$ –0–	–	$ –0–	=	$ 4,000*
2	2,000	–(0)–	4,000	+	3,000	+	–0–	–	–0–	=	7,000*
3	(1,000)	–(0)–	4,000	+	6,000	+	–0–	–	–0–	=	10,000**
4	8,000	3,000	4,000	+	–0–	+	3,000	–	3,000	=	4,000*
5	(200)	–(0)–	4,000	+	–0–	+	–0–	–	300	=	3,700**

*Basis may be determined in gain situations under the alternative method by subtracting the gain not recognized from the fair market value of the new property:

$9,000 – $5,000 = $4,000 for exchange 1.
$9,000 – $2,000 = $7,000 for exchange 2.
$9,000 – $5,000 = $4,000 for exchange 4.

**In loss situations, basis may be determined by adding the loss not recognized to the fair market value of the new property:

$9,000 + $1,000 = $10,000 for exchange 3.
$3,500 + $200 = $3,700 for exchange 5.
The basis of the boot received is the boot's fair market value. ∎

If the taxpayer either assumes a liability or takes property subject to a liability, the amount of the liability is treated as boot given. For the taxpayer whose liability is assumed or whose property is taken subject to the liability, the amount of the liability is treated as boot received. Example 12 illustrates the effect of such a liability. In addition, the example illustrates the tax consequences for both parties involved in the like-kind exchange.

EXAMPLE 12

Jane and Leo exchange real estate investments. Jane gives up property with an adjusted basis of $250,000 (fair market value of $400,000) that is subject to a mortgage of $75,000 (assumed by Leo). In return for this property, Jane receives property with a fair market value of $300,000 (adjusted basis of $200,000) and cash of $25,000.

- Jane's realized gain is $150,000. She gave up property with an adjusted basis of $250,000. Jane received $400,000 from the exchange ($300,000 fair market value of like-kind property plus $100,000 boot received). The boot received consists of the $25,000 cash received from Leo and Jane's mortgage of $75,000, which Leo assumes.
- Jane's recognized gain is $100,000. The realized gain of $150,000 is recognized to the extent of boot received.
- Jane's basis in the real estate received from Leo is $250,000. This basis can be computed by subtracting the postponed gain ($50,000) from the fair market value of the real estate received ($300,000). It can also be computed by adding the recognized gain ($100,000) to the adjusted basis of the real estate given up ($250,000) and subtracting the boot received ($100,000).
- Leo's realized gain is $100,000. Leo gave up property with an adjusted basis of $200,000 plus boot of $100,000 ($75,000 mortgage assumed + $25,000 cash) or a total of $300,000. Leo received $400,000 from the exchange (fair market value of like-kind property received).
- Leo has no recognized gain because he did not receive any boot. The entire realized gain of $100,000 is postponed.

- Leo's basis in the real estate received from Jane is $300,000. This basis can be computed by subtracting the postponed gain ($100,000) from the fair market value of the real estate received ($400,000). It can also be computed by adding the boot given ($75,000 mortgage assumed by Leo + $25,000 cash) to the adjusted basis of the real estate given up ($200,000).[8] ∎

Reporting Considerations

Section 1031 transactions are reported on Form 8824 (Like-Kind Exchanges). This form should be used even though the like-kind exchange transaction results in no recognized gain or loss. It must be filed with the regular return for the tax year in which the taxpayer transfers property in a like-kind exchange.

If the like-kind exchange is with a related party, additional Forms 8824 must be filed for the following two years.

Involuntary Conversions—§ 1033

LO.3

Explain the nonrecognition provisions available on the involuntary conversion of property.

Section 1033 provides that a taxpayer who suffers an involuntary conversion of property may postpone recognition of *gain* realized from the conversion. The objective of this provision is to provide relief to the taxpayer who has suffered hardship and does not have the wherewithal to pay the tax on any gain realized from the conversion. Postponement of realized gain is permitted to the extent that the taxpayer *reinvests* the amount realized from the conversion in replacement property. The rules for nonrecognition of gain are as follows:

- If the amount reinvested in replacement property *equals or exceeds* the amount realized, realized gain is *not recognized.*
- If the amount reinvested in replacement property is *less than* the amount realized, realized gain *is recognized* to the extent of the deficiency.

If a *loss* occurs on an involuntary conversion, § 1033 does not modify the normal rules for loss recognition. That is, if a realized loss would otherwise be recognized, § 1033 does not change the result.

Involuntary Conversion Defined

An **involuntary conversion** results from the destruction (complete or partial), theft, seizure, requisition or condemnation, or sale or exchange under threat or imminence of requisition or condemnation of the taxpayer's property.[9] To prove the existence of a threat or imminence of condemnation, the taxpayer must obtain confirmation that there has been a decision to acquire the property for public use. In addition, the taxpayer must have reasonable grounds to believe the property will be taken.[10] The property does not have to be sold to the authority threatening to condemn it to qualify for § 1033 postponement. If the taxpayer satisfies the confirmation and reasonable grounds requirements, he or she can sell the property to another party.[11] Likewise, the sale of property to a condemning authority by a taxpayer who acquired the property from its former owner with the knowledge that the property was under threat of condemnation also qualifies as an involuntary conversion under § 1033.[12] A voluntary act, such as a taxpayer destroying the property by arson, is not an involuntary conversion.[13]

[8]Example (2) of Reg. § 1.1031(d)–2 illustrates a special situation in which both the buyer and the seller transfer liabilities that are assumed by the other party or both parties acquire property that is subject to a liability.
[9]§ 1033(a) and Reg. §§ 1.1033(a)–1(a) and –2(a).
[10]Rev.Rul. 63–221, 1963–2 C.B. 332, and *Joseph P. Balistrieri*, 38 TCM 526, T.C.Memo. 1979–115.
[11]Rev.Rul. 81–180, 1981–2 C.B. 161.
[12]Rev.Rul. 81–181, 1981–2 C.B. 162.
[13]Rev.Rul. 82–74, 1982–1 C.B. 110.

Computing the Amount Realized

The amount realized from the condemnation of property usually includes only the amount received as compensation for the property.[14] Any amount received that is designated as severance damages by both the government and the taxpayer is not included in the amount realized. *Severance awards* usually occur when only a portion of the property is condemned (e.g., a strip of land is taken to build a highway). Severance damages are awarded because the value of the taxpayer's remaining property has declined as a result of the condemnation. Such damages reduce the basis of the property. However, if either of the following requirements is satisfied, the nonrecognition provision of § 1033 applies to the severance damages:

- The severance damages are used to restore the usability of the remaining property.
- The usefulness of the remaining property is destroyed by the condemnation, and the property is sold and replaced at a cost equal to or exceeding the sum of the condemnation award, severance damages, and sales proceeds.

E X A M P L E 13	The government condemns a portion of Ron's farmland to build part of an interstate highway. Because the highway denies his cattle access to a pond and some grazing land, Ron receives severance damages in addition to the condemnation proceeds for the land taken. Ron must reduce the basis of the property by the amount of the severance damages. If the amount of the severance damages received exceeds the adjusted basis, Ron recognizes gain. ∎
E X A M P L E 14	Assume the same facts as in the previous example, except that Ron uses the proceeds from the condemnation and the severance damages to build another pond and to clear woodland for grazing. Therefore, all the proceeds are eligible for § 1033 treatment. There is no possibility of gain recognition as the result of the amount of the severance damages received exceeding the adjusted basis. ∎

Replacement Property

The requirements for replacement property generally are more restrictive than those for like-kind property under § 1031. The basic requirement is that the replacement property be similar or related in service or use to the involuntarily converted property.[15]

Different interpretations of the phrase *similar or related in service or use* apply depending on whether the involuntarily converted property is held by an *owner-user* or by an *owner-investor* (e.g., lessor). A taxpayer who uses the property in his or her trade or business is subject to a more restrictive test in terms of acquiring replacement property. For an owner-user, the *functional use test* applies, and for an owner-investor, the *taxpayer use test* applies.

Taxpayer Use Test.
The taxpayer use test for owner-investors provides the taxpayer with more flexibility in terms of what qualifies as replacement property than does the functional use test for owner-users. Essentially, the properties must be used by the taxpayer (the owner-investor) in similar endeavors. For example, rental property held by an owner-investor qualifies if replaced by other rental property, regardless of the type of rental property involved. The test is met when an investor replaces a manufacturing plant with a wholesale grocery warehouse if both properties are held for the production of rent income.[16] The replacement of a rental residence with a personal residence does not meet the test.[17]

---

[14]*Pioneer Real Estate Co.*, 47 B.T.A. 886 (1942), *acq.* 1943 C.B. 18.
[15]§ 1033(a) and Reg. § 1.1033(a)–1.

[16]*Loco Realty Co. v. Comm.*, 62–2 USTC ¶9657, 10 AFTR2d 5359, 306 F.2d 207 (CA–8, 1962).
[17]Rev.Rul. 70–466, 1970–2 C.B. 165.

Under eminent domain, governmental units have the right to take private property for public use. As fair compensation must be paid, disagreement often arises over the fair market value of condemned property.

In recent years, there has also been controversy over what constitutes "public use." Courts have expanded the definition of public use beyond the traditional public projects (such as roads, bridges, schools, hospitals, and slum clearance) to allow the taking of unblighted property for commercial development purposes. The objective in taking such property is to create jobs and increase tax revenues by means of new office parks, big box stores, racetracks, and other businesses.

The U.S. Supreme Court addressed this issue of what constitutes "public use" in its 2005 decision in *Kelo v. City of New London* (125 S.Ct. 2655 [USSC, 2005]). The Court, in a 5-to-4 decision, ruled that the "takings clause" in the Fifth Amendment to the U.S. Constitution permits the condemna-

tion of private property for uses that are primarily commercial, as long as such use serves a demonstrated "public use." Here, the City of New London condemned 15 properties to enable the construction of a resort hotel and facilities for a major pharmaceutical company. "Public use" in this case was deemed to occur because benefits would accrue to the city in the form of new jobs and increased tax revenues.

Some have criticized the decision because it leaves few limits on the ability of local governments to take private property. In addition, for those property owners whose property is either condemned or threatened with condemnation, the decision may impair their ability to receive fair compensation. The only way available to limit this government condemnation power is for the states to enact laws restricting its use. Although the laws tend to differ in terms of the definition of "public use," a number of states have now enacted legislation that limits this "taking power" of government entities.

Functional Use Test. The functional use test applies to owner-users (e.g., a manufacturer whose manufacturing plant is destroyed by fire is required to replace the plant with another facility of similar functional use). Under this test, the taxpayer's use of the replacement property and of the involuntarily converted property must be the same. Replacing a manufacturing plant with a wholesale grocery warehouse does not meet this test. Neither does replacing a rental residence with a personal residence.

Special Rules. Under one set of circumstances, the broader replacement rules for like-kind exchanges are substituted for the narrow replacement rules normally used for involuntary conversions. This beneficial provision applies if business real property or investment real property is condemned. This provision gives the taxpayer substantially more flexibility in selecting replacement property. For example, improved real property can be replaced with unimproved real property.

The rules concerning the nature of replacement property are illustrated in Concept Summary 15–1.

Time Limitation on Replacement

The taxpayer normally has a two-year period after the close of the taxable year in which gain is realized from an involuntary conversion to replace the property (*the latest date*).[18] This rule affords as much as three years from the date of realization of gain to replace the property if the realization of gain took place on the first day of the taxable year.[19] If the involuntary conversion involved the condemnation of real property used in a trade or business or held for investment, a three-year period is substituted for the normal two-year period. In this case, the taxpayer can actually have as much as four years from the date of realization of gain to replace the property.

---

[18]§§ 1033(a)(2)(B) and (g)(4) and Reg. § 1.1033(a)–2(c)(3).

[19]The taxpayer can apply for an extension of this time period anytime before its expiration [Reg. § 1.1033(a)–2(c)(3)]. Also, the period for filing the application for extension can be extended if the taxpayer shows reasonable cause.

CONCEPT SUMMARY 15–1

Replacement Property Tests

Type of Property and User	Like-Kind Test	Taxpayer Use Test	Functional Use Test
Land used by a manufacturing company is condemned by a local government authority.	X		
Apartment and land held by an investor are sold due to the threat or imminence of condemnation.	X		
An investor's rented shopping mall is destroyed by fire; the mall may be replaced by other rental properties (e.g., an apartment building).		X	
A manufacturing plant is destroyed by fire; replacement property must consist of another manufacturing plant that is functionally the same as the property converted.			X
Personal residence of taxpayer is condemned by a local government authority; replacement property must consist of another personal residence.			X

EXAMPLE 15

Megan's warehouse is destroyed by fire on December 16, 2007. The adjusted basis is $325,000. Megan receives $400,000 from the insurance company on January 10, 2008. She is a calendar year taxpayer. The latest date for replacement is December 31, 2010 (the end of the taxable year in which realized gain occurred plus two years). The critical date is not the date the involuntary conversion occurred, but rather the date of gain realization. ∎

EXAMPLE 16

Assume the same facts as in the previous example, except that Megan's warehouse is condemned. The latest date for replacement is December 31, 2011 (the end of the taxable year in which realized gain occurred plus three years). ∎

The *earliest date* for replacement typically is the date the involuntary conversion occurs. However, if the property is condemned, it is possible to replace the condemned property before this date. In this case, the earliest date is the date of the threat or imminence of requisition or condemnation of the property. The purpose of this provision is to enable the taxpayer to make an orderly replacement of the condemned property.

EXAMPLE 17

Assume the same facts as in Example 16. Megan can replace the warehouse before December 16, 2007 (the condemnation date). The earliest date for replacement is the date of the threat or imminence of requisition or condemnation of the warehouse. ∎

Nonrecognition of Gain

Nonrecognition of gain can be either mandatory or elective, depending on whether the conversion is direct (into replacement property) or indirect (into money).

Direct Conversion. If the conversion is directly into replacement property rather than into money, nonrecognition of realized gain is *mandatory*. In this case, the basis of the replacement property is the same as the adjusted basis of the converted property. Direct conversion is rare in practice and usually involves condemnations.

EXAMPLE 18

Lupe's property, with an adjusted basis of $20,000, is condemned by the state. Lupe receives property with a fair market value of $50,000 as compensation for the property taken. Since the nonrecognition of realized gain is mandatory for direct conversions, Lupe's realized gain of $30,000 is not recognized, and the basis of the replacement property is $20,000 (adjusted basis of the condemned property). ■

Conversion into Money. If the conversion is into money, at the election of the taxpayer, the realized gain is recognized only to the extent the amount realized from the involuntary conversion exceeds the cost of the qualifying replacement property.[20] This is the usual case, and nonrecognition (postponement) is *elective.* If the election is not made, the realized gain is recognized.

The basis of the replacement property is the property's cost less postponed (deferred) gain.[21] If the election to postpone gain is made, the holding period of the replacement property includes the holding period of the converted property.

Section 1033 applies *only to gains* and *not to losses.* Losses from involuntary conversions are recognized if the property is held for business or income-producing purposes. Personal casualty losses are recognized, but condemnation losses related to personal use assets (e.g., a personal residence) are neither recognized nor postponed.

EXAMPLE 19

Walt's building (used in his trade or business), with an adjusted basis of $50,000, is destroyed by fire on October 5, 2008. Walt is a calendar year taxpayer. On November 17, 2008, he receives an insurance reimbursement of $100,000 for the loss. Walt invests $80,000 in a new building.

- Walt has until December 31, 2010, to make the new investment and qualify for the non-recognition election.
- Walt's realized gain is $50,000 ($100,000 insurance proceeds received − $50,000 adjusted basis of old building).
- Assuming the replacement property qualifies as similar or related in service or use, Walt's recognized gain is $20,000. He reinvested $20,000 less than the insurance proceeds received ($100,000 proceeds − $80,000 reinvested). Therefore, his realized gain is recognized to that extent.
- Walt's basis in the new building is $50,000. This is the building's cost of $80,000 less the postponed gain of $30,000 (realized gain of $50,000 − recognized gain of $20,000).
- The computation of realization, recognition, and basis would apply even if Walt was a real estate dealer and the building destroyed by fire was part of his inventory. Unlike § 1031, § 1033 generally does not exclude inventory. ■

EXAMPLE 20

Assume the same facts as in the previous example, except that Walt receives only $45,000 of insurance proceeds. He has a realized and recognized loss of $5,000. The basis of the new building is the building's cost of $80,000. If the destroyed building had been held for personal use, the recognized loss would have been subject to the following additional limitations.[22] The loss of $5,000 would have been limited to the decline in fair market value of the property, and the amount of the loss would have been reduced first by $100 and then by 10% of adjusted gross income (refer to Chapter 7). ■

Involuntary Conversion of a Personal Residence

The tax consequences of the involuntary conversion of a personal residence depend on whether the conversion is a casualty or condemnation and whether a realized loss or gain results.

---

[20]§ 1033(a)(2)(A) and Reg. § 1.1033(a)–2(c)(1).   [22]§ 165(c)(3) and Reg. § 1.165–7.
[21]§ 1033(b).

Loss Situations. If the conversion is a condemnation, the realized loss is not recognized. Loss from the condemnation of a personal use asset is never recognized. If the conversion is a casualty (a loss from fire, storm, etc.), the loss is recognized subject to the personal casualty loss limitations (refer to Chapter 7).

Gain Situations. If the conversion is a casualty, theft, or condemnation, the gain may be postponed under § 1033 or excluded under § 121. That is, the taxpayer may treat the involuntary conversion as a sale under the exclusion of gain rules relating to the sale of a personal residence under § 121 (presented subsequently).

Under certain circumstances, the taxpayer may use both the § 121 exclusion of gain and the § 1033 postponement of gain provisions. See the discussion under Involuntary Conversion and Using §§ 121 and 1033 later in this chapter.

Reporting Considerations

Involuntary conversions from casualty and theft are reported first on Form 4684, Casualties and Thefts. Casualty and theft losses on personal use property for the individual taxpayer are carried from Form 4684 to Schedule A of Form 1040. For other casualty and theft items, the Form 4684 amounts are generally reported on Form 4797, Sales of Business Property, unless Form 4797 is not required. In the latter case, the amounts are reported directly on the tax return involved.

Except for personal use property, recognized gains and losses from involuntary conversions other than by casualty and theft are reported on Form 4797. As stated previously, if the property involved in the involuntary conversion (other than by casualty and theft) is personal use property, any realized loss is not recognized. Any realized gain is treated as gain on a voluntary sale.

What procedure should be followed if the taxpayer intends to acquire qualifying replacement property but has not done so by the time the tax return is filed? The taxpayer should elect § 1033 and report all of the details of the transaction on a statement attached to the return. Though a tax form (Form 8824) is available for § 1031 like-kind exchanges, no special form is provided for § 1033 transactions. When the qualifying replacement property is acquired, the taxpayer should attach a statement to the tax return that contains relevant information on the replacement property.

An amended return must be filed if qualified replacement property is not acquired during the statutory time period allowed. An amended return also is required if the cost of the replacement property is less than the amount realized from the involuntary conversion. In this case, the return would recognize the portion of the realized gain that can no longer be deferred.

LO.4

Describe the provision for the permanent exclusion of gain on the sale of a personal residence.

Sale of a Residence—§ 121

A taxpayer's **personal residence** is a personal use asset. Therefore, a realized loss from the sale of a personal residence is not recognized.[23]

A realized gain from the sale of a personal residence is subject to taxation. However, favorable relief from recognition of gain is provided in the form of the **§ 121 exclusion**. Under this provision, a taxpayer can exclude up to $250,000 of realized gain on the sale.[24]

Requirements for Exclusion Treatment

To qualify for exclusion treatment, at the date of the sale, the residence must have been *owned* and *used* by the taxpayer as the principal residence for at least two years during the five-year period ending on the date of the sale.[25]

---

[23]§ 165(c).
[24]§ 121(b).

[25]§ 121(a). However, § 121(d)(10) provides that exclusion treatment does not apply if the residence was acquired in a like-kind exchange within the prior five years of the sale of the residence.

EXAMPLE 21

Alice sells her principal residence on September 18, 2008. She had purchased it on July 5, 2006, and lived in it since then. The sale of Alice's residence qualifies for the § 121 exclusion. ■

The five-year window enables the taxpayer to qualify for the § 121 exclusion even though the property is not his or her principal residence at the date of the sale.

EXAMPLE 22

Benjamin sells his principal residence on August 16, 2008. He had purchased it on April 1, 2000, and lived in it until July 1, 2007, when he converted it to rental property. Even though the property is rental property on August 16, 2008, rather than Benjamin's principal residence, the sale qualifies for the § 121 exclusion.[26] During the five-year period from August 16, 2003, to August 16, 2008, Benjamin owned and used the property as his principal residence for at least two years. ■

Taxpayers might be tempted to make liberal use of the § 121 exclusion as a means of speculating when the price of residential housing is rising. Without any time restriction on its use, § 121 would permit the exclusion of realized gain on multiple sales of principal residences. The Code curbs this approach by denying the application of the § 121 exclusion to sales occurring within two years of its last use.[27]

EXAMPLE 23

Seth sells his principal residence (the first residence) in June 2007 for $150,000 (realized gain of $60,000). He then buys and sells the following (all of which qualify as principal residences):

	Date of Purchase	Date of Sale	Amount Involved
Second residence	July 2007		$160,000
Second residence		April 2008	180,000
Third residence	May 2008		200,000

Because multiple sales have taken place within a period of two years, § 121 does not apply to the sale of the second residence. Thus, the realized gain of $20,000 [$180,000 (selling price) − $160,000 (purchase price)] must be recognized. ■

Exceptions to the Two-Year Ownership Rule

The two-year ownership and use requirement and the "only once every two years" provision could create a hardship for taxpayers in certain situations that are beyond their control. Thus, under the following special circumstances, the requirements are waived:[28]

- Change in place of employment.
- Health.
- To the extent provided in the Regulations, other unforeseen circumstances.

These three exceptions have recently been amplified by the IRS and are discussed in the sections that follow.

Change in Place of Employment. In order for this exception to apply, the distance requirements applicable to the deductibility of moving expenses must be satisfied (see Chapter 9).[29] Consequently, the location of the taxpayer's new

---

[26]However, any realized gain on the sale that is attributable to depreciation is not eligible for the § 121 exclusion. See Example 38.

[27]§ 121(b)(3).

[28]§ 121(c)(2)(B).

[29]Reg. § 1.121–3T(c).

TAX *in the News* — A TAX BREAK FOR THOSE WHO SERVE

To qualify for exclusion treatment on the gain from the sale of a principal residence, a two-year ownership and occupancy requirement during the five-year period preceding the sale must be satisfied. As satisfying this provision was difficult for those in the military, Congress enacted the Military Family Tax Relief Act of 2003 to provide some relief. The two-out-of-five-years requirement still must be satisfied, but at the election of the taxpayer, the running of the five-year period can be suspended during any period that the taxpayer or spouse is serving on qualified official extended duty in the military. Since this extension is limited to 10 years, the maximum period allowed is 15 years. This provision is retroactive to home sales after May 6, 1997.

employment must be at least 50 miles further from the old residence than the old residence was from the old job. The house must be used as the principal residence of the taxpayer at the time of the change in the place of employment. Employment includes the commencement of employment with a new employer, the continuation of employment with the same employer, and the commencement or continuation of self-employment.

EXAMPLE 24

Assume the same facts as in the previous example, except that in March 2008, Seth's employer transfers him to a job in another state that is 400 miles away. Thus, the sale of the second residence and the purchase of the third residence were due to relocation of employment. Consequently, the § 121 exclusion is partially available on the sale of the second residence. ∎

Keep in mind, however, that the change in place of employment exception, or any of the other exceptions noted below, does not make the full amount of the exclusion available. See the discussion under Relief Provision later in this chapter for determining the amount of the partial exclusion allowed.

Health Considerations. For the health exception to apply, health must be the primary reason for the sale or exchange of the residence.[30] A sale or exchange that is merely beneficial to the general health or well-being of the individual will not qualify. A safe harbor applies if there is a physician's recommendation for a change of residence (1) to obtain, provide, or facilitate the diagnosis, cure, mitigation, or treatment of disease, illness, or injury or (2) to obtain or provide medical or personal care for an individual suffering from a disease, illness, or injury. If the safe harbor is not satisfied, then the determination is made using a facts and circumstances approach. Examples that qualify include the following:

- A taxpayer who is injured in an accident is unable to care for herself. She sells her residence and moves in with her daughter.
- A taxpayer's father has a chronic disease. The taxpayer sells his house in order to move into the father's house to provide the care the father requires as a result of the disease.
- A taxpayer's son suffers from a chronic disease. The taxpayer sells his house and moves his family so the son can begin a new treatment recommended by the son's physician that is available at a medical facility 100 miles away.
- A taxpayer suffers from chronic asthma. Her physician recommends that she move to a warm, dry climate. She moves from Minnesota to Arizona.

Unforeseen Circumstances. For the unforeseen circumstances exception to apply, the primary reason for the sale or exchange of the residence must be an event

[30]Reg. § 1.121–3T(d).

TAX *in the News*   **LIVING IN A HIGH-CRIME NEIGHBORHOOD**

Normally, a taxpayer must satisfy the tax year ownership and use requirements and the only once-every-two-years provision to be eligible for the § 121 exclusion. However, under the unforeseen circumstances exception, a taxpayer who does not satisfy these three requirements may be eligible for a reduced § 121 exclusion.

In several letter rulings, the IRS has been sympathetic to crime victims. One ruling involved a taxpayer who was accosted leaving his home, driven to several locations, and forced to withdraw money from an ATM. In another ruling, the taxpayers and their son were hospitalized after being assaulted by neighbors. In both cases, the taxpayers sold their homes. Although the taxpayers had not satisfied the three time period requirements, the IRS held that they were eligible for reduced § 121 exclusion treatment under the unforeseen circumstances exception.

---

that the taxpayer did not anticipate before purchasing and occupying the residence.[31] This requirement is satisfied under a safe-harbor provision by any of the following:

- Involuntary conversion of the residence.
- Natural or human-made disasters or acts of war or terrorism resulting in a casualty to the residence.
- Death of a qualified individual.
- Cessation of employment that results in eligibility for unemployment compensation.
- Change in employment or self-employment that results in the taxpayer being unable to pay housing costs and reasonable basic living expenses for the taxpayer's household.
- Divorce or legal separation.
- Multiple births resulting from the same pregnancy.

If the safe harbor is not satisfied, then the determination is made using a facts and circumstances approach.

EXAMPLE 25

Debra and Roy are engaged and buy a house (sharing the mortgage payments) and live in it as their personal residence. Eighteen months after the purchase, they cancel their wedding plans, and Roy moves out of the house. Because Debra cannot afford to make the payments alone, they sell the house. While the sale does not fit under the safe harbor, the sale does qualify under the unforeseen circumstances exception. ∎

Calculation of the Amount of the Exclusion

General Provisions. The amount of the available § 121 exclusion on the sale of a principal residence is $250,000.[32] If the realized gain does not exceed $250,000, there is no recognized gain.

Realized gain is calculated in the normal manner. The *amount realized* is the selling price less the selling expenses, which include items such as the cost of advertising the property for sale, real estate broker commissions, legal fees in connection with the sale, and loan placement fees paid by the taxpayer as a condition of arranging financing for the buyer. Repairs and maintenance performed by the seller to aid in selling the property are treated neither as selling expenses nor as adjustments to the taxpayer's adjusted basis for the residence.

EXAMPLE 26

Mandy, who is single, sells her personal residence (adjusted basis of $130,000) for $290,000. She has owned and lived in the residence for three years. Her selling expenses are $18,000.

---

[31]Reg. § 1.121–3T(e).   [32]§ 121(b)(1).

Three weeks prior to the sale, Mandy paid a carpenter and a painter $1,000 to make some repairs and paint the two bathrooms. Her recognized gain is calculated as follows:

Amount realized ($290,000 – $18,000)	$ 272,000
Adjusted basis	(130,000)
Realized gain	$ 142,000
§ 121 exclusion	(142,000)
Recognized gain	$ –0–

Since the available § 121 exclusion of $250,000 exceeds Mandy's realized gain of $142,000, her recognized gain is $0. ■

EXAMPLE 27

Assume the same facts as in the previous example, except that the selling price is $490,000.

Amount realized ($490,000 – $18,000)	$ 472,000
Adjusted basis	(130,000)
Realized gain	$ 342,000
§ 121 exclusion	(250,000)
Recognized gain	$ 92,000

Since the realized gain of $342,000 exceeds the § 121 exclusion amount of $250,000, Mandy's recognized gain is $92,000 ($342,000 – $250,000). ■

Effect on Married Couples. If a married couple files a joint return, the $250,000 amount is increased to $500,000 if the following requirements are satisfied:[33]

- Either spouse meets the at-least-two-years *ownership* requirement.
- Both spouses meet the at-least-two-years *use* requirement.
- Neither spouse is ineligible for the § 121 exclusion on the sale of the current principal residence because of the sale of another principal residence within the prior two years.

EXAMPLE 28

Margaret sells her personal residence (adjusted basis of $150,000) for $650,000. She has owned and lived in the residence for six years. Her selling expenses are $40,000. Margaret is married to Ted, and they file a joint return. Ted has lived in the residence since they were married two and one-half years ago.

Amount realized ($650,000 – $40,000)	$ 610,000
Adjusted basis	(150,000)
Realized gain	$ 460,000
§ 121 exclusion	(460,000)
Recognized gain	$ –0–

Since the realized gain of $460,000 is less than the available § 121 exclusion amount of $500,000, no gain is recognized. ■

Starting in 2008, a surviving spouse can continue to use the $500,000 exclusion amount on the sale of a personal residence for the next two years following the year of the deceased spouse's death. If the sale occurs in the year of death, however, a joint return must be filed by the surviving spouse.

If each spouse owns a qualified principal residence, each spouse can separately qualify for the $250,000 exclusion on the sale of his or her own residence even if the couple files a joint return.[34]

---

[33]§ 121(b)(2).   [34]§ 121(b)(1).

EXAMPLE 29

Anne and Samuel are married on August 1, 2008. Each owns a residence that is eligible for the § 121 exclusion. Anne sells her residence on September 7, 2008, and Samuel sells his residence on October 9, 2008. Relevant data on the sales are as follows:

	Anne	Samuel
Selling price	$320,000	$425,000
Selling expenses	20,000	25,000
Adjusted basis	190,000	110,000

Anne and Samuel intend to rent a condo in Florida or Arizona and to travel. The recognized gain of each is calculated as follows:

	Anne	Samuel
Amount realized	$ 300,000	$ 400,000
Adjusted basis	(190,000)	(110,000)
Realized gain	$ 110,000	$ 290,000
§ 121 exclusion	(110,000)	(250,000)
Recognized gain	$ –0–	$ 40,000

Anne has no recognized gain because the available $250,000 exclusion amount exceeds her realized gain of $110,000. Samuel's recognized gain is $40,000 as his realized gain of $290,000 exceeds the $250,000 exclusion amount. The recognized gains calculated above result regardless of whether Anne and Samuel file a joint return or separate returns. ∎

Relief Provision. As discussed earlier in Requirements for Exclusion Treatment, partial § 121 exclusion treatment may be available when not all of the statutory requirements are satisfied. Under the relief provision, the § 121 exclusion amount ($250,000 or $500,000) is multiplied by a fraction, the numerator of which is the number of qualifying months and the denominator of which is 24 months. The resulting amount is the excluded gain.[35]

EXAMPLE 30

On October 1, 2007, Rich and Audrey, who file a joint return and live in Chicago, sell their personal residence, which they have owned and lived in for eight years. The realized gain of $325,000 is excluded under § 121. They purchase another personal residence for $525,000 on October 2, 2007. Audrey's employer transfers her to the Denver office in August 2008. Rich and Audrey sell their Chicago residence on August 2, 2008, and purchase a residence in Denver shortly thereafter. The realized gain on the sale is $300,000.

The $325,000 gain on the first Chicago residence is excluded under § 121. The sale of the second Chicago residence is within the two-year window of the prior sale, but because it resulted from a change in employment, Rich and Audrey can qualify for partial § 121 exclusion treatment as follows:

Realized gain	$ 300,000
§ 121 exclusion:	
$\dfrac{10 \text{ months}}{24 \text{ months}} \times \$500{,}000 = \$208{,}333$	(208,333)
Recognized gain	$ 91,667 ∎

---

[35]§ 121(c)(1).

Basis of New Residence. Because § 121 is an exclusion provision rather than a postponement of gain provision, the basis of a new residence is its cost.[36]

Principal Residence

To be eligible for the § 121 exclusion, the residence must have been owned and used by the taxpayer as the principal residence for at least two years during the five-year window (subject to partial exclusion treatment under the relief provision). Whether property is the taxpayer's principal residence "depends upon all of the facts and circumstances in each case."[37]

E X A M P L E   31

Mitch graduates from college and moves to Boston, where he is employed. He decides to rent an apartment in Boston because of its proximity to his place of employment. He purchases a beach condo in the Cape Cod area that he occupies most weekends. Mitch does not intend to live at the beach condo except on weekends. The apartment in Boston is his principal residence. ∎

A residence does not have to be a house. For example, a houseboat, a house trailer, or a motor home can qualify.[38] Land, under certain circumstances, can qualify for exclusion treatment. The lot on which a house is built obviously qualifies. An adjacent lot can qualify if it is regularly used by the owner as part of the residential property. To qualify, the land must be sold along with the residence or within two years before or after the sale of the residence.

Involuntary Conversion and Using §§ 121 and 1033

As mentioned earlier (see Involuntary Conversion of a Personal Residence), a taxpayer can use both the § 121 exclusion of gain provision and the § 1033 postponement of gain provision.[39] The taxpayer initially can elect to exclude realized gain under § 121 to the extent of the statutory amount. Then a qualified replacement of the residence under § 1033 can be used to postpone the remainder of the realized gain. In applying § 1033, the amount of the required reinvestment is reduced by the amount of the § 121 exclusion.

E X A M P L E   32

Angel's principal residence is destroyed by a tornado. Her adjusted basis for the residence is $140,000. She receives insurance proceeds of $480,000.

If Angel does not elect to use the § 121 exclusion, her realized gain on the involuntary conversion of her principal residence is $340,000 ($480,000 amount realized − $140,000 adjusted basis). Thus, to postpone the $340,000 realized gain under § 1033, she would need to acquire qualifying property costing at least $480,000.

Using the § 121 exclusion enables Angel to reduce the amount of the required reinvestment for § 1033 purposes from $480,000 to $230,000. That is, by using § 121 in conjunction with § 1033, the amount realized, for § 1033 purposes, is reduced to $230,000 ($480,000 − $250,000 § 121 exclusion).

Note that if Angel does not acquire qualifying replacement property for § 1033 purposes, her recognized gain is $90,000 ($480,000 − $140,000 adjusted basis − $250,000 § 121 exclusion). ∎

If § 1033 is used in conjunction with the § 121 exclusion on an involuntary conversion of a principal residence, the holding period of the replacement residence includes the holding period of the involuntarily converted residence. This can be beneficial in satisfying the § 121 two-out-of-five-years ownership and use requirement on a subsequent sale of the replacement residence.

---

[36]§ 1012.
[37]Regulation § 1.121–1(b)(2) includes factors to be considered in determining a taxpayer's principal residence.

[38]Reg. § 1.1034–1(c)(3)(i).
[39]§ 121(d)(5).

Other Nonrecognition Provisions

The typical taxpayer experiences the sale of a personal residence or an involuntary conversion more frequently than the other types of nontaxable exchanges. Several less common nonrecognition provisions are treated briefly in the remainder of this chapter.

Exchange of Stock for Property—§ 1032

Under § 1032, a corporation does not recognize gain or loss on the receipt of money or other property in exchange for its stock (including treasury stock). In other words, a corporation does not recognize gain or loss when it deals in its own stock. This provision is consistent with the accounting treatment of such transactions.

Certain Exchanges of Insurance Policies—§ 1035

Under § 1035, no gain or loss is recognized from the exchange of certain insurance contracts or policies. The rules relating to exchanges not solely in kind and the basis of the property acquired are the same as under § 1031. Exchanges qualifying for nonrecognition include the following:

- The exchange of life insurance contracts.
- The exchange of a life insurance contract for an endowment or annuity contract.
- The exchange of an endowment contract for another endowment contract that provides for regular payments beginning at a date not later than the date payments would have begun under the contract exchanged.
- The exchange of an endowment contract for an annuity contract.
- The exchange of annuity contracts.

Exchange of Stock for Stock of the Same Corporation—§ 1036

Section 1036 provides that a shareholder does not recognize gain or loss on the exchange of common stock solely for common stock in the same corporation or from the exchange of preferred stock for preferred stock in the same corporation. Exchanges between individual shareholders as well as between a shareholder and the corporation are included. The rules relating to exchanges not solely in kind and the basis of the property acquired are the same as under § 1031. For example, a nonrecognition exchange occurs when common stock with different rights, such as voting for nonvoting, is exchanged. A shareholder usually recognizes gain or loss from the exchange of common for preferred or preferred for common even though the stock exchanged is in the same corporation.

Certain Reacquisitions of Real Property—§ 1038

Under § 1038, no loss is recognized from the repossession of real property sold on an installment basis. Gain is recognized to a limited extent.

Transfers of Property between Spouses or Incident to Divorce—§ 1041

Section 1041 provides that transfers of property *between spouses or former spouses incident to divorce* are nontaxable transactions. Therefore, the basis to the recipient is a carryover basis. To be treated as incident to the divorce, the transfer must be related to the cessation of marriage or occur within one year after the date on which the marriage ceases.

Section 1041 also provides for nontaxable exchange treatment on property transfers *between spouses during marriage*. The basis to the recipient spouse is a carryover basis.

Rollovers into Specialized Small Business Investment Companies—§ 1044

A postponement opportunity is available for some sellers of publicly traded securities under § 1044. If the amount realized is reinvested in the common stock or partnership interest of a specialized small business investment company (SSBIC), the realized gain is not recognized. Any amount not reinvested will trigger recognition of the realized gain to the extent of the deficiency. The taxpayer must reinvest the proceeds within 60 days of the date of sale in order to qualify. In calculating the basis of the SSBIC stock, the amount of the purchase price is reduced by the amount of the postponed gain.

Statutory ceilings are imposed on the amount of realized gain that can be postponed for any taxable year as follows:

- For an individual taxpayer, the lesser of:
  - $50,000 ($25,000 for married filing separately).
  - $500,000 ($250,000 for married filing separately) reduced by the amount of such nonrecognized gain in prior taxable years.
- For a corporate taxpayer, the lesser of:
  - $250,000.
  - $1 million reduced by the amount of such nonrecognized gain in prior taxable years.

Investors *ineligible* for this postponement treatment include partnerships, S corporations, estates, and trusts.

Rollover of Gain from Qualified Small Business Stock into Another Qualified Small Business Stock—§ 1045

Under § 1045, realized gain from the sale of qualified small business stock held for more than six months may be postponed if the taxpayer acquires other qualified small business stock within 60 days. Any amount not reinvested will trigger the recognition of the realized gain on the sale to the extent of the deficiency. In calculating the basis of the acquired qualified small business stock, the amount of the purchase price is reduced by the amount of the postponed gain.

Qualified small business stock is stock of a qualified small business that is acquired by the taxpayer at its original issue in exchange for money or other property (excluding stock) or as compensation for services. A qualified small business is a domestic corporation that satisfies the following requirements:

- The aggregate gross assets prior to the issuance of the small business stock do not exceed $50 million.
- The aggregate gross assets immediately after the issuance of the small business stock do not exceed $50 million.

LO.6

Identify tax planning opportunities related to the nonrecognition provisions discussed in the chapter.

Like-Kind Exchanges

Since application of the like-kind exchange provisions is mandatory rather than elective, in certain instances it may be preferable to avoid qualifying for § 1031 nonrecognition. If the like-kind exchange provisions do not apply, the end result may be the recognition of capital gain in exchange for a higher basis in the newly acquired asset. Also, the immediate recognition of gain may be preferable in certain situations. Examples where immediate recognition is beneficial include the following:

- Taxpayer has unused net operating loss carryovers.
- Taxpayer has unused general business credit carryovers.
- Taxpayer has suspended or current passive activity losses.
- Taxpayer expects his or her effective tax rate to increase in the future.

TAX PLANNING
Considerations

Alicia disposes of a machine (used in her business) with an adjusted basis of $3,000 for $4,000. She also acquires a new business machine for $9,000. If § 1031 applies, the $1,000 realized gain is not recognized, and the basis of the new machine is reduced by $1,000 (from $9,000 to $8,000). If § 1031 does not apply, a $1,000 gain is recognized and may receive favorable capital gain treatment to the extent that the gain is not recognized as ordinary income due to the depreciation recapture provisions (see Chapter 17). In addition, the basis for depreciation on the new machine is $9,000 rather than $8,000 since there is no unrecognized gain. ■

The application of § 1031 nonrecognition treatment should also be avoided when the adjusted basis of the property being disposed of exceeds the fair market value.

Assume the same facts as in the previous example, except that the fair market value of the machine is $2,500. If § 1031 applies, the $500 realized loss is not recognized. To recognize the loss, Alicia should sell the old machine and purchase the new one. The purchase and sale transactions should be with different taxpayers. ■

On the other hand, the like-kind exchange procedure can be utilized to control the amount of recognized gain.

Rex has property with an adjusted basis of $40,000 and a fair market value of $100,000. Sandra wants to buy Rex's property, but Rex wants to limit the amount of recognized gain on the proposed transaction. Sandra acquires other like-kind property (from an outside party) for $80,000. She then exchanges this property and $20,000 cash for Rex's property. Rex has a realized gain of $60,000 ($100,000 amount realized − $40,000 adjusted basis). His recognized gain is only $20,000, the lower of the $20,000 boot received or the $60,000 realized gain. Rex's basis for the like-kind property is $40,000 ($40,000 adjusted basis + $20,000 gain recognized − $20,000 boot received). If Rex had sold the property to Sandra for its fair market value of $100,000, the result would have been a $60,000 recognized gain ($100,000 amount realized − $40,000 adjusted basis) to him. It is permissible for Rex to identify the like-kind property that he wants Sandra to purchase.[40] ■

Involuntary Conversions

In certain cases, a taxpayer may prefer to recognize gain from an involuntary conversion. Keep in mind that § 1033, unlike § 1031 (dealing with like-kind exchanges), generally is an elective provision.

Ahmad has a $40,000 realized gain from the involuntary conversion of an office building. He reinvests the entire proceeds of $450,000 in a new office building. He does not elect to postpone gain under § 1033, however, because of an expiring net operating loss carryover that is offset against the gain. Therefore, none of the realized gain of $40,000 is postponed. Because Ahmad did not elect § 1033 postponement, his basis in the replacement property is the property's cost of $450,000 rather than $410,000 ($450,000 reduced by the $40,000 realized gain). ■

Sale of a Principal Residence

Election to Forgo. The § 121 exclusion automatically applies if the taxpayer is eligible. That is, the taxpayer does not have to make an election. However, if the taxpayer wishes to avoid § 121 exclusion treatment on an otherwise eligible sale, the taxpayer may elect to do so.[41]

---

[40]*Franklin B. Biggs*, 69 T.C. 905 (1978); Rev.Rul. 73–476, 1973–2 C.B. 300; and *Starker v. U.S.*, 79–2 USTC ¶9541, 44 AFTR2d 79–5525, 602 F.2d 1341 (CA–9, 1979).

[41]§ 121(f).

TAX *in the News*   **SALE OF A RESIDENCE AND THE HOME OFFICE DEDUCTION**

If various requirements are satisfied, a taxpayer who uses his or her residence for business may claim a deduction for the expenses attributable to such use. But what effect, if any, does claiming an office in the home deduction have on a later sale of the residence? Do the sale proceeds still qualify for nonrecognition of gain treatment under § 121?

Until recently, the answers to these questions were unknown. In fact, concern that the § 121 exclusion might be denied may have deterred some taxpayers from claiming legitimate office in the home deductions. Such caution appears to have been unnecessary. The IRS has clarified its position. Only the depreciation deducted on the office portion of the residence after May 5, 1997, is not eligible for the § 121 exclusion.

EXAMPLE 37

George owns two personal residences that satisfy the two-year ownership and use test with respect to the five-year window. The Elm Street residence has appreciated by $25,000, and the Maple Street residence has appreciated by $230,000. He intends to sell both of them and move into rental property. He sells the Elm Street residence in December 2008 and expects to sell the Maple Street residence early next year.

Unless George elects not to apply the § 121 exclusion to the sale of the Elm Street residence, he will exclude the $25,000 realized gain on that residence in 2008. In 2009, however, he will have a recognized gain of $230,000 on the sale of the Maple Street residence.

If George makes the election to forgo, he will report a recognized gain of $25,000 on the sale of the Elm Street residence in 2008. But by using the § 121 exclusion in 2009, he will eliminate the recognized gain of $230,000 on the sale of the Maple Street residence. ∎

Negative Effect of Renting or Using as a Home Office. The residence does not have to be the taxpayer's principal residence at the date of sale to qualify for the § 121 exclusion. During part of the five-year window, it could have been rental property (e.g., either a vacation home or entirely rental property). In addition, the taxpayer can have used part of the principal residence as a qualifying home office.

In either the rental or the home office setting, the taxpayer will have deducted depreciation. Any realized gain on the sale that is attributable to depreciation claimed after May 5, 1997, is not eligible for the § 121 exclusion.[42]

EXAMPLE 38

On December 5, 2008, Amanda sells her principal residence, which qualifies for the § 121 exclusion. Her realized gain is $190,000. From January through November 2007, she was temporarily out of town on a job assignment in another city and rented the residence to a college student. For this period, she deducted MACRS cost recovery of $7,000. Without the depreciation provision, Amanda could exclude the $190,000 realized gain. However, the depreciation taken requires her to recognize $7,000 of the realized gain. ∎

Qualification for § 121 Exclusion. The key requirement for the § 121 exclusion is that the taxpayer must have *owned* and *used* the property as a principal residence for at least two years during the five-year window. As taxpayers advance in age, they quite frequently make decisions such as the following:

- Sell the principal residence and buy a smaller residence or rent the principal residence.
- Sell vacation homes they own.
- Sell homes they are holding as rental property.

These properties may have experienced substantial appreciation during the ownership period. Clearly, the sale of the principal residence is eligible for the § 121

---

[42]§ 121(d)(6).

exclusion. Less clear, however, is that proper planning can make it possible for a vacation home or rental property to qualify for the exclusion. Although this strategy may require taxpayers to be flexible about where they live, it can result in substantial tax savings.

EXAMPLE 39

Thelma and David are approaching retirement. They have substantial appreciation on their principal residence and on a house they own at the beach (about two hours away). After retirement, they plan to move to Florida. They have owned and lived in the principal residence for 28 years and have owned the beach house for 9 years. If they sell their principal residence, it qualifies for the § 121 exclusion. At retirement, they could move into their beach house for two years and make it eligible for the exclusion. If the beach house were not so far away, they could sell the principal residence now and move into the beach house to start the running of the two-year use period. Note that any realized gain on the beach house attributable to depreciation is not eligible for the § 121 exclusion. ■

Record Keeping. Since the amount of the available exclusion ($250,000 or $500,000) for most taxpayers will exceed the realized gain on the sale of the residence, the IRS has discontinued the form that previously was used to report the sale of a principal residence. If the sale of the residence does result in a gain that is not excluded from gross income, the gain is reported on Schedule D of Form 1040 (Capital Gains and Losses).

However, it is a good idea for all taxpayers who own residences to continue to maintain records on the adjusted basis of the residence including the original cost, any capital improvements, and any deductions that decrease basis (e.g., depreciation on a home office or on rental use) for the following reasons:

- The sale of the residence may not qualify for the § 121 exclusion.
- The realized gain may exceed the § 121 exclusion amount.
- The residence may be converted to rental or business use.
- If part of the residence has been rental or business use property (e.g., a qualifying home office) and depreciation has been deducted, the realized gain is recognized to the extent of the depreciation deducted.

Chapter 15 has covered certain situations in which realized gains or losses are not recognized (nontaxable exchanges). Chapters 16 and 17 are concerned with the *classification* of recognized gains and losses. That is, if a gain or loss is recognized, is it an ordinary or a capital gain or loss? Chapter 16 discusses the tax consequences of capital gains and losses.

KEY TERMS

Boot, 15–7	Like-kind exchanges, 15–3	Personal residence, 15–16
Involuntary conversion, 15–11	Nontaxable exchange, 15–2	Section 121 exclusion, 15–16

PROBLEM MATERIALS

DISCUSSION QUESTIONS

1. What is the justification for nontaxable exchange treatment?

2. Distinguish between a loss that is not recognized on a nontaxable exchange and a loss that is not recognized on the sale or exchange of a personal use asset.

3. What are the three requirements that must be satisfied for a transaction to qualify for nontaxable exchange treatment under § 1031?

4. Can the exchange of personal use property for property held for productive use in a trade or business qualify for like-kind exchange treatment? Explain.

5. Why might a taxpayer want to avoid like-kind exchange treatment?

6. Which of the following qualify as like-kind exchanges under § 1031?
   a. Improved for unimproved real estate.
   b. Vending machine (used in business) for inventory.
   c. Rental house for personal residence.
   d. Business equipment for securities.
   e. Warehouse for office building (both used for business).
   f. Truck for computer (both used in business).
   g. Rental house for land (both held for investment).
   h. Ten shares of stock in Blue Corporation for 10 shares of stock in Red Corporation.
   i. Office furniture for office equipment (both used in business).
   j. Unimproved land in Jackson, Mississippi, for unimproved land in Toledo, Spain.
   k. General partnership interest for a general partnership interest.

Issue ID

7. a. Melissa owns a residential lot in Spring Creek that has appreciated substantially in value. She holds the lot for investment. She is considering exchanging the lot with her father for a residential lot in McComb that she also will hold for investment. Identify the relevant tax issues for Melissa.
   b. Assume instead that the lot Melissa receives from her father is located in Paris, France. Identify the relevant tax issues for Melissa.

Issue ID

8. Ross would like to dispose of some land that he acquired five years ago because he believes that it will not continue to appreciate. Its value has increased by $50,000 over the five-year period. He also intends to sell stock that has declined in value by $50,000 during the eight-month period he has owned it. Ross has four offers to acquire the stock and land:

   Buyer number 1:   Exchange land.
   Buyer number 2:   Purchase land for cash.
   Buyer number 3:   Exchange stock.
   Buyer number 4:   Purchase stock for cash.

   Identify the tax issues relevant to Ross in disposing of this land and stock.

9. Under what circumstances can the exchange of partnership interests qualify for like-kind exchange treatment?

10. The receipt of boot in a § 1031 exchange triggers the recognition of realized gain, and any gain recognized will affect the basis of the property received.
    a. What is the tax result if the boot received is greater than the realized gain?
    b. If the boot received is less than the realized gain?
    c. What effect does the recognition of gain have on the basis of the like-kind property received? Of the boot received?

11. In connection with like-kind exchanges, discuss each of the following:
    a. Realized gain.
    b. Realized loss.
    c. Recognized gain.
    d. Recognized loss.
    e. Postponed gain.
    f. Postponed loss.
    g. Basis of like-kind property received.
    h. Basis of boot received.

12. What is the holding period of like-kind property received in a like-kind exchange? Why? What is the holding period of any boot received?

13. Mortgaged real estate may be received in a like-kind exchange. If the taxpayer's mortgage is assumed, what effect does the mortgage have on the recognition of realized gain? On the basis of the real estate received?

14. Bev's retail store building (basis of $270,000) is destroyed by a fire. She receives insurance proceeds of $250,000 (the appraised value of the building prior to its

destruction). How much can Bev reinvest in another retail store building and still recognize a $20,000 loss?

15. What constitutes an involuntary conversion?

16. Ed receives severance damages from the state government for a public road built across his property. Under what circumstances can the § 1033 involuntary conversion provision apply to prevent the recognition of gain?

17. Distinguish between the taxpayer use test and the functional use test for involuntary conversions. When does each test apply?

18. On June 5, 2008, Amber, Inc., a calendar year taxpayer, receives cash of $680,000 from the county upon condemnation of its warehouse building (adjusted basis of $400,000 and fair market value of $680,000).
    a. What must Amber do to qualify for § 1033 postponement of gain treatment?
    b. How would your advice to Amber differ if the adjusted basis were $700,000?

19. In January 2008, Stanley's warehouse (basis of $570,000) is destroyed by fire. Two months later, Stanley collects insurance proceeds of $610,000.
    a. If Stanley is a calendar year taxpayer, what is the latest date that he can reinvest the insurance proceeds and avoid recognition of gain?
    b. Suppose the warehouse was condemned by the city (instead of being destroyed by fire). What would be the latest date for reinvestment to avoid recognition of gain?

20. Bob is notified by the city public housing authority on May 3, 2008, that his apartment building is going to be condemned as part of an urban renewal project. On June 1, 2008, Carol offers to buy the building from Bob. Bob sells the building to Carol on June 30, 2008. Condemnation occurs on September 1, 2008, and Carol receives the condemnation proceeds from the city. Assume both Bob and Carol are calendar year taxpayers.
    a. What is the earliest date on which Bob can dispose of the building and qualify for § 1033 postponement treatment?
    b. Does the sale to Carol qualify as a § 1033 involuntary conversion?
    c. What is the latest date on which Carol can acquire qualifying replacement property and qualify for postponement of the realized gain?
    d. What type of property will be qualifying replacement property?

21. A warehouse owned by Martha and used in her business (i.e., to store inventory) is being condemned by the city to provide a right of way for a highway. The warehouse has appreciated by $100,000 based on Martha's estimate of its fair market value. In the negotiations, the city is offering $40,000 less than what Martha believes the property is worth. Alan, a real estate broker, has offered to purchase Martha's property for $25,000 more than the city's offer. Martha plans to invest the proceeds she will receive in an office building that she will lease to various tenants. Identify the relevant tax issues for Martha. *Issue ID*

22. When does the holding period begin for replacement property acquired in an involuntary conversion?

23. Samantha wants to retire, sell the house that she has occupied as her residence, and travel. She would have a $50,000 realized loss on the sale of the residence.
    a. Can Samantha recognize the loss?
    b. Would the answer in (a) be different if the realized loss was, instead, a $50,000 realized gain?

24. Maria owns two homes. The first home was her principal residence from January 1, 2003, to December 31, 2006, and is sold on April 5, 2008. The second home has been her principal residence since January 1, 2007, and is sold on June 1, 2009. Do both sales qualify for the § 121 exclusion?

25. Sandy owns a personal residence in which she has lived since she acquired it. It has appreciated by $90,000 during this period. Now, however, the school board has redrawn the boundaries for the school districts, and her son will have to transfer to a different high school for his senior year. Sandy is considering selling her residence and buying another one that will enable her son to remain in the same high school. Without this reason, she would not sell the house. Identify the relevant tax issues for Sandy. *Issue ID*

26. Define each of the following items that are associated with the sale of a principal residence:
    a. Amount realized.
    b. Selling expenses.
    c. Realized gain.
    d. Recognized gain.
    e. § 121 excluded gain.
    f. Basis of a new residence.

27. What is a principal residence? Can a taxpayer have several principal residences at the same time?

28. On May 5, 2008, Nancy sells her stock (adjusted basis of $13,000) in Lime, Inc., a publicly traded company, for $17,000. On May 31, 2008, she pays $20,000 for stock in Rose, Inc., a specialized small business investment company. Nancy believes that her adjusted basis for the Rose stock is $10,000.
    a. Evaluate Nancy's calculation of the adjusted basis for her Rose stock.
    b. How would your answer change if Nancy purchased the replacement stock on July 15 rather than on May 31?

PROBLEMS

29. Catherine owns undeveloped land with an adjusted basis of $250,000. She exchanges it for other undeveloped land worth $310,000.
    a. What are Catherine's realized and recognized gain or loss?
    b. What is Catherine's basis in the undeveloped land she receives?

30. Kareem owns an automobile that he uses exclusively in his business. The adjusted basis is $19,000, and the fair market value is $16,000. Kareem exchanges the car for a car that he will use exclusively in his business.
    a. What are Kareem's realized and recognized gain or loss?
    b. What is his basis in the new car?
    c. What are the tax consequences to Kareem in (a) and (b) if he used the old car and will use the new car exclusively for personal purposes?

Decision Making

Communications

31. Tex Watson owns undeveloped land (basis of $350,000) held as an investment. On October 8, 2008, he exchanges the land with his 27-year-old daughter, Porchia, for other undeveloped land also to be held as an investment. The appraised value of Porchia's land is $500,000.
    a. On February 15, 2009, Tex sells the land to Baxter, a real estate broker, for $600,000. Calculate Tex's realized and recognized gain or loss from the exchange with Porchia and on the subsequent sale of the land to Baxter.
    b. Calculate Tex's realized and recognized gain or loss on the exchange with Porchia if Tex does not sell the land. Instead, on February 15, 2009, Porchia sells the land received from Tex. Calculate Tex's basis for the land on October 8, 2008, and on February 15, 2009.
    c. Write a letter to Tex advising him on how he could avoid any recognition of gain associated with the October 8, 2008 exchange. His address is The Corral, El Paso, TX 79968.

32. Beatrice owns a personal computer (adjusted basis of $4,000) that she uses exclusively in her business. Beatrice transfers the computer and cash of $2,000 to Green Computers for a laser printer (worth $7,000) also to be used in her business.
    a. Calculate Beatrice's recognized gain or loss on the exchange.
    b. Calculate Beatrice's basis for the printer.

Decision Making

33. Clarence exchanges a light-duty truck used in his business for one to be similarly used. The adjusted basis of the old truck is $17,000 (fair market value of $11,000).
    a. Calculate Clarence's recognized gain or loss on the exchange.
    b. What is Clarence's basis in the new truck?
    c. How could the transaction have been structured to produce better tax results?
    d. How would your answers in (a), (b), and (c) change if the fair market value of the original truck was $19,000 and the fair market value of the replacement truck was $25,000 (i.e., cash payment of $6,000 was required from Clarence)?

34. Samantha owns a truck that she uses exclusively for personal purposes. Its original cost was $29,000, and the fair market value is $22,000. She exchanges the truck and $11,000 cash for a new truck.
    a. Calculate Samantha's realized and recognized gain or loss.
    b. Calculate Samantha's basis for the new truck.
    c. Determine when Samantha's holding period for the new truck begins.

35. Cary owns undeveloped land (adjusted basis of $150,000) that he exchanges for $40,000 cash and an office building (fair market value of $175,000) to be used in his business.
    a. What is Cary's realized gain or loss?
    b. His recognized gain or loss?
    c. His basis in the office building?

36. Ed owns investment land with an adjusted basis of $35,000. Polly has offered to purchase the land from Ed for $175,000 for use in a real estate development. The amount offered by Polly is $10,000 in excess of what Ed perceives as the fair market value of the land. Ed would like to dispose of the land to Polly but does not want to incur the tax liability that would result. He identifies an office building with a fair market value of $175,000 that he would like to acquire. Polly purchases the office building and then exchanges the office building for Ed's land.
    a. Calculate Ed's realized and recognized gain on the exchange and his basis for the office building.
    b. Calculate Polly's realized and recognized gain on the exchange and her basis in the land.

37. What is the basis of the new property in each of the following exchanges?
    a. Apartment building held for investment (adjusted basis of $145,000) for office building to be held for investment (fair market value of $225,000).
    b. Land and building used as a barber shop (adjusted basis of $190,000) for land and building used as a grocery store (fair market value of $350,000).
    c. Office building (adjusted basis of $45,000) for bulldozer (fair market value of $42,000), both held for business use.
    d. IBM common stock (adjusted basis of $20,000) for ExxonMobil common stock (fair market value of $28,000).
    e. Rental house (adjusted basis of $90,000) for mountain cabin to be held for rental use (fair market value of $225,000).

38. Norm owns Machine A (adjusted basis of $12,000; fair market value of $18,000), which he uses in his business. Norm is considering two options for the disposal of Machine A. Under the first option, he will transfer Machine A and $3,000 cash to Joan, a dealer, in exchange for Machine B (fair market value of $21,000). Under the second option, he will sell Machine A for $18,000 to Tim, another dealer, and then purchase Machine B from Joan for $21,000. Machines A and B qualify as like-kind property.   *Decision Making*
    a. Calculate Norm's recognized gain or loss and the basis of Machine B under the first option.
    b. Calculate Norm's recognized gain or loss and the basis of Machine B under the second option.
    c. Advise Norm on which option is preferable.

39. Greg exchanges real estate held for investment plus stock for real estate to be held for investment. The stock transferred has an adjusted basis of $30,000 and a fair market value of $35,000. The real estate transferred has an adjusted basis of $40,000 and a fair market value of $112,000. The real estate acquired has a fair market value of $147,000.
    a. What is Greg's realized gain or loss?
    b. His recognized gain or loss?
    c. The basis of the newly acquired real estate?

40. Audrey exchanges a warehouse with Dixon for an office building. Audrey's adjusted basis for her warehouse is $500,000. The fair market value of Dixon's office building is $545,000. Audrey's property has a $100,000 mortgage that Dixon assumes.   *Decision Making*
    a. Calculate Audrey's realized and recognized gain or loss.
    b. What is her adjusted basis for the office building?
    c. As an alternative, Dixon has proposed that he will transfer cash of $100,000 rather than assume the mortgage. Audrey would use the cash to pay off the mortgage. Advise Audrey on whether this alternative would be beneficial to her from a tax perspective.

41. Determine the realized, recognized, and postponed gain or loss and the new basis for each of the following like-kind exchanges:

	Adjusted Basis of Old Machine	Boot Given	Fair Market Value of New Asset	Boot Received
a.	$ 7,000	$ –0–	$12,000	$4,000
b.	14,000	2,000	15,000	–0–
c.	3,000	7,000	8,000	500
d.	22,000	–0–	32,000	–0–
e.	10,000	–0–	11,000	1,000
f.	10,000	–0–	8,000	–0–

42. Shontelle owns an apartment house that has an adjusted basis of $950,000 but is subject to a mortgage of $240,000. She transfers the apartment house to Dave and receives from him $150,000 in cash and an office building with a fair market value of $975,000 at the time of the exchange. Dave assumes the $240,000 mortgage on the apartment house.
   a. What is Shontelle's realized gain or loss?
   b. What is her recognized gain or loss?
   c. What is the basis of the newly acquired office building?

43. Melanie's warehouse (adjusted basis of $410,000) is destroyed by a flood. Since Melanie has excess warehouse space, she decides not to replace the building. Instead, she adds the proceeds to the working capital of her business. What is Melanie's recognized gain or loss if the insurance proceeds are:
   a. $440,000?
   b. $390,000?

44. Albert owns 100 acres of land on which he grows spruce Christmas trees. His adjusted basis for the land is $100,000. He receives condemnation proceeds of $10,000 when the city's new beltway takes 5 acres along the eastern boundary of his property. He also receives a severance award of $6,000 associated with the possible harmful effects of exhaust fumes on his Christmas trees. Albert invests the $16,000 in a growth mutual fund. Determine the tax consequences to Albert of the:
   a. Condemnation proceeds.
   b. Severance award.

45. For each of the following involuntary conversions, indicate whether the property acquired qualifies as replacement property, the recognized gain, and the basis for the property acquired:
   a. Frank owns a warehouse that is destroyed by a tornado. The space in the warehouse was rented to various tenants. The adjusted basis was $470,000. Frank uses all of the insurance proceeds of $700,000 to build a shopping mall in a neighboring community where no property has been damaged by tornadoes. The shopping mall is rented to various tenants.
   b. Ivan owns a warehouse that he uses in his business. The adjusted basis is $300,000. The warehouse is destroyed by fire. Because of economic conditions in the area, Ivan decides not to rebuild the warehouse. Instead, he uses all of the insurance proceeds of $400,000 to build a warehouse to be used in his business in another state.
   c. Ridge's personal residence is condemned as part of a local government project to widen the highway from two lanes to four lanes. The adjusted basis is $170,000. Ridge uses all of the condemnation proceeds of $200,000 to purchase another personal residence.
   d. Juanita owns a building that she uses in her retail business. The adjusted basis is $250,000. The building is destroyed by a hurricane. Because of an economic downturn in the area caused by the closing of a military base, Juanita decides to rent space for her retail outlet rather than to replace the building. She uses all of the insurance proceeds of $300,000 to buy a four-unit apartment building in another city. A realtor in that city will handle the rental of the apartments for her.
   e. Susan and Rick's personal residence is destroyed by a tornado. They had owned it for 15 months. The adjusted basis was $170,000. Since they would like to travel, they decide not to acquire a replacement residence. Instead, they invest all of the insurance proceeds of $200,000 in a duplex, which they rent to tenants.

46. The building that houses LaToya's designer clothing store is destroyed in a mud slide associated with a flood on June 27, 2008. LaToya had anticipated the flood and moved her inventory, furniture, and fixtures to a warehouse outside the floodplain on June 20, 2008. Her adjusted basis for the building is $215,000, and she receives insurance proceeds of $240,000 on July 15, 2008. LaToya intends to purchase another building for her store, but would like to have time to find one in a safer location. Her taxable year ends on March 31.

    a. What are the earliest and latest dates that LaToya can make a qualified replacement?

    b. Assuming LaToya makes a qualified replacement costing $240,000, what are her realized gain, recognized gain, and basis for the replacement property?

    c. What are the earliest and latest dates that LaToya can make a qualified replacement if the form of the involuntary conversion is a condemnation by a governmental authority? She was officially notified of the pending condemnation on June 1, 2008, and the condemnation occurred on June 27, 2008.

47. Leslie's office building (adjusted basis of $325,000) is destroyed by a hurricane in November 2008. Leslie, a calendar year taxpayer, receives insurance proceeds of $450,000 in January 2009. Calculate Leslie's realized gain or loss, recognized gain or loss, and basis for the replacement property if she:

    a. Acquires a new office building for $460,000 in January 2009.

    b. Acquires a new office building for $430,000 in January 2009.

    c. Does not acquire replacement property.

48. Cabel's warehouse, which has an adjusted basis of $380,000 and a fair market value of $450,000, is condemned by an agency of the Federal government to make way for a highway interchange. The initial condemnation offer is $410,000. After substantial negotiations, the agency agrees to transfer to Cabel a surplus warehouse that he believes is worth $450,000. Cabel is a calendar year taxpayer. The condemnation and related asset transfer occur during September 2008. *Decision Making*

    a. What are the recognized gain or loss and the basis of the replacement warehouse if Cabel's objective is to recognize as much gain as possible?

    b. Advise Cabel regarding what he needs to do by what date in order to achieve his objective.

49. What are the *maximum* postponed gain or loss and the basis for the replacement property for the following involuntary conversions?

	Property	Type of Conversion	Amount Realized	Adjusted Basis	Amount Reinvested
a.	Drugstore (business)	Casualty	$160,000	$130,000	$110,000
b.	Apartments (investment)	Condemned	100,000	125,000	175,000
c.	Grocery store (business)	Casualty	400,000	300,000	450,000
d.	Residence (personal)	Casualty	16,000	18,000	17,000
e.	Vacant lot (investment)	Condemned	240,000	160,000	220,000
f.	Residence (personal)	Casualty	20,000	18,000	19,000
g.	Residence (personal)	Condemned	18,000	20,000	26,000
h.	Apartments (investment)	Condemned	150,000	100,000	200,000

50. Rental property owned by Faye, a calendar year taxpayer, is destroyed by a tornado on January 1, 2008. Faye had originally paid $150,000 for the property ($125,000 allocated to the building and $25,000 allocated to the land). During the time Faye owned the property, MACRS deductions of $46,250 were claimed. MACRS deductions of $57,500 would have been claimed, except that Faye chose to forgo $11,250 one year when she had a net operating loss. Faye receives insurance proceeds of $60,000 in November 2008. As a result of continuing negotiations with the insurance company, Faye receives additional proceeds of $35,000 in August 2009. *Decision Making*

    a. What is Faye's adjusted basis for the property?

    b. What is Faye's realized gain or loss on the involuntary conversion in 2008? In 2009?

c.   What is the latest date that Faye can replace the involuntarily converted property to qualify for § 1033 postponement?

d.   What is the latest date that Faye can replace the involuntarily converted property to qualify for § 1033 postponement if the form of the involuntary conversion is a condemnation?

e.   What should Faye do regarding the omitted MACRS deductions of $11,250?

Decision Making

51.   On February 2, 2008, Kay sells her principal residence for $235,000. During 2006, she had lived in the residence as a tenant under a lease with an option to buy clause and had purchased it on January 2, 2007, for $180,000. On February 5, 2008, Kay purchases a new residence for $190,000.

a.   What is Kay's recognized gain? Her basis for the new residence?

b.   Assume instead that Kay purchased her original residence on January 2, 2006, rather than on January 2, 2007. What is Kay's recognized gain? Her basis for the new residence?

c.   What could you recommend to Kay to minimize her recognized gain in (a)?

52.   Taylor has owned and occupied her personal residence (adjusted basis of $190,000) for four years. In April 2008, she sells the residence for $300,000 (selling expenses are $20,000). On the same day as the sale, Taylor purchases another house for $350,000. Because of noisy neighbors, she sells the new house after just 10 months. The selling price is $483,000 (selling expenses are $18,000).

a.   What is Taylor's recognized gain on the sale of the first residence?

b.   What is Taylor's basis for her second residence?

c.   What is Taylor's recognized gain on the sale of the second residence?

d.   Assume instead that the sale of the second residence was due to Taylor's job transfer to another state. What is her recognized gain on the sale of the second residence?

53.   Milton, who is single, listed his personal residence with a realtor on March 3, 2008, at a price of $250,000. He rejected several offers in the $200,000 range during the summer. Finally, on August 16, 2008, he and the purchaser signed a contract to sell for $245,000. The sale (i.e., closing) took place on September 7, 2008. The closing statement showed the following disbursements:

Realtor's commission	$ 14,000
Appraisal fee	500
Exterminator's certificate	300
Recording fees	400
Mortgage to First Bank	180,000
Cash to seller	49,800

Milton's adjusted basis for the house is $150,000. He owned and occupied the house for eight years. On October 1, 2008, Milton purchases another residence for $210,000.

a.   Calculate Milton's recognized gain on the sale.

b.   What is Milton's adjusted basis for the new residence?

c.   Assume instead that the selling price is $735,000. What is Milton's recognized gain? His adjusted basis for the new residence?

54.   Assuming § 121 applies, what are the realized, recognized, and excluded gain or loss and the new basis in each of the following cases?

a.   Susan sold her residence for $390,000. The adjusted basis was $55,000. The selling expenses were $15,000. Repair expenses incurred to get the house ready to sell were $3,000. She did not reinvest in a new residence.

b.   Rocky sold his residence for $270,000. The adjusted basis was $120,000. The selling expenses were $9,000. Repair expenses incurred to get the house ready to sell were $6,000. Rocky reinvested $260,000 in a new residence.

c.   Veneia sold her residence for $465,000. The adjusted basis was $35,000. The selling expenses were $17,000. Repair expenses incurred to get the house ready to sell were $2,000. She reinvested $400,000 in a new residence.

d.   Barry sold his residence for $70,000. The adjusted basis was $65,000. The selling expenses were $6,000. He reinvested $80,000 in a new residence.

e. Carl sold his residence for $100,000 in cash, and his mortgage is assumed by the buyer. The adjusted basis was $80,000; the mortgage, $50,000. The selling expenses were $4,000. Repair expenses incurred to get the house ready to sell were $2,000. He reinvested $120,000 in a new residence.

55. Jill bought a house in April 2004 for $190,000. She lived in it until September 2006 when she moved to Mack's new home. Mack and Jill got married and filed a joint return in 2007 and subsequent years. In January 2008, Jill sells her house for $300,000 (selling expenses are $18,000).

a. Do Mack and Jill qualify for the § 121 exclusion? What is the maximum amount of exclusion available on the sale of Jill's house? What is her recognized gain?

b. On June 22, 2009, Mack and Jill sell Mack's house for $600,000. Selling expenses are $24,000, and Mack's adjusted basis is $260,000. What is the maximum amount of the § 121 exclusion available on the sale of Mack's home? What is the recognized gain?

c. Would the result in part (b) change if Mack's house is not sold until June 2010?

56. Nell, Nina, and Nora Sanders, who are sisters, sell their principal residence (owned as tenants in common) in which they have lived for the past 20 years. The youngest of the sisters is age 58. The selling price is $750,000, selling expenses and legal fees are $75,000, and the adjusted basis is $60,000 (the fair market value of the residence when inherited from their parents 20 years ago). Since the sisters are going to live in rental housing, they do not plan to acquire another residence. Nell has contacted you on behalf of the three sisters regarding the tax consequences of the sale.

Communications

a. Write a letter to Nell advising her of the tax consequences and how taxes can be minimized. Nell's address is 100 Oak Avenue, Billings, MT 59101.

b. Prepare a memo for the tax files.

57. Ben owns a beach house (five years) and a cabin in the mountains (four years). His adjusted basis is $280,000 in the beach house and $315,000 in the mountain cabin. Ben also rents a townhouse in the city where he is employed. During the year, he occupies each of the three residences as follows:

Decision Making

Townhouse	120 days
Beach house	170 days
Mountain cabin	75 days

The beach house is close enough to the city so that he can commute to work during the spring and early fall. While this level of occupancy may vary slightly from year to year, it is representative during the time period that Ben has owned the two residences.

As Ben plans on retiring in several years, he sells both residences. The mountain cabin is sold on March 3, 2008, for $540,000 (related selling expenses of $30,000). The beach house is sold on December 10, 2008, for $600,000 (related selling expenses of $36,000).

a. Calculate Ben's lowest recognized gain on the sale of the two residences.

b. Assume instead that both residences satisfy the two-year ownership and use tests as Ben's principal residence. Since the mountain cabin is sold first, is it possible for Ben to apply the § 121 exclusion to the sale of the beach house?

58. Cisco, a calendar year taxpayer who is age 63, owns a residence in which he has lived for 28 years. The residence is destroyed by fire on August 8, 2008. The adjusted basis is $130,000, and the fair market value is $300,000. Cisco receives insurance proceeds of $300,000 for the residence on September 1, 2008. He is trying to decide whether to purchase a comparable house. He anticipates that he will retire in two years and will move to a warmer climate where he will rent in case he decides to live in different places.

Decision Making

a. Advise Cisco of the tax consequences of replacing versus not replacing the residence.

b. Which do you recommend to him?

c. How would your answer in (a) change if the fair market value and insurance proceeds received were $500,000?

59. Jeff and Jill are divorced on August 1, 2008. According to the terms of the divorce decree, Jeff's ownership interest in the house is to be transferred to Jill in exchange for

Decision Making

the release of marital rights. The house was separately owned by Jeff and on the date of the transfer has an adjusted basis of $175,000 and a fair market value of $200,000.

    a.   Does the transfer cause recognized gain to either Jeff or Jill?

    b.   What is the basis of the house to Jill?

    c.   If instead Jeff sold the house to Jill for $200,000 two months prior to the divorce, would either Jeff or Jill have recognized gain?

    d.   Which transaction, (a) or (c), would be preferable for Jeff?

60.   On September 1, 2008, Marsha sells stock in Orange, Inc., for $60,000. The stock is qualified small business stock and was purchased on August 16, 2007, for $42,000. On September 30, 2008, Marsha purchases $58,000 of Blue, Inc., also qualified small business stock.

    a.   What is Marsha's realized and recognized gain (or loss) on the sale of the Orange stock?

    b.   What is Marsha's basis in the Blue stock?

CUMULATIVE PROBLEMS

Tax Return Problem

61.   Arnold Young, age 39, is single. He lives at 1507 Iris Lane, Albuquerque, NM 87131. His Social Security number is 299–55–2000. Arnold does not wish to have $3 go to the Presidential Election Campaign Fund.

    Arnold was divorced in 2003 after 15 years of marriage. He pays alimony of $30,000 a year to his former spouse, Carol. Carol's Social Security number is 999–33–3000. Arnold's son, Tom, who is age 16, resides with Carol. Arnold pays child support of $12,000 per year. Carol has provided Arnold with a signed Form 8332 in which she releases the dependency deduction to him for 2007. Tom's Social Security number is 399–09–1000.

    Arnold owns a sole proprietorship for which he uses the accrual method of accounting. His revenues and expenses for 2007 are as follows:

Sales revenue	$650,000
Cost of goods sold	395,000
Salary expense	80,000
Rent expense	30,000
Utilities	9,000
Telephone	5,000
Advertising	4,000
Bad debts	6,000
Depreciation	21,000
Health insurance*	10,000
Accounting and legal fees	7,000
Supplies	1,000

*$6,000 for employees and $4,000 for Arnold.

Other income received by Arnold includes the following:

Dividend income:	
Swan, Inc.	$ 8,000
Wren, Inc.	4,000
Interest income:	
First Bank	6,000
Second Bank	2,500
City of Asheville bonds	15,000
Lottery winnings (tickets purchased cost $500)	8,000

During the year, Arnold and his sole proprietorship had the following property transactions:

a. Sold Blue, Inc. stock for $39,000 on March 12, 2007. He had purchased the stock on September 5, 2004, for $46,000.

b. Received an inheritance of $150,000 from his Uncle Henry. Arnold used the $150,000 to purchase Green, Inc. stock on May 15, 2007.

c. Received Orange, Inc. stock worth $9,500 as a gift from his Aunt Jane on June 17, 2007. Her adjusted basis for the stock was $5,000. No gift taxes were paid on the transfer. Aunt Jane had purchased the stock on April 1, 2001. Arnold sold the stock on July 1, 2007, for $20,000.

d. On July 15, 2007, Arnold sold one-half of the Green, Inc. stock for $60,000.

e. Arnold was notified on August 1, 2007, that Yellow, Inc. stock he purchased from a colleague on September 1, 2006, for $42,500 had become worthless. While he perceived that the investment was risky, he did not anticipate that the corporation would declare bankruptcy.

f. On August 15, 2007, Arnold received a parcel of land in Phoenix worth $180,000 in exchange for a parcel of land he owned in Tucson. Since the Tucson parcel was worth $200,000, he also received $20,000 cash. Arnold's adjusted basis for the Tucson parcel was $175,000. He originally purchased it on September 18, 2004.

g. On December 1, 2007, Arnold sold the condominium in which he had been living for the past 10 years. The sales price was $480,000, selling expenses were $28,500, and repair expenses related to the sale were $9,000. Arnold and Carol had purchased the condominium as joint owners for $180,000. Arnold had received Carol's ownership interest as part of the divorce proceedings. The fair market value at that time was $240,000.

Arnold's potential itemized deductions, exclusive of the aforementioned information, are as follows:

Medical expenses (before the 7.5% floor)	$ 8,000
Property taxes on residence	5,500
State income taxes	3,000
Charitable contributions	11,000
Mortgage interest on residence	8,500
Sales taxes paid	4,000

During the year, Arnold makes estimated Federal income tax payments of $18,000.

Compute Arnold's lowest net tax payable or refund due for 2007, assuming he makes any available elections that will reduce the tax. If you use tax forms for your computations, you will need Forms 1040, 8332, and 8824 and Schedules A, B, C, D, and SE. Suggested software: Tax Cut.

62. Tammy Walker, age 37, is a self-employed accountant. Tammy's Social Security number is 333–40–1111. Her address is 101 Glass Road, Richmond, VA 23236. Her income and expenses associated with her accounting practice for 2008 are as follows:

Tax Computation Problem

Decision Making

Communications

Revenues (cash receipts during 2008)	$322,000
Expenses	
Salaries	$ 85,000
Office supplies	2,100
Postage	2,900
Depreciation of equipment	30,000
Telephone	800
	$120,800

Since Tammy is a cash method taxpayer, she does not record her receivables as revenue until she receives cash payment. At the beginning of 2008, her accounts receivable were $82,000, and the balance had decreased to $20,000 by the end of the year. The balance on December 31, 2008, would have been $23,000, except that an account for $3,000 had become uncollectible in November.

Tammy used one room in her 10-room house as the office for her accounting practice (300 square feet out of a total square footage of 3,000). She paid the following expenses related to the house during 2008:

Utilities	$3,900
Insurance	1,800
Property taxes	5,000
Repairs	2,700

Tammy had purchased the house on September 1, 2007, for $280,000 (exclusive of land cost).

Tammy has one child, Thomas, age 16. Thomas lives with his father during the summer and with Tammy for the rest of the year. Tammy can document that she spent $26,000 during 2008 for the child's support. The father normally provides about $9,000 per year, but this year he gave Thomas a new car for Christmas. The cost of the car was $20,000. The divorce decree is silent regarding the dependency exemption for Thomas. Tammy does not provide her former spouse with a signed Form 8332 for 2008.

Under the terms of the divorce decree, Tammy is to receive alimony of $10,000 per month. The payments will terminate at Tammy's death or at her remarriage.

Tammy provides part of the support of her mother, age 67. The total support in 2008 for her mother was as follows:

Social Security benefits	$5,200
From Tammy	2,900
From Bob, Tammy's brother	2,000
From Susan, Tammy's sister	1,900

Bob and Susan have both indicated their willingness to sign a multiple support waiver form if it will benefit Tammy.

Tammy's deductible itemized deductions during 2008, excluding any itemized deductions related to the house, were $18,000. She made estimated tax payments of $98,000.

Part 1—Tax Computation
Compute Tammy's lowest net tax payable or refund due for 2008.

Part 2—Tax Planning
Tammy and her former husband have been discussing the $10,000 alimony he pays her each month. Because his new wife has a health problem, he does not feel that he can afford to continue to pay the $10,000 each month. He is in the 15% tax bracket. If Tammy will agree to decrease the amount by 25%, he will agree that the amount paid is not alimony for tax purposes. Assume that the other data used in calculating Tammy's taxable income for 2008 will apply for her 2009 tax return. Write a letter to Tammy that contains your advice on whether she should agree to her former husband's proposal. Also prepare a memo for the tax files.

RESEARCH PROBLEMS

Note: Solutions to Research Problems can be prepared by using the **RIA Checkpoint®
Student Edition** online research product, which is available to accompany this text. It is
also possible to prepare solutions to the Research Problems by using tax research materials found in a standard tax library.

Research Problem 1.   Penelope and Stuart have been married for nine years. For the past six years, they have lived in the house Penelope owns at 100 Oriena Avenue. In July 2007, Stuart purchases the house from Penelope for $350,000. Her adjusted basis for the house is $130,000. No closing costs are incurred.

Penelope and Stuart continue to live in the house until February 2008 when Stuart sells it for $390,000. Selling expenses are $12,000. Penelope and Stuart file separate returns in 2008. Determine if Stuart is eligible for the § 121 exclusion and, if so, the amount of the exclusion. Also determine his recognized gain.

Partial list of research aids:

§ 121(d)(3)(A).

Research Problem 2.   For three years, Amos, a calendar year taxpayer, has owned stock that is qualified small business stock under § 1045. The stock has an adjusted basis of $10,000. On July 2, 2008, he sells the stock for $100,000. On August 3, 2008, he uses the sales proceeds of $100,000 to purchase other qualified small business stock. If possible, Amos would like to defer any recognized gain on the sale of the stock. Advise Amos on the tax consequences of the sale and the subsequent purchase and the procedure he must follow to achieve his deferral objective.

Research Problem 3.   April owned an annuity contract (cash balance of $250,000) issued by Teal Insurance Company. She decides to switch to an annuity contract issued by Brown Insurance Company. To make the change, April instructed Teal to cash out her annuity by issuing a check to Brown. Teal refused to do so and issued a check for $250,000 payable to April.

   April intended that the exchange of annuity contracts qualify for tax deferral treatment under § 1035(a)(3). Consequently, rather than depositing or cashing the check from Teal, she endorsed it and sent it to Brown.

   On audit, an IRS agent contends that the transaction does not qualify under § 1035(a)(3). For tax deferral to apply, the initial annuity contract must be directly exchanged for the new annuity contract. Evaluate the positions of the parties.

Research Problem 4.   Asa operated his business in a building on Mason Drive. Due to changing residential housing patterns in the city, he decided to move the business to a new location on Leigh Lane. His adjusted basis for the Mason Drive property is $120,000, and the fair market value is $500,000. He purchased the Leigh Lane property for $500,000 on September 1, 2008. Asa quitclaimed title to the Leigh Lane property to Ivory Enterprises on September 1, 2008, in exchange for a nonrecourse and non-interest-bearing single payment note for $500,000 (to be paid at the second closing). Ivory was to have a building constructed on the Leigh Lane property in accordance with specifications provided by Asa. The construction of the building was financed by a $700,000 note that was guaranteed by Asa and was nonrecourse to Ivory.

   Another agreement provided that Asa would convey the Mason Drive property to Ivory on completion of the building in exchange for the Leigh Lane property and the new building. At that time, Asa would assume the $700,000 note.

   On December 1, the Leigh Lane property was conveyed to Asa, the Mason Drive property was conveyed to Ivory, and Ivory paid the $500,000 note to Asa (the second closing). Asa assumed the $700,000 note associated with the construction and reported his recognized gain as follows:

	Exchange of Mason Drive	Sale of Leigh Lane
Amount realized	$ 500,000	$ 1,210,000
Basis	(120,000)	(1,200,000)
Realized gain	$ 380,000	$ 10,000
Recognized gain	$ –0–*	$ 10,000

*§ 1031 like-kind exchange.

   An IRS agent treated the transactions as the sale of the Mason Drive property and a § 1031 exchange of the Leigh Lane property, producing a recognized gain of $380,000 rather than $10,000.

   Evaluate the position of the IRS and of Asa.

Research Problem 5.   Taylor owns a 150-unit motel that was constructed in the late 1960s. It is located on 10 acres on the main highway leading into the city. Taylor renovated the motel three years ago.

Taylor's motel is condemned by the city, which is going to use 2 of the 10 acres for a small park. The other 8 acres are to be sold to a timeshare developer who intends to build 400 units on the property. The developer has already secured approval from the city planning commission.

Taylor's attorney advises him not to contest the condemnation of the 2 acres for the park. Under the eminent domain provision, the city does have the right to take "private property for public use." However, the attorney advises Taylor to contest the condemnation of the remaining property. According to the attorney, the city does not have the right to take "private property for private use."

The city's position is that the condemnation will result in a substantial number of new jobs and additional tax revenue for the city.

Will Taylor be successful if he follows the attorney's advice?

Internet *Activity*

Use the tax resources of the Internet to address the following questions. Do not restrict your search to the World Wide Web, but include a review of newsgroups and general reference materials, practitioner sites and resources, primary sources of the tax law, chat rooms and discussion groups, and other opportunities.

Research Problem 6.   Find two newspaper stories about transactions to which you believe the involuntary conversion rules could apply. Do not limit your search to individual taxpayers.

Research Problem 7.   A number of public policy think tanks, taxpayer unions, and other private interest groups have proposed changes to the tax rules that apply to like-kind exchanges of realty. Summarize several of these proposals, including your assessment of the motivations underlying the suggested changes.

Research Problem 8.   Find and print a Form 8824, Like Kind Exchanges. Fill in the form as part of the requirements for Problem 35.

CHAPTER 16

Property Transactions: Capital Gains and Losses

OUTLINE

General Considerations, 16–2
Rationale for Separate Reporting of Capital Gains and Losses, 16–2
General Scheme of Taxation, 16–3
Capital Assets, 16–3
Definition of a Capital Asset, 16–3
Effect of Judicial Action, 16–6
Statutory Expansions, 16–6
Sale or Exchange, 16–8
Worthless Securities and § 1244 Stock, 16–8
Special Rule—Retirement of Corporate Obligations, 16–9
Options, 16–9
Patents, 16–11
Franchises, Trademarks, and Trade Names, 16–12
Lease Cancellation Payments, 16–13
Holding Period, 16–14
Review of Special Holding Period Rules, 16–15
Special Rules for Short Sales, 16–16

Tax Treatment of Capital Gains and Losses of Noncorporate Taxpayers, 16–19
Capital Gain and Loss Netting Process, 16–20
Qualified Dividend Income, 16–23
Alternative Tax on Net Capital Gain, 16–23
Treatment of Capital Losses, 16–24
Reporting Procedures, 16–27
Tax Treatment of Capital Gains and Losses of Corporate Taxpayers, 16–31
Tax Planning Considerations, 16–31
Importance of Capital Asset Status, 16–31
Planning for Capital Asset Status, 16–31
Effect of Capital Asset Status in Transactions Other Than Sales, 16–32
Stock Sales, 16–33
Maximizing Benefits, 16–33
Year-End Planning, 16–34

LO.1
Understand the rationale for separate reporting of capital gains and losses.

General Considerations

Rationale for Separate Reporting of Capital Gains and Losses

Fourteen years ago, a taxpayer purchased 100 shares of IBM stock for $17 a share. This year the taxpayer sells the shares for $118 a share. Should the $101 per share gain receive any special tax treatment? The $101 gain has built up over 14 years, so it may not be fair to tax it the same as income that was all earned this year.

What if the stock had been purchased for $118 per share and sold for $17 a share? Should the $101 loss be fully deductible? The tax law has an intricate approach to answering these investment activity–related questions.

As you study this chapter, keep in mind that how investment-related gains and losses are taxed can dramatically affect whether taxpayers make investments and which investments are made. Except for a brief discussion in Chapter 3, earlier chapters dwelt on how to determine the amount of gain or loss from a property disposition, but did not discuss the classification of gains and losses. This chapter will focus on that topic.

The tax law requires **capital gains** and **capital losses** to be separated from other types of gains and losses. There are two reasons for this treatment. First, long-term capital gains may be taxed at a lower rate than ordinary gains. An *alternative tax computation* is used to determine the tax when taxable income includes net long-term capital gain. Capital gains and losses must therefore be matched with one another to see if a net long-term capital gain exists. The alternative tax computation is discussed later in the chapter under Tax Treatment of Capital Gains and Losses of Noncorporate Taxpayers.

The second reason the Code requires separate reporting of gains and losses and a determination of their tax character is that a net capital loss is only deductible up to $3,000 per year. Excess loss over the annual limit carries over and may be deductible in a future tax year. Capital gains and losses must be matched with one another to see if a net capital loss exists.

For these reasons, capital gains and losses must be distinguished from other types of gains and losses. Most of this chapter and the next chapter describe the intricate rules for determining what type of gains and losses the taxpayer has.

As a result of the need to distinguish and separately match capital gains and losses, the individual tax forms include very extensive reporting requirements for capital gains and losses. This chapter explains the principles underlying the forms. The forms are illustrated with an example at the end of the chapter.

General Scheme of Taxation

Recognized gains and losses must be properly classified. Proper classification depends upon three characteristics:

- The tax status of the property.
- The manner of the property's disposition.
- The holding period of the property.

The three possible tax statuses are capital asset, § 1231 asset, or ordinary asset. Property disposition may be by sale, exchange, casualty, theft, or condemnation.

There are two holding periods: short term and long term. The short-term holding period is one year or less. The long-term holding period is more than one year.

The major focus of this chapter is capital gains and losses. Capital gains and losses usually result from the disposition of a capital asset. The most common disposition is a sale of the asset. Capital gains and losses can also result from the disposition of § 1231 assets, which is discussed in Chapter 17.

Capital Assets

Definition of a Capital Asset

LO.2
Distinguish capital assets from ordinary assets.

Personal use assets and investment assets are the most common capital assets owned by individual taxpayers. Personal use assets usually include items such as clothing, recreational equipment, a residence, and automobiles. Investment assets usually include investments in mutual funds, corporate stocks and bonds, government bonds, and vacant land. Remember, however, that losses from the sale or exchange of personal use assets are not recognized. Therefore, the classification of such losses as capital losses can be ignored.

Due to the historical preferential treatment of capital gains, taxpayers have preferred that gains be capital gains rather than ordinary gains. As a result, a great many statutes, cases, and rulings have accumulated in the attempt to define what is and what is not a capital asset.

Capital assets are not directly defined in the Code. Instead, § 1221(a) defines what is *not* a capital asset. A **capital asset** is property held by the taxpayer (whether or not it is connected with the taxpayer's business) that is *not* any of the following:

- Inventory or property held primarily for sale to customers in the ordinary course of a business. The Supreme Court, in *Malat v. Riddell*, defined *primarily* as meaning *of first importance* or *principally*.[1]
- Accounts and notes receivable acquired from the sale of inventory or acquired for services rendered in the ordinary course of business.
- Depreciable property or real estate used in a business.
- Certain copyrights; literary, musical, or artistic compositions; or letters, memoranda, or similar property held by (1) a taxpayer whose efforts created the property; (2) in the case of a letter, memorandum, or similar property, a taxpayer for whom it was produced; or (3) a taxpayer in whose hands the basis of the property is determined, for purposes of determining gain from a sale or exchange, in whole or in part by reference to the basis of such property in the hands of a taxpayer described in (1) or (2). When a sale or exchange involves musical compositions or copyrights in musical works either (1) created by the taxpayer's personal efforts or (2) having a basis determined by reference to the basis in the hands of a taxpayer whose personal efforts created the compositions or copyrights, the taxpayer may elect to treat the sale or exchange as the disposition of a capital asset.[2]
- U.S. government publications that are (1) received by a taxpayer from the U.S. government other than by purchase at the price at which they are offered for sale to the public or (2) held by a taxpayer whose basis, for purposes of determining gain from a sale or exchange, is determined by reference to a taxpayer described in (1).
- Supplies of a type regularly used or consumed in the ordinary course of a business.

The Code defines what is not a capital asset. From the preceding list, it is apparent that inventory, accounts and notes receivable, supplies, and most fixed assets of a business are not capital assets. Often, the only business asset that is a capital asset is goodwill. The following discussion provides further detail on each part of the capital asset definition.

Inventory. What constitutes inventory is determined by the taxpayer's business.

EXAMPLE 1	Green Company buys and sells used cars. Its cars are inventory. Its gains from the sale of the cars are ordinary income. ∎

EXAMPLE 2	Soong sells her personal use automobile at a $500 gain. The automobile is a personal use asset and, therefore, a capital asset. The gain is a capital gain. ∎

Accounts and Notes Receivable. Collection of an accrual basis account receivable usually does not result in a gain or loss because the amount collected equals the receivable's basis. The sale of an account or note receivable may generate a gain or loss, and the gain or loss is ordinary because the receivable is not a capital asset. The sale of an accrual basis receivable may result in a gain or loss because it will probably be sold for more or less than its basis. A cash basis account receivable has no basis. Sale of such a receivable generates a gain. Collection of a cash basis receivable generates ordinary income rather than a gain. A gain usually requires a sale of the receivable. See the discussion of Sale or Exchange later in this chapter.

---

[1]66–1 USTC ¶9317, 17 AFTR2d 604, 86 S.Ct. 1030 (USSC, 1966).   [2]§ 1221(b)(3).

Oriole Company has accounts receivable of $100,000. Because it needs working capital, it sells the receivables for $83,000 to a financial institution. If Oriole is an accrual basis taxpayer, it has a $17,000 ordinary loss. Revenue of $100,000 would have been recorded and a $100,000 basis would have been established when the receivable was created. If Oriole is a cash basis taxpayer, it has $83,000 of ordinary income because it would not have recorded any revenue earlier; thus, the receivable has no tax basis. ■

Business Fixed Assets.
Depreciable personal property and real estate (both depreciable and nondepreciable) used by a business are not capital assets. Thus, *business fixed assets* are generally not capital assets.

The Code has a very complex set of rules pertaining to such property. One of these rules is discussed under Real Property Subdivided for Sale in this chapter; the remainder of the rules are discussed in Chapter 17. Although business fixed assets are not capital assets, a long-term capital gain can sometimes result from their sale. Chapter 17 discusses the potential capital gain treatment for business fixed assets under § 1231.

Copyrights and Creative Works.
Generally, the person whose efforts led to the copyright or creative work has an ordinary asset, not a capital asset. *Creative works* include the works of authors, composers, and artists. Also, the person for whom a letter, memorandum, or other similar property was created has an ordinary asset. Finally, a person receiving a copyright, creative work, letter, memorandum, or similar property by gift from the creator or the person for whom the work was created has an ordinary asset. Note the exception mentioned earlier that permits the taxpayer to elect to treat the sale or exchange of a musical composition or a copyright of a musical work as the disposition of a capital asset.

Wanda is a part-time music composer. A music publisher purchases one of her songs for $5,000. Wanda has a $5,000 ordinary gain from the sale of an ordinary asset unless she elects to treat the gain as a capital gain. ■

Ed received a letter from the President of the United States in 1982. In the current year, Ed sells the letter to a collector for $300. Ed has a $300 ordinary gain from the sale of an ordinary asset (because the letter was created for Ed). ■

Isabella gives a song she composed to her son. The son sells the song to a music publisher for $5,000. The son has a $5,000 ordinary gain from the sale of an ordinary asset unless he elects to treat the gain as a capital gain. If the son inherits the song from Isabella, his basis for the song is its fair market value at Isabella's death. In this situation, the song is a capital asset because the son's basis is not related to Isabella's basis for the song. ■

(Patents are subject to special statutory rules discussed later in the chapter.)

ETHICAL and EQUITABLE *Considerations*   INVENTORY OR CAPITAL ASSET?

Mathias has been the sole proprietor of a clothing store for many years. He intends to retire after holding a "liquidation sale." He wants to avoid ordinary income from the sale of the business inventory, so he shuts down the store for one month and then begins the liquidation sale. Mathias tells you (his tax return preparer) to report the liquidation sale proceeds as capital gain because he was no longer using those assets in a business at the time of the sale, but was holding them for investment. Evaluate the propriety of Mathias's plan.

U.S. Government Publications. U.S. government publications received from the U.S. government (or its agencies) for a reduced price are not capital assets. This prevents a taxpayer from later donating the publications to charity and claiming a charitable contribution equal to the fair market value of the publications. A charitable contribution of a capital asset generally yields a deduction equal to the fair market value. A charitable contribution of an ordinary asset generally yields a deduction equal to less than the fair market value. If such property is received by gift from the original purchaser, the property is not a capital asset to the donee. (For a more comprehensive explanation of charitable contributions of property, refer to Chapter 10.)

Effect of Judicial Action

Court decisions play an important role in the definition of capital assets. Because the Code only lists categories of what are *not* capital assets, judicial interpretation is sometimes required to determine whether a specific item fits into one of those categories. The Supreme Court follows a literal interpretation of the categories. For instance, corporate stock is not mentioned in § 1221. Thus, corporate stock is *usually* a capital asset. However, what if corporate stock is purchased for resale to customers? Then it is *inventory* and not a capital asset because inventory is one of the categories in § 1221. (See the discussion of Dealers in Securities below.)

A Supreme Court decision was required to distinguish between capital asset and non-capital asset status when a taxpayer who normally did not acquire stock for resale to customers acquired stock with the intention of resale.[3] The Court decided that since the stock was not acquired primarily for sale to customers (the taxpayer did not sell the stock to its regular customers), the stock was a capital asset.

Often the crux of the capital asset determination hinges on whether the asset is held for investment purposes (capital asset) or business purposes (ordinary asset). The taxpayer's *use* of the property often provides objective evidence.

EXAMPLE 7

David's business buys an expensive painting. If the painting is used to decorate David's office and is not of investment quality, the painting is depreciable and, therefore, not a capital asset. If David's business is buying and selling paintings, the painting is inventory and, therefore, an ordinary asset. If the painting is of investment quality and the business purchased it for investment, the painting is a capital asset, even though it serves a decorative purpose in David's office. *Investment quality* generally means that the painting is expected to appreciate in value. If David depreciates the painting, that would be objective evidence that the painting is held for use in his business, is not being held for investment or as inventory, and is not a capital asset. ∎

Because of the uncertainty associated with capital asset status, Congress has enacted several Code Sections to clarify the definition. These statutory expansions of the capital asset definition are discussed in the following section.

Statutory Expansions

Congress has often expanded the § 1221 general definition of what is *not* a capital asset.

Dealers in Securities. As a general rule, securities (stocks, bonds, and other financial instruments) held by a dealer are considered to be inventory and are, therefore, not subject to capital gain or loss treatment. A *dealer in securities* is a merchant (e.g., a brokerage firm) that regularly engages in the purchase and resale of securities to customers. The dealer must identify any securities being held for investment. Generally, if a dealer clearly identifies certain securities as held for investment purposes by the close of business on the acquisition date, gain from the

---

[3] *Arkansas Best v. Comm.*, 88–1 USTC ¶9210, 61 AFTR2d 88–655, 108 S.Ct. 971 (USSC, 1988).

securities' sale will be capital gain. However, the gain will not be capital gain if the dealer ceases to hold the securities for investment prior to the sale. Losses are capital losses if at any time the securities have been clearly identified by the dealer as held for investment.[4]

EXAMPLE 8

Tracy is a securities dealer. She purchases 100 shares of Swan stock. If Tracy takes no further action, the stock is inventory and an ordinary asset. If she designates in her records that the stock is held for investment, the stock is a capital asset. Tracy must designate the investment purpose by the close of business on the acquisition date. If Tracy maintains her investment purpose and later sells the stock, the gain or loss is capital gain or loss. If Tracy redesignates the stock as held for resale (inventory) and then sells it, any gain is ordinary, but any loss is capital loss. Stock designated as held for investment and then sold at a loss always yields a capital loss. ■

Real Property Subdivided for Sale. Substantial real property development activities may result in the owner being considered a dealer for tax purposes. Income from the sale of real estate property lots is treated as the sale of inventory (ordinary income) if the owner is considered to be a dealer. However, § 1237 allows real estate investors capital gain treatment if they engage *only* in *limited* development activities. To be eligible for § 1237 treatment, the following requirements must be met:

- The taxpayer may not be a corporation.
- The taxpayer may not be a real estate dealer.
- No substantial improvements may be made to the lots sold. *Substantial* generally means more than a 10 percent increase in the value of a lot. Shopping centers and other commercial or residential buildings are considered substantial, while filling, draining, leveling, and clearing operations are not.
- The taxpayer must have held the lots sold for at least 5 years, except for inherited property. The substantial improvements test is less stringent if the property is held at least 10 years.

If the preceding requirements are met, all gain is capital gain until the tax year in which the *sixth* lot is sold. Sales of contiguous lots to a single buyer in the same transaction count as the sale of one lot. Beginning with the tax year the *sixth* lot is sold, some of the gain may be ordinary income. Five percent of the revenue from lot sales is potential ordinary income. That potential ordinary income is offset by any selling expenses from the lot sales. Practically, sales commissions often are at least 5 percent of the sales price, so none of the gain is treated as ordinary income.

Section 1237 does not apply to losses. A loss from the sale of subdivided real property is an ordinary loss unless the property qualifies as a capital asset under § 1221. The following example illustrates the application of § 1237.

EXAMPLE 9

Jack owns a large tract of land and subdivides it for sale. Assume Jack meets all the requirements of § 1237 and during the tax year sells the first 10 lots to 10 different buyers for $10,000 each. Jack's basis in each lot sold is $3,000, and he incurs total selling expenses of $4,000 on the sales. Jack's gain is computed as follows:

Selling price (10 × $10,000)	$100,000	
Less: Selling expenses (10 × $400)	(4,000)	
Amount realized		$ 96,000
Basis (10 × $3,000)		(30,000)
Realized and recognized gain		$ 66,000

---

[4]§§ 1236(a) and (b) and Reg. § 1.1236–1(a).

Classification of recognized gain:		
Ordinary income		
Five percent of selling price (5% × $100,000)	$ 5,000	
Less: Selling expenses	(4,000)	
Ordinary gain		1,000
Capital gain		$65,000

Nonbusiness Bad Debts. A loan not made in the ordinary course of business is classified as a nonbusiness receivable. In the year the receivable becomes completely worthless, it is a *nonbusiness bad debt*, and the bad debt is treated as a short-term capital loss. Even if the receivable was outstanding for more than one year, the loss is still a short-term capital loss. Chapter 7 discusses nonbusiness bad debts more thoroughly.

Sale or Exchange

LO.3

Understand the relevance of a sale or exchange to classification as a capital gain or loss and apply the special rules for the capital gain or loss treatment of the retirement of corporate obligations, options, patents, franchises, and lease cancellation payments.

Recognition of capital gain or loss usually requires a sale or exchange of a capital asset. The Code uses the term **sale or exchange**, but does not define it. Generally, a property sale involves the receipt of money by the seller and/or the assumption by the purchaser of the seller's liabilities. An exchange involves the transfer of property for other property. Thus, an involuntary conversion (casualty, theft, or condemnation) is not a sale or exchange. In several situations, the determination of whether a sale or exchange has taken place has been clarified by the enactment of Code Sections that specifically provide for sale or exchange treatment.

Recognized gains or losses from the cancellation, lapse, expiration, or any other termination of a right or obligation with respect to personal property (other than stock) that is or would be a capital asset in the hands of the taxpayer are capital gains or losses.[5] See the discussion under Options later in the chapter for more details.

Worthless Securities and § 1244 Stock

Occasionally, securities such as stock and, especially, bonds may become worthless due to the insolvency of their issuer. If such a security is a capital asset, the loss is deemed to have occurred as the result of a sale or exchange on the *last day* of the tax year.[6] This last-day rule may have the effect of converting what otherwise would have been a short-term capital loss into a long-term capital loss. (See Treatment of Capital Losses later in this chapter.) Worthless securities are discussed in Chapter 7 at pages 7–6, 7–7, and 7–26.

Section 1244 allows an ordinary deduction on disposition of stock at a loss. The stock must be that of a small business company, and the ordinary deduction is limited to $50,000 ($100,000 for married individuals filing jointly) per year. For a more detailed discussion, refer to Chapter 7.

[5]§ 1234A.   [6]§ 165(g)(1).

Special Rule—Retirement of Corporate Obligations

A debt obligation (e.g., a bond or note payable) may have a tax basis in excess of or less than its redemption value because it may have been acquired at a premium or discount. Consequently, the collection of the redemption value may result in a loss or gain. Generally, the collection of a debt obligation is *treated* as a sale or exchange.[7] Therefore, any loss or gain can be a capital loss or capital gain because a sale or exchange has taken place. However, if the debt obligation was issued by a human being prior to June 9, 1997, and/or purchased by the taxpayer prior to June 9, 1997, the collection of the debt obligation is not a sale or exchange.

EXAMPLE 10

Fran acquires $1,000 of Osprey Corporation bonds for $980 in the open market. If the bonds are held to maturity, the $20 difference between Fran's collection of the $1,000 redemption value and her cost of $980 is treated as capital gain. If the obligation had been issued to Fran by an individual prior to June 9, 1997, her $20 gain would be ordinary, since she did not sell or exchange the debt. ■

Original Issue Discount. The benefit of the sale or exchange exception that allows a capital gain from the collection of certain obligations is reduced when the obligation has original issue discount. **Original issue discount (OID)** arises when the issue price of a debt obligation is less than the maturity value of the obligation. OID must generally be amortized over the life of the debt obligation using the effective interest method. The OID amortization increases the basis of the bond. Most new publicly traded bond issues do not carry OID since the stated interest rate is set to make the market price on issue the same as the bond's face amount. In addition, even if the issue price is less than the face amount, the difference is not considered to be OID if the difference is less than one-fourth of 1 percent of the redemption price at maturity multiplied by the number of years to maturity.[8]

In the case where OID does exist, it may or may not have to be amortized, depending upon the date the obligation was issued. When OID is amortized, the amount of gain upon collection, sale, or exchange of the obligation is correspondingly reduced. The obligations covered by the OID amortization rules and the method of amortization are presented in §§ 1272–1275. Similar rules for other obligations can be found in §§ 1276–1288.

EXAMPLE 11

Jerry purchases $10,000 of newly issued White Corporation bonds for $6,000. The bonds have OID of $4,000. Jerry must amortize the discount over the life of the bonds. The OID amortization *increases* his interest income. (The bonds were selling at a discount because the market rate of interest was greater than the bonds' interest rate.) After Jerry has amortized $1,800 of OID, he sells the bonds for $8,000. Jerry has a capital gain of $200 [$8,000 − ($6,000 cost + $1,800 OID amortization)]. The OID amortization rules prevent him from converting ordinary interest income into capital gain. Without the OID amortization, Jerry would have capital gain of $2,000 ($8,000 − $6,000 cost). ■

Options

Frequently, a potential buyer of property wants some time to make the purchase decision, but wants to control the sale and/or the sale price in the meantime. **Options** are used to achieve these objectives. The potential purchaser (grantee) pays the property owner (grantor) for an option on the property. The grantee then becomes the option holder. The option usually sets a price at which the grantee can buy the property and expires after a specified period of time.

[7]§ 1271.   [8]§ 1273(a)(3).

Sale of an Option. A grantee may sell or exchange the option rather than exercising it or letting it expire. Generally, the grantee's sale or exchange of the option results in capital gain or loss if the option property is (or would be) a capital asset to the grantee.[9]

EXAMPLE 12

Rosa wants to buy some vacant land for investment purposes. She cannot afford the full purchase price. Instead, she convinces the landowner (grantor) to sell her the right to purchase the land for $100,000 anytime in the next two years. Rosa (grantee) pays $3,000 to obtain this option to buy the land. The option is a capital asset for Rosa because if she actually purchased the land, the land would be a capital asset. Three months after purchasing the option, Rosa sells it for $7,000. She has a $4,000 ($7,000 − $3,000) short-term capital gain on this sale since she held the option for one year or less. ∎

Failure to Exercise Options. If an option holder (grantee) fails to exercise the option, the lapse of the option is considered a sale or exchange on the option expiration date. Thus, the loss is a capital loss if the property subject to the option is (or would be) a capital asset in the hands of the grantee.

The grantor of an option on *stocks, securities, commodities, or commodity futures* receives short-term capital gain treatment upon the expiration of the option. Options on property other than stocks, securities, commodities, or commodity futures result in ordinary income to the grantor when the option expires. For example, an individual investor who owns certain stock (a capital asset) may sell a call option, entitling the buyer of the option to acquire the stock at a specified price higher than the value at the date the option is granted. The writer of the call receives a premium (e.g., 10 percent) for writing the option. If the price of the stock does not increase during the option period, the option will expire unexercised. Upon the expiration of the option, the grantor must recognize short-term capital gain. These provisions do not apply to options held for sale to customers (the inventory of a securities dealer).

Exercise of Options by Grantee. If the option is exercised, the amount paid for the option is added to the optioned property's selling price. This increases the gain (or reduces the loss) to the grantor resulting from the sale of the property. The grantor's gain or loss is capital or ordinary depending on the tax status of the property. The grantee adds the cost of the option to the basis of the property purchased.

EXAMPLE 13

On September 1, 2004, Wes purchases 100 shares of Eagle Company stock for $5,000. On April 1, 2008, he writes a call option on the stock, giving the grantee the right to buy the stock for $6,000 during the following six-month period. Wes (the grantor) receives a call premium of $500 for writing the call.

- If the call is exercised by the grantee on August 1, 2008, Wes has $1,500 ($6,000 + $500 − $5,000) of long-term capital gain from the sale of the stock. The grantee has a $6,500 ($500 option premium + $6,000 purchase price) basis for the stock.
- Assume that Wes decides to sell his stock prior to exercise for $6,000 and enters into a closing transaction by purchasing a call on 100 shares of Eagle Company stock for $5,000. Since the Eagle stock is selling for $6,000, Wes must pay a call premium of $1,000. He recognizes a $500 short-term capital loss [$1,000 (call premium paid) − $500 (call premium received)] on the closing transaction. On the actual sale of the Eagle stock, Wes has a long-term capital gain of $1,000 [$6,000 (selling price) − $5,000 (cost)]. The grantee is not affected by Wes's closing transaction. The original option is still in existence, and the grantee's tax consequences will depend on what action the grantee takes—exercising the option, letting the option expire, or selling the option.
- Assume that the original option expired unexercised. Wes has a $500 short-term capital gain equal to the call premium received for writing the option. This gain is not

---

[9]§ 1234(a) and Reg. § 1.1234–1(a)(1). Stock options are discussed in Chapter 19.

CONCEPT SUMMARY   16–1

Options

| Event | Effect on | |
	Grantor	Grantee
Option is granted.	Receives value and has a contract obligation (a liability).	Pays value and has a contract right (an asset).
Option expires.	Has a short-term capital gain if the option property is stocks, securities, commodities, or commodity futures. Otherwise, gain is ordinary income.	Has a loss (capital loss if option property would have been a capital asset for the grantee).
Option is exercised.	Amount received for option increases proceeds from sale of the option property.	Amount paid for option becomes part of the basis of the option property purchased.
Option is sold or exchanged by grantee.	Result depends upon whether option later expires or is exercised (see above).	Could have gain or loss (capital gain or loss if option property would have been a capital asset for the grantee).

recognized until the option expires. The grantee has a loss from expiration of the option. The nature of the loss will depend upon whether the option was a capital asset or an ordinary asset. ■

Concept Summary 16–1 summarizes the rules for options.

Patents

Transfer of a **patent** is treated as the sale or exchange of a long-term capital asset when all substantial rights to the patent (or an undivided interest that includes all such rights) are transferred by a holder.[10] The transferor/holder may receive payment in virtually any form. Lump-sum or periodic payments are most common. The amount of the payments may also be contingent on the transferee/purchaser's productivity, use, or disposition of the patent. If the transfer meets these requirements, any gain or loss is *automatically a long-term* capital gain or loss. Whether the asset was a capital asset for the transferor, whether a sale or exchange occurred, and how long the transferor held the patent are not relevant.

This special long-term capital gain or loss treatment for patents is intended to encourage technological progress. Ironically, authors, composers, and artists are not eligible for capital gain treatment when their creations are transferred. Books, songs, and artists' works may be copyrighted, but copyrights and the assets they represent are not capital assets. Thus, the disposition of those assets by their creators usually results in ordinary gain or loss (unless the exception for musical compositions applies, as noted earlier). The following example illustrates the special treatment for patents.

EXAMPLE 14

Diana, a druggist, invents a pill-counting machine, which she patents. In consideration of a lump-sum payment of $200,000 plus $10 per machine sold, Diana assigns the patent to Drug Products, Inc. Assuming Diana has transferred all substantial rights, the question of whether the transfer is a sale or exchange of a capital asset is not relevant. Diana automatically has a long-term capital gain from both the lump-sum payment and the $10 per machine royalty to the extent these proceeds exceed her basis for the patent. ■

---

[10]§ 1235.

Substantial Rights. To receive favorable capital gain treatment, all *substantial rights* to the patent (or an undivided interest in it) must be transferred. All substantial rights to a patent means all rights (whether or not then held by the grantor) that are valuable at the time the patent rights (or an undivided interest in the patent) are transferred. All substantial rights have not been transferred when the transfer is limited geographically within the issuing country or when the transfer is for a period less than the remaining life of the patent. The circumstances of the entire transaction, rather than merely the language used in the transfer instrument, are to be considered in deciding whether all substantial rights have been transferred.[11]

EXAMPLE 15

Assume Diana, the druggist in Example 14, only licensed Drug Products, Inc., to manufacture and sell the invention in Michigan. She retained the right to license the machine elsewhere in the United States. Diana has retained a substantial right and is not eligible for automatic long-term capital gain treatment. ∎

Holder Defined. The *holder* of a patent must be an *individual* and is usually the invention's creator. A holder may also be an individual who purchases the patent rights from the creator before the patented invention is reduced to practice. However, the creator's employer and certain parties related to the creator do not qualify as holders. Thus, in the common situation where an employer has all rights to an employee's inventions, the employer is not eligible for long-term capital gain treatment. More than likely, the employer will have an ordinary asset because the patent was developed as part of its business.

Franchises, Trademarks, and Trade Names

A mode of operation, a widely recognized brand name (trade name), and a widely known business symbol (trademark) are all valuable assets. These assets may be licensed (commonly known as franchising) by their owner for use by other businesses. Many fast-food restaurants (such as McDonald's and Taco Bell) are franchises. The franchisee usually pays the owner (franchisor) an initial fee plus a contingent fee. The contingent fee is often based upon the franchisee's sales volume.

For Federal income tax purposes, a **franchise** is an agreement that gives the franchisee the right to distribute, sell, or provide goods, services, or facilities within a specified area.[12] A franchise transfer includes the grant of a franchise, a transfer by one franchisee to another person, or the renewal of a franchise.

A franchise transfer is generally not a sale or exchange of a capital asset. Section 1253 provides that a transfer of a franchise, trademark, or trade name is not a transfer of a capital asset when the transferor retains any significant power, right, or continuing interest in the property transferred.

Significant Power, Right, or Continuing Interest. *Significant powers, rights, or continuing interests* include control over assignment, quality of products and services, and sale or advertising of other products or services, and the right to require that substantially all supplies and equipment be purchased from the transferor. Also included are the right to terminate the franchise at will and the right to substantial contingent payments. Most modern franchising operations involve some or all of these powers, rights, or continuing interests.

In the unusual case where no significant power, right, or continuing interest is retained by the transferor, a sale or exchange may occur, and capital gain or loss treatment may be available. For capital gain or loss treatment to be available, the asset transferred must qualify as a capital asset.

---

[11]Reg. § 1.1235–2(b)(1).   [12]§ 1253(b)(1).

EXAMPLE 16

Orange, Inc., a franchisee, sells the franchise to a third party. Payments to Orange are not contingent, and all significant powers, rights, and continuing interests are transferred. The gain (payments – adjusted basis) on the sale is a capital gain to Orange. ∎

Noncontingent Payments. When the transferor retains a significant power, right, or continuing interest, the transferee's noncontingent payments to the transferor are ordinary income to the transferor. The franchisee capitalizes the payments and amortizes them over 15 years. The amortization is subject to recapture under § 1245.[13]

EXAMPLE 17

Grey Company signs a 10-year franchise agreement with DOH Donuts. Grey (the franchisee) makes payments of $3,000 per year for the first 8 years of the franchise agreement—a total of $24,000. Grey cannot deduct $3,000 per year as the payments are made. Instead, Grey may amortize the $24,000 total over 15 years. Thus, Grey may deduct $1,600 per year for each of the 15 years of the amortization period. The same result would occur if Grey made a $24,000 lump-sum payment at the beginning of the franchise period. Assuming DOH Donuts (the franchisor) retains significant powers, rights, or a continuing interest, it will have ordinary income when it receives the payments from Grey. ∎

Contingent Payments. Whether or not the transferor retains a significant power, right, or continuing interest, contingent franchise payments are ordinary income for the franchisor and an ordinary deduction for the franchisee. For this purpose, a payment qualifies as a contingent payment only if the following requirements are met:

- The contingent amounts are part of a series of payments that are paid at least annually throughout the term of the transfer agreement.
- The payments are substantially equal in amount or are payable under a fixed formula.

EXAMPLE 18

TAK, a spicy chicken franchisor, transfers an eight-year franchise to Otis. TAK retains a significant power, right, or continuing interest. Otis, the franchisee, agrees to pay TAK 15% of sales. This contingent payment is ordinary income to TAK and a business deduction for Otis as the payments are made. ∎

Sports Franchises. Professional sports franchises (e.g., the Detroit Tigers) are covered by § 1253.[14] Player contracts are usually one of the major assets acquired with a sports franchise. These contracts last only for the time stated in the contract. By being classified as § 197 intangibles, the player contracts and other intangible assets acquired in the purchase of the sports franchise are amortized over a statutory 15-year period.[15]

Concept Summary 16–2 summarizes the rules for franchises.

Lease Cancellation Payments

The tax treatment of payments received for canceling a lease depends on whether the recipient is the **lessor** or the **lessee** and whether the lease is a capital asset or not.

Lessee Treatment. Lease cancellation payments received by a lessee are treated as an exchange.[16] Thus, these payments are capital gains if the lease is a capital asset. Generally, a lessee's lease is a capital asset if the property (either personalty or realty) is used for the lessee's personal use (e.g., his or her residence). A lessee's lease is an ordinary asset if the property is used in the lessee's trade or business and the lease has existed for one year or less when it is canceled. A lessee's lease is a

---

[13]See Chapter 17 for a discussion of the recapture provisions.
[14]§ 1253(e).
[15]§ 197(a).
[16]§ 1241 and Reg. § 1.1241–1(a).

CONCEPT SUMMARY 16–2

Franchises

| | Effect on | |
Event	Franchisor	Franchisee
Franchisor Retains Significant Powers and Rights		
Noncontingent payment	Ordinary income.	Capitalized and amortized over 15 years as an ordinary deduction; if franchise is sold, amortization is subject to recapture under § 1245.
Contingent payment	Ordinary income.	Ordinary deduction.
Franchisor Does *Not* Retain Significant Powers and Rights		
Noncontingent payment	Ordinary income if franchise rights are an ordinary asset; capital gain if franchise rights are a capital asset (unlikely).	Capitalized and amortized over 15 years as an ordinary deduction; if the franchise is sold, amortization is subject to recapture under § 1245.
Contingent payment	Ordinary income.	Ordinary deduction.

§ 1231 asset if the property is used in the lessee's trade or business and the lease has existed for more than a year when it is canceled.[17]

EXAMPLE 19

Mark owns an apartment building that he is going to convert into an office building. Vicki is one of the apartment tenants and receives $1,000 from Mark to cancel the lease. Vicki has a capital gain of $1,000 (which is long term or short term depending upon how long she has held the lease). Mark has an ordinary deduction of $1,000. ■

Lessor Treatment. Payments received by a lessor for a lease cancellation are always ordinary income because they are considered to be in lieu of rental payments.[18]

EXAMPLE 20

Floyd owns an apartment building near a university campus. Hui-Fen is one of the tenants. Hui-Fen is graduating early and offers Floyd $800 to cancel the apartment lease. Floyd accepts the offer. Floyd has ordinary income of $800. Hui-Fen has a nondeductible payment since the apartment was personal use property. ■

LO.4

Determine whether the holding period for a capital asset is long term or short term.

Holding Period

Property must be held more than one year to qualify for long-term capital gain or loss treatment.[19] Property not held for the required long-term period results in short-term capital gain or loss. To compute the **holding period**, start counting on the day after the property was acquired and include the day of disposition.

---

[17]Reg. § 1.1221–1(b) and PLR 200045019.

[18]*Hort v. Comm.*, 41–1 USTC ¶9354, 25 AFTR 1207, 61 S.Ct. 757 (USSC, 1941).

[19]§ 1222.

TAX *in the News*   HOW LONG WAS THE HOLDING PERIOD FOR THAT PROPERTY?

An individual taxpayer exchanged rental real estate in Michigan that she had owned for 16 years for rental real estate in Florida. The transaction qualified as a nontaxable like-kind exchange. Within eight months of acquiring the Florida property, the taxpayer sold it when she received a very substantial unsolicited offer for the property. The local newspaper highlighted the transaction as an example of how out-of-state taxpayers were driving up real estate prices by buying and quickly reselling Florida property. Even though the taxpayer actually owned the Florida property for only eight months, her holding period for Federal income tax purposes was 16 years and eight months because the holding period of the property given up in the like-kind exchange is tacked on to the holding period of the property acquired in the exchange.

EXAMPLE 21

Marge purchases a capital asset on January 15, 2007, and sells it on January 16, 2008. Marge's holding period is more than one year. If Marge had sold the asset on January 15, 2008, the holding period would have been exactly one year, and the gain or loss would have been short term. ■

To be held for more than one year, a capital asset acquired on the last day of any month must not be disposed of until on or after the first day of the thirteenth succeeding month.[20]

EXAMPLE 22

Leo purchases a capital asset on February 28, 2007. If Leo sells the asset on February 28 or 29, 2008, the holding period is one year, and Leo will have a short-term capital gain or loss. If Leo sells the asset on March 1, 2008, the holding period is more than one year, and he will have a long-term capital gain or loss. ■

Review of Special Holding Period Rules

There are several special holding period rules.[21] The application of these rules depends on the type of asset and how it was acquired.

Nontaxable Exchanges. The holding period of property received in a like-kind exchange includes the holding period of the former asset if the property that has been exchanged is a capital asset or a § 1231 asset. In certain nontaxable transactions involving a substituted basis, the holding period of the former property is *tacked on* to the holding period of the newly acquired property.

EXAMPLE 23

Vern exchanges a business truck for another truck in a like-kind exchange. The holding period of the exchanged truck tacks on to the holding period of the new truck. ■

Certain Nontaxable Transactions Involving a Carryover of Another Taxpayer's Basis. A former owner's holding period is tacked on to the present owner's holding period if the transaction is nontaxable and the former owner's basis carries over to the present owner.

EXAMPLE 24

Kareem acquires 100 shares of Robin Corporation stock for $1,000 on December 31, 2004. He transfers the shares by gift to Megan on December 31, 2007, when the stock is worth $2,000. Kareem's basis of $1,000 becomes the basis for determining gain or loss on a subsequent sale by Megan. Megan's holding period begins with the date the stock was acquired by Kareem. ■

---

[20]Rev.Rul. 66–7, 1966–1 C.B. 188.   [21]§ 1223.

EXAMPLE 25	Assume the same facts as in Example 24, except that the fair market value of the shares is only $800 on the date of the gift. The holding period begins on the date of the gift if Megan sells the stock for a loss. The value of the shares at the date of the gift is used in the determination of her basis for loss. If she sells the shares for $500 on April 1, 2008, Megan has a $300 recognized capital loss, and the holding period is from December 31, 2007, to April 1, 2008 (thus, the loss is short term). ∎

Certain Disallowed Loss Transactions. Under several Code provisions, realized losses are disallowed. When a loss is disallowed, there is no carryover of holding period. Losses can be disallowed under § 267 (sale or exchange between related taxpayers) and § 262 (sale or exchange of personal use assets) as well as other Code Sections. Taxpayers who acquire property in a disallowed loss transaction will have a new holding period begin and will have a basis equal to the purchase price.

EXAMPLE 26	Janet sells her personal automobile at a loss. She may not deduct the loss because it arises from the sale of personal use property. Janet purchases a replacement automobile for more than the selling price of her former automobile. Janet has a basis equal to the cost of the replacement automobile, and her holding period begins when she acquires the replacement automobile. ∎

Inherited Property. The holding period for inherited property is treated as long term no matter how long the property is actually held by the heir. The holding period of the decedent or the decedent's estate is not relevant for the heir's holding period.[22]

EXAMPLE 27	Shonda inherits Blue Company stock from her father. She receives the stock on April 1, 2008, and sells it on November 1, 2008. Even though Shonda did not hold the stock more than one year, she receives long-term capital gain or loss treatment on the sale. ∎

Special Rules for Short Sales

General. The Code provides special rules for determining the holding period of property sold short.[23] A **short sale** occurs when a taxpayer sells borrowed property and repays the lender with substantially identical property either held on the date of the sale or purchased after the sale. Short sales usually involve corporate stock. The seller's objective is to make a profit in anticipation of a decline in the stock's price. If the price declines, the seller in a short sale recognizes a profit equal to the difference between the sales price of the borrowed stock and the price paid for the replacement stock.

A *short sale against the box* occurs when the stock is borrowed from a broker by a seller who already owns the same stock. The box is the safe deposit box where stock owners routinely used to keep stock certificates. Although today stockbrokers generally keep stock certificates for their customers, the terminology "short sale against the box" is still used.

EXAMPLE 28	Chris does not own any shares of Brown Corporation. However, Chris sells 30 shares of Brown. The shares are borrowed from Chris's broker and must be replaced within 45 days. Chris has a short sale because he was short the shares he sold. He will *close* the short sale by purchasing Brown shares and delivering them to his broker. If the original 30 shares were sold for $10,000 and Chris later purchases 30 shares for $8,000, he has a gain of $2,000. Chris's hunch that the price of Brown stock would decline was correct. Chris was able to profit from selling high and buying low. If Chris had to purchase Brown shares for $13,000 to

---

[22]In 2010, there will be no estate tax, and not all inherited assets will receive an automatic long-term holding period. Some inherited assets will have a "carryover" basis and holding period that are calculated similarly to the basis and holding period for property received by gift. See § 1022 after the effective date for this provision in the Tax Relief Reconciliation Act of 2001.

[23]§ 1233.

GLOBAL
Tax Issues

TRADING ADRs ON U.S. STOCK EXCHANGES

Many non-U.S. companies now have subsidiaries that were formerly U.S. companies. For instance, until 2007 Chrysler Corporation was a subsidiary of DaimlerChrysler (formed when the German company Daimler-Benz acquired Chrysler). Shares in such foreign companies generally cannot be traded directly on U.S. stock exchanges. Instead, the foreign companies issue instruments called American Depository Receipts (ADRs) that can be traded on U.S. stock exchanges. Purchases and sales of ADRs are treated for tax purposes as though the ADRs were shares in the corporation that issued them.

close the short sale, he would have a loss of $3,000. In this case, Chris would have sold low and bought high—not the result he wanted! Chris would be making a short sale against the box if he borrowed shares from his broker to sell and then closed the short sale by delivering other Brown shares he owned at the time he made the short sale. ■

A short sale gain or loss is a capital gain or loss to the extent that the short sale property constitutes a capital asset of the taxpayer. The gain or loss is not recognized until the short sale is closed. Generally, the holding period of the short sale property is determined by how long the property used to close the short sale was held. However, if *substantially identical property* (e.g., other shares of the same stock) is held by the taxpayer, the short-term or long-term character of the short sale gain or loss may be affected:

- If substantially identical property has *not* been held for the long-term holding period on the short sale date, the short sale *gain or loss* is short term.
- If substantially identical property has *been* held for the long-term holding period on the short sale date, the short sale *gain* is long term if the substantially identical property is used to close the short sale and short term if it is not used to close the short sale.
- If substantially identical property has *been* held for the long-term holding period on the short sale date, the short sale *loss* is long term whether or not the substantially identical property is used to close the short sale.
- If substantially identical property is acquired *after* the short sale date and on or before the closing date, the short sale *gain or loss* is short term.

Concept Summary 16–3 summarizes the short sale rules. These rules are intended to prevent the conversion of short-term capital gains into long-term capital gains and long-term capital losses into short-term capital losses.

Disposition Rules for Short Sales against the Box. In a short sale against the box, the taxpayer either owns securities that are substantially identical to the securities sold short at the short sale date or acquires such securities before the closing date. To remove the taxpayer's flexibility as to when the short sale gain must be reported, a constructive sale approach is used. If the taxpayer has not closed the short sale by delivering the short sale securities to the broker *before* January 31 of the year following the short sale, the short sale is deemed to have been closed on the *earlier* of two events:

- On the short sale date if the taxpayer owned substantially identical securities at that time.
- On the date during the year of the short sale that the taxpayer acquired substantially identical securities.[24]

The basis of the shares in the deemed transfer of shares is used to compute the gain or loss on the short sale. Later, when shares are *actually* transferred to the

---

[24]§ 1259.

CONCEPT SUMMARY 16–3

Short Sales of Securities

Has the taxpayer held substantially identical securities for the required long-term holding period at the date of the short sale?

— Yes —

To the extent of the number of shares sold short, any loss arising from the closing of the short sale is long-term loss regardless of the holding period of the securities used to close the short sale.

If the securities held for the required long-term holding period are used to close the short sale, any gain is long term.

— No —

Any gain or loss from the close of the short sale is short term.

— And —   — And —

For the number of shares sold short, the holding period of substantially identical securities not held long term at the short sale date or acquired after the short sale date and before the closing date begins with the earlier of the date of sale of those securities or the closing date of the short sale. This holding period rule applies in the order of the acquisition dates of the substantially identical property.

broker to close the short sale, there may be a gain or loss because the shares transferred will have a basis equal to the short sale date price and the value at the *actual* short sale closing date may be different from the short sale date price.

Illustrations. The following examples illustrate the treatment of short sales and short sales against the box.

EXAMPLE 29	On January 4, 2008, Donald purchases five shares of Osprey Corporation common stock for $100. On April 14, 2008, he engages in a short sale of five shares of the same stock for $150. On August 15, Donald closes the short sale by repaying the borrowed stock with the five shares purchased on January 4. Donald has a $50 short-term capital gain from the short sale because he had not held substantially identical shares for the long-term holding period on the short sale date. ∎
EXAMPLE 30	Assume the same facts as in the previous example, except that Donald closes the short sale on January 28, 2009, by repaying the borrowed stock with five shares purchased on January 27, 2009, for $200. The stock used to close the short sale was not the property purchased on January 4, 2008, but since Donald held short-term property at the April 14, 2008 short sale date, the gain or

loss from closing the short sale is short term. Donald has a $50 short-term capital loss ($200 cost of stock purchased on January 27, 2009, and a short sale selling price of $150). ■

On January 18, 2007, Rita purchases 200 shares of Owl Corporation stock for $1,000. On November 11, 2008, she sells short for $1,300 200 shares of Owl Corporation stock that she borrows from her broker. On February 10, 2009, Rita closes the short sale by delivering the 200 shares of Owl Corporation stock that she had acquired in 2007. On that date, Owl Corporation stock had a market price of $3 per share. Since Rita owned substantially identical stock on the date of the short sale and did not close the short sale before January 31, 2009, she is *deemed* to have closed the short sale on November 11, 2008 (the date of the short sale). On her 2008 tax return, she reports a $300 long-term capital gain ($1,300 short sale price – $1,000 basis). On February 10, 2009, Rita has a $700 short-term capital loss [$600 short sale closing date price (200 shares × $3 per share) – $1,300 basis] because the holding period of the shares used to close the short sale commences with the date of the short sale. ■

Assume the same facts as in Example 31, except that Rita did not own any Owl Corporation stock on the short sale date and acquired the 200 shares of Owl Corporation stock for $1,000 on December 12, 2008 (after the November 11, 2008 short sale date). The *deemed* closing of the short sale is December 12, 2008, because Rita held substantially identical shares at the end of 2008 and did not close the short sale before January 31, 2009. Her 2008 short sale gain is a *short-term* gain of $300 ($1,300 short sale price – $1,000 basis), and she still has a short-term capital loss of $700 on February 10, 2009. ■

Tax Treatment of Capital Gains and Losses of Noncorporate Taxpayers

> **LO.5**
>
> Describe the beneficial tax treatment for capital gains and the detrimental tax treatment for capital losses for noncorporate taxpayers.

All taxpayers net their capital gains and losses. Short-term gains and losses (if any) are netted against one another, and long-term gains and losses (if any) are netted against one another. The results will be net short-term gain or loss and net long-term gain or loss. If these two net positions are of opposite sign (one is a gain and one is a loss), they are netted against one another.

Six possibilities exist for the result after all possible netting has been completed. Three of these final results are gains, and three are losses. One possible result is a net long-term capital gain (NLTCG). Net long-term capital gains of noncorporate taxpayers are subject to beneficial treatment. A second possibility is a net short-term capital gain (NSTCG). Third, the netting may result in both NLTCG and NSTCG.

The NLTCG portion of these results is eligible for an alternative tax calculation. As many as four different tax rates may be used in the calculation—0, 15, 25, and 28 percent. (For tax years before 2008, the 0 percent alternative rate was 5 percent.) The tax savings from the alternative tax calculation range from a low of 10 percentage points (10 percent regular tax rate – 0 percent alternative tax rate) to a high of 20 percentage points (35 percent regular tax rate – 15 percent alternative tax rate). The alternative tax computation is discussed later in the chapter under Alternative Tax on Net Capital Gain.

The last three results of the capital gain and loss netting process are losses. Thus, a fourth possibility is a net long-term capital loss (NLTCL). A fifth result is a net short-term capital loss (NSTCL). Finally, a sixth possibility includes both an NLTCL and an NSTCL. Neither NLTCLs nor NSTCLs are treated as ordinary losses. Treatment as an ordinary loss generally is preferable to capital loss treatment since ordinary losses are deductible in full while the deductibility of capital losses is subject to certain limitations. An individual taxpayer may deduct a maximum of $3,000 of net capital losses for a taxable year.[25]

---

[25]§ 1211(b).

Capital Gain and Loss Netting Process

Holding Periods for Capital Gain and Loss Netting Purposes. As mentioned earlier in this chapter, there are two holding periods for purposes of the capital gain and loss netting process:

- *Short term*—Assets held one year or less.
- *Long term*—Assets held more than one year.

Net short-term capital gain is not eligible for any special tax rate. It is taxed at the same rate as the taxpayer's other taxable income. *Net long-term capital gain* is eligible for one or more of *four* alternative tax rates: 0 percent, 15 percent, 25 percent, and 28 percent. The 25 percent and 28 percent rates are used only in somewhat unusual circumstances, so the discussion below concentrates more heavily on the other two rates. The net long-term capital gain components are referred to as the *0%/15% gain*, the *25% gain*, and the *28% gain*.

The *25% gain* is technically called the **unrecaptured § 1250 gain** and is related to gain from disposition of § 1231 assets. Gains and losses from disposition of § 1231 assets are discussed in Chapter 17. In this chapter, the discussion will focus only on how the *25% gain* is taxed and not how it is determined. The *28% gain* relates to collectibles and § 1202 gain (see Chapter 5). Collectibles gain is discussed later in this chapter.

The *0% gain* portion of the *0%/15% gain* applies when the taxable income before taxing the *0%/15% gain* does not put the taxpayer out of the 15 percent bracket. Once the taxable income (including any portion of the *0%/15% gain* taxed at 0 percent) puts the taxpayer above the 15 percent bracket, the remaining portion of the *0%/15% gain* is taxed at 15 percent rather than at the regular tax rate.

When the long-term capital gain exceeds short-term capital loss, a **net capital gain (NCG)** exists. Net capital gain qualifies for beneficial alternative tax treatment (see the coverage later in the chapter).[26]

Since there are both short- and long-term capital gains and losses and because the long-term capital gains may be taxed at various rates, an *ordering procedure* is required. The ordering procedure tends to preserve the lowest tax rate long-term capital gain when there is a net long-term capital gain. This ordering procedure is explained in the steps below and then illustrated by several examples.

Step 1. Group all gains and losses into short term and 28%, 25%, and 0%/15% long term.

Step 2. Net the gains and losses within each group.

Step 3. Offset the net 28% and net 25% amounts if they are of opposite sign.

Step 4. Offset the results after step 3 against the 0%/15% amount if they are of opposite sign. If the 0%/15% amount is a loss, offset it against the *highest taxed gain first*. After this step, there is a net long-term capital gain or loss. If there is a net long-term capital gain, it may consist of only 28% gain, only 25% gain, only 0%/15% gain, or some combination of all of these gains. If there is a net long-term capital loss, it is simply a net long-term capital loss.

Step 5. Offset the net short-term amount against the results of step 4 if they are of opposite sign. The netting rules offset net short-term capital loss against the *highest taxed gain first*. Consequently, if there is a net short-term capital loss and a net gain from step 4, the short-term capital loss offsets first the 28% gain, then the 25% gain, and finally the 0%/15% gain.

If the result of step 5 is *only* a short-term capital gain, the taxpayer is not eligible for a reduced tax rate. If the result of step 5 is a loss, the taxpayer may be eligible for a *capital loss deduction* (discussed later in this chapter). If there was no offsetting in step 5 because the short-term and step 4 results were both gains *or* if the result of

---

[26]§ 1222(11).

the offsetting is a long-term gain, a net capital gain exists, and the taxpayer may be eligible for a reduced tax rate. The net capital gain may consist of *28% gain, 25% gain*, and/or *0%/15% gain*.

The five steps outlined above can have many unique final results. See Concept Summary 16–5 later in the chapter for a summary of the netting rules and how capital gains and losses are taxed. The following series of examples illustrates the capital gain and loss netting process.

EXAMPLE 33

This example shows how a net short-term capital gain may result from the netting process.

Step	Short Term	Long-Term Gains and Losses 28%	25%	0%/15%	Comment
1	$13,000	$ 12,000		$ 3,000	
	(2,000)	(20,000)			
2	$11,000	($ 8,000)		$ 3,000	
3					No 28%/25% netting because no opposite sign.
4		3,000 →		(3,000)	Netted because of
		($ 5,000)		$ –0–	opposite sign.
5	(5,000) ←	5,000			The net short-term
	$ 6,000	$ –0–			capital gain is taxed
	Net short-term capital gain				as ordinary income.

EXAMPLE 34

This example shows how a net long-term capital gain may result from the netting process.

Step	Short Term	Long-Term Gains and Losses 28%	25%	0%/15%	Comment
1	$ 3,000	$15,000	$4,000	$ 3,000	
	(5,000)	(7,000)		(8,000)	
2	($ 2,000)	$ 8,000	$4,000	($ 5,000)	
3					No 28%/25% netting because no opposite sign.
4		(5,000) ←		5,000	Netted because of opposite sign. Net 0%/15% loss is netted against 28% gain first.
		$ 3,000		$ –0–	
5	2,000 →	(2,000)			The net short-term capital loss is netted against 28% gain first. The net long-term capital gain is $5,000 ($1,000 + $4,000).
	$ –0–	$ 1,000	$4,000		
		Net 28% gain	Net 25% gain		

EXAMPLE 35

This example shows how a net long-term capital loss may result from the netting process.

		Long-Term Gains and Losses			
Step	Short Term	28%	25%	0%/15%	Comment
1	$ 3,000	$ 1,000		$ 3,000	
				(8,000)	
2	$ 3,000	$ 1,000		($ 5,000)	
3					No 28%/25% netting because no opposite sign.
4		(1,000) →		1,000	Netted because of opposite sign.
		$ –0–		($ 4,000)	
5	(3,000)	→	→	3,000	The net short-term capital gain is netted against the net long-term capital loss, and the remaining loss is eligible for the capital loss deduction.
	$ –0–			($ 1,000)	
				Net long-term capital loss	

Use of Capital Loss Carryovers. A short-term capital loss carryover to the current year retains its character as short term and is combined with the short-term items of the current year. A long-term net capital loss carries over as a long-term capital loss and is combined with the current-year long-term items. The long-term loss carryover is first offset with 28% gain of the current year, then 25% gain, and then 0%/15% gain until it is absorbed.

EXAMPLE 36

In 2008, Abigail has a $4,000 short-term capital gain, a $36,000 28% long-term capital gain, and a $13,000 0%/15% long-term capital gain. She also has a $3,000 short-term capital loss carryover and a $2,000 long-term capital loss carryover from 2007. This produces a $1,000 net short-term capital gain ($4,000 − $3,000), a $34,000 net 28% long-term capital gain ($36,000 − $2,000), and a $13,000 net 0%/15% long-term capital gain for 2008. ∎

Definition of Collectibles. Capital assets that are collectibles, even though they are held long term, are not eligible for the *0%/15%* alternative tax rate. Instead, a 28 percent alternative tax rate applies.

For capital gain or loss purposes, **collectibles** include:[27]

- Any work of art.
- Any rug or antique.
- Any metal or gem.
- Any stamp.
- Any alcoholic beverage.
- Most coins.
- Any historical objects (documents, clothes, etc.).

[27]§ 408(m) and Reg. § 1.408–10(b).

ETHICAL and EQUITABLE *Considerations* — HOW MUCH GAIN HAS TO BE REPORTED?

Selma has a $50,000 short-term capital loss carryforward to 2008 and an $87,000 capital gain from sale of inherited stock in 2008. Because she is going to get married in early 2009 and will have to reveal her 2008 tax return as part of prenuptial financial negotiations with her future spouse, she wants her tax return preparer to show on her 2008 tax return only the $37,000 net gain ($87,000 2008 capital gain less the $50,000 carryforward loss). She is embarrassed about the large loss carryforward and does not want her future husband to know how large the gain from the sale of the inherited stock really was. Is there anything wrong with her approach?

Qualified Dividend Income

Dividends paid from current or accumulated earnings and profits of domestic and certain foreign corporations are eligible to be taxed at the 0%/15% long-term capital gain rates if they are **qualified dividend income**. The question of which dividends constitute qualified dividend income is discussed more fully in Chapter 4. Here the discussion focuses on how the qualified dividend income is taxed.

After the net capital gain or loss has been determined, the qualified dividend income is added to the net long-term capital gain portion of the net capital gain and is taxed as *0%/15% gain*. If there is a net capital loss, the net capital loss is still deductible *for* AGI up to $3,000 per year with the remainder of the loss (if any) carrying forward. In this case, the qualified dividend income is still eligible to be treated as *0%/15% gain* in the alternative tax calculation (it is *not* offset by the net capital loss).

Refer to Example 34, but assume there is qualified dividend income of $2,500 in addition to the items shown. The qualified dividend income *is not* netted against the capital gains and losses. Instead, the taxpayer has $1,000 of 28% gain, $4,000 of 25% gain, *and* $2,500 of qualified dividend income taxed at 0%/15%. ■	*E X A M P L E 37*

Refer to Example 35, but assume there is qualified dividend income of $2,500 in addition to the items shown. The qualified dividend income *is not* netted against the net capital loss. The taxpayer has a $1,000 capital loss deduction *and* $2,500 of qualified dividend income taxed at 0%/15%. ■	*E X A M P L E 38*

Alternative Tax on Net Capital Gain

Section 1 contains the statutory provisions that enable the *net capital gain* to be taxed at special rates (0, 15, 25, and 28 percent). This calculation is referred to as the **alternative tax** on net capital gain.[28] The alternative tax applies only if taxable income includes some long-term capital gain (there is net capital gain). Taxable income includes *all* of the net capital gain unless taxable income is less than the net capital gain. In addition, the net capital gain is taxed *last*, after other taxable income (including any short-term capital gain).

Joan, an unmarried taxpayer, has 2008 taxable income of $98,000, including a $12,000 net capital gain. The last $12,000 of her $98,000 taxable income is the layer related to the net capital gain. The first $86,000 ($98,000 − $12,000) of her taxable income is not subject to any special tax rate, so it is taxed using the regular tax rates. ■	*E X A M P L E 39*

---

[28]§ 1(h) Note: Examples 40, 41, and 42 use the 2008 Tax Rate Schedules rather than the 2008 Tax Table to calculate the tax on the non-long-term capital gain portion of taxable income. This approach is used to better illustrate the concepts under discussion. The actual tax on the non-long-term portion of taxable income would be calculated using the Tax Tables since that income is less than $100,000.

Since the net capital gain may be made up of various *rate layers*, it is important to know in what order those layers will be taxed. For *each* of the layers, the taxpayer compares the regular tax rate on that layer of income and the alternative tax rate on that portion of the net capital gain. The layers are taxed in the following order: *25% gain, 28% gain,* the 0 percent portion of the *0%/15% gain,* and then the 15 percent portion of the *0%/15% gain.* As a result of this layering, the taxpayer will benefit from the 0 percent portion of the net capital gain if the tax-payer is still in the 10 percent or 15 percent regular rate bracket after taxing other taxable income and the 25 percent and 28 percent portions of the net capital gain.

EXAMPLE 40

Assume that Joan's $12,000 net capital gain in Example 39 is made up of $10,000 *25% gain* and $2,000 *0%/15% gain.* Examination of the 2008 tax rates reveals that $86,000 of taxable income for a single individual puts Joan at a marginal tax rate of 28%. Conse-quently, she will use the alternative tax on both the $10,000 gain and the $2,000 gain. Her alternative tax liability for 2008 is $20,858 [$18,058 (tax on $86,000 of taxable income) + $2,500 ($10,000 × .25) + $300 ($2,000 × .15)]. Since the combination of the $86,000 taxable income and her $10,000 *25% gain* puts her above the 15% regular tax bracket, none of the $2,000 *0%/15% gain* is taxed at 0%. Her regular tax liability on $98,000 would be $21,418. Thus, Joan saves $560 ($21,418 − $20,858) by using the alter-native tax calculation. ∎

EXAMPLE 41

Joan, an unmarried taxpayer, has 2008 taxable income of $25,000. Of this amount, $12,000 is net capital gain, and $13,000 is other taxable income. The net capital gain is made up of $8,300 of *25% gain* and $3,700 of *0%/15% gain* (including $1,000 of quali-fied dividend income). Her alternative tax liability for 2008 is $2,794 [$1,549 (tax on $13,000 of taxable income) + $1,245 (tax on $8,300 *25% gain* at 15%) + $0 (tax on $3,700 *0%/15% gain* at 0%)]. Since her marginal rate is still 15% after taxing the $13,000 of other taxable income, she uses the 15% regular tax rate rather than the 25% alternative tax rate on the $8,300 *25% gain.* After taxing the $13,000 and the $8,300, a total of $21,300 of the $25,000 taxable income has been taxed. Since her marginal rate is still 15%, she uses the 0% alternative rate for the $3,700 of *0%/15% gain.* The $1,000 qualified dividend income is included in the $3,700 and, thus, is also taxed at 0%. Joan's regular tax liability on $25,000 would be $3,348. Thus, she saves $554 ($3,348 − $2,794) by using the alternative tax calculation. ∎

The alternative tax computation allows the taxpayer to receive the *lower of* the regular tax or the alternative tax on *each layer* of net capital gain or *portion of each layer* of net capital gain.

EXAMPLE 42

Assume the same facts as in Example 41 except that Joan's taxable income is $33,000, consist-ing of $12,000 of net capital gain and $21,000 of other taxable income. Not all of the $3,700 of *0%/15% gain* is taxed at 0% because Joan's taxable income exceeds $32,550, taking her out of the 15% bracket. Consequently, the last $450 ($33,000 − $32,550) of the $3,700 of *0%/15% gain* is taxed at 15% rather than 0%. Her tax liability using the alternative tax com-putation is $4,062 [$2,749 (tax on $21,000 of taxable income) + $1,245 (tax on $8,300 *25% gain* at 15%) + $0 (tax on $3,250 of *0%/15% gain* at 0%) + $68 (tax on $450 of *0%/15% gain* at 15%)]. Joan's regular tax liability on $33,000 would be $4,594. Thus, she saves $532 ($4,594 − $4,062) by using the alternative tax calculation. ∎

Concept Summary 16–4 summarizes the alternative tax computation.

Treatment of Capital Losses

Computation of Net Capital Loss. A **net capital loss (NCL)** results if capital losses exceed capital gains for the year. An NCL may be all long term, all short term, or

CONCEPT SUMMARY 16-4

Income Layers for Alternative Tax on Capital Gain Computation

Compute tax on:	Ordinary taxable income (including net short-term capital gain) using the regular tax rates.
Compute tax on:	Each of the layers below using the *lower* of the alternative tax rate or the regular tax rate for that layer (or portion of a layer) of taxable income.
+	25% long-term capital gain (unrecaptured § 1250 gain) portion of taxable income
+	28% long-term capital gain
+	0% long-term capital gain (portion of 0%/15% capital gain that is taxed at 0%; available only if ordinary taxable income plus 25% and 28% capital gain layers do not put the taxpayer above the 15% bracket; 0% rate is no longer available once income including the portion of the gain taxed at 0% puts the taxpayer out of the 15% bracket)*
+	15% long-term capital gain (remaining portion of 0%/15% capital gain)*
=	Alternative tax on taxable income

*May include qualified dividend income.

part long and part short term.[29] The characterization of an NCL as long or short term is important in determining the capital loss deduction (discussed later in this chapter).

EXAMPLE 43

Three different individual taxpayers have the following capital gains and losses during the year:

Taxpayer	LTCG	LTCL	STCG	STCL	Result of Netting	Description of Result
Robert	$1,000	($ 2,800)	$1,000	($ 500)	($ 1,300)	NLTCL
Carlos	1,000	(500)	1,000	(2,800)	(1,300)	NSTCL
Troy	400	(1,200)	500	(1,200)	(1,500)	NLTCL ($800)
						NSTCL ($700)

Robert's NCL of $1,300 is all long term. Carlos's NCL of $1,300 is all short term. Troy's NCL is $1,500, $800 of which is long term and $700 of which is short term. ∎

Treatment of Net Capital Loss. An NCL is deductible from gross income to the extent of $3,000 per tax year.[30] Capital losses exceeding the loss deduction limits carry forward indefinitely. Thus, although there may or may not be beneficial treatment for capital gains, there is *unfavorable* treatment for capital losses in terms of the $3,000 annual limitation on deducting NCL against ordinary income. If the NCL includes both long-term and short-term capital loss, the short-term capital loss is counted first toward the $3,000 annual limitation.

EXAMPLE 44

Burt has an NCL of $5,500, of which $2,000 is STCL and $3,500 is LTCL. Burt has a capital loss deduction of $3,000 ($2,000 of STCL and $1,000 of LTCL). He has an LTCL carryforward of $2,500 ($3,500 − $1,000). ∎

---

[29]Section 1222(10) defines a net capital loss as the net loss after the capital loss deduction. However, that definition confuses the discussion of net capital loss. Therefore, net capital loss is used here to mean the result after netting capital gains and losses and before considering the capital loss deduction.

The capital loss deduction is discussed under Treatment of Net Capital Loss in this chapter.

[30]§ 1211(b)(1). Married persons filing separate returns are limited to a $1,500 deduction per tax year.

TAX *in the News*   COSTLESS CAPITAL GAINS

Legislation enacted in 2003 created the four alternative tax rates on long-term capital gains. Through 2007 the lowest of the four rates was 5 percent. However, the 2003 legislation prospectively reduced this 5 percent rate to 0 percent starting in 2008. Thus, in 2008 taxpayers pay no tax if their total taxable income does not get them out of the regular 15 percent bracket and consists *only* of long-term capital gain. For instance, a single taxpayer with $32,550 or less of taxable income that is all net long-term capital gain owes no tax. (It is possible that the taxpayer might owe some alternative minimum tax.) In late 2007, numerous tax planning articles began to appear on the Internet suggesting how to take advantage of these "costless" capital gains.

Carryovers. Taxpayers are allowed to carry over unused capital losses indefinitely. The short-term capital loss (STCL) retains its character as STCL. Likewise the long-term capital loss retains its character as LTCL.

EXAMPLE 45

In 2008, Mark incurred $1,000 of STCL and $11,000 of LTCL. In 2009, Mark has a $400 LTCG.

- Mark's NCL for 2008 is $12,000. Mark deducts $3,000 ($1,000 STCL and $2,000 LTCL). He has $9,000 of LTCL carried forward to 2009.
- Mark combines the $9,000 LTCL carryforward with the $400 LTCG for 2009. He has an $8,600 NLTCL for 2009. Mark deducts $3,000 of LTCL in 2009 and carries forward $5,600 of LTCL to 2010. ∎

When a taxpayer has both a capital loss deduction and negative taxable income, a special computation of the capital loss carryover is required.[31] Specifically, the capital loss carryover is the NCL minus the lesser of:

- The capital loss deduction claimed on the return.
- The negative taxable income increased by the capital loss deduction claimed on the return and the personal and dependency exemption deduction.

Without this provision, some of the tax benefit of the capital loss deduction would be wasted when the deduction drives taxable income below zero. However, the capital loss deduction is not reduced if taxable income before the exemption deduction is a positive number or zero. In that situation, it is the exemption deduction, and not the capital loss deduction, that is creating the negative taxable income.

EXAMPLE 46

In 2008, Joanne has a $13,000 NCL (all long term), a $3,500 personal exemption deduction, and $4,000 negative taxable income. The negative taxable income includes a $3,000 capital loss deduction. The capital loss carryover to 2009 is $10,500 computed as follows:

- The $4,000 negative taxable income is treated as a negative number, but the capital loss deduction and personal exemption deduction are treated as positive numbers.
- The normal ceiling on the capital loss deduction is $3,000.
- However, if the $3,000 capital loss deduction and the $3,500 exemption deduction are added back to the $4,000 negative taxable income, only $2,500 of the $3,000 capital loss deduction is needed to make taxable income equal to zero.
- Therefore, this special computation results in only $2,500 of the $13,000 NCL being consumed. The LTCL carryforward is $10,500 ($13,000 − $2,500). ∎

Concept Summary 16–5 summarizes the rules for noncorporate taxpayers' treatment of capital gains and losses.

---

[31]§ 1212(b).

CONCEPT SUMMARY 16–5

Some Possible Final Results of the Capital Gain and Loss Netting Process and How They Are Taxed

Result	Maximum Tax Rate	Comments
Net short-term capital loss	—	Eligible for capital loss deduction ($3,000 maximum per year).
Net long-term capital loss	—	Eligible for capital loss deduction ($3,000 maximum per year).
Net short-term capital loss *and* net long-term capital loss	—	Eligible for capital loss deduction ($3,000 maximum per year). Short-term capital losses are counted first toward the deduction.
Net short-term capital gain	10–35%	Taxed as ordinary income.
Net long-term capital gain	0–28%	The net long-term capital gain may have as many as four tax rate components: 25%, 28%, and 0%/15%.
• The net long-term capital gain is the *last* portion of taxable income.		The components are taxed in the following order: 25%, 28%, 0%, 15%. They are taxed *after* the non-long-term capital gain portion of taxable income has been taxed. The 0%/15% component may include qualified dividend income.
• Each net long-term capital gain component of taxable income is taxed at the *lower* of the regular tax on that component or the alternative tax.		The alternative tax on net long-term capital gain can never increase the tax on taxable income, but it can reduce the tax on taxable income.
Net short-term capital gain *and* net long-term capital gain	10–35% on net short-term capital gain; 0–28% on net long-term capital gain	The net short-term capital gain is taxed as ordinary income; the net long-term capital gain is taxed as discussed above for just net long-term capital gain.

Reporting Procedures

The following discusses the 2007 tax forms because the 2008 tax forms were not available at the time of this writing.

Capital gains and losses are reported on Schedule D of the 2007 Form 1040 (reproduced on pages 16–28 and 16–29 using the data from Example 47). Part I of Schedule D is used to report short-term capital gains and losses. Part II of Schedule D is used to report long-term capital gains and losses. Part III summarizes the results of Parts I and II and indicates whether the taxpayer has a net capital gain or a net capital loss. Part III then helps determine which alternative tax worksheet is used to calculate the alternative tax on long-term capital gains and qualified dividends. If the taxpayer has a net long-term capital gain that does not include any 28% or 25% long-term capital gain, then the alternative tax is calculated using the Qualified Dividends and Capital Gain Worksheet from the Form 1040 instructions. If the taxpayer has a net long-term capital gain that does include either 28% or 25% long-term capital gain, then the alternative tax is calculated using the Schedule D Tax Worksheet from the Schedule D instructions. These worksheets do not have to be filed with the tax return, but are kept for the taxpayer's records.

SCHEDULE D
(Form 1040)

Department of the Treasury
Internal Revenue Service

Capital Gains and Losses

► Attach to Form 1040 or Form 1040NR.   ► See Instructions for Schedule D (Form 1040).

► Use Schedule D-1 to list additional transactions for lines 1 and 8.

OMB No. 1545-0074

2007

Attachment
Sequence No. **12**

Name(s) shown on return
Joan Rapson

Your social security number
467 37 8383

Part I   Short-Term Capital Gains and Losses—Assets Held One Year or Less

(a) Description of property (Example: 100 sh. XYZ Co.)	(b) Date acquired (Mo., day, yr.)	(c) Date sold (Mo., day, yr.)	(d) Sales price (see page D-7 of the instructions)	(e) Cost or other basis (see page D-7 of the instructions)	(f) Gain or (loss) Subtract (e) from (d)
1 *100 shares Blue stock*	01/21/07	11/11/07	11,000	17,000	(6,000)

2 Enter your short-term totals, if any, from Schedule D-1, line 2 . . . . **2**

3 **Total short-term sales price amounts.** Add lines 1 and 2 in column (d) **3** 11,000

4 Short-term gain from Form 6252 and short-term gain or (loss) from Forms 4684, 6781, and 8824 . . . **4**

5 Net short-term gain or (loss) from partnerships, S corporations, estates, and trusts from Schedule(s) K-1 . . . . **5**

6 Short-term capital loss carryover. Enter the amount, if any, from line 10 of your **Capital Loss Carryover Worksheet** on page D-7 of the instructions . . . . **6** (   )

7 **Net short-term capital gain or (loss).** Combine lines 1 through 6 in column (f) **7** (6,000)

Part II   Long-Term Capital Gains and Losses—Assets Held More Than One Year

(a) Description of property (Example: 100 sh. XYZ Co.)	(b) Date acquired (Mo., day, yr.)	(c) Date sold (Mo., day, yr.)	(d) Sales price (see page D-7 of the instructions)	(e) Cost or other basis (see page D-7 of the instructions)	(f) Gain or (loss) Subtract (e) from (d)
8 *100 shares Yellow stock*	09/12/02	10/12/07	36,000	20,000	16,000
100 shares Purple stock	03/14/05	10/12/07	14,000	12,000	2,000

9 Enter your long-term totals, if any, from Schedule D-1, line 9 . . . . **9**

10 **Total long-term sales price amounts.** Add lines 8 and 9 in column (d) **10** 50,000

11 Gain from Form 4797, Part I; long-term gain from Forms 2439 and 6252; and long-term gain or (loss) from Forms 4684, 6781, and 8824 . . . . **11**

12 Net long-term gain or (loss) from partnerships, S corporations, estates, and trusts from Schedule(s) K-1 . . . . **12**

13 Capital gain distributions. See page D-2 of the instructions **13**

14 Long-term capital loss carryover. Enter the amount, if any, from line 15 of your **Capital Loss Carryover Worksheet** on page D-7 of the instructions . . . . **14** (   )

15 **Net long-term capital gain or (loss).** Combine lines 8 through 14 in column (f). Then go to Part III on the back **15** 18,000

For Paperwork Reduction Act Notice, see Form 1040 or Form 1040NR instructions.   Cat. No. 11338H   **Schedule D (Form 1040) 2007**

Part III   **Summary**

16 Combine lines 7 and 15 and enter the result **16**   *12,000*

If line 16 is:
- A **gain**, enter the amount from line 16 on Form 1040, line 13, or Form 1040NR, line 14. Then go to line 17 below.
- A **loss**, skip lines 17 through 20 below. Then go to line 21. Also be sure to complete line 22.
- **Zero**, skip lines 17 through 21 below and enter -0- on Form 1040, line 13, or Form 1040NR, line 14. Then go to line 22.

17 Are lines 15 and 16 **both** gains?
  ☒ **Yes.** Go to line 18.
  ☐ **No.** Skip lines 18 through 21, and go to line 22.

18 Enter the amount, if any, from line 7 of the **28% Rate Gain Worksheet** on page D-8 of the instructions . . . . ▶ **18**   *0*

19 Enter the amount, if any, from line 18 of the **Unrecaptured Section 1250 Gain Worksheet** on page D-9 of the instructions . . . . ▶ **19**   *0*

20 Are lines 18 and 19 **both** zero or blank?
  ☒ **Yes.** Complete Form 1040 through line 43, or Form 1040NR through line 40. Then complete the **Qualified Dividends and Capital Gain Tax Worksheet** on page 35 of the Instructions for Form 1040 (or in the Instructions for Form 1040NR). **Do not** complete lines 21 and 22 below.

  ☐ **No.** Complete Form 1040 through line 43, or Form 1040NR through line 40. Then complete the **Schedule D Tax Worksheet** on page D-10 of the instructions. **Do not** complete lines 21 and 22 below.

21 If line 16 is a loss, enter here and on Form 1040, line 13, or Form 1040NR, line 14, the **smaller** of:

- The loss on line 16 or
- ($3,000), or if married filing separately, ($1,500)   . . . . **21** (   )

Note. When figuring which amount is smaller, treat both amounts as positive numbers.

22 Do you have qualified dividends on Form 1040, line 9b, or Form 1040NR, line 10b?
  ☒ **Yes.** Complete Form 1040 through line 43, or Form 1040NR through line 40. Then complete the **Qualified Dividends and Capital Gain Tax Worksheet** on page 35 of the Instructions for Form 1040 (or in the Instructions for Form 1040NR).

  ☐ **No.** Complete the rest of Form 1040 or Form 1040NR.

Schedule D (Form 1040) 2007

During 2007, Joan Rapson (Social Security number 467–37–8383) had the following sales of capital assets. In addition, she has other taxable income of $66,000, including $300 of qualified dividend income.

E X A M P L E   47

Description	Acquired On	Date Sold	Sales Price	Tax Basis	Gain or Loss	Character
100 shares Blue stock	1/21/07	11/11/07	$11,000	$17,000	($ 6,000)	STCL
100 shares Yellow stock	9/12/02	10/12/07	36,000	20,000	16,000	LTCG
100 shares Purple stock	3/14/05	10/12/07	14,000	12,000	2,000	LTCG

Qualified Dividends and Capital Gain Tax Worksheet—Line 44

Keep for Your Records

Before you begin: ✓	See the instructions for line 44 that begin on page 33 to see if you can use this worksheet to figure your tax.
✓	If you do not have to file Schedule D and you received capital gain distributions, be sure you checked the box on line 13 of Form 1040.

1. Enter the amount from Form 1040, line 43 . . . .   **1.**   78,000

2. Enter the amount from Form 1040, line 9b **2.**   300

3. Are you filing Schedule D?

    ☒ **Yes.** Enter the **smaller** of line 15 or 16 of
          Schedule D. If either line 15 or line 16 is a
          loss, enter -0-   }   **3.**   12,000
    ☐ **No.** Enter the amount from Form 1040, line 13

4. Add lines 2 and 3 . . . .   **4.**   12,300

5. If you are claiming investment interest expense on Form
    4952, enter the amount from line 4g of that form.
    Otherwise, enter -0- **5.**   0

6. Subtract line 5 from line 4. If zero or less, enter -0- **6.**   12,300

7. Subtract line 6 from line 1. If zero or less, enter -0- **7.**   65,700

8. Enter the **smaller** of:
    ● The amount on line 1, or
    ● $31,850 if single or married filing separately,
       $63,700 if married filing jointly or qualifying widow(er),   } **8.**   31,850
       $42,650 if head of household.

9. Is the amount on line 7 equal to or more than the amount on line 8?
    ☒ **Yes.** Skip lines 9 through 11; go to line 12 and check the "No" box.
    ☐ **No.** Enter the amount from line 7 . . . .   **9.**

10. Subtract line 9 from line 8 . . . .   **10.**

11. Multiply line 10 by 5% (.05) . . . .   **11.**

12. Are the amounts on lines 6 and 10 the same?
    ☐ **Yes.** Skip lines 12 through 15; go to line 16.
    ☒ **No.** Enter the **smaller** of line 1 or line 6 . . . .   **12.**   12,300

13. Enter the amount from line 10 (if line 10 is blank, enter -0-) **13.**   0

14. Subtract line 13 from line 12 . . . .   **14.**   12,300

15. Multiply line 14 by 15% (.15) **15.**   1,845

16. Figure the tax on the amount on line 7. Use the Tax Table or Tax Computation Worksheet,
    whichever applies **16.**   12,858

17. Add lines 11, 15, and 16 . . . .   **17.**   14,703

18. Figure the tax on the amount on line 1. Use the Tax Table or Tax Computation Worksheet,
    whichever applies **18.**   15,930

19. **Tax on all taxable income.** Enter the **smaller** of line 17 or line 18. Also include this amount on
    Form 1040, line 44 . . . .   **19.**   14,703

Joan has a net capital gain of $12,000 ($16,000 *5%/15% gain* + $2,000 *5%/15% gain* − $6,000 short-term capital loss). Consequently, all of the net capital gain is composed of *5%/15% gain.* Joan's $78,000 taxable income includes $65,700 ($66,000 − $300) of other taxable income. This example is filled in on the Schedule D on pages 16–28 through 16–30. Joan's total stock sales were reported to her on Form 1099–B by her stockbroker. ∎

Tax Treatment of Capital Gains and Losses of Corporate Taxpayers

LO.6

Describe the tax treatment for capital gains and the detrimental tax treatment for capital losses for corporate taxpayers.

The treatment of a corporation's net capital gain or loss differs from the rules for individuals. Briefly, the differences are as follows:

- There is an NCG alternative tax rate of 35 percent.[32] However, since the maximum corporate tax rate is 35 percent, the alternative tax is not beneficial.
- Capital losses offset only capital gains. No deduction of capital losses is permitted against ordinary taxable income (whereas a $3,000 deduction is allowed to individuals).[33]
- Corporations may carry back net capital losses (whether long term or short term) as short-term capital losses for three years; if losses still remain after the carryback, the remaining losses may be carried forward five years.[34] Individuals may carry forward unused capital losses indefinitely, but there is no carryback.

EXAMPLE 48

Sparrow Corporation has a $15,000 NLTCL for the current year and $57,000 of ordinary taxable income. Sparrow may not offset the $15,000 NLTCL against its ordinary income by taking a capital loss deduction. The $15,000 NLTCL becomes a $15,000 STCL for carryback and carryover purposes. This amount may be offset by capital gains in the three-year carryback period or, if not absorbed there, offset by capital gains in the five-year carryforward period. ■

The rules applicable to corporations are discussed in greater detail in Chapter 20.

Importance of Capital Asset Status

LO.7

Identify tax planning opportunities arising from the sale or exchange of capital assets.

Why is capital asset status important? Capital asset status enables the taxpayer to be eligible for the alternative tax on net capital gain. For a taxpayer in the 25, 28, 33, or 35 percent regular tax bracket, a 15 percent rate is available on assets held longer than one year. For a taxpayer in the 10 or 15 percent regular tax bracket, a 0 percent rate is available on assets held longer than one year. Thus, individuals who can receive income in the form of long-term capital gains or qualified dividend income have an advantage over taxpayers who cannot receive income in these forms.

Capital asset status is also important because capital gains must be offset by capital losses. If a net capital loss results, the maximum deduction is $3,000 per year.

Consequently, capital gains and losses must be segregated from other types of gains and losses and must be reported separately on Schedule D of Form 1040.

TAX PLANNING *Considerations*

Planning for Capital Asset Status

It is important to keep in mind that capital asset status often is a question of objective evidence. Thus, property that is not a capital asset to one party may qualify as a capital asset to another party.

EXAMPLE 49

Diane, a real estate dealer, transfers by gift a tract of land to Jeff, her son. The land was recorded as part of Diane's inventory (it was held for resale) and was therefore not a capital asset to her. Jeff, however, treats the land as an investment. The land is a capital asset in Jeff's hands, and any later taxable disposition of the property by him will yield a capital gain or loss. ■

If proper planning is carried out, even a dealer may obtain long-term capital gain treatment on the sale of the type of property normally held for resale.

[32]§ 1201.
[33]§ 1211(a).
[34]§ 1212(a)(1).

GLOBAL Tax Issues

CAPITAL GAIN TREATMENT IN THE UNITED STATES AND OTHER COUNTRIES

The United States currently requires a very complex tax calculation when taxable income includes net long-term capital gain. However, the alternative tax on net long-term capital gain can generate tax savings even when the taxpayer is in the lowest regular tax bracket (10 percent) because there is an alternative tax rate of 0 percent. Many other countries do not have an alternative tax rate on long-term capital gains. Instead, those gains are taxed the same as other income. Consequently, even though the U.S. system is complex, it may be preferable because of the lower tax rates and because the lower rates are available to taxpayers in all tax brackets.

EXAMPLE 50

Jim, a real estate dealer, segregates tract A from the real estate he regularly holds for resale and designates the property as being held for investment purposes. The property is not advertised for sale and is disposed of several years later. The negotiations for the subsequent sale were initiated by the purchaser and not by Jim. Under these circumstances, it would appear that any gain or loss from the sale of tract A should be a capital gain or loss.[35] ■

When a business is being sold, one of the major decisions usually concerns whether a portion of the sales price is for goodwill. For the seller, goodwill generally represents the disposition of a capital asset. Goodwill has no basis and represents a residual portion of the selling price that cannot be allocated reasonably to the known assets. The amount of goodwill thus represents capital gain.

From a legal perspective, the buyer may prefer that the residual portion of the purchase price be allocated to a covenant not to compete (a promise that the seller will not compete against the buyer by conducting a business similar to the one that the buyer has purchased). Both purchased goodwill and a covenant not to compete are § 197 intangibles. Thus, both must be capitalized and can be amortized over a 15-year statutory period.

To the seller, a covenant produces ordinary income. Thus, the seller would prefer that the residual portion of the selling price be allocated to goodwill—a capital asset. If the buyer does not need the legal protection provided by a covenant, the buyer is neutral regarding whether the residual amount be allocated to a covenant or to goodwill. Since the seller would receive a tax advantage from labeling the residual amount as goodwill, the buyer should factor this into the negotiation of the purchase price.

EXAMPLE 51

Marcia is buying Jack's dry cleaning proprietorship. An appraisal of the assets indicates that a reasonable purchase price would exceed the value of the known assets by $30,000. If the purchase contract does not specify the nature of the $30,000, the amount will be for goodwill, and Jack will have a long-term capital gain of $30,000. Marcia will have a 15-year amortizable $30,000 asset. If Marcia is paying the extra $30,000 to prevent Jack from conducting another dry cleaning business in the area (a covenant not to compete), Jack will have $30,000 of ordinary income. Marcia will have a $30,000 deduction over the statutory 15-year amortization period rather than over the actual life of the covenant (e.g., 5 years). ■

Effect of Capital Asset Status in Transactions Other Than Sales

The nature of an asset (capital or ordinary) is important in determining the tax consequences that result when a sale or exchange occurs. It may, however, be just as

---

[35] *Toledo, Peoria & Western Railroad Co.*, 35 TCM 1663, T.C.Memo. 1976–366.

significant in circumstances other than a taxable sale or exchange. When a capital asset is disposed of, the result is not always a capital gain or loss. Rather, in general, the disposition must be a sale or exchange. Collection of a debt instrument having a basis less than the face value results in a capital gain if the debt instrument is a capital asset. The collection is a sale or exchange. Sale of the debt shortly before the due date for collection will produce a capital gain.[36] If selling the debt in such circumstances could produce a capital gain but collecting could not, the consistency of what constitutes a capital gain or loss would be frustrated. Another illustration of the sale or exchange principle involves a donation of certain appreciated property to a qualified charity. Recall that in certain circumstances, the measure of the charitable contribution is fair market value when the property, if sold, would have yielded a long-term capital gain [refer to Chapter 10 and the discussion of § 170(e)].

E X A M P L E   52

Sharon wants to donate a tract of unimproved land (basis of $40,000 and fair market value of $200,000) held for the required long-term holding period to State University (a qualified charitable organization). However, Sharon currently is under audit by the IRS for capital gains she reported on certain real estate transactions during an earlier tax year. Although Sharon is not a licensed real estate broker, the IRS agent conducting the audit is contending that she has achieved dealer status by virtue of the number and frequency of the real estate transactions she has conducted. Under these circumstances, Sharon would be well-advised to postpone the donation to State University until her status is clarified. If she has achieved dealer status, the unimproved land may be inventory (refer to Example 50 for another possible result), and Sharon's charitable contribution deduction would be limited to $40,000. If not, and if the land is held as an investment, Sharon's deduction is $200,000 (the fair market value of the property). ■

Stock Sales

The following rules apply in determining the date of a stock sale:

- The date the sale is executed is the date of the sale. The execution date is the date the broker completes the transaction on the stock exchange.
- The settlement date is the date the cash or other property is paid to the seller of the stock. This date is *not* relevant in determining the date of sale.

E X A M P L E   53

Lupe, a cash basis taxpayer, sells stock that results in a gain. The sale was executed on December 29, 2007. The settlement date is January 2, 2008. The date of sale is December 29, 2007 (the execution date). The holding period for the stock sold ends with the execution date. ■

Maximizing Benefits

Ordinary losses generally are preferable to capital losses because of the limitations imposed on the deductibility of net capital losses and the requirement that capital losses be used to offset capital gains. The taxpayer may be able to convert what would otherwise have been capital loss to ordinary loss. For example, business (but not nonbusiness) bad debts, losses from the sale or exchange of small business investment company stock, and losses from the sale or exchange of small business company stock all result in ordinary losses.[37]

Although capital losses can be carried over indefinitely, *indefinite* becomes definite when a taxpayer dies. Any loss carryovers not used by the taxpayer are permanently lost. That is, no tax benefit can be derived from the carryovers subsequent to death.[38] Therefore, the potential benefit of carrying over capital losses diminishes when dealing with older taxpayers.

---

[36]§ 1271(b).
[37]§§ 166(d), 1242, and 1244. Refer to the discussion in Chapter 7.
[38]Rev.Rul. 74–175, 1974–1 C.B. 52.

It is usually beneficial to spread gains over more than one taxable year. In some cases, this can be accomplished through the installment sales method of accounting.

Year-End Planning

The following general rules can be applied for timing the recognition of capital gains and losses near the end of a taxable year:

- If the taxpayer already has recognized more than $3,000 of capital loss, sell assets to generate capital gain equal to the excess of the capital loss over $3,000.

EXAMPLE 54

Kevin has already incurred a $7,000 STCL. Kevin should generate $4,000 of capital gain. The gain will offset $4,000 of the loss. The remaining loss of $3,000 can be deducted against ordinary income. ∎

- If the taxpayer already has recognized capital gain, sell assets to generate capital loss equal to the capital gain. The gain will not be taxed, and the loss will be fully *deductible* against the gain.
- Generally, if the taxpayer has a choice between recognizing short-term capital gain or long-term capital gain, long-term capital gain should be recognized because it has the lower tax rate.

KEY TERMS

Alternative tax, 16–23	Holding period, 16–14	Original issue discount (OID), 16–9
Capital asset, 16–3	Lessee, 16–13	Patent, 16–11
Capital gains, 16–2	Lessor, 16–13	Qualified dividend income, 16–23
Capital losses, 16–2	Net capital gain (NCG), 16–20	Sale or exchange, 16–8
Collectibles, 16–22	Net capital loss (NCL), 16–24	Short sale, 16–16
Franchise, 16–12	Options, 16–9	Unrecaptured § 1250 gain, 16–20

PROBLEM MATERIALS

DISCUSSION QUESTIONS

Issue ID

1. Sheila inherited 200 shares of stock, 100 shares of Magenta and 100 shares of Purple. She has a stockbroker sell the shares for her, uses the proceeds for personal expenses, and thinks nothing further about the transactions. What issues does she face when she prepares her Federal income tax return?

Issue ID

2. Jeremy is a sole proprietor running a video store. A large national chain has made an offer to purchase all of his store assets. What issues does Jeremy face in determining what the results of this sale would be?

Issue ID

3. Melissa is a songwriter part-time and a waitress full-time. To her great surprise, a "song broker" has offered to purchase all of Melissa's rights to a song she wrote. What issues does Melissa face if she accepts this offer?

4. Joanne buys and sells cloth as an Internet-based sole proprietor. She shipped cloth to a regular customer, received electronic confirmation of the receipt of the cloth by the customer, and received an electronic affirmation of the customer's willingness to pay the amount due within 30 days. Since Joanne needed cash to buy additional cloth for resale, she sold the receivable electronically the same day. She received $200 less for the receivable than its face value. What are the tax consequences of this transaction?

5. Why are business fixed assets not capital assets?

6. A retail rug store company hired an interior decorator to refurbish its store. The decorator felt that the store needed to impress customers, so the company purchased "investment-grade" art at the decorator's suggestion. The decorator assures the company that the art will increase in value over time. Is the art a fixed asset, inventory, or something else?

7. Jorge is a trader on Wall Street. He buys and sells the stock of high-tech companies as a trader. Occasionally, he decides to hold certain stocks for his own investment account rather than purchasing them for resale. What does Jorge have to do to make sure such investments are treated as capital assets?

8. Anwar owns vacant land that he purchased many years ago as an investment. After getting approval to subdivide it into 35 lots, he made minimal improvements and then sold the entire property to a real estate developer. Anwar's recognized gain on the sale was $1.2 million. Is this transaction eligible for the "real property subdivided for sale" provisions?

9. What is the difference between a "worthless security" and "§ 1244 stock"?

10. Feng-Shu purchased an original issue discount bond several years ago. He paid $68,000 for the $100,000 face value bond. He sold the bond this year for $83,000. Is all of Feng-Shu's gain long-term capital gain? Why or why not?

11. Kashif receives $38,000 from a real estate developer for an option to purchase land Kashif is holding for investment. Fourteen months later, the option expires unexercised. How is the $38,000 taxed to Kashif?

12. Hubert purchases all the rights in a patent from the inventor who developed the patented product. After holding the patent for two years, Hubert sells all the rights in the patent for a substantial gain. What issues does Hubert face if he wants to treat the gain as a long-term capital gain?

Issue ID

13. Angelo has purchased rights for a Donut Delite franchise in the Phoenix area. Angelo paid $45,000 for the franchise rights and will also pay a fee of $.002 per donut sold to the franchisor. Does Angelo have a capital asset?

14. Juan purchased corporate stock for $10,000 on April 10, 2006. On July 14, 2008, when the stock was worth $7,000, he gave it to his son, Miguel. What has to happen to the value of the property while Miguel holds it if Miguel is to tack Juan's holding period on to his own holding period?

Issue ID

15. Near the end of 2008, Byron realizes that he has a net short-term capital loss of $13,000 for the year. Byron has taxable income (not including the loss) of $123,000 and is single. He owns numerous stocks that could be sold for a long-term capital gain. What should he do before the end of 2008?

Issue ID

PROBLEMS

16. During the year, Eric had the four property transactions summarized below. Eric is a collector of antique automobiles and occasionally sells one to get funds to buy another. What are the amount and nature of the gain or loss from each of these transactions?

Property	Date Acquired	Date Sold	Adjusted Basis	Sale Price
Antique truck	06/18/98	05/23/08	$47,000	$35,000
Blue Growth Fund (100 shares)	12/23/00	11/22/08	12,000	23,000
Orange bonds	02/12/01	04/11/08	34,000	42,000*
Green stock (100 shares)	02/14/08	11/23/08	13,000	11,000

*The sales price included $750 of accrued interest.

17. Revez owns an antique shop. He buys property from estates, often at much less than the retail value of the property. Recently, Revez sold for $4,000 an antique clock for which he had paid $1,250. Revez had held the clock in his shop for 36 months before selling it. Revez would like the gain on the sale of the clock to be a long-term capital gain. How can he achieve that objective?

18. Patricia is in the business of lending money at very high interest rates to financially disadvantaged consumers. She decides to move out-of-state due to pressure from various competitors. She sells all of her receivables to a finance company. She receives $320,000 for receivables that have an adjusted basis of $400,000. She had held all of the receivables for more than a year. What is the nature of her gain or loss?

19. Magenta, Inc., purchases used equipment at auction, refurbishes it, and then resells it at a profit. Magenta purchased a 500,000-pound metal-grinding machine for $1.8 million, spent $600,000 refurbishing it over two years, and then sold it for $4 million. What is the nature of the gain or loss from this transaction?

20. Connie is a songwriter who has had many hit songs over the years. She was hired to write a song for a national awards show, and the song was very well received. A music publishing company offered to buy all of Connie's interest in the song for $33,000. Connie had not capitalized any costs of writing the song. What is the nature of the gain or loss from the disposition of the song if Connie wants to minimize her taxes?

21. Indicate whether each of the following is a capital asset:
    a. Savings account obligations of a commercial lending bank.
    b. Personal savings accounts of an individual bank depositor.
    c. Business savings accounts of a commercial laundry company.

22. All of the following assets are held by Charisa, who is not in business. Which ones are capital assets?
    a. Ten shares of Green Motors common stock.
    b. A note receivable Charisa received when she loaned $3,000 to a friend.
    c. Charisa's personal use automobile.
    d. A letter written by President Theodore Roosevelt that Charisa purchased at an auction. Charisa is a collector of Teddy Roosevelt memorabilia.

23. For many years Brown Company (a manufacturer of large industrial engines) has owned a steam engine that was used as a decoration on its business premises. When the steam engine was originally purchased in 1950, it was depreciated, and it has had a zero basis since 1958. This year Brown Company sold the steam engine for $330,000 to a collector of such engines. Brown would like to offset any gain from the disposition of the steam engine against capital losses it has incurred this year. May it do so?

24. Brenda Reynolds is a dealer in securities. She has spotted a fast-rising company and would like to buy and hold its stock for investment. The stock is currently selling for $145 per share, and Brenda thinks it will climb to $200 a share within two years. Brenda's co-workers have told her that there is "no way" she can get long-term capital gain treatment when she purchases stock because she is a securities dealer. Brenda has asked you to calculate her potential gain and tell her whether her co-workers are right. Draft a letter to Brenda responding to her request. Her address is 200 Morningside Drive, Hattiesburg, MS 39406.

25. Sue Ellen meets all the requirements of § 1237 (subdivided realty). In 2008, she begins selling lots and sells four separate lots to four different purchasers. She also sells two contiguous lots to another purchaser. The sale price of each lot is $20,000. Sue Ellen's basis for each lot is $15,000. Selling expenses are $500 per lot.
    a. What is the realized and recognized gain?
    b. Explain the nature of the gain (i.e., ordinary income or capital gain).
    c. Would your answers change if, instead, the lots sold to the fifth purchaser were not contiguous? If so, how?

26. Sue has had a bad year with her investments. She lent a friend $3,700; the friend did not repay the loan when it was due and then declared bankruptcy. The loan is totally uncollectible. Sue also was notified by her broker that the Willow corporate bonds she owned became worthless on October 13, 2008. She had purchased the bonds for

$12,000 on November 10, 2007. Sue also had a $30,000 loss on the disposition of § 1244 corporate stock that she purchased several years ago. Sue is single.

a. What are the nature and amount of Sue's losses?

b. What is Sue's AGI for 2008 assuming she has $65,000 of ordinary gross income from sources other than those discussed above?

c. What are the nature and amount of Sue's loss carryforwards?

27. Albert purchased $400,000 of Brown Corporation face value bonds for $320,000 on November 13, 2007. The bonds had been issued with $80,000 of original issue discount because Brown was in financial difficulty in 2007. On December 3, 2008, Albert sold the bonds for $383,000 after amortizing $1,000 of the original issue discount. What are the nature and amount of Albert's gain or loss?

28. Frank is an investor in vacant land. When he thinks he has identified property that would be a good investment, he approaches the landowner, pays the landowner for a "right of first refusal" to purchase the land, records this right in the property records, and then waits to see if the land increases in value. The right of first refusal is valid for four years. Fourteen months ago, Frank paid a landowner $4,000 for a right of first refusal. The land was selected as the site of a new shopping center, and the landowner was offered $4 million for the land. In its title search on the land, the buyer discovered Frank's right of first refusal and involved him in the purchase negotiations. Ultimately, the landowner paid Frank $120,000 to give up his right of first refusal; the landowner then sold the land to the buyer for $4,120,000. Frank has a marginal tax rate of 35%.

Decision Making

a. What difference does it make whether or not Frank treats the right of first refusal as an option to purchase the land?

b. What difference does it make whether or not Frank is a "dealer" in land?

29. Celia was the owner of vacant land that she was holding for investment. She paid $1 million for the land in 2003. Ichiro was an investor in vacant land. He thought Celia's land might be the site of an exit ramp from a new freeway. Ichiro gave Celia $420,000 for an option on her land. The option was good for three years and gave Ichiro the ability to purchase Celia's land for $4,765,000. The freeway was not approved by the government, and Ichiro's option expired in 2008. Does Celia have $420,000 of long-term capital gain upon the expiration of the option?

30. Maria purchased all the rights to a patent on a new brush-cutting tool developed by a friend of hers who was an amateur inventor. The inventor had obtained the patent rights, set up a manufacturing company to produce and sell the brush-cutting tool, and produced substantial quantities of the tool, but he then became discouraged when no large garden tool company would agree to distribute the tool for him. Maria purchased the patent rights (but not the manufacturing company) for $320,000 on October 24, 2007. Maria had never engaged in such a transaction before, but she is a salesperson in the garden tool industry and thought she could succeed where her friend had failed. On June 27, 2008, she sold all the patent rights to Green Garden Tool Company for $1,233,000. Green Garden Tool will manufacture the brush-cutting tool in its own factory and sell it to its customers. What is the nature of Maria's gain from this transaction?

31. Mateen, an inventor, obtained a patent on a chemical process to clean old aluminum siding so that it can be easily repainted. Mateen has no tax basis in the patent. Mateen does not have the capital to begin manufacturing and selling this product, so he has done nothing with the patent since obtaining it two years ago. Now a group of individuals has approached him and offered two alternatives. Under one alternative, they will pay Mateen $600,000 (payable evenly over the next 15 years) for the exclusive right to manufacture and sell the product. Under the other, they will form a business and contribute capital to it to begin manufacturing and selling the product; Mateen will receive 20% of the company's shares of stock in exchange for all of his patent rights. Discuss which alternative is better for Mateen.

Decision Making

32. Freys, Inc., sells a 12-year franchise to Reynaldo. The franchise contains many restrictions on how Reynaldo may operate his store. For instance, Reynaldo cannot use less than Grade 10 Idaho potatoes, must fry the potatoes at a constant 410 degrees, dress store personnel in Freys-approved uniforms, and have a Freys sign that meets detailed specifications on size, color, and construction. When the franchise contract is signed,

Reynaldo makes a noncontingent $160,000 payment to Freys. During the same year, Reynaldo pays Freys $300,000—14% of Reynaldo's sales. How does Freys treat each of these payments? How does Reynaldo treat each of the payments?

33. Tricia owns numerous office buildings. A major tenant of one of the buildings wished to cancel its lease because it was moving to another city. After lengthy negotiations, the tenant paid Tricia $500,000 to cancel its obligations under the lease. If the tenant had fulfilled the lease terms, Tricia would have received rent of $1.8 million. What factors should Tricia consider to determine the amount and character of her income from these circumstances?

34. Che held vacant land that qualified as a capital asset. He purchased the vacant land in 2004. In 2008 he exchanged the vacant land for an apartment building in a qualifying like-kind exchange. He is curious as to whether his holding period for the apartment building begins on its acquisition date (November 10, 2008) or on the acquisition date of the vacant land (April 14, 2004). Which is correct?

35. Ken inherited 100 shares of Yellow common stock when his father, Arthur, died. Arthur had acquired the shares for a total of $40,000 on April 11, 2002. Arthur died on May 18, 2007, when the shares were worth a total of $43,000. Ken took ownership of the shares on November 5, 2007, and sold the shares for a total of $22,000 on February 12, 2008. How much gain or loss does Ken have, and what is the nature of that gain or loss?

36. Dennis sells short 100 shares of ARC stock at $20 per share on January 15, 2008. He buys 200 shares of ARC stock on April 1, 2008, at $25 per share. On May 2, 2008, he closes the short sale by delivering 100 of the shares purchased on April 1.
    a. What are the amount and nature of Dennis's loss upon closing the short sale?
    b. When does the holding period for the remaining 100 shares begin?
    c. If Dennis sells (at $27 per share) the remaining 100 shares on January 20, 2009, what will be the nature of his gain or loss?

37. Elaine Case (single with no dependents) has the following transactions in 2008:

AGI (exclusive of capital gains and losses)	$240,000
Long-term capital gain	22,000
Long-term capital loss	(5,000)
Short-term capital gain	19,000
Short-term capital loss	(23,000)

What is Elaine's net capital gain or loss? Draft a letter to Elaine describing how the net capital gain or loss will be treated on her tax return. Assume Elaine's income from other sources puts her in the 35% bracket. Elaine's address is 300 Ireland Avenue, Shepherdstown, WV 25443.

38. In 2008, Betty (head of household with three dependents) had an $18,000 loss from the sale of a personal residence. She also purchased from an individual inventor for $8,000 (and resold in two months for $7,000) a patent on a rubber bonding process. The patent had not yet been reduced to practice. Betty purchased the patent as an investment. Additionally, she had the following capital gains and losses from stock transactions:

Long-term capital loss	($ 3,000)
Long-term capital loss carryover from 2007	(12,000)
Short-term capital gain	21,000
Short-term capital loss	(6,000)

What is Betty's net capital gain or loss? Draft a letter to Betty explaining the tax treatment of the sale of her personal residence. Assume Betty's income from other sources puts her in the 35% bracket. Betty's address is 1120 West Street, Ashland, OR 97520.

39. Bridgette is known as the "doll lady." She started collecting dolls as a child, always received one or more dolls as gifts on her birthday, never sold any dolls, and eventually owned 600 dolls. She is retiring and moving to a small apartment and has decided to sell her collection. She lists the dolls on an Internet auction site and, to her great surprise, receives an offer from another doll collector of $45,000 for the entire collection.

Bridgette sells the entire collection, except for five dolls that she purchased during the last year. She had owned all the dolls sold for more than a year. What tax factors should Bridgette consider in deciding how to report the sale?

40. Phil and Susan are married, filing a joint return. The couple have two dependent children. Susan has wages of $34,000 in 2008. Phil does not work due to a disability, but he is a buyer and seller of stocks on the Internet. He generally buys and holds for long-term gain, but occasionally gets in and out of a stock quickly. The couple's 2008 stock transactions are detailed below. In addition, they have $2,300 of qualifying dividends.

Item	Date Acquired	Date Sold	Cost	Sales Price
Black stock	11/10/07	03/12/08	$ 2,000	$ 5,000
Blue stock	12/13/06	05/23/08	36,000	32,000
Puce stock	12/14/03	07/14/08	13,000	14,500
Ecru stock	06/29/07	05/18/08	26,000	27,000
Red stock	05/15/07	10/18/08	67,000	67,800
Gray stock	04/23/06	10/18/08	89,000	88,200

What is Phil and Susan's AGI?

41. For 2008, Ashley has gross income of $8,300 and a $5,000 long-term capital loss. She claims the standard deduction. Ashley is 35 years old and single with two dependent children. How much of Ashley's $5,000 capital loss carries over to 2009?

42. Jane and Blair are married filing jointly and have 2008 taxable income of $97,000. The taxable income includes $5,000 of gain from a capital asset held for five years, $2,100 of gain from a capital asset held seven months, and $13,000 of gain from a capital asset held four years. All the capital assets were stock in publicly traded corporations. Jane and Blair also have qualified dividend income of $3,000. What is the couple's tax on taxable income?

43. For 2008, Wilma has properly determined taxable income of $36,000, including $3,000 of unrecaptured § 1250 gain and $6,200 of 0%/15% gain. Wilma qualifies for head-of-household filing status. Compute Wilma's tax liability and the tax savings from the alternative tax on net capital gain.

44. Asok's AGI for 2008 is $133,050. Included in this AGI is a $45,000 25% long-term capital gain and a $13,000 0%/15% long-term capital gain. Asok is single, uses the standard deduction, and has only his personal exemption. Compute his taxable income, the tax liability, and the tax savings from the alternative tax on net capital gain.

45. Chartreuse, Inc., a C corporation, has taxable income from operations of $1,432,000 for 2008. It also has a net long-term capital loss of $455,000 from the sale of a subsidiary's stock. The year 2008 is the first year in the last 10 years that Chartreuse has not had at least $500,000 per year of net long-term capital gains. What is Chartreuse's 2008 taxable income, and what, if anything, can it do with any unused capital losses?

46. Hsui, who is single, is the owner of a sole proprietorship. Two years ago, Hsui developed a process for preserving fresh fruit that gives the fruit a much longer shelf life. The process is not patented or copyrighted, but only Hsui knows how it works. Hsui has been approached by a company that would like to buy the process. Hsui insists that she receive a long-term employment contract with the acquiring company as well as be paid for the rights to the process. The acquiring company offers Hsui a choice of two options: (1) $850,000 in cash for the process and a 10-year covenant not to compete at $45,000 per year or (2) $850,000 in cash for a 10-year covenant not to compete and $45,000 per year for 10 years in payment for the process. Which option should Hsui accept? What is the tax effect on the acquiring company of each approach?

Decision Making

CUMULATIVE PROBLEMS

47. Sue Lowe lives at 1310 Meadow Lane, Lima, OH 23412, and her Social Security number is 312–55–8000. Sue is single and has a 20-year-old son, Kania. His Social Security number is 480–01–9030. Kania lives with Sue, and she fully supports him. Kania spent 2007 traveling in Europe and was not a college student. He had gross income of $4,355 in 2007.

   Sue owns the Lowe Enterprises sole proprietorship, a data processing service (38–1234567), which is located at 456 Hill Street, Lima, OH 23401. The business activity code is 514210. Her 2007 Form 1040, Schedule C for Lowe Enterprises shows revenues of $355,000, office expenses of $166,759, employee salary of $23,000, employee payroll taxes of $1,760, meals and entertainment expenses (before the 50% reduction) of $18,000, and rent expense of $44,000. The rent expense includes payments related to renting an office ($32,000) and payments related to renting various equipment ($12,000). There is no depreciation because all depreciable equipment owned has been fully depreciated in previous years. No fringe benefits are provided to the employee. Sue personally purchases health insurance on herself and Kania. The premiums are $23,000 per year.

   Sue has an extensive stock portfolio and has prepared the following analysis:

Stock	Number of Shares	Date Purchased	Date Sold	Per Share Cost	Per Share Selling Price	Total Dividends
Blue	10	10/18/06	10/11/07	$80	$ 72	$30
Green	30	10/11/98	10/11/07	43	157	70
Purple	15	3/10/07	8/11/07	62	33	45

NOTE: The per share cost includes commissions, and the per share selling price is net of commissions. Also, the dividends are the actual dividends received in 2007.

   Sue had $800 of interest income from State of Ohio bonds and $600 of interest income on her Lima Savings Bank account. She also received $5,000 of alimony payments.

   Sue itemizes her deductions and had the following items, which may be relevant to her return:

Item	Amount	Comment
Unreimbursed medical expenses for Sue (all for visits to doctors)	$1,786	Does not include health insurance premiums.
State income taxes paid	1,830	
Real property taxes on personal residence	3,230	
Interest paid on home mortgage (Form 1098)	8,137	The loan is secured by the residence and was incurred when the home was purchased.
Charitable contributions	940	Cash paid to Sue's church.
Sales taxes	619	Amount per sales tax table.

   Sue made a $29,500 estimated Federal income tax payment, does not wish any of her taxes to finance presidential elections, has no foreign bank accounts or trusts, and wishes any refund to be applied against her 2008 taxes.

   Compute Sue's net tax payable or refund due for 2007. If you use tax forms for your computations, you will need Form 1040 and Schedules A, B, C, D, and SE. Suggested software: Tax Cut.

48. Paul Barrone is a graduate student at State University. His 10-year-old son, Jamie, lives with him, and Paul is Jamie's sole support. Paul's wife died in 2007, and Paul has not

remarried. Paul received $320,000 of life insurance proceeds (related to his wife's death) in early 2008 and immediately invested the entire amount as shown below:

Item	Date Acquired	Cost	Date Sold	Selling Price	Dividends/ Interest
1,000 shares Blue	01/23/08	$ 14,000	12/03/08	$ 3,500	None
400 shares Magenta	01/23/08	23,000			$750
600 shares Orange	01/23/08	230,000			$2,300
100 shares Brown	06/23/03	2,800	01/23/08	14,000	None
Green bonds	01/23/08	23,000			$1,200
Gold money market fund	01/23/08	30,000			$600

Paul had $32,000 of taxable graduate assistant earnings from State University and also received a $10,000 scholarship. He used $8,000 of the scholarship to pay his tuition and fees for the year and $2,000 for Jamie's day care. Jamie attended Little Kids Daycare Center, a state certified child care facility. Paul received a statement related to the Green bonds saying that there was $45 of original issue discount amortization during 2008. Paul maintains the receipts for the sales taxes he paid of $735.

Paul lives at 1610 Cherry Lane, State College, MD 34212, and his Social Security number is 452–78–0004. Jamie's Social Security number is 480–01–9030. The university withheld $3,000 of Federal income tax from Paul's salary. Paul is not itemizing his deductions.

Part 1—Tax Computation
Compute Paul's lowest tax liability for 2008.

Part 2—Tax Planning
Paul is concerned because the Green bonds were worth only $18,000 at the end of 2008, $5,000 less than he paid for them. He is an inexperienced investor and wants to know if this $5,000 is deductible. The bonds had original issue discount of $2,000 when he purchased them, and he is also curious about how that affects his investment in the bonds. The bonds had 20 years left to maturity when he purchased them. Draft a brief letter to Paul explaining how to handle these items. Also, prepare a memo for Paul's tax file.

RESEARCH PROBLEMS

Note: Solutions to Research Problems can be prepared by using the **RIA Checkpoint®** **Student Edition** online research product, which is available to accompany this text. It is also possible to prepare solutions to the Research Problems by using tax research materials found in a standard tax library.

Research Problem 1. Ali owns 100 shares of Brown Corporation stock. He purchased the stock at five different times and at five different prices per share as indicated:

Share Block	Number of Shares	Per Share Price	Purchase Date
A	10	$60	10/10/95
B	20	20	8/11/96
C	15	15	10/24/96
D	35	30	4/23/98
E	20	25	7/28/98

On April 28, 2008, Ali will sell 40 shares of Brown stock for $40 per share. All of Ali's shares are held by his stockbroker. The broker's records track when the shares were purchased. May Ali designate the shares he sells, and, if so, which shares should he sell? Assume Ali wants to maximize his gain because he has a capital loss carryforward.

Communications

Research Problem 2.   Clean Corporation runs a chain of dry cleaners. Borax is used heavily in Clean's dry cleaning process and has been in short supply several times in the past. Clean Corporation buys a controlling interest in Dig Corporation—a borax mining concern. Clean's sole reason for purchasing the Dig stock is to assure Clean of a continuous supply of borax if another shortage develops. Although borax must be refined before it is usable for dry cleaning purposes, a well-established commodities market exists for trading unrefined borax for refined borax. After owning the Dig stock for several years, Clean sells the stock at a loss because Dig is in difficult financial straits. Clean no longer needs to own Dig because Clean has obtained an alternative source of borax. What is the nature of Clean's loss on the disposition of the Dig Corporation stock? Write a letter to the controller, Salvio Guitterez, that contains your advice and prepare a memo for the tax files. The mailing address of Clean Corporation is 4455 Whitman Way, San Mateo, CA 44589.

Research Problem 3.   Clyde had worked for many years as the chief executive of Red Industries, Inc., and had also been a major shareholder. Clyde and the company had a falling out, and Clyde was terminated. Clyde and Red executed a document under which Clyde's stock in Red would be redeemed and Clyde would agree not to compete against Red in its geographic service area. After extensive negotiations between the parties, Clyde agreed to surrender his Red stock in exchange for $600,000. Clyde's basis in his shares was $143,000, and he had held the shares for 17 years. The agreement made no explicit allocation of any of the $600,000 to Clyde's agreement not to compete against Red. How should Clyde treat the $600,000 payment on his 2008 tax return?

Research Problem 4.   Mobley is a retired high school teacher. He has $65,000 of AGI from his retirement income. He is an avid player of the stock market. During 2008, he made 3,000 transactions buying and selling stocks. All the sales involved stocks held short term. His net loss for the year was $17,000. He incurred $7,000 of expenses for subscriptions to various publications dealing with how to buy and sell stocks. He has two questions. (1) Is the loss a short-term capital loss or an ordinary loss? (2) Is the $7,000 of expenses deductible *for* or *from* AGI?

Partial list of research aids:
Marlowe King, 89 T.C. 445 (1987), *acq.* 1988–2 C.B. 1.
Frederick Mayer, T.C.Memo. 1994–209 (1994), 67 TCM 2949.

 **Internet** *Activity*

Use the tax resources of the Internet to address the following questions. Do not restrict your search to the World Wide Web, but include a review of newsgroups and general reference materials, practitioner sites and resources, primary sources of the tax law, chat rooms and discussion groups, and other opportunities.

Research Problem 5.   Find a Web site that discusses the income tax in Canada. Determine whether Australia has an alternative tax on net long-term capital gains similar to that in the United States.

Research Problem 6.   Find a Web site, other than the IRS Web site, that discusses the taxation of subdivided real property.

CHAPTER 17

Property Transactions: § 1231 and Recapture Provisions

OUTLINE

Section 1231 Assets, 17–3
Relationship to Capital Assets, 17–3
Justification for Favorable Tax Treatment, 17–4
Property Included, 17–4
Property Excluded, 17–5
Special Rules for Certain § 1231 Assets, 17–5
General Procedure for § 1231 Computation, 17–8
Section 1245 Recapture, 17–11
Section 1245 Property, 17–13
Observations on § 1245, 17–14
Section 1250 Recapture, 17–14
Computing Recapture on Nonresidential
  Real Property, 17–15
Computing Recapture on Residential Rental
  Housing, 17–16
Section 1250 Recapture Situations, 17–16
Unrecaptured § 1250 Gain (Real Estate 25% Gain), 17–17

**Considerations Common to §§ 1245
and 1250, 17–19**
Exceptions, 17–19
Other Applications, 17–20
Special Recapture Provisions, 17–21
Special Recapture for Corporations, 17–21
Gain from Sale of Depreciable Property between Certain
  Related Parties, 17–21
Intangible Drilling Costs, 17–21
Reporting Procedures, 17–22
Tax Planning Considerations, 17–25
Timing of § 1231 Gain, 17–25
Timing of Recapture, 17–25
Postponing and Shifting Recapture, 17–29
Avoiding Recapture, 17–30

Generic Motors Corporation sold machinery, office furniture, and unneeded production plants for $100 million last year. The corporation's disposition of these assets resulted in $60 million of gains and $13 million of losses. How are these gains and losses treated for tax purposes? Do any special tax rules apply? Could any of the gains and losses receive capital gain or loss treatment? This chapter answers these questions by explaining how to *classify* gains and losses from the disposition of assets that are used in the business rather than held for resale. Chapter 8 discussed how to *depreciate* such assets. Chapters 14 and 15 discussed how to determine the *adjusted basis* and the *amount* of gain or loss from their disposition.

A long-term capital gain was defined in Chapter 16 as the recognized gain from the sale or exchange of a capital asset held for the required long-term holding period.[1] Long-term capital assets are capital assets held more than one year.

This chapter is concerned with classification under § 1231, which applies to the sale or exchange of business properties and to certain involuntary conversions. The business properties are not capital assets because they are depreciable and/or real property used in business or for the production of income. Section 1221(a)(2) provides that such assets are not capital assets. Nonetheless, these business properties may be held for long periods of time and may be sold at a gain. Congress decided many years ago that such assets deserved *limited* capital gain–type treatment. Unfortunately, this limited capital gain–type treatment is very complex and difficult to understand.

Because the limited capital gain–type treatment sometimes gives too much tax advantage if assets are eligible for depreciation (or cost recovery), certain recapture rules may prevent the capital gain treatment when depreciation is taken. Thus, this chapter also covers the recapture provisions that tax as ordinary income certain gains that might otherwise qualify for long-term capital gain treatment.

---

[1]§ 1222(3). To be eligible for any beneficial tax treatment, the holding period must be more than one year.

Section 1231 Assets

Relationship to Capital Assets

Depreciable property and real property used in business are not capital assets.[2] Thus, the recognized gains from the disposition of such property (principally machinery, equipment, buildings, and land) would appear to be ordinary income rather than capital gain. Due to § 1231, however, *net gain* from the disposition of such property is sometimes *treated* as *long-term capital gain.* A long-term holding period requirement must be met; the disposition must generally be from a sale, exchange, or involuntary conversion; and certain recapture provisions must be satisfied for this result to occur. Section 1231 may also apply to involuntary conversions of capital assets. Since an involuntary conversion is not a sale or exchange, such a disposition normally would not result in a capital gain.

If the disposition of depreciable property and real property used in business results in a *net loss,* § 1231 *treats* the *loss* as an *ordinary loss* rather than as a capital loss. Ordinary losses are fully deductible *for* adjusted gross income (AGI). Capital losses are offset by capital gains, and, if any loss remains, the loss is deductible to the extent of $3,000 per year for individuals and currently is not deductible at all by regular corporations. It seems, therefore, that § 1231 provides the *best* of both potential results: net gain may be treated as long-term capital gain, and net loss is treated as ordinary loss.

> Roberto sells business land and a building at a $5,000 gain and business equipment at a $3,000 loss. Both properties were held for the long-term holding period. Roberto's net gain is $2,000, and that net gain may (depending on various recapture rules discussed later in this chapter) be treated as a long-term capital gain under § 1231. ∎

EXAMPLE 1

> Samantha sells business equipment at a $10,000 loss and business land at a $2,000 gain. Both properties were held for the long-term holding period. Samantha's net loss is $8,000, and that net loss is an ordinary loss. ∎

EXAMPLE 2

The rules regarding § 1231 treatment do *not* apply to *all* business property. Important in this regard are the holding period requirements and the fact that the property must be either depreciable property or real estate used in business. Nor is § 1231 necessarily limited to business property. Transactions involving certain capital assets may fall into the § 1231 category. Thus, § 1231 singles out only some types of business property.

As discussed in Chapter 16, long-term capital gains receive beneficial tax treatment. Section 1231 requires netting of **§ 1231 gains and losses**. If the result is a gain, it may be treated as a long-term capital gain. The net gain is added to the "real" long-term capital gains (if any) and netted with capital losses (if any). Thus,

LO.1

Understand the rationale for and the nature and treatment of gains and losses from the disposition of business assets.

---

[2]§ 1221(a)(2).

the net § 1231 gain may eventually be eligible for beneficial capital gain treatment or help avoid the unfavorable net capital loss result. The § 1231 gain and loss netting may result in a loss. In this case, the loss is an ordinary loss and is deductible *for* AGI. Finally, § 1231 assets are treated the same as capital assets for purposes of the appreciated property charitable contribution provisions (refer to Chapter 10).

Justification for Favorable Tax Treatment

The favorable capital gain/ordinary loss treatment sanctioned by § 1231 can be explained by examining several historical developments. Before 1938, business property had been included in the definition of capital assets. Thus, if such property was sold for a loss (not an unlikely possibility during the depression years of the 1930s), a capital loss resulted. If, however, the property was depreciable and could be retained for its estimated useful life, much (if not all) of its costs could be recovered in the form of depreciation. Because the allowance for depreciation was fully deductible whereas capital losses were not, the tax law favored those who did not dispose of an asset. Congress recognized this inequity when it removed business property from the capital asset classification. During the period 1938–1942, therefore, all such gains and losses were ordinary gains and losses.

With the advent of World War II, two developments in particular forced Congress to reexamine the situation regarding business assets. First, the sale of business assets at a gain was discouraged because the gain would be ordinary income. Gains were common because the war effort had inflated prices. Second, taxpayers who did not want to sell their assets often were required to because the government acquired them through condemnation. Often, as a result of the condemnation awards, taxpayers who were forced to part with their property experienced large gains and were deprived of the benefits of future depreciation deductions. Of course, the condemnations constituted involuntary conversions, so taxpayers could defer the gain by timely reinvestment in property that was "similar or related in service or use." But where was such property to be found in view of wartime restrictions and other governmental condemnations? The end result did not seem equitable: a large ordinary gain due to government action and no possibility of deferral due to government restrictions.

In recognition of these conditions, in 1942, Congress eased the tax bite on the disposition of some business property by allowing preferential capital gain treatment. Thus, the present scheme of § 1231 and the dichotomy of capital gain/ordinary loss treatment evolved from a combination of economic considerations existing in 1938 and 1942.

Property Included

> **LO.2**
>
> Distinguish § 1231 assets from ordinary assets and capital assets and calculate the § 1231 gain or loss.

Section 1231 property generally includes the following assets if they are held for more than one year:

- Depreciable or real property used in business or for the production of income (principally machinery and equipment, buildings, and land).
- Timber, coal, or domestic iron ore to which § 631 applies.
- Livestock held for draft, breeding, dairy, or sporting purposes.
- Unharvested crops on land used in business.
- Certain *purchased* intangible assets (such as patents and goodwill) that are eligible for amortization.

These assets are ordinary assets until they have been held for more than one year. Only then do they become § 1231 assets.

Property Excluded

Section 1231 property generally does *not* include the following:

- Property not held for the long-term holding period. Since the benefit of § 1231 is long-term capital gain treatment, the holding period must correspond to the more-than-one-year holding period that applies to capital assets. Livestock must be held at least 12 months (24 months in some cases). Unharvested crops do not have to be held for the required long-term holding period, but the land must be held for the long-term holding period.
- Nonpersonal use property where casualty losses exceed casualty gains for the taxable year. If a taxpayer has a net casualty loss, the individual casualty gains and losses are treated as ordinary gains and losses.
- Inventory and property held primarily for sale to customers.
- Copyrights; literary, musical, or artistic compositions, etc.; and certain U.S. government publications.
- Accounts receivable and notes receivable arising in the ordinary course of the trade or business.

Special Rules for Certain § 1231 Assets

A rather diverse group of assets is included under § 1231. The following discussion summarizes the special rules for some of those assets.

Timber. Congress has provided preferential treatment relative to the natural growth value of timber, which takes a relatively long time to mature. Congress believed that this preferential treatment would encourage reforestation of timber lands. A taxpayer disposing of timber held for the long-term holding period has a long-term capital gain or loss if the timber was held for investment, has a § 1231 gain or loss if the timber was used in a trade or business, but, without special statutory treatment, would have ordinary income or loss if the timber was held as inventory. Section 631(a) allows the taxpayer to *elect* to treat the cutting of timber as a sale or exchange and, if the election is made, to treat the sale as the disposition of a § 1231 asset.[3]

The recognized § 1231 gain or loss is determined at the time the timber is cut and is equal to the difference between the timber's fair market value as of the *first day* of the taxable year and the adjusted basis for depletion. If a taxpayer sells the timber for more or less than the fair market value as of the first day of the taxable year in which it is cut, the difference is ordinary income or loss.

EXAMPLE 3

Several years ago, Tom, a timber dealer, purchased a tract of land with a substantial stand of trees on it. The land cost $40,000, and the timber cost $100,000. On the first day of 2008, the timber was appraised at $250,000. In August 2008, Tom cut the timber and sold it for $265,000. Tom elects to treat the cutting as a sale or exchange under § 1231. He has a $150,000 § 1231 gain ($250,000 − $100,000) and a $15,000 ordinary gain ($265,000 − $250,000).

What if the timber had been sold for $235,000? Tom would still have a $150,000 § 1231 gain, but he would also have a $15,000 ordinary loss. The price for computing § 1231 gain is the price at the beginning of the tax year. Any difference between that price and the sales price is ordinary gain or loss. Here, since the price declined by $15,000, Tom has an ordinary loss in that amount. ■

---

[3]§ 631(a) and Reg. § 1.631–1. To receive § 631 treatment, the holding period for the timber must be greater than one year.

Livestock. Cattle and horses must be held 24 months or more and other livestock must be held 12 months or more to qualify under § 1231.[4] The primary reason for enacting this provision was the considerable amount of litigation over the character of livestock [whether livestock was held primarily for sale to customers (ordinary income) or for use in a trade or business (§ 1231 property)]. Poultry is not livestock for purposes of § 1231.

Section 1231 Assets Disposed of by Casualty or Theft.

When § 1231 assets are disposed of by casualty or theft, a special netting rule is applied. For simplicity, the term *casualty* is used to mean both casualty and theft dispositions. First, the casualty gains and losses from § 1231 assets *and* the casualty gains and losses from **long-term nonpersonal use capital assets** are determined. A nonpersonal use capital asset might be an investment painting or a baseball card collection held by a nondealer in baseball cards.

Next, the § 1231 asset casualty gains and losses and the nonpersonal use capital asset casualty gains and losses are netted together (see Concept Summary 17–1) . If the result is a *net loss*, the § 1231 casualty gains and the nonpersonal use capital asset casualty gains are treated as ordinary gains, the § 1231 casualty losses are deductible *for* AGI, and the nonpersonal use capital asset casualty losses are deductible *from* AGI subject to the 2 percent-of-AGI limitation.

If the result of the netting is a *net gain*, the net gain is treated as a § 1231 gain. Thus, a § 1231 asset disposed of by casualty may or may not get § 1231 treatment, depending on whether the netting process results in a gain or a loss. Also, a nonpersonal use capital asset disposed of by casualty may get § 1231 treatment or ordinary treatment, but will not get capital gain or loss treatment!

Personal use property casualty gains and losses are not subject to the § 1231 rules. If the result of netting these gains and losses is a gain, the net gain is a capital gain. If the netting results in a loss, the net loss is a deduction *from* AGI to the extent it exceeds 10 percent of AGI.

Casualties, thefts, and condemnations are *involuntary conversions*. Involuntary conversion gains may be deferred if conversion proceeds are reinvested; involuntary conversion losses are recognized currently (refer to Chapter 15) regardless of whether the conversion proceeds are reinvested. Thus, the special netting process discussed above for casualties and thefts would not include gains that are not currently recognizable because the insurance proceeds are reinvested.

---

[4]Note that the holding period is "12 months or more" and not "more than 12 months."

CONCEPT SUMMARY 17–1

Section 1231 Netting Procedure

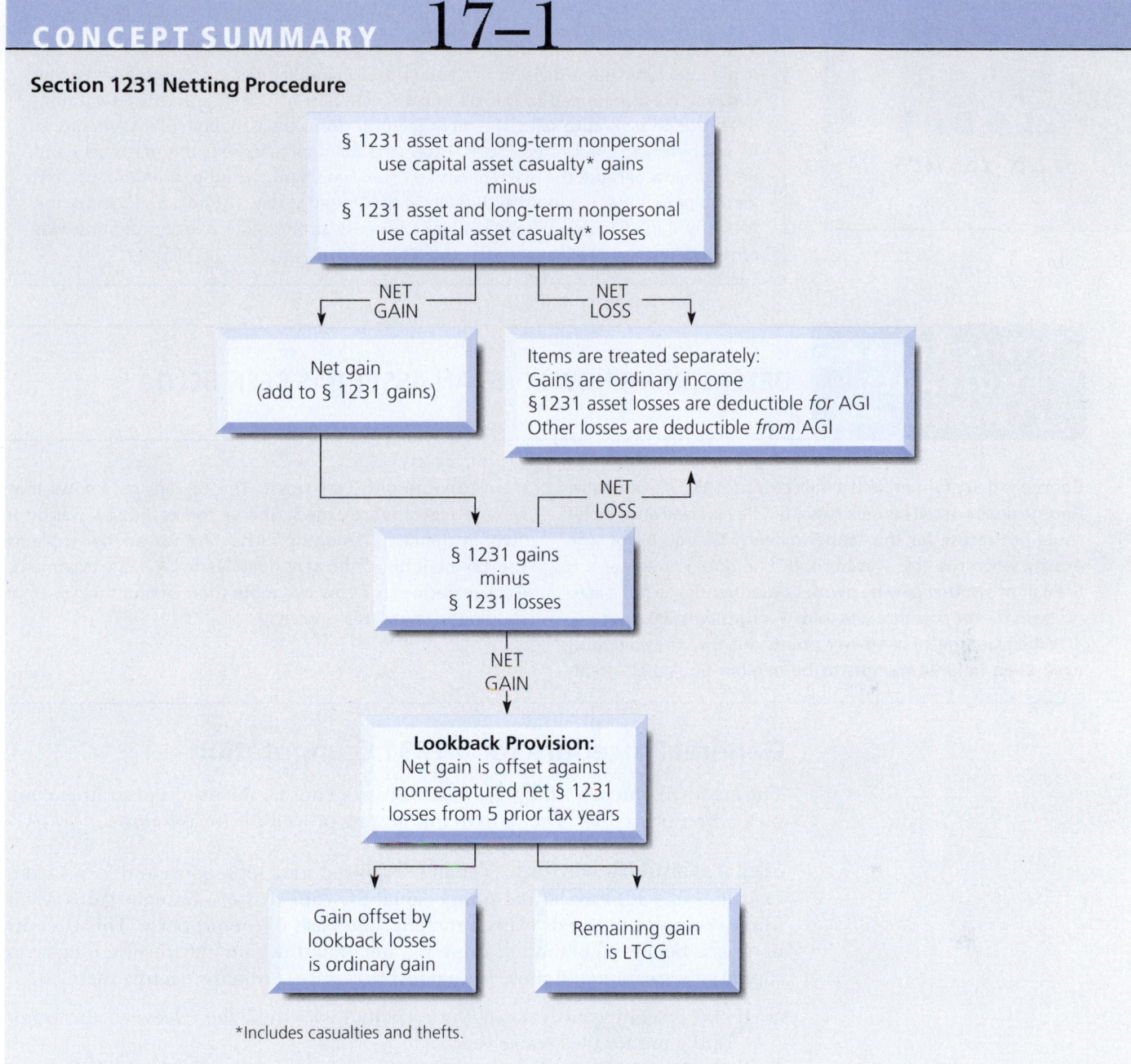

§ 1231 asset and long-term nonpersonal
use capital asset casualty* gains
minus
§ 1231 asset and long-term nonpersonal
use capital asset casualty* losses

NET GAIN   NET LOSS

Net gain
(add to § 1231 gains)

Items are treated separately:
Gains are ordinary income
§1231 asset losses are deductible *for* AGI
Other losses are deductible *from* AGI

NET LOSS

§ 1231 gains
minus
§ 1231 losses

NET GAIN

Lookback Provision:
Net gain is offset against
nonrecaptured net § 1231
losses from 5 prior tax years

Gain offset by
lookback losses
is ordinary gain

Remaining gain
is LTCG

*Includes casualties and thefts.

The special netting process for casualties and thefts also does not include condemnation gains and losses. Consequently, a § 1231 asset disposed of by condemnation will receive § 1231 treatment. This variation between recognized casualty and condemnation gains and losses sheds considerable light on what § 1231 is all about. Section 1231 has no effect on whether or not *realized* gain or loss is recognized. Instead, § 1231 merely dictates how such *recognized* gain or loss is *classified* (ordinary, capital, or § 1231) under certain conditions.

Personal use property condemnation gains and losses are not subject to the § 1231 rules. The gains are capital gains (because personal use property is a capital asset), and the losses are nondeductible because they arise from the disposition of personal use property.

GLOBAL
Tax Issues

CANADIAN SLOW DEPRECIATION

A manufacturer has a division in Canada that manufactures auto components. The components are shipped to Detroit and become part of U.S.-manufactured automobiles. Due to slow auto sales, the manufacturer closes the Canadian plant and moves its machinery to the United States. Later, the manufacturer sells the machinery and has a tax loss because the machinery's adjusted basis is much higher than that of similar equipment that was used exclusively in the United States. The adjusted basis of the formerly Canadian equipment is higher because straight-line tax depreciation was required for the Canadian property (see Chapter 8).

ETHICAL and EQUITABLE
Considerations

DETERMINING HOW LONG AN ASSET HAS BEEN HELD

George, a dairy farmer, sells a milk cow for $35,000. Normally, George does not sell his milk cows, but he received an offer he could not refuse for this "super milker." George is not sure exactly when the cow was born, but he does know that it is the calf of another cow he owns. Consequently, he has a zero tax basis for the cow that was sold. George owns 500 cows.

When George's tax adviser points out that the cow must have been held 24 months to be eligible for § 1231 treat-ment, George gets very upset. The tax adviser knows that George's records are a mess. George thinks the cow was born "within the last 27 months." After the tax adviser explains the tax benefits if the sale qualifies for § 1231 treatment, George decides the cow was more than 24 months old. How should the tax adviser proceed?

General Procedure for § 1231 Computation

The tax treatment of § 1231 gains and losses depends on the results of a rather complex *netting* procedure. The steps in this netting procedure are as follows.

Step 1: Casualty Netting. Net all recognized long-term gains and losses from casualties of § 1231 assets and nonpersonal use capital assets. Casualty gains result when insurance proceeds exceed the adjusted basis of the property. This casualty netting is beneficial because if there is a net gain, the gain may receive long-term capital gain treatment. If there is a net loss, it receives ordinary loss treatment.

a. If the casualty gains exceed the casualty losses, add the excess to the other § 1231 gains for the taxable year.

b. If the casualty losses exceed the casualty gains, exclude all casualty losses and gains from further § 1231 computation. If this is the case, all casualty gains are ordinary income. Section 1231 asset casualty losses are deductible *for* AGI. Other casualty losses are deductible *from* AGI.

Step 2: § 1231 Netting. After adding any net casualty gain from Step 1a to the other § 1231 gains and losses (including recognized § 1231 asset condemnation gains and losses), net all § 1231 gains and losses.

a. If the gains exceed the losses, the net gain is offset by the "lookback" nonrecaptured § 1231 losses (see below) from the five prior tax years. To the extent of this offset, the net § 1231 gain is classified as ordinary gain. Any remaining gain is long-term capital gain.

b. If the losses exceed the gains, all gains are ordinary income. Section 1231 asset losses are deductible *for* AGI. Other casualty losses are deductible *from* AGI.

Step 3: § 1231 Lookback Provision. The net § 1231 gain from Step 2a is offset by the nonrecaptured net § 1231 losses for the five preceding taxable years. For 2008, the lookback years are 2003, 2004, 2005, 2006, and 2007. To the extent of the nonrecaptured net § 1231 loss, the current-year net § 1231 gain is ordinary income. The *nonrecaptured* net § 1231 losses are those that have not already been used to offset net § 1231 gains. Only the net § 1231 gain exceeding this net § 1231 loss carryforward is given long-term capital gain treatment. Concept Summary 17–1 summarizes the § 1231 computational procedure. Examples 6 and 7 illustrate the **§ 1231 lookback** provision.

Examples 4 through 7 illustrate the application of the § 1231 computation procedure.

During 2008, Ross had $125,000 of AGI before considering the following recognized gains and losses:

E X A M P L E 4

Capital Gains and Losses	
Long-term capital gain	$3,000
Long-term capital loss	(400)
Short-term capital gain	1,000
Short-term capital loss	(200)
Casualties	
Theft of diamond ring (owned four months)	($ 800)*
Fire damage to personal residence (owned 10 years)	(400)*
Gain from insurance recovery on fire loss to business building (owned two years)	200
§ 1231 Gains and Losses from Depreciable Business Assets Held Long Term	
Asset A	$ 300
Asset B	1,100
Asset C	(500)
Gains and Losses from Sale of Depreciable Business Assets Held Short Term	
Asset D	$ 200
Asset E	(300)

*As adjusted for the $100 floor on personal casualty losses.

Ross had no net § 1231 losses in tax years before 2008.

Disregarding the recapture of depreciation (discussed later in the chapter), Ross's gains and losses receive the following tax treatment:

- The diamond ring and the residence are personal use assets. Therefore, these casualties are not § 1231 transactions. The $800 (ring) plus $400 (residence) losses are potentially deductible *from* AGI. However, the total loss of $1,200 does not exceed 10% of AGI. Thus, only the business building (a § 1231 asset) casualty gain remains. The netting of the § 1231 asset and nonpersonal use capital asset casualty gains and losses contains only one item—the $200 gain from the business building. Consequently, there is a net gain and that gain is treated as a § 1231 gain (added to the § 1231 gains).
- The gains from § 1231 transactions (Assets A, B, and C and the § 1231 asset casualty gain) exceed the losses by $1,100 ($1,600 − $500). This excess is a long-term capital gain and is added to Ross's other long-term capital gains.
- Ross's net long-term capital gain is $3,700 ($3,000 + $1,100 from § 1231 transactions − $400 long-term capital loss). Ross's net short-term capital gain is $800 ($1,000 − $200). The result is capital gain net income of $4,500. The $3,700 net long-term capital gain portion is eligible for beneficial capital gain treatment [assume all the gain is 0%/15%

gain (see the discussion in Chapter 16)]. The $800 net short-term capital gain is subject to tax as ordinary income.[5]

- Ross treats the gain and loss from Assets D and E (depreciable business assets held for less than the long-term holding period) as ordinary gain and loss.

Results of the Gains and Losses on Ross's Tax Computation

NLTCG	$ 3,700
NSTCG	800
Ordinary gain from sale of Asset D	200
Ordinary loss from sale of Asset E	(300)
AGI from other sources	125,000
AGI	$129,400

- Ross will have personal use property casualty losses of $1,200 [$800 (diamond ring) + $400 (personal residence)]. A personal use property casualty loss is deductible only to the extent it exceeds 10% of AGI. Thus, none of the $1,200 is deductible ($129,400 × 10% = $12,940). ■

EXAMPLE 5

Assume the same facts as in Example 4, except the loss from Asset C was $1,700 instead of $500.

- The treatment of the casualty losses is the same as in Example 4.
- The losses from § 1231 transactions now exceed the gains by $100 ($1,700 − $1,600). As a result, the gains from Assets A and B and the § 1231 asset casualty gain are ordinary income, and the loss from Asset C is a deduction *for* AGI (a business loss). The same result can be achieved by simply treating the $100 net loss as a deduction *for* AGI.
- Capital gain net income is $3,400 ($2,600 long term + $800 short term). The $2,600 net long-term capital gain portion is eligible for beneficial capital gain treatment, and the $800 net short-term capital gain is subject to tax as ordinary income.

Results of the Gains and Losses on Ross's Tax Computation

NLTCG	$ 2,600
NSTCG	800
Net ordinary loss on Assets A, B, and C and § 1231 casualty gain	(100)
Ordinary gain from sale of Asset D	200
Ordinary loss from sale of Asset E	(300)
AGI from other sources	125,000
AGI	$128,200

- None of the personal use property casualty losses will be deductible since $1,200 does not exceed 10% of $128,200. ■

EXAMPLE 6

Assume the same facts as in Example 4, except that Ross has a $700 nonrecaptured net § 1231 loss from 2007.

- The treatment of the casualty losses is the same as in Example 4.
- The 2008 net § 1231 gain of $1,100 is treated as ordinary income to the extent of the 2007 nonrecaptured § 1231 loss of $700. The remaining $400 net § 1231 gain is a long-term capital gain and is added to Ross's other long-term capital gains.

---

[5]Ross's taxable income (unless the itemized deductions and the personal exemption and dependency deductions are extremely large) will put him in at least the 28% bracket. Thus, the alternative tax computation will yield a lower tax. See Example 40 in Chapter 16.

- Ross's net long-term capital gain is $3,000 ($3,000 + $400 from § 1231 transactions − $400 long-term capital loss). Ross's net short-term capital gain is still $800 ($1,000 − $200). The result is capital gain net income of $3,800. The $3,000 net long-term capital gain portion is eligible for beneficial capital gain treatment, and the $800 net short-term capital gain is subject to tax as ordinary income.

Results of the Gains and Losses on Ross's Tax Computation

NLTCG	$ 3,000
NSTCG	800
Ordinary gain from recapture of § 1231 losses	700
Ordinary gain from sale of Asset D	200
Ordinary loss from sale of Asset E	(300)
AGI from other sources	125,000
AGI	$129,400

- None of the personal use property casualty losses will be deductible since $1,200 does not exceed 10% of $129,400. ∎

Assume the same facts as in Example 4, except that Ross had a net § 1231 loss of $2,700 in 2006 and a net § 1231 gain of $300 in 2007.

- The treatment of the casualty losses is the same as in Example 4.
- The 2006 net § 1231 loss of $2,700 will have carried over to 2007 and been offset against the 2007 net § 1231 gain of $300. Thus, the $300 gain will have been classified as ordinary income, and $2,400 of nonrecaptured 2006 net § 1231 loss will carry over to 2008. The 2008 net § 1231 gain of $1,100 will be offset against this loss, resulting in $1,100 of ordinary income. The nonrecaptured net § 1231 loss of $1,300 ($2,400 − $1,100) carries over to 2009.
- Capital gain net income is $3,400 ($2,600 net long-term capital gain + $800 net short-term capital gain). The $2,600 net long-term capital gain portion is eligible for beneficial capital gain treatment, and the $800 net short-term capital gain is subject to tax as ordinary income.

EXAMPLE 7

Results of the Gains and Losses on Ross's Tax Computation

NLTCG	$ 2,600
NSTCG	800
Ordinary gain from recapture of § 1231 losses	1,100
Ordinary gain from sale of Asset D	200
Ordinary loss from sale of Asset E	(300)
AGI from other sources	125,000
AGI	$129,400

- None of the personal use property casualty losses will be deductible since $1,200 does not exceed 10% of $129,400. ∎

Section 1245 Recapture

LO.3

Determine when § 1245 recapture applies and how it is computed.

Now that the basic rules of § 1231 have been introduced, it is time to add some complications. The Code contains two major *recapture* provisions—§§ 1245 and 1250. These provisions cause *gain* to be treated *initially* as ordinary gain. Thus, what may appear to be a § 1231 gain is ordinary gain instead. These recapture provisions may also cause a gain in a nonpersonal use casualty to be *initially* ordinary gain rather

TAX *in the News*

ASK THE CPA ABOUT RECAPTURE

A local newspaper includes a column called "Ask the CPA." A subscriber asked whether there were any differences between § 1245 recapture related to depreciable tangible personal property and that related to amortizable intangible personal property. The CPA wrote back that accelerated depreciation is usually used for tangible personal property, whereas straight-line amortization is used for intangible per-

sonal property. Consequently, the adjusted basis for the tangible personal property tends to be lower than that of the intangible personal property. If the properties had the same original cost and the same fair market value when they were sold, the tangible personal property would result in the larger gain and, therefore, the larger amount subject to recapture as ordinary income under § 1245.

---

than casualty gain. Classifying gains (and losses) properly initially is important because improper initial classification may lead to incorrect mixing and matching of gains and losses. This section discusses the § 1245 recapture rules, and the next section discusses the § 1250 recapture rules.

Section 1245 requires taxpayers to treat all gain as ordinary gain unless the property is disposed of for more than was paid for it. This result is accomplished by requiring that all gain be treated as ordinary gain to the extent of the depreciation taken on the property disposed of. Section 1231 gain results only when the property is disposed of for more than its original cost. The excess of the sales price over the original cost is § 1231 gain. Section 1245 applies *primarily* to non-real-estate property such as machinery, trucks, and office furniture. Section 1245 does not apply if property is disposed of at a loss. Generally, the loss will be a § 1231 loss unless the form of the disposition is a casualty.

EXAMPLE 8

Alice purchased a $100,000 business machine and deducted $70,000 depreciation before selling it for $80,000. If it were not for § 1245, the $50,000 gain would be § 1231 gain ($80,000 amount realized – $30,000 adjusted basis). Section 1245 prevents this potentially favorable result by treating as ordinary income (not as § 1231 gain) any gain to the extent of depreciation taken. In this example, the entire $50,000 gain would be ordinary income. If Alice had sold the machine for $120,000, she would have a gain of $90,000 ($120,000 amount realized – $30,000 adjusted basis). The § 1245 gain would be $70,000 (equal to the depreciation taken), and the § 1231 gain would be $20,000 (equal to the excess of the sales price over the original cost). ■

Section 1245 recapture provides, in general, that the portion of recognized gain from the sale or other disposition of § 1245 property that represents depreciation (including § 167 depreciation, § 168 cost recovery, § 179 immediate expensing, and § 197 amortization) is *recaptured* as ordinary income. Thus, in Example 8, $50,000 of the $70,000 depreciation taken is recaptured as ordinary income when the business machine is sold for $80,000. Only $50,000 is recaptured rather than $70,000 because Alice is only required to recognize § 1245 recapture ordinary gain equal to the lower of the depreciation taken or the gain recognized.

The method of depreciation (e.g., accelerated or straight-line) does not matter. All depreciation taken is potentially subject to recapture. Thus, § 1245 recapture is often referred to as *full recapture*. Any remaining gain after subtracting the amount recaptured as ordinary income will usually be § 1231 gain. If the property is disposed of in a casualty event, however, the remaining gain will be casualty gain. If the business machine in Example 8 had been disposed of by casualty and the $80,000 received had been an insurance recovery, Alice would still have a gain of $50,000, and the gain would still be recaptured by § 1245 as ordinary gain. The § 1245 recapture rules apply before there is any casualty gain. Since all the $50,000 gain is recaptured, no casualty gain arises from the casualty.

The following examples illustrate the general application of § 1245.

On January 1, 2008, Gary sold for $13,000 a machine acquired several years ago for $12,000. He had taken $10,000 of depreciation on the machine.

EXAMPLE 9

- The recognized gain from the sale is $11,000. This is the amount realized of $13,000 less the adjusted basis of $2,000 ($12,000 cost − $10,000 depreciation taken).
- Depreciation taken is $10,000. Therefore, since § 1245 recapture gain is the lower of depreciation taken or gain recognized, $10,000 of the $11,000 recognized gain is ordinary income, and the remaining $1,000 gain is § 1231 gain.
- The § 1231 gain of $1,000 is also equal to the excess of the sales price over the original cost of the property ($13,000 − $12,000 = $1,000 § 1231 gain). ■

Assume the same facts as in the previous example, except the asset is sold for $9,000 instead of $13,000.

EXAMPLE 10

- The recognized gain from the sale is $7,000. This is the amount realized of $9,000 less the adjusted basis of $2,000.
- Depreciation taken is $10,000. Therefore, since the $10,000 depreciation taken exceeds the recognized gain of $7,000, the entire $7,000 recognized gain is ordinary income.
- The § 1231 gain is zero. There is no § 1231 gain because the selling price ($9,000) does not exceed the original purchase price ($12,000). ■

Assume the same facts as in Example 9, except the asset is sold for $1,500 instead of $13,000.

EXAMPLE 11

- The recognized loss from the sale is $500. This is the amount realized of $1,500 less the adjusted basis of $2,000.
- Since there is a loss, there is no depreciation recapture. All of the loss is § 1231 loss. ■

If § 1245 property is disposed of in a transaction other than a sale, exchange, or involuntary conversion, the maximum amount recaptured is the excess of the property's fair market value over its adjusted basis. See the discussion under Considerations Common to §§ 1245 and 1250 later in the chapter.

Section 1245 Property

Generally, **§ 1245 property** includes all depreciable personal property (e.g., machinery and equipment), including livestock. Buildings and their structural components generally are not § 1245 property. The following property is *also* subject to § 1245 treatment:

- Amortizable personal property such as goodwill, patents, copyrights, and leaseholds of § 1245 property. Professional baseball and football player contracts are § 1245 property.
- Amortization of reforestation expenditures.
- Expensing of costs to remove architectural and transportation barriers that restrict the handicapped and/or elderly.
- Section 179 immediate expensing of depreciable tangible personal property costs.
- Elevators and escalators acquired before January 1, 1987.
- Certain depreciable tangible real property (other than buildings and their structural components) employed as an integral part of certain activities such as manufacturing and production. For example, a natural gas storage tank where the gas is used in the manufacturing process is § 1245 property.
- Pollution control facilities, railroad grading and tunnel bores, on-the-job training, and child care facilities on which amortization is taken.
- Single-purpose agricultural and horticultural structures and petroleum storage facilities (e.g., a greenhouse or silo).

- Fifteen-year, 18-year, and 19-year nonresidential real estate for which accelerated cost recovery is used is subject to the § 1245 recapture rules, although it is technically not § 1245 property. Such property would have been placed in service after 1980 and before 1987.

EXAMPLE 12

James acquired nonresidential real property on December 1, 1986, for $100,000. He used the statutory percentage method to compute the ACRS cost recovery. He sells the asset on January 15, 2008, for $120,000. The amount and nature of James's gain are computed as follows:

Amount realized		$120,000
Adjusted basis		
Cost	$ 100,000	
Less cost recovery: 1986–2007	(100,000)	
2008	(–0–)	
January 15, 2008 adjusted basis		(–0–)
Gain realized and recognized		$120,000

The gain of $120,000 is treated as ordinary income to the extent of *all* depreciation taken because the property is 19-year nonresidential real estate for which accelerated depreciation was used. Thus, James reports ordinary income of $100,000 and § 1231 gain of $20,000 ($120,000 – $100,000). ∎

Observations on § 1245

- In most instances, the total depreciation taken will exceed the recognized gain. Therefore, the disposition of § 1245 property usually results in ordinary income rather than § 1231 gain. Thus, generally, no § 1231 gain will occur unless the § 1245 property is disposed of for more than its original cost. Refer to Examples 9 and 10.
- Recapture applies to the total amount of depreciation allowed or allowable regardless of the depreciation method used.
- Recapture applies regardless of the holding period of the property. Of course, the entire recognized gain would be ordinary income if the property were held for less than the long-term holding period because § 1231 would not apply.
- Section 1245 does not apply to losses, which receive § 1231 treatment.
- Gains from the disposition of § 1245 assets may also be treated as passive activity gains (see Chapter 11).

LO.4

Determine when § 1250 recapture applies and how it is computed.

Section 1250 Recapture

Generally, **§ 1250 property** is depreciable real property (principally buildings and their structural components) that is not subject to § 1245.[6] Intangible real property, such as leaseholds of § 1250 property, is also included.

Section 1250 recapture rarely applies since only the amount of *additional depreciation* is subject to recapture. To have additional depreciation, accelerated depreciation must have been taken on the asset. Straight-line depreciation is not recaptured (except for property held one year or less). Since depreciable real property placed in service after 1986 can generally only be depreciated using the straight-line method, there will usually be *no § 1250 depreciation recapture* on such property. Nor does § 1250 apply if the real property is sold at a loss.

---

[6]As noted above, in one limited circumstance, § 1245 does apply to nonresidential real estate. If the nonresidential real estate was placed in service after 1980 and before 1987 and accelerated depreciation was used, the § 1245 recapture rules rather than the § 1250 recapture rules apply.

If depreciable real property has been held for many years before it is sold, however, the § 1250 recapture rules may apply and are therefore discussed here. **Additional depreciation** is the excess of the accelerated depreciation actually deducted over depreciation that would have been deductible if the straight-line method had been used. Section 1250 recapture may apply when either (1) residential rental real property was acquired after 1975 and before 1987 and accelerated depreciation was taken or (2) nonresidential real property was acquired before 1981 and accelerated depreciation was taken after December 31, 1969.

If § 1250 property with additional depreciation is disposed of in a transaction other than a sale, exchange, or involuntary conversion, the depreciation recapture is limited to the excess of the property's fair market value over the adjusted basis. For instance, if a corporation distributes real property to its shareholders as a dividend and the fair market value of the real property is greater than its adjusted basis, the corporation will recognize a gain. If accelerated depreciation was taken on the property, § 1250 recapture will apply.

It is important to know what assets are defined as § 1250 property because even when there is no additional depreciation, the gain from such property may be subject to a special 25 percent tax rate. See the discussion of Unrecaptured § 1250 Gain later in this chapter.

The discussion below describes the computational steps when § 1250 recapture applies and indicates how that recapture is reflected on Form 4797 (Sales of Business Property).

Computing Recapture on Nonresidential Real Property

For § 1250 property other than residential rental property, the potential recapture is equal to the amount of additional depreciation taken since December 31, 1969. This nonresidential real property includes buildings such as offices, warehouses, factories, and stores. (The definition of and rules for residential rental housing are discussed later in the chapter.) The lower of the potential § 1250 recapture amount or the recognized gain is ordinary income. The following general rules apply:

- Additional depreciation is depreciation taken in excess of straight-line after December 31, 1969, on property that was acquired before 1981.
- If the property is held for one year or less (usually not the case), all depreciation taken, even under the straight-line method, is additional depreciation.

The following procedure is used to compute recapture on nonresidential real property that was acquired before 1981 and for which accelerated depreciation was taken after December 31, 1969, under § 1250:

- Determine the recognized gain from the sale or other disposition of the property.
- Determine the additional depreciation (if any).
- The lower of the recognized gain or the additional depreciation is ordinary income.
- If any recognized gain remains (total recognized gain less recapture), it is § 1231 gain. However, it would be casualty gain if the disposition was by casualty.

The following example shows the application of the § 1250 computational procedure.

EXAMPLE 13

On January 3, 1980, Larry acquired a new building at a cost of $200,000 for use in his business. The building had an estimated useful life of 50 years and no estimated salvage value. Depreciation has been taken under the 150% declining-balance method through December 31, 2007. Pertinent information with respect to depreciation taken follows:

Year	Undepreciated Balance (Beginning of the Year)	Current Depreciation Provision	Straight-Line Depreciation	Additional Depreciation
1980–2006	$200,000	$113,020	$108,000	$5,020
2007	86,980	3,070	4,000	(930)
Total 1980–2007		$116,090	$112,000	$4,090

On January 2, 2008, Larry sold the building for $180,000. Compute the amount of his § 1250 ordinary income and § 1231 gain.

- Larry's recognized gain from the sale is $96,090. This is the difference between the $180,000 amount realized and the $83,910 adjusted basis ($200,000 cost − $116,090 depreciation taken).
- Additional depreciation is $4,090.
- The amount of ordinary income is $4,090. Since the additional depreciation of $4,090 is less than the recognized gain of $96,090, the entire gain is not recaptured.
- The remaining $92,000 ($96,090 − $4,090) gain is § 1231 gain. ■

Computing Recapture on Residential Rental Housing

Section 1250 recapture sometimes applies to the sale or other disposition of residential rental housing. Property qualifies as *residential rental housing* only if at least 80 percent of gross rent income is rent income from dwelling units.[7] The rules are the same as for other § 1250 property, except that only the post-1975 additional depreciation may be recaptured on property acquired before 1987. If any of the recognized gain is not absorbed by the recapture rules pertaining to the post-1975 period, the remaining gain is § 1231 gain.

EXAMPLE 14

Assume the same facts as in the previous example, except the building is residential rental housing.

- Post-1975 ordinary income is $4,090 (post-1975 additional depreciation of $4,090).
- The remaining $92,000 ($96,090 − $4,090) gain is § 1231 gain. ■

Under § 1250, when straight-line depreciation is used, there is no § 1250 recapture potential unless the property is disposed of in the first year of use. Generally, however, the § 1250 recapture rules do not apply to depreciable real property unless the property is disposed of in the first year of use.

EXAMPLE 15

Sanjay acquires a residential rental building on January 1, 2007, for $300,000. He receives an offer of $450,000 for the building in 2008 and sells it on December 23, 2008.

- Sanjay takes $20,909 {($300,000 × .03485) + [$300,000 × .03636 × (11.5/12)] = $20,909} of total depreciation for 2007 and 2008, and the adjusted basis of the property is $279,091 ($300,000 − $20,909).
- Sanjay's recognized gain is $170,909 ($450,000 − $279,091).
- All of the gain is § 1231 gain. ■

Section 1250 Recapture Situations

The § 1250 recapture rules apply to the following property for which accelerated depreciation was used:

---

[7]§ 168(e)(2)(A). Note that there may be residential, nonrental housing (e.g., a bunkhouse on a cattle ranch). Such property is commonly regarded as "non-residential real estate." The rules for such property were discussed in the previous section.

CONCEPT SUMMARY 17–2

Comparison of § 1245 and § 1250 Depreciation Recapture

	§ 1245	§ 1250
Property affected	All depreciable personal property, but also nonresidential real property acquired after December 31, 1980, and before January 1, 1987, for which accelerated cost recovery was used. Also includes miscellaneous items such as § 179 expense and § 197 amortization of intangibles such as goodwill, patents, and copyrights.	Nonresidential real property acquired after December 31, 1969, and before January 1, 1981, on which accelerated depreciation was taken. Residential rental real property acquired after December 31, 1975, and before January 1, 1987, on which accelerated depreciation was taken.
Depreciation recaptured	Potentially all depreciation taken. If the selling price is greater than or equal to the original cost, all depreciation is recaptured. If the selling price is between the adjusted basis and the original cost, only some depreciation is recaptured.	Additional depreciation (the excess of accelerated cost recovery over straight-line cost recovery or the excess of accelerated depreciation over straight-line depreciation).
Limit on recapture	Lower of depreciation taken or gain recognized.	Lower of additional depreciation or gain recognized.
Treatment of gain exceeding recapture gain	Usually § 1231 gain.	Usually § 1231 gain.
Treatment of loss	No depreciation recapture; loss is usually § 1231 loss.	No depreciation recapture; loss is usually § 1231 loss.

- Residential rental real estate acquired before 1987.
- Nonresidential real estate acquired before 1981.
- Real property used predominantly outside the United States.
- Certain government-financed or low-income housing.[8]

Concept Summary 17–2 compares and contrasts the § 1245 and § 1250 depreciation recapture rules.

Unrecaptured § 1250 Gain (Real Estate 25% Gain)

This section will explain what gain is eligible for the 25 percent tax rate on **unrecaptured § 1250 gain**. This gain is used in the alternative tax computation for net capital gain discussed in Chapter 16. Unrecaptured § 1250 gain (25% gain) is some or all of the § 1231 gain that is treated as long-term capital gain and relates to a sale of depreciable real estate.

The maximum amount of this 25% gain is the depreciation taken on real property sold at a recognized gain. That maximum amount is reduced in one or more of the following ways:

- The recognized gain from disposition is less than the depreciation taken. The 25% gain is reduced to the recognized gain amount. Refer to Example 13. The depreciation taken was $116,090, but the recognized gain was only

---

[8]Described in § 1250(a)(1)(B).

$96,090. Consequently, *all* of the recognized gain is potential 25% § 1231 gain.

- There is § 1250 depreciation recapture because the property is residential real estate acquired before 1987 on which accelerated depreciation was taken. The § 1250 recapture reduces the 25% gain. Refer to Example 14. Of the $96,090 recognized gain, $4,090 was recaptured by § 1250 as ordinary income, leaving $92,000 of the potential 25% § 1231 gain.
- There is § 1245 depreciation recapture because the property is nonresidential real estate acquired in 1981–1986 on which accelerated depreciation was taken. No 25% § 1231 gain will be left because § 1245 will recapture all of the depreciation or the recognized gain, whichever is less. Refer to Example 12. Depreciation of $100,000 was taken, but all of it was recaptured as ordinary income by § 1245. Thus, there is no remaining potential 25% § 1231 gain. The entire $20,000 § 1231 gain in Example 12 is potential 0%/15% gain.
- Section 1231 loss from disposition of other § 1231 assets held long term reduces the gain from real estate.
- Section 1231 lookback losses convert some or all of the potential 25% § 1231 gain to ordinary income.

Special 25% Gain Netting Rules. Where there is a § 1231 gain from real estate and that gain includes both potential *25% gain* and potential *0%/15% gain*, any § 1231 loss from disposition of other § 1231 assets *first offsets* the *0%/15%* portion of the § 1231 gain and then offsets the *25%* portion of the § 1231 gain. Also, any § 1231 lookback loss *first recharacterizes* the *25%* portion of the § 1231 gain and then recharacterizes the *0%/15%* portion of the § 1231 gain as ordinary income.

Net § 1231 Gain Limitation. The amount of unrecaptured § 1250 gain may not exceed the net § 1231 gain that is eligible to be treated as long-term capital gain. The unrecaptured § 1250 gain is the *lesser of* the unrecaptured § 1250 gain or the net § 1231 gain that is treated as capital gain. Thus, if there is a net § 1231 gain, but it is all recaptured by the five-year § 1231 lookback loss provision, there is no surviving § 1231 gain or unrecaptured § 1250 gain.

Refer to Example 6. There was $200 of § 1231 gain from the building fire that would also be potential *25% gain* if at least $200 of depreciation was taken. The net § 1231 gain was $1,100 including the $200 building gain. (The $500 loss from Asset C would offset the potential *0%/15%* § 1231 gain and not the potential *25% gain*, so all of the potential *25% gain* of $200 is in the $1,100 net § 1231 gain.) However, the $700 of § 1231 lookback losses would *first* absorb the $200 building gain, so the $400 of § 1231 gain that is treated as long-term capital gain includes no *25% gain*.

Section 1250 Property for Purposes of the Unrecaptured § 1250 Gain. Section 1250 property includes any real property (other than § 1245 property) that is or has been depreciable. Land is *not* § 1250 property because it is not depreciable.

EXAMPLE 16

Bill is a single taxpayer with 2008 taxable income of $84,000 composed of:

- $64,000 ordinary taxable income,
- $3,000 short-term capital loss,
- $15,000 long-term capital gain from sale of stock, and
- $8,000 § 1231 gain that is all unrecaptured § 1250 gain (the actual unrecaptured gain was $11,000, but net § 1231 gain is only $8,000).

Bill's net capital gain is $20,000 ($15,000 long-term capital gain + $8,000 unrecaptured § 1250 gain/net § 1231 gain − $3,000 short-term capital loss). The $3,000 short-term capital loss is offset against the $8,000 unrecaptured § 1250 gain, reducing that gain to $5,000 (see the discussion in Chapter 16 concerning netting of capital losses). Bill's adjusted net capital

EXCHANGE FOR FOREIGN PROPERTY YIELDS RECOGNIZED RECAPTURE GAIN

Tangible personal property used in a trade or business may be the subject of a § 1031 like-kind exchange, and the postponed gain is most likely postponed § 1245 gain. However, tangible personal property used predominantly within the United States cannot be exchanged for tangible personal property used predominantly outside the United States. Thus, such an exchange would cause recognized gain, and, as long as the fair market value of the property given up does not exceed its original cost, all of the gain is § 1245 depreciation recapture gain.

GLOBAL *Tax Issues*

gain is $15,000 ($20,000 net capital gain − $5,000 unrecaptured § 1250 gain). Bill's total tax (using the alternative tax calculation discussed in Chapter 16) is $15,844 [$12,344 (tax on ordinary taxable income) + $1,250 ($5,000 unrecaptured § 1250 gain × 25%) + $2,250 ($15,000 adjusted net capital gain × 15%)]. ∎

Considerations Common to §§ 1245 and 1250

LO.5

Understand considerations common to §§ 1245 and 1250.

Exceptions

Recapture under §§ 1245 and 1250 does not apply to the following transactions.

Gifts. The recapture potential carries over to the donee.[9]

EXAMPLE 17

Wade gives his daughter, Helen, § 1245 property with an adjusted basis of $1,000. The amount of recapture potential is $700. Helen uses the property in her business and claims further depreciation of $100 before selling it for $1,900. Helen's recognized gain is $1,000 ($1,900 amount realized − $900 adjusted basis), of which $800 is recaptured as ordinary income ($100 depreciation taken by Helen + $700 recapture potential carried over from Wade). The remaining gain of $200 is § 1231 gain. Even if Helen used the property for personal purposes, the $700 recapture potential would still be carried over. ∎

Death. Although not a very attractive tax planning approach, death eliminates all recapture potential.[10] In other words, any recapture potential does not carry over from a decedent to an estate or heir.

EXAMPLE 18

Assume the same facts as in Example 17, except Helen receives the property as a result of Wade's death. The $700 recapture potential from Wade is extinguished. Helen has a basis for the property equal to the property's fair market value (assume $1,700) at Wade's death. She will have a $300 gain when the property is sold because the selling price ($1,900) exceeds the property's adjusted basis of $1,600 ($1,700 original basis to Helen − $100 depreciation) by $300. Because of § 1245, $100 is ordinary income. The remaining gain of $200 is § 1231 gain. ∎

Charitable Transfers. The recapture potential reduces the amount of the charitable contribution deduction under § 170.[11]

EXAMPLE 19

Kanisha donates to her church § 1245 property with a fair market value of $10,000 and an adjusted basis of $7,000. Assume that the amount of recapture potential is $2,000 (the

---

[9]§§ 1245(b)(1) and 1250(d)(1) and Reg. §§ 1.1245–4(a)(1) and 1.1250–3(a)(1).
[10]§§ 1245(b)(2) and 1250(d)(2).

[11]§ 170(e)(1)(A) and Reg. § 1.170A–4(b)(1). In certain circumstances, § 1231 gain also reduces the amount of the charitable contribution. See § 170(e)(1)(B).

amount of recapture that would occur if the property were sold). Her charitable contribution deduction (subject to the limitations discussed in Chapter 10) is $8,000 ($10,000 fair market value − $2,000 recapture potential). ■

Certain Nontaxable Transactions. In certain transactions, the transferor's adjusted basis of property carries over to the transferee.[12] The recapture potential also carries over to the transferee.[13] Included in this category are transfers of property pursuant to the following:

- Nontaxable incorporations under § 351.
- Certain liquidations of subsidiary companies under § 332.
- Nontaxable contributions to a partnership under § 721.
- Nontaxable reorganizations.

Gain may be recognized in these transactions if boot is received. If gain is recognized, it is treated as ordinary income to the extent of the recapture potential or recognized gain, whichever is lower.[14]

Like-Kind Exchanges (§ 1031) and Involuntary Conversions (§ 1033).

Realized gain will be recognized to the extent of boot received under § 1031. Realized gain also will be recognized to the extent the proceeds from an involuntary conversion are not reinvested in similar property under § 1033. Such recognized gain is subject to recapture as ordinary income under §§ 1245 and 1250. The remaining recapture potential, if any, carries over to the property received in the exchange. Realized losses are not recognized in like-kind exchanges, but are recognized in involuntary conversions (see Chapter 15).

EXAMPLE 20	Anita exchanges § 1245 property with an adjusted basis of $300 for § 1245 property with a fair market value of $6,000. The exchange qualifies as a like-kind exchange under § 1031. Anita also receives $1,000 cash (boot). Her realized gain is $6,700 ($7,000 amount realized − $300 adjusted basis of property). Assuming the recapture potential is $7,500, Anita recognizes § 1245 gain of $1,000 because she received boot of $1,000. The remaining recapture potential of $6,500 carries over to the like-kind property received. ■

Other Applications

Sections 1245 and 1250 apply notwithstanding any other provisions in the Code.[15] That is, the recapture rules under these Sections *override* all other Sections. Special applications include installment sales and property dividends.

Installment Sales. Recapture gain is recognized in the year of the sale regardless of whether gain is otherwise recognized under the installment method.[16] All gain is ordinary income until the recapture potential is fully absorbed. Nonrecapture (§ 1231) gain is recognized under the installment method as cash is received.

EXAMPLE 21	Seth sells § 1245 property for $20,000, to be paid in 10 annual installments of $2,000 each plus interest at 10%. Seth realizes a $6,000 gain from the sale, of which $4,000 is attributable to depreciation taken. If Seth uses the installment method, he recognizes the entire $4,000 of recapture gain as ordinary income in the year of the sale. The $2,000 of nonrecapture (§ 1231) gain will be recognized at the rate of $200 per year for 10 years. ■

---

[12]§§ 1245(b)(3) and 1250(d)(3) and Reg. §§ 1.1245–4(c) and 1.1250–3(c).

[13]Reg. §§ 1.1245–2(a)(4) and −2(c)(2) and 1.1250–2(d)(1) and (3) and −3(c)(3).

[14]§§ 1245(b)(3) and 1250(d)(3) and Reg. §§ 1.1245–4(c) and 1.1250–3(c). Some of these special corporate problems are discussed in Chapter 20. Partnership contributions are also discussed in Chapter 20.

[15]§§ 1245(d) and 1250(i).

[16]§ 453(i). The installment method of reporting gains on the sale of property is discussed in Chapter 18.

Gain is also recognized on installment sales in the year of the sale in an amount equal to the § 179 (immediate expensing) deduction taken with respect to the property sold.

Property Dividends. A corporation generally recognizes gain if it distributes appreciated property as a dividend. Recapture under §§ 1245 and 1250 applies to the extent of the lower of the recapture potential or the excess of the property's fair market value over the adjusted basis.[17]

Emerald Corporation distributes § 1245 property as a dividend to its shareholders. The amount of the recapture potential is $300, and the excess of the property's fair market value over the adjusted basis is $800. Emerald recognizes $300 of ordinary income and $500 of § 1231 gain. ■

Concept Summary 17–3 integrates the depreciation recapture rules with the § 1231 netting process. It is an expanded version of Concept Summary 17–1.

Special Recapture Provisions

> **LO.6**
>
> Apply the special recapture provisions for related parties and IDC and be aware of the special recapture provision for corporations.

Special Recapture for Corporations

Corporations selling depreciable real estate may have ordinary income in addition to that required by § 1250.[18] See the discussion of this topic in Chapter 20.

Gain from Sale of Depreciable Property between Certain Related Parties

When the sale or exchange of property, which in the hands of the *transferee* is depreciable property (principally machinery, equipment, and buildings, but not land), is between certain related parties, any gain recognized is ordinary income.[19] This provision applies to both direct and indirect sales or exchanges. A **related party** is defined as an individual and his or her controlled corporation or partnership or a taxpayer and any trust in which the taxpayer (or the taxpayer's spouse) is a beneficiary.

Isabella sells a personal use automobile (therefore nondepreciable) to her controlled corporation. The automobile, which was purchased two years ago, originally cost $5,000 and is sold for $7,000. The automobile is to be used in the corporation's business. If the related-party provision did not exist, Isabella would realize a $2,000 long-term capital gain. The income tax consequences would be favorable because Isabella's controlled corporation is entitled to depreciate the automobile based upon the purchase price of $7,000. Under the related-party provision, Isabella's $2,000 gain is ordinary income. ■

Intangible Drilling Costs

Taxpayers may elect to either *expense or capitalize* intangible drilling and development costs for oil, gas, or geothermal properties.[20] **Intangible drilling and development costs (IDC)** include operator (one who holds a working or operating interest in any tract or parcel of land) expenditures for wages, fuel, repairs, hauling, and supplies. These expenditures must be incident to and necessary for the drilling of wells and preparation of wells for production. In most instances, taxpayers elect to expense IDC to maximize tax deductions during drilling.

---

[17]§ 311(b) and Reg. §§ 1.1245–1(c) and –6(b) and 1.1250–1(a)(4), –1(b)(4), and –1(c)(2).
[18]§ 291(a)(1).
[19]§ 1239.
[20]§ 263(c).

CONCEPT SUMMARY   17–3

Depreciation Recapture and § 1231 Netting Procedure

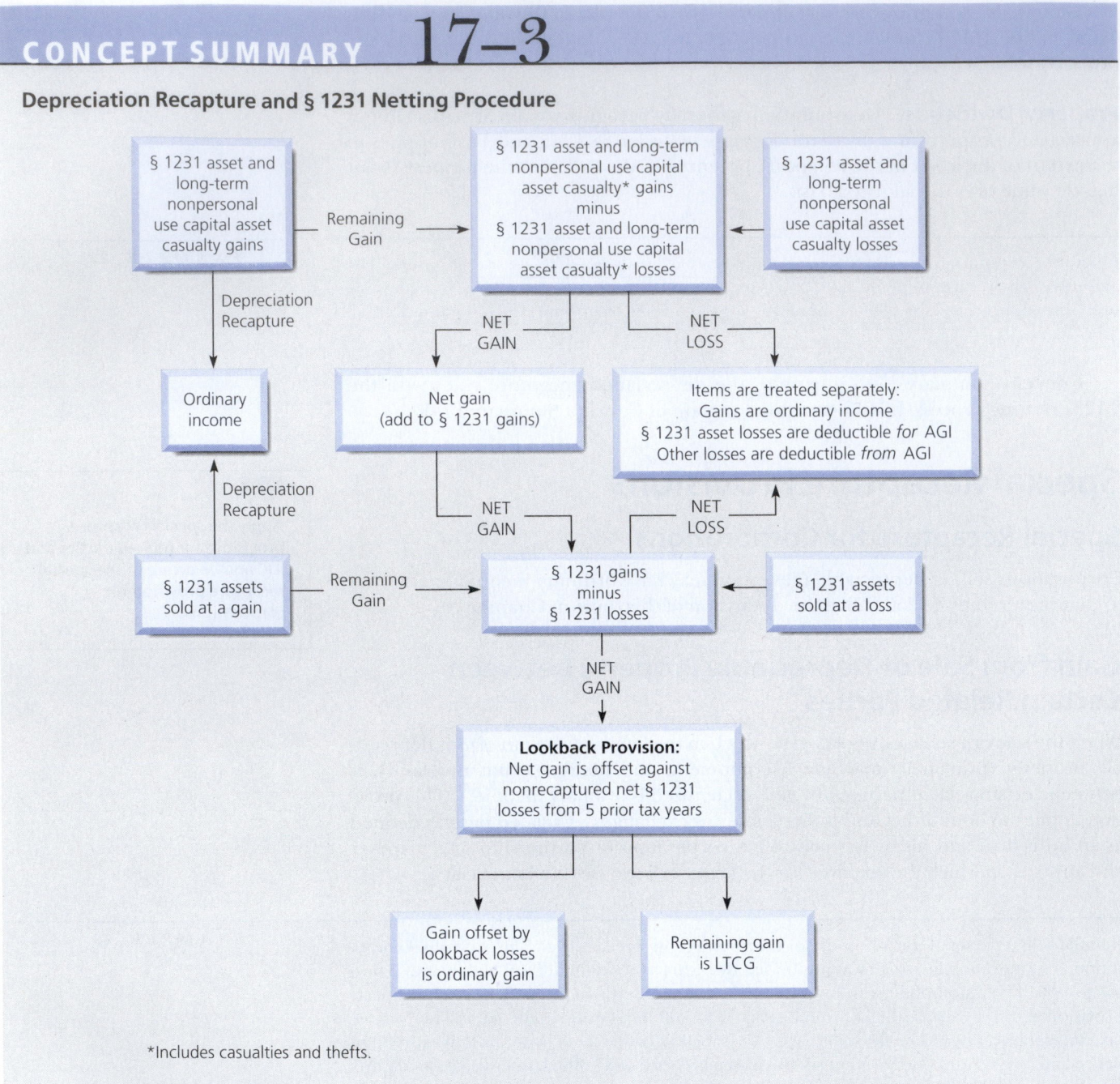

*Includes casualties and thefts.

Intangible drilling and development costs are subject to § 1254 recapture when the property is disposed of. The gain on the disposition of the property is subject to recapture as ordinary income.

LO.7

Describe and apply the reporting procedures for §§ 1231, 1245, and 1250.

Reporting Procedures

Noncapital gains and losses are reported on Form 4797, Sales of Business Property. Before filling out Form 4797, however, Form 4684, Casualties and Thefts, Part B, must be completed to determine whether any casualties will enter into the § 1231 computation procedure. Recall that gains from § 1231 asset casualties may be recaptured by § 1245 or § 1250. These gains will not appear on Form 4684. The § 1231 gains and nonpersonal use long-term capital gains are netted against § 1231

DEPRECIATION RECAPTURE IN OTHER COUNTRIES

The rules for dispositions of depreciated property are more complex in the United States than in any other country. Most countries treat the gain or loss from the disposition of business depreciable assets as ordinary income or loss. Consequently, although the U.S. rules are more complex, they can be more beneficial than those of other countries because at least some gains from the disposition of depreciable business property may be taxed at the lower capital gain rates.

GLOBAL
Tax Issues

losses and nonpersonal use long-term capital losses on Form 4684 to determine if there is a net gain to transfer to Form 4797, Part I.

Because the 2008 tax forms were unavailable at this writing, 2007 tax forms are used in the remainder of the discussion.

Form 4797 is divided into four parts, summarized as follows:

Part	Function
I	To report regular § 1231 gains and losses [including recognized gains and losses from certain involuntary conversions (condemnations)].
II	To report ordinary gains and losses.
III	To determine the portion of the gain that is subject to recapture (e.g., §§ 1245 and 1250 gain).
IV	Computation of recapture amounts under §§ 179 and 280F when business use of depreciable property drops to 50% or less.

Generally, the best approach to completing Form 4797 is to start with Part III. Once the recapture amount has been determined, it is transferred to Part II. The balance of any gain remaining after the recapture has been accounted for is transferred from Part III to Part I. Also transferred to Part I is any net gain from certain casualties and thefts as reported on Form 4684, Part B (refer to above and Chapter 15). If the netting process in Form 4797, Part I, results in a gain, it is reduced by the nonrecaptured net § 1231 losses from prior years (line 8 of Part I). Any remaining gain is shifted to Schedule D, Capital Gains and Losses, of Form 1040. If the netting process in Part I of Form 4797 results in a loss, it goes to Part II to be treated as an ordinary loss.

The complex rules for the alternative tax on net capital gain for individuals, estates, and trusts affect the reporting of gains and losses from the disposition of business and rental assets. S corporations, partnerships, individuals, estates, and trusts that use Form 4797 must provide information sufficient to determine what portion of the gain surviving Form 4797, Part I (the gain that goes to Schedule D) is 28% gain, 25% gain, or 0%/15% gain.

The process explained below is based upon an analysis of Form 1040, Schedule D, and Form 4797 and their instructions. One key point to remember is that all the gains and losses that end up being treated as ordinary gains and losses (and, therefore, end up in Part II of Form 4797) are not eligible for any of the special tax rates for net capital gain. Another key point is that the gain that goes from Part I of Form 4797 to Schedule D will go to line 11 of Schedule D (long-term capital gains and losses). The entire gain from Form 4797 goes in column 11(f).

The 25% gain (if any) from Form 4797 is part of the Schedule D, line 11(f) gain. *Nothing on the face of Form 4797 or Schedule D identifies this gain.* Only when the alternative tax on net capital gain is computed is the 25% gain portion of the Form 4797 net gain specifically mentioned on line 19.

Also remember that § 1231 assets are assets held more than one year. Therefore, no gain or loss is reportable on Form 4797, Part I, unless that holding period requirement is satisfied.

EXAMPLE 24

For 2007, Troy Williams, a single taxpayer (Social Security number 467–85–3036), has taxable income of $133,000 *including* the following recognized gains and losses (a 2007 example has been used since 2008 forms were unavailable):

Sale of Depreciable Business Assets Held Long Term	
Asset A (Note 1)	$36,500
Asset B (Note 2)	20,126
Asset C (Note 3)	(880)
Sale of Depreciable Business Assets Held Short Term	
Asset D (Note 4)	($ 600)
Capital Assets	
Long-term gain (Note 5)	$ 3,000
Short-term loss (Note 6)	(200)

Note 1. Asset A was acquired on June 23, 2004, for $50,000. It was five-year MACRS property, and four years' cost recovery allowances totaled $38,480. The property was sold for $48,020 on August 31, 2007.

Note 2. Asset B was purchased on May 10, 1997, for $37,000. It was 27.5-year residential rental real estate, and straight-line depreciation totaled $14,126. Asset B was sold for $43,000 on November 10, 2007.

Note 3. Asset C was purchased on December 9, 2004, for $16,000. It was five-year MACRS property, and four years' cost recovery totaled $12,314. The property was sold for $2,806 on December 30, 2007.

Note 4. Asset D was purchased for $7,000 on July 27, 2007. It was five-year MACRS property but proved unsuitable to Troy's business. Troy sold it for $6,400 on November 3, 2007.

Note 5. The LTCG resulted from the sale of 100 shares of Orange Corporation stock purchased for $10,000 on April 5, 2005. The shares were sold on October 21, 2007, for $13,223. Expenses of sale were $223.

Note 6. The STCL resulted from the sale of 50 shares of Blue Corporation stock purchased for $350 on March 14, 2007. The shares were sold for $170 on August 20, 2007. Expenses of sale were $20.

The sale of asset A at a gain results in the recapture of cost recovery deductions. That recapture is shown in Part III of Form 4797. The gain from the sale of asset B is carried from line 32 to Part I, line 6, of Form 4797. On line 2, the loss from asset C appears. Part I is where the § 1231 netting process takes place. Assume Troy Williams has no nonrecaptured net § 1231 losses from prior years. The net gain on line 7 is transferred to Schedule D, line 11. In Part II of Form 4797, the ordinary gains are accumulated. On line 13, the recapture from line 31 (Part III) is shown. On line 10, the loss from asset D is shown. The net gain on line 18 is ordinary income and is transferred to Form 1040, line 14.

Schedule D, Part I, line 1, reports the short-term capital loss from the Blue Corporation stock. Part II of Schedule D has the net § 1231 gain transferred from Form 4797 on line 11 and the Orange Corporation gain on line 8. The net capital gain is determined on line 16, Part III. The capital gain is then carried to line 13 of Form 1040.

On Form 4797, Part III, the $20,126 § 1231 gain from Asset B is made up of $14,126 (equals depreciation taken) of potential 25% gain and $6,000 of potential 5%/15% gain. The $880 § 1231 loss from Form 4797, Part I, line 2, offsets the potential 5%/15% portion of the $20,126 § 1231 gain on Form 4797, Part I, line 6. Consequently, of the $19,246 § 1231 gain that goes from Form 4797, Part I, line 7, to Schedule D, line 11, $14,126 is 25% gain and $5,120 is 5%/15% gain. Schedule D, Part III, line 19, shows an unrecaptured § 1250 gain of $13,926. This gain results from the $14,126 25% gain being reduced by the $200 short-term capital loss from Schedule D, line 7. Troy's 2007 tax liability is $29,878 using the alternative tax on net capital gain method. ■

The 2007 tax form solution for Example 24 appears on the following pages.

TO DEPRECIATE OR NOT TO DEPRECIATE

A staff accountant for a CPA firm is hurriedly finalizing depreciation and gain computations for a 2008 calendar year client's disposition of various business buildings. If the client's return is not finished quickly, a filing extension will be necessary, and the staff accountant will be blamed for it. All of the buildings were acquired three years ago, are 39-year MACRS real property, and were disposed of in April 2008. Rather than compute depreciation for the year of disposition, the staff accountant uses the beginning-of-the-year adjusted basis for the buildings to compute the disposition gain or loss. Could this approach make any difference on the client's return? (Assume the client is an individual taxpayer.)

Timing of § 1231 Gain

Although §§ 1245 and 1250 recapture much of the gain from the disposition of business property, sometimes § 1231 gain is still substantial. For instance, land held as a business asset will generate either § 1231 gain or § 1231 loss. If the taxpayer already has a capital loss for the year, the sale of land at a gain should be postponed so that the net § 1231 gain is not netted against the capital loss. The capital loss deduction will therefore be maximized for the current tax year, and the capital loss carryforward (if any) may be offset against the gain when the land is sold. If the taxpayer already has a § 1231 loss, § 1231 gains might be postponed to maximize the ordinary loss deduction this year. However, the carryforward of unrecaptured § 1231 losses will make the § 1231 gain next year an ordinary gain.

TAX PLANNING *Considerations*

EXAMPLE 25

Mark has a $2,000 net STCL for 2008. He could sell business land held 27 months for a $3,000 § 1231 gain. He will have no other capital gains and losses or § 1231 gains and losses in 2008 or 2009. He has no nonrecaptured § 1231 losses from prior years. Mark is in the 28% tax bracket in 2008 and will be in the 25% bracket in 2009. If he sells the land in 2008, he will have a $1,000 net LTCG ($3,000 § 1231 gain − $2,000 STCL) and will pay a tax of $150 ($1,000 × 15%). If Mark sells the land in 2009, he will have a 2008 tax savings of $560 ($2,000 capital loss deduction × 28% tax rate on ordinary income). In 2009, he will pay tax of $450 ($3,000 × 15%). By postponing the sale for a year, Mark will have the use of $710 ($560 + $150). ■

EXAMPLE 26

Beth has a $15,000 § 1231 loss in 2008. She could sell business equipment held 30 months for a $20,000 § 1231 gain and a $12,000 § 1245 gain. Beth is in the 28% tax bracket in 2008 and will be in the 25% bracket in 2009. She has no nonrecaptured § 1231 losses from prior years. If she sells the equipment in 2008, she will have a $5,000 net § 1231 gain and $12,000 of ordinary gain. Her tax would be $4,110 [($5,000 § 1231 gain × 15%) + ($12,000 ordinary gain × 28%)].

If Beth postpones the equipment sale until 2009, she would have a 2008 ordinary loss of $15,000 and tax savings of $4,200 ($15,000 × 28%). In 2009, she would have $5,000 of § 1231 gain (the 2008 § 1231 loss carries over and recaptures $15,000 of the 2009 § 1231 gain as ordinary income) and $27,000 of ordinary gain. Her tax would be $7,500 [($5,000 § 1231 gain × 15%) + ($27,000 ordinary gain × 25%)]. By postponing the equipment sale, Beth has the use of $8,310 ($4,200 + $4,110). ■

Timing of Recapture

Since recapture is usually not triggered until the property is sold or disposed of, it may be possible to plan for recapture in low-bracket or loss years. If a taxpayer has net operating loss (NOL) carryovers that are about to expire, the recognition of ordinary income from recapture may be advisable to absorb the loss carryovers.

Form **4797**

Department of the Treasury
Internal Revenue Service   (99)

Sales of Business Property

(Also Involuntary Conversions and Recapture Amounts
Under Sections 179 and 280F(b)(2))

" Attach to your tax return."   See separate instructions.

OMB No. 1545-0184

2007

Attachment
Sequence No. **27**

Name(s) shown on return

Troy Williams

Identifying number

467 - 85 - 3036

1   Enter the gross proceeds from sales or exchanges reported to you for 2007 on Form(s) 1099-B or 1099-S (or substitute statement) that you are including on line 2, 10, or 20 (see instructions). | **1** |

Part I   Sales or Exchanges of Property Used in a Trade or Business and Involuntary Conversions From Other Than Casualty or Theft—Most Property Held More Than 1 Year (see instructions)

(a) Description of property	(b) Date acquired (mo., day, yr.)	(c) Date sold (mo., day, yr.)	(d) Gross sales price	(e) Depreciation allowed or allowable since acquisition	(f) Cost or other basis, plus improvements and expense of sale	(g) Gain or (loss) Subtract (f) from the sum of (d) and (e)
2 *Asset C*	*12/09/04*	*12/30/07*	*2,806*	*12,314*	*16,000*	*(880)*

3 Gain, if any, from Form 4684, line 39	**3**
4 Section 1231 gain from installment sales from Form 6252, line 26 or 37	**4**
5 Section 1231 gain or (loss) from like-kind exchanges from Form 8824	**5**
6 Gain, if any, from line 32, from other than casualty or theft	**6** *20,126*
7 Combine lines 2 through 6. Enter the gain or (loss) here and on the appropriate line as follows:	**7** *19,246*

Partnerships (except electing large partnerships) and S corporations. Report the gain or (loss) following the instructions for Form 1065, Schedule K, line 10, or Form 1120S, Schedule K, line 9. Skip lines 8, 9, 11, and 12 below.

Individuals, partners, S corporation shareholders, and all others. If line 7 is zero or a loss, enter the amount from line 7 on line 11 below and skip lines 8 and 9. If line 7 is a gain and you did not have any prior year section 1231 losses, or they were recaptured in an earlier year, enter the gain from line 7 as a long-term capital gain on the Schedule D filed with your return and skip lines 8, 9, 11, and 12 below.

8 Nonrecaptured net section 1231 losses from prior years (see instructions)	**8**
9 Subtract line 8 from line 7. If zero or less, enter -0-. If line 9 is zero, enter the gain from line 7 on line 12 below. If line 9 is more than zero, enter the amount from line 8 on line 12 below and enter the gain from line 9 as a long-term capital gain on the Schedule D filed with your return (see instructions).	**9**

Part II   Ordinary Gains and Losses (see instructions)

10   Ordinary gains and losses not included on lines 11 through 16 (include property held 1 year or less):

Asset D	*07/27/07*	*11/03/07*	*6,400*	*0*	*7,000*	*(600)*

11 Loss, if any, from line 7	**11** ( )
12 Gain, if any, from line 7 or amount from line 8, if applicable	**12**
13 Gain, if any, from line 31	**13** *36,500*
14 Net gain or (loss) from Form 4684, lines 31 and 38a	**14**
15 Ordinary gain from installment sales from Form 6252, line 25 or 36	**15**
16 Ordinary gain or (loss) from like-kind exchanges from Form 8824	**16**
17 Combine lines 10 through 16	**17** *35,900*

18   For all except individual returns, enter the amount from line 17 on the appropriate line of your return and skip lines a and b below. For individual returns, complete lines a and b below:

a   If the loss on line 11 includes a loss from Form 4684, line 35, column (b)(ii), enter that part of the loss here. Enter the part of the loss from income-producing property on Schedule A (Form 1040), line 28, and the part of the loss from property used as an employee on Schedule A (Form 1040), line 23. Identify as from "Form 4797, line 18a." See instructions | **18a** |

b   Redetermine the gain or (loss) on line 17 excluding the loss, if any, on line 18a. Enter here and on Form 1040, line 14 | **18b**   *35,900* |

For Paperwork Reduction Act Notice, see separate instructions.   Cat. No. 13086I   Form **4797** (2007)

Form 4797 (2007)   Page **2**

Part III Gain From Disposition of Property Under Sections 1245, 1250, 1252, 1254, and 1255 (see instructions)

19	(a) Description of section 1245, 1250, 1252, 1254, or 1255 property:	(b) Date acquired (mo., day, yr.)	(c) Date sold (mo., day, yr.)
A	*Asset A*	06/23/04	08/31/07
B	*Asset B*	05/10/97	11/10/07
C			
D			

	These columns relate to the properties on lines 19A through 19D.		Property A	Property B	Property C	Property D
20	Gross sales price (**Note:** *See line 1 before completing.*)	20	48,020	43,000		
21	Cost or other basis plus expense of sale	21	50,000	37,000		
22	Depreciation (or depletion) allowed or allowable	22	38,480	14,126		
23	Adjusted basis. Subtract line 22 from line 21	23	11,520	22,874		
24	Total gain. Subtract line 23 from line 20	24	36,500	20,126		
25	**If section 1245 property:**					
a	Depreciation allowed or allowable from line 22	25a	38,480			
b	Enter the **smaller** of line 24 or 25a	25b	36,500			
26	**If section 1250 property:** If straight line depreciation was used, enter -0- on line 26g, except for a corporation subject to section 291.					
a	Additional depreciation after 1975 (see instructions)	26a				
b	Applicable percentage multiplied by the **smaller** of line 24 or line 26a (see instructions)	26b				
c	Subtract line 26a from line 24. If residential rental property **or** line 24 is not more than line 26a, skip lines 26d and 26e	26c				
d	Additional depreciation after 1969 and before 1976	26d				
e	Enter the **smaller** of line 26c or 26d	26e				
f	Section 291 amount (corporations only)	26f				
g	Add lines 26b, 26e, and 26f	26g		0		
27	**If section 1252 property:** Skip this section if you did not dispose of farmland or if this form is being completed for a partnership (other than an electing large partnership).					
a	Soil, water, and land clearing expenses	27a				
b	Line 27a multiplied by applicable percentage (see instructions)	27b				
c	Enter the **smaller** of line 24 or 27b	27c				
28	**If section 1254 property:**					
a	Intangible drilling and development costs, expenditures for development of mines and other natural deposits, and mining exploration costs (see instructions)	28a				
b	Enter the **smaller** of line 24 or 28a	28b				
29	**If section 1255 property:**					
a	Applicable percentage of payments excluded from income under section 126 (see instructions)	29a				
b	Enter the **smaller** of line 24 or 29a (see instructions)	29b				

Summary of Part III Gains. Complete property columns A through D through line 29b before going to line 30.

30	Total gains for all properties. Add property columns A through D, line 24	30	56,626
31	Add property columns A through D, lines 25b, 26g, 27c, 28b, and 29b. Enter here and on line 13	31	36,500
32	Subtract line 31 from line 30. Enter the portion from casualty or theft on Form 4684, line 33. Enter the portion from other than casualty or theft on Form 4797, line 6	32	20,126

Part IV Recapture Amounts Under Sections 179 and 280F(b)(2) When Business Use Drops to 50% or Less (see instructions)

			(a) Section 179	(b) Section 280F(b)(2)
33	Section 179 expense deduction or depreciation allowable in prior years	33		
34	Recomputed depreciation (see instructions)	34		
35	Recapture amount. Subtract line 34 from line 33. See the instructions for where to report	35		

Form **4797** (2007)

| SCHEDULE D
(Form 1040)
Department of the Treasury
Internal Revenue Service | **Capital Gains and Losses**
Attach to Form 1040 or Form 1040NR.   See Instructions for Schedule D (Form 1040).
Use Schedule D-1 to list additional transactions for lines 1 and 8. | OMB No. 1545-0074
2007
Attachment
Sequence No. **12** |

Name(s) shown on return   *Troy Williams*

Your social security number   467 85 3036

Part I   Short-Term Capital Gains and Losses—Assets Held One Year or Less

(a) Description of property (Example: 100 sh. XYZ Co.)	(b) Date acquired (Mo., day, yr.)	(c) Date sold (Mo., day, yr.)	(d) Sales price (see page D-7 of the instructions)	(e) Cost or other basis (see page D-7 of the instructions)	(f) Gain or (loss) Subtract (e) from (d)
1 *Blue Corp. (50 shares)*	03/14/07	08/20/07	170	370	(200)

2 Enter your short-term totals, if any, from Schedule D-1, line 2	**2**	
3 Total short-term sales price amounts. Add lines 1 and 2 in column (d)	**3**	*170*
4 Short-term gain from Form 6252 and short-term gain or (loss) from Forms 4684, 6781, and 8824	**4**	
5 Net short-term gain or (loss) from partnerships, S corporations, estates, and trusts from Schedule(s) K-1	**5**	
6 Short-term capital loss carryover. Enter the amount, if any, from line 10 of your **Capital Loss Carryover Worksheet** on page D-7 of the instructions	**6** (	)
7 **Net short-term capital gain or (loss).** Combine lines 1 through 6 in column (f)	**7**	*(200)*

Part II   Long-Term Capital Gains and Losses—Assets Held More Than One Year

(a) Description of property (Example: 100 sh. XYZ Co.)	(b) Date acquired (Mo., day, yr.)	(c) Date sold (Mo., day, yr.)	(d) Sales price (see page D-7 of the instructions)	(e) Cost or other basis (see page D-7 of the instructions)	(f) Gain or (loss) Subtract (e) from (d)
8 *Orange Corp. (100 shares)*	04/05/05	10/21/07	13,223	10,223	3,000

9 Enter your long-term totals, if any, from Schedule D-1, line 9	**9**	
10 Total long-term sales price amounts. Add lines 8 and 9 in column (d)	**10**	*13,223*
11 Gain from Form 4797, Part I; long-term gain from Forms 2439 and 6252; and long-term gain or (loss) from Forms 4684, 6781, and 8824	**11**	*19,246*
12 Net long-term gain or (loss) from partnerships, S corporations, estates, and trusts from Schedule(s) K-1	**12**	
13 Capital gain distributions. See page D-2 of the instructions	**13**	
14 Long-term capital loss carryover. Enter the amount, if any, from line 15 of your **Capital Loss Carryover Worksheet** on page D-7 of the instructions	**14** (	)
15 **Net long-term capital gain or (loss).** Combine lines 8 through 14 in column (f). Then go to Part III on the back	**15**	*22,246*

For Paperwork Reduction Act Notice, see Form 1040 or Form 1040NR instructions.   Cat. No. 11338H   Schedule D (Form 1040) 2007

Part III   **Summary**

16 Combine lines 7 and 15 and enter the result **16**   *22,046*

If line 16 is:

" A **gain**, enter the amount from line 16 on Form 1040, line 13, or Form 1040NR, line 14. Then go to line 17 below.

" A **loss**, skip lines 17 through 20 below. Then go to line 21. Also be sure to complete line 22.

" **Zero**, skip lines 17 through 21 below and enter -0- on Form 1040, line 13, or Form 1040NR, line 14. Then go to line 22.

17 Are lines 15 and 16 **both** gains?

☐ **Yes.** Go to line 18.

☐ **No.** Skip lines 18 through 21, and go to line 22.

18 Enter the amount, if any, from line 7 of the **28% Rate Gain Worksheet** on page D-8 of the instructions . . . . "   **18**   *0*

19 Enter the amount, if any, from line 18 of the **Unrecaptured Section 1250 Gain Worksheet** on page D-9 of the instructions . . . . "   **19**   *13,926*

20 Are lines 18 and 19 **both** zero or blank?

☐ **Yes.** Complete Form 1040 through line 43, or Form 1040NR through line 40. Then complete the **Qualified Dividends and Capital Gain Tax Worksheet** on page 35 of the Instructions for Form 1040 (or in the Instructions for Form 1040NR). **Do not** complete lines 21 and 22 below.

☐ **No.** Complete Form 1040 through line 43, or Form 1040NR through line 40. Then complete the **Schedule D Tax Worksheet** on page D-10 of the instructions. **Do not** complete lines 21 and 22 below.

21 If line 16 is a loss, enter here and on Form 1040, line 13, or Form 1040NR, line 14, the **smaller** of:

" The loss on line 16 or
" ($3,000), or if married filing separately, ($1,500)   }   . . . .   **21** (   )

Note. When figuring which amount is smaller, treat both amounts as positive numbers.

22 Do you have qualified dividends on Form 1040, line 9b, or Form 1040NR, line 10b?

☐ **Yes.** Complete Form 1040 through line 43, or Form 1040NR through line 40. Then complete the **Qualified Dividends and Capital Gain Tax Worksheet** on page 35 of the Instructions for Form 1040 (or in the Instructions for Form 1040NR).

☐ **No.** Complete the rest of Form 1040 or Form 1040NR.

Schedule D (Form 1040) 2007

EXAMPLE 27

Ahmad has a $15,000 NOL carryover that will expire this year. He owns a machine that he plans to sell in the early part of next year. The expected gain of $17,000 from the sale of the machine will be recaptured as ordinary income under § 1245. Ahmad sells the machine before the end of this year and offsets $15,000 of the ordinary income against the NOL carryover. ∎

Postponing and Shifting Recapture

It is also possible to postpone recapture or to shift the burden of recapture to others. For example, recapture is avoided upon the disposition of a § 1231 asset if the taxpayer replaces the property by entering into a like-kind exchange. In this instance, recapture potential is merely carried over to the newly acquired property (refer to Example 20).

Recapture can be shifted to others through the gratuitous transfer of § 1245 or § 1250 property to family members. A subsequent sale of such property by the donee will trigger recapture to the donee rather than the donor (refer to Example 17). This procedure would be advisable only if the donee is in a lower income tax bracket than the donor.

Avoiding Recapture

The immediate expensing election (§ 179) is subject to § 1245 recapture. If the election is not made, the § 1245 recapture potential will accumulate more slowly (refer to Chapter 8). Since using the immediate expense deduction complicates depreciation and book accounting for the affected asset, not taking the deduction may make sense even though the time value of money might indicate it should be taken.

KEY TERMS

Additional depreciation, 17–15	Section 1231 gains and losses, 17–3	Section 1245 recapture, 17–12
Intangible drilling and development costs (IDC), 17–21	Section 1231 lookback, 17–9	Section 1250 property, 17–14
Long-term nonpersonal use capital assets, 17–6	Section 1231 property, 17–4	Section 1250 recapture, 17-14
Related party, 17–21	Section 1245 property, 17–13	Unrecaptured § 1250 gain, 17–17

PROBLEM MATERIALS

DISCUSSION QUESTIONS

1. If there is a net loss from § 1231 transactions, what is the character of the loss, and how is it deducted (*for* or *from* AGI)?

2. If there is a net § 1231 gain that is treated as a long-term capital gain, how would a net short-term capital loss affect the computation of the net long-term capital gain?

3. When is land a § 1231 asset?

4. A taxpayer elects to treat the cutting of timber held for use in her business as a sale or exchange. The timber had been held for the long-term holding period. How is the § 1231 gain measured?

Issue ID
5. Ahmad, a farmer, is thinking about raising ostriches. Ostrich meat is very high in protein, low in calories, and low in fat. Ahmad would like to know what tax issues he would face if he decides to raise ostriches in addition to the cattle he is currently raising.

Issue ID
6. Aretha has a loss of $4,000 on a § 1231 asset and a gain of $16,000 on sale of vacant land. Under what circumstances could the gain from the sale of the land offset the loss?

Issue ID
7. Harold's business building was destroyed by fire, but was not insured. His adjusted basis for the building was substantial, but was less than he had paid for the building in 2004. The building was Harold's only asset damaged by the fire. How should Harold handle this situation?

Issue ID
8. Sabath began a sole proprietorship in 2000. He sold § 1231 assets at a loss in 2006 and 2007. He had not sold any § 1231 assets before 2006. In 2008, he could sell a § 1231 asset at a gain and would like to have the gain taxed as a long-term capital gain. What issues must Sabath deal with?

9. As a result of a casualty event, Tricia disposed of tangible personal property (a § 1231 asset) at a realized and recognized gain. At the time of the casualty, the property was worth substantially less than Tricia had paid for it and had an adjusted basis of zero. This was her only business casualty, and she has no § 1231 lookback loss. Is the resulting gain a casualty gain taxed as a long-term capital gain, a gain taxed as an ordinary gain, or a casualty gain taxed as a § 1231 gain?

10. An individual taxpayer had a net § 1231 loss in 2005 and a net § 1231 gain in 2006, 2007, and 2008. What factors will influence whether any of the 2008 net § 1231 gain will be treated as long-term capital gain?

    Issue ID

11. Review Examples 4 and 6 in the text. In both examples, the taxpayer's AGI is $129,400 even though in Example 6 there is $700 of nonrecaptured § 1231 loss from 2007. Explain why the two AGI amounts are the same.

12. A taxpayer owns depreciable business equipment held for the long-term holding period. What would have to be true for the equipment to generate a § 1231 loss when it is sold?

13. A depreciable business machine has been owned for four years and is no longer useful to the taxpayer. What would have to be true for the disposition of the machine to generate at least some § 1231 gain?

14. Sylvia owns two items of business equipment. They were both purchased in 2004 for $100,000, both have a seven-year recovery period, and both have an adjusted basis of $37,490. Sylvia is considering selling these assets in 2008. One of them is worth $40,000, and the other is worth $23,000. Since both items were used in her business, Sylvia simply assumes that the loss on one will be offset against the gain from the other and the net gain or loss will increase or reduce her business income. Is she correct?

    Issue ID

15. If depreciable equipment used in a business is sold at a recognized gain on July 10, 2008, and it was purchased on August 21, 2007, does § 1245 depreciation recapture apply to the asset?

16. A professional football player's contract is sold at a gain after it has been held for two years. What issues should the team consider in determining the nature of this gain?

    Issue ID

17. A farmer's silo is destroyed by a tornado, but is insured for its replacement cost. Consequently, the farmer has a $40,000 gain after receiving the insurance proceeds. The silo is not replaced because the farmer spends the insurance proceeds on additional cattle. What is the nature of the gain if the silo originally cost $100,000 three years ago and had an adjusted basis of $60,000 at the time of its destruction?

18. Residential real estate is sold at a gain. In what year(s) would it have to have been acquired in order for some of the gain to be recaptured as ordinary income by § 1250?

19. Residential real estate was acquired in 1993. What is the maximum amount of unrecaptured § 1250 gain from the disposition of the real estate if the real estate is sold at a gain?

20. Nonresidential real estate was acquired in 2006. What is the maximum amount of unrecaptured § 1250 gain from the disposition of the real estate if the building is sold for a loss and the land is sold for a gain?

21. An individual taxpayer has $25,000 of § 1231 gain from the disposition of nonresidential real estate. Straight-line depreciation of $43,000 was deducted on the real estate. The taxpayer also has a § 1231 loss of $56,000 from the sale of equipment. How much of the § 1231 gain is taxed as unrecaptured § 1250 gain?

22. Meredith receives tangible personal property as a gift. The property was depreciated by the donor, and Meredith will also depreciate it. At the date of the gift, the property was worth more than the donor's adjusted basis. What is the impact of these facts on Meredith when she sells the property at a gain several years after she acquired it?

23. Thomas receives tangible personal property as an inheritance. The property was depreciated by the deceased, and Thomas will also depreciate it. At the date of the deceased's death, the property was worth more than the deceased's adjusted basis. What is the impact of these facts on Thomas when he sells the property at a gain several years after he acquired it?

24. Dino contributes to charity some tangible personal property that he had used in his business and depreciated. At the date of the donation, the property has a fair market value greater than its adjusted basis, but less than the original cost. What is the impact of these facts on Dino's charitable contribution?

25. Desiree contributes to her wholly owned corporation some tangible personal property that she had used in her sole proprietorship business and depreciated. At the date of the contribution, the property has a fair market value greater than its adjusted basis. What is the impact of these facts on the corporation?

26. A corporation distributes a truck it has owned for three years to its sole shareholder. The shareholder will use the truck for personal use activity. The truck's fair market value at the time of the distribution is greater than its adjusted basis, but less than its original cost. Does the corporation recognize a gain? If so, what is the character of the gain?

27. A corporation distributes a truck it has owned for three years to its sole shareholder. The shareholder will use the truck for business activity. The truck's fair market value at the time of the distribution is greater than its adjusted basis, but less than its original cost. Does the corporation recognize a gain? If so, what is the character of the gain?

28. Refer to Form 4797 at the end of this chapter. Where would a § 1231 loss be entered on the form?

29. Refer to Form 4797 at the end of this chapter. Where would a § 1231 gain on the disposition of business land be entered on the form?

30. Refer to Form 4797 at the end of this chapter. Where would a § 1231 lookback loss be entered on the form?

PROBLEMS

31. Sue-Jen purchased timber on a 100-acre tract of land in South Dakota in March 2005 for $100,000. On January 1, 2007, the timber had a fair market value of $130,000. Because of careless cutting in November 2007, when the fair market value was $145,000, the wood was sold on January 30, 2008, for $78,000.
    a. What gain (loss) was recognized in 2006, 2007, and 2008 if Sue-Jen elects to treat the cutting as a sale?
    b. What was the nature of the gains (losses) in (a)?
    c. Does the answer change if the timber was sold in December 2007? Why?
    d. If the timber was worth only $48,000 on January 1, 2007, was cut in November when worth $21,000, and was sold in December for $49,000, how would the answers to (a) and (b) change?

32. Bob owns a farming sole proprietorship. During the year, Bob sold a milk cow that he had owned for 15 months and a workhorse that he had owned for 66 months. The cow had an adjusted basis of $28,000 and was sold for $25,000. The horse had an adjusted basis of $750 and was sold for $4,000. Bob also has a $200 long-term capital loss from the sale of corporate stock. He has $55,000 of other AGI (not associated with the items above) for the year. He has $4,000 nonrecaptured § 1231 losses from the previous five years. What is the nature of the gains or losses from the disposition of the farm animals, and what is Bob's AGI for the year?

Communications

33. A painting that Kwan Lee held for investment was destroyed in a flood. The painting was insured, and Kwan had a $60,000 gain from this casualty. He also had a $27,000 loss from an uninsured antique vase that was destroyed by the flood. The vase was also held for investment. Kwan had no other property transactions during the year and has no nonrecaptured § 1231 losses from prior years. Both the painting and the vase had been held more than one year when the flood occurred. Compute Kwan's net gain or loss and identify how it would be treated. Also, write a letter to Kwan explaining the nature of the gain or loss. Kwan's address is 2367 Meridian Road, Hannibal Point, MO 34901.

34. Vicki has the following net § 1231 results for each of the years shown. What would be the nature of the net gains in 2007 and 2008?

Tax Year	Net § 1231 Loss	Net § 1231 Gain
2003	$18,000	
2004	33,000	
2005	32,000	
2006		$42,000
2007		30,000
2008		41,000

35. Yoshida owns two parcels of business land (§ 1231 assets). One parcel can be sold at a loss of $50,000, and the other parcel can be sold at a gain of $70,000. Yoshida has no nonrecaptured § 1231 losses from prior years. The parcels could be sold at any time because potential purchasers are abundant. Yoshida has a $25,000 short-term capital loss carryover from a prior tax year and no capital assets that could be sold to generate long-term capital gains. Both the land parcels have been held more than one year. What should Yoshida do based upon these facts? (Assume tax rates are constant and ignore the present value of future cash flow.)

Decision Making

36. Gray Industries (a sole proprietorship) sold three § 1231 assets during 2008. Data on these property dispositions are as follows:

Asset	Cost	Acquired	Depreciation	Sold for	Sold on
Rack	$100,000	10/10/04	$70,000	$75,000	10/10/08
Forklift	35,000	10/16/05	23,000	5,000	10/10/08
Bin	87,000	03/12/07	34,000	60,000	10/10/08

a. Determine the amount and the character of the recognized gain or loss from the disposition of each asset.
b. Assuming Gray has no nonrecaptured net § 1231 losses from prior years, how much of the 2008 recognized gains is treated as capital gains?

37. Green Industries (a sole proprietorship) sold three § 1231 assets during 2008. Data on these property dispositions are as follows:

Asset	Cost	Acquired	Depreciation	Sold for	Sold on
Rack	$100,000	10/10/04	$100,000	$135,000	10/10/08
Forklift	35,000	10/16/05	23,000	5,000	10/10/08
Bin	87,000	03/12/07	34,000	60,000	10/10/08

a. Determine the amount and the character of the recognized gain or loss from the disposition of each asset.
b. Assuming Green has $5,000 nonrecaptured net § 1231 losses from the five prior years, how much of the 2008 recognized gains is treated as capital gains?

38. Magenta Industries (a sole proprietorship) sold three § 1231 assets during 2008. Data on these property dispositions are as follows:

Asset	Cost	Acquired	Depreciation	Sold for	Sold on
Rack	$110,000	10/10/05	$60,000	$55,000	10/10/08
Forklift	45,000	10/16/04	23,000	15,000	10/10/08
Bin	97,000	03/12/07	34,000	60,000	10/10/08

a. Determine the amount and the character of the recognized gain or loss from the disposition of each asset.
b. Assuming Magenta has $2,000 nonrecaptured net § 1231 losses from prior years, how much of the 2008 recognized gains is treated as capital gains?

Communications

39. On December 1, 2006, Gray Manufacturing Company (a corporation) purchased another company's assets, including a patent. The patent was used in Gray's manufacturing operations; $40,500 was allocated to the patent, and it was amortized at the rate of $225 per month. On July 30, 2008, Gray sold the patent for $70,000. Twenty months of amortization had been taken on the patent. What are the amount and nature of the gain Gray recognizes on the disposition of the patent? Write a letter to Gray discussing the treatment of the gain. Gray's address is 6734 Grover Street, Back Bay Harbor, ME 23890. The letter should be addressed to Siddim Sadatha, Controller.

40. On June 1, 2004, Sparrow Enterprises (not a corporation) acquired a retail store for $500,000 (with $100,000 being allocated to the land). The store was 39-year real property, and the straight-line cost recovery method was used. The property was sold on June 21, 2008, for $385,000.
    a. Compute the cost recovery and adjusted basis for the store using Table 8–6 from Chapter 8.
    b. What are the amount and nature of Sparrow's gain or loss from disposition of the store? What amount, if any, of the gain is unrecaptured § 1250 gain?

41. On May 2, 1986, Moad acquired residential rental real estate for $450,000. Of the cost, $100,000 was allocated to the land and $350,000 to the building. On January 20, 2008, the building, which then had an adjusted basis of $0, was sold for $345,000 and the land for $500,000.
    a. Determine the amount and character of the recognized gain from the sale of the building.
    b. Determine the amount and character of the recognized gain from the sale of the land.

42. Dave is the sole proprietor of a trampoline shop. During 2008, the following transactions occurred:

    • Unimproved land adjacent to the store was condemned by the city on February 1. The condemnation proceeds were $25,000. The land, acquired in 1984, had an allocable basis of $40,000. Dave has additional parking across the street and plans to use the condemnation proceeds to build his inventory.

    • A truck used to deliver trampolines was sold on January 2 for $3,500. The truck was purchased on January 2, 2004, for $6,000. On the date of sale, the adjusted basis was $2,509.

    • Dave sold an antique rowing machine at an auction. Net proceeds were $3,900. The rowing machine was purchased as used equipment 17 years ago for $5,200 and is fully depreciated.

    • Dave sold an apartment building for $200,000 on September 1. The rental property was purchased on September 1, 2005, for $150,000 and was being depreciated over a 27.5-year life using the straight-line method. At the date of sale, the adjusted basis was $124,783.

    • Dave's personal yacht was stolen on September 5. The yacht had been purchased in August at a cost of $25,000. The fair market value immediately preceding the theft was $20,000. Dave was insured for 50% of the original cost, and he received $12,500 on December 1.

    • Dave sold a Buick on May 1 for $9,600. The vehicle had been used exclusively for personal purposes. It was purchased on September 1, 2004, for $20,800.

    • Dave's trampoline stretching machine (owned two years) was stolen on May 5, but the business's insurance company will not pay any of the machine's value because Dave failed to pay the insurance premium. The machine had a fair market value of $8,000 and an adjusted basis of $6,000 at the time of theft.

    • Dave had AGI of $402,000 from sources other than those described above.

    • Dave has no nonrecaptured § 1231 lookback losses.

    a. For each transaction, what are the amount and nature of recognized gain or loss?
    b. What is Dave's 2008 AGI?

Communications

43. On January 1, 1999, Cora Hassant acquired depreciable real property for $50,000. She used straight-line depreciation to compute the asset's cost recovery. The asset was sold for $89,000 on January 3, 2008, when its adjusted basis was $38,000.

a.   What are the amount and nature of the gain if the real property was residential?

b.   Cora is curious about how the recapture rules differ for residential rental real estate acquired in 1986 and for residential rental real estate acquired in 1987 and thereafter. Write a letter to Cora explaining the differences. Her address is 2345 Westridge Street #23, Homer, MT 67342.

Decision Making

44. Joanne is in the 35% tax bracket and owns depreciable business equipment that she purchased several years ago for $135,000. She has taken $100,000 of depreciation on the equipment, and it is worth $85,000. Joanne's niece, Susan, is starting a new business and is short of cash. Susan has asked Joanne to gift the equipment to her so that Susan can use it in her business. Joanne no longer needs the equipment. Identify the alternatives available to Joanne if she wishes to help Susan and the tax effects of those alternatives. (Assume all alternatives involve the business equipment in one way or another, and ignore the gift tax.)

45. Harriet received tangible personal property with a fair market value of $45,000 as a gift in 2006. The donor had purchased the property for $67,000 and taken $67,000 of depreciation. Harriet used the property in her business. Harriet sells the property for $13,000 in 2008. What are the tax status of the property and the nature of the recognized gain when she sells the property?

46. Trent receives tangible personal property as an inheritance. The property was depreciated by the deceased (Trent's father), and Trent will also depreciate it. At the date of the deceased's death, the property was worth $432,000. The deceased had purchased it for $800,000 and taken $623,000 of depreciation on the property. Trent takes $123,000 of depreciation on the property before selling it for $382,000 in 2008. What are the tax status of the property and the nature of the recognized gain when Trent sells the property?

47. David contributes to charity some tangible personal property that he had used in his business and depreciated. At the date of the donation, the property has a fair market value of $233,000 and an adjusted basis of zero; it was originally acquired for $400,000. What is the amount of David's charitable contribution?

48. Dedriea contributes to her wholly owned corporation some tangible personal property that she had used in her sole proprietorship business and depreciated. She had acquired the property for $566,000 and taken $431,000 of depreciation on it before contributing it to the corporation. At the date of the contribution, the property had a fair market value of $289,000. The corporation took $100,000 of depreciation on the property and then sold it for $88,000 in 2008. What are the tax status of the property to the corporation and the nature of the recognized gain or loss when the corporation sells the property?

49. Magenta Corporation purchased depreciable tangible personal property for $100,000 in 2005 and immediately expensed the entire cost under § 179. In 2008, when the property was worth $40,000, Magenta distributed it as a dividend to the corporation's sole shareholder. What was the tax status of this property for Magenta, and what is the nature of the recognized gain or loss from the distribution of the property?

50. Albert, a single taxpayer, has 2008 ordinary taxable income of $335,000 *before* considering the following items: $45,000 gain from disposition of depreciable real property (straight-line depreciation taken on the building was $67,000), $14,000 loss on disposition of depreciable business equipment, and $32,000 gain from disposition of a stock investment. All of the assets disposed of had been held for more than 12 months. Albert has a § 1231 lookback loss of $23,000. What are Albert's taxable income and his tax on taxable income?

51. Carlotta owned rental real estate that she sold to her tenant in an installment sale. Carlotta acquired the property in 1998 for $400,000, took $178,000 of depreciation on it, and sold it for $210,000, receiving $25,000 and the balance (plus interest at a market rate) in equal payments of $18,500 for 10 years. What is the nature of the recognized gain or loss from this transaction?

52. Terri provided depreciable furniture in a furnished rental apartment she owned. She sold the furniture after owning it for two years and had a $4,000 loss on the disposition. What is the nature of the loss, and where is it reported on Form 4797?

53. Is a § 1245 gain that is reported on Form 4797, Part II, line 18(b) included on Form 1040, Schedule D? Is it included in AGI?

Decision Making

54. Jay sold three items of business equipment for a total of $300,000. None of the equipment was appraised to determine its value. Jay's cost and adjusted basis for the assets are as follows:

Asset	Cost	Adjusted Basis
Skidder	$230,000	$ 40,000
Driller	120,000	60,000
Platform	620,000	–0–
Total	$970,000	$100,000

Jay has been unable to establish the fair market values of the three assets. All he can determine is that combined they were worth $300,000 to the buyer in this arm's length transaction. How should Jay allocate the sales price and figure the gain or loss on the sale of the three assets?

CUMULATIVE PROBLEMS

Tax Return Problem

55. Justin Stone was an employee of DataCare Services, Inc. His salary was $47,000 through November 10, 2007, when he was laid off. He received $14,000 of unemployment compensation from November 11, 2007, through December 31, 2007. FICA withholdings were as follows: Social Security of $2,914 ($47,000 × 6.2%) and Medicare of $682 ($47,000 × 1.45%). Justin lives at 112 Green Road, Sandusky, ID 45623. His Social Security number is 567–89–1234. Justin owned an apartment building until November 22, 2007, when he sold it for $200,000. For 2007, he had rent revenue of $23,000. He incurred and paid expenses as follows: $4,568 of repairs, $12,000 of mortgage interest, and $1,000 of miscellaneous expenses. He had purchased the building on January 2, 2001, for $125,000. The building generated an operating profit each year that Justin owned it.

Other information follows:

- On November 22, 2007, Justin sold for $14,000 equipment that had been used for repairing various items in the apartments. The equipment was purchased for $25,000 on July 10, 2000, and was fully depreciated prior to 2007.
- Justin has no unrecaptured § 1231 losses from prior years.
- Justin is age 38, single, divorced, and has custody of his nine-year-old son, Flint. Justin provides more than 50% of Flint's support. Flint's Social Security number is 098–77–6543.
- Justin had $5,000 interest income from Blue Corporation bonds.
- Justin had $3,000 interest income from a State Bank certificate of deposit.
- Justin had a $2,000 5%/15% long-term capital gain distribution from the Brown Stock Investment Fund.
- Justin had the following itemized deductions: $5,600 real estate taxes on his home; $8,900 mortgage interest on his home; $760 charitable contributions (all in cash, properly documented, and no single contribution exceeded $25); $2,300 state income tax withholding during 2007; $2,000 state estimated income tax payments during 2007; $2,600 sales taxes paid.
- Justin does not wish to donate to the Presidential Election Campaign Fund.
- He had $5,000 of Federal income tax withholding during 2007 and made total Federal estimated income tax payments of $25,000 during 2007.

Compute Justin's 2007 net tax payable or refund due. If you use tax forms for your computations, you will need Form 1040 and Schedules A, B, D, and E. You will also need Form 4797, but ignore Form 6251. Suggested software: TaxCut.

56. Glen and Diane Okumura are married, file a joint return, and live at 39 Kaloa Street, Honolulu, HI 56790. Glen's Social Security number is 777–88–2000 and Diane's is 888–77–1000. The Okumuras have two dependent children, Amy (age 15) and John (age 9). Glen works for the Hawaii Public Works Department, and Diane works in a retail dress shop. The Okumuras had the following transactions during 2008:

    a. Glen earned $97,000 in wages and had Federal income tax withholding of $13,000.

    b. Diane earned $68,000 in wages from the dress shop and had Federal income tax withholding of $11,000.

    c. The Okumuras sold a small apartment building for $199,980 on November 15, 2008. The building was acquired in October 2002 for $300,000; cost recovery was $86,820.

    d. The Okumuras received $3,000 in qualified dividends on various domestic corporation stocks that they own.

    e. The Okumuras sold stock on November 5 for a $7,000 long-term capital gain and other stock on December 10 at a $2,000 short-term capital loss.

    f. The Okumuras had the following itemized deductions: $11,000 unreimbursed medical expenses; $10,500 personal use real property taxes; $7,000 qualified residence interest; $1,500 of Glen's unreimbursed employee business expenses; $535 of investment-related expenses; $2,700 of state income taxes paid; and $1,061 of sales taxes from the sales tax table.

    g. The Okumuras spent $3,000 on qualifying child care expenses during the year.

    Compute the Okumuras' 2008 net tax payable or refund due. Also write a letter to the Okumuras describing how the sale of the apartment building affects their return.

Tax Computation Problem

Communications

RESEARCH PROBLEMS

Note: Solutions to Research Problems can be prepared by using the **RIA Checkpoint®** **Student Edition** online research product, which is available to accompany this text. It is also possible to prepare solutions to the Research Problems by using tax research materials found in a standard tax library.

Research Problem 1.   Sidney owns a professional football franchise. He has received an offer of $80 million for the franchise, all the football equipment, the rights to concession receipts, the rights to a stadium lease, and the rights to all the player contracts he owns. Most of the players have been with the team for quite a long time and have contracts that were signed several years ago. The contracts have been substantially depreciated. Sidney is concerned about potential § 1245 recapture when the contracts are sold. He has heard about "previously unrecaptured depreciation with respect to initial contracts" and would like to know more about it. Find a definition for that phrase and write an explanation of it.

Communications

Research Problem 2.   Walter is both a real estate developer and the owner and manager of residential rental real estate. Walter is retiring and is going to sell both the land he is holding for future development and the rental properties he owns. Straight-line depreciation was used to depreciate the rental real estate. The rental properties will be sold at a substantial loss, and the development property will be sold at a substantial gain. What is the nature of these gains and losses?

Partial list of research aids:
§§ 1221 and 1231.
Zane R. Tollis, 65 TCM 1951, T.C.Memo. 1993–63.

Research Problem 3.   Brown Corporation, a software development company, was formed in 1996 and has always been an S corporation. In 2008, due to rapid growth, it sold its office building for a $70,000 gain and bought a larger building. Brown did not do a like-kind exchange. How does § 291 affect the character of this gain?

Research Problem 4.   In 2005, a taxpayer made leasehold improvements that were eligible for a 15-year MACRS life. Straight-line depreciation was taken on the improvements. Will these improvements be subject to either § 1245 or § 1250 depreciation recapture if they are eventually disposed of at a recognized gain?

Internet Activity

Use the tax resources of the Internet to address the following questions. Do not restrict your search to the World Wide Web, but include a review of newsgroups and general reference materials, practitioner sites and resources, primary sources of the tax law, chat rooms and discussion groups, and other opportunities.

Research Problem 5.   Summarize tax planning strategies related to each of the following topics that are presented on the Internet by tax advisers looking for clients:

a.   A strategy for maximizing gains that are eligible for the 0%/15% alternative tax rate rather than the 25% rate.

b.   A strategy for maximizing gains that are eligible for the 0%/15% alternative tax rate rather than the 28% rate.

Research Problem 6.   Determine whether Ireland has an equivalent to § 1231 treatment for gains from the disposition of business depreciable assets.

Research Problem 7.   Find a state Web site that has tax forms and instructions for that state. Let's call that state "X." Find a discussion in those sources that reveals whether state X taxes gains from the sale of real estate that is located in state Y when the taxpayer is an individual and is a full-time resident of state X.

PART 6

Accounting Periods, Accounting Methods, and Deferred Compensation

Part VI provides a more comprehensive examination of the accounting periods and accounting methods that were introduced in Part II. A discussion of special accounting methods is also included. Part VI concludes with an analysis of the tax consequences of deferred compensation transactions.

CHAPTER 18
Accounting Periods and Methods

CHAPTER 19
Deferred Compensation

Accounting Periods and Methods

LEARNING OBJECTIVES

After completing Chapter 18, you should be able to:

LO.1

Understand the relevance of the accounting period concept, the different types of accounting periods, and the limitations on their use.

LO.2

Apply the cash method, accrual method, and hybrid method of accounting.

LO.3

Utilize the procedure for changing accounting methods.

LO.4

Determine when the installment method of accounting can be utilized and apply the related calculation techniques.

LO.5

Understand the alternative methods of accounting for long-term contracts (the completed contract method and the percentage of completion method) including the limitations on the use of the completed contract method.

LO.6

Know when accounting for inventories must occur, recognize the types of costs that must be included in inventories, and apply the LIFO method.

LO.7

Identify tax planning opportunities related to accounting periods and accounting methods.

OUTLINE

Accounting Periods, 18–3
In General, 18–3
Specific Provisions for Partnerships, S Corporations, and
  Personal Service Corporations, 18–3
Making the Election, 18–6
Changes in the Accounting Period, 18–6
Taxable Periods of Less Than One Year, 18–7
Mitigation of the Annual Accounting Period
  Concept, 18–9

Accounting Methods, 18–10
Permissible Methods, 18–10
Cash Receipts and Disbursements Method—Cash
  Basis, 18–10
Accrual Method, 18–13
Hybrid Method, 18–16
Change of Method, 18–16

Special Accounting Methods, 18–19
Installment Method, 18–19
Disposition of Installment Obligations, 18–24
Interest on Deferred Taxes, 18–24
Electing Out of the Installment Method, 18–24
Long-Term Contracts, 18–25

Inventories, 18–29
Determining Inventory Cost, 18–30
The LIFO Election, 18–35
Special Inventory Methods Relating to Farming and
  Ranching, 18–36

Tax Planning Considerations, 18–36
Taxable Year, 18–36
Cash Method of Accounting, 18–36
Installment Method, 18–36
Completed Contract Method, 18–37
Inventories, 18–37

Tax practitioners must deal with the issue of *when* particular items of income and expense are recognized as well as the basic issue of *whether* the items are includible in taxable income. Earlier chapters discussed the types of income subject to tax (gross income and exclusions) and allowable deductions (the *whether* issue).[1] This chapter focuses on the related issue of the periods in which income and deductions are reported (the *when* issue). Generally, a taxpayer's income and deductions must be assigned to particular 12-month periods—calendar years or fiscal years.

Income and deductions are placed within particular years through the use of tax accounting methods. The basic accounting methods are the cash method, accrual method, and hybrid method. Other special purpose methods, such as the installment method and the methods used for long-term construction contracts, are available for specific circumstances or types of transactions.

Over the long run, the accounting period used by a taxpayer will not affect the aggregate amount of reported taxable income. However, taxable income for any particular year may vary significantly due to the use of a particular reporting period. Also, through the choice of accounting methods or accounting periods, it is possible to postpone the recognition of taxable income and to enjoy the benefits from deferring the related tax. This chapter discusses the taxpayer's alternatives for accounting periods and accounting methods.

TAX *in the News* | **DOMESTIC PRODUCTION ACTIVITIES DEDUCTION CREATED TAX PLANNING OPPORTUNITIES**

Under the American Jobs Creation Act of 2004, producers are allowed a deduction equal to a percentage of their income from qualified production activities: 3 percent in 2005 and 2006, 6 percent in 2007 through 2009, and 9 percent in 2010. Thus, assuming the tax rate was the same between years, a producer would prefer to take the deduction in 2010, rather than in 2009. Taking the deduction in 2009 would reduce the producer's taxable income by $.06 for each dollar of production activities income whereas taking the deduction in 2010 reduces the producer's taxable income by $.09 on the dollar.

---

[1] See Chapters 4, 5, and 6.

Accounting Periods

LO.1

Understand the relevance of the accounting period concept, the different types of accounting periods, and the limitations on their use.

In General

A taxpayer who keeps adequate books and records may be permitted to elect a **fiscal year**, a 12-month period ending on the *last day* of a month other than December, for the **accounting period**. Otherwise, a *calendar year* must be used.[2] Frequently, corporations can satisfy the record-keeping requirements and elect to use a fiscal year.[3] Often the fiscal year conforms to a natural business year (e.g., a summer resort's fiscal year may end on September 30, after the close of the season). Individuals seldom use a fiscal year because they do not maintain the necessary books and records and because complications can arise as a result of changes in the tax law (e.g., often the transition rules and effective dates differ for fiscal year taxpayers).

Generally, a taxable year may not exceed 12 calendar months. However, if certain requirements are met, a taxpayer may elect to use an annual period that varies from 52 to 53 weeks.[4] In that case, the year-end must be on the same day of the week (e.g., the Tuesday falling closest to October 31 or the last Tuesday in October). The day of the week selected for ending the year will depend upon business considerations. For example, a retail business that is not open on Sundays may end its tax year on a Sunday so that it can take an inventory without interrupting business operations.

EXAMPLE 1

Wade is in the business of selling farm supplies. His natural business year terminates at the end of October with the completion of harvesting. At the end of the fiscal year, Wade must take an inventory, which is most easily accomplished on a Tuesday. Therefore, Wade could adopt a 52–53 week tax year ending on the Tuesday closest to October 31. If Wade selects this method, the year-end date may fall in the following month if that Tuesday is closer to October 31. The tax year ending in 2008 will contain 52 weeks beginning on Wednesday, October 31, 2007, and ending on Tuesday, October 28, 2008. The tax year ending in 2009 will have 53 weeks beginning on Wednesday, October 29, 2008, and ending on Tuesday, November 3, 2009. ■

Specific Provisions for Partnerships, S Corporations, and Personal Service Corporations

Partnerships and S Corporations. When a partner's tax year and the partnership's tax year differ, the partner will enjoy a deferral of income. This results because the partner reports his or her share of the partnership's income and deductions for the partnership's tax year ending within or with the partner's tax year.[5] For example, if the tax year of the partnership ends on January 31, a calendar year partner will not report partnership profits for the first 11 months of the partnership tax year until the following year. Therefore, partnerships are subject to special tax year requirements.

In general, the partnership tax year must be the same as the tax year of the majority interest partners. The **majority interest partners** are the partners who own a greater-than-50 percent interest in the partnership capital and profits. If there are no majority interest partners, the partnership must adopt the same tax year as its principal partners. A **principal partner** is a partner with a 5 percent or more interest in the partnership capital or profits.[6]

---

[2]§ 441(c) and Reg. § 1.441–1(b)(1)(ii).
[3]Reg. § 1.441–1(e)(2).
[4]§ 441(f).

[5]Reg. § 1.706–1(a).
[6]§§ 706(b)(1)(B) and 706(b)(3).

EXAMPLE 2

The RST Partnership is owned equally by Rose Corporation, Silver Corporation, and Tom. The partners have the following tax years.

	Partner's Tax Year Ending
Rose	June 30
Silver	June 30
Tom	December 31

The partnership's tax year must end on June 30. If Silver Corporation's as well as Tom's year ended on December 31, the partnership would be required to adopt a calendar year. ■

If the principal partners do not all have the same tax year and no majority of partners have the same tax year, the partnership must use a year that results in the *least aggregate deferral* of income.[7] Under the **least aggregate deferral method**, the different tax years of the principal partners are tested to determine which produces the least aggregate deferral. This is calculated by first multiplying the combined percentages of the principal partners with the same tax year by the months of deferral for the test year. Once this is done for each set of principal partners with the same tax year, the resulting products are summed to produce the aggregate deferral. After calculating the aggregate deferral for each of the test years, the test year with the smallest summation (the least aggregate deferral) is the tax year for the partnership.

EXAMPLE 3

The DE Partnership is owned equally by Diane and Emily. Diane's fiscal year ends on March 31, and Emily's fiscal year ends on August 31. The partnership must use the partner's fiscal year that will result in the least aggregate deferral of income. Therefore, the fiscal years ending March 31 and August 31 must both be tested.

	Test for Fiscal Year Ending March 31			
Partner	Year Ends	Profit %	Months of Deferral	Product
Diane	3–31	50	0	0
Emily	8–31	50	5	2.5
Aggregate deferral months				2.5

Thus, with a year ending March 31, Emily would be able to defer her half of the income for five months. That is, Emily's share of the partnership income for the fiscal year ending March 31, 2009, would not be included in her income until August 31, 2009.

	Test for Fiscal Year Ending August 31			
Partner	Year Ends	Profit %	Months of Deferral	Product
Diane	3–31	50	7	3.5
Emily	8–31	50	0	0
Aggregate deferral months				3.5

---

[7]Reg. § 1.706–1(b)(3).

Thus, with a year ending August 31, Diane would be able to defer her half of the income for seven months. That is, Diane's share of the partnership income for the fiscal year ending August 31, 2009, would not be included in her income until March 31, 2010.

The year ending March 31 must be used because it results in the least aggregate deferral of income. ∎

Generally, S corporations must adopt a calendar year.[8] However, partnerships and S corporations may *elect* an otherwise *impermissible year* under any of the following conditions:

- A business purpose for the year can be demonstrated.[9]
- The partnership's or S corporation's year results in a deferral of not more than three months' income, and the entity agrees to make required tax payments.[10]
- The entity retains the same year as was used for the fiscal year ending in 1987, provided the entity agrees to make required tax payments.

Business Purpose. The only business purpose for a fiscal year that the IRS has acknowledged is the need to conform the tax year to the natural business year of a business.[11] Generally, only seasonal businesses have a natural business year. For example, the natural business year for a department store may end on January 31, after Christmas returns have been processed and clearance sales have been completed.

Required Tax Payments. Under the required payments system, tax payments are due from a fiscal year partnership or S corporation by April 15 of each tax year.[12] The amount due is computed by applying the highest individual tax rate plus 1 percentage point to an estimate of the deferral period income. The deferral period runs from the close of the fiscal year to the end of the calendar year. Estimated income for this period is based on the average monthly earnings for the previous fiscal year. The amount due is reduced by the amount of required tax payments for the previous year.[13]

EXAMPLE 4

Brown, Inc., an S corporation, elected a fiscal year ending September 30. Bob is the only shareholder. For the fiscal year ending September 30, 2008, Brown earned $100,000. The required tax payment for the previous year was $5,000. The corporation must pay $4,000 by April 15, 2009, calculated as follows:

$$(\$100,000 \times \text{}^3/_{12} \times 36\%*) - \$5,000 = \$4,000$$

*Maximum § 1 rate of 35% + 1%. ∎

ETHICAL and EQUITABLE *Considerations*

WHO BENEFITS FROM THE CHANGE IN TAX YEAR?

A public accounting sole practitioner has reached a breaking point. All of his clients use the calendar year to report income. Many of the clients are S corporations and partnerships. His workload the first four months of the year is so heavy that it is putting the quality of his work at risk. He is considering asking some of his S corporations and partnerships to switch to a fiscal year ending September 30. The accountant believes that he can convince the shareholders and partners to make the change. Although the shareholders and partners would be subject to the "required tax payments" rules, the accountant will sell the plan by promising better service. Evaluate the plan proposed by the accountant.

---

[8]§§ 1378(a) and (b).
[9]§§ 706(b)(1)(C) and 1378(b)(2).
[10]§ 444.
[11]Rev.Rul. 87–57, 1987–2 C.B. 117.

[12]§§ 444(c) and 7519. No payment is required if the calculated amount is $500 or less.
[13]§ 7519(b).

Personal Service Corporations. A **personal service corporation (PSC)** is a corporation whose shareholder-employees provide personal services (e.g., medical, dental, legal, accounting, engineering, actuarial, consulting, or performing arts). Generally, a PSC must use a calendar year.[14] However, a PSC can *elect* a fiscal year under any of the following conditions:

- A business purpose for the year can be demonstrated.
- The PSC year results in a deferral of not more than three months' income, the corporation pays the shareholder-employee's salary during the portion of the calendar year after the close of the fiscal year, and the salary for that period is at least proportionate to the shareholder-employee's salary received for the preceding fiscal year.[15]
- The PSC retains the same year it used for the fiscal year ending in 1987, provided it satisfies the latter two requirements in the preceding option.

E X A M P L E 5	Nancy's corporation paid Nancy a salary of $120,000 during its fiscal year ending September 30, 2008. The corporation cannot satisfy the business purpose test for a fiscal year. The corporation can continue to use its fiscal year without any negative tax effects, provided Nancy receives at least $30,000 [(3 months/12 months) × $120,000] as salary during the period October 1 through December 31, 2008. ∎

If the salary test is not satisfied, the PSC can retain the fiscal year, but the corporation's deduction for salary for the fiscal year is limited to the following:

$$A + A(F/N)$$

Where   A = Amount paid after the close of the fiscal year.
F = Number of months in the fiscal year minus number of months from the end of the fiscal year to the end of the ongoing calendar year.
N = Number of months from the end of the fiscal year to the end of the ongoing calendar year.

E X A M P L E 6	Assume the corporation in the previous example paid Nancy $10,000 of salary during the period October 1 through December 31, 2008. The deduction for Nancy's salary for the corporation's fiscal year ending September 30, 2009, is thus limited to $40,000 calculated as follows:

$$\$10,000 + \left[\$10,000\left(\frac{12 - 3}{3}\right)\right] = \$10,000 + \$30,000 = \$40,000 \qquad ∎$$

Making the Election

A taxpayer elects to use a calendar or fiscal year by the timely filing of his or her initial tax return. For all subsequent years, the taxpayer must use this same period unless approval for change is obtained from the IRS.[16]

Changes in the Accounting Period

A taxpayer must obtain consent from the IRS before changing the tax year.[17] This power to approve or not to approve a change is significant in that it permits the IRS to issue authoritative administrative guidelines that must be met by taxpayers who wish to change their accounting period. An application for permission to change

---

[14]§ 441(i).
[15]§§ 444 and 280H.
[16]Reg. §§ 1.441–1(b)(3) and 1.441–1(b)(4).

[17]§ 442. Under certain conditions, corporations are allowed to change tax years without obtaining IRS approval. See Reg. § 1.442–1(c)(1).

tax years must be made on Form 1128, Application for Change in Accounting Period. The application must be filed on or before the fifteenth day of the second calendar month following the close of the short period that results from the change in accounting period.[18]

EXAMPLE 7

Beginning in 2008, Gold Corporation, a calendar year taxpayer, would like to switch to a fiscal year ending March 31. The corporation must file Form 1128 by May 15, 2008. ∎

IRS Requirements. The IRS will not grant permission for the change unless the taxpayer can establish a substantial business purpose for the request. One substantial business purpose is to change to a tax year that coincides with the *natural business year* (the completion of an annual business cycle). The IRS applies an objective gross receipts test to determine if the entity has a natural business year. At least 25 percent of the entity's gross receipts for the 12-month period must be realized in the final two months of the 12-month period for three consecutive years.[19]

EXAMPLE 8

A Virginia Beach motel had gross receipts as follows:

	2006	2007	2008
July–August receipts	$ 300,000	$250,000	$ 325,000
September 1–August 31 receipts	1,000,000	900,000	1,250,000
Receipts for final 2 months divided by receipts for 12 months	30.0%	27.8%	26.0%

Since it satisfies the natural business year test, the motel will be allowed to use a fiscal year ending August 31. ∎

The IRS usually establishes certain conditions that the taxpayer must accept if the approval for change is to be granted. In particular, if the taxpayer has a net operating loss (NOL) for the short period, the IRS requires that the loss be carried forward; the loss cannot be carried back to prior years.[20] As you may recall (refer to Chapter 7), NOLs are ordinarily carried back for 2 years and forward for 20 years.

EXAMPLE 9

Parrot Corporation changed from a calendar year to a fiscal year ending September 30. The short-period return for the nine months ending September 30, 2008, reflected a $60,000 NOL. The corporation had taxable income for 2006 and 2007. As a condition for granting approval, the IRS requires Parrot to carry the loss forward rather than carrying the loss back to the two preceding years (the usual order for applying an NOL). ∎

Taxable Periods of Less Than One Year

A **short taxable year** (or **short period**) is a period of less than 12 calendar months. A taxpayer may have a short year for (1) the first income tax return, (2) the final income tax return, or (3) a change in the tax year. If the short period results from a change in the taxpayer's annual accounting period, the taxable income for the period must be annualized. Due to the progressive tax rate structure, taxpayers

---

[18]Reg. § 1.442–1(b)(1). In Example 7, the first period after the change in accounting period (January 1, 2008 through March 31, 2008) is less than a 12-month period and is referred to as a *short period*.

[19]Rev.Proc. 87–32, 1987–1 C.B. 131, and Rev.Rul. 87–57, 1987–2 C.B. 117.
[20]Rev.Proc. 2002–39, 2002–1 C.B. 1046.

could reap benefits from a short-period return if some adjustments were not required. Thus, the taxpayer is required to do the following:

1. Annualize the short-period income.

$$\text{Annualized income} = \text{Short-period income} \times \frac{12}{\text{Number of months in the short period}}$$

2. Compute the tax on the annualized income.
3. Convert the tax on the annualized income to a short-period tax.

$$\text{Short-period income} = \text{Tax on annualized income} \times \frac{\text{Number of months in the short period}}{12}$$

EXAMPLE 10

Gray Corporation obtained permission to change from a calendar year to a fiscal year ending September 30, beginning in 2008. For the short period January 1 through September 30, 2008, the corporation's taxable income was $48,000. The relevant tax rates and the resultant short-period tax are as follows:

Amount of Taxable Income	Tax Rates
$1–$50,000	15% of taxable income
$50,001–$75,000	$7,500 plus 25% of taxable income in excess of $50,000

Calculation of Short-Period Tax

Annualized income
  ($48,000 × 12/9) = **$64,000**
Tax on annualized income
  $7,500 + .25($64,000 − $50,000) =
    $7,500 + $3,500 = **$11,000**
Short-period tax = ($11,000 × 9/12) = **$8,250**
Annualizing the income increased the tax by $1,050:

Tax with annualizing	$ 8,250
Tax without annualizing (.15 × $48,000)	(7,200)
	$ 1,050

Rather than annualize the short-period income, the taxpayer can (1) elect to calculate the tax for a 12-month period beginning on the first day of the short period and (2) convert the tax in (1) to a short-period tax as follows:[21]

$$\frac{\text{Taxable income for short period}}{\text{Taxable income for the 12-month period}} \times \text{Tax on the 12 months of income}$$

EXAMPLE 11

Assume Gray Corporation's taxable income for the calendar year 2008 was $60,000. The tax on the full 12 months of income would have been $10,000 [$7,500 + .25($60,000 − $50,000)]. The short-period tax would be $8,000 [($48,000/$60,000) × $10,000]. Thus, if the corporation utilized this option, the tax for the short period would be $8,000 (rather than $8,250, as calculated in Example 10). ■

---

[21]§§ 443(b)(1) and (2).

For individuals, annualizing requires some special adjustments:[22]

- Deductions must be itemized for the short period (the standard deduction is not allowed).
- Personal and dependency exemptions must be prorated.

Fortunately, individuals rarely change tax years.

Mitigation of the Annual Accounting Period Concept

Several provisions in the Code are designed to give the taxpayer relief from the seemingly harsh results that may be produced by the combined effects of an arbitrary accounting period and a progressive rate structure. For example, under the NOL carryback and carryover rules, a loss in one year can be carried back and offset against taxable income for the preceding two years. Unused NOLs are then carried over for 20 years.[23] In addition, the Code provides special relief provisions for casualty losses pursuant to a disaster and for the reporting of insurance proceeds from destruction of crops.[24]

Farm Relief. Farmers and fishermen are often subject to wide fluctuations in income between years, some of which are due to the weather. Congress has provided these taxpayers a special method of computing their tax on income from farming or fishing. In the high-income years, these taxpayers can elect to compute their tax on income from farming or fishing as though it were earned equally in the three previous years.[25] Thus, the tax on the farming or fishing income for the year is the sum of the additional tax that would have been due in the three previous years if one-third of the income had been earned in each of those years. This averaging system enables the taxpayer to avoid the higher marginal tax rates associated with a large amount of income received in one year.

The income pattern for farmers can also be disrupted by natural disasters that are covered by insurance. The disaster may occur and the **crop insurance proceeds** may be received in a year before the income from the crop would have been realized. Under these circumstances, § 451(d) permits the farmer to defer reporting the income until the year following the disaster. Section 451(e) provides similar relief when livestock must be sold on account of drought or other weather-related conditions.

Restoration of Amounts Received under a Claim of Right. The court-made **claim of right doctrine** applies when the taxpayer receives property as income and treats it as his or her own but a dispute arises over the taxpayer's rights to the income.[26] According to the doctrine, the taxpayer must include the amount as income in the year of receipt. The rationale for the doctrine is that the Federal government cannot await the resolution of all disputes before exacting a tax. As a corollary to the doctrine, if the taxpayer is later required to repay the funds, generally a deduction is allowed in the year of repayment.[27]

E X A M P L E   1 2

In 2008, Pedro received a $5,000 bonus computed as a percentage of profits. In 2009, Pedro's employer determined that the 2008 profits had been incorrectly computed, and Pedro had to refund the $5,000 in 2009. Pedro was required to include the $5,000 in his 2008 gross income, but he can claim a $5,000 deduction in 2009. ∎

In Example 12 the transactions were a wash; that is, the income and deduction were the same ($5,000). Suppose, however, that Pedro was in the 35 percent tax

---

[22]§ 443(b)(3), § 443(c), and Reg. § 1.443–1(b).

[23]§ 172. Refer to Chapter 7.

[24]§§ 165(i) and 451(d). Refer to Chapter 7.

[25]§ 1301. The tax is calculated on Schedule J.

[26]*North American Consolidated Oil Co. v. Burnet,* 3 USTC ¶943, 11 AFTR 16, 52 S.Ct. 613 (USSC, 1932).

[27]*U.S. v. Lewis,* 51–1 USTC ¶9211, 40 AFTR 258, 71 S.Ct. 522 (USSC, 1951).

bracket in 2008 but in the 15 percent bracket in 2009. Without some relief provision, the mistake would be costly to Pedro. He paid $1,750 tax in 2008 (.35 × $5,000), but the deduction reduced his tax liability in 2009 by only $750 (.15 × $5,000). The Code does provide the needed relief in such cases. Under § 1341, when income that has been taxed under the claim of right doctrine must later be repaid, in effect, the taxpayer gets to apply to the deduction the tax rate of the year that will produce the greatest tax benefit. Thus, in Example 12, the repayment in 2009 would reduce Pedro's 2009 tax liability by the higher 2008 rate (.35) applied to the $5,000. However, relief is provided only in cases where the tax is significantly different; that is, when the deduction for the amount previously included in income exceeds $3,000.

Accounting Methods

LO.2

Apply the cash method, accrual method, and hybrid method of accounting.

Permissible Methods

Section 446 requires the taxpayer to compute taxable income using the method of accounting regularly employed in keeping his or her books, provided the method clearly reflects income. The Code recognizes the following as generally permissible **accounting methods**:

- The cash receipts and disbursements method.
- The accrual method.
- A hybrid method (a combination of cash and accrual).

The Regulations refer to these alternatives as *overall methods* and add that the term *method of accounting* includes not only the taxpayer's overall method of accounting but also the accounting treatment of any item.[28]

Generally, any of the three methods of accounting may be used if the method is consistently employed and clearly reflects income. However, in most cases the taxpayer is required to use the accrual method for sales and cost of goods sold if inventories are an income-producing factor to the business.[29] Other situations in which the accrual method is required are discussed later. Special methods are also permitted for installment sales, long-term construction contracts, and farmers.

A taxpayer who has more than one trade or business may use a different method of accounting for each trade or business activity. Furthermore, a taxpayer may use one method of accounting to determine income from a trade or business and use another method to compute nonbusiness items of income and deductions.[30]

EXAMPLE 13

Linda operates a grocery store and owns stock and bonds. The sales and cost of goods sold from the grocery store must be computed by the accrual method because inventories are material. However, Linda can report her dividends and interest from the stocks and bonds under the cash method. ∎

The Code grants the IRS broad powers to determine whether the taxpayer's accounting method *clearly reflects income*. Thus, if the method employed does not clearly reflect income, the IRS has the power to prescribe the method to be used by the taxpayer.[31]

Cash Receipts and Disbursements Method—Cash Basis

Most individuals and many businesses use the cash basis to report income and deductions. The popularity of this method can largely be attributed to its simplicity and flexibility.

---

[28]Reg. § 1.446–1(a)(1).
[29]Reg. § 1.446–1(a)(4)(i).

[30]§ 446(d) and Reg. § 1.446–1(c)(1)(iv)(b).
[31]§ 446(b).

TAX *in the News*   WHO WANTS TO BE A PRODUCER?

For many years, small businesses wanted to be considered service providers rather than producers of products. Service provider classification meant that the cash method could be used. Now, however, classification as a producer can be advantageous. As a result of the American Jobs Creation Act of 2004, producers can deduct 6 percent of their production activities income in calculating taxable income for 2007 through 2009 (3 percent in 2005–2006 and 9 percent in 2010). Thus, a company that develops advertising materials might argue that it is a producer rather than a provider of advertising services.

Under the **cash method**, income is not recognized until the taxpayer actually receives, or constructively receives, cash or its equivalent. Cash is constructively received if it is available to the taxpayer.[32] Generally, a cash equivalent is anything with a fair market value, including a note receivable from a customer.

EXAMPLE 14

Don, a dentist, does not accept credit cards. He requires that his patients either pay cash at the time the services are performed or give him a note receivable with interest at the market rate. Generally, the notes can be sold to the local banks for 95% of their face amount. At the end of 2008, Don has $60,000 in notes receivable from patients. The notes receivable are a cash equivalent and have a fair market value of $57,000 ($60,000 × 95%). Therefore, Don must include the $57,000 in his gross income for 2008. ∎

Deductions are generally permitted in the year of payment. Thus, year-end accounts receivable, accounts payable, and accrued income and deductions are not included in the determination of taxable income.

In many cases, a taxpayer using the cash method can choose the year in which a deduction is claimed simply by postponing or accelerating the payment of expenses. For fixed assets, however, the cash basis taxpayer claims deductions through depreciation or amortization, the same as an accrual basis taxpayer does. In addition, prepaid expenses must be capitalized and amortized if the life of the asset extends substantially beyond the end of the tax year.[33] Most courts have applied the one-year rule (**one-year rule for prepaid expenses**) to determine whether capitalization and amortization are required. According to this rule, capitalization is required only if the asset has a life that extends beyond the tax year following the year of payment.[34]

Restrictions on Use of the Cash Method. Using the cash method to measure income from a merchandising or manufacturing operation would often yield a distorted picture of the results of operations. Income for the period would largely be a function of when payments were made for goods or materials. Thus, the Regulations prohibit the use of the cash method (and require the accrual method) to measure sales and cost of goods sold if inventories are material to the business.[35]

The prohibition on the use of the cash method if inventories are material and the rules regarding prepaid expenses (discussed above) are intended to assure that annual income is clearly reflected. However, certain taxpayers may not use the cash method of accounting for Federal income tax purposes regardless of whether inventories are material. The accrual basis must be used to report the income earned by (1) a

---

[32]Reg. § 1.451–1(a). Refer to Chapter 4 for a discussion of constructive receipt.

[33]Reg. § 1.461–1(a)(1).

[34]*Zaninovich v. Comm.*, 80–1 USTC ¶9342, 45 AFTR2d 80–1442, 616 F.2d 429 (CA–9, 1980), *rev'g* 69 T.C. 605 (1978); *U.S. Freightways Corp. v. Comm.*, 2001–2 USTC ¶50,731, 88 AFTR2d 2001–6703, 270 F.3d 1137 (CA–7, 2001), *rev'g*

113 T.C. 329 (1999). Refer to Chapter 6 for further discussion of the one-year rule. See also Reg. § 1.263(a)–4(f) for the application of the one-year rule to prepayments for intangibles.

[35]Reg. § 1.446–1(a)(4)(i).

corporation (other than an S corporation), (2) a partnership with a corporate partner, and (3) a tax shelter. This accrual basis requirement has three exceptions:[36]

- A farming business.
- A qualified personal service corporation (a corporation performing services in health, law, engineering, architecture, accounting, actuarial science, performing arts, or consulting).
- An entity that is not a tax shelter whose average annual gross receipts for the most recent three-year period are $5 million or less.

As a matter of administrative convenience, the IRS will permit any entity with average annual gross receipts of not more than $1 million for the most recent three-year period to use the cash method. This applies even if the taxpayer is buying and selling inventory. Also as a matter of administrative convenience, the IRS will permit certain entities whose average annual gross receipts are greater than $1 million but are not more than $10 million for the most recent three-year period to use the cash method. However, under the $10 million exception, inventory on hand at the end of the tax year cannot be deducted until the inventory is sold (i.e., must be capitalized). Not eligible for the cash method under the $10 million exception are entities whose principal business activity (the activity producing the largest percentage of gross receipts) is selling goods, manufacturing, mining, and certain publishing activities. Also not eligible are the C corporations, partnerships, and tax shelters discussed above that must use the accrual method. The major beneficiaries of the $10 million exception are small construction companies and small service businesses that sell some goods in conjunction with the services provided.[37]

Special Rules for Small Farmers.

Although inventories are material to farming operations and the accrual method would appear to be required, the IRS long ago created an exception to the general rule that allows small farmers to use the cash method of accounting.[38] The purpose of the exception is to relieve the small farmer from the bookkeeping burden of accrual accounting. Generally, this exception applies to unincorporated farms and closely held farming corporations with gross receipts for the year of less than $25 million.[39]

Cash method farmers must nevertheless capitalize their costs of raising trees that have a preproduction period of more than two years.[40] Thus, an apple farmer generally must capitalize the costs of raising the trees until they produce apples in merchantable quantities. However, to simplify the farmer's tax accounting, the cash method farmer is given an option: the preproduction cost of the trees can be expensed if the taxpayer elects to use the alternative depreciation system (refer to Chapter 8) for all the farming assets.

Farmers who produce crops that take more than a year from planting to harvesting (e.g., pineapples) can elect to use the crop method to report the income. Under the **crop method**, the costs of raising the crop are capitalized as those costs are incurred and then deducted in the year the income from the crop is realized.[41] This method is analogous to the completed contract method used by contractors (discussed later in this chapter).

Generally, a cash basis farmer must capitalize the purchase price of an animal, whether it is acquired for sale or for breeding. However, the cost of raising the animal can be expensed.[42]

---

[36]§§ 448(a) and 448(b). For this purpose, the hybrid method of accounting is considered the same as the cash method.

[37]Rev.Proc. 2001–10, 2001–1 C.B. 272 and Rev.Proc. 2002–28, 2002–1 C.B. 815.

[38]Reg. § 1.471–6(a).

[39]See §§ 447(c) and 464.

[40]§ 263A(d).

[41]Reg. §§ 1.61–4 and 1.162–12(a).

[42]Reg. § 1.162–12(a).

TAX ACCOUNTING METHODS AS AN INCENTIVE TO GO FOREIGN

Some foreign countries allow a corporation to defer income by using tax accounting methods that are not permitted in the United States. For example, a producer or retailer may be allowed to use the cash method of accounting even though inventory is present. Under the cash method, the cost of goods sold is deducted in the tax year the goods are paid for, and income is not recognized until receivables are collected. Thus, if a U.S. corporation creates a foreign subsidiary to produce in a country that permits the cash method in association with inventory, tax savings occur that would not be available in the United States. The corporation obtains additional deductions in the first year equal to the ending inventory and additional deferrals equal to the ending accounts receivable. The company would continue to benefit until it has no more receivables or inventory.

GLOBAL
Tax Issues

Accrual Method

All Events Test for Income.

Under the **accrual method**, an item is generally included in gross income for the year in which it is earned, regardless of when the income is collected. An item of income is earned when (1) all the events have occurred to fix the taxpayer's right to receive the income and (2) the amount of income (the amount the taxpayer has a right to receive) can be determined with reasonable accuracy.[43]

EXAMPLE 15

Andre, a calendar year taxpayer who uses the accrual basis of accounting, was to receive a bonus equal to 6% of Blue Corporation's net income for its fiscal year ending each June 30. For the fiscal year ending June 30, 2008, Blue Corporation had net income of $240,000, and for the six months ending December 31, 2008, the corporation's net income was $150,000. Andre will report $14,400 (.06 × $240,000) for 2008 because his right to the amount became fixed when Blue Corporation's year closed. However, Andre would not accrue income based on the corporation's profits for the last six months of 2008 since his right to the income does not accrue until the close of the corporation's tax year. ■

An accrual basis taxpayer's amount of income and the tax year the income is recognized are based on his or her right to receive the income. Thus, the fair market value of a receivable is irrelevant.

EXAMPLE 16

Marcey, an accrual basis taxpayer, has provided services to clients and has the right to receive $60,000. The clients have signed notes receivable to Marcey that have a fair market value of $57,000. Marcey must include $60,000, the amount she has the right to receive, in her gross income, rather than the fair market value of the notes of $57,000. ■

As discussed in Chapter 4, when an accrual basis taxpayer receives prepaid income that will not all be earned by the end of the tax year following the tax year of receipt, generally the income that is not earned by the end of the year of receipt must be allocated to the following year.

EXAMPLE 17

Troy sells computers and two-year service contracts on the computers. On November 1, 2008, Troy sold a 24-month service contract and received $240. He recognizes $20 gross income in 2008 ($240 × 2/24) and $220 ($240 − $20) in 2009. ■

---

[43]Reg. § 1.451–1(a). Refer to Chapter 4 for further discussion of the accrual basis.

GLOBAL
Tax Issues

CHANGES IN THE TAX RATES LEAD TO INCOME SHIFTING

In 2006, the statistical evidence indicated that the German economy was booming. On further analysis of the data, however, it became clear that businesses were taking steps to shift their income from 2007 to 2006. Generally, businesses do not wish to accelerate their income because their taxes on the income will also be accelerated. In this case, though, German income tax rates were to increase in 2007. For many companies, the tax savings were worth the earlier-than-necessary recognition of the income.

Source: *Adapted from Brian Wesbury, "A One-Year Wonder; Germany Is Booming, Pulling the Rest of Europe Along. Or Is It?" Newsweek, International Edition, March 12, 2007.*

However, the deferral of prepaid income is not available for prepaid rent and prepaid interest.

In a situation where the accrual basis taxpayer's right to income is being contested and the income has not yet been collected, generally no income is recognized until the dispute has been settled.[44] Before the settlement, "all of the events have not occurred that fix the right to receive the income."

All Events and Economic Performance Tests for Deductions. An **all events test** applies to accrual basis deductions. A deduction cannot be claimed until (1) all the events have occurred to create the taxpayer's liability and (2) the amount of the liability can be determined with reasonable accuracy.[45] Once these requirements are satisfied, the deduction will be permitted only if economic performance has occurred.[46]

The **economic performance test** addresses situations in which the taxpayer has either of the following obligations:

1. To pay for services or property to be provided in the future.
2. To provide services or property (other than money) in the future.

When services or property are to be provided to the taxpayer in the future (situation 1), economic performance occurs when the property or services are actually provided by the other party.

EXAMPLE 18

An accrual basis calendar year taxpayer, JAB, Inc., promoted a boxing match held in the company's arena on December 31, 2008. CLN, Inc., had contracted to clean the arena for $5,000, but did not actually perform the work until January 1, 2009. JAB, Inc., did not pay the $5,000 until 2010. Although financial accounting would require JAB, Inc., to accrue the $5,000 cleaning expense in 2008 to match the revenues from the fight, the economic performance test was not satisfied until 2009, when CLN, Inc., performed the service. Thus, JAB, Inc., must deduct the expense in 2009. ■

If the taxpayer is obligated to provide property or services (situation 2), economic performance occurs (and thus the deduction is allowed) in the year the taxpayer provides the property or services.

EXAMPLE 19

Copper Corporation, an accrual basis taxpayer, is in the strip mining business. According to the contract with the landowner, the company must reclaim the land. The estimated cost of reclaiming land mined in 2008 was $500,000, but the land was not actually reclaimed until 2010. The all events test was satisfied in 2008. The obligation existed, and the amount of the

---

[44]*Burnet v. Sanford & Brooks Co.*, 2 USTC ¶636, 9 AFTR 603, 51 S.Ct. 150 (USSC, 1931).

[45]§ 461(h)(4).

[46]§ 461(h).

liability could be determined with reasonable accuracy. However, the economic performance test was not satisfied until 2010. Therefore, the deduction is not allowed until 2010.[47] ■

The economic performance test is waived, and thus year-end accruals can be deducted, if all the following conditions (*recurring item exception*) are met:

- The obligation exists and the amount of the liability can be reasonably estimated.
- Economic performance occurs within a reasonable period (but not later than 8½ months after the close of the taxable year).
- The item is recurring in nature and is treated consistently by the taxpayer.
- Either the accrued item is not material, or accruing it results in a better matching of revenues and expenses.

EXAMPLE 20

Green Corporation often sells goods that are on hand but cannot be shipped for another week. Thus, the sales account usually includes revenues for some items that have not been shipped at year-end. Green Corporation is obligated to pay shipping costs. Although the company's obligation for shipping costs can be determined with reasonable accuracy, economic performance is not satisfied until Green (or its agent) actually delivers the goods. However, accruing shipping costs on sold items will better match expenses with revenues for the period. Therefore, the company should be allowed to accrue the shipping costs on items sold but not shipped at year-end. ■

The economic performance test as set forth in the Code does not address all possible accrued expenses. That is, in some cases, the taxpayer incurs cost even though no property or services were received. In these instances, according to the Regulations, economic performance generally is not satisfied until the liability is paid. The following liabilities are cases in which payment is generally the only means of satisfying economic performance:[48]

1. Workers' compensation.
2. Torts.
3. Breach of contract.
4. Violation of law.
5. Rebates and refunds.
6. Awards, prizes, and jackpots.
7. Insurance, warranty, and service contracts.[49]
8. Taxes.

EXAMPLE 21

Yellow Corporation sold defective merchandise that injured a customer. Yellow admitted liability in 2008, but did not pay the claim until January 2009. The customer's tort claim cannot be deducted until it is paid. ■

However, items (5) through (8) above are eligible for the aforementioned recurring item exception.

EXAMPLE 22

Pelican Corporation filed its 2008 state income tax return in March 2009. At the time the return was filed, Pelican was required to pay an additional $5,000. The state taxes are eligible for the recurring item exception. Thus, the $5,000 of state income taxes can be deducted on the corporation's 2008 Federal tax return. The deduction is allowed because all the events had occurred to fix the liability as of the end of 2008, the payment was made within 8½ months after the end of the tax year, the item is recurring in nature, and allowing the deduction in 2008 produces a good matching of revenues and expenses. ■

---

[47]See § 468 for an elective method for reporting reclamation costs.
[48]Reg. §§ 1.461–4(g)(2)–(6) and 1.461–5(c).
[49]This item applies to contracts the taxpayer enters into for his or her own protection, rather than the taxpayer's liability as insurer, warrantor, or service provider.

Reserves. Generally, the all events and economic performance tests will prevent the use of reserves (e.g., for product warranty expense) frequently used in financial accounting to match expenses with revenues. However, small banks are allowed to use a bad debt reserve.[50] Furthermore, an accrual basis taxpayer in a service business is permitted to not accrue revenue that appears uncollectible based on experience. In effect, this approach indirectly allows a reserve.[51]

Hybrid Method

A **hybrid method** of accounting involves the use of more than one method. For example, a taxpayer who uses the accrual basis to report sales and cost of goods sold but uses the cash basis to report other items of income and expense is employing a hybrid method. The Code permits the use of a hybrid method provided the taxpayer's income is clearly reflected.[52] A taxpayer who uses the accrual method for business expenses must also use the accrual method for business income (the cash method may not be used for income items if the taxpayer's expenses are accounted for under the accrual method).

It may be preferable for a business that is required to report sales and cost of goods sold on the accrual method to report other items of income and expense under the cash method. The cash method permits greater flexibility in the timing of income and expense recognition.

Change of Method

LO.3

Utilize the procedure for changing accounting methods.

The taxpayer, in effect, makes an election to use a particular accounting method when an initial tax return is filed using that method. If a subsequent change in method is desired, the taxpayer must obtain the permission of the IRS. The request for change is made on Form 3115, Application for Change in Accounting Method. Generally, the form must be filed within the taxable year of the desired change.[53]

As previously mentioned, the term *accounting method* encompasses not only the overall accounting method used by the taxpayer (the cash or accrual method) but also the treatment of any material item of income or deduction.[54] Thus, a change in the method of deducting property taxes from a cash basis to an accrual basis that results in a deduction for taxes in a different year constitutes a change in an accounting method. Another example of an accounting method change is a change involving the method or basis used in the valuation of inventories. However, a change in treatment resulting from a change in the underlying facts does not constitute a change in the taxpayer's method of accounting.[55] For example, a change in employment contracts so that an employee accrues one day of vacation pay for each month

---

[50]§ 585.
[51]§ 448(d)(5).
[52]§ 446(c).

[53]Rev.Proc. 99–49, 1999–2 C.B. 725.
[54]Reg. § 1.446–1(a)(1).
[55]Reg. § 1.446–1(e)(2)(ii).

of service rather than 12 days of vacation pay for a full year of service is a change in the underlying facts and is therefore not an accounting method change.

Correction of an Error. A change in accounting method should be distinguished from the *correction of an error*. The taxpayer can correct an error (by filing amended returns) without permission, and the IRS can simply adjust the taxpayer's liability if an error is discovered on audit of the return. Some examples of errors are incorrect postings, errors in the calculation of tax liability or tax credits, deductions of business expense items that are actually personal, and omissions of income and deductions.[56] Unless the taxpayer or the IRS corrects the error within the statute of limitations, the taxpayer's total lifetime taxable income will be overstated or understated by the amount of the error.

Change from an Incorrect Method. An *incorrect accounting method* is the consistent (year-after-year) use of an incorrect rule to report an item of income or expense. The incorrect accounting method generally will not affect the taxpayer's total lifetime income (unlike the error). That is, an incorrect method has a self-balancing mechanism. For example, deducting freight on inventory in the year the goods are purchased, rather than when the inventory is sold, is an incorrect accounting method. The total cost of goods sold over the life of the business is not affected, but the year-to-year income is incorrect.[57]

If a taxpayer is employing an incorrect method of accounting, permission must be obtained from the IRS to change to a correct method. An incorrect method is not treated as a mechanical error that can be corrected by merely filing an amended tax return.

The tax return preparer as well as the taxpayer will be subject to penalties if the tax return is prepared using an incorrect method of accounting and permission for a change to a correct method has not been requested.[58]

Net Adjustments Due to Change in Accounting Method. In the year of a change in accounting method, some items of income and expense may have to be adjusted to prevent the change from distorting taxable income.

EXAMPLE 23

In 2008, White Corporation, with consent from the IRS, switched from the cash to the accrual basis for reporting sales and cost of goods sold. The corporation's accrual basis gross profit for the year was computed as follows:

Sales		$100,000
Beginning inventory	$ 15,000	
Purchases	60,000	
Less: Ending inventory	(10,000)	
Cost of goods sold		(65,000)
Gross profit		$ 35,000

At the end of the previous year, White Corporation had accounts receivable of $25,000 and accounts payable for merchandise of $34,000. The accounts receivable from the previous year in the amount of $25,000 were never included in gross income since White was on the cash basis and did not recognize the uncollected receivables. In the current year, the $25,000 was not included in the accrual basis sales since the sales were made in a prior year. Therefore, a $25,000 adjustment to income is required to prevent the receivables from being omitted from income.

---

[56]Reg. § 1.446–1(e)(2)(ii)(b).

[57]But see *Korn Industries v. U.S.*, 76–1 USTC ¶9354, 37 AFTR2d 76–1228, 532 F.2d 1352 (Ct.Cls., 1976).

[58]§ 446(f). See *South-Western Federal Taxation: Corporations, Partnerships, Estates, and Trusts*, Chapter 16.

The corollary of the failure to recognize a prior year's receivables is the failure to recognize a prior year's accounts payable. The beginning of the year's accounts payable were not included in the current or prior year's purchases. Thus, a deduction for the $34,000 was not taken in either year and is therefore included as an adjustment to income for the period of change.

An adjustment is also required to reflect the $15,000 beginning inventory that White deducted (due to the use of a cash method of accounting) in the previous year. In this instance, the cost of goods sold during the year of change was increased by the beginning inventory and resulted in a double deduction.

The net adjustment due to the change in accounting method is computed as follows:

Beginning inventory (deducted in prior and current year)	$ 15,000
Beginning accounts receivable (omitted from income)	25,000
Beginning accounts payable (omitted from deductions)	(34,000)
Net increase in taxable income	$ 6,000

∎

ETHICAL and EQUITABLE *Considerations*

CHANGE IN ACCOUNTING METHOD

Your new client has consistently deducted items that should have been included in the cost of the ending inventory. You have advised the client that it will be necessary to change accounting methods, which requires filing a Form 3115, increasing the beginning inventory balance, and creating a positive adjustment to income. The client will have a net operating loss for the year. The client agrees to the change, but he wants to do it his way: valuing the ending inventory for the year correctly without mentioning the change to the IRS. The client maintains that the necessary adjustment will be accomplished without formally filing a Form 3115 and having to deal with spreading the adjustment. Therefore, why undergo the additional expense of re-computing the beginning inventory and filing Form 3115? What should you do?

Disposition of the Net Adjustment. Required changes in accounting methods are the result of an IRS examination. The IRS usually will examine all years that are open under the statute of limitations. Generally, this means that the three preceding years are examined. The IRS will not require a change unless the net adjustment is positive. That adjustment generally must be included in gross income for the year of the change. Additional tax and interest on the tax will be due. However, if the adjustment is greater than $3,000, the taxpayer can elect to calculate the tax by spreading the adjustment over one or more previous years.[59] The election is beneficial if the taxpayer's marginal tax rate for the prior years is lower than the marginal tax rate for the year of the change.

To encourage taxpayers to *voluntarily* change from incorrect methods and to facilitate changes from one correct method to another, the IRS generally allows the taxpayer to spread a positive adjustment into future years. One-fourth of the adjustment is applied to the year of the change, and one-fourth of the adjustment is applied to each of the next three taxable years. A negative adjustment can be deducted in the year of the change.[60]

EXAMPLE 24	White Corporation in Example 23 voluntarily changed from an incorrect method (the cash basis was incorrect because inventories were material to the business) to a correct method. The company must add $1,500 (¼ × $6,000 positive adjustment) to its 2008, 2009, 2010, and 2011 income. ∎

---

[59]§ 481(b). See also Notice 98–31, 1998–1 C.B. 1165.

[60]Rev.Proc. 99–49, 1999–2 C.B. 725 and Rev.Proc. 2002–19, 2002–1 C.B. 696.

Special Accounting Methods

Generally, accrual basis taxpayers recognize income when goods are sold and shipped to the customer. Cash basis taxpayers generally recognize income from a sale on the collection of cash from the customer. The tax law provides special accounting methods for certain installment sales and long-term contracts. These special methods were enacted, in part, to assure that the tax will be due when the taxpayer is best able to pay the tax.

Installment Method

Under the general rule for computing the gain or loss from the sale of property, the taxpayer recognizes the entire amount of gain or loss upon the sale or other disposition of the property.

> **LO.4**
>
> Determine when the installment method of accounting can be utilized and apply the related calculation techniques.

EXAMPLE 25

Mark sells property to Fran for $10,000 cash plus Fran's note (fair market value and face amount of $90,000). Mark's basis for the property was $15,000. Gain or loss is computed under either the cash or accrual basis as follows:

Selling price	
Cash down payment	$ 10,000
Note receivable	90,000
	$100,000
Basis in the property	(15,000)
Realized gain	$ 85,000

■

In Example 25, the general rule for recognizing gain or loss requires Mark to pay a substantial amount of tax on the gain in the year of sale even though he received only $10,000 cash. Congress enacted the installment sales provisions to prevent this sort of hardship by allowing the taxpayer to spread the gain from installment sales over the collection period. The installment method is a very important planning tool because of the tax deferral possibilities.

Eligibility and Calculations. The **installment method** applies to *gains* (but not losses) from the sale of property by a taxpayer who will receive at least one payment *after* the year of sale. For many years, practically all gains from the sale of property were eligible for the installment method. However, over the years, the Code has been amended to *deny* the use of the installment method for the following:[61]

- Gains on property held for sale in the ordinary course of business.
- Depreciation recapture under § 1245 or § 1250.
- Gains on stocks or securities traded on an established market.

As an exception to the first item, the installment method may be used to report gains from sales of the following:[62]

- Time-share units (e.g., the right to use real property for two weeks each year).
- Residential lots (if the seller is not to make any improvements).
- Any property used or produced in the trade or business of farming.

The Nonelective Aspect. As a general rule, eligible sales *must* be reported by the installment method.[63] A special election is required to report the gain by any other method of accounting (see the discussion in a subsequent section of this chapter).

---

[61]§§ 453(b), (i), and (l).
[62]§ 453(l)(2).
[63]§ 453(a).

Computing the Gain for the Period. The gain reported on each sale is computed by the following formula:

$$\frac{\text{Total gain}}{\text{Contract price}} \times \text{Payments received} = \text{Recognized gain}$$

The taxpayer must compute each variable as follows:

1. *Total gain* is the selling price reduced by selling expenses and the adjusted basis of the property. The selling price is the total consideration received by the seller, including notes receivable from the buyer and the seller's liabilities assumed by the buyer.
2. *Contract price* is the selling price less the seller's liabilities that are assumed by the buyer. Generally, the contract price is the amount, other than interest, the seller will receive from the purchaser.
3. *Payments received* are the collections on the contract price received in the tax year. This generally is equal to the cash received less the interest income collected for the period. If the buyer pays any of the seller's expenses, the seller regards the amount paid as a payment received.

EXAMPLE 26

The seller is not a dealer, and the facts are as follows:

Sales price		
Cash down payment	$ 1,000	
Seller's mortgage assumed	3,000	
Notes payable to the seller	13,000	$ 17,000
Selling expenses		(500)
Seller's basis		(10,000)
Total gain		$ 6,500

The contract price is $14,000 ($17,000 − $3,000). Assuming the $1,000 is the only payment in the year of sale, the recognized gain in that year is computed as follows:

$$\frac{\$6,500 \text{ total gain}}{\$14,000 \text{ contract price}} \times \$1,000 = \$464 \text{ (gain recognized in year of sale)} \qquad \blacksquare$$

If the sum of the seller's basis and selling expenses is less than the liabilities assumed by the buyer, the difference must be added to the contract price and to the payments (treated as *deemed payments*) received in the year of sale.[64] This adjustment to the contract price is required so that the ratio of total gain to contract price will not be greater than one. The adjustment also accelerates the reporting of income from the deemed payments.

EXAMPLE 27

Assume the same facts as in Example 26, except that the seller's basis in the property is only $2,000. The total gain, therefore, is $14,500 [$17,000 − ($2,000 + $500)]. Payments in the year of sale are $1,500 and are calculated as follows:

Down payment	$1,000
Excess of mortgage assumed over seller's basis and selling expenses ($3,000 − $2,000 − $500)	500
	$1,500

The contract price is $14,500 [$17,000 (selling price) − $3,000 (seller's mortgage assumed) + $500 (excess of mortgage assumed over seller's basis and selling expenses)]. The gain recognized in the year of sale is computed as follows:

[64]Temp.Reg. § 15a.453–1(b)(3)(i).

$$\frac{\$14{,}500 \text{ total gain}}{\$14{,}500 \text{ contract price}} \times \$1{,}500 = \$1{,}500$$

In subsequent years, all amounts the seller collects on the note principal ($13,000) will be recognized gain ($13,000 × 100%). ■

As previously discussed, gains attributable to ordinary income recapture under §§ 1245 and 1250 are *ineligible* for installment reporting. Therefore, the § 1245 or § 1250 gain realized must be recognized in the year of sale, and the installment sale gain is the remaining gain.

E X A M P L E   2 8

Olaf sold an apartment building for $50,000 cash and a $75,000 note due in two years. Olaf's basis in the property was $25,000, and he recaptured $40,000 ordinary income under § 1250.

Olaf's realized gain is $100,000 ($125,000 − $25,000), and the $40,000 recapture must be recognized in the year of sale. Of the $60,000 remaining § 1231 gain, $24,000 must be recognized in the year of sale:

$$\frac{\S\ 1231 \text{ gain}}{\text{Contract price}} \times \text{Payments received} = \frac{\$125{,}000 - \$25{,}000 - \$40{,}000}{\$125{,}000} \times \$50{,}000$$

$$= \frac{\$60{,}000}{\$125{,}000} \times \$50{,}000 = \$24{,}000$$

The remaining realized gain of $36,000 ($60,000 − $24,000) will be recognized as the $75,000 note is collected. ■

Imputed Interest. If a deferred payment contract for the sale of property with a selling price greater than $3,000 does not contain a reasonable interest rate, a reasonable rate is imputed.[65] The imputing of interest effectively restates the selling price of the property to equal the sum of the payments at the date of the sale and the discounted present value of the future payments. The difference between the present value of a future payment and the payment's face amount is taxed as interest income, as discussed in the following paragraphs. Thus, the **imputed interest** rules prevent sellers of capital assets from increasing the selling price to reflect the equivalent of unstated interest on deferred payments and thereby converting ordinary (interest) income into long-term capital gains. In addition, the imputed interest rules are important because they affect the timing of income recognition.

Generally, if the contract does not charge at least the Federal rate, interest will be imputed at the Federal rate. The Federal rate is the interest rate the Federal government pays on new borrowing and is published monthly by the IRS.[66]

As a general rule, the buyer and seller must account for interest on the accrual basis with semiannual compounding.[67] Requiring the use of the accrual basis assures that the seller's interest income and the buyer's interest expense are reported in the same tax year. Under pre-1984 law, the cash basis seller did not report interest income until it was actually collected, but an accrual basis buyer could deduct the interest as it accrued. The following example illustrates the calculation and amortization of imputed interest.

E X A M P L E   2 9

Peggy, a cash basis taxpayer, sold land on January 1, 2008, for $200,000 cash and $6 million due on December 31, 2009, with 5% interest payable December 31, 2008, and December 31, 2009. At the time of the sale, the Federal rate was 8% (compounded semiannually). Because

---

[65]§§ 483 and 1274.

[66]§ 1274(d)(1). There are three Federal rates: short term (not over three years), midterm (over three years but not over nine years), and long term (over nine years).

[67]§§ 1274(a), 1273(a), and 1272(a).

Peggy did not charge at least the Federal rate, interest will be imputed at 8% (compounded semiannually).

Date	Payment	Present Value (at 8%) on 1/1/2008	Imputed Interest
12/31/2008	$ 300,000	$ 277,500	$ 22,500
12/31/2009	6,300,000	5,386,500	913,500
	$6,600,000	$5,664,000	$936,000

Thus, the selling price will be restated to $5,864,000 ($200,000 + $5,664,000) rather than $6,200,000 ($200,000 + $6,000,000), and Peggy will recognize interest income in accordance with the following amortization schedule:

	Beginning Balance	Interest Income (at 8%)*	Received	Ending Balance
2008	$5,664,000	$462,182	$ 300,000	$5,826,182
2009	5,826,182	473,818	6,300,000	–0–

*Compounded semiannually.   ∎

Congress has created several exceptions regarding the rate at which interest is imputed and the method of accounting for the interest income and expense. The general rules and exceptions are summarized in Concept Summary 18–1.

Related-Party Sales of Nondepreciable Property.

If the Code did not contain special rules, a taxpayer could make an installment sale of property to a related party (e.g., a family member) who would obtain a basis in the property equal to the purchase price (the fair market value of the property). Then, the purchasing family member could immediately sell the property to an unrelated party for cash with no recognized gain or loss (the amount realized would equal the basis). The related-party purchaser would not pay the installment note to the selling family member until a later year or years. The net result would be that the family has the cash, but no taxable gain is recognized until the intrafamily transfer of the cash (when the purchasing family member makes payments on the installment note).

Under special rules designed to combat the scheme described above, the proceeds from the subsequent sale (the second sale) by the purchasing family member are treated as though they were used to pay the installment note due the selling family member (the first sale). As a result, the recognition of gain from the original sale between the related parties is accelerated.[68]

However, even with these special rules, Congress did not eliminate the benefits of all related-party installment sales.

- Related parties include the first seller's brothers, sisters, ancestors, lineal descendants, controlled corporations, and partnerships, trusts, and estates in which the seller has an interest.[69]
- There is no acceleration if the second disposition occurs more than two years after the first sale.[70]

Thus, if the taxpayer can sell the property to an unrelated party (not a related party) or patient family member, the intrafamily installment sale is still a powerful tax planning tool. Other exceptions also can be applied in some circumstances.[71]

---

[68]§ 453(e).
[69]§ 453(f)(1), cross-referencing §§ 267(b) and 318(a). Although spouses are related parties, the exemption of gain between spouses (§ 1041) makes the

second-disposition rules inapplicable when the first sale was between spouses.
[70]§ 453(e)(2). But see § 453(e)(2)(B) for extensions of the two-year period.
[71]See §§ 453(e)(6) and (7).

CONCEPT SUMMARY 18–1

Interest on Installment Sales

	Imputed Interest Rate
General rule	Federal rate
Exceptions:	
• Principal amount not over $2.8 million.[1]	Lesser of Federal rate or 9%
• Sale of land (with a calendar year ceiling of $500,000) between family members (the seller's spouse, brothers, sisters, ancestors, or lineal descendants).[2]	Lesser of Federal rate or 6%

	Method of Accounting for Interest	
	Seller's Interest Income	Buyer's Interest Expense
General rule[3]	Accrual	Accrual
Exceptions:		
• Total payments under the contract are $250,000 or less.[4]	Taxpayer's overall method	Taxpayer's overall method
• Sale of a farm (sales price of $1 million or less).[5]	Taxpayer's overall method	Taxpayer's overall method
• Sale of a principal residence.[6]	Taxpayer's overall method	Taxpayer's overall method
• Sale for a note with a principal amount of not over $2 million, the seller is on the cash basis, the property sold is not inventory, and the buyer agrees to report expense by the cash method.[7]	Cash	Cash

[1] § 1274A(b). This amount is adjusted annually for inflation. For 2008, the amount is $4,913,400.

[2] §§ 1274(c)(3)(F) and 483(e).

[3] §§ 1274(a) and 1272(a)(3).

[4] §§ 1274(c)(3)(C) and 483.

[5] §§ 1274(c)(3)(A) and 483.

[6] §§ 1274(c)(3)(B) and 483.

[7] § 1274A(c). This amount is adjusted annually for inflation. For 2008, the amount is $3,509,600.

Related-Party Sales of Depreciable Property. The installment method cannot be used to report a gain on the sale of depreciable property to a controlled entity. The purpose of this rule is to prevent the seller from deferring gain (until collections are received) while the related purchaser is enjoying a stepped-up basis for depreciation purposes.[72]

The prohibition on the use of the installment method applies to sales between the taxpayer and a partnership or corporation in which the taxpayer holds a more-than-50 percent interest. Constructive ownership rules are used in applying the ownership test (e.g., the taxpayer is considered to own stock owned by a spouse and certain other family members).[73] However, if the taxpayer can establish that tax avoidance was not a principal purpose of the transaction, the installment method can be used to report the gain.

EXAMPLE 30

Alan purchased an apartment building from his controlled corporation, Emerald Corporation. Alan was short of cash at the time of the purchase (December 2008), but was to collect a large cash payment in January 2009. The agreement required Alan to pay the entire arm's length price in January 2009. Alan had good business reasons for acquiring the building. Emerald Corporation should be able to convince the IRS that tax avoidance was not a

---

[72] § 453(g).

[73] §§ 1239(b) and (c).

principal purpose for the installment sale because the tax benefits are not overwhelming. The corporation will report all of the gain in the year following the year of sale, and the building must be expensed over 27.5 years (the cost recovery period). ■

Disposition of Installment Obligations

Generally, a taxpayer must recognize the deferred profit from an installment sale when the obligation is transferred to another party or otherwise relinquished. The rationale for accelerating the gain is that the deferral should continue for no longer than the taxpayer owns the installment obligation.[74]

The gift or cancellation of an installment note is treated as a taxable disposition by the donor. The amount realized from the cancellation is the face amount of the note if the parties (obligor and obligee) are related to each other.[75]

EXAMPLE 31	Liz cancels a note issued by Tina (Liz's daughter) that arose in connection with the sale of property. At the time of the cancellation, the note had a basis to Liz of $10,000, a face amount of $25,000, and a fair market value of $20,000. Presuming the initial sale by Liz qualified as an installment sale, the cancellation results in gain of $15,000 ($25,000 − $10,000) to Liz. ■

Certain exceptions to the recognition of gain provisions are provided for transfers of installment obligations pursuant to tax-free incorporations under § 351, contributions of capital to a partnership, certain corporate liquidations, transfers due to the taxpayer's death, and transfers between spouses or incident to divorce.[76] In such situations, the deferred profit is merely shifted to the transferee, who is responsible for the payment of tax on the subsequent collections of the installment obligations.

Interest on Deferred Taxes

With the installment method, the seller earns interest on the receivable. The receivable includes the deferred gain. Thus, one could argue that the seller is earning interest on the deferred taxes. Some commentators reason that the government is, in effect, making interest-free loans to taxpayers who report gains by the installment method. Following the argument that the amount of the deferred taxes is a loan, the taxpayer is required to pay interest on the deferred taxes in some situations.[77]

The taxpayer is required to pay interest on the deferred taxes only if *both* of the following requirements are met:

- The installment obligation arises from the sale of property (other than farming property) for more than $150,000.
- Such installment obligations outstanding at the close of the tax year exceed $5 million.

Interest on the deferred taxes is payable only for the portion of the taxes that relates to the installment obligations in *excess* of $5 million. The interest is calculated using the underpayment rate in § 6621.

Electing Out of the Installment Method

A taxpayer can *elect not to use* the installment method. The election is made by reporting on a timely filed return the gain computed by the taxpayer's usual method of accounting (cash or accrual).[78] However, the Regulations provide that the amount realized by a cash basis taxpayer cannot be less than the value of the

---

[74]§ 453B(a).

[75]§ 453B(f)(2).

[76]§§ 453B(c), (d), and (g). See Chapter 20 for a discussion of some of these subjects.

[77]§ 453A.

[78]§ 453(d) and Temp.Reg. § 15a.453–1(d). See also Rev.Rul. 82–227, 1982–2 C.B. 89.

property sold. This rule differs from the usual cash basis accounting rules (discussed earlier),[79] which measure the amount realized in terms of the fair market value of the property received. The net effect of the Regulations is to allow the cash basis taxpayer to report his or her gain as an accrual basis taxpayer. The election is frequently applied to year-end sales by taxpayers who expect to be in a higher tax bracket in the following year.

E X A M P L E   32

On December 31, 2008, Kurt sold land to Jodie for $20,000 (fair market value). He had owned the land for 7 years. The cash was to be paid on January 4, 2009. Kurt is a cash basis taxpayer, and his basis in the land is $8,000. Kurt has a large casualty loss which when combined with his other income in 2008 puts him in a marginal tax rate in 2008 of 15%. He expects his tax rate to increase to 35% in 2009.

The transaction constitutes an installment sale because a payment will be received in a tax year after the tax year of disposition. Jodie's promise to pay Kurt is an installment obligation, and under the Regulations, the value of the installment obligation is equal to the value of the property sold ($20,000). If Kurt elects out of the installment method, he would shift $12,000 of gain ($20,000 − $8,000) from the expected higher rate in 2009 of 15% to the 0% rate for long-term capital gains in 2008. The expected tax savings based on the rate differentials may exceed the benefit of the tax deferral available with the installment method. ∎

Revocation of the Election. Permission of the IRS is required to revoke an election not to use the installment method.[80] The stickiness of the election is an added peril.

ETHICAL and EQUITABLE *Considerations*   ELECTING OUT OF ELECTING OUT OF THE INSTALLMENT SALE METHOD

The general rule is that gain on a transaction eligible to use the installment sale method is to be reported by that method. However, the taxpayer can elect not to use the installment method. What if the taxpayer elects not to use the installment method but later discovers he or she has made an improvident election (e.g., the taxpayer thought he or she would have a loss to offset the gain)? Generally, the taxpayer cannot revoke the election.

If the election was "inadvertent," however, the IRS will grant permission to amend the return and to use the installment method. For example, the IRS has frequently allowed revocation when the taxpayer's accountant prepared the tax return without using the installment method (reporting the entire gain in the year of sale), and the taxpayer filed the return not realizing that the election to forgo the use of the installment method had been made.

Martha, the tax adviser for Swan Partnership, analyzed Swan's situation and incorrectly concluded that the partnership should elect out of the installment method. Martha had discussed the tax return with Swan's CFO when she presented the tax return to him. Upon discovering her error in "electing out," Martha contacts Swan's new CFO (the CFO with whom she discussed the tax return has died), informs him of the benefit of amending the election out, and tells him that when she tried to discuss the tax return with the deceased CFO, he said, "I have complete confidence in you and do not need to discuss any aspect of the tax return." Evaluate what Martha has done.

Long-Term Contracts

A **long-term contract** is a building, installation, construction, or manufacturing contract that is entered into but not completed within the same tax year. However, a *manufacturing* contract is long term *only* if the contract is to manufacture (1) a unique item not normally carried in finished goods inventory or (2) items that normally require more than 12 calendar months to complete.[81] An item is *unique* if it is designed to meet the customer's particular needs and is not suitable for use by

LO.5

Understand the alternative methods of accounting for long-term contracts (the completed contract method and the percentage of completion method) including the limitations on the use of the completed contract method.

---

[79]Refer to Chapter 4, Example 6.
[80]§ 453(d)(3) and Temp.Reg. § 15a.453–1(d)(4).

[81]§ 460(f) and Reg. § 1.451–3(b).

others. A contract to perform services (e.g., auditing or legal services) is not considered a contract for this purpose and thus cannot qualify as a long-term contract.

EXAMPLE 33

Rocky, a calendar year taxpayer, entered into two contracts during the year. One contract was to construct a building foundation. Work was to begin in October 2008 and was to be completed by June 2009. The contract is long term because it will not be entered into and completed in the same tax year. The fact that the contract requires less than 12 calendar months to complete is not relevant because the contract is not for manufacturing. The second contract was for architectural services to be performed over two years. These services will not qualify for long-term contract treatment because the taxpayer will not build, install, construct, or manufacture a product. ■

Generally, the taxpayer must accumulate all of the direct and indirect costs incurred under a contract. This means the production costs must be accumulated and allocated to individual contracts. Furthermore, mixed services costs, costs that benefit contracts as well as the general administrative operations of the business, must be allocated to production. Exhibit 18–1 lists the types of costs that must be accumulated and allocated to contracts. The taxpayer must develop reasonable bases for cost allocations.[82]

EXAMPLE 34

Falcon, Inc., uses detailed cost accumulation records to assign labor and materials to its contracts in progress. The total cost of fringe benefits is allocated to a contract on the following basis:

$$\frac{\text{Labor on the contract}}{\text{Total salaries and labor}} \times \text{Total cost of fringe benefits}$$

Similarly, storage and handling costs for materials are allocated to contracts on the following basis:

$$\frac{\text{Contract materials}}{\text{Materials purchases}} \times \text{Storage and handling costs}$$

The cost of the personnel operations, a mixed services cost, is allocated between production and general administration based on the number of employees in each function. The personnel cost allocated to production is allocated to individual contracts on the basis of the formula used to allocate fringe benefits. ■

The accumulated costs are deducted when the revenue from the contract is recognized. Generally, two methods of accounting are used in varying circumstances to determine when the revenue from a contract is recognized:[83]

- The completed contract method.
- The percentage of completion method.

The *completed contract method may be used* for (1) home construction contracts (contracts in which at least 80 percent of the estimated costs are for dwelling units in buildings with four or fewer units) and (2) certain other real estate construction contracts. Other real estate contracts can qualify for the completed contract method if the following requirements are satisfied:

- The contract is expected to be completed within the two-year period beginning on the commencement date of the contract.
- The contract is performed by a taxpayer whose average annual gross receipts for the three taxable years preceding the taxable year in which the contract is entered into do not exceed $10 million.

All other contractors must use the percentage of completion method.

---

[82]Reg. §§ 1.263A–1T(b)(3)(iii)(A)(1) and 1.451–3(d)(9).   [83]§ 460.

EXHIBIT 18–1	Contract Costs, Mixed Services Costs, and Current Expense Items for Contracts

	Contracts Eligible for the Completed Contract Method	Other Contracts
Contract costs:		
Direct materials (a part of the finished product).	Capital	Capital
Indirect materials (consumed in production but not in the finished product, e.g., grease and oil for equipment).	Capital	Capital
Storage, handling, and insurance on materials.	Expense	Capital
Direct labor (worked on the product).	Capital	Capital
Indirect labor (worked in the production process but not directly on the product, e.g., a construction supervisor).	Capital	Capital
Fringe benefits for direct and indirect labor (e.g., vacation, sick pay, unemployment, and other insurance).	Capital	Capital
Pension costs for direct and indirect labor:		
Current cost.	Expense	Capital
Past service costs.	Expense	Capital
Depreciation on production facilities:		
For financial statements.	Capital	Capital
Tax depreciation in excess of financial statements.	Expense	Capital
Depreciation on idle facilities.	Expense	Expense
Property taxes, insurance, rent, and maintenance on production facilities.	Capital	Capital
Bidding expenses—successful.	Expense	Capital
Bidding expenses—unsuccessful.	Expense	Expense
Interest to finance real estate construction.	Capital	Capital
Interest to finance personal property:		
Production period of one year or less.	Expense	Expense
Production period exceeds one year and costs exceed $1 million.	Capital	Capital
Production period exceeds two years.	Capital	Capital
Mixed services costs:		
Personnel operations.	Expense	Allocate
Data processing.	Expense	Allocate
Purchasing.	Expense	Allocate
Selling, general, and administrative expenses (including an allocated share of mixed services).	Expense	Expense
Losses.	Expense	Expense

Completed Contract Method. Under the **completed contract method**, no revenue from the contract is recognized until the contract is completed and accepted. However, a taxpayer may not delay completion of a contract for the principal purpose of deferring tax.[84]

In some situations, the original contract price may be disputed, or the buyer may want additional work to be done on a long-term contract. If the disputed amount is substantial (it is not possible to determine whether a profit or loss will ultimately be realized on the contract), the Regulations provide that no amount of

---
[84]Reg. § 1.451–3(b)(2).

income or loss is recognized until the dispute is resolved. In all other cases, the profit or loss (reduced by the amount in dispute) is recognized in the current period on completion of the contract. However, additional work may need to be performed with respect to the disputed contract. In this case, the difference between the amount in dispute and the actual cost of the additional work is recognized in the year the work is completed rather than in the year in which the dispute is resolved.[85]

EXAMPLE 35

Ted, a calendar year taxpayer utilizing the completed contract method of accounting, constructed a building for Brad under a long-term contract. The gross contract price was $500,000. Ted finished construction in 2008 at a cost of $475,000. When Brad examined the building, he insisted that the building be repainted or the contract price be reduced. The estimated cost of repainting is $10,000. Since under the terms of the contract, Ted is assured of a profit of at least $15,000 ($500,000 − $475,000 − $10,000) even if the dispute is ultimately resolved in Brad's favor, Ted must include $490,000 ($500,000 − $10,000) in gross income and is allowed deductions of $475,000 for 2008.

In 2009, Ted and Brad resolve the dispute, and Ted repaints certain portions of the building at a cost of $6,000. Ted must include $10,000 in 2009 gross income and may deduct the $6,000 expense in that year. ■

EXAMPLE 36

Assume the same facts as in the previous example, except the estimated cost of repainting the building is $50,000. Since the resolution of the dispute completely in Brad's favor would mean a net loss on the contract for Ted ($500,000 − $475,000 − $50,000 = $25,000 loss), Ted does not recognize any income or loss until the year the dispute is resolved. ■

Frequently, a contractor receives payment at various stages of completion. For example, when the contract is 50 percent complete, the contractor may receive 50 percent of the contract price less a retainage. The taxation of these payments is generally governed by Regulation § 1.451–5, "advance payments for goods and long-term contracts" (discussed in Chapter 4). Generally, contractors are permitted to defer the advance payments until the payments are recognized as income under the taxpayer's method of accounting.

ETHICAL and EQUITABLE *Considerations*

INTENTIONAL DELAY

Clear Home Contracting, Inc., uses the completed contract method to report the income from long-term contracts. The company schedules work so that contracts will be completed shortly after the end of the year, although it would be feasible to complete them before year-end. The customers generally do not object to the later completion date because it is difficult to move at the end of the year. Evaluate the policy adopted by Clear. Should the tax law require the taxpayer to complete the contracts as soon as feasible?

Percentage of Completion Method. The percentage of completion method must be used to account for long-term contracts unless the taxpayer qualifies for one of the two exceptions that permit the completed contract method to be used (home construction contracts and certain other real estate construction contracts).[86] Under the **percentage of completion method**, a portion of the gross

---

[85]Reg. §§ 1.451–3(d)(2)(ii)–(vii), Example (2).
[86]Certain residential construction contracts that do not qualify for the completed contract method may nevertheless use that method to account for

30% of the profit from the contract, with the remaining 70% reported by the percentage of completion method.

contract price is included in income during each period as the work progresses. The revenue accrued each period (except for the final period) is computed as follows:[87]

$$\frac{C}{T} \times P$$

Where C = Contract costs incurred during the period.
       T = Estimated total cost of the contract.
       P = Contract price.

All of the costs allocated to the contract during the period are deductible from the accrued revenue.[88] The revenue reported in the final period is simply the unreported revenue from the contract. Because T in this formula is an estimate that frequently differs from total actual costs, which are not known until the contract has been completed, the profit on a contract for a particular period may be overstated or understated.

EXAMPLE 37

Tan, Inc., entered into a contract that was to take two years to complete, with an estimated cost of $2,250,000. The contract price was $3,000,000. Costs of the contract for 2007, the first year, totaled $1,350,000. The gross profit reported by the percentage of completion method for 2007 was $450,000 [($1,350,000/$2,250,000 × $3,000,000) − $1,350,000]. The contract was completed at the end of 2008 at a total cost of $2,700,000. In retrospect, 2007 profit should have been $150,000 [($1,350,000/$2,700,000 × $3,000,000) − $1,350,000]. Thus, taxes were overpaid for 2007. ■

A *de minimis* rule enables the contractor to delay the recognition of income for a particular contract under the percentage of completion method. If less than 10 percent of the estimated contract costs have been incurred by the end of the taxable year, the taxpayer can elect to defer the recognition of income and the related costs until the taxable year in which cumulative contract costs are at least 10 percent of the estimated contract costs.[89]

Lookback Provisions. In the year a contract is completed, a *lookback* provision requires the recalculation of annual profits reported on the contract under the percentage of completion method. Interest is paid to the taxpayer if taxes were overpaid, and interest is payable by the taxpayer if there was an underpayment.[90] For a corporate taxpayer, the lookback interest paid by the taxpayer is deductible, but for an individual taxpayer, it is nondeductible personal interest associated with a tax liability.

EXAMPLE 38

Assume Tan, Inc., in Example 37, was in the 35% tax bracket in both years and the relevant interest rate was 10%. For 2007, the company paid excess taxes of $105,000 [($450,000 − $150,000) × .35]. When the contract is completed at the end of 2008, Tan, Inc., should receive interest of $10,500 for one year on the tax overpayment ($105,000 × .10). ■

Inventories

LO.6

Know when accounting for inventories must occur, recognize the types of costs that must be included in inventories, and apply the LIFO method.

Generally, tax accounting and financial accounting for inventories are much the same:

- The use of inventories is necessary to clearly reflect the income of any business engaged in the production and sale or purchase and sale of goods.[91]
- The inventories should include all finished goods, goods in process, and raw materials and supplies that will become part of the product (including containers).

---

[87]§ 460(b)(1)(A).
[88]Reg. § 1.451–3(c)(3).
[89]§ 460(b)(5).

[90]§§ 460(b)(2) and (6). The taxpayer can elect to not apply the lookback method in situations where the cumulative taxable income as of the close of each prior year is within 10% of the correct income for each prior year.
[91]§ 471(a) and Reg. §§ 1.471–1 and –2.

- Inventory rules must give effect to the *best* accounting practice of a particular trade or business, and the taxpayer's method should be consistently followed from year to year.
- All items included in inventory should be valued at either (1) cost or (2) the lower of cost or market value.

The following are *not* acceptable methods or practices in valuing inventories:

- A deduction for a reserve for anticipated price changes.
- The use of a constant price or nominal value for a so-called normal quantity of materials or goods in stock (e.g., the base stock method).
- The inclusion in inventory of stock in transit to which title is not vested in the taxpayer.
- The direct costing approach (excluding fixed indirect production costs from inventory).
- The prime costing approach (excluding all indirect production costs from inventory).

The reason for the similarities between tax and financial accounting for inventories is that § 471 sets forth what appears to be a two-prong test. Under this provision "inventories shall be taken . . . on such basis . . . as conforming as nearly as may be to the *best accounting practice* in the trade or business and as most *clearly reflecting the income*." The best accounting practice is synonymous with generally accepted accounting principles (hereafter referred to as GAAP). However, the IRS determines whether an inventory method clearly reflects income.

In *Thor Power Tool Co. v. Comm.*, there was a conflict between the two tests.[92] The taxpayer's method of valuing obsolete parts was in conformity with GAAP. The IRS, however, successfully argued that the clear reflection of income test was not satisfied because the taxpayer's procedures for valuing its inventories were contrary to the Regulations. Under the taxpayer's method, inventories for parts in excess of estimated future sales were written off (expensed), although the parts were kept on hand and their asking prices were not reduced. [Under Regulation § 1.471–4(b), inventories cannot be written down unless the selling prices also are reduced.] The taxpayer contended that conformity to GAAP creates a presumption that the method clearly reflects income. The Supreme Court disagreed, concluding that the clear reflection of income test was *paramount*. Moreover, it is the opinion of the IRS that controls in determining whether the method of inventory clearly reflects income. Thus, the best accounting practice test was rendered practically meaningless. It follows that the taxpayer's method of inventory must strictly conform to the Regulations regardless of what GAAP may require.

Determining Inventory Cost

For merchandise purchased, cost is the invoice price less trade discounts plus freight and other handling charges.[93] Cash discounts approximating a fair interest rate can be deducted or capitalized at the taxpayer's option, providing the method used is consistently applied.

Uniform Capitalization (UNICAP). Section 263A provides that for inventory and property produced by the taxpayer, "(A) the direct cost of such property, and (B) such property's share of those indirect costs (including taxes) part or all of which are allocable to such property" must be capitalized. The Committee Reports observe that Congress is attempting to achieve a set of capitalization rules that will apply to all

---

[92]79–1 USTC ¶9139, 43 AFTR2d 79–362, 99 S.Ct. 773 (USSC, 1979).   [93]Reg. § 1.471–3(b).

types of businesses: contractors, manufacturers, farmers, wholesalers, and retailers.[94] Congress has labeled the system the **uniform capitalization (UNICAP) rules**, and practitioners refer to the rules as a *super-full absorption costing system.*

To value inventory under the UNICAP rules, a *producer* must apply the following steps:

- Classify all costs into three categories: (1) production, (2) general administrative expense, and (3) mixed services.
- Allocate mixed services costs to production and general administrative expenses.[95]
- Allocate the production costs between the cost of goods sold and the ending inventory.

Exhibit 18–1 (see the "Other Contracts" column) lists typical items that are included in the three classes of costs. The mixed services costs should be allocated to production on a rational basis. For example, the costs of operating the personnel department may be allocated between production and general administration based on the number of applications processed or the number of employees. In lieu of allocating each mixed services cost, the taxpayer can elect a *simplified method* whereby the total of all mixed services costs is allocated to production as follows:[96]

$$\text{MSP} = \frac{\text{TP}}{\text{TC}} \times \text{TMS}$$

Where MSP = Mixed services costs allocated to production.
        TP = Total production costs, other than interest and mixed services.
        TC = Total costs, other than interest; state, local, or foreign income taxes; and mixed services costs.
    TMS = Total mixed services costs.

The usual cost accounting techniques (e.g., average cost per equivalent unit) can be used to allocate the costs between the cost of goods sold and the ending inventory.

Alternatively, the producer can elect to allocate mixed services costs to production on the basis of labor charges only (production labor as a percentage of total labor costs).

The costs included in the inventory of *wholesalers and retailers* are comparable to those of the producer. However, many of these costs are captured in the price these taxpayers pay for the goods. The following additional costs must be capitalized by these taxpayers:

- All storage costs for wholesalers.
- Offsite storage costs for retailers.
- Purchasing costs (e.g., buyers' wages or salaries).
- Handling, processing, assembly, and repackaging.
- The portion of mixed services costs allocable to these functions.

Mixed services costs must be allocated to offsite storage, purchasing, and packaging on the basis of direct labor costs of these departments as a percentage of total payroll. Thus, the storage, purchasing, and packaging costs allocated to ending inventory include some mixed services costs.

The UNICAP rules may result in some costs being capitalized for tax purposes but not for financial accounting purposes. For example, a wholesaler's or a manufacturer's storage costs are generally expensed for financial reporting purposes, but are capitalized for tax purposes. Also, the taxpayer may capitalize

---

[94]H. Rep. 99–841, 99th Cong., 2nd Sess., 1986, pp. 302–309. See also Reg. § 1.263A–1(a).

[95]Producers with mixed services costs of less than $200,000 for the year are not required to allocate mixed services costs if the simplified method is used to allocate their production costs. Reg. § 1.263A–1(b)(12).

[96]Reg. § 1.263A–1(h)(5).

GLOBAL
Tax Issues

INVENTORY ACQUIRED FROM A FOREIGN SUBSIDIARY

Generally, a parent corporation and its foreign subsidiaries are treated as separate corporations. If a foreign subsidiary is producing goods in a country whose tax rates are lower than the U.S. tax rates, tax savings can accrue to the group if the foreign subsidiary's prices to the U.S. parent are as high as permissible. This will increase the income in the foreign country, but will reduce taxable income subject to the higher U.S. rates. Section 482 is the IRS's weapon against such income shifting. Under § 482, the prices charged on transactions between related parties must be equal to an "arm's length price."

straight-line depreciation of production equipment for financial accounting purposes, but the total tax depreciation must be capitalized under uniform capitalization.

The Farmer's Exemption. A farmer who is permitted to use the cash method (see Special Rules for Small Farmers above) is not required to apply the UNICAP rules to (1) any animals or (2) any plants with a preproduction period of two years or less that the farmer produces. In exchange for this concession, the farmer is required to use the alternative depreciation system (see Chapter 8) for property used in the farming business.[97]

Lower of Cost or Market. Except for those taxpayers who use the LIFO method, inventories may be valued at the **lower of cost or market (replacement cost)**.[98] Taxpayers using LIFO must value inventory at cost. However, the write-down of damaged or shopworn merchandise and goods that are otherwise unsalable at normal prices is not considered to be an application of the lower of cost or market method. Such items should be valued at bona fide selling price less direct cost of disposal.[99]

In the case of excess inventories (as in *Thor Power Tool Co.*, discussed previously), the goods can be written down only to the taxpayer's offering price. If the offering price on the goods is not reduced, the goods must be valued at cost.

EXAMPLE 39

The Cardinal Publishing Company invested $50,000 in printing 10,000 copies of a book. Although only 7,000 copies were sold in the first 3 years and none in the next 5 years, management is convinced that the book will become a classic in 20 years. Cardinal leaves the price the same as it was when the book was first distributed ($15 per copy). The remaining 3,000 books must be valued at cost ($15,000). Note that the tax law provides an incentive for the taxpayer to destroy or abandon its excess inventory and obtain an immediate deduction rather than wait for the event of future sales. ■

In applying the lower of cost or market method, *each* item included in the inventory must be valued at the lower of its cost or market value.[100]

EXAMPLE 40

The taxpayer's ending inventory is valued as follows:

Item	Cost	Market	Lower of Cost or Market
A	$5,000	$ 4,000	$4,000
B	3,000	2,000	2,000
C	1,500	6,000	1,500
	$9,500	$12,000	$7,500

---

[97]§§ 263A(d) and (e)(3).
[98]Reg. § 1.472–4.

[99]Reg. § 1.471–2(c).
[100]Reg. § 1.471–4(c).

Under the lower of cost or market method, the taxpayer's inventory is valued at $7,500 rather than $9,500. ∎

Inventory Shrinkage.
The difference between the inventory per physical count and according to the company's records is referred to as *inventory shrinkage*. Inventory shrinkage is the result of accidents, theft, and errors in recording. Many companies take physical inventories at times other than the last day of the tax year and adjust their inventory per books to agree with the physical count. The inventory of the last day of the tax year, which is used to compute cost of goods sold, is based on the perpetual records. Such companies often adjust the ending inventory for the estimated shrinkage that has occurred between the date of the physical inventory and the last day of the tax year. The adjustment is often based on the historical relationship between inventory shrinkage and sales.[101]

Determining Cost—Specific Identification, FIFO, and LIFO.
In some cases, it is feasible to determine the cost of the particular item sold. For example, an automobile dealer can easily determine the specific cost of each automobile that has been sold. However, in most businesses it is necessary to resort to a flow of goods assumption such as *first in, first out (FIFO)*, *last in, first out (LIFO)*, or an *average cost* method. A taxpayer may use any of these methods, provided the method selected is consistently applied from year to year.

During a period of rising prices, LIFO will generally produce a lower ending inventory valuation and will result in a greater cost of goods sold than would be obtained under the FIFO method. The following example illustrates how LIFO and FIFO affect the computation of the cost of goods sold.

On January 1, 2008, the taxpayer opened a retail store to sell refrigerators. At least 10 refrigerators must be carried in inventory to satisfy customer demands. The initial investment in the 10 refrigerators is $5,000. During the year, 10 refrigerators were sold at $750 each and were replaced at a cost of $6,000 ($600 each). Gross profit under the LIFO and FIFO methods is computed as follows:

EXAMPLE 41

	FIFO		LIFO	
Sales (10 × $750)		$ 7,500		$ 7,500
Beginning inventory	$ 5,000		$ 5,000	
Purchases	6,000		6,000	
	$11,000		$11,000	
Ending inventory				
10 × $600	(6,000)			
10 × $500	_____		(5,000)	
Cost of goods sold		(5,000)		(6,000)
Gross profit		$ 2,500		$ 1,500

∎

Dollar-Value LIFO.
In the previous example, the taxpayer was buying and selling a single product, a particular model of a refrigerator. The taxpayer employed the specific goods LIFO technique. Under the specific goods approach, if the identical items are not on hand at the end of the period, the LIFO inventory is depleted, and all of the deferred profit must be recaptured. Thus, taxpayers who frequently change the items carried in inventory would realize little benefit from LIFO. However, the dollar-value LIFO technique avoids the LIFO depletion problem associated with the specific goods technique.

---

[101]§ 471(b).

TAX *in the News*   **LIFO AS A SOURCE OF EARNINGS**

The Securities and Exchange Commission (SEC) recently filed criminal charges against corporate officers for their alleged deceptive reporting of the company's earnings. The company had in the past deferred a substantial amount of income from tax through the use of the LIFO inventory method. To give earnings a boost, the company allowed the inventory to be depleted, thus bringing the LIFO deferral into current income. Contrary to SEC regulations, management failed to disclose that the depletion of the LIFO layers substantially enhanced the reported earnings for the year.

Under **dollar-value LIFO**, each inventory item is assigned to a pool. A *pool* is a collection of similar items and is treated as a separate inventory. Determining whether items are similar involves considerable judgment. In general, however, the taxpayer would prefer broad pools so that when a particular item is sold out, it can be replaced by increases in other items in the same pool. Generally, all products manufactured at a particular plant can be treated as a pool.[102] A department store may have a separate pool for each department. An automobile dealer may have separate pools for new cars, lightweight trucks, heavy-duty trucks, and car and truck parts.

At the end of the period, the ending inventory must be valued at the current-year prices and then at the LIFO base period (the year LIFO was adopted). The ratio of the ending inventory at current prices to the ending inventory at base period prices is the *LIFO index*. If the total current inventory at base period prices is greater than the base period inventory at base period prices, a LIFO layer must be added. The LIFO index is applied to the LIFO layer to convert it to current prices.

EXAMPLE 42

Black Company adopted LIFO effective January 1, 2008. The base LIFO inventory (from December 31, 2007) was $1,000,000. On December 31, 2008, the inventory was $1,320,000 at end-of-2008 prices and $1,200,000 at end-of-2007 (the base period) prices. Thus, Black added a 2008 layer of $200,000 ($1,200,000 − $1,000,000) at base period prices. The layer must be converted to 2008 prices as follows:

$$\text{LIFO index} = \$1,320,000/\$1,200,000 = 1.10$$
$$2008 \text{ layer} \times \text{LIFO index} = \$200,000 \times 1.10 = \$220,000$$

Therefore, the 2008 ending inventory is $1,000,000 + $220,000 = $1,220,000.

The inventory on December 31, 2009, is $1,325,000 using 2009 prices and $1,250,000 using base period prices. Thus, the LIFO index for 2009 is $1,325,000/$1,250,000 = 1.06. The LIFO inventory is $1,273,000, computed as follows:

BLACK COMPANY
LIFO Inventory
December 31, 2009

	Base Period Cost	LIFO Index	LIFO Layers
Base inventory	$1,000,000	1.00	$1,000,000
2008 layer	200,000	1.10	220,000
2009 layer	50,000	1.06	53,000
	$1,250,000		$1,273,000

---

[102]See, generally, Reg. § 1.472–8.

Blanch Corporation has been using the dollar-value LIFO inventory method for 20 years. The company maintains one inventory pool that includes raw materials, goods in process, and finished goods. The LIFO deferral is several million dollars. At the end of the current year, the corporation's inventory of finished goods was almost depleted because the company's major competitor had to recall a substantial portion of its products. Blanch's management is aware that if the inventory is not replenished, the corporation will be required to recognize income that has been deferred for the past 20 years. The controller has suggested that the company buy sufficient raw materials to substitute for the depleted finished goods. This will require having on hand at the end

of the year the raw materials required for the next 18 months, when ordinarily the company has only a three-month supply on hand. The controller argues that the cost of carrying the additional inventory is much less than the additional taxes that will be due if the inventories are allowed to decrease.

The operations manager has suggested that the company buy the raw materials before the end of the year and have the supplier store the materials. Furthermore, the supplier would act as Blanch's agent to sell the excess materials. This would minimize the actual investment in inventory. Do you think the corporation should follow either proposal?

The LIFO Election

A taxpayer may adopt LIFO by merely using the method in the tax return for the year of the change and by attaching Form 970 (Application to Use LIFO Inventory Method) to the tax return. Thus, a taxpayer does not have to request approval for the change. Once the election is made, it cannot be revoked. However, a prospective change from LIFO to any other inventory method can be made only if the consent of the IRS is obtained.[103]

The beginning inventory valuation for the first year LIFO is used is computed by the costing method employed in the preceding year. Thus, the beginning LIFO inventory is generally the same as the closing inventory for the preceding year. However, since lower of cost or market cannot be used in conjunction with LIFO, previous write-downs to market for items included in the beginning inventory must be restored to income. The amount the inventories are written up is an adjustment due to a change in accounting method.[104] However, the usual rules for disposition of the adjustments under Revenue Procedure 99–49 are not applicable.[105] The taxpayer is allowed to spread the adjustment ratably over the year of the change and the two succeeding years.

EXAMPLE 43

In 2007, Paul used the lower of cost or market FIFO inventory method. The FIFO cost of his ending inventory was $30,000, and the market value of the inventory was $24,000. Therefore, the ending inventory for 2007 was $24,000. Paul switched to LIFO in 2008 and was required to write up the beginning inventory to $30,000. Paul must add $2,000 ($6,000 ÷ 3) to his income for each of the years 2008, 2009, and 2010. ∎

Congress added this provision to the Code to overrule the previous IRS policy of requiring the taxpayer to include the entire adjustment in income for the year preceding the change to LIFO.[106]

Once the LIFO election is made for tax purposes, the taxpayer's financial reports to owners and creditors must also be prepared on the basis of LIFO.[107] The

---

[103]Reg. §§ 1.472–3(a) and 1.472–5 and Rev.Proc. 84–74, 1984–2 C.B. 736 at 742.

[104]Reg. § 1.472–2(c). In Rev.Rul. 76–282, 1976–2 C.B. 137, the IRS required the restoration of write-downs for damaged and shopworn goods when the taxpayer switched to LIFO.

[105]1999–2 C.B. 725.

[106]§ 472(d), overruling the IRS position cited in Footnote 104.

[107]§ 472(c).

conformity of financial reports to tax reporting is specifically required by the Code and is strictly enforced by the IRS. However, the Regulations permit the taxpayer to make a footnote disclosure of the net income computed by another method of inventory valuation (e.g., FIFO).[108]

Special Inventory Methods Relating to Farming and Ranching

Farmers who do not use the cash method and therefore account for inventories may elect to use the **farm price method** or the **unit-livestock-price method** rather than one of the inventory methods discussed above. Under the farm price method, the inventory is valued at its market price less disposition costs (e.g., transportation and selling expenses).[109] If the taxpayer uses the unit-livestock-price method, the animals are valued at a standard cost, which is based on the average cost of raising an animal with the characteristics of the animals included in the ending inventory.[110] The farmer can also elect to use the lower of cost or market inventory method.

LO.7

Identify tax planning opportunities related to accounting periods and accounting methods.

TAX PLANNING
Considerations

Taxable Year

Under the general rules for tax years, partnerships and S corporations frequently will be required to use a calendar year. However, if the partnership or S corporation can demonstrate a business purpose for a fiscal year, the IRS will allow the entity to use the requested year. The advantage to a fiscal year is that the calendar year partners and S corporation shareholders may be able to defer from tax the income earned from the close of the fiscal year until the end of the calendar year. Tax advisers for these entities should apply the IRS's gross receipts test described in Revenue Procedure 87–32 to determine if permission for the fiscal year will be granted.[111]

Cash Method of Accounting

The cash method of accounting gives the taxpayer considerable control over the recognition of expenses and some control over the recognition of income. This method can be used by proprietorships, partnerships, and small corporations (gross receipts of $5 million or less) that provide services (inventories are not material to the service business). Farmers (except certain farming corporations) can also use the cash method.

Installment Method

Unlike the cash and accrual methods, the installment method often results in an interest-free loan (of deferred taxes) from the government. The installment method is not available for the sale of inventory. Nevertheless, the installment method is an important tax planning technique and should be considered when a sale of eligible property is being planned. That is, if the taxpayer can benefit from deferring the tax, the terms of sale can be arranged so that the installment method rules apply. If, on the other hand, the taxpayer expects to be in a higher tax bracket when the payments will be received, he or she can elect not to use the installment method.

Related Parties. Intrafamily installment sales can still be a useful family tax planning tool. If the related party holds the property more than two years, a subsequent

---

[108]Reg. § 1.472–2(e).
[109]Reg. § 1.471–6(d).

[110]Reg. § 1.471–6(e). See also IRS Pub. 225 (Farmers Tax Guide), p. 7.
[111]See also Rev. Proc. 2002–38, 2002–1 C.B. 1037.

sale will not accelerate the gain from the first disposition. Patience and forethought are rewarded.

The 6 percent limitation on imputed interest on sales of land between family members (see Concept Summary 18–1) enables the seller to convert ordinary income into capital gain or make what is, in effect, a nontaxable gift. If the selling price is raised to adjust for the low interest rate charges on an installment sale, the seller has more capital gain but less ordinary income than would be realized from a sale to an unrelated party. If the selling price is not raised and the specified interest of 6 percent is charged, the seller enables the relative to have the use of the property without having to pay its full market value. As an additional benefit, the bargain sale is not a taxable gift.

Disposition of Installment Obligations. A disposition of an installment obligation is also a serious matter. Gifts of the obligations will accelerate income to the seller. The list of taxable and nontaxable dispositions of installment obligations should not be trusted to memory. In each instance where transfers of installment obligations are contemplated, the practitioner should conduct research to be sure he or she knows the consequences.

Completed Contract Method

Generally, large contractors must use the percentage of completion method of accounting for reporting the income from long-term contracts. Under the percentage of completion method, the taxpayer must recognize profit in each period costs are incurred. Profit is reported in proportion to the cost incurred for the period as a proportion of the total contract cost. However, small contractors (average annual gross receipts do not exceed $10 million) working on contracts that are completed within a two-year period can elect to use the completed contract method and defer profit until the year in which the contract is completed.

Inventories

Lower of Cost or Market. Generally, under tax accounting rules, a deduction cannot be taken for a loss before the loss is realized. Inventories with a replacement cost below their original cost are the major exception to this rule. The rationale for the lower of cost or market method is that when the replacement cost of the goods has decreased, the taxpayer's selling price must likewise be reduced. Under the lower of cost or market method, the taxpayer is allowed to anticipate a reduction in the expected selling price of the goods by taking a deduction in the period the replacement cost decreases, rather than waiting until the goods are actually sold. Thus, the lower of cost or market method is a tax deferral technique.

LIFO. While the lower of cost or market method defers tax when replacement costs are declining, LIFO defers tax when prices are rising. However, when some goods are increasing in value while others are decreasing, the taxpayer cannot use the lower of cost or market method for the goods declining in value and LIFO for the goods whose replacement costs are rising. That is, LIFO cannot be used in conjunction with the lower of cost or market method. Assuming that prices generally are rising, the taxpayer generally should elect LIFO. The only major disadvantage to LIFO is the financial-tax conformity requirement. However, even this disadvantage can be overcome through footnote disclosure of earnings as computed under FIFO.

KEY TERMS

Accounting methods, 18–10

Accounting period, 18–3

Accrual method, 18–13

All events test, 18–14

Cash method, 18–11

Claim of right doctrine, 18–9

Completed contract method, 18–27

Crop insurance proceeds, 18–9

Crop method, 18–12

Dollar-value LIFO, 18–34

Economic performance test, 18–14

Farm price method, 18–36

Fiscal year, 18–3

Hybrid method, 18–16

Imputed interest, 18–21

Installment method, 18–19

Least aggregate deferral method, 18–4

Long-term contract, 18–25

Lower of cost or market (replacement cost), 18–32

Majority interest partners, 18–3

One-year rule for prepaid expenses, 18–11

Percentage of completion method, 18–28

Personal service corporation (PSC), 18–6

Principal partner, 18–3

Short taxable year (short period), 18–7

Uniform capitalization (UNICAP) rules, 18–31

Unit-livestock-price method, 18–36

PROBLEM MATERIALS

DISCUSSION QUESTIONS

1. Why would December 31 be an inappropriate year-end for a department store?

2. In the case of a profitable S corporation, what would be the advantage to using a tax year ending January 31 if this was permissible?

Decision Making

3. A medical practice was incorporated on January 1, 2008, and expects to earn $25,000 per month before deducting the doctor's salary. The doctor owns 100% of the stock. The corporation and the doctor both use the cash method of accounting. The corporation does not need to retain any of the earnings in the business; thus, the salary of the doctor (a calendar year taxpayer) will equal the corporation's net income before salary expense. If the corporation could choose any tax year it wished and pay the doctor's salary at the time that would be the most tax efficient (but at least once every 12 months), what tax year should the corporation choose, and when should the salary be paid each year?

4. Pale Motel, Inc., was a C corporation using a fiscal year ending April 30 for tax purposes for all tax years through April 30, 2008. In May 2008, the corporation made an S election. What are the implications of the election for Pale's tax year?

5. Freda is a cash basis farmer. She was in the 35% marginal tax bracket in 2007, the 15% marginal tax bracket in 2008, and the 35% marginal tax bracket in 2009. In 2007, she received $10,000 from the sale of produce. The customer complained that the produce was unfit for consumption, and in 2008 Freda refunded the $10,000. Also in 2008, Freda paid her farmers' cooperative $50,000 for seeds and fertilizer. In 2009, the cooperative paid Freda a dividend of $5,000 based on the cooperative's 2008 earnings.
    a. What are the tax consequences of the payment to the customer in 2008?
    b. What are the tax consequences of the refund from the cooperative in 2009?
    c. Were the tax accounting rules "kind" to Freda?

6. Discuss the provision in the tax law that provides tax relief for farmers whose income fluctuates from year to year.

7. A cash basis taxpayer owns rental properties. The insurance on the properties is renewed each January 1. On December 30, 2008, the taxpayer paid the premium of

$24,000 for the period January 1, 2009, through December 31, 2009. Can the taxpayer deduct the premium of $24,000 in 2008?

8. In 2008, the taxpayer became eligible to switch from the accrual to the cash method of accounting. At the beginning of the year, accounts receivable totaled $50,000, inventory was $100,000, and accounts payable for merchandise totaled $40,000. What is the amount of the adjustment due to the change in accounting method?

9. Osprey Corporation, an accrual basis taxpayer, had taxable income for 2008. The company filed its 2008 state income tax return in August 2009 and paid the $6,000 state income tax due for 2008. In December 2008, the company received a notice from the state tax commission that an additional $2,000 of income tax was due for 2007 because of an error on the return. The company acknowledged the error in December 2008 and paid the additional $2,000 in tax in February 2009. Can the $6,000 and $2,000 in state income tax be deducted on Osprey's 2008 Federal income tax return?

10. Compare the cash basis and accrual basis of accounting as applied to the following:
    a. Fixed assets.
    b. Prepaid rent income.
    c. Prepaid interest expense.
    d. A note received for services performed if the market value and face amount of the note differ.

11. Edgar uses the cash method to report the income from his software consulting business. A large publicly held corporation has offered to invest in Edgar's business as a limited partner. What tax accounting complications would be created if Edgar and the corporation become partners?

Decision Making

12. In January 2008, a taxpayer purchased for $1,800 a three-year service contract on business equipment. What is the cash basis taxpayer's 2008 deduction associated with the cost of the service contract?

13. Ruby, Inc., is an automobile dealer. This year the company makes a special offer. The purchaser of a new car will get free gas for the first year the car is owned. The company can accurately predict the cost of gas that will be used by the customer next year for cars sold this year. Therefore, the company's financial statements reflect the estimated future costs of such gas. Explain how Ruby must account for the gas costs for tax purposes.

14. Irene has made Sara an offer on the purchase of a capital asset. Irene will pay (1) $200,000 cash or (2) $50,000 cash and a 6% installment note for $150,000 guaranteed by City Bank of New York. If Sara sells for $200,000 cash, she will invest the after-tax proceeds in certificates of deposit yielding 6% interest. Sara's cost of the asset is $25,000. Why would Sara prefer the installment sale?

Decision Making

15. Arnold gave land to his son, Bruce. Arnold's basis in the land was $50,000, and its fair market value at the date of the gift was $60,000. Bruce borrowed $120,000 that he used to improve the property. He sold the property to Della for $270,000. Della paid Bruce $60,000 in cash, assumed his $120,000 mortgage, and agreed to pay $90,000 in two years. Bruce's selling expenses were $10,000. Della is going to pay adequate interest. What is Bruce's installment sale gain in the year of sale?

16. A seller and buyer agree that the sales/purchase price for land is $100,000 down and five payments of $50,000 each. In addition, the seller would like the contract to read that the total selling price is $322,600 and that the five payments of $50,000 each include interest at 4%, which is the current Federal intermediate-term rate. The buyer counters that the price should be stated as $310,600, with a 6% stated rate on the five payments of $50,000 each. The land is a capital asset to the seller, and the holding period is four years. Because the total amount received by the seller and the amount paid by the buyer are the same [$100,000 + 5($50,000) = $350,000], why does it matter how the price and interest rate are stated in the contract?

17. On June 1, 2006, Father sold land to Son for $200,000. Father reported the gain by the installment method, with the gain to be spread over five years. In May 2008, Son received an offer of $300,000 for the land, to be paid over three years. What would be the tax consequences of Son's sale? How could the tax consequences be improved?

Decision Making

Decision Making

18. In December 2008, Juan Corporation sold land it held as an investment. The corporation received $50,000 in 2008 and a note payable (with adequate interest) for $150,000 to be paid in 2010. Juan Corporation's cost of the land was $80,000. The corporation has a $90,000 net capital loss carryover that will expire in 2008. Should Juan Corporation report the sale in 2008 or use the installment method to report the income as payments are received?

19. What are the similarities between the crop method used for farming and the completed contract method used for long-term construction?

20. Nathan uses the percentage of completion method to report income from his real estate construction contracts. A contract was begun in 2008 and completed in 2009. In 2008, Nathan reported gross income from the partial completion of the contract. In 2009, however, costs had risen above the original estimate. The contract was completed with the actual profit on the contract being less than the income from the contract reported in 2008. What mechanism should be used to correct for the overpayment of tax in 2008?

21. Neal used the percentage of completion method to report income from a contract that began in the previous year and was completed in the current year. The actual total cost of completing the contract was greater than the estimate of total cost made at the end of the previous year. How will the lookback rules affect Neal?

22. The Eagle Corporation builds yachts. All vessels are practically identical and sell for more than $2 million. Production does not begin until the company has a contract to sell the vessel. The company has recently changed its production techniques to reduce the time for producing a yacht from 15 months to 9 months. What are the tax implications of the change?

Issue ID

23. Largo Company is an engineering consulting business that uses the accrual method of accounting for its services. Mango Company manufactures nuts and bolts and also uses the accrual method to account for its sales. Each company has a personnel department. How should the cost of personnel operations be treated by each of the two companies?

Issue ID

24. For over 20 years, Pearl Parts Company has produced parts using brass as the only material. This year the company started making some of the component parts from plastic. This change substantially reduced production costs. What are the inventory valuation issues for Pearl, which has used the dollar-value LIFO inventory method for 10 years?

Issue ID

25. Pearl, Inc., is about to make its first attempt to borrow from a local bank. The company uses LIFO for tax purposes, solely to defer taxes, and believes that income computed using the FIFO method would better reflect its income. The company also uses the double-declining balance method of depreciation for tax, although the straight-line method better reflects the actual depreciation. The company would like to present its financial position in the most favorable light. Therefore, Pearl's CEO intends to provide the bank with an income statement prepared using the FIFO inventory method and straight-line depreciation. What types of problems will presenting the income statement to the bank in this fashion cause for Pearl?

Issue ID

26. Blue and Gold are competitors in the automotive supply business. In calculating its ending inventory at the end of the tax year, Blue includes an estimate of inventory shrinkage, but Gold does not. What could account for this difference?

PROBLEMS

27. Red, White, and Blue are unrelated corporations engaged in real estate development. The three corporations formed a joint venture (treated as a partnership) to develop a tract of land. Assuming the venture does not have a natural business year, what tax year must the joint venture adopt under the following circumstances?

		Tax Year Ending	Interest in Joint Venture
a.	Red	March 31	60%
	Blue	June 30	20%
	White	October 31	20%
b.	Red	October 31	30%
	White	June 30	40%
	Blue	January 31	30%

28. The Cardinal Wholesale Company is an S corporation that began business on March 1, 2008. Robert, a calendar year taxpayer, owns 100% of the Cardinal stock. He has $400,000 taxable income from other sources each year. Robert will work approximately 30 hours a week for the corporation. Cardinal sells swimming pool supplies, and its natural business year ends in September. Approximately 80% of Cardinal's gross receipts occur in June through September.   *Decision Making*
    a. What tax year should Cardinal elect, assuming that Robert anticipates the company will produce a net profit for all years?
    b. What tax year should Cardinal elect, assuming it will lose $10,000 a month for the first 12 months and an average of $5,000 a month for the next 12 months? In the third year, the corporation will earn taxable income.

29. Zack conducted his professional practice through Zack, Inc. The corporation uses a fiscal year ending September 30 even though the business purpose test for a fiscal year cannot be satisfied. For the year ending September 30, 2008, the corporation paid Zack a salary of $180,000, and during the period January through September 2008, the corporation paid him a salary of $150,000.   *Decision Making*
    a. How much salary should Zack receive during the period October 1 through December 31, 2008?
    b. Assume Zack received only $30,000 salary during the period October 1 through December 31, 2008. What would be the consequences to Zack, Inc.?

30. Mauve Corporation began operations as a farm supplies business and used a fiscal year ending September 30. The company gradually went out of the farm supplies business and into the mail-order Christmas gifts business. The company has received permission from the IRS to change to a fiscal year ending January 31, effective for the year ending January 31, 2008. For the short period October 1, 2007, through January 31, 2008, Mauve earned $25,000. Calculate Mauve's tax liability for the short period October 1, 2007, through January 31, 2008.

31. In 2007, Juan entered into a contract to write a book. The publisher advanced Juan $30,000, which was to be repaid out of future royalties. If the book was not completed by the end of 2008, however, Juan would be required to repay the publisher for the advance. Juan did not complete the book in 2008, and in accordance with the agreement, he repaid the $30,000 to the publisher in 2009. Juan is a cash basis taxpayer. His marginal tax rate was 35% in 2007 and 15% in 2009. What are the tax consequences to Juan of the repayment?

32. Gold, Inc., is an accrual basis taxpayer. In 2008, an employee accidentally spilled hazardous chemicals on leased property. The chemicals destroyed trees on neighboring property, resulting in $30,000 of damages. In 2008, the owner of the property sued Gold, Inc., for the $30,000. Gold's attorney feels that it is liable and the only issue is whether the neighbor will also seek punitive damages that could be as much as three times the actual damages. In addition, as a result of the spill, Gold was in violation of its lease and was therefore required to pay the landlord $15,000. However, the amount due for the lease violation is not payable until the termination of the lease in 2011. None of these costs were covered by insurance. Jeff Stuart, the president of Gold, Inc., is generally familiar with the accrual basis tax accounting rules and is concerned about when the company will be allowed to deduct the amounts the company is required to pay as a result of this environmental disaster. Write Mr. Stuart a letter explaining these issues. Gold's address is 200 Elm Avenue, San Jose, CA 95192.   *Communications*

33. Compute the taxpayer's income or deductions for 2008 using (1) the cash basis and (2) the accrual basis for each of the following:

    a. In March 2008, the taxpayer purchased a copying machine for $250,000. The taxpayer paid $25,000 in cash and gave a $225,000 interest-bearing note for the balance. The copying machine has an MACRS cost recovery period of five years, and the § 179 election was not made.

    b. In December 2008, the taxpayer collected $10,000 for January 2009 rents. In January 2009, the taxpayer collected $2,000 for December 2008 rents.

    c. In December 2008, the taxpayer paid office equipment insurance premiums of $30,000 for January–June 2009.

    d. In June 2008, the taxpayer purchased office furniture for $200,000. The taxpayer paid $36,000 in cash and gave a $144,000 interest-bearing note for the balance. The office furniture has an MACRS cost recovery period of seven years. The taxpayer made the § 179 election.

34. What accounting method (cash or accrual) would you recommend for the following businesses?

    a. An incorporated retail hardware store with annual gross receipts of $4.5 million.

    b. An incorporated engineering firm with annual gross receipts of $12 million.

    c. A dry wall subcontractor who works on residences and has annual gross receipts of $3 million.

    d. An incorporated insurance agency with annual gross receipts of $6 million.

Decision Making

35. Pink Company, an architectural firm, has a bookkeeper who maintains a cash receipts and disbursements journal. At the end of the year, the company hires you to convert the cash receipts and disbursements into accrual basis revenues and expenses. The total cash receipts are summarized as follows:

Cash sales	$120,000
Collections on accounts receivable	350,000
Bank loan	30,000
Total cash receipts	$500,000

    The accounts receivable from customers at the end of the year are $190,000. You note that the accounts receivable at the beginning of the year were $150,000. The cash sales included $30,000 of prepayments for services to be provided over the next 36 months (i.e., 12 months of such services relate to 2008).

    a. Compute the company's accrual basis gross income for 2008.

    b. Would you recommend that Pink use the cash method or the accrual method?

    c. The company does not maintain an allowance for uncollectible accounts. Would you recommend that such an allowance be established for tax purposes?

36. How do the all events and economic performance requirements apply to the following transactions by an accrual basis taxpayer?

    a. The company guarantees its products for six months. At the end of 2008, customers had made valid claims for $600,000 that were not paid until 2009. Also, the company estimates that another $400,000 in claims from 2008 sales will be filed and paid in 2009.

    b. The accrual basis taxpayer reported $200,000 in corporate taxable income for 2008. The state income tax rate was 6%. The corporation paid $7,000 in estimated state income taxes in 2008 and paid $2,000 on 2007 state income taxes when it filed its 2007 state income tax return in March 2008. The company filed its 2008 state income return in March 2009 and paid the remaining $5,000 of its 2008 state income tax liability.

    c. An employee was involved in an accident while making a sales call. The company paid the injured victim $15,000 in 2008 and agreed to pay the victim $15,000 a year for the next nine years.

37. Moss Company is a computer consulting firm. The company also sells equipment to its clients. The sales of equipment account for approximately 40% of the company's gross receipts. The company has consistently used the cash method to report its income from services and the accrual method to report its income from the sale of inventory. In June of the current year, Moss's accountant discovered that as a small business the company qualifies to use the cash method for all of its activities. The company is a calendar year

taxpayer. As of the beginning of the current year, the company had $80,000 of inventory on hand and $40,000 of accounts receivable from the sales of equipment and $60,000 of receivables from the consulting services.

a.   Compute the adjustment due to the change in accounting method.

b.   Is the adjustment positive or negative? Explain.

c.   When can the adjustment be taken into account in computing taxable income?

38. Crow Finance Company experiences bad debts of about 3% of its outstanding loans. At the end of the year, the company had outstanding receivables of $30 million. This balance included $2 million of accrued interest receivable. Crow's loan loss reserve for the year was computed as follows:

Decision Making

Balance, January 1, 2008	$850,000
Accounts written off as uncollectible	
Loans made in 2008	(60,000)
Loans made in prior years	(15,000)
Collections on loans previously written off	25,000
Adjustment to required balance	100,000
Balance, December 31, 2008	$900,000

a.   Determine the effects of the above on Crow's taxable income for 2008.

b.   Assume that Crow has used the reserve method to compute its taxable income for the 10 years the company has been in existence. In 2008, you begin preparing Crow's tax return. What should be done with regard to the reserve?

39. Jeffrey Boyd, the president of Eagle Furniture Company (average annual gross receipts of $4 million), has prepared the company's financial statements and income tax returns for the past 15 years. In July 2009, however, he hired you to prepare the 2008 corporate income tax return because he has not studied taxes for over 20 years and suspects the rules may have changed. Eagle uses the accrual method of accounting. Based on an initial examination of Eagle's trial balance and some account analyses, you have determined that the following items may require adjustments:

Communications

- The company uses the FIFO inventory method, as valued at cost. However, all freight expenses on incoming merchandise have been expensed for the 15 years the company has been in business.

- The company experiences inventory shrinkage (due to breakage and theft) of about 1% of sales each year. The shrinkage is not taken into account until the company takes a physical inventory each October, but the corporation's fiscal year ends January 31.

- The company has used an allowance for uncollectible accounts, which has a balance of $60,000. In the past, the company has been able to accurately predict its actual bad debt expense.

- The company sells a three-year service contract on its appliances. The company treats 1/36 of the contract price as earned each month. At the beginning of the year, the company had $120,000 in its account for unearned revenues from the service contracts.

- The company deducts its state income tax in the year paid. Thus, the 2008 state income tax expense includes the estimated taxes paid in 2008 and the additional amount paid in 2008 on 2007 taxes.

Write a letter to Mr. Boyd explaining what adjustments will be required and how they will be implemented. The address of Eagle Furniture Company is 1000 East Maryland Street, Evansville, IL 47722.

40. Floyd, a cash basis taxpayer, has received an offer to purchase his land. The buyer will either pay him $100,000 at closing or pay $50,000 at closing and $52,000 one year after the date of closing. If Floyd recognizes the entire gain in the current year, his marginal tax rate will be 35% (combined Federal and state rates). However, if he spreads the gain over the two years, his marginal tax rate on the gain will be only 25%. Floyd does not consider the buyer a credit risk, but he realizes that the deferred payment will, in effect, earn only 4% interest ($2,000/$50,000 = 4%). Floyd believes he can earn a 10% before-tax rate of return on his after-tax cash. Floyd's adjusted basis for the land is $25,000, the

Decision Making

buyer is also a cash basis taxpayer, and the short-term Federal rate is 4%. Floyd has asked you to evaluate the two alternatives on an after-tax basis.

41. Tom, a cash basis taxpayer, sold his unincorporated accounting practice for $600,000. The bases and fair market values of the assets sold were as follows:

Assets	Fair Market Value	Basis	
Office equipment	$ 70,000	Cost	$ 120,000
		Less: Depreciation	(100,000)
Office building	180,000	Cost	220,000
		Less: Depreciation	(100,000)
Land	80,000	Cost	40,000
Goodwill	270,000	Cost	–0–
Total	$600,000	Total	$ 180,000

The buyer paid $240,000 at closing and agreed to pay the balance with interest at 8% (exceeds the Federal rate) over 10 years. The office building was depreciated using the straight-line method. Thus, there is no § 1250 gain.
a. Compute Tom's recognized gain in the year of the sale.
b. Determine the character of the gain recognized in the year of the sale.

42. Kay, who is not a dealer, sold an apartment house to Polly during the current year (2008). The closing statement for the sale is as follows:

Total selling price		$ 150,000
Add: Polly's share of property taxes (6 months) paid by Kay		2,500
Less: Kay's 8% mortgage assumed by Polly	$55,000	
Polly's refundable binder ("earnest money") paid in 2007	1,000	
Polly's 8% installment note given to Kay	80,000	
Kay's real estate commissions and attorney's fees	7,500	(143,500)
Cash paid to Kay at closing		$ 9,000
Cash due from Polly = $9,000 + $7,500 expenses		$ 16,500

During 2008, Kay collected $4,000 in principal on the installment note and $2,000 of interest. Kay's basis in the property was $70,000 [$85,000 − $15,000 (depreciation)], and there was $9,000 in potential depreciation recapture under § 1250. The Federal rate is 6%.
a. Compute the following:
   1. Total gain.
   2. Contract price.
   3. Payments received in the year of sale.
   4. Recognized gain in the year of sale and the character of such gain.
   (*Hint:* Think carefully about the manner in which the property taxes are handled before you begin your computations.)
b. Same as (a)(2) and (3), except Kay's basis in the property was $45,000.

Decision Making

43. On June 30, 2008, Kelly sold property for $250,000 cash and a $750,000 note due on September 30, 2009. The note will also pay 6% interest, which is slighty higher than the Federal rate. Kelly's cost of the property was $400,000. She is concerned that Congress may increase the tax rate that will apply when the note is collected. Kelly's after-tax rate of return on investments is 7%.
a. What can Kelly do to avoid the expected higher tax rate?
b. Assuming Kelly's marginal combined Federal and state tax rate is 20% in 2008, how much would the tax rates need to increase to make the option identified in (a) advisable?

Decision Making

44. On December 30, 2007, Maud sold land to her son, Charles, for $50,000 cash and a 7% installment note for $350,000, payable over 10 years. Maud's cost of the land was $150,000. In October 2009, after Charles had paid $60,000 on the principal of the note, he received an offer to sell the land for $500,000 cash. What advice can you provide Charles that will minimize the present value of the tax liability for Maud and Charles?

45. George sold land to an unrelated party in 2007. His basis in the land was $40,000, and the selling price was $100,000—$25,000 payable at closing and $25,000 (plus 10% interest) due January 1, 2008, 2009, and 2010. What would be the tax consequences of the following? [Treat each part independently and assume (1) George did not elect out of the installment method and (2) the installment obligations have values equal to their face amounts.]
    a. In 2008, George gave to his daughter the right to collect all future payments on the installment obligations.
    b. In 2008, after collecting the payment due on January 1, George transferred the installment obligation to his 100%-controlled corporation in exchange for additional shares of stock.
    c. On December 31, 2008, George received the payment due on January 1, 2009. On December 15, 2009, George died, and the remaining installment obligation was transferred to his estate. The estate collected the amount due on January 1, 2010.

46. The Dove Construction Company reports its income by the completed contract method. At the end of 2008, the company completed a contract to construct a building at a total cost of $800,000. The contract price was $1.2 million. However, the customer refused to accept the work and would not pay anything on the contract because he claimed the roof did not meet specifications. Dove's engineers estimated it would cost $140,000 to bring the roof up to the customer's standards. In 2009, the dispute was settled in the customer's favor; the roof was improved at a cost of $165,000, and the customer accepted the building and paid the $1.2 million.
    a. What would be the effects of the above on Dove's taxable income for 2008 and 2009?
    b. Same as (a), except Dove had $1.1 million accumulated cost under the contract at the end of 2008.

47. Rust Company is a real estate construction company with average annual gross receipts of $4 million. Rust uses the completed contract method, and the contracts require 18 months to complete. *Communications*
    a. Which of the following costs would be allocated to construction in progress by Rust?
       1. The payroll taxes on direct labor.
       2. The current services pension costs for employees whose wages are included in direct labor.
       3. Accelerated depreciation on equipment used on contracts.
       4. Freight charges on materials assigned to contracts.
       5. The past service costs for employees whose wages are included in direct labor.
       6. Bidding expenses for contracts awarded.
    b. Assume that Rust generally builds commercial buildings under contracts with the owners and reports the income by the completed contract method. The company is considering building a series of similar stores for a retail chain. The gross profit margin would be a low percentage, but the company's gross receipts would triple. Write a letter to your client, Rust Company, explaining the tax accounting implications of entering into these contracts. Rust's mailing address is P.O. Box 1000, Harrisonburg, VA 22807.

48. Explain why the taxpayer may not be required to use the percentage of completion method in each of the following situations:
    a. The taxpayer agrees to build six aircraft. It takes six months to complete each aircraft, the price is $1.5 million per aircraft, and it will take 18 months to complete all six aircraft.
    b. A contract to produce and sell hot dogs at the Superbowl for the next two years.
    c. A contract to build an office building. The contractor's average annual gross receipts are approximately $3 million.

49. Ostrich Company makes gasoline storage tanks. Everything produced is under contract (that is, the company does not produce until it gets a contract for a product). Ostrich makes three basic models. However, the tanks must be adapted to each individual customer's location and needs (e.g., the location of the valves, the quality of the materials and insulation). Discuss the following issues relative to Ostrich's operations:

a.   An examining IRS agent contends that each of the company's contracts is to pro-duce a "unique product." What difference does it make whether the product is unique or a "shelf item"?

b.   Producing one of the tanks takes over one year from start to completion, and the total cost is in excess of $1 million. What costs must be capitalized for this contract that are not subject to capitalization for a contract with a shorter duration and lower cost?

c.   What must Ostrich do with the costs of bidding on contracts?

d.   Ostrich frequently makes several cost estimates for a contract, using various esti-mates of materials costs. These costs fluctuate almost daily. Assuming Ostrich must use the percentage of completion method to report the income from the contract, what will be the consequence if the company uses the highest estimate of a con-tract's cost and the actual cost is closer to the lowest estimated cost?

Communications

50. Swallow Company is a large real estate construction company that reports its income by the percentage of completion method. In 2009, the company completed a contract at a total cost of $1.9 million. The contract price was $2.4 million. At the end of 2008, the year the contract was begun, Swallow estimated the total cost of the contract would be $2.1 million, and total accumulated costs on the contract at the end of 2008 were $1.4 million. The relevant tax rate is 34%, and the relevant Federal interest rate is 7%. Assume that all returns were filed and taxes were paid on March 15 following the close of the calendar tax year.

a.   Compute the gross profit on the contract for 2008 and 2009.

b.   Compute the lookback interest due with the 2009 return.

c.   Before bidding on a contract, Swallow generally makes three estimates of total contract costs: (1) optimistic, (2) pessimistic, and (3) most likely (based on a blend-ing of optimistic and pessimistic assumptions). The company has asked you to write a letter explaining which of these estimates should be used for percentage of completion purposes. In writing your letter, you should consider the fact that Swallow is incorporated and has made an S corporation election; therefore, the income and deductions flow through to the shareholders who are all individuals in the 35% marginal tax bracket. The relevant Federal interest rate is 8%. Swallow's mailing address is 400 Front Avenue, Ashland, OR 97520.

51. Bluebird Company is a furniture retailer whose average annual gross receipts for the three preceding years exceeded $10 million. In the current tax year, the company purchased merchandise with an invoice price of $12 million, less a 2% discount for early payment. However, the company had to borrow on a bank line of credit to take advantage of the discount for early payment. Freight on the merchandise totaled $360,000. The company has three stores and operates a warehouse where it stores goods. The cost of operating the warehouse was $300,000. The $300,000 includes labor, depreciation, taxes, and insurance on the building. The cost of the purchasing operations totaled $420,000. The jurisdiction where the company operates imposes a tax on inventories on hand as of January 1. The inventory tax for this year is $24,000. The invoice cost of goods on hand at the end of the year is $3 million. Compute Bluebird's ending inventory using the FIFO method.

Decision Making

52. Lavender Manufacturing Company began business in the current year. The company uses the simplified method to allocate mixed services costs to production. The company's costs and expenses for the year were as follows:

Direct labor	$1,750,000
Direct materials	2,500,000
Factory supervision	400,000
Personnel department	125,000
Computer operations	120,000
General administration	150,000
Marketing	100,000
Interest	25,000
	$5,170,000

a. Determine Lavender's total production costs for the year.
b. What suggestions can you offer regarding the allocation of the company's mixed services costs?

53. Silver Creek Ranch, LLC, is a small, family-owned cattle ranch that began operations in the current year. The ranch will grow hay that will be fed to its purebred cattle. It will take approximately three years to build up the herd and to begin producing a positive cash flow. The owners' other income will equal their deductions, so they will not be able to utilize farm losses for the first three years. The owners have asked you to discuss the tax accounting issues related to their cattle business.

Issue ID

54. In 2008, Gail changed from the lower of cost or market FIFO method to the LIFO inventory method. The ending inventory for 2007 was computed as follows:

Item	FIFO Cost	Replacement Cost	Lower of Cost or Market
A	$21,000	$15,000	$15,000
B	50,000	55,000	50,000
C	30,000	6,000	6,000
			$71,000

Item C was damaged goods, and the replacement cost used was actually the estimated selling price of the goods. The actual cost to replace item C was $32,000.
a. What is the correct beginning inventory for 2008 under the LIFO method?
b. What immediate tax consequences (if any) will result from the switch to LIFO?

55. Wren Manufacturing Company's 2008 Federal income tax return was examined by an IRS agent. One of the proposed adjustments was for the $140,000 cost of rebuilding some production equipment. Wren deducted the $140,000 as a repair expense, but the agent thinks the cost should be capitalized and depreciated as seven-year property. What would be the consequences of the agent's adjustment under the following circumstances?
a. The taxpayer uses the FIFO inventory method, and 25% of goods produced during the period were included in the ending inventory.
b. The taxpayer uses the LIFO inventory method, and no new LIFO layer was added during the current year.

56. Amber Company has used the dollar-value LIFO technique for the past three years. The company has only one inventory pool. Its beginning inventory for the current year was computed as follows:

	Base Period Cost	LIFO Index	LIFO Layer
Base inventory	$1,250,000	1.0	$1,250,000
Year 1 layer	500,000	1.05	525,000
Year 2 layer	200,000	1.08	216,000
	$1,950,000		$1,991,000

The ending inventory is $1,955,000 at current period prices and $1,750,000 at base period prices. Determine the company's LIFO inventory value as of the end of the current year.

57. Your client, Bob Young, is negotiating a sale of investment real estate for $12 million. Bob believes that the buyer would pay cash of $8 million and a note for $4 million, or $3 million cash and a note for $9 million. The notes will pay interest at slightly above the market rate. Bob realizes that the second option involves more risks of collection, but he is willing to accept that risk if the tax benefits of the installment sale are substantial. Write a letter to Bob advising him of the tax consequences of choosing the lower down payment and larger note option, assuming he has no other installment receivables. Bob's address is 200 Jerdone, Gettysburg, PA 17325.

Decision Making

Communications

RESEARCH PROBLEMS

Note: Solutions to Research Problems can be prepared by using the **RIA Checkpoint®
Student Edition** online research product, which is available to accompany this text. It is
also possible to prepare solutions to the Research Problems by using tax research materials found in a standard tax library.

Research Problem 1.   Your client is not permitted to deduct a year-end accrual for vacation
pay earned but not paid. This result occurs because the tax law considers this to be
deferred compensation that is ineligible for the recurring item exception, unless it is paid
by March 15 of the year following the accrual [see §§ 404(a)(5) and (6)]. Your client has
asked whether the related accrued Social Security taxes on the vacation pay can be
accrued under the general recurring item exception because these taxes will be paid by
the fifteenth day of the ninth month after the close of the tax year.

Research Problem 2.   Your client is an accrual basis taxpayer. For 2008 the company had a
$600,000 net operating loss, which can be carried back to 2006. The loss can also be
carried back to the 2006 state income tax return and will create a $36,000 refund of state
income taxes for that year. The IRS agent insists that the state income tax refund must be
included in 2008 gross income (under the tax benefit rule) and thus will reduce the 2008
Federal income tax loss available for carryback by $36,000. When does the income from
the state tax refund accrue?

Research Problem 3.   Your client is a small business with average annual gross receipts of
$5 million. The company sells shirts with team emblems. The client surveys customers
to estimate the demand for different kinds and sizes of shirts. Then the client contracts to
have the shirts produced by a local print screen operator who buys the shirts and adds the
emblems. The client would like to know whether the company is subject to the uniform
capitalization requirements for its inventory.

Research Problem 4.   Your client is a manufacturer. For several years, the company buried
empty paint cans on its property. The paint was used in the production process. Recently,
a state environmental agency informed the company that it was required to dig up the
paint cans and decontaminate the land. The company spent a substantial amount for this
environmental cleanup in the current year. An IRS agent contends that the cost must be
added to the basis in the land because the cleanup improved the land. The company's
CFO has asked you to determine if any authority exists that would support a current
deduction for these costs.

Research Problem 5.   In 2008, your client, Clear Corporation, changed from the cash to the
accrual method of accounting for its radio station. The company had a positive § 481
adjustment of $2.4 million as a result of the change and began amortizing the adjustment
in 2008. In 2009, Clear received an offer to purchase the assets of the radio station
business (this would be considered a sale of a trade or business under § 1060). If the offer
is accepted, Clear plans to purchase a satellite television business. Clear has asked you to
explain the consequences of the sale of the radio station on the amortization of the § 481
adjustment.

**Internet
Activity**

Use the tax resources of the Internet to address the following questions. Do not restrict
your search to the World Wide Web, but include a review of newsgroups and general
reference materials, practitioner sites and resources, primary sources of the tax law,
chat rooms and discussion groups, and other opportunities.

Research Problem 6.   What tax form is used to compute the lookback interest income or
expense under the percentage of completion method for long-term contracts?

Research Problem 7.   Use the Internet to determine which countries in the European
Union permit the use of the LIFO inventory method to compute taxable income.

CHAPTER 19

Deferred Compensation

LEARNING OBJECTIVES

After completing Chapter 19, you should be able to:

LO.1

Distinguish between qualified (defined contribution and defined benefit) and nonqualified compensation arrangements.

LO.2

Identify the qualification requirements for qualified plans.

LO.3

Discuss the tax consequences of qualified plans.

LO.4

Calculate the limitations on contributions to and benefits from qualified plans.

LO.5

Understand the qualified plan (Keogh plan) available to a self-employed person.

LO.6

Describe the benefits of the different types of Individual Retirement Accounts (IRAs).

LO.7

Understand the rationale for nonqualified deferred compensation plans and the related tax treatment.

LO.8

Explain the value of restricted property plans.

LO.9

Differentiate the tax treatment of qualified and nonqualified stock options.

LO.10

Identify tax planning opportunities available with deferred compensation.

OUTLINE

Qualified Pension, Profit Sharing, and Stock Bonus Plans, 19–4
Types of Plans, 19–4
Qualification Requirements, 19–7
Tax Consequences to the Employee and
    Employer, 19–12
Limitations on Contributions to and Benefits from
    Qualified Plans, 19–13
§ 401(k) Plans, 19–15

Retirement Plans for Self-Employed Individuals, 19–19
Coverage Requirements, 19–19
Contribution Limitations, 19–19

Individual Retirement Accounts (IRAs), 19–20
General Rules, 19–20
Penalty Taxes for Excess Contributions, 19–26
Taxation of Benefits, 19–26

Nonqualified Deferred Compensation Plans, 19–29
Underlying Rationale for Tax Treatment, 19–29
Tax Treatment to the Employer and Employee, 19–30

Restricted Property Plans, 19–33
General Provisions, 19–33
Substantial Risk of Forfeiture, 19–34
Special Election Available, 19–34
Employer Deductions, 19–35

Stock Options, 19–36
In General, 19–36
Incentive Stock Options, 19–36
Nonqualified Stock Options, 19–38

Tax Planning Considerations, 19–39
Deferred Compensation, 19–39
Qualified Plans, 19–40
Self-Employed Retirement Plans, 19–40
Individual Retirement Accounts, 19–40
Comparison of § 401(k) Plan with IRA, 19–40
Nonqualified Deferred Compensation (NQDC)
    Plans, 19–41
Stock Options, 19–42
Flexible Benefit Plans, 19–43
Liquidating Retirement Assets, 19–43

Compensation is important in any type of organization. If you have not chosen a career, consider becoming a professional golfer, basketball player, or boxer. According to *Sports Illustrated*,[1] half of the 50 top-earning American athletes in 2007 were basketball players, along with 12 baseball players, 5 football players, and 3 NASCAR drivers. But golfer Tiger Woods with $112 million was at the top of the list followed by boxer Oscar De La Hoya. The average National Football League player earned about one-third as much as the average NBA player. In order, the top 10 athletes were as follows:

1. Tiger Woods, $112 million.
2. Oscar De La Hoya, $55 million.
3. Golfer Phil Mickelson, $51 million.
4. Miami Heat's Shaquille O'Neal, $35 million.
5. L.A. Lakers' Kobe Bryant, $34 million.
6. Cleveland Cavaliers' LeBron James, $31 million.
7. Minnesota Timberwolves' Kevin Garnett, $29 million.
8. N.Y. Yankees' Derek Jeter, $29 million.
9. N.Y. Yankees' Alex Rodriguez, $28 million.
10. Auto racer Dale Earnhardt Jr., $27 million.

For comparison, a second lieutenant in the U.S. Army receives approximately $45,000 (after factoring in the exclusion benefit for the meal and housing allowance), and an entry-level accountant earns approximately $55,000.

Compensation, however, whether in sports or otherwise does not guarantee commensurate performance. Consider the salary (plus bonus) and actual performance of the five top running backs in terms of rushing yards in the National Football League in 2006:

---

[1]Adapted from Jonah Freedman, SI.com, 2007.

Players	Total Salary	Touchdowns	Rushing Yards	Cost per Yard Gained	Cost per Touchdown
1. LaDainian Tomlinson (16)*	$6,317,436	28	1,815	$3,481	$225,623
2. Larry Johnson (16)*	791,000	17	1,789	442	46,529
3. Frank Gore (16)*	353,300	8	1,695	208	44,162
4. Tiki Barber (16)*	4,250,000	5	1,662	2,557	850,000
5. Steven Jackson (16)*	502,500	13	1,528	329	38,654

*Number of games played.

Thus, based on cost per yard gained, the San Francisco 49ers' Frank Gore at $208 per yard was most effective, followed by the St. Louis Rams' Steven Jackson at $329 per yard. Of these two, Jackson was more effective on a per touchdown basis. The San Diego Chargers' LaDainian Tomlinson scored more touchdowns, but his high salary caused his cost per touchdown to remain high. The N.Y. Giants' Tiki Barber also had bad numbers when compared to his salary, which may help explain why he retired at the end of the 2006 season.

Before you decide to give up your future career in accounting, education, or the military and jump into major league sports, also consider the tax consequences. A professional athlete's lifetime sports income is compressed into about 10 years. For example, tennis star Pete Sampras, a 14-time Grand Slam winner, retired in 2003 at the age of 32. Andre Agassi, another tennis star, retired in 2006 at age 36. Yet income averaging is not allowed for Federal income tax purposes. As a result, the athlete will lose a larger portion of lifetime earned income in the form of taxes than someone with a comparable amount of earned income over a typical work/life cycle. The athlete does, however, have a method available for reducing the Federal income tax liability in the form of deferred compensation.

This chapter discusses the various types of deferred compensation arrangements available to employees and self-employed individuals. With **deferred compensation**, an employee receives compensation for services in a later period than that in which the services were performed—quite often during retirement years. The tax law encourages employers to offer deferred compensation plans to their employees to supplement the Federal Social Security retirement system.

Qualified deferred compensation plans receive particularly favorable tax treatment. The amounts that may be deferred under these plans are limited, so they might not be perfect for Tiger Woods or Oscar De La Hoya. For employers and more traditional employees, however, they provide tax advantages that are exceedingly helpful. For example, contributors to qualified pension, profit sharing, or stock bonus plans receive three major tax advantages:

- Contributions are immediately deductible by the employer.
- Employees are not taxed until these funds are distributed to them.
- Income earned by the plan trust, which has received the contributions, is not subject to tax until made available to the employees, and thus grows at a tax-free rate.
- Employer contributions to and benefits payable under qualified plans generally are not subject to FICA and FUTA taxes.

Compared to nonqualified plans, though, qualified plans have some disadvantages including the following:

- The employer must make contributions for most employees on a nondiscriminatory basis.
- There are a number of limits on contributions to defined contribution plans and on benefits that may be paid under defined benefit plans.
- Qualified plans have higher startup and administrative costs.

A variety of deferred compensation arrangements are being offered to employees, including the following:

- Qualified profit sharing plans.
- Qualified pension plans.
- Cash or deferred arrangement plans.
- SIMPLE IRAs and § 401(k) plans.
- Tax-deferred annuities.
- Incentive stock option plans.
- Nonqualified deferred compensation plans.
- Restricted property plans.
- Cafeteria benefit plans.
- Employee stock purchase plans.

In addition to the various types of deferred compensation, employees may receive other valuable fringe benefits, some of which may be tax-free. Examples of such benefits include group term life insurance, medical reimbursement plans, company-supplied automobiles, education expense reimbursement plans, qualified transportation benefits, and group legal services.[2]

LO.1

Distinguish between qualified (defined contribution and defined benefit) and nonqualified compensation arrangements.

Qualified Pension, Profit Sharing, and Stock Bonus Plans

To ensure that retired people will not be dependent solely on government programs, the Federal government encourages private pension and profit sharing plans. Therefore, the Federal tax law provides substantial tax benefits for plans that meet certain requirements (qualified plans). The major requirement for qualification is that a plan not discriminate in favor of highly compensated employees.

Types of Plans

Qualified plans can be conveniently divided into four groups: pension, profit sharing, stock bonus, and cash balance plans.

Pension Plans. A **pension plan** is a deferred compensation arrangement that provides for systematic payments of definitely determinable retirement benefits to employees who meet the requirements set forth in the plan. Employer contributions under a qualified pension plan must *not* depend on profits. A pension plan normally must pay benefits out as lifetime annuities to provide retirement income to retired employees.

There are basically two types of qualified pension plans: defined benefit plans and defined contribution plans.

A **defined benefit plan** includes a formula that defines the benefits employees are to receive.[3] Benefits are generally measured by and based on such factors as years of service and employee compensation. Under such a plan, an employer must

---

[2]Refer to the discussions in Chapters 4 and 5.   [3]§ 414(j).

TAX *in the News*   COMPENSATION AND PERFORMANCE

When one or several employees have huge salaries compared to the other employees, the business may not succeed in achieving its mission. Matt Bloom, a management professor at the University of Notre Dame, says that the bigger the pay difference between a Major League Baseball team's stars and scrubs, the worse its record. According to Bloom, more parity in performance pay will result in a better baseball team. Big pay differentials sow the seeds of discord rather than promoting team unity.

An interesting measure of performance for a Major League Baseball team is its "payroll cost per win" for the regular season. The results for some teams may be surprising. For the eight teams making the playoffs in 2007, the "payroll cost per win" was as follows (with their payroll ranking in brackets):

Arizona Diamondbacks (26th)	$ 578,528
Colorado Rockies (25th)	604,711
Cleveland Indians (23rd)	642,430
Philadelphia Phillies (13th)	1,004,811
Chicago Cubs (8th)	$1,172,592
Los Angeles Angels (4th)	1,162,248
Boston Red Sox (2nd)	1,490,231
New York Yankees (1st)	2,017,436

Five of the top 13 payroll teams made the playoffs, but three of the bottom 8 teams also made the playoffs (out of a total of 30 teams). The highly efficient Rockies and the second highest "payroll cost per win" Red Sox made it to the World Series. The highly paid Red Sox (with a total payroll of $143 million) swept the Cinderella Rockies (with a total payroll of only $53 million) in four straight games. The salaries of just 4 Red Sox players amounted to more than the total for the entire 25-player Rockies' team.

Some of the big spenders per win did not make it to the playoffs—the New York Mets ($1,309,451) and Chicago White Sox ($1,509,331).

Source: *Adapted from Gordon Fairclough, "Listen Up, Managers; Fat Paychecks Don't Always Guarantee Success," The Wall Street Journal, March 23, 1999, p. B1.*

make annual contributions based upon actuarial computations that will be sufficient to fund the retirement benefits. If a plan document permits, employees may make contributions to the pension fund. A separate account is not maintained for each participant. A defined benefit plan provides some sense of security for employees since the benefits may be expressed in fixed dollar amounts. In a defined benefit plan, the employer (not the employee) assumes the market risk because the employer promises to pay fixed benefits. Since an expense is not deductible for tax purposes until paid, there often will be a book-tax difference because the employer accounts for the expense on an accrual basis for accounting purposes.

A **defined contribution pension plan** (or money purchase plan) defines the amount the employer is required to contribute (e.g., a flat dollar amount, an amount based on a special formula, or an amount equal to a certain percentage of compensation). A separate account must be maintained for each participant. Benefits are based solely on (1) the amount contributed and (2) income from the fund that accrues to the participant's account.[4] Consequently, actuarial calculations are not required to determine the employer's annual contribution. Upon retirement, an employee's pension amount depends on the value of his or her account. Although it is not mandatory, a plan may require or permit employee contributions to the pension fund. Since employers record the expense for both tax and accounting purposes when funding an employee's account, book-tax differences do not often occur.

---

[4]§ 414(i).

CONCEPT SUMMARY 19–1

Defined Benefit Plan and Defined Contribution Plan Compared

Defined Benefit Plan	Defined Contribution Plan
Includes a pension plan.	Includes profit sharing, stock bonus, money purchase, target benefit, qualified cash or deferred compensation, employee stock ownership plans, and some pension plans.
Determinable benefits based upon years of service and average compensation. Benefits calculated by a formula.	An account for each participant. Ultimate benefits depend upon contributions and investment performance.
Maximum annual *benefits* payable may not exceed the smaller of (1) $185,000 (in 2008)* or (2) 100% of the participant's average earnings in the three highest years of employment.	Maximum annual *contribution* to an account may not exceed the smaller of (1) $46,000** (in 2008) or (2) 100% of the participant's compensation (25% for a profit sharing plan, money purchase plan, or stock bonus plan).
Employer bears the investment risk and reward.	Employee bears the investment risk and reward.
Forfeitures must reduce subsequent funding costs and cannot increase the benefits any participant can receive under the plan.	Forfeitures may be allocated to the accounts of remaining participants.
Subject to minimum funding requirement in order to avoid penalties.	Exempt from funding requirements.
Greater administrative and actuarial costs and greater reporting requirements.	Costs and reporting requirements less burdensome.
Subject to Pension Benefit Guaranty Corporation (PBGC) plan termination insurance rules.	Not subject to PBGC plan termination insurance rules.
More favorable to employees who are older when plan is adopted since it is possible to fund higher benefits over a shorter period.	More favorable to younger employees since, over a longer period, higher benefits may result.

*This amount is subject to indexing annually in $5,000 increments.

**This amount is subject to indexing annually in $1,000 increments.

EXAMPLE 1

The qualified pension plan of Rose Company calls for both the employer and the employee to contribute annually to the pension trust an amount equal to 5% of the employee's compensation. Since the employer's rate of contribution is fixed, this pension plan is a defined contribution plan. If the plan called for contributions sufficient to provide retirement benefits equal to 30% of the employee's average salary for the last five years of employment, it would be a defined benefit plan. ■

Concept Summary 19–1 compares and contrasts a defined benefit plan and a defined contribution plan.

Profit Sharing Plans. A **profit sharing plan** is a deferred compensation arrangement established and maintained by an employer to provide for employee participation in the company's profits. Contributions are paid from the employer to a trustee and are commingled in a single trust fund. Despite the name, an employer does not have to have current or accumulated profits to make a contribution. The contribution formula can be based on compensation, earnings, gross sales, or any other measurement chosen by the employer.

In a profit sharing plan, a separate account is maintained for each participant. The plan must provide a definite, predetermined formula for allocating the contributions made to the trustee among the participants. Likewise, it must include a definite, predetermined formula for distributing the accumulated funds after a fixed number of years, on the attainment of a stated age, or on the occurrence of certain events such as illness, layoff, retirement, or termination of the plan. A company is not required to contribute a definite, predetermined amount to the plan every year, although substantial and recurring contributions must be made to meet the permanency requirement. Forfeitures arising under this plan may be used to increase the individual accounts of the remaining participants as long as these increases do not result in prohibited discrimination.[5] Benefits to employees may normally be distributed through lump-sum payouts in a profit sharing plan. A § 401(k) cash or deferred arrangement plan is the most common type of profit sharing plan.

Stock Bonus Plans. A **stock bonus plan** is another form of deferred compensation. The employer establishes and maintains the plan in order to contribute shares of its stock. The contributions need not be dependent on the employer's profits. A stock bonus plan is subject to the same requirements as a profit sharing plan for purposes of allocating and distributing the stock among the employees.[6] Also, as with profit sharing plans, benefits are paid out of each separate account, and participants bear the investment risks and rewards. Any benefits of the plan normally are distributable in the form of stock of the employer company, except that distributable fractional shares may be paid in cash. Employee stock ownership plans (ESOPs) may be either profit sharing or stock bonus plans.

Cash Balance Plans. A **cash balance plan** is a controversial hybrid form of pension plan that is similar in many aspects to a defined benefit plan. These plans are funded by the employer, and the employer bears the investment risks and rewards. Thus, the employer bears the mortality risk if an employee elects to receive benefits in the form of a lifetime annuity and lives beyond normal life expectancy. But like defined contribution plans, a cash balance plan accrues benefits to individual accounts. The benefits for an employee depend on how much builds up over time in the employee's account and not on a formula based on years of service and preretirement pay. Cash balance plans are better for younger, mobile employees, and the companies save money by reducing pension payouts for older and longer-service employees.

ETHICAL and EQUITABLE *Considerations*

DO CASH BALANCE PLANS DISCRIMINATE AGAINST OLDER EMPLOYEES?

Older employees often suffer under both state and Federal laws when employers convert traditional pension plans to cash balance plans. Under a traditional pension plan, a company adopts a formula that calculates pension benefits by multiplying years of service by a factor based on average salary, which causes benefits to escalate rapidly in value in later years. Should companies be allowed to reduce a long-term employee's expected benefits significantly by converting to a cash balance plan?

Qualification Requirements

LO.2

Identify the qualification requirements for qualified plans.

To be *qualified*, and thereby to receive favorable tax treatment, a plan generally must satisfy the following requirements:

- Exclusive benefit requirement.
- Nondiscrimination requirements.

---

[5]Reg. §§ 1.401–1(b) and 1.401–4(a)(1)(iii).   [6]Reg. § 1.401–1(b)(1)(iii).

- Participation and coverage requirements.
- Vesting requirements.
- Distribution requirements.
- Minimum funding requirements.

These qualification rules are highly technical and numerous. As a result, the IRS maintains a staggered determination letter request process that allows plan sponsors to file a plan document with the IRS for approval. A favorable determination letter (similar to a letter ruling) indicates that the form of the plan meets the qualification requirements and that the form of the plan's trust meets the requirements for exemption. However, the ultimate qualification of the plan depends upon its actual administration and operations. Therefore, the operations of the plan should be reviewed periodically. Favorable determination letters have an expiration date with individually designed plans on a five-year schedule and preapproved plans on a six-year schedule.

The IRS has an Employee Plans Compliance Resolution System (EPCRS) that allows sponsors of retirement plans to correct failures to satisfy requirements for a period of time. By using this system to correct failures, plan sponsors can avoid disqualification and continue to provide employees with retirement benefits on a taxfavored basis. The components of EPCRS include the Self-Correction Program (SCP), the Voluntary Correction Program (VCP), and the Audit Closing Agreement Program (Audit CAP).

Nondiscrimination Requirements. The contributions and benefits under a plan must *not discriminate* in favor of highly compensated employees. A plan is not considered discriminatory merely because contributions and benefits are proportional to compensation.[7] For example, a pension plan that provides for the allocation of employer contributions based upon a flat 3 percent of each employee's compensation would not be discriminatory solely because highly paid employees receive greater benefits.

Participation and Coverage Requirements. A qualified plan must provide, at a minimum, that all employees in the covered group who are 21 years of age are eligible to participate after completing one year of service. A year of service is generally defined as the completion of 1,000 hours of service within a measuring period of 12 consecutive months. As an alternative, where the plan provides that 100 percent of an employee's accrued benefits will be vested upon entering the plan, the employee's participation may be postponed until the later of age 21 or two years from the date of employment. Once the age and service requirements are met, an employee must begin participating no later than the *earlier* of the following:

- The first day of the first plan year beginning after the date on which the requirements were satisfied.
- Six months after the date on which the requirements were satisfied.[8]

| EXAMPLE 2 | Coffee Corporation has a calendar year retirement plan covering its employees. The corporation adopts the most restrictive eligibility rules permitted. Wilma, age 21, is hired on January 31, 2007, and meets the service requirement over the next 12 months (completes at least 1,000 hours by January 31, 2008). Wilma must be included in this plan no later than July 31, 2008, because the six-month limitation would be applicable. If the company had adopted the two-year participation rule, Wilma must be included in the plan no later than July 31, 2009. ∎ |

---

[7]§§ 401(a)(4) and (5).   [8]§§ 410(a)(1)(A) and (B) and 410(a)(4).

Since a qualified plan must be primarily for the benefit of employees and be nondiscriminatory, the plan has to cover a reasonable percentage of the company employees. A plan will be qualified only if it satisfies one of the following tests:[9]

- The plan benefits a percentage of non-highly compensated employees equal to at least 70 percent of the percentage of highly compensated employees benefiting under the plan (the *ratio percentage test*).
- The plan meets the *average benefits test*, which is described below.

If a company has no highly compensated employees, the retirement plan will automatically satisfy the coverage rules.

To satisfy the *average benefits test*, the plan must benefit any employees who qualify under a classification set up by the employer and found by the Secretary of the Treasury not to be discriminatory in favor of highly compensated employees (the classification test). In addition, the average benefit percentage for non-highly compensated employees must be at least 70 percent of the average benefit percentage for highly compensated employees. The *average benefit percentage* means, with respect to any group of employees, the average of the benefit percentages calculated separately for each employee in the group. The term *benefit percentage* means the employer-provided contributions (including forfeitures) or benefits of an employee under all qualified plans of the employer, expressed as a percentage of that employee's compensation.

An employee is a **highly compensated employee** if, at any time during the year or the preceding year, the employee satisfies *either* of the following:[10]

- Was a 5 percent owner of the company.
- Received more than $105,000 (in 2008) in annual compensation from the employer *and* was a member of the top-paid group of the employer.[11] The top-paid group clause is applicable only if the employer elects to have it apply. An employee whose compensation is in the top 20 percent of the employees is a member of the top-paid group.

An additional *minimum participation test* must also be met for some plans. A plan must cover at least 40 percent of all employees or, if fewer, at least 50 employees on one representative day of the plan year. In determining all employees, nonresident aliens, certain union members, and employees not fulfilling the minimum age or years-of-service requirement of the plan may be excluded.[12]

E X A M P L E   3

Assume that Rust Corporation's retirement plan automatically meets the 70% test (the ratio percentage test) because 70% of all non-highly compensated employees benefit. The company has 100 employees, but only 38 of these employees are covered by the plan. Therefore, this retirement plan does not meet the minimum participation requirement. ■

Vesting Requirements. The purpose of the **vesting requirements** is to protect an employee who has worked a reasonable period of time for an employer from losing employer contributions because of being fired or changing jobs. An employee's right to accrued benefits derived from his or her own contributions to a defined benefit plan must be nonforfeitable from the date of contribution. The accrued benefits derived from employer contributions must be nonforfeitable in accordance with one of *two alternative minimum vesting schedules* or an even more generous vesting schedule.

To satisfy the *first alternative*, a participant must have a nonforfeitable right to 100 percent of his or her accrued benefits derived from employer contributions upon completion of not more than five years of service (five-year or cliff vesting).

---

[9]§ 410(b).
[10]§§ 401(a)(4) and 414(q).
[11]The $105,000 amount is indexed annually in $5,000 increments.
[12]§§ 401(a)(26) and 410(b)(3) and (4).

TABLE 19–1	Three- to Seven-Year Vesting

Years of Service	Nonforfeitable Percentage
3	20%
4	40%
5	60%
6	80%
7 or more	100%

TABLE 19–2	Two- to Six-Year Vesting

Years of Service	Nonforfeitable Percentage
2	20%
3	40%
4	60%
5	80%
6 or more	100%

The *second alternative* is satisfied if a participant has a nonforfeitable right at least equal to a percentage of the accrued benefits derived from employer contributions as depicted in Table 19–1 (graded vesting). Of the two alternatives, cliff vesting minimizes administration expenses for a company and provides more vesting for a long-term employee.

EXAMPLE 4

Mitch has six years of service completed as of February 2, 2008, his employment anniversary date. If his defined benefit plan has a five-year (cliff) vesting schedule, 100% of Mitch's accrued benefits are vested. If the plan uses the graded vesting rule, Mitch's nonforfeitable percentage is 80%. ∎

After 2006, defined contribution plans also must satisfy one of the following minimum vesting schedules: two- to six-year graded vesting as shown in Table 19–2, three-year cliff vesting, or an even more generous vesting schedule.

EXAMPLE 5

Millie has five years of service completed as of February 2, 2008, her employment anniversary date. If her defined contribution plan uses three-year cliff vesting, Millie must be 100% vested. Under a two- to six-year vesting plan, Millie must be 80% vested. ∎

Distribution Requirements. Uniform *minimum distribution rules* exist for all qualified defined benefit and defined contribution plans, traditional Individual Retirement Accounts (IRAs) and annuities, unfunded deferred compensation plans of state and local governments and tax-exempt employers, and tax-sheltered custodial accounts and annuities. Distributions to a participant must begin by April 1 of the calendar year *following the later* of (1) the calendar year in which the employee attains age 70½ or (2) the calendar year in which the employee retires. Thus, an employee can delay receiving distributions until retirement. However, distributions to a 5 percent owner or a traditional IRA holder must begin no later than April 1 of the calendar year *following* the year in which the 5 percent owner or the IRA holder

TAX *in the News*   DEFINED BENEFIT PLANS DECLINING?

The Pension Protection Act of 2006 will probably not stem the decline of defined benefit pension plans as large companies end them or freeze their benefits. Northwest Airlines, Delta Airlines, Motorola, Inc., and Hewlett-Packard are only a few of the companies freezing benefits. Companies freeze benefits by locking out new employees or halting new enrollments and stopping the accrual of benefits to current employees.

Other companies will follow IBM, which converted its defined benefit plan into a cash balance plan. Maintaining a defined benefit plan is expensive, and a hard freeze can reduce the expected annual retirement benefits to an employee by more than one-half.

Ironically, as larger companies eliminate their defined benefit plans, sole practitioners and small-business owners—attorneys, doctors, consultants—are adopting them. Defined benefit plans are attractive for a business with few or no employees or a young, low-paid, transient staff.

Adapted from S. D. Jones, "Pensions Likely to Stay Dying Breed," The Wall Street Journal, August 29, 2006, p. C3; T. S. Bernard, "A Rapid Build-up," The Wall Street Journal, May 8, 2006, p. R4.

---

reaches age 70½.[13] A holder of a Roth IRA does *not* have to take a distribution by April 1 of the calendar year following the calendar year in which the holder attains age 70½. That is, the holder of a Roth IRA is not required to begin receiving distributions at any point in time during his or her life.

Minimum annual distributions must be made over the life of the participant or the lives of the participant and a designated individual beneficiary. The amount of the required minimum distribution for a particular year is determined by dividing the account balance as of December 31 of the prior year by the applicable life expectancy. The life expectancy of the owner and his or her beneficiary is based upon the expected return multiples in the Regulations, using ages attained within the calendar year the participant reaches age 70½.[14]

EXAMPLE 6

Beth reaches age 70½ in 2008, and she will also be age 71 in 2008. Her retirement account has a balance of $120,000 on December 31, 2007. If Beth is retired, a 5% owner, or the holder of a traditional IRA, she must withdraw $7,843 for the 2008 calendar year, assuming her multiple is 15.3 ($120,000 ÷ 15.3). This distribution need not be made until April 1, 2009, but a second distribution must be made by December 31, 2009. ■

Failure to make a minimum required distribution to a particular participant results in a *50 percent nondeductible excise tax* on the excess in any taxable year of the amount that should have been distributed over the amount that actually was distributed. The tax is imposed on the individual required to take the distribution (the payee).[15] The Secretary of the Treasury is authorized to waive the tax for a given taxpayer year if the taxpayer is able to establish that the shortfall is due to reasonable error and that reasonable steps are being taken to remedy the shortfall.

If a taxpayer receives an *early distribution* from a qualified retirement plan, a 10 percent additional tax is levied on the full amount of any distribution includible in gross income.[16] For this purpose, the term *qualified retirement plan* includes a qualified defined benefit plan or defined contribution plan, a tax-sheltered annuity or custodial account, or a traditional IRA. The following distributions, however, are *not* treated as early distributions:

- Distributions made on or after the date the employee attains age 59½.
- Distributions made to a beneficiary (or the estate of an employee) on or after the death of the employee.

---

[13]§ 401(a)(9).
[14]Reg. § 1.72–9. Refer to Chapter 4.

[15]§ 4974(a).
[16]§ 72(t). See Ltr.Rul. 8837071.

GLOBAL *Tax Issues*

COVERING EXPATRIATE EMPLOYEES

Can an employer cover individuals employed outside the United States in a qualified retirement plan? This question often arises when an employee is transferred from the United States to a foreign affiliate of the employer.

The hurdle to overcome is the exclusive benefit rule in § 401(a): the qualified plan must be maintained for the exclusive benefit of the employees of the company that sponsors the plan.

If a company conducts its foreign operations through branches that are part of the U.S. entity, the employee can qualify for the plan. Likewise, all employees of all corporations that are members of a controlled group of corporations can be covered. A controlled group would include both a brother-sister group and a parent-subsidiary group.

- Distributions attributable to the employee's being disabled.
- Distributions made as part of a scheduled series of substantially equal periodic payments (made not less frequently than annually) for the life of the participant (or the joint lives of the participant and the participant's beneficiary).
- Distributions made to an employee after separation from service because of early retirement under the plan after attaining age 55. This exception to early distribution treatment does not apply to a traditional IRA.
- Distributions used to pay medical expenses to the extent that the expenses are deductible under § 213 (determined regardless of whether or not the taxpayer itemizes deductions).
- IRA distributions that are used to pay qualified higher education expenses of the taxpayer, the spouse, or any child or grandchild of the taxpayer or the taxpayer's spouse.
- IRA distributions up to $10,000 that are used to pay expenses incurred by qualified first-time home buyers.

Minimum Funding Requirements. Minimum funding requirements apply to defined benefit plans, money purchase plans, and target benefit plans to regulate the amount that an employer must contribute to ensure that the plan is properly funded. The amount of contributions required for a plan year is the amount needed to fund benefits earned during a plan year (e.g., normal costs) plus the portion of other liabilities that are amortized over a period of years (e.g., investment losses). A special account called a funding standard account is required, and contribution amounts are determined under one of several acceptable actuarial cost methods. A tax equal to 10 percent of the aggregate unpaid required contribution is imposed on a single-employer plan (5 percent for a multiemployer plan). If an accumulated funding deficit is not corrected, a 100 percent tax is imposed.[17]

LO.3

Discuss the tax consequences of qualified plans.

Tax Consequences to the Employee and Employer

In General. Although employer contributions to qualified plans are generally deductible immediately (subject to contribution and deductibility rules), these amounts are not subject to taxation until distributed to employees.[18] If benefits are paid with respect to an employee (to a creditor of the employee, a child of the employee, etc.), the benefits paid are treated as if paid to the employee. When benefits are distributed to employees, or paid with respect to an employee, the employer does not receive another deduction.

---

[17]§ 412.   [18]§ 402(a)(1).

The tax benefit to the employee amounts to a substantial tax deferral and may be viewed as an interest-free loan from the government to the trust fund. Another advantage of a qualified plan is that any income earned by the trust is not taxable to the trust.[19] Employees, in effect, are taxed on such earnings when they receive the retirement benefits.

The taxation of amounts received by employees in periodic or installment payments is generally subject to the annuity rules in § 72 (refer to Chapter 4). In any situation where employee contributions have been subject to tax previously, they are included in the employee's *investment in the contract*. Two other alternative options generally are available for benefit distributions. A taxpayer may (1) receive the distribution in a lump-sum payment or (2) roll over the benefits into an IRA or another qualified employer retirement plan.

Lump-Sum Distributions from Qualified Plans. A **lump-sum distribution** occurs when an employee receives his or her entire payout from a qualified plan in a single payment rather than receiving the amount in installments. The annuity rules do not apply to a lump-sum distribution. All such payments are thrown into one year. Since lump-sum payments have been accumulated over a number of years, bunching retirement benefits into one taxable year may impose a high tax burden because of progressive rates. To overcome this bunching effect, for many years the tax law has provided favorable treatment for certain lump-sum distributions. Major changes were made in the lump-sum distribution rules by TRA of 1986. Transitional provisions allow a participant who reached age 50 before January 1, 1986 (born before 1936), to elect the pre-1987 rules on a limited basis. These pre-1987 rules permit a 10-year forward averaging technique and a limited capital gain allocation.[20]

Rollover Treatment. A taxpayer who receives a distribution can avoid current taxation by rolling the distribution into another qualified employer retirement plan or into an IRA.[21] The taxation of the distribution is deferred until distributions are made from the recipient's qualified employer retirement plan or IRA. The rollover can be *direct* with the balance in the account going directly from a qualified employer retirement plan to another qualified employer retirement plan or an IRA (sometimes called a conversion). The rollover can be *indirect* with the proceeds going to the taxpayer who has 60 days to transfer the proceeds into another qualified employer retirement plan or an IRA. One can use an indirect rollover to borrow from an IRA, but the "loan" must be fully reinvested in another retirement plan or IRA within the 60-day window. A benefit of the direct rollover is that it is not subject to the 20 percent withholding applicable to indirect rollovers.[22]

Limitations on Contributions to and Benefits from Qualified Plans

> **LO.4**
>
> Calculate the limitations on contributions to and benefits from qualified plans.

In General. The annual limitations on contributions to and benefits from qualified plans appearing in § 415 must be written into a qualified plan. Section 404 sets the limits on deductibility applicable to the employer. The limit on the amount deductible under § 404 may have an impact on the amount the employer is willing to contribute. In fact, a defined benefit plan or defined contribution plan is not allowed a deduction for the amount that exceeds the § 415 limitations.[23]

Defined Contribution Plans. Under a *defined contribution plan*, the annual addition to an employee's account cannot exceed the smaller of $46,000 (in 2008) or

---

[19]§ 501(a).
[20]§ 402(e)(1)(C) of the IRC of 1954.
[21]§ 402(c).

[22]§ 3405(c).
[23]§ 404(j).

100 percent of the employee's compensation.[24] However, this individual percentage limitation of 100 percent normally is not attainable for small plans because the employer's deduction limit cannot exceed 25 percent of eligible compensation for all participants. The $46,000 amount is indexed (in $1,000 increments).[25]

Defined Benefit Plans. Under a *defined benefit plan,* the annual benefit payable to an employee is limited to the smaller of $185,000 (in 2008)[26] or 100 percent of the employee's average compensation for the highest three years of employment. This benefit limit is subject to a $10,000 *de minimis* floor. The $185,000 limitation is reduced actuarially if the benefits begin before the Social Security normal retirement age (currently age 65 and 10 months) and is increased actuarially if the benefits begin after the Social Security normal retirement age. The dollar limit on annual benefits ($185,000) is reduced by one-tenth for each year of *participation* under 10 years by the employee. Furthermore, the 100 percent of compensation limitation and the $10,000 *de minimis* floor are reduced proportionately for a participant who has less than 10 years of *service* with the employer.[27]

EXAMPLE 7	Adam's average compensation for the highest three years of employment is $87,000. The defined benefit plan would not qualify if the plan provides for benefits in excess of the smaller of (1) $87,000 or (2) $185,000 for Adam in 2008 (assuming normal retirement age). ∎

EXAMPLE 8	Peggy has participated for four years in a defined benefit plan and has six years of service with her employer. Her average compensation for the three highest years is $60,000. Her four years of participation reduce her dollar limitation to $74,000 ($185,000 × ⁴⁄₁₀). Her six years of service reduce her 100% of compensation limitation to 60%. Therefore, her limit on annual benefits is $36,000 ($60,000 × 60%). ∎

The amount of compensation that may be taken into account under any plan is limited to $230,000 (in 2008).[28] Thus, the benefits highly compensated individuals receive may be smaller as a percentage of their pay than those received by non-highly compensated employees.

EXAMPLE 9	Swan Corporation has a defined contribution plan with a 10% contribution formula. An employee earning less than $230,000 in 2008 would not be affected by this includible compensation limitation. However, an employee earning $460,000 in 2008 would have only 5% of compensation allocated to his or her account because of the $230,000 limit on includible compensation. ∎

The maximum deduction a corporation is permitted for contributions to pension plans may be determined by either of two methods. First, an aggregate cost method allows an actuarially determined deduction based on a level amount, or a level percentage, of compensation over the remaining future service of covered participants. Second, the employer is permitted to deduct the so-called normal cost plus no more than 10 percent of the past service costs. The *normal cost* represents the estimated contribution required associated with work performed by employees in the current year. *Past service costs* are costs relating to the inception of the plan and costs that result from changes in the retirement plan.

The employer's contribution is deductible in the tax year such amounts are allocated or credited to the pension trust. However, both cash and accrual basis employers may defer the payment of contributions with respect to any tax year until the date fixed for filing the taxpayer's Federal income tax return for that year

---

[24]§§ 415(c) and (d).
[25]§ 415(d)(4).
[26]This amount is indexed annually in $5,000 increments.

[27]§ 415(b).
[28]§§ 401(a)(17) and 404(l). This amount is indexed in $5,000 increments.

(including extensions).[29] In effect, the corporation is allowed a deduction to the extent it is compelled to make such contributions to satisfy the funding requirement. If an amount in excess of the allowable amount is contributed in any tax year, the excess may be carried forward and deducted in succeeding tax years (to the extent the carryover plus the succeeding year's contribution does not exceed the deductible limitation for that year).[30]

E X A M P L E   1 0

During 2008, Green Corporation contributes $17,500 to its qualified pension plan. Normal cost for this year is $7,200, and the amount necessary to pay retirement benefits on behalf of employee services before 2008 is $82,000 (past service costs). The corporation's maximum deduction is $15,400. This amount consists of the $7,200 normal cost plus 10% ($8,200) of the past service costs. The corporation has a $2,100 [$17,500 (contribution) − $15,400 (deduction)] contribution carryover. ∎

E X A M P L E   1 1

Assume in the previous example that Green Corporation has normal cost of $7,200 in 2009 and contributes $10,000 to the pension trust. The corporation's maximum deduction would be $15,400. Green Corporation may deduct $12,100, composed of this year's contribution ($10,000) plus the $2,100 contribution carryover. ∎

A 10 percent excise tax is imposed on nondeductible contributions. The tax is levied on the employer making the contribution. The tax applies to nondeductible contributions for the current year and any nondeductible contributions for the preceding year that have not been eliminated by the end of the current year (as a carryover or by being returned to the employer in the current year).[31]

Profit Sharing and Stock Bonus Plan Limitations. The maximum deduction permitted to an employer each year for contributions to profit sharing and stock bonus plans is 25 percent of the compensation paid or accrued with respect to plan participants in the aggregate. The maximum amount of compensation for an employee that may be taken into account under a plan for deduction calculations or any other purposes is $230,000 (in 2008), and the maximum deduction allowed is $46,000 (in 2008). Any nondeductible excess, a so-called contribution carryover, may be carried forward indefinitely and deducted in subsequent years. The maximum deduction in any succeeding year is 25 percent of all compensation paid or accrued in the aggregate during that taxable year.[32]

§ 401(k) Plans

General. A **§ 401(k) plan** allows participants to elect either to receive up to $15,500 (in 2008)[33] in cash (taxed currently) or to have a contribution made on their behalf to a profit sharing or stock bonus plan. The plan may also be in the form of a salary-reduction agreement between an eligible participant and an employer under which a contribution will be made only if the participant elects to reduce his or her compensation or to forgo an increase in compensation.

Any pretax amount elected by the employee as a plan contribution is not includible in gross income in the year of deferral and is 100 percent vested. Any employer contributions are tax deferred until distributed, as are earnings on contributions in the plan.

---

[29]§§ 404(a)(1) and (6).
[30]§ 404(a)(1)(D).
[31]§ 4972.
[32]§§ 404(a)(3)(A) and (a)(7).

[33]§§ 402(g)(1) and (4). Starting in 2003, this amount was increased in $1,000 increments until it reached $15,000 in 2006. It is indexed in $500 increments in years after 2006. The amount was $12,000 for 2003; $13,000 for 2004; $14,000 for 2005; $15,000 for 2006; and $15,500 for 2007.

GLOBAL Tax Issues

GLOBAL REMUNERATION APPROACH

A multinational firm may find it desirable to develop a global remuneration strategy. According to Bowker Consulting International, a nonglobal remuneration approach has several disadvantages:

- U.S. compensation and benefit programs are imposed worldwide, without regard to local laws, employee expectations, and competitive practices.
- U.S. compensation and benefit programs are layered on top of local programs, resulting in a confusing and often overly generous total remuneration package.
- Perceived "U.S." philosophy and principles that might have important global application if properly communicated may be rejected in favor of local programs that do not reflect overall business objectives, performance standards, and corporate values.
- An "us against them" attitude may develop between the corporation and local employees, preventing constructive dialogue in creating and implementing an appropriate rewards structure for a particular country.

Source: *Adapted from* **http://www.bowkerconsulting.com/services**.

EXAMPLE 12

Sam participates in a § 401(k) plan of his employer. The plan permits the participants to choose between a full salary or a reduced salary where the reduction becomes a before-tax contribution to a retirement plan. Sam elects to contribute 10% of his annual compensation of $30,000 to the plan. Income taxes are paid on only $27,000. No income taxes are paid on the $3,000—or on any earnings—until it is distributed from the plan to Sam. The main benefit of a § 401(k) plan is that Sam can shift a portion of his income to a later taxable year. ∎

The maximum annual elective contribution to a § 401(k) plan is $15,500 (in 2008), but that amount is reduced dollar for dollar by other salary-reduction contributions to tax-sheltered annuities, simplified employee pension plans, and § 401(k) plans. Elective contributions in excess of the maximum limitation are taxable in the year of deferral. These amounts may be refunded from the plan tax-free before April 15 of the following year. Excess amounts not timely distributed will be double-taxed because they will be taxable in the year of distribution, even though they were included in income in the year of deferral. Annual elective contributions are also limited by complicated nondiscrimination requirements designed to encourage participation by non-highly compensated employees and by the general defined contribution plan limitations.

A person who has attained age 50 by the end of the tax year can make catch-up contributions of $1,000 for 2002, $2,000 for 2003, $3,000 for 2004, $4,000 for 2005, and $5,000 for 2006 and thereafter.[34]

EXAMPLE 13

Heather is age 57 in 2008. Heather is able to make additional catch-up elective deferrals of $1,000 for 2002 (beyond the $11,000 limit), $2,000 for 2003 (beyond the $12,000 limit), $3,000 for 2004 (beyond the $13,000 limit), $4,000 for 2005 (beyond the $14,000 limit), $5,000 for 2006 (beyond the $15,000 limit), $5,000 for 2007 (beyond the $15,500 limit), and $5,000 for 2008 (beyond the $15,500 limit). ∎

A 10 percent excise tax is imposed on the employer for excess elective deferral contributions not withdrawn from the plan within 2½ months after the close of the

---

[34]The $5,000 amount is indexed in $500 increments in 2007 and thereafter. For 2007 and 2008, the amount remains at $5,000.

plan year. The plan may lose its qualified status if these excess contributions (and any related income) are not withdrawn by the end of the plan year following the plan year in which the excess contributions were made.[35]

Carmen, age 36, is an employee of a manufacturing corporation. She defers $17,500 in a § 401(k) plan in 2008. The $2,000 excess over the $15,500 limit, along with the appropriate earnings, must be returned to Carmen by April 15, 2009. This $2,000 excess amount plus related income is taxable to her in 2008 and will be taxed again upon distribution (if made after April 15, 2009). There will be a 10% tax on Carmen's employer on any excess contributions not returned within 2½ months after the close of the plan year. ■

For self-employed individuals, matching contributions are not treated as elective contributions under a cash or deferred election.[36] Beginning in 2008, there is a qualified automatic enrollment arrangement (QAEA), whereby companies may automatically enroll employees in a § 401(k) plan with a prescribed percentage (not to exceed 10 percent) of the employee's pay automatically withdrawn from each paycheck (unless the employee elects otherwise). This stated percentage must be applied uniformly to all eligible employees.

If certain requirements are met, the plan administrator may choose the investments for the participants and be protected from liability involving investment choices. A § 401(k) plan consisting solely of contributions made under a QAEA also is exempt from the top-heavy rules.[37] Finally, after 2009, small employers may establish a combined defined benefit/§ 401(k) plan (a DB/K plan); the § 401(k) component of the DB/K plan must have automatic enrollment, with an employee being treated as having elected to make deferrals of 4 percent of pay, and must provide a minimum match of 50 percent of elective deferrals up to 4 percent of pay.[38]

SIMPLE Plans. Employers with 100 or fewer employees who do not maintain another qualified retirement plan may establish a *savings incentive match plan for employees* (SIMPLE plan).[39] The plan can be in the form of a § 401(k) plan or an IRA. A SIMPLE § 401(k) plan is not subject to the nondiscrimination rules that are normally applicable to § 401(k) plans.

All employees who received at least $5,000 in compensation from the employer during any two preceding years and who reasonably expect to receive at least $5,000 in compensation during the current year must be eligible to participate in the plan. The decision to participate is up to the employee. A self-employed individual may also participate in the plan.

The contributions made by the employee (a salary-reduction approach) must be expressed as a percentage of compensation rather than as a fixed dollar amount. The SIMPLE plan must not permit the SIMPLE elective employee contribution for the year to exceed $10,500 (in 2008).[40] The SIMPLE elective deferral limit is increased under the catch-up provision for employees age 50 and over. The amount is $500 for 2002, $1,000 for 2003, $1,500 for 2004, $2,000 for 2005, and $2,500 for 2006 and thereafter. The $2,500 amount is indexed for inflation in $500 increments beginning in 2007 (remains at $2,500 for 2007 and 2008).

Generally, the employer must either match elective employee contributions up to 3 percent of the employee's compensation or provide nonmatching contributions of 2 percent of compensation for each eligible employee. Thus, the maximum amount that may be contributed to the plan for an employee under age 50 for 2008

---

[35]§ 4979(a).

[36]Prop.Reg. § 1.401(k)–1(a)(6)(ii).

[37]§§ 401(a)(3)(G), 401(k)(8)(E), 401(k)(13), 401(m)(6)(A), 401(m)(12), and 414(w).

[38]§ 414(x) and ERISA § 210(e).

[39]§ 408(p).

[40]For 2004, the limit was $9,000. The $10,000 amount for 2005 is indexed for inflation in $500 increments in 2006 and thereafter. For 2006, the amount remained at $10,000. For 2007, it increased to $10,500. § 408(p)(2)(E)(i).

is $17,400 [$10,500 employee contributions + $6,900 ($230,000 compensation ceiling × 3%) employer match].

No other contributions may be made to the plan other than the employee elective contribution and the required employer matching contribution (or nonmatching contribution under the 2 percent rule). All contributions are fully vested. An employer is required to make the required matching or nonmatching contributions to a SIMPLE § 401(k) plan once it is established, whereas an employer's contributions to a traditional § 401(k) plan generally may be discretionary.

An employer's deduction for contributions to a SIMPLE § 401(k) plan is limited to the greater of 25 percent of the compensation paid or accrued or the amount that the employer is required to contribute to the plan. Thus, an employer may deduct contributions to a SIMPLE § 401(k) plan in excess of 25 percent of the $230,000 salary cap. A traditional § 401(k) plan is limited to 25 percent of the total compensation of plan participants for the year (excluding age 50 catch-ups).

An employer is allowed a deduction for matching contributions only if the contributions are made by the due date (including extensions) for the employer's tax return. Contributions to a SIMPLE plan are excludible from the employee's gross income, and the SIMPLE plan is tax-exempt.

EXAMPLE 15

The Mauve Company has a SIMPLE plan for its employees under which it provides nonmatching contributions of 2% of compensation for each eligible employee. The maximum amount that can be added to each participant's account in 2008 is $15,100, composed of the $10,500 employee salary reduction plus an employer contribution of $4,600 ($230,000 × 2%). ∎

Distributions from a SIMPLE plan are taxed under the IRA rules. Tax-free rollovers can be made from one SIMPLE account to another. A SIMPLE account can be rolled over to an IRA tax-free after the expiration of a two-year period since the individual first participated in the plan. Withdrawals of contributions during the two-year period beginning on the date an employee first participates in the SIMPLE plan are subject to a 25 percent early withdrawal tax rather than the 10 percent early withdrawal tax that otherwise would apply.

Designated Roth Contributions. Starting in 2006, § 401(k) plans and § 403(b) plans may be amended to permit employees to irrevocably designate some or all of their future salary deferral contributions as Roth § 401(k) or Roth § 403(b) contributions.[41] These designated amounts are currently includible in the employee's gross income and are maintained in a separate plan account. The earnings on these elective contributions build up in the plan on a tax-free basis. Future qualified distributions made from designated contributions are excludible from gross income. The adjusted gross income (AGI) limitation (discussed later in the chapter) does not apply to these designated contributions, so a Roth § 401(k) should be attractive to highly paid officers and employees.

Roth § 401(k)s must comply with the nondiscrimination requirements. The contributions are treated like regular § 401(k) contributions for other purposes and may not exceed the annual limitation ($15,500 in 2008) without regard to any catch-up contributions. A person should be able to roll a designated Roth contributions (DRCs) account into another designated Roth account or into a Roth IRA to preserve the tax-free nature of the account after age 70½ and to avoid the minimum distribution requirements. A "qualified distribution" from a designated Roth account is a distribution that is made after the person has participated for five years and that occurs on or after the date the person attains age 59½, dies, or becomes disabled. If a distribution is not a qualified distribution, such a distribution is taxable to the participant (or a beneficiary) to the extent it consists of earnings (in a pro rata manner).

[41]§ 402A.

A designated Roth account has $18,800 of DRCs and $1,200 of earnings. If a qualified distribution of $10,000 is made to the participant, the entire amount is excluded from gross income. However, if the distribution is not a qualified distribution, $9,400 is a return of capital (excluded from gross income), but a pro rata amount of $600 is included in gross income [($10,000 ÷ $20,000) × $1,200]. ■

Retirement Plans for Self-Employed Individuals

LO.5

Understand the qualified plan (Keogh plan) available to a self-employed person.

Self-employed individuals (e.g., partners and sole proprietors) and their employees are eligible to receive qualified retirement benefits under the SIMPLE plans described previously or under what are known as **H.R. 10 (Keogh) plans**. Because of contribution limitations and other restrictions, self-employed plans previously were less attractive than corporate plans. Contributions and benefits of a self-employed person now are subject to the general corporate provisions, putting self-employed persons on a parity with corporate employees. Consequently, Keogh plans can provide a self-employed person with an adequate retirement base.

A variety of funding vehicles can be used for Keogh investments, such as mutual funds, annuities, real estate shares, certificates of deposit, debt instruments, commodities, securities, and personal properties. Investment in most collectibles is not allowed in a self-directed plan. When an individual decides to make all investment decisions, a self-directed retirement plan is established. However, the individual may prefer to invest the funds with a financial institution such as a broker, a bank, or a savings and loan institution.

Coverage Requirements

Generally, the corporate coverage rules apply to Keogh plans. Thus, the ratio percentage and average benefits tests previously discussed also apply to self-employed plans.[42] An individual covered under a qualified corporate plan as an employee may also establish a Keogh plan for earnings from self-employment.

Contribution Limitations

A self-employed individual may annually contribute the smaller of $46,000 (in 2008) or 100 percent of earned income to a *defined contribution* Keogh plan.[43] However, if the defined contribution plan is a profit sharing plan or stock bonus plan, a 25 percent deduction limit applies. Under a *defined benefit* Keogh plan, the annual benefit payable to an employee is limited to the smaller of $185,000 (in 2008) or 100 percent of the employee's average compensation for the three highest years of employment.[44] An employee includes a self-employed person.

Earned income refers to net earnings from self-employment as defined in § 1402(a).[45] Net earnings from self-employment means the gross income derived by an individual from any trade or business carried on by that individual, less appropriate deductions, plus the distributive share of income or loss from a partnership.[46] Earned income is reduced by contributions to a Keogh plan on the individual's behalf and by 50 percent of any self-employment tax.[47]

[42]§ 401(d).
[43]§ 415(c)(1).
[44]§ 415(b)(1). This amount is indexed annually.
[45]§ 401(c)(2).
[46]§ 1402(a).
[47]§§ 401(c)(2)(A)(v) and 164(f).

TABLE 19–3	Phaseout of IRA Deduction of an Active Participant in 2008	
AGI Filing Status	**Phaseout Begins***	**Phaseout Ends**
Single and head of household	$53,000	$63,000
Married, filing joint return	85,000	95,000
Married, filing separate return	–0–	10,000

*These amounts are indexed annually for inflation.

EXAMPLE 17

Pat, a partner, has earned income of $150,000 in 2008 (after the deduction for one-half of self-employment tax). The maximum contribution Pat may make to a defined contribution Keogh plan is $46,000, the lesser of $150,000 or $46,000. ■

For discrimination purposes, the 25 percent limitation on the employee contribution to a profit sharing plan or stock bonus plan is computed on the first $230,000 (in 2008) of earned income. Thus, the maximum contribution in 2008 is $46,000 ($230,000 − .25X = X; X = $184,000). Therefore, $230,000 − $184,000 = $46,000. Alternatively, this can be calculated by multiplying $230,000 by 20 percent.

EXAMPLE 18

Terry, a self-employed accountant, has a profit sharing plan with a contribution rate of 15% of compensation. Terry's earned income after the deduction of one-half of self-employment tax, but before the Keogh contribution, is $250,000. Terry's contribution is limited to $30,000 ($230,000 − .15X = X), since X = $200,000 and .15 × $200,000 = $30,000. ■

Although a Keogh plan must be established before the end of the year in question, contributions may be made up to the normal filing date for that year.

LO.6

Describe the benefits of the different types of Individual Retirement Accounts (IRAs).

Individual Retirement Accounts (IRAs)

General Rules

Employees not covered by another qualified plan can establish their own tax-deductible **Individual Retirement Accounts (IRAs)**. For years 2005–2007, the contribution ceiling was the smaller of $4,000 (or $8,000 for spousal IRAs) or 100 percent of compensation. For 2008, the contribution ceiling is the smaller of $5,000 (or $10,000 for spousal IRAs) or 100 percent of compensation.[48] The contribution ceiling applies to all types of IRAs (traditional deductible, traditional nondeductible, and Roth).

An individual who attains the age of 50 by the end of the tax year can make additional catch-up IRA contributions. The maximum contribution limit is increased by $500 for the period 2002 through 2005 and $1,000 for years after 2005.

The amount accumulated in an IRA can be substantial. For example, if a husband and wife each contribute only $4,000 annually to an IRA from age 25 to age 65 (and earn 6 percent annually), their account balances together would be approximately $1.4 million at retirement. If the taxpayer is an *active participant* in a qualified plan, the traditional IRA deduction limitation is phased out *proportionately* between certain AGI ranges, as shown in Table 19–3.[49]

---

[48]§§ 219(b)(1) and (c)(2). The ceiling was $3,000 for 2002–2004. After 2008, the limit is adjusted annually for inflation in $500 increments.

[49]§ 219(g).

AGI is calculated taking into account any § 469 passive losses and § 86 taxable Social Security benefits and ignoring any § 911 foreign income exclusion, § 135 savings bonds interest exclusion, and the IRA deduction. There is a $200 floor on the IRA deduction limitation for individuals whose AGI is not above the phaseout range.

EXAMPLE 19

Dan, who is single, has compensation income of $59,000 in 2008. He is an active participant in his employer's qualified retirement plan. Dan contributes $5,000 to a traditional IRA. The deductible amount is reduced from $5,000 by $3,000 because of the phaseout mechanism:

$$\frac{\$6,000}{\$10,000} \times \$5,000 = \$3,000 \text{ reduction}$$

Therefore, of the $5,000 contribution, Dan can deduct only $2,000 ($5,000 − $3,000). ∎

EXAMPLE 20

Ben, an unmarried individual, is an active participant in his employer's qualified retirement plan in 2008. With AGI of $62,800, he would normally have an IRA deduction limit of $100 {$5,000 − [($62,800 − $53,000)/$10,000 × $5,000]}. However, because of the special floor provision, Ben is allowed a $200 IRA deduction. ∎

An individual is not considered an active participant in a qualified plan merely because the individual's spouse is an active participant in such a plan for any part of a plan year. Thus, most homemakers may take a full $5,000 deduction regardless of the participation status of their spouse, unless the couple has AGI above $159,000. If their AGI is above $159,000, the phaseout of the deduction begins at $159,000 and ends at $169,000 (phaseout over the $10,000 range) rather than beginning and ending at the phaseout amounts in Table 19–3.[50]

EXAMPLE 21

Nell is covered by a qualified employer retirement plan at work. Her husband, Nick, is not an active participant in a qualified plan. If Nell and Nick's combined AGI is $135,000, Nell cannot make a deductible IRA contribution because she exceeds the income threshold for an active participant in Table 19–3. However, since Nick is not an active participant, and their combined AGI does not exceed $159,000, he can make a deductible contribution of $5,000 to an IRA. ∎

To the extent that an individual is ineligible to make a deductible contribution to an IRA, *nondeductible contributions* can be made to separate accounts.[51] The nondeductible contributions are subject to the same dollar limits as deductible contributions ($5,000 of earned income, $10,000 for a spousal IRA). Income in the account accumulates tax-free until distributed. Only the account earnings are taxed upon distribution because the account basis equals the contributions made by the taxpayer. A taxpayer may elect to treat deductible IRA contributions as nondeductible. If an individual has no taxable income for the year after taking into account other deductions, the election would be beneficial. The election is made on the individual's tax return for the taxable year to which the designation relates.

Starting in 2002, there is a nonrefundable credit for contributions to a traditional IRA or elective deferrals for a § 401(k) plan (see Chapter 13).

For distributions made in tax years 2006 and 2007, an exclusion from gross income is available for traditional IRA distributions made to charity.[52] The amount of the distribution that is eligible for this beneficial exclusion treatment is limited to $100,000.

---

[50]§ 219(g)(7). However, a special rule in § 219(g)(4) allows a married person filing a separate return to avoid the phaseout rules even though the spouse is an active participant. The individual must live apart from the spouse at all times during the taxable year and must not be an active participant in another qualified plan.

[51]§ 408(o).

[52]§ 408(d)(8)(A). This provision may be extended by Congress.

EXAMPLE 22

Amber has a traditional deductible IRA, so her basis is $0 (see the later discussion under Taxation of Benefits). Therefore, in 2007 she can have an IRA distribution of $100,000 made to a charity and exclude the $100,000 from her gross income. Assume instead that Amber has a traditional nondeductible IRA with a basis of $75,000. So, if she has a $100,000 IRA distribution made to a charity, she can exclude $25,000 ($100,000 − $75,000) from her gross income. ■

Roth IRAs. Introduced by Congress to encourage individual savings, a **Roth IRA** is a *nondeductible* alternative to the traditional deductible IRA. Earnings inside a Roth IRA are not taxable, and all qualified distributions from a Roth IRA are tax-free.[53] The maximum allowable annual contribution to a Roth IRA for 2008 is the smaller of $5,000 ($10,000 for spousal IRAs) or 100 percent of the individual's compensation for the year. Contributions to a Roth IRA must be made by the due date (excluding extensions) of the taxpayer's tax return. Roth IRAs are not subject to the minimum distribution rules that apply to traditional IRAs. Contributions to a Roth IRA (unlike a traditional IRA) may continue beyond age 70½ so long as the person generates compensation income and is not barred by the AGI limits.

A taxpayer can make tax-free withdrawals from a Roth IRA after an initial five-year holding period if any of the following requirements is satisfied:

- The distribution is made on or after the date on which the participant attains age 59½.
- The distribution is made to a beneficiary (or the participant's estate) on or after the participant's death.
- The participant becomes disabled.
- The distribution is used to pay for qualified first-time home buyer's expenses (statutory ceiling of $10,000).

EXAMPLE 23

Edith establishes a Roth IRA at age 42 and contributes $5,000 per year for 20 years. The account is now worth $149,400, consisting of $100,000 of nondeductible contributions and $49,400 in accumulated earnings that have not been taxed. Edith may withdraw the $149,400 tax-free from the Roth IRA because she is over age 59½ and has met the five-year holding period requirement. ■

If the taxpayer receives a distribution from a Roth IRA and does not satisfy the aforementioned requirements, the distribution may be taxable. If the distribution represents a return of capital, it is not taxable. Conversely, if the distribution represents a payout of earnings, it is taxable. Under the ordering rules for Roth IRA distributions, distributions are treated as first made from contributions (return of capital).

EXAMPLE 24

Assume the same facts as in the previous example, except that Edith is only age 50 and receives a distribution of $55,000. Since her adjusted basis for the Roth IRA is $100,000 (contributions made), the distribution is tax-free, and her adjusted basis is reduced to $45,000 ($100,000 − $55,000). ■

Roth IRAs are subject to income limits. In 2008, the maximum annual contribution of $5,000 is phased out beginning at AGI of $101,000 for single taxpayers and $159,000 for married couples who file a joint return. The phaseout range is $10,000 for married filing jointly and $15,000 for single taxpayers. For a married taxpayer filing separately, the phaseout begins with AGI of $0 and is phased out over a $10,000 range.[54]

---

[53]§ 408A.

[54]The income limits for Roth IRA contributions are indexed for tax years after 2006.

TAX *in the News*   ROTH 401 (k) PLAN ADOPTIONS RISING

Since Congress has eliminated the 2010 sunset provision for Roth § 401 (k) plans, employees now may choose between a traditional § 401 (k) or a Roth § 401 (k). A traditional § 401 (k) plan is funded with pretax amounts that grow tax-free until withdrawn. Thus, the amount withdrawn is included in the employee's gross income.

If the contributions are Roth § 401 (k) contributions, the amount so elected is included in the employee's gross income, but the earnings are tax-exempt. The Roth § 401 (k) plan is not limited by the income rules applicable to Roth IRAs. Further, the maximum allowable contributions to a Roth § 401 (k) are much higher—$15,500 (in 2008) or $20,500 for age 50 or older versus $5,000 for a Roth IRA ($6,000 if 50 or older). Young, recently hired employees are more likely than older employees to adopt Roth § 401 (k) plans.

Source: *Adapted from D. L. Chesser, C. E. Davis, and T. S. Thomasson, "To Roth or Not to Roth,"* Journal of Accountancy, *February 2007, pp. 64–67.*

EXAMPLE 25

Bev, who is single, would like to contribute $5,000 to her Roth IRA. However, her AGI is $111,000, so her contribution is limited to $1,667 ($5,000 − $3,333) calculated as follows:

$$\frac{\$10,000}{\$15,000} \times \$5,000 = \$3,333 \text{ reduction}$$

∎

For distributions made in tax years 2006 and 2007, an exclusion from gross income is available for Roth IRA distributions made to charity.[55] This exclusion treatment is beneficial for Roth IRA distributions that otherwise are not eligible for Roth IRA exclusion treatment.

Coverdell Education Savings Accounts (CESAs).

Distributions from a **Coverdell Education Savings Account (CESA)** to pay for qualified education expenses receive favorable tax treatment.[56] Qualified education expenses include tuition, fees, books, supplies, and related equipment. Room and board qualify if the student's course load is at least one-half of the full-time course load. If the CESA is used to pay the qualified education expenses of the designated beneficiary, the withdrawals are tax-free. To the extent the distributions during a tax year exceed qualified education expenses, part of the excess is treated as a return of capital (the contributions), and part is treated as a distribution of earnings under the § 72 annuity rules. Thus, the distribution is presumed to be pro rata from each category. The exclusion for the distribution of earnings part is calculated as follows:

$$\frac{\text{Qualified education expenses}}{\text{Total distributions}} \times \text{Earnings} = \text{Exclusion}$$

EXAMPLE 26

Meg receives a $2,500 distribution from her CESA. She uses $2,000 to pay for qualified education expenses. On the date of the distribution, Meg's CESA balance is $10,000, $6,000 of which represents her contributions. Since 60% ($6,000/$10,000) of her account balance represents her contributions, $1,500 ($2,500 × 60%) of the distribution is a return of capital, and $1,000 ($2,500 × 40%) is a distribution of earnings. The excludible amount of the earnings is calculated as follows:

$$\frac{\$2,000}{\$2,500} \times \$1,000 = \$800$$

Thus, Meg must include $200 ($1,000 − $800) in her gross income. ∎

---

[55]§ 408(d)(8)(A). This provision may be extended by Congress.   [56]§ 530.

The maximum amount that can be contributed annually to a CESA for a beneficiary is $2,000. A beneficiary must be an individual and cannot be a group of children or an unborn child. The contributions are not deductible. A CESA is subject to income limits. The maximum annual contribution is phased out beginning at $95,000 for single taxpayers and $190,000 for married couples who file a joint return. The phaseout range is $30,000 for married filing jointly and $15,000 for single taxpayers. Contributions cannot be made to a CESA after the date on which the designated beneficiary attains age 18. Thus, a total of up to $36,000 can be contributed for each beneficiary—$2,000 in the year of birth and in each of the following 17 years. A 6 percent excise tax is imposed on excess contributions to a CESA. A 10 percent excise tax is imposed on any distributions that are included in gross income.

The balance in a CESA must be distributed within 30 days after the death of the beneficiary or within 30 days after the beneficiary reaches age 30. Any balance at the close of either 30-day period is considered to be distributed at such time, and the earnings portion is included in the beneficiary's gross income. Before a beneficiary reaches age 30, any balance can be rolled over tax-free into another CESA for a member of the beneficiary's family who is under age 30.

The CESA exclusion may be available in a tax year in which the beneficiary claims the HOPE credit or the lifetime learning credit (see Chapter 13). However, any excluded amount of the CESA distribution cannot be used for the same educational expenses for which the HOPE credit or the lifetime learning credit is claimed.

Contributions cannot be made to a beneficiary's CESA during any year in which contributions are made to a qualified tuition program on behalf of the same beneficiary (see Chapter 5).

Simplified Employee Pension Plans.

An employer may contribute to an IRA covering an employee an amount equal to the lesser of $46,000 (in 2008) or 25 percent of the employee's earned income. In such a plan, the employer must make contributions for *each* employee who has reached age 21, has performed service for the employer during the calendar year and at least three of the five preceding calendar years, and has received at least $500 (in 2008) in compensation from the employer for the year.[57] Known as **simplified employee pension (SEP) plans**, these plans are subject to many of the same restrictions applicable to qualified plans (e.g., age and period-of-service requirements, and nondiscrimination limitations). Concept Summary 19–2 compares a SEP with a Keogh plan.

EXAMPLE 27

In 2008, Ryan's compensation before his employer's contribution to a SEP is $30,000. Ryan's employer may contribute and deduct up to $7,500 ($30,000 × 25%) for 2008. ∎

The amounts contributed to a SEP by an employer on behalf of an employee and the elective deferrals of an employee under a SEP are excludible from gross income. Elective deferrals under a SEP are subject to a statutory ceiling of $15,500 (in 2008),[58] which is increased under the catch-up provision for employees at least 50 years of age by the end of the tax year. Only $230,000 (in 2008) in compensation may be taken into account in making the SEP computation. An employer is permitted to elect to use its taxable year rather than the calendar year for purposes of determining contributions to a SEP.[59]

---

[57]§§ 408(j) and (k)(2). This amount is indexed annually. For 2007, the amount was $500.

[58]Elective deferrals by an employee were repealed by the Small Business Job Protection Act of 1996 effective after December 31, 1996. However, if the employer plan was established before January 1, 1997, contributions can continue to be made under the pre-repeal provisions.

[59]§ 404(h)(1)(A). The $15,500 and $230,000 amounts are indexed annually. The elective deferral amount was increased in $1,000 annual increments until it reached $15,000 and then became subject to indexing.

CONCEPT SUMMARY 19–2

Keogh Plan and SEP Compared

	Keogh	SEP
Form	Trust.	IRA.
Establishment	By end of year.	By extension due date of employer.
Type of plan	Qualified.	Qualified.
Contributions to plan	By extension due date.	By extension due date of employer.
Vesting rules	Qualified plan rules.	100% immediately.
Participants' rules	Flexible.	Stricter.
Lump-sum distributions and averaging	Yes, favorable 10-year forward averaging.	No, ordinary income.
Deduction limitation	Varies.*	Smaller of $46,000 (in 2008) or 25% of earned income.**
Self as trustee	Yes.	No.

*For a defined contribution pension plan, the limit is the smaller of $46,000 (in 2008) or 100% of self-employment income (after one-half of self-employment tax is deducted). A defined contribution profit sharing plan has a 25% deduction limit. A defined benefit Keogh plan's limit is the smaller of $185,000 (in 2008) or 100% of the employee's average compensation for the highest three years of employment.

**Only $230,000 of income can be taken into consideration.

Simple IRA. A SIMPLE plan can be in the form of an IRA. See the earlier discussion under SIMPLE Plans.

Spousal IRA. If both spouses work, each can individually establish an IRA. Deductible IRA contributions of up to $5,000 may be made by each spouse if the combined compensation of both spouses is at least equal to the contributed amount. Thus, if each spouse has compensation of at least $5,000, they each may contribute a maximum of $5,000. Likewise, if only one spouse is employed, they each may contribute a maximum of $5,000 if the employed spouse has compensation of at least $10,000. Finally, if both spouses are employed, but one has compensation of less than $5,000, they each may contribute a maximum of $5,000 if their combined compensation is at least $10,000.

For the spousal IRA provision to apply, a joint return must be filed.[60] The spousal IRA deduction is also proportionately reduced for active participants whose AGI exceeds the above target ranges.

EXAMPLE 28

Tony, who is married, is eligible to establish an IRA. He received $30,000 in compensation in 2008, and his spouse does not work outside the home. Tony can contribute up to $10,000 to two IRAs, to be divided in any manner between the two spouses, except that no more than $5,000 can be allocated to either spouse. ■

EXAMPLE 29

Assume the same facts as in the previous example, except that Tony's wife has compensation income of $2,200. Without the spousal IRA provision, Tony could contribute $5,000 to his IRA, and his spouse could contribute only $2,200 to her IRA. With the spousal IRA provision, they both can contribute $5,000 to their IRAs. ■

---

[60]§ 219(c).

Alimony is considered to be earned income for purposes of IRA contributions. Thus, a person whose only income is alimony can contribute to an IRA.

Timing of Contributions. Contributions (both deductible and nondeductible) can be made to an IRA anytime before the due date of the individual's tax return.[61] For example, an individual can establish and contribute to an IRA through April 15, 2009 (the return due date), and deduct this amount on his or her tax return for 2008. IRA contributions that are made during a tax return extension period do not satisfy the requirement of being made by the return due date. An employer can make contributions up until the time of the due date for filing the return (including extensions) and treat those amounts as a deduction for the prior year.[62] As noted earlier, a similar rule applies to Keogh plans. However, the Keogh plan must be established before the end of the tax year. Contributions to the Keogh plan may then be made anytime before the due date of the individual's tax return.

Penalty Taxes for Excess Contributions

A cumulative, nondeductible 6 percent excise penalty tax is imposed on the smaller of (1) any excess contributions or (2) the market value of the plan assets determined as of the close of the tax year. *Excess contributions* are any contributions that exceed the maximum limitation and contributions that are made to a traditional IRA during or after the tax year in which the individual reaches age 70½.[63] Contributions can be made to a Roth IRA during or after the tax year in which the individual reaches age 70½. A taxpayer is not allowed a deduction for excess contributions. If the excess is corrected by contributing less than the deductible amount for a later year, a deduction then is allowable in the later year as a *makeup* deduction.

An excess contribution is taxable annually until returned to the taxpayer or reduced by the underutilization of the maximum contribution limitation in a subsequent year. The 6 percent penalty tax can be avoided if the excess amounts are returned.[64]

EXAMPLE 30

Nancy, age 45, establishes a traditional IRA in 2008 and contributes $5,300 in cash to the plan. She has earned income of $22,000. Nancy is allowed a $5,000 deduction *for* AGI for 2008. Assuming the market value of the plan assets is at least $300, there is a nondeductible 6% excise penalty tax of $18 ($300 × 6%). The $300 may be subject to an additional penalty tax in future years if it is not returned to Nancy or reduced by underutilization of the $5,000 maximum contribution limitation (ignoring any catch-up contributions). ∎

Taxation of Benefits

A participant has a zero basis in the *deductible* contributions of a traditional IRA because the contributions were deducted.[65] Therefore, all withdrawals from a deductible IRA are taxed as ordinary income in the year of receipt. They are not eligible for the 10-year averaging allowed for certain lump-sum distributions.

A participant has a basis equal to the contributions made for a *nondeductible* traditional IRA. Therefore, only the earnings component of withdrawals is included in gross income. Such amounts are taxed as ordinary income in the year of receipt and are not eligible for the 10-year averaging allowed for certain lump-sum distributions.

In addition to being included in gross income, payments from IRAs made to a participant before age 59½ are subject to a nondeductible 10 percent penalty tax

---

[61]§ 219(f)(3).
[62]§ 404(h)(1)(B).
[63]§§ 4973(a)(1) and (b).
[64]§§ 408(d)(4) and 4973(b)(2).
[65]§ 408(d)(1).

on such actual, or constructive, payments.[66] However, an individual may make penalty-free withdrawals to pay for medical expenses in excess of 7.5 percent of AGI, to pay for qualified higher education expenses, and to pay for qualified, first-time home buyer expenses (up to $10,000). Note that a qualified first-time home buyer is defined as an individual (and spouse) who has not owned a principal residence in the two-year period preceding the date of acquisition of a principal residence. Further, an individual who has received unemployment compensation for at least 12 consecutive weeks may use IRA withdrawals to pay for health insurance for himself or herself, the spouse, and dependents without incurring the 10 percent penalty tax.[67]

All traditional IRAs of an individual are treated as one contract, and all distributions during a taxable year are treated as one distribution. See the earlier discussion of the special rules for distributions from Roth IRAs and traditional IRAs. If an individual who previously has made both deductible and nondeductible IRA contributions makes a withdrawal from a traditional IRA during a taxable year, the excludible amount must be calculated. The amount excludible from gross income for the taxable year is calculated by multiplying the amount withdrawn by a percentage. The percentage is calculated by dividing the individual's aggregate nondeductible IRA contributions by the aggregate balance of all of his or her traditional IRAs (including rollover IRAs and SEPs).[68]

Carl, age 59, has a $12,000 deductible traditional IRA and a $2,000 nondeductible traditional IRA (without any earnings). Carl withdraws $1,000 from the nondeductible IRA. The excludible portion is $143 [($2,000/$14,000) × $1,000], and the includible portion is $857 [($12,000/$14,000) × $1,000]. Carl must also pay a 10% penalty tax on the prorated portion considered withdrawn from the deductible IRA and earnings in either type of IRA. Thus, the 10% penalty tax is $85.70 (10% × $857). ∎	*E X A M P L E 31*

Rollovers: General Provisions. As introduced earlier, an IRA may be the recipient of a rollover from another qualified plan, including another IRA. Such a distribution from a qualified plan is not included in gross income if it is transferred within 60 days of receipt to an IRA or another qualified plan. For a series of distributions that constitute a lump-sum distribution, the 60-day period does not begin until the last distribution. Amounts received from IRAs may be rolled over tax-free only once in a 12-month period. If a person has more than one IRA, the one-year waiting period applies separately to each IRA.[69]

Nonemployer stock worth $60,000 is distributed to an employee from a qualified retirement plan. Hubert, the employee, sells the stock within 60 days for $60,000 and transfers one-half of the proceeds to a traditional IRA. Hubert has $30,000 of ordinary income, which is not eligible for 10-year forward averaging or for capital gain treatment under the pre-1987 rules. One-half of the distribution, or $30,000, does escape taxation because of the rollover. ∎	*E X A M P L E 32*

A tax-free rollover for distributions from qualified plans is an alternative to the taxable 10-year forward averaging technique. Any rollover amount in a traditional IRA may later be rolled over into another qualified plan if the IRA consists of only the amounts from the original plan and the receiving plan permits it. The amount of nondeductible employee contributions included in a distribution may not be rolled over, but that amount is tax-free because the contributions were made with after-tax dollars. Partial rollovers are allowed, but the maximum amount that may be rolled over may not exceed the portion of the distribution that is otherwise

---

[66]§ 72(t). There are limited exceptions to the penalty on early distributions.

[67]§§ 72(t)(2)(B), (D), (E), and (F). For purposes of the unemployment provision, a self-employed individual who otherwise would have been eligible for unemployment compensation will qualify.

[68]§ 408(d)(2).

[69]§ 408(d)(3)(B) and Reg. § 1.408–4(b)(4).

CONCEPT SUMMARY 19–3

Comparison of IRAs

	Traditional		Roth IRA	Coverdell Education Savings Account (CESA)
	Deductible IRA	Nondeductible IRA		
Maximum contribution (per year)	$5,000*	$5,000*	$5,000*	$2,000
Tax-deductible contribution	Yes	No	No	No
Tax-free growth of income	Yes	Yes	Yes	Yes
Beginning of AGI phaseout for active participant (2008)	$53,000 single, $85,000 joint	N/A	$101,000 single, $159,000 joint	$95,000 single, $190,000 joint
Income tax on distributions	Yes, for entire distribution	Yes, for the earnings portion	No, if satisfy 5-year holding period**	No, if used for education expenses
50% excise tax: age 70½ minimum distributions	Yes	Yes	No	No
10% early withdrawal penalty (before age 59½)	Yes, with exceptions†	Yes, with exceptions†	Yes, with exceptions†	Yes††

*The total of deductible, nondeductible, and Roth IRA contributions may not exceed $5,000 per year.

**In addition, the distribution must satisfy one of the following: after age 59½, for qualified first-time home buyer expenses, participant is disabled, or made to a beneficiary on or after the participant's death.

†Qualified education and first-time home buyer costs (up to $10,000) avoid the 10% penalty.

††On early withdrawals not used for education costs. Qualified first-time home buyer costs (up to $10,000) avoid 10% penalty.

includible in gross income. Rollovers are not available for required distributions under the minimum distribution rules once age 70½ is reached.

EXAMPLE 33

Jane withdraws $1,500 from her traditional IRA on May 2, 2008, but she redeposits it in the same IRA on June 28, 2008. Although the withdrawal and redeposit was a partial rollover and Jane may have used the funds for a limited time, this is a tax-free rollover.[70] ■

A rollover is different from a direct transfer of funds from a qualified plan to an IRA or another qualified plan by a trustee or issuer. A direct transfer is not subject to the one-year waiting period and the withholding rules.[71] Further, in many states, IRA amounts are subject to claims of creditors, which is not the case for some employer plans.

An employer must withhold 20 percent of any lump-sum distributions unless the transfer is a direct transfer to an IRA or another qualified plan.[72]

EXAMPLE 34

Kay receives a distribution from a qualified retirement plan. The amount of the distribution would have been $20,000, but Kay receives only $16,000 ($20,000 − $4,000) as a result of the 20% withholding provision. After several weeks, Kay decides to contribute $20,000 (the gross amount of the distribution) to her traditional IRA. Since she received only $16,000, she will need to contribute $4,000 from another source in order to make a $20,000 contribution. Kay will be able to claim a refund for the $4,000 that was withheld when she files her tax return for the year. ■

---

[70]Ltr.Rul. 9010007.
[71]Reg. § 35.3405–1.

[72]§ 3405(c).

Distributions from a traditional IRA are generally not eligible for 10-year averaging or capital gain treatment. An exception applies in the case of a *conduit IRA*, where the sole assets of a qualified plan are rolled over into an IRA, and the assets are then rolled into a qualified plan. With a conduit IRA, the lump-sum distribution from the original plan is still eligible for the special tax treatments.

Rollovers and Conversions: Roth IRAs. A Roth IRA may be rolled over tax-free into another Roth IRA.[73]

A traditional IRA may be rolled over or converted to a Roth IRA. A conversion occurs when the taxpayer notifies the IRA trustee that the IRA is now a Roth IRA. A rollover or conversion of a traditional IRA to a Roth IRA can occur only if the following requirements are satisfied:[74]

- The participant's AGI does not exceed $100,000 (excluding the amount included in gross income resulting from the rollover or conversion).
- The participant is not married filing a separate return.
- The rollover occurs within 60 days of the IRA distribution.

The $100,000 AGI limitation for conversions and rollovers temporarily goes away in 2010. Thus, contributions made to a traditional IRA can be converted to a Roth IRA in 2010. Taxes will be due on the conversion amount in 2010, but these taxes can be spread over two years.[75] Further, unlike a traditional IRA, which requires withdrawals at age 70½, there are no required withdrawals from a Roth IRA. Thus, money can be accumulated over the taxpayer's lifetime and then passed to heirs without tax penalties.

When a traditional IRA is rolled over or converted to a Roth IRA, the tax consequences depend on whether the traditional IRA was deductible or nondeductible. If deductible, then the basis for the IRA is zero. Thus, the entire amount of the rollover or conversion is included in gross income. If nondeductible, then the basis for the IRA is equal to the sum of the contributions. Thus, only the IRA earnings included in the rollover or conversion are included in gross income. The 10 percent penalty tax will not apply in either case.[76]

Starting in 2008, distributions from qualified retirement plans, § 403(b) annuities, and governmental § 457 plans can be rolled over into a Roth IRA.[77] However, for this rollover to be permitted, the $100,000 AGI limit must be satisfied. Note that, as mentioned previously, the $100,000 limit is scheduled to go away in 2010. Although this rollover is a taxable transaction, it enables subsequent earnings to be excluded from gross income.

Nonqualified Deferred Compensation Plans

LO.7

Understand the rationale for nonqualified deferred compensation plans and the related tax treatment.

Underlying Rationale for Tax Treatment

Nonqualified deferred compensation (NQDC) plans provide a flexible way for taxpayers, particularly those in the 35 percent tax bracket, to defer income taxes on income payments until a potentially lower tax bracket year. When the deferred compensation is credited with annual earnings until payment, the entire deferred compensation, not just the after-tax amount, is generating investment income. Also, most NQDC plans do not have to meet the discrimination, funding, coverage, and other requirements of qualified plans. In addition to these advantages for the

---

[73]§ 408A(c)(3)(B).
[74]§ 408A(c)(3)(B).
[75]§ 408A(d)(3)(A).

[76]§ 408A(d)(3)(A)(ii).
[77]§ 402(c)(8)(B).

employee, the employer may not have a current cash outflow. The IRS will issue rulings on deferred compensation plans.

Tax Treatment to the Employer and Employee

New rules apply after 2004 to nonqualified arrangements that defer the receipt of compensation income to a year later than that in which it is earned. During a taxable year in which an NQDC plan does not meet certain conditions in § 409A or is not operating in accordance with these conditions, all amounts deferred under the arrangement will be included in the participant's gross income to the extent they are not subject to a substantial risk of forfeiture. In addition, a 20 percent penalty tax is imposed on such income along with interest at the underpayment rate plus 1 percent.[78]

A three-pronged analysis determines whether a plan to defer compensation faces these punitive actions. First, does the deferred compensation fall within the NQDC provisions under § 409A? Second, are the benefits subject to a substantial risk of forfeiture (SRF)? SRF is discussed later in this chapter under Restricted Property Plans, but the definition of SRF for NQDCs differs from the normal definition. For example, a covenant not to compete can never be an SRF under § 409A, nor will conditions under the discretionary control of the employee be an SRF under § 409A. Also, an elective extension of a forfeiture period will generally be disregarded as an SRF unless there are substantial additional considerations for such an extension. Third, at the time the arrangement is not covered by an SRF, has the plan suffered a "plan failure"?

Certain compensation arrangements do not fall within § 409A, including a qualified employer plan, any bona fide vacation leave, sick leave, educational benefits, legal settlements, indemnification arrangements, compensatory time, disability pay, and a death benefit plan.[79] Excluded qualified employer plans include tax-qualified pension, profit sharing, or § 401(k) plans; a § 403(b) tax-deferred annuity; a simplified employee pension plan; or an eligible § 457(b) plan for state, government, or tax-exempt employees.

In general, a § 409A deferral occurs where an employee has a legally binding right to compensation that has been deferred to the future. The section casts a wide net and may even cover nonqualified stock options and stock appreciation rights (SARs). These rules do not cover restricted property under § 83, as well as nondiscounted stock options, nondiscounted SARs, and statutory stock options. Discounted stock options, discounted SARs, phantom stock, and restricted stock units are covered.

Generally, funded NQDC plans must be forfeitable to keep the compensation payments from being taxable immediately. In most instances, employees prefer to have some assurance that they will ultimately receive benefits from the NQDC (that the plan provides for nonforfeitable benefits). In such instances, the plan will have to be unfunded to prevent immediate taxation to the employee. Note that most funded NQDC plans are subject to many of the provisions that apply to qualified plans, including the nondiscrimination requirements, and are impractical as a result.

To be effective, an unfunded deferred compensation plan must meet and comply with the following requirements under § 409A.[80]

- The NQDC plan may not distribute the deferred compensation to the employee except in these six situations: separation of service, disability, death, specified time or fixed schedule, change in employer control, or unforeseeable emergency.

---

[78]§409A(a)(1).

[79]§409A(d)(1).

[80]§409A(a)(2),(3), and (4).

- The plan must not permit any participant to accelerate the time or scheduled date of distributions (subject to some exceptions).
- A participant must elect to postpone the compensation for the current year no later than the close of the preceding tax year (initial deferral election).
- The employee must decide on the form and time of the benefits (e.g., installment payments or lump sum) when the deferral election is made if the plan permits an election between alternatives, or the NQDC plan must specify the form and time of distribution when the deferral election is made.
- A participant must not change the time or form of benefits unless the employee does so at least 12 months before the scheduled distribution date and also postpones the scheduled distribution date by at least five years.
- The plan should specify the amount payable (or the terms of the formula determining the amount), along with the payment schedule or triggering events that result in payment.
- Publicly held companies must provide for a six-month delay requirement for the top 50 officers with incomes of at least $130,000 (along with certain owner-employees).

EXAMPLE 35

Eagle Corporation and Bill, a cash basis employee, enter into an employment agreement that provides an annual salary of $120,000 to Bill. Of this amount, $100,000 is paid in current monthly installments, and $20,000 is to be paid in 10 annual installments beginning at Bill's retirement or death. Although Eagle Corporation maintains a separate account for Bill, that account is not funded. Bill is merely an unsecured creditor of the corporation. The $20,000 is not considered constructively received and is deferred. Compensation of $100,000 is currently taxable to Bill and deductible to Eagle. The other $20,000 will be taxable and deductible when paid in future years. ∎

A deferred compensation arrangement occurs when an employee receives compensation after the 2½-month period following the end of an employer's corporate tax year in which such services were performed.[81] An employer's deduction of NQDC must be delayed to match the employee's recognition of income regardless of the employer's method of accounting.[82]

EXAMPLE 36

Beige, Inc., a calendar year employer, has an accrued NQDC liability of $300,000 on December 31, 2007. During 2008, the company accrues another $60,000 of NQDC. On February 13, 2009, the company pays the entire $360,000 to the employee. Since the $60,000 was paid within 2½ months after the end of 2008, only $300,000 ever met the requirement for deferred compensation. The entire $360,000 may be deducted by the company only in the year ending December 31, 2009, when the employee receives the cash and recognizes the income. ∎

When to Use an NQDC Arrangement.

As a general rule, NQDC plans are more appropriate for executives in a financially secure company. Because of the need for currently disposable income, such plans are usually not appropriate for young employees.

An NQDC plan can reduce an employee's overall tax payments by deferring the taxation of income to later years (possibly when the employee is in a lower tax bracket). In effect, these plans may produce a form of income averaging. Further, unfunded NQDC plans may discriminate in favor of shareholders, officers, specific highly compensated key employees, or a single individual.

Certain disadvantages should be noted, however. As mentioned earlier, nonqualified plans are usually required to be unfunded, which means that an employee is not assured that funds ultimately will be available to pay the benefits. In other words, the deferred amounts are recorded as a liability on the company's

---

[81]Temp.Reg. § 1.404(b)–1T.   [82]§ 404(a)(5); Reg. § 1.404(a)–12(b)(1).

books, and the employee will be an unsecured creditor in the event of the firm's bankruptcy.

Golden Parachute Arrangements. Golden parachute arrangements promise monetary benefits to key employees if they lose their jobs as a result of a change in ownership of the corporation. In essence, these are unfunded NQDC plans that do not vest until the change in ownership. These payments may be unreasonable or not really for services rendered. The term **golden parachute payments**, as used in the Code, means *excess severance pay*.

These excessive severance payments to employees are penalized. The Code denies a deduction to an employer who makes a payment of cash or property to an employee or independent contractor that satisfies both of the following conditions:

- The payment is contingent on a change of ownership of a corporation through a stock or asset acquisition.
- The aggregate present value of the payment equals or exceeds three times the employee's (or independent contractor's) average annual compensation.[83]

The disallowed amount is the excess of the payment over a statutory base amount (a five-year average of taxable compensation if the taxpayer was an employee for the entire five-year period). Further, a 20 percent excise tax is imposed on the recipient on the receipt of these parachute payments; the tax is withheld at the time of payment.[84]

EXAMPLE 37

Irene, an executive, receives a golden parachute payment of $380,000 from her employer. Her average annual compensation for the most recent five tax years is $120,000. The corporation will be denied a deduction for $260,000 ($380,000 payment − $120,000 base amount). Irene's excise tax is $52,000 ($260,000 × 20%). ■

Golden parachute payments do not include payments to or from qualified pension, profit sharing, stock bonus, annuity, or simplified employee pension plans. Also excluded is the amount of the payment that, in fact, represents reasonable compensation for personal services actually rendered or to be rendered. Such excluded payments are not taken into account when determining whether the threshold (the aggregate present value calculation) is exceeded.

S corporations are not subject to the golden parachute rules. Generally, corporations that do not have stock that is readily tradable on an established securities market or elsewhere are also exempt.

Publicly Held Companies' Compensation Limitation. For purposes of both the regular income tax and the alternative minimum tax, the deductible compensation for the top five executives of publicly traded companies is limited to $1 million for each executive. A company is publicly held if the corporation has common stock listed on a national securities exchange.[85] This $1 million deduction limitation is decreased by any nondeductible golden parachute payments made to the employee during the same year.

This deduction limitation applies when the compensation deduction would otherwise be taken. For example, in the case of a nonqualified stock option (NQSO), which is discussed later in this chapter, the deduction is normally taken in the year the NQSO is exercised, even though the option was granted with respect to services performed in a prior year.

Certain types of compensation are *not* subject to this deduction limit and are not taken into account in determining whether other compensation exceeds $1 million:

[83]§ 280G.
[84]§ 4999.
[85]§ 162(m).

- Compensation payable on a commission basis.
- Compensation payable solely on account of the attainment of one or more performance goals when certain requirements involving the approval of outside directors and shareholders are met.
- Payments to a tax-qualified retirement plan (including salary-reduction contributions).
- Amounts that are excludible from an executive's gross income (such as employer-provided health benefits and miscellaneous fringe benefits).

The most important exception is performance-based compensation. Compensation qualifies for this exception only if the following conditions are satisfied:

- The compensation is paid solely on account of the attainment of one or more performance goals.
- The performance goals are established by a compensation committee consisting solely of two or more outside directors.
- The material terms under which the compensation is to be paid (including the performance goals) are disclosed to and approved by the shareholders in a separate vote prior to payment.
- Prior to payment, the compensation committee certifies that the performance goals and any other material terms were in fact satisfied.

Compensation (other than stock options or other stock appreciation rights) is not treated as paid solely on account of the attainment of one or more performance goals unless the compensation is paid to the particular executive under a preestablished objective performance formula or standard that precludes discretion. In essence, a third party with knowledge of the relevant performance results could calculate the amount to be paid to the particular executive. A performance goal is broadly defined and includes, for example, any objective performance standard that is applied to the individual executive, a business unit (e.g., a division or a line of business), or the corporation as a whole. Performance standards could include increases in stock price, market share, sales, or earnings per share.

ETHICAL and EQUITABLE *Considerations* — **UNEVEN COMPENSATION PLAYING FIELD**

The top five executives of publicly traded corporations are subject to a $1 million limit each on deductible compensation. Many other highly paid individuals are not subject to this $1 million cap on deductibility.

Among those to whom the cap does not apply are Oprah Winfrey, who gets $225 million annually; Dr. Phil, who gets $45 million; and David Letterman, who gets $40 million. Tom Cruise, Mel Gibson, and Will Smith receive $25 million for six weeks' work on a film. Basketball's Kevin Garnett and Shaquille

O'Neal make $20 million annually. Baseball's Derek Jeter and Alex Rodriguez earn, respectively, $29 million and $28 million. Even a University of Florida basketball coach makes $3 million, and a University of Alabama football coach makes $4 million.

Discuss the fairness of a tax policy that subjects the compensation of certain business executives to a limitation on deductibility by their corporate employers while allowing compensation paid to entertainers, sports stars, and others to be exempt from this limitation.

Restricted Property Plans

General Provisions

A **restricted property plan** is an arrangement whereby an employer transfers property (e.g., stock of the employer-corporation) to an employee or other provider of services at no cost or at a bargain price. The usual purpose of a restricted stock plan

LO.8

Explain the value of restricted property plans.

is to retain the services of key employees who might otherwise leave. The employer hopes that such compensation arrangements will encourage company growth and attainment of performance objectives. Section 83 was enacted in 1969 to provide rules for the taxation of incentive compensation arrangements, which previously were governed by judicial and administrative interpretations. Although the following discussion refers to an employee as the provider of the services, the services may be performed by an independent contractor.

As a general rule, if an employee performs services and receives property (e.g., stock), the fair market value of that property in excess of any amount paid by the employee is includible in his or her gross income. The time for inclusion is the earlier of (1) the time the property is no longer subject to a substantial risk of forfeiture or (2) the time the property is transferable by the employee. The fair market value of the property is determined without regard to any restriction, except a restriction that by its terms will never lapse.[86] Since the amount of the compensation is determined at the date that the restrictions lapse or when the property is transferable, the opportunity to generate capital gain treatment on the property is denied during a period when the ordinary income element is being deferred.

EXAMPLE 38	On October 1, 2004, Blue Corporation sold 100 shares of its stock to Ahmad, an employee, for $10 per share. At the time of the sale, the fair market value of the stock was $100 per share. Under the terms of the sale, each share of stock was nontransferable and subject to a substantial risk of forfeiture (which was not to lapse until October 1, 2008). Evidence of these restrictions was stamped on the face of the stock certificates. On October 1, 2008, the fair market value of the stock was $250 per share. Since the stock was nontransferable and was subject to a substantial risk of forfeiture, Ahmad did not include any compensation in gross income during 2004 (assuming no special election was made). Instead, Ahmad was required to include $24,000 of compensation in gross income [100 shares × ($250 − $10 per share)] during 2008. If for some reason the forfeiture had occurred (e.g., the plan required Ahmad to surrender the stock to the corporation if he voluntarily terminated his employment with the company before October 1, 2008) and Ahmad never received the stock certificates, he would have been allowed a capital loss of $1,000 (the extent of his investment). ■

Substantial Risk of Forfeiture

A **substantial risk of forfeiture (SRF)** exists if a person's rights to full enjoyment of property are conditioned upon the future performance, or the refraining from the performance, of substantial services by that individual.[87] For example, if an employee must return the property (receiving only his or her original cost, if any) should there be a failure to complete a substantial period of service (for any reason), the property is subject to an SRF. Another such situation exists when an employer can compel an employee to return the property due to a breach of a substantial covenant not to compete. Any SRF should be stated on the face of the stock certificates. Assuming that an SRF does not exist, the property received is valued at its fair market value, ignoring any restrictions, except for one instance dealing with closely held stock.

Special Election Available

An employee may elect within 30 days after the receipt of restricted property to recognize immediately as ordinary income the fair market value in excess of the amount paid for the property. Any appreciation in the value of the property after receipt is classified as capital gain instead of ordinary income. No deduction is allowed to the employee

---

[86]§ 83(a)(1); *Miriam Sakol*, 67 T.C. 986 (1977); *T. M. Horwith*, 71 T.C. 932 (1979).   [87]§ 83(c). Regulation § 1.83–3(c)(2) includes several examples of restricted property arrangements.

for taxes paid on the original amount included in income if the property is subsequently forfeited.[88] The employee is permitted to take a capital loss for any amounts that were actually paid for the property. Furthermore, in such a case, the employer must repay taxes saved by any compensation deduction taken in the earlier year.[89]

Any increase in value between the time the property is received and the time it becomes either nonforfeitable or transferable is taxed as ordinary income if the employee does not make this special election. However, if the employee elects to be taxed immediately on the difference between the cost and fair market value on the date of issue, any future appreciation is treated as capital gain. In determining whether the gain is long term or short term, the holding period starts when the employee is taxed on the ordinary income.[90]

E X A M P L E 39

On July 1, 1998, Sparrow Company sold 100 shares of its preferred stock, worth $15 per share, to Diane (an employee) for $5 per share. The sale was subject to Diane's agreement to resell the preferred shares to the company for $5 per share if she terminated her employment during the following 10 years. The stock had a value of $25 per share on July 1, 2008, and Diane sold the stock for $30 per share on October 10, 2008. Diane made the special election to include the original spread (between the value of $15 in 1998 and the amount paid of $5) in income for 1998. Diane was required to recognize $1,000 of compensation income in 1998 ($15 − $5 = $10 × 100 shares), at which time her holding period in her stock began. Diane's tax basis in the stock was $1,500 ($1,000 + $500). When the preferred stock was sold in 2008, Diane recognized a $1,500 long-term capital gain ($30 × 100 shares − $1,500). ∎

E X A M P L E 40

Assume the same facts as in the previous example, except that Diane sells the stock in 2009 (rather than 2008). She would not recognize any gain in 2008 when the SRF lapses. Instead, Diane would recognize the $1,500 long-term capital gain in 2009. ∎

This special provision is usually not elected since it results in an immediate recognition of income and adverse tax consequences result from a subsequent forfeiture. However, the special election may be attractive in the following situations:

- The bargain element is relatively small.
- Substantial appreciation is expected in the future.
- A high probability exists that the restrictions will be met.

Employer Deductions

At the time the employee is required to include the compensation in income, the employer is allowed a tax deduction for the same amount. The employer must withhold on this amount in accordance with § 3402. In the no-election situation, the deduction is limited to the fair market value of the restricted property (without regard to the restrictions) at the time the restrictions lapse, reduced by the amount originally paid for the property by the employee.[91] When the employee elects to be taxed immediately, the corporate deduction also is accelerated and deductible in like amount. In cases of deferred income recognition, the employer can receive a sizable deduction if the property has appreciated.

E X A M P L E 41

On March 14, 2006, Gold Corporation sold to Harry, an employee, 10 shares of Gold common stock for $100 per share. Both the corporation and Harry were calendar year taxpayers. The common stock was subject to an SRF and was nontransferable; both conditions were to lapse on March 14, 2008. At the time of the sale, the fair market value of the common stock (without considering the restrictions) was $1,000 per share. On March 14, 2008, when the fair market value of the stock is $2,000 per share, the restrictions lapse. Harry did not make

[88]§ 83(b).
[89]Reg. §§ 1.83–6(c) and 2(a).
[90]§ 1223(6).
[91]Reg. § 1.83–6(a).

the special election. In 2008, Harry realizes ordinary income of $19,000 (10 shares at $2,000 per share less the $100 per share he had paid). Likewise, Gold Corporation is allowed a $19,000 compensation deduction in 2008. ∎

EXAMPLE 42

In the previous example, assume that Harry had made the special election. Since he was taxed on $9,000 in 2006, the corporation was allowed to deduct a like amount in 2006. No deduction would be available in 2008. ∎

LO.9

Differentiate the tax treatment of qualified and nonqualified stock options.

Stock Options

In General

Various equity types of stock option programs are available for an employee's compensation package. Some authorities believe that some form of *equity kicker* is needed to attract new management, convert key officers into *partners* by giving them a share of the business, and retain the services of executives who might otherwise leave. Encouraging the managers of a business to have a proprietary interest in its successful operation should provide executives with a key motive to expand the company and improve its profits. In addition, under certain conditions, stock options may fall outside the $1 million limitation on the salaries of the top five executives of publicly traded companies. Sometimes an executive's stock option income may far exceed cash salaries and bonuses. For example, in 2006 CEO Barry Diller of InterActiveCorp received a $730,000 salary and exercised stock options valued at approximately $290.2 million.

A **stock option** gives an individual the right to purchase a stated number of shares of stock from a corporation at a certain price within a specified period of time. The optionee must be under no obligation to purchase the stock, and the option may be revocable by the corporation. The option must be in writing, and its terms must be clearly expressed.[92]

Incentive Stock Options

An equity type of stock option called an *incentive stock option (ISO)* is available. There are no tax consequences for either the issuing corporation or the recipient when the option is granted. However, the *spread* (the excess of the fair market value of the share at the date of exercise over the option price)[93] is a tax preference item to the recipient for purposes of the alternative minimum tax. The determination of fair market value is made without regard to any lapse restrictions (a restriction that will expire after a period of time). After the option is exercised and when the stock is sold, any gain from the sale is taxed as a long-term capital gain if certain holding period requirements are met. For a gain to qualify as a long-term capital gain, the employee must not dispose of the stock within two years after the option is granted or within one year after acquiring the stock.[94] If the employee meets the holding period requirements, none of these transactions generates any business deduction for the employer.[95] If the employee pays anything for the option and does not exercise the option, any amount paid is recognized as a capital loss.

EXAMPLE 43

Wren Corporation granted an ISO for 100 shares of its stock to Rocky, an employee, on March 18, 2005. The option price was $100, and the fair market value was $100 on the date of the grant. Rocky exercised the option on April 1, 2007, when the fair market value of the stock was $200 per share. He sells the stock on April 6, 2008, for $300 per share. Rocky did not recognize any ordinary income on the date of the grant or the exercise date since the

---

[92]Reg. §§ 1.421–1(a)(1) and –7(a)(1).

[93]§§ 422(a), 421(a)(1), 57(a)(3), and 1234(a)(1) and (2).

[94]§ 422(a)(1).

[95]§ 421(a)(2).

option qualified as an ISO. Wren received no compensation deduction. Rocky has a $10,000 tax preference item on the exercise date. He has a long-term capital gain of $20,000 [($300 − $100) × 100] on the sale of the stock in 2008, because the one-year and two-year holding periods and other requirements have been met. ■

As a further requirement for ISO treatment, the option holder must be an employee of the issuing corporation from the date the option is granted until 3 months (12 months if disabled) before the date of exercise. The holding period and the employee-status rules just described (the one-year, two-year, and three-month requirements) are waived in the case of the death of an employee.[96]

EXAMPLE 44

Assume the same facts as in the previous example, except that Rocky was not employed by Wren Corporation for six months before the date he exercised the options. Rocky must recognize ordinary income to the extent of the spread, assuming there was no SRF. Thus, Rocky recognizes $10,000 [($200 − $100) × 100] of ordinary income on the exercise date, because he was not an employee of Wren Corporation at all times during the period beginning on the grant date and ending three months before the exercise date. Wren is allowed a deduction at the same time that Rocky reports the ordinary income. ■

If the holding period requirements are not satisfied but all other conditions are met, the tax is still deferred to the point of the sale. However, the difference between the option price and the value of the stock at the date the option was exercised is treated as ordinary income. The difference between the amount realized for the stock and the value of the stock at the date of exercise is short-term or long-term capital gain, depending on the holding period of the stock itself. The employer is allowed a deduction equal to the amount recognized by the employee as ordinary income. The employee does not have a tax preference for alternative minimum tax purposes.

EXAMPLE 45

Assume the same facts as in Example 43, except that Rocky sells the stock on March 22, 2008, for $290 per share. Since Rocky did not hold the stock itself for more than one year, $10,000 of the gain is treated as ordinary income in 2008, and Wren Corporation is allowed a $10,000 compensation deduction in 2008. The remaining $9,000 is a short-term capital gain ($29,000 − $20,000). ■

Qualification Requirements for Incentive Stock Option Plans. An **incentive stock option (ISO)** is an option to purchase stock of a corporation granted to an individual for any reason connected with his or her employment that meets specific qualification requirements.[97] The option is granted by the employer-corporation or by a parent or subsidiary corporation of the employer-corporation. An ISO plan may permit an employee to use company stock to pay for the exercise of the option without disqualifying the ISO plan.

For an option to qualify as an ISO, the terms of the option must identify it as an ISO and meet the following conditions:

- The option must be granted under a plan specifying the number of shares of stock to be issued and the employees or class of employees eligible to receive the options. The plan must be approved by the shareholders of the corporation within 12 months before or after the plan is adopted.
- The option must be granted within 10 years of the date the plan is adopted or of the date the plan is approved by the shareholders, whichever date is earlier.
- The option must by its terms be exercisable only within 10 years of the date it is granted.

---

[96]§§ 422(a)(2) and (c)(3). Exceptions are made for parent and subsidiary situations, corporate reorganizations, and liquidations. Also, in certain situations involving an insolvent employee, the holding period rules are modified.

[97]§ 422(b).

- The option price must equal or exceed the fair market value of the stock at the time the option is granted. This requirement is deemed satisfied if there has been a good faith attempt to value the stock accurately, even if the option price is less than the stock value.
- The option by its terms must be nontransferable other than at death and must be exercisable during the employee's lifetime only by the employee.
- The employee must not, immediately before the option is granted, own stock representing more than 10 percent of the voting power or value of all classes of stock in the employer-corporation or its parent or subsidiary. (Here, the attribution rules of § 267 are applied in modified form.) However, the stock ownership limitation will be waived if the option price is at least 110 percent of the fair market value (at the time the option is granted) of the stock subject to the option and the option by its terms is not exercisable more than five years from the date it is granted.[98]

An overall limitation is imposed on the amount of ISOs that can be first exercisable in one year by an employee. This limit is set at $100,000 per year based on the value of the stock determined at the time the option is granted. For example, an ISO plan may permit acquisition of up to $600,000 worth of stock if it provides that the options are exercisable in six installments, each of which becomes exercisable in a different year and does not exceed $100,000.

Because of these regulatory conditions and the fact that a company may never receive a tax deduction, employers may view ISOs less favorably than nonqualified stock options.

Nonqualified Stock Options

A **nonqualified stock option (NQSO)** does not satisfy the statutory requirements for ISOs. In addition, a stock option that otherwise would qualify as an ISO will be treated as an NQSO if the terms of the stock option provide that it is not an ISO. If the NQSO has a readily ascertainable fair market value (e.g., the option is traded on an established exchange), the value of the option must be included in the employee's income at the date of grant. Thereafter, capital gain or loss is recognized only upon the disposal of the optioned stock. The employee's basis is the amount paid for the stock plus any amount reported as ordinary income. The employer obtains a corresponding tax deduction at the same time and to the extent that ordinary income is recognized by the employee.[99]

EXAMPLE 46

On February 1, 2007, Janet was granted an NQSO to purchase 100 shares of stock from her employer at $10 per share. On this date, the option was selling for $2 on an established exchange. Janet exercised the option on March 30, 2008, when the stock was worth $20 per share. On November 5, 2008, Janet sold the optioned stock for $22 per share.

- Janet must report ordinary income of $200 ($2 × 100 shares) on the date of grant (February 1, 2007), because the option has a readily ascertainable fair market value.
- Janet's adjusted basis for the stock is $1,200 ($1,000 cost + $200 recognized gain).
- Upon the sale of the stock (November 5, 2008), Janet must report a long-term capital gain of $1,000 [($22 − $12) × 100 shares].
- At the date of grant (February 1, 2007), the employer receives a tax deduction of $200, the amount of ordinary income reported by Janet. ∎

If an NQSO does not have a readily ascertainable fair market value, an employee does not recognize income at the grant date. However, as a general rule, ordinary income must then be reported in the year of exercise (the difference

---

[98]§ 422(c)(5).   [99]Reg. §§ 1.421–6(c), (d), (e), and (f); Reg. § 1.83–7.

between the fair market value of the stock at the exercise date and the option price).[100] The amount paid by the employee for the stock plus the amount reported as ordinary income becomes the basis. Any appreciation above that basis is taxed as a long-term capital gain upon disposition (assuming the stock is held for the required long-term holding period after exercise). The corporation receives a corresponding tax deduction at the same time and to the extent that ordinary income is recognized by the employee.

EXAMPLE 47

On February 3, 2006, Maria was granted an NQSO for 100 shares of common stock at $10 per share. On the date of the grant, there was no readily ascertainable fair market value for the option. Maria exercised the options on January 3, 2007, when the stock was selling for $15 per share. She sold one-half of the shares on April 15, 2007, and the other half on September 17, 2008. The sale price on both dates was $21 per share. Maria would not recognize any income on the grant date (February 3, 2006) but would recognize $500 ($1,500 − $1,000) of ordinary income on the exercise date (January 3, 2007). She would recognize a short-term capital gain of $300 on the sale of the first half in 2007 and a $300 long-term capital gain on the sale of the second batch of stock in 2008 [½($2,100 − $1,500)]. ∎

The major *advantages* of NQSOs can be summarized as follows:

- A tax deduction is available to the corporation without a cash outlay.
- The employee receives capital gain treatment on any appreciation in the stock starting either at the exercise date if the option does not have a readily ascertainable fair market value or at the date of grant if the option has a readily ascertainable fair market value.
- Options can be issued at more flexible terms than under ISO plans (e.g., longer exercise period and granted to nonemployees).

A major *disadvantage* is that the employee must recognize ordinary income on the exercise of the option or at the date of grant without receiving cash to pay the tax. Another negative factor is that the exercise price for NQSOs must not be lower than the underlying stock's fair market value on the grant date because of § 409A restrictions.

> **LO.10**
>
> Identify tax planning opportunities available with deferred compensation.

Deferred Compensation

TAX PLANNING
Considerations

With the individual tax rate being as high as 35 percent in 2008, taxpayers are motivated to try to lower their tax burden by participating in more deferred compensation arrangements. The $1 million annual limit on the compensation deduction

---

[100]Reg. § 1.83–7(a); Reg. § 1.421–6(d).

for the top five executives of publicly traded companies may cause a shift into § 401(k) plans, qualified retirement plans, and especially nonqualified deferred compensation arrangements. However, only $230,000 of compensation can be taken into consideration for purposes of calculating contributions or benefits under a qualified pension or profit sharing plan. The $5,000 allowed for traditional IRAs and Roth IRAs should encourage more participation in retirement vehicles. The spousal IRA option should expand retirement coverage even further.

Qualified Plans

Qualified plans provide maximum tax benefits for employers, because the employer receives an immediate tax deduction for contributions to a plan's trust and the income that is earned on the contributions is not taxable to the employer. The employer's contributions and the trust earnings are not taxed to the employees until those funds are made available to them.

Qualified plans are most appropriate where it is desirable to provide benefits for a cross section of employees. In some closely held corporations, the primary objective is to provide benefits for the officer-shareholder group and other highly paid personnel. The nondiscrimination requirements that must be met in a qualified plan may prevent such companies from attaining these objectives. Thus, a nonqualified arrangement may be needed as a supplement to, or used in lieu of, the qualified plan.

Cash balance plans are better for younger, mobile employees, and the converting company saves money by reducing pension payouts for older and longer-service employees. If a participant moves or retires, he or she can roll over the lump-sum payment into an IRA or another qualified plan.

Although defined benefit plans are being eliminated by larger companies, many small-business owners with few or no employees (or a young, low-paid, transient staff) are adopting them.

Self-Employed Retirement Plans

A Keogh or traditional deductible IRA participant may make a deductible contribution for a tax year up to the time prescribed for filing the individual's tax return. A Keogh plan must have been established by the end of the tax year (e.g., December 31) to obtain a current deduction for the contribution made in the subsequent year. An individual can establish an IRA after the end of the tax year and still receive a current deduction for the contribution made in the subsequent year. However, since the deductibility of contributions to IRAs has been restricted for many middle-income and upper-income taxpayers, Keogh plans are likely to become more important.

Individual Retirement Accounts

Unlike a traditional IRA, which defers taxes on the entire account, a Roth IRA allows the earnings to accumulate completely tax-free. All ordinary income and capital gains earned inside a Roth IRA are never taxed (assuming the five-year holding period provision is satisfied). Thus, a Roth IRA runs contrary to the general principle that it is usually better for a taxpayer to postpone the payment of any tax. In many situations, a retirement plan participant will earn more wealth with a Roth IRA than with a traditional IRA. This potential for tax-free growth is so advantageous that taxpayers who have substantial traditional IRA balances and are eligible should evaluate converting at least some of their traditional IRA balances into a Roth IRA.

Comparison of § 401(k) Plan with IRA

Most employees will find a § 401(k) plan more attractive than an IRA. Probably the biggest limitation of an IRA is the $5,000 maximum shelter in 2008 (ignoring the catch-up provision). Under § 401(k), employees are permitted to shelter

CONCEPT SUMMARY 19–4

Section 401(k) Plan and IRA Compared

	§ 401(k) Plan	IRA
Deduction limitation	Smaller of $15,500 (in 2008) or approximately 100% of total earnings. Limited by antidiscrimination requirements of § 401(k)(3).	$5,000 or 100% of compensation.
Distributions	Early withdrawal possible if for early retirement (55 or over) or to pay medical expenses.	10% penalty for early withdrawals, except for withdrawals to pay for certain medical expenses and health insurance, qualified education expenses, and qualified first-time home buyer expenses.
Effect on gross earnings	Gross salary reduction, which may reduce profit sharing contributions, Social Security benefits, and group life insurance.	No effect.
Employer involvement	Must keep records; monitor for compliance with antidiscrimination test.	Minimal.
Lump-sum distributions	Favorable 10-year forward averaging under limited circumstances.	Ordinary income.
Timing of contribution	Within 30 days of plan year-end or due date of employer's return.*	Grace period up to due date of tax return (not including extensions).
Loans from plan	Yes.	No.

*Elective contributions must be made to the plan no later than 30 days after the end of the plan year, and nonelective contributions no later than the due date of the tax return (including extensions).

compensation up to $15,500 (in 2008).[101] The restrictions on deducting contributions to IRAs for many middle-income and upper-income taxpayers may cause many employees to utilize § 401(k) plans more frequently.

Another difference between § 401(k) plans and IRAs is the manner in which the money is treated. Money placed in an IRA may be tax deductible, whereas dollars placed in a § 401(k) plan are considered to be deferred compensation. Thus, a § 401(k) reduction may reduce profit sharing payments, group life insurance, and Social Security benefits. Finally, many employers "match or partially match" employee elective deferrals with employer money. Concept Summary 19–4 compares a § 401(k) plan with an IRA.

Nonqualified Deferred Compensation (NQDC) Plans

Nonqualified deferred compensation arrangements such as restricted property plans can be useful to attract executive talent or to provide substantial retirement benefits for executives. A restricted property plan may be used to retain a key employee of a closely held company when management continuity problems are anticipated. Without such employees, the untimely death or disability of one of the owners might cause a disruption of the business with an attendant loss in value for his or her heirs. Such plans may discriminate in favor of officers and other highly paid employees. The employer, however, does not receive a tax deduction until the

---

[101]These amounts are being increased through a phase-in approach. See Footnotes 33 and 48.

CONCEPT SUMMARY   19–5

Incentive Stock Options and Nonqualified Stock Options Compared

	ISO	NQSO
Granted at any price	No	Yes
May have any duration	No	Yes
Governing Code Section	§ 422	§ 83
Spread subject to alternative minimum tax	Yes	No
Deduction to employer for spread	No	Yes
Type of gain/loss on disposal	Capital	Capital
Statutory amount ($100,000) limitation	Yes	No

employee is required to include the deferred compensation in income (upon the lapse of the restrictions).

The principal advantage of NQDC plans over current compensation is that the employee can defer the recognition of income to future periods when his or her income tax bracket may be lower (e.g., during retirement years). The time value benefits from the deferral of income should also be considered. If the trend toward decreasing rates continues, an executive with a deferred compensation arrangement entered into in a prior year might wish to continue to delay the income into future years since individual tax rates in future years may be even lower. However, if future rates are projected to rise, a different decision would be appropriate.

The principal disadvantage of NQDC plans could be the bunching effect that takes place on the expiration of the period of deferral. In some cases, planning can alleviate this result.

EXAMPLE 48

During 2008, Kelly, an executive, enters into an agreement to postpone a portion of her payment for current services until retirement. The deferred amount is not segregated from the company's general assets and is subject to normal business risk. The entire payment, not the after-tax amount, is invested in securities and variable annuity contracts. Kelly is not taxed on the payment in 2008, and the company receives no deduction in 2008. If Kelly receives the deferred payment in a lump sum when she retires, the tax rates might be higher and more progressive than in 2008. Thus, Kelly may wish to arrange for a number of payments to be made to her or a designated beneficiary over a number of years. ■

Stock Options

Rather than paying compensation in the form of corporate stock, a corporation may issue options to purchase stock at a specific price to an employee. Stock option plans are used more frequently by publicly traded companies than by closely held companies. This difference is due to the problems of determining the value of the stock of a company that is not publicly held, which is a practical requirement now in order to avoid negative treatment under § 409A.

Nonqualified stock options (NQSOs) are more flexible and less restrictive than incentive stock options (ISOs). For example, the holding period for an NQSO is not as long as that for an ISO. However, the option price of an NQSO cannot be less than the fair market value of the stock at the time the option is granted because of § 409A. An NQSO creates an employer deduction that lowers the cost of the NQSO to the employer. The employer may pass along this tax savings to the employee in the form of a cash payment. Both the employer and the employee may be better off by combining NQSOs with additional cash payments rather than using ISOs. See Concept Summary 19–5.

For tax purposes, most companies are able to deduct the expense of options and thereby reduce their taxes. Generally, options carry an exercise price (strike price) equal to the fair market value on the date the options are approved by the board of directors. The Financial Accounting Standards Board (FASB) now requires stock options to be expensed, which lowers a company's earnings. Companies must measure the economic value of the options on the grant date and then amortize this cost equally over the vesting period of the options. Also, § 409A effectively forces stock options to be granted with an exercise price equal to the stock's fair market value.

Stock options are an effective compensation device as long as share prices are rising. When stock prices fall, the options become unexercisable and possibly worthless. In an upmarket, options are great. But during a downturn in the market, these underwater options can be ugly.

Stock options are likely to be a less dominant form of executive compensation in the future. The backdating scandals and the required expensing of stock options for financial statement purposes are causing businesses to turn to other forms of compensation. Performance-based bonuses and § 401(k) plans probably will become more popular.

Flexible Benefit Plans

Employees may be permitted to choose from a package of employer-provided fringe benefits.[102] In these so-called **cafeteria benefit plans**, some of the benefits chosen by an employee may be taxable, and some may be statutory nontaxable benefits (e.g., health and accident insurance and group term life insurance).

Under general tax rules, providing a choice to employees would result in all benefits (both taxable and nontaxable) under the cafeteria benefit plan to be taxable. However, if the cafeteria plan rules are met, a special provision applies to prevent this tax result from occurring.

Employer contributions made to a flexible plan are included in an employee's gross income only to the extent that the employee actually elects the taxable benefits. Certain nondiscrimination standards with respect to coverage, eligibility for participation, contributions, and benefits must be met. Thus, such a plan must cover a fair cross section of employees. Also, a flexible plan cannot include an election to defer compensation, and a key employee is not exempt from taxation on the taxable benefits made available where more than 25 percent of the statutory nontaxable benefits are provided to key employees.

Liquidating Retirement Assets

If a person has funds from sources other than retirement assets, which retirement assets should an individual spend first? The most tax-efficient result is to postpone the income tax obligation for as long as possible. Generally, retirement assets should be taken from assets or accounts in the following order so that the tax-deferred growth continues:

- Taxable accounts.
- Section 457 accounts of government employees since no penalties apply once the employee is separated from employment.
- Section 401(k) and nonprofit § 403(b) plans because the age 55 separation rule may apply.
- Traditional IRAs since a taxpayer must be at least age 59½ to obtain penalty-free withdrawals.
- Roth IRAs since no required minimum distribution rules apply.[103]

---

[102]§ 125.

[103]David M. Maloney and James E. Smith, "Distribution Options for Defined Contribution Plans, Part II," *The Tax Adviser,* June 2007, pp. 340 and 341.

KEY TERMS

Cafeteria benefit plans, 19–43

Cash balance plan, 19–7

Coverdell Education Savings Account (CESA), 19–23

Deferred compensation, 19–3

Defined benefit plan, 19–4

Defined contribution pension plan, 19–5

Golden parachute payments, 19–32

Highly compensated employee, 19–9

H.R. 10(Keogh) plans, 19–19

Incentive stock option (ISO), 19–37

Individual Retirement Accounts (IRAs), 19–20

Lump-sum distribution, 19–13

Nonqualified deferred compensation (NQDC), 19–29

Nonqualified stock option (NQSO), 19–38

Pension plan, 19–4

Profit sharing plan, 19–6

Restricted property plan, 19–33

Roth IRA, 19–22

Section 401(k) plan, 19–15

Simplified employee pension (SEP) plans, 19–24

Stock bonus plan, 19–7

Stock option, 19–36

Substantial risk of forfeiture (SRF), 19–34

Vesting requirements, 19–9

PROBLEM MATERIALS

DISCUSSION QUESTIONS

1. Provide a definition for deferred compensation.

2. List some types of deferred compensation arrangements.

3. Determine whether each of the following independent statements best applies to a defined contribution plan *(DCP)*, a defined benefit plan *(DBP)*, both *(B)*, or neither *(N)*:
    a. The amount to be received at retirement depends on actuarial calculations.
    b. Forfeitures can be allocated to the remaining participants' accounts.
    c. Requires greater reporting requirements and more actuarial and administrative costs.
    d. Forfeitures can revert to the employer.
    e. More favorable to employees who are older at the time the plan is adopted.
    f. Employee forfeitures can be used to reduce future contributions by the employer.
    g. May exclude employees who begin employment within five years of normal retirement age.
    h. Annual addition to each employee's account may not exceed the smaller of $46,000 or 100% of the employee's salary.
    i. The final benefit to a participant depends upon investment performance.
    j. To avoid penalties, the amount of annual contributions must meet minimum funding requirements.

4. Indicate whether the following statements apply to a pension plan *(P)*, a profit sharing plan *(PS)*, both *(B)*, or neither *(N)*:
    a. Forfeited amounts can be used to reduce future contributions by the employer.
    b. Allocation of forfeitures may discriminate in favor of the prohibited group (highly compensated employees).
    c. Forfeitures can revert to the employer.
    d. Forfeitures can be allocated to participants and increase plan benefits.
    e. An annual benefit of $60,000 could be payable on behalf of a participant.
    f. More favorable to employees who are older at the time the qualified plan is adopted.

5. What is a pension plan?

6. What are the two types of qualified pension plans?

7. Describe a defined contribution pension plan.

8. List the requirements that must be satisfied in order for a retirement plan to be a qualified plan and receive favorable tax treatment.

9. Why is a determination letter needed for a new qualified retirement plan?

10. When must an employee be eligible to participate in a qualified retirement plan?

11. Jenny plans to retire in 2008 at age 70. Identify any issues facing Jenny with respect to distributions from her qualified retirement plan.

    Issue ID

12. Harvey Maxwell, who is age 71, is going to receive a lump-sum distribution from a qualified plan in 2008. He has asked you to provide him with a description of the alternatives available to him for taxing the lump-sum distribution. Draft a letter to Harvey in which you respond. He resides at 3000 East Glenn, Tulsa, OK 74104.

    Issue ID

    Communications

13. Which of the following would be considered a tax benefit or advantage of a qualified retirement plan?
    a. Certain lump-sum distributions may be subject to capital gain treatment.
    b. Employer contributions are deductible by the employer in the year of contribution.
    c. Employee contributions are deductible by the employee in the year of contribution.
    d. The qualified trust is tax-exempt as to all income (other than unrelated business income).

14. Sally is retiring and wishes to know her alternatives for receiving payments from her qualified retirement plan.

    Decision Making

15. Explain the contribution limitations for a defined contribution Keogh plan and for a defined benefit Keogh plan.

16. Should a 29-year-old self-employed woman establish a traditional deductible IRA, a traditional nondeductible IRA, or a Roth IRA? She has two children, ages 11 and 9.

    Decision Making

17. Nick is not covered by another qualified plan and earns $103,000 at his job in 2008. How much can he contribute to a traditional IRA or to a Roth IRA in 2008?

18. Jim White calls you and asks about "designated Roth contributions." Prepare a memo for the tax files about your response.

    Communications

19. A beneficiary of a Coverdell Education Savings Account (CESA) reaches age 30 in 2008. The plan balance of $6,000 consists of $4,000 of contributions and $2,000 of earnings. Discuss any tax consequences.

20. When is it appropriate to use a nonqualified deferred compensation arrangement?

21. During his senior year in college, Mark is drafted by the Los Angeles Dodgers. When he graduates, he expects to sign a five-year contract in the range of $1.8 million per year. Mark plans to marry his girlfriend before he reports to the Dodger farm team in California. Identify the relevant tax issues facing this left-handed pitcher.

    Issue ID

22. How are golden parachute payments treated by the payor and by the recipient?

23. What is a substantial risk of forfeiture, and what effect does it have on the taxpayer's gross income?

24. Sammy is retiring and wishes to know the most tax-efficient sequence for liquidating his retirement assets. What do you tell him?

PROBLEMS

25. Red Corporation has a total of 1,000 employees, of whom 700 are non-highly compensated. The retirement plan covers 300 non-highly compensated employees and 200 highly compensated employees. Does this plan satisfy the minimum coverage test?

26. Cardinal Corporation's pension plan benefits 620 of its 1,000 highly compensated employees. How many of its 620 non-highly compensated employees must benefit to meet the ratio percentage test for the minimum coverage requirement?

27. A retirement plan covers 72% of the non-highly compensated individuals. The plan benefits 48 of the 131 employees. Determine if the participation requirement is met.

28. Ryan, Inc., uses a three- to seven-year graded vesting approach in its retirement plan. Calculate the nonforfeitable percentage for each of the following participants based on the years of service completed:

Participant	Years of Service
Murphy	2
Sam	3
Sally	5
Heather	8

29. Jackie participates in a defined benefit plan that uses a fixed formula providing an employee with a benefit of 2% for each year of service, up to a maximum of 30 years. The total percentage accumulated before retirement is applied to the average of her three highest years of salary. Jackie works for 21 years, and the average of her three highest years of salary is $290,000. Calculate the amount of retirement benefits she will receive each year.

Decision Making

30. Iris has worked for Yellow Corporation for four and one-half years, but she has an offer to move to Red Corporation for a moderate increase in salary. Her average salary for Yellow has been $210,000, and she receives a 2% benefit for each year of service in her retirement plan. The company uses a five-year vesting schedule. Advise Iris as to this possible switch in jobs.

31. Heather has been an active participant in a defined benefit plan for 19 years. During her last 6 years of employment, Heather earned $42,000, $48,000, $56,000, $80,000, $89,000, and $108,000, respectively (representing her highest-income years).
    a. Calculate Heather's maximum allowable benefits from her qualified plan (assume there are fewer than 100 participants).
    b. Assume that Heather's average compensation for her three highest years is $196,700. Calculate her maximum allowable benefits.

32. Determine the maximum annual benefits payable to a participant from a defined benefit plan in the following independent situations:
    a. Frank, age 66, has been a participant for 17 years, and his highest average compensation for 3 years is $127,300.
    b. Ellen, age 65, has been a participant for 9 years (11 years of service), and her highest average compensation for 3 years is $102,600.

33. In 2008, Magenta Corporation paid compensation of $45,300 to the participants in a profit sharing plan. During 2008, Magenta Corporation contributed $13,200 to the plan.
    a. Calculate Magenta's deductible amount for 2008.
    b. Calculate the amount of any contribution carryover from 2008.

Decision Making

34. Amber's employer, Lavender, Inc., has a § 401(k) plan that permits salary deferral elections by its employees. Amber's salary is $95,000, and her marginal tax rate is 33%.
    a. What is the maximum amount Amber can elect for salary deferral treatment for 2008?
    b. If Amber elects salary deferral treatment for the amount in (a), how much can she save in taxes?
    c. What amount would you recommend that Amber elect for salary deferral treatment for 2008?

35. Sally, a single individual, participates in her employer's SIMPLE § 401(k) plan. The plan permits participants to contribute a percentage of their salary. Sally elects to contribute 5% of her annual salary of $111,000 to the plan. On what amount of her salary does Sally pay income taxes in 2008?

36. In 2008, Susan's sole proprietorship earns $240,000 of self-employment net income (after the deduction for one-half of self-employment tax).
    a. Calculate the maximum amount that Susan can deduct for contributions to a defined contribution Keogh plan.
    b. Suppose Susan contributes more than the allowable amount to the Keogh plan. What are the consequences to her?
    c. Can Susan retire and begin receiving Keogh payments at age 55 without incurring a penalty?

37. Adam is a self-employed attorney with earned income from the business of $120,000 (after the deduction for one-half of his self-employment tax). He has a profit sharing plan (e.g., defined contribution Keogh plan). What is the maximum amount Adam can contribute to his retirement plan in 2008?

38. Molly, age 29, is unmarried and is an active participant in a qualified retirement plan. Her modified AGI is $58,000 in 2008.
    a. Calculate the amount that Molly can contribute to a traditional IRA and the amount she can deduct.
    b. Assume instead that Molly is a participant in a SIMPLE IRA and that she elects to contribute 4% of her compensation to the account, while her employer contributes 3%. What amount will be contributed for 2008? What amount will be vested?

39. Answer the following independent questions with respect to a deductible IRA and § 401(k) contributions for 2008:
    a. Govind, age 31, earns a salary of $26,000 and is not an active participant in any other qualified plan. His wife has $600 of compensation income. What is the maximum total deductible contribution to their IRAs?
    b. Danos is a participant in a SIMPLE § 401(k) plan. He contributes 6% of his salary of $31,000, and his employer contributes 3%. What amount will be contributed for the year? What amount will be vested?

40. Answer the following independent questions with respect to traditional IRA contributions for 2008:
    a. Juan, age 41, earns a salary of $28,000 and is not an active participant in any other qualified plan. His wife, Agnes, has no earned income. What is the maximum total deductible contribution to their IRAs? Juan wishes to contribute as much as possible to his own IRA.
    b. Abby, age 29, has earned income of $25,000, and her husband has earned income of $2,600. They are not active participants in any other qualified plan. What is the maximum contribution to their IRAs?
    c. Leo's employer makes a contribution of $3,500 to Leo's simplified employee pension plan. If Leo is single, has earned income of $32,000, and has AGI of $29,000, what amount, if any, can he contribute to an IRA?

41. Stuart established a Roth IRA at age 26 and contributed a total of $92,600 to it over 39 years. The account is now worth $193,200. How much of these funds can Stuart withdraw tax-free?

42. Dana, age 51, has a traditional deductible IRA with an account balance of $224,300, of which $160,400 represents contributions and $63,900 represents earnings. In 2008, she converts her traditional IRA into a Roth IRA. What amount, if any, must Dana include in her gross income in 2008?

43. Karli and Jacob, age 34 and 35, have been married for 12 years and are both active participants in employer qualified retirement plans. Their total AGI in 2008 is $166,000, and they earn salaries of $85,000 and $81,000, respectively. What amount can Karli and Jacob:
    a. Contribute to traditional IRAs?
    b. Deduct for their contributions in (a)?
    c. Contribute to Roth IRAs?
    d. Deduct for their contributions in (c)?
    e. Contribute to Coverdell Education Savings Accounts for their two children?

44. Heather is a participant in a SIMPLE IRA plan of her employer. During 2008, she contributes 9% of her $52,000 salary, and her employer contributes 3%. What amount will be vested in her account at the end of 2008?

45. In 2013, Joyce receives a $4,000 distribution from her Coverdell Education Savings Account, which has a fair market value of $10,000. Total contributions to her CESA have been $7,000. Joyce's AGI is $25,000.
    a. Joyce uses the entire $4,000 to pay for qualified education expenses. What amount should she include in her gross income?
    b. Assume instead that Joyce uses only $2,500 of the $4,000 distribution for qualified education expenses. What amount should she include in her gross income?

46. Gene, age 34, and Beth, age 32, have been married for nine years. Gene, who is a college student, works part-time and earns $1,500. Beth is a high school teacher and earns a salary of $34,000. Their AGI is $37,000.
    a. What is the maximum amount Gene can contribute to an IRA in 2008?
    b. What is the maximum amount Beth can contribute to an IRA in 2008?

Decision Making

47. Samuel, age 32, loses his job in a corporate downsizing. As a result of his termination, he receives a distribution of the balance in his § 401(k) account of $20,000 ($25,000 − $5,000 withholding) on May 1, 2008. Samuel's marginal tax rate is 28%.
    a. What effect will the distribution have on Samuel's gross income and tax liability if he invests the $20,000 received in a mutual fund?
    b. Same as (a) except that Samuel invests the $20,000 received in a traditional IRA within 60 days of the distribution.
    c. Same as (a) except that Samuel invests the $20,000 received in a Roth IRA within 60 days of the distribution.
    d. How could Samuel have received better tax consequences in (b)?

48. Red, Inc., a calendar year employer, has an accrued NQDC liability of $400,000 on December 31, 2007. During 2008, the company accrues another $70,000 of NQDC. On February 12, 2009, the company pays the entire $470,000 to an employee.
    a. What amount is considered to be deferred compensation?
    b. When and what amount, if any, can the corporation deduct?

49. Elba is an officer of a local company that merges with a public company, resulting in a change of ownership. She loses her job as a result of the merger, but she receives a cash settlement of $680,000 from her employer under her golden parachute. Her average annual compensation for the past five tax years is $230,000.
    a. What are the tax consequences to Elba and to the company as a result of the $680,000 payment?
    b. Assume instead that Elba's five-year average annual compensation was $130,000, and she receives $420,000 in the settlement. What are the tax consequences to Elba?

Decision Making

50. On February 20, 2008, Tim (an executive of Hawk Corporation) purchased 100 shares of Hawk stock (selling at $20 a share) for $10. A condition of the transaction was that Tim must resell the stock to Hawk at cost if he voluntarily leaves the company within five years of receiving the stock (assume this represents a substantial risk of forfeiture).
    a. Assuming that no special election is made under § 83(b), what amount, if any, is taxable to Tim in 2008?
    b. Five years later when the stock is selling for $40 a share, Tim is still employed by Hawk. What amount of ordinary income, if any, is taxable to Tim?
    c. What amount, if any, is deductible by Hawk as compensation expense five years later?
    d. Should Tim make the § 83(b) special election in 2008? What amount would be taxable in 2008 if he makes the special election?
    e. In (d), what amount would be deductible by Hawk five years later?
    f. Under (d), assume Tim sold all the stock six years later for $65 per share. How much capital gain is included in his gross income?
    g. In (d), what loss is available to Tim if he voluntarily resigns in 2011 before the five-year period and does not sell the stock back to the corporation?
    h. In (g), in the year Tim resigns, what amount, if any, would be taxable to Hawk Corporation?

51. On July 2, 2006, Black Corporation sold 1,000 of its common shares (worth $14 per share) to Earl, an employee, for $5 per share. The sale was subject to Earl's agreement to resell the shares to the corporation for $5 per share if his employment is terminated within the following four years. The shares had a value of $24 per share on July 2, 2010. Earl sells the shares for $31 per share on September 16, 2010. No special election under § 83(b) is made.
    a. What amount, if any, is taxed to Earl on July 2, 2006?
    b. On July 2, 2010?
    c. On September 16, 2010?
    d. What deduction, if any, will Black Corporation obtain? When?
    e. Assume the same facts, except that Earl makes an election under § 83(b). What amount, if any, will be taxed to Earl on July 2, 2006, July 2, 2010, and September 16, 2010?
    f. Will the assumption made in (e) have any effect on any deduction Black Corporation will receive? Explain.

52. Rosa exercises ISOs for 100 shares of Copper Corporation common stock at the option price of $100 per share on May 21, 2007, when the fair market value is $120 per share. She sells the 100 shares of common stock three and one-half years later for $140.
    a. Calculate the long-term capital gain and the ordinary income on the sale.
    b. Assume Rosa holds the stock only seven months and sells the shares for $140 per share. Calculate the capital gain and ordinary income on the sale.
    c. In (b), what amount can Copper Corporation deduct? When?
    d. Assume instead that Rosa holds the stock for two years and sells the shares for $115 per share. Calculate any capital gain and ordinary income on this transaction.
    e. In (a), assume the options are nonqualified stock options with a nonascertainable fair market value on the date of the grant. Calculate the long-term capital gain and ordinary income on the date of the sale.
    f. In (e), assume that each option has an ascertainable fair market value of $10 on the date of the grant and that no substantial risk of forfeiture exists. Calculate the long-term capital gain and the ordinary income on the date of the sale.

53. On November 19, 2006, Rex is granted a nonqualified stock option to purchase 100 shares of Tan Company. On that date, the stock is selling for $8 per share, and the option price is $9 per share. Rex exercises the option on August 21, 2007, when the stock is selling for $10 per share. Five months later, Rex sells the shares for $11.50 per share.
    a. What amount is taxable to Rex in 2006?
    b. What amount is taxable to Rex in 2007?
    c. What amount and type of gain are taxable to Rex in 2008?
    d. What amount, if any, is deductible by Tan Company in 2007?
    e. What amount, if any, is recognized in 2008 if the stock is sold for $9.50 per share?

54. Sara Reid, age 35, is the owner of a small business. She is trying to decide whether to have a § 401(k) plan or a simplified employee pension plan. She is not interested in a SIMPLE § 401(k) plan. Her salary will be approximately $49,000, and she will have no employees. She asks you to provide her with information on the advantages and disadvantages of both types of plans and your recommendation. Draft a letter to Sara that contains your response. Her address is 1000 Canal Avenue, New Orleans, LA 70148.

Decision Making

Communications

55. Lou's employer provides a qualified cafeteria plan under which he can choose cash of $10,000 or health and accident insurance premiums worth approximately $7,000. If Lou is in the 35% tax bracket, advise him of his tax alternatives.

Decision Making

56. Suppose a company pays an executive a $300,000 salary. Social Security taxes are 6.2%, and Medicare taxes are 1.45%. Assume the marginal tax rate of the company is 34%. Calculate the after-tax cost to the company of providing this cash salary.

RESEARCH PROBLEMS

Note: Solutions to Research Problems can be prepared by using the **RIA Checkpoint**® **Student Edition** online research product, which is available to accompany this text. It is also possible to prepare solutions to the Research Problems by using tax research materials found in a standard tax library.

Research Problem 1.   Why do some argue that age discrimination occurs when a company converts a traditional defined benefit plan into a cash balance plan? How did the Pension Protection Act of 2006 deal with this issue?

Research Problem 2.   Shelly and Austin were divorced in 2008. Since they lived in a community property state, the judgment dissolving the marriage ordered that Austin's traditional deductible IRA be divided equally between Shelly and him. Austin accordingly withdrew $125,000 from his IRA and transferred $112,000 to Shelly. Discuss the tax consequences for Shelly and for Austin.

Partial list of research aids:
§§ 72(t), 408(d)(1), 408(d)(6), 408(g), and 6662(a).

Research Problem 3.   Billy Donovan, the basketball coach for the University of Florida, walks into your office with a problem. In May 2007, he signed a five-year, $27.5 million contract to be the new coach of the professional Orlando Magic team.

Within days, Donovan changed his mind, and eventually he and the Magic organization reached an agreement that allowed him to walk away and remain the coach at the University of Florida. He has an approximately $3 million contract with the University of Florida. The Magic contract stated that "we have the legal right to hold Billy [Donovan] to the contract he signed."

Assume that Donovan signed a noncompete clause restricting him from coaching in the NBA for the next five years. Assume (1) the Magic released Donovan without receiving any compensation from him, (2) the Magic canceled a $2 million buyout provision, and (3) Donovan signed the noncompete clause.

Does Coach Donovan have any taxable income from this separation agreement?

Research Problem 4.   Jim Raby transfers one-half of his compensatory stock options (ISOs and nonqualified stock options) to his ex-wife as part of a divorce settlement. Discuss the tax aspects of this transfer.

Research Problem 5.   Are stock appreciation rights covered by the new statutory framework for nonqualified deferred compensation in § 409A?

Internet Activity

Use the tax resources of the Internet to address the following questions. Do not restrict your search to the World Wide Web, but include a review of newsgroups and general reference materials, practitioner sites and resources, primary sources of the tax law, chat rooms and discussion groups, and other opportunities.

Research Problem 6.   Locate and download an Internet retirement calculator. Use this program to help you answer the questions in Problems 38 and 39.

Research Problem 7.   Search the Internet to determine what happens when annual limitations on contributions and benefits from a qualified retirement plan are not met. How can an employer correct such a problem?

Research Problem 8.   Using newspapers and magazine articles, determine the latest positions of the AICPA, SEC, PCAOB, and other groups with respect to the backdating of stock options. Determine if any executives have been convicted of backdating stock options.

PART 7

Corporations and Partnerships

The primary orientation of this text is toward basic tax concepts and the individual taxpayer. Although many of these tax concepts also apply to corporations and partnerships, numerous tax concepts apply specifically to corporations or partnerships. An overview of these provisions is presented in Part VII. Comprehensive coverage of these topics appears in South-Western Federal Taxation: Corporations, Partnerships, Estates, & Trusts.

CHAPTER 20
Corporations and Partnerships

CHAPTER **20**

Corporations and Partnerships

LEARNING OBJECTIVES

After completing Chapter 20, you should be able to:

LO.1
Identify those entities that are treated as corporations for Federal income tax purposes.

LO.2
Contrast the income tax treatment of individuals with that applicable to corporations.

LO.3
Recognize and calculate the tax deductions available only to corporations.

LO.4
Determine the corporate tax liability and comply with various procedural and reporting requirements.

LO.5
Understand the tax rules governing the formation of corporations.

LO.6
Work with the tax rules governing the operation of corporations.

LO.7
Recognize the tax rules governing the liquidation of corporations.

LO.8
Appreciate the utility and effect of the Subchapter S election.

LO.9
Understand the tax consequences of forming and operating a partnership.

LO.10
Evaluate the advantages and disadvantages of the various forms for conducting a business.

OUTLINE

What Is a Corporation?, 20–2
Compliance with State Law, 20–2
Entity Classification prior to 1997, 20–3
Entity Classification after 1996, 20–4
Income Tax Considerations, 20–4
General Tax Consequences of Different Forms
    of Business Entities, 20–4
Individuals and Corporations Compared—An
    Overview, 20–4
Specific Provisions Compared, 20–6
Deductions Available Only to Corporations, 20–11
Determination of Corporate Tax Liability, 20–14
Corporate Filing Requirements, 20–14
Reconciliation of Corporate Taxable Income
    and Accounting Income, 20–15
Forming the Corporation, 20–17
Capital Contributions, 20–17
Transfers to Controlled Corporations, 20–17
Operating the Corporation, 20–21
Dividend Distributions, 20–21
Stock Redemptions, 20–24

Liquidating the Corporation, 20–24
General Rule of § 331, 20–24
Exception to the General Rule, 20–25
Basis Determination—§§ 334 and 338, 20–25
Effect of the Liquidation on the Corporation, 20–26
The S Election, 20–26
Qualification for S Status, 20–26
Operational Rules, 20–28
Partnerships, 20–31
Nature of Partnership Taxation, 20–31
Partnership Formation, 20–32
Partnership Operation, 20–34
Tax Planning Considerations, 20–36
Corporate versus Noncorporate Forms
    of Business Organization, 20–36
Regular Corporation versus S Status, 20–38
Use of an Entity to Reduce the Family
    Income Tax Burden, 20–39

Until now this text has concentrated on the Federal income taxation of individual taxpayers. However, even the most basic business decisions require some awareness of the tax implications of other business forms.

EXAMPLE 1

Gina and Tom are contemplating entering into a new business venture that will require additional capital investment by other parties. As the venture will involve financial risk, both Gina and Tom are concerned about personal liability. Further, they would prefer to avoid any income taxes at the entity level. Both Gina and Tom would like to take advantage of any losses the venture may generate during its formative period. ■

In choosing the form for the venture, Gina and Tom will have to consider using a corporation. The corporate form limits a shareholder's liability to the amount invested in the stock. Regular corporations, however, are subject to the corporate income tax. Furthermore, losses incurred by corporations do not pass through to the shareholders. Perhaps the ideal solution would be to use the corporate form and elect to be taxed as an S corporation. The election would avoid the corporate income tax and permit the pass-through of losses while providing limited liability for the shareholders.

Although the resolution of the problem posed by Example 1 seems simple enough, it did not consider the possible use of a partnership or limited liability company. More important, the decision required *some* knowledge of corporations and the S corporation election. This chapter is intended to provide such knowledge by briefly reviewing the tax consequences of the various forms of business organization.

LO.1

Identify those entities that are treated as corporations for Federal income tax purposes.

What Is a Corporation?

Compliance with State Law

A company must comply with the specific requirements for corporate status under state law. For example, it is necessary to draft articles of incorporation and file them with the state regulatory agency, be granted a charter, and issue stock to share-holders.

Compliance with state law, although important, is not the only requirement that must be met to qualify for corporate *tax* status. For example, a corporation qualifying under state law may be disregarded as a taxable entity if it is a mere sham lacking in economic substance. The key consideration is the degree of business activity conducted at the corporate level.

EXAMPLE 2

Gene and Mike are joint owners of a tract of unimproved real estate that they wish to protect from future creditors. Gene and Mike form Falcon Corporation and transfer the land to it in return for all of the corporation's stock. The corporation merely holds title to the land and conducts no other activities. In all respects, Falcon Corporation meets the legal requirements of a corporation under applicable state law. Nevertheless, Falcon might not be recognized as a separate entity for corporate tax purposes under these facts.[1] ∎

EXAMPLE 3

Assume the same facts as in Example 2. In addition to holding title to the land, Falcon Corporation leases the property, collects rents, and pays the property taxes. Falcon probably would be treated as a corporation for Federal income tax purposes because of the scope of its activities. ∎

In some instances, the IRS has attempted to disregard (or collapse) a corporation in order to make the income taxable directly to the shareholders.[2] In other cases, the IRS has asserted that the corporation is a separate taxable entity so as to assess tax at the corporate level and to tax corporate distributions to shareholders as dividend income (double taxation).[3]

Entity Classification prior to 1997

Can an organization not qualifying as a corporation under state law still be treated as such for Federal income tax purposes? Unfortunately, the tax law defines a corporation as including "associations, joint stock companies, and insurance companies."[4] As the Code contains no definition of an "association," the issue became the subject of frequent litigation.[5]

It was finally determined that an entity would be treated as a corporation if it had a majority of the characteristics common to corporations.[6] For this purpose, the relevant characteristics are:

- Continuity of life.
- Centralized management.
- Limited liability.
- Free transferability of interests.

These criteria did not resolve all of the problems that continued to arise over corporate classification. When a new type of business entity, the **limited liability company**, was developed, the IRS was deluged with inquiries about its tax status. As the limited liability company became increasingly popular with professional groups, all states enacted statutes allowing some form of this entity. The statutes invariably permitted the corporate characteristic of limited liability and, often, that of centralized management. Because continuity of life and free transferability of interests were absent, it was hoped that the entity would be classified as a partnership.

---

[1]See *Paymer v. Comm.*, 45–2 USTC ¶9353, 33 AFTR 1536, 150 F.2d 334 (CA–2, 1945).

[2]*Floyd Patterson*, 25 TCM 1230, T.C.Memo. 1966–239, *aff'd* in 68–2 USTC ¶9471, 22 AFTR2d 5810 (CA–2, 1968).

[3]*Raffety Farms Inc. v. U.S.*, 75–1 USTC ¶9271, 35 AFTR2d 75–811, 511 F.2d 1234 (CA–8, 1975).

[4]§ 7701(a)(3).

[5]See, for example, *U.S. v. Kintner*, 54–2 USTC ¶9626, 46 AFTR 995, 216 F.2d 418 (CA–5, 1954).

[6]See Reg. § 301.7701–2(a) prior to repeal.

This treatment would avoid the double taxation result inherent in the corporate form.

Entity Classification after 1996

In late 1996, the IRS issued its so-called **check-the-box Regulations**.[7] Effective beginning in 1997, these Regulations enable taxpayers to classify a business entity for tax purposes without regard to its corporate (or noncorporate) characteristics. These rules have simplified tax administration considerably and eliminated the litigation that arose with regard to association (corporation) status.

Under the rules, an entity with more than one owner can elect to be classified as either a partnership or a corporation. An entity with only one owner can elect to be classified as a corporation or a sole proprietorship. In the event of default (no election is made), entities with multiple owners will be classified as partnerships and single-person businesses as sole proprietorships.

The election is not available to entities that are actually incorporated under state law or to entities that are required to be corporations under Federal law (e.g., certain publicly traded partnerships). For purposes of these prohibitions, limited liability companies not incorporated under state law can elect either corporation or partnership status.

Eligible entities make the election as to tax status by filing Form 8832 (Entity Classification Election).[8] New elections are permitted, but only after a 60-month waiting period.

Income Tax Considerations

LO.2

Contrast the income tax treatment of individuals with that applicable to corporations.

General Tax Consequences of Different Forms of Business Entities

A business operation may be conducted as a sole proprietorship, as a partnership, or in corporate form.

- Sole proprietorships are not separate taxable entities. The owner of the business reports all business transactions on his or her individual income tax return.
- Partnerships are not subject to the income tax. Under the *conduit* concept, the various tax attributes of the partnership's operations flow through to the individual partners to be reported on their personal income tax returns.
- The regular corporate form (known as a **C corporation**) of doing business carries with it the imposition of the corporate income tax. The corporation is recognized as a separate taxpaying entity. Income is taxed to the corporation as earned and taxed again to the shareholders as dividends when distributed.
- A regular corporation (C corporation) may elect to be taxed as an S corporation. This special treatment follows the conduit concept and is similar (although not identical) to the partnership rules. Income tax is generally avoided at the corporate level, and shareholders are taxed currently on the taxable income of the S corporation.

Individuals and Corporations Compared—An Overview

Similarities between Corporate and Individual Tax Rules. The gross income of a corporation is determined in much the same manner as for individuals. Both individuals and corporations are entitled to exclusions from gross income, such as interest on municipal bonds. Gains and losses from property

---

[7]Reg. §§ 301.7701–1 through –4, and –7. [8]Reg. § 301.7701–3(c).

transactions are also treated similarly. For example, whether a gain or loss is capital or ordinary depends on the nature and use of the asset rather than the type of taxpayer. Upon the sale or other taxable disposition of depreciable personalty, the recapture rules of § 1245 make no distinction between corporate and noncorporate taxpayers. In the case of the recapture of depreciation on real property (§ 1250), however, corporate taxpayers experience more severe tax consequences. As illustrated later, corporations must recognize as additional ordinary income 20 percent of the excess of the amount that would be recaptured under § 1245 over the amount recaptured under § 1250.

In cases involving nontaxable exchanges and certain transactions allowing the deferral of gain recognition, many of the rules are the same. Thus, both individuals and corporations can utilize the like-kind exchange provisions of § 1031 and the deferral allowed by § 1033 for involuntary conversions. In contrast, the § 121 exclusion for gain from the sale of a principal residence is a relief measure available only to individual taxpayers.

The business deductions of corporations parallel those available to individuals. Corporate deductions are allowed for all ordinary and necessary expenses paid or incurred in carrying on a trade or business. Corporations may also deduct interest, certain taxes, losses, bad debts, depreciation, cost recovery, charitable contributions subject to corporate limitation rules, net operating losses, research and experimental expenditures, and other less common deductions.

Many of the tax credits available to individuals, such as the foreign tax credit, can be claimed by corporations. Not available to corporations are certain credits that are personal in nature. Examples of credits not available to corporations include the credit for child and dependent care expenses, the credit for the elderly or disabled, and the earned income credit.

Corporations usually have the same choices of accounting periods as do individuals. Like an individual, a corporation may choose a calendar year or a fiscal year for reporting purposes. Corporations do enjoy greater flexibility in the election of a tax year. For example, corporations usually can have different tax years from those of their shareholders. Also, a newly formed corporation generally has a free choice of any approved accounting period without having to obtain the consent of the IRS. As noted in Chapter 18, however, personal service corporations are subject to severe restrictions on the use of a fiscal year.

In terms of methods of accounting, both individuals and corporations must use the *accrual* method in determining cost of goods sold if they maintain inventory for sale to customers. The *accrual* method must also be used by *large* corporations (annual gross receipts in excess of $5 million). The *cash method* of accounting, however, is available to *small* corporations and in the following additional situations:

- An S election is in effect.
- The trade or business is farming or timber.
- A qualified personal service corporation is involved.
- A qualified service provider (e.g., plumbing business) is involved, and annual gross receipts (for the past three years) do not exceed $10 million. This exception applies even if the service provider is buying and selling inventory.

Dissimilarities. Both noncorporate and corporate taxpayers are subject to progressive income tax rates. For individuals, the rates for 2008 are 10, 15, 25, 28, 33, and 35 percent. For corporations, the rates are 15, 25, 34, and 35 percent. Corporate taxpayers lose the benefits of the lower brackets (using a phaseout approach) once taxable income reaches a certain level. Noncorporate taxpayers, however, continue to enjoy the benefits of the lower brackets even though they have reached the higher taxable income levels.

Commencing in 2003, qualified dividends received by individual shareholders are subject to preferential tax rates. For those shareholders in the top four tax brackets

ARE CORPORATE TAXES TOO HIGH?

A recent Treasury report shows that the average statutory corporate tax rate in the United States is 39 percent when both Federal and state income taxes are considered. In contrast, average rates for the European Union and the Asia-Pacific region are 26 percent and 30 percent, respectively. Currently, the United States is second only to Japan in top rates, and that country is planning a rate reduction. The recent downward trend in corporate income tax rates has been particularly prevalent in European countries (e.g., from 34 to 28 percent in France, from 35 to 30 percent in Spain, and from 39 to just under 30 percent in Germany). Meanwhile, in the United States the Federal tax rates on corporations have remained unchanged since they were substantially lowered in 1986!

If the United States is to compete worldwide for investment capital, the applicable income tax rates are one of the factors that will influence the outcome. To enable the United States to compete with low-tax European countries, the Treasury report recommends that the top Federal tax rate on corporations be cut from 35 to 27 percent. To make up for the loss of revenue that the cut will cause, the report suggests that the curtailment or elimination of a number of tax benefits including the following: the domestic production activities deduction (DPAD), the exclusion for interest on state and local bonds, the research activities tax credit, the low-income housing tax credit, and percentage depletion on minerals.

Regardless of its merits, the Treasury report is not likely to be implemented in the near future. In an election year, lowering the corporate income tax rates has little popular appeal. Furthermore, some of the suggested revenue offsets (e.g., eliminating the research activities tax credit and the exclusion of interest on state and local bonds) would generate strong opposition among certain politically influential groups.

Source: Treasury Conference on Business Taxation and Global Competitiveness, *U.S. Department of the Treasury, July 23, 2007.*

(25, 28, 33, and 35 percent), the maximum rate is 15 percent; for those in the bottom two brackets (10 and 15 percent), the rate is 0 percent (5 percent for 2007). As discussed later, corporate shareholders enjoy the alternative of the dividends received deduction.

Many corporate and all noncorporate taxpayers are subject to the alternative minimum tax (AMT). For AMT purposes, many adjustments and tax preference items are the same for both, but other adjustments and tax preferences apply only to corporations or only to individuals. Also, certain small business corporations are effectively exempt from the corporate AMT. Corporate tax rates are discussed later in the chapter. The AMT is discussed at length in Chapter 12. See also the coverage in *South-Western Federal Taxation: Corporations, Partnerships, Estates, and Trusts.*

All allowable corporate deductions are treated as business expenses. The determination of adjusted gross income, so essential for individuals, has no relevance to corporations. Corporations need not be concerned with classifying deductions into *deduction for* and *deduction from* categories.

Specific Provisions Compared

Corporate and individual tax rules also differ in the following areas:

- Capital gains and losses.
- Recapture of depreciation.

- Charitable contributions.
- Domestic production activities deduction.
- Net operating losses.
- Special deductions for corporations.

Capital Gains and Losses. Both corporate and noncorporate taxpayers are required to aggregate gains and losses from the taxable sale or exchange of capital assets. (Refer to Chapter 16 for a description of the netting process that takes place after the aggregation has been completed.) For long-term capital gains (including gains from collectibles and unrecaptured § 1250 gain), individuals enjoy an advantage. Called the alternative tax, the maximum applicable tax rate is 28 percent for collectibles, 25 percent for unrecaptured § 1250 gain, and 15 percent for other capital gains. For the last category, the tax rate is reduced to 0 percent (5 percent for 2007) if the taxpayer is in the 15 percent (or lower) tax bracket. In the case of corporations, all capital gains are taxed using the rates for ordinary income. Therefore, the net long-term capital gain of a corporation could be taxed at a rate of 35 percent (the highest rate applicable to corporations).

Significant differences exist in the treatment of capital losses for income tax purposes. Individuals, for example, can annually deduct up to $3,000 of net capital losses against ordinary income. If an individual has both net short-term and net long-term capital losses, the short-term capital losses are used first in arriving at the $3,000 ordinary loss deduction. Corporations are not permitted to use net capital losses to offset ordinary income. Net capital losses can be used only to offset past or future capital gains.[9] Unlike individuals, corporations are not allowed an unlimited carryover period for capital losses. Instead, they may carry back excess capital losses to the three preceding years, applying the losses initially to the earliest year. If not exhausted by the carryback, remaining unused capital losses may be carried forward for a period of five years from the year of the loss.[10]

When carried back or forward, *both* short-term capital losses and long-term capital losses are treated as short-term capital losses by corporate taxpayers. For noncorporate taxpayers, carryovers of capital losses retain their identity as short or long term.

EXAMPLE 4

Hawk Corporation, a calendar year taxpayer, incurs a long-term net capital loss of $5,000 for 2008. None of the capital loss may be deducted in 2008. Hawk may, however, carry the loss back to years 2005, 2006, and 2007 (in this order) and offset any capital gains recognized in these years. If the carryback does not exhaust the loss, the loss may be carried forward to 2009, 2010, 2011, 2012, and 2013 (in this order). Such capital loss carrybacks or carryovers are treated as short-term capital losses. ∎

Recapture of Depreciation. Corporations selling depreciable real estate may have ordinary income in addition to that required by § 1250. Under § 291, the additional ordinary income element is 20 percent of the excess of the § 1245 recapture potential over the § 1250 recapture. As a result, the § 1231 gain is correspondingly decreased by the additional recapture.

Under § 1250, the excess of accelerated depreciation over straight-line depreciation is recaptured as ordinary income as to residential real property. Since all real property purchased since 1986 is depreciated using only the straight-line method, after 2005 the § 1250 amount is zero because the depreciation period (19 years in 1986) has expired and such buildings are fully depreciated.

---

[9] §§ 1211(a) and (b).   [10] § 1212(a).

EXAMPLE 5

Condor Corporation purchases residential real property on November 3, 1996, for $300,000. Straight-line cost recovery is taken in the amount of $121,808 before the property is sold on January 5, 2008, for $250,000.

First, determine the recognized gain:

Sales price		$ 250,000
Less adjusted basis:		
Cost of property	$300,000	
Less cost recovery	(121,808)	(178,192)
Recognized gain		$ 71,808

Second, determine the § 1245 recapture potential. This is the lesser of $71,808 (recognized gain) or $121,808 (cost recovery claimed).

Third, determine the § 1250 recapture amount:

Cost recovery taken	$ 121,808
Less straight-line cost recovery	(121,808)
§ 1250 ordinary income	$ –0–

Fourth, because the taxpayer is a corporation, determine the additional § 291 amount:

§ 1245 recapture potential	$ 71,808
Less § 1250 recapture amount	(–0–)
Excess § 1245 recapture potential	$ 71,808
Apply § 291 percentage	× 20%
Additional ordinary income under § 291	$ 14,362

Condor Corporation's recognized gain of $71,808 is accounted for as follows:

Ordinary income under § 1250	$ –0–
Ordinary income under § 291	14,362
§ 1231 gain	57,446
Total recognized gain	$ 71,808

■

Charitable Contributions. Generally, a charitable contribution deduction is allowed only for the tax year in which the payment is made. However, an important exception is made for accrual basis corporations. The deduction may be claimed in the tax year *preceding* payment if the following conditions are satisfied:

- The contribution is authorized by the board of directors by the end of that tax year *and*
- The contribution is paid on or before the fifteenth day of the third month of the next tax year.[11]

EXAMPLE 6

On December 29, 2008, the board of directors of Dove Corporation, a calendar year, accrual basis taxpayer, authorizes a $5,000 donation to a qualified charity. The donation is paid on March 13, 2009. Dove Corporation may claim the $5,000 donation as a deduction for 2008. As an alternative, Dove may claim the deduction in 2009 (the year of payment). ■

Like individuals, corporations are not permitted an unlimited charitable contribution deduction. In any one year, a corporate taxpayer is limited to 10 percent of taxable income. For this purpose, taxable income is computed without regard to the charitable contribution deduction, any net operating loss carryback or capital

---

[11]§ 170(a)(2).

loss carryback, or the dividends received deduction.[12] Any contributions in excess of the 10 percent limitation are carried forward to the five succeeding tax years. Any carryover must be added to subsequent contributions and is subject to the 10 percent limitation. In applying the limitation, the most recent contributions must be deducted first.[13]

EXAMPLE 7

During 2008, Eagle Corporation (a calendar year taxpayer) had the following income and expenses:

Income from operations	$140,000
Expenses from operations	110,000
Dividends received	10,000
Charitable contributions made in 2008	5,000

For purposes of the 10% limitation only, Eagle's taxable income is $40,000 ($140,000 − $110,000 + $10,000). Consequently, the allowable charitable contribution deduction for 2008 is $4,000 (10% × $40,000). The $1,000 unused portion of the contribution is carried forward to 2009, 2010, 2011, 2012, and 2013 (in that order) until exhausted. ∎

EXAMPLE 8

Assume the same facts as in Example 7. In 2009, Eagle Corporation has taxable income (after adjustments) of $50,000 and makes a charitable contribution of $4,800. The maximum deduction allowed for 2009 is $5,000 (10% × $50,000). The first $4,800 of the allowed deduction must be allocated to the 2009 contribution, and the $200 excess is allocated to the carryover from 2008. The remaining $800 of the 2008 contribution is carried over to 2010, etc. ∎

As noted in Chapter 10, the deduction for charitable contributions of ordinary income property is limited to the lesser of the fair market value or the adjusted basis of the property. A special rule provides an exception that permits a corporation to contribute inventory (ordinary income property) to certain charitable organizations and receive a deduction equal to the adjusted basis plus one-half of the difference between the fair market value and the adjusted basis of the property. In no event, however, may the deduction exceed twice the adjusted basis of the property. To qualify for this exception, the inventory must be used by the charity in its exempt purpose for the care of *children*, the *ill*, or the *needy*.

EXAMPLE 9

In the current year, Robin Company (a retail clothier) donates sweaters and overcoats to Sheltering Arms (a qualified charity caring for the homeless). The clothing is inventory and has a basis of $10,000 and a fair market value of $14,000. If Robin is a corporation, the charitable contribution that results is $12,000 [$10,000 (basis) + $2,000 (50% of the appreciation of $4,000)]. In contrast, if Robin is not a corporation, the charitable contribution is limited to $10,000 (basis). ∎

The special rule allowing the inventory exception also provides further exceptions for gifts of scientific property and computer technology and equipment to be used for educational purposes. If certain conditions are met, 50 percent of the appreciation on such property is allowed as an additional charitable deduction.[14]

Domestic Production Activities Deduction. As noted in Chapter 7, § 199 was designed to replace various export tax benefits that our world trading partners deemed discriminatory. Known as the domestic production activities deduction (DPAD), the provision is equally applicable to C corporations. In the case of C corporations, however, the limitation is based on taxable income, rather than AGI

---

[12]§ 170(b)(2).
[13]§ 170(d)(2).

[14]These conditions are set forth in §§ 170(e)(4) and (6). The inventory exception is prescribed by § 170(e)(3).

(both computed without considering the deduction). Thus, the DPAD is 6 percent of the *lesser* of qualified production activities income (QPAI) or taxable income. (The DPAD was 3 percent prior to 2007 and will increase to 9 percent in 2010.) As with individual taxpayers, the DPAD cannot exceed 50 percent of the W–2 wages involved (those subject to withholding plus certain elective deferrals). Domestic gross receipts from manufacturing activities are a major source of QPAI. These gross receipts are adjusted by cost of goods sold and other assignable expenses to arrive at QPAI.

For corporations that are members of an affiliated group (based on 50 percent common control), the deduction is determined by treating the group as a single taxpayer. In effect, therefore, each member of the group is treated as being engaged in the activities of every other member. The deduction is then allocated among the members in proportion to each member's respective amount of QPAI.[15]

EXAMPLE 10	Mallard and Pintail Corporations are members of an affiliated group but do not file a consolidated return. Mallard manufactures a machine at a cost of $300 and sells it to Pintail for $500. Pintail incurs additional cost of $100 for marketing and then sells the machine to an unrelated customer for $700. The QPAI deduction is based on $300 ($700 − $300 − $100) even though the seller (Pintail) did not perform any manufacturing.[16] Note that this is the same result that would have been reached if Pintail had not been involved and Mallard had conducted its own marketing function. ∎

EXAMPLE 11	Assume the same facts as in Example 10 except that the parties are not related. Under these circumstances, Mallard has QPAI of $200 ($500 − $300) and Pintail has none. Pintail's activities, when considered alone, are not QPAI because they involve marketing and not manufacturing. ∎

In the case of pass-through entities (e.g., partnerships, S corporations, trusts, and estates), special rules apply for handling the DPAD.[17] Because the deduction is determined at the owner level, each partner or shareholder must make the computation separately. Thus, the entity allocates to each owner his or her share of QPAI. The QPAI that is passed through is then combined with any qualifying activities that the owner has from other sources (e.g., a partner also conducts a manufacturing activity on his or her own).

The DPAD can be claimed in computing the alternative minimum tax (including adjusted current earnings). The deduction allowed is the lesser of QPAI or alternative minimum taxable income (AMTI). In the case of an individual taxpayer, AGI is substituted for AMTI in determining the limitation on the amount allowed as a deduction.[18]

Net Operating Losses.   The computation of a net operating loss (NOL) for individuals was discussed in Chapter 7. Corporations are not subject to the complex adjustments required for individuals (e.g., a corporation has no adjustments for nonbusiness deductions or capital gains and losses). Corporations are subject to fewer adjustments than individuals are because a corporation's loss more clearly approximates a true economic loss. Artificial deductions (e.g., personal and dependency exemptions) that merely generate paper losses are not permitted for corporations.

In computing the NOL of a corporation, the dividends received deduction (discussed below) can be claimed in determining the amount of the loss. Generally, NOLs generated after 1998 may be carried back 2 years and forward 20 years (or

---

[15]§ 199(d)(4).
[16]Reg. § 1.199–7(c).

[17]§ 199(d)(1).
[18]§ 199(d)(6).

TAX *in the News*   **VARIATIONS IN MITIGATING THE EFFECT OF MULTIPLE TAXATION**

When a corporation receives a dividend from another corporation, multiple taxation of the same income is eased (or avoided) by allowing the corporate shareholder a dividends received deduction. But what happens when these funds are later passed through to the individual shareholders? Until recently, such distributions were fully taxed as ordinary income.

This problem of double taxation of corporate distributions at the individual shareholder level was addressed by Congress in 2003. The solution arrived at, however, is different from that used for corporate shareholders. Instead of allowing a deduction for some (or all) of the dividends received, relief is provided through the application of a lower tax rate. Thus, qualified dividends are taxed at the same preferential tax rate available to net capital gains.

In summary, the possible triple taxation of corporate-source income is mitigated by the combination of a deduction (available to corporate shareholders) and a lower tax rate (available to individual shareholders).

---

taxpayers may elect to forgo the carryback period) to offset taxable income for those years.[19]

EXAMPLE 12

In 2008, Wren Corporation has gross income of $200,000 and deductions of $300,000, excluding the dividends received deduction. Wren received taxable dividends of $100,000 from ExxonMobil stock. Wren has an NOL of $170,000, computed as follows:

Gross income (including ExxonMobil dividends)		$ 200,000
Less: Business deductions	$300,000	
Dividends received deduction (70% × $100,000)	70,000	(370,000)
Taxable income (loss)		($ 170,000) ∎

EXAMPLE 13

Assume the same facts as in Example 12 and that Wren Corporation had taxable income of $40,000 in 2006. The NOL of $170,000 is carried back to 2006 (unless Wren elects not to carry back the loss to that year). The carryover to 2007 is $130,000, computed as follows:

Taxable income for 2006	$ 40,000
Less: NOL carryback from 2008	(170,000)
Carryover of unabsorbed 2008 loss	($ 130,000) ∎

In Example 13, the carryback to 2006 might have been ill-advised if Wren Corporation had little, if any, taxable income in 2007 and if it anticipated large amounts of taxable income in the immediate future. In that case, the *election to forgo* the carryback might generate greater tax savings. In this regard, three points should be considered. First, the time value of the tax refund that is lost by not using the carryback procedure must be considered. Second, the election to forgo an NOL carryback is irrevocable. Thus, it cannot be changed later if the future high profits do not materialize. Third, future increases or decreases in corporate income tax rates that can reasonably be anticipated should be considered.

Deductions Available Only to Corporations

LO.3

Recognize and calculate the tax deductions available only to corporations.

Dividends Received Deduction. The purpose of the **dividends received deduction** is to prevent triple taxation. Without the deduction, income paid to a corporation in the form of a dividend would be subject to taxation for a second time (after being taxed first to the distributing corporation) with no corresponding

---

[19]§ 172(b).

deduction to the distributing corporation. A third level of tax would be assessed on the shareholders when the recipient corporation distributed the income to its shareholders. Since the dividends received deduction may be less than 100 percent, the law provides only partial relief.

The amount of the dividends received deduction depends upon the percentage of ownership the recipient corporate shareholder holds in the corporation making the dividend distribution.[20] For dividends received or accrued, the *deduction percentage* is summarized as follows:

Percentage of Ownership by Corporate Shareholder	Deduction Percentage
Less than 20%	70%
20% or more (but less than 80%)	80%
80% or more	100%

The dividends received deduction may be limited to a percentage of the taxable income of a corporation computed without regard to the NOL deduction, the dividends received deduction, the DPAD, or any capital loss carryback to the current tax year. The percentage of taxable income limitation corresponds to the deduction percentage. Thus, if a corporate shareholder owns less than 20 percent of the stock in the distributing corporation, the dividends received deduction is limited to 70 percent of taxable income (as previously defined). However, this limitation does not apply if the corporation has an NOL for the current taxable year.[21]

In working with these myriad rules, the following steps need to be taken:

1. Multiply the dividends received by the deduction percentage.
2. Multiply the taxable income (as previously defined) by the deduction percentage.
3. The deduction is limited to the lesser of step 1 or step 2, unless subtracting the amount derived from step 1 from taxable income (as previously defined) generates a negative number. If so, the amount derived in step 1 should be used.

EXAMPLE 14

Crane, Osprey, and Gull Corporations, three unrelated calendar year corporations, have the following transactions for 2008:

	Crane Corporation	Osprey Corporation	Gull Corporation
Gross income from operations	$ 400,000	$ 320,000	$ 260,000
Expenses from operations	(340,000)	(340,000)	(340,000)
Dividends received from domestic corporations (less than 20% ownership)	200,000	200,000	200,000
Taxable income before the dividends received deduction	$ 260,000	$ 180,000	$ 120,000

In determining the dividends received deduction, use the step procedure just described:

[20]§ 243(a).   [21]§ 246(b).

	Crane Corporation	Osprey Corporation	Gull Corporation
Step 1: (70% × $200,000)	$140,000	$140,000	$140,000
Step 2:			
70% × $260,000 (taxable income)	$182,000		
70% × $180,000 (taxable income)		$126,000	
70% × $120,000 (taxable income)			$ 84,000
Step 3:			
Lesser of step 1 or step 2	$140,000	$126,000	
Generates an NOL			$140,000

Osprey Corporation is subject to the 70 percent of taxable income limitation. It does not qualify for the loss rule treatment, since subtracting $140,000 (step 1) from $180,000 does not yield a loss. Gull Corporation qualifies for the loss rule treatment because subtracting $140,000 (step 1) from $120,000 does yield a loss. In summary, each corporation has the following dividends received deduction for 2008: $140,000 for Crane, $126,000 for Osprey, and $140,000 for Gull. If a corporation already has an NOL before any dividends received deduction is claimed, the full dividends received deduction (as calculated in step 1) is allowed.

Deduction of Organizational Expenditures. Under § 248, a corporation may elect to amortize organizational expenses over a period of 15 years or more. A special exception allows the corporation to immediately expense the first $5,000 of these costs.[22] The exception, however, is phased out on a dollar-for-dollar basis when these expenses exceed $50,000.

EXAMPLE 15

Kingbird Corporation, a calendar year taxpayer, is formed on June 1, 2008. In connection with its formation, it incurs organizational expenditures of $52,000. If Kingbird wants to claim as much of these expenses as soon as possible, its deduction for 2008 is—

$$\text{Expense: } \$5,000 - (\$52,000 - \$50,000) = \$3,000$$

$$\text{Amortization: } \frac{\$52,000 - \$3,000}{180 \text{ months}} \times 7 \text{ (months)} = \$1,906$$

Kingbird deducts a total of $4,906 ($3,000 + $1,906) for 2008. ■

If the election is not made on a timely basis, the expenditures cannot be deducted until the corporation ceases to conduct business and liquidates. The election is made in a statement attached to the corporation's return for its first taxable year. The election covers all qualifying expenses *incurred* in the corporation's first tax year. Thus, a cash basis taxpayer need not have paid the expenses as long as they were incurred.

Organizational expenditures include the following:

- Legal services incident to organization (e.g., drafting the corporate charter, bylaws, minutes of organizational meetings, terms of original stock certificates).
- Necessary accounting services.
- Expenses of temporary directors and of organizational meetings of directors and shareholders.
- Fees paid to the state of incorporation.

---

[22]Organizational expenditures incurred before October 23, 2004, could not be immediately expensed but could be amortized over a period of 60 months or more.

Expenditures connected with issuing or selling shares of stock or other securities (e.g., commissions, professional fees, and printing costs) or with the transfer of assets to a corporation do not qualify. These expenditures are generally added to the capital account and are not subject to amortization.

Determination of Corporate Tax Liability

LO.4

Determine the corporate tax liability and comply with various procedural and reporting requirements.

Income Tax Rates. The rate brackets for corporations are as follows:[23]

Taxable Income	Tax Rate
Not over $50,000	15%
Over $50,000 but not over $75,000	25%
Over $75,000 but not over $100,000	34%
Over $100,000 but not over $335,000	39%*
Over $335,000 but not over $10,000,000	34%
Over $10,000,000 but not over $15,000,000	35%
Over $15,000,000 but not over $18,333,333	38%**
Over $18,333,333	35%

*Five percent of this rate represents a phaseout of the benefits of the lower tax rates on the first $75,000 of taxable income.

**Three percent of this rate represents a phaseout of the benefits of the lower tax rate (34% rather than 35%) on the first $10 million of taxable income.

EXAMPLE 16

A calendar year corporation has taxable income of $90,000 for the current year. The income tax liability is $18,850, determined as follows: $7,500 (15% × $50,000) + $6,250 (25% × $25,000) + $5,100 (34% × $15,000). ■

Qualified personal service corporations are taxed at a flat 35 percent rate on all taxable income. They do not enjoy the tax savings of the lower brackets. For this purpose, a *qualified* **personal service corporation** is one that is substantially employee owned and engages in one of the following activities: health, law, engineering, architecture, accounting, actuarial science, performing arts, or consulting.

Alternative Minimum Tax. Corporations are subject to an alternative minimum tax (AMT) that is structured in the same manner as that applicable to individuals. The AMT for corporations, as for individuals, defines a more expansive tax base than for the regular tax. Like individuals, corporations are required to apply a minimum tax rate to the expanded base and pay the difference between the tentative AMT liability and the regular tax. Many of the adjustments and tax preference items necessary to arrive at alternative minimum taxable income (AMTI) are the same for individuals and corporations. Although the objective of the AMT is the same for individuals and for corporations, the rate and exemptions are different. As noted in Chapter 12, certain small business corporations are effectively exempt from the corporate AMT.

Corporate Filing Requirements

A corporation must file a return whether it has taxable income or not.[24] A corporation that was not in existence throughout an entire annual accounting period is required to file a return for the fraction of the year during which it was in existence. In addition, the corporation must file a return even though it has ceased to do

[23]§ 11(b).   [24]§ 6012(a)(2).

business if it has valuable claims for which it will bring suit. It is relieved of filing returns once it ceases business and dissolves.

The corporate return is filed on Form 1120. [Note: The shorter Form 1120-A was discontinued for tax years beginning in 2007.] Corporations making the S corporation election (discussed later in the chapter) file on Form 1120S.

Corporations with less than $250,000 of gross receipts and less than $250,000 in assets do not have to complete Schedule L (balance sheet) and Schedules M–1 and M–2 (see below) of Form 1120. Similar omissions are allowed for Form 1120S. These rules are intended to ease the compliance burden on small business.

The return must be filed on or before the fifteenth day of the third month following the close of the corporation's tax year. Corporations can receive an automatic extension of six months for filing the corporate return by filing Form 7004 by the due date of the return. However, the IRS may terminate an extension by mailing a 10-day notice to the taxpayer corporation.[25]

A corporation must make payments of estimated tax unless its tax liability can reasonably be expected to be less than $500.[26] The payments must equal the lesser of 100 percent of the corporation's final tax or 100 percent of the last year's tax. These payments may be made in four installments due on or before the fifteenth day of the fourth, sixth, ninth, and twelfth months of the corporate taxable year. The full amount of the unpaid tax is due on the date of the return. Failure to make the required estimated tax prepayments will result in a nondeductible penalty being imposed on the corporation. The penalty can be avoided, however, if any of various exceptions apply.[27]

Reconciliation of Corporate Taxable Income and Accounting Income

Taxable income and accounting net income are seldom the same amount. For example, a difference may arise if the corporation uses accelerated depreciation for tax purposes and straight-line depreciation for accounting purposes.

Many items of income for accounting purposes, such as proceeds from a life insurance policy on the death of a corporate officer and interest on municipal bonds, may not be includible in calculating taxable income. Some expense items for accounting purposes, such as expenses to produce tax-exempt income, estimated warranty reserves, a net capital loss, and Federal income taxes, are not deductible for tax purposes.

Schedule M–1 on the last page of Form 1120 is used to reconcile accounting net income (net income after Federal income taxes) with taxable income (as computed on the corporate tax return before the deduction for an NOL and the dividends received deduction). In the left-hand column of Schedule M–1, net income per books is added to the following: the Federal income tax liability for the year, the excess of capital losses over capital gains (which cannot be deducted in the current year), income for tax purposes that is not income in the current year for accounting purposes, and expenses recorded on the books that are not deductible on the tax return. In the right-hand column, income recorded on the books that is not currently taxable or is tax-exempt and deductions for tax purposes that are not expenses for accounting purposes are totaled and subtracted from the left-hand column total to arrive at taxable income (before the NOL or dividends received deductions).

---

[25]§ 6081.

[26]§ 6655(f).

[27]See § 6655 for the penalty involved and the various exceptions.

EXAMPLE 17

During the current year, Crow Corporation had the following transactions:

Net income per books (after tax)	$92,400
Taxable income	50,000
Federal income tax liability (15% × $50,000)	7,500
Interest income from tax-exempt bonds	5,000
Interest paid on loan, the proceeds of which were used to purchase the tax-exempt bonds	500
Life insurance proceeds received as a result of the death of a key employee	50,000
Premiums paid on key employee life insurance policy	2,600
Excess of capital losses over capital gains	2,000

For book and tax purposes, Crow determines depreciation under the straight-line method. Crow's Schedule M–1 for the current year follows.

Schedule M-1 Reconciliation of Income (Loss) per Books With Income per Return

Note: Schedule M-3 required instead of Schedule M-1 if total assets are $10 million or more—see instructions

1	Net income (loss) per books	92,400	7	Income recorded on books this year not included on this return (itemize):	
2	Federal income tax per books	7,500			
3	Excess of capital losses over capital gains .	2,000		Tax-exempt interest $ _5,000_	
4	Income subject to tax not recorded on books this year (itemize):			_Life insurance proceeds on key employee $50,000_	55,000
			8	Deductions on this return not charged against book income this year (itemize):	
5	Expenses recorded on books this year not deducted on this return (itemize):			a Depreciation . . . . $	
a	Depreciation . . . . $			b Charitable contributions $	
b	Charitable contributions $				
c	Travel and entertainment $				
	Prem.–life ins. $2,600; Int.–exempt bonds $500	3,100	9	Add lines 7 and 8	55,000
6	Add lines 1 through 5	105,000	10	Income (page 1, line 28)—line 6 less line 9	50,000

Schedule M–2 reconciles unappropriated retained earnings at the beginning of the year with unappropriated retained earnings at year-end. Beginning balance plus net income per books, as entered on line 1 of Schedule M–1, less dividend distributions during the year equals ending retained earnings. Other sources of increases or decreases in retained earnings are also listed on Schedule M–2.

EXAMPLE 18

Assume the same facts as in Example 17. Crow Corporation's beginning balance in unappropriated retained earnings is $125,000, and Crow distributed a cash dividend of $30,000 to its shareholders during the year. Based on these further assumptions, Crow has the following Schedule M–2 for the current year.

Schedule M-2 Analysis of Unappropriated Retained Earnings per Books (Line 25, Schedule L)

1	Balance at beginning of year . , ...	125,000	5	Distributions:	a Cash	30,000
2	Net income (loss) per books	92,400			b Stock	
3	Other increases (itemize):				c Property . . .	
	--		6	Other decreases (itemize):		
	--		7	Add lines 5 and 6		30,000
4	Add lines 1, 2, and 3	217,400	8	Balance at end of year (line 4 less line 7)		187,400

Effective for taxable years ending on or after December 31, 2004, certain corporations have to file **Schedule M–3**.[28] This schedule, designated "Net Income (Loss) Reconciliation for Corporations With Total Assets of $10 Million or More," is in lieu of Schedule M–1. It has to be filed when the assets reported on Schedule L of Form 1120 total or exceed $10 million. Because it reveals significant differences between book and taxable income, Schedule M–3 will enable the IRS to more quickly identify possible abusive transactions (e.g., use of tax shelter schemes).

Forming the Corporation

Capital Contributions

<table>
<tr><td>**LO.5**</td></tr>
<tr><td>Understand the tax rules governing the formation of corporations.</td></tr>
</table>

The receipt of money or property in exchange for capital stock produces neither recognized gain nor loss to the recipient corporation.[29] Gross income of a corporation does not include shareholders' contributions of money or property to the capital of the corporation.[30] Contributions by nonshareholders are also excluded from the gross income of a corporation.[31] The basis of the property (capital transfers by nonshareholders) to the corporation is zero.

A city donates land worth $200,000 to Cardinal Corporation as an inducement for it to locate in the city. The receipt of the land does not represent gross income. The land's basis to the corporation is zero. ■

E X A M P L E   1 9

Thin Capitalization. The advantages of capitalizing a corporation with debt may be substantial. Interest on debt is deductible by the corporation, while dividend payments are not. Further, the shareholders are not taxed on loan repayments unless the payments exceed basis.

In certain instances, the IRS will contend that debt is really an equity interest (**thin capitalization**) and will deny the shareholders the tax advantages of debt financing. If the debt instrument has too many features of stock, it may be treated as a form of stock, and principal and interest payments are treated as dividends.[32]

The form of the instrument will not assure debt treatment, but failure to observe certain formalities in creating the debt may lead to an assumption that the purported debt is a form of stock. The debt should be in proper legal form, bear a legitimate rate of interest, have a definite maturity date, and be repaid on a timely basis. Payments should not be contingent upon earnings. Further, the debt should not be subordinated to other liabilities, and proportionate holdings of stock and debt should be avoided or minimized.

The preferential treatment allowed for qualified dividend income has added another dimension to the thin capitalization issue. Although a corporation would prefer to pay out profits in the form of interest (deductible as an expense) rather than as dividends (nondeductible), the shareholders have the opposite tax position. Interest income is ordinary income, while qualified dividends are subject to beneficial net capital gain rates. Nevertheless, the repayment of the debt is not taxed at all as it is a return of capital. Hence, the thin capitalization incentive will continue to exist.

Transfers to Controlled Corporations

Without special provisions in the Code, a transfer of property to a corporation in exchange for its stock would be a sale or exchange of property and would constitute

---

[28]Rev.Proc. 2004–45, 2004–2 C.B. 140. Schedule M–3 satisfies some of the disclosure requirements set forth in Reg. § 1.6011–4 when significant book-tax differences occur.

[29]§ 1032.

[30]§ 118.

[31]*Edwards v. Cuba Railroad Co.*, 1 USTC ¶139, 5 AFTR 5398, 45 S.Ct. 614 (USSC, 1925).

[32]Section 385 lists several factors that might be used to determine whether a debtor-creditor relationship or a shareholder-corporation relationship exists.

CONCEPT SUMMARY 20–1

Summary of Income Tax Consequences

	Individuals	Corporations
Computation of gross income	§ 61.	§ 61.
Computation of taxable income	§§ 62, 63(b) through (h).	§ 63(a). Concept of AGI has no relevance.
Deductions	Trade or business (§ 162); nonbusiness (§ 212); some personal and employee expenses (generally deductible as itemized deductions).	Trade or business (§ 162).
Charitable contributions	Limited in any tax year to 50% of AGI; 30% for long-term capital gain property unless election is made to reduce fair market value of gift; 20% for long-term capital gain property contributed to private nonoperating foundations.	Limited in any tax year to 10% of taxable income computed without regard to the charitable contribution deduction, net operating loss or capital loss carryback, and dividends received deduction.
	Time of deduction—year in which payment is made.	Time of deduction—year in which payment is made unless accrual basis taxpayer. Accrual basis corporation may take deduction in year preceding payment if contribution was authorized by board of directors by end of that year and contribution is paid by fifteenth day of third month of following year.
	Contribution of ordinary income property is limited to the lesser of adjusted basis or fair market value.	Contribution of certain ordinary income property can include one-half of any appreciation on the property.
	Excess charitable contributions can be carried over for a period of up to five years.	Excess charitable contributions can be carried over for a period of up to five years.
Casualty losses	$100 floor on nonbusiness casualty and theft losses; nonbusiness casualty and theft losses deductible only to extent losses exceed 10% of AGI.	Deductible in full.
Depreciation recapture for § 1250 property	Recaptured to extent accelerated depreciation exceeds straight-line.	20% of excess of amount that would be recaptured under § 1245 over amount recaptured under § 1250 is additional ordinary income under § 291.
Domestic production activities deduction	6% of the lesser of QPAI or AGI.	6% of the lesser of QPAI or taxable income.
Net operating loss	Adjusted for nonbusiness deductions over nonbusiness income and for personal and dependency exemptions.	Generally no adjustments.
Dividends received	Qualified dividends are taxed at the same rate applicable to net long-term capital gains.	Deduction allowed (70%, 80%, or 100%) as to dividends received.

	Individuals	Corporations
Long-term capital gains	Generally taxed at a rate no higher than 15% [0% in 2008 (5% in 2007) if taxpayer is in the 15% or lower tax bracket].	Taxed using regular corporate rates.
Capital losses	Only $3,000 of capital loss can offset ordinary income; loss is carried forward indefinitely to offset capital gains or ordinary income up to $3,000; carryovers of short-term losses remain short term; long-term losses carry over as long term.	Can offset only capital gains; carried back three years and forward five years; carrybacks and carryovers are treated as short-term losses.
Passive activity losses	Generally deductible only against income from passive activities.	For regular corporations, no limitation on deductibility. Personal service corporations and certain closely held corporations, however, are subject to same limitations as imposed on individuals. A closely held corporation is one where five or fewer individuals own more than 50% of the stock either directly or indirectly.
Alternative minimum tax	Applied at a graduated rate schedule of 26% and 28% to AMT base (taxable income as modified by certain adjustments plus preference items minus exemption amount); exemption allowed depending on filing status; exemption phaseout begins when AMTI reaches a certain amount (e.g., $150,000 for married filing jointly).	Applied at a 20% rate to AMT base (taxable income as modified by certain adjustments plus preference items minus exemption amount); $40,000 exemption allowed but phaseout begins once AMTI reaches $150,000; adjustments and tax preference items similar to those applicable to individuals but also include 75% of adjusted current earnings (ACE) over AMTI. Certain small business corporations are exempt from the AMT.
Tax rates	Progressive with six rates in 2008 (10%, 15%, 25%, 28%, 33%, and 35%).	Progressive with four rates (15%, 25%, 34%, and 35%); lower brackets phased out at higher levels.

a taxable transaction to the transferor shareholder. Section 351 provides for the nonrecognition of gain or loss upon such transfers of property if the transferors are in control of the corporation immediately after the transfer. Gain or loss is merely postponed in a manner similar to a like-kind exchange (see Chapter 15). The following requirements must be met to qualify under § 351:

- The transferors must be in control of the corporation immediately after the exchange. *Control* is defined as ownership of at least 80 percent of the total combined voting power of all classes of stock entitled to vote and at least 80 percent of the total number of shares of all other classes of stock.[33]
- Realized gain (but not loss) is recognized to the extent that the transferors receive property other than stock. Such nonqualifying property is commonly referred to as *boot.*

---

[33] § 368(c).

If the requirements of § 351 are satisfied and no boot is involved, nonrecognition of gain or loss is *mandatory*.

Basis Considerations and Computation of Gain.

The nonrecognition of gain or loss is accompanied by a carryover of basis. The basis of stock received in a §351 transfer is determined as follows:

- Start with the adjusted basis of the property transferred by the shareholder.
- Add any gain recognized by the shareholder as a result of the transfer.
- Subtract the fair market value of any boot received by the shareholder from the corporation.[34]

Shareholders who receive noncash boot have a basis in the property equal to the fair market value.

The basis of properties received by the corporation is the basis in the hands of the transferor increased by the amount of any gain recognized to the transferor shareholder.[35]

EXAMPLE 20	Ann and Lori form Bluejay Corporation. Ann transfers property with an adjusted basis of $30,000 and a fair market value of $60,000 for 50% of the stock. Lori transfers property with an adjusted basis of $40,000 and a fair market value of $60,000 for the remaining 50% of the stock. The realized gain ($30,000 for Ann and $20,000 for Lori) is not recognized on the transfer because the transfer qualifies under § 351. The basis of the stock to Ann is $30,000, and the basis of the stock to Lori is $40,000. Bluejay Corporation has a basis of $30,000 in the property transferred by Ann and a basis of $40,000 in the property transferred by Lori. ∎

EXAMPLE 21	Mike and John form Condor Corporation with the following investments: Mike transfers property (adjusted basis of $30,000 and fair market value of $70,000), and John transfers cash of $60,000. Each receives 50 shares of the Condor stock, but Mike also receives $10,000 in cash. Assume each share of the Condor stock is worth $1,200. Mike's realized gain is $40,000, determined as follows:

Value of the Condor stock received	
[50 (shares) × $1,200 (value per share)]	$ 60,000
Cash received	10,000
Amount realized	$ 70,000
Less basis of property transferred	(30,000)
Realized gain	$ 40,000

Mike's recognized gain is $10,000, the lesser of the realized gain ($40,000) or the fair market value of the boot received ($10,000). Mike's basis in the Condor stock is $30,000, computed as follows:

Basis in the property transferred	$ 30,000
Plus recognized gain	10,000
	$ 40,000
Less boot received	(10,000)
Basis to Mike of the Condor stock	$ 30,000

Condor Corporation's basis in the property transferred by Mike is $40,000 [$30,000 (basis of the property to Mike) + $10,000 (gain recognized by Mike)]. John neither realizes nor recognizes gain or loss and will have a basis of $60,000 in the Condor stock. ∎

---

[34]§ 358(a).   [35]§ 362(a).

The receipt of stock for the performance of *services* always results in ordinary
income to the transferor shareholder. An example might be an attorney who does
not charge a fee for incorporating a business but instead receives the value equivalent in stock of the newly formed corporation. The basis of stock received for the
performance of services is equal to the fair market value of the services.

Operating the Corporation

Dividend Distributions

Corporate distributions of cash or property to shareholders are treated as dividend
income to the extent the corporation has accumulated *or* current earnings and
profits (E & P).[36] In determining the source of the distribution, a dividend is
deemed to have been made initially from current E & P.

> **LO.6**
>
> Work with the tax rules governing
> the operation of corporations.

EXAMPLE 22

As of January 1, 2008, Teal Corporation has a deficit in accumulated E & P of $30,000. For
tax year 2008, it has current E & P of $10,000. In 2008, the corporation distributes $5,000 to
its shareholders. The $5,000 distribution is treated as a dividend, since it is deemed to have
been made from current E & P. This is the case even though Teal still has a deficit in its accumulated E & P at the end of 2008. ∎

Qualified dividend income is taxed like net long-term capital gain.[37] Consequently, the tax rate on such income cannot exceed 15 percent (0 percent in 2008
for individual shareholders in the 15 percent or lower tax bracket).[38]

If a corporate distribution is not covered by E & P (either current or past), it is
treated as a return of capital (refer to the discussion of the recovery of capital doctrine in Chapter 4). Because this treatment allows the shareholder to apply the
amount of the distribution against the basis of the stock investment, the distribution represents a nontaxable return of capital. Any amount received in excess of
the stock basis is classified as a capital gain (if the stock is a capital asset in the hands
of the shareholder).

EXAMPLE 23

When Mallard Corporation has no E & P (either current or accumulated), it distributes
cash of $30,000 to its sole shareholder, Helen. The basis of Helen's stock investment is
$20,000. Based on these facts, the $30,000 distribution Helen receives is accounted for as
follows:

---

[36]§ 316.

[37]Qualified dividend income is defined in § 1(h)(11)(B) and is discussed in
Chapter 4.

[38]§ 1(h)(1). See the discussion in Chapter 3. Prior to 2008, the rate was 5%
rather than 0% for taxpayers in the 15% or lower tax bracket.

GLOBAL
Tax Issues

TRANSFERRING ASSETS TO FOREIGN CORPORATIONS—FORGET § 351?

Otherwise tax-deferred transfers to controlled corporations under § 351 may generate current taxation when those transfers cross national borders. When a U.S. person transfers appreciated assets to a foreign corporation, the United States may lose its ability to tax the deferred gain on those assets (as well as the future income generated by the assets). To protect the U.S. taxing jurisdiction, § 367 provides that transfers of assets outside the U.S. tax net are generally taxable, in spite of the provisions of § 351.

Return of capital (nontaxable)	$20,000
Capital gain	10,000
Total amount of distribution	$30,000

After the distribution, Helen has a basis of zero in her stock investment. ∎

Concept of Earnings and Profits. The term **earnings and profits** is not defined in the Code, but § 312 does include certain transactions that affect E & P. Although E & P and the accounting concept of retained earnings have certain similarities, they differ in numerous respects. For example, a nontaxable stock dividend is treated as a capitalization of retained earnings for accounting purposes, yet it does not decrease E & P for tax purposes. Taxable dividends do reduce E & P but cannot yield a deficit. Referring to Example 23, after the distribution Mallard Corporation's E & P remains zero rather than being a negative amount.

E & P is an account that reflects a corporation's economic ability to pay dividends to its shareholders. Thus, in converting a corporation's taxable income for any one year to *current E & P*, certain adjustments need to be made. For example, one adjustment is to add back any tax-exempt interest received. Although such interest is not included in taxable income, it is available for distribution as dividends. Some of the other adjustments to taxable income to arrive at current E & P include the following:

As additions—

- Dividends received deduction.
- Domestic production activities deduction.
- Proceeds of life insurance policies on key employees.

As subtractions—

- Federal income taxes paid.
- Charitable contributions in excess of the 10 percent limitation.
- Excess capital losses (no carryback available).
- Nondeductible items (e.g., fines, penalties, losses between related parties).

Accumulated E & P is the sum of the corporation's past current E & P that has not been distributed as dividends. A more detailed discussion of the concept of E & P is beyond the scope of this chapter.

Property Dividends. A distribution of property to a shareholder is measured by the fair market value of the property on the date of distribution. The shareholder's basis in the property received is also the fair market value.[39]

---

[39]§ 301.

Drake Corporation has E & P of $60,000. It distributes land with a fair market value of $50,000 (adjusted basis of $30,000) to its sole shareholder, Art. Art has a taxable dividend of $50,000 and a basis in the land of $50,000. ∎

A corporation that distributes appreciated property to its shareholders as a dividend must recognize the amount of the appreciation as gain.[40]

Assume the same facts as in Example 24. Drake Corporation must recognize a gain of $20,000 on the distribution it made to Art. ∎

However, if the property distributed has a basis in excess of its fair market value, the distributing corporation cannot recognize any loss.

Constructive Dividends. Many taxpayers mistakenly assume that dividend consequences do not take place unless the distribution carries the formalities of a dividend (declaration date, record date, payment date). They further assume that dividends must be paid out to all shareholders on a pro rata basis. This may not be the case when closely held corporations are involved. Here, the key to dividend treatment depends upon whether the shareholders derive a benefit from the corporation that cannot be otherwise classified (e.g., as reasonable salary). The following are examples of **constructive dividends**:

- Salaries paid to shareholder-employees that are not reasonable (refer to Example 6 in Chapter 6).
- Interest on debt owed by the corporation to shareholders that is reclassified as equity because the corporation is thinly capitalized (refer to the earlier discussion in this chapter).
- Excessive rent paid by a corporation for the use of shareholder property. The arm's length standard is used to test whether the rent is excessive (refer to Example 22 in Chapter 1) .
- Advances to shareholders that are not bona fide loans.
- Interest-free (or below-market) loans to shareholders. In this situation, the dividend component is the difference between the interest provided for, if any, and that calculated using the market rate.
- Shareholder use of corporate property for less than an arm's length rate.
- Absorption by the corporation of a shareholder's personal expenses.
- Bargain purchase of corporate property by shareholders.

Like regular dividends, constructive dividends must be covered by E & P to carry dividend income consequences to the shareholders. As noted above, however, constructive dividends need not be available to all shareholders on a pro rata basis.

Although dividends reduce the E & P of a corporation, they are not deductible for income tax purposes. In this regard, certain constructive dividends could have subtle tax consequences for all parties concerned.

Grouse Corporation makes a loan to one of its shareholders, Hal. No interest is provided for, but application of the market rate would produce $20,000 of interest for the term of the loan. Presuming the loan is bona fide, the following results occur:

- Hal has dividend income of $20,000.
- Grouse Corporation has interest income of $20,000.
- Hal might obtain an interest deduction of $20,000.

---

[40]The tax consequences to a corporation of nonliquidating distributions to shareholders are covered in § 311.

Not only does Grouse Corporation have to recognize income of $20,000, but it also obtains no income tax deduction for the $20,000 constructive dividend. ■

EXAMPLE 27

Assume the same facts as in Example 26, except that the loan to Hal was not bona fide. In this event, the full amount of the loan is regarded as a dividend to Hal. Therefore, the interest element is not a factor since no bona fide loan ever existed. ■

Stock Redemptions

If a corporation redeems a shareholder's stock (a **stock redemption**), one of two possible outcomes occurs:

- The redemption may qualify as a sale or exchange under § 302 or § 303. In that case, capital gain or loss treatment usually applies to the qualifying shareholders.
- The redemption will be treated as a dividend under § 301, provided the distributing corporation has E & P.

EXAMPLE 28

Reba owns 300 shares of Snipe Corporation stock as an investment. The shares have a basis to Reba of $100 each, for a total of $30,000. When the fair market value of a share is $300, Snipe redeems 200 of Reba's shares. If the redemption qualifies for sale or exchange treatment, the result is a capital gain to Reba of $40,000 [$60,000 (redemption price) − $20,000 (basis in 200 shares)]. Reba's basis in the remaining 100 shares is $10,000 [$30,000 (basis in the original shares) − $20,000 (basis in the shares redeemed)]. ■

EXAMPLE 29

Assume the same facts as in Example 28, except that the redemption does not qualify for sale or exchange treatment. Presuming adequate E & P, the redemption results in $60,000 dividend income. Reba's basis in the remaining 100 shares now becomes $30,000, or $300 per share. ■

Because dividend income is taxed at the rate applicable to net long-term capital gain, the difference between Examples 28 and 29 is in the amount of recognized gain that is eligible for the beneficial capital gain rate. In Example 29, an extra $20,000 of such gain occurs, since the redeemed stock's basis of $20,000 is not part of the recognized gain calculation.

A stock redemption qualifies as a sale or exchange if it meets any of the safe harbors of § 302 or § 303.

LO.7

Recognize the tax rules governing the liquidation of corporations.

Liquidating the Corporation

Unlike dividend distributions or stock redemptions, where the distributing corporation continues its operations, **liquidating distributions** occur during the termination of the business. All debts are paid, and any remaining corporate assets are distributed pro rata to the shareholders in exchange for their stock. Once these distributions are completed, the corporation undergoing liquidation will cease to be a separate tax entity.

General Rule of § 331

Under the general rule, the shareholders recognize gain or loss in a corporate liquidation. The amount of recognized gain or loss is measured by the difference between the fair market value of the assets received from the corporation and the adjusted basis of the stock surrendered. The shareholders recognize capital gain or loss if the stock is a capital asset.[41]

---

[41]If the stock is held as an investment, which is usually the case, gain or loss will be capital. Stock owned by a broker probably will be inventory and therefore will not constitute a capital asset. Thus, the gain or loss on this type of stock is ordinary and not capital.

EXAMPLE 30

Pursuant to a complete liquidation, Starling Corporation distributes $100,000 in cash to Edna, one of its shareholders. If Edna's basis in the stock surrendered is $40,000, she must recognize a gain of $60,000. If Edna held the stock as an investment, the $60,000 gain is capital gain—either short term or long term (depending on the holding period). ■

ETHICAL and EQUITABLE *Considerations*

ELIMINATING BURDENSOME PAPERWORK

For many years, Sophie has owned and operated several apartment buildings. In 1995 and upon the advice of her attorney, Sophie transferred the apartment buildings to a newly created corporation. Her main reason for incorporating the business was to achieve limited liability.

Every year since 1995, Sophie has prepared and filed a Form 1120 for the corporation. No corporate income tax has been paid because, after the deduction of various expenses (including Sophie's "management fee"), the corporation has zero taxable income.

In 2008, Sophie decides that filing Form 1120 is a waste of time and serves no useful purpose. Instead, she plans to report all of the financial activities of the apartment business on her own individual Form 1040.

Comment on the propriety of what Sophie plans to do.

Exception to the General Rule

Section 332 is an exception to the general rule that the shareholder recognizes gain or loss on a corporate liquidation. If a parent corporation liquidates a subsidiary corporation in which it owns at least 80 percent of the voting power and value of the stock, no gain or loss is recognized by the parent company. The subsidiary must distribute all of its property in complete liquidation of all of its stock within the taxable year or within three years from the close of the tax year in which the first distribution occurred.

Basis Determination—§§ 334 and 338

General Rule. Where gain or loss is recognized upon the complete liquidation of a corporation, the basis of the property received by the shareholders is the property's fair market value.[42]

Subsidiary Liquidation Basis Rules. The general rule is that the property received by the parent corporation in a complete liquidation of its subsidiary under § 332 has the same basis it had in the hands of the subsidiary (a carryover basis).[43] The parent's basis in the stock of the liquidated subsidiary disappears.

EXAMPLE 31

Swallow, the parent corporation, has a basis of $20,000 in the stock of Shrike Corporation, a subsidiary in which it owns 85% of all classes of stock. Swallow purchased the stock of Shrike Corporation 10 years ago. In the current year, Swallow liquidates Shrike Corporation and receives assets worth $50,000 with a tax basis to Shrike of $40,000. Swallow Corporation will have a basis of $40,000 in the assets, with a potential gain upon sale of $10,000. Swallow's original $20,000 basis in the Shrike stock disappears. ■

An exception to the carryover of basis rule is provided in § 338. Under this exception, the parent company may elect to receive a basis for the assets equal to the adjusted basis of the stock of the subsidiary. In effect, the initial acquisition of

---

[42]§ 334(a).

[43]§ 334(b)(1).

the subsidiary is treated as if the parent company had acquired the assets (rather than the stock) of the subsidiary.

Effect of the Liquidation on the Corporation

At the corporate level, § 336 applies to dictate the tax consequences to the corporation being liquidated. Under § 336, the distributing corporation recognizes gain or loss upon complete liquidation. In this regard, it does not matter whether the corporation distributes the property in kind (*as is*) to the shareholders or first sells the property and then distributes the proceeds.

EXAMPLE 32

Pursuant to a complete liquidation, Grackle Corporation distributes the following assets to its shareholders: undeveloped land held as an investment (basis of $150,000 and fair market value of $140,000) and marketable securities (basis of $160,000 and fair market value of $200,000). Since Grackle is treated as if it had sold the property, a gain of $40,000 results from the securities, and a loss of $10,000 results from the land. ■

The deductibility of losses may be restricted by the related-party rules (refer to Chapter 6) if certain conditions exist (e.g., the distributions are not pro rata).[44]

A wholly owned subsidiary corporation does not recognize gain or loss when the parent corporation uses the carryover basis option of § 334(b)(1). The reason for the special treatment is that the subsidiary's basis (and all other tax attributes) in the assets carries over to the parent corporation.

LO.8

Appreciate the utility and effect of the Subchapter S election.

The S Election

Numerous nontax reasons exist for operating a business in the corporate form (e.g., limited liability). Consequently, the existence of income tax disadvantages (e.g., double taxation of corporate income and shareholder dividends) should not deter businesspeople from using the corporate form. To prevent tax considerations from interfering with the exercise of sound business judgment, Congress enacted Subchapter S of the Code. The Subchapter S election enables taxpayers to use the corporate form for conducting a business without being taxed as a corporation.

Qualification for S Status

To achieve S corporation status, the corporation must meet certain requirements and make an effective election.

Qualifying for the Election. To qualify for **S corporation** status, the corporation must be a **small business corporation**. This includes any corporation that has the following characteristics:

- Is a domestic corporation.
- Has no more than 100 shareholders.
- Has as its shareholders only individuals, estates, and certain trusts.
- Does not have a nonresident alien as a shareholder.
- Has only one class of stock outstanding.

Effective for tax years beginning after 2004, the members of a family who own stock are treated as a single shareholder. Members of a family include all lineal descendants of a shareholder and spouse (or ex-spouse) and the spouses (or ex-spouses) of such lineal descendants.[45]

---

[44]§ 336(d).   [45]§ 1361(c)(1).

EXAMPLE 33

Harry, a shareholder in an S corporation dies, and under his will, his stock is distributed among three children and eight grandchildren. The 11 new shareholders are treated as one shareholder for purposes of the 100-shareholder limitation. ■

These characteristics must continue to exist if an electing S corporation is to maintain S status.

Making the Election. The election is made by filing Form 2553, and *all* shareholders must consent. For this purpose, husbands and wives are counted as a single shareholder.

To be effective for the current year, the election must be filed anytime during the preceding taxable year or on or before the fifteenth day of the third month of the current year.[46]

EXAMPLE 34

Heron, a calendar year taxpayer, is a regular corporation that wishes to elect S status for 2008. If the election is filed anytime from January 1, 2007, through March 17, 2008, it will be effective for 2008. [March 15, 2008, falls on a Saturday.] ■

The IRS has the authority to waive invalid S elections (e.g., inadvertent failure to obtain all the necessary shareholder consents to the original election) and to treat late elections as timely.

Loss of the Election. The S election may be terminated *voluntarily* (a majority of the shareholders file to revoke the election) or *involuntarily*. An involuntary termination may occur in *any* of the following ways:

- The corporation ceases to qualify as a small business corporation (e.g., the number of shareholders exceeds 100, or a partnership becomes a shareholder).
- The corporation has passive investment income (e.g., interest, dividends) in excess of 25 percent of gross receipts for a period of three consecutive years. This possibility applies only if the corporation was previously a regular corporation and has E & P from that period.

If the holders of a *majority* of the shares consent to a voluntary revocation of S status, the election to revoke must be made on or before the fifteenth day of the third month of the tax year to be effective for that year.

EXAMPLE 35

The shareholders of Stork Corporation, a calendar year S corporation, elect to revoke the election on January 3, 2008. Assuming the election is duly executed and timely filed, Stork will become a regular corporation for calendar year 2008. If the election to revoke is not made until June 2008, Stork will not become a regular corporation until calendar year 2009. ■

Suppose the shareholders in Example 35 file the election to revoke on January 3, 2008, but do not want the revocation to take place until 2009. If the election so specifies, Stork Corporation will cease to have S status as of January 1, 2009.

In the case where S status is lost because of a disqualifying act (involuntarily), the loss of the election takes effect as of the date on which the event occurs.

EXAMPLE 36

Crow Corporation has been a calendar year S corporation for several years. On August 14, 2008, one of its shareholders sells her stock to Kite Corporation. Since Crow Corporation no

[46]§ 1362.

longer satisfies the definition of a small business corporation (it has another corporation as a shareholder), the election has been involuntarily terminated. For calendar year 2008, therefore, Crow will be an S corporation through August 13 and a regular corporation from August 14 through December 31, 2008. ■

In the event the election is lost through a violation of the passive investment income limitation, the loss of S status starts at the beginning of the next tax year.

Barring certain exceptions, the loss of the election places the corporation in a five-year holding period before S status can be reelected.

Operational Rules

The S corporation is primarily a tax-reporting rather than a taxpaying entity. In this respect, the entity is taxed much like a partnership.[47] Under the conduit concept, the taxable income and losses of an S corporation flow through to the shareholders who report them on their personal income tax returns.

To ascertain the annual tax consequences to each shareholder, it is necessary to carry out two steps at the S corporation level. First, all corporate transactions that will flow through to the shareholders on an *as is* basis under the conduit approach must be set aside. Second, what remains is aggregated as the taxable income of the S corporation and is allocated to each shareholder on a per-share and per-day of stock ownership basis.[48]

Separately Stated Items.
The following are some of the items that do not lose their identity as they pass through the S corporation and are therefore picked up by each shareholder on an *as is* basis:

- Tax-exempt income.
- Long-term and short-term capital gains and losses.
- Section 1231 gains and losses.
- Charitable contributions.
- Domestic production activities deduction.
- Qualified dividend income.
- Foreign tax credits.
- Depletion.
- Nonbusiness income or loss under § 212.
- Intangible drilling costs.
- Investment interest, income, and expenses covered under § 163(d).
- Certain portfolio income.
- Passive activity gains, losses, and credits under § 469.
- AMT adjustments and tax preference items.

In the case of the DPAD, the individual components needed to determine the deduction at the shareholder level must be broken out. These components include each shareholder's pro rata portion of QPAI and the W–2 wages paid by the corporation. This information is listed on line 12 of Schedule K–1 (Form 1120S) and is picked up by the shareholder on his or her Form 8903 (Domestic Production Activities Deduction).

The items listed above are separately stated because each may lead to a different tax result when combined with a particular shareholder's other transactions.

---

[47]This is not to imply that an S corporation is always free from the income tax. For example, a tax may be imposed on certain built-in gains or certain excessive passive investment income.

[48]§ 1366.

TAX *in the News*	S CORPORATIONS AND SALARIES: MORE TRAUMA ON THE WAY!

Devising the most beneficial salary structure has always presented a supreme challenge for many S corporations. The owner-shareholders may want to receive enough salary to be covered under Social Security and private retirement plans. Too much, however, will aggravate the employment tax cost (particularly the Medicare portion, which does not have a cap). (Note that nonsalary distributions to a shareholder are not subject to self-employment tax.) Not infrequently, common sense disappears, and shareholders work for free just to avoid payroll taxes.

Finding the right salary mix has become even more complicated with the enactment of the domestic production activities deduction (DPAD). Two new variables have been added with both detrimental and beneficial effects. The bad news is that salary is an expense and will reduce the QPAI that passes through. The good news is that salary is a Form W–2 item and will increase the wage limitation on deducting QPAI.

When the benefits of the DPAD are fully phased in at 9 percent, the salary structure of an S corporation will become even more significant.

EXAMPLE 37

Arnold and Jean are equal shareholders in Lark Corporation (an S corporation). For calendar year 2008, each must account for one-half of a corporate short-term capital gain of $6,000. Arnold has no other capital asset transactions, and Jean has a short-term capital loss of $3,000 from the sale of stock in IBM Corporation. In terms of overall effect, the difference between the two taxpayers is significant. Although both must report the short-term capital gain pass-through, Jean will neutralize its inclusion in gross income by offsetting it with the $3,000 short-term capital loss from the sale of the IBM stock. For Arnold, the short-term capital gain pass-through results in a $3,000 increase in his taxable income. ■

Taxable Income. After the separately stated items have been removed, the balance represents the taxable income of the S corporation. In arriving at taxable income, the dividends received deduction, the DPAD, and the NOL deduction are not allowed. An S corporation does come under the regular corporate rules, however, for purposes of amortization of organizational expenditures.

Once taxable income has been determined, it passes through to each shareholder as of the last day of the S corporation's tax year.

EXAMPLE 38

Harrier Corporation, a calendar year S corporation, had the following transactions during the current year:

Sales		$ 40,000
Cost of goods sold		(23,000)
Other income		
*Tax-exempt interest	$ 300	
*Long-term capital gain	500	800
Other expenses		
*Charitable contributions	$ 400	
Advertising expense	1,500	
Other operating expenses	2,000	
*Short-term capital loss	150	(4,050)
Net income per books		$ 13,750

When the items that are to be separately stated (those preceded by an asterisk [*]) and shown *as is* by each shareholder are withdrawn, Harrier has the following taxable income:

Sales		$ 40,000
Cost of goods sold		(23,000)
Other expenses		
Advertising expense	$1,500	
Other operating expenses	2,000	(3,500)
Taxable income		$ 13,500

∎

EXAMPLE 39

If Oscar owned 10% of the stock in Harrier Corporation (refer to Example 38) during all of the current year, he must account for the following:

Separately stated items	
Tax-exempt interest	$ 30
Long-term capital gain	50
Charitable contributions	40
Short-term capital loss	15
Taxable income (10% of $13,500)	1,350

Some of the separately stated items (e.g., the tax-exempt interest) must be reported on Oscar's individual income tax return but may not lead to tax consequences. Oscar picks up his share of Harrier's taxable income ($1,350) as ordinary income. ∎

Treatment of Losses. As previously noted, separately stated loss items (e.g., capital losses, § 1231 losses) flow through to the shareholders on an *as is* basis. Their treatment by a shareholder depends on the shareholder's individual income tax position. If the S corporation's taxable income determination results in an operating loss, it also passes through to the shareholders. As is the case with separately stated items, the amount of the loss each shareholder receives depends on the stock ownership during the year.

EXAMPLE 40

In 2008, Oriole Corporation (a calendar year S corporation) incurred an operating loss of $36,600. During 2008, Jason's ownership in Oriole was 20% for 200 days and 30% for 166 days. Jason's share of the loss is determined as follows:

[$36,600 × (200/366)] × 20% =	$4,000
[$36,600 × (166/366)] × 30% =	4,980
Total loss for Jason	$8,980

Presuming the basis limitation does not come into play (see the following discussion), Jason deducts $8,980 in arriving at adjusted gross income. ∎

Basis Determination. A shareholder's *basis* in the stock of an S corporation, like that of a regular corporation, is the original investment plus additional capital contributions less return of capital distributions. At this point, however, the symmetry disappears. Generally, basis is increased by the pass-through of income items (including those separately stated) and decreased by the loss items (including those separately stated).[49]

EXAMPLE 41

In 2008, Warbler Corporation is formed with an investment of $100,000, of which Janice contributed $20,000 for a 20% stock interest. A timely S election is made, and for 2008, Warbler earns taxable income of $15,000. Janice's basis in her stock investment now becomes $23,000

[49]§ 1367.

[$20,000 (original capital contribution) + $3,000 (the 20% share of the corporation's taxable income assigned to Janice)]. ■

Distributions by an S corporation reduce the basis of a shareholder's stock investment. However, if the amount of the distribution exceeds basis, the excess normally receives capital gain treatment.

As previously noted, operating losses of an S corporation pass through to the shareholders and reduce the basis in their stock investment. Because the basis of the stock cannot fall below zero, an excess loss is then applied against the basis of any loans the shareholder may have made to the corporation.

EXAMPLE 42

Flamingo Corporation, a calendar year S corporation, has an operating loss of $60,000 for 2008. Norman, a 50% shareholder, has an adjusted basis of $25,000 in his stock investment and has made loans to the corporation of $5,000. Based on these facts, Norman may take full advantage of the $30,000 loss (50% of $60,000) on his 2008 individual income tax return. Norman's basis in the stock and the loans must be reduced accordingly, and both will be zero after the pass-through. ■

In the event the basis limitation precludes an operating loss from being absorbed, the loss can be carried forward and deducted when and if it is covered by basis.

EXAMPLE 43

Assume the same facts as in Example 42, except that Norman had not made any loans to Flamingo Corporation. Further assume that Flamingo has taxable income of $15,000 in the following year (2009). Norman's tax situation for 2008 and 2009 is summarized as follows:

Ordinary loss for 2008	$25,000
Income to be reported in 2009 (50% of $15,000)	7,500
Restoration of stock basis in 2009 (50% of $15,000)	7,500
Loss allowed for 2009 ($30,000 − $25,000)	5,000
Basis in stock account after 2009 ($7,500 − $5,000)	2,500

Thus, Norman's unabsorbed loss of $5,000 from 2008 carries over to 2009 and is applied against the $7,500 of ordinary income for that year. ■

Partnerships

Nature of Partnership Taxation

LO.9

Understand the tax consequences of forming and operating a partnership.

Unlike corporations, partnerships are not considered separate taxable entities. Each member of a partnership is subject to income tax on his or her distributive share of the partnership's income, even if an actual distribution is not made. The tax return (Form 1065) required of a partnership serves only to provide information necessary in determining the character and amount of each partner's distributive share of the partnership's income and expense. Because a partnership acts as a conduit, items that pass through to the partners do not lose their identity. For example, tax-exempt income earned by a partnership is picked up by the partners as tax-exempt income. In this regard, partnerships function in much the same fashion as S corporations, which also serve as conduits.

A partnership is considered a separate taxable entity for purposes of making various elections and selecting its taxable year, method of depreciation, and accounting method. A partnership is also treated as a separate legal entity under civil law with the right to own property in its own name and to transact business free from the personal debts of its partners.

Partnership Formation

Recognition of Gain or Loss. The general rule is that no gain or loss is recognized by a partnership or any of its partners on the contribution of property in exchange for a capital interest in the partnership.[50] The general rule also applies to all subsequent contributions of property.

There are certain exceptions to the nonrecognition of gain or loss rule including the following:

- If a partner transfers property to the partnership and receives money or other consideration (boot) as a result, the transaction will be treated as a sale or exchange rather than as a contribution of capital. Realized gain is recognized to the extent of the fair market value of the boot received.
- If a partnership interest is received in exchange for services rendered or to be rendered by the partner to the partnership, the fair market value of the transferred capital interest is regarded as compensation for services rendered. In such cases, the recipient of the capital interest must recognize the amount as ordinary income in the year actually or constructively received.
- If property that is subject to a liability in excess of its basis is contributed to a partnership, the contributing partner may recognize gain.

Basis of a Partnership Interest. The contributing *partner's basis* in the partnership interest received is the sum of money contributed plus the adjusted basis of any other property transferred to the partnership.[51]

EXAMPLE 44

In return for the contribution of property (with a basis of $50,000 and a fair market value of $80,000) and cash of $10,000 to the Brown Partnership, Marcia receives a 10% capital interest worth $90,000. Although Marcia has a realized gain of $30,000 ($90,000 − $60,000) on the transfer, none of the gain is recognized. The basis of her interest in the Brown Partnership is $60,000 [$50,000 (basis of property contributed) + $10,000 (cash contribution)]. ∎

A partner's basis in the partnership interest is determined without regard to any amount reflected on the partnership's books as capital, equity, or a similar account.

EXAMPLE 45

Marge and Clyde form the equal Blue Partnership with a cash contribution of $30,000 from Marge and a property contribution (adjusted basis of $18,000 and fair market value of $30,000) from Clyde. Although the books of the Blue Partnership may reflect a credit of $30,000 to each partner's capital account, only Marge has a tax basis of $30,000 in her partnership interest. Clyde's tax basis in his partnership interest is $18,000, the amount of his tax basis in the property contributed to the partnership. ∎

After its initial determination, the basis of a partnership interest is subject to continuous fluctuations. A partner's basis is increased by additional contributions and the sum of his or her current and prior years' distributive share of the following:

- Taxable income of the partnership, including capital gains.
- Tax-exempt income of the partnership.
- The excess of the deductions for depletion over the basis of the partnership's property subject to depletion.[52]

Similarly, the basis of a partner's interest is decreased, but not below zero, by distributions of partnership property and by the sum of the current and prior years' distributive share of the following:

---

[50]§ 721.
[51]§ 722.

[52]§ 705(a).

- Partnership losses, including capital losses.
- Partnership expenditures that are not deductible in computing taxable income or loss and that are not capital expenditures.

Changes in the liabilities (including trade accounts payable, bank loans, etc.) of a partnership also affect the basis of a partnership interest. A partner's basis is increased by his or her assumption of partnership liabilities and by his or her pro rata share of liabilities incurred by the partnership. Likewise, the partner's basis is decreased by the amount of any personal liabilities assumed by the partnership and by the pro rata share of any decreases in the liabilities of the partnership.

EXAMPLE 46

Tony, Martha, and Carolyn form the Orange Partnership with the following contributions: cash of $50,000 from Tony for a 50% interest in capital and profits, cash of $25,000 from Martha for a 25% interest, and property valued at $33,000 from Carolyn for a 25% interest. The property contributed by Carolyn has an adjusted basis of $15,000 and is subject to a mortgage of $8,000, which is assumed by the partnership. Carolyn's basis in her interest in the Orange Partnership is $9,000, determined as follows:

Adjusted basis of Carolyn's contributed property	$15,000
Less portion of mortgage assumed by Tony and Martha and treated as a distribution of money to Carolyn (75% of $8,000)	(6,000)
Basis of Carolyn's interest in Orange Partnership	$ 9,000

EXAMPLE 47

Assuming the same facts as in Example 46, Tony and Martha have a basis in their partnership interests of $54,000 and $27,000, respectively.

	Tony	Martha
Cash contribution	$50,000	$25,000
Plus portion of mortgage assumed and treated as an additional cash contribution:		
(50% of $8,000)	4,000	
(25% of $8,000)		2,000
Basis of interest in Orange Partnership	$54,000	$27,000

Partnership's Basis in Contributed Property. The *basis of property* contributed to a partnership by a partner is the adjusted basis of the property to the contributing partner at the time of the contribution.[53] Additionally, the holding period of the property for the partnership includes the period during which the property was held by the contributing partner. This is logical, since the partnership's basis in the property is the same basis the property had in the hands of the partner.[54]

EXAMPLE 48

In 2008, Roger contributed equipment with an adjusted basis of $10,000 and fair market value of $30,000 to the Red Partnership in exchange for a one-third interest in the partnership. No gain or loss is recognized by Roger. The Red Partnership's basis in the equipment is $10,000. If Roger had acquired the equipment in 1999, the partnership's holding period would include the period from 1999 through 2008.

---

[53]§ 723.   [54]§ 1223(2).

Partnership Operation

Measuring and Reporting Partnership Income. Although a partnership is not subject to Federal income taxation, it is required to determine its taxable income and file an income tax return for information purposes.[55] The tax return, Form 1065, is due on the fifteenth day of the fourth month following the close of the taxable year of the partnership.

In measuring and reporting partnership income, certain transactions must be segregated and reported separately on the partnership return. Items such as charitable contributions, the domestic production activities deduction, capital gains and losses, qualified dividend income, and foreign taxes are excluded from partnership taxable income and are allocated separately to the partners.[56] These items must be segregated and allocated separately because they affect the computation of various exclusions, deductions, and credits at the individual partner level. For example, one of the partners may have made personal charitable contributions in excess of the ceiling limitations on his or her individual tax return. Therefore, partnership charitable contributions are excluded from partnership taxable income and are reported separately on the partnership return.

Similar to the procedure for an S corporation, the individual components needed to determine the DPAD at the partner level must be separated. These components include each partner's pro rata portion of QPAI and the W–2 wages paid by the partnership. This information is listed on line 13 of Schedule K–1 (Form 1065) and is picked up by the partner on his or her Form 8903 (Domestic Production Activities Deduction).

The separate stating of certain attributes of the partnership is essential as they may result in differing tax consequences when passed through to the various partners.

EXAMPLE 49

Alyssa, Madison, and Brad are equal partners in the Yellow Partnership. All parties use the calendar year for tax purposes. Among other transactions, Yellow had the following separately stated items for 2008: $30,000 in QPAI, $15,000 in long-term capital gains, and $6,000 in charitable contributions. The pass-through of these items generates the following results: Alyssa cannot use all of her $10,000 share of QPAI because of the AGI limitation; Madison's $5,000 long-term capital gain is not subject to tax (i.e., she is in a 15% or lower tax bracket); and Brad cannot benefit from his $2,000 share of the charitable contribution as he chooses not to itemize (i.e., claims the standard deduction). Thus, the pass-through of these separately stated items caused different tax consequences to the partners. ■

A second step in the measurement and reporting process is the computation of the partnership's ordinary income or loss. The taxable income of a partnership is computed in the same manner as the taxable income of an individual taxpayer. However, a partnership is not allowed the following deductions:[57]

- The deduction for personal and dependency exemptions.
- The deduction for taxes paid to foreign countries or possessions of the United States.
- The deduction for charitable contributions.
- The deduction for net operating losses.
- The additional itemized deductions allowed individuals in §§ 211 through 219.

The partnership's ordinary income or loss and each of the items requiring separate treatment are reported in the partnership's information return and allocated to the partners in accordance with their distributive shares.

---

[55]§ 6031.
[56]§ 702(a).
[57]§ 703(a).

Limitation on Partner's Share of Losses.

A partner's deduction of the distributive share of partnership losses (including capital losses) could be limited. The limitation is the adjusted basis of the partnership interest at the end of the partnership year in which the losses were incurred.

The limitation for partnership loss deductions is similar to that applicable to losses of S corporations. Like S corporation losses, partnership losses may be carried forward by the partner and utilized against future increases in the basis of the partnership interest. Such increases might result from additional capital contributions to the partnership, from additional partnership liabilities, or from future partnership income.

EXAMPLE 50

Florence and Donald do business as the Green Partnership, sharing profits and losses equally. All parties use the calendar year for tax purposes. As of January 1, 2008, Florence's basis in her partnership interest is $25,000. The partnership sustained an operating loss of $80,000 in 2008 and earned a profit of $70,000 in 2009. For the calendar year 2008, Florence may claim only $25,000 of her $40,000 distributive share of the partnership loss (one-half of the $80,000 loss). As a result, the basis in her partnership interest is reduced to zero as of January 1, 2009, and she must carry forward the remaining $15,000 of partnership losses. ■

EXAMPLE 51

Assuming the same facts as in Example 50, what are the income tax consequences for Florence in 2009? Since the partnership earned a profit of $70,000 for the calendar year 2009, Florence reports income from the partnership of $20,000 ($35,000 distributive share of income for 2009 less the $15,000 loss not allowed for 2008). The adjusted basis of her partnership interest now becomes $20,000. ■

Transactions between Partner and Partnership.

A partner engaging in a transaction with the partnership is generally regarded as a nonpartner or outsider. However, the Code includes certain exceptions to prevent unwarranted tax avoidance in related-party situations. For instance, losses from the sale or exchange of property are disallowed if they arise in either of the following cases:

- Between a partnership and a person whose direct or indirect interest in the capital or profits of the partnership is more than 50 percent.
- Between two partnerships in which the same persons own more than a 50 percent interest in the capital or profits.[58]

An indirect interest includes those owned by family members (e.g., parents, children, brothers, and sisters).

EXAMPLE 52

Michael, Samantha, and Sarah (brother and sisters) are equal partners in the Beige Partnership. For purposes of the 50% related-party rules described above, each partner indirectly owns the interests of the others. Thus, Michael has a 100% interest (i.e., his one-third *direct* interest plus the two-thirds *indirect* interests of his sisters) in the Beige Partnership. ■

In a related-party situation, if one of the purchasers later sells the property, any gain realized will be recognized only to the extent that it exceeds the loss previously disallowed.

EXAMPLE 53

Pat owns a 60% interest in the capital and profits of the Rose Partnership. In the current year, Pat sells property with an adjusted basis of $50,000 to the partnership for its fair market value of $35,000. The $15,000 loss is not deductible since Pat's ownership interest is more than 50%. If the Rose Partnership later sells the property for $40,000, none of the $5,000 gain (sale price of $40,000 less adjusted basis to partnership of $35,000) will be recognized

---

[58] § 707(b)(1).

since it is offset by $5,000 of the previously disallowed loss of $15,000. The unused loss of $10,000, however, is of no tax benefit either to the partnership or to Pat. ■

Payments made by a partnership to one of its partners for services rendered or for the use of capital, to the extent they are determined without regard to the income of the partnership, are treated by the partnership in the same manner as payments made to a person who is not a partner. Referred to as **guaranteed payments**, these are generally deductible by the partnership as a business expense.[59] The payments must be reported as ordinary income by the receiving partner. Their deductibility distinguishes guaranteed payments from a partner's distributive share of income that is not deductible by the partnership.

EXAMPLE 54

Under the terms of the Silver Partnership agreement, Kim is entitled to a fixed annual salary of $18,000 without regard to the income of the partnership. He is also to share in the profits and losses of the partnership as a one-third partner. After deducting the guaranteed payment, the partnership has $36,000 of ordinary income. Kim must include $30,000 as ordinary income on his income tax return for his tax year with or within which the partnership tax year ends ($18,000 guaranteed payment + $12,000 one-third distributive share of partnership income). ■

Other Partnership Considerations. Complex tax provisions involving liquidating and nonliquidating distributions and the sale of a partnership interest are beyond the scope of this text and are discussed in depth in *South-Western Federal Taxation: Corporations, Partnerships, Estates, and Trusts.*

LO.10

Evaluate the advantages and disadvantages of the various forms for conducting a business.

TAX PLANNING
Considerations

Corporate versus Noncorporate Forms of Business Organization

Nontax Considerations. The decision of which entity to use in conducting a trade or business must be weighed carefully. Of prime importance are nontax considerations, including the legal attributes of the business entity chosen. For the corporate form, those commonly include limited liability, continuity of life, free transferability of interests, and centralized management. Many, if not all, of these attributes can also be obtained through the use of a limited liability company. When evaluating nontax considerations, close attention must be paid to applicable state law. Many states, for example, place severe restrictions on the use of corporations to practice certain professions (e.g., medicine, law). Likewise, the legal attributes of a limited liability company may vary from one state to another and may not be identical to those of corporations.

Tax Considerations. The applicable income tax rates will affect the choice of the form of doing business. Because of the wide range of possibilities (10 to 35 percent for individuals in 2008 and 15 to 35 percent for corporations), this factor must be evaluated on a case-by-case basis. For example, the corporate form is very appealing if the anticipated taxable income falls within the 25 percent corporate bracket and the shareholder's individual bracket is 35 percent. Here, the time value of the taxes saved could make operating a business as a corporation advantageous. Do not, moreover, overlook the potential impact of state and local income taxes applicable to individuals and corporations. Also, in those states that do not have an income tax, a franchise tax can pose an added tax burden on corporations (see Chapter 1).

Unless an election is made under Subchapter S, operating as a corporation yields a potential double tax result. Corporate-source income will be taxed twice—

---

[59]§ 707(c).

TAXING THE INCOME OF FOREIGN CORPORATIONS

Are foreign corporations subject to the U.S. corporate income tax? If the income is from U.S. sources, the answer is *yes*! This presumes that the income is not insulated from U.S. taxation by a provision in a tax treaty between the United States and the country of incorporation.

The manner of taxation depends upon the nature of the income involved. If the income is fixed, determinable, annual, or periodic (known as FDAP income), it is taxed at 30 percent on the *gross* amount. The tax is collected by virtue of required withholding imposed on the payor. FDAP income generally includes passive income (e.g., dividends, interest, rents, royalties, annuities) that is not effectively connected with a U.S. trade or business.

If, however, the income comes from the conduct of a U.S. trade or business, it is taxed at *net* in much the same manner as the income of domestic corporations. Any FDAP income effectively connected with the trade or business is taxed in the same manner as the business *net* income.

GLOBAL
Tax Issues

once as earned by the corporation and again when distributed to the shareholders. The payment of a dividend does not result in a deduction to the corporation, and the receipt of a dividend generally results in income to a shareholder. In the case of closely held corporations, therefore, a strong incentive exists to avoid the payment of dividends. Instead, a premium is put on bailing out profits in some manner that is deductible by the corporation. This can be accomplished by categorizing the distributions as salaries, interest, or rent—all of which are deductible by the corporation. If not properly structured, however, these devices can generate a multitude of problems. Excessive debt, for example, can lead to its reclassification as equity (under the thin capitalization approach) with a resulting disallowance of any interest deduction. Large salaries could fail the reasonableness test, and rent payments must meet an arm's length standard.

Changes in the tax treatment of qualified dividends have interjected an additional variable that must be taken into account when structuring corporation-shareholder dealings. Prior to 2003, it made little tax difference to an individual shareholder whether a corporate distribution was classified as a dividend, interest, salary, or rent—all were fully taxed as ordinary income. After 2002, however, qualified dividends are taxed in the same manner as net long-term capital gain.[60] Thus, the maximum rate cannot exceed 15 percent (0 percent in some cases—5 percent in 2007). In light of this preferential treatment of qualified dividends, effective planning becomes a matter of deciding who most needs the tax benefit. If it is the corporation, try to pay out profits in a deductible form (i.e., interest, salaries, rents). If it is the shareholder, distribute the profits as dividends. These rules apply only to *qualified* dividends and are subject to a sunset provision.[61]

Other tax considerations having a bearing on the choice of the corporate form to operate a business are summarized below:

- Corporate-source income loses its identity as it passes through the corporation to the shareholders. Thus, items possessing preferential tax treatment (e.g., interest on municipal bonds) are not taxed as such to the shareholders.
- As noted earlier, it may be difficult for shareholders to recover some or all of their investment in the corporation without a dividend income result. Recall that most corporate distributions are treated as dividends to the extent of the

---

[60]§ 1(h)(3)(B).

[61]After December 31, 2010, dividend income will be taxed at ordinary income rates (i.e., pre-2003 tax treatment is reinstated).

corporation's E & P. Structuring the capital of the corporation to include debt is a partial solution to this problem. Thus, the shareholder-creditor could recoup part of his or her investment through the tax-free payment of principal. Too much debt, however, may lead to the debt being reclassified as equity.

- Corporate losses cannot be passed through to the shareholders.
- The domestic production activities deduction generated by the corporation is not available to its shareholders. The deduction will become even more attractive as the applicable rate progresses from the current 6 percent to 9 percent.
- The liquidation of a corporation may generate tax consequences to both the corporation and its shareholders.
- The corporate form provides the shareholders with the opportunity to be treated as employees for tax purposes if they render services to the corporation. This status makes a number of attractive tax-sheltered fringe benefits available (e.g., group term life insurance). These benefits are not available to partners and sole proprietors.

ETHICAL and EQUITABLE *Considerations*

A YEAR-END CHANGE IN CORPORATE POLICY

Allison and Derek are the key employees and the sole shareholders of Garnet Company, a calendar year C corporation. In early 2008, they have Garnet adopt a policy that travel and entertainment expenses on behalf of the company shall be absorbed by the employee incurring the expense. Allison and Derek believe this policy will shift the deductibility of these expenses to themselves where it will provide a greater tax benefit.

In late December of 2008, Allison and Derek confer with their accountant and are appalled to learn that the employee expenses they were planning to deduct are subject to severe restrictions. First, they must be claimed as itemized deductions. Second, they are reduced by the 2 percent-of-AGI floor. Third, they are subject to a partial phaseout. As a result, it is decided to have Garnet claim these expenses. The corporate policy adopted in January is rescinded, and Garnet reimburses Allison and Derek for the expenses they paid. Garnet deducts the expenses on its Form 1120, and Allison and Derek do not report any of the reimbursement on their individual returns.

Comment on the propriety of what has occurred.

Regular Corporation versus S Status

Due to the pass-through concept, the use of S status generally avoids the income tax at the corporate level, bringing the individual income tax into play. As noted in the previous section, the differential between the rates applicable to noncorporate and corporate taxpayers makes this a factor to be considered. The S election enables a business to operate in the corporate form, avoid the corporate income tax, and, depending on taxable income, possibly take advantage of the lower rates usually applicable to individuals. Also, losses incurred at the corporate level pass through to the shareholders, who will utilize them on their individual returns.

Electing S status can present several problems, however. First, the election is available only to small business corporations. Consequently, many corporations will not qualify for the election. Second, S corporations are subject to the rules governing regular corporations unless otherwise specified in the Code. For example, § 351 applies on the formation of an S corporation. Likewise, if the S corporation later carries out a stock redemption or is liquidated, the rules governing regular corporations apply. Third, some states do not recognize S status for purposes of state and local taxation. Therefore, an S corporation might be subject to a state franchise tax or a state or local income tax.

Use of an Entity to Reduce the Family Income Tax Burden

One objective of tax planning is to keep the income from a business within the family unit but to disperse the income in such a manner as to minimize the overall tax burden. To the extent feasible, therefore, income should be shifted from higher-bracket to lower-bracket family members.

Several recent legislative changes, however, have raised major obstacles to shifting income to children. The first change, effective for 2007, makes the kiddie tax applicable to children under age 18. (Previously, it applied only to those under age 14.) The second change occurred shortly thereafter and goes even further. Beginning in 2008, the kiddie tax applies to all children under age 19 *and* to those who are full-time students under age 24.[62] As a result, shifting investment income (or capital gains) to a child provides no benefit to the extent that the income is taxed at the parents' tax rate.

Unfortunately, the income from property (a business) cannot be shifted to another without also transferring an interest in the property. If, for example, a father wants to assign income from his sole proprietorship to his children, he must form a partnership or incorporate the business. In either case, the transfer of the interest may be subject to the Federal gift tax. But any potential gift tax can be eliminated or controlled through judicious use of the annual exclusion, the election to split gifts (for married donors), and the unified tax credit (refer to the discussion of the Federal gift tax in Chapter 1).

Consequently, the first problem to be resolved becomes which form of business organization will best fit the objective of income shifting. For the partnership form, one major obstacle arises. Family partnership rules preclude the assignment of income to a family member unless capital is a material income-producing factor.[63] If not, the family member must contribute substantial or vital services. Ordinarily, capital is not a material income-producing factor if the income of the business consists principally of compensation for personal services performed by members or employees of the partnership. Conversely, capital is a material income-producing factor if the operation of the business entails a substantial investment in physical assets (e.g., inventory, plant, machinery, or equipment).

ETHICAL and EQUITABLE *Considerations*   **SHARING THE FAMILY BUSINESS**

Several years ago, Don Parker incorporated his car dealership and immediately made an election under Subchapter S. In 2005, he made gifts of 30 percent of the stock to his three children (10 percent each). After completing the corporation's Form 1120S and his own Form 1040 for 2006, Don put the children on the corporation's payroll. For years 2007 and 2008, they are paid salaries for participating in TV commercials. The amounts paid approximate their share of the corporation's earnings for year 2006. No payroll taxes are withheld from their salaries as Don has heard that children under age 18 who work for a parent are not subject to FICA.

What is Don trying to accomplish? Will it work?

Income shifting through the use of a partnership, therefore, may be ineffectual if a personal service business is involved. In fact, it could be hopeless if the

---

[62]The kiddie tax is restricted to *unearned* income (e.g., interest, dividends) and does not apply to *earned* income (e.g., wages, salaries). See the discussion of § 1(g) in Chapter 3.

[63]§ 704(e).

assignees are minors. The use of the corporate form usually involves no such impediment. Regardless of the nature of the business, a gift of stock carries with it the attributes of ownership. Thus, dividends paid on stock are taxed to the owner of the stock.

But what if the corporate form is utilized and the S election is made? A new hurdle arises. The Code authorizes the IRS to make adjustments in situations where shareholders are not being adequately compensated for the value of their services or capital provided to an S corporation in a family setting.[64] Thus, an S corporation suffers from the same vulnerability that exists with family partnerships.

A further factor that favors the corporate form (either a regular or an S corporation) as a device for income splitting is the ease with which it can be carried out. Presuming the entity already exists, the transfer of stock merely requires an entry in the corporation's stock ledger account. In contrast, a gift of a partnership interest probably requires an amendment to the articles of copartnership.

Regardless of the form of organization used for the business, income shifting will not take place unless the transfer is complete.[65] If the donor continues to exercise control over the interest transferred and does not recognize and protect the ownership rights of the donee, the IRS may argue that the transfer is ineffective for tax purposes. In that case, the income from the transferred interest continues to be taxed to the donor.

KEY TERMS

C corporation, 20–4	Guaranteed payments, 20–36	S corporation, 20–26
Check-the-box Regulations, 20–4	Limited liability company, 20–3	Schedule M–1, 20–15
Constructive dividends, 20–23	Liquidating distributions, 20–24	Schedule M–3, 20–17
Dividends received deduction, 20–11	Organizational expenditures, 20–13	Small business corporation, 20–26
Earnings and profits, 20–22	Personal service corporation, 20–14	Stock redemption, 20–24
		Thin capitalization, 20–17

PROBLEM MATERIALS

DISCUSSION QUESTIONS

1. What is the role of state law in determining whether an entity will be classified as a corporation for Federal income tax purposes?

2. Under what circumstances might the disregard of the corporate entity produce a favorable result for the IRS?

3. Why are limited liability companies advantageous?

4. What purpose is served by the check-the-box Regulations?

5. Presuming no election is made under the check-the-box Regulations, how will the following businesses be treated for Federal income tax purposes?
   a. A one-person entity not incorporated under state law.
   b. A one-person entity incorporated under state law.

---

[64]§ 1366(e).

[65]*Ginsberg v. Comm.*, 74–2 USTC ¶9660, 34 AFTR2d 74–5760, 502 F.2d 965 (CA–6, 1974), and *Michael F. Beirne*, 61 T.C. 268 (1973).

   c.   A multi-owner entity not incorporated under state law and possessing all of the characteristics common to corporations (i.e., continuity of life, centralized management, limited liability, and free transferability of interests).

6. Partnerships and S corporations are treated similarly for Federal income tax purposes. Explain this statement.

7. Is the cash method of accounting available to all C corporations? Explain.

8. Compare the income tax treatment of individuals and C corporations as to each of the following:
   a.   Recapture of depreciation on the disposition of business real property.
   b.   Availability of nontaxable exchange treatment as to certain property transactions.
   c.   Tax credits that are allowed.
   d.   The tax rates that apply.
   e.   The tax year (i.e., fiscal, calendar) allowed.
   f.   The special treatment of qualified dividend income.
   g.   The allowance of deductions *from* AGI (i.e., itemized deductions).
   h.   The availability of the domestic production activities deduction.

9. Taupe Corporation (a C corporation) invests and trades in real estate. During the year, it sells a tract of land for a substantial loss. Since the land was held both for resale and as an investment, the loss could arguably be classified as ordinary or capital.   **Issue ID**
   a.   In most cases, which classification will be preferable?
   b.   Under what circumstances might the classification of the loss not make any immediate difference?

10. A taxpayer has an unused capital loss carried over from a prior year. Discuss the income tax ramifications of the loss if the taxpayer is:
   a.   An individual.
   b.   A C corporation.

11. In late December 2008, Gray Corporation (a calendar year C corporation) pledges a $50,000 donation to a local relief agency formed to fight AIDS in Africa. Although Gray's board of directors authorized the donation in 2008, the payment is not made until March 2009. What are the issues involved?   **Issue ID**

12. Regarding the 10% limitation on the charitable contributions of a C corporation, how do the following affect the determination of taxable income?
   a.   Charitable contribution deduction.
   b.   Net operating loss carryback.
   c.   Capital loss carryback.
   d.   Dividends received deduction.

13. Someone has told you that C corporations can deduct the fair market value of any inventory they donate to charity. Do you agree? Why or why not?

14. In connection with the domestic production activities deduction, comment on the following:
   a.   In applying the limitation on the deduction, the difference between individual and corporate taxpayers.
   b.   How the deduction is determined in the case of an affiliated group of corporations.
   c.   What pass-through situations are, why they are necessary, and how they work.
   d.   Relevance to the imposition of the AMT.

15. What factors should be considered before making the election to forgo the carryback of a net operating loss?

16. Corey is a shareholder in Olive Corporation (a C corporation), which owns some stock in IBM. From its earnings, IBM declares and pays a dividend. Using its share of the dividend it receives from IBM, Olive distributes a dividend to its shareholders.
   a.   How many times has the dividend Corey receives been subject to taxation? Explain.
   b.   How does the tax law provide relief in this type of situation?
   c.   Does the relief completely eliminate the effect of multiple taxation? Why or why not?

Issue ID

17. Mallard Corporation was formed in December 2007 and plans to use the cash basis of accounting. Mallard incurred one-half of its organizational expenses in December 2007 and one-half in January 2008. The payment of these expenses also occurred in these two months. Do you recognize any income tax problem?

Issue ID

18. Personal service corporations frequently pay out all of their profits to their shareholder-employees in the form of salaries. Is there a reason for doing this? Explain.

19. Concerning the filing requirements for C corporations, comment on the following:
    a. When an income tax return must be filed.
    b. When a corporation must make payments of estimated tax.
    c. The purpose of Schedules M–1, M–2, and M–3 of Form 1120.

20. In view of the current preferential treatment of qualified dividends, the thin capitalization procedure is no longer as tax advantageous as it was previously.
    a. Why is this so?
    b. In what respects, if any, is thin capitalization still advantageous?

Decision Making

21. A group of developers is planning to form a new corporation to construct and operate a shopping center. Pam, who is to contribute a specific tract of land to the venture, would like to recognize the loss on its decline in value. In view of the rules governing the application of § 351, what do you suggest?

22. Harvey, an attorney, is retained to incorporate a new real estate venture. Instead of charging cash for his work, Harvey requests and receives stock in the new corporation. He does this in order to avoid recognizing any income from the performance of his services. Is Harvey correct in his assumption? Why or why not?

23. How do the following transactions affect the E & P of a corporation?
    a. A nontaxable stock dividend issued to the shareholders.
    b. Term life insurance proceeds received by the corporation on the death of its CEO.
    c. Federal corporate income tax liability.
    d. Domestic production activities deduction.
    e. Excess capital losses (no carryback available).
    f. Dividends received deduction for cash dividends received on an investment in Boeing Company stock.

24. A C corporation makes a cash distribution to its shareholders. Describe the tax effect on the shareholders if the distribution is:
    a. A qualified dividend.
    b. A return of capital that does not exceed the basis in the stock investment.
    c. A return of capital that exceeds the basis in the stock investment.
    d. What causes the "return of capital" result described in parts (b) and (c) above?

25. When a corporation distributes property as a dividend, what are the tax effects on the corporation and its shareholders under the following assumptions?
    a. The property has declined in value.
    b. The property has appreciated in value.

Issue ID

26. The stock of Grouse Corporation (a C corporation) is owned equally by a sister and two brothers: Mary, Rex, and Orson. During the year, the following transactions occur:
    a. Mary sells property to Grouse Corporation.
    b. Orson buys property from Grouse Corporation.
    c. Rex leases property to Grouse Corporation.
    d. Grouse Corporation pays for Orson's medical bills.
    e. All shareholders use an airplane owned by Grouse Corporation.
    f. Orson borrows money from Grouse Corporation.
    g. All shareholders are paid salaries by Grouse Corporation.
    h. Grouse Corporation has no E & P (earnings and profits).

Discuss any potential tax problems that these transactions might present.

27. As opposed to a corporate distribution that results in dividend income, what is the advantage of the sale or exchange treatment of a stock redemption? Doesn't capital gain treatment result in both situations?

28. Angie is the sole shareholder of Rust Corporation. If the corporation is liquidated, what are the tax effects on:
    a. Rust Corporation?
    b. Angie?

29. Nighthawk Corporation maintains an election under Subchapter S. What effect, if any, will the following events have on its S status?
    a. The number of shareholders increases from 99 to 102.
    b. A French national who lives in New York City becomes a shareholder.
    c. Nighthawk Corporation becomes a general partner in a real estate venture.
    d. A shareholder dies, and her stock in Nighthawk passes to her estate.
    e. Nighthawk decides to move from New York City to Dublin, Ireland.

30. Noah, Brandi, and Emma are equal shareholders in Oro (a calendar year S corporation). For 2008, Oro Corporation had qualified production activities income (with related W–2 wages), realized a net long-term capital gain, and made charitable contributions. As to these transactions, explain the following results: *Issue ID*
    a. Brandi cannot deduct all of her share of the domestic production activities deduction.
    b. Noah's share of the long-term capital gain does not generate any additional tax.
    c. Emma cannot claim her share of the charitable contributions.

31. Compare the nonrecognition of gain or loss on contributions to a partnership with the similar provision found in corporate formation (§ 351). What are the major differences and similarities?

32. Under what circumstances does the receipt of a partnership interest result in the recognition of ordinary income? What is the effect of this on the partnership and the other partners?

33. How do changes in the liabilities of a partnership affect the basis of a partnership interest?

34. Indicate whether each of the following will increase (+), decrease (−), or have no effect (*NE*) on a partner's basis in a partnership interest:
    a. Operating loss of the partnership.
    b. Capital gains of the partnership.
    c. Tax-exempt income of the partnership.
    d. Partnership expenditures that are not deductible in computing taxable income.

35. Blaine, Cassie, and Kirstin are equal partners in the Maize Partnership. During the year, Maize has qualified dividends, charitable contributions, and a domestic production activities deduction. Explain the following results: *Issue ID*
    a. Blaine pays less tax than Cassie and Kirstin on his share of the qualified dividends.
    b. Cassie cannot deduct any of her share of the charitable contributions.
    c. Kirstin has a larger domestic production activities deduction than either Blaine or Cassie.

36. To what extent can a partner deduct his or her distributive share of partnership losses? What happens to any unused losses?

37. Blanche and her two brothers are equal partners in the Rose Partnership. During the year, Blanche sells land (adjusted basis of $220,000) to Rose for its fair market value of $200,000. Do you perceive any tax problems as to this transfer? Explain.   *Issue ID*

38. What are guaranteed payments? When might such payments be used?

PROBLEMS

39. Ruby has the following capital asset transactions during 2008:

Long-term capital gain	$12,000
Short-term capital gain	10,000

Further, Ruby has an excess capital loss carryforward of $11,000 from 2007.

 a. What are the tax consequences of these transactions if the $11,000 loss is long term and Ruby is an individual? Ruby is a C corporation?
 b. What are the tax consequences of these transactions if the $11,000 loss is short term and Ruby is an individual? Ruby is a C corporation?

40. Penguin Corporation has a net short-term capital loss of $20,000 and a net long-term capital loss of $30,000 during 2008. Taxable income from other sources is $620,000. Capital transactions for prior years are as follows:

2004	Net long-term capital gain	$10,000
2005	Net short-term capital gain	25,000
2006	No capital asset transactions	–0–
2007	Net long-term capital gain	15,000

 a. How are the capital asset transactions handled on Penguin's 2008 tax return?
 b. Determine the capital loss carrybacks, if any.
 c. What, if any, is the capital loss carryover?

41. On December 8, 2008, Pintail Company (a calendar year taxpayer) authorizes a cash contribution of $20,000 to the United Way of Providence. The contribution is carried out as follows: $8,000 on December 9, 2008; $9,000 on March 10, 2009; and $3,000 on April 10, 2009. Regarding the year of deduction, what are the options if Pintail is:
 a. An accrual basis partnership?
 b. An accrual basis corporation?
 c. Would your answer to parts (a) and (b) change if Pintail uses the cash basis (rather than the accrual basis) of accounting? Explain.

42. During 2008, Avocet Corporation had the following transactions:

Income from operations	$700,000
Expenses from operations	610,000
Dividends from domestic corporations (less than 20% ownership)	30,000
Dividends received deduction (70% × $30,000)	21,000
Unused short-term capital loss from 2006 (there are no capital gains in 2007 and 2008)	3,000
NOL carryover from 2007	50,000

In June 2008, Avocet made a contribution to a qualified charitable organization of $13,000 in cash (not included in any of the items listed above).

 a. How much, if any, of the contribution can be claimed as a deduction for 2008?
 b. What happens to any portion not deductible for 2008?

43. Auburn Company manufactures and sells furnishings for hospitals (e.g., special needs bathroom fixtures). In the current year, it donates some of its inventory to a newly constructed hospice. The hospice is adjacent to a cancer treatment center and is intended to care for indigent and terminal patients. The property donated has an adjusted basis of $40,000 and a fair market value of $90,000. What is the amount of the charitable contribution deduction if Auburn is a:
 a. Sole proprietorship?
 b. C corporation?
 c. Would your answer to part (b) change if the fair market value of the property is $121,000 (not $90,000)?

44. For each of the following *independent* situations, determine the domestic production activities deduction (DPAD) for 2008.

Corporation	Qualified Production Activities Income	Taxable Income (without Any DPAD)	Relevant W-2 Wages
Peacock	$600,000	$900,000	$200,000
Owl	500,000	450,000	100,000
Flycatcher	400,000	500,000	40,000

45. Determine the dividends received deduction for each of the following independent situations. Assume the percentage of stock owned in the corporation paying the dividend is 30% for Warbler Corporation and less than 20% for Tern Corporation and Sparrow Corporation.

	Tern Corporation	Sparrow Corporation	Warbler Corporation
Income from operations	$6,000,000	$4,500,000	$4,000,000
Expenses of operations	5,400,000	4,800,000	4,200,000
Qualified dividends received	1,200,000	150,000	1,000,000

46. Khaki Corporation was formed on July 1, 2008, and incurred qualifying organizational expenditures. It uses a calendar year and wants to accelerate any deductions that are available. Based on this assumption, what is Khaki Corporation's deduction for 2008 if its organizational expenditures are:
    a. $4,000?
    b. $35,000?
    c. $54,000?
    d. $57,000?

47. In each of the following *independent* situations, determine the C corporation's Federal income tax liability for calendar year 2008.

Corporation	Taxable Income
Partridge	$ 22,000
Pheasant	51,000*
Junco	73,000**
Crossbill	115,000
Petrel	360,000
Flicker (a personal service corporation)	80,000

    *Does not include a short-term capital loss of $2,000.
    **Does not include a long-term capital gain of $3,000.

48. Using the legend provided below, classify each statement.

Legend
I = Applies *only* to the income taxation of individuals
C = Applies *only* to the income taxation of corporations
B = Applies to the income taxation of *both* individuals and C corporations
N = Applies to the income taxation of *neither* individuals nor C corporations

    a. The determination of AGI.
    b. The deduction of charitable contributions is subject to percentage limitation(s).
    c. On the contribution of inventory to charity, the full amount of any appreciation can be claimed as a deduction.
    d. Excess charitable contributions can be carried forward indefinitely.
    e. Excess capital losses can be carried back.

f.   A net short-term capital gain is subject to the same tax rate as ordinary income.

g.   A domestic production activities deduction may be available.

h.   A dividends received deduction may be available.

i.   The like-kind provisions of § 1031 are available.

j.   The involuntary conversion provisions of § 1033 are not available.

k.   No exemption amount is allowed for AMT purposes.

49. Elton, Neil, Courtney, and Zelma form Ecru Corporation with the following investments:

	Basis to Transferor	Fair Market Value	Number of Shares Issued
From Elton—Cash	$ 200,000	$ 200,000	200
From Neil—Inventory	230,000	270,000	260
From Courtney—Machinery and equipment	400,000	370,000	350
From Zelma—Land and building ,	1,270,000	1,300,000	1,200

In addition to its stock, Ecru distributes cash as follows: $10,000 to Neil, $20,000 to Courtney, and $100,000 to Zelma. Assume that each share of Ecru stock is worth $1,000. Regarding these transactions, provide the following information:

a.   Neil's realized and recognized gain (or loss).

b.   Neil's basis in the Ecru stock.

c.   Ecru's basis in the inventory.

d.   Courtney's realized and recognized gain (or loss).

e.   Courtney's basis in the Ecru stock.

f.   Ecru's basis in the machinery and equipment.

g.   Zelma's realized and recognized gain (or loss).

h.   Zelma's basis in the Ecru stock.

i.   Ecru's basis in the land and building.

50. Amelia is the sole shareholder of Emerald Corporation. At a time when Emerald has a deficit in accumulated E & P of $80,000 and current E & P of $40,000, it distributes a cash dividend of $70,000. If Amelia's basis in her stock is $25,000, what are the tax consequences of the distribution to:

a.   Amelia?

b.   Emerald Corporation?

Decision Making

Communications

51. The stock of Sandpiper Corporation is held equally by Russ and Erlyne. The shareholders would like to receive, as a dividend, value of $200,000 each. The corporation has the following assets it can spare:

Asset	Adjusted Basis to Sandpiper Corporation	Fair Market Value
Land (parcel A)	$ 120,000	$200,000
Land (parcel B)	260,000	200,000

Both assets are held as investments. Sandpiper Corporation has a capital loss carryover from the previous year of $20,000 and has accumulated E & P in excess of $1 million.

    Russ and Erlyne have come to you for advice. Suggest an attractive tax plan to carry out what the parties want. Write a letter (addressed to Sandpiper Corporation at P.O. Box 1150, St. Louis, MO 63130) describing your plan and its tax consequences.

52. In the current year, Carmine Corporation is liquidated under the general rules of § 331 and §336. It has cash of $200,000 and undeveloped land (basis of $100,000 and fair market value of $400,000). After taxes, Carmine distributes all remaining assets to Amy, its sole share-holder. Amy's basis in the Carmine stock is $50,000.

a.   What are Carmine Corporation's income tax consequences?

b.   What are Amy's income tax consequences?

c.   What basis will Amy have in the land?

53. Ten years ago, Rose Corporation purchased all of the stock of Fuchsia Corporation for $200,000. In the current year, Fuchsia has a basis in its assets of $600,000 and a fair market value of $800,000. Rose liquidates Fuchsia Corporation and receives all of its assets. The exception to the carryover basis rule does not apply.
    a. Does Rose Corporation recognize any gain as a result of the liquidation?
    b. What is Rose Corporation's basis for the assets it receives from Fuchsia Corporation?

54. During 2008, Gold (a calendar year, accrual basis S corporation) has the following transactions:

Sales	$640,000
Cost of goods sold	310,000
Bad debts (trade accounts receivable deemed to be uncollectible)	11,000
Long-term capital gain	40,000
Short-term capital loss	22,000
Rent expense	38,000
Qualified dividends	15,000
Charitable contribution	8,000
Salaries	110,000
Interest on State of Missouri bonds	12,000
Organizational expenditures	1,800
Advertising expense	24,000
§ 1231 gain	18,000

    a. Determine Gold Corporation's separately stated items.
    b. Determine Gold Corporation's taxable income.

55. Julius Walker owns all of the stock of Mockingbird Corporation, a calendar year S corporation. For calendar year 2008, Mockingbird anticipates an operating loss of $20,000 and could, if deemed worthwhile, sell a stock investment that would generate a $3,000 long-term capital loss. Julius has an adjusted basis of $5,000 in the Mockingbird stock. He anticipates no capital asset transactions and expects to be in the 33% tax bracket in 2008.

Decision Making

Communications

    a. Can you recommend a course of action that can save Julius taxes for 2008?
    b. Write a letter to Julius explaining your recommendations. Julius's address is Box 429, Normal, AL 35762.

56. Jennifer owns 30% of the stock in Blond, a calendar year S corporation. Blond Corporation has an operating loss of $400,000 in 2008 and an operating profit of $300,000 in 2009. Jennifer withdraws $30,000 in cash from the corporation in 2009. As of January 1, 2008, Jennifer's basis in the Blond Corporation stock is $100,000.
    a. What are Jennifer's tax consequences as to 2008?
    b. 2009?
    c. What is Jennifer's basis in the Blond Corporation stock as of January 1, 2009?
    d. January 1, 2010?

57. Guy, Alma, and Kara form the Rust Partnership. In exchange for a 30% capital interest, Guy transfers property (basis of $200,000; fair market value of $400,000) subject to a liability of $100,000. The liability is assumed by the partnership. Alma transfers property (basis of $350,000; fair market value of $300,000) for a 30% capital interest. Kara invests cash of $400,000 for the remaining 40% capital interest. Concerning these transactions, provide the following information:
    a. Guy's recognized gain.
    b. Guy's basis in the partnership interest.
    c. Alma's recognized loss.
    d. Alma's basis in the partnership interest.
    e. Kara's basis in the partnership interest.
    f. Rust Partnership's basis in the property transferred by Guy and Alma.

58. As of January 1, 2007, Norman has a basis of $90,000 in his 30% capital interest in the Plata Partnership. He and the partnership use the calendar year for tax purposes. The

Decision Making

partnership incurs an operating loss of $450,000 for 2007 and a profit of $270,000 for 2008.

   a.   How much, if any, loss may Norman recognize for 2007?
   b.   How much income must Norman recognize for 2008?
   c.   What basis will Norman have in his partnership interest as of January 1, 2008?
   d.   What basis will Norman have in his partnership interest as of January 1, 2009?
   e.   What year-end tax planning would you suggest to ensure that a partner could deduct all of his or her share of any partnership losses?

59.   Vicky owns a 55% interest in the capital and profits of the Green Partnership. In 2008, Vicky sells property (adjusted basis of $100,000) to Green for its fair market value of $90,000. In 2009, Green Partnership sells the same property to an outside party for $105,000.

   a.   What are Vicky's tax consequences on the 2008 sale?
   b.   What are Green Partnership's tax consequences on the 2009 sale?
   c.   Would the answers to parts (a) and (b) change if Vicky owns only a 45% interest and the other 55% interest is owned by her mother? Explain.

RESEARCH PROBLEMS

Note: Solutions to Research Problems can be prepared by using the **RIA Checkpoint**® **Student Edition** online research product, which is available to accompany this text. It is also possible to prepare solutions to the Research Problems by using tax research materials found in a standard tax library.

Research Problem 1.   In 2003, Rhoda forms Madison Healthcare Center, LLC, to own and operate several nursing homes. Madison is a limited liability company with Rhoda as its sole owner. Rhoda *did not* elect under the "check-the-box" Regulations to have Madison treated as a corporation for Federal income tax purposes.

   In 2008 and after several years of Madison's failure to pay taxes, the IRS assesses Rhoda for the delinquency. Because Madison is a sole proprietorship, Rhoda is directly liable for the tax obligations of the business. Under the check-the-box Regulations, a one-owner limited liability company is a sole proprietorship in a default situation (i.e., failure to elect otherwise) [Reg. § 301.7701–3(b)(1)(iii)].

   Rhoda maintains that Madison is a corporation and that, as a shareholder, she is not liable for its obligations. She says that Madison is a corporation because it meets the definition of a corporation under § 7701(a)(2). Included in the definition is an "association," which is an entity that possesses a preponderance of corporate attributes—continuity of life, centralized management, limited liability, and free transferability of interests. Consequently, says Rhoda, the check-the-box Regulations are an unnecessary and invalid interpretation of the Code.

   Which party will prevail?

Partial list of research aids:
§§ 7701(a)(2) and (3).
Reg. § 301.7701–2. The "Kintner" Regulations issued in 1960 and effective prior to January 1, 1997.
Reg. §§ 301.7701–1 through –3. The check-the-box Regulations, effective after 1996.
Littriello v. U.S., 2005–1 USTC ¶50,385, 95 AFTR2d 2005–2581 (D.Ct.Ky., 2005).

Research Problem 2.   Cynthia and Lindsey (mother and daughter) started Pottery Shed in the early 1990s. Shortly after beginning business, Pottery Shed was incorporated with stock issued as follows: 700 shares to Cynthia and 300 to Lindsey. The business has proved successful and by 2008 is in dire need of additional space for customer parking. Fortunately, Cynthia owns property adjacent to the business, which she purchased many years ago (cost basis of $20,000 and current value of $200,000). To be suitable for parking, however, the property must be cleared and paved at a cost of $50,000. To carry out this objective, the parties are considering the three following alternatives:

   (1)   Cynthia makes a capital contribution of the property to Pottery Shed. To make the needed improvements, Pottery Shed borrows $50,000 from a bank.

(2) Cynthia transfers the property to Pottery Shed in exchange for 200 shares of its stock. To make the improvements, Pottery Shed borrows $50,000 from a bank.

(3) Cynthia transfers the property to Pottery Shed in exchange for 200 shares of its stock, while Lindsey invests cash of $50,000 for 50 shares.

Evaluate the tax ramifications of each of these alternatives.

Partial list of research aids:
§§ 118, 351, and 1032.
Reg. §§ 1.351–1(a)(1)(ii) and (b)(1).

Research Problem 3. In anticipation that a dividend will be declared, Garnet Corporation purchases $300,000 worth of common stock of Magenta Corporation. Of the $300,000 purchase price, $200,000 is borrowed from a bank. After the dividend is declared and paid, Garnet sells the Magenta stock for a loss. Earlier in the year, Garnet realized a capital gain from the sale of a different investment.

a. What are the hoped-for tax advantages of these transactions?

b. What can go wrong?

Research Problem 4. In 1996, Claude received a distribution of $50,000 from Swallow Corporation that purported to be a return of capital. Since Claude's basis in the stock was $80,000, he reduced the basis to $30,000 and recognized no income as to the distribution. In 2003, it was determined that Swallow Corporation has been miscalculating its E & P for a number of years. As a result, the 1996 distribution it made should have been taxed to the shareholders as a dividend. Due to the expiration of the three-year statute of limitations, Claude made no adjustment to his income tax return for 1996.

Communications

In 2008, Claude sells his stock in Swallow for $300,000. He feels that he should recognize a gain of only $220,000 from the sale. Since the 1996 distribution was a dividend and not a return of capital, his stock basis should not have been reduced and should remain at the original $80,000. Claude seeks your advice on this matter.

Write a letter to Claude Romano, Box 1340, Clinton, MS 39058, explaining his position. Use layperson terminology, as your client is not well versed in tax matters.

Use the tax resources of the Internet to address the following questions. Do not restrict your search to the World Wide Web, but include a review of newsgroups and general reference materials, practitioner sites and resources, primary sources of the tax law, chat rooms and discussion groups, and other opportunities.

Internet Activity

Research Problem 5. Does your state permit CPAs to practice public accounting in the corporate form? If not, can they form limited liability companies? What, if any, special restrictions are imposed?

Research Problem 6. Does your state recognize a Subchapter S election for state tax purposes? If so, does it treat out-of-state shareholders in the same way as resident shareholders?

Research Problem 7. To report its transactions for the year, a partnership must file a Form 1065 with the IRS.

a. When is this return due?

b. As is the case with individuals and corporations, can a partnership obtain an automatic six-month extension for filing the Form 1065?

c. Does a partnership need to include a Schedule M–3 with its Form 1065? Explain.

APPENDIX A

TAX RATE SCHEDULES AND TABLES

(The 2008 Tax Tables and 2008 Sales Tax Tables can be accessed at the IRS
web site: [**http://www.irs.gov**] when released.)

2007	Income Tax Rate Schedules	A–2
2008	Income Tax Rate Schedules	A–2
2007	Tax Tables	A–3
2007	Sales Tax Tables	A–15

2007 Tax Rate Schedules

Single—Schedule X

If taxable income is: Over—	But not over—	The tax is:	of the amount over—
$ 0	$ 7,825	........10%	$ 0
7,825	31,850	$ 782.50 + 15%	7,825
31,850	77,100	4,386.25 + 25%	31,850
77,100	160,850	15,698.75 + 28%	77,100
160,850	349,700	39,148.75 + 33%	160,850
349,700	....	101,469.25 + 35%	349,700

Head of household—Schedule Z

If taxable income is: Over—	But not over—	The tax is:	of the amount over—
$ 0	$ 11,200	........10%	$ 0
11,200	42,650	$ 1,120.00 + 15%	11,200
42,650	110,100	5,837.50 + 25%	42,650
110,100	178,350	22,700.00 + 28%	110,100
178,350	349,700	41,810.00 + 33%	178,350
349,700	....	98,355.50 + 35%	349,700

Married filing jointly or Qualifying widow(er)—Schedule Y–1

If taxable income is: Over—	But not over—	The tax is:	of the amount over—
$ 0	$ 15,650	........10%	$ 0
15,650	63,700	$ 1,565.00 + 15%	15,650
63,700	128,500	8,772.50 + 25%	63,700
128,500	195,850	24,972.50 + 28%	128,500
195,850	349,700	43,830.50 + 33%	195,850
349,700	....	94,601.00 + 35%	349,700

Married filing separately—Schedule Y–2

If taxable income is: Over—	But not over—	The tax is:	of the amount over—
$ 0	$ 7,825	........10%	$ 0
7,825	31,850	$ 782.50 + 15%	7,825
31,850	64,250	4,386.25 + 25%	31,850
64,250	97,925	12,486.25 + 28%	64,250
97,925	174,850	21,915.25 + 33%	97,925
174,850	....	47,300.50 + 35%	174,850

2008 Tax Rate Schedules

Single—Schedule X

If taxable income is: Over—	But not over—	The tax is:	of the amount over—
$ 0	$ 8,025	........10%	$ 0
8,025	32,550	$ 802.50 + 15%	8,025
32,550	78,850	4,481.25 + 25%	32,550
78,850	164,550	16,056.25 + 28%	78,850
164,550	357,700	40,052.25 + 33%	164,550
357,700	....	103,791.75 + 35%	357,700

Head of household—Schedule Z

If taxable income is: Over—	But not over—	The tax is:	of the amount over—
$ 0	$ 11,450	........10%	$ 0
11,450	43,650	$ 1,145.00 + 15%	11,450
43,650	112,650	5,975.00 + 25%	43,650
112,650	182,400	23,225.00 + 28%	112,650
182,400	357,700	42,755.00 + 33%	182,400
357,700	....	100,604.00 + 35%	357,700

Married filing jointly or Qualifying widow(er)—Schedule Y–1

If taxable income is: Over—	But not over—	The tax is:	of the amount over—
$ 0	$ 16,050	........10%	$ 0
16,050	65,100	$ 1,605.00 + 15%	16,050
65,100	131,450	8,962.50 + 25%	65,100
131,450	200,300	25,550.00 + 28%	131,450
200,300	357,700	44,828.00 + 33%	200,300
357,700	....	96,770.00 + 35%	357,700

Married filing separately—Schedule Y–2

If taxable income is: Over—	But not over—	The tax is:	of the amount over—
$ 0	$ 8,025	........10%	$ 0
8,025	32,550	$ 802.50 + 15%	8,025
32,550	65,725	4,481.25 + 25%	32,550
65,725	100,150	12,775.00 + 28%	65,725
100,150	178,850	22,414.00 + 33%	100,150
178,850	....	48,385.00 + 35%	178,850

2007 Tax Table

See the instructions for line 44 that begin on page 33 to see if you must use the Tax Table below to figure your tax.

Example. Mr. and Mrs. Brown are filing a joint return. Their taxable income on Form 1040, line 43, is $25,300. First, they find the $25,300–25,350 taxable income line. Next, they find the column for married filing jointly and read down the column. The amount shown where the taxable income line and filing status column meet is $3,016. This is the tax amount they should enter on Form 1040, line 44.

Sample Table

At least	But less than	Single	Married filing jointly	Married filing separately	Head of a household
			Your tax is—		
25,200	25,250	3,393	3,001	3,393	3,224
25,250	25,300	3,400	3,009	3,400	3,231
25,300	25,350	3,408	(3,016)	3,408	3,239
25,350	25,400	3,415	3,024	3,415	3,246

If line 43 (taxable income) is— At least	But less than	Single	Married filing jointly*	Married filing separately	Head of a household
			Your tax is—		
0	5	0	0	0	0
5	15	1	1	1	1
15	25	2	2	2	2
25	50	4	4	4	4
50	75	6	6	6	6
75	100	9	9	9	9
100	125	11	11	11	11
125	150	14	14	14	14
150	175	16	16	16	16
175	200	19	19	19	19
200	225	21	21	21	21
225	250	24	24	24	24
250	275	26	26	26	26
275	300	29	29	29	29
300	325	31	31	31	31
325	350	34	34	34	34
350	375	36	36	36	36
375	400	39	39	39	39
400	425	41	41	41	41
425	450	44	44	44	44
450	475	46	46	46	46
475	500	49	49	49	49
500	525	51	51	51	51
525	550	54	54	54	54
550	575	56	56	56	56
575	600	59	59	59	59
600	625	61	61	61	61
625	650	64	64	64	64
650	675	66	66	66	66
675	700	69	69	69	69
700	725	71	71	71	71
725	750	74	74	74	74
750	775	76	76	76	76
775	800	79	79	79	79
800	825	81	81	81	81
825	850	84	84	84	84
850	875	86	86	86	86
875	900	89	89	89	89
900	925	91	91	91	91
925	950	94	94	94	94
950	975	96	96	96	96
975	1,000	99	99	99	99

1,000

At least	But less than	Single	Married filing jointly*	Married filing separately	Head of a household
1,000	1,025	101	101	101	101
1,025	1,050	104	104	104	104
1,050	1,075	106	106	106	106
1,075	1,100	109	109	109	109
1,100	1,125	111	111	111	111
1,125	1,150	114	114	114	114
1,150	1,175	116	116	116	116
1,175	1,200	119	119	119	119
1,200	1,225	121	121	121	121
1,225	1,250	124	124	124	124
1,250	1,275	126	126	126	126
1,275	1,300	129	129	129	129

At least	But less than	Single	Married filing jointly*	Married filing separately	Head of a household
1,300	1,325	131	131	131	131
1,325	1,350	134	134	134	134
1,350	1,375	136	136	136	136
1,375	1,400	139	139	139	139
1,400	1,425	141	141	141	141
1,425	1,450	144	144	144	144
1,450	1,475	146	146	146	146
1,475	1,500	149	149	149	149
1,500	1,525	151	151	151	151
1,525	1,550	154	154	154	154
1,550	1,575	156	156	156	156
1,575	1,600	159	159	159	159
1,600	1,625	161	161	161	161
1,625	1,650	164	164	164	164
1,650	1,675	166	166	166	166
1,675	1,700	169	169	169	169
1,700	1,725	171	171	171	171
1,725	1,750	174	174	174	174
1,750	1,775	176	176	176	176
1,775	1,800	179	179	179	179
1,800	1,825	181	181	181	181
1,825	1,850	184	184	184	184
1,850	1,875	186	186	186	186
1,875	1,900	189	189	189	189
1,900	1,925	191	191	191	191
1,925	1,950	194	194	194	194
1,950	1,975	196	196	196	196
1,975	2,000	199	199	199	199

2,000

At least	But less than	Single	Married filing jointly*	Married filing separately	Head of a household
2,000	2,025	201	201	201	201
2,025	2,050	204	204	204	204
2,050	2,075	206	206	206	206
2,075	2,100	209	209	209	209
2,100	2,125	211	211	211	211
2,125	2,150	214	214	214	214
2,150	2,175	216	216	216	216
2,175	2,200	219	219	219	219
2,200	2,225	221	221	221	221
2,225	2,250	224	224	224	224
2,250	2,275	226	226	226	226
2,275	2,300	229	229	229	229
2,300	2,325	231	231	231	231
2,325	2,350	234	234	234	234
2,350	2,375	236	236	236	236
2,375	2,400	239	239	239	239
2,400	2,425	241	241	241	241
2,425	2,450	244	244	244	244
2,450	2,475	246	246	246	246
2,475	2,500	249	249	249	249
2,500	2,525	251	251	251	251
2,525	2,550	254	254	254	254
2,550	2,575	256	256	256	256
2,575	2,600	259	259	259	259
2,600	2,625	261	261	261	261
2,625	2,650	264	264	264	264
2,650	2,675	266	266	266	266
2,675	2,700	269	269	269	269

At least	But less than	Single	Married filing jointly*	Married filing separately	Head of a household
2,700	2,725	271	271	271	271
2,725	2,750	274	274	274	274
2,750	2,775	276	276	276	276
2,775	2,800	279	279	279	279
2,800	2,825	281	281	281	281
2,825	2,850	284	284	284	284
2,850	2,875	286	286	286	286
2,875	2,900	289	289	289	289
2,900	2,925	291	291	291	291
2,925	2,950	294	294	294	294
2,950	2,975	296	296	296	296
2,975	3,000	299	299	299	299

3,000

At least	But less than	Single	Married filing jointly*	Married filing separately	Head of a household
3,000	3,050	303	303	303	303
3,050	3,100	308	308	308	308
3,100	3,150	313	313	313	313
3,150	3,200	318	318	318	318
3,200	3,250	323	323	323	323
3,250	3,300	328	328	328	328
3,300	3,350	333	333	333	333
3,350	3,400	338	338	338	338
3,400	3,450	343	343	343	343
3,450	3,500	348	348	348	348
3,500	3,550	353	353	353	353
3,550	3,600	358	358	358	358
3,600	3,650	363	363	363	363
3,650	3,700	368	368	368	368
3,700	3,750	373	373	373	373
3,750	3,800	378	378	378	378
3,800	3,850	383	383	383	383
3,850	3,900	388	388	388	388
3,900	3,950	393	393	393	393
3,950	4,000	398	398	398	398

4,000

At least	But less than	Single	Married filing jointly*	Married filing separately	Head of a household
4,000	4,050	403	403	403	403
4,050	4,100	408	408	408	408
4,100	4,150	413	413	413	413
4,150	4,200	418	418	418	418
4,200	4,250	423	423	423	423
4,250	4,300	428	428	428	428
4,300	4,350	433	433	433	433
4,350	4,400	438	438	438	438
4,400	4,450	443	443	443	443
4,450	4,500	448	448	448	448
4,500	4,550	453	453	453	453
4,550	4,600	458	458	458	458
4,600	4,650	463	463	463	463
4,650	4,700	468	468	468	468
4,700	4,750	473	473	473	473
4,750	4,800	478	478	478	478
4,800	4,850	483	483	483	483
4,850	4,900	488	488	488	488
4,900	4,950	493	493	493	493
4,950	5,000	498	498	498	498

*This column must also be used by a qualifying widow(er).

(Continued on next page)

2007 Tax Table–*Continued*

If line 43 (taxable income) is— At least	But less than	Single	Married filing jointly*	Married filing separately	Head of a household
5,000					
5,000	5,050	503	503	503	503
5,050	5,100	508	508	508	508
5,100	5,150	513	513	513	513
5,150	5,200	518	518	518	518
5,200	5,250	523	523	523	523
5,250	5,300	528	528	528	528
5,300	5,350	533	533	533	533
5,350	5,400	538	538	538	538
5,400	5,450	543	543	543	543
5,450	5,500	548	548	548	548
5,500	5,550	553	553	553	553
5,550	5,600	558	558	558	558
5,600	5,650	563	563	563	563
5,650	5,700	568	568	568	568
5,700	5,750	573	573	573	573
5,750	5,800	578	578	578	578
5,800	5,850	583	583	583	583
5,850	5,900	588	588	588	588
5,900	5,950	593	593	593	593
5,950	6,000	598	598	598	598
6,000					
6,000	6,050	603	603	603	603
6,050	6,100	608	608	608	608
6,100	6,150	613	613	613	613
6,150	6,200	618	618	618	618
6,200	6,250	623	623	623	623
6,250	6,300	628	628	628	628
6,300	6,350	633	633	633	633
6,350	6,400	638	638	638	638
6,400	6,450	643	643	643	643
6,450	6,500	648	648	648	648
6,500	6,550	653	653	653	653
6,550	6,600	658	658	658	658
6,600	6,650	663	663	663	663
6,650	6,700	668	668	668	668
6,700	6,750	673	673	673	673
6,750	6,800	678	678	678	678
6,800	6,850	683	683	683	683
6,850	6,900	688	688	688	688
6,900	6,950	693	693	693	693
6,950	7,000	698	698	698	698
7,000					
7,000	7,050	703	703	703	703
7,050	7,100	708	708	708	708
7,100	7,150	713	713	713	713
7,150	7,200	718	718	718	718
7,200	7,250	723	723	723	723
7,250	7,300	728	728	728	728
7,300	7,350	733	733	733	733
7,350	7,400	738	738	738	738
7,400	7,450	743	743	743	743
7,450	7,500	748	748	748	748
7,500	7,550	753	753	753	753
7,550	7,600	758	758	758	758
7,600	7,650	763	763	763	763
7,650	7,700	768	768	768	768
7,700	7,750	773	773	773	773
7,750	7,800	778	778	778	778
7,800	7,850	783	783	783	783
7,850	7,900	790	788	790	788
7,900	7,950	798	793	798	793
7,950	8,000	805	798	805	798

If line 43 (taxable income) is— At least	But less than	Single	Married filing jointly*	Married filing separately	Head of a household
8,000					
8,000	8,050	813	803	813	803
8,050	8,100	820	808	820	808
8,100	8,150	828	813	828	813
8,150	8,200	835	818	835	818
8,200	8,250	843	823	843	823
8,250	8,300	850	828	850	828
8,300	8,350	858	833	858	833
8,350	8,400	865	838	865	838
8,400	8,450	873	843	873	843
8,450	8,500	880	848	880	848
8,500	8,550	888	853	888	853
8,550	8,600	895	858	895	858
8,600	8,650	903	863	903	863
8,650	8,700	910	868	910	868
8,700	8,750	918	873	918	873
8,750	8,800	925	878	925	878
8,800	8,850	933	883	933	883
8,850	8,900	940	888	940	888
8,900	8,950	948	893	948	893
8,950	9,000	955	898	955	898
9,000					
9,000	9,050	963	903	963	903
9,050	9,100	970	908	970	908
9,100	9,150	978	913	978	913
9,150	9,200	985	918	985	918
9,200	9,250	993	923	993	923
9,250	9,300	1,000	928	1,000	928
9,300	9,350	1,008	933	1,008	933
9,350	9,400	1,015	938	1,015	938
9,400	9,450	1,023	943	1,023	943
9,450	9,500	1,030	948	1,030	948
9,500	9,550	1,038	953	1,038	953
9,550	9,600	1,045	958	1,045	958
9,600	9,650	1,053	963	1,053	963
9,650	9,700	1,060	968	1,060	968
9,700	9,750	1,068	973	1,068	973
9,750	9,800	1,075	978	1,075	978
9,800	9,850	1,083	983	1,083	983
9,850	9,900	1,090	988	1,090	988
9,900	9,950	1,098	993	1,098	993
9,950	10,000	1,105	998	1,105	998
10,000					
10,000	10,050	1,113	1,003	1,113	1,003
10,050	10,100	1,120	1,008	1,120	1,008
10,100	10,150	1,128	1,013	1,128	1,013
10,150	10,200	1,135	1,018	1,135	1,018
10,200	10,250	1,143	1,023	1,143	1,023
10,250	10,300	1,150	1,028	1,150	1,028
10,300	10,350	1,158	1,033	1,158	1,033
10,350	10,400	1,165	1,038	1,165	1,038
10,400	10,450	1,173	1,043	1,173	1,043
10,450	10,500	1,180	1,048	1,180	1,048
10,500	10,550	1,188	1,053	1,188	1,053
10,550	10,600	1,195	1,058	1,195	1,058
10,600	10,650	1,203	1,063	1,203	1,063
10,650	10,700	1,210	1,068	1,210	1,068
10,700	10,750	1,218	1,073	1,218	1,073
10,750	10,800	1,225	1,078	1,225	1,078
10,800	10,850	1,233	1,083	1,233	1,083
10,850	10,900	1,240	1,088	1,240	1,088
10,900	10,950	1,248	1,093	1,248	1,093
10,950	11,000	1,255	1,098	1,255	1,098

If line 43 (taxable income) is— At least	But less than	Single	Married filing jointly*	Married filing separately	Head of a household
11,000					
11,000	11,050	1,263	1,103	1,263	1,103
11,050	11,100	1,270	1,108	1,270	1,108
11,100	11,150	1,278	1,113	1,278	1,113
11,150	11,200	1,285	1,118	1,285	1,118
11,200	11,250	1,293	1,123	1,293	1,124
11,250	11,300	1,300	1,128	1,300	1,131
11,300	11,350	1,308	1,133	1,308	1,139
11,350	11,400	1,315	1,138	1,315	1,146
11,400	11,450	1,323	1,143	1,323	1,154
11,450	11,500	1,330	1,148	1,330	1,161
11,500	11,550	1,338	1,153	1,338	1,169
11,550	11,600	1,345	1,158	1,345	1,176
11,600	11,650	1,353	1,163	1,353	1,184
11,650	11,700	1,360	1,168	1,360	1,191
11,700	11,750	1,368	1,173	1,368	1,199
11,750	11,800	1,375	1,178	1,375	1,206
11,800	11,850	1,383	1,183	1,383	1,214
11,850	11,900	1,390	1,188	1,390	1,221
11,900	11,950	1,398	1,193	1,398	1,229
11,950	12,000	1,405	1,198	1,405	1,236
12,000					
12,000	12,050	1,413	1,203	1,413	1,244
12,050	12,100	1,420	1,208	1,420	1,251
12,100	12,150	1,428	1,213	1,428	1,259
12,150	12,200	1,435	1,218	1,435	1,266
12,200	12,250	1,443	1,223	1,443	1,274
12,250	12,300	1,450	1,228	1,450	1,281
12,300	12,350	1,458	1,233	1,458	1,289
12,350	12,400	1,465	1,238	1,465	1,296
12,400	12,450	1,473	1,243	1,473	1,304
12,450	12,500	1,480	1,248	1,480	1,311
12,500	12,550	1,488	1,253	1,488	1,319
12,550	12,600	1,495	1,258	1,495	1,326
12,600	12,650	1,503	1,263	1,503	1,334
12,650	12,700	1,510	1,268	1,510	1,341
12,700	12,750	1,518	1,273	1,518	1,349
12,750	12,800	1,525	1,278	1,525	1,356
12,800	12,850	1,533	1,283	1,533	1,364
12,850	12,900	1,540	1,288	1,540	1,371
12,900	12,950	1,548	1,293	1,548	1,379
12,950	13,000	1,555	1,298	1,555	1,386
13,000					
13,000	13,050	1,563	1,303	1,563	1,394
13,050	13,100	1,570	1,308	1,570	1,401
13,100	13,150	1,578	1,313	1,578	1,409
13,150	13,200	1,585	1,318	1,585	1,416
13,200	13,250	1,593	1,323	1,593	1,424
13,250	13,300	1,600	1,328	1,600	1,431
13,300	13,350	1,608	1,333	1,608	1,439
13,350	13,400	1,615	1,338	1,615	1,446
13,400	13,450	1,623	1,343	1,623	1,454
13,450	13,500	1,630	1,348	1,630	1,461
13,500	13,550	1,638	1,353	1,638	1,469
13,550	13,600	1,645	1,358	1,645	1,476
13,600	13,650	1,653	1,363	1,653	1,484
13,650	13,700	1,660	1,368	1,660	1,491
13,700	13,750	1,668	1,373	1,668	1,499
13,750	13,800	1,675	1,378	1,675	1,506
13,800	13,850	1,683	1,383	1,683	1,514
13,850	13,900	1,690	1,388	1,690	1,521
13,900	13,950	1,698	1,393	1,698	1,529
13,950	14,000	1,705	1,398	1,705	1,536

*This column must also be used by a qualifying widow(er).

(Continued on next page)

2007 Tax Table–*Continued*

14,000

At least	But less than	Single	Married filing jointly *	Married filing separately	Head of a house-hold
14,000	14,050	1,713	1,403	1,713	1,544
14,050	14,100	1,720	1,408	1,720	1,551
14,100	14,150	1,728	1,413	1,728	1,559
14,150	14,200	1,735	1,418	1,735	1,566
14,200	14,250	1,743	1,423	1,743	1,574
14,250	14,300	1,750	1,428	1,750	1,581
14,300	14,350	1,758	1,433	1,758	1,589
14,350	14,400	1,765	1,438	1,765	1,596
14,400	14,450	1,773	1,443	1,773	1,604
14,450	14,500	1,780	1,448	1,780	1,611
14,500	14,550	1,788	1,453	1,788	1,619
14,550	14,600	1,795	1,458	1,795	1,626
14,600	14,650	1,803	1,463	1,803	1,634
14,650	14,700	1,810	1,468	1,810	1,641
14,700	14,750	1,818	1,473	1,818	1,649
14,750	14,800	1,825	1,478	1,825	1,656
14,800	14,850	1,833	1,483	1,833	1,664
14,850	14,900	1,840	1,488	1,840	1,671
14,900	14,950	1,848	1,493	1,848	1,679
14,950	15,000	1,855	1,498	1,855	1,686

15,000

At least	But less than	Single	Married filing jointly *	Married filing separately	Head of a house-hold
15,000	15,050	1,863	1,503	1,863	1,694
15,050	15,100	1,870	1,508	1,870	1,701
15,100	15,150	1,878	1,513	1,878	1,709
15,150	15,200	1,885	1,518	1,885	1,716
15,200	15,250	1,893	1,523	1,893	1,724
15,250	15,300	1,900	1,528	1,900	1,731
15,300	15,350	1,908	1,533	1,908	1,739
15,350	15,400	1,915	1,538	1,915	1,746
15,400	15,450	1,923	1,543	1,923	1,754
15,450	15,500	1,930	1,548	1,930	1,761
15,500	15,550	1,938	1,553	1,938	1,769
15,550	15,600	1,945	1,558	1,945	1,776
15,600	15,650	1,953	1,563	1,953	1,784
15,650	15,700	1,960	1,569	1,960	1,791
15,700	15,750	1,968	1,576	1,968	1,799
15,750	15,800	1,975	1,584	1,975	1,806
15,800	15,850	1,983	1,591	1,983	1,814
15,850	15,900	1,990	1,599	1,990	1,821
15,900	15,950	1,998	1,606	1,998	1,829
15,950	16,000	2,005	1,614	2,005	1,836

16,000

At least	But less than	Single	Married filing jointly *	Married filing separately	Head of a house-hold
16,000	16,050	2,013	1,621	2,013	1,844
16,050	16,100	2,020	1,629	2,020	1,851
16,100	16,150	2,028	1,636	2,028	1,859
16,150	16,200	2,035	1,644	2,035	1,866
16,200	16,250	2,043	1,651	2,043	1,874
16,250	16,300	2,050	1,659	2,050	1,881
16,300	16,350	2,058	1,666	2,058	1,889
16,350	16,400	2,065	1,674	2,065	1,896
16,400	16,450	2,073	1,681	2,073	1,904
16,450	16,500	2,080	1,689	2,080	1,911
16,500	16,550	2,088	1,696	2,088	1,919
16,550	16,600	2,095	1,704	2,095	1,926
16,600	16,650	2,103	1,711	2,103	1,934
16,650	16,700	2,110	1,719	2,110	1,941
16,700	16,750	2,118	1,726	2,118	1,949
16,750	16,800	2,125	1,734	2,125	1,956
16,800	16,850	2,133	1,741	2,133	1,964
16,850	16,900	2,140	1,749	2,140	1,971
16,900	16,950	2,148	1,756	2,148	1,979
16,950	17,000	2,155	1,764	2,155	1,986

17,000

At least	But less than	Single	Married filing jointly *	Married filing separately	Head of a house-hold
17,000	17,050	2,163	1,771	2,163	1,994
17,050	17,100	2,170	1,779	2,170	2,001
17,100	17,150	2,178	1,786	2,178	2,009
17,150	17,200	2,185	1,794	2,185	2,016
17,200	17,250	2,193	1,801	2,193	2,024
17,250	17,300	2,200	1,809	2,200	2,031
17,300	17,350	2,208	1,816	2,208	2,039
17,350	17,400	2,215	1,824	2,215	2,046
17,400	17,450	2,223	1,831	2,223	2,054
17,450	17,500	2,230	1,839	2,230	2,061
17,500	17,550	2,238	1,846	2,238	2,069
17,550	17,600	2,245	1,854	2,245	2,076
17,600	17,650	2,253	1,861	2,253	2,084
17,650	17,700	2,260	1,869	2,260	2,091
17,700	17,750	2,268	1,876	2,268	2,099
17,750	17,800	2,275	1,884	2,275	2,106
17,800	17,850	2,283	1,891	2,283	2,114
17,850	17,900	2,290	1,899	2,290	2,121
17,900	17,950	2,298	1,906	2,298	2,129
17,950	18,000	2,305	1,914	2,305	2,136

18,000

At least	But less than	Single	Married filing jointly *	Married filing separately	Head of a house-hold
18,000	18,050	2,313	1,921	2,313	2,144
18,050	18,100	2,320	1,929	2,320	2,151
18,100	18,150	2,328	1,936	2,328	2,159
18,150	18,200	2,335	1,944	2,335	2,166
18,200	18,250	2,343	1,951	2,343	2,174
18,250	18,300	2,350	1,959	2,350	2,181
18,300	18,350	2,358	1,966	2,358	2,189
18,350	18,400	2,365	1,974	2,365	2,196
18,400	18,450	2,373	1,981	2,373	2,204
18,450	18,500	2,380	1,989	2,380	2,211
18,500	18,550	2,388	1,996	2,388	2,219
18,550	18,600	2,395	2,004	2,395	2,226
18,600	18,650	2,403	2,011	2,403	2,234
18,650	18,700	2,410	2,019	2,410	2,241
18,700	18,750	2,418	2,026	2,418	2,249
18,750	18,800	2,425	2,034	2,425	2,256
18,800	18,850	2,433	2,041	2,433	2,264
18,850	18,900	2,440	2,049	2,440	2,271
18,900	18,950	2,448	2,056	2,448	2,279
18,950	19,000	2,455	2,064	2,455	2,286

19,000

At least	But less than	Single	Married filing jointly *	Married filing separately	Head of a house-hold
19,000	19,050	2,463	2,071	2,463	2,294
19,050	19,100	2,470	2,079	2,470	2,301
19,100	19,150	2,478	2,086	2,478	2,309
19,150	19,200	2,485	2,094	2,485	2,316
19,200	19,250	2,493	2,101	2,493	2,324
19,250	19,300	2,500	2,109	2,500	2,331
19,300	19,350	2,508	2,116	2,508	2,339
19,350	19,400	2,515	2,124	2,515	2,346
19,400	19,450	2,523	2,131	2,523	2,354
19,450	19,500	2,530	2,139	2,530	2,361
19,500	19,550	2,538	2,146	2,538	2,369
19,550	19,600	2,545	2,154	2,545	2,376
19,600	19,650	2,553	2,161	2,553	2,384
19,650	19,700	2,560	2,169	2,560	2,391
19,700	19,750	2,568	2,176	2,568	2,399
19,750	19,800	2,575	2,184	2,575	2,406
19,800	19,850	2,583	2,191	2,583	2,414
19,850	19,900	2,590	2,199	2,590	2,421
19,900	19,950	2,598	2,206	2,598	2,429
19,950	20,000	2,605	2,214	2,605	2,436

20,000

At least	But less than	Single	Married filing jointly *	Married filing separately	Head of a house-hold
20,000	20,050	2,613	2,221	2,613	2,444
20,050	20,100	2,620	2,229	2,620	2,451
20,100	20,150	2,628	2,236	2,628	2,459
20,150	20,200	2,635	2,244	2,635	2,466
20,200	20,250	2,643	2,251	2,643	2,474
20,250	20,300	2,650	2,259	2,650	2,481
20,300	20,350	2,658	2,266	2,658	2,489
20,350	20,400	2,665	2,274	2,665	2,496
20,400	20,450	2,673	2,281	2,673	2,504
20,450	20,500	2,680	2,289	2,680	2,511
20,500	20,550	2,688	2,296	2,688	2,519
20,550	20,600	2,695	2,304	2,695	2,526
20,600	20,650	2,703	2,311	2,703	2,534
20,650	20,700	2,710	2,319	2,710	2,541
20,700	20,750	2,718	2,326	2,718	2,549
20,750	20,800	2,725	2,334	2,725	2,556
20,800	20,850	2,733	2,341	2,733	2,564
20,850	20,900	2,740	2,349	2,740	2,571
20,900	20,950	2,748	2,356	2,748	2,579
20,950	21,000	2,755	2,364	2,755	2,586

21,000

At least	But less than	Single	Married filing jointly *	Married filing separately	Head of a house-hold
21,000	21,050	2,763	2,371	2,763	2,594
21,050	21,100	2,770	2,379	2,770	2,601
21,100	21,150	2,778	2,386	2,778	2,609
21,150	21,200	2,785	2,394	2,785	2,616
21,200	21,250	2,793	2,401	2,793	2,624
21,250	21,300	2,800	2,409	2,800	2,631
21,300	21,350	2,808	2,416	2,808	2,639
21,350	21,400	2,815	2,424	2,815	2,646
21,400	21,450	2,823	2,431	2,823	2,654
21,450	21,500	2,830	2,439	2,830	2,661
21,500	21,550	2,838	2,446	2,838	2,669
21,550	21,600	2,845	2,454	2,845	2,676
21,600	21,650	2,853	2,461	2,853	2,684
21,650	21,700	2,860	2,469	2,860	2,691
21,700	21,750	2,868	2,476	2,868	2,699
21,750	21,800	2,875	2,484	2,875	2,706
21,800	21,850	2,883	2,491	2,883	2,714
21,850	21,900	2,890	2,499	2,890	2,721
21,900	21,950	2,898	2,506	2,898	2,729
21,950	22,000	2,905	2,514	2,905	2,736

22,000

At least	But less than	Single	Married filing jointly *	Married filing separately	Head of a house-hold
22,000	22,050	2,913	2,521	2,913	2,744
22,050	22,100	2,920	2,529	2,920	2,751
22,100	22,150	2,928	2,536	2,928	2,759
22,150	22,200	2,935	2,544	2,935	2,766
22,200	22,250	2,943	2,551	2,943	2,774
22,250	22,300	2,950	2,559	2,950	2,781
22,300	22,350	2,958	2,566	2,958	2,789
22,350	22,400	2,965	2,574	2,965	2,796
22,400	22,450	2,973	2,581	2,973	2,804
22,450	22,500	2,980	2,589	2,980	2,811
22,500	22,550	2,988	2,596	2,988	2,819
22,550	22,600	2,995	2,604	2,995	2,826
22,600	22,650	3,003	2,611	3,003	2,834
22,650	22,700	3,010	2,619	3,010	2,841
22,700	22,750	3,018	2,626	3,018	2,849
22,750	22,800	3,025	2,634	3,025	2,856
22,800	22,850	3,033	2,641	3,033	2,864
22,850	22,900	3,040	2,649	3,040	2,871
22,900	22,950	3,048	2,656	3,048	2,879
22,950	23,000	3,055	2,664	3,055	2,886

*This column must also be used by a qualifying widow(er).

(Continued on next page)

2007 Tax Table–*Continued*

23,000

At least	But less than	Single	Married filing jointly*	Married filing separately	Head of a house-hold
23,000	23,050	3,063	2,671	3,063	2,894
23,050	23,100	3,070	2,679	3,070	2,901
23,100	23,150	3,078	2,686	3,078	2,909
23,150	23,200	3,085	2,694	3,085	2,916
23,200	23,250	3,093	2,701	3,093	2,924
23,250	23,300	3,100	2,709	3,100	2,931
23,300	23,350	3,108	2,716	3,108	2,939
23,350	23,400	3,115	2,724	3,115	2,946
23,400	23,450	3,123	2,731	3,123	2,954
23,450	23,500	3,130	2,739	3,130	2,961
23,500	23,550	3,138	2,746	3,138	2,969
23,550	23,600	3,145	2,754	3,145	2,976
23,600	23,650	3,153	2,761	3,153	2,984
23,650	23,700	3,160	2,769	3,160	2,991
23,700	23,750	3,168	2,776	3,168	2,999
23,750	23,800	3,175	2,784	3,175	3,006
23,800	23,850	3,183	2,791	3,183	3,014
23,850	23,900	3,190	2,799	3,190	3,021
23,900	23,950	3,198	2,806	3,198	3,029
23,950	24,000	3,205	2,814	3,205	3,036

24,000

At least	But less than	Single	Married filing jointly*	Married filing separately	Head of a house-hold
24,000	24,050	3,213	2,821	3,213	3,044
24,050	24,100	3,220	2,829	3,220	3,051
24,100	24,150	3,228	2,836	3,228	3,059
24,150	24,200	3,235	2,844	3,235	3,066
24,200	24,250	3,243	2,851	3,243	3,074
24,250	24,300	3,250	2,859	3,250	3,081
24,300	24,350	3,258	2,866	3,258	3,089
24,350	24,400	3,265	2,874	3,265	3,096
24,400	24,450	3,273	2,881	3,273	3,104
24,450	24,500	3,280	2,889	3,280	3,111
24,500	24,550	3,288	2,896	3,288	3,119
24,550	24,600	3,295	2,904	3,295	3,126
24,600	24,650	3,303	2,911	3,303	3,134
24,650	24,700	3,310	2,919	3,310	3,141
24,700	24,750	3,318	2,926	3,318	3,149
24,750	24,800	3,325	2,934	3,325	3,156
24,800	24,850	3,333	2,941	3,333	3,164
24,850	24,900	3,340	2,949	3,340	3,171
24,900	24,950	3,348	2,956	3,348	3,179
24,950	25,000	3,355	2,964	3,355	3,186

25,000

At least	But less than	Single	Married filing jointly*	Married filing separately	Head of a house-hold
25,000	25,050	3,363	2,971	3,363	3,194
25,050	25,100	3,370	2,979	3,370	3,201
25,100	25,150	3,378	2,986	3,378	3,209
25,150	25,200	3,385	2,994	3,385	3,216
25,200	25,250	3,393	3,001	3,393	3,224
25,250	25,300	3,400	3,009	3,400	3,231
25,300	25,350	3,408	3,016	3,408	3,239
25,350	25,400	3,415	3,024	3,415	3,246
25,400	25,450	3,423	3,031	3,423	3,254
25,450	25,500	3,430	3,039	3,430	3,261
25,500	25,550	3,438	3,046	3,438	3,269
25,550	25,600	3,445	3,054	3,445	3,276
25,600	25,650	3,453	3,061	3,453	3,284
25,650	25,700	3,460	3,069	3,460	3,291
25,700	25,750	3,468	3,076	3,468	3,299
25,750	25,800	3,475	3,084	3,475	3,306
25,800	25,850	3,483	3,091	3,483	3,314
25,850	25,900	3,490	3,099	3,490	3,321
25,900	25,950	3,498	3,106	3,498	3,329
25,950	26,000	3,505	3,114	3,505	3,336

26,000

At least	But less than	Single	Married filing jointly*	Married filing separately	Head of a house-hold
26,000	26,050	3,513	3,121	3,513	3,344
26,050	26,100	3,520	3,129	3,520	3,351
26,100	26,150	3,528	3,136	3,528	3,359
26,150	26,200	3,535	3,144	3,535	3,366
26,200	26,250	3,543	3,151	3,543	3,374
26,250	26,300	3,550	3,159	3,550	3,381
26,300	26,350	3,558	3,166	3,558	3,389
26,350	26,400	3,565	3,174	3,565	3,396
26,400	26,450	3,573	3,181	3,573	3,404
26,450	26,500	3,580	3,189	3,580	3,411
26,500	26,550	3,588	3,196	3,588	3,419
26,550	26,600	3,595	3,204	3,595	3,426
26,600	26,650	3,603	3,211	3,603	3,434
26,650	26,700	3,610	3,219	3,610	3,441
26,700	26,750	3,618	3,226	3,618	3,449
26,750	26,800	3,625	3,234	3,625	3,456
26,800	26,850	3,633	3,241	3,633	3,464
26,850	26,900	3,640	3,249	3,640	3,471
26,900	26,950	3,648	3,256	3,648	3,479
26,950	27,000	3,655	3,264	3,655	3,486

27,000

At least	But less than	Single	Married filing jointly*	Married filing separately	Head of a house-hold
27,000	27,050	3,663	3,271	3,663	3,494
27,050	27,100	3,670	3,279	3,670	3,501
27,100	27,150	3,678	3,286	3,678	3,509
27,150	27,200	3,685	3,294	3,685	3,516
27,200	27,250	3,693	3,301	3,693	3,524
27,250	27,300	3,700	3,309	3,700	3,531
27,300	27,350	3,708	3,316	3,708	3,539
27,350	27,400	3,715	3,324	3,715	3,546
27,400	27,450	3,723	3,331	3,723	3,554
27,450	27,500	3,730	3,339	3,730	3,561
27,500	27,550	3,738	3,346	3,738	3,569
27,550	27,600	3,745	3,354	3,745	3,576
27,600	27,650	3,753	3,361	3,753	3,584
27,650	27,700	3,760	3,369	3,760	3,591
27,700	27,750	3,768	3,376	3,768	3,599
27,750	27,800	3,775	3,384	3,775	3,606
27,800	27,850	3,783	3,391	3,783	3,614
27,850	27,900	3,790	3,399	3,790	3,621
27,900	27,950	3,798	3,406	3,798	3,629
27,950	28,000	3,805	3,414	3,805	3,636

28,000

At least	But less than	Single	Married filing jointly*	Married filing separately	Head of a house-hold
28,000	28,050	3,813	3,421	3,813	3,644
28,050	28,100	3,820	3,429	3,820	3,651
28,100	28,150	3,828	3,436	3,828	3,659
28,150	28,200	3,835	3,444	3,835	3,666
28,200	28,250	3,843	3,451	3,843	3,674
28,250	28,300	3,850	3,459	3,850	3,681
28,300	28,350	3,858	3,466	3,858	3,689
28,350	28,400	3,865	3,474	3,865	3,696
28,400	28,450	3,873	3,481	3,873	3,704
28,450	28,500	3,880	3,489	3,880	3,711
28,500	28,550	3,888	3,496	3,888	3,719
28,550	28,600	3,895	3,504	3,895	3,726
28,600	28,650	3,903	3,511	3,903	3,734
28,650	28,700	3,910	3,519	3,910	3,741
28,700	28,750	3,918	3,526	3,918	3,749
28,750	28,800	3,925	3,534	3,925	3,756
28,800	28,850	3,933	3,541	3,933	3,764
28,850	28,900	3,940	3,549	3,940	3,771
28,900	28,950	3,948	3,556	3,948	3,779
28,950	29,000	3,955	3,564	3,955	3,786

29,000

At least	But less than	Single	Married filing jointly*	Married filing separately	Head of a house-hold
29,000	29,050	3,963	3,571	3,963	3,794
29,050	29,100	3,970	3,579	3,970	3,801
29,100	29,150	3,978	3,586	3,978	3,809
29,150	29,200	3,985	3,594	3,985	3,816
29,200	29,250	3,993	3,601	3,993	3,824
29,250	29,300	4,000	3,609	4,000	3,831
29,300	29,350	4,008	3,616	4,008	3,839
29,350	29,400	4,015	3,624	4,015	3,846
29,400	29,450	4,023	3,631	4,023	3,854
29,450	29,500	4,030	3,639	4,030	3,861
29,500	29,550	4,038	3,646	4,038	3,869
29,550	29,600	4,045	3,654	4,045	3,876
29,600	29,650	4,053	3,661	4,053	3,884
29,650	29,700	4,060	3,669	4,060	3,891
29,700	29,750	4,068	3,676	4,068	3,899
29,750	29,800	4,075	3,684	4,075	3,906
29,800	29,850	4,083	3,691	4,083	3,914
29,850	29,900	4,090	3,699	4,090	3,921
29,900	29,950	4,098	3,706	4,098	3,929
29,950	30,000	4,105	3,714	4,105	3,936

30,000

At least	But less than	Single	Married filing jointly*	Married filing separately	Head of a house-hold
30,000	30,050	4,113	3,721	4,113	3,944
30,050	30,100	4,120	3,729	4,120	3,951
30,100	30,150	4,128	3,736	4,128	3,959
30,150	30,200	4,135	3,744	4,135	3,966
30,200	30,250	4,143	3,751	4,143	3,974
30,250	30,300	4,150	3,759	4,150	3,981
30,300	30,350	4,158	3,766	4,158	3,989
30,350	30,400	4,165	3,774	4,165	3,996
30,400	30,450	4,173	3,781	4,173	4,004
30,450	30,500	4,180	3,789	4,180	4,011
30,500	30,550	4,188	3,796	4,188	4,019
30,550	30,600	4,195	3,804	4,195	4,026
30,600	30,650	4,203	3,811	4,203	4,034
30,650	30,700	4,210	3,819	4,210	4,041
30,700	30,750	4,218	3,826	4,218	4,049
30,750	30,800	4,225	3,834	4,225	4,056
30,800	30,850	4,233	3,841	4,233	4,064
30,850	30,900	4,240	3,849	4,240	4,071
30,900	30,950	4,248	3,856	4,248	4,079
30,950	31,000	4,255	3,864	4,255	4,086

31,000

At least	But less than	Single	Married filing jointly*	Married filing separately	Head of a house-hold
31,000	31,050	4,263	3,871	4,263	4,094
31,050	31,100	4,270	3,879	4,270	4,101
31,100	31,150	4,278	3,886	4,278	4,109
31,150	31,200	4,285	3,894	4,285	4,116
31,200	31,250	4,293	3,901	4,293	4,124
31,250	31,300	4,300	3,909	4,300	4,131
31,300	31,350	4,308	3,916	4,308	4,139
31,350	31,400	4,315	3,924	4,315	4,146
31,400	31,450	4,323	3,931	4,323	4,154
31,450	31,500	4,330	3,939	4,330	4,161
31,500	31,550	4,338	3,946	4,338	4,169
31,550	31,600	4,345	3,954	4,345	4,176
31,600	31,650	4,353	3,961	4,353	4,184
31,650	31,700	4,360	3,969	4,360	4,191
31,700	31,750	4,368	3,976	4,368	4,199
31,750	31,800	4,375	3,984	4,375	4,206
31,800	31,850	4,383	3,991	4,383	4,214
31,850	31,900	4,393	3,999	4,393	4,221
31,900	31,950	4,405	4,006	4,405	4,229
31,950	32,000	4,418	4,014	4,418	4,236

*This column must also be used by a qualifying widow(er).

(Continued on next page)

2007 Tax Table–*Continued*

If line 43 (taxable income) is—		And you are—			
At least	But less than	Single	Married filing jointly *	Married filing separately	Head of a household
		Your tax is—			

32,000

At least	But less than	Single	MFJ	MFS	HoH
32,000	32,050	4,430	4,021	4,430	4,244
32,050	32,100	4,443	4,029	4,443	4,251
32,100	32,150	4,455	4,036	4,455	4,259
32,150	32,200	4,468	4,044	4,468	4,266
32,200	32,250	4,480	4,051	4,480	4,274
32,250	32,300	4,493	4,059	4,493	4,281
32,300	32,350	4,505	4,066	4,505	4,289
32,350	32,400	4,518	4,074	4,518	4,296
32,400	32,450	4,530	4,081	4,530	4,304
32,450	32,500	4,543	4,089	4,543	4,311
32,500	32,550	4,555	4,096	4,555	4,319
32,550	32,600	4,568	4,104	4,568	4,326
32,600	32,650	4,580	4,111	4,580	4,334
32,650	32,700	4,593	4,119	4,593	4,341
32,700	32,750	4,605	4,126	4,605	4,349
32,750	32,800	4,618	4,134	4,618	4,356
32,800	32,850	4,630	4,141	4,630	4,364
32,850	32,900	4,643	4,149	4,643	4,371
32,900	32,950	4,655	4,156	4,655	4,379
32,950	33,000	4,668	4,164	4,668	4,386

33,000

At least	But less than	Single	MFJ	MFS	HoH
33,000	33,050	4,680	4,171	4,680	4,394
33,050	33,100	4,693	4,179	4,693	4,401
33,100	33,150	4,705	4,186	4,705	4,409
33,150	33,200	4,718	4,194	4,718	4,416
33,200	33,250	4,730	4,201	4,730	4,424
33,250	33,300	4,743	4,209	4,743	4,431
33,300	33,350	4,755	4,216	4,755	4,439
33,350	33,400	4,768	4,224	4,768	4,446
33,400	33,450	4,780	4,231	4,780	4,454
33,450	33,500	4,793	4,239	4,793	4,461
33,500	33,550	4,805	4,246	4,805	4,469
33,550	33,600	4,818	4,254	4,818	4,476
33,600	33,650	4,830	4,261	4,830	4,484
33,650	33,700	4,843	4,269	4,843	4,491
33,700	33,750	4,855	4,276	4,855	4,499
33,750	33,800	4,868	4,284	4,868	4,506
33,800	33,850	4,880	4,291	4,880	4,514
33,850	33,900	4,893	4,299	4,893	4,521
33,900	33,950	4,905	4,306	4,905	4,529
33,950	34,000	4,918	4,314	4,918	4,536

34,000

At least	But less than	Single	MFJ	MFS	HoH
34,000	34,050	4,930	4,321	4,930	4,544
34,050	34,100	4,943	4,329	4,943	4,551
34,100	34,150	4,955	4,336	4,955	4,559
34,150	34,200	4,968	4,344	4,968	4,566
34,200	34,250	4,980	4,351	4,980	4,574
34,250	34,300	4,993	4,359	4,993	4,581
34,300	34,350	5,005	4,366	5,005	4,589
34,350	34,400	5,018	4,374	5,018	4,596
34,400	34,450	5,030	4,381	5,030	4,604
34,450	34,500	5,043	4,389	5,043	4,611
34,500	34,550	5,055	4,396	5,055	4,619
34,550	34,600	5,068	4,404	5,068	4,626
34,600	34,650	5,080	4,411	5,080	4,634
34,650	34,700	5,093	4,419	5,093	4,641
34,700	34,750	5,105	4,426	5,105	4,649
34,750	34,800	5,118	4,434	5,118	4,656
34,800	34,850	5,130	4,441	5,130	4,664
34,850	34,900	5,143	4,449	5,143	4,671
34,900	34,950	5,155	4,456	5,155	4,679
34,950	35,000	5,168	4,464	5,168	4,686

35,000

At least	But less than	Single	MFJ	MFS	HoH
35,000	35,050	5,180	4,471	5,180	4,694
35,050	35,100	5,193	4,479	5,193	4,701
35,100	35,150	5,205	4,486	5,205	4,709
35,150	35,200	5,218	4,494	5,218	4,716
35,200	35,250	5,230	4,501	5,230	4,724
35,250	35,300	5,243	4,509	5,243	4,731
35,300	35,350	5,255	4,516	5,255	4,739
35,350	35,400	5,268	4,524	5,268	4,746
35,400	35,450	5,280	4,531	5,280	4,754
35,450	35,500	5,293	4,539	5,293	4,761
35,500	35,550	5,305	4,546	5,305	4,769
35,550	35,600	5,318	4,554	5,318	4,776
35,600	35,650	5,330	4,561	5,330	4,784
35,650	35,700	5,343	4,569	5,343	4,791
35,700	35,750	5,355	4,576	5,355	4,799
35,750	35,800	5,368	4,584	5,368	4,806
35,800	35,850	5,380	4,591	5,380	4,814
35,850	35,900	5,393	4,599	5,393	4,821
35,900	35,950	5,405	4,606	5,405	4,829
35,950	36,000	5,418	4,614	5,418	4,836

36,000

At least	But less than	Single	MFJ	MFS	HoH
36,000	36,050	5,430	4,621	5,430	4,844
36,050	36,100	5,443	4,629	5,443	4,851
36,100	36,150	5,455	4,636	5,455	4,859
36,150	36,200	5,468	4,644	5,468	4,866
36,200	36,250	5,480	4,651	5,480	4,874
36,250	36,300	5,493	4,659	5,493	4,881
36,300	36,350	5,505	4,666	5,505	4,889
36,350	36,400	5,518	4,674	5,518	4,896
36,400	36,450	5,530	4,681	5,530	4,904
36,450	36,500	5,543	4,689	5,543	4,911
36,500	36,550	5,555	4,696	5,555	4,919
36,550	36,600	5,568	4,704	5,568	4,926
36,600	36,650	5,580	4,711	5,580	4,934
36,650	36,700	5,593	4,719	5,593	4,941
36,700	36,750	5,605	4,726	5,605	4,949
36,750	36,800	5,618	4,734	5,618	4,956
36,800	36,850	5,630	4,741	5,630	4,964
36,850	36,900	5,643	4,749	5,643	4,971
36,900	36,950	5,655	4,756	5,655	4,979
36,950	37,000	5,668	4,764	5,668	4,986

37,000

At least	But less than	Single	MFJ	MFS	HoH
37,000	37,050	5,680	4,771	5,680	4,994
37,050	37,100	5,693	4,779	5,693	5,001
37,100	37,150	5,705	4,786	5,705	5,009
37,150	37,200	5,718	4,794	5,718	5,016
37,200	37,250	5,730	4,801	5,730	5,024
37,250	37,300	5,743	4,809	5,743	5,031
37,300	37,350	5,755	4,816	5,755	5,039
37,350	37,400	5,768	4,824	5,768	5,046
37,400	37,450	5,780	4,831	5,780	5,054
37,450	37,500	5,793	4,839	5,793	5,061
37,500	37,550	5,805	4,846	5,805	5,069
37,550	37,600	5,818	4,854	5,818	5,076
37,600	37,650	5,830	4,861	5,830	5,084
37,650	37,700	5,843	4,869	5,843	5,091
37,700	37,750	5,855	4,876	5,855	5,099
37,750	37,800	5,868	4,884	5,868	5,106
37,800	37,850	5,880	4,891	5,880	5,114
37,850	37,900	5,893	4,899	5,893	5,121
37,900	37,950	5,905	4,906	5,905	5,129
37,950	38,000	5,918	4,914	5,918	5,136

38,000

At least	But less than	Single	MFJ	MFS	HoH
38,000	38,050	5,930	4,921	5,930	5,144
38,050	38,100	5,943	4,929	5,943	5,151
38,100	38,150	5,955	4,936	5,955	5,159
38,150	38,200	5,968	4,944	5,968	5,166
38,200	38,250	5,980	4,951	5,980	5,174
38,250	38,300	5,993	4,959	5,993	5,181
38,300	38,350	6,005	4,966	6,005	5,189
38,350	38,400	6,018	4,974	6,018	5,196
38,400	38,450	6,030	4,981	6,030	5,204
38,450	38,500	6,043	4,989	6,043	5,211
38,500	38,550	6,055	4,996	6,055	5,219
38,550	38,600	6,068	5,004	6,068	5,226
38,600	38,650	6,080	5,011	6,080	5,234
38,650	38,700	6,093	5,019	6,093	5,241
38,700	38,750	6,105	5,026	6,105	5,249
38,750	38,800	6,118	5,034	6,118	5,256
38,800	38,850	6,130	5,041	6,130	5,264
38,850	38,900	6,143	5,049	6,143	5,271
38,900	38,950	6,155	5,056	6,155	5,279
38,950	39,000	6,168	5,064	6,168	5,286

39,000

At least	But less than	Single	MFJ	MFS	HoH
39,000	39,050	6,180	5,071	6,180	5,294
39,050	39,100	6,193	5,079	6,193	5,301
39,100	39,150	6,205	5,086	6,205	5,309
39,150	39,200	6,218	5,094	6,218	5,316
39,200	39,250	6,230	5,101	6,230	5,324
39,250	39,300	6,243	5,109	6,243	5,331
39,300	39,350	6,255	5,116	6,255	5,339
39,350	39,400	6,268	5,124	6,268	5,346
39,400	39,450	6,280	5,131	6,280	5,354
39,450	39,500	6,293	5,139	6,293	5,361
39,500	39,550	6,305	5,146	6,305	5,369
39,550	39,600	6,318	5,154	6,318	5,376
39,600	39,650	6,330	5,161	6,330	5,384
39,650	39,700	6,343	5,169	6,343	5,391
39,700	39,750	6,355	5,176	6,355	5,399
39,750	39,800	6,368	5,184	6,368	5,406
39,800	39,850	6,380	5,191	6,380	5,414
39,850	39,900	6,393	5,199	6,393	5,421
39,900	39,950	6,405	5,206	6,405	5,429
39,950	40,000	6,418	5,214	6,418	5,436

40,000

At least	But less than	Single	MFJ	MFS	HoH
40,000	40,050	6,430	5,221	6,430	5,444
40,050	40,100	6,443	5,229	6,443	5,451
40,100	40,150	6,455	5,236	6,455	5,459
40,150	40,200	6,468	5,244	6,468	5,466
40,200	40,250	6,480	5,251	6,480	5,474
40,250	40,300	6,493	5,259	6,493	5,481
40,300	40,350	6,505	5,266	6,505	5,489
40,350	40,400	6,518	5,274	6,518	5,496
40,400	40,450	6,530	5,281	6,530	5,504
40,450	40,500	6,543	5,289	6,543	5,511
40,500	40,550	6,555	5,296	6,555	5,519
40,550	40,600	6,568	5,304	6,568	5,526
40,600	40,650	6,580	5,311	6,580	5,534
40,650	40,700	6,593	5,319	6,593	5,541
40,700	40,750	6,605	5,326	6,605	5,549
40,750	40,800	6,618	5,334	6,618	5,556
40,800	40,850	6,630	5,341	6,630	5,564
40,850	40,900	6,643	5,349	6,643	5,571
40,900	40,950	6,655	5,356	6,655	5,579
40,950	41,000	6,668	5,364	6,668	5,586

*This column must also be used by a qualifying widow(er).

(Continued on next page)

2007 Tax Table—*Continued*

41,000

At least	But less than	Single	Married filing jointly*	Married filing separately	Head of a household
41,000	41,050	6,680	5,371	6,680	5,594
41,050	41,100	6,693	5,379	6,693	5,601
41,100	41,150	6,705	5,386	6,705	5,609
41,150	41,200	6,718	5,394	6,718	5,616
41,200	41,250	6,730	5,401	6,730	5,624
41,250	41,300	6,743	5,409	6,743	5,631
41,300	41,350	6,755	5,416	6,755	5,639
41,350	41,400	6,768	5,424	6,768	5,646
41,400	41,450	6,780	5,431	6,780	5,654
41,450	41,500	6,793	5,439	6,793	5,661
41,500	41,550	6,805	5,446	6,805	5,669
41,550	41,600	6,818	5,454	6,818	5,676
41,600	41,650	6,830	5,461	6,830	5,684
41,650	41,700	6,843	5,469	6,843	5,691
41,700	41,750	6,855	5,476	6,855	5,699
41,750	41,800	6,868	5,484	6,868	5,706
41,800	41,850	6,880	5,491	6,880	5,714
41,850	41,900	6,893	5,499	6,893	5,721
41,900	41,950	6,905	5,506	6,905	5,729
41,950	42,000	6,918	5,514	6,918	5,736

42,000

At least	But less than	Single	Married filing jointly*	Married filing separately	Head of a household
42,000	42,050	6,930	5,521	6,930	5,744
42,050	42,100	6,943	5,529	6,943	5,751
42,100	42,150	6,955	5,536	6,955	5,759
42,150	42,200	6,968	5,544	6,968	5,766
42,200	42,250	6,980	5,551	6,980	5,774
42,250	42,300	6,993	5,559	6,993	5,781
42,300	42,350	7,005	5,566	7,005	5,789
42,350	42,400	7,018	5,574	7,018	5,796
42,400	42,450	7,030	5,581	7,030	5,804
42,450	42,500	7,043	5,589	7,043	5,811
42,500	42,550	7,055	5,596	7,055	5,819
42,550	42,600	7,068	5,604	7,068	5,826
42,600	42,650	7,080	5,611	7,080	5,834
42,650	42,700	7,093	5,619	7,093	5,844
42,700	42,750	7,105	5,626	7,105	5,856
42,750	42,800	7,118	5,634	7,118	5,869
42,800	42,850	7,130	5,641	7,130	5,881
42,850	42,900	7,143	5,649	7,143	5,894
42,900	42,950	7,155	5,656	7,155	5,906
42,950	43,000	7,168	5,664	7,168	5,919

43,000

At least	But less than	Single	Married filing jointly*	Married filing separately	Head of a household
43,000	43,050	7,180	5,671	7,180	5,931
43,050	43,100	7,193	5,679	7,193	5,944
43,100	43,150	7,205	5,686	7,205	5,956
43,150	43,200	7,218	5,694	7,218	5,969
43,200	43,250	7,230	5,701	7,230	5,981
43,250	43,300	7,243	5,709	7,243	5,994
43,300	43,350	7,255	5,716	7,255	6,006
43,350	43,400	7,268	5,724	7,268	6,019
43,400	43,450	7,280	5,731	7,280	6,031
43,450	43,500	7,293	5,739	7,293	6,044
43,500	43,550	7,305	5,746	7,305	6,056
43,550	43,600	7,318	5,754	7,318	6,069
43,600	43,650	7,330	5,761	7,330	6,081
43,650	43,700	7,343	5,769	7,343	6,094
43,700	43,750	7,355	5,776	7,355	6,106
43,750	43,800	7,368	5,784	7,368	6,119
43,800	43,850	7,380	5,791	7,380	6,131
43,850	43,900	7,393	5,799	7,393	6,144
43,900	43,950	7,405	5,806	7,405	6,156
43,950	44,000	7,418	5,814	7,418	6,169

44,000

At least	But less than	Single	Married filing jointly*	Married filing separately	Head of a household
44,000	44,050	7,430	5,821	7,430	6,181
44,050	44,100	7,443	5,829	7,443	6,194
44,100	44,150	7,455	5,836	7,455	6,206
44,150	44,200	7,468	5,844	7,468	6,219
44,200	44,250	7,480	5,851	7,480	6,231
44,250	44,300	7,493	5,859	7,493	6,244
44,300	44,350	7,505	5,866	7,505	6,256
44,350	44,400	7,518	5,874	7,518	6,269
44,400	44,450	7,530	5,881	7,530	6,281
44,450	44,500	7,543	5,889	7,543	6,294
44,500	44,550	7,555	5,896	7,555	6,306
44,550	44,600	7,568	5,904	7,568	6,319
44,600	44,650	7,580	5,911	7,580	6,331
44,650	44,700	7,593	5,919	7,593	6,344
44,700	44,750	7,605	5,926	7,605	6,356
44,750	44,800	7,618	5,934	7,618	6,369
44,800	44,850	7,630	5,941	7,630	6,381
44,850	44,900	7,643	5,949	7,643	6,394
44,900	44,950	7,655	5,956	7,655	6,406
44,950	45,000	7,668	5,964	7,668	6,419

45,000

At least	But less than	Single	Married filing jointly*	Married filing separately	Head of a household
45,000	45,050	7,680	5,971	7,680	6,431
45,050	45,100	7,693	5,979	7,693	6,444
45,100	45,150	7,705	5,986	7,705	6,456
45,150	45,200	7,718	5,994	7,718	6,469
45,200	45,250	7,730	6,001	7,730	6,481
45,250	45,300	7,743	6,009	7,743	6,494
45,300	45,350	7,755	6,016	7,755	6,506
45,350	45,400	7,768	6,024	7,768	6,519
45,400	45,450	7,780	6,031	7,780	6,531
45,450	45,500	7,793	6,039	7,793	6,544
45,500	45,550	7,805	6,046	7,805	6,556
45,550	45,600	7,818	6,054	7,818	6,569
45,600	45,650	7,830	6,061	7,830	6,581
45,650	45,700	7,843	6,069	7,843	6,594
45,700	45,750	7,855	6,076	7,855	6,606
45,750	45,800	7,868	6,084	7,868	6,619
45,800	45,850	7,880	6,091	7,880	6,631
45,850	45,900	7,893	6,099	7,893	6,644
45,900	45,950	7,905	6,106	7,905	6,656
45,950	46,000	7,918	6,114	7,918	6,669

46,000

At least	But less than	Single	Married filing jointly*	Married filing separately	Head of a household
46,000	46,050	7,930	6,121	7,930	6,681
46,050	46,100	7,943	6,129	7,943	6,694
46,100	46,150	7,955	6,136	7,955	6,706
46,150	46,200	7,968	6,144	7,968	6,719
46,200	46,250	7,980	6,151	7,980	6,731
46,250	46,300	7,993	6,159	7,993	6,744
46,300	46,350	8,005	6,166	8,005	6,756
46,350	46,400	8,018	6,174	8,018	6,769
46,400	46,450	8,030	6,181	8,030	6,781
46,450	46,500	8,043	6,189	8,043	6,794
46,500	46,550	8,055	6,196	8,055	6,806
46,550	46,600	8,068	6,204	8,068	6,819
46,600	46,650	8,080	6,211	8,080	6,831
46,650	46,700	8,093	6,219	8,093	6,844
46,700	46,750	8,105	6,226	8,105	6,856
46,750	46,800	8,118	6,234	8,118	6,869
46,800	46,850	8,130	6,241	8,130	6,881
46,850	46,900	8,143	6,249	8,143	6,894
46,900	46,950	8,155	6,256	8,155	6,906
46,950	47,000	8,168	6,264	8,168	6,919

47,000

At least	But less than	Single	Married filing jointly*	Married filing separately	Head of a household
47,000	47,050	8,180	6,271	8,180	6,931
47,050	47,100	8,193	6,279	8,193	6,944
47,100	47,150	8,205	6,286	8,205	6,956
47,150	47,200	8,218	6,294	8,218	6,969
47,200	47,250	8,230	6,301	8,230	6,981
47,250	47,300	8,243	6,309	8,243	6,994
47,300	47,350	8,255	6,316	8,255	7,006
47,350	47,400	8,268	6,324	8,268	7,019
47,400	47,450	8,280	6,331	8,280	7,031
47,450	47,500	8,293	6,339	8,293	7,044
47,500	47,550	8,305	6,346	8,305	7,056
47,550	47,600	8,318	6,354	8,318	7,069
47,600	47,650	8,330	6,361	8,330	7,081
47,650	47,700	8,343	6,369	8,343	7,094
47,700	47,750	8,355	6,376	8,355	7,106
47,750	47,800	8,368	6,384	8,368	7,119
47,800	47,850	8,380	6,391	8,380	7,131
47,850	47,900	8,393	6,399	8,393	7,144
47,900	47,950	8,405	6,406	8,405	7,156
47,950	48,000	8,418	6,414	8,418	7,169

48,000

At least	But less than	Single	Married filing jointly*	Married filing separately	Head of a household
48,000	48,050	8,430	6,421	8,430	7,181
48,050	48,100	8,443	6,429	8,443	7,194
48,100	48,150	8,455	6,436	8,455	7,206
48,150	48,200	8,468	6,444	8,468	7,219
48,200	48,250	8,480	6,451	8,480	7,231
48,250	48,300	8,493	6,459	8,493	7,244
48,300	48,350	8,505	6,466	8,505	7,256
48,350	48,400	8,518	6,474	8,518	7,269
48,400	48,450	8,530	6,481	8,530	7,281
48,450	48,500	8,543	6,489	8,543	7,294
48,500	48,550	8,555	6,496	8,555	7,306
48,550	48,600	8,568	6,504	8,568	7,319
48,600	48,650	8,580	6,511	8,580	7,331
48,650	48,700	8,593	6,519	8,593	7,344
48,700	48,750	8,605	6,526	8,605	7,356
48,750	48,800	8,618	6,534	8,618	7,369
48,800	48,850	8,630	6,541	8,630	7,381
48,850	48,900	8,643	6,549	8,643	7,394
48,900	48,950	8,655	6,556	8,655	7,406
48,950	49,000	8,668	6,564	8,668	7,419

49,000

At least	But less than	Single	Married filing jointly*	Married filing separately	Head of a household
49,000	49,050	8,680	6,571	8,680	7,431
49,050	49,100	8,693	6,579	8,693	7,444
49,100	49,150	8,705	6,586	8,705	7,456
49,150	49,200	8,718	6,594	8,718	7,469
49,200	49,250	8,730	6,601	8,730	7,481
49,250	49,300	8,743	6,609	8,743	7,494
49,300	49,350	8,755	6,616	8,755	7,506
49,350	49,400	8,768	6,624	8,768	7,519
49,400	49,450	8,780	6,631	8,780	7,531
49,450	49,500	8,793	6,639	8,793	7,544
49,500	49,550	8,805	6,646	8,805	7,556
49,550	49,600	8,818	6,654	8,818	7,569
49,600	49,650	8,830	6,661	8,830	7,581
49,650	49,700	8,843	6,669	8,843	7,594
49,700	49,750	8,855	6,676	8,855	7,606
49,750	49,800	8,868	6,684	8,868	7,619
49,800	49,850	8,880	6,691	8,880	7,631
49,850	49,900	8,893	6,699	8,893	7,644
49,900	49,950	8,905	6,706	8,905	7,656
49,950	50,000	8,918	6,714	8,918	7,669

*This column must also be used by a qualifying widow(er).

(Continued on next page)

2007 Tax Table–*Continued*

If line 43 (taxable income) is— At least	But less than	Single	Married filing jointly *	Married filing separately	Head of a household
50,000					
50,000	50,050	8,930	6,721	8,930	7,681
50,050	50,100	8,943	6,729	8,943	7,694
50,100	50,150	8,955	6,736	8,955	7,706
50,150	50,200	8,968	6,744	8,968	7,719
50,200	50,250	8,980	6,751	8,980	7,731
50,250	50,300	8,993	6,759	8,993	7,744
50,300	50,350	9,005	6,766	9,005	7,756
50,350	50,400	9,018	6,774	9,018	7,769
50,400	50,450	9,030	6,781	9,030	7,781
50,450	50,500	9,043	6,789	9,043	7,794
50,500	50,550	9,055	6,796	9,055	7,806
50,550	50,600	9,068	6,804	9,068	7,819
50,600	50,650	9,080	6,811	9,080	7,831
50,650	50,700	9,093	6,819	9,093	7,844
50,700	50,750	9,105	6,826	9,105	7,856
50,750	50,800	9,118	6,834	9,118	7,869
50,800	50,850	9,130	6,841	9,130	7,881
50,850	50,900	9,143	6,849	9,143	7,894
50,900	50,950	9,155	6,856	9,155	7,906
50,950	51,000	9,168	6,864	9,168	7,919
51,000					
51,000	51,050	9,180	6,871	9,180	7,931
51,050	51,100	9,193	6,879	9,193	7,944
51,100	51,150	9,205	6,886	9,205	7,956
51,150	51,200	9,218	6,894	9,218	7,969
51,200	51,250	9,230	6,901	9,230	7,981
51,250	51,300	9,243	6,909	9,243	7,994
51,300	51,350	9,255	6,916	9,255	8,006
51,350	51,400	9,268	6,924	9,268	8,019
51,400	51,450	9,280	6,931	9,280	8,031
51,450	51,500	9,293	6,939	9,293	8,044
51,500	51,550	9,305	6,946	9,305	8,056
51,550	51,600	9,318	6,954	9,318	8,069
51,600	51,650	9,330	6,961	9,330	8,081
51,650	51,700	9,343	6,969	9,343	8,094
51,700	51,750	9,355	6,976	9,355	8,106
51,750	51,800	9,368	6,984	9,368	8,119
51,800	51,850	9,380	6,991	9,380	8,131
51,850	51,900	9,393	6,999	9,393	8,144
51,900	51,950	9,405	7,006	9,405	8,156
51,950	52,000	9,418	7,014	9,418	8,169
52,000					
52,000	52,050	9,430	7,021	9,430	8,181
52,050	52,100	9,443	7,029	9,443	8,194
52,100	52,150	9,455	7,036	9,455	8,206
52,150	52,200	9,468	7,044	9,468	8,219
52,200	52,250	9,480	7,051	9,480	8,231
52,250	52,300	9,493	7,059	9,493	8,244
52,300	52,350	9,505	7,066	9,505	8,256
52,350	52,400	9,518	7,074	9,518	8,269
52,400	52,450	9,530	7,081	9,530	8,281
52,450	52,500	9,543	7,089	9,543	8,294
52,500	52,550	9,555	7,096	9,555	8,306
52,550	52,600	9,568	7,104	9,568	8,319
52,600	52,650	9,580	7,111	9,580	8,331
52,650	52,700	9,593	7,119	9,593	8,344
52,700	52,750	9,605	7,126	9,605	8,356
52,750	52,800	9,618	7,134	9,618	8,369
52,800	52,850	9,630	7,141	9,630	8,381
52,850	52,900	9,643	7,149	9,643	8,394
52,900	52,950	9,655	7,156	9,655	8,406
52,950	53,000	9,668	7,164	9,668	8,419

If line 43 (taxable income) is— At least	But less than	Single	Married filing jointly *	Married filing separately	Head of a household
53,000					
53,000	53,050	9,680	7,171	9,680	8,431
53,050	53,100	9,693	7,179	9,693	8,444
53,100	53,150	9,705	7,186	9,705	8,456
53,150	53,200	9,718	7,194	9,718	8,469
53,200	53,250	9,730	7,201	9,730	8,481
53,250	53,300	9,743	7,209	9,743	8,494
53,300	53,350	9,755	7,216	9,755	8,506
53,350	53,400	9,768	7,224	9,768	8,519
53,400	53,450	9,780	7,231	9,780	8,531
53,450	53,500	9,793	7,239	9,793	8,544
53,500	53,550	9,805	7,246	9,805	8,556
53,550	53,600	9,818	7,254	9,818	8,569
53,600	53,650	9,830	7,261	9,830	8,581
53,650	53,700	9,843	7,269	9,843	8,594
53,700	53,750	9,855	7,276	9,855	8,606
53,750	53,800	9,868	7,284	9,868	8,619
53,800	53,850	9,880	7,291	9,880	8,631
53,850	53,900	9,893	7,299	9,893	8,644
53,900	53,950	9,905	7,306	9,905	8,656
53,950	54,000	9,918	7,314	9,918	8,669
54,000					
54,000	54,050	9,930	7,321	9,930	8,681
54,050	54,100	9,943	7,329	9,943	8,694
54,100	54,150	9,955	7,336	9,955	8,706
54,150	54,200	9,968	7,344	9,968	8,719
54,200	54,250	9,980	7,351	9,980	8,731
54,250	54,300	9,993	7,359	9,993	8,744
54,300	54,350	10,005	7,366	10,005	8,756
54,350	54,400	10,018	7,374	10,018	8,769
54,400	54,450	10,030	7,381	10,030	8,781
54,450	54,500	10,043	7,389	10,043	8,794
54,500	54,550	10,055	7,396	10,055	8,806
54,550	54,600	10,068	7,404	10,068	8,819
54,600	54,650	10,080	7,411	10,080	8,831
54,650	54,700	10,093	7,419	10,093	8,844
54,700	54,750	10,105	7,426	10,105	8,856
54,750	54,800	10,118	7,434	10,118	8,869
54,800	54,850	10,130	7,441	10,130	8,881
54,850	54,900	10,143	7,449	10,143	8,894
54,900	54,950	10,155	7,456	10,155	8,906
54,950	55,000	10,168	7,464	10,168	8,919
55,000					
55,000	55,050	10,180	7,471	10,180	8,931
55,050	55,100	10,193	7,479	10,193	8,944
55,100	55,150	10,205	7,486	10,205	8,956
55,150	55,200	10,218	7,494	10,218	8,969
55,200	55,250	10,230	7,501	10,230	8,981
55,250	55,300	10,243	7,509	10,243	8,994
55,300	55,350	10,255	7,516	10,255	9,006
55,350	55,400	10,268	7,524	10,268	9,019
55,400	55,450	10,280	7,531	10,280	9,031
55,450	55,500	10,293	7,539	10,293	9,044
55,500	55,550	10,305	7,546	10,305	9,056
55,550	55,600	10,318	7,554	10,318	9,069
55,600	55,650	10,330	7,561	10,330	9,081
55,650	55,700	10,343	7,569	10,343	9,094
55,700	55,750	10,355	7,576	10,355	9,106
55,750	55,800	10,368	7,584	10,368	9,119
55,800	55,850	10,380	7,591	10,380	9,131
55,850	55,900	10,393	7,599	10,393	9,144
55,900	55,950	10,405	7,606	10,405	9,156
55,950	56,000	10,418	7,614	10,418	9,169

If line 43 (taxable income) is— At least	But less than	Single	Married filing jointly *	Married filing separately	Head of a household
56,000					
56,000	56,050	10,430	7,621	10,430	9,181
56,050	56,100	10,443	7,629	10,443	9,194
56,100	56,150	10,455	7,636	10,455	9,206
56,150	56,200	10,468	7,644	10,468	9,219
56,200	56,250	10,480	7,651	10,480	9,231
56,250	56,300	10,493	7,659	10,493	9,244
56,300	56,350	10,505	7,666	10,505	9,256
56,350	56,400	10,518	7,674	10,518	9,269
56,400	56,450	10,530	7,681	10,530	9,281
56,450	56,500	10,543	7,689	10,543	9,294
56,500	56,550	10,555	7,696	10,555	9,306
56,550	56,600	10,568	7,704	10,568	9,319
56,600	56,650	10,580	7,711	10,580	9,331
56,650	56,700	10,593	7,719	10,593	9,344
56,700	56,750	10,605	7,726	10,605	9,356
56,750	56,800	10,618	7,734	10,618	9,369
56,800	56,850	10,630	7,741	10,630	9,381
56,850	56,900	10,643	7,749	10,643	9,394
56,900	56,950	10,655	7,756	10,655	9,406
56,950	57,000	10,668	7,764	10,668	9,419
57,000					
57,000	57,050	10,680	7,771	10,680	9,431
57,050	57,100	10,693	7,779	10,693	9,444
57,100	57,150	10,705	7,786	10,705	9,456
57,150	57,200	10,718	7,794	10,718	9,469
57,200	57,250	10,730	7,801	10,730	9,481
57,250	57,300	10,743	7,809	10,743	9,494
57,300	57,350	10,755	7,816	10,755	9,506
57,350	57,400	10,768	7,824	10,768	9,519
57,400	57,450	10,780	7,831	10,780	9,531
57,450	57,500	10,793	7,839	10,793	9,544
57,500	57,550	10,805	7,846	10,805	9,556
57,550	57,600	10,818	7,854	10,818	9,569
57,600	57,650	10,830	7,861	10,830	9,581
57,650	57,700	10,843	7,869	10,843	9,594
57,700	57,750	10,855	7,876	10,855	9,606
57,750	57,800	10,868	7,884	10,868	9,619
57,800	57,850	10,880	7,891	10,880	9,631
57,850	57,900	10,893	7,899	10,893	9,644
57,900	57,950	10,905	7,906	10,905	9,656
57,950	58,000	10,918	7,914	10,918	9,669
58,000					
58,000	58,050	10,930	7,921	10,930	9,681
58,050	58,100	10,943	7,929	10,943	9,694
58,100	58,150	10,955	7,936	10,955	9,706
58,150	58,200	10,968	7,944	10,968	9,719
58,200	58,250	10,980	7,951	10,980	9,731
58,250	58,300	10,993	7,959	10,993	9,744
58,300	58,350	11,005	7,966	11,005	9,756
58,350	58,400	11,018	7,974	11,018	9,769
58,400	58,450	11,030	7,981	11,030	9,781
58,450	58,500	11,043	7,989	11,043	9,794
58,500	58,550	11,055	7,996	11,055	9,806
58,550	58,600	11,068	8,004	11,068	9,819
58,600	58,650	11,080	8,011	11,080	9,831
58,650	58,700	11,093	8,019	11,093	9,844
58,700	58,750	11,105	8,026	11,105	9,856
58,750	58,800	11,118	8,034	11,118	9,869
58,800	58,850	11,130	8,041	11,130	9,881
58,850	58,900	11,143	8,049	11,143	9,894
58,900	58,950	11,155	8,056	11,155	9,906
58,950	59,000	11,168	8,064	11,168	9,919

*This column must also be used by a qualifying widow(er).

(Continued on next page)

2007 Tax Table—Continued

59,000

At least	But less than	Single	Married filing jointly *	Married filing separately	Head of a household
59,000	59,050	11,180	8,071	11,180	9,931
59,050	59,100	11,193	8,079	11,193	9,944
59,100	59,150	11,205	8,086	11,205	9,956
59,150	59,200	11,218	8,094	11,218	9,969
59,200	59,250	11,230	8,101	11,230	9,981
59,250	59,300	11,243	8,109	11,243	9,994
59,300	59,350	11,255	8,116	11,255	10,006
59,350	59,400	11,268	8,124	11,268	10,019
59,400	59,450	11,280	8,131	11,280	10,031
59,450	59,500	11,293	8,139	11,293	10,044
59,500	59,550	11,305	8,146	11,305	10,056
59,550	59,600	11,318	8,154	11,318	10,069
59,600	59,650	11,330	8,161	11,330	10,081
59,650	59,700	11,343	8,169	11,343	10,094
59,700	59,750	11,355	8,176	11,355	10,106
59,750	59,800	11,368	8,184	11,368	10,119
59,800	59,850	11,380	8,191	11,380	10,131
59,850	59,900	11,393	8,199	11,393	10,144
59,900	59,950	11,405	8,206	11,405	10,156
59,950	60,000	11,418	8,214	11,418	10,169

60,000

At least	But less than	Single	Married filing jointly *	Married filing separately	Head of a household
60,000	60,050	11,430	8,221	11,430	10,181
60,050	60,100	11,443	8,229	11,443	10,194
60,100	60,150	11,455	8,236	11,455	10,206
60,150	60,200	11,468	8,244	11,468	10,219
60,200	60,250	11,480	8,251	11,480	10,231
60,250	60,300	11,493	8,259	11,493	10,244
60,300	60,350	11,505	8,266	11,505	10,256
60,350	60,400	11,518	8,274	11,518	10,269
60,400	60,450	11,530	8,281	11,530	10,281
60,450	60,500	11,543	8,289	11,543	10,294
60,500	60,550	11,555	8,296	11,555	10,306
60,550	60,600	11,568	8,304	11,568	10,319
60,600	60,650	11,580	8,311	11,580	10,331
60,650	60,700	11,593	8,319	11,593	10,344
60,700	60,750	11,605	8,326	11,605	10,356
60,750	60,800	11,618	8,334	11,618	10,369
60,800	60,850	11,630	8,341	11,630	10,381
60,850	60,900	11,643	8,349	11,643	10,394
60,900	60,950	11,655	8,356	11,655	10,406
60,950	61,000	11,668	8,364	11,668	10,419

61,000

At least	But less than	Single	Married filing jointly *	Married filing separately	Head of a household
61,000	61,050	11,680	8,371	11,680	10,431
61,050	61,100	11,693	8,379	11,693	10,444
61,100	61,150	11,705	8,386	11,705	10,456
61,150	61,200	11,718	8,394	11,718	10,469
61,200	61,250	11,730	8,401	11,730	10,481
61,250	61,300	11,743	8,409	11,743	10,494
61,300	61,350	11,755	8,416	11,755	10,506
61,350	61,400	11,768	8,424	11,768	10,519
61,400	61,450	11,780	8,431	11,780	10,531
61,450	61,500	11,793	8,439	11,793	10,544
61,500	61,550	11,805	8,446	11,805	10,556
61,550	61,600	11,818	8,454	11,818	10,569
61,600	61,650	11,830	8,461	11,830	10,581
61,650	61,700	11,843	8,469	11,843	10,594
61,700	61,750	11,855	8,476	11,855	10,606
61,750	61,800	11,868	8,484	11,868	10,619
61,800	61,850	11,880	8,491	11,880	10,631
61,850	61,900	11,893	8,499	11,893	10,644
61,900	61,950	11,905	8,506	11,905	10,656
61,950	62,000	11,918	8,514	11,918	10,669

62,000

At least	But less than	Single	Married filing jointly *	Married filing separately	Head of a household
62,000	62,050	11,930	8,521	11,930	10,681
62,050	62,100	11,943	8,529	11,943	10,694
62,100	62,150	11,955	8,536	11,955	10,706
62,150	62,200	11,968	8,544	11,968	10,719
62,200	62,250	11,980	8,551	11,980	10,731
62,250	62,300	11,993	8,559	11,993	10,744
62,300	62,350	12,005	8,566	12,005	10,756
62,350	62,400	12,018	8,574	12,018	10,769
62,400	62,450	12,030	8,581	12,030	10,781
62,450	62,500	12,043	8,589	12,043	10,794
62,500	62,550	12,055	8,596	12,055	10,806
62,550	62,600	12,068	8,604	12,068	10,819
62,600	62,650	12,080	8,611	12,080	10,831
62,650	62,700	12,093	8,619	12,093	10,844
62,700	62,750	12,105	8,626	12,105	10,856
62,750	62,800	12,118	8,634	12,118	10,869
62,800	62,850	12,130	8,641	12,130	10,881
62,850	62,900	12,143	8,649	12,143	10,894
62,900	62,950	12,155	8,656	12,155	10,906
62,950	63,000	12,168	8,664	12,168	10,919

63,000

At least	But less than	Single	Married filing jointly *	Married filing separately	Head of a household
63,000	63,050	12,180	8,671	12,180	10,931
63,050	63,100	12,193	8,679	12,193	10,944
63,100	63,150	12,205	8,686	12,205	10,956
63,150	63,200	12,218	8,694	12,218	10,969
63,200	63,250	12,230	8,701	12,230	10,981
63,250	63,300	12,243	8,709	12,243	10,994
63,300	63,350	12,255	8,716	12,255	11,006
63,350	63,400	12,268	8,724	12,268	11,019
63,400	63,450	12,280	8,731	12,280	11,031
63,450	63,500	12,293	8,739	12,293	11,044
63,500	63,550	12,305	8,746	12,305	11,056
63,550	63,600	12,318	8,754	12,318	11,069
63,600	63,650	12,330	8,761	12,330	11,081
63,650	63,700	12,343	8,769	12,343	11,094
63,700	63,750	12,355	8,779	12,355	11,106
63,750	63,800	12,368	8,791	12,368	11,119
63,800	63,850	12,380	8,804	12,380	11,131
63,850	63,900	12,393	8,816	12,393	11,144
63,900	63,950	12,405	8,829	12,405	11,156
63,950	64,000	12,418	8,841	12,418	11,169

64,000

At least	But less than	Single	Married filing jointly *	Married filing separately	Head of a household
64,000	64,050	12,430	8,854	12,430	11,181
64,050	64,100	12,443	8,866	12,443	11,194
64,100	64,150	12,455	8,879	12,455	11,206
64,150	64,200	12,468	8,891	12,468	11,219
64,200	64,250	12,480	8,904	12,480	11,231
64,250	64,300	12,493	8,916	12,493	11,244
64,300	64,350	12,505	8,929	12,507	11,256
64,350	64,400	12,518	8,941	12,521	11,269
64,400	64,450	12,530	8,954	12,535	11,281
64,450	64,500	12,543	8,966	12,549	11,294
64,500	64,550	12,555	8,979	12,563	11,306
64,550	64,600	12,568	8,991	12,577	11,319
64,600	64,650	12,580	9,004	12,591	11,331
64,650	64,700	12,593	9,016	12,605	11,344
64,700	64,750	12,605	9,029	12,619	11,356
64,750	64,800	12,618	9,041	12,633	11,369
64,800	64,850	12,630	9,054	12,647	11,381
64,850	64,900	12,643	9,066	12,661	11,394
64,900	64,950	12,655	9,079	12,675	11,406
64,950	65,000	12,668	9,091	12,689	11,419

65,000

At least	But less than	Single	Married filing jointly *	Married filing separately	Head of a household
65,000	65,050	12,680	9,104	12,703	11,431
65,050	65,100	12,693	9,116	12,717	11,444
65,100	65,150	12,705	9,129	12,731	11,456
65,150	65,200	12,718	9,141	12,745	11,469
65,200	65,250	12,730	9,154	12,759	11,481
65,250	65,300	12,743	9,166	12,773	11,494
65,300	65,350	12,755	9,179	12,787	11,506
65,350	65,400	12,768	9,191	12,801	11,519
65,400	65,450	12,780	9,204	12,815	11,531
65,450	65,500	12,793	9,216	12,829	11,544
65,500	65,550	12,805	9,229	12,843	11,556
65,550	65,600	12,818	9,241	12,857	11,569
65,600	65,650	12,830	9,254	12,871	11,581
65,650	65,700	12,843	9,266	12,885	11,594
65,700	65,750	12,855	9,279	12,899	11,606
65,750	65,800	12,868	9,291	12,913	11,619
65,800	65,850	12,880	9,304	12,927	11,631
65,850	65,900	12,893	9,316	12,941	11,644
65,900	65,950	12,905	9,329	12,955	11,656
65,950	66,000	12,918	9,341	12,969	11,669

66,000

At least	But less than	Single	Married filing jointly *	Married filing separately	Head of a household
66,000	66,050	12,930	9,354	12,983	11,681
66,050	66,100	12,943	9,366	12,997	11,694
66,100	66,150	12,955	9,379	13,011	11,706
66,150	66,200	12,968	9,391	13,025	11,719
66,200	66,250	12,980	9,404	13,039	11,731
66,250	66,300	12,993	9,416	13,053	11,744
66,300	66,350	13,005	9,429	13,067	11,756
66,350	66,400	13,018	9,441	13,081	11,769
66,400	66,450	13,030	9,454	13,095	11,781
66,450	66,500	13,043	9,466	13,109	11,794
66,500	66,550	13,055	9,479	13,123	11,806
66,550	66,600	13,068	9,491	13,137	11,819
66,600	66,650	13,080	9,504	13,151	11,831
66,650	66,700	13,093	9,516	13,165	11,844
66,700	66,750	13,105	9,529	13,179	11,856
66,750	66,800	13,118	9,541	13,193	11,869
66,800	66,850	13,130	9,554	13,207	11,881
66,850	66,900	13,143	9,566	13,221	11,894
66,900	66,950	13,155	9,579	13,235	11,906
66,950	67,000	13,168	9,591	13,249	11,919

67,000

At least	But less than	Single	Married filing jointly *	Married filing separately	Head of a household
67,000	67,050	13,180	9,604	13,263	11,931
67,050	67,100	13,193	9,616	13,277	11,944
67,100	67,150	13,205	9,629	13,291	11,956
67,150	67,200	13,218	9,641	13,305	11,969
67,200	67,250	13,230	9,654	13,319	11,981
67,250	67,300	13,243	9,666	13,333	11,994
67,300	67,350	13,255	9,679	13,347	12,006
67,350	67,400	13,268	9,691	13,361	12,019
67,400	67,450	13,280	9,704	13,375	12,031
67,450	67,500	13,293	9,716	13,389	12,044
67,500	67,550	13,305	9,729	13,403	12,056
67,550	67,600	13,318	9,741	13,417	12,069
67,600	67,650	13,330	9,754	13,431	12,081
67,650	67,700	13,343	9,766	13,445	12,094
67,700	67,750	13,355	9,779	13,459	12,106
67,750	67,800	13,368	9,791	13,473	12,119
67,800	67,850	13,380	9,804	13,487	12,131
67,850	67,900	13,393	9,816	13,501	12,144
67,900	67,950	13,405	9,829	13,515	12,156
67,950	68,000	13,418	9,841	13,529	12,169

*This column must also be used by a qualifying widow(er).

(Continued on next page)

2007 Tax Table–*Continued*

If line 43 (taxable income) is—		And you are—			
At least	But less than	Single	Married filing jointly *	Married filing separately	Head of a household
		Your tax is—			

68,000

At least	But less than	Single	MFJ	MFS	HoH
68,000	68,050	13,430	9,854	13,543	12,181
68,050	68,100	13,443	9,866	13,557	12,194
68,100	68,150	13,455	9,879	13,571	12,206
68,150	68,200	13,468	9,891	13,585	12,219
68,200	68,250	13,480	9,904	13,599	12,231
68,250	68,300	13,493	9,916	13,613	12,244
68,300	68,350	13,505	9,929	13,627	12,256
68,350	68,400	13,518	9,941	13,641	12,269
68,400	68,450	13,530	9,954	13,655	12,281
68,450	68,500	13,543	9,966	13,669	12,294
68,500	68,550	13,555	9,979	13,683	12,306
68,550	68,600	13,568	9,991	13,697	12,319
68,600	68,650	13,580	10,004	13,711	12,331
68,650	68,700	13,593	10,016	13,725	12,344
68,700	68,750	13,605	10,029	13,739	12,356
68,750	68,800	13,618	10,041	13,753	12,369
68,800	68,850	13,630	10,054	13,767	12,381
68,850	68,900	13,643	10,066	13,781	12,394
68,900	68,950	13,655	10,079	13,795	12,406
68,950	69,000	13,668	10,091	13,809	12,419

69,000

At least	But less than	Single	MFJ	MFS	HoH
69,000	69,050	13,680	10,104	13,823	12,431
69,050	69,100	13,693	10,116	13,837	12,444
69,100	69,150	13,705	10,129	13,851	12,456
69,150	69,200	13,718	10,141	13,865	12,469
69,200	69,250	13,730	10,154	13,879	12,481
69,250	69,300	13,743	10,166	13,893	12,494
69,300	69,350	13,755	10,179	13,907	12,506
69,350	69,400	13,768	10,191	13,921	12,519
69,400	69,450	13,780	10,204	13,935	12,531
69,450	69,500	13,793	10,216	13,949	12,544
69,500	69,550	13,805	10,229	13,963	12,556
69,550	69,600	13,818	10,241	13,977	12,569
69,600	69,650	13,830	10,254	13,991	12,581
69,650	69,700	13,843	10,266	14,005	12,594
69,700	69,750	13,855	10,279	14,019	12,606
69,750	69,800	13,868	10,291	14,033	12,619
69,800	69,850	13,880	10,304	14,047	12,631
69,850	69,900	13,893	10,316	14,061	12,644
69,900	69,950	13,905	10,329	14,075	12,656
69,950	70,000	13,918	10,341	14,089	12,669

70,000

At least	But less than	Single	MFJ	MFS	HoH
70,000	70,050	13,930	10,354	14,103	12,681
70,050	70,100	13,943	10,366	14,117	12,694
70,100	70,150	13,955	10,379	14,131	12,706
70,150	70,200	13,968	10,391	14,145	12,719
70,200	70,250	13,980	10,404	14,159	12,731
70,250	70,300	13,993	10,416	14,173	12,744
70,300	70,350	14,005	10,429	14,187	12,756
70,350	70,400	14,018	10,441	14,201	12,769
70,400	70,450	14,030	10,454	14,215	12,781
70,450	70,500	14,043	10,466	14,229	12,794
70,500	70,550	14,055	10,479	14,243	12,806
70,550	70,600	14,068	10,491	14,257	12,819
70,600	70,650	14,080	10,504	14,271	12,831
70,650	70,700	14,093	10,516	14,285	12,844
70,700	70,750	14,105	10,529	14,299	12,856
70,750	70,800	14,118	10,541	14,313	12,869
70,800	70,850	14,130	10,554	14,327	12,881
70,850	70,900	14,143	10,566	14,341	12,894
70,900	70,950	14,155	10,579	14,355	12,906
70,950	71,000	14,168	10,591	14,369	12,919

71,000

At least	But less than	Single	MFJ	MFS	HoH
71,000	71,050	14,180	10,604	14,383	12,931
71,050	71,100	14,193	10,616	14,397	12,944
71,100	71,150	14,205	10,629	14,411	12,956
71,150	71,200	14,218	10,641	14,425	12,969
71,200	71,250	14,230	10,654	14,439	12,981
71,250	71,300	14,243	10,666	14,453	12,994
71,300	71,350	14,255	10,679	14,467	13,006
71,350	71,400	14,268	10,691	14,481	13,019
71,400	71,450	14,280	10,704	14,495	13,031
71,450	71,500	14,293	10,716	14,509	13,044
71,500	71,550	14,305	10,729	14,523	13,056
71,550	71,600	14,318	10,741	14,537	13,069
71,600	71,650	14,330	10,754	14,551	13,081
71,650	71,700	14,343	10,766	14,565	13,094
71,700	71,750	14,355	10,779	14,579	13,106
71,750	71,800	14,368	10,791	14,593	13,119
71,800	71,850	14,380	10,804	14,607	13,131
71,850	71,900	14,393	10,816	14,621	13,144
71,900	71,950	14,405	10,829	14,635	13,156
71,950	72,000	14,418	10,841	14,649	13,169

72,000

At least	But less than	Single	MFJ	MFS	HoH
72,000	72,050	14,430	10,854	14,663	13,181
72,050	72,100	14,443	10,866	14,677	13,194
72,100	72,150	14,455	10,879	14,691	13,206
72,150	72,200	14,468	10,891	14,705	13,219
72,200	72,250	14,480	10,904	14,719	13,231
72,250	72,300	14,493	10,916	14,733	13,244
72,300	72,350	14,505	10,929	14,747	13,256
72,350	72,400	14,518	10,941	14,761	13,269
72,400	72,450	14,530	10,954	14,775	13,281
72,450	72,500	14,543	10,966	14,789	13,294
72,500	72,550	14,555	10,979	14,803	13,306
72,550	72,600	14,568	10,991	14,817	13,319
72,600	72,650	14,580	11,004	14,831	13,331
72,650	72,700	14,593	11,016	14,845	13,344
72,700	72,750	14,605	11,029	14,859	13,356
72,750	72,800	14,618	11,041	14,873	13,369
72,800	72,850	14,630	11,054	14,887	13,381
72,850	72,900	14,643	11,066	14,901	13,394
72,900	72,950	14,655	11,079	14,915	13,406
72,950	73,000	14,668	11,091	14,929	13,419

73,000

At least	But less than	Single	MFJ	MFS	HoH
73,000	73,050	14,680	11,104	14,943	13,431
73,050	73,100	14,693	11,116	14,957	13,444
73,100	73,150	14,705	11,129	14,971	13,456
73,150	73,200	14,718	11,141	14,985	13,469
73,200	73,250	14,730	11,154	14,999	13,481
73,250	73,300	14,743	11,166	15,013	13,494
73,300	73,350	14,755	11,179	15,027	13,506
73,350	73,400	14,768	11,191	15,041	13,519
73,400	73,450	14,780	11,204	15,055	13,531
73,450	73,500	14,793	11,216	15,069	13,544
73,500	73,550	14,805	11,229	15,083	13,556
73,550	73,600	14,818	11,241	15,097	13,569
73,600	73,650	14,830	11,254	15,111	13,581
73,650	73,700	14,843	11,266	15,125	13,594
73,700	73,750	14,855	11,279	15,139	13,606
73,750	73,800	14,868	11,291	15,153	13,619
73,800	73,850	14,880	11,304	15,167	13,631
73,850	73,900	14,893	11,316	15,181	13,644
73,900	73,950	14,905	11,329	15,195	13,656
73,950	74,000	14,918	11,341	15,209	13,669

74,000

At least	But less than	Single	MFJ	MFS	HoH
74,000	74,050	14,930	11,354	15,223	13,681
74,050	74,100	14,943	11,366	15,237	13,694
74,100	74,150	14,955	11,379	15,251	13,706
74,150	74,200	14,968	11,391	15,265	13,719
74,200	74,250	14,980	11,404	15,279	13,731
74,250	74,300	14,993	11,416	15,293	13,744
74,300	74,350	15,005	11,429	15,307	13,756
74,350	74,400	15,018	11,441	15,321	13,769
74,400	74,450	15,030	11,454	15,335	13,781
74,450	74,500	15,043	11,466	15,349	13,794
74,500	74,550	15,055	11,479	15,363	13,806
74,550	74,600	15,068	11,491	15,377	13,819
74,600	74,650	15,080	11,504	15,391	13,831
74,650	74,700	15,093	11,516	15,405	13,844
74,700	74,750	15,105	11,529	15,419	13,856
74,750	74,800	15,118	11,541	15,433	13,869
74,800	74,850	15,130	11,554	15,447	13,881
74,850	74,900	15,143	11,566	15,461	13,894
74,900	74,950	15,155	11,579	15,475	13,906
74,950	75,000	15,168	11,591	15,489	13,919

75,000

At least	But less than	Single	MFJ	MFS	HoH
75,000	75,050	15,180	11,604	15,503	13,931
75,050	75,100	15,193	11,616	15,517	13,944
75,100	75,150	15,205	11,629	15,531	13,956
75,150	75,200	15,218	11,641	15,545	13,969
75,200	75,250	15,230	11,654	15,559	13,981
75,250	75,300	15,243	11,666	15,573	13,994
75,300	75,350	15,255	11,679	15,587	14,006
75,350	75,400	15,268	11,691	15,601	14,019
75,400	75,450	15,280	11,704	15,615	14,031
75,450	75,500	15,293	11,716	15,629	14,044
75,500	75,550	15,305	11,729	15,643	14,056
75,550	75,600	15,318	11,741	15,657	14,069
75,600	75,650	15,330	11,754	15,671	14,081
75,650	75,700	15,343	11,766	15,685	14,094
75,700	75,750	15,355	11,779	15,699	14,106
75,750	75,800	15,368	11,791	15,713	14,119
75,800	75,850	15,380	11,804	15,727	14,131
75,850	75,900	15,393	11,816	15,741	14,144
75,900	75,950	15,405	11,829	15,755	14,156
75,950	76,000	15,418	11,841	15,769	14,169

76,000

At least	But less than	Single	MFJ	MFS	HoH
76,000	76,050	15,430	11,854	15,783	14,181
76,050	76,100	15,443	11,866	15,797	14,194
76,100	76,150	15,455	11,879	15,811	14,206
76,150	76,200	15,468	11,891	15,825	14,219
76,200	76,250	15,480	11,904	15,839	14,231
76,250	76,300	15,493	11,916	15,853	14,244
76,300	76,350	15,505	11,929	15,867	14,256
76,350	76,400	15,518	11,941	15,881	14,269
76,400	76,450	15,530	11,954	15,895	14,281
76,450	76,500	15,543	11,966	15,909	14,294
76,500	76,550	15,555	11,979	15,923	14,306
76,550	76,600	15,568	11,991	15,937	14,319
76,600	76,650	15,580	12,004	15,951	14,331
76,650	76,700	15,593	12,016	15,965	14,344
76,700	76,750	15,605	12,029	15,979	14,356
76,750	76,800	15,618	12,041	15,993	14,369
76,800	76,850	15,630	12,054	16,007	14,381
76,850	76,900	15,643	12,066	16,021	14,394
76,900	76,950	15,655	12,079	16,035	14,406
76,950	77,000	15,668	12,091	16,049	14,419

*This column must also be used by a qualifying widow(er).

(Continued on next page)

2007 Tax Table–*Continued*

77,000

At least	But less than	Single	Married filing jointly *	Married filing separately	Head of a household
77,000	77,050	15,680	12,104	16,063	14,431
77,050	77,100	15,693	12,116	16,077	14,444
77,100	77,150	15,706	12,129	16,091	14,456
77,150	77,200	15,720	12,141	16,105	14,469
77,200	77,250	15,734	12,154	16,119	14,481
77,250	77,300	15,748	12,166	16,133	14,494
77,300	77,350	15,762	12,179	16,147	14,506
77,350	77,400	15,776	12,191	16,161	14,519
77,400	77,450	15,790	12,204	16,175	14,531
77,450	77,500	15,804	12,216	16,189	14,544
77,500	77,550	15,818	12,229	16,203	14,556
77,550	77,600	15,832	12,241	16,217	14,569
77,600	77,650	15,846	12,254	16,231	14,581
77,650	77,700	15,860	12,266	16,245	14,594
77,700	77,750	15,874	12,279	16,259	14,606
77,750	77,800	15,888	12,291	16,273	14,619
77,800	77,850	15,902	12,304	16,287	14,631
77,850	77,900	15,916	12,316	16,301	14,644
77,900	77,950	15,930	12,329	16,315	14,656
77,950	78,000	15,944	12,341	16,329	14,669

78,000

At least	But less than	Single	Married filing jointly *	Married filing separately	Head of a household
78,000	78,050	15,958	12,354	16,343	14,681
78,050	78,100	15,972	12,366	16,357	14,694
78,100	78,150	15,986	12,379	16,371	14,706
78,150	78,200	16,000	12,391	16,385	14,719
78,200	78,250	16,014	12,404	16,399	14,731
78,250	78,300	16,028	12,416	16,413	14,744
78,300	78,350	16,042	12,429	16,427	14,756
78,350	78,400	16,056	12,441	16,441	14,769
78,400	78,450	16,070	12,454	16,455	14,781
78,450	78,500	16,084	12,466	16,469	14,794
78,500	78,550	16,098	12,479	16,483	14,806
78,550	78,600	16,112	12,491	16,497	14,819
78,600	78,650	16,126	12,504	16,511	14,831
78,650	78,700	16,140	12,516	16,525	14,844
78,700	78,750	16,154	12,529	16,539	14,856
78,750	78,800	16,168	12,541	16,553	14,869
78,800	78,850	16,182	12,554	16,567	14,881
78,850	78,900	16,196	12,566	16,581	14,894
78,900	78,950	16,210	12,579	16,595	14,906
78,950	79,000	16,224	12,591	16,609	14,919

79,000

At least	But less than	Single	Married filing jointly *	Married filing separately	Head of a household
79,000	79,050	16,238	12,604	16,623	14,931
79,050	79,100	16,252	12,616	16,637	14,944
79,100	79,150	16,266	12,629	16,651	14,956
79,150	79,200	16,280	12,641	16,665	14,969
79,200	79,250	16,294	12,654	16,679	14,981
79,250	79,300	16,308	12,666	16,693	14,994
79,300	79,350	16,322	12,679	16,707	15,006
79,350	79,400	16,336	12,691	16,721	15,019
79,400	79,450	16,350	12,704	16,735	15,031
79,450	79,500	16,364	12,716	16,749	15,044
79,500	79,550	16,378	12,729	16,763	15,056
79,550	79,600	16,392	12,741	16,777	15,069
79,600	79,650	16,406	12,754	16,791	15,081
79,650	79,700	16,420	12,766	16,805	15,094
79,700	79,750	16,434	12,779	16,819	15,106
79,750	79,800	16,448	12,791	16,833	15,119
79,800	79,850	16,462	12,804	16,847	15,131
79,850	79,900	16,476	12,816	16,861	15,144
79,900	79,950	16,490	12,829	16,875	15,156
79,950	80,000	16,504	12,841	16,889	15,169

80,000

At least	But less than	Single	Married filing jointly *	Married filing separately	Head of a household
80,000	80,050	16,518	12,854	16,903	15,181
80,050	80,100	16,532	12,866	16,917	15,194
80,100	80,150	16,546	12,879	16,931	15,206
80,150	80,200	16,560	12,891	16,945	15,219
80,200	80,250	16,574	12,904	16,959	15,231
80,250	80,300	16,588	12,916	16,973	15,244
80,300	80,350	16,602	12,929	16,987	15,256
80,350	80,400	16,616	12,941	17,001	15,269
80,400	80,450	16,630	12,954	17,015	15,281
80,450	80,500	16,644	12,966	17,029	15,294
80,500	80,550	16,658	12,979	17,043	15,306
80,550	80,600	16,672	12,991	17,057	15,319
80,600	80,650	16,686	13,004	17,071	15,331
80,650	80,700	16,700	13,016	17,085	15,344
80,700	80,750	16,714	13,029	17,099	15,356
80,750	80,800	16,728	13,041	17,113	15,369
80,800	80,850	16,742	13,054	17,127	15,381
80,850	80,900	16,756	13,066	17,141	15,394
80,900	80,950	16,770	13,079	17,155	15,406
80,950	81,000	16,784	13,091	17,169	15,419

81,000

At least	But less than	Single	Married filing jointly *	Married filing separately	Head of a household
81,000	81,050	16,798	13,104	17,183	15,431
81,050	81,100	16,812	13,116	17,197	15,444
81,100	81,150	16,826	13,129	17,211	15,456
81,150	81,200	16,840	13,141	17,225	15,469
81,200	81,250	16,854	13,154	17,239	15,481
81,250	81,300	16,868	13,166	17,253	15,494
81,300	81,350	16,882	13,179	17,267	15,506
81,350	81,400	16,896	13,191	17,281	15,519
81,400	81,450	16,910	13,204	17,295	15,531
81,450	81,500	16,924	13,216	17,309	15,544
81,500	81,550	16,938	13,229	17,323	15,556
81,550	81,600	16,952	13,241	17,337	15,569
81,600	81,650	16,966	13,254	17,351	15,581
81,650	81,700	16,980	13,266	17,365	15,594
81,700	81,750	16,994	13,279	17,379	15,606
81,750	81,800	17,008	13,291	17,393	15,619
81,800	81,850	17,022	13,304	17,407	15,631
81,850	81,900	17,036	13,316	17,421	15,644
81,900	81,950	17,050	13,329	17,435	15,656
81,950	82,000	17,064	13,341	17,449	15,669

82,000

At least	But less than	Single	Married filing jointly *	Married filing separately	Head of a household
82,000	82,050	17,078	13,354	17,463	15,681
82,050	82,100	17,092	13,366	17,477	15,694
82,100	82,150	17,106	13,379	17,491	15,706
82,150	82,200	17,120	13,391	17,505	15,719
82,200	82,250	17,134	13,404	17,519	15,731
82,250	82,300	17,148	13,416	17,533	15,744
82,300	82,350	17,162	13,429	17,547	15,756
82,350	82,400	17,176	13,441	17,561	15,769
82,400	82,450	17,190	13,454	17,575	15,781
82,450	82,500	17,204	13,466	17,589	15,794
82,500	82,550	17,218	13,479	17,603	15,806
82,550	82,600	17,232	13,491	17,617	15,819
82,600	82,650	17,246	13,504	17,631	15,831
82,650	82,700	17,260	13,516	17,645	15,844
82,700	82,750	17,274	13,529	17,659	15,856
82,750	82,800	17,288	13,541	17,673	15,869
82,800	82,850	17,302	13,554	17,687	15,881
82,850	82,900	17,316	13,566	17,701	15,894
82,900	82,950	17,330	13,579	17,715	15,906
82,950	83,000	17,344	13,591	17,729	15,919

83,000

At least	But less than	Single	Married filing jointly *	Married filing separately	Head of a household
83,000	83,050	17,358	13,604	17,743	15,931
83,050	83,100	17,372	13,616	17,757	15,944
83,100	83,150	17,386	13,629	17,771	15,956
83,150	83,200	17,400	13,641	17,785	15,969
83,200	83,250	17,414	13,654	17,799	15,981
83,250	83,300	17,428	13,666	17,813	15,994
83,300	83,350	17,442	13,679	17,827	16,006
83,350	83,400	17,456	13,691	17,841	16,019
83,400	83,450	17,470	13,704	17,855	16,031
83,450	83,500	17,484	13,716	17,869	16,044
83,500	83,550	17,498	13,729	17,883	16,056
83,550	83,600	17,512	13,741	17,897	16,069
83,600	83,650	17,526	13,754	17,911	16,081
83,650	83,700	17,540	13,766	17,925	16,094
83,700	83,750	17,554	13,779	17,939	16,106
83,750	83,800	17,568	13,791	17,953	16,119
83,800	83,850	17,582	13,804	17,967	16,131
83,850	83,900	17,596	13,816	17,981	16,144
83,900	83,950	17,610	13,829	17,995	16,156
83,950	84,000	17,624	13,841	18,009	16,169

84,000

At least	But less than	Single	Married filing jointly *	Married filing separately	Head of a household
84,000	84,050	17,638	13,854	18,023	16,181
84,050	84,100	17,652	13,866	18,037	16,194
84,100	84,150	17,666	13,879	18,051	16,206
84,150	84,200	17,680	13,891	18,065	16,219
84,200	84,250	17,694	13,904	18,079	16,231
84,250	84,300	17,708	13,916	18,093	16,244
84,300	84,350	17,722	13,929	18,107	16,256
84,350	84,400	17,736	13,941	18,121	16,269
84,400	84,450	17,750	13,954	18,135	16,281
84,450	84,500	17,764	13,966	18,149	16,294
84,500	84,550	17,778	13,979	18,163	16,306
84,550	84,600	17,792	13,991	18,177	16,319
84,600	84,650	17,806	14,004	18,191	16,331
84,650	84,700	17,820	14,016	18,205	16,344
84,700	84,750	17,834	14,029	18,219	16,356
84,750	84,800	17,848	14,041	18,233	16,369
84,800	84,850	17,862	14,054	18,247	16,381
84,850	84,900	17,876	14,066	18,261	16,394
84,900	84,950	17,890	14,079	18,275	16,406
84,950	85,000	17,904	14,091	18,289	16,419

85,000

At least	But less than	Single	Married filing jointly *	Married filing separately	Head of a household
85,000	85,050	17,918	14,104	18,303	16,431
85,050	85,100	17,932	14,116	18,317	16,444
85,100	85,150	17,946	14,129	18,331	16,456
85,150	85,200	17,960	14,141	18,345	16,469
85,200	85,250	17,974	14,154	18,359	16,481
85,250	85,300	17,988	14,166	18,373	16,494
85,300	85,350	18,002	14,179	18,387	16,506
85,350	85,400	18,016	14,191	18,401	16,519
85,400	85,450	18,030	14,204	18,415	16,531
85,450	85,500	18,044	14,216	18,429	16,544
85,500	85,550	18,058	14,229	18,443	16,556
85,550	85,600	18,072	14,241	18,457	16,569
85,600	85,650	18,086	14,254	18,471	16,581
85,650	85,700	18,100	14,266	18,485	16,594
85,700	85,750	18,114	14,279	18,499	16,606
85,750	85,800	18,128	14,291	18,513	16,619
85,800	85,850	18,142	14,304	18,527	16,631
85,850	85,900	18,156	14,316	18,541	16,644
85,900	85,950	18,170	14,329	18,555	16,656
85,950	86,000	18,184	14,341	18,569	16,669

*This column must also be used by a qualifying widow(er).

(Continued on next page)

2007 Tax Table–*Continued*

If line 43 (taxable income) is— At least	But less than	And you are— Single	Married filing jointly*	Married filing separately	Head of a household
86,000					
86,000	86,050	18,198	14,354	18,583	16,681
86,050	86,100	18,212	14,366	18,597	16,694
86,100	86,150	18,226	14,379	18,611	16,706
86,150	86,200	18,240	14,391	18,625	16,719
86,200	86,250	18,254	14,404	18,639	16,731
86,250	86,300	18,268	14,416	18,653	16,744
86,300	86,350	18,282	14,429	18,667	16,756
86,350	86,400	18,296	14,441	18,681	16,769
86,400	86,450	18,310	14,454	18,695	16,781
86,450	86,500	18,324	14,466	18,709	16,794
86,500	86,550	18,338	14,479	18,723	16,806
86,550	86,600	18,352	14,491	18,737	16,819
86,600	86,650	18,366	14,504	18,751	16,831
86,650	86,700	18,380	14,516	18,765	16,844
86,700	86,750	18,394	14,529	18,779	16,856
86,750	86,800	18,408	14,541	18,793	16,869
86,800	86,850	18,422	14,554	18,807	16,881
86,850	86,900	18,436	14,566	18,821	16,894
86,900	86,950	18,450	14,579	18,835	16,906
86,950	87,000	18,464	14,591	18,849	16,919
87,000					
87,000	87,050	18,478	14,604	18,863	16,931
87,050	87,100	18,492	14,616	18,877	16,944
87,100	87,150	18,506	14,629	18,891	16,956
87,150	87,200	18,520	14,641	18,905	16,969
87,200	87,250	18,534	14,654	18,919	16,981
87,250	87,300	18,548	14,666	18,933	16,994
87,300	87,350	18,562	14,679	18,947	17,006
87,350	87,400	18,576	14,691	18,961	17,019
87,400	87,450	18,590	14,704	18,975	17,031
87,450	87,500	18,604	14,716	18,989	17,044
87,500	87,550	18,618	14,729	19,003	17,056
87,550	87,600	18,632	14,741	19,017	17,069
87,600	87,650	18,646	14,754	19,031	17,081
87,650	87,700	18,660	14,766	19,045	17,094
87,700	87,750	18,674	14,779	19,059	17,106
87,750	87,800	18,688	14,791	19,073	17,119
87,800	87,850	18,702	14,804	19,087	17,131
87,850	87,900	18,716	14,816	19,101	17,144
87,900	87,950	18,730	14,829	19,115	17,156
87,950	88,000	18,744	14,841	19,129	17,169
88,000					
88,000	88,050	18,758	14,854	19,143	17,181
88,050	88,100	18,772	14,866	19,157	17,194
88,100	88,150	18,786	14,879	19,171	17,206
88,150	88,200	18,800	14,891	19,185	17,219
88,200	88,250	18,814	14,904	19,199	17,231
88,250	88,300	18,828	14,916	19,213	17,244
88,300	88,350	18,842	14,929	19,227	17,256
88,350	88,400	18,856	14,941	19,241	17,269
88,400	88,450	18,870	14,954	19,255	17,281
88,450	88,500	18,884	14,966	19,269	17,294
88,500	88,550	18,898	14,979	19,283	17,306
88,550	88,600	18,912	14,991	19,297	17,319
88,600	88,650	18,926	15,004	19,311	17,331
88,650	88,700	18,940	15,016	19,325	17,344
88,700	88,750	18,954	15,029	19,339	17,356
88,750	88,800	18,968	15,041	19,353	17,369
88,800	88,850	18,982	15,054	19,367	17,381
88,850	88,900	18,996	15,066	19,381	17,394
88,900	88,950	19,010	15,079	19,395	17,406
88,950	89,000	19,024	15,091	19,409	17,419

If line 43 (taxable income) is— At least	But less than	And you are— Single	Married filing jointly*	Married filing separately	Head of a household
89,000					
89,000	89,050	19,038	15,104	19,423	17,431
89,050	89,100	19,052	15,116	19,437	17,444
89,100	89,150	19,066	15,129	19,451	17,456
89,150	89,200	19,080	15,141	19,465	17,469
89,200	89,250	19,094	15,154	19,479	17,481
89,250	89,300	19,108	15,166	19,493	17,494
89,300	89,350	19,122	15,179	19,507	17,506
89,350	89,400	19,136	15,191	19,521	17,519
89,400	89,450	19,150	15,204	19,535	17,531
89,450	89,500	19,164	15,216	19,549	17,544
89,500	89,550	19,178	15,229	19,563	17,556
89,550	89,600	19,192	15,241	19,577	17,569
89,600	89,650	19,206	15,254	19,591	17,581
89,650	89,700	19,220	15,266	19,605	17,594
89,700	89,750	19,234	15,279	19,619	17,606
89,750	89,800	19,248	15,291	19,633	17,619
89,800	89,850	19,262	15,304	19,647	17,631
89,850	89,900	19,276	15,316	19,661	17,644
89,900	89,950	19,290	15,329	19,675	17,656
89,950	90,000	19,304	15,341	19,689	17,669
90,000					
90,000	90,050	19,318	15,354	19,703	17,681
90,050	90,100	19,332	15,366	19,717	17,694
90,100	90,150	19,346	15,379	19,731	17,706
90,150	90,200	19,360	15,391	19,745	17,719
90,200	90,250	19,374	15,404	19,759	17,731
90,250	90,300	19,388	15,416	19,773	17,744
90,300	90,350	19,402	15,429	19,787	17,756
90,350	90,400	19,416	15,441	19,801	17,769
90,400	90,450	19,430	15,454	19,815	17,781
90,450	90,500	19,444	15,466	19,829	17,794
90,500	90,550	19,458	15,479	19,843	17,806
90,550	90,600	19,472	15,491	19,857	17,819
90,600	90,650	19,486	15,504	19,871	17,831
90,650	90,700	19,500	15,516	19,885	17,844
90,700	90,750	19,514	15,529	19,899	17,856
90,750	90,800	19,528	15,541	19,913	17,869
90,800	90,850	19,542	15,554	19,927	17,881
90,850	90,900	19,556	15,566	19,941	17,894
90,900	90,950	19,570	15,579	19,955	17,906
90,950	91,000	19,584	15,591	19,969	17,919
91,000					
91,000	91,050	19,598	15,604	19,983	17,931
91,050	91,100	19,612	15,616	19,997	17,944
91,100	91,150	19,626	15,629	20,011	17,956
91,150	91,200	19,640	15,641	20,025	17,969
91,200	91,250	19,654	15,654	20,039	17,981
91,250	91,300	19,668	15,666	20,053	17,994
91,300	91,350	19,682	15,679	20,067	18,006
91,350	91,400	19,696	15,691	20,081	18,019
91,400	91,450	19,710	15,704	20,095	18,031
91,450	91,500	19,724	15,716	20,109	18,044
91,500	91,550	19,738	15,729	20,123	18,056
91,550	91,600	19,752	15,741	20,137	18,069
91,600	91,650	19,766	15,754	20,151	18,081
91,650	91,700	19,780	15,766	20,165	18,094
91,700	91,750	19,794	15,779	20,179	18,106
91,750	91,800	19,808	15,791	20,193	18,119
91,800	91,850	19,822	15,804	20,207	18,131
91,850	91,900	19,836	15,816	20,221	18,144
91,900	91,950	19,850	15,829	20,235	18,156
91,950	92,000	19,864	15,841	20,249	18,169

If line 43 (taxable income) is— At least	But less than	And you are— Single	Married filing jointly*	Married filing separately	Head of a household
92,000					
92,000	92,050	19,878	15,854	20,263	18,181
92,050	92,100	19,892	15,866	20,277	18,194
92,100	92,150	19,906	15,879	20,291	18,206
92,150	92,200	19,920	15,891	20,305	18,219
92,200	92,250	19,934	15,904	20,319	18,231
92,250	92,300	19,948	15,916	20,333	18,244
92,300	92,350	19,962	15,929	20,347	18,256
92,350	92,400	19,976	15,941	20,361	18,269
92,400	92,450	19,990	15,954	20,375	18,281
92,450	92,500	20,004	15,966	20,389	18,294
92,500	92,550	20,018	15,979	20,403	18,306
92,550	92,600	20,032	15,991	20,417	18,319
92,600	92,650	20,046	16,004	20,431	18,331
92,650	92,700	20,060	16,016	20,445	18,344
92,700	92,750	20,074	16,029	20,459	18,356
92,750	92,800	20,088	16,041	20,473	18,369
92,800	92,850	20,102	16,054	20,487	18,381
92,850	92,900	20,116	16,066	20,501	18,394
92,900	92,950	20,130	16,079	20,515	18,406
92,950	93,000	20,144	16,091	20,529	18,419
93,000					
93,000	93,050	20,158	16,104	20,543	18,431
93,050	93,100	20,172	16,116	20,557	18,444
93,100	93,150	20,186	16,129	20,571	18,456
93,150	93,200	20,200	16,141	20,585	18,469
93,200	93,250	20,214	16,154	20,599	18,481
93,250	93,300	20,228	16,166	20,613	18,494
93,300	93,350	20,242	16,179	20,627	18,506
93,350	93,400	20,256	16,191	20,641	18,519
93,400	93,450	20,270	16,204	20,655	18,531
93,450	93,500	20,284	16,216	20,669	18,544
93,500	93,550	20,298	16,229	20,683	18,556
93,550	93,600	20,312	16,241	20,697	18,569
93,600	93,650	20,326	16,254	20,711	18,581
93,650	93,700	20,340	16,266	20,725	18,594
93,700	93,750	20,354	16,279	20,739	18,606
93,750	93,800	20,368	16,291	20,753	18,619
93,800	93,850	20,382	16,304	20,767	18,631
93,850	93,900	20,396	16,316	20,781	18,644
93,900	93,950	20,410	16,329	20,795	18,656
93,950	94,000	20,424	16,341	20,809	18,669
94,000					
94,000	94,050	20,438	16,354	20,823	18,681
94,050	94,100	20,452	16,366	20,837	18,694
94,100	94,150	20,466	16,379	20,851	18,706
94,150	94,200	20,480	16,391	20,865	18,719
94,200	94,250	20,494	16,404	20,879	18,731
94,250	94,300	20,508	16,416	20,893	18,744
94,300	94,350	20,522	16,429	20,907	18,756
94,350	94,400	20,536	16,441	20,921	18,769
94,400	94,450	20,550	16,454	20,935	18,781
94,450	94,500	20,564	16,466	20,949	18,794
94,500	94,550	20,578	16,479	20,963	18,806
94,550	94,600	20,592	16,491	20,977	18,819
94,600	94,650	20,606	16,504	20,991	18,831
94,650	94,700	20,620	16,516	21,005	18,844
94,700	94,750	20,634	16,529	21,019	18,856
94,750	94,800	20,648	16,541	21,033	18,869
94,800	94,850	20,662	16,554	21,047	18,881
94,850	94,900	20,676	16,566	21,061	18,894
94,900	94,950	20,690	16,579	21,075	18,906
94,950	95,000	20,704	16,591	21,089	18,919

*This column must also be used by a qualifying widow(er).

(Continued on next page)

2007 Tax Table–*Continued*

If line 43 (taxable income) is—		And you are—			
At least	But less than	Single	Married filing jointly *	Married filing separately	Head of a house-hold
			Your tax is—		

95,000

At least	But less than	Single	MFJ *	MFS	HoH
95,000	95,050	20,718	16,604	21,103	18,931
95,050	95,100	20,732	16,616	21,117	18,944
95,100	95,150	20,746	16,629	21,131	18,956
95,150	95,200	20,760	16,641	21,145	18,969
95,200	95,250	20,774	16,654	21,159	18,981
95,250	95,300	20,788	16,666	21,173	18,994
95,300	95,350	20,802	16,679	21,187	19,006
95,350	95,400	20,816	16,691	21,201	19,019
95,400	95,450	20,830	16,704	21,215	19,031
95,450	95,500	20,844	16,716	21,229	19,044
95,500	95,550	20,858	16,729	21,243	19,056
95,550	95,600	20,872	16,741	21,257	19,069
95,600	95,650	20,886	16,754	21,271	19,081
95,650	95,700	20,900	16,766	21,285	19,094
95,700	95,750	20,914	16,779	21,299	19,106
95,750	95,800	20,928	16,791	21,313	19,119
95,800	95,850	20,942	16,804	21,327	19,131
95,850	95,900	20,956	16,816	21,341	19,144
95,900	95,950	20,970	16,829	21,355	19,156
95,950	96,000	20,984	16,841	21,369	19,169

96,000

At least	But less than	Single	MFJ *	MFS	HoH
96,000	96,050	20,998	16,854	21,383	19,181
96,050	96,100	21,012	16,866	21,397	19,194
96,100	96,150	21,026	16,879	21,411	19,206
96,150	96,200	21,040	16,891	21,425	19,219
96,200	96,250	21,054	16,904	21,439	19,231
96,250	96,300	21,068	16,916	21,453	19,244
96,300	96,350	21,082	16,929	21,467	19,256
96,350	96,400	21,096	16,941	21,481	19,269
96,400	96,450	21,110	16,954	21,495	19,281
96,450	96,500	21,124	16,966	21,509	19,294
96,500	96,550	21,138	16,979	21,523	19,306
96,550	96,600	21,152	16,991	21,537	19,319
96,600	96,650	21,166	17,004	21,551	19,331
96,650	96,700	21,180	17,016	21,565	19,344
96,700	96,750	21,194	17,029	21,579	19,356
96,750	96,800	21,208	17,041	21,593	19,369
96,800	96,850	21,222	17,054	21,607	19,381
96,850	96,900	21,236	17,066	21,621	19,394
96,900	96,950	21,250	17,079	21,635	19,406
96,950	97,000	21,264	17,091	21,649	19,419

97,000

At least	But less than	Single	MFJ *	MFS	HoH
97,000	97,050	21,278	17,104	21,663	19,431
97,050	97,100	21,292	17,116	21,677	19,444
97,100	97,150	21,306	17,129	21,691	19,456
97,150	97,200	21,320	17,141	21,705	19,469
97,200	97,250	21,334	17,154	21,719	19,481
97,250	97,300	21,348	17,166	21,733	19,494
97,300	97,350	21,362	17,179	21,747	19,506
97,350	97,400	21,376	17,191	21,761	19,519
97,400	97,450	21,390	17,204	21,775	19,531
97,450	97,500	21,404	17,216	21,789	19,544
97,500	97,550	21,418	17,229	21,803	19,556
97,550	97,600	21,432	17,241	21,817	19,569
97,600	97,650	21,446	17,254	21,831	19,581
97,650	97,700	21,460	17,266	21,845	19,594
97,700	97,750	21,474	17,279	21,859	19,606
97,750	97,800	21,488	17,291	21,873	19,619
97,800	97,850	21,502	17,304	21,887	19,631
97,850	97,900	21,516	17,316	21,901	19,644
97,900	97,950	21,530	17,329	21,915	19,656
97,950	98,000	21,544	17,341	21,932	19,669

98,000

At least	But less than	Single	MFJ *	MFS	HoH
98,000	98,050	21,558	17,354	21,948	19,681
98,050	98,100	21,572	17,366	21,965	19,694
98,100	98,150	21,586	17,379	21,981	19,706
98,150	98,200	21,600	17,391	21,998	19,719
98,200	98,250	21,614	17,404	22,014	19,731
98,250	98,300	21,628	17,416	22,031	19,744
98,300	98,350	21,642	17,429	22,047	19,756
98,350	98,400	21,656	17,441	22,064	19,769
98,400	98,450	21,670	17,454	22,080	19,781
98,450	98,500	21,684	17,466	22,097	19,794
98,500	98,550	21,698	17,479	22,113	19,806
98,550	98,600	21,712	17,491	22,130	19,819
98,600	98,650	21,726	17,504	22,146	19,831
98,650	98,700	21,740	17,516	22,163	19,844
98,700	98,750	21,754	17,529	22,179	19,856
98,750	98,800	21,768	17,541	22,196	19,869
98,800	98,850	21,782	17,554	22,212	19,881
98,850	98,900	21,796	17,566	22,229	19,894
98,900	98,950	21,810	17,579	22,245	19,906
98,950	99,000	21,824	17,591	22,262	19,919

99,000

At least	But less than	Single	MFJ *	MFS	HoH
99,000	99,050	21,838	17,604	22,278	19,931
99,050	99,100	21,852	17,616	22,295	19,944
99,100	99,150	21,866	17,629	22,311	19,956
99,150	99,200	21,880	17,641	22,328	19,969
99,200	99,250	21,894	17,654	22,344	19,981
99,250	99,300	21,908	17,666	22,361	19,994
99,300	99,350	21,922	17,679	22,377	20,006
99,350	99,400	21,936	17,691	22,394	20,019
99,400	99,450	21,950	17,704	22,410	20,031
99,450	99,500	21,964	17,716	22,427	20,044
99,500	99,550	21,978	17,729	22,443	20,056
99,550	99,600	21,992	17,741	22,460	20,069
99,600	99,650	22,006	17,754	22,476	20,081
99,650	99,700	22,020	17,766	22,493	20,094
99,700	99,750	22,034	17,779	22,509	20,106
99,750	99,800	22,048	17,791	22,526	20,119
99,800	99,850	22,062	17,804	22,542	20,131
99,850	99,900	22,076	17,816	22,559	20,144
99,900	99,950	22,090	17,829	22,575	20,156
99,950	100,000	22,104	17,841	22,592	20,169

$100,000
or over —
use the
Tax Rate
Schedules
on page A-2

*This column must also be used by a qualifying widow(er)

2007 Optional Sales Tax Tables

When Used. The election to deduct state and local general sales taxes requires that the taxpayer forgo any deduction for state and local income taxes. Whether this is advisable or not depends on a comparison of the amounts involved. In making the choice, however, the outcome could be influenced by the additional sales tax incurred due to any "big ticket" purchases that were made. For example, a taxpayer who chose to deduct state and local income taxes for 2006 might well prefer the sales tax deduction in 2007 if a new family automobile was purchased during the year. To make the sales tax election, the taxpayer must enter the amount on Schedule A, line 5, with the notation "**ST**" on the dotted line to the left of the line 5 entry space.

If the sales tax election is made, the amount of the deduction can be determined by use of the *actual expense method* or the *optional sales tax tables* issued by the IRS. The actual expense method can be used only when the taxpayer has actual receipts to support the deduction claimed. In the absence of receipts, the usual case with most taxpayers, resorting to the optional sales tax tables is necessary. Under neither method, however, is the purchase of items used in a taxpayer's trade or business to be considered.

Adjustments Necessary. The optional sales tax tables are based on a number of assumptions that require adjustments to be made. As the starting point for the use of the tables is AGI, nontaxable receipts have not been included. Examples of receipts that should be added include: tax-exempt interest, veterans' benefits, nontaxable combat pay, public assistance payments, workers' compensation, nontaxable Social Security and other retirement benefits. But do not include any large nontaxable items that are not likely to be spent. For example, a $100,000 inheritance should not be added if it was invested in a certificate of deposit.

The tables represent the sales tax on the average (and recurring) expenditures based on level of income by family size and do not include exceptional purchases. Therefore, add to the table amount any sales taxes on major purchases (such as motor vehicles, aircraft, boats, and home building materials, etc.).

When the optional sales tax tables are utilized, special adjustments may be needed when a taxpayer has lived in more than one taxing jurisdiction (e.g., state, county, city) during the year. The adjustments involve apportionment of taxes based on days involved and are illustrated in IRS Publication 600 (*State and Local General Sales Taxes*), pages 3 and 4.

Local Sales Taxes. Local sales taxes (i.e., those imposed by counties, cities, transit authorities) may or may not require a separate determination. In those states where they are not imposed (such as Connecticut, Hawaii, Indiana, and others), no further computations are necessary. This is also the case where the local taxes are uniform and are incorporated into the state sales tax table (Virginia). In other situations, another step is necessary to arrive at the optional sales tax table deduction. Depending on where the taxpayer lives, one of two procedures needs to be used. In one procedure, the local sales tax is arrived at by using the **state table** amount—see the Example 1 worksheet. In the other procedure, special **local tables** issued by the IRS for enumerated state and local jurisdictions are modified (if necessary) and used—see the Example 2 worksheet.

Use Illustrated.

EXAMPLE 1 The Archers file a joint return for 2007 reflecting AGI of $88,000 and claiming three exemptions. They have tax-exempt interest of $3,000, and during the year they incurred sales tax of $1,650 on the purchase of an automobile for their dependent teenage son. They live in Bellaire, Texas, where the general sales tax rates are 6.25% for state and 2% for local. Since the IRS *has not issued* optional local sales tax tables for Texas, use the Worksheet below to arrive at the Archers' general sales tax deduction of $3,114.

Sales Tax Deduction Worksheet
(To be used when *no* IRS Optional Local Sales Tax Table Available)

Adjusted Gross Income (AGI) as listed on line 38 of Form 1040	$88,000
Add nontaxable items	3,000
Table income to be used for purposes of line 1 below	$91,000

1. Use table income to determine table amount—go to state of residence and find applicable range of table income and exemption column* for *state* sales tax		$ 1,109
2a. Enter local general sales tax rate	2.0	
2b. Enter state general sales tax rate	6.25	
2c. Divide 2a by 2b	0.32	
2d. Multiply line 1 by line 2c for the local sales tax		355
3. Enter general sales tax on large purchases		1,650
4. Deduction for general sales tax (add lines 1 + 2d + 3) and report on line 5 of Schedule A of Form 1040		$ 3,114

*Use total of personal and dependency exemptions as reported in item 6d of Form 1040.

EXAMPLE 2 The Hardys file a joint return for 2007, reporting AGI of $40,000 and claiming four exemptions (two personal and two dependency). They received $30,000 in nontaxable pension benefits. Although the Hardys do not keep sales tax receipts, they can prove that they paid $4,800 in sales tax on the purchase of a new RV in 2007. The Hardys are residents of Paulding County, Georgia, and live in a jurisdiction that imposes a 2% local sales tax. Since the IRS *has issued* optional local sales tax tables for Georgia, use the Worksheet below to arrive at the Hardys' general sales tax deduction of $5,799.

Sales Tax Deduction Worksheet
[To be used for Alaska, Arizona, Arkansas (Texarkana), California (Los Angeles County), Colorado, Georgia, Illinois, Louisiana, New York State, and North Carolina]

Adjusted Gross Income (AGI) as listed on line 38 of Form 1040	$40,000
Add nontaxable income	30,000
Table income to be used for purpose of line 1 below	$70,000

1. Use the table income to determine *state* sales tax amount—go to table for state of residence and find applicable income range and exemption column*		$ 587
2a. Enter local general sales tax rate	2.0	
2b. Enter IRS *local* sales tax table amount (based on 1%)	$206	
2c. Multiply line 2b by 2a for the local sales tax		412
3. Enter general sales tax on large purchases		4,800
4. Deduction for general sales tax (add lines 1 + 2c + 3) and report on line 5 of Schedule A of Form 1040		$ 5,799

*Use total of personal and dependency exemptions as reported in item 6d of Form 1040

2007 Optional State and Certain Local Sales Tax Tables

Alabama 4.0000%

Income: At least	Income: But less than	Exemptions: 1	2	3	4	5	Over 5
$0	$20,000	199	249	283	311	335	368
20,000	30,000	300	374	425	466	501	550
30,000	40,000	351	436	496	543	583	641
40,000	50,000	395	490	556	609	654	717
50,000	60,000	434	538	610	668	716	786
60,000	70,000	469	581	659	721	773	848
70,000	80,000	503	622	705	771	827	906
80,000	90,000	534	660	748	818	876	960
90,000	100,000	564	696	788	862	923	1011
100,000	120,000	603	744	842	919	985	1078
120,000	140,000	657	809	915	999	1070	1170
140,000	160,000	704	866	979	1068	1144	1251
160,000	180,000	751	923	1043	1138	1217	1331
180,000	200,000	794	975	1101	1200	1284	1403
200,000 or more		1010	1236	1392	1515	1619	1766

Arizona 5.6000%

Income: At least	Income: But less than	Exemptions: 1	2	3	4	5	Over 5
$0	$20,000	208	245	270	289	304	326
20,000	30,000	345	406	446	478	504	540
30,000	40,000	417	491	539	577	608	651
40,000	50,000	480	565	621	664	699	749
50,000	60,000	538	632	695	743	782	838
60,000	70,000	591	694	763	815	859	919
70,000	80,000	642	753	828	885	932	997
80,000	90,000	689	809	888	950	1000	1070
90,000	100,000	735	862	946	1011	1065	1140
100,000	120,000	795	932	1023	1094	1151	1232
120,000	140,000	879	1030	1130	1208	1271	1360
140,000	160,000	953	1116	1225	1309	1377	1473
160,000	180,000	1027	1203	1320	1410	1484	1587
180,000	200,000	1095	1283	1407	1502	1581	1691
200,000 or more		1443	1688	1850	1974	2077	2219

Arkansas 6.0000%

Income: At least	Income: But less than	Exemptions: 1	2	3	4	5	Over 5
$0	$20,000	310	376	421	456	485	526
20,000	30,000	486	587	656	710	755	819
30,000	40,000	576	694	775	838	891	966
40,000	50,000	652	786	877	948	1008	1091
50,000	60,000	721	868	968	1046	1111	1204
60,000	70,000	783	942	1051	1135	1206	1306
70,000	80,000	842	1013	1129	1220	1295	1402
80,000	90,000	897	1078	1201	1297	1378	1491
90,000	100,000	949	1140	1270	1371	1456	1575
100,000	120,000	1017	1221	1360	1468	1558	1686
120,000	140,000	1111	1333	1483	1601	1699	1837
140,000	160,000	1193	1430	1591	1717	1822	1969
160,000	180,000	1275	1527	1699	1832	1944	2101
180,000	200,000	1349	1615	1796	1937	2054	2220
200,000 or more		1719	2053	2279	2456	2603	2811

California[1] 7.2500%

Income: At least	Income: But less than	Exemptions: 1	2	3	4	5	Over 5
$0	$20,000	248	292	321	344	363	389
20,000	30,000	413	486	534	572	603	645
30,000	40,000	501	588	647	692	729	780
40,000	50,000	577	678	745	797	839	899
50,000	60,000	647	760	835	892	940	1006
60,000	70,000	712	835	917	981	1033	1105
70,000	80,000	774	907	996	1065	1121	1200
80,000	90,000	831	975	1070	1144	1204	1288
90,000	100,000	887	1039	1141	1219	1283	1373
100,000	120,000	960	1125	1235	1319	1388	1485
120,000	140,000	1062	1244	1365	1458	1535	1641
140,000	160,000	1153	1350	1481	1581	1664	1779
160,000	180,000	1244	1456	1597	1705	1794	1918
180,000	200,000	1328	1553	1703	1818	1913	2045
200,000 or more		1755	2050	2246	2396	2520	2692

Colorado 2.9000%

Income: At least	Income: But less than	Exemptions: 1	2	3	4	5	Over 5
$0	$20,000	95	113	124	134	141	152
20,000	30,000	156	185	204	219	231	248
30,000	40,000	188	223	246	264	278	299
40,000	50,000	217	256	282	302	319	343
50,000	60,000	242	286	315	338	357	383
60,000	70,000	266	314	346	371	391	419
70,000	80,000	289	340	375	402	424	454
80,000	90,000	310	365	402	431	454	487
90,000	100,000	330	389	428	459	484	519
100,000	120,000	357	420	463	496	522	560
120,000	140,000	394	464	511	547	576	618
140,000	160,000	428	503	553	592	624	669
160,000	180,000	461	542	596	638	672	720
180,000	200,000	491	578	635	679	716	767
200,000 or more		648	760	834	892	939	1005

Connecticut 6.0000%

Income: At least	Income: But less than	Exemptions: 1	2	3	4	5	Over 5
$0	$20,000	210	241	261	277	290	307
20,000	30,000	348	399	433	458	479	508
30,000	40,000	421	482	522	553	578	612
40,000	50,000	484	554	600	635	664	703
50,000	60,000	541	619	671	710	741	785
60,000	70,000	594	679	735	778	813	861
70,000	80,000	644	736	797	843	880	933
80,000	90,000	690	789	854	903	944	999
90,000	100,000	735	840	909	961	1004	1063
100,000	120,000	793	907	981	1037	1083	1147
120,000	140,000	875	999	1081	1143	1193	1263
140,000	160,000	946	1081	1168	1235	1290	1365
160,000	180,000	1018	1162	1256	1328	1387	1467
180,000	200,000	1083	1236	1336	1412	1474	1560
200,000 or more		1412	1610	1739	1837	1917	2028

District of Columbia 5.7500%

Income: At least	Income: But less than	Exemptions: 1	2	3	4	5	Over 5
$0	$20,000	176	204	223	238	250	266
20,000	30,000	292	339	370	393	413	440
30,000	40,000	354	410	447	475	498	531
40,000	50,000	408	472	514	546	573	610
50,000	60,000	456	528	575	611	641	682
60,000	70,000	501	580	631	671	703	748
70,000	80,000	544	629	685	728	763	811
80,000	90,000	585	675	735	781	818	870
90,000	100,000	623	719	783	832	871	927
100,000	120,000	674	778	847	899	942	1001
120,000	140,000	744	859	935	992	1039	1105
140,000	160,000	807	931	1012	1074	1125	1196
160,000	180,000	870	1003	1090	1157	1212	1288
180,000	200,000	927	1068	1161	1232	1291	1371
200,000 or more		1219	1403	1523	1616	1691	1796

Florida 6.0000%

Income: At least	Income: But less than	Exemptions: 1	2	3	4	5	Over 5
$0	$20,000	217	261	290	314	333	360
20,000	30,000	355	426	474	511	542	585
30,000	40,000	428	512	570	614	651	703
40,000	50,000	491	588	653	703	746	805
50,000	60,000	549	656	728	785	831	897
60,000	70,000	602	719	798	859	911	982
70,000	80,000	653	779	864	931	986	1063
80,000	90,000	700	835	926	997	1056	1139
90,000	100,000	745	888	985	1061	1123	1211
100,000	120,000	805	959	1064	1145	1212	1306
120,000	140,000	888	1058	1172	1261	1335	1438
140,000	160,000	962	1145	1268	1364	1444	1555
160,000	180,000	1036	1232	1365	1468	1553	1672
180,000	200,000	1104	1312	1453	1562	1652	1779
200,000 or more		1449	1719	1901	2042	2158	2322

Georgia 4.0000%

Income: At least	Income: But less than	Exemptions: 1	2	3	4	5	Over 5
$0	$20,000	143	168	184	197	207	221
20,000	30,000	235	274	301	321	338	361
30,000	40,000	283	330	362	386	406	434
40,000	50,000	324	379	415	443	466	497
50,000	60,000	363	423	463	494	520	555
60,000	70,000	398	464	508	542	569	608
70,000	80,000	431	503	550	587	617	658
80,000	90,000	462	539	590	629	661	706
90,000	100,000	492	574	628	669	703	751
100,000	120,000	532	620	678	723	759	810
120,000	140,000	587	684	748	797	837	893
140,000	160,000	636	740	810	863	906	967
160,000	180,000	685	797	872	928	975	1040
180,000	200,000	730	849	928	988	1038	1107
200,000 or more		958	1114	1216	1295	1359	1449

Hawaii 4.0000%

Income: At least	Income: But less than	Exemptions: 1	2	3	4	5	Over 5
$0	$20,000	232	284	320	348	371	405
20,000	30,000	359	438	493	536	572	622
30,000	40,000	424	516	580	630	672	731
40,000	50,000	478	582	654	710	757	823
50,000	60,000	528	641	720	781	833	906
60,000	70,000	572	695	780	846	902	980
70,000	80,000	614	746	836	907	966	1051
80,000	90,000	653	792	888	963	1026	1115
90,000	100,000	690	837	937	1017	1083	1177
100,000	120,000	738	895	1002	1087	1157	1257
120,000	140,000	805	974	1091	1182	1259	1367
140,000	160,000	863	1044	1168	1266	1347	1463
160,000	180,000	920	1113	1245	1349	1435	1558
180,000	200,000	972	1175	1314	1423	1515	1644
200,000 or more		1232	1485	1658	1794	1908	2069

Idaho 6.0000%

Income: At least	Income: But less than	Exemptions: 1	2	3	4	5	Over 5
$0	$20,000	300	373	423	464	498	546
20,000	30,000	457	566	642	702	753	825
30,000	40,000	537	663	752	821	880	964
40,000	50,000	605	747	845	923	989	1082
50,000	60,000	666	821	929	1014	1086	1188
60,000	70,000	721	889	1005	1097	1174	1284
70,000	80,000	774	953	1077	1175	1257	1374
80,000	90,000	823	1012	1143	1247	1334	1458
90,000	100,000	869	1068	1206	1315	1407	1537
100,000	120,000	931	1143	1290	1406	1503	1642
120,000	140,000	1015	1245	1404	1529	1635	1785
140,000	160,000	1089	1334	1504	1638	1750	1910
160,000	180,000	1163	1424	1604	1746	1865	2035
180,000	200,000	1231	1505	1694	1844	1969	2147
200,000 or more		1570	1912	2149	2335	2491	2712

Illinois 6.2500%

Income: At least	Income: But less than	Exemptions: 1	2	3	4	5	Over 5
$0	$20,000	246	292	323	346	366	394
20,000	30,000	400	474	523	561	592	636
30,000	40,000	480	568	627	672	710	762
40,000	50,000	550	650	717	769	812	872
50,000	60,000	613	725	799	857	905	971
60,000	70,000	671	793	875	938	989	1062
70,000	80,000	727	858	946	1014	1070	1149
80,000	90,000	779	919	1013	1086	1146	1229
90,000	100,000	828	977	1077	1154	1218	1306
100,000	120,000	894	1054	1162	1245	1313	1408
120,000	140,000	985	1161	1279	1370	1445	1550
140,000	160,000	1065	1255	1382	1480	1561	1674
160,000	180,000	1146	1350	1486	1591	1678	1799
180,000	200,000	1219	1436	1581	1692	1784	1913
200,000 or more		1595	1875	2063	2207	2326	2492

Indiana 6.0000%

Income: At least	Income: But less than	Exemptions: 1	2	3	4	5	Over 5
$0	$20,000	230	272	301	322	340	365
20,000	30,000	373	440	485	519	548	588
30,000	40,000	447	527	580	621	655	702
40,000	50,000	511	602	662	709	748	802
50,000	60,000	569	670	737	789	831	891
60,000	70,000	622	732	805	862	908	973
70,000	80,000	673	791	870	931	981	1051
80,000	90,000	720	846	930	995	1049	1123
90,000	100,000	765	899	988	1056	1113	1192
100,000	120,000	824	968	1064	1137	1198	1283
120,000	140,000	906	1064	1169	1249	1316	1409
140,000	160,000	979	1148	1261	1348	1419	1519
160,000	180,000	1051	1232	1353	1446	1523	1630
180,000	200,000	1117	1309	1437	1536	1617	1730
200,000 or more		1450	1697	1861	1987	2091	2236

Iowa 5.0000%

Income: At least	Income: But less than	Exemptions: 1	2	3	4	5	Over 5
$0	$20,000	208	245	269	288	304	325
20,000	30,000	340	399	438	468	493	528
30,000	40,000	408	478	525	561	591	632
40,000	50,000	467	547	601	642	675	723
50,000	60,000	520	609	669	714	752	804
60,000	70,000	569	666	731	781	821	878
70,000	80,000	616	720	790	843	888	949
80,000	90,000	659	771	845	902	949	1015
90,000	100,000	700	818	897	958	1008	1077
100,000	120,000	754	882	966	1031	1085	1160
120,000	140,000	829	969	1062	1133	1191	1273
140,000	160,000	895	1045	1145	1222	1285	1373
160,000	180,000	961	1122	1229	1311	1379	1473
180,000	200,000	1021	1191	1305	1392	1463	1563
200,000 or more		1323	1541	1686	1798	1889	2017

Kansas 5.3000%

Income: At least	Income: But less than	Exemptions: 1	2	3	4	5	Over 5
$0	$20,000	287	352	398	434	464	507
20,000	30,000	443	543	612	666	711	776
30,000	40,000	522	638	719	782	835	910
40,000	50,000	589	720	810	881	940	1025
50,000	60,000	650	793	891	969	1034	1127
60,000	70,000	705	859	965	1049	1119	1219
70,000	80,000	756	921	1035	1124	1199	1306
80,000	90,000	804	979	1099	1194	1273	1386
90,000	100,000	849	1033	1160	1259	1343	1462
100,000	120,000	909	1105	1240	1346	1435	1561
120,000	140,000	991	1203	1349	1464	1560	1697
140,000	160,000	1062	1288	1444	1567	1670	1816
160,000	180,000	1133	1374	1539	1670	1779	1933
180,000	200,000	1197	1450	1625	1762	1877	2039
200,000 or more		1517	1833	2050	2220	2363	2565

Kentucky 6.0000%

Income: At least	Income: But less than	Exemptions: 1	2	3	4	5	Over 5
$0	$20,000	218	257	283	303	320	343
20,000	30,000	352	415	456	488	514	551
30,000	40,000	422	497	546	584	616	659
40,000	50,000	483	568	624	668	703	753
50,000	60,000	539	633	695	743	783	838
60,000	70,000	590	692	760	813	856	916
70,000	80,000	638	749	822	879	925	990
80,000	90,000	684	802	880	941	990	1060
90,000	100,000	727	852	935	999	1052	1126
100,000	120,000	784	919	1009	1078	1134	1213
120,000	140,000	864	1012	1110	1186	1248	1334
140,000	160,000	934	1094	1200	1281	1348	1441
160,000	180,000	1005	1176	1290	1377	1449	1549
180,000	200,000	1070	1251	1372	1464	1540	1647
200,000 or more		1399	1634	1790	1909	2007	2144

Louisiana 4.0000%

Income: At least	Income: But less than	Exemptions: 1	2	3	4	5	Over 5
$0	$20,000	160	186	203	217	227	243
20,000	30,000	263	306	334	356	373	398
30,000	40,000	317	368	402	428	449	479
40,000	50,000	364	423	461	491	515	549
50,000	60,000	407	472	515	548	575	613
60,000	70,000	446	517	564	600	630	671
70,000	80,000	483	561	611	650	682	726
80,000	90,000	518	601	655	697	731	778
90,000	100,000	551	639	697	741	777	827
100,000	120,000	596	690	752	800	839	893
120,000	140,000	656	760	828	880	923	983
140,000	160,000	710	822	895	952	998	1062
160,000	180,000	764	884	963	1023	1073	1142
180,000	200,000	813	940	1024	1088	1141	1214
200,000 or more		1061	1226	1334	1417	1485	1579

Maine 5.0000%

Income: At least	Income: But less than	Exemptions: 1	2	3	4	5	Over 5
$0	$20,000	145	171	188	202	213	228
20,000	30,000	241	284	312	334	352	377
30,000	40,000	292	343	377	403	425	455
40,000	50,000	337	395	434	464	489	523
50,000	60,000	378	443	487	520	548	586
60,000	70,000	416	487	535	571	602	644
70,000	80,000	452	529	581	621	653	699
80,000	90,000	486	569	624	667	702	750
90,000	100,000	518	607	665	711	748	800
100,000	120,000	561	657	720	769	809	865
120,000	140,000	621	727	797	851	895	957
140,000	160,000	675	789	865	923	971	1038
160,000	180,000	729	852	933	996	1047	1119
180,000	200,000	778	909	996	1062	1117	1194
200,000 or more		1032	1203	1317	1404	1476	1576

Maryland 5.0000%

Income: At least	Income: But less than	Exemptions: 1	2	3	4	5	Over 5
$0	$20,000	186	218	239	256	269	288
20,000	30,000	308	361	396	423	445	475
30,000	40,000	372	436	478	510	537	574
40,000	50,000	428	501	549	586	617	659
50,000	60,000	479	560	614	656	690	737
60,000	70,000	526	615	674	719	756	808
70,000	80,000	571	667	731	780	820	876
80,000	90,000	612	716	784	836	880	940
90,000	100,000	652	762	835	890	936	1000
100,000	120,000	705	823	902	962	1012	1081
120,000	140,000	778	908	995	1061	1116	1192
140,000	160,000	842	984	1077	1149	1208	1290
160,000	180,000	907	1059	1160	1237	1300	1388
180,000	200,000	966	1128	1235	1317	1384	1478
200,000 or more		1267	1477	1616	1723	1811	1932

Massachusetts 5.0000%

Income: At least	Income: But less than	Exemptions: 1	2	3	4	5	Over 5
$0	$20,000	161	187	204	217	228	242
20,000	30,000	266	308	336	358	375	399
30,000	40,000	322	372	406	431	452	481
40,000	50,000	370	428	467	496	520	553
50,000	60,000	415	479	522	555	581	619
60,000	70,000	455	527	573	609	638	679
70,000	80,000	494	571	622	661	692	736
80,000	90,000	531	613	668	709	743	790
90,000	100,000	566	654	711	755	791	841
100,000	120,000	612	707	769	816	855	909
120,000	140,000	677	781	849	901	944	1003
140,000	160,000	734	846	920	977	1023	1087
160,000	180,000	792	912	992	1052	1102	1171
180,000	200,000	844	973	1057	1121	1174	1247
200,000 or more		1113	1280	1390	1474	1543	1638

Michigan 6.0000%

Income: At least	Income: But less than	Exemptions: 1	2	3	4	5	Over 5
$0	$20,000	224	261	286	305	320	341
20,000	30,000	373	434	474	505	531	566
30,000	40,000	452	525	574	611	641	683
40,000	50,000	520	605	660	703	738	786
50,000	60,000	583	677	739	787	826	880
60,000	70,000	640	744	812	864	907	966
70,000	80,000	695	807	881	938	984	1049
80,000	90,000	747	867	946	1007	1057	1126
90,000	100,000	796	924	1008	1073	1126	1199
100,000	120,000	861	1000	1091	1160	1218	1297
120,000	140,000	952	1105	1205	1282	1345	1432
140,000	160,000	1032	1198	1306	1389	1457	1552
160,000	180,000	1113	1291	1408	1498	1571	1672
180,000	200,000	1187	1376	1501	1596	1674	1782
200,000 or more		1565	1812	1975	2099	2201	2343

Minnesota 6.5000%

Income: At least	Income: But less than	Exemptions: 1	2	3	4	5	Over 5
$0	$20,000	209	241	262	278	292	310
20,000	30,000	354	408	443	469	491	522
30,000	40,000	431	496	538	570	597	633
40,000	50,000	498	573	621	658	689	731
50,000	60,000	560	643	697	739	773	820
60,000	70,000	616	707	767	813	850	902
70,000	80,000	670	769	834	883	924	980
80,000	90,000	721	827	896	949	993	1053
90,000	100,000	769	882	956	1012	1059	1122
100,000	120,000	833	955	1035	1096	1146	1215
120,000	140,000	922	1057	1145	1212	1267	1343
140,000	160,000	1000	1146	1242	1314	1374	1456
160,000	180,000	1079	1236	1339	1417	1481	1570
180,000	200,000	1151	1318	1428	1511	1579	1673
200,000 or more		1518	1736	1878	1987	2076	2198

Mississippi 7.0000%

Income: At least	Income: But less than	Exemptions: 1	2	3	4	5	Over 5
$0	$20,000	387	473	533	579	619	674
20,000	30,000	598	729	819	890	950	1034
30,000	40,000	704	857	963	1045	1115	1213
40,000	50,000	795	967	1085	1178	1255	1365
50,000	60,000	877	1065	1194	1296	1381	1501
60,000	70,000	950	1154	1293	1403	1495	1624
70,000	80,000	1020	1237	1386	1503	1601	1740
80,000	90,000	1085	1315	1472	1597	1700	1847
90,000	100,000	1146	1388	1554	1685	1794	1948
100,000	120,000	1226	1484	1661	1800	1916	2081
120,000	140,000	1336	1616	1808	1958	2084	2262
140,000	160,000	1432	1731	1935	2096	2230	2420
160,000	180,000	1528	1845	2062	2233	2376	2577
180,000	200,000	1614	1948	2177	2356	2506	2719
200,000 or more		2045	2461	2746	2970	3156	3420

Missouri 4.2250%

Income: At least	Income: But less than	Exemptions: 1	2	3	4	5	Over 5
$0	$20,000	160	194	218	236	252	274
20,000	30,000	255	309	346	375	399	433
30,000	40,000	304	368	412	446	474	514
40,000	50,000	347	419	469	507	540	585
50,000	60,000	386	466	520	563	598	649
60,000	70,000	421	508	568	614	652	707
70,000	80,000	455	549	612	662	704	762
80,000	90,000	487	586	654	707	751	814
90,000	100,000	517	622	694	750	797	863
100,000	120,000	557	670	747	807	857	927
120,000	140,000	612	736	820	885	940	1017
140,000	160,000	661	794	884	955	1013	1096
160,000	180,000	710	852	949	1024	1087	1175
180,000	200,000	755	905	1007	1087	1153	1247
200,000 or more		983	1175	1305	1407	1491	1610

Nebraska 5.5000%

Income: At least	Income: But less than	Exemptions: 1	2	3	4	5	Over 5
$0	$20,000	230	266	290	307	322	342
20,000	30,000	381	439	478	507	531	564
30,000	40,000	459	530	576	611	640	680
40,000	50,000	527	608	661	701	734	780
50,000	60,000	589	679	738	783	820	870
60,000	70,000	646	744	809	858	898	954
70,000	80,000	700	806	876	929	972	1033
80,000	90,000	750	864	938	995	1042	1106
90,000	100,000	798	919	998	1058	1108	1176
100,000	120,000	861	992	1077	1142	1195	1269
120,000	140,000	949	1092	1186	1257	1316	1397
140,000	160,000	1026	1180	1281	1359	1422	1509
160,000	180,000	1103	1269	1377	1460	1528	1621
180,000	200,000	1173	1349	1464	1552	1624	1723
200,000 or more		1527	1755	1904	2017	2110	2238

(Continued on next page)

2007 Optional State and Certain Local Sales Tax Tables *(Continued)*

Nevada[2] 6.5000%

Income: At least	But less than	Exemptions 1	2	3	4	5	Over 5
$0	$20,000	242	281	307	327	343	366
20,000	30,000	398	462	504	536	563	600
30,000	40,000	479	557	607	646	678	722
40,000	50,000	551	639	697	742	778	829
50,000	60,000	616	714	779	829	870	926
60,000	70,000	676	784	855	909	953	1015
70,000	80,000	733	850	927	985	1033	1100
80,000	90,000	786	911	994	1057	1108	1180
90,000	100,000	837	970	1058	1125	1180	1256
100,000	120,000	905	1049	1143	1215	1274	1356
120,000	140,000	999	1157	1261	1341	1406	1496
140,000	160,000	1082	1253	1366	1452	1522	1619
160,000	180,000	1166	1350	1471	1563	1639	1743
180,000	200,000	1243	1438	1566	1665	1745	1856
200,000 or more		1633	1888	2055	2183	2288	2433

New Jersey[4] 7.0000%

Income: At least	But less than	Exemptions 1	2	3	4	5	Over 5
$0	$20,000	252	290	315	334	350	371
20,000	30,000	416	478	518	549	575	610
30,000	40,000	501	576	624	662	692	734
40,000	50,000	576	661	716	759	793	842
50,000	60,000	643	737	799	847	885	939
60,000	70,000	705	808	876	927	969	1028
70,000	80,000	763	875	948	1004	1049	1112
80,000	90,000	818	937	1015	1075	1124	1191
90,000	100,000	870	997	1080	1143	1194	1266
100,000	120,000	939	1075	1164	1232	1288	1365
120,000	140,000	1034	1184	1282	1356	1417	1501
140,000	160,000	1118	1279	1385	1465	1531	1621
160,000	180,000	1202	1375	1488	1574	1644	1742
180,000	200,000	1278	1461	1581	1672	1747	1850
200,000 or more		1663	1899	2053	2170	2266	2399

New Mexico 5.0000%

Income: At least	But less than	Exemptions 1	2	3	4	5	Over 5
$0	$20,000	223	259	282	300	315	335
20,000	30,000	367	425	463	493	517	550
30,000	40,000	442	512	558	593	622	662
40,000	50,000	507	587	639	680	713	758
50,000	60,000	566	655	713	758	795	845
60,000	70,000	620	717	781	830	870	926
70,000	80,000	671	776	846	898	942	1001
80,000	90,000	719	832	905	962	1008	1072
90,000	100,000	765	884	962	1022	1071	1139
100,000	120,000	825	954	1038	1102	1155	1228
120,000	140,000	908	1049	1142	1213	1271	1351
140,000	160,000	981	1133	1233	1310	1372	1459
160,000	180,000	1055	1218	1325	1407	1474	1567
180,000	200,000	1121	1294	1408	1495	1566	1665
200,000 or more		1456	1680	1826	1938	2030	2157

New York 4.0000%

Income: At least	But less than	Exemptions 1	2	3	4	5	Over 5
$0	$20,000	144	166	180	191	200	212
20,000	30,000	238	274	297	315	329	349
30,000	40,000	287	330	358	379	397	421
40,000	50,000	330	379	411	435	455	482
50,000	60,000	369	423	459	486	508	538
60,000	70,000	404	464	502	532	556	590
70,000	80,000	438	502	544	576	602	638
80,000	90,000	470	538	583	617	645	684
90,000	100,000	500	572	620	656	686	727
100,000	120,000	539	618	669	708	740	784
120,000	140,000	594	680	736	779	814	862
140,000	160,000	643	735	796	842	879	932
160,000	180,000	691	790	855	904	945	1001
180,000	200,000	735	840	909	961	1004	1064
200,000 or more		956	1092	1181	1248	1304	1380

North Carolina 4.2500%

Income: At least	But less than	Exemptions 1	2	3	4	5	Over 5
$0	$20,000	171	202	223	239	252	271
20,000	30,000	278	328	362	388	409	439
30,000	40,000	334	394	434	465	490	526
40,000	50,000	383	451	496	531	560	601
50,000	60,000	427	502	553	592	624	669
60,000	70,000	467	549	605	647	682	731
70,000	80,000	505	594	654	700	737	790
80,000	90,000	541	636	699	748	789	845
90,000	100,000	575	676	743	795	838	898
100,000	120,000	620	728	801	857	903	967
120,000	140,000	682	801	880	942	992	1062
140,000	160,000	737	865	951	1016	1071	1146
160,000	180,000	792	929	1021	1091	1149	1231
180,000	200,000	842	987	1084	1159	1221	1307
200,000 or more		1094	1282	1407	1503	1582	1692

North Dakota 5.0000%

Income: At least	But less than	Exemptions 1	2	3	4	5	Over 5
$0	$20,000	183	218	242	260	275	296
20,000	30,000	302	358	396	425	449	483
30,000	40,000	364	431	476	511	540	581
40,000	50,000	418	495	547	587	620	666
50,000	60,000	468	553	611	655	692	743
60,000	70,000	513	607	670	718	758	814
70,000	80,000	557	658	726	778	822	882
80,000	90,000	598	706	778	834	881	945
90,000	100,000	637	752	829	888	937	1006
100,000	120,000	689	812	895	959	1012	1086
120,000	140,000	761	897	988	1058	1116	1197
140,000	160,000	825	972	1070	1145	1208	1295
160,000	180,000	890	1047	1152	1233	1300	1394
180,000	200,000	948	1115	1227	1313	1385	1484
200,000 or more		1250	1467	1611	1723	1815	1944

Ohio 5.5000%

Income: At least	But less than	Exemptions 1	2	3	4	5	Over 5
$0	$20,000	222	256	279	296	310	330
20,000	30,000	367	423	460	489	512	544
30,000	40,000	442	511	555	589	617	656
40,000	50,000	509	587	638	677	709	753
50,000	60,000	569	656	713	756	792	841
60,000	70,000	624	719	781	829	868	922
70,000	80,000	676	779	847	898	940	999
80,000	90,000	725	836	908	963	1008	1071
90,000	100,000	772	889	966	1025	1073	1139
100,000	120,000	834	960	1043	1106	1158	1229
120,000	140,000	920	1059	1150	1219	1276	1355
140,000	160,000	996	1146	1244	1319	1380	1465
160,000	180,000	1072	1233	1338	1419	1484	1575
180,000	200,000	1141	1312	1424	1509	1579	1676
200,000 or more		1491	1713	1858	1969	2059	2185

Oklahoma 4.5000%

Income: At least	But less than	Exemptions 1	2	3	4	5	Over 5
$0	$20,000	222	271	305	332	355	386
20,000	30,000	349	426	479	520	555	604
30,000	40,000	414	505	567	616	656	714
40,000	50,000	471	573	643	698	744	809
50,000	60,000	521	634	711	772	822	894
60,000	70,000	568	690	773	839	894	972
70,000	80,000	612	743	833	903	962	1045
80,000	90,000	653	792	888	962	1025	1113
90,000	100,000	692	839	940	1019	1085	1178
100,000	120,000	744	901	1009	1093	1164	1264
120,000	140,000	816	987	1104	1196	1273	1381
140,000	160,000	879	1062	1188	1286	1369	1485
160,000	180,000	942	1138	1272	1377	1464	1588
180,000	200,000	999	1206	1348	1459	1551	1682
200,000 or more		1291	1553	1732	1872	1989	2154

Pennsylvania 6.0000%

Income: At least	But less than	Exemptions 1	2	3	4	5	Over 5
$0	$20,000	199	229	248	263	275	292
20,000	30,000	335	384	416	441	461	489
30,000	40,000	406	466	505	535	559	593
40,000	50,000	469	538	583	617	645	684
50,000	60,000	526	603	653	692	723	766
60,000	70,000	579	663	718	760	795	842
70,000	80,000	629	721	780	826	863	914
80,000	90,000	676	774	838	887	927	982
90,000	100,000	721	825	893	945	988	1046
100,000	120,000	781	893	967	1023	1068	1132
120,000	140,000	863	987	1068	1130	1180	1250
140,000	160,000	936	1070	1158	1225	1279	1354
160,000	180,000	1010	1154	1248	1320	1378	1459
180,000	200,000	1077	1230	1330	1406	1468	1554
200,000 or more		1417	1616	1747	1846	1927	2038

Rhode Island 7.0000%

Income: At least	But less than	Exemptions 1	2	3	4	5	Over 5
$0	$20,000	243	277	298	314	327	346
20,000	30,000	406	460	495	522	544	574
30,000	40,000	491	556	599	631	657	693
40,000	50,000	565	640	689	726	756	797
50,000	60,000	633	717	771	812	846	892
60,000	70,000	695	787	846	891	928	978
70,000	80,000	754	854	918	967	1006	1061
80,000	90,000	809	916	985	1037	1080	1138
90,000	100,000	862	976	1049	1104	1150	1212
100,000	120,000	932	1054	1134	1193	1242	1309
120,000	140,000	1029	1164	1251	1317	1370	1444
140,000	160,000	1114	1260	1354	1425	1483	1563
160,000	180,000	1200	1357	1458	1534	1596	1682
180,000	200,000	1278	1444	1552	1633	1699	1790
200,000 or more		1674	1890	2030	2136	2221	2339

South Carolina[3] 5.5863%

Income: At least	But less than	Exemptions 1	2	3	4	5	Over 5
$0	$20,000	243	291	323	348	369	399
20,000	30,000	393	469	521	560	594	640
30,000	40,000	471	561	622	670	709	764
40,000	50,000	538	640	710	764	808	871
50,000	60,000	598	712	789	849	898	968
60,000	70,000	654	778	862	927	980	1056
70,000	80,000	706	840	930	1000	1058	1140
80,000	90,000	755	898	994	1069	1131	1217
90,000	100,000	802	953	1055	1134	1200	1291
100,000	120,000	864	1026	1135	1220	1291	1389
120,000	140,000	949	1127	1246	1339	1416	1524
140,000	160,000	1024	1215	1344	1443	1526	1642
160,000	180,000	1099	1304	1441	1548	1636	1760
180,000	200,000	1167	1384	1529	1642	1736	1867
200,000 or more		1511	1788	1974	2119	2238	2405

South Dakota 4.0000%

Income: At least	But less than	Exemptions 1	2	3	4	5	Over 5
$0	$20,000	222	271	306	333	356	388
20,000	30,000	343	419	471	512	547	595
30,000	40,000	405	493	554	602	642	699
40,000	50,000	457	556	625	678	723	787
50,000	60,000	504	613	688	747	796	866
60,000	70,000	547	664	745	809	862	937
70,000	80,000	587	712	799	867	924	1004
80,000	90,000	624	757	849	921	981	1066
90,000	100,000	659	799	896	972	1035	1125
100,000	120,000	705	855	958	1038	1106	1202
120,000	140,000	769	931	1043	1130	1203	1307
140,000	160,000	824	998	1116	1210	1288	1398
160,000	180,000	880	1064	1190	1289	1372	1489
180,000	200,000	930	1123	1256	1360	1448	1571
200,000 or more		1178	1420	1586	1716	1824	1978

Tennessee 7.0000%

Income: At least	But less than	Exemptions 1	2	3	4	5	Over 5
$0	$20,000	358	438	493	537	573	625
20,000	30,000	557	679	763	829	884	962
30,000	40,000	658	801	899	976	1040	1132
40,000	50,000	745	905	1015	1101	1174	1276
50,000	60,000	822	998	1119	1213	1293	1405
60,000	70,000	893	1083	1213	1315	1401	1522
70,000	80,000	959	1163	1302	1412	1503	1633
80,000	90,000	1021	1237	1385	1501	1598	1735
90,000	100,000	1080	1307	1463	1585	1687	1832
100,000	120,000	1157	1400	1566	1696	1805	1959
120,000	140,000	1264	1527	1707	1848	1966	2134
140,000	160,000	1357	1638	1830	1981	2107	2286
160,000	180,000	1450	1749	1953	2114	2248	2437
180,000	200,000	1534	1849	2064	2233	2375	2574
200,000 or more		1956	2351	2620	2831	3007	3256

Texas 6.2500%

Income: At least	But less than	Exemptions 1	2	3	4	5	Over 5
$0	$20,000	252	298	328	352	371	398
20,000	30,000	414	487	537	575	606	650
30,000	40,000	498	586	645	691	728	781
40,000	50,000	571	672	739	791	834	894
50,000	60,000	637	749	824	881	929	995
60,000	70,000	698	820	901	964	1016	1089
70,000	80,000	755	887	975	1043	1099	1178
80,000	90,000	809	950	1044	1116	1176	1260
90,000	100,000	860	1009	1109	1186	1250	1338
100,000	120,000	927	1088	1196	1278	1347	1442
120,000	140,000	1021	1197	1315	1406	1480	1585
140,000	160,000	1103	1293	1420	1517	1598	1710
160,000	180,000	1185	1389	1524	1629	1716	1836
180,000	200,000	1260	1476	1620	1731	1822	1950
200,000 or more		1636	1914	2099	2241	2359	2523

Utah 4.7500%

Income: At least	But less than	Exemptions 1	2	3	4	5	Over 5
$0	$20,000	226	270	300	323	342	368
20,000	30,000	362	431	477	513	543	585
30,000	40,000	432	513	568	611	646	696
40,000	50,000	492	584	647	695	735	791
50,000	60,000	546	648	717	770	815	876
60,000	70,000	596	707	781	839	887	955
70,000	80,000	643	762	842	905	956	1028
80,000	90,000	687	814	899	965	1020	1097
90,000	100,000	728	862	953	1023	1081	1162
100,000	120,000	783	927	1024	1099	1161	1248
120,000	140,000	859	1016	1122	1203	1271	1366
140,000	160,000	925	1094	1207	1295	1368	1469
160,000	180,000	992	1172	1293	1387	1464	1573
180,000	200,000	1052	1242	1370	1469	1551	1666
200,000 or more		1355	1598	1760	1886	1990	2135

Vermont 6.0000%

Income: At least	But less than	Exemptions 1	2	3	4	5	Over 5
$0	$20,000	158	176	186	195	201	210
20,000	30,000	269	298	316	330	341	356
30,000	40,000	327	363	385	402	415	433
40,000	50,000	379	420	445	465	480	501
50,000	60,000	426	472	501	522	540	563
60,000	70,000	470	520	552	575	595	621
70,000	80,000	511	566	600	626	647	675
80,000	90,000	550	609	646	674	696	727
90,000	100,000	587	650	690	719	743	776
100,000	120,000	637	705	748	780	806	841
120,000	140,000	705	780	828	864	892	931
140,000	160,000	766	848	899	938	969	1011
160,000	180,000	827	915	971	1013	1046	1092
180,000	200,000	883	977	1036	1081	1117	1165
200,000 or more		1169	1292	1371	1429	1476	1540

Virginia[5] 5.0000%

Income: At least	But less than	Exemptions 1	2	3	4	5	Over 5
$0	$20,000	198	239	267	289	307	332
20,000	30,000	315	380	423	457	486	526
30,000	40,000	376	452	504	544	578	625
40,000	50,000	429	515	573	619	657	710
50,000	60,000	476	572	636	687	729	788
60,000	70,000	520	624	694	749	794	858
70,000	80,000	562	673	749	808	857	925
80,000	90,000	600	719	800	862	915	988
90,000	100,000	637	763	848	915	970	1047
100,000	120,000	686	821	913	984	1043	1126
120,000	140,000	754	902	1001	1079	1144	1234
140,000	160,000	814	973	1080	1163	1232	1330
160,000	180,000	874	1044	1158	1247	1321	1425
180,000	200,000	929	1108	1230	1324	1402	1512
200,000 or more		1208	1437	1592	1712	1812	1952

Washington 6.5000%

Income: At least	But less than	Exemptions 1	2	3	4	5	Over 5
$0	$20,000	269	313	342	364	383	408
20,000	30,000	445	517	564	601	631	672
30,000	40,000	536	623	680	724	760	809
40,000	50,000	616	715	780	830	872	929
50,000	60,000	688	799	871	927	973	1036
60,000	70,000	755	875	955	1016	1066	1135
70,000	80,000	818	948	1034	1100	1154	1229
80,000	90,000	876	1016	1108	1178	1236	1316
90,000	100,000	932	1081	1178	1253	1315	1400
100,000	120,000	1006	1166	1271	1352	1418	1510
120,000	140,000	1109	1284	1400	1488	1561	1662
140,000	160,000	1199	1388	1513	1608	1687	1795
160,000	180,000	1289	1492	1626	1729	1813	1929
180,000	200,000	1371	1587	1729	1838	1927	2050
200,000 or more		1785	2064	2247	2388	2503	2662

West Virginia 6.0000%

Income: At least	But less than	Exemptions 1	2	3	4	5	Over 5
$0	$20,000	307	368	410	442	469	507
20,000	30,000	485	579	644	694	735	794
30,000	40,000	575	687	762	821	870	939
40,000	50,000	653	779	864	931	986	1063
50,000	60,000	723	862	956	1029	1090	1175
60,000	70,000	787	937	1039	1119	1184	1277
70,000	80,000	847	1009	1118	1203	1274	1373
80,000	90,000	903	1075	1191	1281	1356	1462
90,000	100,000	956	1138	1261	1356	1435	1546
100,000	120,000	1027	1221	1352	1454	1538	1657
120,000	140,000	1123	1335	1478	1588	1680	1809
140,000	160,000	1208	1435	1587	1706	1805	1943
160,000	180,000	1293	1534	1697	1824	1929	2076
180,000	200,000	1369	1624	1796	1930	2040	2196
200,000 or more		1754	2077	2294	2462	2601	2797

Wisconsin 5.0000%

Income: At least	But less than	Exemptions 1	2	3	4	5	Over 5
$0	$20,000	207	240	261	278	291	310
20,000	30,000	342	395	430	456	478	508
30,000	40,000	412	476	517	549	575	612
40,000	50,000	473	546	593	630	660	701
50,000	60,000	528	609	662	703	736	782
60,000	70,000	578	667	725	770	806	856
70,000	80,000	626	722	785	833	872	927
80,000	90,000	671	774	841	892	934	992
90,000	100,000	714	823	894	948	993	1055
100,000	120,000	770	887	964	1023	1071	1137
120,000	140,000	848	977	1061	1126	1178	1251
140,000	160,000	916	1055	1147	1216	1273	1352
160,000	180,000	985	1134	1232	1306	1367	1452
180,000	200,000	1047	1206	1309	1388	1453	1543
200,000 or more		1362	1566	1700	1802	1886	2001

Wyoming 4.0000%

Income: At least	But less than	Exemptions 1	2	3	4	5	Over 5
$0	$20,000	156	183	201	214	226	242
20,000	30,000	256	300	329	351	370	396
30,000	40,000	309	361	396	423	445	476
40,000	50,000	354	414	454	485	510	545
50,000	60,000	396	463	507	541	569	608
60,000	70,000	434	507	555	593	623	666
70,000	80,000	470	549	601	642	675	721
80,000	90,000	504	588	644	687	723	772
90,000	100,000	536	626	685	731	768	820
100,000	120,000	579	675	739	788	829	885
120,000	140,000	638	744	814	868	912	974
140,000	160,000	690	804	880	938	986	1052
160,000	180,000	743	865	946	1008	1060	1131
180,000	200,000	790	920	1006	1072	1127	1202
200,000 or more		1032	1199	1310	1395	1465	1563

Note. Alaska does not have a state sales tax. Alaska residents should follow the instructions on the next page to determine their local sales tax amount.

1 The California table includes the 1% uniform local sales tax rate in additon to the 6.25% state sales tax rate.
2 The Nevada table includes the 2.25% uniform local sales tax rate in addition to the 4.25% state sales tax rate.
3 The rate for South Carolina increased during 2007, so the rate given is averaged over the year.
4 Residents of Salem County should deduct only half of the amount in the state table.
5 The state and local general sales taxes are combined in the Virginia table.

Which Optional Local Sales Tax Table Should I Use?

IF you live in the state of...	AND you live in...	THEN use Local Table...
Alaska	Any locality	C
Arizona	Any locality	C
Arkansas	Texarkana	B
California	Los Angeles County	B
Colorado	City of Denver	B
	Arvada, Aurora, City of Boulder, Centennial, Colorado Springs, Fort Collins, Greeley, Jefferson County, Lakewood, Longmont, City of Pueblo, Thornton, or Westminster	C
	Boulder County, Denver County, Pueblo County, or any other locality	A
Georgia	DeKalb County, Rockdale County, Taliaferro County, or Webster	B
	Any other locality	C
Illinois	Any locality	C
Louisiana	Any locality	C
New York	New York City, or one of the following counties: Albany, Allegany, Cattaraugus, Cayuga, Chemung, Clinton, Cortland, Erie, Essex, Franklin, Fulton, Genesee, Herkimer, Jefferson, Lewis, Livingston, Madison, Monroe, Montgomery, Nassau, Niagara, Oneida, Onondaga, Ontario, Orange, Orleans, Oswego, Otsego, Putnam, Rensselaer, Rockland, St. Lawrence, Saratoga, Schenectady, Schoharie, Seneca, Steuben, Suffolk, Sullivan, Tompkins, Ulster, Warren, Washington, Westchester, Wyoming, or Yates	B
	Any other locality	D
North Carolina	Any locality	C

2007 Optional Local Sales Tax Tables for Certain Local Jurisdictions

(Based on a local sales tax rate of 1 percent)

Income At least	But less than	Local Table A 1	2	3	4	5	Over 5	Local Table B 1	2	3	4	5	Over 5
$0	$20,000	33	39	43	46	49	52	40	48	53	57	61	66
20,000	30,000	54	64	70	75	80	86	65	77	86	93	98	106
30,000	40,000	65	77	85	91	96	103	78	93	103	111	117	126
40,000	50,000	75	88	97	104	110	118	89	106	117	126	134	144
50,000	60,000	84	99	109	117	123	132	99	118	130	140	148	160
60,000	70,000	92	108	119	128	135	145	108	129	143	153	162	175
70,000	80,000	100	117	129	139	146	157	117	139	154	165	175	188
80,000	90,000	107	126	139	149	157	168	125	149	165	177	187	201
90,000	100,000	114	134	148	158	167	179	133	158	175	188	199	214
100,000	120,000	123	145	160	171	180	193	143	170	188	202	214	230
120,000	140,000	136	160	176	189	199	213	158	187	207	222	235	252
140,000	160,000	147	173	191	204	215	231	170	202	223	239	253	272
160,000	180,000	159	187	206	220	232	248	183	217	239	257	271	292
180,000	200,000	169	199	219	234	247	264	194	230	254	273	288	310
200,000 or more		223	262	288	308	324	347	252	298	329	352	372	400

Income At least	But less than	Local Table C 1	2	3	4	5	Over 5	Local Table D 1	2	3	4	5	Over 5
$0	$20,000	53	65	74	80	86	93	36	42	45	48	50	53
20,000	30,000	82	100	112	122	131	142	60	69	74	79	82	87
30,000	40,000	96	117	132	143	153	167	72	83	90	95	99	105
40,000	50,000	108	132	149	161	172	188	83	95	103	109	114	121
50,000	60,000	119	145	163	178	189	206	92	106	115	122	127	135
60,000	70,000	129	157	177	192	205	223	101	116	126	133	139	148
70,000	80,000	139	169	190	206	220	239	110	126	136	144	151	160
80,000	90,000	147	179	201	219	233	254	118	135	146	154	161	171
90,000	100,000	156	189	213	231	246	267	125	143	155	164	172	182
100,000	120,000	167	203	227	247	263	286	135	155	167	177	185	196
120,000	140,000	182	221	247	268	286	311	149	170	184	195	204	216
140,000	160,000	195	237	265	287	306	332	161	184	199	211	220	233
160,000	180,000	208	252	283	306	326	354	173	198	214	226	236	250
180,000	200,000	220	267	298	323	344	374	184	210	227	240	251	266
200,000 or more		280	338	378	409	435	472	239	273	295	312	326	345

APPENDIX B

TAX FORMS

(Tax forms can be obtained from the IRS web site: http://www.irs.gov)

Form 1040	U.S. Individual Income Tax Return	B–2
Schedules A & B	Itemized Deductions; Interest and Ordinary Dividends	B–4
Schedule C	Profit or Loss from Business	B–6
Schedule D	Capital Gains and Losses	B–8
Schedule E	Supplemental Income and Loss	B–10
Schedule F	Profit or Loss from Farming	B–12
Schedule SE	Self-Employment Tax	B–14

Form **1040**

Department of the Treasury—Internal Revenue Service

U.S. Individual Income Tax Return 2007   IRS Use Only—Do not write or staple in this space.

For the year Jan. 1–Dec. 31, 2007, or other tax year beginning _____ , 2007, ending _____ , 20 ___   OMB No. 1545-0074

Label

(See instructions on page 12.)

Use the IRS label. Otherwise, please print or type.

L A B E L H E R E		
Your first name and initial	Last name	Your social security number
If a joint return, spouse's first name and initial	Last name	Spouse's social security number
Home address (number and street). If you have a P.O. box, see page 12.	Apt. no.	▲ You **must** enter your SSN(s) above. ▲
City, town or post office, state, and ZIP code. If you have a foreign address, see page 12.		Checking a box below will not change your tax or refund.

Presidential Election Campaign ▶ Check here if you, or your spouse if filing jointly, want $3 to go to this fund (see page 12) ▶   ☐ **You** ☐ **Spouse**

Filing Status

Check only one box.

1 ☐ Single
2 ☐ Married filing jointly (even if only one had income)
3 ☐ Married filing separately. Enter spouse's SSN above and full name here. ▶
4 ☐ Head of household (with qualifying person). (See page 13.) If the qualifying person is a child but not your dependent, enter this child's name here. ▶ _____
5 ☐ Qualifying widow(er) with dependent child (see page 14)

Exemptions

6a ☐ **Yourself.** If someone can claim you as a dependent, **do not** check box 6a . . . . .
b ☐ **Spouse** . . . .

c **Dependents:**

(1) First name Last name	(2) Dependent's social security number	(3) Dependent's relationship to you	(4) ✔ if qualifying child for child tax credit (see page 15)
			☐
			☐
			☐
			☐

If more than four dependents, see page 15.

Boxes checked on 6a and 6b _____
No. of children on 6c who:
• lived with you _____
• did not live with you due to divorce or separation (see page 16) _____
Dependents on 6c not entered above _____
Add numbers on lines above ▶ ☐

d Total number of exemptions claimed . . . .

Income

Attach Form(s) W-2 here. Also attach Forms W-2G and 1099-R if tax was withheld.

If you did not get a W-2, see page 19.

Enclose, but do not attach, any payment. Also, please use **Form 1040-V.**

7	Wages, salaries, tips, etc. Attach Form(s) W-2	7
8a	**Taxable** interest. Attach Schedule B if required	8a
b	**Tax-exempt** interest. **Do not** include on line 8a . . .	8b
9a	Ordinary dividends. Attach Schedule B if required	9a
b	Qualified dividends (see page 19)	9b
10	Taxable refunds, credits, or offsets of state and local income taxes (see page 20) . .	10
11	Alimony received	11
12	Business income or (loss). Attach Schedule C or C-EZ	12
13	Capital gain or (loss). Attach Schedule D if required. If not required, check here ▶ ☐	13
14	Other gains or (losses). Attach Form 4797	14
15a	IRA distributions . .	15a	b Taxable amount (see page 21)	15b
16a	Pensions and annuities	16a	b Taxable amount (see page 22)	16b
17	Rental real estate, royalties, partnerships, S corporations, trusts, etc. Attach Schedule E	17
18	Farm income or (loss). Attach Schedule F	18
19	Unemployment compensation	19
20a	Social security benefits	20a	b Taxable amount (see page 24)	20b
21	Other income. List type and amount (see page 24) _____	21
22	Add the amounts in the far right column for lines 7 through 21. This is your **total income** ▶	22

Adjusted Gross Income

23	Educator expenses (see page 26)	23
24	Certain business expenses of reservists, performing artists, and fee-basis government officials. Attach Form 2106 or 2106-EZ	24
25	Health savings account deduction. Attach Form 8889 . .	25
26	Moving expenses. Attach Form 3903	26
27	One-half of self-employment tax. Attach Schedule SE . .	27
28	Self-employed SEP, SIMPLE, and qualified plans . . .	28
29	Self-employed health insurance deduction (see page 26) .	29
30	Penalty on early withdrawal of savings	30
31a	Alimony paid b Recipient's SSN ▶ _____	31a
32	IRA deduction (see page 27)	32
33	Student loan interest deduction (see page 30)	33
34	Tuition and fees deduction. Attach Form 8917	34
35	Domestic production activities deduction. Attach Form 8903	35
36	Add lines 23 through 31a and 32 through 35	36
37	Subtract line 36 from line 22. This is your **adjusted gross income** . . . . . . ▶	37

For Disclosure, Privacy Act, and Paperwork Reduction Act Notice, see page 83.   Cat. No. 11320B   Form **1040** (2007)

Form 1040 (2007)   Page **2**

Tax and Credits				38	
	38	Amount from line 37 (adjusted gross income)			
	39a	Check if: ☐ **You** were born before January 2, 1943, ☐ Blind. ☐ **Spouse** was born before January 2, 1943, ☐ Blind. } Total boxes checked ▶ **39a**			

Standard Deduction for—

- People who checked any box on line 39a or 39b **or** who can be claimed as a dependent, see page 31.

- All others:

Single or Married filing separately, $5,350

Married filing jointly or Qualifying widow(er), $10,700

Head of household, $7,850

b	If your spouse itemizes on a separate return or you were a dual-status alien, see page 31 and check here ▶**39b** ☐			
40	**Itemized deductions** (from Schedule A) **or** your **standard deduction** (see left margin) . .		**40**	
41	Subtract line 40 from line 38		**41**	
42	If line 38 is $117,300 or less, multiply $3,400 by the total number of exemptions claimed on line 6d. If line 38 is over $117,300, see the worksheet on page 33		**42**	
43	**Taxable income.** Subtract line 42 from line 41. If line 42 is more than line 41, enter -0-		**43**	
44	**Tax** (see page 33). Check if any tax is from: **a** ☐ Form(s) 8814 **b** ☐ Form 4972 **c** ☐ Form(s) 8889		**44**	
45	**Alternative minimum tax** (see page 36). Attach Form 6251		**45**	
46	Add lines 44 and 45 . . . . ▶		**46**	
47	Credit for child and dependent care expenses. Attach Form 2441	**47**		
48	Credit for the elderly or the disabled. Attach Schedule R .	**48**		
49	Education credits. Attach Form 8863	**49**		
50	Residential energy credits. Attach Form 5695	**50**		
51	Foreign tax credit. Attach Form 1116 if required . . .	**51**		
52	Child tax credit (see page 39). Attach Form 8901 if required	**52**		
53	Retirement savings contributions credit. Attach Form 8880 .	**53**		
54	Credits from: **a** ☐ Form 8396 **b** ☐ Form 8859 **c** ☐ Form 8839	**54**		
55	Other credits: **a** ☐ Form 3800 **b** ☐ Form 8801 **c** ☐ Form____	**55**		
56	Add lines 47 through 55. These are your **total credits**		**56**	
57	Subtract line 56 from line 46. If line 56 is more than line 46, enter -0- . . . . . ▶		**57**	

Other Taxes				
58	Self-employment tax. Attach Schedule SE		**58**	
59	Unreported social security and Medicare tax from: **a** ☐ Form 4137 **b** ☐ Form 8919 . .		**59**	
60	Additional tax on IRAs, other qualified retirement plans, etc. Attach Form 5329 if required . .		**60**	
61	Advance earned income credit payments from Form(s) W-2, box 9		**61**	
62	Household employment taxes. Attach Schedule H		**62**	
63	Add lines 57 through 62. This is your **total tax** . . . . ▶		**63**	

Payments				
64	Federal income tax withheld from Forms W-2 and 1099 . .	**64**		
65	2007 estimated tax payments and amount applied from 2006 return	**65**		

If you have a qualifying child, attach Schedule EIC.

66a	**Earned income credit (EIC)**	**66a**		
b	Nontaxable combat pay election ▶ **66b**			
67	Excess social security and tier 1 RRTA tax withheld (see page 59)	**67**		
68	Additional child tax credit. Attach Form 8812	**68**		
69	Amount paid with request for extension to file (see page 59)	**69**		
70	Payments from: **a** ☐ Form 2439 **b** ☐ Form 4136 **c** ☐ Form 8885 .	**70**		
71	Refundable credit for prior year minimum tax from Form 8801, line 27	**71**		
72	Add lines 64, 65, 66a, and 67 through 71. These are your **total payments** . . . . ▶		**72**	

Refund				
73	If line 72 is more than line 63, subtract line 63 from line 72. This is the amount you **overpaid**		**73**	
74a	Amount of line 73 you want **refunded to you.** If Form 8888 is attached, check here ▶ ☐		**74a**	

Direct deposit?
See page 59 and fill in 74b, 74c, and 74d, or Form 8888.

▶ **b**	Routing number	▶ **c** Type: ☐ Checking ☐ Savings
▶ **d**	Account number	
75	Amount of line 73 you want **applied to your 2008 estimated tax** ▶	**75**

Amount You Owe				
76	**Amount you owe.** Subtract line 72 from line 63. For details on how to pay, see page 60 ▶		**76**	
77	Estimated tax penalty (see page 61)	**77**		

Third Party Designee

Do you want to allow another person to discuss this return with the IRS (see page 61)? ☐ **Yes.** Complete the following. ☐ **No**

Designee's name ▶	Phone no. ▶ ( )	Personal identification number (PIN) ▶

Sign Here

Under penalties of perjury, I declare that I have examined this return and accompanying schedules and statements, and to the best of my knowledge and belief, they are true, correct, and complete. Declaration of preparer (other than taxpayer) is based on all information of which preparer has any knowledge.

Joint return? See page 13.
Keep a copy for your records.

Your signature	Date	Your occupation	Daytime phone number ( )
Spouse's signature. If a joint return, **both** must sign.	Date	Spouse's occupation	

Paid Preparer's Use Only

Preparer's signature ▶	Date	Check if self-employed ☐	Preparer's SSN or PTIN
Firm's name (or yours if self-employed), address, and ZIP code ▶		EIN	
		Phone no. ( )	

Form **1040** (2007)

SCHEDULES A&B
(Form 1040)

Department of the Treasury
Internal Revenue Service

Schedule A—Itemized Deductions

(Schedule B is on back)

► **Attach to Form 1040.**   ► **See Instructions for Schedules A&B (Form 1040).**

OMB No. 1545-0074

2007

Attachment
Sequence No. **07**

Name(s) shown on Form 1040

Your social security number

Medical and Dental Expenses	**1**	**Caution.** Do not include expenses reimbursed or paid by others. Medical and dental expenses (see page A-1) . . .	**1**	
	2	Enter amount from Form 1040, line 38 ⌊ **2** ⌋		
	3	Multiply line 2 by 7.5% (.075).	**3**	
	4	Subtract line 3 from line 1. If line 3 is more than line 1, enter -0-	**4**	
Taxes You Paid (See page A-2.)	**5**	State and local **(check only one box):** **a** ☐ Income taxes, **or** **b** ☐ General sales taxes	**5**	
	6	Real estate taxes (see page A-5)	**6**	
	7	Personal property taxes	**7**	
	8	Other taxes. List type and amount ► _____	**8**	
	9	Add lines 5 through 8	**9**	
Interest You Paid (See page A-5.) **Note.** Personal interest is not deductible.	**10**	Home mortgage interest and points reported to you on Form 1098	**10**	
	11	Home mortgage interest not reported to you on Form 1098. If paid to the person from whom you bought the home, see page A-6 and show that person's name, identifying no., and address ► _____	**11**	
	12	Points not reported to you on Form 1098. See page A-6 for special rules	**12**	
	13	Qualified mortgage insurance premiums (See page A-7) .	**13**	
	14	Investment interest. Attach Form 4952 if required. (See page A-7.)	**14**	
	15	Add lines 10 through 14	**15**	
Gifts to Charity If you made a gift and got a benefit for it, see page A-8.	**16**	Gifts by cash or check. If you made any gift of $250 or more, see page A-8 . . .	**16**	
	17	Other than by cash or check. If any gift of $250 or more, see page A-8. You **must** attach Form 8283 if over $500	**17**	
	18	Carryover from prior year	**18**	
	19	Add lines 16 through 18	**19**	
Casualty and Theft Losses	**20**	Casualty or theft loss(es). Attach Form 4684. (See page A-9.)	**20**	
Job Expenses and Certain Miscellaneous Deductions (See page A-9.)	**21**	Unreimbursed employee expenses—job travel, union dues, job education, etc. Attach Form 2106 or 2106-EZ if required. (See page A-9.) ► _____	**21**	
	22	Tax preparation fees.	**22**	
	23	Other expenses—investment, safe deposit box, etc. List type and amount ► _____	**23**	
	24	Add lines 21 through 23	**24**	
	25	Enter amount from Form 1040, line 38 ⌊ **25** ⌋		
	26	Multiply line 25 by 2% (.02)	**26**	
	27	Subtract line 26 from line 24. If line 26 is more than line 24, enter -0-	**27**	
Other Miscellaneous Deductions	**28**	Other—from list on page A-10. List type and amount ► _____	**28**	
Total Itemized Deductions	**29**	Is Form 1040, line 38, over $156,400 (over $78,200 if married filing separately)? ☐ **No.** Your deduction is not limited. Add the amounts in the far right column for lines 4 through 28. Also, enter this amount on Form 1040, line 40. ⎬► ☐ **Yes.** Your deduction may be limited. See page A-10 for the amount to enter.	**29**	
	30	If you elect to itemize deductions even though they are less than your standard deduction, check here ► ☐		

For Paperwork Reduction Act Notice, see Form 1040 instructions.   Cat. No. 11330X   **Schedule A (Form 1040) 2007**

Schedules A&B (Form 1040) 2007   OMB No. 1545-0074   Page **2**

Name(s) shown on Form 1040. Do not enter name and social security number if shown on other side.

Your social security number

Schedule B—Interest and Ordinary Dividends

Attachment Sequence No. **08**

		Amount

Part I
Interest

(See page B-1 and the instructions for Form 1040, line 8a.)

Note. If you received a Form 1099-INT, Form 1099-OID, or substitute statement from a brokerage firm, list the firm's name as the payer and enter the total interest shown on that form.

1 List name of payer. If any interest is from a seller-financed mortgage and the buyer used the property as a personal residence, see page B-1 and list this interest first. Also, show that buyer's social security number and address ▶

1

2 Add the amounts on line 1 . . . .   **2**

3 Excludable interest on series EE and I U.S. savings bonds issued after 1989. Attach Form 8815 . . . .   **3**

4 Subtract line 3 from line 2. Enter the result here and on Form 1040, line 8a ▶   **4**

Note. If line 4 is over $1,500, you must complete Part III.

		Amount

Part II
Ordinary
Dividends

(See page B-1 and the instructions for Form 1040, line 9a.)

Note. If you received a Form 1099-DIV or substitute statement from a brokerage firm, list the firm's name as the payer and enter the ordinary dividends shown on that form.

5 List name of payer ▶

5

6 Add the amounts on line 5. Enter the total here and on Form 1040, line 9a . ▶   **6**

Note. If line 6 is over $1,500, you must complete Part III.

Part III
Foreign
Accounts
and Trusts

(See page B-2.)

You must complete this part if you **(a)** had over $1,500 of taxable interest or ordinary dividends; or **(b)** had a foreign account; or **(c)** received a distribution from, or were a grantor of, or a transferor to, a foreign trust.

	Yes	No

7a At any time during 2007, did you have an interest in or a signature or other authority over a financial account in a foreign country, such as a bank account, securities account, or other financial account? See page B-2 for exceptions and filing requirements for Form TD F 90-22.1. . . . . . .

b If "Yes," enter the name of the foreign country ▶

8 During 2007, did you receive a distribution from, or were you the grantor of, or transferor to, a foreign trust? If "Yes," you may have to file Form 3520. See page B-2 . . . .

For Paperwork Reduction Act Notice, see Form 1040 instructions.   Schedule B (Form 1040) 2007

SCHEDULE C
(Form 1040)

Department of the Treasury
Internal Revenue Service   (99)

Profit or Loss From Business
(Sole Proprietorship)

▶ Partnerships, joint ventures, etc., must file Form 1065 or 1065-B.

▶ **Attach to Form 1040, 1040NR, or 1041.**   ▶ See Instructions for Schedule C (Form 1040).

OMB No. 1545-0074

2007

Attachment
Sequence No. **09**

Name of proprietor

Social security number (SSN)

A   Principal business or profession, including product or service (see page C-2 of the instructions)

B Enter code from pages C-8, 9, & 10
▶

C   Business name. If no separate business name, leave blank.

D Employer ID number (EIN), if any

E   Business address (including suite or room no.) ▶
City, town or post office, state, and ZIP code

F   Accounting method: **(1)** ☐ Cash   **(2)** ☐ Accrual   **(3)** ☐ Other (specify) ▶

G   Did you "materially participate" in the operation of this business during 2007? If "No," see page C-3 for limit on losses   ☐ Yes   ☐ No

H   If you started or acquired this business during 2007, check here   . . . . ▶ ☐

Part I   Income

1	Gross receipts or sales. **Caution.** If this income was reported to you on Form W-2 and the "Statutory employee" box on that form was checked, see page C-3 and check here . . . . . . ▶ ☐	1	
2	Returns and allowances	2	
3	Subtract line 2 from line 1	3	
4	Cost of goods sold (from line 42 on page 2)	4	
5	**Gross profit.** Subtract line 4 from line 3	5	
6	Other income, including federal and state gasoline or fuel tax credit or refund (see page C-3) . . .	6	
7	**Gross income.** Add lines 5 and 6 . . . . ▶	7	

Part II   Expenses. Enter expenses for business use of your home **only** on line 30.

8	Advertising	8		18	Office expense	18	
9	Car and truck expenses (see page C-4)	9		19	Pension and profit-sharing plans	19	
10	Commissions and fees . .	10		20	Rent or lease (see page C-5):		
11	Contract labor (see page C-4)	11		a	Vehicles, machinery, and equipment .	20a	
12	Depletion	12		b	Other business property . . .	20b	
13	Depreciation and section 179 expense deduction (not included in Part III) (see page C-4)	13		21	Repairs and maintenance . .	21	
				22	Supplies (not included in Part III) .	22	
				23	Taxes and licenses	23	
				24	Travel, meals, and entertainment:		
				a	Travel	24a	
14	Employee benefit programs (other than on line 19). .	14		b	Deductible meals and entertainment (see page C-6)	24b	
15	Insurance (other than health) .	15		25	Utilities	25	
16	Interest:			26	Wages (less employment credits) .	26	
a	Mortgage (paid to banks, etc.) .	16a		27	Other expenses (from line 48 on page 2)	27	
b	Other	16b					
17	Legal and professional services	17					

28	**Total expenses** before expenses for business use of home. Add lines 8 through 27 in columns . ▶	28	
29	Tentative profit (loss). Subtract line 28 from line 7	29	
30	Expenses for business use of your home. Attach **Form 8829**	30	
31	**Net profit or (loss).** Subtract line 30 from line 29.		
	• If a profit, enter on both **Form 1040, line 12,** and **Schedule SE, line 2,** or on **Form 1040NR, line 13** (statutory employees, see page C-7). Estates and trusts, enter on Form 1041, line 3. • If a loss, you **must** go to line 32.	31	
32	If you have a loss, check the box that describes your investment in this activity (see page C-7).		
	• If you checked 32a, enter the loss on both **Form 1040, line 12,** and **Schedule SE, line 2,** or on **Form 1040NR, line 13** (statutory employees, see page C-7). Estates and trusts, enter on Form 1041, line 3. • If you checked 32b, you **must** attach **Form 6198.** Your loss may be limited.	32a ☐ All investment is at risk. 32b ☐ Some investment is not at risk.	

Paperwork Reduction Act Notice, see page C-8 of the instructions.   Cat. No. 11334P   Schedule C (Form 1040) 2007

Schedule C (Form 1040) 2007 — Page **2**

Part III   Cost of Goods Sold (see page C-7)

33	Method(s) used to value closing inventory: **a** ☐ Cost **b** ☐ Lower of cost or market **c** ☐ Other (attach explanation)	
34	Was there any change in determining quantities, costs, or valuations between opening and closing inventory? If "Yes," attach explanation . . . . ☐ **Yes** ☐ **No**	
35	Inventory at beginning of year. If different from last year's closing inventory, attach explanation . .	**35**
36	Purchases less cost of items withdrawn for personal use	**36**
37	Cost of labor. Do not include any amounts paid to yourself	**37**
38	Materials and supplies	**38**
39	Other costs	**39**
40	Add lines 35 through 39	**40**
41	Inventory at end of year	**41**
42	**Cost of goods sold.** Subtract line 41 from line 40. Enter the result here and on page 1, line 4 . .	**42**

Part IV   Information on Your Vehicle. Complete this part **only** if you are claiming car or truck expenses on line 9 and are not required to file Form 4562 for this business. See the instructions for line 13 on page C-4 to find out if you must file Form 4562.

43 When did you place your vehicle in service for business purposes? (month, day, year) ▶ _____ / _____ / _____

44 Of the total number of miles you drove your vehicle during 2007, enter the number of miles you used your vehicle for:

a Business _____ **b** Commuting (see instructions) _____ **c** Other _____

45 Do you (or your spouse) have another vehicle available for personal use?. . . . . ☐ **Yes** ☐ **No**

46 Was your vehicle available for personal use during off-duty hours? . . . . ☐ **Yes** ☐ **No**

47a Do you have evidence to support your deduction? . . . . ☐ **Yes** ☐ **No**

b If "Yes," is the evidence written? . . . . ☐ **Yes** ☐ **No**

Part V   Other Expenses. List below business expenses not included on lines 8–26 or line 30.

----------------------------------	
48 Total other expenses. Enter here and on page 1, line 27	**48**

Schedule C (Form 1040) 2007

SCHEDULE D
(Form 1040)

Department of the Treasury
Internal Revenue Service

Capital Gains and Losses

▶ Attach to Form 1040 or Form 1040NR.   ▶ See Instructions for Schedule D (Form 1040).

▶ Use Schedule D-1 to list additional transactions for lines 1 and 8.

OMB No. 1545-0074

2007

Attachment
Sequence No. **12**

Name(s) shown on return

Your social security number

Part I   Short-Term Capital Gains and Losses—Assets Held One Year or Less

	(a) Description of property (Example: 100 sh. XYZ Co.)	(b) Date acquired (Mo., day, yr.)	(c) Date sold (Mo., day, yr.)	(d) Sales price (see page D-7 of the instructions)	(e) Cost or other basis (see page D-7 of the instructions)	(f) Gain or (loss) Subtract (e) from (d)
1						

2 Enter your short-term totals, if any, from Schedule D-1, line 2	**2**	
3 **Total short-term sales price amounts.** Add lines 1 and 2 in column (d)	**3**	

4 Short-term gain from Form 6252 and short-term gain or (loss) from Forms 4684, 6781, and 8824	**4**	
5 Net short-term gain or (loss) from partnerships, S corporations, estates, and trusts from Schedule(s) K-1	**5**	
6 Short-term capital loss carryover. Enter the amount, if any, from line 10 of your **Capital Loss Carryover Worksheet** on page D-7 of the instructions	**6**	( )
7 **Net short-term capital gain or (loss).** Combine lines 1 through 6 in column (f)	**7**	

Part II   Long-Term Capital Gains and Losses—Assets Held More Than One Year

	(a) Description of property (Example: 100 sh. XYZ Co.)	(b) Date acquired (Mo., day, yr.)	(c) Date sold (Mo., day, yr.)	(d) Sales price (see page D-7 of the instructions)	(e) Cost or other basis (see page D-7 of the instructions)	(f) Gain or (loss) Subtract (e) from (d)
8						

9 Enter your long-term totals, if any, from Schedule D-1, line 9	**9**	
10 **Total long-term sales price amounts.** Add lines 8 and 9 in column (d)	**10**	

11 Gain from Form 4797, Part I; long-term gain from Forms 2439 and 6252; and long-term gain or (loss) from Forms 4684, 6781, and 8824	**11**	
12 Net long-term gain or (loss) from partnerships, S corporations, estates, and trusts from Schedule(s) K-1	**12**	
13 Capital gain distributions. See page D-2 of the instructions	**13**	
14 Long-term capital loss carryover. Enter the amount, if any, from line 15 of your **Capital Loss Carryover Worksheet** on page D-7 of the instructions	**14**	( )
15 **Net long-term capital gain or (loss).** Combine lines 8 through 14 in column (f). Then go to Part III on the back	**15**	

For Paperwork Reduction Act Notice, see Form 1040 or Form 1040NR instructions.   Cat. No. 11338H   Schedule D (Form 1040) 2007

Part III   **Summary**

16   Combine lines 7 and 15 and enter the result. **16**

  If line 16 is:
  - A **gain**, enter the amount from line 16 on Form 1040, line 13, or Form 1040NR, line 14. Then go to line 17 below.
  - A **loss**, skip lines 17 through 20 below. Then go to line 21. Also be sure to complete line 22.
  - **Zero**, skip lines 17 through 21 below and enter -0- on Form 1040, line 13, or Form 1040NR, line 14. Then go to line 22.

17   Are lines 15 and 16 **both** gains?
  ☐ **Yes.** Go to line 18.
  ☐ **No.** Skip lines 18 through 21, and go to line 22.

18   Enter the amount, if any, from line 7 of the **28% Rate Gain Worksheet** on page D-8 of the instructions . . . . ▶   **18**

19   Enter the amount, if any, from line 18 of the **Unrecaptured Section 1250 Gain Worksheet** on page D-9 of the instructions . . . . ▶   **19**

20   Are lines 18 and 19 **both** zero or blank?
  ☐ **Yes.** Complete Form 1040 through line 43, or Form 1040NR through line 40. Then complete the **Qualified Dividends and Capital Gain Tax Worksheet** on page 35 of the Instructions for Form 1040 (or in the Instructions for Form 1040NR). **Do not** complete lines 21 and 22 below.

  ☐ **No.** Complete Form 1040 through line 43, or Form 1040NR through line 40. Then complete the **Schedule D Tax Worksheet** on page D-10 of the instructions. **Do not** complete lines 21 and 22 below.

21   If line 16 is a loss, enter here and on Form 1040, line 13, or Form 1040NR, line 14, the **smaller** of:

  - The loss on line 16 or
  - ($3,000), or if married filing separately, ($1,500)   } . . . .   **21** (   )

  Note. When figuring which amount is smaller, treat both amounts as positive numbers.

22   Do you have qualified dividends on Form 1040, line 9b, or Form 1040NR, line 10b?
  ☐ **Yes.** Complete Form 1040 through line 43, or Form 1040NR through line 40. Then complete the **Qualified Dividends and Capital Gain Tax Worksheet** on page 35 of the Instructions for Form 1040 (or in the Instructions for Form 1040NR).

  ☐ **No.** Complete the rest of Form 1040 or Form 1040NR.

SCHEDULE E	Supplemental Income and Loss	OMB No. 1545-0074
(Form 1040)	(From rental real estate, royalties, partnerships, S corporations, estates, trusts, REMICs, etc.)	2007
Department of the Treasury Internal Revenue Service	▶ Attach to Form 1040, 1040NR, or Form 1041. ▶ See Instructions for Schedule E (Form 1040).	Attachment Sequence No. 13

Name(s) shown on return | Your social security number

Part I   Income or Loss From Rental Real Estate and Royalties   **Note.** If you are in the business of renting personal property, use **Schedule C** or **C-EZ** (see page E-3). If you are an individual, report farm rental income or loss from **Form 4835** on page 2, line 40.

1	List the type and location of each **rental real estate property**:	2 For each rental real estate property listed on line 1, did you or your family use it during the tax year for personal purposes for more than the greater of: • 14 days **or** • 10% of the total days rented at fair rental value? (See page E-3)	Yes	No
A			A	
B			B	
C			C	

Income:

			Properties			Totals (Add columns A, B, and C.)
			A	B	C	
3	Rents received	3				3
4	Royalties received	4				4

Expenses:

5	Advertising	5				
6	Auto and travel (see page E-4) .	6				
7	Cleaning and maintenance . . .	7				
8	Commissions	8				
9	Insurance	9				
10	Legal and other professional fees	10				
11	Management fees	11				
12	Mortgage interest paid to banks, etc. (see page E-4)	12				12
13	Other interest	13				
14	Repairs	14				
15	Supplies	15				
16	Taxes	16				
17	Utilities	17				
18	Other (list) ▶	18				
19	Add lines 5 through 18	19				19
20	Depreciation expense or depletion (see page E-5)	20				20
21	Total expenses. Add lines 19 and 20	21				
22	Income or (loss) from rental real estate or royalty properties. Subtract line 21 from line 3 (rents) or line 4 (royalties). If the result is a (loss), see page E-5 to find out if you must file **Form 6198** . . .	22				
23	Deductible rental real estate loss. **Caution.** Your rental real estate loss on line 22 may be limited. See page E-5 to find out if you must file **Form 8582.** Real estate professionals must complete line 43 on page 2	23	( )	( )	( )	
24	**Income.** Add positive amounts shown on line 22. **Do not** include any losses				24	
25	**Losses.** Add royalty losses from line 22 and rental real estate losses from line 23. Enter total losses here.				25	( )
26	**Total rental real estate and royalty income or (loss).** Combine lines 24 and 25. Enter the result here. If Parts II, III, IV, and line 40 on page 2 do not apply to you, also enter this amount on Form 1040, line 17, or Form 1040NR, line 18. Otherwise, include this amount in the total on line 41 on page 2 . .				26	

For Paperwork Reduction Act Notice, see page E-7 of the instructions.   Cat. No. 11344L   **Schedule E (Form 1040) 2007**

Schedule E (Form 1040) 2007   Attachment Sequence No. **13**   Page **2**

Name(s) shown on return. Do not enter name and social security number if shown on other side. | Your social security number

Caution. The IRS compares amounts reported on your tax return with amounts shown on Schedule(s) K-1.

Part II **Income or Loss From Partnerships and S Corporations**   **Note.** If you report a loss from an at-risk activity for which **any** amount is **not** at risk, you **must** check the box in column **(e)** on line 28 and attach **Form 6198.** See page E-1.

27 Are you reporting any loss not allowed in a prior year due to the at-risk or basis limitations, a prior year unallowed loss from a passive activity (if that loss was not reported on Form 8582), or unreimbursed partnership expenses? ☐ **Yes** ☐ **No**
    If you answered "Yes," see page E-6 before completing this section.

28	**(a)** Name	**(b)** Enter **P** for partnership; **S** for S corporation	**(c)** Check if foreign partnership	**(d)** Employer identification number	**(e)** Check if any amount is not at risk
A			☐		☐
B			☐		☐
C			☐		☐
D			☐		☐

	Passive Income and Loss		Nonpassive Income and Loss		
	(f) Passive loss allowed (attach **Form 8582** if required)	**(g)** Passive income from **Schedule K–1**	**(h)** Nonpassive loss from **Schedule K–1**	**(i)** Section 179 expense deduction from **Form 4562**	**(j)** Nonpassive income from **Schedule K–1**
A					
B					
C					
D					
29a Totals					
b Totals					

30	Add columns (g) and (j) of line 29a	30	
31	Add columns (f), (h), and (i) of line 29b	31	( )
32	**Total partnership and S corporation income or (loss).** Combine lines 30 and 31. Enter the result here and include in the total on line 41 below	32	

Part III **Income or Loss From Estates and Trusts**

33	**(a)** Name	**(b)** Employer identification number
A		
B		

	Passive Income and Loss		Nonpassive Income and Loss	
	(c) Passive deduction or loss allowed (attach **Form 8582** if required)	**(d)** Passive income from **Schedule K–1**	**(e)** Deduction or loss from **Schedule K–1**	**(f)** Other income from **Schedule K–1**
A				
B				
34a Totals				
b Totals				

35	Add columns (d) and (f) of line 34a	35	
36	Add columns (c) and (e) of line 34b	36	( )
37	**Total estate and trust income or (loss).** Combine lines 35 and 36. Enter the result here and include in the total on line 41 below	37	

Part IV **Income or Loss From Real Estate Mortgage Investment Conduits (REMICs)—Residual Holder**

38	**(a)** Name	**(b)** Employer identification number	**(c)** Excess inclusion from **Schedules Q,** line 2c (see page E-7)	**(d)** Taxable income (net loss) from **Schedules Q,** line 1b	**(e)** Income from **Schedules Q,** line 3b

| 39 | Combine columns (d) and (e) only. Enter the result here and include in the total on line 41 below | 39 | |

Part V **Summary**

| 40 | Net farm rental income or (loss) from **Form 4835.** Also, complete line 42 below . . . . . . | 40 | |
| 41 | **Total income or (loss).** Combine lines 26, 32, 37, 39, and 40. Enter the result here and on Form 1040, line 17, or Form 1040NR, line 18 ▶ | 41 | |

42 **Reconciliation of farming and fishing income.** Enter your **gross** farming and fishing income reported on Form 4835, line 7; Schedule K-1 (Form 1065), box 14, code B; Schedule K-1 (Form 1120S), box 17, code T; and Schedule K-1 (Form 1041), line 14, code F (see page E-7) . . . . | **42** | |

43 **Reconciliation for real estate professionals.** If you were a real estate professional (see page E-2), enter the net income or (loss) you reported anywhere on Form 1040 or Form 1040NR from all rental real estate activities in which you materially participated under the passive activity loss rules . | **43** | |

Schedule E (Form 1040) 2007

SCHEDULE F
(Form 1040)

Department of the Treasury
Internal Revenue Service

Profit or Loss From Farming

► Attach to Form 1040, Form 1040NR, Form 1041, Form 1065, or Form 1065-B.

► See Instructions for Schedule F (Form 1040).

OMB No. 1545-0074

2007

Attachment
Sequence No. **14**

Name of proprietor

Social security number (SSN)

A Principal product. Describe in one or two words your principal crop or activity for the current tax year.

B Enter code from Part IV

D Employer ID number (EIN), if any

C Accounting method: (1) ☐ Cash   (2) ☐ Accrual

E Did you "materially participate" in the operation of this business during 2007? If "No," see page F-2 for limit on passive losses.   ☐ Yes   ☐ No

| **Part I** | **Farm Income—Cash Method.** Complete Parts I and II (Accrual method. Complete Parts II and III, and Part I, line 11.) |
| | Do not include sales of livestock held for draft, breeding, sport, or dairy purposes. Report these sales on Form 4797. |

1	Sales of livestock and other items you bought for resale	1			
2	Cost or other basis of livestock and other items reported on line 1 . . .	2			
3	Subtract line 2 from line 1			3	
4	Sales of livestock, produce, grains, and other products you raised			4	
5a	Cooperative distributions (Form(s) 1099-PATR) .	5a		5b Taxable amount	5b	
6a	Agricultural program payments (see page F-3) .	6a		6b Taxable amount	6b	
7	Commodity Credit Corporation (CCC) loans (see page F-3):				
a	CCC loans reported under election			7a	
b	CCC loans forfeited	7b		7c Taxable amount	7c	
8	Crop insurance proceeds and federal crop disaster payments (see page F-3):				
a	Amount received in 2007	8a		8b Taxable amount	8b	
c	If election to defer to 2008 is attached, check here ► ☐		8d Amount deferred from 2006 .	8d	
9	Custom hire (machine work) income			9	
10	Other income, including federal and state gasoline or fuel tax credit or refund (see page F-3)			10	
11	**Gross income.** Add amounts in the right column for lines 3 through 10. If you use the accrual method, enter the amount from Part III, line 51 . . . . ►			11	

| **Part II** | **Farm Expenses—Cash and Accrual Method.** |
| | Do not include personal or living expenses such as taxes, insurance, or repairs on your home. |

12	Car and truck expenses (see page F-4). Also attach **Form 4562** . .	12		25	Pension and profit-sharing plans	25	
13	Chemicals	13		26	Rent or lease (see page F-6):		
14	Conservation expenses (see page F-4)	14		a	Vehicles, machinery, and equipment	26a	
15	Custom hire (machine work) .	15		b	Other (land, animals, etc.) . .	26b	
16	Depreciation and section 179 expense deduction not claimed elsewhere (see page F-5) . .	16		27	Repairs and maintenance . .	27	
				28	Seeds and plants	28	
				29	Storage and warehousing . .	29	
17	Employee benefit programs other than on line 25	17		30	Supplies	30	
18	Feed	18		31	Taxes	31	
19	Fertilizers and lime	19		32	Utilities	32	
20	Freight and trucking. . . .	20		33	Veterinary, breeding, and medicine	33	
21	Gasoline, fuel, and oil . . .	21		34	Other expenses (specify):		
22	Insurance (other than health) .	22		a	....	34a	
23	Interest:			b	....	34b	
a	Mortgage (paid to banks, etc.)	23a		c	....	34c	
b	Other	23b		d	....	34d	
24	Labor hired (less employment credits)	24		e	....	34e	
				f	....	34f	

35	**Total expenses.** Add lines 12 through 34f. If line 34f is negative, see instructions . . . . ►	35	
36	**Net farm profit or (loss).** Subtract line 35 from line 11.		
	• If a profit, enter the profit on **Form 1040, line 18,** and **also** on **Schedule SE, line 1.** If you file Form 1040NR, enter the profit on **Form 1040NR, line 19.** }	36	
	• If a loss, you **must** go to line 37. Estates, trusts, and partnerships, see page F-6.		
37	If you have a loss, you **must** check the box that describes your investment in this activity (see page F-7).		
	• If you checked 37a, enter the loss on **Form 1040, line 18,** and **also** on **Schedule SE, line 1.** If you file Form 1040NR, enter the loss on **Form 1040NR, line 19.** }	37a ☐ All investment is at risk.	
	• If you checked 37b, you **must** attach **Form 6198.** Your loss may be limited.	37b ☐ Some investment is not at risk.	

Paperwork Reduction Act Notice, see page F-7 of the instructions.   Cat. No. 11346H

Part III **Farm Income—Accrual Method** (see page F-7).

Do not include sales of livestock held for draft, breeding, sport, or dairy purposes. Report these sales on Form 4797 and do not include this livestock on line 46 below.

38	Sales of livestock, produce, grains, and other products	**38**	
39a	Cooperative distributions (Form(s) 1099-PATR) . **39a** [____] **39b** Taxable amount	**39b**	
40a	Agricultural program payments . . . . . **40a** [____] **40b** Taxable amount	**40b**	
41	Commodity Credit Corporation (CCC) loans:		
a	CCC loans reported under election	**41a**	
b	CCC loans forfeited . . . . **41b** [____] **41c** Taxable amount	**41c**	
42	Crop insurance proceeds	**42**	
43	Custom hire (machine work) income	**43**	
44	Other income, including federal and state gasoline or fuel tax credit or refund	**44**	
45	Add amounts in the right column for lines 38 through 44	**45**	
46	Inventory of livestock, produce, grains, and other products at beginning of the year . . . . **46** [____]		
47	Cost of livestock, produce, grains, and other products purchased during the year . . . . **47** [____]		
48	Add lines 46 and 47 . . . . **48** [____]		
49	Inventory of livestock, produce, grains, and other products at end of year **49** [____]		
50	Cost of livestock, produce, grains, and other products sold. Subtract line 49 from line 48*	**50**	
51	**Gross income.** Subtract line 50 from line 45. Enter the result here and on Part I, line 11 . . . . ▶	**51**	

*If you use the unit-livestock-price method or the farm-price method of valuing inventory and the amount on line 49 is larger than the amount on line 48, subtract line 48 from line 49. Enter the result on line 50. Add lines 45 and 50. Enter the total on line 51 and on Part I, line 11.

Part IV **Principal Agricultural Activity Codes**

 File Schedule C (Form 1040) or Schedule C-EZ (Form 1040) instead of Schedule F if (a) your principal source of income is from providing agricultural services such as soil preparation, veterinary, farm labor, horticultural, or management for a fee or on a contract basis, or (b) you are engaged in the business of breeding, raising, and caring for dogs, cats, or other pet animals.

These codes for the Principal Agricultural Activity classify farms by their primary activity to facilitate the administration of the Internal Revenue Code. These six-digit codes are based on the North American Industry Classification System (NAICS).

Select the code that best identifies your primary farming activity and enter the six digit number on page 1, line B.

Crop Production

111100	Oilseed and grain farming
111210	Vegetable and melon farming
111300	Fruit and tree nut farming
111400	Greenhouse, nursery, and floriculture production
111900	Other crop farming

Animal Production

112111	Beef cattle ranching and farming
112112	Cattle feedlots
112120	Dairy cattle and milk production
112210	Hog and pig farming
112300	Poultry and egg production
112400	Sheep and goat farming
112510	Aquaculture
112900	Other animal production

Forestry and Logging

113000	Forestry and logging (including forest nurseries and timber tracts)

SCHEDULE SE
(Form 1040)

Department of the Treasury
Internal Revenue Service

Self-Employment Tax

▶ **Attach to Form 1040.** ▶ **See Instructions for Schedule SE (Form 1040).**

OMB No. 1545-0074

20**07**

Attachment
Sequence No. **17**

Name of person with **self-employment** income (as shown on Form 1040)

Social security number of person
with **self-employment** income ▶

Who Must File Schedule SE

You must file Schedule SE if:

- You had net earnings from self-employment from **other than** church employee income (line 4 of Short Schedule SE or line 4c of Long Schedule SE) of $400 or more, **or**
- You had church employee income of $108.28 or more. Income from services you performed as a minister or a member of a religious order **is not** church employee income (see page SE-1).

Note. Even if you had a loss or a small amount of income from self-employment, it may be to your benefit to file Schedule SE and use either "optional method" in Part II of Long Schedule SE (see page SE-4).

Exception. If your only self-employment income was from earnings as a minister, member of a religious order, or Christian Science practitioner **and** you filed Form 4361 and received IRS approval not to be taxed on those earnings, **do not** file Schedule SE. Instead, write "Exempt–Form 4361" on Form 1040, line 58.

May I Use Short Schedule SE or Must I Use Long Schedule SE?

Note. Use this flowchart **only if** you must file Schedule SE. If unsure, see Who Must File Schedule SE, above.

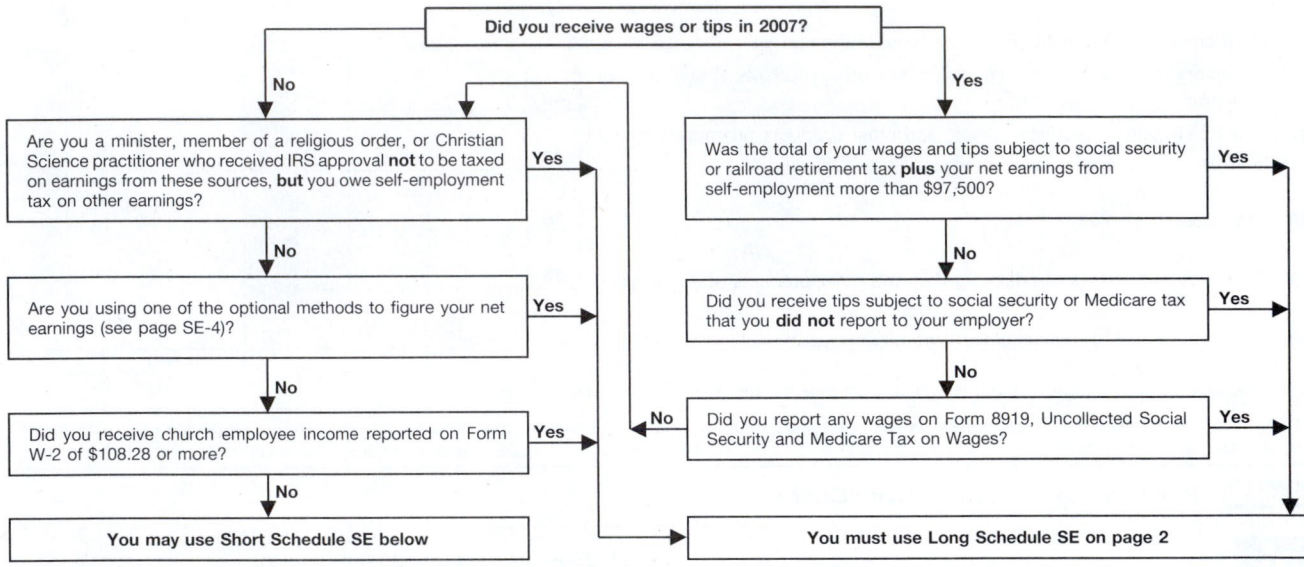

Section A—Short Schedule SE. Caution. Read above to see if you can use Short Schedule SE.

1	Net farm profit or (loss) from Schedule F, line 36, and farm partnerships, Schedule K-1 (Form 1065), box 14, code A	**1**	
2	Net profit or (loss) from Schedule C, line 31; Schedule C-EZ, line 3; Schedule K-1 (Form 1065), box 14, code A (other than farming); and Schedule K-1 (Form 1065-B), box 9, code J1. Ministers and members of religious orders, see page SE-1 for amounts to report on this line. See page SE-3 for other income to report	**2**	
3	Combine lines 1 and 2	**3**	
4	**Net earnings from self-employment.** Multiply line 3 by 92.35% (.9235). If less than $400, **do not** file this schedule; you do not owe self-employment tax . . . . ▶	**4**	
5	**Self-employment tax.** If the amount on line 4 is: • $97,500 or less, multiply line 4 by 15.3% (.153). Enter the result here and on **Form 1040, line 58.** • More than $97,500, multiply line 4 by 2.9% (.029). Then, add $12,090 to the result. Enter the total here and on **Form 1040, line 58**	**5**	
6	**Deduction for one-half of self-employment tax.** Multiply line 5 by 50% (.5). Enter the result here and on **Form 1040, line 27** . . .	**6**	

For Paperwork Reduction Act Notice, see Form 1040 instructions.   Cat. No. 11358Z   **Schedule SE (Form 1040) 2007**

Name of person with **self-employment** income (as shown on Form 1040)	Social security number of person with **self-employment** income ▶		

Section B—Long Schedule SE

Part I   Self-Employment Tax

Note. If your only income subject to self-employment tax is **church employee income,** skip lines 1 through 4b. Enter -0- on line 4c and go to line 5a. Income from services you performed as a minister or a member of a religious order **is not** church employee income. See page SE-1.

A   If you are a minister, member of a religious order, or Christian Science practitioner **and** you filed Form 4361, but you had $400 or more of **other** net earnings from self-employment, check here and continue with Part I . . . . . . ▶ ☐

1	Net farm profit or (loss) from Schedule F, line 36, and farm partnerships, Schedule K-1 (Form 1065), box 14, code A. **Note.** Skip this line if you use the farm optional method (see page SE-4)	**1**		
2	Net profit or (loss) from Schedule C, line 31; Schedule C-EZ, line 3; Schedule K-1 (Form 1065), box 14, code A (other than farming); and Schedule K-1 (Form 1065-B), box 9, code J1. Ministers and members of religious orders, see page SE-1 for amounts to report on this line. See page SE-3 for other income to report. **Note.** Skip this line if you use the nonfarm optional method (see page SE-4)	**2**		
3	Combine lines 1 and 2	**3**		
4a	If line 3 is more than zero, multiply line 3 by 92.35% (.9235). Otherwise, enter amount from line 3	**4a**		
b	If you elect one or both of the optional methods, enter the total of lines 15 and 17 here . . .	**4b**		
c	Combine lines 4a and 4b. If less than $400, **stop;** you do not owe self-employment tax. **Exception.** If less than $400 and you had **church employee income,** enter -0- and continue. . . . . . ▶	**4c**		
5a	Enter your **church employee income** from Form W-2. See page SE-1 for definition of church employee income **5a**			
b	Multiply line 5a by 92.35% (.9235). If less than $100, enter -0-	**5b**		
6	**Net earnings from self-employment.** Add lines 4c and 5b	**6**		
7	Maximum amount of combined wages and self-employment earnings subject to social security tax or the 6.2% portion of the 7.65% railroad retirement (tier 1) tax for 2007	**7**	97,500	00
8a	Total social security wages and tips (total of boxes 3 and 7 on Form(s) W-2) and railroad retirement (tier 1) compensation. If $97,500 or more, skip lines 8b through 10, and go to line 11 . . . . **8a**			
b	Unreported tips subject to social security tax (from Form 4137, line 10) **8b**			
c	Wages subject to social security tax (from Form 8919, line 10) . . . **8c**			
d	Add lines 8a, 8b, and 8c	**8d**		
9	Subtract line 8d from line 7. If zero or less, enter -0- here and on line 10 and go to line 11 . ▶	**9**		
10	Multiply the **smaller** of line 6 or line 9 by 12.4% (.124)	**10**		
11	Multiply line 6 by 2.9% (.029)	**11**		
12	**Self-employment tax.** Add lines 10 and 11. Enter here and on **Form 1040, line 58**	**12**		
13	**Deduction for one-half of self-employment tax.** Multiply line 12 by 50% (.5). Enter the result here and on **Form 1040, line 27** **13**			

Part II   Optional Methods To Figure Net Earnings (see page SE-4)

Farm Optional Method. You may use this method **only** if **(a)** your gross farm income[1] was not more than $2,400, **or (b)** your net farm profits[2] were less than $1,733.

14	Maximum income for optional methods	**14**	1,600	00
15	Enter the **smaller** of: two-thirds (⅔) of gross farm income[1] (not less than zero) or $1,600. Also include this amount on line 4b above	**15**		

Nonfarm Optional Method. You may use this method **only** if **(a)** your net nonfarm profits[3] were less than $1,733 and also less than 72.189% of your gross nonfarm income,[4] **and (b)** you had net earnings from self-employment of at least $400 in 2 of the prior 3 years.

Caution. You may use this method no more than five times.

16	Subtract line 15 from line 14	**16**		
17	Enter the **smaller** of: two-thirds (⅔) of gross nonfarm income[4] (not less than zero) **or** the amount on line 16. Also include this amount on line 4b above	**17**		

[1] From Sch. F, line 11, and Sch. K-1 (Form 1065), box 14, code B.

[2] From Sch. F, line 36, and Sch. K-1 (Form 1065), box 14, code A.

[3] From Sch. C, line 31; Sch. C-EZ, line 3; Sch. K-1 (Form 1065), box 14, code A; and Sch. K-1 (Form 1065-B), box 9, code J1.

[4] From Sch. C, line 7; Sch. C-EZ, line 1; Sch. K-1 (Form 1065), box 14, code C; and Sch. K-1 (Form 1065-B), box 9, code J2.

The words and phrases in this glossary have been defined to reflect their conventional use in the field of taxation. The definitions may therefore be incomplete for other purposes.

A

Abandoned spouse. The abandoned spouse provision enables a married taxpayer with a dependent child whose spouse did not live in the taxpayer's home during the last six months of the tax year to file as a head of household rather than as married filing separately.

Accelerated cost recovery system (ACRS). A method in which the cost of tangible property is recovered over a prescribed period of time. Enacted by the Economic Recovery Tax Act (ERTA) of 1981 and substantially modified by the Tax Reform Act (TRA) of 1986 (the modified system is referred to as MACRS), the approach disregards salvage value, imposes a period of cost recovery that depends upon the classification of the asset into one of various recovery periods, and prescribes the applicable percentage of cost that can be deducted each year. § 168.

Accelerated death benefits. The amount received from a life insurance policy by the insured who is terminally ill or chronically ill. Any realized gain may be excluded from the gross income of the insured if the policy is surrendered to the insurer or is sold to a licensed viatical settlement provider. § 101(g).

Accelerated depreciation. Various methods of depreciation that yield larger deductions in the earlier years of the life of an asset than the straight-line method. Examples include the double declining-balance and the sum-of-the-years' digits methods of depreciation. § 167.

Accident and health benefits. Employee fringe benefits provided by employers through the payment of health and accident insurance premiums or the establishment of employer-funded medical reimbursement plans. Employers generally are entitled to a deduction for such payments, whereas employees generally exclude the fringe benefits from gross income. §§ 105 and 106.

Accountable plan. An accountable plan is a type of expense reimbursement plan that requires an employee to render an adequate accounting to the employer and return any excess reimbursement or allowance. If the expense qualifies, it will be treated as a deduction *for* AGI.

Accounting income. The accountant's concept of income is generally based upon the realization principle. Financial accounting income may differ from taxable income (e.g., accelerated depreciation might be used for Federal income tax and straight-line depreciation for financial accounting purposes). Differences are included in a reconciliation of taxable and accounting income on Schedule M–1 or Schedule M–3 of Form 1120 for corporations. Seventy-five percent of the excess of adjusted current earnings over alternative minimum taxable income is an adjustment for alternative minimum tax purposes for a corporation. See also *alternative minimum tax* and *economic income*.

Accounting method. The method under which income and expenses are determined for tax purposes. Major accounting methods are the cash basis and the accrual basis. Special methods are available for the reporting of gain on installment sales, recognition of income on construction projects (the completed contract and percentage of completion methods), and the valuation of inventories (last-in, first-out and first-in, first-out). §§ 446–474. See also *accrual method, cash receipts method, completed contract method, percentage of completion method*, etc.

Accounting period. The period of time, usually a year, used by a taxpayer for the determination of tax liability. Unless a fiscal year is chosen, taxpayers must determine and pay their income tax liability by using the calendar year (January 1 through December 31) as the period of measurement. An example of a fiscal year is July 1 through June 30. A change in accounting period (e.g., from a calendar year to a fiscal year) generally requires the consent of the IRS. A new taxpayer, such as a newly formed corporation or an estate created upon the death of an individual taxpayer, is free to select either a calendar or a fiscal year without the consent of the IRS. Limitations exist on the accounting period that may be selected by a partnership, an S corporation, and a personal service corporation. §§ 441–444.

Accrual basis. See *accrual method*.

Accrual method. A method of accounting that reflects expenses incurred and income earned for any one tax year. In contrast to the cash basis of accounting, expenses do not have to be paid to be deductible nor does income have to be received to be taxable. Unearned income (e.g., prepaid interest and rent) generally is taxed in the year of receipt regardless of the method of accounting used by the taxpayer. § 446(c)(2). See also *accounting method, cash receipts method,* and *unearned income.*

Accumulated earnings tax. A special tax imposed on corporations that accumulate (rather than distribute) their earnings beyond the reasonable needs of the business. The tax is imposed on accumulated taxable income and is imposed in addition to the corporate income tax. §§ 531–537.

ACE adjustment. See *adjusted current earnings (ACE) adjustment.*

Acquiescence. In agreement with the result reached. The IRS follows a policy of either acquiescing (*A, Acq.*) or nonacquiescing (*NA, Nonacq.*) in the results reached in certain judicial decisions.

Acquisition indebtedness. Debt incurred in acquiring, constructing, or substantially improving a qualified residence of the taxpayer. The interest on such loans is deductible as *qualified residence interest.* However, interest on such debt is deductible only on the portion of the indebtedness that does not exceed $1,000,000 ($500,000 for married persons filing separate returns). § 163(h)(3). See also *home equity loans.*

ACRS. See *accelerated cost recovery system.*

Active income. Active income includes wages, salary, commissions, bonuses, profits from a trade or business in which the taxpayer is a material participant, gain on the sale or other disposition of assets used in an active trade or business, and income from intangible property if the taxpayer's personal efforts significantly contributed to the creation of the property. The passive activity loss rules require classification of income and losses into three categories with active income being one of them.

Active participation. A term that is relevant for both the at-risk rules and the passive activity loss rules associated with rental real estate activities. For the at-risk rules, the following factors indicate active participation: (1) making decisions involving the operation or management of the activity, (2) performing services for the activity, and (3) hiring and discharging employees. For the passive activity loss rules, the taxpayer must participate in the making of management decisions in a significant and bona fide sense.

Ad valorem tax. A tax imposed on the value of property. The most familiar ad valorem tax is that imposed by states, counties, and cities on real estate. Ad valorem taxes can, however, be imposed upon personal property (e.g., a motor vehicle tax based on the value of an automobile). §§ 164(a)(1) and (2).

Additional depreciation. The excess of the amount of depreciation actually deducted over the amount that would have been deducted had the straight-line method been used. § 1250(b). See also *Section 1250 recapture.*

Additional first-year depreciation. See *Fifty percent additional first-year depreciation.*

Adjusted basis. The cost or other basis of property reduced by depreciation (cost recovery) allowed or allowable and increased by capital improvements. See also *basis* and *realized gain or loss.*

Adjusted current earnings (ACE) adjustment. An adjustment in computing corporate alternative minimum taxable income (AMTI), computed at 75 percent of the excess of adjusted current earnings and profits computations over unadjusted AMTI. ACE computations reflect longer and slower cost recovery deductions and other restrictions on the timing of certain recognition events. Exempt interest, life insurance proceeds, and other receipts that are included in earnings and profits but not in taxable income also increase the ACE adjustment. If unadjusted AMTI exceeds adjusted current earnings and profits, the ACE adjustment is negative. The negative adjustment is limited to the aggregate of the positive adjustments under ACE for prior years, reduced by any previously claimed negative adjustments. See also *alternative minimum tax* and *earnings and profits.*

Adjusted gross income (AGI). A determination peculiar to individual taxpayers. Generally, it represents gross income less business expenses, expenses attributable to the production of rent or royalty income, the allowed capital loss deduction, and certain personal expenses (deductions *for* AGI). § 62. See also *gross income.*

Adoption expenses credit. A provision intended to assist taxpayers who incur nonrecurring costs directly associated with the adoption process such as legal costs, social service review costs, and transportation costs. Up to $11,650 ($11,650 for a child with special needs regardless of the actual adoption expenses) of costs incurred to adopt an eligible child qualify for the credit. A taxpayer may claim the credit in the year qualifying expenses are paid or incurred if the expenses are paid during or after the year in which the adoption is finalized. For qualifying expenses paid or incurred in a tax year prior to the year the adoption is finalized, the credit must be claimed in the tax year following the tax year during which the expenses are paid or incurred. § 23.

Advance payments. In general, prepayments for services or goods are includible in gross income upon receipt of the advance payments (for both accrual and cash basis taxpayers). However, Revenue Procedure 2004–34, I.R.B. No. 22, 991, provides guidelines for the deferral of tax on certain advance payments providing specific conditions are met.

AFTR. Published by Research Institute of America (formerly by Prentice-Hall), *American Federal Tax Reports* contains all of the Federal tax decisions issued by the U.S. District Courts, U.S. Court of Federal Claims, U.S. Courts of Appeals, and U.S. Supreme Court.

AFTR2d. The second series of the *American Federal Tax Reports.*

AFTR3d. The third series of the *American Federal Tax Reports.*

Alimony and separate maintenance payments. Alimony and separate maintenance payments are includible in the gross income of the recipient and are deductible by the payor. The payments must be made in discharge of a legal obligation arising from a marital or family relationship. Child support and voluntary payments are not treated as alimony. Alimony is deductible *for* AGI. §§ 62(10), 71, and 215. See also *child support payments.*

Alimony recapture. The amount of alimony that previously has been included in the gross income of the recipient and deducted by the payor that now is deducted by the recipient and included in the gross income of the payor as the result of front-loading. § 71(f).

All events test. For accrual method taxpayers, income is earned when (1) all the events have occurred that fix the right to receive the income and (2) the amount can be determined with reasonable accuracy. Accrual of income cannot be postponed simply because a portion of the income may have to be returned in a subsequent period. The all events test also is utilized to determine when expenses can be deducted by an accrual basis taxpayer. The application of the test could cause a variation between the treatment of an item for accounting and for tax purposes. For example, a reserve for warranty expense may be properly accruable under generally accepted accounting principles but not be deductible under the Federal income tax law. Because of the application of the all events test, the deduction becomes available in the year the warranty obligation becomes fixed and the amount is determinable with reasonable certainty. See also *economic performance test*. Reg. §§ 1.446–1(c)(1)(ii) and 1.461–1(a)(2).

Alternate valuation date. Property passing from a person by reason of death may be valued for death tax purposes as of the date of death or the alternate valuation date. The alternate valuation date is six months from the date of death or the date the property is disposed of by the estate, whichever comes first. To use the alternate valuation date, the executor or administrator of the estate must make an affirmative election. The election of the alternate valuation date is not available unless it decreases both the amount of the gross estate *and* the estate tax liability. §§ 1014(a) and 2032.

Alternative depreciation system (ADS). A cost recovery system that produces a smaller deduction than would be calculated under ACRS or MACRS. The alternative system must be used in certain instances and can be elected in other instances. § 168(g). See also *cost recovery allowance*.

Alternative minimum tax (AMT). The alternative minimum tax is imposed only to the extent it exceeds the regular income tax (in effect, the tax liability is the greater of the tax liability calculated using the AMT rules and that calculated using the regular income tax rules). The AMT rates (26 and 28 percent for the individual taxpayer and 20 percent for the corporate taxpayer) are applied to the AMT base. The AMT base is calculated by modifying taxable income as follows: (1) add tax preferences, (2) add certain adjustments, (3) deduct certain adjustments, and (4) deduct the exemption amount. §§ 55–59. See also *adjusted current earnings (ACE) adjustment*.

Alternative minimum tax credit. The AMT can result from timing differences that give rise to positive adjustments in calculating the AMT base. To provide equity for the taxpayer when these timing differences reverse, the regular tax liability may be reduced by a tax credit for prior year's minimum tax liability attributable to timing differences. § 53.

Alternative tax. An option that is allowed in computing the tax on net capital gain. For the corporate taxpayer, the rate is 35 percent (the same as the highest regular corporate tax rate). Thus, for corporate taxpayers, the alternative tax does not produce a beneficial result. For noncorporate taxpayers, the rate is usually 15 percent (but it is 25 percent for unrecaptured § 1250 gain and is 28 percent for collectibles and § 1202 gain). However, if the noncorporate taxpayer is in either the 10 percent or the 15 percent tax bracket, the alternative tax rate is 0 percent in 2008 and 5 percent in 2007 and prior years (rather than 15 percent). §§ 1(h) and 1201. See also *collectibles, net capital gain* and *unrecaptured § 1250 gain (25 percent gain)*.

Alternative tax NOL deduction (ATNOLD). In calculating the AMT, the taxpayer is allowed to deduct NOL carryovers and carrybacks. A special calculation, referred to as the ATNOLD, is required for this purpose. The regular income tax is modified for AMT adjustments and preferences to produce the ATNOLD. § 56(d).

Amortization. The allocation (and charge to expense) of the cost or other basis of an intangible asset over a statutory period of 15 years. Examples of amortizable intangibles include patents, copyrights, covenants not to compete, acquired goodwill, and leasehold interests. See also *estimated useful life* and *goodwill*. § 197.

Amount realized. The amount received by a taxpayer on the sale or other disposition of property. The amount realized is the sum of the cash and the fair market value of any property or services received, plus any related debt assumed by the buyer. Determining the amount realized is the starting point for arriving at realized gain or loss. The amount realized is defined in § 1001(b) and the related Regulations. See also *realized gain or loss* and *recognized gain or loss*.

AMT adjustments. In calculating AMTI, certain adjustments are added to or deducted from taxable income. These adjustments generally reflect timing differences. § 56.

AMT exclusions. A credit that can be used to reduce the regular tax liability in future tax years is available in connection with the AMT (*AMT credit*). The credit is applicable only with respect to the AMT that results from timing differences. It is not available in connection with AMT exclusions, which include the standard deduction, personal exemptions, medical expenses deductible in calculating the regular income tax that are not deductible in computing the AMT, other itemized deductions that are not allowable for AMT purposes, excess percentage depletion, and tax-exempt interest on specified private activity bonds.

Annuity. A fixed sum payable to a person at specified intervals for a specific period of time or for life. Payments represent a partial return of capital and a return (interest) on the capital investment. Therefore, an exclusion ratio must be used to compute the amount of nontaxable income. The exclusion ratio is used until the annuitant has recovered his or her investment in the annuity contract. Thereafter, all of the annuity payments received are included in gross income. If the annuitant dies before his or her investment is recovered, a deduction is allowed. § 72. See also *qualified pension or profit sharing plan*.

Appellate court. For Federal tax purposes, appellate courts include the Courts of Appeals and the Supreme Court. If the party losing in the trial (or lower) court is dissatisfied with the result, the dispute may be carried to the appropriate appellate court. See also *Court of Appeals* and *trial court*.

Archer medical savings account. See *medical savings account*.

Arm's length transaction. The standard under which unrelated parties would determine an exchange price for a transaction. Suppose, for example, Cardinal Corporation sells property to its sole shareholder for $10,000. In testing whether the $10,000 is an "arm's length" price, one would ascertain the price that would have been negotiated between the corporation and an unrelated party in a bargained exchange.

Asset Depreciation Range (ADR) system. A system of estimated useful lives for categories of tangible assets prescribed by the IRS. The system provides a range for each category that extends from 20 percent above to 20 percent below the guideline class lives prescribed by the IRS.

Assignment of income. A procedure whereby a taxpayer attempts to avoid the recognition of income by assigning the property that generates the income to another. Such a procedure will not avoid the recognition of income by the taxpayer making the assignment if it can be said that the income was earned at the point of the transfer. In this case, usually referred to as an anticipatory assignment of income, the income will be taxed to the person who earns it.

Association. An organization treated as a corporation for Federal tax purposes even though it may not qualify as such under applicable state law. An entity designated as a trust or a partnership, for example, may be classified as an association if it clearly possesses corporate attributes. Corporate attributes include centralized management, continuity of life, free transferability of interests, and limited liability. When the check-the-box Regulations were finalized, the association Regulations were withdrawn. Thus, for most entities, reclassification as an association is unlikely. § 7701(a)(3). See also *check-the-box Regulations.*

At-risk limitation. Under the at-risk rules, a taxpayer's deductible losses from an activity for any taxable year are limited to the amount the taxpayer has at risk at the end of the taxable year. The initial amount considered at risk is generally the sum of the amount of cash and the adjusted basis of property contributed to the activity and amounts borrowed for use in the activity for which the taxpayer is personally liable or has pledged as security property not used in the activity. § 465.

Attribution. Under certain circumstances, the tax law applies attribution (construction ownership) rules to assign to one taxpayer the ownership interest of another taxpayer. If, for example, the stock of Gold Corporation is held 60 percent by Marsha and 40 percent by Sid, Marsha may be deemed to own 100 percent of Gold Corporation if she and Sid are mother and son. In that case, the stock owned by Sid is attributed to Marsha. See, for example, §§ 267 and 318.

Audit. Inspection and verification of a taxpayer's return or other transactions possessing tax consequences. See also *correspondence audit, field audit,* and *office audit.*

Automatic mileage method. See *automobile expenses.*

Automobile expenses. Automobile expenses are generally deductible only to the extent the automobile is used in business or for the production of income. Personal commuting expenses are not deductible. The taxpayer may deduct actual expenses (including depreciation and insurance), or the standard (automatic) mileage rate may be used (50.5 cents for 2008 and 48.5 cents for 2007). Automobile expenses incurred for medical purposes or in connection with job-related moving expenses are deductible to the extent of actual out-of-pocket expenses or at the rate of 19 cents per mile in 2008 (20 cents per mile in 2007). For charitable activities, the rate is 14 cents per mile. See also *transportation expenses.*

B

Bad debts. A deduction is permitted if a business account receivable subsequently becomes partially or completely worthless, providing the income arising from the debt previously was included in income. Available methods are the specific charge-off method and the reserve method. However, except for certain financial institutions, TRA of 1986 repealed the use of the reserve method for 1987 and thereafter. If the reserve method is used, partially or totally worthless accounts are charged to the reserve. A nonbusiness bad debt deduction is allowed as a short-term capital loss if the loan did not arise in connection with the creditor's trade or business activities. Loans between related parties (family members) generally are classified as nonbusiness. § 166. See also *nonbusiness bad debts.*

Basis. The acquisition cost assigned to an asset for income tax purposes. For assets acquired by purchase, the basis is the cost (§ 1012). Special rules govern the basis of property received by virtue of another's death (§ 1014) or by gift (§ 1015), the basis of stock received on a transfer of property to a controlled corporation (§ 358), the basis of the property transferred to the corporation (§ 362), and the basis of property received upon the liquidation of a corporation (§§ 334 and 338). See also *adjusted basis.*

Book value. The net amount of an asset after reduction by a related reserve. The book value of accounts receivable, for example, is the face amount of the receivables less the reserve for bad debts. The book value of a building is the cost less the accumulated depreciation.

Boot. Cash or property of a type not included in the definition of a nontaxable exchange. The receipt of boot will cause an otherwise nontaxable transfer to become taxable to the extent of the lesser of the fair market value of such boot or the realized gain on the transfer. Examples of nontaxable exchanges that could be partially or completely taxable due to the receipt of boot include transfers to controlled corporations [§ 351(b)] and like-kind exchanges [§ 1031(b)]. See also *realized gain or loss* and *recognized gain or loss.*

Bribes and illegal payments. Section 162 denies a deduction for bribes or kickbacks, fines, and penalties paid to a government official or employee for violation of law, and two-thirds of the treble damage payments made to claimants for violation of the antitrust law. Denial of a deduction for bribes and illegal payments is based upon the judicially established principle that allowing such payments would be contrary to public policy.

B.T.A. The Board of Tax Appeals was a trial court that considered Federal tax matters. This court is now the U.S. Tax Court.

Burden of proof. The requirement in a lawsuit to show the weight of evidence and thereby gain a favorable decision. Except in cases of tax fraud, the burden of proof in a tax case generally is on the taxpayer.

Business bad debt. A debt created or acquired in connection with a trade or business of the taxpayer, or a debt the loss from the worthlessness of which is incurred in the taxpayer's trade or business. A business bad debt is deducted as an ordinary deduction. § 166.

Business expenses. See *trade or business expenses.*

Business gifts. Business gifts are deductible only to the extent that each gift does not exceed $25 per person per year. Exceptions are made for gifts costing $4 or less and for certain employee awards. § 274(b).

C

C corporation. A corporation that has not elected conduit treatment under § 1361. See also *S corporation status*.

Cafeteria benefit plan. An employee benefit plan under which an employee is allowed to select from among a variety of employer-provided fringe benefits. Some of the benefits may be taxable and some may be statutory nontaxable benefits (e.g., health and accident insurance and group term life insurance). The employee is taxed only on the taxable benefits selected. A cafeteria benefit plan is also referred to as a flexible benefit plan. § 125.

Cafeteria plan. See *cafeteria benefit plan*.

Canons of taxation. Criteria used in the selection of a tax base that were originally discussed by Adam Smith in *The Wealth of Nations*. Canons of taxation include equality, convenience, certainty, and economy.

Capital asset. Broadly speaking, all assets are capital except those specifically excluded by the Code. Major categories of noncapital assets include property held for resale in the normal course of business (inventory), trade accounts and notes receivable, and depreciable property and real estate used in a trade or business (§ 1231 assets). § 1221. See also *capital gain* and *capital loss*.

Capital contributions. Various means by which a shareholder makes additional funds available to the corporation (placed at the risk of the business) without the receipt of additional stock. Such contributions are added to the basis of the shareholder's existing stock investment and do not generate income to the corporation. § 118.

Capital expenditure. An expenditure that should be added to the basis of the property improved. For income tax purposes, this generally precludes a full deduction for the expenditure in the year paid or incurred. Any capital recovery in the form of a tax deduction must come in the form of depreciation. § 263.

Capital gain. The gain from the sale or exchange of a capital asset. See also *capital asset* and *net capital gain*.

Capital gain net income. If the total capital gains for the tax year exceed the total capital losses, the result is capital gain net income. Note that the term does not distinguish between the long-term and short-term gains. § 1222(9). See also *net capital gain*.

Capital gain or loss holding period. The period of time that a capital asset is held by the taxpayer. To qualify for long-term treatment, the asset must be held for more than one year. If held for one year or less, the holding period is short term. See also *holding period*.

Capital gain property. Property contributed to a charitable organization that, if sold rather than contributed, would have resulted in long-term capital gain to the donor. See also *ordinary income property*.

Capital loss. The loss from the sale or exchange of a capital asset. See also *capital asset*.

Cash balance plan. A hybrid form of pension plan similar in some aspects to a defined benefit plan. Such a plan is funded by the employer, and the employer bears the investment risks and rewards. But like defined contribution plans, a cash balance plan establishes allocations to individual employee accounts, and the payout for an employee depends on investment performance.

Cash basis. See *accounting method* and *cash receipts method*.

Cash equivalent doctrine. Generally, a cash basis taxpayer does not report income until cash is constructively or actually received. Under the cash equivalent doctrine, cash basis taxpayers are required to report income if they receive the equivalent of cash (e.g., property is received) in a taxable transaction.

Cash method. See *cash receipts method*.

Cash receipts method. A method of accounting under which the taxpayer generally reports income when cash is collected and reports expenses when cash payments are made. However, for fixed assets, the cash basis taxpayer claims deductions through depreciation or amortization in the same manner as an accrual basis taxpayer. Prepaid expenses must be capitalized and amortized if the life of the asset extends "substantially beyond" the end of the tax year. See also *constructive receipt*.

Casualty loss. A casualty is defined as "the complete or partial destruction of property resulting from an identifiable event of a sudden, unexpected or unusual nature" (e.g., floods, storms, fires, auto accidents). Individuals may deduct a casualty loss only if the loss is incurred in a trade or business or in a transaction entered into for profit or arises from fire, storm, shipwreck, or other casualty or from theft. Individuals usually deduct personal casualty losses as itemized deductions subject to a $100 nondeductible amount and to an annual floor equal to 10 percent of adjusted gross income that applies after the $100 per casualty floor has been applied. Special rules are provided for the netting of certain casualty gains and losses. § 165. See also *disaster area loss* and *Section 1231 gains and losses*.

Cert. den. By denying the Writ of Certiorari, the U.S. Supreme Court refuses to accept an appeal from a U.S. Court of Appeals. The denial of certiorari does not, however, mean that the U.S. Supreme Court agrees with the result reached by the lower court.

Certiorari. Appeal from a U.S. Court of Appeals to the U.S. Supreme Court is by Writ of Certiorari. The Supreme Court does not have to accept the appeal and usually does not (*cert. den.*) unless there is a conflict among the lower courts that needs to be resolved or a constitutional issue is involved.

Change in accounting method. A change in the taxpayer's method of accounting (e.g., from FIFO to LIFO) generally requires prior approval from the IRS. Generally, a request must be filed within the taxable year of the desired change. In some instances, the permission for change will not be granted unless the taxpayer agrees to certain adjustments prescribed by the IRS.

Change in accounting period. A taxpayer must obtain the consent of the IRS before changing his or her tax year. Income for the short period created by the change must be annualized.

Charitable contributions. Contributions are deductible (subject to various restrictions and ceiling limitations) if made to qualified nonprofit charitable organizations. A cash basis taxpayer is entitled to a deduction solely in the year of payment. Accrual basis corporations may accrue contributions at year-end if payment is properly authorized before the end of the year and payment is made within two and one-half months after the end of the year. § 170.

Check-the-box Regulations. These Regulations enable taxpayers to classify the tax status of a business entity without regard to its corporate or noncorporate characteristics. An entity with more than one owner can elect to be classified either as a partnership or as a corporation. An entity with only one owner can elect to be classified as a sole proprietorship or as a corporation. These Regulations should simplify tax administration and taxpayer compliance and reduce tax litigation.

Child and dependent care expenses credit. A tax credit ranging from 20 percent to 35 percent of employment-related expenses (child and dependent care expenses) for amounts of up to $6,000 is available to individuals who are employed (or deemed to be employed) and maintain a household for a dependent child under age 13, disabled spouse, or disabled dependent. § 21.

Child support payments. Payments for child support do not constitute alimony and are therefore not includible in gross income by the recipient or deductible as alimony by the payor. Generally, none of the amounts paid are regarded as child support unless the divorce decree or separation agreement specifically calls for child support payments, However, if the amount of the payment to the former spouse would be reduced upon the happening of a contingency related to a child (e.g., the child attains age 21 or dies), the amount of the future reduction in the payment will be deemed child support for post-1984 agreements and decrees. § 71(c). See also *alimony and separate maintenance payments.*

Child tax credit. A tax credit based solely on the number of qualifying children under age 17. The maximum credit available is $1,000 per child through 2010. A qualifying child must be claimed as a dependent on a parent's tax return in order to qualify for the credit. Taxpayers who qualify for the child tax credit may also qualify for a supplemental credit. The supplemental credit is treated as a component of the earned income credit and is therefore refundable. The credit is phased out for higher-income taxpayers. § 24.

Circuit Court of Appeals. See *Court of Appeals.*

Circulation expenditures. Expenditures of establishing or increasing the circulation of a periodical that may be either expensed or capitalized. If such expenses are expensed, an adjustment will occur for AMT purposes, since the expenses are deducted over a three-year period for AMT purposes. Over the three-year period, both positive and negative AMT adjustments will be produced. § 173. See also *AMT adjustments.*

Citator. A tax research resource that presents the judicial history of a court case and traces the subsequent references to the case. When these references include the citing case's evaluations of the cited case's precedents, the research can obtain some measure of the efficacy and reliability of the original holding.

Claim of right doctrine. A judicially imposed doctrine applicable to both cash and accrual basis taxpayers that holds that an amount is includible in income upon actual or constructive receipt if the taxpayer has an unrestricted claim to the payment. For the tax treatment of amounts repaid when previously included in income under the claim of right doctrine, see § 1341.

Claims Court. One of three Federal trial courts that consider Federal tax controversies. Now known as the U.S. Court of Federal Claims, appeal from this court (formerly to the U.S. Supreme Court) now goes to the Court of Appeals for the Federal Circuit. See also *trial court.*

Clear reflection of income. The IRS has the authority to redetermine a taxpayer's income using a method that clearly reflects income if the taxpayer's method does not do so. § 446(b). In addition, the IRS may apportion or allocate income among various related businesses if income is not "clearly reflected." § 482.

Closely held corporation. A corporation where the stock ownership is not widely dispersed. Instead, a few shareholders are in control of corporate policy and are in a position to benefit personally from that policy.

Collectibles. A special type of capital asset, the gain from which is taxed at a maximum rate of 28 percent if the holding period is more than one year. Examples include art, rugs, antiques, gems, metals, stamps, some coins and bullion, and alcoholic beverages held for investment.

Community property. Louisiana, Texas, New Mexico, Arizona, California, Washington, Idaho, Nevada, and Wisconsin have community property systems. In Alaska, spouses can choose to have the community property rules apply. The rest of the states are classified as common law jurisdictions. The difference between common law and community property systems centers around the property rights possessed by married persons. In a common law system, each spouse owns whatever he or she earns. Under a community property system, one-half of the earnings of each spouse is considered owned by the other spouse. Assume, for example, Alice and Jeff are husband and wife and their only income is the $50,000 annual salary Jeff receives. If they live in New York (a common law state), the $50,000 salary belongs to Jeff. If, however, they live in Texas (a community property state), the $50,000 salary is divided equally, in terms of ownership, between Jeff and Alice. See also *separate property.*

Compensatory damages. Damages received or paid by the taxpayer can be classified as compensatory damages or as punitive damages. Compensatory damages are those paid to compensate one for harm caused by another. Compensatory damages are excludible from the recipient's gross income. See also *punitive damages.*

Completed contract method. A method of reporting gain or loss on certain long-term contracts. Under this method of accounting, gross income and expenses are recognized in the tax year in which the contract is completed. Reg. § 1.451–3. Limitations exist on a taxpayer's ability to use the completed contract method. § 460. See also *long-term contract* and *percentage of completion method.*

Component depreciation. The process of dividing an asset (e.g., a building) into separate components or parts for the purpose of calculating depreciation. The advantage of dividing an asset into components is to use shorter depreciation lives for selected components under § 167. Generally, the same cost recovery period must be used for all the components of an asset under § 168.

Condemnation. The taking of property by a public authority. The property is condemned as the result of legal action, and the owner is compensated by the public authority. The power to condemn property is known as the right of eminent domain.

Conduit concept. An approach assumed by the tax law in the treatment of certain entities and their owners. Specific tax characteristics pass through the entity without losing their identity. For example, items of income and expense, capital gains and losses, tax credits, etc., realized by a partnership pass through the partnership (a conduit) and are subject to taxation at the partner level. Also, in an S corporation, certain items pass through and are reported on the returns of the shareholders.

Constructive dividends. In addition to dividends formally declared by the board of directors of a corporation (i.e., declaration date, record date, and payment date), a shareholder may receive a distribution that does not have the formalities of a dividend but is treated as a dividend. Examples include salaries paid to shareholder-employees that are not reasonable and the shareholder use of corporate property for less than an arm's length rate.

Constructive ownership. See *attribution*.

Constructive receipt. If income is unqualifiedly available, it will be subject to the income tax even though it is not physically in the taxpayer's possession. An example is accrued interest on a savings account. Under the constructive receipt of income concept, the interest will be taxed to a depositor in the year it is available rather than the year actually withdrawn. The fact that the depositor uses the cash basis of accounting for tax purposes is irrelevant. See Reg. § 1.451–2.

Consumer interest. Interest expense of the taxpayer of a personal nature (not trade or business interest, investment interest, qualified residence interest, or passive activity interest) is not deductible. § 163(h). See also *interest on student loans* and *qualified residence interest*.

Contributions to the capital of a corporation. See *capital contributions*.

Convention expenses. Travel expenses incurred in attending a convention are deductible if the meetings are related to a taxpayer's trade or business or job-related activities. If, however, the convention trip is primarily for pleasure, no deduction is permitted for transportation expenses. Likewise, if the expenses are for attending a convention related to the production of income (§ 212), no deduction is permitted. Specific limitations are provided for foreign convention expenses. See § 274(n) for the limitations on the deductions for meals. § 274(h).

Correspondence audit. An audit conducted by the IRS by mail. Typically, the IRS writes to the taxpayer requesting the verification of a particular deduction, exemption, or credit. The completion of a special form or the remittance of copies of records or other support is all that is requested of the taxpayer. To be distinguished from a *field audit* or an *office audit*.

Cost depletion. Depletion that is calculated based on the adjusted basis of the asset. The adjusted basis is divided by the expected recoverable units to determine the depletion per unit. The depletion per unit is multiplied by the units sold during the tax year to calculate cost depletion. See also *percentage depletion*.

Cost recovery allowance. The portion of the cost of an asset written off under ACRS (or MACRS), which replaced the depreciation system as a method for writing off the cost of an asset for most assets placed in service after 1980 (after 1986 for MACRS). § 168. See also *alternative depreciation system* and *thirty percent additional first-year depreciation*.

Cost recovery period. A period specified in the Code for writing off the cost of an asset under ACRS or MACRS.

Court of Appeals. Any of 13 Federal courts that consider tax matters appealed from the U.S. Tax Court, U.S. Court of Federal Claims, or a U.S. District Court. Appeal from a U.S. Court of Appeals is to the U.S. Supreme Court by Writ of Certiorari. See also *appellate court*.

Court of Federal Claims. See *Claims Court*.

Court of original jurisdiction. The Federal courts are divided into courts of original jurisdiction and appellate courts. A dispute between a taxpayer and the IRS is first considered by a court of original jurisdiction (i.e., a trial court). The four Federal courts of original jurisdiction are the U.S. Tax Court, U.S. District Court, the Court of Federal Claims, and the Small Cases Division of the U.S. Tax Court. See also *Court of Appeals*.

Coverdell Education Savings Account (CESA). A savings account established to pay for qualified education expenses (i.e., tuition, fees, books, supplies, related equipment, room and board if the student's course load is at least one-half of the full-time course load). The maximum annual contribution to the savings account of a beneficiary is $2,000. The maximum annual contribution is subject to phaseout beginning at $95,000 for single taxpayers and $150,000 for married couples who file a joint return. Contributions are not deductible and cannot be made to a savings account once the beneficiary attains age 18. Distributions used to pay for qualified education expenses for a designated beneficiary are tax free. § 530.

Credit for certain retirement plan contributions. A nonrefundable credit is available based on eligible contributions of up to $2,000 to certain qualified retirement plans, such as traditional and Roth IRAs and § 401(k) plans, for taxable years beginning after 2001. The benefit provided by this credit is in addition to any deduction or exclusion that otherwise is available resulting from the qualifying contribution. The amount of the credit depends on the taxpayer's AGI and filing status. § 25B.

Credit for child and dependent care expenses. See *child and dependent care expenses credit*.

Credit for employer-provided child care. A nonrefundable credit is available to employers who provide child care facilities to their employees during normal working hours. The credit, limited to $150,000, is comprised of two components. The portion of the credit for qualified child care expenses is equal to 25 percent of these expenses while the portion of the credit for qualified child care resource and referral services is equal to 10 percent of these expenses. Any qualifying expenses otherwise deductible by the taxpayer must be reduced by the amount of the credit. In addition, the taxpayer's basis for any property used for qualifying purposes is reduced by the amount of the credit. § 45F.

Credit for small employer pension plan startup costs. A nonrefundable credit available to small businesses based on administrative costs associated with establishing and maintaining certain qualified plans. While such qualifying costs generally are deductible as ordinary and necessary business expenses, the availability of the credit is intended to lower the costs of starting a qualified retirement program, and therefore encourage qualifying businesses to establish retirement plans for their employees. The credit is available for eligible employers at the rate of 50 percent of qualified startup costs. The maximum credit is $500 (based on a maximum $1,000 of qualifying expenses). § 45E.

Crop insurance proceeds. The proceeds received when an insured crop is destroyed. Section 451(d) permits the farmer to defer reporting the income from the insurance proceeds until the tax year following the taxable year of the destruction.

Crop method. A method of accounting for agricultural crops that are planted in one year but harvested in a subsequent year. Under this method, the costs of raising the crop are accumulated as inventory and are deducted when the income from the crop is realized.

D

Death benefit. A payment made by an employer to the beneficiary or beneficiaries of a deceased employee on account of the death of the employee.

Death tax. See *estate tax.*

Declaration of estimated tax. A procedure whereby individuals and corporations are required to make quarterly installment payments of estimated tax. Individuals are required to make the declaration and file quarterly payments of the estimated tax if certain requirements are met. In 2007, a declaration is not required for an individual whose estimated tax is reasonably expected to be less than $1,000.

Deduction for qualified tuition and related expenses. Taxpayers are allowed a deduction of up to $4,000 for higher education expenses. Certain taxpayers are not eligible for the deduction: those whose AGI exceeds a specified amount and those who can be claimed as a dependent by another taxpayer. These expenses are classified as a deduction *for* AGI and they need not be employment related. § 222.

Deductions for adjusted gross income. See *adjusted gross income.*

Deductions from adjusted gross income. See *itemized deductions.*

Deferred compensation. Compensation that will be taxed when received or upon the removal of certain restrictions on receipt and not when earned. Contributions by an employer to a qualified pension or profit sharing plan on behalf of an employee are an example. The contributions will not be taxed to the employee until the funds are made available or distributed to the employee (e.g., upon retirement). See also *qualified pension or profit sharing plan.*

Deficiency. Additional tax liability owed by a taxpayer and assessed by the IRS. See also *statutory notice of deficiency.*

Defined benefit plan. Qualified plans can be dichotomized into defined benefit plans and defined contribution plans. Under a defined benefit plan, a formula defines the benefits employees are to receive. The formula usually includes years of service, employee compensation, and some stated percentage. The employer must make annual contributions based on actuarial computations that will be sufficient to pay the vested retirement benefits. See also *defined contribution plan* and *pension plan.*

Defined contribution plan. Qualified plans can be dichotomized into defined benefit plans and defined contribution plans. Under a defined contribution plan, a separate account is maintained for each covered employee. The employee's benefits under the plan are based solely on (1) the amount contributed and (2) income from the fund that accrues to the employee's account. The plan defines the amount the employer is required to contribute (e.g., a flat dollar amount, an amount based on a special formula, or an amount equal to a certain percentage of compensation). See also *defined benefit plan* and *pension plan.*

Defined contribution pension plan. See *defined contribution plan.*

De minimis fringe. Benefits provided to employees that are too insignificant to warrant the time and effort required to account for the benefits received by each employee and the value of those benefits. Such amounts are excludible from the employee's gross income. § 132.

Dependency exemption. See *personal and dependency exemptions.*

Depletion. The process by which the cost or other basis of a natural resource (e.g., an oil or gas interest) is recovered upon extraction and sale of the resource. The two ways to determine the depletion allowance are the cost and percentage (or statutory) methods. Under the cost method, each unit of production sold is assigned a portion of the cost or other basis of the interest. This is determined by dividing the cost or other basis by the total units expected to be recovered. Under the percentage (or statutory) method, the tax law provides a special percentage factor for different types of minerals and other natural resources. This percentage is multiplied by the gross income from the interest to arrive at the depletion allowance. §§ 613 and 613A.

Depreciation. The deduction of the cost or other basis of a tangible asset over the asset's estimated useful life. § 167. For intangible assets, see *amortization.* For natural resources, see *depletion.* Also see *estimated useful life.* The depreciation system was replaced by ACRS for most assets placed in service after 1980 (by MACRS for most assets placed in service after 1986) but still applies for assets placed in service before 1981. See also *recapture of depreciation.*

Determination letter. Upon the request of a taxpayer, a District Director will comment on the tax status of a completed transaction. Determination letters are most frequently used to clarify employee versus self-employed status, to determine whether a pension or profit sharing plan qualifies under the Code, and to determine the tax-exempt status of certain nonprofit organizations.

Direct charge-off method. See *specific charge-off method.*

Disabled access credit. A tax credit designed to encourage small businesses to make their facilities more accessible to disabled individuals. The credit is equal to 50 percent of the eligible expenditures that exceed $250 but do not exceed $10,250. Thus, the maximum amount for the credit is $5,000. The adjusted basis for depreciation is reduced by the amount of the credit. To qualify, the facility must have been placed in service before November 6, 1990. § 44. See also *general business credit.*

Disaster area loss. A casualty sustained in an area designated as a disaster area by the President of the United States. In such an event, the disaster loss may be treated as having occurred in the taxable year immediately preceding the year in which the disaster actually occurred. Thus, immediate tax benefits are provided to victims of a disaster. § 165(i). See also *casualty loss*.

Dissent. To disagree with the majority. If, for example, Judge Brown disagrees with the result reached by Judges Charles and Davis (all of whom are members of the same court), Judge Brown could issue a dissenting opinion.

District Court. A Federal District Court is a trial court for purposes of litigating (among others) Federal tax matters. It is the only trial court where a jury trial can be obtained. See also *trial court*.

Dividends received deduction. A deduction allowed a shareholder that is a corporation for dividends received from a domestic corporation. The percentage applied in calculating the dividends received deduction varies according to the percentage of stock ownership. If the stock ownership percentage is less than 20 percent, the percentage is 70 percent of the dividends received. If the stock ownership percentage is at least 20 percent but less than 80 percent, the percentage is 80 percent. If the stock ownership percentage is at least 80 percent, the percentage is 100 percent. §§ 243–246A.

Dollar value LIFO. An inventory technique that focuses on the dollars invested in the inventory rather than the particular items on hand each period. Each inventory item is assigned to a pool. A pool is a collection of similar items and is treated as a separate inventory. At the end of the period, each pool is valued in terms of prices at the time LIFO was adopted (base period prices), whether or not the particular items were actually on hand in the year LIFO was adopted, to compare with current prices to determine if there has been an increase or decrease in inventories.

Domestic production activities deduction (DPAD). See also *production activities deduction (PAD)*.

Domestic production gross receipts (DPGR). A key component in computing the domestic production activities deduction (DPAD). Includes receipts from the sale and other disposition of qualified production property produced in significant part within the U.S. DPGR is defined in § 199(c)(4). See also *production activities deduction (PAD)*.

E

Earned income. Income from personal services as distinguished from income generated by property. See §§ 32 and 911 and the related Regulations.

Earned income credit. A refundable tax credit designed to provide assistance to certain low-income individuals. To receive the most beneficial treatment, the taxpayer must have qualifying children. However, it is possible to qualify for the credit without having a child. To calculate the credit for a taxpayer with one or more children for 2008, a statutory rate of 34.0 percent for one child (40.0 percent for two or more children) is multiplied by the earned income (subject to a statutory maximum of $8,580 with one qualifying child or $12,060 with two or more qualifying children). Once the earned income exceeds certain thresholds, the credit is phased out using a 15.98 percent rate for one qualifying child and a 21.06 percent rate for two or more qualifying children. For the qualifying taxpayer without children, the credit is calculated on a maximum earned income of $5,720 applying a 7.65 percent rate with the phaseout beginning at later applying the same rate. § 32.

Earnings and profits. A tax concept peculiar to corporate taxpayers that measures economic capacity to make a distribution to shareholders that is not a return of capital. Such a distribution will result in dividend income to the shareholders to the extent of the corporation's current and accumulated earnings and profits.

Economic income. The change in the taxpayer's net worth, as measured in terms of market values, plus the value of the assets the taxpayer consumed during the year. Because of the impracticality of this income model, it is not used for tax purposes. See also *accounting income*.

Economic performance test. One of the requirements that must be satisfied in order for an accrual basis taxpayer to deduct an expense. The accrual basis taxpayer first must satisfy the all events test. That test is not deemed satisfied until economic performance occurs. This occurs when property or services are provided to the taxpayer or, in the case in which the taxpayer is required to provide property or services, whenever the property or services are actually provided by the taxpayer. See also *all events test*.

Education expenses. Employees may deduct education expenses that are incurred either (1) to maintain or improve existing job-related skills or (2) to meet the express requirements of the employer or the requirements imposed by law to retain employment status. The expenses are not deductible if the education is required to meet the minimum educational standards for the taxpayer's job or if the education qualifies the individual for a new trade or business. Reg. § 1.162–5. See also *HOPE scholarship credit* and *lifetime learning credit*.

Educational savings bonds. U.S. Series EE bonds whose proceeds are used for qualified higher educational expenses for the taxpayer, the taxpayer's spouse, or a dependent. The interest may be excluded from gross income, provided the taxpayer's adjusted gross income does not exceed certain amounts. § 135.

e-file. The electronic filing of a tax return. The filing is either direct or indirect. As to direct, the taxpayer goes online using a computer and tax return preparation software. Indirect filing occurs when a taxpayer utilizes an authorized IRS e-file provider. The provider often is the tax return preparer.

Employee expenses. The deductions *for* adjusted gross income include reimbursed expenses and certain expenses of performing artists. All other employee expenses are deductible *from* AGI. § 62. See also *trade or business expenses*.

Employment taxes. Employment taxes are those taxes that an employer must pay on account of its employees. Employment taxes include FICA (Federal Insurance Contributions Act) and FUTA (Federal Unemployment Tax Act) taxes. Employment taxes are paid to the IRS in addition to income tax withholdings at specified intervals. Such taxes can be levied on the employees, the employer, or both. See also *FICA tax* and *FUTA tax*.

Entertainment expenses. These expenses are deductible only if they are directly related to or associated with a trade or business. Various restrictions and documentation requirements have been imposed upon the deductibility of entertainment expenses to prevent abuses by taxpayers. See, for example, the provision contained in § 274(n) that disallows 50 percent of entertainment expenses. § 274.

Estate tax. A tax imposed on the right to transfer property by reason of death. Thus, an estate tax is levied on the decedent's estate and not on the heir receiving the property. §§ 2001 and 2002. See also *inheritance tax*.

Estimated tax. The amount of tax (including alternative minimum tax and self-employment tax) an individual expects to owe for the year after subtracting tax credits and income tax withheld. The estimated tax must be paid in installments at designated intervals (e.g. for the individual taxpayer, by April 15, June 15, September 15, and January 15 of the following year).

Estimated useful life. The period over which an asset will be used by a particular taxpayer. Although the period cannot be longer than the estimated physical life of an asset, it could be shorter if the taxpayer does not intend to keep the asset until it wears out. Assets such as goodwill do not have an estimated useful life. The estimated useful life of an asset is essential to measuring the annual tax deduction for depreciation and amortization. An asset subject to ACRS or MACRS is written off over a specified cost recovery period rather than over its estimated useful life. In addition, most intangibles are now amortized over a 15-year statutory period.

Excise tax. A tax on the manufacture, sale, or use of goods or on the carrying on of an occupation or activity. Also, a tax on the transfer of property. Thus, the Federal estate and gift taxes are, theoretically, excise taxes.

Extraordinary personal services. These are services provided by individuals where the customers' use of the property is incidental to their receipt of the services. For example, a patient's use of a hospital bed is incidental to his or her receipt of medical services. This is one of the six exceptions to determine whether an activity is a passive rental activity. § 469.

F

Fair market value. The amount at which property would change hands between a willing buyer and a willing seller, neither being under any compulsion to buy or sell and both having reasonable knowledge of the relevant facts. Reg. §§ 1.1001–1(a) and 20.2031–1(b).

Farm price method. A method of accounting for agricultural crops. The inventory of crops is valued at its market price less the estimated cost of disposition (e.g., freight and selling expense.)

Federal district court. See *district court*.

FICA tax. An abbreviation for Federal Insurance Contributions Act, commonly referred to as the Social Security tax. The FICA tax is comprised of the Social Security tax (old age, survivors, and disability insurance) and the Medicare tax (hospital insurance) and is imposed on both employers and employees. The employer is responsible for withholding from the employee's wages the Social Security tax at a rate of 6.2 percent on a maximum wage base of $102,000 (for 2008) and the Medicare tax at a rate of 1.45 percent (no maximum wage base). The employer is required to match the employee's contribution. See also *employment taxes*.

Field audit. An audit by the IRS conducted on the business premises of the taxpayer or in the office of the tax practitioner representing the taxpayer. To be distinguished from a *correspondence audit* or an *office audit*.

Fifty percent additional first-year depreciation. This provision, which was effective for property acquired after May 5, 2003 and placed in service before January 1, 2005, provided for an additional cost recovery deduction of fifty percent in the tax year the qualified property is placed in service. Qualified property included most types of new property other than buildings. The taxpayer could elect to forgo this bonus depreciation. The taxpayer also could elect to use thirty percent bonus depreciation rather than the fifty percent bonus depreciation. The Economic Stimulus Act of 2008 reinstated the 50 percent additional first-year depreciation for 2008. See also *cost recovery allowance* and *thirty percent additional first-year depreciation*.

Finalized Regulation. See *regulations*.

First-in, first-out (FIFO). An accounting method for determining the cost of inventories. Under this method, the inventory on hand is deemed to be the sum of the cost of the most recently acquired units. See also *last-in, first-out (LIFO)*.

Fiscal year. A fiscal year is a 12-month period ending on the last day of a month other than December. In certain circumstances, a taxpayer is permitted to elect a fiscal year instead of being required to use a calendar year. See also *accounting period* and *taxable year*.

Flat tax. In its pure form, it would replace the graduated income tax rates with a single rate (e.g., 17 percent). All deductions are eliminated, and a large personal exemption is allowed to remove low-income and many middle-income taxpayers from the application of the tax.

Flexible spending plan. An employee benefit plan that allows the employee to take a reduction in salary in exchange for the employer paying benefits that can be provided by the employer without the employee being required to recognize income (e.g., medical and child care benefits).

Foreign earned income exclusion. The foreign earned income exclusion is a relief provision that applies to U.S. citizens working in a foreign country. To qualify for the exclusion, the taxpayer must be either a bona fide resident of the foreign country or present in the country for 330 days during any 12 consecutive months. The exclusion is limited to $87,600 per year for 2008 ($85,700 in 2007). § 911.

Foreign tax credit or deduction. Both individual taxpayers and corporations may claim a foreign tax credit on income earned and subject to tax in a foreign country or U.S. possession. As an alternative to the credit, a deduction may be taken for the foreign taxes paid. §§ 27, 164, and 901–905.

Franchise. An agreement that gives the transferee the right to distribute, sell, or provide goods, services, or facilities within a specified area. The cost of obtaining a franchise may be amortized over a statutory period of 15 years. In general, the franchisor's gain on the sale of franchise rights is an ordinary gain because the franchisor retains a significant power, right, or continuing interest in the subject of the franchise. §§ 197 and 1253.

Franchise tax. A tax levied on the right to do business in a state as a corporation. Although income considerations may come into play, the tax usually is based on the capitalization of the corporation.

Fringe benefits. Compensation or other benefits received by an employee that are not in the form of cash. Some fringe benefits (e.g., accident and health plans, group term life insurance) may be excluded from the employee's gross income and therefore are not subject to the Federal income tax.

Fruit and tree metaphor. The courts have held that an individual who earns income from property or services cannot assign that income to another. For example, a father cannot assign his earnings from commissions to his child and escape income tax on those amounts.

F.3d. An abbreviation for the Third Series of the *Federal Reporter*, the official series where decisions of the U.S. Claims Court (before October 1982) and the U.S. Courts of Appeals are published.

F.Supp. The abbreviation for the *Federal Supplement*, the official series where the reported decisions of the U.S. District Courts are published.

FUTA tax. An employment tax levied on employers. Jointly administered by the Federal and state governments, the tax provides funding for unemployment benefits. FUTA applies at a rate of 6.2 percent on the first $7,000 of covered wages paid during the year for each employee. The Federal government allows a credit for FUTA paid (or allowed under a merit rating system) to the state. The credit cannot exceed 5.4 percent of the covered wages. See also *employment taxes*.

G

General business credit. The summation of various nonrefundable business credits, including the tax credit for rehabilitation expenditures, business energy credit, work opportunity credit, research activities credit, low-income housing credit, and disabled access credit. The amount of general business credit that can be used to reduce the tax liability is limited to the taxpayer's net income tax reduced by the greater of (1) the tentative minimum tax or (2) 25 percent of the net regular tax liability that exceeds $25,000. Unused general business credits can be carried back 1 year and forward 20 years.

Gift. A transfer of property for less than adequate consideration. Gifts usually occur in a personal setting (such as between members of the same family). Gifts are excluded from the income tax but may be subject to the *gift tax*.

Gift tax. A tax imposed on the transfer of property by gift. The tax is imposed upon the donor of a gift and is based upon the fair market value of the property on the date of the gift. §§ 2501–2524.

Golden parachute payment. A severance payment to employees that meets the following requirements: (1) the payment is contingent on a change of ownership of a corporation through a stock or asset acquisition and (2) the aggregate present value of the payment equals or exceeds three times the employee's average annual compensation. To the extent the severance payment meets these conditions, a deduction is disallowed to the employer for the excess of the payment over a statutory base amount (a five-year average of compensation if the taxpayer was an employee for the entire five-year period). In addition, a 20 percent excise tax is imposed on the employee who receives the excess severance pay. §§ 280G and 4999.

Goodwill. The ability of a business to generate income in excess of a normal rate on assets due to superior managerial skills, market position, new product technology, etc. In the purchase of a business, goodwill represents the difference between the purchase price and the fair market value of the net assets acquired. Goodwill is an intangible asset that possesses an indefinite life. However, since acquired goodwill is a § 197 intangible asset, it is amortized over a 15-year statutory period. Self-created goodwill cannot be amortized. Reg. § 1.167(a)–3. See also *amortization*.

Government bonds issued at a discount. Certain U.S. government bonds (Series EE) are issued at a discount and do not pay interest during the life of the bonds. Instead, the bonds are redeemable at increasing fixed amounts. Thus, the difference between the purchase price and the amount received upon redemption represents interest income to the holder. A cash basis taxpayer may defer recognition of gross income until the bonds are redeemed. For Series EE savings bonds issued after 1989, the interest otherwise taxable at redemption can be excluded if the bonds are qualified educational savings bonds. As an alternative to deferring recognition of gross income until the bonds are redeemed, the taxpayer may elect to include in gross income on an annual basis the annual increase in the value of the bonds. § 454.

Gross income. Income subject to the Federal income tax. Gross income does not include income for which the Code permits exclusion treatment (e.g., interest on municipal bonds). For a manufacturing or merchandising business, gross income means gross profit (gross sales or gross receipts less cost of goods sold). § 61 and Reg. § 1.61–3(a).

Group term life insurance. Life insurance coverage permitted by an employer for a group of employees. Such insurance is renewable on a year-to-year basis and does not accumulate in value (i.e., no cash surrender value is built up). The premiums paid by the employer on the insurance are not taxed to an employee on coverage of up to $50,000 per person. § 79 and Reg. § 1.79–1(a).

Guaranteed payments. Payments made by a partnership to one of its partners for services rendered or for the use of capital, to the extent the payments are determined without regard to the income of the partnership. Such payments generally are deductible by the partnership as a business expense and are reported as ordinary income by the recipient partner. § 707(c).

H

Half-year convention. The half-year convention is a cost recovery convention that assumes all property is placed in service at mid-year and thus provides for a half-year's cost recovery for that year.

Head of household. An unmarried individual who maintains a household for another and satisfies certain conditions set forth in § 2(b). Such status enables the taxpayer to use a set of income tax rates [see § 1(b)] that are lower than those applicable to other unmarried individuals [§ 1(c)] but higher than those applicable to surviving spouses and married persons filing a joint return [§ 1(a)]. See also *tax rate schedules*.

Health savings account. A medical savings account created in legislation enacted in December 2003 that is designed to replace and expand Archer Medical Savings Accounts. See also *medical savings account*.

Highly compensated employee. The employee group is generally divided into two categories for fringe benefit (including pension and profit sharing plans) purposes. These are (1) highly compensated employees and (2) non-highly compensated employees. For most fringe benefits, if the fringe benefit plan discriminates in favor of highly compensated employees, it will not be a qualified plan with respect, at a minimum, to the highly compensated employees.

Hobby loss. A nondeductible loss arising from a personal hobby as contrasted with an activity engaged in for profit. Generally, the law provides a rebuttable presumption that an activity is engaged in for profit if profits are earned during any three or more years during a five-year period. § 183. See also *vacation home.*

Holding period. The period of time property has been held for income tax purposes. The holding period is crucial in determining whether gain or loss from the sale or exchange of a capital asset is long term or short term. § 1223. See also *capital gain or loss holding period.*

Home equity loans. Loans that utilize the personal residence of the taxpayer as security. The interest on such loans is deductible as *qualified residence interest.* However, interest is deductible only on the portion of the loan that does not exceed the lesser of (1) the fair market value of the residence, reduced by the *acquisition indebtedness,* or (2) $100,000 ($50,000 for married persons filing separate returns). A major benefit of a home equity loan is that there are no tracing rules regarding the use of the loan proceeds. § 163(h)(3).

Home office expenses. See *office-in-the-home expenses.*

HOPE scholarship credit. A tax credit for qualifying expenses paid for the first two years of postsecondary education. Room, board, and book costs are ineligible for the credit. The maximum credit available is $1,800 per year per student, computed as 100 percent of the first $1,200 of qualifying expenses, plus 50 percent of the second $1,200 of qualifying expenses. Eligible students include the taxpayer, taxpayer's spouse, and taxpayer's dependents. To qualify for the credit, a student must take at least one-half the full-time course load for at least one academic term at a qualifying educational institution. The credit is phased out for higher-income taxpayers. § 25A.

H.R 10 (Keogh) plan. See *self-employment retirement plan.*

Hybrid method. A combination of the accrual and cash methods of accounting. That is, the taxpayer may account for some items of income on the accrual method (e.g., sales and cost of goods sold) and other items (e.g., interest income) on the cash method.

I

Imputed interest. For certain long-term sales of property, the IRS can convert some of the gain from the sale into interest income if the contract does not provide for a minimum rate of interest to be paid by the purchaser. The application of this procedure has the effect of forcing the seller to recognize less long-term capital gain and more ordinary income (interest income). §§ 483 and 1274 and the Regulations thereunder. In addition, interest income and interest expense are imputed (deemed to exist) on interest-free or below-market rate loans between certain related parties. § 7872. See also *interest-free loans.*

Incentive stock option (ISO). A type of stock option that receives favorable tax treatment. If various qualification requirements can be satisfied, there are no recognition tax consequences when the stock option is granted. However, the spread (the excess of the fair market value at the date of exercise over the option price) is a tax preference item for purposes of the alternative minimum tax. The gain on disposition of the stock resulting from the exercise of the stock option will be classified as long-term capital gain if certain holding period requirements are met (the employee must not dispose of the stock within two years after the option is granted or within one year after acquiring the stock). § 422. See also *nonqualified stock option (NQSO).*

Income. For tax purposes, an increase in wealth that has been realized.

Independent contractor. A self-employed person as distinguished from one who is employed as an employee.

Individual retirement account (IRA). A type of retirement plan to which an individual with earned income can contribute a maximum of $3,000 ($3,000 each in the case of a married couple with a spousal IRA) per tax year for 2002–2004. The maximum amount increases to $4,000 in 2005 and to $5,000 in 2008. IRAs can be classified as traditional IRAs or Roth IRAs. With a traditional IRA, an individual can contribute and deduct a maximum of $5,000 per tax year in 2008. The deduction is a deduction *for* AGI. However, if the individual is an active participant in another qualified retirement plan, the deduction is phased out proportionally between certain AGI ranges (note that the phase-out limits the amount of the deduction and not the amount of the contribution). With a Roth IRA, an individual can contribute a maximum of $5,000 per tax year in 2008. No deduction is permitted. However, if a five-year holding period requirement is satisfied and if the distribution is a qualified distribution, the taxpayer can make tax-free withdrawals from a Roth IRA. The maximum annual contribution is phased out proportionally between certain AGI ranges. §§ 219 and 408A. See also *simplified employee pension plan.*

Inheritance tax. An excise tax levied on the heir based on the value of property received from a decedent. See also *estate tax.*

Installment method. A method of accounting enabling a taxpayer to spread the recognition of gain on the sale of property over the payout period. Under this procedure, the seller computes the gross profit percentage from the sale (the gain divided by the contract price) and applies it to each payment received to arrive at the gain to be recognized. §§ 453 and 453A.

Intangible drilling and development costs (IDC). Taxpayers may elect to expense or capitalize (subject to amortization) intangible drilling and development costs. However, ordinary income recapture provisions apply to oil and gas properties on a sale or other disposition if the expense method is elected. §§ 263(c) and 1254(a).

Interest-free loans. Bona fide loans that carry no interest (or a below-market rate). If made in a nonbusiness setting, the imputed interest element is treated as a gift from the lender to the borrower. If made by a corporation to a shareholder, a constructive dividend could result. In either event, the lender may recognize interest income, and the borrower may be able to deduct interest expense. § 7872.

Interest on student loans. A limited ability exists to deduct interest on student loans used to pay qualified higher education expenses (i.e., tuition, fees, books, supplies, room and board). The ceiling on the deduction is $2,500. The deduction is a deduction *for* AGI. § 221. See also *consumer interest.*

Interpretive Regulation. A Regulation issued by the Treasury Department that purports to explain the meaning of a particular Code Section. An interpretive Regulation is given less deference than a legislative Regulation. See also *legislative regulation* and *procedural regulation.* § 7805.

Investigation of a new business. Expenditures incurred in the evaluation of prospective business activities by taxpayers who are not engaged in a trade or business (to acquire an existing business or enter into a new trade or business). If the expenditures are general, it is the position of the IRS that no deduction is permitted even if the investigation is abandoned because the taxpayer is not engaged in a trade or business. The courts, however, have permitted a loss deduction providing the expenditures were specific.

Investment income. Gross income from interest, dividends, annuities, and royalties not derived in the ordinary course of a trade or business. Net capital gain attributable to the disposition of property producing these types of income and qualified dividend income normally are not included in investment income. However, a taxpayer may elect to include the capital gains as investment income if the net capital gain qualifying for the *alternative tax* is reduced by an equivalent amount. A similar election can be made for qualified dividends. See also *investment interest.*

Investment indebtedness. If funds are borrowed by non-corporate taxpayers for the purpose of purchasing or continuing to hold investment property, some portion of the interest expense deduction may be disallowed. The interest deduction is generally limited to net investment income. Amounts that are disallowed may be carried forward and treated as investment interest of the succeeding year. § 163(d).

Investment interest. Payment for the use of funds used to acquire assets that produce investment income. The deduction for investment interest is limited to *net investment income* for the tax year. See also *investment income.*

Investment tax credit (ITC). A tax credit that usually was equal to 10 percent (unless a reduced credit was elected) of the qualified investment in tangible personalty used in a trade or business. If the tangible personalty had a recovery period of five years or more, the full cost of the property qualified for the credit. Only 60 percent of cost qualified for property with a recovery period of three years. However, the regular investment tax credit was repealed by TRA of 1986 for property placed in service after December 31, 1985. §§ 46–48. See also *general business credit and recapture of investment tax credit.*

Involuntary conversion. The loss or destruction of property through theft, casualty, or condemnation. Any gain realized on an involuntary conversion can, at the taxpayer's election, be postponed (deferred) for Federal income tax purposes if the owner reinvests the proceeds within a prescribed period of time in property that is similar or related in service or use. § 1033. See also *nontaxable exchange.*

IRA. See *individual retirement account.*

Itemized deductions. Certain personal expenditures allowed by the Code as deductions *from* adjusted gross income. Examples include certain medical expenses, interest on home mortgages, state income taxes, and charitable contributions. Itemized deductions are reported on Schedule A of Form 1040. Certain miscellaneous itemized deductions are reduced by 2 percent of the taxpayer's adjusted gross income. In addition, a taxpayer whose adjusted gross income exceeds $100,000 ($50,000 for married filing separately) must reduce the itemized deductions by 3 percent of the excess of adjusted gross income over $100,000. For 2008, the indexed amount for the $100,000 is $159,950, and the indexed amount for the $50,000 is $79,975. Medical, casualty and theft, and investment interest deductions are not subject to the 3 percent reduction. The 3 percent reduction may not reduce itemized deductions that are subject to the reduction to below 20 percent of their initial amount. Beginning in 2006, this reduction is subject to partial phaseout. §§ 63(d), 67, and 68.

K

Keogh plan. See *self-employment retirement plan.*

Kiddie tax. To reduce the tax savings that result from shifting income from parents to children, the net unearned income of a child under age 19 (or under age 24 if a full-time student) is taxed at the marginal tax rate of the parent(s). For the provision to apply, the child must have at least one living parent and unearned income of more than $1,800 for the tax year. § 1(g). See also *unearned income.*

L

Last-in, first-out (LIFO). An accounting method for valuing inventories for tax purposes. Under this method, it is assumed that the inventory on hand is valued at the cost of the earliest acquired units. § 472 and the related Regulations. See also *first-in, first-out (FIFO).*

Least aggregate deferral method. An algorithm set forth in the Regulations to determine the tax year for a partnership with partners whose tax years differ. The tax year that produces the least aggregate deferral of income for the partners is selected.

Legislative Regulation. Some Code Sections give the Secretary of the Treasury or his delegate the authority to prescribe Regulations to carry out the details of administration or to otherwise complete the operating rules. Regulations issued pursuant to this type of authority truly possess the force and effect of law. In effect, Congress is almost delegating its legislative powers to the Treasury Department. See also *interpretive regulation* and *procedural regulation.*

Lessee. One who rents property from another. In the case of real estate, the lessee is also known as the tenant.

Lessor. One who rents property to another. In the case of real estate, the lessor is also known as the landlord.

Letter rulings. Issued upon a taxpayer's request, by the National Office of the IRS, they describe how the IRS will treat a proposed transaction for tax purposes. They apply only to the taxpayer who asks for and obtains the ruling, but post-1984 rulings may be substantial authority for purposes of avoiding the accuracy-related penalties. The IRS limits the issuance of letter rulings to restricted, preannounced areas of taxation.

Life insurance proceeds. Generally, life insurance proceeds paid to a beneficiary upon the death of the insured are exempt from Federal income tax. An exception is provided when a life insurance contract has been transferred for valuable consideration to another individual who assumes ownership rights. In that case, the proceeds are income to the assignee to the extent that the proceeds exceed the amount paid for the policy plus any subsequent premiums paid. Insurance proceeds may be subject to the Federal estate tax if the decedent retained any incidents of ownership in the policy before death or if the proceeds are payable to the decedent's estate. §§ 101 and 2042.

Lifetime learning credit. A tax credit for qualifying expenses for taxpayers pursuing education beyond the first two years of postsecondary education. Individuals who are completing their last two years of undergraduate studies, pursuing graduate or professional degrees, or otherwise seeking new job skills or maintaining existing job skills are all eligible for the credit. Eligible individuals include the taxpayer, taxpayer's spouse, and taxpayer's dependents. The maximum credit is 20 percent of the first $10,000 of qualifying expenses and is computed per taxpayer. The credit is phased out for higher-income taxpayers. § 25A.

Like-kind exchange. An exchange of property held for productive use in a trade or business or for investment (except inventory, stocks and bonds, and partnership interests) for other investment or trade or business property. Unless non-like-kind property is received (boot), the exchange will be nontaxable. § 1031. See also *boot* and *nontaxable exchange*.

Limited expensing. See *Section 179 expensing*.

Limited liability company. An organization that combines the corporate characteristic of limited liability with treatment as a partnership for Federal income tax purposes.

Liquidating distribution. A distribution of assets by a corporation associated with the termination of the business. See also *liquidation of a corporation*.

Liquidation of a corporation. In a complete or partial liquidation of a corporation, amounts received by the shareholders in exchange for their stock are usually treated as a sale or exchange of the stock resulting in capital gain or loss treatment. § 331. Special rules apply to the liquidation of a subsidiary under § 332. Generally, a liquidation is a taxable event to the corporation. § 336. Special rules apply to a parent corporation that is liquidating a subsidiary. § 337.

Listed property. The term listed property includes (1) any passenger automobile, (2) any other property used as a means of transportation, (3) any property of a type generally used for purposes of entertainment, recreation, or amusement, (4) any computer or peripheral equipment (with an exception for exclusive business use), (5) any cellular telephone (or other similar telecommunications equipment), and (6) any other property of a type specified in the Regulations. If listed property is predominantly used for business, the taxpayer is allowed to use the statutory percentage method of cost recovery. Otherwise, the straight-line cost recovery method must be used. § 280F.

Long-term care insurance. Insurance that helps pay the cost of care when the insured is unable to care for himself or herself. Such insurance is generally thought of as insurance against the cost of an aged person entering a nursing home. The employer can provide the insurance, and the premiums may be excluded from the employee's gross income. § 7702B.

Long-term contract. A building, installation, construction, or manufacturing contract that is entered into but not completed within the same tax year. A manufacturing contract is a long-term contract only if the contract is to manufacture (1) a unique item not normally carried in finished goods inventory or (2) items that normally require more than 12 calendar months to complete. The two available methods to account for long-term contracts are the percentage of completion method and the completed contract method. The completed contract method can be used only in limited circumstances. § 460. See also *completed contract method* and *percentage of completion method*.

Long-term nonpersonal use capital assets. Includes investment property with a long-term holding period. Such property disposed of by casualty or theft may receive § 1231 treatment. See also *Section 1231 gains and losses*.

Lower of cost or market. An elective inventory method, whereby the taxpayer may value inventories at the lower of the taxpayer's actual cost or the current replacement cost of the goods. This method cannot be used in conjunction with the LIFO inventory method.

Low-income housing. Low-income housing is rental housing that is a dwelling unit for low- or moderate-income individuals or families. Beneficial tax treatment is in the form of the *low-income housing credit*. § 42. See also *accelerated cost recovery system (ACRS)*.

Low-income housing credit. Beneficial treatment to owners of low-income housing is provided in the form of a tax credit. The calculated credit is claimed in the year the building is placed in service and in the following nine years. § 42. See also *general business credit*.

Lump-sum distribution. Payment of the entire amount due at one time rather than in installments. Such distributions often occur from qualified pension or profit sharing plans upon the retirement or death of a covered employee. The recipient of a lump-sum distribution may recognize both long-term capital gain and ordinary income upon the receipt of the distribution. The ordinary income portion may be subject to a special 10-year income averaging provision. § 402(e).

M

MACRS. See *accelerated cost recovery system (ACRS)*.

Majority interest partners. Partners who have more than a 50 percent interest in partnership profits and capital, counting only those partners who have the same taxable year, are referred to as majority interest partners. The term is of significance in determining the appropriate taxable year of a partnership. § 706(b). See also *accounting period* and *principal partner*.

Marital deduction. A deduction allowed upon the transfer of property from one spouse to another. The deduction is allowed under the Federal gift tax for lifetime (inter vivos) transfers or under the Federal estate tax for death (testamentary) transfers. §§ 2056 and 2523.

Marriage penalty. The additional tax liability that results for a married couple compared with what their tax liability would be if they were not married and filed separate returns.

Material participation. If an individual taxpayer materially participates in a nonrental trade or business activity, any loss from that activity is treated as an active loss that can be offset against active income. Material participation is achieved by meeting any one of seven tests provided in the Regulations. § 469(h).

Medical expenses. Medical expenses of an individual, spouse, and dependents are allowed as an itemized deduction to the extent that such amounts (less insurance reimbursements) exceed 7.5 percent of adjusted gross income. § 213.

Medical savings account. A plan available to employees of small firms (50 or fewer employees) with high-deductible health insurance. The employee can place money in the fund and then deduct the contributions (within limits) from gross income. If the employer contributes to the fund, the employee can exclude the contribution from gross income. Income earned from the fund and withdrawals for medical care are not subject to tax. §§ 106(b) and 220.

Mid-month convention. A cost recovery convention that assumes property is placed in service in the middle of the month that it is actually placed in service.

Mid-quarter convention. A cost recovery convention that assumes property placed in service during the year is placed in service at the middle of the quarter in which it is actually placed in service. The mid-quarter convention applies if more than 40 percent of the value of property (other than eligible real estate) is placed in service during the last quarter of the year.

Miscellaneous itemized deductions. A special category of itemized deductions that includes such expenses as professional dues, tax return preparation fees, job-hunting costs, unreimbursed employee business expenses, and certain investment expenses. Such expenses are deductible only to the extent they exceed 2 percent of adjusted gross income. § 67. See also *itemized deductions.*

Mitigation of the annual accounting period concept. Various tax provisions that provide relief from the effect of the finality of the annual accounting period concept. For example, the *net operating loss* provisions provide relief to a taxpayer whose business profits and losses for different taxable years fluctuate. See also *accounting period.*

Modified accelerated cost recovery system (MACRS). See *accelerated cost recovery system (ACRS).*

Modified adjusted gross income. A key determinant in computing the domestic production activities deduction (DPAD). The deduction is limited to a percentage of the *lesser of* qualified production activities income (QPAI) or modified adjusted gross income. Aside from limited changes required by § 199(d)(2)(A), modified adjusted gross income is AGI as usually determined but without any

domestic production activities deduction (DPAD). See also *production activities deduction (PAD).*

Moving expenses. A deduction *for* AGI is permitted to employees and self-employed individuals provided certain tests are met. The taxpayer's new job must be at least 50 miles farther from the old residence than the old residence was from the former place of work. In addition, an employee must be employed on a full-time basis at the new location for 39 weeks in the 12-month period following the move. Deductible moving expenses include the cost of moving the household and personal effects, transportation, and lodging expenses during the move. The cost of meals during the move are not deductible. Qualified moving expenses that are paid (or reimbursed) by the employer can be excluded from the employee's gross income. In this case, the related deduction by the employee is not permitted. §§ 62(a)(15), 132(a)(6), and 217.

Multiple support agreement. To qualify for a dependency exemption, the support test must be satisfied. This requires that over 50 percent of the support of the potential dependent be provided by the taxpayer. Where no one person provides more than 50 percent of the support, a multiple support agreement enables a taxpayer to still qualify for the dependency exemption. Any person who contributed more than 10 percent of the support is entitled to claim the exemption if each person in the group who contributed more than 10 percent files a written consent (Form 2120). Each person who is a party to the multiple support agreement must meet all the other requirements for claiming the dependency exemption. § 152(c). See also *personal and dependency exemptions.*

N

National sales tax. Intended as a replacement for the current Federal income tax. Unlike a value added tax (VAT), which is levied on the manufacturer, it would be imposed on the consumer upon the final sale of goods and services. To keep the tax from being regressive, low-income taxpayers would be granted some kind of credit or exemption.

Necessary. Appropriate and helpful in furthering the taxpayer's business or income-producing activity. §§ 162(a) and 212. See also *ordinary.*

Net capital gain. The excess of the net long-term capital gain for the tax year over the net short-term capital loss. The net capital gain of an individual taxpayer is eligible for the alternative tax. § 1222(11). See also *alternative tax.*

Net capital loss. The excess of the losses from sales or exchanges of capital assets over the gains from sales or exchanges of such assets. Up to $3,000 per year of the net capital loss may be deductible by noncorporate taxpayers against ordinary income. The excess net capital loss carries over to future tax years. For corporate taxpayers, the net capital loss cannot be offset against ordinary income, but it can be carried back three years and forward five years to offset net capital gains. §§ 1211, 1212, and 1221(10).

Net investment income. The excess of *investment income* over investment expenses. Investment expenses are those deductible expenses directly connected with the production of investment income. Investment expenses do not include investment interest. The deduction for *investment interest* for the tax year is limited to net investment income. § 163(d).

Net operating loss. To mitigate the effect of the annual accounting period concept, § 172 allows taxpayers to use an excess loss of one year as a deduction for certain past or future years. In this regard, a carryback period of 2 years and a carryforward period of 20 years are allowed. See also *mitigation of the annual accounting period concept.*

Net worth method. An approach used by the IRS to reconstruct the income of a taxpayer who fails to maintain adequate records. Under this approach, the gross income for the year is the increase in net worth of the taxpayer (assets in excess of liabilities) with appropriate adjustment for nontaxable receipts and nondeductible expenditures. The net worth method often is used when tax fraud is suspected.

Ninety-day letter. See *statutory notice of deficiency.*

No-additional-cost services. Services that the employer may provide the employee at no additional cost to the employer. Generally, the benefit is the ability to utilize the employer's excess capacity (vacant seats on an airliner). Such amounts are excludible from the recipient's gross income. § 132.

Nonaccountable plan. An expense reimbursement plan that does not have an accountability feature. The result is that employee expenses must be claimed as deductions *from* AGI. An exception is moving expenses, which are deductions *for* AGI. See also *accountable plan.*

Nonacquiescence. Announcement of disagreement by the IRS on the result reached in certain judicial decisions. Sometimes abbreviated *Nonacq.* or *NA.* See also *acquiescence.*

Nonbusiness bad debts. A bad debt loss not incurred in connection with a creditor's trade or business. The loss is deductible as a short-term capital loss and is allowed only in the year the debt becomes entirely worthless. In addition to family loans, many investor losses fall into the classification of nonbusiness bad debts. § 166(d). See also *bad debts.*

Nonqualified deferred compensation (NQDC) plans. Compensation arrangements that are frequently offered to executives. Such plans may include stock options, restricted stock, etc. Often, an executive may defer the recognition of taxable income. The employer, however, does not receive a tax deduction until the employee is required to include the compensation in income. See also *restricted property plan.*

Nonqualified stock option (NQSO). A type of stock option that does not satisfy the statutory requirements of an incentive stock option. If the NQSO has a readily ascertainable fair market value (e.g., the option is traded on an established exchange), the value of the option must be included in the employee's gross income at the date of the grant. Otherwise, the employee does not recognize income at the grant date. Instead, ordinary income is recognized in the year of exercise of the option. See also *incentive stock option (ISO).*

Nonrecourse debt. An obligation on which the endorser is not personally liable. An example of a nonrecourse debt is a mortgage on real estate acquired by a partnership without the assumption of any liability on the mortgage by the partnership or any of the partners. The acquired property generally is pledged as collateral for the loan.

Nonrefundable credit. A nonrefundable credit is a credit that is not paid if it exceeds the taxpayer's tax liability. Some nonrefundable credits qualify for carryback and carryover treatment. See also *refundable credit.*

Nontaxable exchange. A transaction in which realized gains or losses are not recognized. The recognition of gain or loss is postponed (deferred) until the property received in the nontaxable exchange is subsequently disposed of in a taxable transaction. Examples are § 1031 like-kind exchanges and § 1033 involuntary conversions. See also *involuntary conversion* and *like-kind exchange.*

O

Occupational tax. A tax imposed on various trades or businesses. A license fee that enables a taxpayer to engage in a particular occupation.

Office audit. An audit by the IRS of a taxpayer's return that is conducted in the agent's office. To be distinguished from a *correspondence audit* or a *field audit.*

Office-in-the-home expenses. Employment and business-related expenses attributable to the use of a residence (e.g., den or office) are allowed only if the portion of the residence is exclusively used on a regular basis as a principal place of business of the taxpayer or as a place of business that is used by patients, clients, or customers. If the expenses are incurred by an employee, the use must be for the convenience of the employer as opposed to being merely appropriate and helpful. § 280A.

One-year rule for prepaid expenses. Taxpayers who use the cash method are required to use the accrual method for deducting certain prepaid expenses (i.e., must capitalize the item and can deduct only when used). If a prepayment will not be consumed or expire by the end of the tax year following the year of payment, the prepayment must be capitalized and prorated over the benefit period. Conversely, if the prepayment will be consumed by the end of the tax year following the year of payment, it can be expensed when paid. To obtain the current deduction under the one-year rule, the payment must be a required payment rather than a voluntary payment.

Open transaction. A judicially imposed doctrine that allows the taxpayer to defer all gain until he or she has collected an amount equal to the adjusted basis of assets transferred pursuant to an exchange transaction. This doctrine has been applied where the property received in an exchange has no ascertainable fair market value due to the existence of contingencies. The method is permitted only in very limited circumstances. See also *recovery of capital doctrine.*

Options. The sale or exchange of an option to buy or sell property results in capital gain or loss if the property is a capital asset. Generally, the closing of an option transaction results in short-term capital gain or loss to the writer of the call and the purchaser of the call option. § 1234.

Ordinary. Common and accepted in the general industry or type of activity in which the taxpayer is engaged. It comprises one of the tests for the deductibility of expenses incurred or paid in connection with a trade or business; for the production or collection of income; for the management, conservation, or maintenance of property held for the production of income; or in connection with the determination, collection, or refund of any tax. §§ 162(a) and 212. See also *necessary*.

Ordinary and necessary. See *necessary* and *ordinary*.

Ordinary income property. Property contributed to a charitable organization that, if sold rather than contributed, would have resulted in other than long-term capital gain to the donor (i.e., ordinary income property and short-term capital gain property). Examples are inventory and capital assets held for less than the long-term holding period.

Organizational expenditures. A corporation may elect to immediately expense the first $5,000 (subject to phaseout) of organizational expenses and generally amortize the balance over a period of 180 months. Certain expenses of organizing a company do not qualify for amortization (e.g., expenditures connected with issuing or selling stock or other securities). § 248.

Original issue discount (OID). The difference between the issue price of a debt obligation (e.g., a corporate bond) and the maturity value of the obligation when the issue price is *less than* the maturity value. OID represents interest and must be amortized over the life of the debt obligation using the effective interest method. The difference is not considered to be original issue discount for tax purposes when it is less than one-fourth of 1 percent of the redemption price at maturity multiplied by the number of years to maturity. §§ 1272 and 1273(a)(3).

Outside salesperson. An outside salesperson solicits business away from the employer's place of business on a full-time basis. The employment-related expenses of an outside salesperson are itemized deductions unless reimbursed by the employer. If reimbursed, such expenses are deductible *for* AGI.

P

Partnerships. A partnership is treated as a conduit and is not subject to taxation. Various items of partnership income, expenses, gains, and losses flow through to the individual partners and are reported on the partners' personal income tax returns. §§ 701 and 702.

Passive activity. A trade or business activity in which the taxpayer does not materially participate is subject to limitations on the deduction of losses and credits. Rental activities (subject to exceptions) and limited partnership interests are inherently passive. Relief from passive activity limitation treatment is provided in certain situations, such as for certain rental real estate, if the taxpayer actively participates in the activity. The annual ceiling on this rental real estate relief is $25,000. Relief also is provided for material participation in a real estate trade or business. § 469. See also *passive loss* and *portfolio income*.

Passive investment income. As defined in § 1362(d)(3)(D), passive investment income means gross receipts from royalties, certain rents, dividends, interest, annuities, and gains from the sale or exchange of stock and securities. Revocation of the S corporation election may occur in certain cases when the S corporation has passive investment income in excess of 25 percent of gross receipts for a period of three consecutive years.

Passive loss. Any loss from (1) activities in which the taxpayer does not materially participate or (2) rental activities (subject to certain exceptions). Net passive losses cannot be used to offset income from nonpassive sources. Rather, they are suspended until the taxpayer either generates net passive income (and a deduction of the losses is allowed) or disposes of the underlying property (at which time the loss deductions are allowed in full). One relief provision allows landlords who actively participate in the rental activities to deduct up to $25,000 of passive losses annually. However, a phaseout of the $25,000 amount commences when the landlord's AGI exceeds $100,000. Another relief provision applies for material participation in a real estate trade or business. See also *passive activity* and *portfolio income*.

Patent. A patent is an intangible asset that may be amortized over a statutory 15-year period as a § 197 intangible. The sale of a patent usually results in favorable long-term capital gain treatment. §§ 197 and 1235.

Pension plan. A type of deferred compensation arrangement that provides for systematic payments of definitely determinable retirement benefits to employees who meet the requirements set forth in the plan. See also *defined benefit plan* and *defined contribution plan*.

Percentage depletion. Percentage depletion is depletion based on a statutory percentage applied to the gross income from the property. The taxpayer deducts the greater of cost depletion or percentage depletion. § 613. See also *cost depletion*.

Percentage of completion method. A method of reporting gain or loss on certain long-term contracts. Under this method of accounting, the gross contract price is included in income as the contract is being completed. § 460 and Reg. § 1.451–3. See also *completed contract method* and *long-term contract*.

Permanent and total disability. A person is considered permanently and totally disabled if he or she is unable to engage in any substantial gainful activity due to a physical or mental impairment. In addition, this impairment must be one that can be expected to result in death or that has lasted or can be expected to last for a continuous period of not less than 12 months. The taxpayer generally must provide the IRS a physician's statement documenting this condition.

Personal and dependency exemptions. The tax law provides an exemption for each individual taxpayer and an additional exemption for the taxpayer's spouse if a joint return is filed. An individual may also claim a dependency exemption for each dependent, provided certain tests are met. The amount of the personal and dependency exemptions is $3,400 in 2007 and $3,500 in 2008. The amount is indexed for inflation. The exemption is subject to phaseout once adjusted gross income exceeds certain statutory threshold amounts. This phaseout provision is subject to partial phaseout beginning in 2006. §§ 151 and 152. See also *qualifying child* and *qualifying relative*.

Personal casualty gain. The recognized gain from any involuntary conversion of personal use property arising from fire, storm, shipwreck, or other casualty, or from theft. See also *personal casualty loss*.

Personal casualty loss. The recognized loss from any involuntary conversion of personal use property arising from fire, storm, shipwreck, or other casualty, or from theft. See also *personal casualty gain.*

Personal exemption. See *personal and dependency exemptions.*

Personal expenses. Expenses of an individual for personal reasons that are not deductible unless specifically provided for under the tax law. § 262.

Personal property. Generally, all property other than real estate. It is sometimes referred to as personalty when real estate is termed realty. Personal property also can refer to property that is not used in a taxpayer's trade or business or held for the production or collection of income. When used in this sense, personal property can include both realty (e.g., a personal residence) and personalty (e.g., personal effects such as clothing and furniture).

Personal residence. See *sale of principal residence.*

Personal service corporation (PSC). A corporation the principal activity of which is the performance of personal services (e.g., health, law, engineering, architecture, accounting, actuarial science, performing arts, or consulting), with such services being substantially performed by the employee-owners. The 35 percent statutory rate applies to PSCs.

Personalty. All property other than realty (real estate). Personalty usually is categorized as tangible or intangible property. Tangible personalty includes such assets as machinery and equipment, automobiles and trucks, and office equipment. Intangible personalty includes stocks and bonds, goodwill, patents, trademarks, and copyrights. See also *personal property.*

Points. Loan origination fees that may be deductible as interest by a buyer of property. A seller of property who pays points reduces the selling price by the amount of the points paid for the buyer. While the seller is not permitted to deduct this amount as interest, the buyer may do so. See *prepaid interest* for the timing of the interest deduction.

Pollution control facilities. A certified pollution control facility, the cost of which may be amortized over a 60-month period if the taxpayer elects. § 169.

Portfolio income. The term is relevant in applying the limitation on passive activity losses and credits. Although normally considered passive in nature, for this purpose portfolio income is treated as nonpassive. Therefore, net passive losses and credits cannot be offset against portfolio income. Examples of portfolio income are interest, dividends, annuities, and certain royalties. § 469. See also *passive activity.*

Precedent. A previously decided court decision that is recognized as authority for the disposition of future decisions.

Prepaid expenses. Cash basis as well as accrual basis taxpayers usually are required to capitalize prepayments for rent, insurance, etc., that cover more than one year. Deductions are taken during the period the benefits are received.

Prepaid interest. In effect, the Code places cash basis taxpayers on an accrual basis for purposes of recognizing a deduction for prepaid interest. Thus, interest paid in advance is deductible as an interest expense only as it accrues. The one exception to this rule involves the interest element when a cash basis taxpayer pays points to obtain financing for the purchase of a principal residence (or to make improvements thereto) if the payment of points is an established business practice in the area in which the indebtedness is incurred and the amount involved is not excessive. § 461(g). See also *points.*

Principal partner. A partner with a 5 percent or greater interest in partnership capital or profits. § 706(b)(3). See also *majority interest partners.*

Private activity bond. Interest on state and local bonds is excludible from gross income. § 103. Certain such bonds are labeled private activity bonds. Although the interest on such bonds is excludible for regular income tax purposes, it is treated as a tax preference in calculating the AMT. See also *alternative minimum tax (AMT).*

Prizes and awards. The fair market value of a prize or award generally is includible in gross income. However, exclusion is permitted if the prize or award is made in recognition of religious, charitable, scientific, educational, artistic, literary, or civic achievement, and the recipient transfers the award to a qualified governmental unit or a nonprofit organization. In that case, the recipient must be selected without any action on his or her part to enter a contest or proceeding, and the recipient must not be required to render substantial future services as a condition of receiving the prize or award. § 74.

Procedural Regulation. A Regulation issued by the Treasury Department that is a housekeeping-type instruction indicating information that taxpayers should provide the IRS as well as information about the internal management and conduct of the IRS itself. See also *interpretive regulation* and *legislative regulation.*

Production activities deduction (PAD). A deduction based on 3% of the lesser of qualified production activities income (QPAI) or modified adjusted gross income but not to exceed 50% of the W-2 wages paid. In the case of a corporate taxpayer, taxable income is substituted for modified AGI. The deduction rate increases to 6% for 2007 to 2009 and to 9% for 2010 and thereafter. §199. See also *qualified production activities income (QPAI).*

Profit sharing plan. A deferred compensation plan established and maintained by an employer to provide for employee participation in the company's profits. Contributions are paid from the employer's current or accumulated profits to a trustee. Separate accounts are maintained for each participant employee. The plan must provide a definite, predetermined formula for allocating the contributions among the participants. It also must include a definite, predetermined formula for distributing the accumulated funds after a fixed number of years, on the attainment of a stated age, or on the occurrence of certain events such as illness, layoff, or retirement.

Proposed Regulation. A Regulation issued by the Treasury Department in proposed, rather than final, form. The interval between the proposal of a Regulation and its finalization permits taxpayers and other interested parties to comment on the propriety of the proposal. See also *regulations* and *temporary regulation.*

Public policy limitation. See *bribes and illegal payments.*

Punitive damages. Damages received or paid by the taxpayer can be classified as compensatory damages or as punitive damages. Punitive damages are those awarded to punish the defendant for gross negligence or the intentional infliction of harm. Such damages are includible in gross income. § 104. See also *compensatory damages.*

Q

Qualified dividend income. Dividends that are eligible for the beneficial 0 percent (5% prior to 2008) or 15 percent tax rate. Excluded are certain dividends from foreign corporations, dividends from tax-exempt entities, and dividends that do not satisfy the holding period requirement. A dividend from a foreign corporation is eligible for qualified dividend status only if one of the following requirements are met: (1) the foreign corporation's stock is traded on an established U.S. securities market, or (2) the foreign corporation is eligible for the benefits of a comprehensive income tax treaty between its country of incorporation and the United States. To satisfy the holding period requirement, the stock on which the dividend is paid must have been held for more than 60 days during the 120-day period beginning 60 days before the ex-dividend date.

Qualified employee discounts. Discounts offered employees on merchandise or services that the employer ordinarily sells or provides to customers. The discounts must be generally available to all employees. In the case of property, the discount cannot exceed the employer's gross profit (the sales price cannot be less than the employer's cost). In the case of services, the discounts cannot exceed 20 percent of the normal sales price. § 132.

Qualified pension or profit sharing plan. An employer-sponsored plan that meets the requirements of § 401. If these requirements are met, none of the employer's contributions to the plan will be taxed to the employee until distributed to him or her (§ 402). The employer will be allowed a deduction in the year the contributions are made (§ 404). See also *annuity* and *deferred compensation*.

Qualified production activities income (QPAI). A key determinant in computing the domestic production activities deduction (DPAD). It consists of domestic production gross receipts (DPGR) reduced by cost of goods sold and other assignable expenses. Thus, QPAI represents the profit derived from production activities. § 199. See also *production activities deduction (PAD)* and *domestic production gross receipts (DPGR)*.

Qualified real property business indebtedness. Indebtedness that was incurred or assumed by the taxpayer in connection with real property used in a trade or business and is secured by such real property. The taxpayer must not be a C corporation. For qualified real property business indebtedness, the taxpayer may elect to exclude some or all of the income realized from cancellation of debt on qualified real property. If the election is made, the basis of the property must be reduced by the amount excluded. The amount excluded cannot be greater than the excess of the principal amount of the outstanding debt over the fair market value (net of any other debt outstanding on the property) of the property securing the debt. § 108(c).

Qualified residence interest. A term relevant in determining the amount of interest expense the individual taxpayer may deduct as an itemized deduction for what otherwise would be disallowed as a component of personal interest (consumer interest). Qualified residence interest consists of interest paid on qualified residences (principal residence and one other residence) of the taxpayer. Debt that qualifies as qualified residence interest is limited to $1 million of debt to acquire, construct, or substantially improve qualified residences (acquisition indebtedness) plus $100,000 of other debt secured by qualified residences (home equity indebtedness). The home equity indebtedness may not exceed the fair market value of a qualified residence reduced by the acquisition indebtedness for that residence. § 163(h)(3). See also *consumer interest* and *home equity loans*.

Qualified transportation fringes. Transportation benefits provided by the employer to the employee. Such benefits include (1) transportation in a commuter highway vehicle between the employee's residence and the place of employment, (2) a transit pass, and (3) qualified parking. Qualified transportation fringes are excludible from the employee's gross income to the extent categories (1) and (2) above do not exceed $115 per month in 2008 ($110 in 2007) and category (3) does not exceed $220 per month in 2008 ($215 in 2007). These amounts are indexed annually for inflation. § 132.

Qualified tuition program. A program that allows college tuition to be prepaid for a beneficiary. When amounts in the plan are used, nothing is included in gross income provided they are used for qualified higher education expenses. § 529.

Qualified tuition reduction plan. A type of fringe benefit plan that is available to employees of nonprofit educational institutions. Such employees (and the spouse and dependent children) are allowed to exclude from gross income a tuition waiver pursuant to a qualified tuition reduction plan. The exclusion applies to undergraduate tuition. In limited circumstances, the exclusion also applies to the graduate tuition of teaching and research assistants. § 117(d).

Qualifying child. An individual who, as to the taxpayer, satisfies the relationship, abode, and age tests. To be claimed as a dependent, such an individual must also meet the citizenship and joint return tests and not be self-supporting. §§ 152(a)(1) and (c). See also *personal and dependency exemptions*.

Qualifying relative. An individual who, as to the taxpayer, satisfies the relationship, gross income, support, citizenship, and joint return tests. Such an individual can be claimed as a dependent of the taxpayer. §§ 152(a)(2) and (d). See also *personal and dependency exemptions*.

R

RAR. A Revenue Agent's Report, which reflects any adjustments made by the agent as a result of an audit of the taxpayer. The RAR is mailed to the taxpayer along with the 30-day letter, which outlines the appellate procedures available to the taxpayer.

Realized gain or loss. The difference between the amount realized upon the sale or other disposition of property and the adjusted basis of the property. § 1001. See also *adjusted basis* and *recognized gain or loss*.

Realty. All real estate, including land and buildings. Permanent improvements to a building (fixtures) become realty if their removal would cause significant damage to the property. An example of a fixture is the installation of a central air conditioning or heating system to a building.

Thus, personalty can become realty through the fixture reclassification.

Reasonable needs of the business. See *accumulated earnings tax.*

Reasonableness. The Code includes a reasonableness requirement with respect to the deduction of salaries and other compensation for services. What constitutes reasonableness is a question of fact. If an expense is unreasonable, the amount that is classified as unreasonable is not allowed as a deduction. The question of reasonableness generally arises with respect to closely held corporations where there is no separation of ownership and management. § 162(a)(1).

Recapture. To recover the tax benefit of a deduction or a credit previously taken.

Recapture of depreciation. Upon the disposition of depreciable property used in a trade or business, gain or loss is measured by the difference between the consideration received (the amount realized) and the adjusted basis of the property. Before the enactment of the recapture of depreciation provisions of the Code, any such gain recognized could be § 1231 gain and usually qualified for long-term capital gain treatment. The recapture provisions of the Code (e.g., §§ 1245 and 1250) may operate to convert some or all of the previous § 1231 gain into ordinary income. The justification for recapture of depreciation is that it prevents a taxpayer from deducting depreciation at ordinary income rates and having the related gain on disposition taxed at capital gain rates. The recapture of depreciation rules do not apply when the property is disposed of at a loss. See also *residential rental property, Section 1231 gains and losses, Section 1245 recapture,* and *Section 1250 recapture.*

Recapture of investment tax credit. When investment tax credit property is disposed of or ceases to be used in the trade or business of the taxpayer, some or all of the investment tax credit claimed on the property may be recaptured as additional tax liability. The amount of the recapture is the difference between the amount of the credit originally claimed and what should be claimed in light of the length of time the property was actually held or used for qualifying purposes. § 50. See also *investment tax credit.*

Recapture potential. Reference is to property that, if disposed of in a taxable transaction, would result in the recapture of depreciation (§§ 1245 or 1250) and/or of the investment tax credit (§ 50).

Recognized gain or loss. The portion of realized gain or loss that is considered in computing taxable income. See also *realized gain or loss.*

Recovery of capital doctrine. When a taxable sale or exchange occurs, the seller may be permitted to recover his or her investment (or other adjusted basis) in the property before gain or loss is recognized. See also *open transaction.*

Refundable credit. A refundable credit is a credit that is paid to the taxpayer even if the amount of the credit (or credits) exceeds the taxpayer's tax liability. See also *nonrefundable credit.*

Regulations. Treasury Department Regulations represent the position of the IRS as to how the Internal Revenue Code is to be interpreted. Their purpose is to provide taxpayers and IRS personnel with rules of general and specific application to the various provisions of the tax law. Regulations are published in the *Federal Register* and in all tax services. See also *interpretive regulation, legislative regulation, procedural regulation,* and *proposed regulation.*

Rehabilitation expenditures credit. A credit that is based on expenditures incurred to rehabilitate industrial and commercial buildings and certified historic structures. The credit is intended to discourage businesses from moving from older, economically distressed areas to newer locations and to encourage the preservation of historic structures. § 47. See also *rehabilitation expenditures credit recapture.*

Rehabilitation expenditures credit recapture. When property that qualifies for the rehabilitation expenditures credit is disposed of or ceases to be used in the trade or business of the taxpayer, some or all of the tax credit claimed on the property may be recaptured as additional tax liability. The amount of the recapture is the difference between the amount of the credit claimed originally and what should have been claimed in light of the length of time the property was actually held or used for qualifying purposes. § 50. See also *rehabilitation expenditures credit.*

Related party. Includes certain family members and controlled entities (i.e., partnerships and corporations). §§ 267, 707(b), and 1239. See also *related-party transactions.*

Related-party transactions. The tax law places restrictions upon the recognition of gains and losses between related parties because of the potential for abuse. For example, restrictions are placed on the deduction of losses from the sale or exchange of property between related parties. In addition, under certain circumstances, related-party gains that would otherwise be classified as capital gain are classified as ordinary income. §§ 267, 707(b), and 1239. See also *related party.*

Rental activity. Any activity where payments are received principally for the use of tangible property is a rental activity. Temporary Regulations provide that in certain circumstances activities involving rentals of real and personal property are not to be *treated* as rental activities. The Temporary Regulations list six exceptions.

Research activities credit. A tax credit whose purpose is to encourage research and development. It consists of three components: the incremental research activities credit, the basic research credit, and the energy credit. The incremental research activities credit is equal to 20 percent of the excess of qualified research expenditures over the base amount. The basic research credit is equal to 20 percent of the excess of basic research payments over the base amount. § 41. See also *general business credit.*

Research and experimental expenditures. The Code provides three alternatives for the tax treatment of research and experimentation expenditures. They may be expensed in the year paid or incurred, deferred subject to amortization, or capitalized. If the taxpayer does not elect to expense such costs or to defer them subject to amortization (over 60 months), the expenditures must be capitalized. § 174. Three types of research activities credits are available: the basic research credit, the incremental research activities credit and the energy credit. The rate for each type is 20 percent. § 41. See also *research activities credit.*

Reserve for bad debts. A method of accounting whereby an allowance is permitted for estimated uncollectible accounts. Actual write-offs are charged to the reserve, and recoveries of amounts previously written off are credited to the reserve. The Code permits only certain financial institutions to use the reserve method. § 166. See also *specific charge-off method.*

Reserve method. See *reserve for bad debts.*

Reserves for estimated expenses. Except in the limited case for bad debts, reserves for estimated expenses (e.g., warranty service costs) are not permitted for tax purposes even though such reserves are appropriate for financial accounting purposes. See also *all events test.*

Residential rental property. Buildings for which at least 80 percent of the gross rents are from dwelling units (e.g., an apartment building). This type of building is distinguished from nonresidential (commercial or industrial) buildings in applying the recapture of depreciation provisions. The term also is relevant in distinguishing between buildings that are eligible for a 27.5-year life versus a 39-year (or 31.5-year) life for MACRS purposes. Generally, residential buildings receive preferential treatment. §§ 168(e)(2) and 1250. See also *recapture of depreciation.*

Residential rental real estate. See *residential rental property.*

Restricted property plan. An arrangement whereby an employer transfers property (usually stock) to an employee at a bargain price (for less than the fair market value). If the transfer is accompanied by a substantial risk of forfeiture and the property is not transferable, no compensation results to the employee until the restrictions disappear. An example of a substantial risk of forfeiture would be a requirement that the employee return the property if his or her employment is terminated within a specified period of time. § 83. See also *nonqualified deferred compensation (NQDC) plans* and *substantial risk of forfeiture.*

Retirement of corporate obligations. The retirement of corporate and certain government obligations is considered to be a sale or exchange. Gain or loss, upon the retirement of a corporate obligation, therefore, is treated as capital gain or loss rather than as ordinary income or loss. §§ 1271–1275.

Return of capital doctrine. See *recovery of capital doctrine.*

Revenue neutrality. A description that characterizes tax legislation when it neither increases nor decreases the revenue result. Thus, any tax revenue losses are offset by tax revenue gains.

Revenue Procedure. A matter of procedural importance to both taxpayers and the IRS concerning the administration of the tax law is issued by the National Office of the IRS as a Revenue Procedure (abbreviated Rev.Proc.). A Revenue Procedure is first published in an *Internal Revenue Bulletin* (I.R.B.) and later transferred to the appropriate *Cumulative Bulletin* (C.B.). Both the *Internal Revenue Bulletin* and the *Cumulative Bulletin* are published by the U.S. Government Printing Office.

Revenue Ruling. A Revenue Ruling (abbreviated Rev.Rul.) is issued by the National Office of the IRS to express an official interpretation of the tax law as applied to specific transactions. It is more limited in application than a Regulation. A Revenue Ruling is first published in an *Internal Revenue Bulletin* (I.R.B.) and later transferred to the appropriate *Cumulative Bulletin* (C.B.). Both the *Internal Revenue*

Bulletin and the *Cumulative Bulletin* are published by the U.S. Government Printing Office.

S

S corporation. See *S corporation status.*

S corporation status. An elective provision permitting certain small business corporations (§ 1361) and their shareholders to elect (§ 1362) to be treated for income tax purposes in accordance with the operating rules of §§ 1363–1379. Of major significance are the facts that S status avoids the corporate income tax and corporate losses can be claimed by the shareholders. See also *C corporation.*

Sale of principal residence. If a residence has been owned and used by the taxpayer as the principal residence for at least two years during the five-year period ending on the date of sale, up to $250,000 of realized gain is excluded from gross income. For a married couple filing a joint return, the $250,000 is increased to $500,000 if either spouse satisfies the ownership requirement and both spouses satisfy the use requirement. § 121.

Sale or exchange. A requirement for the recognition of capital gain or loss. Generally, the seller of property must receive money or relief from debt in order to have sold the property. An exchange involves the transfer of property for other property. Thus, collection of a debt is neither a sale nor an exchange. The term *sale or exchange* is not defined by the Code.

Sales tax. A transaction tax imposed upon the sale of goods. It usually is based on a specified percentage of the value of the property sold. A sales tax differs from an excise tax, in that a sales tax applies to a broad variety of commodities.

Salvage value. The estimated amount a taxpayer will receive upon the disposition of an asset used in the taxpayer's trade or business. Salvage value is relevant in calculating depreciation under § 167, but is not relevant in calculating cost recovery under § 168.

Schedule M-1. On the Form 1120, a reconciliation of book net income with Federal taxable income. Accounts for timing and permanent differences in the two computations, such as depreciation differences, exempt income, and nondeductible items. On Forms 1120S and 1065, the Schedule M-1 reconciles book income with the owners' aggregate ordinary taxable income.

Schedule M-3. An *expanded* reconciliation of book net income with Federal taxable income (refer to *Schedule M-1* above). Applies to corporations with total assets of $10 million or more.

Scholarships. Scholarships are generally excluded from the gross income of the recipient unless the payments are a disguised form of compensation for services rendered. However, the Code imposes restrictions on the exclusion. The recipient must be a degree candidate. The excluded amount is limited to amounts used for tuition, fees, books, supplies, and equipment required for courses of instruction. Amounts received for room and board are not eligible for the exclusion. § 117.

Section 121 exclusion. See *sale of principal residence.*

Section 179 expensing. The ability to deduct a capital expenditure in the year an asset is placed in service rather than over the asset's useful life or cost recovery period. The annual ceiling on the deduction is $250,000 for 2008 ($125,000 for 2007). However, the deduction is reduced dollar for dollar when § 179 property placed in service during the taxable year exceeds $800,000 in 2008 ($500,000 in 2007). In addition, the amount expensed under § 179 cannot exceed the aggregate amount of taxable income derived from the conduct of any trade or business by the taxpayer.

Section 401(k) plan. A cash or deferred arrangement plan that allows participants to elect to receive up to $15,500 in 2008 ($15,500 in 2007) in cash (taxed currently) or to have a contribution made on their behalf to a profit sharing or stock bonus plan (excludible from gross income). The plan may also be in the form of a salary reduction agreement between the participant and the employer.

Section 1231 assets. Depreciable assets and real estate used in a trade or business and held for the required long-term holding period. Under certain circumstances, the classification also includes timber, coal, domestic iron ore, livestock (held for draft, breeding, dairy, or sporting purposes), and unharvested crops. § 1231(b).

Section 1231 gains and losses. If the net result of the combined gains and losses from the taxable dispositions of § 1231 assets plus the net gain from the involuntary conversion of nonpersonal use assets is a gain, the gains and losses from § 1231 assets are treated as long-term capital gains and losses. In arriving at § 1231 gains, however, the depreciation recapture provisions (e.g., §§ 1245 and 1250) are first applied to produce ordinary income. If the net result of the combination is a loss, the gains and losses from § 1231 assets are treated as ordinary gains and losses. § 1231(a). See also *recapture of depreciation*.

Section 1231 lookback. In order for gain to be classified as § 1231 gain, the gain must survive the § 1231 lookback. To the extent of nonrecaptured § 1231 losses for the five prior tax years, the gain is classified as ordinary income. § 1231(c).

Section 1231 property. See *Section 1231 assets*.

Section 1244 stock. Stock issued under § 1244 by qualifying small business corporations. If § 1244 stock is disposed of at a loss or becomes worthless, the shareholders may claim an ordinary loss rather than the usual capital loss. The annual ceiling on the ordinary loss treatment is $50,000 ($100,000 for married individuals filing jointly). See also *worthless securities*.

Section 1245 property. Property that is subject to the recapture of depreciation under § 1245. For a definition of § 1245 property, see § 1245(a)(3). See also *Section 1245 recapture*.

Section 1245 recapture. Upon a taxable disposition of § 1245 property, all depreciation claimed on the property is recaptured as ordinary income (but not to exceed the recognized gain from the disposition). See also *recapture of depreciation*.

Section 1250 property. Real estate that is subject to the recapture of depreciation under § 1250. For a definition of § 1250 property, see § 1250(c). See also *Section 1250 recapture*.

Section 1250 recapture. Upon a taxable disposition of § 1250 property, some or all of the additional depreciation claimed on the property may be recaptured as ordinary income. Various recapture rules apply depending upon the type of property (residential or nonresidential real estate) and the date acquired. Generally, the additional depreciation is recaptured in full to the extent of the gain recognized. See also *additional depreciation* and *recapture of depreciation*.

Self-employment retirement plan. A designation for retirement plans available to self-employed taxpayers. Also referred to as H.R. 10 and Keogh plans. Under such plans, in 2008, a taxpayer may deduct each year up to either 100 percent of net earnings from self-employment or $46,000, whichever is less. If the plan is a profit sharing plan, the percentage is 25 percent.

Self-employment tax. In 2008, a tax of 12.4 percent is levied on individuals with net earnings from self-employment (up to $102,000) to provide Social Security benefits (i.e., the old age, survivors, and disability insurance portion) for such individuals. In addition, in 2008, a tax of 2.9 percent is levied on individuals with net earnings from self-employment (with no statutory ceiling) to provide Medicare benefits (i.e., the hospital insurance portion) for such individuals. If a self-employed individual also receives wages from an employer that are subject to FICA, the self-employment tax will be reduced if total income subject to Social Security is more than $102,000 in 2008. A partial deduction is allowed in calculating the self-employment tax. Individuals with net earnings of $400 or more from self-employment are subject to this tax. §§ 1401 and 1402.

Separate property. In a community property jurisdiction, separate property is the property that belongs entirely to one of the spouses. Generally, it is property acquired before marriage or acquired after marriage by gift or inheritance. See also *community property*.

Severance tax. A tax imposed upon the extraction of natural resources.

Short sale. A short sale occurs when a taxpayer sells borrowed property (usually stock) and repays the lender with substantially identical property either held on the date of the short sale or purchased after the sale. No gain or loss is recognized until the short sale is closed, and such gain or loss is generally short term. § 1233.

Short taxable year (short period). A tax year that is less than 12 months. A short taxable year may occur in the initial reporting period, in the final tax year, or when the taxpayer changes tax years.

Significant participation activity. There are seven tests to determine whether an individual has achieved material participation in an activity, one of which is based on more than 500 hours of participation in significant participation activities. A significant participation activity is one in which the individual's participation exceeds 100 hours during the year. Temp.Reg. § 1.469–5T.

Simplified employee pension (SEP) plan. An employer may make contributions to an employee's IRA in amounts not exceeding the lesser of 15 percent of compensation or $46,000 per individual in 2008. These employer-sponsored simplified employee pensions are permitted only if the contributions are nondiscriminatory and are made on behalf of all employees who have attained age 21 and have worked for the employer during at least three of the five preceding calendar years. § 219(b). See also *individual retirement account (IRA)*.

Small business corporation. A corporation that satisfies the definition of § 1361(b), § 1244(c)(3), or both. Satisfaction of § 1361(b) permits an S corporation election, and satisfaction of § 1244 enables the shareholders of the corporation to claim an ordinary loss. See also *S corporation status* and *Section 1244 stock*.

Small business stock. See *small business corporation*.

Small cases division. A subsidiary division of the U.S. Tax Court. The jurisdiction of the Small Cases division is limited to small claims (i.e., claims of $50,000 or less). The proceedings of the Small Cases Division are informal, and the findings cannot be appealed.

Specific charge-off method. A method of accounting for bad debts in which a deduction is permitted only when an account becomes partially or completely worthless. See also *reserve for bad debts*.

Standard deduction. The individual taxpayer can either itemize deductions or take the standard deduction. The amount of the standard deduction depends on the taxpayer's filing status (single, head of household, married filing jointly, surviving spouse, or married filing separately). For 2008, the amount of the standard deduction ranges from $5,450 to $10,900. Additional standard deductions of either $1,050 (for married taxpayers) or $1,350 (for single taxpayers) are available if the taxpayer is either blind or age 65 or over. Limitations exist on the amount of the standard deduction of a taxpayer who is another taxpayer's dependent. The standard deduction amounts are adjusted for inflation each year. § 63(c).

Startup expenditures. Expenditures paid or incurred associated with the creation of a business prior to the beginning of business. Examples of such expenditures include advertising, salaries and wages, travel and other expenses incurred in lining up prospective distributors, suppliers, or customers, and salaries and fees to executives, consultants, and professional service providers. A taxpayer may elect to immediately expense the first $5,000 (subject to phaseout) of startup expenditures and generally amortize the balance over a period of 180 months.

Statute of limitations. Provisions of the law that specify the maximum period of time in which action may be taken on a past event. Code §§ 6501–6504 contain the limitation periods applicable to the IRS for additional assessments, and §§ 6511–6515 relate to refund claims by taxpayers.

Statutory employee. Statutory employees are considered self-employed independent contractors for purposes of reporting income and expenses on their tax returns. Generally, a statutory employee must meet three tests:

- It is understood from a service contract that the services will be performed by the person.
- The person does not have a substantial investment in facilities (other than transportation used to perform the services).
- The services involve a continuing relationship with the person for whom they are performed.

For further information on statutory employees, see Circular E, *Employer's Tax Guide*, IRS Publication 15.

Statutory notice of deficiency. Commonly referred to as the 90-day letter, this notice is sent to a taxpayer upon request, upon the expiration of the 30-day letter, or upon exhaustion by the taxpayer of his or her administrative remedies before the IRS. The notice gives the taxpayer 90 days in which to file a petition with the U.S. Tax Court. If a petition is not filed, the IRS will issue a demand for payment of the assessed deficiency. §§ 6211–6216. See also *thirty-day letter*.

Stock bonus plan. A type of deferred compensation plan in which the employer establishes and maintains the plan and contributes employer stock to the plan for the benefit of employees. The contributions need not be dependent on the employer's profits. Any benefits of the plan are distributable in the form of employer stock, except that distributable fractional shares may be paid in cash.

Stock option. The right to purchase a stated number of shares of stock from a corporation at a certain price within a specified period of time. §§ 421 and 422. See also *incentive stock option (ISO)* and *nonqualified stock option (NQSO)*.

Stock redemption. The redemption of the stock of a shareholder by the issuing corporation is treated as a sale or exchange of the stock if the redemption is not a dividend. §§ 301 and 302.

Substantial risk of forfeiture. A term that is associated with a restricted property plan. Generally, an employee who receives property (e.g., stock of the employer-corporation) from the employer at a bargain price or at no cost must include the bargain element in gross income. However, the employee currently does not have to do so if there is a substantial risk of forfeiture. A substantial risk of forfeiture exists if a person's rights to full enjoyment of property are conditioned upon the future performance, or the refraining from the performance, of substantial services by the individual. § 83. See also *restricted property plan*.

Sunset provision. A provision attached to new tax legislation that will cause such legislation to expire at a specified date. Sunset provisions are attached to tax cut bills for long-term budgetary reasons in order to make their effect temporary. Once the sunset provision comes into play, the tax cut is rescinded and former law is reinstated. An example of a sunset provision is the one contained in the Tax Relief Reconciliation Act of 2001, which relates to the estate tax. After the estate tax is phased out by 2010, a sunset provision reinstates the estate tax as on January 1, 2011.

Super-full absorption costing rules. See *uniform capitalization rules*.

Surviving spouse. The joint return tax rates apply for a surviving spouse. Such rates apply for the two tax years after the tax year of the death of the spouse. To qualify as a surviving spouse, the taxpayer must maintain a household for a dependent child. § 2.

T

Targeted jobs tax credit. See *work opportunity tax credit*.

Taxable year. The annual period over which income is measured for income tax purposes. Most individuals use a calendar year, but many businesses use a fiscal year based on the natural business year. See also *accounting period* and *fiscal year*.

Tax avoidance. The minimization of one's tax liability by taking advantage of legally available tax planning opportunities. Tax avoidance can be contrasted with tax evasion, which entails the reduction of tax liability by illegal means.

Tax benefit rule. A provision that limits the recognition of income from the recovery of an expense or loss properly deducted in a prior tax year to the amount of the deduction that generated a tax benefit. § 111.

Tax Court. The U.S. Tax Court is one of three trial courts of original jurisdiction that decides litigation involving Federal income, estate, or gift taxes. It is the only trial court where the taxpayer need not first pay the deficiency assessed by the IRS. The Tax Court will not have jurisdiction over a case unless the statutory notice of deficiency (90-day letter) has been issued by the IRS and the taxpayer files the petition for hearing within the time prescribed.

Tax credits. Tax credits are amounts that directly reduce a taxpayer's tax liability. The tax benefit received from a tax credit is not dependent on the taxpayer's marginal tax rate, whereas the benefit of a tax deduction or exclusion is dependent on the taxpayer's tax bracket.

Tax credit for the elderly or disabled. An elderly (age 65 and over) or disabled taxpayer may receive a tax credit amounting to 15 percent of $5,000 ($7,500 for qualified married individuals filing jointly). This amount is reduced by Social Security benefits, excluded pension benefits, and one-half of the taxpayer's adjusted gross income in excess of $7,500 ($10,000 for married taxpayers filing jointly). § 22.

Tax-free exchange. Transfers of property specifically exempted from Federal income tax consequences. Examples are a transfer of property to a controlled corporation under § 351(a) and a like-kind exchange under § 1031(a). The recognition of gain or loss is postponed, rather than being permanently excluded, through the assignment of a carryover basis to the replacement property. See also *nontaxable exchange.*

Tax home. Since travel expenses of an employee are deductible only if the taxpayer is away from home, the deductibility of such expenses rests upon the definition of tax home. The IRS position is that tax home is the business location, post, or station of the taxpayer. If an employee is temporarily reassigned to a new post for a period of one year or less, the taxpayer's home should be his or her personal residence, and the travel expenses should be deductible. If the assignment is for more than two years, the IRS position is that it is indefinite or permanent and the taxpayer is therefore not in travel status. If the assignment is for between one and two years, the IRS position is that the location of the tax home will be determined on the basis of the facts and circumstances. The courts are in conflict regarding what constitutes a person's home for tax purposes. The taxpayer will not be treated as temporarily away from home if the employment period exceeds one year. Thus, in this situation, the tax home will be the place of employment. See also *travel expenses.*

Tax preferences. Those items set forth in § 57 that may result in the imposition of the alternative minimum tax. See also *alternative minimum tax (AMT).*

Tax rate schedules. Rate schedules appearing in Appendix A that are used by upper-income taxpayers and those not permitted to use the tax table. Separate rate schedules are provided for married individuals filing jointly, head of household, single taxpayers, estates and trusts, and married individuals filing separate returns. § 1.

Tax research. The method used to determine the best available solution to a situation that possesses tax consequences. Both tax and nontax factors are considered.

Tax shelters. The typical tax shelter generated large losses in the early years of the activity. Investors would offset these losses against other types of income and, therefore, avoid paying income taxes on this income. These tax shelter investments could then be sold after a few years and produce capital gain income, which is taxed at a lower rate than ordinary income. The passive activity loss rules and the at-risk rules now limit tax shelter deductions.

Tax table. A tax table appearing in Appendix A that is provided for taxpayers with less than $100,000 of taxable income. Separate columns are provided for single taxpayers, married taxpayers filing jointly, head of household, and married taxpayers filing separately. § 3.

Technical advice memoranda (TAMs). TAMs are issued by the National Office of the IRS in response to questions raised by IRS field personnel during audits. They deal with completed rather than proposed transactions and are often requested for questions related to exempt organizations and employee plans.

Temporary Regulation. A Regulation issued by the Treasury Department in temporary form. When speed is critical, the Treasury Department issues Temporary Regulations, which take effect immediately. These Regulations have the same authoritative value as final Regulations and may be cited as precedent for three years. Temporary Regulations are also issued as Proposed Regulations. See also *proposed regulation* and *regulations.*

Theft loss. A loss from larceny, embezzlement, and robbery. It does not include misplacement of items. See also *casualty loss.*

Thin capitalization. When debt owed by a corporation to its shareholders is large relative to its capital structure (stock and shareholder equity), the IRS may contend that the corporation is thinly capitalized. In effect, this means that some or all of the debt will be reclassified as equity. The immediate result is to disallow any interest deduction to the corporation on the reclassified debt. To the extent of the corporation's earnings and profits, interest payments and loan repayments on the reclassified debt are treated as dividends to the shareholders. § 385.

Thirty-day letter. A letter that accompanies a Revenue Agent's Report (RAR) issued as a result of an IRS audit of a taxpayer (or the rejection of a taxpayer's claim for refund). The letter outlines the taxpayer's appeal procedure before the IRS. If the taxpayer does not request any such procedures within the 30-day period, the IRS will issue a *statutory notice of deficiency* (the 90-day letter).

Thirty percent additional first-year depreciation. This provision, which was effective for property acquired after September 10, 2001 and before September 11, 2004, provided for an additional cost recovery deduction of 30 percent in the tax year that qualified property was placed in service. Qualified property included most types of new property other than buildings. The property had to be placed in service before January 1, 2005. § 168(k). See also *cost recovery allowance* and *fifty percent additional first-year depreciation*.

Timber. Special rules apply to the recognition of gain from the sale of timber. A taxpayer may elect to treat the cutting of timber that is held for sale or use in a trade or business as a sale or exchange. If the holding period requirements are met, the gain is recognized as § 1231 gain and may therefore receive long-term capital gain treatment. § 631.

Trade or business expenses. Deductions *for* AGI that are attributable to a taxpayer's business or profession. Some employee expenses may also be treated as trade or business expenses. See also *employee expenses*.

Transportation expenses. Transportation expenses for an employee include only the cost of transportation (taxi fares, automobile expenses, etc.) in the course of employment when the employee is not away from home in travel status. Commuting expenses are not deductible. See also *automobile expenses*.

Travel expenses. Travel expenses include meals (generally subject to a 50 percent disallowance) and lodging and transportation expenses while away from home in the pursuit of a trade or business (including that of an employee). See also *tax home*.

Trial court. The court of original jurisdiction; the first court to consider litigation. In Federal tax controversies, trial courts include U.S. District Courts, the U.S. Tax Court, and the U.S. Court of Federal Claims. See also *appellate court*.

U

Unearned income. Also referred to as investment income, it includes such income as interest, dividends, capital gains, rents, royalties, and pension and annuity income. See also *kiddie tax*.

Unearned (prepaid) income. For tax purposes, prepaid income (e.g., rent) is taxable in the year of receipt. In certain cases involving advance payments for goods and services, income may be deferred. See Revenue Procedure 2004–34 (2004–22 I.R.B. 13, 991) and Reg. § 1.451–5. See also *accrual method*.

Uniform capitalization (UNICAP) rules. Under § 263A, the Regulations provide a set of rules that all taxpayers (regardless of the particular industry) can use to determine the items of cost (and means of allocating those costs) that must be capitalized with respect to the production of tangible property.

Unit-livestock-price method. A method of accounting for the cost of livestock. The livestock are valued using a standard cost of raising an animal with the characteristics of that animal to the same age as the animals on hand.

Unreasonable compensation. Under § 162(a)(1), a deduction is allowed for "reasonable" salaries or other compensation for personal services actually rendered. To the extent compensation is excessive ("unreasonable"), no deduction will be allowed. The problem of unreasonable compensation usually is limited to closely held corporations where the motivation is to pay out profits in some form deductible to the corporation. Deductible compensation, therefore, becomes an attractive substitute for nondeductible dividends when the shareholders are also employees of the corporation.

Unrecaptured § 1250 gain (25 percent gain). Gain from the sale of depreciable real estate held more than one year. The gain is equal to or less than the depreciation taken on such property and is reduced by § 1245 gain and § 1250 gain. See also *alternative tax*.

U.S. Court of Federal Claims. See *Claims Court*.

U.S. Supreme Court. The highest appellate court or the court of last resort in the Federal court system and in most states. Only a small number of tax decisions of the U.S. Courts of Appeal are reviewed by the U.S. Supreme Court under its certiorari procedure. The Supreme Court usually grants certiorari to resolve a conflict among the Courts of Appeal (e.g., two or more appellate courts have assumed opposing positions on a particular issue) or when the tax issue is extremely important (e.g., size of the revenue loss to the Federal government).

U.S. Tax Court. See *Tax Court*.

Use tax. A use tax is an ad valorem tax, usually at the same rate as the sales tax, on the use or consumption of tangible personalty. The purpose of a use tax is to prevent the avoidance of a sales tax.

USTC. Published by Commerce Clearing House, *U.S. Tax Cases* contain all of the Federal tax decisions issued by the U.S. District Courts, U.S. Court of Federal Claims, U.S. Courts of Appeals, and the U.S. Supreme Court.

V

Vacation home. The Code places restrictions upon taxpayers who rent their residences or vacation homes for part of the tax year. The restrictions may result in a scaling down of expense deductions for the taxpayers. § 280A. See also *hobby loss*.

Value added tax (VAT). A national sales tax that taxes the increment in value as goods move through the production process. A VAT is much used in other countries, but has not yet been incorporated as part of the U.S. Federal tax structure.

Vesting requirements. A qualified deferred compensation arrangement must satisfy a vesting requirement. Under this provision, an employee's right to accrued plan benefits derived from employer contributions must be nonforfeitable in accordance with one of two vesting time period schedules (or two required alternate vesting schedules for certain employer matching contributions).

W

W–2 wages. The production activities deduction (PAD) cannot exceed 50% of the W–2 wages paid for any particular year. Prop.Reg. § 199–2(f)(2) provides several methods for calculating the W–2 wages, but the payments must involve common law employees. To qualify, however, they need not be involved in the production process. § 199. See also *production activities deduction (PAD)*.

Wash sale. A loss from the sale of stock or securities that is disallowed because the taxpayer within 30 days before or after the sale has acquired stock or securities that are substantially identical to those sold. § 1091.

Welfare-to-work credit. A tax credit available to employers hiring individuals who have been long-term recipients of family assistance welfare benefits. In general, long-term recipients are those individuals who are certified by a designated local agency as being members of a family receiving assistance under a public aid program for at least an 18-month period ending on the hiring date. The welfare-to-work credit is available for qualified wages paid in the first two years of employment. The maximum credit is equal to $9,000 per qualified employee, computed as 40 percent of the first $10,000 of qualified wages paid in the first year of employment, plus 50 percent of the first $10,000 of qualified wages paid in the second year of employment. Starting in 2007, the welfare-to-work credit becomes part of the work opportunity tax credit. § 51A. See also *general business credit* and *work opportunity tax credit*.

Wherewithal to pay. This concept recognizes the inequity of taxing a transaction when the taxpayer lacks the means with which to pay the tax. Under it, there is a correlation between the imposition of the tax and the ability to pay the tax. It is particularly suited to situations in which the taxpayer's economic position has not changed significantly as a result of the transaction.

Withholding allowances. The number of withholding allowances serves as the basis for determining the amount of income taxes withheld from an employee's salary or wages. The more withholding allowances claimed, the less income tax withheld by an employer. An employee may claim withholding allowances for personal exemptions for self and spouse (unless claimed as a dependent of another person), dependency exemptions, and special withholding allowances.

Working condition fringe. A type of fringe benefit received by the employee that is excludible from the employee's gross income. It consists of property or services provided (paid or reimbursed) by the employer for which the employee could take a tax deduction if the employee had paid for them. § 132.

Work opportunity tax credit. Employers are allowed a tax credit equal to 40 percent of the first $6,000 of wages (per eligible employee) for the first year of employment. Eligible employees include certain hard-to-employ individuals (e.g., qualified ex-felons, high-risk youth, food stamp recipients, and veterans). For an employer to qualify for the 40 percent credit, the employees must (1) be certified by a designated local agency as being members of one of the targeted groups and (2) have completed at least 400 hours of service to the employer. For employees who meet the first condition but not the second, the credit rate is reduced to 25 percent provided the employees meet a minimum employment level of 120 hours of service to the employer. The employer's deduction for wages is reduced by the amount of the credit taken. For qualified summer youth employees, the 40 percent rate is applied to the first $3,000 of qualified wages. See the *welfare-to-work credit* for the calculation for long-term recipients of family assistance welfare benefits. §§ 51 and 52.

Worthless securities. A loss (usually capital) is allowed for a security that becomes worthless during the year. The loss is deemed to have occurred on the last day of the year. Special rules apply to securities of affiliated companies and small business stock. § 165. See also *Section 1244 stock*.

Writ of certiorari. See *certiorari*.

[See Title 26 U.S.C.A.]

I.R.C. Sec.	This Work Page	I.R.C. Sec.	This Work Page
1	2–7, 16–23	25A(f)	9–16
1(a)	3–29	25A(h)(2)(A)	13–24
1(g)	20–39	25B	13–25, 13–29
1(g)(2)	3–23	25B(e)	13–25
1(h)	16–23	26(a)(2)	12–8
1(h)(1)	3–33, 20–21	27	13–18, 13–29
1(h)(3)(B)	20–37	31	13–28
1(h)(11)(B)	20–21	32	13–15, 13–28
1(i)	3–21	32(a)(2)(B)	13–15
2	2–7, 2–8	32(i)	13–15
2(a)	2–6, 3–30	38	13–29
2(a)(1)(A)	2–6, 2–7	38(c)	13–6
2(b)	3–31	39(a)(1)	13–6
2(b)(1)(B)	3–31	41	7–15, 13–10, 13–27, 13–29
2(b)(3)(B)	3–31	41(b)(3)(A)	13–11
5	2–6	41(b)(3)(D)	13–11
6	2–6	41(c)(4)	13–10
7	2–6	41(c)(5)	13–10
8	2–6	41(d)	13–11
9	2–6	42	13–13, 13–29
10	2–6	44	13–13, 13–27, 13–29
11	2–6	45E	13–14, 13–29
11(b)	20–14	45E(d)(1)	13–14
12(d)	2–7	45E(c)(1)	13–14
21	13–21, 13–28	45F	13–14, 13–30
21(c)	13–24	45F(d)	13–15
21(d)	13–22	47	13–7, 13–29
22	13–17, 13–28	50(c)	13–7
22(e)(3)	3–12	51	13–9, 13–30
23	13–20, 13–28	51A	13–10
23(b)(1)	13–20	51(d)(1)(I)	13–10
23(b)(2)	13–21	53	12–24
23(d)(3)	13–20	55	12–2
24	13–21, 13–28	55(b)(1)	12–7
24(a)	3–20, 13–21	55(b)(1)(B)	12–26
24(b)	13–21	55(d)	12–7
25A	9–17, 9–32, 13–24, 13–28	55(d)(2)	12–26
25A(d)	13–24	55(d)(3)	12–26

I.R.C. Sec.	This Work Page	I.R.C. Sec.	This Work Page
55(e)(1)(A)	12–26	71	4–20
55(e)(1)(B)	12–26	71–90	4–20
55(e)(1)(C)	12–26	71(b)(1)	4–21
56	12–4	71(c)(2)	4–23
56(a)(1)	12–11	71(f)	4–21
56(a)(2)	12–12	71(f)(5)(A)	4–22
56(a)(3)	12–12	71(f)(5)(C)	4–22
56(a)(4)	12–15	72	19–13, 19–23
56(a)(5)	12–11	72(b)	4–30
56(a)(6)	12–13	72(d)	4–30
56(b)(1)(A)	12–16	72(e)(3)	4–28
56(b)(1)(B)	12–16	72(q)	4–28
56(b)(1)(C)	12–17	72(t)	19–11, 19–27, 19–50
56(b)(1)(D)	12–16	72(t)(2)(B)	19–27
56(b)(1)(E)	12–19	72(t)(2)(D)	19–27
56(b)(1)(F)	12–16, 12–41	72(t)(2)(E)	9–27
56(b)(2)(A)(i)	12–9	72(t)(2)(F)	19–27
56(b)(3)	12–13	73	4–14
56(c)	12–27	74	4–31
56(g)	12–27	74(b)	4–31
56(g)(1)	12–28	74(c)	4–31, 5–3
56(g)(2)	12–28	79	4–31, 4–41, 5–3, 5–40
56(g)(6)	12–27	79(d)	4–32, 5–25
57	12–5	83	19–30, 19–34, 19–42
57(a)(1)	12–20	83(a)	4–11
57(a)(2)	12–20	83(a)(1)	19–34
57(a)(3)	19–36	83(b)	19–35, 19–48, 19–49
57(a)(5)	12–20	83(c)	19–34
57(a)(6)	12–21	85	4–33
57(a)(7)	12–22	86	4–33, 5–3, 19–21
59(e)(2)(A)	12–9	101	5–3, 7–17, 14–28
59(e)(2)(D)	12–12	101 through 150	5–4
59(e)(2)(E)	12–12	101(a)	5–6
61	4–2, 4–3, 20–18	101(a)(1)	14–28
61(a)	3–3, 4–2	101(g)	5–3, 5–7
61(a)(3)	14–6	101(h)	5–3
61(a)(12)	5–33	102	5–3, 5–5
62	3–5, 6–3, 6–4, 20–18	102(a)	14–11
62(a)(1)	6–30, 7–13	102(c)	5–5
62(a)(2)	9–26	103	5–3, 6–28
62(a)(2)(A)	6–30	103(a)	5–28
62(a)(2)(B)	6–30, 10–27	104	5–3
62(a)(2)(D)	6–30, 9–24	104(a)(1)	5–13
62(a)(3)	6–30	104(a)(2)	5–11
62(a)(4)	6–4, 6–30, 7–13	104(a)(3)	5–13
62(a)(15)	6–30, 9–13	105	5–3, 5–14
62(a)(18)	6–30	105(a)	5–13
62(b)	9–26	105(b)	5–13
63(a)	20–18	105(c)	5–13
63(b) through (h)	20–18	105(h)	5–14, 5–25
63(c)(1)	3–7	106	5–3, 5–13
63(c)(5)	3–10	106(d)	5–3, 5–14
63(c)(6)	3–9	107	5–3, 5–17
63(d)	6–4	108	5–3, 5–33
66	4–19	108(a)	5–34
67	4–18, 5–22, 9–28	108(b)	5–34
67(b)(3)	7–13	108(c)	5–34
68	10–30, 12–41	108(e)	5–34

I.R.C. Sec.	This Work Page
108(e)(5)	5–34
108(e)(6)	5–34
108(f)	5–34
108(g)	5–34
109	5–3, 5–4, 14–23
110	5–3
111	5–3, 5–32, 12–41
111(a)	5–32
112	5–3
117	4–31, 5–3, 9–17
117(a)	2–36, 5–9
117(b)	5–9
117(c)	13–30
117(d)	5–10
118	20–17, 20–49
119	5–3, 5–15, 5–21
119(a)	5–15
119(b)(4)	5–17
119(d)	5–17
121	5–3, 10–15, 14–7, 14–19, 14–20, 15–2, 15–3, 15–15, 15–16, 15–17, 15–18, 15–19, 15–20, 15–22, 15–25, 15–26, 15–27, 15–29, 15–30, 15–34, 15–35, 15–39, 20–5
121(a)	15–16
121(b)	15–16
121(b)(1)	15–19, 15–20
121(b)(2)	15–20
121(b)(3)	15–17
121(c)(1)	15–21
121(c)(2)(B)	15–17
121(d)(3)(A)	15–39
121(d)(5)	15–22
121(d)(6)	15–26
121(d)(10)	15–16
121(f)	15–25
123	5–3
125	5–3, 5–19, 19–43
125(f)	5–19
127	5–3, 5–18, 9–17
127(b)(2)	5–25
129	5–3, 5–18
131	5–3
132	5–3, 5–20
132(m)	5–24
132(a)(6)	9–12
132(a)(7)	5–24
132(c)	5–21
132(d)	5–22
132(e)	5–23
132(f)	5–23
132(g)	9–12
132(j)(1)	5–24, 5–25
132(j)(3)	5–22
132(j)(4)	5–18
132(m)(2)	5–24
134	5–3, 5–18
135	5–3, 5–30, 19–21
137	5–3, 5–18
139	5–3, 5–4, 5–5

I.R.C. Sec.	This Work Page
141	12–21
151(b)	3–11
151(d)	2–28
151(d)(2)	2–34, 2–36
151(d)(3)	3–18
151(e)(1)	3–50
151(e)(2)	3–50
152(a)	2–36
152(b)(2)	2–33, 2–36, 3–17
152(b)(3)	3–17
152(c)	2–29, 3–12
152(c)(1)(D)	2–29, 2–36
152(c)(4)	3–12
152(d)	2–29, 3–14
152(d)(1)(B)	2–36
152(d)(2)	2–28
152(d)(2)(H)	3–14
152(d)(3)	3–15
152(e)(2)	3–17
152(e)(5)	3–17
152(f)(1)	3–32
152(f)(2)	3–12
152(f)(3)	2–47
152(f)(3)	3–14
152(f)(5)	2–29, 2–36, 3–12
152(f)(6)	3–12
162	6–3, 6–5, 6–12, 6–30, 6–44, 11–27, 13–14, 20–18
162(a)	6–5, 6–24, 6–30, 6–44, 9–8
162(a)(1)	6–6
162(a)(2)	6–30, 9–44
162(c)	6–11
162(c)(1)	6–5
162(c)(2)	9–44, 9–45
162(e)	6–14
162(f)	6–11, 6–24
162(g)	6–11
162(l)	10–7
162(m)	6–14, 6–45, 19–32
163	6–30
163(a)	6–30, 8–24
163(d)	6–30, 20–28
163(h)	6–30
163(h)(3)	10–15
163(h)(3)(E)(i)	10–16
163(i)(8)(B)	8–12
164	6–30, 8–24, 10–11, 13–18
164(a)(1)	6–30
164(a)(2)	6–30
164(a)(3)	6–30
164(b)(5)	6–30
164(f)	13–40, 19–19
165	6–7, 7–37
165(a)	14–6
165(c)	7–8, 15–16
165(c)(1)	6–30, 11–2
165(c)(2)	11–2
165(c)(3)	6–30, 7–11, 15–15
165(g)	7–6

I.R.C. Sec.	This Work Page
165(g)(1)	11–26, 16–8
165(h)	7–10, 7–14
165(h)(4)(E)	7–11
165(i)	7–11, 18–9
165(k)	7–10
166	6–30
166(a)	7–3
166(d)	16–33
167	14–23, 17–12
168	8–2, 14–23, 17–12
168(b)	8–7, 8–10
168(b)(2)(B)	8–11
168(b)(3)(E)	8–11
168(b)(5)	8–11
168(c)	8–10
168(d)(3)	8–9
168(d)(4)(A)	8–7
168(e)	8–5, 8–10
168(e)(2)(A)	17–16
168(e)(3)	8–20
168(e)(3)(D)(ii)	8–11
168(g)	8–20
168(g)(3)(B)	8–20
168(k)	8–7
168(k)(2)(F)(i)	8–16
168(k)(2)(G)	8–21
170	6–30, 10–18, 17–19
170(a)(2)	20–8
170(b)(2)	20–9
170(c)	10–19, 10–20
170(d)(2)	20–9
170(e)	16–33
170(e)(1)(A)	17–19
170(e)(1)(B)	17–19
170(e)(1)(B)(i)	10–24
170(e)(1)(B)(ii)	10–24
170(e)(3)	20–9
170(e)(4)	20–9
170(e)(5)	10–24
170(e)(6)	20–9
170(f)(8)	10–21
170(f)(11)	10–21
170(i)	10–20
170(j)	10–20
170(l)	10–19
171(c)	14–5
172	7–19, 18–9
172(b)	20–11
172(d)	7–21
173(a)	12–9
174	7–15, 7–37, 8–24, 13–11
174(b)(2)	7–16
179	1–2, 1–25, 1–38, 8–1, 8–13, 8–14, 8–16, 8–17, 8–21, 8–32, 8–38, 8–39, 8–40, 8–41, 8–42, 8–43, 9–6, 9–31, 9–37, 12–34, 13–51, 14–23, 17–12, 17–13, 17–17, 17–21, 17–23, 17–30, 17–35, 18–42
179(b)	8–13
179(b)(6)	8–17

I.R.C. Sec.	This Work Page
179(d)	8–13
183	2–16, 2–17, 6–17, 6–31
183(b)(2)	6–16, 11–27
183(d)	6–17
195	6–15, 8–23, 8–41, 8–42, 8–43
195(a)	8–23
195(b)	6–15, 8–23
195(b)(1)(A)	8–23
195(b)(1)(B)	8–23
195(c)	8–24
195(c)(1)(A)	8–23
195(c)(1)(B)	8–23
195(d)	8–23
197	6–25, 8–22, 8–23, 8–38, 14–38, 16–13, 16–32, 17–12, 17–17
197(a)	8–22, 16–13
199	7–17, 11–37, 20–9
199(a)	7–17
199(b)	7–17
199(c)	7–18
199(c)(4)	7–18
199(d)(1)	20–10
199(d)(2)	7–17
199(d)(4)	20–10
199(d)(6)	20–10
211	2–6
211 through 219	20–34
212	3–6, 6–3, 6–4, 6–5, 6–6, 6–28, 6–30, 9–29, 10–27, 20–18, 20–28
212(1)	2–6
212(2)	11–27
212(3)	10–5
213	6–30, 19–12
213(a)	6–23
213(d)(1)(A)	10–3
213(d)(2)	10–6
213(d)(10)	5–15
215	4–20
217	5–24, 5–26
217(a)	9–11
217(b)	9–12
219	6–4, 9–25, 20–34
219(b)(1)	19–20
219(c)	19–25
219(c)(2)	19–20
219(f)(3)	19–26
219(g)	19–20
219(g)(4)	19–21
219(g)(7)	19–21
221	9–17, 10–14
221(b)(2)(C)	10–14
222	6–4, 6–30, 9–14, 9–16, 9–17, 9–29, 9–32, 9–35, 9–39
222(b)(2)(C)	9–15
222(c)	9–16
222(d)	9–16
223	5–14, 10–9
223(b)	5–14
223(b)(2)	10–10

I.R.C. Sec.	This Work Page	I.R.C. Sec.	This Work Page
223(c)(2)	10–9	280H	18–6
223(d)	5–14, 10–10	291	17–37, 20–7, 20–8, 20–18
223(f)	10–10	291(a)(1)	17–21
241	2–6	301	20–22, 20–24
243(a)	20–12	301(c)	5–29
246(b)	20–12	302	20–24
248	8–24, 20–13	303	20–24
262	6–24, 6–30, 10–2, 10–27, 16–16	305(a)	5–30, 14–10
263	8–43	305(b)	5–30
263(a)(1)	6–24	307(a)	14–10
263A	18–30	307(b)	14–10
263A(e)(3)	18–32	311	20–23
263A(d)	18–12, 18–32	311(b)	17–21
263A(d)(3)(A)	8–12	312	20–22
263A(e)(4)	8–11	316	20–21
263(c)	17–21	316(a)	5–29
265	2–40, 6–28	318(a)	18–22
265(a)(2)	10–17	331	20–24, 20–46
267	6–26, 6–35, 14–16, 14–17, 14–25, 16–16, 19–38	332	17–20, 20–25
267(a)(1)	6–26, 14–7	334	20–25
267(b)	15–5, 18–22	334(a)	20–25
267(d)	14–17	334(b)(1)	20–25, 20–26
269	2–11	336	20–26
269A(b)(2)	11–9	336(d)	20–26
274	8–19	338	20–2, 20–25
274(a)	9–20	341(e)	2–30
274(a)(1)(A)	9–19	351	17–20, 18–24, 20–19, 20–20, 20–22, 20–38, 20–42, 20–43, 20–49
274(a)(3)	9–20	358(a)	20–20
274(b)(1)	9–21	362(a)	20–20
274(c)	9–10	367	20–22
274(d)	8–19, 9–26	368(c)	20–19
274(e)(4)	9–19	385	20–17
274(e)(7)	9–20	401(a)	19–12
274(h)(1)	9–8	401(a)(3)(G)	19–17
274(i)	8–19	401(a)(4)	19–8, 19–9
274(j)	4–31	401(a)(5)	19–8
274(k)	9–19	401(a)(9)	19–11
274(l)	9–21	401(a)(17)	19–14
274(m)(2)	9–9	401(a)(26)	19–9
274(m)(3)	9–9	401(c)	9–25
274(n)	9–18	401(c)(2)	19–19
275	10–11	401(c)(2)(A)(v)	19–19
276	6–13	401(d)	19–19
280A	6–19, 11–27	401(k)	6–14, 9–25, 13–25, 13–26, 13–49, 19–4, 19–7, 19–15, 19–16, 19–17, 19–18, 19–21, 19–23, 19–30, 19–39, 19–40, 19–41, 19–43, 19–46, 19–47, 19–48, 19–49
280A through 280H	2–6		
280A(c)(1)	9–22	401(k)(3)	19–41
280A(d)	6–20, 6–22	401(k)(8)(E)	19–17
280A(g)	6–19	401(k)(13)	19–17
280C(c)	13–11	401(m)(6)(A)	19–17
280E	6–13	401(m)(12)	19–17
280F	8–15, 17–23	402A	19–18
280F(a)(1)	8–16	402(a)(1)	19–12
280F(b)(1)	8–18	402(c)	19–13
280F(b)(2)	8–18	402(c)(8)(B)	19–29
280F(b)(3)	8–15	402(e)(1)(C)	19–13
280F(d)(1)	8–16	402(g)(1)	19–15
280F(d)(5)	8–16		
280G	19–32		

I.R.C. Sec.	This Work Page	I.R.C. Sec.	This Work Page
402(g)(4)	19–15	421(a)(2)	19–36
403(b)	19–18, 19–29, 19–30, 19–43	422	19–42
404	19–13	422(a)	19–36
404(a)(1)	19–15	422(a)(1)	19–36
404(a)(1)(D)	19–15	422(a)(2)	19–37
404(a)(3)(A)	19–15	422(b)	19–37
404(a)(5)	18–48, 19–31	422(c)(3)	19–37
404(a)(6)	18–48, 19–15	422(c)(5)	19–38
404(a)(7)	19–15	441(a)	4–7
404(h)(1)(A)	19–24	441(c)	18–3
404(h)(1)(B)	19–26	441(d)	4–7
404(j)	19–13	441(f)	18–3
404(l)	19–14	441(i)	18–6
408	9–25	442	18–6
408A	9–25, 19–22	443(b)(1)	18–8
408A(c)(3)(B)	19–29	443(b)(2)	18–8
408A(d)(3)(A)	19–29	443(b)(3)	18–9
408A(d)(3)(A)(ii)	19–29	443(c)	18–9
408(d)(1)	19–26, 19–50	444	18–5, 18–6
408(d)(2)	19–27	444(c)	18–5
408(d)(3)(B)	19–27	446	18–10
408(d)(4)	19–26	446(a)	6–8
408(d)(6)	19–50	446(b)	4–8, 4–13, 6–8, 18–10
408(d)(8)(A)	19–21, 19–23	446(c)	18–16
408(g)	19–50	446(d)	18–10
408(j)	19–24	446(e)	4–8, 6–8
408(k)(2)	19–24	446(f)	18–17
408(m)	16–22	447(c)	18–12
408(o)	19–21	448	6–9
408(p)	19–17	448(a)	18–12
408(p)(2)(E)(i)	19–17	448(b)	18–12
409A	19–30, 19–39, 19–42, 19–43, 19–50	448(d)(2)(A)	11–9
409A(a)(1)	19–30	448(d)(5)	18–16
409A(a)(2)(3)	19–30	451(d)	18–9
409A(a)(4)	19–30	451(e)	18–9
409A(d)(1)	19–30	453	2–38, 4–8
410(a)(1)(A)	19–8	453(a)	18–19
410(a)(1)(B)	19–8	453A	18–24
410(a)(4)	19–8	453(b)	18–19
410(b)	19–9	453B(a)	18–24
410(b)(4)	19–9	453B(c)	18–24
410(b)(3)	19–9	453B(d)	18–24
412	19–12	453B(f)(2)	18–24
414(e)	2–41	453B(g)	18–24
414(i)	19–5	453(d)	18–24
414(j)	19–4	453(d)(3)	18–25
414(q)	19–9	453(e)	18–22
414(w)	19–17	453(e)(2)	18–22
414(x)	19–17	453(e)(2)(B)	18–22
415	19–13	453(e)(6)	18–22
415(b)	19–14	453(e)(7)	18–22
415(b)(1)	19–19	453(f)(1)	18–22
415(c)	19–14	453(g)	18–23
415(c)(1)	19–19	453(i)	17–20, 18–19
415(d)	19–14	453(l)	18–19
415(d)(4)	19–14	453(l)(2)	18–19
421(a)	12–13	454(a)	4–12
421(a)(1)	19–36	457	7–17, 9–25, 19–29, 19–43

I.R.C. Sec.	This Work Page
457(b)	19–30
460	4–8, 18–26
460(b)(1)(A)	18–29
460(b)(2)	18–29
460(b)(5)	18–29
460(b)(6)	18–29
460(f)	18–25
461(g)(1)	10–17
461(g)(2)	10–16
461(h)	6–10, 18–14
461(h)(3)(A)	6–10
461(h)(4)	18–14
464	18–12
465(b)(1)	11–4
465(b)(6)	11–4
465(e)	11–5
468	18–15
469	11–5, 11–10, 11–13, 11–37, 19–21, 20–28
469(a)	11–8
469(b)	11–7
469(c)(2)	11–16
469(c)(7)	11–19
469(c)(7)(B)	11–19
469(d)(2)	11–7
469(f)	11–8
469(g)(2)	11–22
469(g)(3)	11–23
469(i)	11–20
469(i)(6)	11–20
469(j)(2)	11–9
469(j)(5)	11–21
469(j)(6)	11–23
469(j)(8)	11–16
471	18–30
471(a)	18–29
471(b)	18–33
472(c)	12–27, 18–35
472(d)	18–35
474	2–39
481	18–48
481(b)	18–18
482	18–32
483	18–21
501	10–20
501(a)	19–13
529	5–3, 5–31, 5–36, 9–17, 13–53
530	5–3, 5–31, 9–17, 9–30, 19–23
585	18–16
611(a)	8–25
612	8–25
613	8–28
613(a)	8–26, 12–20
613A	8–26
613A(c)	12–20
616(a)	12–12
617(a)	12–12
631	17–4, 17–5
631(a)	17–5

I.R.C. Sec.	This Work Page
652(a)	4–18
662(a)	4–18
702(a)	20–34
703(a)	20–34
704(e)	20–39
705(a)	20–32
706(a)	4–17
706(b)(1)(B)	18–3
706(b)(1)(C)	18–5
706(b)(3)	18–3
707	14–17
707(b)(1)	20–35
707(c)	20–36
721	11–24, 17–20, 20–32
722	20–32
723	20–33
742	5–29
901–908	13–18
904	13–19
904(c)	13–20
911	5–3, 5–27, 5–31, 19–21
911(a)	5–25
911(c)	5–27
911(d)	5–25
1001	2–40
1001(a)	14–3
1001(b)	14–3
1001(c)	14–6
1011	14–14
1011(a)	14–4
1012	14–8, 15–22
1014	14–38, 14–39
1014(a)	14–14
1014(b)(6)	14–15
1014(e)	14–15
1015(a)	14–12
1015(d)(6)	14–12
1016(a)	14–4
1016(a)(2)	14–5
1016(a)(4)	14–5
1016(a)(5)	14–5
1017	5–33
1022	16–16
1031	11–24, 14–7, 14–8, 15–2, 15–4, 15–5, 15–7, 15–8, 15–10, 15–11, 15–12, 15–15, 15–16, 15–23, 15–24, 15–25, 15–27, 15–28, 15–28, 15–39, 17–19, 17–20, 20–5, 20–46
1031(a)	15–3
1032	15–23, 20–17, 20–49
1033	14–7, 15–2, 15–2, 15–11, 15–12, 15–15, 15–16, 15–22, 15–25, 15–29, 15–34, 17–20, 20–5, 20–46
1033(a)	15–11, 15–12
1033(a)(2)(A)	15–15
1033(a)(2)(B)	15–13
1033(b)	15–15
1033(g)(4)	15–13
1035	15–23
1035(a)(3)	15–39

I.R.C. Sec.	This Work Page
1036	15–23
1038	15–23
1041	4–21, 14–17, 15–23, 18–22
1044	15–24
1045	15–24, 15–39
1060	14–9, 18–48
1091	14–17, 14–38
1091(a)	14–17
1091(b)	14–18
1091(d)	14–18
1201	16–31
1202	5–3, 12–6, 12–22, 16–20
1211	11–26
1211(a)	16–31, 20–7
1211(b)	7–6, 16–19, 20–7
1211(b)(1)	16–25
1212	11–26
1212(a)	20–7
1212(a)(1)	16–31
1212(b)	16–26
1221	3–33, 16–6, 16–7, 17–37
1221(a)	16–3
1221(a)(2)	17–2, 17–3
1221(b)(3)	16–4
1222	16–14
1222(1)	2–6
1222(3)	17–2
1222(10)	16–25
1222(11)	16–20
1223	16–15
1223(1)	15–9
1223(2)	14–13, 14–17, 20–33
1223(4)	14–18
1223(5)	14–10, 14–11
1223(6)	19–35
1223(11)	14–16
1231	6–25, 10–23, 14–9, 15–9, 16–3, 16–5, 16–13, 16–14, 16–15, 16–20, 17–1, 17–2, 17–3, 17–4, 17–5, 17–6, 17–7, 17–8, 17–9, 17–10, 17–11, 17–12, 17–13, 17–14, 17–15, 17–16, 17–17, 17–18, 17–19, 17–20, 17–21, 17–22, 17–23, 17–24, 17–25, 17–29, 17–30, 17–31, 17–32, 17–33, 17–34, 17–35, 17–36, 17–37, 17–38, 18–21, 20–7, 20–8, 20–28, 20–30, 20–47
1233	16–16
1233(a)	2–38
1233(b)(2)	2–38
1234A	16–8
1234(a)	16–10
1234(a)(1)	19–36
1234(a)(2)	19–36
1235	16–11
1236(a)	16–7
1236(b)	16–7
1237	16–7, 16–36
1239	17–21
1239(b)	18–23
1239(c)	18–23
1241	16–13

I.R.C. Sec.	This Work Page
1242	16–33
1244	7–1, 7–6, 7–7, 7–26, 7–27, 7–28, 7–30, 7–34, 7–35, 7–36, 7–37, 11–26, 16–2, 16–8, 16–33, 16–35, 16–37
1245	16–13, 16–14, 17–1, 17–2, 17–11, 17–12, 17–13, 17–14, 17–17, 17–18, 17–19, 17–20, 17–21, 17–22, 17–23, 17–25, 17–29, 17–30, 17–31, 17–35, 17–36, 17–37, 18–19, 18–21, 20–5, 20–7, 20–8, 20–18
1245(b)(1)	17–19
1245(b)(2)	17–19
1245(b)(3)	17–20
1245(d)	17–20
1250	3–33, 16–20, 16–25, 16–34, 16–39, 17–1, 17–2, 17–11, 17–12, 17–13, 17–14, 17–15, 17–16, 17–17, 17–18, 17–19, 17–20, 17–21, 17–22, 17–23, 17–24, 17–25, 17–30, 17–31, 17–34, 17–37, 18–19, 18–21, 18–44, 20–5, 20–7, 20–8, 20–18
1250(a)(1)(B)	17–17
1250(d)(1)	17–19
1250(d)(2)	17–19
1250(d)(3)	17–20
1250(i)	17–20
1253	16–12, 16–13
1253(b)(1)	16–12
1253(e)	16–13
1254	17–22
1259	16–17
1271	16–9
1271(b)	16–33
1272–1275	16–9
1272(a)	18–21
1272(a)(2)	4–11
1272(a)(3)	4–11
1273(a)	4–11, 18–21
1273(a)(3)	16–9
1274	18–21
1274(a)	18–21
1274(d)	4–24
1274(d)(1)	18–21
1276–1288	16–9
1301	18–9
1341	18–10
1361–1379	2–6
1361(a)	4–18
1361(c)(1)	20–26
1362	20–27
1366	4–18, 20–28
1366(e)	20–40
1367	20–30
1378(a)	18–5
1378(b)	18–5
1378(b)(2)	18–5
1402(a)	19–19
1402(a)(12)	13–40
2032(a)	14–37
2032(a)(1)	14–14
2032(c)	14–14
2040(b)	14–16
3121(d)(3)	9–4

I.R.C. Sec.	This Work Page
3401	13–33
3402	3–22, 13–33, 19–35
3403	13–26
3405(c)	19–13, 19–28
3406(a)	13–38
3507	13–17
4972	19–15
4973(b)	19–26
4973(a)(1)	19–26
4973(b)(2)	19–26
4974(a)	19–11
4979(a)	19–17
4999	19–32
6012(a)(1)	3–25
6012(a)(2)	20–14
6013(a)(1)	3–30
6013(d)(3)	3–51
6013(g)	3–30
6015	3–51
6017	13–40
6031	20–34
6072(a)	3–27
6081	20–15
6110	2–10
6110(j)(3)	2–11
6428	13–27
6621	18–24
6654	3–22, 13–26
6654(b)(2)	13–39
6654(b)(3)	13–39
6654(c)(1)	13–39

I.R.C. Sec.	This Work Page
6654(e)(1)	13–39
6655	20–15
6655(f)	20–15
6656	13–26
6662	2–33
6662(a)	2–30, 19–50
6662(b)(1)	2–30
6662(b)(3)	10–47
6662(c)	2–31
7436	9–4
7482(a)	2–16
7482(c)	2–16
7502(f)	3–28
7519	18–5
7519(b)	18–5
7701(a)(2)	20–48
7701(a)(3)	20–3, 20–48
7702B	5–3, 5–15
7703(b)	3–31
7805	2–7
7805(a)	2–8
7805(e)	2–8
7852(d)	2–21
7872(a)(1)	4–24
7872(b)(2)	4–24
7872(c)	4–25
7872(c)(2)	4–26
7872(c)(3)	4–27
7872(d)	4–26
7872(f)(2)	4–24

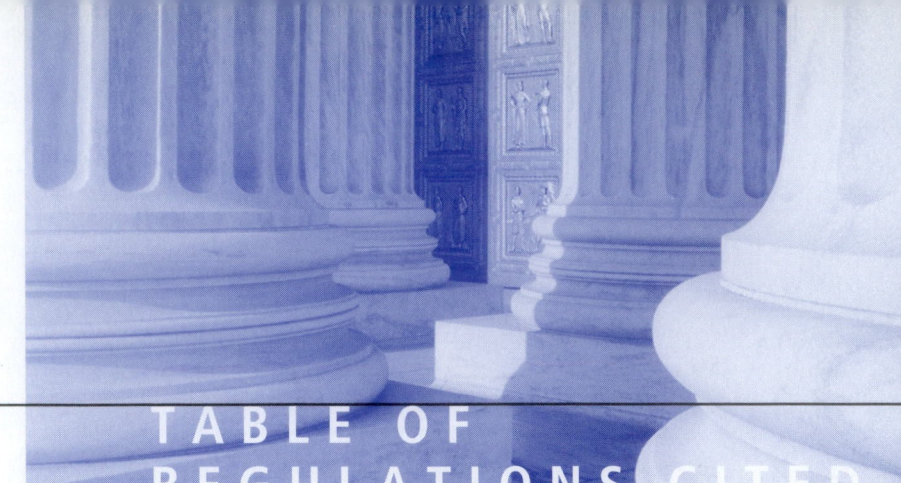

TABLE OF
REGULATIONS CITED

Temporary Treasury Regulations

Temp.Reg. Sec.	This Work Page
1.2	2–8
1.67–1T(a)(1)(iv)	6–18
1.101–7T	5–9
1.117–6(b)(2)	5–10
1.117–6(c)(3)(i)	5–9
1.117–6(d)	5–10
1.117–6(h)	5–9
1.121–3T(c)	15–17
1.121–3T(d)	15–18
1.121–3T(e)	15–19
1.152–4T	3–17
1.163–8T(c)	11–36
1.199–8T	2–8
1.263A–1T(b)(3)(iii)(A)(1)	18–26
1.274–5T(c)(3)	9–26, 9–44
1.280A–3(c)	6–20
1.280A–3(c)(4)	2–41
1.280A–3(d)(4)	6–21
1.280F–6T(e)	8–15
1.469–1T(e)(3)(ii)	11–16, 11–36
1.469–1T(e)(3)(iv)	11–17
1.469–1T(e)(3)(vi)(B) through (D)	11–17
1.469–5T(a)	11–13
1.469–5T(b)(2)	11–15
1.469–5T(e)(3)(ii)	11–16
1.469–5T(f)(3)	11–15
1.469–5T(f)(4)	11–20
1.7872–2(b)(1)(i)	4–25
15a.453–1(b)(3)(i)	18–20
15a.453–1(d)	18–24
15a.453–1(d)(4)	18–25

Treasury Regulations

Reg. Sec.	This Work Page
1.2	2–7
1.25A–1(f)	13–53
1.61–1(a)	4–6

Treasury Regulations

Reg. Sec.	This Work Page
1.61–12	4–6
1.61–2(d)(2)(i)	14–8
1.61–3(a)	6–13
1.61–4	18–12
1.61–6(a)	14–6, 14–9
1.61–9(c)	4–16
1.61–21(d)	5–24
1.72–7(c)(1)	5–9
1.72–9	4–28, 19–11
1.79–3(d)(2)	4–32
1.83–2(a)	19–35
1.83–3(c)(2)	19–34
1.83–6(a)	19–35
1.83–6(c)	19–35
1.83–7	19–38
1.83–7(a)	19–39
1.106–1	5–13
1.107–1	5–17
1.117–2(a)	5–9
1.119–1(c)(1)	5–16
1.119–1(f)	5–16
1.121–1(b)(2)	15–22
1.132–1(b)	5–21
1.132–2	5–21
1.152–1(a)	3–50
1.152–1(c)	2–29, 2–36, 3–50
1.162–2(b)(1)	9–9
1.162–2(e)	9–44
1.162–5(b)(2)	9–13
1.162–5(b)(2)(iii)	9–14
1.162–5(b)(3)	9–13
1.162–5(b)(3)(ii)	9–14
1.162–8	6–7
1.162–12(a)	18–12
1.162–17(b)(4)	9–26
1.162–21(b)	6–44
1.164–4(a)	10–12
1.165–1(a)	14–6
1.165–1(d)(2)	7–9

Treasury Regulations

Reg. Sec.	This Work Page
1.165–1(d)(2)(i)	7–9
1.165–7	15–15
1.165–7(a)(2)(ii)	7–11
1.165–8(a)(2)	7–9
1.165–8(d)	7–9
1.165–9(b)(2)	14–19
1.166–1(e)	7–3
1.166–5(d)	7–5
1.166–5(e)	7–3
1.167(g)–1	14–14, 14–19
1.170A–1(e)	10–47
1.170A–4(b)(1)	17–19
1.170A–4(b)(3)(ii)(b)	10–24
1.170A–13(c)(2)	10–48
1.172–3(a)	7–21
1.174–2(a)(1)	7–15
1.179–1(e)	8–15
1.183–1(b)(1)	6–18
1.183–2(b)(1) through (9)	6–16
1.199–7(c)	20–10
1.212–1(d)	6–6
1.212–1(f)	9–14
1.212–1(g)	6–4
1.213–1(e)(1)(iii)	10–5
1.213–1(e)(1)(v)	10–3
1.263A–1(a)	18–31
1.263A–1(b)(12)	18–31
1.263A–1(h)(5)	18–31
1.263A–4(d)(4)(ii)	8–12
1.263(a)–1(b)	6–25
1.263(a)–4(f)	18–11
1.267(d)–1(a)	14–17
1.267(d)–1(c)(3)	14–17
1.274–4	9–10
1.280F–7(a)	8–19
1.301–1(j)	14–8
1.307–1(a)	14–10
1.351–1(a)(1)(ii)	20–49
1.351–1(b)(1)	20–49
1.401–1(b)	19–7
1.401–1(b)(1)(iii)	19–7
1.401–4(a)(1)(iii)	19–7
1.401(k)–1(a)(6)(ii)	19–17
1.408–4(b)(4)	19–27
1.408–10(b)	16–22
1.41–1 through 1.41–7	13–11
1.421–1(a)(1)	19–36
1.421–6(c)	19–38
1.421–6(d)	19–38, 19–39
1.421–6(e)	19–38
1.421–6(f)	19–38
1.421–7(a)(1)	19–36
1.441–1(b)(1)(ii)	18–3
1.441–1(b)(3)	18–6
1.441–1(b)(4)	18–6
1.441–1(e)(2)	18–3

Reg. Sec.	This Work Page
1.442–1(b)(1)	18–7
1.442–1(c)(1)	18–6
1.443–1(b)	18–9
1.446–1(a)(1)	18–10, 18–16
1.446–1(a)(2)	6–8
1.446–1(a)(3)	4–8
1.446–1(a)(4)(i)	18–10, 18–11
1.446–1(c)(1)(i)	4–8
1.446–1(c)(1)(iv)(b)	18–10
1.446–1(c)(2)(i)	4–8
1.446–1(e)(2)(ii)	18–16
1.446–1(e)(2)(ii)(b)	18–17
1.451–1(a)	4–9, 18–11, 18–13
1.451–2(a)	4–10
1.451–2(b)	4–10
1.451–3(b)	18–25
1.451–3(b)(2)	18–27
1.451–3(c)(3)	18–29
1.451–3(d)(2)(ii)–(vii)	18–28
1.451–3(d)(9)	18–26
1.451–5	4–36, 18–28
1.451–5(b)	4–13
1.451–5(c)	4–13
1.461–1(a)	6–9
1.461–1(a)(1)	18–11
1.461–4(g)(2)–(6)	18–15
1.461–5(c)	18–15
1.469–4	11–11
1.469–4(c)(3)	11–11
1.469–4(d)	11–11
1.469–4(f)	11–11
1.469–9	11–19
1.471–1	18–29
1.471–2	18–29
1.471–2(c)	18–32
1.471–3(b)	18–30
1.471–4(b)	18–30
1.471–4(c)	18–32
1.471–6(a)	18–12
1.471–6(d)	18–36
1.471–6(e)	18–36
1.472–2(c)	18–35
1.472–2(e)	18–36
1.472–3(a)	18–35
1.472–4	18–32
1.472–5	18–35
1.472–8	18–34
1.611–1(b)	8–24
1.631–1	17–5
1.702–1(a)(8)	2–40
1.706–1(a)	18–3
1.706–1(a)(1)	4–17
1.706–1(b)(3)	18–4
1.864(b)–1(b)(2)(ii)(E)	2–46
1.871–2(b)	5–25
1.901–1(a)(3)(i)	13–20

Treasury Regulations

Reg. Sec.	This Work Page
1.904–2(g)	13–20
1.1001–1(a)	14–3
1.1001–1(b)	14–3
1.1001–1(b)(2)	14–4
1.1001–1(c)(1)	14–3
1.1001–2(a)	5–33
1.1002–1(a)	14–6
1.1002–1(c)	15–2
1.1011–1	14–4, 14–14
1.1012–1(a)	14–8
1.1012–1(b)	14–4
1.1012–1(c)(1)	14–8
1.1015–1(a)(1)	14–12
1.1015–1(a)(3)	14–12
1.1015–5(c)(2)	14–12
1.1016–1	14–4
1.1016–3(a)(1)(i)	14–5
1.1016–5(a)	14–5
1.1016–5(b)	14–5
1.1016–6(a)	14–5
1.1031(a)–1(a)	15–3
1.1031(a)–1(b)	15–3
1.1031(d)–2	15–11
1.1031(j)–1	15–5
1.1033(a)–1	15–12
1.1033(a)–1(a)	15–11
1.1033(a)–2(a)	15–11
1.1033(a)–2(c)(1)	15–15
1.1033(a)–2(c)(3)	15–13
1.1034–1(c)(3)(i)	15–22
1.1091–1(a)	14–17, 14–18
1.1091–1(c)	14–18
1.1091–1(f)	14–17
1.1091–2(a)	14–18
1.1221–1(b)	16–14
1.1223–1(a)	15–9
1.1223–1(b)	14–13

Treasury Regulations

Reg. Sec.	This Work Page
1.1223–1(d)	14–18
1.1223–1(e)	14–10, 14–11
1.1223–1(f)	14–11
1.1234–1(a)(1)	16–10
1.1235–2(b)(1)	16–12
1.1236–1(a)	16–7, 16–13
1.1245–1(c)	17–21
1.1245–2(a)(4)	15–9, 17–20
1.1245–2(c)(2)	17–20
1.1245–4(a)(1)	17–19
1.1245–4(c)	17–20
1.1245–6(b)	17–21
1.1250–1(a)(4)	17–21
1.1250–1(b)(4)	17–21
1.1250–1(c)(2)	17–21
1.1250–2(d)(1)	15–9, 17–20
1.1250–2(d)(3)	17–20
1.1250–3(a)(1)	17–19
1.1250–3(c)	17–20
1.1250–3(c)(3)	17–20
1.6011–4	20–17
1.6013–1(a)(1)	3–36
1.6081–4	3–28
1.6661–3(b)(2)	2–33
31.3401(c)–(1)(b)	9–3
35.3405–1	19–28
301.6114–1	2–21
301.6712–1	2–21
301.7701–1	20–4
301.7701–2	20–4, 20–48
301.7701–2(a)	20–3
301.7701–3	20–4, 20–48
301.7701–3(b)(1)(iii)	20–48
301.7701–3(c)	20–4
301.7701–4	20–4
301.7701–7	20–4
301.7701(b)(7)	2–21

Revenue Procedures

Rev.Proc.	This Work Page
84–74	18–35
87–1	2–32
87–32	18–7, 18–36
87–56	8–5, 12–11
87–57	8–34, 8–35, 8–36, 15–5
92–71	6–27
94–27	10–16, 10–33
99–49	18–16, 18–18, 18–35
2001–10	18–12
2002–19	18–18
2002–28	4–8
2002–33	8–8
2002–38	18–36
2002–39	18–7
2004–2	20–17
2004–34	4–13, 4–14, 4–36
2004–45	20–17
2005–50	2–46
2007–70	9–6
2008–1	2–10

Revenue Rulings

Rev.Rul.	This Work Page
53–61	4–4
53–80	5–16
54–567	2–34
56–60	14–14
56–406	14–18
57–345	10–11
57–418	6–15
58–67	3–50
59–86	14–13

Revenue Rulings

Rev.Rul.	This Work Page
60–345	2–47
61–119	15–6
61–221	9–44
62–102	5–6
63–221	15–11
63–232	7–9
65–34	2–34, 2–36
66–7	16–15
67–297	10–16
68–662	6–12
69–292	9–14
70–466	15–12
70–622	10–11
71–190	10–13
71–425	5–3
72–545	6–24
72–592	7–8
73–300	2–47
73–476	15–25
73–539	9–8
74–78	9–14
74–175	16–33
75–14	6–18
75–168	9–7
75–448	5–10
76–282	18–35
77–318	5–47
78–39	6–9
78–340	10–4
79–379	4–17
80–52	4–10
80–335	6–9
81–180	15–11
81–181	15–11
82–74	15–11
82–196	5–13

Revenue Rulings

Rev.Rul.	This Work Page
82–202	5–33
82–208	10–13
82–227	18–24
87–22	10–16
87–41	9–3
87–57	18–5

Revenue Rulings

Rev.Rul.	This Work Page
87–57	18–7
87–106	10–6
99–7	9–44
2007–28	9–10
2007–49	2–9

CITATOR EXAMPLE

Illustration of the Use of the Citator

Background

A *Citator* provides the history of a legal case and lists subsequently published opinions that refer to the case being assessed. Reviewing these references enables the tax researcher to determine whether the decision in question has been reversed, affirmed, followed by other courts, or distinguished in some way. Chapter 2 introduces the *Citator* as an invaluable reference in tax research. The major citators are published by Commerce Clearing House (CCH), RIA, and Shepard's Citation, Inc. The use of the RIA citator is illustrated in the discussion that follows.

The *RIA Federal Tax Citator* is a separate multivolume service with monthly supplements that may be used to determine the tax status of tax case decisions, Revenue Rulings, and Revenue Procedures. A similar citation process is available with the online research system.[1] Cases that are traced by the *Citator* are divided into the issues involved. Since the researcher may be interested in only one issue, only those cases involving that issue need to be checked.

The *Citator* includes the following volumes, each of which covers a particular period of time:

- Volume 1 (1863–1941)
- Volume 2 (1942–1948)
- Volume 3 (1948–1954)
- Volume 1, Second Series (1954–1977)
- Volume 2, Second Series (1978–1989)
- Volume 3, Second Series (1990–1996)
- Volume 4, Second Series (1997–2002)
- Volume 5, Second Series (2003–2006).
- Annual and monthly cumulative paperback supplements

Through the use of symbols, the *Citator* indicates whether a decision has been followed, explained, criticized, questioned, or overruled by a later court decision. These symbols are reproduced in Figure E–1.

Example

Determine the background and validity of *Adda v. Comm.*, 37 AFTR 654, 171 F.2d 457 (CA–4, 1948).

---

[1]Features in the *RIA Citator* that do not appear in the CCH *Citator* include the following: (1) distinguishes between the various issues in the case, (2) lists all court decisions that cite the court decision being researched, (3) indicates the relationship (e.g., explained, criticized, followed, or overruled) between the court decision being researched and subsequent decisions, and (4) pinpoints the exact page on which one court decision is cited by another court decision. Prior to the acquisition of Prentice-Hall Information Services, the *Federal Tax Citator* was published by Prentice-Hall. The *Citator 2nd Series* is now published by Research Institute of America.

FIGURE E–1	RIA Citator Symbols

Citator Symbols*
COURT DECISIONS
Judicial History of the Case

a	affirmed (by decision of a higher court)
d	dismissed (appeal to a higher court dismissed)
m	modified (decision modified by a higher court, or on rehearing)
r	reversed (by a decision of a higher court)
s	same case (e.g., on rehearing)
rc	related case (companion cases and other cases arising out of the same subject matter are so designated)
x	certiorari denied (by the Supreme Court of the United States)
(C or G)	The Commissioner or Solicitor General has made the appeal
(T)	Taxpayer has made the appeal
(A)	decision acquiesced in by Commissioner
(NA)	decision nonacquiesced in by Commissioner
sa	same case affirmed (by the cited case)
sd	same case dismissed (by the cited case)
sm	same case modified (by the cited case)
sr	same case reversed (by the cited case)
sx	same case—certiorari denied

Syllabus of the Cited Case

iv	four (on all fours with the cited case)
f	followed (the cited case followed)
e	explained (comment generally favorable, but not to a degree that indicates the cited case is followed)
k	reconciled (the cited case reconciled)
n	dissenting opinion (cited in a dissenting opinion)
g	distinguished (the cited case distinguished either in law or on the facts)
l	limited (the cited case limited to its facts. Used when an appellate court so limits a prior decision, or a lower court states that in its opinion the cited case should be so limited)
c	criticized (adverse comment on the cited case)
q	questioned (the cited case not only criticized, but its correctness questioned)
o	overruled

*Reprinted from RIA *Citator 2nd Series* Volume 1 © 1992, Thomson/RIA. Reprinted with permission.

Solution

The headnote for *Adda* summarizes the holding of the court and lists the two main issues involved (designated "1" and "2") in the case. As noted previously, the issue designation procedure facilitates the use of the *Citator*.

Refer to Volume 3 of the First Series (covering the period from October 7, 1948, through July 29, 1954) of the *Citator*. Information about the case reference is located in the excerpt reproduced in Figure E–2.

FIGURE E–2   **Excerpt from Volume 3, First Series**

```
ADDA v COMM., 171 F(2d) 457, 37 AFTR 654,
    1948 P.-H. ¶ 72,655 (CCA 4, Dec 3, 1948)
Cert. filed, March 1, 1949 (T)
No cert. (G) 1949 P-H ¶ 71,050
x—Adda v Comm., 336 US 952, 69 S Ct 883,
    93 L Ed 1107, April 18, 1949 (T)
sa—Adda, Fernand C. A., 10 TC 273 (No.
    33), ¶ 10.33 P.-H. TC 1948
iv—Milner Hotels, Inc., N. Y., 173 F (2d)
    567, 37 AFTR 1170, 1949 P.-H. page 72,528
    (CCA 6)
1—Nubar; Comm. v, 185 F(2d) 588, 39 AFTR
    1315, 1950 P.-H. page 73,423 (CCA 4)
g-1—Scottish Amer. Invest. Co., Ltd.,
    The, 12 TC 59, 12-1949 P.-H. TC 32
g-1—Nubar, Zareh, 13 TC 579, 13-1949
    P.-H. TC 318
```

Reprinted from *RIA Citator 1st Series* Volume 3
© 1955, Thomson/RIA. Reprinted with permission.

Correlating the symbols in Figure E–1 with the excerpt in Figure E–2 reveals the following information about *Adda v. Comm.*:

- Application for certiorari (appeal to the U.S. Supreme Court) filed by the taxpayer (T) on March 1, 1949.
- Certiorari was denied (x) by the U.S. Supreme Court on April 18, 1949.
- The trial court decision is reported in 10 T.C. 273 and was affirmed on appeal (sa) to the Fourth Court of Appeals.
- During the time frame of Volume 3 of the *Citator* (October 7, 1948, through July 29, 1954), one decision (*Milner Hotels, Inc.*) has agreed "on all fours with the cited case" (iv). One decision (*Comm. v. Nubar*) has cited the first issue in *Adda* without comment and two decisions (*The Scottish American Investment Co., Ltd.* and *Zareh Nubar*) have distinguished the cited case on issue number one (g–1).

Reference to Volume 1 of the *Citator 2nd Series* (covering the period from 1954 through 1977) shows the *Adda v. Comm.* case which is reproduced in Figure E–3.

FIGURE E–3   **Excerpt from Volume 1, Second Series**

```
ADDA v COMM., 171 F2d 457, 37 AFTR 654 (USCA 4)
Rev. Rul. 56-145, 1956-1 CB 613
1—Balanovski; U.S. v, 236 F2d 304, 49 AFTR 2013
    (USCA 2)
1—Liang, Chang Hsiao, 23 TC 1045, 23-1955 P-H TC
    624
f-1—Asthmanefrin Co., Inc., 25 TC 1141, 25-1956 P-H
    TC 639
g-1—de Vegvar, Edward A. Neuman, 28 TC 1061,
    28-1957 P-H TC 599
g-1—Purvis, Ralph E. & Patricia Lee, 1974 P-H TC
    Memo 74-669
k-1—deKrause, Piedad Alvarado, 1974 P-H TC Memo
    74-1291
1—Rev. Rul. 56-392, 1956-2 CB 971
```

Reprinted from *RIA Citator 2nd Series* Volume 1
© 1992, Thomson/RIA. Reprinted with permission.

Correlating the symbols in Figure E–1 with the excerpt in Figure E–3 reveals the following additional information about *Adda v. Comm.*:

- The case was cited without comment in two rulings and two cases: Rev. Rul. 56–145, Rev.Rul. 56–392, *Balanovski*, and *Liang*.

FIGURE E–4	Excerpt from Volume 2, Second Series

ADDA v COMM., 171 F2d 457, 37 AFTR 654 (USCA 4)
1—Connelly, Judith C., 1982 PH TC Memo 82-2866
1—Cleveland, Robert E., 1983 PH TC Memo 83-1223

Reprinted from *RIA Citator 2nd Series* Volume 2
© 1992, Thomson/RIA. Reprinted with permission.

- It was followed in *Asthmanefrin Co.* (f–1).
- It was distinguished in *de Vegvar* and *Purvis* (g–1).
- It was reconciled in *deKrause* (k–1).

Reference to the "Court Decisions" section of Volume 2, *Citator 2nd Series* (covering the period from 1978 through 1989) shows that *Adda v. Comm.* was cited in *Judith C. Connelly* and *Robert E. Cleveland*, as to the first issue in *Adda* without comment. See the excerpt which is reproduced in Figure E–4.

No citations appear in Volume 3, *Citator Second Series* (which covers the period from 1990 through 1996), in Volume 4, *Citator Second Series* (which covers 1997 through 2002), or in Volume 5, *Citator Second Series* (which covers 2003 through 2006) for *Adda v. Comm.*

The *Citator* includes a cumulative supplement, and a cumulative monthly paperback supplement is published each month. Be sure to refer to these supplements, or very recent citations might be overlooked. No citations appear in the supplements for *Adda v. Comm.*

Except as otherwise noted, it appears that *Adda v. Comm.* has withstood the test of time.

Problem 1

Sidney (Sid) T. and Arlene S. Rice (ages 44 and 43) are married and live at 1431 Hawthorn Street, Springfield, MO 65801. Sid is a self-employed insurance claims adjuster (business activity code 524290), and Arlene is the dietitian for the local school district.

1. Sid represents several national casualty insurance companies on a contract basis. He is paid a retainer and receives additional compensation if the claims for the year exceed a specified number. As an independent contractor, he is responsible for whatever expenses he incurs. Sid maintains an office near his residence at 810 Dogwood Lane. He shares Suite 604 with a financial consultant, and operating expenses are divided equally between them. The suite has a common waiting room with a receptionist furnished and paid by the landlord. Sid's *one-half share* of the 2007 expenses that he paid appears below:

Office rent	$12,200
Utilities (includes telephone and fax)	4,300
Renters' insurance (covers personal liability, casualty, theft)	1,200
Replacement of waiting room furniture on May 1	3,600
New Xerox copier (less trade-in on old machine) on January 17	300
Waiting room magazine subscriptions	140
Waiting room coffee service (catered)	240
Office expense (supplies, postage meter)	720

For his own business use, Sid purchased a notebook computer for $1,400 on January 17 and a Kodak camera for $1,900 on February 5. Except for his automobile (see item 2 below), Sid follows a policy of avoiding claiming depreciation by utilizing the § 179 write-off option.

2. On January 2, 2007, Sid paid $38,000 (including sales tax) to purchase an Infiniti crossover SUV that he uses 95% of the time for business. No trade-in was involved, and he did not claim any § 179 expensing. Under the actual operating cost method, he uses 200% declining-balance with a half-year convention. His expenses relating to the Infiniti for 2007 are as follows:

Gasoline	$2,100
Oil and lubrication	80
Auto insurance	1,500
Auto club dues	190
Interest on car loan	820
License and registration	45

In connection with the business use, Sid paid $310 for parking and $350 in fines for traffic violations.

In 2007, Sid drove the Infiniti 14,250 miles for business and 750 miles for personal use (includes commuting).

3. Sid handles most claim applications locally, but on occasion he must travel out of town. Expenses in connection with these business trips during 2007 were $630 for lodging and $840 for meals. He also paid $510 for entertainment (business dinners) of several visiting executives of insurance companies with whom he does business. Sid's other business-related expenses for 2007 are listed below:

Birthday gift for receptionist ($25 box of Godiva chocolates plus $2 for gift wrap)	$ 27
State and local occupation fee	480
Premiums on disability insurance policy (pays for loss of income in the event Sid is disabled and cannot work)	1,300
Premiums on medical insurance covering family (spouse and children)	3,600
Contribution to H.R. 10 (Keogh) retirement plan	8,000

4. Arlene is employed by the Springfield School District as a dietitian at an annual salary of $28,000. The job she holds, manager of the school lunch program, is not classified as full-time. Consequently, she is not eligible to participate in the teacher retirement or health insurance programs. Arlene's expenses for 2007 are summarized as follows:

Job hunting expense	$ 720
Subscription to *Nutrition Today*	120
Membership dues to the National Association of Dietitians	90
Continuing education program	150
Contribution to traditional IRA	4,000

In order to work full-time and earn a larger salary, Arlene applied for a position as chief dietitian for a chain of nursing homes. According to the director of the recruiting service she hired, the position has not yet been filled, and Arlene is one of the leading candidates. The continuing education program was sponsored by the National Association of Dietitians and consisted of a one-day seminar on special diets for seniors. Arlene drove the family Chevrolet Suburban 1,200 miles on job-related use, out of a total of 8,000 miles driven for the year. As to the car, purchased July 11, 2005, the automatic mileage method is utilized in determining any available deduction.

5. Arlene's widowed mother, Grace Strong, has been supported by the Rices for several years and has been claimed by them as a dependent. On December 30, 2006, Grace suffered a heart attack and was taken by ambulance to St. Paul's Memorial Hospital. Grace died in the intensive care unit on January 2, 2007. On behalf of Grace, the Rices paid the following expenses: $11,200 medical ($6,000 incurred in 2006 and $5,200 in 2007) and $5,700 funeral. [The Rices' medical insurance (see item 3 above) does not cover parents.] These expenses were paid in January and February 2007. Grace's will named Arlene as executor and sole heir of the estate.

6. Upon the advice of the financial consultant who shares office space with Sid, the Rices decided to convert Grace's home into a furnished rental house. After several minor repairs (e.g., replace window screen, pressure wash brick exterior), the property was advertised for rent in the classified section of the local newspaper on March 1, 2007. The repairs cost $720, and the newspaper ad was $360.

Based on reconstructed records and appraisal estimates, information about the property is summarized below:

	Original Cost	Fair Market Value 1/2/07
House	$40,000	$220,000
Land	10,000	50,000
Furniture and appliances	21,000	14,000

7. Grace's property was rented almost immediately with occupancy commencing April 1, 2007, under the following terms: one-year lease, $2,400 per month, first and last month's rent in advance, $2,000 damage deposit, lawn care included but not utilities. The tenant complied with all terms except that the December rent payment was not made until January 1, 2008—the tenant took an extended Christmas holiday trip.

   Expenses in connection with the property were as follows: property taxes, $2,600; repairs, $320; lawn maintenance, $540; insurance, $1,800; and street paving assessment, $2,100. The property is located at 1220 Algonquin Drive, Springfield, MO 65801.

8. In early December 2006, a friend advised Sid to buy stock in Crimson Mining Corporation. Crimson was in serious financial straits and was headed toward bankruptcy. Nevertheless, according to Sid's friend, the value of its underlying assets was such that the shareholders were bound to recover considerably more than the current market price of $0.50 per share. Delighted at the chance for a sure profit, on December 15, 2006, Sid purchased 20,000 shares for $10,000. In September 2007, the trustee in bankruptcy announced that the stock was worthless and that even some of Crimson's preferred creditors would not be paid.

9. On June 19, 2007, the Rices decided to sell 500 shares of Garnet Corporation for $17,500 ($35 per share). They owned 1,000 shares, acquired as follows: 500 shares on November 5, 2003, for $25 a share and 500 shares on August 5, 2005, for $30 a share. Their broker was not instructed as to which 500 shares to sell.

10. One month before he died on April 3, 2002, John Strong (Arlene's father) gave Arlene a coin collection. Based on careful records that John kept, the collection had a cost basis of $9,000 and a fair market value of $18,000. On February 12, 2007, the Rice residence was burglarized, and the coin collection was stolen. The Rices filed a claim with the carrier of their homeowner's insurance policy for $24,000 (the current value of the collection). All they were able to collect, however, was $10,000, which was the maximum amount allowed for valuables (e.g., jewelry, antiques) without a special rider.

11. In his will, John Strong (see item 10) left Arlene a vacant lot on Joplin Road. John had paid $15,000 for the property, and it had a value of $19,000 when he died. John had bought the lot because it was adjacent to a school that he expected to expand. By 2007, it has become clear that the Joplin Road area of Springfield is not growing and that no school expansion will take place. Consequently, on June 1, 2007, Arlene sold the lot for $19,000. Not included in this price are back property taxes (and interest) of $700 on the lot, which the purchaser assumed and later paid.

12. Every year around Christmas, Sid receives cards from various car repair facilities (including dealerships), expressing thanks for the business referrals and enclosing cash. Sid has no arrangement, contractual or otherwise, that requires any compensation for the referrals he makes. Concerned about the legality of such "gifts," Sid previously consulted an attorney about the matter. Without passing judgment on the status of the payors, the attorney found that Sid's acceptance of the payments does not violate state or local law. Sid sincerely believes that the payments he receives have no effect on the referrals he makes. During December 2007, Sid received cards containing $7,200. One card containing $900, however, was delayed in the mail and was not received by Sid until January 2, 2008.

13. Several years ago the Rices established a Coverdell Education Savings Account (CESA) for each of their two children. The custodian of the CESAs is Green County State Bank, which is approved for this purpose by the IRS. In 2007, the Rices contributed $4,000 ($2,000 per child) to the CESAs.

14. In addition to those previously noted, the Rices' receipts during 2007 are summarized below:

Payments to Sid for services rendered (as reported on Forms 1099 issued by several payor insurance companies) pursuant to contractual arrangement		$82,000
Income tax refunds for tax year 2006—		
Federal	$ 210	
State	90	300
Interest income—		
State of Missouri general-purpose bonds	$1,400	
GE corporate bonds	1,100	
Certificate of deposit at Springfield National Bank	900	3,400
Qualified dividends (Duke Energy)		600
Proceeds from garage sale (see item 15 below)		9,200
Cash gifts from Sid's parents		24,000
Sid's net state lottery gains (winnings were $1,000, while losses were $900)		100

15. On June 23 and 24, 2007, the Rices held a garage sale to dispose of unwanted furniture, appliances, books, bicycles, clothes, and one boat (including trailer). The estimated basis of the items sold is $25,500. All were personal use property.

16. Expenditures during 2007, not mentioned elsewhere, are as follows:

Medical—		
Copayment portion of medical expenses	$1,300	
Dental (orthodontist)	1,200	$2,500
Taxes—		
State income tax (see item 18 below)	$3,456	
Property taxes on personal residence	3,800	7,256
Interest on home mortgage		4,200
Charitable contributions		3,600

The medical insurance the Rices have does not cover dental services. Between the sales tax and state income tax options, the income tax deduction provides a greater benefit. The Rices' church pledge is $1,200 per year. In 2007, they paid the pledges for 2006–2008. During 2007, the Rices drove the Suburban 250 miles for medical purposes (e.g., trips to the hospital, doctor and dentist offices) and 300 miles for charitable purposes (delivering meals to the poor under a church-sponsored program).

17. The Rices have two daughters who live with them: Alexis (age 17) and Tracy (age 18). Both are full-time students. Tracy is an accomplished singer and made $4,200 during the year performing at special events (e.g., weddings, anniversaries, civic functions). Tracy deposits her earnings in a savings account intended to help cover future college expenses.

18. The Form W–2 Arlene receives from her employer reflects wages of $28,000. Appropriate amounts for Social Security and Medicare taxes were deducted. Income tax withholdings were $1,320 for Federal and $1,056 for state. The Rices made quarterly tax payments of $2,200 for Federal and $600 for state. Relevant Social Security numbers are noted below:

Name	Social Security Number	Birth Date
Sidney T. Rice	486–52–4592	06/06/1963
Arlene S. Rice	488–36–7843	08/14/1964
Grace Strong	487–21–0592	03/12/1934
Alexis Rice	499–48–6588	09/13/1990
Tracy Rice	499–82–1892	07/20/1989

Requirements

Prepare an income tax return (with appropriate schedules) for the Rices for 2007. In doing this, utilize the following guidelines:

- Make necessary assumptions for information not given in the problem but needed to complete the return.
- The taxpayers are preparing their own return (i.e., no preparer is involved).
- The taxpayers have the necessary substantiation (e.g., records, receipts) to support the transactions involved.
- If any refund is due, the Rices want it sent to them.
- The Rices had itemized deductions *from* AGI for 2006 of $18,000, of which $1,500 was for state and local income tax.
- The Rices do not want to contribute to the Presidential Election Campaign Fund.

Problem 2

William (Bill) S. and Sandra K. Bond, ages 68 and 67, are husband and wife and live at 462 Bluebonnet Lane, Denton, TX 76201. Bill is a retired petroleum engineer, and Sandra is a portrait artist.

1. When he retired at age 65, Bill was chief of offshore operations at Pelican Exploration Corporation. While employed, Bill participated in Pelican's contributory qualified pension plan, to which he had contributed $250,000 (in after-tax dollars). Under one of the plan options, in 2004 he chose a life-annuity payout of $60,000 per year over his life. Due to Bill's expertise in Gulf of Mexico offshore operations, Pelican continues to use his services on a consulting basis (see item 3 below).

2. Sandra, an accomplished artist, is well known regionally for oil portraits. She is very meticulous in her work and refuses to accept deadlines. Consequently, her output averages one portrait per month. Her fee of $3,000 per portrait was set several years ago and never varies. As this is quite reasonable for a good quality oil portrait, she has a long waiting list of clients who have not yet been scheduled for sittings. She does all of her work in the studio the Bonds maintain in their personal residence (see item 6 below).

3. During 2007, Bill made seven trips on behalf of Pelican. On a typical trip, Bill flies by commercial airline to New Orleans, Houston, or Corpus Christi, and then takes a company helicopter to the offshore platform. If necessary, he rents a room at a local motel. Sometimes offsite consultations can solve the problem, and a trip to the rig is not necessary. His expenses for these trips are as follows:

Airfare	$ 5,100
Meals	2,200
Lodging	3,100
Ground transportation (taxis, limos, rental cars)	750
Total	$11,150

After each trip, Bill recovers his expenses when he is paid by Pelican for the services rendered. Pelican does not require an accounting for the expenses and reimburses Bill based on the amount he says he spent.

4. During 2007, Sandra completed 14 portraits, 11 of which were delivered and paid for. Two portraits were delivered but were not paid for until 2008. One portrait was commissioned by the CEO of a company that has since entered bankruptcy. Since the CEO has been indicted for securities fraud, Sandra feels certain that she will not be paid for the work. In December she accepted $3,000 as a payment for a portrait to be done in 2008. Although she did not like the arrangement, the corporation said the prepayment was motivated by anticipated cash-flow considerations. In early January 2007, Sandra was paid for three portraits she painted and delivered in 2006.

5. Sandra keeps all her receipts for expenses but does not classify them by category. Her total for 2007 was $3,010 for canvases, brushes, oil paints, smocks, palettes, and other art supplies. As frames are a matter of personal taste and depend on the setting where the painting is exhibited, the framing of the finished portrait is left to the customer.

6. For convenience and security reasons, Sandra prefers to work at home. The Bonds had this in mind when they constructed their present residence. One-fourth of the 4,000-square-foot living area is devoted to Sandra's studio. The home was built at a cost of $350,000 on a lot previously acquired for $100,000, and they moved in on June 15, 2004. As to business use, depreciation has been based on MACRS (using the mid-month convention) applicable to 39-year nonresidential realty. Besides home mortgage interest and property taxes (see item 20 below), residence expenses for 2007 are summarized below:

Utilities	$4,200
Homeowner's insurance	1,100
Service fee for home security system	1,600
Molly Maid cleaning service	2,800
Repairs to studio skylight	340
Removal of stains from studio flooring	1,100

7. While on a business trip to South Texas to acquire some oil leases, Bill attended a mortgage foreclosure auction. At the auction (held on February 4, 1997), he acquired an abandoned sugarcane farm near Pearland, known as the Broussard Place. Bill financed most of the $30,000 purchase through a local farm credit union. In view of the expansion trend in nearby Houston, he regarded the purchase as a good investment. Early in 2007, Bill was contacted by a Houston real estate developer who offered $250,000 for Broussard Place. Horrified at the prospect of a $220,000 taxable gain, Bill ultimately arranged for an exchange transaction by written notice on May 10. In exchange for several vacant lots on Padre Island (TX) worth $240,000 and cash of $10,000, Bill transferred Broussard Place to the developer. The exchange took place at an attorney's office in Houston on June 20, 2007.

8. On another business trip to South Texas, Bill purchased unimproved land near Nederland (TX) for $18,200 at an estate sale held on April 17, 1986. Described as Block 46, the property was adjacent to a modest prison rice farm owned by the Texas Department of Corrections (TDC). Bill bought the property based on a hunch that the TDC might someday wish to expand its Nederland prison facility. In late 2006, the TDC contacted Bill and offered him $140,000 for Block 46. After repeated threats of a condemnation proceeding, Bill transferred the property to the TDC on June 28, 2007, for $180,000. On December 17, 2007, Bill reinvested $175,000 in vacant land located near Texas State University in San Marcos. Bill does not plan to reinvest any more of the amount received from the TDC.

9. The Bonds had always thought that taking extended road trips in an RV would be fun. Therefore, in June 2007, they bought a new Republic Coach RV for $106,250 [$100,000 (discounted list price) + $6,250 (state sales tax)]. Two weeks on the road was enough, however, and the road trip was over. In July 2007, they sold the RV to a neighbor for $90,000. The neighbor made a $20,000 cash down payment and paid the balance of $70,000 in early December 2007. No interest is provided for.

10. On May 9, 1997, Bill's father gave him 400 shares of Carmine Corporation common stock as a birthday present. The stock had cost his father $16,000 ($40 a share) and was worth $20,000 on the date of the gift. In 2003, when the stock was worth $140 per share, Carmine declared a 2-for-1 stock split. On July 27, 2007, Bill sold 400 shares for $20,000 ($50 a share). For sentimental reasons (they were a gift from his father), Bill wanted to keep 400 shares.

11. On December 21, 2007, the Bonds sold 500 shares of Flamingo Power common stock for $40,000 ($80 a share); the stock was purchased on February 1, 2007, for $50,000 ($100 a share). They wanted to generate a loss to offset some of the capital gain recognized during the year. Because the Bonds considered the stock to be a good

investment, they repurchased 500 shares of Flamingo on February 20, 2008, for $45,000 ($90 a share).

12. On March 2, 2005, Sandra was contacted by Laura Turner, a former college roommate. Over lunch Laura asked Sandra for a loan of $6,000 to help finance a new venture. Because the venture, a summer art camp in Santa Fe (NM), sounded interesting, Sandra made the loan. Laura signed a note due in two years at 10% interest. In late 2007, Sandra learned that Laura had disappeared after being charged by New Mexico authorities with grand theft. Even worse, Laura is wanted in Arkansas for parole violation from a prior felony conviction. Laura has never paid any interest on the note she gave Sandra.

13. The Bonds have a long-term capital loss carryover of $7,000 from 2006.

14. On May 9, 2003, Bill's favorite uncle, Cornelius Bond, gave him the family antique gun collection. Based on family records and educated estimates, the collection had an adjusted basis to Cornelius of $4,200 and was worth $13,000 on the date of the gift. Since Sandra abhors guns, Bill has been under heavy pressure to get rid of the collection. After Cornelius died in early 2007, Bill donated the collection to the Alamo Siege Museum (a qualified charity). The transfer was made on December 5, 2007; at that time, several qualified appraisers valued the collection at $16,000. The museum plans to add the collection to the other firearms it exhibits to visitors.

15. While walking the dog in late December 2006, Sandra was hit by an out-of-control delivery truck. The mishap sent Sandra to the hospital for several days of observation and medical evaluation. Aside from severe bruises, she suffered no permanent injury. Once apprehended, the driver of the truck was ticketed for DUI. The owner of the truck, a local distributor for a national brewery, was quite concerned about the adverse publicity that would result if Sandra filed a lawsuit. Consequently, it paid all her medical expenses and offered Sandra a settlement if she would sign a release. Under the settlement, Sandra would receive $126,000—$6,000 for loss of income and $120,000 for personal injury. On January 31, 2007, Sandra signed the release and was immediately paid $126,000.

16. In August 2006, Bill was rear-ended while stopped for a red light. Since the driver who caused the accident left the scene, Bill was forced to use his insurance to repair the damage to his car. As a result, Bill was subject to the $1,000 deductible provision in the policy. In 2007, the insurance company (Falcon Casualty) located the driver at fault and recovered the amount paid for repairs. Consequently, in April 2007, Bill received a check from Falcon refunding the $1,000 deductible he had paid. The Bonds did not claim any deduction as to the accident on their 2006 income tax return.

17. Sandra's parents (Roger and Betty Knight) have lived with her for several years. In fact, the Bonds built their current home with a garage apartment to allow the parents some measure of privacy and independence. Roger and Betty do not pay rent or otherwise contribute to their own support. Consequently, they are rightfully claimed by the Bonds as dependents. During 2007, Roger's heart condition deteriorated to the point that he was having great difficulty handling the stairs to the apartment. To resolve the problem, the Bonds had an elevator installed at a cost of $11,000. A real estate appraiser determined that the addition of the elevator increased the value of the Bonds' property by $5,000. The elevator was operational on July 6, 2007, and Bill paid the contractor on the same day.

18. After an acrimonious divorce, the Bonds' only daughter (Pamela Martin) moved back home in January 2007. She brought her twins (Madison and Lindsay, age 4) with her. Pamela (age 28) has no income for the year except the $4,200 she received for two months of child support. Under the divorce decree, Pamela was given custody of the children and awarded child support of $2,100 a month. The decree does not indicate who is entitled to the dependency exemptions for the children. Pamela plans to initiate legal proceeding against her ex-husband for delinquent child support.

19. Besides the items already mentioned, the Bonds have the following receipts for 2007:

Social Security benefits (Bill, $12,000; Sandra, $6,000)		$18,000
Consulting income paid by Pelican (including expense reimbursement of $11,150—see item 3)		35,000
Life insurance proceeds (see below)		50,000
Qualified dividend income—		
Carmine Corporation	$1,200	
Flamingo Power	400	1,600
Interest income—		
IBM bonds	$ 600	
CD at First National Bank of Denton	400	
Wells Fargo money market fund	300	
City of Beaumont (TX) general-purpose bonds	9,000	10,300

The life insurance proceeds concerned a policy owned by Cornelius Bond (see item 14), which named Bill as the beneficiary. The receipt of the proceeds came as a complete surprise to Bill as he never knew the policy existed.

20. Expenditures for 2007 not already mentioned are as follows:

Payment of Pamela's legal fees and court costs incident to her divorce		$9,000
Medical—		
Medicare B insurance premiums	$2,244	
Dental implants for Betty Knight	8,000	10,244
Taxes on personal residence		3,600
Interest on home mortgage		2,200
Church pledge		1,200
Professional journals—		
Oil and gas related (Bill)	$ 160	
Art related (Sandra)	120	280
Dues to professional organizations (Bill)		140
State professional license fee (Bill)		250
Tax return preparation fee [50%, equally divided between Bill and Sandra and relates to their business transactions]		900

Texas does not impose an income tax, so the Bonds choose the state and local sales tax option. The local sales tax rate is 2% (1.5% city; 0.5% county). They do not keep track of sales tax expenditures for routine purchases (e.g., clothes, prepared foods) but can verify the sales tax on exceptional items (i.e., big-ticket purchases).

21. Relevant information for 2007 appears below:

2006 tax refund applied toward 2007 income tax	$ 800
Amount withheld by trustee of Bill's retirement plan	6,500
Quarterly payments made to the IRS ($2,500 each payment)	10,000

Name	Social Security Number	Birth Date
William S. Bond	466–36–4524	09/15/1939
Sandra K. Bond	465–29–8431	12/03/1940
Roger Knight	449–32–8642	04/20/1918
Betty Knight	450–29–6124	02/29/1920
Pamela Martin	628–92–5784	10/19/1979
Madison Martin	629–53–6583	06/25/2003
Lindsay Martin	629–53–6584	06/25/2003

The business activity code for Bill is 541330, and for Sandra it is 711510.

Requirements

Prepare an income tax return (with appropriate schedules) for the Bonds for 2007. In doing this, utilize the following guidelines:

- Make necessary assumptions for information not given in the problem but needed to complete the return.
- The taxpayers have the necessary substantiation (e.g., records, receipts) to support the transaction involved.
- If any refund is due, the Bonds want it applied to next year's tax liability.
- The Bonds do not want to contribute to the Presidential Election Campaign Fund.

APPENDIX G

TABLE OF CASES CITED

A

Adelson, U.S. v., 2–47
Allen, Mary Francis, 7–9
Anderson, Comm. v., 5–16
Anton, M. G., 4–16
Arcade Realty Co., 10–17
Argo Sales Co. v. Comm., 2–44
Arkansas Best v. Comm., 16–6
Armantrout Richard T., 5–10
Armstrong v. Phinney, 5–16
Arnett v. Comm., 5–28
Arrigoni v. Comm., 7–37
Augustus v. Comm., 2–30

B

Baist, George A., 9–31
Balistrieri, Joseph P., 15–11
Barry, Frederick J., 9–44
Baxter v. Comm., 4–10
Bedell v. Comm., 4–8
Beirne, Michael F., 20–40
Bhalla, C. P., 5–9
Biggs, Franklin B., 15–25
Bingler v. Johnson, 5–9
Bissonnette, Marc G., 9–44
Bolton v. Comm., 6–21
Bonaire Development Co. v. Comm., 6–9
Bright v. U.S., 4–9
Brockman, Richard M., 9–44
Brody, Clifford L., 7–37
Broudo v. Dura Pharmaceutical, Inc., 2–47
Brown v. Helvering, 4–9
Bruun, Helvering v., 5–4
Burnet v. Sanford and Brooks, 4–9, 18–14

C

Carr, Jack D., 2–18, 2–44
Carter, Sydney J., Estate of v. Comm., 5–6
Caruth Corp. v. U.S., 4–17
Cheshire, Kathryn, 3–51
Cohen, Theodore H., 4–11
Comm. v. (see opposing party)

Continental Trust Co., 10–17
Correll, U.S. v., 9–7
Cowden v. Comm., 4–11
Crane v. Comm., 14–3

D

Daly, D. R., Estate of, 5–5
Davidson, Collin J., 9–14
Davis, v. U.S., 14–4
DeClerk, Barbara J., 7–37
Delman, Estate of v. Comm., 5–33
Deputy v. DuPont, 6–6
Diaz, Teresita T., 9–44
Doak, Comm. v., 5–16
Doyle v. Mitchell Bros. Co., 4–6
Dreicer v. Comm., 2–16
Duberstein, Comm. v., 2–16, 5–5, 10–19
Dunn and McCarthy, Inc. v. Comm., 6–6
Dura Pharmaceuticals, Inc. v. Broudo, 2–47
Dyer, J. Raymond, 6–6

E

Edwards v. Cuba Railroad Co., 20–17
Eisner v. Macomber, 4–5, 5–30
Estate of (see name of party)
Evans, D. L, 2–42
Evans, Donald L., 2–46

F

F. W. Woolworth Co., 2–8
Faulconer, Sr. v. Comm., 6–31
Fausner v. Comm., 9–5
Fay v. Helvering, 7–8
Fischer, L. M., 4–10
Flint v. Stone Tracy Co., 1–3
Flora, 2–47
Frank, Morton, 6–15
FRGC Investment, 2–46

G

Galligan, Steven, 9–16
Galt v. Comm., 4–15

Garwood Irrigation Co. v. Comm., 2–44
Generes, U.S. v., 7–37
Gilmore v. U.S., 10–47
Ginsberg v. Comm., 20–40
Goldberg, Harry H., 6–24
Golsen, Jack E., 2–16
Grabske, U.S. v., 2–47
Groetzinger v. Comm., 7–2
Guenther, Kenneth W., 9–32

H

H. Pulvers v. Comm., 7–9
Harris M. Miller, 2–8
Harris v. Comm., 2–44
Hawkins, C. A., 5–11
Heininger, Comm. v, 6–6
Helvering v. (see opposing party)
Hillsboro National Bank v. Comm., 6–9
Horst, Helvering v., 4–15
Hort v. Comm., 16–14
Horwith, T. M, 19–34
Hospital Corporation of America, 2–47

I

Industrial Valley Bank & Trust Co., 2–32

J

Jacobson v. Comm., 5–34
James v. U.S., 2–42, 4–3
J. W. Yarbro v. Comm., 2–44

K

Kahler, Charles F., 4–9
Keller v. Comm., 6–9
Kelo v. City of New London, 15–13
Kennedy, Jr. v. Comm., 6–6
Kieselbach v. Comm., 5–28
King, Jeffrey R., 3–50
King, Marlowe, 16–42
Kintner, U.S. v., 20–3
Kirby Lumber Co v. U.S., 4–6, 5–33
Kluger Associates, Inc., 14–8
Korn Industries v. U.S., 18–17
Kowalski, Comm. v., 5–16

L

Lesslie, Thomas E., 10–34
Lewis, U.S. v., 18–9
Lincoln Electric Co. Comm. v., 6–6
Lindeman, J. B, 5–16
Littriello v. U.S., 20–48
Loco Realty Co. v. Comm., 15–12
Lucas v. Earl, 4–14
Lucas v. North Texas Lumber Co., 4–9
Lynch v. Turrish, 14–3

M

Maac v. Resource Design & Construction, Inc., 2–47
Malat v. Riddell, 16–4

Mantell, John, 4–13
Marshman, Comm. v., 14–3
Martin, Evelyn M., 2–42, 3–51
Mayer, Frederick, 16–42
McAdams, Thomas W., 4–33
McCauley, Philip J., 2–36
McWilliams v. Comm., 6–26, 14–18
Mellon Bank v. U.S., 2–47
Merchants Loan and Trust Co. v. Smietanka, 4–3
Mulherin, Brian C., 9–31
Murphy v. IRS, 5–11

N

National Muffler Dealers Assn., Inc., 2–31
Neuhoff, Ann R., 2–32
New Colonial Ice Co. v. Helvering, 6–2
Newman, Comm. v., 2–36
Newman, Commissioner v., 2–35
Nico, Severino R. Jr., 2–32
Nielsen, James A., 2–19
North American Consolidated Oil Co. v. Burnet, 18–9

O

O'Malley v. Ames, 14–3
O'Neill, William J., 2–47
Old Colony Railroad Co. v. Comm., 10–14
Olis, U.S. v., 2–47

P

Page v. Rhode Island Trust Co., Exr., 6–9
Papineau, G. A., 5–16
Patterson, Floyd, 20–3
Pauli, Karl, 2–18
Paymer v. Comm., 20–3
Pfeifer, Donald R., 10–4
Pioneer Real Estate Co., 15–12
Pollock v. Farmers' Loan and Trust Co., 1–3, 5–28

R

Raffety Farms Inc. v. U.S., 20–3
Ramirez-Ota v. Comm., 2–46
Rapoport, Herbert M., Estate of, 7–37
Reimels v. Comm., 5–47
Riach v. Frank, 10–5
Robertson v. U.S., 5–5
Rogers, U.S. v., 7–8
Rose, Erie H., 10–12
Rosenberg v. Comm., 7–8
Rowan Companies, Inc. v. U.S., 5–15
Rubnitz, Alan A., 10–33
Rutkin v. U.S., 4–4

S

Sakol, Miriam, 19–34
Sargent v. Comm., 4–14
Selig, Bruce, 8–42
Seymour, John L., 10–47
Sherman, Stephen G., 9–31

Shopmaker v. U.S., 7–8
Simons-Eastern Co. v. U.S., 2–19, 2–23
Simpson v. U.S., 5–6
Snow v. Comm., 7–16
Soliman, Comm. v., 9–22
Solomon, S. L., 7–9
South Carolina v. Baker III, 5–28
Stark, Nelda C., 2–32
Starker v. U.S., 15–25
Strauss, Julia A., 2–42, 4–8
Sullivan, Comm. v., 6–12
Sundby, Dale H., 7–37

T

Tank Truck Rentals, Inc. v. Comm., 6–11
Tellier, Comm. v., 6–12
Thor Power Tool Co. v. Comm., 18–30
Toledo, Peoria & Western Railroad Co., 16–32
Tollis, Zane R., 17–37
Tomerlin, James O. Trust, 2–8
Tougher v. Comm., 5–16
Tufts, Comm. v., 14–3
Tyler, W. David, 9–26

U

U.S. Freightways Corp. v. Comm., 18–11
U.S. Trust Co. of New York v. Anderson, 5–28

United States v. (see opposing party)
Untermann John T., 2–47

V

Vogel Fertilizer Co., U.S. v., 2–31

W

Ward, Dwight A., 6–15
Washington, Alexander, 4–21
Washington, Jerry, 2–45
Welch v. Helvering, 6–6
Whitaker, William T., 9–26
Whittington v. Jones, 2–44
Wilkerson, Donald L., 10–33
William L. Rudkin Testamentary Trust, 2–47
Wisconsin Cheeseman, Inc, The v. U.S., 6–28
Withers, LaVar M., 10–34

Y

York v. Comm., 6–15
Young v. Comm., 7–26

Z

Zaninovich v. Comm., 6–9, 18–11
Zarin v. Comm., 2–42, 4–2

DEPRECIATION

Introduction

Cost recovery, amortization, and depletion are presented in Chapter 8. For most fixed assets (e.g., machinery, equipment, furniture, fixtures, buildings) placed in service after December 31, 1980, the Economic Recovery Tax Act of 1981 (ERTA) has replaced the depreciation system with the cost recovery system.[1] The general relationship between the depreciation system and the cost recovery system is summarized in Exhibit H–1.

Despite ERTA, a discussion of § 167 depreciation is still relevant for two reasons. First, assets that were placed in service prior to 1981 are still in use. Second, certain assets placed in service after 1980 are not eligible to use the cost recovery system (ACRS and MACRS) and therefore must be depreciated. They include property placed in service after 1980 whose life is not based on years (e.g., units-of-production method).

Depreciation

Section 167 permits a depreciation deduction in the form of a reasonable allowance for the exhaustion, wear and tear, and obsolescence of business property and property held for the production of income (e.g., rental property held by an investor).[2] Obsolescence refers to normal technological change due to reasonably foreseeable economic conditions. If rapid or abnormal obsolescence occurs, a taxpayer may change to a shorter estimated useful life if there is a "clear and convincing

EXHIBIT H–1	Depreciation and Cost Recovery: Relevant Time Periods

System	Date Property Is Placed in Service
§ 167 depreciation	Before January 1, 1981, and *certain* property placed in service after December 31, 1980.
Original accelerated cost recovery system (ACRS)	After December 31, 1980, and before January 1, 1987.
Modified accelerated cost recovery system (MACRS)	After December 31, 1986.

---

[1] Depreciation is covered in § 167, and cost recovery (ACRS and MACRS) is covered in § 168.

[2] § 167(a) and Reg. § 1.167(a)–1.

basis for the redetermination." Depreciation deductions are *not* permitted for personal use property.

The taxpayer must adopt a reasonable and consistent plan for depreciating the cost or other basis of assets over the estimated useful life of the property (e.g., the taxpayer cannot arbitrarily defer or accelerate the amount of depreciation from one year to another). The basis of the depreciable property must be reduced by the depreciation allowed and by not less than the allowable amount.[3] The *allowed* depreciation is the depreciation actually taken, whereas the *allowable* depreciation is the amount that could have been taken under the applicable depreciation method. If the taxpayer does not claim any depreciation on property during a particular year, the basis of the property still must be reduced by the amount of depreciation that should have been deducted (the allowable depreciation).

EXAMPLE 1

On January 1, Ted paid $7,500 for a truck to be used in his business. He chose a five-year estimated useful life, no salvage value, and straight-line depreciation. Thus, the allowable depreciation deduction was $1,500 per year. However, depreciation actually taken (allowed) was as follows:

Year 1	$1,500
Year 2	–0–
Year 3	–0–
Year 4	1,500
Year 5	1,500

The adjusted basis of the truck must be reduced by the amount of allowable depreciation of $7,500 ($1,500 × 5 years) even though Ted claimed only $4,500 depreciation during the five-year period. Therefore, if Ted sold the truck at the end of Year 5 for $1,000, he would recognize a $1,000 gain, since the adjusted basis of the truck is zero. ∎

Qualifying Property and Basis for Depreciation

The use rather than the character of property determines whether a depreciation deduction is permitted. Property must be used in a trade or business or held for the production of income to qualify as depreciable.

EXAMPLE 2

Carol is a self-employed CPA who maintains her office in a room in her home. The room, which is used exclusively for her business, comprises 20% of the square footage of her house. Carol is permitted a depreciation deduction only for the business use part of the house. No depreciation deduction is permitted for the 80% of the square footage of her house that is used as her residence. ∎

The basis for depreciation generally is the adjusted cost basis used to determine gain if the property is sold or otherwise disposed of.[4] However, if personal use assets are converted to business or income-producing use, the basis for depreciation *and* for loss is the *lower* of the adjusted basis or fair market value at the time of the conversion of the property.[5] As a result of this lower of basis rule, losses that occurred while the property was personal use property will not be recognized for tax purposes through the depreciation of the property.

---

[3]§ 1016(a)(2) and Reg. § 1.167(a)–10(a).
[4]§ 167(c).

[5]Reg. § 1.167(g)–1.

EXAMPLE 3

Hans acquires a personal residence for $130,000. Four years later, when the fair market value is only $125,000, he converts the property to rental use. The basis for depreciation is $125,000, since the fair market value is less than the adjusted basis. The $5,000 decline in value is deemed to be personal (since it occurred while the property was held for personal use) and therefore nondeductible. ■

The Regulations provide that tangible property is depreciable only to the extent that the property is subject to wear and tear, decay or decline from natural causes, exhaustion, and obsolescence.[6] Thus, land and inventory are not depreciable, but land improvements are depreciable (e.g., paved surfaces, fences, landscaping).

Other Depreciation Considerations

In determining the amount of the depreciation deduction, the following additional considerations need to be addressed:

- The salvage value of the asset.
- The choice of depreciation methods.
- The useful life of the asset.

For property subject to depreciation under § 167, taxpayers generally must take into account the **salvage value** (assuming there is a salvage value) of an asset in calculating depreciation. An asset cannot be depreciated below its salvage value. However, the Code permits a taxpayer to disregard salvage value for amounts up to 10 percent of the basis in the property. This provision applies to tangible personal property (other than livestock) with an estimated useful life of three years or more.[7]

EXAMPLE 4

Green Company acquired a machine for $10,000 in 1980 with an estimated salvage value of $3,000 after 19 years. The company may disregard salvage value to the extent of $1,000 and compute the machine's depreciation based upon a cost of $10,000 less $2,000 salvage value. The adjusted basis may be reduced to $2,000 (depreciation of $8,000 may be taken) even though the actual salvage value is $3,000. ■

This provision was incorporated into the law to reduce the number of IRS-taxpayer disputes over the amount of the salvage value that should be used.

Another consideration is the *choice of depreciation methods* from among the several allowed. The following alternative depreciation methods are permitted for property placed into service before January 1, 1981, and for the aforementioned property placed in service after December 31, 1980, for which cost recovery is not permitted:

- The straight-line (SL) method (cost basis less salvage value ÷ estimated useful life).
- The declining-balance method (DB) using a rate not to exceed twice the straight-line rate. Common methods include 200 percent DB (double-declining balance), 150 percent DB, and 125 percent DB. Salvage value is not taken into account under any of the declining-balance methods. However, no further depreciation can be claimed once net book value (cost minus depreciation) and salvage value are the same.
- The sum-of-the-years' digits method (SYD).
- Any other consistent method that does not result in greater total depreciation being claimed during the first two-thirds of the useful life than would have been allowable under the double-declining balance method. Permissible methods include machine hours and the units-of-production method.

---

[6]Reg. § 1.167(a)–2.   [7]Reg. §§ 1.167(a)–1(c) and (f)–1.

EXAMPLE 5

On January 1, 1980, Diego acquired a new machine to be used in his business. The asset cost $10,000 with an estimated salvage value of $2,000 and a four-year estimated useful life.[8] The following amounts of depreciation could be deducted, depending on the method of depreciation used:

	1980	1981	1982	1983
1. Straight-line:				
$10,000 cost less ($2,000 salvage value reduced by 10% of cost) ÷ 4 years	$2,250	$2,250	$2,250	$2,250
2. Double-declining balance:				
a. $10,000 × 50% (twice the straight-line rate)	5,000			
b. ($10,000 − $5,000) × 50%		2,500		
c. ($10,000 − $5,000 − $2,500) × 50%			1,250	
d. ($10,000 − $5,000 − $2,500 − $1,250) × 50%				250[9]
3. Sum-of-the-years' digits:*				
$10,000 cost less ($2,000 salvage value reduced by 10% of cost) or $9,000				
a. $9,000 × 4/10	3,600			
b. $9,000 × 3/10		2,700		
c. $9,000 × 2/10			1,800	
d. $9,000 × 1/10				900

*The formula for the sum-of-the-years' digits (SYD) method is

$$\text{Cost} - \text{Salvage value} \times \frac{\text{Remaining life at the beginning of the year}}{\text{Sum-of-the-years' digits of the estimated life}}$$

In this example, the denominator for SYD is $1 + 2 + 3 + 4$, or 10. The numerator is 4 for Year 1 (the number of years left at the beginning of Year 1), 3 for Year 2, etc. The denominator can be calculated by the following formula:

$$S = \frac{Y(Y + 1)}{2} \text{ where } Y = \text{estimated useful life}$$

$$S = \frac{4(4 + 1)}{2} = 10$$

■

EXAMPLE 6

Using the depreciation calculations in Example 5, the depreciation reserve (accumulated depreciation) and net book value at the end of 1983 are as follows:

	Cost	− Depreciation	= Net Book Value*
Straight-line	$10,000	$9,000	$1,000
Double-declining balance	10,000	9,000	1,000
Sum-of-the-years' digits	10,000	9,000	1,000

*Note that an asset may not be depreciated below its salvage value even when a declining-balance method is used.

■

In 1969, Congress placed certain restrictions on the use of accelerated methods for new and used realty that are subject to the depreciation rules under § 167. These restrictions were imposed to reduce the opportunities for using real estate

---

[8] A four-year life is used to illustrate the different depreciation methods. Note that an asset placed in service in 1980 must have a useful life of at least 29 years in order for depreciation to be deducted in 2008.

[9] Total depreciation taken cannot exceed cost minus estimated salvage value ($1,000 in this example).

investments as tax shelters. The use of accelerated depreciation frequently resulted in the recognition of ordinary tax losses on economically profitable real estate ventures.

The following methods were permitted for residential and nonresidential real property:

	Nonresidential Real Property (Commercial and Industrial Buildings, Etc.)	Residential Real Property (Apartment Buildings, Etc.)
New property acquired after July 24, 1969, and generally before January 1, 1981	150% DB, SL	200% DB, SYD, 150% DB, or SL
Used property acquired after July 24, 1969, and generally before January 1, 1981	SL	125% DB (if estimated useful life is 20 years or greater) or SL

Congress chose to permit accelerated methods (200 percent declining-balance and sum-of-the-years' digits) for new residential rental property. Presumably, the desire to stimulate construction of new housing units justified the need for such accelerated methods.

Restrictions on the use of accelerated methods were not imposed on new tangible personalty (e.g., machinery, equipment, and automobiles). However, the 200 percent declining-balance and sum-of-the-years' digits methods were not permitted for used tangible personal property. The depreciation methods permitted for *used* tangible personal property were as follows:

	Useful Life of Three Years or More	Useful Life of Less Than Three Years
Used tangible personal property acquired after July 24, 1969, and generally before January 1, 1981	150% DB, SL	SL

Since the acquisition of used property does not result in any net addition to gross private investment in our economy, Congress chose not to provide as rapid accelerated depreciation for used property.

The determination of a *useful life* for a depreciable asset often led to disagreement between taxpayers and the IRS. One source of information was the company's previous experience and policy with respect to asset maintenance and utilization. Another source was the guideline lives issued by the IRS.[10] In 1971, the IRS guideline life system was modified and liberalized by the enactment of the **Asset Depreciation Range (ADR) system.**[11]

KEY TERMS

Asset Depreciation Range (ADR) system, H–5

Salvage value, H–3

[10]Rev.Proc. 72–10, 1972–1 C.B. 721, superseded by Rev.Proc. 83–35, 1983–1 C.B. 745.   [11]Reg. § 1.167(a)–11.

INDEX

A

Abandoned spouse rules, **3**:29, **3**:31–32
Abode test, qualifying child, **3**:12
Above-the-line deductions, **3**:5
Accelerated cost recovery system (ACRS), **8**:2–3, **8**:22, **8**:31–32
  characteristics of, **8**:22
  relevant time periods, **8**:3
  See also Modified accelerated cost recovery system
Accelerated death benefits, **5**:7
Access expenditures, eligible for disabled access credit, **13**:13–14
Accident and health benefits, 5:13
  long-term care insurance benefits, employer-sponsored, **5**:15
  medical reimbursement plans, employer-sponsored, **5**:14
  purchased by the taxpayer, **5**:13
  See also Employee fringe benefits
Accountable plan, **9**:26–27
Accountant's Index, **2**:21
Accounting & Tax Index, The, **2**:21
Accounting concept of income, **4**:4–5
  and tax concepts, comparison of, **4**:5
Accounting income, **4**:4
  reconciliation of corporate taxable income and, **20**:15–17
Accounting method, **4**:7–10, **6**:8, **18**:10–18
  accrual method, **18**:13–16
  cash receipts and disbursements method—cash basis, **18**:10–12
  change from an incorrect method, **18**:17
  change of method, **18**:16–18
  correction of an error, **18**:17
  determined by the IRS, **18**:10
  disposition of installment obligations, **18**:24
  disposition of the net adjustment, **18**:18
  electing out of the installment method, **18**:24–25
  hybrid method, **18**:16
  installment method, **18**:19–24
  interest on deferred taxes, **18**:24
  long-term contracts, **18**:25–29

  net adjustments due to change in, **18**:17–18
  prescribed by the IRS, **4**:8
  special methods, **18**:19–29
  timing of expense recognition, **6**:8–9
  tax planning for, **18**:36–37
  See also Accrual method, Cash receipts method, Completed contract method, Hybrid method, Installment method, and Percentage of completion method
Accounting periods, **18**:3–10
  business purpose, **18**:5
  changes in, **18**:6–7
  IRS requirements for changes in, **18**:7
  making the election, **18**:6
  mitigation of the annual accounting period concept, **18**:9–10
  partnerships, **18**:3–5
  personal service corporations, **18**:6
  required tax payments, **18**:5
  S corporations, **18**:3–5
  tax planning for, **18**:36–37
  taxable periods of less than one year, **18**:7–9
Accounts and notes receivable, as definition of capital asset, **16**:4–5
Accrual basis requirement exceptions, **18**:12
Accrual basis taxpayers, exceptions applicable to, **4**:13–14
Accrual method, **4**:7, **4**:9, **18**:13–16
  exceptions applicable to, **4**:13–14
  reserves, **18**:16
  timing of expense recognition, **6**:10
Accumulated earnings and profits (E & P), **20**:21, **20**:22
  dividends from, **5**:29
ACE (adjusted current earnings) adjustment, **12**:27–29
Acquiescence ("A" or "Acq."), **2**:18
Acquisition indebtedness, **10**:15
ACRS. *See* accelerated cost recovery system
Action on Decision, **2**:18, **2**:32
Active income, **11**:5
Active participant in qualified plan, **19**:20
Active participation in real estate rental activities, **11**:20

Actual cost method, computation of automobile expenses, **9**:7
Ad valorem taxes, **1**:6, **10**:11
  on personalty, **1**:8
  on realty, **1**:6–7
Additional depreciation, **17**:14, **17**:15
Additional first-year depreciation, **8**:7–8
  limits on cost recovery for automobiles, **8**:16
Additional standard deduction (age 65 or older or blind), **3**:7–8, **3**:25, **3**:26
Adjusted basis, **14**:4, **14**:20–21
Adjusted gross income (AGI), **1**:14, **3**:6
  classification of interest expense, **10**:18
  election to claim certain unearned income of children under age 19 on parent's return and, **3**:24
  phaseout of dependency exemptions and, **3**:18–19
  Roth IRAs and, **19**:22
  spousal IRAs and, **19**:25
  tax credit for the elderly or disabled, **13**:17–18
  two percent floor, **9**:28–29
  See also Deductions for AGI; Deductions from AGI
Adjusted gross income threshold
  adoption expenses credit, **13**:21
  child and dependent care expenses, **13**:22–23
  child tax credit, **13**:21
  education tax credits, **13**:24
  saver's credit rate and, **13**:26
Adjustments
  AMT formula for individuals, **12**:4–5
  summary of basis, **14**:22
  to basis, **14**:23–24
Administrative feasibility, influence of IRS, **1**:32
Administrative sources of the tax law, **2**:7–11
  assessing the validity of other, **2**:32
  letter rulings, **2**:10
  other administrative pronouncements, **2**:10–11
  Revenue Rulings and Revenue Procedures, **2**:8–10
  Treasury Department Regulations, **2**:7–8

Adoption assistance program, employee
    fringe benefits, **5**:18
Adoption expenses credit, **13**:20–21,
    13:28
Age, additional standard deduction for
    65 or older, **3**:7–8, **3**:25
Age test, qualifying child, **3**:12
Agent, income received by, **4**:17
Alimony
    and spousal IRAs, **19**:24
    recapture, **4**:21–22
    tax planning for, **4**:37–38
Alimony and separate maintenance
    payments, **4**:20–23
    child support, **4**:23
    front-loading, **4**:21–23
    inclusion in gross income, **4**:20–23
    post-1984 agreements and decrees,
        4:21
All events test, **6**:10, **18**:14
    for deductions, **18**:14–15
    for income, **18**:13–14
Allocable parental tax, **3**:23
Alternate valuation amount, **14**:14
Alternate valuation date, **14**:14
Alternative deprecation system (ADS),
    8:7, **8**:12, **8**:20–22, **12**:9, **12**:11
    individual and corporate AMT
        adjustments, **12**:27
    tables, **8**:36–37
Alternative minimum tax (AMT), **12**:2,
    20:6
    corporate, **12**:26–30, **20**:14
        AMT adjustments, **12**:27–29
        exemption, **12**:29
        formula, **12**:26
        other aspects of, **12**:29–30
        repeal of AMT for small
            corporations, **12**:26
        tax preferences, **12**:29
    individual **12**:2–26
        AMT adjustments, **12**:8–20
        AMT credit, **12**:24
        AMT exclusions, **12**:24
        AMT formula, **12**:2–6, **12**:6–8
        AMT preferences, **12**:20–22
        AMT rate schedule, **12**:7
        exemption amount, **12**:7
        Form 6251, **12**:25
        formula, **12**:6
        illustration of AMT computation,
            12:23–24
        regular tax liability, **12**:8
        summary of income tax consequences,
            20:29
        table, **8**:35
        tax planning for, **12**:30–31
Alternative minimum tax credit, **12**:24
Alternative minimum taxable income
    (AMTI), **12**:2–26, **20**:10
    AMT formula for individuals, **12**:2–6
Alternative minimum vesting schedules,
    19:9
Alternative tax, **16**:23
    computation, **3**:33, **16**:2

on capital gain computation, income
    layers for, **16**:25
Alternative tax NOL deduction
    (ATNOLD), **12**:15–16
    individual and corporate AMT
        adjustments, **12**:27
American Depository Receipts (ADRs),
    16:17
American Federal Tax Reports (AFTR), **2**:19
American Institute of Certified Public
    Accountants (AICPA), **1**:5
    ethical guidelines, **1**:23
American Jobs Creation Act of 2004
    (AJCA), **1**:30, **2**:3, **4**:3, **7**:17, **8**:17,
    18:2, **18**:11
Americans with Disabilities Act, **13**:3
Amnesty programs, **1**:15
Amortizable bond premium as capital
    recovery, **14**:5–6
Amortizable Section 197 intangibles, **8**:22
Amortization, **8**:3, **8**:22–24
    Form 4562, **8**:28, **8**:29
    of research and experimental
        expenditures, **7**:16
    tax planning for, **8**:32
Amount realized, **14**:3–4, **14**:20
    in Section 121 sale, **15**:19
AMT adjustments, **12**:4
    applicable only to corporations,
        12:27–29
    individuals, **12**:22, **12**:27
        adjusted gain or loss, **12**:13–14
        alternative tax net operating loss
            deduction (ATNOLD), **12**:15–16
        circulation expenditures, **12**:9
        cutback adjustment, **12**:16
        depreciation of post-1986 personal
            property, **12**:10–11
        depreciation of post-1986 real
            property, **12**:9–10
        direction of, **12**:8–9
        expenditures requiring 10-year
            write-off for AMT purposes, **12**:12
        housing interest, **12**:18
        incentive stock options, **12**:12–13
        interest in general, **12**:17
        investment interest, **12**:18–19
        itemized deductions, **12**:16–19
        medical expenses, **12**:16–17
        other adjustments, **12**:19–20
        passive activity losses, **12**:14–15
        pollution control facilities, **12**:11
        use of completed contract method of
            accounting, **12**:12
    tax planning for, **12**:30–31
AMT exclusions, **12**:24
AMT preferences
    depreciation, **12**:21
    fifty percent exclusion for certain small
        business stock, **12**:21–22
    individual, **12**:20–22
    intangible drilling costs, **12**:20
    interest on private activity bonds,
        12:20–21
    percentage depletion, **12**:20

    tax planning for, **12**:30–31
AMT rate schedule, **12**:7
AMT/regular tax rate differential, tax
    planning for, **12**:30–31
Annual accounting period concept, **1**:29
    farm relief, **18**:9
    mitigation of, **18**:9–10
Annual exclusion per donee, **1**:12
Annuity, **4**:27
    exclusion amount, **4**:28
    exclusion ratio, **4**:30
    expected return, **4**:29
    income from, **4**:27–30
    number of anticipated monthly
        payments under the simplified
        method, **4**:30
    one life–expected return multiples,
        4:29
    simplified method for annuity
        distributions from qualified
        retirement plans, **4**:30
    tax-deferred, **19**:4
    term certain, **4**:29
Antitrust law violations, **6**:11
Appeals, **2**:14
Appeals Division of the IRS, **1**:20
Appellate courts, **2**:15–17
    See also Courts
Appreciated property, determining the
    deduction for contributions of by
    individuals, **10**:26
Appropriate economic unit, **11**:11
Archipelago Holdings, Inc., **16**:3
Arm's length concept, **1**:33
Assets
    amortization of Section 197 intangible,
        8:22
    capital, **16**:3–8
    classification and use of, **1**:8, **8**:3
    disposition of business, **17**:2
    expenditures for intangible, **6**:25
    expenditures for tangible, **6**:25
    expensing of, **8**:13–15
    general business asset class, **15**:5
    in a lump-sum purchase, allocation of
        cost among multiple, **14**:9
    investment, **16**:3
    liquidating retirement, **19**:43
    ordinary, **16**:3
    personal use, **8**:3, **16**:3
    sale, exchange, or condemnation of
        personal use assets, **14**:7
    Section 1231, **16**:3, **17**:3–11
    tangible and intangible, **8**:3
    valuation of, **4**:3–4
Assignment of income, **4**:14
Athletic facilities, employee fringe
    benefits, **5**:18
At-risk amount, calculation of, **11**:5
At-risk limitation, **11**:3
At-risk limits, **11**:4–5
Audit Closing Agreement Program
    (AuditCAP), **19**:8
Audit process, **1**:19–20
    selection of returns for audit, **1**:19–20

Audit process (contd.)
  settlement procedures, 1:20
  types of audits, 1:20
Automatic mileage method, 9:6, 9:12
Automobiles
  business and personal use of, 8:15–19
  change from predominantly business
    use, 8:18–19
  computation of expenses, 9:6–7
  leased, 8:19
  limits on cost recovery for, 8:16–17
  not used predominantly in business,
    8:17–18
  passenger, 8:16
  substantiation requirements, 8:19
  used predominantly in business, 8:15
Average benefit percentage, 19:9
Average benefits test for qualified plans,
  19:9
Average cost method, 18:33
Average tax rate, 3:21
Awards, income from, 4:31
Away-from-home requirement
  determining the tax home, 9:8
  temporary assignments, 9:7–8
  travel expenses, 9:7–8

B

Backup withholding, 13:38
Bad debt deductions, 7:7
Bad debts, 7:3–6
  business vs. nonbusiness, 7:4–5
  loans between related parties, 7:5–6
  nonbusiness, 16:8
  specific charge-off method, 7:3–4
Bankruptcy, 2:14, 7:4
Basic research, 13:12
  credit, 13:12
  payments, 13:12
Basic standard deduction, 3:7–8
Basis
  adjusted, 14:4, 14:20–21
  adjustments to, 14:22, 14:23–24
  effect of expensing of assets on,
    8:14–15
  for depreciating the converted
    property, 14:19
  partnership's basis in contributed
    property, 20:33
  stepped-down, 14:14
  stepped-up, 14:14
Basis considerations, 14:8–22
  additional complexities in determining
    realized gain or loss, 14:20–21
  and computation of gain, transfers to
    controlled corporations, 20:20–21
  conversion of property from personal
    use to business or income-producing
    use, 14:19–20
  determination of cost basis, 14:8–11
  disallowed losses, 14:16–18
  gift basis, 14:11–14
  property acquired from a decedent,
    14:14–16

summary of basis adjustments, 14:22
Basis determination
  in S corporation, 20:30–31
  Sections 334 and 338 (liquidating the
    corporation), 20:25–26
  subsidiary liquidation basis rules,
    20:25–26
Basis of
  boot in like-kind exchanges, 15:8–11
  inherited property, effect of 2001 tax
    legislation on, 14:16
  partnership interest, 20:32–33
  property received in like-kind
    exchanges, 15:8–11
Below-market loans, 4:25
  effect of on the lender and borrower,
    4:25
  exceptions to imputed interest rules
    for, 4:27
Beneficiaries of estates and trusts, 4:18
Benefit percentage, 19:9
Benefit received rule, 10:19
Benefits
  general classes of excluded, 5:26
  tax planning for maximizing, 16:33–34
Bequests
  inheritances and, 5:5
  tax planning for selection of property,
    14:25
Blindness, additional standard deduction
  for, 3:7–8
Board of Tax Appeals, 2:18
Boot, 15:7–8, 20:19
  given as appreciated or depreciated
    property, 15:8
  giving of, 15:8
  receipt of, 15:7
Bracket creep, 1:30
Bribes, 6:11
  disallowance of deduction for, in other
    countries, 6:13
  Section 162 exclusion, 6:5
Business and personal use of automobiles
  and other listed property, 8:15–19
  change from predominantly business
    use, 8:18–19
  leased automobiles, 8:19
  limits on cost recovery for automobiles,
    8:16–17
  not used predominantly in business,
    8:17–18
  special limitation, 8:17
  substantiation requirements, 8:19
  used predominantly in business, 8:14
Business assets
  disposition of, 17:2
  See also Section 1231 assets
Business bad debt, 7:2, 7:4–5
Business, costs of investigating, 6:16
Business entities
  corporate filing requirements,
    20:14–15
  deductions available only to
    corporations, 20:11–11

determination of corporate tax liability,
  20:14
general tax consequences of different
  forms of, 20:4
individuals and corporations compared, 20:4–6
reconciliation of corporate taxable
  income and accounting income,
  20:15–17
specific provisions compared, 20:6–11
tax planning for, 20:36–40
use of an entity to reduce the family
  income tax burden, 20:39–40
Business expenses, 6:5–7
Business fixed assets, as definition of
  capital asset, 16:4, 16:5
Business gifts, deductibility restrictions
  for, 9:21
Business losses, 6:7
Business meals, deductibility restrictions
  for, 9:19–20
Business supplies, as definition of capital
  asset, 16:4
Business Use of Your Home (Publication
  587), 9:23
Business year, natural, 18:7

C

C corporation, 20:4
Cafeteria benefit plan, 19:4, 19:43
Cafeteria plan, 5:19
Calendar year, 4:7, 18:3
  personal service corporations, 18:6
  S corporations, 18:5
Canons of taxation, 1:4–5
Capital additions, 14:4
Capital asset status, tax planning for,
  16:31–33
Capital assets, 16:3–8
  accounts and notes receivable, as
    definition of, 16:4–5
  business fixed assets, as definition of,
    16:5
  copyrights and creative works, as
    definition of, 16:5
  definition of, 3:33, 16:3–6
  effect of judicial action, 16:6
  franchises, trademarks, and trade
    names, 16:12–13
  holding period, 16:14–19
  inventory, as definition of, 16:4
  long-term nonpersonal use, 17:6
  relationship to Section 1231 assets,
    17:3–4
  sale or exchange, 16:8–14
  statutory expansions, 16:6–8
  U.S. government publications, as
    definition of, 16:6
Capital contributions, thin capitalization,
  20:17
Capital doctrine, recovery of, 4:6–7
Capital expenditures
  capitalization vs. expense, 6:25
  disallowance of deductions for, 6:24–25

Capital expenditures (*contd.*)
  for medical purposes, **10**:5–6
  tax planning for, **6**:32
Capital gain computation, income layers
    for alternative tax, **16**:25
Capital gain confusion, **17**:3
Capital gain netting process, some
    possible final results and how they
    are taxed, **16**:27
Capital gain property, **10**:23–25
Capital gains, **16**:2
  alternative tax on net capital gain,
    16:23–24
  determination of net, **3**:34
  from property transactions, **3**:33–34
  net nonbusiness, **7**:21–22
  netting process, **16**:20–22
  rationale for separate reporting of,
    16:2–3
  reporting procedures, **16**:27–30
  Schedule D of Form 1040, **16**:27,
    16:28–29, **17**:23, **17**:28–29
  summary of income tax consequences
    for long-term, **20**:29
  tax planning for, **16**:31–34
  tax treatment of corporate taxpayers,
    16:31, **20**:7
  tax treatment of noncorporate tax-
    payers, **16**:19–30, **20**:7
  taxation of net, **3**:33–34
  treatment in the U.S. and other coun-
    tries, **16**:32
  See also Net Capital gain; Net long-term
    capital gain; Net short-term capital
    gain
Capital loss deduction, **16**:20
Capital losses, **16**:2
  carryovers, **16**:22, **16**:26
  from property transactions, **3**:33–34
  netting process, **16**:20–22, **16**:23, **16**:27
  rationale for separate reporting of,
    16:2–3
  short term, **7**:2
  summary of income tax consequences,
    20:29
  tax planning for, **16**:31–34
  tax treatment of corporate taxpayers,
    16:31, **20**:7
  tax treatment of noncorporate
    taxpayers, **16**:19–30, **20**:7
  worthless securities as, **7**:6–7
  See also Net capital loss; Net long-term
    capital loss; Net short-term capital
    loss
Capital recoveries, **14**:4–6
Capital, recovery of, **4**:18, **14**:4
Carryback and carryover periods
  election to forgo carryback, **7**:21
  net operating losses (NOLs), **7**:20–21
  sequence of use of NOLs, **7**:20
Carryover provision of some
    nonrefundable credits, **13**:5
Carryovers, capital loss, **16**:22
Cash balance plans, **19**:7

See also Qualified plans
Cash method, **18**:11, **18**:36
  timing of expense recognition, **6**:9
  See also Cash receipts and
    disbursements method
Cash or deferred arrangement plans, **19**:4
Cash receipts and disbursements method,
    4:7
  cash basis, **18**:10–12
  restrictions on use of, **18**:11–12
  special rules for small farmers, **18**:12
  See also Cash method
Cash receipts method, **4**:8–9, **4**:36
  exceptions applicable to, **4**:10–13
Casualty gains, **7**:14
Casualty loss, **7**:8, **7**:14, **7**:26–27
  AMT allowable deductions for, **12**:16
  as capital recovery, **14**:5
  events that are not casualties, **7**:8–9
  measuring the amount of loss, **7**:10–12
  personal casualty gains and losses,
    7:13–14
  reduction for $100 and 10
    percent-of-AGI floors, **7**:11
  Section 1231 assets, **17**:6–7
  statutory framework for deducting
    losses of individuals, **7**:13
  summary of income tax consequences,
    20:18
  when to deduct, **7**:9–10
  See also Theft losses
Casualty netting, **17**:8
Catchup contribution, **10**:10
CCH's Tax Research Consultant, **2**:23
CD-ROM services, **2**:24
Change in form, not in substance, **15**:2–3
Charitable contribution deduction
  capital gain property, **10**:23–25
  contribution carryovers, **10**:26–27
  fifty percent ceiling, **10**:25
  limitations on, **10**:22–27
  ordinary income property, **10**:22–23
  thirty percent ceiling, **10**:25–26
  twenty percent ceiling, **10**:26
Charitable contributions, **10**:18–27,
    10:34–35
  AMT allowable deductions for, **12**:16
  benefit received rule, **10**:19
  corporate and individual treatment
    compared, **20**:8–9
  criteria for a gift, **10**:19–20
  defined, **10**:19
  Form 8283, Noncash Charitable
    Contributions, **10**:21
  nondeductible items, **10**:20
  of services, **10**:19–20
  or gifts, Section 162 exclusion, **6**:5
  qualified organizations, **10**:20
  recapture potential of, **17**:19–20
  record-keeping and valuation
    requirements, **10**:21–22
  summary of income tax consequences,
    20:18
  time of deduction, **10**:20–21
  valuation requirement for, **10**:21–22

Charity, act of affection or, **5**:6
Check-the-box regulations, **20**:4
Chicago Board of Trade, **16**:3
Child
  care resource and referral services,
    13:15
  credit for employer-provided care,
    13:14–15
  personal services of, **4**:14
  support, **4**:23
  See also Kiddie tax
Child and dependent care expenses,
    13:22–23, **13**:42–44
  dependent care assistance program,
    13:23–24
  earned income ceiling, **13**:22
  eligibility for, **13**:22
  eligible employment-related expenses,
    13:22
  employee fringe benefits, **5**:18
  reporting requirements, **13**:24
  special rule for medical expenses of
    noncustodial parent, **10**:6
  tax credit for, **13**:2, **13**:21–24
Child tax credit, **3**:19–20, **13**:21, **13**:28
  maximum credit and phaseouts, **13**:21
Children of divorced or separated
    parents, support test for, **3**:16–17
Chronically ill, accelerated death benefits
    and, **5**:7
Circuit Court of Appeals, **2**:15–17
  See also Courts
Circular E, *Employer's Tax Guide*
    (Publication 15), **13**:30
Circulation expenditures, **12**:4
  individual AMT adjustments, **12**:9
Citations, general judicial, **2**:17
Citator, **2**:32
Citizenship test, dependency exemptions
    3:17
Civil fraud penalty, **1**:22
Claim for refund, **1**:21
Claim of right doctrine, **4**:9, **18**:9–10
  deduction for repayment of amounts
    under, **10**:28
  restoration of amounts received under,
    18:9–10
Claims Court Reporter, **2**:19
Clear business purpose test, **9**:20
Client letter, **2**:37
Closely held corporation, **11**:9–10
Clothing, deductibility of special, **9**:23–24
Club dues, deductibility restrictions for,
    9:20–21
Code of Professional Conduct, **1**:23
Collectibles, **3**:33, **16**:22
Commerce Clearing House (CCH),
    2:18
Commissioner of Internal Revenue, **1**:19
Common law employees, **9**:3
Common law property system,
    1:31, **4**:18
Common law states
  rates for married individuals, **3**:29
  survivor's share of property, **14**:16

Community property, **1**:30–31, **4**:18–20
  foreign earned income exclusion
    5:25–27
  ramifications for dependency
    exemptions, **3**:36
  survivor's share of, **14**:15
  tax planning for, **4**:37
Community property states
  income in, **4**:18–20
  innocent spouse relief, **4**:20
  rates for married individuals, **3**:29
  spouses living apart, **4**:19–20
Commuter highway vehicle, **5**:23
Commuting expenses, **9**:4–5
  See also Travel expenses
Compensation, **19**:2–4
  deferred, **19**:3
  excessive executive, **6**:14–15, **6**:29–31
  performance and, **19**:5
  plans, nonqualified deferred, **19**:4
  unreasonable, tax planning for, **6**:29
Compensation for injuries and sickness,
  5:11–13
  accident and health insurance benefits,
    5:13
  damages, **5**:11–12
  workers' compensation, **5**:13
Compensation-related loans, **4**:25, **4**:27
Compensatory damages, **5**:11
Completed contract method, **4**:8, **18**:26,
  18:27–28, **18**:37
  individual AMT adjustments for, **12**:12
Comps, Section 274 exception, **9**:20
Conformity of financial reports, LIFO
  election, **18**:36
Congress, intent of, **2**:4
Constructive dividends, **20**:23–24
Constructive ownership, **6**:27
  rules, **18**:23
Constructive receipt, **4**:10–11, **18**:10
  doctrine, **4**:36
Consumer interest, **10**:14
Consumption tax, **1**:6
Contingent payments, **16**:13
Contract costs, **18**:26, **18**:27
Contract price, **18**:20
Contracts, current expense items for,
  18:27
Control, **20**:19
Controlled corporations, transfers to,
  20:17–21
  basis considerations and computation
    of gain, **20**:20–21
Convenience of the employer test for
  office in the home, **9**:22
Convention rules, foreign, **9**:10
Conventions, travel expenses restrictions
  on, **9**:8–9
Conversion chart for 2008, **13**:36
Copyrights, **8**:22
  and creative works, as definition of
    capital asset, **16**:4, **16**:5
Corporate Distributions and
  Adjustments, Subchapter C, **2**:6
Corporate income tax, **1**:6

Corporate stock, as capital asset or
  inventory, **16**:6
Corporate taxpayers, tax treatment of
  capital gains and losses, **16**:31
Corporations, **20**:2–4
  alternative minimum tax, **20**:14
  capital contributions, **20**:17
  compliance with state law, **20**:2–3
  deduction of organizational
    expenditures, **20**:13–14
  deductions available only to, **20**:11–14
  determination of tax liability, **20**:14
  distributions as capital recovery, **14**:5
  dividend distributions, **20**:21–24
  dividends received deduction, **20**:11–13
  entity classification after 1996, **20**:4
  entity classification prior to 1997,
    20:3–4
  filing requirements, **20**:14–15
  formation of, **20**:17–21
  income tax rates, **20**:14
  liquidating. *See* Liquidations
  operations of, **20**:21–24
  reconciliation of corporate taxable
    income and accounting income,
    20:15–17
  regular vs. S status, tax planning for,
    20:38
  retirement of obligation, original issue
    discount, **16**:9
  special recapture for, **17**:21
  stock redemptions, **20**:24
  tax consequences compared to
    individual taxpayers, **20**:4–6
  transferring assets to foreign
    corporations, **20**:22
  See also C corporations; Personal service
    corporations; S corporations
Corporation-shareholder loans, **4**:25, **4**:27
Correspondence audit, **1**:20
Cosmetic surgery, deductible medical
  expenses, **10**:3
Cost basis
  allocation problems, **14**:9–11
  determination of, **14**:8–11
  identification problems, **14**:8
Cost depletion, **8**:25–26
Cost identification and documentation
  considerations, tax planning for,
    14:24
Cost of repairs, **7**:11
Cost recovery, **8**:2
  allowances, as capital recovery, **14**:4–5
  and depreciation: relevant time
    periods, **8**:3
  periods for farming assets, **8**:12
  recapture, **8**:18
  reporting procedures, **8**:28
  tables, **8**:33–37
  See also Accelerated cost recovery system
    (ACRS); Modified accelerated cost
    recovery system (MACRS)
Courts,
  appellate courts, **2**:15–17
  Circuit Court of Appeals, **2**:15–17

Court of original jurisdiction, **2**:12
  District courts, jurisdiction of, **2**:13
  influence of on the tax law, **1**:32–33
  trial, **2**:12, **2**:13–14
  U.S. Court of Appeals, **2**:14, **2**:15–17,
    2:19–20
  U.S. Court of Federal Claims, **2**:12,
    2:13, **2**:14, **2**:15–17, **2**:19–20
  U.S. District Court, **2**:12, **2**:14, **2**:15–17,
    2:19–20
  U.S. Supreme Court, **2**:16, **2**:20
  U.S. Tax Court, **2**:12, **2**:13, **2**:14,
    2:15–17, **2**:17–19
  Small Cases Division of, **2**:12
Covenants not to compete, **8**:22
Coverdell Education Savings Account
  (CESA), **2**:4, **9**:17, **13**:25, **19**:23–24,
  19:28
CPA examination, taxation on, **2**:39–40
Credit for certain retirement plan
  contributions, **13**:25–26, **13**:29
Credit for child and dependent care
  expenses, **13**:21–24, **13**:28
  Form 2441, **13**:24
Credit for employer-provided child care,
  13:14–15, **13**:30
Credit for small employer pension plan
  startup costs, **13**:14, **13**:29
Credits
  carryovers of passive, **11**:8
  nonrefundable personal, **12**:8
  passive, **11**:7–8
  See also Tax credits
Criminal fraud penalty, **1**:23
Crop insurance proceeds, **18**:9
Crop method, **18**:12
Cumulative Bulletin (*C.B.*), **2**:9, **2**:10,
  2:17–18
Cumulative effect of Federal gift tax, **1**:13
Current earnings and profits (E & P),
  20:21, **20**:22
  dividends from, **5**:29
Current participation tests, **11**:13–14
Current Tax Payment Act, **1**:4
Customs duties, **1**:3
  federal, **1**:17
Cutback adjustment, **10**:28
  for entertainment expenses, **9**:18–19
  individual AMT adjustments, **12**:16
Cutback rule for entertainment expenses,
  9:18–19

D

Daily Tax Reports, **2**:10
Damages, **5**:11–12
  compensatory, **5**:11
  personal injury, **5**:11–12
  punitive, **5**:11
  taxation of, **5**:12
Data warehousing reduces global taxes,
  2:28
De minimis exception, lobbying
  expenditures, **6**:14

De minimis floor, defined benefit plans, **19**:14

De minimis fringe, **5**:20, **5**:23, **5**:24, **5**:26
  benefit rule, cutback adjustment, **9**:19

De minimis rule, percentage of completion method of accounting, **18**:29

Dealers in securities, **16**:6–7

Death
  disposition of passive activity at, **11**:22
  recapture potential of, **17**:19

Death benefits, **5**:6
  accelerated, **5**:7

Death tax, **1**:10–12

Deathbed gifts, **14**:15

Debt, income from discharge of, **5**:33–34

Decedent, unrecovered investment in an annuity contract, **10**:28

Deductions for adjusted gross income (AGI), **3**:5–6, **6**:2, **6**:3–4, **7**:2
  casualty and theft losses of trade or business, **7**:13
  expenses of self-employed persons, **9**:3
  home office expenses, **9**:22
  interest on qualified education loans, **10**:14
  IRAs, **9**:25
  Keogh (H.R. 10) plans, **9**:25
  legal fees, **6**:12
  medical insurance premiums of the self-employed, **10**:7
  NOL, **7**:23
  ordinary losses, **17**:3–4
  qualified moving expenses, **9**:13
  qualified tuition and related expenses, **9**:15
  reimbursed employee expenses under an accountable plan, **9**:25–26, **9**:27
  reporting procedures, **6**:7
  Section 1231 asset casualty losses, **17**:8
  Section 1231 asset losses, **17**:8
  Section 1231 casualty losses, **17**:6
  self-employment tax, **13**:41

Deductions from adjusted gross income, **3**:5, **6**:2, **7**:2
  casualty losses, **17**:8
  employee expenses, **9**:3
  hobby losses, **6**:18–19
  itemized deductions, **10**:2
  legal expenses, **6**:12
  nonpersonal use capital asset casualty losses, **17**:6
  reimbursed employee expenses under a nonaccountable plan, **9**:26, **9**:27
  reporting procedures, **6**:7
  unreimbursed employee expenses, **9**:26, **9**:27
  unreimbursed employment-related transportation expenses, **9**:4

Deductions
  above-the-line, **3**:5
  additional standard (age 65 or older or blind), **3**:7–8, **3**:25, **3**:26
  all events and economic performance tests for, **18**:14–15
  business and nonbusiness losses, **6**:7

classification of, **6**:2–8
disallowance possibilities, **6**:11–29
for qualified tuition and related expenses, **9**:15
itemized, **3**:6–7, **6**:4–5
limitations on charitable contribution, **10**:22–27
limitations on itemized, **9**:28–29
nonbusiness, **7**:22
partial list of itemized, **3**:7
reporting procedures, **6**:7
standard, **3**:7–8, **3**:9, **3**:25, **3**:26
tax planning for itemized, **10**:32–35
timing of expense recognition, **6**:8–10
trade or business expenses and production of income expenses, **6**:5–7

Deemed payments, **18**:20

Deemed substantiation, accountable plan for reimbursement of employee expenses, **9**:26–27

Deemed to be long term, holding period of property acquired from a decedent, **14**:16

Defendant, **2**:17

Defense of Marriage Act (P.L. 104–199), **3**:11

Deferral and amortization method, research and experimental expenditures, **7**:16

Deferred compensation, **19**:3, **19**:39–40
  Individual Retirement Accounts (IRAs), **19**:20–29
  nonqualified deferred compensation plans, **19**:29–33
  qualified pension, profit sharing, and stock bonus plans, **19**:4–19
  restricted property plans, **19**:33–36
  retirement plans for self-employed individuals, **19**:19–20
  stock options, **19**:36–39

Deferred taxes, interest on, **18**:24

Deficiency, payment of, **2**:14

Defined benefit Keogh plan, **19**:19

Defined benefit plan, **19**:4, **19**:14–15
  compared to defined contribution plan, **19**:6
  declining, **19**:11

Defined benefit/Section 401(k) plan (DF/K plan), **19**:17 .

Defined contribution Keogh plan, **19**:19

Defined contribution pension plan, **19**:5

Defined contribution plans, **19**:13–14
  compared to defined benefit plan, **19**:6

Department of the Treasury, **1**:19

Dependency exemptions, **3**:9, **3**:11–20, **3**:35–37
  child tax credit, **3**:19–20
  comparison of categories for, **3**:18
  other rules for, **3**:17
  phaseout of, **3**:18–19
  qualifying child, **3**:11–13
  qualifying relative, **3**:13–17
  release by custodial parent (Form 8332), **3**:17
  tests for, **3**:19

Dependent care assistance program, **13**:23–24

Dependent care expenses, tax credit for child and, **13**:2

Dependents
  child care expenses, **13**:21–24, **13**:42–44
  filing requirements for, **3**:25–26
  medical expenses incurred for, **6**:23, **10**:6
  special limitations for individuals who can be claimed as, **3**:9–10

Depletion, **8**:3, **8**:24–28, **8**:32–33
  intangible drilling and development costs (IDC), **8**:25

Depletion methods, **8**:25–28
  cost depletion, **8**:25–26
  effect of intangible drilling costs on depletion, **8**:27–28
  percentage depletion, **8**:26–27

Depreciation, **8**:2, **8**:3
  additional, **17**:14, **17**:15
  additional first-year, **8**:7–8
  as capital recovery, **14**:4–5
  concepts relating to, **8**:3–4
  cost recovery allowed or allowable, **8**:3–4
  cost recovery basis for personal use assets converted to business or income-producing use, **8**:4
  Form 4562, **8**:28, **8**:29
  gift basis for **14**:14
  individual AMT preferences, **12**:21
  nature of property, **8**:3
  placed in service requirement, **8**:3

Depreciation and cost recovery: relevant time periods, **8**:3

Depreciation of post-1986 personal property, individual AMT adjustments, **12**:10–11

Depreciation of post-1986 real property, individual AMT adjustments, **12**:9–10

Depreciation recapture
  and Section 1231 netting procedure, **17**:22
  corporate and individual treatment compared, **20**:7–8
  for Section 1250 property, summary of income tax consequences, **20**:18
  in other countries, **17**:23

Depreciation rules, **8**:2–3

Depreciation write-offs, **1**:25

Designated Roth contributions, **19**:18–19

Determination letters, **2**:11

Digital Daily, **2**:25, **2**:26

Directly related to business test for entertainment expenses, **9**:19

Disabled access credit, **13**:3–4, **13**:13–14, **13**:29

Disabled taxpayers
  base and threshold amounts for tax credit for elderly and, **13**:18
  tax credit for, **13**:2–3, **13**:17–18

Disallowance possibilities
 deductions for capital expenditures, **6**:24–25
 excessive executive compensation, **6**:14–15
 expenditures incurred for taxpayer's benefit or taxpayer's obligation, **6**:22–24
 expenses and interest relating to tax-exempt income, **6**:28–29
 hobby losses, **6**:16–19
 investigation of a business, **6**:15–16
 personal expenditures, **6**:24
 political contributions and lobbying activities, **6**:13–14
 public policy limitation, **6**:11–13
 related parties transactions, **6**:26–27
 rental of vacation homes, **6**:19–22
 substantiation requirements, **6**:27
Disallowed losses, **14**:16–18, **14**:25–26
 holding period of certain transactions, **16**:16
 related taxpayers, **14**:16–17
 wash sales, **14**:17–18
Disaster area losses, **7**:10
Discharge of indebtedness, income from, **5**:33–34
Discriminant Information Function (DIF) score, **1**:19
Discrimination awards, **5**:11
Disinterested generosity test, **10**:19
Distribution requirements from qualified plans, **19**:10–12
District Court, **2**:14, **2**:15–17
 jurisdiction of, **2**:13
 See also Courts
Dividend distributions
 concept of earnings and profits, **20**:22
 constructive dividends, **20**:23–24
 corporate, **20**:21–24
 property dividends, **20**:22–23
Dividend taxation, beneficiaries and victims of changes in, **5**:30
Dividends, **5**:29
 constructive, **20**:23–24
 income from, **4**:15–17
 property, **20**:22–23
 recapture potential of property, **17**:21
 stock dividends, **5**:30
Dividends received
 deduction, **20**:11–13
 summary of income tax consequences, **20**:18
Divorce
 agreements and decrees, tax treatment of payments and transfers pursuant to Post-1984, **4**:22
 deduction of legal fees incurred in connection with, **6**:24
 tax issues, **4**:20–23
Divorced parents with children, special rule for medical expenses of noncustodial parent, **10**:6

Documentation and cost identification considerations, tax planning for, **14**:24
Dollar-value LIFO, **18**:33–34
Domestic production activities deduction (DPAD), **7**:17–19, **20**:6
 calculation of, **7**:17–18
 changes to, **7**:18
 corporate and individual treatment compared, **20**:9–10
 created tax planning opportunities, **18**:2
 eligible taxpayers, **7**:18–19
 Form 8903, **20**:28, **20**:34
 operational rules, **7**:17–19
 summary of income tax consequences, **20**:18
Domestic production gross receipts (DPGR), **7**:18
Domestic travel. *See* Travel expenses
Double taxation, **1**:6
Drug dealers, deduction of expenses, **6**:13
Dual basis property, **14**:12
Dual reporting system in U.S., **19**:39

E

Earned income credit, **13**:3, **13**:15–17, **13**:28
 advance payment, **13**:17
 eligibility requirements, **13**:16
 phaseout percentages and, **13**:16
 qualifying child, **13**:16
 table, **13**:16
 workers without children, **13**:16
Earnings and profits (E & P), **20**:22
 accumulated and current, **5**:29
Easements as capital recovery, **14**:6
Economic concept of income, **4**:3
Economic considerations
 control of the economy, **1**:25
 encouragement of certain activities, **1**:25–26
 encouragement of small business, **1**:26
 tax law, **1**:33
Economic income, **4**:3
Economic loss, **7**:21
Economic performance test, **6**:10, **18**:14
 for deductions, **18**:14–15
 recurring item exception, **18**:15
Economic Stimulus Act of 2008, **8**:7, **13**:26, **13**:27
Education expenses, **9**:13–17, **9**:31–32
 classification of specific items, **9**:14–15
 general requirements, **9**:13–14
 limited deduction approach, **9**:15–16
 maintaining or improving existing skills, **9**:14
 other provisions dealing with education, **9**:16–17
 requirements imposed by law or by the employer for retention of employment, **9**:14
Education tax credits, **13**:24–25, **13**:28

eligible individuals, **13**:24
 income limitations, **13**:24–25
 maximum credit, **13**:24
 restrictions on double tax benefit, **13**:25
Education, travel expenses restrictions on, **9**:9
Educational assistance plans, **5**:18
Educational savings bonds, **5**:30–31
Educator expenses, deductibility of, **9**:24–25
Effective rate (tax planning), **3**:37
E-file, **3**:26–27
Elderly or disabled credit, **13**:2–3, **13**:17–18, **13**:28
 base and threshold amounts for, **13**:18
Election to expense assets. *See* Expensing of assets
Electronic return originator (ERO), **3**:26
Electronic services, **2**:23–26
 CD-ROM services, **2**:24
 Internet, **2**:25–26
 online systems, **2**:24–25
Electronic tax services, **2**:24
Eligible access expenditures, **13**:13
Eligible small business, **13**:13
Employee achievement awards, **4**:31
Employee benefits, tax planning for, **5**:34–35
Employee compensation exclusions, **6**:14–15
Employee death benefits, **5**:6
Employee expenses
 accountable plans, **9**:26–27
 Business Expenses, Form 2106, **9**:27
 classification of, **9**:25–28
 contributions to retirement accounts, **9**:25
 education expenses, **9**:13–17
 educator expenses, **9**:24–25
 entertainment expenses, **9**:17–21
 in general, **9**:4
 limitation on itemized deductions, **9**:28–29
 miscellaneous, **9**:23–25
 moving expenses, **9**:11–13
 nonaccountable plans, **9**:27
 office in the home, **9**:21–23
 other, **9**:21–25
 reporting procedures, **9**:27–28
 seeking employment, **9**:24
 special clothing, **9**:23–24
 transportation expenses, **9**:4–7
 travel expenses, **9**:7–11
Employee fringe benefits, **5**:18–25
 cafeteria plans, **5**:19
 de minimis fringes, **5**:20, **5**:23
 flexible spending plans, **5**:20
 general classes of excluded benefits, **5**:20–24
 no-additional-cost service, **5**:20, **5**:21
 nondiscrimination provisions, **5**:24
 qualified employee discounts, **5**:20, **5**:21–22

Employee fringe benefits (contd.)
   qualified moving expense
      reimbursements, **5:**20, **5:**24
   qualified retirement planning services,
      5:20, **5:**24
   qualified transportation fringes, **5:**20,
      5:23
   specific benefits, **5:**18
   taxable fringe benefits, **5:**24–25
   working condition fringes, **5:**20,
      5:22–23
   See also Accident and health insurance
      benefits
Employee IRAs, **9:**25
Employee or independent contractor
   status, Form SS-8, **9:**4
Employee Plans Compliance Resolution
   System (EPCRS), **19:**8
Employee stock purchase plans, **19:**4
Employees
   common law, **9:**3
   gifts to, **5:**5
   highly compensated, **19:**9
   of educational institutions, housing
      exclusions, **5:**17
   personal services of, **4:**14
   statutory, **9:**4
   vs. self-employed, **9:**2–4
   Withholding Allowance Certificate,
      Form W-4, **13:**33
Employer
   accident and health plans sponsored
      by, **5:**13–15
   Annual Federal Unemployment
      (FUTA) Tax Return, Form 940 or
      940 EZ, **13:**37–38
   Quarterly Federal Tax Return, Form
      941, **13:**37–38
Employer-employee relationship, **9:**3
Employment taxes, **1:**15–17, **13:**26
   amount of FICA taxes, **13:**30–33
   amount of income tax withholding,
      13:33–38
   backup withholding, **13:**38
   coverage requirements, **13:**30
   reporting and payment procedures,
      13:37–38
Employment-related expenses, child and
   dependent care expenses, **13:**22
En banc, **2:**32
Energy Advancement and Investment Act
   of 2007, **8:**27
Energy research credit, **13:**12
Energy Tax Incentives Act of 2005, **2:**3,
   13:4
Entertainment expenses, **9:**17–21,
   9:32–33
   associated with business test for, **9:**19,
      9:32
   classification of, **9:**19
   cutback adjustment, **9:**18–19
   restrictions upon deductibility, **9:**19–21
Entertainment expenses restrictions
   business gifts, **9:**21
   business meals, **9:**19–20

club dues, **9:**20–21
   ticket purchases for entertainment,
      9:21
Entity classification
   after 1996, **20:**4
   Election, Form 8823, **20:**4
   prior to 1997, **20:**3–4
Equity considerations
   alleviating the effect of multiple
      taxation, **1:**28
   coping with inflation, **1:**29–30
   mitigating effect of the annual
      accounting period concept, **1:**29
   tax law, **1:**33
   the wherewithal to pay concept,
      1:28–29
Estate tax, **1:**11
Estates
   beneficiaries of, **4:**18
   income from, **4:**17–18
Estimated tax, **13:**38
   Form 1040-ES, **3:**22
Ethical guidelines, American Institute of
   CPAs, **1:**23
Excess contributions to IRAs, penalty
   taxes for, **19:**26
Excess cost recovery, **8:**18
Excess severance pay, **19:**32
Excessive executive compensation,
   6:14–15, **6:**29–31
Exchange period, like kind exchanges,
   15:6
Excise taxes, **1:**3, **1:**8
   federal, **1:**8–9
   state and local, **1:**9
Exclusions from income, **3:**3, **3:**4
Exemption amount, individual AMT, **12:**7
Exemptions
   corporate AMT, **12:**29
   dependency, **3:**9, **3:**11–20
   marital status, **3:**11
   personal, **3:**9, **3:**10–11
Expatriate employees, qualified plan,
   19:12
Expenditures
   incurred for taxpayer's benefit or
      taxpayer's obligation, disallowance
      possibilities, **6:**22–24
   nondeductible, **3:**7
Expenses
   and interest relating to tax-exempt
      income, judicial interpretations,
      6:28–29
   Business Use of Your Home, Form
      8829, **9:**23
   classification of, **6:**30
   classification of deductible, **6:**2–8
   general classification of, **10:**2
   in the production of income, **6:**5–7
   nonbusiness, **3:**6
Expensing of assets, **8:**13–15
   annual limitations, **8:**14
   conversion to personal use, **8:**15
   effect on basis, **8:**14–15
Extraordinary personal services, **11:**17

F

Facts and circumstances test, **11:**15
Failure to file and failure to pay penalties,
   1:22
Fair market value, **14:**3
Fair tax, **1:**18
Family tax planning, **13:**43
Farm price method, **18:**36
Farm property under MACRS, **8:**11–12
Farmer's exemption, determining
   inventory cost, **18:**32
Farmers, special rules for small, **18:**12
Farming and ranching, special inventory
   methods relating to, **18:**36
Federal budget receipts—2008, **1:**4
Federal Claims Reporter (Fed.Cl.), **2:**19
Federal Courts of Appeals, **2:**15
   See also Courts
Federal customs duties, **1:**17
Federal District Court, **2:**12
   See also Courts
Federal Emergency Management Agency
   (FEMA), **5:**4
Federal estate tax, **1:**11
   on income in respect of a decedent,
      10:28
Federal excise taxes, **1:**8–9
Federal gift taxes, **1:**12–13
Federal income taxes, **1:**13–14
Federal Income, Gift and Estate Taxation,
   2:23
Federal Insurance Contribution Act, see
   FICA
Federal judicial system, **2:**12
   trial courts, **2:**14
Federal Register, **2:**8
Federal Second Series (F.2d), **2:**19
Federal Supplement Second Series
   (F.Supp.2d), **2:**19
Federal Supplement Series (F.Supp.), **2:**19
Federal Tax Articles, **2:**21
Federal Tax Coordinator 2d, **2:**23
Federal tax law, understanding,
   1:24–34
Federal Third Series (F.3d), **2:**19
Federal Unemployment Tax Act. See
   FUTA
FICA, **1:**16
   rates and base, **13:**32
   taxes, **1:**16, **13:**26
Field audit, **1:**20
Field Service Advice (FSAs), **2:**11
FIFO (first in, first out) method, **18:**33
   applied to carrybacks, carryovers, and
      utilization of tax credits, **13:**7
Fifty percent exclusion for certain small
   business stock, individual AMT
   preferences, **12:**21–22
Fifty percent nondeductible excise tax,
   19:11
Fifty percent organizations, **10:**25
Filing considerations, **3:**25–32
   e-file approach **3:**26–27
   filing levels, **3:**26

Filing considerations (*contd.*)
  filing requirements for individuals, 3:25–28
  filing status, 3:28–32
  mode of payment, 3:28
  requirements for dependents, 3:25–26
  selecting the proper form, 3:26
  when and where to file, 3:27–28
Filing status
  abandoned spouse rules, 3:31–32
  rates for heads of household, 3:30–31
  rates for married individuals, 3:29–30
  rates for single taxpayers, 3:29
Finalized Regulations, 2:8
Financial Accounting Standards Board (FASB), 19:43
Fines and penalties
  paid to a government for violation of law, 6:11
  Section 162 exclusion, 6:5
Fiscal year, 4:7, 18:3
  election, personal service corporations, 18:6
Fixed, determination, annual, or periodic (FDAP) income, 20:37
Fixture, 1:6
Flat tax, 1:17–18
Flexible benefit plans, tax planning for, 19:43
Flexible spending plans, 5:20
Foreign convention rules, travel expenses, 9:10
Foreign corporations, taxing the income of, 20:37
Foreign Corrupt Practices Act of 1977, 6:5, 6:11
Foreign earned income, 5:25–28
  exclusion, 5:25
Foreign income taxes, tax credit neutralizes, 4:12
Foreign property yields recognized recapture gain, exchange for, 17:19
Foreign tax credit (FTC), 13:3, 13:18–20 13:29, 13:42
  carryover provision, 13:5
  computation of, 13:19–20
  overall limitations formula, 13:19
  sourcing of income in cyberspace, 13:19
Foreign taxes, deductibility of, 10:13
Foreign travel. *See* Travel expenses
Foreign withholding tax, 13:38
Form 940 or 940 EZ, Employer's Annual Federal Unemployment (FUTA) Tax Return, 13:37–38
Form 941, Employer's Quarterly Federal Tax Return, 13:37–38
Form 970, Application to Use LIFO Inventory Method, 18:35
Form 1040, 1:3, 6:8
  Schedule A, Itemized Deductions, 9:3, 9:27, 10:18, 10:29
  Schedule C, Profit or Loss from Business, 8:28, 8:30, 9:3, 10:18

Schedule D, Capital Gains and Losses, 16:27, 16:28–29, 17:23, 17:28–29
Schedule E, interest expenses related to rents or royalties, 10:18
Form 1040-ES, Estimated Tax for Individuals, 3:22
Form 1065, partnership, 4:17
Form 1099, backup withholding, 13:38
Form 1120 or Form 1120-A, corporate return, 20:15
Form 1120S, S corporation return, 20:15
Form 1128, Application for Change in Accounting Period, 18:7
Form 2106, Employee Business Expenses, 9:3, 9:27
Form 2106-EZ, Unreimbursed Employee Business Expenses, 9:27
Form 2120, Multiple Support Declaration, 3:16
Form 2441, Credit for Child and Dependent Care Expenses, 13:24
Form 2553, S election, 20:27
Form 3115, Application for Change in Accounting Method, 18:16
Form 3903, qualified moving expenses, 9:13
Form 4562, Depreciation and Amortization, 8:28, 8:29
Form 4684, Casualties and Thefts, 15:16, 17:22–23, 7:26
Form 4797, Sales of Business Property, 15:16, 17:22–24, 17:26–27
Form 4868, Application for Automatic Extension of Time to File U.S. Individual Income Tax Return, 3:28
Form 6251, Alternative Minimum Tax—Individuals, 12:3, 12:25
Form 8283, Noncash Charitable Contributions, 6:27, 10:21
Form 8332, Release of Claim to Exemption for Child of Divorced or Separated Parents, 3:17
Form 8453, U.S. Individual Income Tax Declaration for an IRS *e-file* Return, 3:27
Form 8453–OL, 3:27
Form 8615, 3:23
Form 8814, Parents' Election to Report Child's Interest and Dividends, 3:24
Form 8823, Entity Classification Election, 20:4
Form 8824, Like-Kind Exchanges, 15:4, 15:11
Form 8829, Expenses for Business Use of Your Home, 9:23
Form 8903, Domestic Production Activities Deduction, 7:19, 20:28, 20:34
Form 8917, Tuition and Fees Deduction, 9:16
Form SS-4, Application for Employer Identification Number, 13:37–38
Form SS-8, Determination of Worker Status for Purposes of Federal

Employment Taxes and Income Tax Withholding, 9:4
Form W-2, Wage and Tax Statement, 3:22, 9:27, 13:37–38
Form W-3, Transmittal of Wage and Tax Statements, 13:37–38
Form W-4, Employee's Withholding Allowance Certificate, 13:33
Form W-5, certificate of eligibility for advance payments of the earned income credit, 13:17
Forms of doing business. *See* Business entities
Foundations, private operating and private nonoperating 10:23–24
401(k) plans, 19:4
Franchise tax, 1:3, 1:17
Franchises, 8:22, 16:12–13, 16:14
  contingent payments, 16:13
  noncontingent payments, 16:13
  significant power, right, or continuing interest, 16:12–13
  sports franchises, 16:13
Fraud, 1:22
Fraudulent returns, 1:21
Fringe benefits. *See* Employee fringe benefits
Fruit and tree metaphor, 4:14
Full recapture, 17:12
Functional use test, replacement property, 15:13
Funded NQDC plan, 19:30
FUTA, 1:16
  taxes, 1:16, 13:26

G

GAAP. *See* Generally accepted accounting principles
Gain
  determination of, 14:3–8
  from sale of depreciable property between certain related parties, 17:21
  in involuntary conversion of personal residence, 15:16
  individual AMT adjustments, 12:13–14
  nonrecognition of, 14:6–7, 15:14–15
  rationale for separate reporting of capital loss and, 16:2–3
  realized, 14:3–6, 14:12
  recognition of by partnerships, 20:32
  recognized, 14:6
  recovery of capital doctrine, 14:7–8
  Section 1231, 17:3
  transfers to controlled corporations basis considerations and computation of, 20:20–21
Gain basis, 14:12
  for converted property, 14:19
  rules, holding period for property acquired by gift, 14:13
Gains from property transactions
  capital gains, taxation of net capital gain, 3:33–34
  in general, 3:32

Gambling losses
  AMT allowable deductions for, **12**:16
  miscellaneous deductions, **10**:28
General business asset class, **15**:5
General business credit, **13**:5–6, **13**:29
  treatment of unused, **13**:6–7
General Counsel Memoranda (GCMs), **2**:11
General partner, material participation, **11**:16
General sales taxes, **1**:9–10
Generally accepted accounting principles (GAAP), **18**:30
Gift basis, **14**:11–14
  adjustment for gift tax, **14**:12–13
  basis for depreciation, **14**:14
  gifts made before 1977, **14**:13
  holding period, **14**:13
  rules if no gift tax is paid, **14**:12
Gift loans, **4**:25–26
Gift or loan, related parties, **7**:5–6
Gift splitting, **1**:12
Gift tax, **1**:12–13
  federal, **1**:12–13
  state, **1**:13
Gifts, **5**:4–6
  criteria for, **10**:19–20
  deathbed, **14**:15
  disposition of passive activity by, **11**:23
  recapture potential of, **17**:19
  Section 162 exclusion, **6**:5
  tax planning for selection of property, **14**:24–25
  to employees, **5**:5
Global approach to taxation, **3**:30
Global remuneration approach, **19**:16
Global system approach to taxation, **3**:5
Going-concern value, **8**:22
Golden parachute payments, **19**:32
Golsen rule, **2**:16
Goods, deferral of advance payments, **4**:13
Goodwill, **6**:32, **8**:22, **9**:19, **9**:32, **14**:9
Government Accountability Office, **2**:4, **2**:36
Gross estate, **1**:11
Gross income, **3**:3–5, **4**:2–7
  comparison of the accounting and tax concepts of, **4**:5
  economic and accounting concepts, **4**:3–5
  exclusions from, **3**:4
  form of receipt, **4**:6
  items specifically excluded from, **5**:2–4, **5**:6–9
  items specifically included in, **4**:20–34
  leased automobile inclusion amount, **8**:19
  recovery of capital doctrine, **4**:6–7
  year of inclusion, **4**:7–14
  See also Income
Gross income exclusions
  compensation for injuries and sickness, **5**:11–13
  dividends, **5**:29

educational savings bonds, **5**:30–31
employee death benefits, **5**:6
employer-sponsored accident and health plans, **5**:13–15
foreign earned income, **5**:25–28
gifts and inheritances, **5**:4–6
gifts to employees, **5**:5
income from discharge of indebtedness, **5**:33–34
interest on certain state and local government obligations, **5**:28–30
meals and lodging, **5**:15–17
other employee fringe benefits, **5**:18–25
qualified tuition programs, **5**:31–32
scholarships, **5**:9–10
Section 529 plans, **5**:31–32
statutory authority, **5**:4
tax benefit rule, **5**:32
Gross income test, qualifying relative, **3**:14–15
Gross receipts test, **12**:26
Group term life insurance, **4**:31–32
  Section 79 limited exclusion, **4**:31–32
  uniform premiums for $1,000 of protection, **4**:32
Growth stock vs. income stock, **14**:21
Guaranteed payments, **20**:36

H

H.R. 10 (Keogh) plans, **19**:19
Half-year convention, **8**:7
Handicapped individual, capital expenditures for medical purposes, **10**:5–6
Handicapped person, impairment-related work expenses, **10**:28
Hazard of litigation, **1**:20
Head-of-household, **3**:31
  rates for **3**:30–31
Health insurance benefits
  employer-sponsored, **5**:13–15
  purchased by the taxpayer, **5**:13
  when jobs leave the country, **5**:14
Health Savings Account (HSA), **3**:6, **5**:14, **10**:9–11
  deductible amount, **10**:10–11
  high-deductible plans, **10**:9–10
  tax treatment of HSA contributions and distributions, **10**:10
Highly compensated employee, **19**:9
Hobby losses, **6**:16–19, **6**:31
  determining the amount of the deduction, **6**:17–19
  general rules, **6**:16–17
  presumptive rule of Section 183, **6**:17
Holding, **2**:12
Holding period, **14**:13, **16**:14–19
  certain disallowed loss transactions, **16**:16
  certain nontaxable transactions involving a carryover of another taxpayer's basis, **16**:15–16

for capital gain and loss netting purposes, **16**:20–22
for nontaxable stock dividends, **14**:10
inherited property, **16**:16
nontaxable exchanges, **16**:15
of nontaxable stock rights, **14**:11
of the buyer of related taxpayers, **14**:17
short sales, **16**:16–19
special rules, **16**:15–16
Holding period of property, **16**:3
  acquired by gift, **14**:13
  acquired from a decedent, **14**:16
  received in like-kind exchanges, **15**:8–11
Home equity loans, **10**:15
Home for the aged, deductible medical expenses, **10**:3
Home mortgage interest, **10**:14
Home office expense, **9**:21–23
  tax planning for sale of personal residence, **15**:26
Home sourcing, substantial cost-savings, **9**:24
HOPE scholarship credit, **9**:16, **9**:17, **13**:24, **13**:28, **19**:24
Hospital insurance, **1**:16
House of Representatives, **2**:3–5
House Ways and Means Committee, **2**:3–5
Housekeeping-type instructions, **2**:31
Housing costs, foreign earned income, **5**:27
Housing exclusions, other, **5**:17–18
Housing interest, individual AMT adjustments, **12**:18
Hybrid method, **4**:7, **4**:10, **18**:16

I

Identification period, like kind exchanges, **15**:6
Illegal business, deduction of expenses relating to, **6**:12–13
Imputed interest, **4**:24, **18**:21–22
  exceptions and limitations, **4**:25–27
  rules for below-market loans, exceptions to, **4**:27
  tax avoidance and other below-market loans, **4**:25
Incentive stock options (ISO), **12**:12, **19**:4, **19**:36–38
  and nonqualified stock options compared, **19**:42
  individual AMT adjustments, **12**:12–13
  qualification requirements for, **19**:37–38
Income, **3**:3, **4**:3
  active, **11**:5
  all events test for, **18**:13–14
  alternative minimum taxable (AMTI), **12**:2–26
  assignment of, **4**:13, **4**:18
  comparison of the accounting and tax concepts of gross, **4**:5
  economic and accounting concepts of gross, **4**:3–5

Income (*contd.*)
exclusions from, **3**:3, **3**:4
expenses and interest relating to tax-exempt, **6**:28–29
form of receipt of gross, **4**:6
gross, **4**:2–7
investment, **11**:24
least aggregate deferral method of, **18**:4
measuring and reporting partnership, **20**:34
net investment, **11**:25
nonbusiness, **7**:22
of certain children, tax planning for, **3**:38
of foreign corporations, taxing, **20**:37
passive, **11**:5
portfolio, **11**:5
prepaid, **4**:13, **4**:36
reconciliation of corporate taxable and accounting, **20**:15–17
recovery of capital doctrine of gross, **4**:6–7
unearned of certain children, **3**:23
See also Gross income
Income from discharge of indebtedness, **5**:33–34
Income in respect of a decedent
AMT allowable deductions for estate tax on, **12**:16
Federal estate tax on, **10**:28
Income layers for alternative tax on capital gain computation, **16**:25
Income shifting, changes in tax rates lead to, **18**:14
Income sources, **4**:14–20
income from partnerships, S corporations, trusts, and estates, **4**:17–18
income from property, **4**:15–17
income in community property states, **4**:18–20
income received by an agent, **4**:17
personal services, **4**:14
Income stock vs. growth stock, **14**:21
Income Tax Act of 1913, **5**:4
Income tax consequences, summary of, **20**:18–19
Income tax considerations, **20**:4–17
Income tax rates, corporate, **20**:14
Income tax return as a "use tax" reminder, **1**:15
Income taxes, **1**:3, **1**:13–15
deductibility of state and local, **10**:13–14
federal, **1**:13–14
formula for individuals, **1**:14
history of, **1**:2–4
local, **1**:15
state, **1**:14–15
Income-splitting option, **3**:29
Incremental research activities credit, **13**:10–12
Indebtedness, income from discharge of, **5**:33–34

Independent contractor, **9**:2
or employee status, Form SS-8, **9**:4
See also Self-employed individual
Indexation, **1**:30
Individual Retirement Accounts (IRAs), **1**:26, **2**:4, **3**:5, **19**:10, **19**:20–29, **19**:40
and Section 401(k) plan, compared, **19**:40–41
comparison of, **19**:28
contributions deductible for AGI, **9**:25
deduction, phaseout of, **19**:20
penalty taxes for excess contributions, **19**:26
rollovers and conversions, Roth IRA, **19**:29
Roth IRAs, **9**:25, **19**:22–23
SIMPLE IRA, **19**:4, **19**:25
simplified employee pension plans, **19**:24
spousal IRA, **19**:25–26
taxation of benefits, **19**:26–29
timing of contributions, **19**:26
traditional, **9**:25
Individual Tax Identification Number (ITIN), **3**:27
Inflation, **1**:29–30
Inheritance tax, **1**:11
Inherited property
basis of, **14**:14–16
effect of 2001 tax legislation on basis of, **14**:16
holding period, **14**:16, **16**:16
tax consequences, **5**:4–6
Innocent spouse relief, **4**:20
Installment method, **1**:29, **4**:8, **18**:19–24
computing the gain for the period, **18**:20
disposition of obligations, **18**:24
electing out of, **18**:24–25
eligibility and calculations, **18**:19
imputed interest, **18**:21–22
nonelective aspect, **18**:19
recapture potential of, **17**:20–21
related-party sales of depreciable property, **18**:23–24
related-party sales of nondepreciable property, **18**:22
revocation of the election, **18**:25
tax planning, **2**:38, **18**:36–37
Installment obligation, tax planning for the disposition of, **18**:37
Installment sale of a passive activity, **11**:23
Installment sales, interest on, **18**:23
Insurance
benefits purchased by the taxpayer, accident and health, **5**:13
claim, timeliness of, **7**:11
group term life, **4**:31–32
medical premiums of the self-employed, deductibility of, **10**:7
policies, certain exchanges of (Section 1035), **15**:23
Intangible assets, **8**:3
amortization of, **8**:22
expenditures for, **6**:25

Intangible drilling and development costs (IDC), **8**:24, **17**:21–22
effect on depletion, **8**:27–28
individual AMT preferences, **12**:20
Intent of Congress, **2**:4
Inter vivos gifts, **5**:5
Interest, **10**:14–18
allowed and disallowed items, **10**:14–17
AMT allowable deductions for qualified, **12**:16
classification of interest expense, **10**:18
consumer, **10**:14
deductibility of personal, student loan, investment, and mortgage, **10**:18
home mortgage, **10**:14
imputed, **4**:24, **18**:21–22
income from, **4**:15
individual AMT adjustments, **12**:17
investment, **10**:14, **10**:15, **11**:24–26
mortgage insurance payment, **10**:16
prepaid, **10**:17–18
prepayment penalty, **10**:17
qualified residence, **10**:14, **10**:15–16
restrictions on deductibility and timing considerations, **10**:17–18
tax-exempt securities, **10**:17
taxpayer's obligation, **10**:17
termination of running of, **2**:14
time of deduction, **10**:17
Interest deduction, tax planning for, **10**:33–34
Interest on
certain state and local government obligations, (gross income exclusions), **5**:28–30
deferred taxes, **18**:24
installment sales, **18**:23
private activity bonds, individual AMT preferences, **12**:20–21
qualified education loans, **10**:14–15
Interest paid
for services, **10**:16
to related parties, **10**:17
Interest rates, on taxes and tax refunds, **1**:22–23
Internal Revenue Bulletin (I.R.B.), **2**:8, **2**:9, **2**:10, **2**:18, **7**:27
Internal Revenue Code, **8**:2
arrangement of, **2**:6
citing of, **2**:6–7
interpretation pitfalls, **2**:31
interpreting, **2**:30
of 1939, **1**:3, **2**:3
of 1954, **1**:3, **2**:3
of 1986, **1**:3, **2**:3, **2**:4, **2**:6
origin of, **2**:2–3
Internal Revenue Service, **1**:19
Appeals Division, **1**:20
assessment by, **1**:21
Digital Daily, **2**:25, **2**:26
influence of tax law, **1**:33
influence of, **1**:31–32
Letter Rulings Reports, **2**:10
Publication 970, *Tax Benefits for Education*, **10**:14

Internal Revenue Service (*contd.*)
  Restructuring and Reform Act of 1998, **2**:3
  vs. USCIS (U.S. Citizenship and Immigration Services), **3**:27
Internet, **2**:25–26
Interpretive Regulations, **2**:31
Inventories, **18**:29–36, **18**:37
  acquired from a foreign subsidiary, **18**:32
  as definition of capital asset, **16**:4
  best accounting practice, **18**:30
  clear reflection of income test, **18**:30
  corporate stock, **16**:6
  determining cost—specific identification, FIFO, and LIFO, **18**:33
  determining inventory cost, **18**:30–34
  dollar-value LIFO, **18**:33–34
  farmer's exemption, **18**:32
  inventory shrinkage, **18**:33
  LIFO election, **18**:35–36
  lower of cost or market, **18**:32–33
  uniform capitalization (UNICAP), **18**:30–32
Investigation of a business, expenses incurred in, **6**:15–16
Investment assets, **16**:3
Investment earnings from the reinvestment of life insurance proceeds, **5**:8–9
Investment in the contract, **19**:13
Investment income, **11**:24
  net, **11**:25
  of certain children, **3**:23
  tax planning for, **5**:35–36
Investment interest, **10**:14, **10**:15, **11**:24–26
  individual AMT adjustments, **12**:18–19
Investment losses, other, **11**:26–27
Investments selections, tax planning for, **4**:35
Involuntary conversions, **15**:11–16, **15**:25, **17**:6
  computing the amount realized, **15**:12
  defined, **15**:11
  nonrecognition of gain, **15**:14–15
  of personal residence, gain and loss situations, **15**:16
  recapture potential of, **17**:20
  replacement property, **15**:12–13
  reporting considerations, **15**:16
  time limitation on replacement, **15**:13–14
IRA. *See* Individual retirement account
IRS. *See* Internal Revenue Service
Itemized deductions, **3**:6–7, **6**:4–5, **7**:2
  charitable contributions, **10**:18–27
  cutback adjustment, AMT adjustments, **12**:16
  deductible personal expenses, **6**:5
  housing interest, AMT adjustments, **12**:18
  individual AMT adjustments, **12**:16–19
  interest, **10**:14–18, **12**:17
  investment interest, AMT adjustments, **12**:18–19
  limitation on, **9**:28–29
  medical expenses, **10**:2–11, **12**:16–17
  miscellaneous, **10**:27
  other miscellaneous, **10**:28
  overall limitation on certain itemized, **10**:28–32
  partial list of, **3**:7
  Section 212 expenses, **6**:4
  tax planning for, **10**:32–35
  taxes, **10**:11–14

J

Job Creation and Worker Assistance Act of 2002, **2**:3
Job hunting, miscellaneous employee expenses, **9**:24
Jobs and Growth Tax Relief Reconciliation Act (JGTRRA) of 2003, **2**:3, **3**:21, **3**:29, **4**:15, **14**:21
Jock tax, **1**:15
Joint Committee on Taxation, material participation explained, **11**:12
Joint Conference Committee, **2**:4–5
Joint return test, dependency exemptions **3**:17, **3**:35–36
Judicial citations
  general, **2**:17
  U.S. District Court, Court of Federal Claims, and Court of Appeals, **2**:19–20
  U.S. Supreme Court, **2**:20
  U.S. Tax Court, **2**:17–19
Judicial concepts relating to tax, **1**:32–33
Judicial influence on statutory provisions, **1**:33
Judicial interpretations of expenses and interest relating to tax-exempt income, **6**:28–29
Judicial sources of the tax law, **2**:12–20
  appellate courts, **2**:15–17
  assessing the validity of, **2**:32–33
  judicial citations, **2**:17–19, **2**:19–20
  judicial process in general, **2**:12–13
  trial courts, **2**:13–14
Judicial sources, **2**:21
Jury trial, **2**:14

K

Keogh (H.R. 10), **1**:26
  plan and SEP compared, **19**:25
  plans, **9**:25
Kickbacks, **6**:11
Kiddie tax, **3**:23, **5**:32
  rules, **20**:39

L

Lease cancellation payments, **16**:13–14
  lessee treatment, **16**:13–14
  lessor treatment, **16**:14
Leasehold improvements, **5**:4
  property under MACRS, **8**:12–13
Least aggregate deferral method, **18**:4
Legal expenses incurred in defense of civil or criminal penalties, **6**:12
Legislative process, **2**:3–5
Legislative Regulations, **2**:31
Lessee, **16**:13–14
Lessor, **16**:13, **16**:14
Letter Ruling Review, **2**:10
Letter rulings, **2**:10
Life insurance proceeds, **5**:6–9, **5**:34
  accelerated death benefits, **5**:7
  transfer for valuable consideration, **5**:8–9
Lifetime learning credit, **9**:16, **9**:17, **13**:24, **13**:28, **19**:24
LIFO (last in, first out), **18**:33, **18**:37
  as a source of earnings, **18**:34
  dollar-value, **18**:33–34
LIFO election, **18**:35–36
  special inventory methods relating to farming and ranching, **18**:36
LIFO index, **18**:34
Like-kind exchanges, **15**:3–11, **15**:24–25
  basis and holding period of property received, **15**:8–11
  boot, **15**:7–8
  exchange period, **15**:6
  exchange requirement, **15**:6–7
  Form 8824, **15**:11
  identification period, **15**:6
  like-kind property, **15**:3–6
  recapture potential of (Section 1031), **17**:20
  reporting considerations, **15**:11
Limited liability company, **20**:3
Limited partners, material participation, **11**:16
Liquidating distributions, **20**:24
Liquidating retirement assets, **19**:43
Liquidations, **20**:24–26
  basis determination—Sections 334 and 338, **20**:25–26
  effect of on the corporation, **20**:26
  exception to the general rule, **20**:25
  general rule of Section 331, **20**:24–25
Listed property, **8**:15
  business and personal use of, **8**:15–19
  change from predominantly business use, **8**:18–19
  cost recovery, **8**:21
  not used predominantly in business, **8**:17–18
  substantiation requirements, **8**:19
  used predominantly in business, **8**:15
Livestock, as Section 1231 asset, **17**:6
Loans
  below-market, **4**:25
  between related parties, **7**:5–6
  compensation-related, **4**:25, **4**:27
  corporation-shareholder, **4**:25, **4**:27
  gift, **4**:25–26
  tax avoidance, **4**:25
  to executives prohibited, **4**:26

Lobbying expenditures, **6**:13–14
Lodging exclusion, **5**:15–17
Lodging for medical treatment, deductible medical expenses, **10**:6–7
Long-term capital gain, **17**:3–4
    alternative tax computation, **3**:33
    summary of income tax consequences, **20**:29
Long-term care insurance, **5**:15
Long-term contracts, **18**:25–29
    completed contract method, **18**:27–28
    lookback provisions, **18**:29
    percentage of completion method, **18**:28–29
Long-term family assistance recipient, **13**:10
Long-term nonpersonal use capital assets, **17**:6
Lookback provision
    long-term contracts, **18**:29
    Section 1231, **17**:9–11
Loss basis, **14**:12
    rules, holding period for property acquired by gift, **14**:13
Loss on personal use assets, original basis for, **14**:19
Loss(es)
    amount of, **7**:10–11
    business and nonbusiness, **6**:7
    carryovers of suspended, **11**:7
    determination of, **14**:3–8
    disallowed, **14**:16–18, **14**:25–26
    impact of suspended, **11**:6–7
    in involuntary conversion of personal residence, **15**:16
    in related party transactions, **6**:26
    individual AMT adjustments, **12**:13–14
    limitation on partner's share of, **20**:35
    nonrecognition of, **14**:6–7
    sale, exchange, or condemnation of personal use assets, nonrecognition of, **14**:7
    ordinary, **7**:7
    other investment, **11**:26–27
    rationale for separate reporting of capital gains and, **16**:2–3
    realized, **14**:12, **14**:3–6
    recognition of by partnerships, **20**:32
    recognized, **14**:6
    recovery of capital doctrine, **14**:7–8
    S corporation treatment of, **20**:30
    Section 1231, **17**:3
    timing for recognition of, **7**:9
    timing of expense recognition, **6**:8–10
    See also Capital losses; Net capital loss; Realized loss; Recognized loss
Losses from property transactions
    capital losses, definition of a capital asset, **3**:33
    capital losses, treatment of net capital loss, **3**:34
    in general, **3**:32
Losses of individuals, **7**:7–14
    events that are not casualties, **7**:8–9
    measuring the amount of loss, **7**:10–12

personal casualty gains and losses, **7**:13–14
    statutory framework for deducting, **7**:13
    theft losses, **7**:9
    when to deduct casualty losses, **7**:9–10
Lower of cost or market (replacement cost), **18**:32, **18**:37
Low-income housing credit, **13**:13, **13**:29
Lump-sum distribution, **19**:13
Lump-sum purchase, allocation problems with, **14**:9

M

MACRS. *See* Modified accelerated cost recovery system
Majority interest partners, **18**:3
Manufactured, produced, grown, or extracted (MPGE) in the U.S., **7**:18
Manufacturing contract, **18**:25
Marginal tax rate, **3**:21
Marital deduction, **1**:11, **1**:12
Marital status for exemption purposes, **3**:11
Marriage penalty, **3**:29
Married couples, effect of Section 121 residence sales on, **15**:20–21
Married individuals, rates for **3**:29–30
Mass tax, **1**:4
Matching provision, related-party transactions, **6**:26
Material participation, **11**:12–16
    in a real property trade or business, **11**:19–20
    in real estate rental activities, **11**:20
    limited partners, **11**:16
    participation defined, **11**:15–16
    test based on facts and circumstances, **11**:15
    tests based on current participation, **11**:13–14
    tests based on prior participation, **11**:14–15
Meals and lodging, **5**:15–17
    for medical treatment, deductible medical expenses, **10**:6–7
    for the convenience of the employer, **5**:16–17
    furnished by the employer, **5**:16
    furnished for the convenience of the employer, **5**:15–17
    on the employer's business premises, **5**:16
    other housing exclusions, **5**:17–18
    required as a condition of employment, **5**:17
Medical care, defined, **10**:3–4
Medical expense deduction, tax planning for dependency exemptions, **3**:36–37
Medical expenses, **10**:2–11, **10**:32–33
    capital expenditures for medical purposes, **10**:5–6
    defined, **10**:3–4

examples of deductible and nondeductible, **10**:4
    for a dependent, **6**:23
    health savings accounts, **10**:9–11
    in excess of 10 percent of AGI, AMT allowable deductions for, **12**:16
    incurred for spouse and dependents, **10**:6
    individual AMT adjustments, **12**:16–17
    medical insurance premiums deductible as, **10**:7
    reimbursements, **10**:8–9
    transportation, meal, and lodging expenses for medical treatment, **10**:6–7
    year of deduction, **10**:8
Medical reimbursement plans, **5**:14
Medicare tax (hospital insurance), **1**:16, **13**:30
Memorandum decisions, **2**:17, **2**:32
Mertens Law of Federal Income Taxation, **2**:23
Mid-month convention, **8**:10
Mid-quarter convention, **8**:9–10
Military Family Tax Relief Act of 2003, **3**:28, **9**:30, **15**:18
Military personnel, housing exclusions, **5**:18
Millionaires provision, **6**:14
Minimum distribution rules, **19**:10
Minimum funding requirements, **19**:12
Minimum participation test for qualified plans, **19**:9
Mining exploration and development costs, **12**:12
Ministers of the gospel, housing exclusions, **5**:17–18
Miscellaneous itemized deductions, **10**:27
Mixed service costs, **18**:26, **18**:27
Modified accelerated cost recovery system (MACRS), **8**:2–3, **8**:4–19, **8**:31–32
    alternative depreciation system (ADS), **8**:20–22
    business and personal use of automobiles and other listed property, **8**:15–19
    election to expense assets, **8**:13–15
    farm property, **8**:11–12
    individual and corporate AMT adjustments, **12**:27
    leasehold improvement property, **8**:12–13
    personalty: cost recovery periods and methods, **8**:5–8
    property, **12**:9, **12**:10–11
    realty: recovery periods and methods, **8**:10–11
    relevant time periods, **8**:3
    statutory percentage method under, **8**:10
    straight-line election under, **8**:11, **8**:14
    tables, **8**:34–36
    See also Accelerated cost recovery system (ACRS)

Modified adjusted gross income (MAGI), 4:33–34, 5:31, 7:17, 10:14
Money purchase plan, 19:5
Moving expense deduction, expatriates and, 9:13
Moving expenses, 9:11–13, 9:31
    distance test for, 9:11
    time test, 9:11–12
    treatment of, 9:12–13
Multiple assets in a lump-sum purchase, allocation of cost among, 14:9
Multiple support agreement, 3:15–16
    Form 2120, 3:16
    tax planning for dependency exemptions, 3:37
Municipal bonds, tax free, 12:21

N

National Association of Realtor's annual survey for 2006, 6:19
National sales tax, 1:18
Natural business year, 18:7
Natural resources, 8:3, 8:24
Negligence penalty, 1:22
Net capital gain (NCG), 16:20
    alternative tax on, 16:23–24
    determination of, 3:34
    taxation of, 3:33–34
Net capital loss (NCL), 16:2, 16:24
    computation of, 16:24–25
    treatment of, 3:34, 16:24–26
Net earnings from self-employment, 13:42
Net gain, 17:3–4
Net income tax, 13:6
Net investment income, 11:25
Net long-term capital gain (NLTCG), 3:34, 16:2, 16:19, 16:20
Net long-term capital loss (NLTCL), 16:19
Net loss, 17:3–4
Net nonbusiness capital gains, 7:21–22
Net operating losses (NOL), 7:17, 7:19–25, 7:27
    calculation of the remaining NOL, 7:24–25
    carryback and carryover periods, 7:20–21
    computation of, 7:21–23, 7:25
    corporate and individual treatment compared, 20:10–11
    new incentives, 7:21
    recomputation of tax liability for year to which NOL is carried, 7:23–24
    summary of income tax consequences, 20:18
Net regular tax liability, 13:6
Net Section 1231 gain limitation, 17:18
Net short-term capital gain (NSTCG), 16:19, 16:20
Net short-term capital loss (NSTCL), 3:34, 16:19
Net unearned income of a dependent child, 3:23

Netting process, capital gain and loss, 16:20–22
    capital loss carryovers, 16:22
    definition of collectibles, 16:22
    holding periods, 16:20–22
    qualified dividend income, 16:23
New York Stock Exchange (NYSE), private entity becomes a public corporation, 16:3
No-additional-cost service, 5:20, 5:21, 5:26
Nonaccountable plans, 9:27
    failure to comply with accountable plan requirements, 9:27
    unreimbursed employee expenses, 9:27
Nonacquiescence ("NA" or "Nonacq."), 2:18
Nonbusiness bad debt, 7:2, 7:4–5, 16:8
Nonbusiness deductions, 7:22
Nonbusiness expenses, 3:6
Nonbusiness income, 7:22
Nonbusiness losses, 6:7
Noncontingent payments, 16:13
Noncorporate taxpayers, tax treatment of capital gains and losses of, 16:19–30
Noncustodial parent, deductibility of medical expenses, 10:6–7
Nondeductible contributions and IRAs, 19:20
Nondeductible items, charitable contributions, 10:20
Nondiscrimination provisions, employee fringe benefits, 5:24
Nondiscrimination requirements, qualified plans, 19:8
Nonoperating private foundations, 10:24
Nonqualified deferred compensation (NQDC) plans, 19:4, 19:29–33, 19:41–42
    golden parachute arrangements, 19:32
    publicly held companies' compensation limitation, 19:32–33
    tax treatment to the employer and employee, 19:30–33
    underlying rationale for tax treatment, 19:29–30
    when to use NQDC arrangement, 19:31–32
Nonqualified stock options (NQSO), 19:38–39, 19:32
    advantages of, 19:39
    and incentive stock options compared, 19:42
    disadvantage of, 19:39
Nonrecaptured net Section 1231 losses, 17:9
Nonrecognition of gain
    conversion into money, 15:15
    direct conversion, 15:14–15
Nonrecourse financing, qualified, 11:4
Nonrefundable credits, 13:5
    carryover provision, 13:5
Nonresidential real property, computing Section 1250 recapture on, 17:15–16
Nontaxable economic benefits, tax planning for, 4:34

Nontaxable exchanges, 15:2–3
    certain exchanges of insurance policies—Section 1035, 15:23
    certain reacquisitions of real property—Section 1038, 15:23
    exchange of stock for property—Section 1032, 15:23
    exchange of stock for stock of the same corporation—Section 1036, 15:23
    general concept of, 15:2–3
    holding period rules, 16:15
    involuntary conversions—Section 1033, 15:11–16
    like-kind exchanges—Section 1031, 15:3–11
    of a passive activity, 11:23–24
    other nonrecognition provisions of, 15:23–24
    rollover of gain from qualified small business stock into another qualified small business stock—Section 1045, 15:24
    rollovers into specialized small business investment companies—Section 1044, 15:24
    sale of personal residence, 15:16–22
    transfers of property between spouses or incident to divorce—Section 1041, 15:23
Nontaxable stock dividends, 14:10
    holding period for, 14:10
Nontaxable stock rights, 14:10
    holding period of, 14:11
Nontaxable transactions, recapture exceptions, 17:20
Normal cost, 19:14
North American Free Trade Agreement of 1993, 5:14
Nursing home care, deductible medical expenses, 10:3

O

Obligation to repay, amounts received under, 4:12–13
Obligations
    disposition of installment, 18:24, 18:37
    retirement of corporate (special rule), 16:9
Occupational taxes, 1:17
OECD. See Organization for Economic Cooperation and Development
Office audit, 1:20
Office in the home expenses, 9:21–23
Offset, right of, 14:17
Old age, survivors, and disability insurance, 1:16
$100 per event floor and a 10 percent-of-AGI aggregate floor, reduction for, 7:11
One-year rule for prepaid expenses, 6:9, 18:11
Online systems, 2:24–25
Online tax services, 2:25

Operational rules, domestic production activities deduction, 7:17–19
Options, 16:9–11
  exercise of by grantee, 16:10–11
  failure to exercise, 16:10
  sale of, 16:10
Ordering procedure, 16:20
Ordinary and necessary, 6:5–6
Ordinary asset, 16:3
Ordinary income property, 10:22–23
Ordinary loss, 7:7, 17:3–4
Organization for Economic Cooperation and Development (OECD), 1:18, 6:13
  Convention on Combating the Bribery of Foreign Public Officials in International Business, 6:13
Organizational expenditures, 20:13–14
Original issue discount (OID), 4:11, 16:9
Outsourcing of tax return preparation, 1:25

P

Participation and coverage requirements, qualified plan, 19:8–9
Partners and Partnerships, Subchapter K, 2:6
Partnership
Partnerships, 4:17, 20:4, 20:31–36
  accounting period for, 18:3–5
  basis of partnership interest, 20:32–33
  Form 1065, 20:31
  formation of, 20:32–33
  income from, 4:17–18
  limitation on partner's share of losses, 20:35
  measuring and reporting partnership income, 20:34
  nature of taxation, 20:31
  operation, 20:34–36
  other partner considerations, 20:36
  partnership's basis in contributed property, 20:33
  recognition of gain or loss, 20:32
  transactions between partner and partnership, 20:35–36
Passenger automobiles, 8:16
Passive activities, 11:3
Passive activity loss rules
  general concepts, 11:24
  individual AMT adjustments, 12:14–15
Passive activity losses (PALs), 11:27
  individual AMT adjustments, 12:14–15
  summary of income tax consequences, 20:29
Passive income and losses
  carryovers of suspended losses, 11:7
  classification of, 11:5–8
  general impact, 11:6
  impact of suspended losses, 11:6–7
  passive activity changes to active, 11:8
  passive credits, 11:7–8
Passive income generators (PIGs), 11:27
Passive income under Section 469, 11:5

Passive interests, dispositions of, 11:22–24
Passive investments, 11:3
Passive loss, 11:3, 11:27–28
Passive loss rules limits, 11:5–24
  classification and impact of passive income and losses, 11:5–8
  closely held C corporations, 11:9–10
  dispositions of passive interests, 11:22–24
  identification of an activity, 11:10–12
  interaction of the at-risk and passive activity limits, 11:18–19
  material participation, 11:12–16, 11:19–20
  passive activities defined, 11:10–18
  personal service corporations, 11:9
  real estate rental activities, 11:20–21
  regrouping of activities, 11:11
  rental activities defined, 11:16–18
  special grouping rules for rental activities, 11:11–12
  special passive activity rules for real estate activities, 11:19–21
  taxpayers subject to, 11:8–10
Past service costs, 19:14
Patent, 8:22, 16:11–12
  holder defined, 16:12
  substantial rights, 16:12
  tax shelter strategies now protected by, 11:19
Patent and Trademark Office, 11:19
Pay-as-you-go tax income tax system, 1:4, 13:3
  tax payment procedures, 13:26
Payments received, 18:20
Payroll period, 13:34
Penalties
  for lack of compliance, 1:22, 13:26
  imposed on tax return preparers, 1:24
  on underpayments of self-employed persons, 13:39–40
  Section 162 exclusion, 6:5
Pension plan, 19:4–6, 9:25
  See also Qualified plans
Pension Protection Act of 2006, 2:3, 19:11
Per diem allowance, 9:27
Percentage depletion, 8:26–27
  individual AMT preferences, 12:20
  rates, sample of, 8:26
Percentage of completion method, 4:8, 18:26, 18:28–29
Permanent and total disability, 13:17
Personal casualty gain, 7:13
Personal casualty loss, 7:13
Personal exemptions, 3:9, 3:10–11
Personal expenditures
  deduction of, 10:2
  disallowance of, 6:24
Personal expenses, deductions of, 6:5
Personal identification number (Self-Select PIN), 3:27
Personal injury, damages for, 5:11–12
Personal residence, 15:16
  involuntary conversion of, 15:15–16

Personal residence, sale of, 15:16–22, 15:25–27
  basis of new residence, 15:22
  calculation of amount of exclusion, 15:19–22
  change in place of employment, 15:17–18
  effect on married couples, 15:20–21
  exceptions to the two-year ownership rule, 15:17–19
  health considerations, 15:18
  involuntary conversion and using Sections 121 and 1033, 15:22
  principal residence, 15:22
  relief provision, 15:21
  requirements for exclusion treatment, 15:16–17
  unforeseen circumstances, 15:18–19
Personal service corporations (PSC), 11:9, 18:6, 20:14
  calendar year, 18:6
  fiscal year election, 18:6
Personal services, 4:14
  of a child, 4:14
  of an employee, 4:14
Personal use assets, 8:3, 16:3
  converted to business or income-producing use, cost recovery basis for, 8:4
  original basis for loss on, 14:19
  sale, exchange, or condemnation of, 14:7
Personal use property, 8:3
  casualty gains and losses, 17:6
  condemnation gains and losses, 17:7
  conversion to business or income-producing use, 14:19–20
Personalty, 1:8, 8:3
  ad valorem taxes on 1:8
  cost recovery periods: MACRS, 8:6
  tangible, 10:24
  recovery periods and methods, 8:5–8, 8:9–10
Petitioner, 2:17
Phaseout of IRA deduction, 19:20
Piggyback approach to state income taxation, 1:14
Plaintiff, 2:17
Points, 10:16
Political considerations
  political expediency situations, 1:30
  special interest legislation, 1:30
  state and local government influences, 1:30–31
  tax law, 1:33
Political contributions, 6:13
Pollution control facilities, individual AMT adjustments, 12:11
Pool, 18:34
Portfolio income, 11:5
Precedents, 2:16
Prepaid expenses, one-year rule for, 6:9
Prepaid income, 4:13, 4:36
Prepaid interest, 10:17–18
Prepayment penalty, 10:17

Primary valuation amount, **14**:14
Principal partner, **18**:3
Principal place of business, defined, **9**:22
Principal residence, **10**:15, **15**:22
Principal-agent, **4**:18
Prior participation tests, **11**:14–15
Private activity bonds, **12**:20–21
Private entity becomes a public
    corporation, **16**:3
Private Letter Rulings, **2**:10
Private nonoperating foundations, **10**:24
Private operating foundations, **10**:23
Prizes and awards, income from, **4**:31
Procedural Regulations, **2**:31
Product class, **15**:5
Production activities, **7**:17
Production of income expenses, **6**:5–7
Profit sharing, **19**:4–19
Profit sharing plan, **19**:4, **19**:6–7
    limitations, **19**:15
    See also Qualified plans
Progressive (graduated) rate structure,
    3:21
Progressive taxes, **1**:5
Property
    adjusted basis of, **14**:4
    amount realized from a sale or other
        disposition of, **14**:3–4
    bargain purchase of, **14**:8
    boot given as appreciated or
        depreciated, **15**:8
    business and personal use of listed,
        8:15–19
    capital gain, **10**:23–25
    cost recovery of listed, **8**:21
    disposed by sale, exchange, casualty,
        theft, or condemnation, **16**:3
    dual basis, **14**:12
    eminent domain, **15**:12
    exchange for foreign yields recognized
        recapture gain, **17**:19
    exchange of stock for (Section 1032),
        15:23
    excluded under Section 1231, **17**:5
    expensing of tangible personal, **8**:13
    fair market value of, **14**:3
    gain basis for converted, **14**:19
    holding periods of, **16**:3, **16**:16
    included under Section 1231, **17**:4
    income from, **4**:15–17
    individual AMT adjustments for depre-
        ciation of post-1986 personal,
        12:10–11
    individual AMT adjustments for
        depreciation of post-1986 real,
        12:9–10
    involuntary conversion of, **15**:11–16
    like-kind, **15**:3–6
    lodging rented for the convenience of
        an employer, **11**:18
    MACRS classification of, **8**:5–7
    ordinary income, **10**:22–23
    partnership's basis in contributed,
        20:33
    personal use, **8**:3

qualified for additional first-year
    depreciation, **8**:7
replacement, **15**:12–13
restricted plans, **19**:4
sales of depreciable between
    related-parties, **18**:23–24
sales of nondepreciable between
    related-parties, **18**:22
Section 1245, **17**:13–14
Section 1250, **17**:14
substantially identical, **16**:17
tax status of, **16**:3
transfers of between spouses or
    incident to divorce, **15**:23
used in a trade or business, **11**:17
Property acquired by gift, holding period
    for, **14**:13
Property acquired from a decedent,
    14:14–16
    deathbed gifts, **14**:15
    holding period, **14**:16
    survivor's share of property, **14**:15–16
Property dividends, **20**:22–23
    recapture potential of, **17**:21
Property held primarily for investment,
    11:17
Property put to unrelated use, **10**:24
Property taxes, **1**:6–8, **10**:11–13
    apportionment between seller and
        purchaser, **10**:12–13
    assessments for local benefits, **10**:11–12
Property transactions
    capital gains and losses, **3**:33–34
    gains and losses from, **3**:32
    tax planning for, **14**:22
Proportional taxes, **1**:5
Proposed Regulations, **2**:8
Public Law No. 107-294, **4**:26
Public policy limitation, **6**:11–13
    expenses relating to an illegal business,
        6:12–13
    justification for denying deductions,
        6:11–12
    legal expenses incurred in defense of
        civil or criminal penalties, **6**:12
Publication 505, *Tax Withholding and
    Estimated Tax*, **13**:44
Publicly held companies' compensation
    limitation, **19**:32–33
Publicly traded partnerships (PTPs), **11**:9
Punitive damages, **5**:11

Q

Qualified automatic enrollment
    arrangement (QAEA), **19**:17
Qualified charitable organizations, **10**:20
Qualified child care expenses, **13**:15
Qualified disaster, Section 139, **5**:4
Qualified dividend income, **16**:23
Qualified Dividends and Capital Gain
    Tax Worksheet, **16**:27, **16**:30
Qualified domestic organization, **10**:18
Qualified employee discount, **5**:20,
    5:21–22, **5**:26

Qualified higher education expenses,
    5:30
Qualified housing interest, **12**:18
Qualified intermediary (QI), selection of,
    15:7
Qualified moving expense
    reimbursements, **5**:20, **5**:24, **5**:26
Qualified nonrecourse financing, **11**:4
Qualified parking, **5**:23
Qualified pension plans, **19**:4–19
Qualified plans
    distribution requirements, **19**:10–12
    limitations on contributions to and
        benefits from, **19**:13–15
    lump-sum distributions from, **19**:13
    minimum funding requirements, **19**:12
    nondiscrimination requirements, **19**:8
    participation and coverage
        requirements, **19**:8–9
    qualification requirements, **19**:7–12
    rollover treatment, **19**:13
    Section 401(k) plans, **19**:15–19
    tax consequences to the employee and
        employer, **19**:12–13
    tax planning for, **19**:40
    types of plans, **19**:4–7
    vesting requirements, **19**:9–10
Qualified production activities income
    (QPAI), **7**:17, **7**:18, **20**:10
Qualified production property (QPP),
    7:18
Qualified profit sharing plans, **19**:4
Qualified property, additional first-year
    depreciation, **8**:7
Qualified real property business
    indebtedness, **5**:33
Qualified residence, **10**:15
    interest, **10**:14, **10**:15–16, **12**:18
Qualified retirement plan, **19**:11
    early distribution, **19**:11
Qualified retirement planning services,
    5:20, **5**:24, **5**:26
Qualified summer youth employee, **13**:9–10
Qualified transportation fringes, **5**:20,
    5:23, **5**:26
Qualified tuition deduction, rules for,
    9:16
Qualified tuition program, **5**:31–32
    (Section 529 plans), **9**:17
Qualified tuition reduction plan, **5**:10
Qualifying child, **3**:11–13
    abode test, **3**:12
    age test, **3**:12
    relationship test, **3**:12
    requirements, **2**:28–29
    support test, **3**:12
    tiebreaker rules, **3**:12–13
Qualifying relative, dependency
    exemptions, **3**:13–17
    gross income test, **3**:14–15
    relationship test, **3**:14
    requirements, **2**:28–29
    support test, **3**:15–17
Quintessential principal-agent
    relationship, **4**:18

R

Ratio percentage test for qualified plans, **19**:9

Real estate activities, special passive activity rules for, **11**:19–21

Real property
certain reacquisitions of (Section 1038), **15**:23
computing Section 1250 recapture on nonresidential, **17**:15–16

Real property trade or business, material participation in, **11**:19–20

Realization principle, **4**:4

Realized gain, **3**:32, **14**:3–6, **14**:12
additional complexities in determining, **14**:20–21
adjusted basis, **14**:4, **14**:20–21
amount realized, **14**:3–4, **14**:20
capital additions, **14**:4
capital recoveries, **14**:4–6
sale or other disposition, **14**:3

Realized loss, **3**:32, **14**:3–6, **14**:12
additional complexities in determining, **14**:20–21
adjusted basis, **14**:4, **14**:20–21
amount realized, **14**:3–4, **14**:20
capital additions, **14**:4
capital recoveries, **14**:4–6
sale or other disposition, **14**:3

Realty, **1**:6, **8**:3
ad valorem taxes on, **1**:6–7
recovery periods and methods, **8**:10–11

Reasonable prospect of full recovery, **7**:9

Reasonable prospect of recovery doctrine, **7**:11

Reasonableness, **6**:6–7

Recapture
alimony, **4**:21–22
Section 1245, **17**:11–14, **17**:17
Section 1250, **17**:14–19, **17**:17
special provisions, **17**:21–22
tax planning for avoiding, **17**:30
tax planning for the postponing and shifting of, **17**:29–30
tax planning for the timing of, **17**:25–29

Recapture exceptions
certain nontaxable transactions, **17**:20
charitable contributions, **17**:19–20
death, **17**:19
gifts, **17**:19
like-kind exchanges and involuntary conversions, **17**:20

Recapture of depreciation, corporate and individual treatment compared, **20**:7–8

Reciprocal agreements, qualified tuition reduction plans, **5**:10

Recognized gain, **3**:32, **14**:6

Recognized loss, **3**:32, **14**:6

Recoveries of capital, **4**:18, **14**:4

Recovery of capital doctrine, **4**:6–7, **14**:7–8

relationship of to the concepts of realization and recognition, **14**:7–8

Recovery rebate credit, **13**:26, **13**:27

Recurring items, **6**:10
exception, **18**:15

Reduced deduction election, **10**:25–26

Refundable credits, **13**:4

Refunds
computation of, **3**:22
limitations on, **1**:21

Regular decisions, **2**:17, **2**:32

Regular tax liability, **13**:6
individual AMT, **12**:8

Regulations. *See* Treasury Department Regulations

Rehabilitation expenditures credit, **13**:7–9, **13**:29

Rehabilitation expenditures credit recapture, **13**:8

Related party, **17**:21
definition of, **6**:27
disallowed losses between, **14**:16–17
installment sales, tax planning for, **18**:36–37
interest paid to, **10**:17
like-kind exchanges between, **15**:5
loans, **7**:5–6, **7**:26
recapture on gain from sale of depreciable property between, **17**:21
sales of depreciable property between, **18**:23–24
sales of nondepreciable property between, **18**:22
tax planning for shifting income to, **4**:36–37

Related party transactions, **6**:26–27
losses, **6**:26
relationships and constructive ownership, **6**:26–27
unpaid expenses and interest, **6**:26

Relationship test
qualifying child, **3**:12
qualifying relative, **3**:14

Rental activity, **11**:16

Rental of vacation homes, **6**:19–22

Rental real estate activities, **11**:20–21

Repairs, cost of, **7**:11

Replacement property tests, **15**:14
functional use test, **15**:13
taxpayer use test, **15**:12

Repossessions of real property, **15**:23

Research activities credit, **7**:15, **13**:10–13, **13**:29
basic research credit, **13**:12
energy research credit, **13**:12
incremental research activities credit, **13**:10–12

Research and experimental expenditures, **7**:15–16, **12**:12, **13**:11
deferral and amortization method, **7**:16
expense method, **7**:15–16

Research Institute of America (RIA), **2**:18

Reserve method, **7**:3

Reserves, **6**:10, **18**:16

Residence. *See* Personal residence

Residency test, dependency exemptions **3**:17

Residential rental housing, computing Section 1250 recapture on, **17**:16

Residential rental real estate, **8**:10

Respondent, **2**:17

Restricted property plan, **19**:4, **19**:33–36
employer deductions, **19**:35–36
special election available, **19**:34–35
substantial risk of forfeiture, **19**:34

Retirement accounts, contributions to, **9**:25
employee IRAs, **9**:25
self-employed Keogh (H.R. 10) plans, **9**:25

Retirement assets, liquidating, **19**:43

Revenue act, **1**:3
of 1913, **1**:3
of 1916, **1**:11
of 1948, **1**:31

Revenue Agent's Report (RAR), **1**:20

Revenue, IRS as protector of, **1**:31–32

Revenue neutrality, **1**:24

Revenue Procedures, **2**:7, **2**:8–10

Revenue Rulings, **2**:7, **2**:8–10

Right of offset, **14**:17

Rollover treatment, qualified plan, **19**:13

Roth 401 (k) plan adoptions, **19**:23

Roth IRA, **9**:25, **19**:11, **19**:22–23, **19**:28
designated contributions, **19**:18–19
rollovers and conversions, **19**:29

S

S corporation, **4**:18, **20**:4, **20**:26
accounting period for, **18**:3–5
and salaries, **20**:29
basis determination, **20**:30–31
calendar year, **18**:5
election, **20**:26–31
impermissible year election, **18**:5
income from, **4**:17–18
loss of election, **20**:27–28
making the election, **20**:27
operational rules, **20**:28–31
qualification for S status, **20**:26–28
separately stated items, **20**:28–29
tax planning for regular vs. S status, **20**:38
taxable income, **20**:29–30
treatment of losses, **20**:30

Safe harbor provisions, **15**:18

Salaries and S corporations, **20**:29

Sale of a residence—Section 121, **15**:16–22

Sale or exchange, **16**:8–14
lease cancellation payments, **16**:13–14
options, **16**:9–11
patents, **16**:11–12
retirement of corporate obligations (special rule), **16**:9
worthless securities and Section 1244 stock, **16**:8

Sales tax, **1:**9, **1:**18
    itemized deduction for sales taxes paid, **10:**14
    national, **1:**18
Sarbanes-Oxley Act of 2002, **4:**26
Saver's credit, **13:**25
    rate and AGI thresholds, **13:**26
Schedule A of Form 1040, Itemized Deductions, **9:**3, **9:**27, **10:**14, **10:**18, **10:**28, **10:**29
Schedule C of Form 1040, Profit or Loss From Business, **8:**28, **8:**30, **9:**3, **10:**18
Schedule D of Form 1040, Capital Gains and Losses, **15:**27, **16:**27, **16:**28–29, **17:**23, **17:**28–29
Schedule E, interest expenses related to rents or royalties, **10:**18
Schedule K-1
    Form 1065, **20:**34
    Form 1120S, **20:**28
Schedule L, **20:**15
Schedule M-1, **20:**15
Schedule M-2, **20:**15, **20:**16
Schedule M-3, **20:**17
Scholarships, **5:**9–10
    disguised compensation, **5:**10
    qualified tuition reduction plans, **5:**10
    timing issues, **5:**10
Section 61 definition of gross income, **4:**2–3
Section 62, deductions for adjusted gross income, **6:**3–4
Section 121 exclusion, **15:**16–17, **15:**17–19, **15:**19–22, **15:**26–27
    Exclusion of Gain from Sale of Principal Residence, **15:**16–22
Section 162 exclusion of trade or business expenses, **6:**5
Section 163, interest, **8:**24
Section 164, taxes, **8:**24
Section 174, research and experimental expenditures, **8:**24
Section 179 expensing, **8:**13
    Election to Expense Certain Depreciable Business Assets, **8:**13
Section 183, Activities Not Engaged in for Profit, **6:**17
Section 195, startup expenditures, **8:**23
Section 197, Amortization of Goodwill and Certain Other Intangibles, **8:**22
Section 212 expenses, **6:**4
Section 267, Losses, Expenses, and Interest with Respect to Transactions between Related Taxpayers, **14:**16–17, **14:**25–26, **15:**5
Section 331, general rule of (corporate liquidation), **20:**24–25
Section 332, exception to the general rule, **20:**25
Section 334, basis determination, **20:**25–26
Section 338, basis determination, **20:**25–26
Section 401(k) plan, **19:**15–19
    and IRA compared, **19:**40–41

Section 446, General Rule for Methods of Accounting, **18:**10
Section 529 plan, **5:**31–32, **9:**17
Section 1031, Exchange of Property Held for Production Use or Investment, **15:**3–11
Section 1032—exchange of stock for property, **15:**23
Section 1033, Involuntary Conversions, **15:**11–16, **15:**22
Section 1035—certain exchanges of insurance policies, **15:**23
Section 1036—exchange of stock for stock of the same corporation, **15:**23
Section 1038—certain reacquisitions of real property, **15:**23
Section 1041—transfers of property between spouses or incident to divorce, **15:**23
Section 1044—rollovers into specialized small business investment companies, **15:**24
Section 1045—rollover of gain from qualified small business stock into another qualified small business stock, **15:**24
Section 1221, Capital Asset Defined, **16:**3–4
Section 1231 asset, **16:**3, **17:**3–11, **17:**22–25
    See also Business assets
Section 1231 gains and losses, **17:**3, **17:**25
Section 1231 lookback, **17:**9–11
Section 1231 netting procedure, **17:**7, **17:**8, **17:**22
Section 1231 property, **17:**4
    Property Used in the Trade or Business and Involuntary Conversions, **17:**3–11
Section 1244 stock, **7:**6–7, **7:**26, **16:**8
    Losses on Small Business Stock, **7:**6–7
Section 1245 property, **17:**13–14, **17:**22–25
Section 1245 recapture, **17:**11–14, **17:**17, **17:**19–20, **17:**20–21, **17:**22–25
Section 1250 property, **17:**14, **17:**18–19, **17:**22–25
Section 1250 recapture, **17:**14–19, **17:**19–20, **17:**20–21, **17:**22–25
Securities
    dealers in, **16:**6–7
    short sales of, **16:**18
    tax-exempt, **10:**17
    worthless, **7:**6–7, **16:**8
Securities and Exchange Commission (SEC), **18:**34
Self-Correction Program (SCP), **19:**8
Self-employed individuals
    contribution limitations for retirement plans, **19:**19–20
    coverage requirements for retirement plans, **19:**19
    deductibility of medical insurance premiums, **10:**7
    employee vs., **9:**2–4

filing requirements, **3:**25–26
    office in the home expenses, **9:**21–23
    retirement plans for, **19:**19–20
    tax planning for, **9:**29–30
Self-employed Keogh (H.R. 10) plans, **9:**25
Self-employed persons, tax payment procedures applicable to, **13:**38–42
    estimated tax for individuals, **13:**38–39
    penalty on underpayments, **13:**39–40
    self-employment tax, **13:**40–42
Self-employed retirement plans, tax planning for, **19:**40
Self-employment, net earnings from, **13:**42
Self-employment tax, **13:**40–42
    Social Security and Medicare portions, **13:**40
    worksheet for 2007, **13:**41
    worksheet for 2008, **13:**40
Senate Finance Committee, **2:**3–5
Separate home for parent or parents, head of household, **3:**31
Separately stated items, **20:**28–29
Series E, **4:**12
Series EE bonds, **4:**12, **4:**35, **4:**36, **5:**30, **5:**35–36
Series HH bonds, **4:**12
Service requirement for depreciation, **8:**3
Services
    contribution of, **10:**19–20
    deferral of advance payments, **4:**13–14
    interest paid for, **10:**16
Severance awards, **15:**12
Severance taxes, **1:**10
Shifting deductions
    between employer and employee, **9:**30
    tax planning for, **6:**31
Short period, **18:**7
Short sale against the box, **2:**38, **16:**16
    disposition rules, **16:**17–18
    treatment illustrations, **16:**18–19
Short sales, **16:**16
    of securities, **16:**18
    treatment illustrations, **16:**18–19
Short taxable year, **18:**7
Significant participation activity, **11:**14
SIMPLE (savings incentive match plan for employees), **19:**4, **19:**17–18, **19:**25
Simplified employee pension (SEP) plans, **19:**24
    and Keogh plans compared, **19:**25
Small Business and Work Opportunity Tax Act of 2007, **2:**3
Small business corporation, **4:**18, **20:**26
Small business, encouragement of, **1:**26
Small business stock, **7:**6–7, **7:**26
    fifty percent exclusion, individual AMT preferences, **12:**21–22
Small Cases Division of the U.S. Tax Court, **2:**12
Social considerations, tax law, **1:**33
Social Security benefits, **4:**33–34
    taxation formula, **4:**33
Social Security tax, **1:**16, **13:**26, **13:**30

Sole proprietors, reporting procedures, **8**:28

Sole proprietorship, **20**:4

Special clothing, deductibility of, **9**:23–24

Special withholding allowance, **13**:34

Specialized small business investment companies (SSBIC), **15**:24

Specific charge-off method, **7**:3–4

Sports franchises, **16**:13

Spousal IRA, **19**:20, **19**:22, **19**:25–26

Spouse(s)
    abandoned spouse rules, **3**:29, **3**:31–32
    innocent, **4**:20
    living apart, **4**:19–20
    medical expenses incurred for, **10**:6
    surviving spouse status, **3**:30
    transfers of property between spouses (or incident to divorce), **15**:23

Spread, stock options and, **19**:36

Standard deduction, **3**:7–8, **3**:25, **3**:26
    individuals not eligible for, **3**:9
    tax planning considerations for, **3**:35

Standard Federal Tax Reporter, **2**:23

Standard mileage method, **9**:6

Startup expenditures, **8**:23

State and local excise taxes, **1**:9

State death taxes, **1**:12

State decisis, doctrine of, **2**:12

State gift taxes, **1**:13

State income taxation, piggyback approach to, **1**:14

State income taxes, **1**:14–15

Statements on Responsibilities in Tax Practice, **1**:23

Statements on Standards for Tax Services, **1**:23

Statute of limitations, **1**:21
    assessment by the IRS, **1**:21
    limitations on refunds, **1**:21

Statutory (nominal) rates, **3**:21

Statutory authority, **5**:4

Statutory employees, **9**:4

Statutory expansions, **16**:6–8
    dealers in securities, **16**:6–7
    nonbusiness bad debts, **16**:8
    real property subdivided for sale, **16**:7–8

Statutory percentage method, **8**:15
    under MACRS, **8**:10

Statutory sources of the tax law, **2**:2–7
    arrangement of the code, **2**:6
    citing the code, **2**:6–7
    legislative process, **2**:3–5
    origin of the internal revenue code, **2**:2–3

Stealth tax, **3**:20

Stepped-down basis, **14**:14

Stepped-up basis, **14**:14

Stock
    exchange of for property (Section 1032), **15**:23
    exchange of for stock of the same corporation, **15**:23
    growth vs. income, **14**:21

rollover of gain from qualified small business stock into another qualified small business stock, **15**:24

Stock appreciation rights (SARs), **19**:30

Stock bonus plan, **19**:7, **19**:4–19
    limitations, **19**:15
    See also Qualified plans

Stock dividends, **5**:30
    holding period for nontaxable, **14**:10
    nontaxable, **14**:10

Stock option, **19**:36–39, **19**:42–43
    incentive stock options (ISO), **19**:36–38
    nonqualified stock options, **19**:38–39

Stock redemptions, **20**:24

Stock rights
    holding period of nontaxable, **14**:11
    nontaxable, **14**:10

Stock sales, tax planning for, **16**:33

Straight-line depreciation election, **8**:7, **8**:12
    under ADS, **8**:21
    under MACRS, **8**:11, **8**:14

Straight-line method, **8**:15

Subchapter C, Corporate Distributions and Adjustments, **2**:6

Subchapter K, Partners and Partnerships, **2**:6

Subchapter S, Tax Treatment of S Corporations and Their Shareholders, **2**:6

Subprime mortgage debacle, **5**:34

Substantial limitations or restrictions, **4**:10–11

Substantial rights, patents, **16**:12

Substantial risk of forfeiture (SRF), **19**:33, **19**:34

Substantially identical (wash sales), **14**:17

Substantially identical property, **16**:17

Substantially rehabilitated, **13**:8

Substantiation
    accountable plan for reimbursement of employee expenses, **9**:26
    requirements, **6**:27, **8**:19

Sunset provision, **1**:12, **1**:24, **19**:23

Super-full absorption costing system, **18**:31

Support test
    children of divorced or separated parents, **3**:16–17
    multiple support agreement, **3**:15–16
    qualifying child, **3**:12
    qualifying relative, **3**:15–17
    tax planning for dependency exemptions, **3**:36

Supreme Court Reporter (S.Ct.), **2**:20

Surviving spouse status, **3**:30

Suspended losses
    carryovers of, **11**:7
    impact of, **11**:6–7

T

Table for percentage method of withholding for wages paid through 2008, **13**:37

Table 4-1, Ordinary life annuities: one life—expected return multiples, **4**:29

Table 4-2, Number of anticipated monthly annuity payments under the simplified method, **4**:30

Table 4-3, Uniform premiums for $1,000 of group term life insurance protection, **4**:32

Tables (MACRS, AMT, and ADS), **8**:33–37

Tangible assets, **8**:3
    expenditures for, **6**:25

Tangible personal property, expensing of, **8**:13

Tangible personalty, **10**:24

Tariffs, **1**:3, **1**:17

Tax accounting methods as an incentive to go foreign, **18**:13

Tax administration, **1**:19–24
    audit process, **1**:19–20
    interest and penalties, **1**:22–23
    Internal Revenue Service, **1**:19
    statute of limitations, **1**:21
    tax practice, **1**:23–24

Tax avoidance, **2**:35–38
    loans, **4**:25

Tax base, **1**:5

Tax benefit rule, **5**:32, **10**:8

Tax concepts of income, comparison of the accounting and, **4**:5

Tax conventions, **2**:20

Tax Court, **2**:14, **2**:15–17
    See also Courts

Tax Court of the United States Reports (T.C.), **2**:17–18

Tax credits, **3**:22, **13**:2, **13**:28–30
    adoption expenses credit, **13**:20–21
    child and dependent care expenses, **13**:2, **13**:21–24
    child tax credit, **13**:21
    credit for certain retirement plan contributions, **13**:25–26
    credit for employer-provided child care, **13**:14–15
    credit for small employer pension plan startup costs, **13**:14
    disabled access credit, **13**:3, **13**:13–14
    earned income credit, **13**:3, **13**:15–17
    education, **13**:24–25
    for elderly or disabled, **13**:2–3, **13**:17–18
    for rehabilitation expenditures, **13**:7–9
    foreign tax credit (FTC), **13**:3, **13**:5, **13**:18–20
    general business credit, **13**:5–6, **13**:6–7
    HOPE scholarship credit, **13**:24
    lifetime learning credit, **13**:24
    low-income housing credit, **13**:13
    neutralizes foreign income taxes, **4**:12
    other, **13**:15–26
    overview and priority of, **13**:4–7
    partial listing of refundable and nonrefundable, **13**:5
    refundable and nonrefundable, **13**:3, **13**:4–5

Tax credits (*contd.*)
  research activities credit, **13**:10–13
  specific business-related provisions, **13**:7–15
  tax policy considerations, **13**:3–4
  work opportunity tax credit, **13**:9–10
Tax deductions, tax planning for the time value of, **6**:29
Tax deferral, tax planning for, **4**:34–36
Tax delinquencies, **1**:21
Tax determination, **3**:20–25
  computation of net taxes payable or refund due, **3**:22
  of a dependent child, **3**:23–24
  tax rate schedule method, **3**:21
  tax table method, **3**:20
  unearned income of children under age 19 taxed at parents' rate, **3**:23–25
Tax evasion, **2**:35–38
Tax file memorandum, **2**:35, **2**:36
Tax filing considerations *See* Filing considerations
Tax formula, **3**:2, **3**:3–10
  adjusted gross income (AGI), **3**:6
  application of, **3**:9
  components of, **3**:3–9
  deductions for adjusted gross income, **3**:5–6
  dependency exemptions, **3**:9
  exclusions, **3**:3
  gross income, **3**:3–5
  income (broadly conceived), **3**:3
  individuals not eligible for the standard deduction, **3**:9
  itemized deductions, **3**:6–7
  nondeductible expenditures, **3**:7
  personal exemptions, **3**:9
  special limitations for individuals who can be claimed as dependents, **3**:9–10
  standard deduction, **3**:7–8
Tax free municipal bonds, **12**:21
Tax Freedom Day, **2**:3
Tax gap, **2**:13, **4**:4
Tax holiday, **1**:7
Tax home, determining, **9**:8
Tax incentives, use of for wind energy, **8**:7
Tax Increase Prevention Act of 2005 (TIPRA), **2**:3, **4**:15
Tax law
  courts influence of, **1**:32–33
  economic considerations, **1**:25–26, **1**:33
  equity considerations, **1**:27–30, **1**:33
  IRS influence of, **1**:31–32, **1**:33
  political considerations, **1**:30–31, **1**:33
  primary sources of, **2**:33
  revenue needs, **1**:24–25
  rules of, **2**:2
  secondary materials, **2**:33
  social considerations, **1**:26–27, **1**:33
  tax planning, **2**:34–39
  tax research, **2**:26–34
  tax research tools, **2**:22–26
  understanding the Federal, **1**:24–34
Tax law sources, **2**:2–22

administrative, **2**:7–11
assessing the validity of other, **2**:33
judicial, **2**:12–20
other, **2**:20–22
statutory, **2**:2–7
Tax loopholes, **1**:31
Tax Management Portfolios, **2**:23
Tax Notes, **2**:10
Tax payment procedures, **13**:26–42
  applicable to employers, **13**:26–38
  applicable to self-employed persons, **13**:38–42
Tax periodicals, **2**:21–22
Tax planning considerations, **2**:34–39, **7**:25–27
  accounting for community property, **4**:37
  adjustments to avoid overwithholding, **13**:44
  adjustments to increase withholding, **13**:44
  alimony, **4**:37–38
  alternative minimum tax, **12**:30–31
  amortization, **8**:32
  avoiding recapture, **17**:30
  business entities, **20**:36–40
  capital asset status, **16**:31–33
  capital expenditures, **6**:32
  capital gains and losses, **16**:31–34
  cash method of accounting, **4**:36, **18**:36
  casualty losses, **7**:26–27
  charitable contribution deduction, **10**:34–35
  child and dependent care expenses, **13**:42–44
  comparison of Section 401(k) plan with IRA, **19**:40–41
  completed contract method, **18**:37
  cost identification and documentation considerations, **14**:24
  cost recovery, **8**:31–32
  deferred compensation, **19**:39–40
  dependency exemptions, **3**:35–37
  depletion, **8**:32–33
  disallowed losses, **14**:25–26
  documentation of related-taxpayer loans, casualty losses, and theft losses, **7**:26
  education expenses, **9**:31–32
  employee benefits, **5**:34–35
  entertainment expenses, **9**:32–33
  excessive executive compensation, **6**:29–31
  flexible benefit plans, **19**:43
  follow-up procedures, **2**:38
  for corporations, regular vs. S status, **20**:38
  for maximizing benefits, **16**:33–34
  for stock sales, **16**:33
  for year-end planning, **16**:34
  foreign tax credit, **13**:42
  hobby losses, **6**:31
  income of certain children, **3**:38
  individual retirement accounts, **19**:40

installment method of accounting, **18**:36–37
interest deduction, **10**:33–34
inventories, **18**:37
investment income, **5**:35–36
involuntary conversions, **15**:25
itemized deductions, **10**:32–35
life insurance, **5**:34
like-kind exchanges, **15**:24–25
maximizing use of standard deduction, **3**:35
medical deductions, **10**:32–33
moving expenses, **9**:31
net operating losses, **7**:27
nonqualified deferred compensation (NQDC) plans, **19**:41–42
nontax considerations, **2**:35
nontaxable economic benefits, **4**:34
postponing and shifting recapture, **17**:29–30
practical application, **2**:38–39
property transactions, **14**:22
qualified plans, **19**:40
sale of a principal residence, **15**:25–27
selection of property for making bequests, **14**:25
selection of property for making gifts, **14**:24–25
self-employed individuals, **9**:29–30
self-employed retirement plans, **19**:40
shifting deductions, **6**:31
shifting deductions between employer and employee, **9**:30
shifting income to relatives, **4**:36–37
small business stock, **7**:26
stock options, **19**:42–43
tax avoidance and tax evasion, **2**:35–38
tax deferral, **4**:34–36
tax rate differentials, **3**:37–38
taxable year, **18**:36
time value of tax deductions, **6**:29
timing of recapture, **17**:25–29
timing of Section 1231 gain, **17**:25
timing the payment of deductible taxes, **10**:33
transportation and travel expenses, **9**:31
unreasonable compensation, **6**:29
unreimbursed employee business expenses, **9**:33
utilizing passive losses, **11**:27–28
worthless securities, **7**:26
Tax practice, **1**:23–24
  ethical guidelines, **1**:23
  statements on responsibilities in, **1**:23
  statutory penalties imposed on tax return preparers, **1**:24
Tax preferences, **12**:4
  AMT formula for individual, **12**:5–6
  corporate AMT, **12**:29
Tax rate differentials, tax planning considerations, **3**:37–38
Tax rate schedules, **3**:21
  for single taxpayers (2008), **3**:21

Tax rates, **1**:5–6
 change lead to income shifting, **18**:14
 corporate income, **20**:14
 summary of income tax consequences, **20**:29
Tax Reform Act (TRA) of 1986, **2**:3
Tax Relief and Health Care Act of 2006, **2**:3
Tax Relief Reconciliation Act of 2001, **1**:11, **1**:13, **2**:3, **14**:16
Tax research, **2**:26–34
 arriving at the solution or at alternative solutions, **2**:33–34
 assessing the validity of the tax law sources, **2**:30–33
 communicating tax research, **2**:34
 identifying the problem, **2**:28
 locating the appropriate tax law sources, **2**:29–30
 refining the problem, **2**:28–29
Tax research process, **2**:29
Tax research tools, **2**:22–26
 electronic services, **2**:23–26
 electronic vs. paper, **2**:22–23
 tax services, **2**:23
Tax return preparation, outsourcing of, **1**:25
Tax services, **2**:23
 statements on standards for, **1**:23
Tax shelters, **11**:2–3
 strategies now protected by patents, **11**:19
Tax structure, **1**:5–6
 criteria used in the selection of, **1**:4–5
 incidence of taxation, **1**:6
 tax base, **1**:5
 tax rates, **1**:5–6
Tax table, **3**:20
Tax treaties, **2**:20–21
Tax Withholding and Estimated Tax, Publication 505, **13**:44
Taxable estate, **1**:11
Taxable income, **1**:5
 S corporation, **20**:29–30
Taxable year, **4**:7, **18**:3, **18**:36
Taxation
 double, **1**:6
 general scheme of, **16**:3
 global system approach, **3**:5
 incidence of, **1**:6
 on the CPA examination, **2**:39–40
 territorial system approach, **3**:5
Tax-deferred annuities, **19**:4
Taxes, **10**:11–14
 ad valorem, **1**:6
 consumption, **1**:6
 corporate income, **1**:6
 data warehousing reduces global taxes, **2**:28
 death taxes, **1**:10–12
 deductibility as, **10**:11
 deductibility of foreign, **10**:13
 deductible and nondeductible, **10**:12
 distinguished from fees, **10**:11
 employment taxes, **1**:15–17

excise, **1**:3, **1**:8
 fair, **1**:18
 Federal estate, **1**:11
 Federal gift, **1**:12–13
 Federal income, **1**:13–14
 FICA, **1**:16, **13**:26
 flat, **1**:17–18
 foreign withholding, **13**:38
 franchise, **1**:3, **1**:17
 FUTA, **1**:16, **13**:26
 general sales, **1**:9–10
 income, **1**:3, **1**:13–15
 inheritance, **1**:11
 interest on deferred, **18**:24
 jock, **1**:15
 major types of, **1**:6–18
 mass, **1**:4
 Medicare, **1**:16
 miscellaneous state and local taxes, **1**:17
 national sales, **1**:18
 occupational, **1**:17
 other U.S., **1**:17
 payable, computation of net, **3**:22
 progressive, **1**:5
 property, **1**:6–8, **10**:11–13
 proportional, **1**:5
 proposed U.S. taxes, **1**:17–18
 sales, **1**:9, **1**:18
 severance, **1**:10
 Social Security, **1**:16
 state and local excise, **1**:9
 state and local income and sales, **10**:13–14
 state death, **1**:12
 state gift, **1**:13
 state income, **1**:14–15, **10**:13–14
 tax planning for timing the payment of deductible, **10**:33
 transaction taxes, **1**:8–10
 value added, **1**:18
Tax-exempt income, expenses and interest relating to, **6**:28–29
Tax-exempt securities, **10**:17
Tax-free transaction, **15**:3
Taxpayer Relief Act (TRA) of 1997, **2**:3, **2**:4
Taxpayer use test, replacement property, **15**:12
Taxpayers eligible for domestic production activities deduction, **7**:18–19
Tax-related Web sites, **2**:27
Technical Advice Memoranda (TAMs), **2**:9, **2**:11
Technical Expedited Advice Memorandums (TEAMs), **2**:11
Temporary assignments, travel expenses, **9**:7–8
Temporary Regulations, **2**:8, **4**:25
Tentative minimum tax, **13**:6
Terminally ill, accelerated death benefits and, **5**:7
Territorial system approach to taxation, **3**:5

Tests based on
 current participation, **11**:13–14
 facts and circumstances, **11**:15
 prior participation, **11**:14–15
Theft losses, **7**:9
 as capital recovery, **14**:5
 personal casualty gains and losses, **7**:13–14
 Section 1231 assets, **17**:6–7
 statutory framework for deducting losses of individuals, **7**:13
 tax planning for documentation of, **7**:26
 See also Casualty loss
Thin capitalization, **20**:17
Tiebreaker rules, qualifying child, **3**:12–13
Timber, as Section 1231 asset, **17**:5
Timing of expense recognition, **6**:8–10
 accrual method requirements, **6**:10
 cash method requirements, **6**:9
 importance of taxpayer's method of accounting, **6**:8–9
Total gain, **18**:20
TRA of 1986, **8**:5, **19**:13
Trade names, **8**:22, **16**:12–13
Trade or business expenses, **6**:5–7
Trade or business expenses and production of income expenses
 ordinary and necessary requirement, **6**:5–6
 reasonableness requirement, **6**:6–7
Trademarks, **8**:22, **16**:12–13
Traditional IRA, **9**:25, **19**:28
 See also Individual retirement account
Transaction taxes, **1**:8–10
Transfer for valuable consideration, life insurance proceeds, **5**:8–9
Transmittal of Wage and Tax Statements, Form W-3, **13**:37–38
Transportation expenses, **9**:4–7, **9**:31
 commuting expenses, **9**:4–5
 computation of automobile expenses, **9**:6–7
 qualified expenditures, **9**:4–5
Transportation for medical treatment, deductible medical expenses, **10**:6–7
Travel expenses, **9**:7–11, **9**:31
 away-from-home requirement, **9**:7–8
 combined business and pleasure travel, **9**:9–11
 definition of travel expenses, **9**:7
 domestic travel, **9**:9–10
 foreign travel, **9**:10–11
 restrictions on, **9**:8–9
Travel status, **9**:4
Treasury Decisions (TDs), **2**:8, **2**:10
Treasury Department Regulations, **2**:7–8
 assessing the validity of, **2**:30–31
Treasury Inspector General for Tax Administration (TIGTA), **6**:17, **15**:4
Trial courts, **2**:12, **2**:13–14
 See also Courts
Trusts
 beneficiaries of, **4**:18

Trusts (*contd.*)
   income from, **4**:17–18
Tuition expenses, deductible medical
      expenses, **10**:4
Two percent floor
   limitation on itemized deductions, **9**:28
   miscellaneous itemized deductions not
      subject to, **9**:29
   miscellaneous itemized deductions
      subject to, **9**:28–29
Two percent-of-AGI floor, **9**:27
Two percent-of-AGI limitation, **17**:6
Two-year ownership rule exceptions, sale
   of personal residence, **15**:17–19

U

U.S. Court of Appeals, **2**:14, **2**:15–17
   See also Courts
U.S. Court of Federal Claims, **2**:12
   See also Courts
U.S. District Court, judicial citations of,
   2:19–20
   See also Courts
U.S. government publications, as
   definition of capital asset, **16**:4,
   16:6
U.S. Supreme Court, **2**:16
   judicial citations of, **2**:20
   See also Courts
U.S. Tax Cases (USTC), **2**:19
U.S. Tax Court, **2**:12
   http://www.ustaxcourt.gov, **2**:18
   judicial citations of, **2**:17–19
   jurisdiction of, **2**:13
   Small Cases Division, **2**:12
   See also Courts
U.S. taxation, history of, **1**:2–4
Undergraduate tuition waivers, **5**:10
Unearned income of children under age
   19 taxed at parents' rate, **3**:23–25
   election to claim certain unearned
      income on parent's return, **3**:24
   net unearned income, **3**:23
   other provisions, **3**:24–25
   tax determination, **3**:23–24
Unearned income, **3**:23
Unemployment compensation, **4**:32–33
Unfunded NQDC plan, **19**:30–31
Unified transfer tax credit, **1**:11

Unified transfer tax schedule, **1**:13
Uniform capitalization (UNICAP) rules,
   18:30–32
Uniform Gifts to Minors Act, **4**:36
United States Board of Tax Appeals Reports
   (B.T.A.), **2**:18
United States Reports, Lawyer's Edition
   (L.Ed.), **2**:20
United States Supreme Court Reports (U.S.),
   2:20
United States Tax Reporter, **2**:23
Unit-livestock-price method, **18**:36
Unreasonable compensation, tax plan-
   ning for, **6**:29
Unrecaptured Section 1250 gain, **16**:20,
   17:17–19
   net Section 1231 gain limitation, **17**:18
   Section 1250 property for purposes of,
      17:18–19
   special 25% gain netting rules, **17**:18
Unreimbursed employee business
   expenses, **9**:28, **9**:33
   Form 2106-EZ, **9**:27
Unreimbursed employee expenses, **9**:27
Unreimbursed employment-related
   expenses, child and dependent care
   expenses, **13**:22
Use or lose plans, **5**:20
Use tax, **1**:9
   using the income tax return as a
      reminder, **1**:15

V

Vacation homes, **6**:19
   conversion to rental property, **6**:22
   personal/rental use, **6**:20–22
   primarily personal use, **6**:19–20
   primarily rental use, **6**:20
   rental of, **6**:19–22
Vacation/rental home, **6**:23
Valuation requirements for charitable
   contributions, **10**:21–22
Value added tax (VAT), **1**:18
Vesting requirements, **19**:9–10
   alternative minimum vesting schedules,
      19:9
   qualified plan, **19**:9–10
Voluntary Correction Program (VCP),
   19:8

W

W-2 wages, **7**:17
   Form W-2, **3**:22, **9**:27, **13**:37–38
Wash sale, **14**:17–18, **14**:26
Web sites, tax-related, **2**:27
Wherewithal to pay, **1**:28
Withholding
   backup, **13**:38
   tax planning for adjustments to avoid
      overwithholding, **13**:44
   tax planning for adjustments to
      increase, **13**:44
Withholding allowances, **13**:33
Withholding classifications, **13**:31
Withholding table, wage bracket, **13**:35
Withholding tax, foreign, **13**:38
Work opportunity tax credit, **13**:9–10,
   13:30
   computation of, **13**:9
   long-term family assistance recipient,
      13:10
   qualified summer youth employees,
      13:9–10
Workers' compensation, **5**:13
Working condition fringes, **5**:20, **5**:22–23,
   5:24, **5**:26
Working Families Tax Relief Act of 2004,
   2:3, **3**:11, **3**:13
Worthless securities, **7**:6–7, **7**:26
   and Section 1244 stock, sale or
      exchange of, **16**:8
   small business stock, **7**:6–7
Writ of Certiorari, **2**:16
Written substantiation, record-keeping
   requirements, **10**:21

Y

Year of deduction, medical expenses,
   10:8
Year of inclusion
   accounting methods, **4**:7–10
   exceptions applicable to accrual basis
      taxpayers, **4**:13–14
   exceptions applicable to cash basis
      taxpayers, **4**:10–13
   taxable year, **4**:7
Year-end planning, tax planning for,
   16:34